Collect
BRITISH
Postmarks

Collect
BRITISH
Postmarks

The Handbook to British Postmarks and their Values

STANLEY GIBBONS LTD
London and Ringwood

By Appointment to Her Majesty The Queen
Stanley Gibbons Ltd, London
Philatelists

Acknowledgements

1st Edition   February 1979
               Reprinted August 1979
2nd edition   (Picton Publishing) May 1980
3rd Edition   (Longman Group Limited) May 1983
4th Edition   (Published by the Author) January 1987
5th Edition   (Published by the Author) January 1990
6th Edition   (Published by the British Postmark Society)
               Summer 1993
7th Edition   (Published by the British Postmark Society)
               Summer 1997
8th Edition   (Published by Stanley Gibbons) November 2011
9th Edition   (Published by Stanley Gibbons) December 2013

Published by Stanley Gibbons Ltd
Editorial, Publications Sales Offices
and Distribution Centre:
7 Parkside, Christchurch Road, Ringwood,
Hants BH24 3SH

© Stanley Gibbons Ltd 2013

Copyright Notice

The contents of this Catalogue, including the numbering system and illustrations, are fully protected by copyright. No part of this publication may be reproduced, stored in a retrieval system, or transmitted in any form or by any means, electronic, mechanical, photocopying, recording or otherwise, without prior permission. Requests for such permission should be addressed to the Catalogue Editor. The "Towns with Krag and Universal machines 1933-1999" list in chapter 10 is the copyright of Colin Peachey. This Catalogue is sold on condition that it is not, by way of trade or otherwise, lent, re-sold, hired out, circulated or otherwise disposed of other than in its complete, original and unaltered form and without a similar condition including this condition being imposed on the subsequent purchaser.

British Library Cataloguing in
Publication Data.
A catalogue record for this book is available from
the British Library.

Errors and omissions excepted. The colour
reproduction of stamps is only as accurate as
the printing process will allow.

ISBN-10: 0-85259-986-3
ISBN-13: 978-0-85259-896-2

Item No. R2786-13

Printed by GraphyCems, Spain

Acknowledgement for illustrations is given to the British Post Office, Mr E W Proud of Proud-Bailey Co Ltd, the Railway Philatelic Group, Robson Lowe and especially to the House of Alcock for illustrations from "The Postmarks of GB and Ireland" by R.C. Alcock and F. C. Holland (1940). The individual numbers of these illustrations are as published in the 5th edition (though we have revised the numbering in the Sixth Edition and again the Seventh edition) and copyright of these is now reserved by Mr E W Proud of Proud-Bailey Co Ltd.

Thanks are also expressed to "Parsons, Peachey and Pearson" for permission to use their reference numbers in chapter 11 "Slogan Postmarks" and to the British Postmark Society for permission to use, in chapter 12, the reference numbers of "Special Event Postmarks of the UK" by G.R. Pearson. (This permission was granted by Colin Peachey, a previous co-editor of this book, at an earlier date.)

We are grateful to all collectors who have been kind enough to submit ideas and material that has helped us produce the Ninth Edition. The following list may not be exhaustive but we extend our thanks to these and to others who have helped with previous editions & this ninth edition :

Patrick Awcock, Grahame Blackman, Paul Carter, Stan Challis, S. F. Cohen, John Cowell, Michael Dobbs, Keith Downing, Patrick Frost, Dr. Tony Goodbody, Martin Grier, John Holman, Alistair Kennedy, David MacDonnell, Glenn Morgan, John Newcomb, Alastair Nixon, Tony Osmond, John Owen, John Parmenter, Brian Purcell, Paul Reynolds, Mike Roberts, Mark Samwell, Ken Smith, Fred Taylor, The Forces Postal History Society, The Railway Philatelic Group, and with particular thanks to the late Michael Goodman whose contributions have had a lasting effect on successive editions of the book.

Lastly, we express an eternal Thank You to the late Dr. Tim Whitney who initiated this book and produced its first five editions.

Special thanks go to Colin Peachey, who has given me assistance at every level in the production of this edition, particularly in the areas of Special Events, Postal Labels, Machine Marks, Postal Rates and much more.

Bill Pipe
November 2013

Foreword

After the success of the 2011 8th edition, the decision was made to expand on this work by including a whole new chapter on Scots Local cancels and massively expanding chapter 5 on early Irish postmarks. This long overdue chapter revision has been completed to an extremely high standard by David MacDonnell of MacDonnell Whyte of Dublin and Stan Challis, to whom I am extremely grateful for the hard work and dedication shown in compiling this work. At this juncture, I would like to thank Colin Peachey who has proof read this edition and has enabled a number of corrections or adjustments to be made throughout this edition to enable easier reference. Finally, I would like to thank my wife, Claire and children for giving me the time & encouragement required to complete this work.

I would like to dedicate this edition to my new son, George William

BILL PIPE
6th November 2013

Contents

Acknowledgements		iv
Foreword		v
Contents		vi
Introduction		ix
	1. Using this book	ix
	2. How to price a cover.	ix
	3. SID handstamps	x

1	The General Post to 1839	1
	Early Stages of the Postal System	1
	The General Post (GPO London)	1

1A	Free Franks	5
	England and Wales	5
	Scotland	6
	Ireland	6

2	London Local Posts to 1839	9
	Dockwra's Post, 1680-82	9
	Government Penny Post, 1682-1794	9
	Reorganised Penny Post, 1794-1801: Twopenny Post 1801-1839	9
	Receiving House and Country Sorting Offices	9

3	Marks of the Provincial Post to 1839 – England and Wales	27

4	Early Scottish Marks to 1839	78
	The General Post (G.P.O. Edinburgh)	78
	Edinburgh Local Posts (Penny Posts)	79
	Outbounds and District Receiving Houses	80
	The Provincial Post	82
	The Additional Halfpenny	93

5	Early Irish Marks	95
	Marks of the Dublin General Post Office	95
	Dublin Paid markings	96
	Marks of the Dublin Penny and Twopenny Posts	96
	Marks applied to mail between Ireland and Britain (and beyond)	97
	Marks associated with the Cork Mailcoaches	97
	Provincial office markings	98
	Provincial Paid markings	98
	Provincial Penny Posts	99
	Undated and Receiving House marks	99
	Ireland - list of offices	100
	Dublin Town Receiving Houses	118

6	The Great Post Office Reforms, 1839-1844	119
	Uniform 4d Post, 5 Dec 1839 - 9 Jan 1840	119
	Uniform 1d Post, from 10 Jan 1840	119
	Maltese Cross Cancellations, 1840 - 1844	122

6A	Scots Local Cancellations	126
	Types of Datestamp (all lettering upper case):	126

7	Numeral, Spoon and Duplex Postmarks	130
	Basic Prices for London, England and Wales	130
	London: Inland Section	130
	London: District Post and Suburban Offices	130
	England and Wales	131
	Scotland	163
	Ireland	167

8	Squared Circle Postmarks	171
	London Head District Offices	173
	London Branch Offices	173
	London Suburban District Offices	173
	Provincial Offices	174
	London Fancy Geometric Postmarks	179

9	Later Circular Handstamps	181
	Single Arcs	181
	Thimbles (small diameter single circles)	181
	Single Circles	181
	Double Circles	182
	Coded time	183
	Skeletons	183
	Hooded Circles	183
	P/PD (Paid) Handstamps (in red)	184
	Rubber handstamps (from 1885)	184
	Rollers	186
	Paid Handstamps (in red)	186
	Other types used for backstamping	187
	Self Inking datestamps (SIDs)	187
	Dumb handstamps	187
	Charity appeal mailing handstamps	188

10	Machine Cancellations	189
	Pearson Hill Experimental Machines, 1857-58	189
	Charles Rideout, from 1858	189
	Pearson Hill, from 1858	189
	Azemar, 1869-72 (or Fischer and Maas)	190
	Sloper, 1870-75	190
	Hoster, 1882-93	190
	Ethridge, September 1886-April 1887	190
	International, 1893-1933 (or Hey & Dolphin, or Flier)	191
	Imperial Mail Marking, 1897	191
	Empire Machine, 1898	191
	Bickerdike, 1897-1907	191
	Boston, 1898-1907	192
	Columbia (single impression machines), 1901-21	192
	Krag (continuous impression machines), from 1905	193
	Sylbe, 1907-08	194
	Columbia (continuous impression machines), 1909-11	194
	Universal, from 1910	194
	Time Mail Marking Machine Company, 1912-13	194
	Alma or Bee, 1912-22 (continuous impression machines)	194
	Krag (single impression machines), from 1923	195
	Klussendorf (or Standard), 1930-37	195
	Totometer, 1957-90 (used for stamping magazines/wrappers)	195
	Machines for stamping "large flats" and/or packets	195
	Universal-style (unified) postmarks from 1933 - Summary	196
	Computer produced Postmarks on Bulk Mailings, from 1993	197
	Ink jet machines, from 1993	197
	Baumann (previously Klussendorf) machines, from 2003	199
	Towns with Krag and Universal machines from 1933 to 1999	199
	Channel Islands and Isle of Man	222
	London missort marks	223
	Index to 'generic' identities	224

11	Slogan Postmarks	226
	Other categories of slogans :	231
	Further reading :	232

12	Special Event Postmarks	233
	Summary from 1862	233
	Exhibition sites	240
	"First Day of Issue" postmarks	240
	Special Occasions	241
	Philatelic handstamps	242
	Relevant Operational handstamps on FDCs	242
	Mobile Post Offices	242
	Operational handstamps used at events	245
	Seasonal Post Offices (ie summer only)	245
	Thematic collecting	246

Contents

13	Railway Postmarks	249
	Stations	249
	Travelling Post Offices (TPO's)	254
	Routes operating in England, Wales and Scotland	254
	Railway Sub Offices	259
	London Distribution Centre (initially known as the "Willesden Hub")	268

13A	Colliery Postmarks	269

14	Maritime Markings	271
	Section II: Packet Letters	278
	Section III: Moveable Box Marks on Mail to France	280
	Section IV: British Coastal Steamers	280
	Section V: Private Cachets	282
	Section VI: Ocean Going Steamers	283
	Section VII: Paquebot	285
	Section VIII: Sea Post Offices	287
	Section IX: Royal Navy	287
	Section X: Special Events	292
	Section XI: Disaster/Wreck and Salvaged Mail	292
	Appendix - Overseas Paquebot marks	292

15	Military and Camp Postmarks	294
	Section I: Early Wars and Campaigns	294
	Section II: First World War: 1914-19	295
	Section III: Between the Two World Wars	303
	Section IV: Second World War 1939-45	304
	Section V: Post War Operations	309
	Section VI: Camps and other military establishments	319
	Section VII: Special Events	324

16	Aviation	325
	Air Mail postmarks	325
	Special Events	325
	Aerodromes and airports	325
	Second World War	326
	RAF and RNAS Establishments	327
	Instructional and other markings	330
	Disaster or Crash cachets	331

17	Islands	332
	The Channel Islands	332
	Isle of Man	337
	Isles of Scilly	340
	Isle of Wight	341
	Other English Islands	343
	Wales	344
	Northern Ireland	347
	Scotland	347

18	Charge, Instructional and Explanatory Marks	353
	Charge Marks	353
	Boxed T shaped	353
	Rectangular types	354
	Boxed marks	355
	Inland Section and Foreign Section	356
	Charge and other marks confined to mail from abroad (incl Channel Is)	358
	Charge Marks used countrywide	358
	Instructional & Explanatory Marks used countrywide	360
	Multipurpose marks explaining non-delivery, framed or unframed	362
	RLB/RLO Handstamps	363

19	Newspaper, Parcel, Registered, Express and Triangular Postmarks	364
	Newspaper Branch	364
	Parcel Postmarks	364
	Registration	366
	Express	367
	Triangular Handstamps	367
	Inspectors' marks	367

20	Posted in Advance for Christmas Postmarks	368

21	Parliamentary	370

22	Royalty	373
	Royal Residences (some for short visits only)	373
	Other Royal Postmarks:	375
	Royal Cachets	375
	Meters at Royal Residences/Estates	376
	Court Post Offices (modern FDCs)	377

23	British Post Offices Abroad	379
	Ovals with codes C,G,M and S	379
	Ovals/duplexes with numeric and alpha-numeric codes	379
	Postmarks in "clear English"	381

24	Tourist Cachets	382
	Beachy Head	382
	Blackpool Tower	382
	Cranmere Pool and other Dartmoor cachets	383
	Island Cachets	383
	Island Cachets - Channel Islands	384
	Island Cachets - Isle of Man	384
	John O'Groats	384
	Land's End	385
	Llanfair P.G.	386
	Snowdon	387
	Ship's cachets	387
	Other cachets – England	387
	Other cachets – Scotland	389
	Other cachets – Wales	389
	Other cachets – Northern Ireland	389

25	Meter Marks	390
	Early meters	390
	New Frank, 1968	392
	New "bar code" Design	393
	Ink-Jet Printed Meters	394
	Delivered by Royal Mail	395
	Parcel post labels	395
	Wilkinson "Penny in the slot" machine	395

26	Printed Postage Impressions	396
	Alternative Carriers – Condition 9	
	Access Mail	398

27	Postal Mechanisation	399
	Transorma Marks	399
	Other Early Sorting marks	399
	Dots representing postcodes and related idents	399
	Bars from OCR process	400
	Mechanisation oriented postmarks	401
	Glossary of some mechanisation-related terms/abbreviations	402

28	Modern Postal Labels	404
	Horizon Labels	404
	Post & Go labels	406
	Fast Stamps	407

29	"A-Z of Interesting Places".	408

30	Postal Rates	416
	Inland Letters Rates 1638-1839	416
	1832 Provincial Penny Posts	417
	1839-1968	417
	1968-2013	418

31	Abbreviations	419

Bibliography		421
	"The Classics"	421
	"The Moderns"	421
	"General"	423

vii

"You can't beat a night at the Opera"

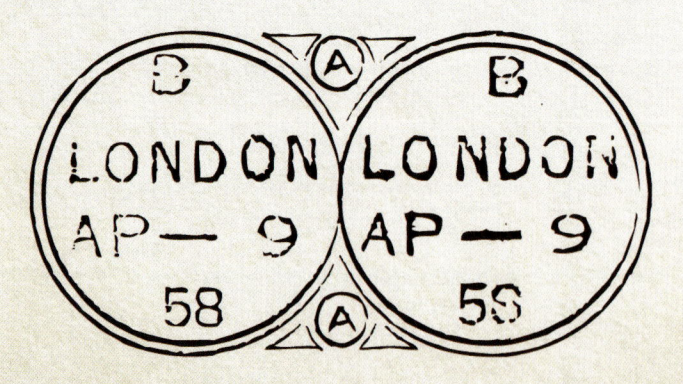

mark bloxham stamps
ESTABLISHED PHILATELISTS FOR OVER 35 YEARS

W: www.philatelic.co.uk   T: +44 (0)1661 871953   E: mark@philatelic.co.uk

Introduction

1. Using this book

In introducing our Ninth Edition, the principle of previous editions remains unchanged, in that the book is designed as a 'Postmarks Simplified'. It can be used by readers with little or no previous knowledge, by the "average level" collector, or by specialists who will find it useful for ready reference or for fields outside their area of specialisation. For the beginner we hope the brief explanatory paragraphs will prove useful. For the specialist we have checked the data carefully, improved it where possible and revised the prices, not always upwards.

It is important to realise that, in many instances, this is a catalogue of postmark types rather than actual postmarks. Behind a single entry there may be several hundred or even thousands of postmarks, varying in value depending on the date and place of use. Even where lists have been given, variations such as punctuation and the size of the mark have been ignored or the lists would be just too long. Thus the price is a minimum for each type of postmark and each price should be treated as though the word 'From' is printed before it.

An important attribute of this edition is the retention of individual listing numbers, whereby EACH entry in the main lists is numbered, not just those that are pictured. Those that ARE pictured have a CBP number in BOLD typeface. We hope thereby to build upon the increased use of "CBP ref numbers" as an "industry standard", used by collectors, dealers and auctioneers alike. In order to achieve this, we have retained the numbers as allocated in the Seventh Edition, and we promise NOT to change them again (unless perhaps a chapter or section receives a wholesale revision) and we acknowledge we will have to use "A" numbers if necessary in future. Numbers remain related to the chapters in which they appear, thus chapter 7 starts with 7/1, 7/2 and so on.

In describing postmarks, where / appears in the list it separates lines of type (though not used universally). All postmarks are in black unless stated otherwise. A postmark on cover may be shown ✉, △ on piece, ○ on loose stamp. The term 'postmark' is used for convenience to describe all kinds of marks applied in the processing of the mails though the function may vary considerably, e.g. cancelling the stamps, giving information, advertising an event, raising a surcharge etc. A cancellation is slightly different in that it is a mark used for cancelling a stamp, thus frequently 'postmark', 'mark' and 'cancellation' can be used synonymously. The term 'cachet' is used to describe explanatory rubber stamps but specifically those that do NOT cancel the stamps. (Note: terminology is different in USA where a special event cover is termed a "cacheted cover").

2. How to price a cover.

2.1 Prices given are generally for clear strikes on a clean card or cover. Exceptions are for parcel marks on "piece", or documents including registration receipts. The latter are worth less than a complete envelope. * (asterisk) denotes "items seldom seen so difficult to value" or "top end of price scale, depends on auction realisations".

Some dealers describe the quality of a mark with a 4-star rating, others attempt more precision by the use of percentages.

Prices stated are for at least Three Star or 85% quality.
- Halve prices for Two Star or 55%
- Quarter prices for One Star or when less than half the mark is clear

Collectors are strongly advised to insist on these standards when purchasing items. Covers in pristine condition or with other attractive features will command a premium above catalogue value. Covers from which stamps have been removed are usually almost worthless, even if with valuable postmarks. "Grubby" or "dog eared" covers, those roughly opened, or those with biro addresses across which the postmark has fallen, are only of one or two star quality and their value is affected accordingly. Accordingly, if you cannot read the postmark, or more importantly, the date, don't buy it!

2.2 Postmarks, in the editor's opinion, should always be collected on full entire, cover or card (or on a piece as large as an envelope in the case of parcel or packet marks).
- Fronts are often worth only one third of Catalogue value.
- Pieces (or 'squares') are worth 20-25% of Catalogue value.
- Loose stamps on which a substantial (at least half) part of the postmark can be positively identified are usually worth only 10% of Catalogue value.

2.3 To assess the basic value of a cover -
- First check the value of all postmarks on the cover in this handbook
- Take the highest value and add to it half the value of other marks priced over £5, ignoring others.
- Then check the value of the stamps in a stamp catalogue. If the market value of the stamp (say one quarter catalogue value) is greater than the postmark then the value of the stamp will prevail, otherwise add a premium to take account of the value of the stamp if above, say, £10.

2.4 One last factor is that of "genuineness". A postal history collector will usually favour an envelope or card that is addressed and appears to have travelled through the mails. A commercial cover, with handwritten or typed address, is normally preferred to a "philatelic" one ie clearly prepared by a collector, and this may be reflected in the price of the cover. Since the discovery & subsequent sale of the George King accumulations, many valuable and very desirable items have been circulated amongst collectors. These "philatelic" covers are an exception to this rule in many cases. "By favour" items, with postmarks stamped on plain unaddressed cards etc., are be viewed with suspicion since forgery is possible.

Introduction

3. SID handstamps

SIDs (Self Inking Datestamps) are now commonplace throughout the U.K., having spread across the country in the 1990s. We do NOT claim to have included them in all the relevant lists of this edition.

> PLEASE REMEMBER: THIS HANDBOOK IS AN OVERALL GUIDE, WE DO NOT PLAN TO INCLUDE EVERY POSTMARK!! SO WRITE TO US WITH VALUES AND IDEAS BY ALL MEANS, BUT NOT TO TELL US ONE POSTMARK IS MISSING!!

All correspondence should be addressed to Bill Pipe, 7, Richard Close, Upton, Poole, Dorset, BH16 5PY. Please send photocopies of any postmark about which you have a query and enclose a SAE or International Reply Coupon if you need a reply.

> 'Please note that the prices given in *Collect British Postmarks* are not Stanley Gibbons' selling prices. Where a specific cancel is priced by SG, it will be found in the relevant volume of the *Great Britain Specialised Catalogue*'

Wouldn't it be nice if you could buy stamps in this catalogue at a price you choose, all guaranteed and no extra premiums to pay?

We've got news for you,

You can ! - plus

You Can Test UPA Free & Take £52 OFF Your Next Purchase

And Usually You'll Have

22,000+ lots to choose from!

You qualify if you're aged over 18 and live in Western Europe, USA, Australia, Canada, New Zealand and have never purchased from UPA before. Request Your Next free UPA Mail-Auction Catalogue today:

www.upastampauctions.co.uk   info@upastampauctions.co.uk

Universal Philatelic Auctions (SG GBPMK OFFER),
4, The Old Coalyard, West End, Northleach, Glos GL54 3HE, UK.
Telephone: 01451 861111, Fax: 01451 861297

AGL

Fine GB Postmarks

Visit our website to view hundreds of fine GB items:
www.andrewglajer.co.uk

Andrew G Lajer Ltd
sales@andrewglajer.co.uk / T: 01189 344151
The Old Post Office, Davis Way, Hurst, Berkshire, RG10 0TR

GBPS   PTS   ASDA Established 1914

1 The General Post to 1839

Early Stages of the Postal System

We include this summary as a brief background to early postal history, and to show the steps that led to the first postal markings shown in the pages of chapter 1 that follow.

Henry I (1100-1135) appointed messengers to carry Government letters. Later, messengers were appointed by Barons, Church dignitaries and others.
Henry III (1216-1272) provided uniforms for King's Messengers.
Edward I (1272-1307) instituted fixed places (Posting Houses) where horses were available for the carriage of letters.
Edward II (1307-1327). The first manuscript postal marking appeared on covers: "Haste, post haste".
Henry VIII (1509-1547) appointed Brian Tuke as "Master of the Postes".
Elizabeth I (1558-1603) appointed Thomas Randolph as "Chief Postmaster" for Inland and Foreign mail.
Charles I (1625-1649) appointed Thomas Witherings as "Chief Postmaster". He set up the nucleus of the modern system with regular post roads, post houses, staff and fixed rates.
Charles II (1660-1685) appointed Henry Bishop as "Postmaster General". Following complaints of delays to letters, the first postal handstamp "Bishop mark" was introduced in April 1661. The "Franking system" also started whereby letters from MPs and others were sent and received free of postal charges.

The General Post (GPO London)

The Postmaster General administered six main post roads which radiated from London to post towns in England and Wales. They were named Bristol, Chester, Kent, North, Western and Yarmouth. Additionally, the Great North Road continued to Holyhead where Packet Boats took mail to Dublin for destinations in Ireland.

Handstamps were struck in London on the date of posting there or on the date of receipt.

Bishop Marks

1/1	London Bishop Marks with month in top section (14mm), 1661-66	£600+
1/2	As above but 1667-1713, sans serif from 1673	£250
1/3	As above but day in top section and larger (19mm), 1713-19	£175
1/4	As above but 1720-87	40.00+

Note: The year can only be determined from contents of the letter.

Later Datestamps

1/5 Double circle type, Jan-April 1787 £225
1/6 Double circle with month, day and year, with or without code letters, 1787-98 12.00
1/7 As above, but with S above for Sunday £600
1/8 New type, single or double rim, 1795-99 8.00
1/9 As above, but year in 3 or 4 figures, 1800-39 5.00
1/10 Coded type, single or double rim, several types, red, 1799-1839. 5.00
1/11 As above but coded S for Sunday £125
1/12 As above but without code for Late Fees £100
1/13 Boxed types for Late Fees, 1797-1839 50.00+
1/14 Sunday stamp, various colours, 1832-39 40.00

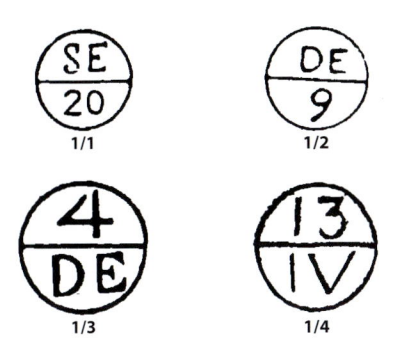

Note: In the example **1/4** I used for J, V for U, thus IV = JU = June

DO YOU COLLECT G.B. POSTAL HISTORY

Are YOU on my mailing list?

I provide a photocopy service of all new stock to clients on my mailing list

New clients will receive photocopies of existing stock which caters for the general collector, the majority being priced at under £100

I have a good range of most GB counties from pre-stamp onwards.

Please drop me a line or phone to advise me of your collecting interests and see what I can offer

BRIAN PURCELL LTD
PO Box 749
WORCHESTER
WR4 0UR
TEL/FAX: 01905 452415

Britannia Albums
The perfect solution for housing stamp from any country

From Afghanistan to Zimbabwe...

Whichever country you collect, the Britannia range of albums contains something suitable for you. The binders are made from the best quality vinyl and come with polypropylene pockets, complete with 160gsm white acid free paper used are top quality products.

Each A4 (210mm x 297mm) page is specifically designed, having a space for each stamp with the date, title, and value of the stamp shown. These albums are compiled using the Scott (rather than SG) numbering system. Binders are available in blue or maroon.

There are over 900 volumes available including single countries, states, used abroad and omnibus issues. If you are looking for something in particular or would like a full list of Britannia albums, please contact us on the details at the bottom of the page and we will do all we can to help.

Please note: Delivery of these items will take a minimum of 21 days and are only printed to order. If you are unsure about the content of these albums, please contact us prior to ordering.

For a list of Britannia albums, visit **www.stanleygibbons.com/britannia**

STANLEY GIBBONS Est 1856

Stanley Gibbons Limited
7 Parkside, Christchurch Road, Ringwood, Hants, BH24 3SH
+44 (0)1425 472 363
www.stanleygibbons.com

The General Post to 1839

Branch Offices

1/15

1/15 Branch offices (with or without PAID) from 1829:

Borough (B)	15.00
Charing Cross (CH, CX or C)	10.00
Lombard St. (LS)	15.00
Old Cavendish Street (O.C.S)	15.00
Vere St. (VS)	15.00

Early Receiving House Miscellaneous Marks

1/16 Send Answer By the Post at the Round House in Love Lane Neare Billinsgate, oval, 1661-63

1/17 The Post For all Kent Goes Every Night From the Round House in Love Lane & Comes Every Mor(ning), circular, 1661-62

1/18 Essex Post Goes and Coms Every Day, circular, 1674-75

1/19 S.X. Post Goes & Comes Every Day, 1675

These marks (not shown to scale) were used to advertise the posts which ran on the Kent and Essex roads. They are very rare and are each worth several thousand pounds. A specimen of **1/18** realised £4,400 at auction in 1989, it would realise £20,000 today.

Receiving Houses

1/20	Initials of Receiver, usually circled, black	30.00+
1/21	as above but red	£175

Surname of Receiver:

1/22	Partington (lower case letters)	£125
1/23	Walter (upper case letters)	£400

1/24 Address with circle or double circle:

Borough	£500
Charles St. Soho	£250
Gt. Knightrider St.	£250
Temple	£250
Tottenham Court Road	£200
Union St. Borough	£500
Vigo Lane	£150
Wapping	£750
Whitechapel	£500

1/25 G.P.O. above Receiving House name:

Finsbury Square	£350
Gt. Surrey St.	£350
King St. Tower Hill	£350
Pall Mall	£500
Wapping	£450
Whitechapel	£350

1/26 Office name within frame, single or double, many types 15.00+

Paid Marks

The General Post to 1839

Early Instructional Markings

1/33

1/27	PD in single circle, 1713-65, black	£100
1/28	POST/PAID in single circle, 1766-91, red	60.00
1/29	As 1/6 but PAID in additional outer circle, 1787-91, red	£200
1/30	As above but two figure year in outer circle, 1791-94, red	40.00
1/31	As above but year in four figures, 1795-1801, red	25.00
1/32	Tombstone Paid marks, single (morning) or double (evening) from 1800, red	3.00
1/33	Large circle types, 1801-39, red	6.00
1/34	Sunday Paid stamps, incorporating S	£125

Foreign Office

1/37  *1/39*

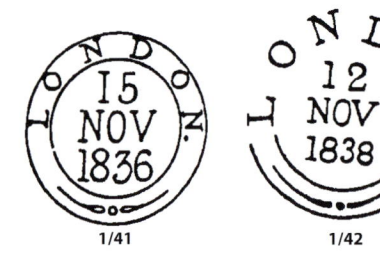

1/41 *1/42*

1/43  *1/51*

1/58

1/43	Addl. ½d, with/without frame	from 10.00+
1/44	British Foreign	45.00
1/45	Crown Inspectors' marks for changes of rate	30.00
1/46	Foreign Paid	60.00
1/47	In All	75.00
1/48	Ireland	£200+
1/49	Missent to London	60.00
1/50	More to Pay (circular)	10.00
1/51	(others)	75.00+
1/52	Not according to the Act	£500
1/53	Not Called for	£250
1/54	Not Paid	30.00
1/55	Postage to London Not Paid	60.00
1/56	Posted after 7 p.m.	£200
1/57	Put in after 6 o'clock	£100
1/58	Put in after 7 o'clock	40.00
1/59	Returned for postage	£125
1/60	Star Inspectors' marks	from 20.00+
1/61	Too Late	from 20.00+
1/62	Wants better direction	£500
1/63	Waterloo Subscription	£750

1/35	Bishop Marks, identical to **1/1** and **1/2**, 1661-1713	from £300+
1/36	As above, also day above month, 1713-97	75.00
1/37	Double circle types, 1797-1806 in black (inward) or red (outward)	35.00
1/38	As above but worded FOREIGN only, 1806-16	60.00
1/39	Dotted circle type, 1816-36, black	10.00
1/40	As above but solid frame, 1822, black	£200
1/41	Double circle, 1836-37, black	40.00
1/42	As above but double arc, unframed, 1838-39	10.00

1A Free Franks

England and Wales

It was as early as 1652 that the Council of State set down rules under which correspondence to and from Members of Parliament and specified Officers of State could be sent without payment of a postal charge. Such letters were known as FRANKS. Initially the local Postmaster had to be able to recognise, from the sender's seal or the recipient's name, the eligibility. Later it became necessary for the sender's place of residence, date and signature to be written on the address panel. Various other restrictions were imposed from time to time, including maximum weight (1 ounce) and daily number of letters received (15) or sent (10).

In 1764 the Franking Office within London Chief Office introduced a FREE handstamp. This was applied to eligible letters arriving or departing London or in transit.

Frank letters were not exempted from provincial Penny Post charges, nor from the London Two Penny Post. Handstamp instructional markings concerning these Posts and other matters first appeared in the early 1800s. They were struck *instead of* a FREE mark.

On 10 January 1840 the Uniform Penny Post was introduced and the Free Franking system abolished. The final date of the FREE system was 11 January to allow for the latest possible eligible posting.

1A/1	Single circle, large F, red, 1764-66	£275
1A/2	as above, but uniform letters, red, 1765-88	50.00
1A/3	Double circle, with stamper's code letter A, C, P or S at centre, brown or red, 1787-92	£250
1A/4	Single circle, with code letter, brown or red, 1789-91	£300
1A/5	Hooded wreath circle, with code letter, purple or red, 1790-91	£500
1A/6	Treble circle, with date & code letter, red, 1791-97	75.00
1A/7	as above, but without code letter, single or double rim, red, 1797-99	£100
1A/8	Fancy Experimental types, with FREE and date, 1799	£300
1A/9	Single circle, crown inside, single or double rim, red, 1800-07	75.00
1A/10	Single circle, crown on top, red, 1807	60.00
1A/11	Single circle, with single rim (morning duty) or double rim (evening duty), crown breaking top of circle, many varieties, red, 1807-39 (see note 4 at end of chapter)	from 15.00+

Free Franks

1A/12	as above, with simple cross below date, red, 1815-39	15.00
1A/13	as above, with Maltese Cross or letter 'E' below date, 1837-39	75.00
1A/14	as above, with letter 'N' below date, 1837-39	£200
1A/15	as above, with space below date, 1838-39	75.00
1A/16	Any of the above, but January 1840	x 2

Scotland

The system was similar to that for England and Wales. However, many fewer letters were routed via the Edinburgh Chief Office and only one FREE handstamp was ever used - during the period 1771 to 1792. Only two handstamp instructional markings are occasionally seen, one of which was used at the Glasgow Branch Office.

1A/17 — TO PAY ONLY D 2

1A/18 — TO PAY 2d ONLY

1A/19 — TO PAY 1D ONLY

1A/20 — To Pay 1d Only

1A/21 — Above Privilege Number (script)

1A/22 — ABOVE NUMBER

1A/23 — Above Weight (script)

1A/24 — ABOVE WEIGHT

1A/25 — FREE / E (single circle)

1A/26 — TO PAY ONE PENNY

1A/27 — To Pay ONE PENNY

1A/25	Single circle with 'E' below FREE, red, 1771-92	*
1A/26	TO PAY ONE PENNY, unframed, black, Edinburgh Chief Office, 1827-39	£200
1A/27	To Pay ONE PENNY, unframed, black, Glasgow Branch Office, 1835-39	£300

Ireland

The system was similar to that for England and Wales. Many letters were routed through the Dublin Chief Office and from there to London, so two different FREE marks may be found on one cover. More than 10 handstamp instructional markings have been recorded, but little is known of them. Readers are invited to send a photocopy of any unlisted mark and of covers which extend the periods of use.

1A/28 — FREE (with shamrock leaves)

1A/29 (two) — Free / FREE

1A/30 — FREE / D

1A/17	TO PAY ONLY D 2, framed, black, 1803-17	£250
1A/18	TO PAY 2d ONLY, framed, several varieties, black, brown or red, 1817-39	30.00
1A/19	TO PAY 1D ONLY, framed, several varieties, black, brown or red, 1817-36	50.00
1A/20	as above, but unframed, 1835-39	£200
1A/21	Above Privilege, Above Privilige Number or Above Number, in script, framed or unframed, black, purple or red, 1797-1830	£400
1A/22	as above, but capitals, black or red, 1819-35	£300
1A/23	Above Weight, script, purple or red, 1814-25	£350
1A/24	as above, but capitals, framed or unframed, black, brown, green, purple or red, 1818-36	£300

1A/28	Single circle, with shamrock leaves above and below FREE, black, 1706-10	*
1A/29	Free, unframed, upper or lower case, black, 1707-84	£450
1A/30	Single circle, with FREE and 'D' (Dublin) below, red or purple, 1769-84	£300
1A/31	as above but unframed, purple, 1783-84	*

| 1A/32 | as above but framed and without 'D', red, 1785-94 | £100 |

1A/33	Double circle, with date and 'DUB', several varieties, black or purple, 1787-1807	£250
1A/34	"Mermaid", single or double frame, several varieties, brown, orange, red or yellow, 1808-14	£450
1A/35	"Mermaid" removed, single or double frame, several varieties, red or yellow, 1813-31	30.00

1A/36	"Shield", several varieties, red or yellow, 1815-32	30.00
1A/37	Double circle with crown on top, red, 1832-35	60.00
	Single circle with crown breaking top of circle, time code letter below year, red, 1835-39	
1A/38	code A - Afternoon	30.00
1A/39	code E - Evening	25.00
1A/40	code F - Forenoon	£150
1A/41	code M - Morning	50.00
1A/42	code * - Noon	50.00
1A/43	as above, but no code, red, 1839	£100
1A/44	Any of the above, but January 1840	x 3
1A/45	Double rim oval with SUNDAY, red, 1820-31	£750
1A/46	Above/Number/Privileged, in red, 1829	£500

Notes:

1. The use of FREE handstamps by the Foreign Branch, other Government Departments and Charities, is not covered in this chapter.
2. During the mid- and late-1830s there developed a craze for collecting autographs by sticking the fronts (address panels) from letters into scrap albums. This has resulted in large numbers of inexpensive FREE FRANK fronts being available for collectors.
3. A detailed, scholarly account, with many illustrations and listings of all known marks is in "Herewith my Frank ." by J W Lovegrove. See bibliography later in this volume.
4. Entry **1A/11** is known with letter "O" below date. It may be counterfeit or may have been used for the "Secret Office of the Post Office".

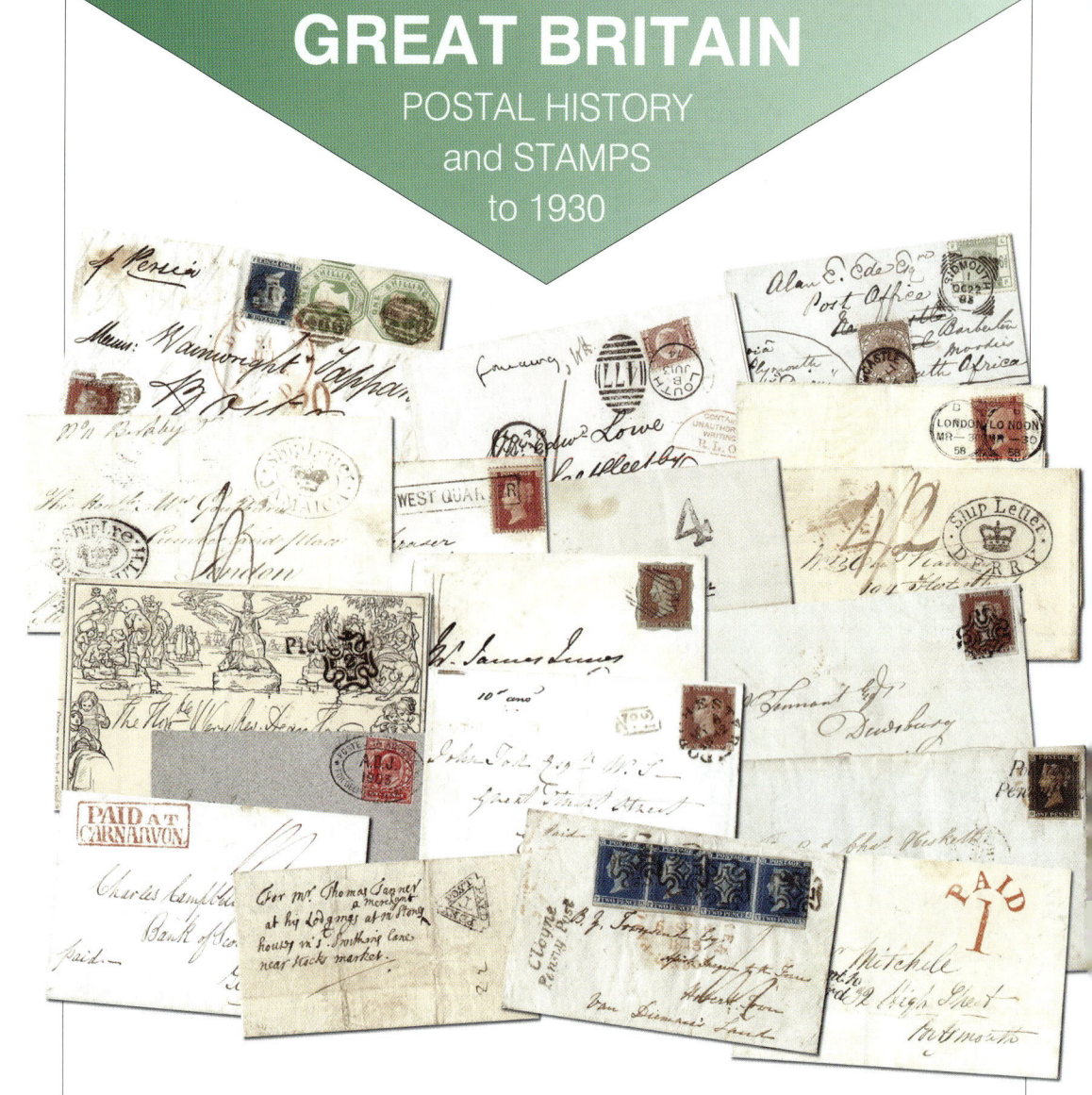

GREAT BRITAIN
POSTAL HISTORY and STAMPS to 1930

PRICE LIST Available free upon request. This list includes selected Postal History from 1300 and Fine Stamps from Queen Victoria to King George V

YOUR WANTS LIST IS WELCOME!

BUYING Collections and single items of Postal History and Fine Stamps

Martin Townsend

Established over 40 years – clients may rely on our reputation and expertise

PO BOX 10, HITCHIN, HERTS SG4 9PE, UK

Tel/Fax: (01462) 420678   E-mail: Martin@MartinTownsend.com

2 London Local Posts to 1839

Dockwra's Post, 1680-82

A private Penny Post organised by William Dockwra for letters within London and its suburbs. Triangular stamps show abbreviations for offices: L for Lime Street, B for Bishopsgate, W for Westminster, P for St. Paul's and T for Temple. Only about twenty-five examples are known, the majority being in archives. In March 1988 an example from the Temple Office sold at auction for £15,400.

Government Penny Post, 1682-1794

Dockwra's post was declared illegal (breach of the Royal monopoly), taken over by the Government and continued until 1794.

2/2	Dockwra-type marks, several types, with office abbreviation and day:		
	B/CH Bishopsgate	see note	
	B Bishopsgate		£400
	G General Office (ie Chief Office)		£155
	H Hermitage		£350
	P St. Paul's		£225
	S Southwark		£300
	T Temple		£275
	W Westminster		£225
2/3	Circular time markings	additional	50.00
2/4	As above but in other shapes (e.g. heart-shaped)	additional	£300

Note: B/CH Bishopsgate valuation "several thousand pounds".

Reorganised Penny Post, 1794-1801: Twopenny Post 1801-1839

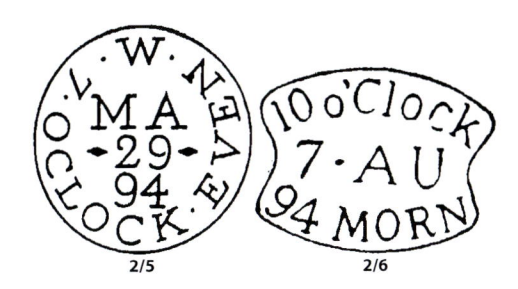

2/5	Experimental circular datestamps, several similar, 1794	£750
2/6	Indented sides types, 1794-1822, red.	25.00
2/7	As above but in black, 1794-1822	£100
2/8	Oval, 1795-1822, red	4.00
2/9	Small oval with double frame, 1824-33, red	4.00
2/10	As above but single frame, 1834-35, red	4.00
2/11	Small stamp with indented sides, 1836-43, red	4.00
2/12	As above but with oval frame, 1836-43, red or black	6.00
2/13	Paid types, red	5.00

Receiving House and Country Sorting Offices

2/14 **A** (with 1, 2, 3, or 4)

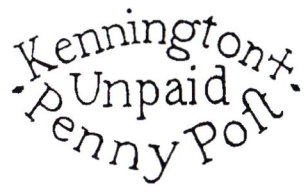

2/15 **B**

London Local Posts to 1839

Penny Post Pd 1d Pentonville
2/16 C

Penny Post Pd 2d Grosvenor Squ
2/17 D

Two-Penny Post Cary St
2/18 E

Two-Penny Pt Paid W.O Chelsea
2/19 F

Two Py Post Unpaid Brompton
2/20 G

Hanwell
2/21 H

T·P Bge St Lambh
2/22 J

T. P. Charles S'West
2/23 K

Fore St 1 py P·Paid
2/24 L

Aldgate 2 py P·Paid
2/25 M

Deptford Bge 3py P·Paid
2/26 N

Hoxton 1D·PAID
2/27 O

Bond St 2D·PAID
2/28 P

Cornhill 3D·PAID
2/29 Q

Devonshire St
2/30 R

PUTNEY EV SP 19 1820
2/31 S

In this basic listing, one entry is given for each district and only major variations in wording are included (eg 8 different offices operated in Oxford Street). Black is the most common colour, thus blue and green are always worth more, red sometimes more. Full details are to be found in Willcocks and Jay.

Many Receiving Houses continued to use their handstamps after 1839. For most examples, values should be reduced to one third.

Acton		
	A	£250
	C	50.00
	G	15.00
	H	15.00
	J	8.00
	K	8.00

London Local Posts to 1839

	M	15.00		K	8.00
	O	8.00		M	8.00
	R	8.00		N	50.00
	S	25.00		O	8.00
	T	8.00		P	8.00
Albany Road	J	10.00		Q	75.00
	N	60.00		R	8.00
Albany St.	J	8.00	Beckenham	G	25.00
	L	8.00		J	15.00
	M	15.00		M	15.00
	R	10.00		N	50.00
Aldersgate St.	A	£250	Beddington	G	20.00
	E	30.00		J	8.00
	F	£125		R	15.00
	G	20.00	Belvedere Place	G	25.00
	J	8.00		J	12.00
	M	75.00		L	12.00
	N	18.00		M	15.00
Aldgate	J	8.00		O	12.00
	L	8.00		P	10.00
	M	15.00		R	10.00
	N	75.00	Berkeley St. West	K	8.00
	O	15.00		R	12.00
	R	10.00	Berkeley Sq.	A	£350
Amwell St.	J	10.00		B	75.00
	L	15.00		C	50.00
	M	18.00	Bermondsey St.	B	60.00
	O	15.00		G	20.00
Aylesbury St.	J	10.00		J	8.00
	M	18.00		R	8.00
	R	10.00	Berners St.	G	15.00
Bagnigge Wells	J	10.00		J	8.00
	O	15.00		L	12.00
	R	10.00		M	12.00
Balham	G	10.00		P	8.00
	J	8.00	Berwick St.	O	12.00
	L	8.00		R	12.00
	M	10.00	Bethnal Green	A	£300
	R	12.00		E	25.00
Balls Pond	O	10.00		J	8.00
	R	12.00		K	10.00
Barbican	J	8.00		O	8.00
	K	8.00		P	8.00
	L	8.00	Bexley	J	8.00
	M	10.00		R	8.00
	O	8.00		T	10.00
	R	8.00	Bexley Heath	K	8.00
Barking	K	8.00	Bishopsgate	A	£300
	N	75.00		C	30.00
Barkingside	L	10.00		E	25.00
Barnes	G	10.00		G	12.00
	J	7.00		J	10.00
	K	7.00		K	8.00
	M	12.00		L	8.00
	N	75.00		M	12.00
	O	8.00		N	50.00
Barnesbury	O	8.00		O	8.00
	R	8.00		P	8.00
Barnesbury Park	R	12.00		R	8.00
Barnet	J	7.00	Blackfriars Rd	J	8.00
	M	10.00		K	7.00
	R	10.00		L	7.00
	T	10.00		N	50.00
Battersea	J	10.00		R	7.00
	K	10.00	Blackheath	D	£100
	M	12.00		G	18.00
Battersea Rise	R	15.00		J	15.00
Battle Bridge	H	18.00		L	8.00
	J	12.00		M	8.00
	L	15.00		N	75.00
	M	12.00		R	12.00
	O	12.00	Blackheath Hill	O	12.00
	R	15.00		R	18.00
Bayswater	J	8.00	Blackman St.	G	12.00
				J	8.00

11

London Local Posts to 1839

	K	12.00	
	L	12.00	
	M	18.00	
	N	75.00	
	O	12.00	
	P	12.00	
	Q	60.00	
	R	12.00	
Blackmoor St.	A	£400	
	B	40.00	
	G	18.00	
	J	7.00	
	L	12.00	
	O	12.00	
Black St.	A	£400	
Blackwell	B	30.00	
	E	30.00	
	G	12.00	
	J	8.00	
	K	8.00	
	M	12.00	
	N	50.00	
	O	12.00	
	R	8.00	
Blandford St.	B	30.00	
	J	12.00	
	R	7.00	
Bloomsbury	A	£300	
	N	60.00	
Bond St.	E	25.00	
	G	18.00	
	J	12.00	
	K	8.00	
	M	15.00	
	N	60.00	
	O	12.00	
	P	12.00	
	R	8.00	
Borough	B	50.00	
	E	50.00	
	G	30.00	
	J	12.00	
	K	12.00	
	O	12.00	
	R	12.00	
Bow	O	12.00	
	R	7.00	
	S	50.00	
	T	18.00	
Brentford	A	£300	
	C	30.00	
	M	12.00	
	S	30.00	
	T	10.00	
Brentford End	H	20.00	
	J	10.00	
	O	12.00	
	R	12.00	
Brewer St.	E	30.00	
	G	12.00	
	J	7.00	
	M	18.00	
Brick Lane	C	25.00	
	E	50.00	
	J	8.00	
	L	8.00	
	M	10.00	
	N	50.00	
	O	12.00	
Bridge Rd, Lambeth	J	12.00	
	R	12.00	
Bridge St., Lambeth	G	12.00	
	J	8.00	
	L	12.00	

	M	12.00	
	N	75.00	
Bridge St., Westminster	E	25.00	
	G	25.00	
	J	12.00	
	K	8.00	
	L	8.00	
	M	25.00	
	O	7.00	
	R	7.00	
Brixton	J	7.00	
	K	7.00	
	N	50.00	
	O	12.00	
	R	7.00	
Brixton Hill	G	8.00	
	J	7.00	
	K	7.00	
	L	7.00	
	M	12.00	
	N	50.00	
Brixton New Rd	J	8.00	
Brixton Rd	J	7.00	
	M	12.00	
	N	30.00	
Broad St., Bloomsbury	E	£100	
	G	12.00	
	J	12.00	
	K	12.00	
	O	7.00	
	R	7.00	
Broad St., Golden Sq.	G	12.00	
	J	7.00	
	Q	50.00	
Broadway, Stratford	G	30.00	
Broadway, Westminster	J	7.00	
	K	12.00	
	O	7.00	
	R	7.00	
Bromley Kent	J	7.00	
	K	7.00	
	N	75.00	
	O	12.00	
	R	12.00	
	T	10.00	
Bromley Middx.	R	7.00	
Brompton	B	30.00	
	G	10.00	
	H	12.00	
	K	7.00	
	N	50.00	
	R	7.00	
	S	60.00	
	T	18.00	
Brompton Row	J	12.00	
	L	12.00	
	O	12.00	
	R	12.00	
Brook St., Grosvenor Sq.	E	35.00	
	G	12.00	
	J	7.00	
	L	7.00	
	M	12.00	
	O	7.00	
	R	7.00	
Bruton St.	O	12.00	
	R	12.00	
Bunhill Row	B	50.00	
	G	25.00	
	J	12.00	
	L	12.00	
	M	12.00	
	O	8.00	
	R	12.00	

London Local Posts to 1839

Cable St.	J	7.00
	O	7.00
	P	10.00
Caledonian Rd	O	12.00
	R	12.00
Camberwell	A	£275
	G	12.00
	J	12.00
	N	25.00
	S	50.00
Camberwell Gr.	B	20.00
	C	30.00
	D	£100
	G	25.00
	J	12.00
	K	25.00
	M	20.00
	N	50.00
	O	10.00
	P	10.00
	R	10.00
Camberwell New Rd	J	7.00
	K	7.00
	L	7.00
	O	7.00
Camberwell Rd	K	7.00
	O	7.00
	R	7.00
Camberwell, Southampton St.	K	12.00
	O	7.00
	R	7.00
Camden Town	G	12.00
	H	12.00
	L	7.00
	N	50.00
	O	7.00
	R	7.00
	S	40.00
Canon St. East	E	25.00
	G	12.00
	M	12.00
Canon St. Rd	J	10.00
Carey St.	B	35.00
	E	30.00
	F	£120
	G	12.00
	J	7.00
	M	12.00
Carshalton	G	12.00
	J	7.00
	N	75.00
	S	50.00
Castle St., Leicester Sq.	G	12.00
	J	7.00
	M	12.00
	R	7.00
Cateaton St.	A	£350
Chadwell	H	40.00
Chancery Lane	B	35.00
	E	25.00
	G	12.00
	J	7.00
	K	7.00
	L	12.00
	M	12.00
	N	30.00
	O	7.00
	P	7.00
	Q	60.00
	R	7.00
Chapel St., Belgrave Sq.	J	12.00
	K	7.00
Chapel St., Grosvenor Pl.	J	7.00
	M	18.00
	R	7.00
Charing Cross	B	20.00
	C	18.00
	D	75.00
	G	8.00
	J	7.00
	K	7.00
	M	8.00
	N	25.00
	O	7.00
	P	7.00
	R	7.00
Charles St., Manchester Sq.	J	12.00
Charles St., Middlesex Hos.	O	12.00
	R	12.00
Charles St., Soho	E	75.00
	G	12.00
	J	7.00
	K	12.00
	M	12.00
	O	12.00
	P	12.00
Charles St., Westminster	G	12.00
	J	7.00
	K	12.00
	L	7.00
	M	12.00
	N	50.00
	O	12.00
	P	12.00
Charlton	J	7.00
	L	7.00
	O	7.00
	R	7.00
Cheam	J	7.00
	R	7.00
Cheapside	G	12.00
	J	7.00
	K	7.00
	M	10.00
	O	7.00
	P	7.00
	R	10.00
Chelsea	A	£300
	D	65.00
	E	25.00
	F	£100
	G	8.00
	H	8.00
	J	10.00
	K	8.00
	L	8.00
	M	8.00
	N	50.00
	Q	35.00
	R	12.00
Chelsea Church St.	N	7.00
Chelsea Common	R	12.00
Chigwell	G	12.00
	H	12.00
	J	7.00
	N	50.00
	S	50.00
	T	20.00
Chigwell Row	G	12.00
	H	12.00
	J	7.00
	L	7.00
	N	75.00
	R	12.00
Chingford	H	18.00
	M	18.00
Chislehurst	N	£100
Chiswell St.	A	£300

13

London Local Posts to 1839

	C	75.00		K	20.00
	E	£100	Commercial Rd	K	12.00
	G	18.00		O	12.00
	J	7.00		R	7.00
Chiswick	G	12.00	Commercial Rd East	J	7.00
	H	12.00		K	12.00
	L	7.00		L	7.00
	M	10.00		O	12.00
	N	75.00	Commercial Rd West	J	12.00
	O	12.00		K	12.00
Circus	G	12.00		L	12.00
	J	7.00		O	7.00
	M	12.00	Commercial Rd, Lambeth	J	7.00
City Road	H	7.00		R	10.00
	J	7.00	Conduit St., Paddington	J	7.00
	M	12.00		R	7.00
	N	30.00	Connaught Terrace	J	12.00
	R	7.00		K	7.00
Clapham	A	£250		M	18.00
	H	8.00		O	12.00
	N	12.00	Coram St.	J	7.00
	S	50.00		K	7.00
	T	10.00		N	50.00
Clapham Comm.	B	45.00		R	7.00
	C	40.00	Cornhill	J	7.00
	G	15.00		K	7.00
	J	7.00		M	9.00
	L	7.00		N	25.00
	M	10.00		O	12.00
	N	30.00		P	7.00
	R	7.00		Q	40.00
Clapham Lower Road	J	10.00		R	7.00
	N	50.00	Covent Gdn.	A	£300
	R	7.00		B	25.00
Clapham Rise	J	12.00	Coventry St.	B	30.00
	N	75.00		E	30.00
	R	7.00		G	12.00
Clapham Rd	J	7.00		J	12.00
	N	50.00		K	12.00
	O	12.00		L	7.00
Clapton	C	30.00		M	15.00
	G	8.00		N	50.00
	N	30.00		O	10.00
	O	12.00		Q	75.00
	R	10.00		R	10.00
Clarendon Sq.	G	12.00	Crawford St.	G	12.00
	K	7.00		J	7.00
	N	50.00		K	7.00
	P	12.00		L	7.00
	R	7.00		M	12.00
Clerkenwell Green	C	£100		N	12.00
	G	8.00		O	7.00
	J	7.00		P	7.00
	L	7.00		R	7.00
	O	10.00	Crawley St.	N	50.00
	R	10.00		R	7.00
Clifton St., Finsbury	J	12.00	Crayford	K	12.00
	K	12.00		L	7.00
Cockspur St.	G	8.00		N	75.00
	M	8.00		O	7.00
	N	75.00	Cromer St.	J	12.00
Cold Harbour Lane	R	12.00		R	12.00
Coleman St.	G	8.00	Crouch End	K	7.00
	J	7.00	Croydon	G	10.00
	M	12.00		K	10.00
	N	30.00		M	12.00
College St., Westminster	G	12.00		O	10.00
	J	7.00		R	7.00
	M	12.00		S	50.00
Collett Place, Commercial Rd	J	30.00		T	10.00
	L	30.00	Croydon Common	J	8.00
	M	40.00		K	8.00
	O	12.00		N	12.00
Colney Hatch	H	30.00	Croydon High St.	G	10.00

14

	J	7.00
	K	7.00
	N	30.00
	R	8.00
Curzon St.	K	7.00
	N	40.00
	R	7.00
Dalston	R	8.00
Denmark Hill	J	8.00
	K	7.00
	L	7.00
	M	12.00
Deptford	A	£250
	G	8.00
	J	7.00
	K	7.00
	M	8.00
	O	10.00
	R	7.00
	S	50.00
	T	12.00
Deptford Bridge	C	50.00
	E	30.00
	G	20.00
	M	18.00
	N	50.00
Deptford Broadway	J	7.00
	K	7.00
	N	50.00
	O	12.00
	R	7.00
Deptford High Street	O	12.00
Devonshire St., Marylebone	B	75.00
	E	25.00
	G	8.00
	J	7.00
	N	50.00
	R	10.00
Dockhead	E	75.00
	G	12.00
	J	7.00
	K	7.00
	M	8.00
	N	75.00
	O	12.00
	R	10.00
Dover Rd	K	9.00
	R	9.00
Drummond St.	K	12.00
	O	12.00
	R	10.00
Drury Lane	B	50.00
	G	12.00
	J	7.00
	L	7.00
	M	12.00
	O	7.00
Duke St., Manchester Sq.	B	75.00
	G	8.00
	J	7.00
	K	7.00
	M	15.00
	R	12.00
Dulwich	S	30.00
	T	8.00
Ealing	A	£300
	G	8.00
	J	7.00
	M	8.00
	N	40.00
	R	10.00
Ealing Common	G	12.00
	J	8.00
	K	7.00
Ealing Town	B	50.00
	C	30.00
	H	10.00
	J	7.00
Earl St., Blackfriars	O	7.00
	R	7.00
East Acton	J	7.00
	N	50.00
East Barnet	G	75.00
	H	30.00
	J	12.00
	K	7.00
	R	7.00
East Ham	H	18.00
	J	12.00
East India Rd	O	7.00
	R	7.00
East Place, Lambeth	K	9.00
	R	7.00
East Sheen	C	75.00
	G	30.00
	K	20.00
	L	15.00
	M	30.00
East Smithfield	G	12.00
	J	7.00
	K	7.00
	L	7.00
Ebury St.	J	7.00
	K	7.00
	L	7.00
	R	10.00
Edgeware	K	9.00
	M	12.00
	N	30.00
	R	7.00
	T	22.00
Edgeware Rd	G	18.00
	H	18.00
	J	9.00
	K	9.00
	M	12.00
	N	40.00
	O	7.00
	P	9.00
	R	9.00
Edmonton	C	30.00
	H	12.00
	J	7.00
	S	50.00
	T	12.00
Elstree	J	7.00
	M	12.00
	O	7.00
	R	7.00
Eltham	C	30.00
	G	18.00
	J	7.00
	K	7.00
	M	18.00
	N	50.00
	R	7.00
	S	50.00
Enfield	A	£300
	B	50.00
	D	20.00
	G	18.00
	H	8.00
	K	7.00
	M	8.00
	N	40.00
	R	7.00
Enfield Highway	G	8.00
	H	8.00

London Local Posts to 1839

	L	7.00			B	30.00
Erith	J	7.00			C	30.00
	L	7.00			D	£100
Euston Sq.	O	12.00			G	12.00
	R	7.00			H	12.00
Euston St.	J	12.00			K	7.00
Exeter St.	G	60.00			L	7.00
Exmouth St.	J	7.00			M	12.00
	M	12.00			N	10.00
	O	12.00			R	7.00
	R	10.00	Gerrard St.	B	40.00
Farringdon St.	K	12.00			C	40.00
	M	12.00			D	£100
	Q	60.00			F	£100
	R	7.00			G	8.00
Fenchurch St.	B	50.00			J	7.00
	E	30.00			M	12.00
	G	12.00			N	12.00
	J	7.00	Golden Hill	A	£350
	L	7.00	Golden Sq.	A	£300
	M	9.00	Goswell Rd	O	8.00
	N	50.00	Goswell St.	G	12.00
	O	7.00			K	7.00
	R	7.00			M	18.00
Fetter Lane	E	50.00			N	7.00
	F	£150			O	12.00
	G	15.00			Q	75.00
	J	7.00	Goswell St. Rd	G	12.00
	K	7.00			H	12.00
	L	7.00	Graces Alley	E	£150
	M	10.00	Grange Rd	K	7.00
	O	7.00			O	7.00
	R	12.00			R	8.00
Finchley	G	10.00	Grays Inn	K	7.00
	G	7.00			O	7.00
	N	8.00			R	8.00
	O	7.00	Great Baker St.	K	9.00
	T	10.00	Great Coram St.	O	9.00
Finchley Common	J	10.00	Great Dover Rd	J	12.00
	K	7.00			M	12.00
	R	10.00			R	7.00
Finsbury Place	E	25.00	Great Eastcheap	K	7.00
	G	12.00			P	7.00
	J	7.00			Q	75.00
	M	12.00	Great James St.	B	40.00
Finsbury Sq.	A	£250	Great Knightrider St.	G	12.00
	O	8.00			M	18.00
	R	8.00	Great Marylebone St.	B	30.00
Fish St. Hill	B	75.00			C	30.00
	E	60.00			E	25.00
	F	£150			F	£125
	G	18.00			G	8.00
	J	8.00			J	7.00
	M	18.00			K	7.00
Fleet Market	G	18.00			L	7.00
Fleet St.	A	£250			M	8.00
	G	8.00			O	7.00
	J	7.00			P	7.00
	K	7.00			R	7.00
	L	7.00	Great Newport St.	L	8.00
	M	8.00			R	7.00
	N	25.00	Great Portland St	C	30.00
	O	7.00			E	30.00
	P	7.00			F	£125
	R	8.00			G	10.00
Foots Cray	J	8.00			J	7.00
Fore St.	J	10.00			M	8.00
	K	10.00			N	50.00
	L	10.00			R	7.00
	M	12.00	Great Russell St., Bloomsbury	B	30.00
	N	50.00			C	30.00
	O	7.00			D	80.00
	R	10.00			E	30.00
Fulham	A	£350			G	12.00

16

London Local Posts to 1839

		J	7.00	Hackney Rd	E	25.00
		K	7.00		F	£125
		L	7.00		G	8.00
		M	8.00		J	7.00
		N	40.00		K	7.00
		O	7.00		M	8.00
		R	10.00		N	50.00
Great Russell St., Covent Garden		G	8.00		O	7.00
		J	7.00		R	10.00
		K	7.00	Ham	C	50.00
		L	7.00		G	30.00
		M	15.00		J	10.00
		O	12.00		M	15.00
		P	7.00		N	10.00
		R	10.00		R	10.00
Great Surrey St.		E	30.00	Hammersmith	A	£250
		F	£125		B	25.00
		G	18.00		C	25.00
		J	7.00		D	60.00
		L	10.00		G	8.00
		M	8.00		H	8.00
		N	40.00		J	12.00
		O	10.00		K	7.00
		R	10.00		M	15.00
Gt. Tower St.		B	40.00		O	7.00
Greek St.		K	7.00		Q	50.00
		R	7.00		R	9.00
Greenford		J	7.00		S	30.00
		O	9.00		T	10.00
		R	9.00	Hammersmith Broadway	K	7.00
Greenwich		A	£300		R	7.00
		B	45.00	Hampstead	A	£300
		E	40.00		B	25.00
		G	18.00		D	65.00
		J	12.00		G	8.00
		K	7.00		J	7.00
		L	7.00		K	7.00
		M	12.00		L	7.00
		N	75.00		M	8.00
		O	7.00		N	30.00
		R	7.00		O	7.00
		S	40.00		P	7.00
		T	25.00		Q	75.00
Greenwich Limekilns		G	50.00		R	10.00
		J	30.00	Hampstead Rd	L	12.00
		M	30.00		O	7.00
		N	75.00		P	9.00
		R	9.00		R	9.00
Grenville St.		G	18.00	Hampton	F	8.00
		J	12.00		J	7.00
		K	7.00		K	7.00
		M	12.00		M	8.00
		N	50.00		O	7.00
		O	7.00		S	50.00
		P	7.00		T	10.00
		R	7.00	Hampton Court	G	£100
Grosvenor Sq.		C	50.00		J	50.00
		D	90.00		K	40.00
Grove St., Deptford		G	18.00		L	40.00
Guildford St.		J	7.00		N	90.00
		K	7.00		R	10.00
		L	7.00	Hampton Wick	J	30.00
		M	10.00		N	75.00
		O	7.00		R	9.00
		P	7.00	Hanwell	G	9.00
Hackney		B	25.00		H	9.00
		G	8.00		K	7.00
		M	8.00		L	7.00
		J	7.00		N	50.00
		K	10.00		O	12.00
		L	8.00	Harrow	J	7.00
		M	8.00		K	7.00
		R	7.00		N	50.00
		S	40.00		O	7.00

17

London Local Posts to 1839

		R	7.00			H	18.00
Harrow Rd		R	30.00			L	10.00
Hayes (Kent)		J	50.00			M	8.00
Hendon		A	£275			O	10.00
		G	8.00			R	9.00
		H	8.00	Hope Town		H	7.00
		M	10.00			L	7.00
		N	40.00			N	50.00
		S	50.00			O	7.00
Heston		J	50.00			R	7.00
Highbury		O	30.00	Hornsey		G	8.00
Highgate		G	8.00			H	8.00
		K	7.00			L	7.00
		L	7.00	Hornsey Down		O	30.00
		M	8.00			R	25.00
		N	50.00	Hornsey Rd		K	7.00
		O	7.00	Hounslow		J	7.00
		R	8.00			N	40.00
		S	30.00			O	7.00
High Holborn		B	25.00			T	12.00
		E	25.00	Hoxton		E	75.00
		G	8.00			F	£125
		J	7.00			G	12.00
		K	7.00			J	7.00
		M	8.00			K	12.00
		N	30.00			O	12.00
		P	7.00	Hoxton New Town		J	7.00
		Q	£100			O	12.00
High St., Borough		J	12.00	Ilford		G	8.00
		M	12.00			H	8.00
		N	30.00			J	7.00
High St., Lambeth		J	7.00			K	7.00
		O	7.00			M	8.00
High St., Marylebone		B	50.00	Isleworth		E	50.00
		E	25.00			G	8.00
High St., St. Giles		K	7.00			H	8.00
		O	7.00			J	7.00
Holborn		K	7.00			K	7.00
		O	7.00			M	8.00
		P	7.00			R	10.00
		R	7.00	Islington		B	75.00
Holborn Bars		B	30.00			C	40.00
		E	30.00			G	8.00
		F	£125			H	8.00
		G	8.00			J	7.00
		J	7.00			K	7.00
		K	7.00			L	7.00
		M	8.00			M	8.00
		N	50.00			N	50.00
		O	7.00			O	7.00
		P	7.00			R	7.00
		Q	60.00			S	50.00
		R	10.00	Islington, Back Rd		J	8.00
Holborn Hill		A	£225			K	8.00
		B	30.00			L	8.00
		C	30.00			O	7.00
		G	8.00			R	7.00
		J	7.00	Islington, Boundary Rd		K	8.00
		K	7.00			O	7.00
		L	7.00			R	10.00
		M	8.00	Islington, Lower Rd		J	7.00
		N	25.00			L	7.00
		O	7.00			O	7.00
		P	7.00	Jermyn St.		G	8.00
		R	7.00			J	7.00
Holloway		H	8.00			M	8.00
		K	7.00			N	40.00
Holloway Rd		J	7.00			O	7.00
		K	7.00			R	7.00
		L	7.00	Jews Row		B	£200
		O	7.00	Judd Place, New Rd		K	10.00
		P	7.00			O	10.00
		R	7.00			R	8.00
Homerton		G	9.00	Kennington		B	30.00

18

London Local Posts to 1839

	G	8.00		P	10.00
	J	10.00		R	10.00
	M	9.00	Kingsland Rd	J	12.00
Kennington "+"	B	50.00		K	10.00
Kennington, Clapham Rd	J	12.00		L	8.00
Kennington Common	K	10.00		M	12.00
	R	7.00		O	7.00
Kennington Cross	G	8.00		R	10.00
	J	7.00	Kings Rd	K	30.00
	K	7.00	Kings Rd, Chelsea	H	8.00
	L	7.00		K	7.00
	N	12.00		L	7.00
	O	12.00		M	8.00
	P	12.00		N	75.00
	R	9.00		O	7.00
Kensington	A	£300		S	50.00
	B	50.00	Kingston	J	7.00
	C	50.00		K	7.00
	F	£150		L	7.00
	G	15.00		M	12.00
	H	12.00		N	50.00
	J	8.00		O	10.00
	K	7.00		T	18.00
	M	8.00	King St., Covent Garden	O	7.00
	N	50.00		P	7.00
	O	7.00		Q	75.00
	R	7.00		R	7.00
	S	75.00	King St., Westminster	B	30.00
	T	10.00		E	30.00
Kensington Gravel Pits	G	15.00		G	12.00
	H	18.00	King William St.	K	8.00
	K	12.00		O	7.00
	N	18.00		P	7.00
	O	12.00		Q	50.00
	Q	60.00		R	7.00
	R	12.00	Knightrider St.	G	12.00
Kensington New Town	D	8.00		J	7.00
Kent Rd	G	9.00		K	7.00
	J	8.00		L	7.00
	K	7.00		M	10.00
	L	7.00		N	50.00
	M	10.00		O	10.00
	N	40.00		P	7.00
	O	7.00		R	9.00
	R	10.00	Knightsbridge	B	40.00
	S	30.00		G	12.00
Kent Street Rd	G	8.00		K	7.00
	J	7.00		M	12.00
	K	7.00		N	50.00
	N	12.00		O	7.00
	P	8.00		R	7.00
Kentish Town	B	25.00	Lambeth	A	£275
	D	£100	Lambs Conduit St.	E	30.00
	G	8.00		G	8.00
	H	8.00		J	7.00
	J	7.00		K	7.00
	M	8.00		L	7.00
	N	8.00		M	8.00
	O	7.00		N	25.00
	R	7.00		O	7.00
Kew	B	75.00		P	7.00
	C	75.00		Q	50.00
	G	8.00		R	10.00
	H	8.00	Leadenhall St.	B	30.00
	J	7.00		E	30.00
	K	7.00		F	£125
Kilburn	H	8.00		G	8.00
	J	7.00		J	7.00
	K	7.00		K	7.00
	R	7.00		L	10.00
Kingsland	B	18.00		M	8.00
	K	7.00		O	7.00
	L	10.00		P	12.00
	O	10.00		R	10.00

19

London Local Posts to 1839

Leather Lane	G	50.00			N	30.00
	J	7.00			O	10.00
	K	7.00			R	12.00
	L	7.00	Long Acre		J	7.00
	M	8.00			K	7.00
	O	7.00	Lothbury		B	30.00
	P	7.00			E	30.00
	R	7.00			F	£125
Lee	K	30.00			G	12.00
	R	20.00	Loughton		H	25.00
Leigh St., Burton Crescent	K	7.00	Lower Brook St.		K	12.00
	O	7.00	Lower Edmonton		K	7.00
	P	7.00			L	8.00
	R	7.00			O	8.00
Leman St.	O	10.00	Lower Tooting		G	15.00
Lewisham	A	£300			K	8.00
	G	8.00			L	8.00
	J	7.00			M	8.00
	L	10.00			O	8.00
	M	18.00			P	8.00
	N	10.00			R	8.00
	R	10.00	Ludgate Hill		C	30.00
Leyton	H	8.00			E	20.00
	J	7.00			F	£110
Leytonstone	C	50.00			G	10.00
	H	8.00			J	8.00
	N	30.00			M	10.00
	S	40.00			N	40.00
Lime Grove	O	10.00			P	8.00
Limehouse	G	12.00	Ludgate St.		E	30.00
	K	7.00			F	£110
	M	9.00			G	20.00
	N	30.00			J	8.00
	O	7.00			M	15.00
	R	12.00			N	50.00
Limehouse Causeway	M	18.00			P	8.00
Lincolns Inn	A	£225	Lyall Place, Eaton Sq.		O	15.00
	G	12.00			R	12.00
	M	12.00	Maddox St.		B	50.00
Lisson Grove	H	12.00			G	15.00
	J	7.00			J	8.00
	K	7.00			L	8.00
	N	30.00			M	12.00
	O	7.00			O	8.00
	P	7.00			R	12.00
	R	7.00	Maida Hill		J	8.00
Little Chelsea	H	12.00			K	8.00
	K	7.00			O	8.00
	L	7.00	Manswell St.		J	8.00
	M	9.00			L	8.00
	N	50.00			O	8.00
	R	12.00	Marchmont St.		G	30.00
Little Ealing	H	15.00			J	20.00
	M	18.00	Marylebone St., Golden Sq.		K	12.00
Little Earl St.	G	12.00			O	12.00
	J	7.00	May Fair		E	50.00
Little Knightrider St.	J	7.00			G	30.00
Little Newport St.	J	7.00			J	9.00
	L	7.00			K	9.00
	O	7.00			L	7.00
	R	12.00			M	12.00
Lombard St.	B	25.00	Merton		J	7.00
	C	35.00			O	7.00
	D	£110	Mile End		G	18.00
	E	25.00			J	12.00
	F	90.00			K	7.00
	G	12.00			L	7.00
	J	7.00			M	12.00
	M	12.00			O	7.00
	N	25.00			R	7.00
London Rd	J	7.00	Milk St.		E	50.00
	K	7.00			F	£125
	L	7.00			G	15.00
	M	18.00			J	7.00

London Local Posts to 1839

	M	12.00		M	12.00
	N	75.00		N	50.00
Mill Hill	B	25.00		R	7.00
	G	18.00	New Cut, Lambeth	J	9.00
	H	12.00		K	7.00
	R	7.00	Newgate St.	G	12.00
Millbank St.	B	30.00		J	7.00
	C	30.00		K	7.00
	D	75.00	Newington	J	7.00
	E	30.00		M	12.00
	G	20.00		S	£100
	J	7.00	Newington Butts	A	£300
	M	7.00		G	12.00
	O	7.00		J	7.00
	R	7.00		K	9.00
Millwall	O	7.00		M	15.00
	R	7.00		R	7.00
Minories	E	35.00		S	£100
	F	£110	Newington Causeway	G	12.00
	G	25.00		J	7.00
	J	10.00		L	7.00
	K	10.00		R	7.00
	L	8.00	Newington Green	D	7.00
	M	15.00		H	12.00
	O	9.00		J	7.00
	P	9.00		M	12.00
Mitcham	S	40.00		N	60.00
	T	12.00	New Kent Rd	J	7.00
Mitcham, Lower	F	50.00		K	7.00
	J	9.00		L	7.00
	O	8.00	New North Rd	R	7.00
Mitcham, Upper	L	7.00	New Park St., Southwark	O	7.00
	M	12.00		R	7.00
	N	50.00	New Road	E	50.00
Mitre Court, Fleet St.	B	30.00		G	12.00
	E	30.00		J	7.00
Moorgate St.	K	7.00		M	12.00
	O	7.00	New St., Covent Garden	E	30.00
	P	7.00		G	12.00
	R	7.00		J	7.00
Morden	J	7.00		L	7.00
Mortlake	A	£300		M	12.00
	C	£125	New St., Vincent Sq.	K	10.00
	G	12.00	North Brixton	J	10.00
	J	7.00		O	9.00
	M	12.00	North End (Fulham Rd)	H	12.00
	N	40.00		N	75.00
	O	7.00		O	7.00
	S	50.00	Norton Folgate	O	7.00
	T	12.00		R	7.00
Mount St., Grosvenor Sq.	E	30.00	Norwood	J	7.00
	G	12.00		K	7.00
	J	7.00		L	7.00
	K	7.00		R	7.00
	L	7.00	Notting Hill	O	7.00
	M	7.00		R	7.00
Mount St., Lambeth	G	12.00	Old Brentford	E	50.00
	J	7.00		G	25.00
	M	15.00		H	12.00
Muswell Hill	J	7.00		J	7.00
	R	9.00		K	7.00
New Bond St.	J	7.00		R	7.00
New Brentford	B	30.00	Old Broad St.	J	7.00
	C	30.00		K	7.00
	E	30.00		L	7.00
	G	12.00		M	12.00
	H	12.00		P	7.00
	K	7.00	Old Brompton	J	7.00
	L	7.00		O	7.00
	M	12.00		R	7.00
	N	50.00	Old St.	J	7.00
	O	10.00		O	7.00
	R	10.00		R	7.00
New Cross	J	9.00	Orford Place	J	7.00

21

London Local Posts to 1839

		K	7.00			R	7.00
Osnaburgh St.		J	7.00			S	75.00
		K	7.00			T	25.00
		N	60.00	Peckham New Town		K	9.00
		Q	55.00			O	7.00
		R	7.00			R	7.00
Oxford St.		B	30.00	Peckham Rye		J	7.00
		E	18.00			N	12.00
		F	£110			O	7.00
		G	8.00			R	7.00
		J	5.00	Pentonville		C	30.00
		K	5.00			D	75.00
		L	7.00			G	12.00
		M	8.00			H	12.00
		N	9.00			J	7.00
		O	7.00			O	7.00
		P	7.00			R	7.00
		R	7.00	Petersham		G	20.00
Oxford & Vere St.		B	75.00			J	9.00
		C	75.00			K	8.00
Paddington		A	£225	Piccadilly		B	50.00
		B	30.00			C	25.00
		G	12.00			D	£100
		J	7.00			E	30.00
		L	7.00			G	12.00
		M	8.00			J	7.00
		N	30.00			K	7.00
		O	7.00			L	7.00
		R	7.00			M	12.00
		S	50.00			N	30.00
		T	9.00			O	7.00
Pall Mall		B	25.00			P	7.00
		C	25.00			R	7.00
		G	10.00	Pimlico		B	25.00
		H	12.00			E	30.00
		J	7.00			F	£125
		K	7.00			G	12.00
		L	7.00			J	7.00
		M	10.00			K	7.00
		N	30.00			L	7.00
		O	7.00			M	9.00
		P	7.00			O	7.00
		Q	35.00			P	7.00
Pancras		H	12.00			R	7.00
		L	7.00	Pitfield St.		E	75.00
		O	7.00			F	£200
		R	7.00	Plaistow		G	10.00
Park St., Camden Town		O	9.00			J	7.00
		R	7.00			M	12.00
Park St., Grosvenor Sq.		B	30.00	Plumstead		K	30.00
		G	18.00			R	40.00
		J	7.00	Poplar		J	7.00
		M	12.00			K	7.00
		R	7.00			M	12.00
Park Terrace		J	7.00			N	75.00
		K	7.00			O	7.00
		O	7.00			P	9.00
		R	9.00			R	9.00
Parson's Green		B	30.00	Portland Sq.		A	£250
		D	£125	Portland St.		A	£250
		J	12.00			B	30.00
		M	12.00	Portland Town		J	7.00
		R	7.00			K	7.00
Paternoster Row		J	7.00			M	12.00
		M	7.00			N	£100
Peckham		A	£350			O	7.00
		C	30.00	Portugal St.		J	7.00
		D	75.00			K	7.00
		F	12.00			L	7.00
		J	7.00			M	10.00
		K	7.00			N	50.00
		M	12.00			O	7.00
		N	50.00			P	7.00
		O	7.00			R	7.00

London Local Posts to 1839

Location	Code	Value
Potters Bar	J	7.00
	M	7.00
Pratt St., Lambeth	E	75.00
	G	50.00
Princes St., Leicester Sq.	O	7.00
	R	7.00
Putney	A	£275
	G	18.00
	J	7.00
	K	7.00
	L	7.00
	M	10.00
	N	15.00
	O	7.00
	R	7.00
	S	50.00
	T	25.00
Queens Elm	H	20.00
	J	8.00
	K	8.00
	L	8.00
	M	10.00
	O	8.00
	R	10.00
Queen St., Cheapside	B	50.00
	G	12.00
	J	7.00
	K	7.00
	L	7.00
	M	10.00
	O	7.00
	P	7.00
Rainham	J	10.00
Ratcliff	J	8.00
	R	10.00
Ratcliff Cross	E	£100
	L	8.00
	M	10.00
Red Lion Sq.	B	75.00
Red Lion St. (Holborn)	K	7.00
	O	7.00
	P	7.00
	R	7.00
Regent St.	J	7.00
	K	7.00
	L	7.00
	O	9.00
	P	7.00
	R	7.00
Regent St., Westminster	J	10.00
	M	10.00
Richmond	A	£300
	B	30.00
	C	30.00
	D	75.00
	E	30.00
	G	12.00
	H	8.00
	M	9.00
	O	7.00
	P	7.00
	S	50.00
	T	10.00
Richmond Hill	J	7.00
Roehampton	J	7.00
	K	7.00
	O	7.00
Romford	J	7.00
	N	12.00
	T	25.00
Rotherhithe	G	12.00
	J	9.00
	K	9.00
	L	7.00

Location	Code	Value
	R	10.00
Royal Arcade	J	7.00
	M	15.00
	N	40.00
St. Agnes Place	G	12.00
	J	7.00
St. George's Fields	J	12.00
St. James' St.	A	£250
	J	12.00
	K	12.00
	L	9.00
	M	10.00
	N	30.00
	O	7.00
	P	9.00
	R	7.00
St. John St.	E	30.00
	G	12.00
	J	7.00
	M	9.00
	N	75.00
	O	7.00
	P	9.00
	R	7.00
St. John's Wood	O	7.00
	R	7.00
St. Martins Lane	J	7.00
	N	18.00
St. Martins le Grand	B	30.00
	E	30.00
	F	£100
	G	12.00
St. Mary at Hill	K	8.00
St. Mary Cray	J	7.00
	O	7.00
St. Paul's Churchyard	B	50.00
	E	30.00
	G	12.00
	N	75.00
Saville Place, Lambeth	J	7.00
	L	7.00
	M	9.00
	O	7.00
Shackelwell	J	7.00
	L	7.00
	O	7.00
	P	12.00
Shadwell	G	30.00
	J	7.00
	L	7.00
	R	9.00
Shepherds Bush	J	7.00
	R	7.00
Shooters Hill	B	50.00
	G	8.00
	J	7.00
	M	8.00
	N	12.00
	R	7.00
Shoreditch	A	£250
	B	30.00
	E	30.00
	G	10.00
	J	7.00
	L	7.00
	M	8.00
	N	30.00
	O	7.00
	P	7.00
	R	7.00
Skinner St.	O	7.00
	R	7.00
Sloane Sq.	B	50.00
Sloane St.	B	50.00

23

London Local Posts to 1839

	G	9.00			R	7.00
	H	9.00			S	10.00
	J	7.00			T	9.00
	K	7.00	Store St.		J	7.00
	M	9.00			L	7.00
	N	30.00			M	12.00
	R	7.00			O	7.00
Smithfield Bars	O	8.00			R	7.00
	R	7.00	Strand		B	18.00
Snaresbrook	C	£100			C	18.00
Snow Hill	B	£125			D	75.00
Somers Town	G	12.00			E	25.00
	H	10.00			F	75.00
	J	7.00			G	7.00
	M	12.00			H	7.00
	S	£100			J	5.00
Southall	J	7.00			K	10.00
	M	8.00			L	5.00
Southampton Court	G	8.00			M	7.00
	J	7.00			N	30.00
	K	7.00			O	5.00
	L	7.00			P	7.00
	N	40.00			Q	50.00
	P	7.00			R	5.00
	Q	40.00	Stratford		B	25.00
	R	7.00			H	12.00
Southampton Row	O	12.00			L	7.00
	R	10.00			M	8.00
South Audley St.	E	50.00			N	40.00
	G	18.00			O	10.00
	J	8.00			S	50.00
	K	7.00			T	20.00
	L	7.00	Stratford S.O.		G	18.00
	O	7.00	Streatham		B	30.00
	R	10.00			G	12.00
South End, Lewisham	E	50.00			J	7.00
	G	12.00			M	10.00
	J	7.00			N	50.00
	R	7.00			R	7.00
Southgate	B	30.00	Sunbury		E	30.00
	G	12.00			J	7.00
	J	7.00			K	7.00
	K	7.00			N	50.00
	N	50.00			O	7.00
South Lambeth	J	9.00			R	10.00
	O	7.00	Sussex Place		K	8.00
	S	75.00			O	7.00
Stamford Hill	J	7.00			R	7.00
	K	7.00	Sutton		K	8.00
	M	12.00			O	7.00
	R	12.00	Swan St		B	50.00
Stanmore	J	9.00			E	30.00
	K	7.00			G	8.00
	R	12.00	Sydenham		G	8.00
Stepney	G	12.00			N	40.00
	J	9.00			S	50.00
	L	9.00			T	12.00
	O	7.00	Tabernacle Sq.		K	10.00
	R	10.00	Tavistock Place		J	7.00
Stockwell	G	8.00			K	7.00
	J	7.00			M	15.00
	K	7.00	Teddington		E	75.00
	M	8.00			G	30.00
	O	7.00			J	7.00
	R	7.00			K	7.00
Stockwell Green	K	7.00			M	9.00
	P	7.00			O	7.00
	Q	40.00			R	8.00
	R	7.00	Temple		K	7.00
Stoke Newington	A	£250			O	7.00
	B	50.00	Thames St.		A	£225
	K	7.00			G	12.00
	M	8.00			J	7.00
	O	7.00			M	12.00

London Local Posts to 1839

		O	7.00		D	90.00
Thayer St.		J	7.00		G	12.00
		L	9.00		H	12.00
		M	12.00		K	7.00
		O	9.00		M	8.00
		R	7.00		N	50.00
Theobalds Rd		B	75.00		O	7.00
Throgmorton St.		O	8.00		R	7.00
		R	7.00	Twickenham	E	25.00
Titchfield Pl.		A	£300		G	8.00
Tooley St.		A	£250		J	7.00
		E	30.00		K	7.00
		G	12.00		M	8.00
		J	7.00		N	30.00
		K	7.00		O	7.00
		L	7.00		R	7.00
		M	12.00	Union St., Southwark	G	8.00
		O	7.00		O	7.00
		R	7.00		R	7.00
Tooting		H	12.00	Upper Baker St.	J	7.00
		J	7.00		K	7.00
		S	£100		P	9.00
		T	18.00		R	7.00
Tooting, Upper		M	12.00	Upper Berkeley St.	G	8.00
		N	50.00		J	7.00
		O	7.00		K	7.00
Torrington Place		J	9.00		M	8.00
		L	9.00		R	7.00
		M	12.00	Upper Clapton	O	9.00
		N	40.00		R	7.00
Tottenham		G	8.00	Upper Edmonton	G	12.00
		H	8.00		L	7.00
		J	7.00		N	50.00
		K	7.00		O	7.00
		L	7.00	Upper Holloway	J	7.00
		M	8.00		M	8.00
		N	9.00		R	9.00
		R	10.00	Upper Seymour St.	B	30.00
		S	75.00		E	30.00
		T	20.00		F	£100
Tottenham Court		E	30.00		M	15.00
		F	£100	Upper St., Islington	H	25.00
		G	8.00	Vauxhall	B	30.00
		J	7.00		G	12.00
		M	8.00		J	7.00
Tottenham Court Rd		A	£300		K	7.00
		D	£125		O	7.00
		E	25.00		R	7.00
		F	£100	Vigo Lane	O	7.00
		G	8.00		P	8.00
		J	7.00		R	7.00
		L	7.00	Vigo St.	P	8.00
		M	8.00	Waddon	J	30.00
		O	7.00	Walcot Place, Lambeth	G	12.00
		R	7.00		J	7.00
Tottenham Court Terrace		E	50.00		K	7.00
		G	12.00	Walham Green	H	20.00
Totteridge		B	£100		J	7.00
		G	30.00		K	7.00
		H	9.00		L	7.00
		K	7.00		N	75.00
		M	8.00		O	7.00
		N	50.00	Waltham Abbey	J	7.00
Tower St.		E	50.00	Walthamstow	G	12.00
		J	7.00		H	12.00
		K	7.00	Walworth	B	30.00
		L	7.00		G	12.00
		M	8.00		J	7.00
		O	7.00		K	7.00
		P	7.00		M	12.00
		R	7.00		N	15.00
Tulse Hill		O	7.00		O	7.00
		R	7.00		R	7.00
Turnham Green		C	50.00		S	75.00

25

London Local Posts to 1839

	T	20.00
Wandsworth	A	£275
	C	£100
	G	15.00
	J	7.00
	K	7.00
	M	12.00
	N	15.00
	Q	£100
	R	9.00
	S	50.00
Wanstead	O	7.00
Wapping	A	£300
	B	25.00
	E	30.00
	G	12.00
	J	7.00
	L	7.00
	M	10.00
	N	12.00
	O	7.00
	R	7.00
Wapping Dock	G	12.00
	J	7.00
	L	7.00
Wardour St.	G	12.00
Watling St.	A	£275
	E	50.00
	O	9.00
	R	7.00
Wellclose Sq.	G	12.00
	M	12.00
Welling	J	7.00
	L	7.00
	R	9.00
West Ham	C	75.00
	G	50.00
	J	7.00
	L	7.00
West Wickham	R	9.00
Whetstone	G	50.00
	R	9.00
	S	50.00
	T	20.00
Whips Cross	G	60.00
	H	25.00
	J	7.00
	L	7.00
	O	7.00
Whitechapel	A	£275
	E	50.00
	G	12.00
	J	7.00
	M	12.00
	N	50.00
	O	7.00
	R	7.00
Whitechapel Rd	G	12.00
	J	7.00
	L	7.00
	M	12.00
	N	60.00
Whitecross St.	J	7.00
	L	7.00
	R	7.00
Whitehall	A	£300
	B	30.00
	C	30.00
	D	75.00
Whitton	H	12.00
	R	7.00
Willisdon	J	7.00
	R	7.00
Wimbledon	B	75.00

	G	12.00
	J	7.00
	K	7.00
	M	12.00
	N	60.00
	R	7.00
Winchmore Hill	J	30.00
	K	20.00
Wood St.	F	£150
	G	15.00
	J	9.00
Woodford	G	12.00
	H	12.00
	M	12.00
	N	75.00
	O	7.00
	P	7.00
	S	75.00
Woodford Bridge	G	12.00
	M	12.00
	R	12.00
Woolwich	A	£225
	B	25.00
	C	40.00
	E	25.00
	F	£100
	G	8.00
	J	7.00
	K	7.00
	L	7.00
	M	8.00
	N	30.00
	O	7.00
	R	7.00
	S	75.00
	T	12.00
Woolwich Common	R	9.00
Worton	H	40.00

Instructional Markings

2/32

2/37

2/39

2/32	Charge Mark 2	8.00
2/33	As above but 3	30.00
2/34	As above but 4	£125
2/35	As above but 5	£225
2/36	As above but 6	£250
2/37	Erasure stamps, stars, spirals etc., overcharge marks	15.00+
2/38	TP rate 2, boxed or unboxed	8.00
2/39	Too late for Morning Post (various types)	£175
2/40	To be delivered by 10 o'clock on Sunday morning (various types)	75.00

26

3 Marks of the Provincial Post to 1839 – England and Wales

Handstamps were struck on letters despatched from or arriving at post towns.

Marks introduced after 1839 are not included. The number of post offices increased dramatically in the 1840s, largely using the sans serif version of type O. Listing of these marks is beyond the scope of this chapter. Towns and counties shown in brackets are given for identification: they do not form part of the postmark. Cross Post marks are excluded.

Values shown in this chapter are not easy to determine. We have examined lists of relative rarity (especially in the County Catalogues of Willcocks and Jay – see Bibliography), dealers' lists and material in Exchange Packets (especially those of the British Postmark Society). Many covers for sale are well below the quality standards which are defined in this volume and for which the prices here apply. We have made efforts to check all the data including archaic spellings, and we show the spellings as they appear in the postmark.

Key to types: (note not all are illustrated)

A	Distinctive town marks, many variations
B	Abbreviated types
C	One straight line, upper or lower case or "script"
D	Divided words, two or three lines
E	Undivided words, two or three lines
F	One straight line, framed by bars, 1720-65
G	Convex or concave arc, 1789-1810
H	Horseshoe, 1789-1801
J	Reversed horseshoe
K	Undulating town name
L	Name & date in two straight lines, 1798–1804
M	Circular undated, with stop
N	Circular undated, with fleurons
O	Circular undated, with single or double arcs and seriffed letters, from 1820
P	Circular dated, double arcs, from 1829
Q	Circular dated, single arc
R	Straight line, mileage below, 1784-95
S	Mileage before name, 1784-95
T	Mileage after name, 1784–95
U	Mileage in horseshoe
V	Mileage boxed beneath, 1801-30
W	Mileage in bars beneath, 1804-40
X	Circular dated mileage types, with or without small circles, stars or arcs, 1804-40
Y	Circular undated mileage types, 1809-28
Z	Penny Post, unframed
AA	Py Post, boxed
BB	Penny Post, boxed
CC	Penny Post, italic letters, unframed or boxed
FF	Fifth Clause Post, several types
HH	Paid At, several types
JJ	Too Late, several types
MM	Missent to, several types
NN	Returned to, several types
OO	Additional ½d, on letters to Scotland, several types
PP	Abbreviated Penny Post, many types

3/1 A

3/2 A

3/3 A

3/4 B AB·N·DON

ALCESTER
3/5 C One straight line, upper or lower case

NOTTING HAM
3/6 D Divided words, two or three lines

BOLTON LEMOORS
3/7 E Undivided words, two or three lines

COSHAM
3/8 G Convex or concave

NORTHAMPTON
3/9 H Horseshoe

SWINDON
3/10 J Reversed Horseshoe

EXETER
3/11 K Undulating

27

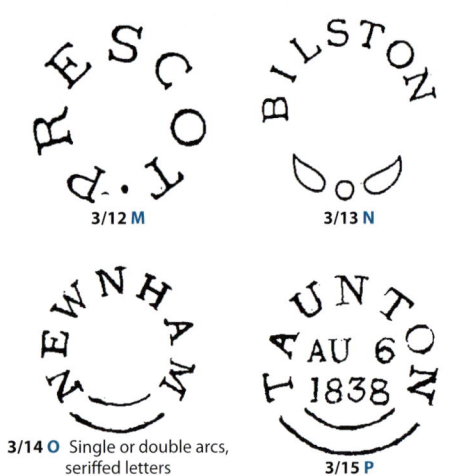

Marks of the Provincial Post to 1839 - England and Wales

3/12 M PRESCOT

3/13 N BILSTON

3/14 O NEWNHAM Single or double arcs, seriffed letters

3/15 P TAUNTON AU 6 1838

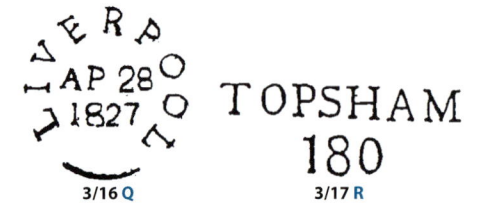

3/16 Q LIVERPOOL AP 28 1827

3/17 R TOPSHAM 180

3/18 S 98 LYMING TON — One or two lines

3/19 U NOTTINGHAM 127

3/20 V MILVERTON 172

3/21 W CANTERBURY 5 6

3/22 X BATH MA 11 1824 109 — With or without small circles, stars or arcs

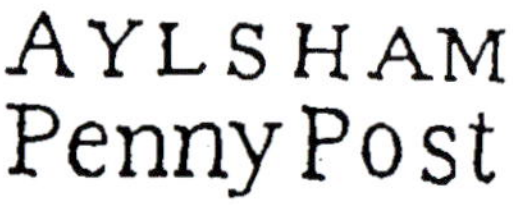

3/23 Z AYLSHAM Penny Post

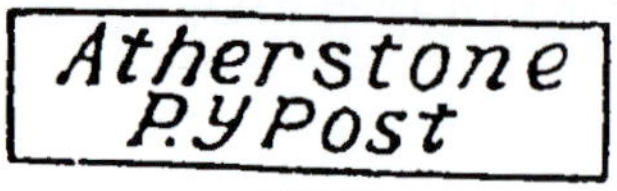

3/24 AA Atherstone P.y Post

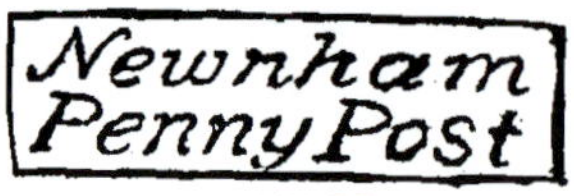

3/25 BB Newnham Penny Post

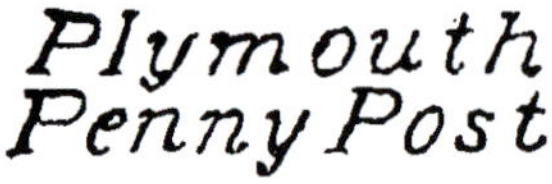

3/26 CC Plymouth Penny Post

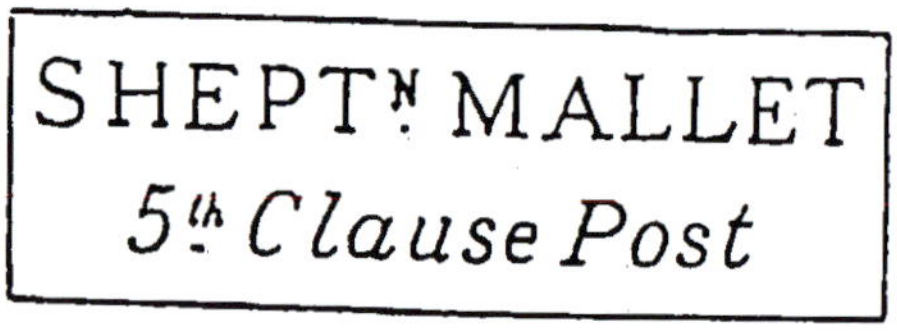

3/27 FF SHEPTN MALLET 5th Clause Post — Several types

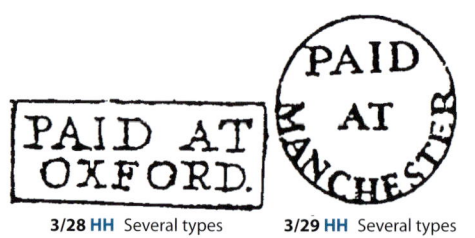

3/28 HH PAID AT OXFORD. — Several types

3/29 HH PAID AT MANCHESTER — Several types

3/30 JJ TOO LATE — Several types

3/31 MM MISSENT TO WARWICK — Several types

3/32 OO Addl ½ — Many types

3/33 PP LEIGH. P.P.

Abbots Bromley	O	40.00
Abbotts Ann	O	60.00
	CC	90.00
Aberayon	W erased	15.00
Aberayron	O	15.00
	W	40.00
Abercarne	CC	20.00
Aberdovey	C	40.00
Aberford	O	40.00
Abergaveney	D	£100
Abergavenney	D	75.00
Abergavenny	D	£100
	H	60.00
	P	8.00
	S	60.00
	V	20.00
	W	15.00
	Y	15.00

Marks of the Provincial Post to 1839 - England and Wales

		Y erased	20.00	Alresford (Hants)		C	40.00
		Z	65.00			D	£100
		BB	40.00			O	40.00
		JJ	£100			P	8.00
Abergele		C	65.00			S	£150
		O	15.00			V	20.00
		V	20.00			W	20.00
		V erased	20.00			Y	20.00
Aberistwith		V	15.00			Y erased	15.00
		W	15.00	Alrewas		C	65.00
		W erased	20.00	Alston		O	20.00
		JJ	£100			Z	£100
Aberystwyth		D	60.00			Z distinctive	£100
		P	5.00			HH	£100
Abingdon		C	40.00	Althorn (Essex)		CC	£250
		D	£100	Althorne		CC	£250
		G	40.00	Alton (Hants)		C	65.00
		O	15.00			G	40.00
		P	4.00			O	40.00
		S	£125			P	8.00
		V	20.00			S	£150
		Y	20.00			V	20.00
		Y erased	20.00			Y	40.00
		BB	65.00			Y erased	40.00
		HH	65.00			Z	65.00
Ab.n.don		B	£500			AA	£100
Accrington		P	6.00			CC	60.00
Acle		R	40.00	Altrincham		C	40.00
		W	65.00			G	60.00
Adderbury		FF	£400			O	40.00
Addingham		C boxed	65.00			P	8.00
		O	40.00			BB	60.00
Addington Place (Ramsgate)		C	65.00	Altringham		C	40.00
Addlestone		CC	40.00	Ambleside		P	4.00
Aigburth (L'pool)		O	40.00			CC	£100
Albrighton		O	40.00	Amersham		C	65.00
Alcester		C	40.00			P	6.00
Aldborough (Durham)		CC	40.00			S	£200
Aldborough (Suffolk)		D	£150			V	20.00
		O	25.00			W	20.00
		V	£100			Y	65.00
Aldborough (Yorks)		CC	70.00			Y erased	40.00
Aldbourn		C	70.00	Amesbury		C	40.00
		W	45.00			P	8.00
		W erased	45.00			S	£150
Aldbourne		O	40.00			V	40.00
Aldeburgh (Suffolk)		O	20.00			V erased	20.00
		P	8.00			CC	65.00
		W	40.00			MM	£225
Alford		C	40.00	Amlwch		CC	65.00
		O	40.00	Ampthill		C	£100
		W	20.00			G	60.00
Alfreton		P	6.00			O	30.00
		V	20.00			P	8.00
		W	8.00			V	20.00
		W erased	8.00	Ancoats/Manchester		E	40.00
Allendale		CC	60.00	Ancoats/Manchr		A	£100
Allesley		O	60.00	Andover		C	65.00
Allonby		O	20.00			G	65.00
Alnewick		C	£100			P	4.00
Alnmouth		CC	60.00			R	£150
Alnwick		C	40.00			V	20.00
		H	40.00			W	15.00
		M	60.00			W erased	20.00
		O	15.00			CC	65.00
		P	8.00	Andover Road		O	40.00
		V	20.00			P	8.00
		W	20.00	Andoversford		O	20.00
		W erased	20.00			Y	40.00
		Y	20.00	Appleby		C	40.00
		Y erased	15.00			H	£100
		BB	£100			P	4.00
		CC	£100			R	£150
Alphington		CC	£100			V	40.00

29

Marks of the Provincial Post to 1839 - England and Wales

	W	20.00		BB	40.00
	W erased	20.00	Attleboro	C	£100
	BB	£100		W	20.00
Appleshaw	O	65.00	Attleborough	D	£100
	CC	£100		O	15.00
Ardwick/Manchester	E	40.00		P	5.00
Ardwick/Manchr	A	80.00		S	£175
Arreton (IOW)	O	60.00		V	20.00
Arrington	O	40.00		Z	£100
	W	65.00		BB	£100
Arundel	C	65.00		JJ	£100
	G	65.00	Attlebro	Z	£100
	P	8.00	Auckland	C	40.00
	S	£150		H	40.00
	W	20.00		O	20.00
	Y	20.00		BB	65.00
	Z	40.00	Aulcester	D	65.00
	AA	20.00		O	15.00
Ashborn	S	£150	Austerlands PP.	AA distinctive	£100
	V	40.00	Aversham	D	40.00
Ashborne	C	£100	Axbridge	C	20.00
	D	60.00		V	20.00
Ashbourn	D	20.00	Axminster	D	£100
	O	20.00		P	8.00
	P	8.00		W	40.00
	V	20.00		Y	20.00
	W	15.00		Z	40.00
	JJ	£150		AA	20.00
Ashbourne	W	20.00	Aycliffe	CC	£100
	Z	£150	Aye	C	£200
Ashburton	D boxed	£150	Aylesbury	D	65.00
	H	£100		G	40.00
	P	6.00		P	8.00
	R	60.00		S	£125
	W	40.00		V	20.00
	Y	20.00		W	20.00
	Y erased	20.00		W erased	40.00
	Z	45.00		AA	40.00
	AA distinctive	40.00	Aylesham	D	£200
Ashby (Leics)	O	65.00	Aylsham	C	60.00
Ashby de la Zouch	C	40.00		D	£200
	O	20.00		O	15.00
	P	6.00		P	4.00
	V	40.00		S	£175
	W	20.00		V	20.00
	BB	65.00		W	15.00
Ashby/Z	D	£150		Z	£100
Ashcott	C	20.00		JJ	90.00
Ashford (Kent)	D	£100	Ayton	CC	65.00
	G	60.00	Backbarrow	O	20.00
	P	4.00	Bacup	O	20.00
	V	20.00	Bagshot	C	40.00
	W	20.00		D	60.00
	W erased	15.00		P	8.00
	Z	40.00		V	40.00
Ashford Kent	S	£200		V erased	40.00
Ashford Kt	C	£150		Z	40.00
Ashtead Row (B'ham)	C	20.00		AA	40.00
Ashton	CC	40.00		BB	40.00
Ashton under Line	P	20.00		CC	£100
	BB	40.00	Bakewell	C	£100
Askrigg	CC	60.00		D	65.00
Aston under L	BB	£150		O	20.00
Athenaeum/Upper Parade				P	5.00
(Leamington Spa)	E two line	75.00		V	40.00
Atherstone	C	40.00		V erased	20.00
	D	£100	Bala	A (circular)	60.00
	O	20.00		C	20.00
	P	4.00		P	5.00
	V	40.00		R	60.00
	W	15.00		V	15.00
	Y	15.00		Y	20.00
	Z	60.00	Baldock	O	40.00
	AA	40.00		P	8.00

30

Marks of the Provincial Post to 1839 - England and Wales

	V	65.00		Y	15.00
	W	40.00		JJ	20.00
Bamborough	CC	65.00		MM	£150
Bampton (Oxon)	CC	65.00	Barnstable	C	£150
Bampton D (Devon)	O	20.00		D	£150
	P	8.00		AA	40.00
	V	60.00	Barnstaple	C	£400
Banbury	D	65.00		D	£100
	F	£100		H	£100
	G	40.00		P	40.00
	P	5.00		V	£100
	S	£150		W	40.00
	V	15.00		X	65.00
	W	15.00		AA	65.00
	X	15.00		BB	65.00
	Y	15.00		CC	65.00
	Z	60.00	Barrow (Lincs)	CC	£100
	JJ	65.00	Barrow (Yorks)	CC	£100
Bangor	C	40.00	Barrow on Humber	C	65.00
	P	5.00	Barrow upon Humber	O	65.00
	R	£150	Bartley	CC	65.00
	V	40.00	Barton (Lincs)	C	65.00
	W	15.00		C framed	£100
	X	15.00		O	65.00
	X erased	40.00		V	40.00
	Z	40.00		W	40.00
	AA	20.00	Barton (Staffs)	C	65.00
	BB	40.00	Barton (Yorks)	D	40.00
	CC	65.00		V	20.00
	HH	£150		W	20.00
	JJ	60.00	Barton on Humber	O	40.00
	MM	£150	Barwick	C	£150
Banstead	O	£100		D	£150
Barford (Wks)	CC	£100	Baschurch	CC	40.00
Barham	O	65.00	Basingstoke	C	65.00
Barkhamsted	D	65.00		D	40.00
	F	£150		G	60.00
Barkley	C	£150		G two lines	75.00
Barmouth	C	70.00		O	60.00
	O	20.00		P	5.00
	P	5.00		V	20.00
	V	40.00		W	15.00
	V erased	65.00		JJ	£100
	Z	40.00	Bath	C	50.00
	BB	40.00		P	5.00
Barnard Castle	D	60.00		R	£150
	W	15.00		S	£200
	W erased	15.00		V	65.00
Barnards Castle	D	60.00		X	20.00
	O	15.00		X erased	20.00
	V	20.00		Z	40.00
Barnard's Castle	P	5.00		Z dated	20.00
Barnby	Z	£100		AA	40.00
Barnd Castle	V	40.00		AA unframed	40.00
Barnds Castle	H	60.00		JJ	75.00
Barnesly	D	£150		MM	£125
	W	20.00		Returned from	£250
Barnet	C	60.00	Batley	O	20.00
	K	£100		P	8.00
	S	£200	Battel	C	£150
	W	20.00		S	£150
	W erased	40.00	Battle	O	20.00
	Z	65.00		P	8.00
	AA	£100		V	65.00
	BB	£100		W	40.00
	CC	£100		Z	£100
	JJ	£125		AA	£100
	MM	£200		CC	£150
Barnsley (Yorks)	C	40.00		MM	£250
	G	65.00	Bautry	C distinctive	£200
	H	65.00	Bawtry	C	40.00
	P	5.00		P	5.00
	V	15.00		R	£100
	W	15.00		V	20.00

31

Marks of the Provincial Post to 1839 - England and Wales

Place	Mark	Price
	W	20.00
	W erased	20.00
	Z	65.00
	Misdirected	£300
B Bridge (Boroughbridge)	C	£200
Beaconsfield	C	£100
	D	65.00
	P	8.00
	W	40.00
	W erased	40.00
	Z	£100
Beaford	CC	40.00
Beaminster	C	40.00
	O	40.00
Beaulieu	CC	65.00
Beaumaris	C	20.00
	O	8.00
	P	5.00
	V	20.00
	W	15.00
	HH	£200
	MM	£250
Beccles	C	65.00
	O	20.00
	V	45.00
Beckington	O	40.00
Beckington-S (Som)	O distinctive	£300
Beconsfield	V	40.00
Bedal	C	65.00
	V	20.00
Bedale	C	40.00
	H	40.00
	O	40.00
	P	5.00
	V	40.00
	W	15.00
	Y	40.00
	Z	40.00
	AA	20.00
	CC	£100
Bedall	C	£125
	D	60.00
Bedfont	O	£150
	CC	£150
Bedford	C	65.00
	G	65.00
	O	20.00
	P	8.00
	S	£150
	V	20.00
	W	20.00
	JJ	£100
	MM	£150
Bedford Place (S'ton)	C	60.00
	O	60.00
Bedlington	CC	65.00
Bedwin	C	65.00
	O	40.00
Bedwin-Gt	V	40.00
Bedworth	O	40.00
Beer	CC	£100
Beeston	O	40.00
	BB	40.00
Belford	C	40.00
	D	65.00
	H	40.00
	O	20.00
	P	8.00
	V	40.00
	W	20.00
	Y	20.00
	JJ	90.00
	MM	£100
Belper	O	60.00

Place	Mark	Price
	P	10.00
Beminster	V	40.00
Benenden	CC	60.00
Bensington	V	40.00
Benson	P	8.00
	CC	65.00
Berkeley	C	£100
	O	20.00
	V	20.00
Berkhempstead	S	£150
	S erased	£100
	V	20.00
	W	40.00
	Y	60.00
	Y erased	60.00
	JJ	£100
Berkhemstead	G	£100
	P	8.00
Bermingam (error)	E	£250
Bernard Castle	D	60.00
Berriew	O	20.00
Berstead Kent (error)	O	50.00
Berwick	C	40.00
	D	60.00
	F in circle	40.00
	M in doub circle	75.00
	P	8.00
	Q	8.00
	R	£100
	R framed	20.00
	V	20.00
	W distinctive Scottish type	40.00
	X	25.00
	X erased	15.00
	Z	40.00
	JJ	£100
	MM	£125
	OO	20.00
Besthorpe	O	£150
Beverley	C	40.00
	D	60.00
	P	5.00
	V	20.00
	W	20.00
	Y	40.00
	Y erased	20.00
	JJ	75.00
Beverly	C	65.00
	H	40.00
Bevois	CC	£100
Bewdley	C	20.00
	F	£100
	G	£150
	J	60.00
	P	5.00
	S	£125
	V	40.00
	W	20.00
	X	20.00
	X erased	15.00
	Y	20.00
	Z	40.00
	AA	20.00
	BB	65.00
	CC	£100
	MM	£150
Bexhill	O	20.00
	V	60.00
Bexley	O	60.00
Bicester	C	65.00
	P	5.00
	S	£150
	V	20.00

32

Marks of the Provincial Post to 1839 - England and Wales

Location	Mark	Price
	W	20.00
	X	15.00
	Y	15.00
Biddeford	H	£100
	V	65.00
Biddenden	C	£100
	O	65.00
	V	45.00
	V erased	20.00
Bideford	C	65.00
	P	8.00
	W	20.00
	W erased	40.00
	Z	£100
Bidford	O	40.00
Biggleswade	D	£100
	O	20.00
	P	8.00
	S	£125
	V	20.00
	W	15.00
Billericay	P	4.00
	W	£100
	W erased	20.00
Billingshurst	O (red)	60.00
	CC	£150
Bilston	C	65.00
	N	£250
Bilstone	O	40.00
	P	8.00
Bingham	C	40.00
	C dated	£150
	O	65.00
Bingley	C	£100
	O	40.00
	P	5.00
	R	40.00
	V	40.00
Birch	CC	65.00
Birchington	CC	40.00
Birkenhead	C	£100
	P	10.00
Birmingham	A (chandelier)	£2500
	A (3 lines inside 21mm circle)	£400
	B	£500
	C	40.00
	D	40.00
	J	40.00
	P	5.00
	R	£150
	S	£200
	V	20.00
	W	65.00
	X	20.00
	AA	65.00
	HH	15.00
	JJ	40.00
	MM	£125
Birstal	O	40.00
	BB	60.00
Bishop Auckland	P	5.00
Bishop Castle	M	15.00
Bishops Auckd	V	20.00
Bishops Auckland	D	60.00
Bishop's Auckland	O	20.00
Bishops Castle	D	60.00
	H	40.00
	V	20.00
	W	15.00
Bishops-Cleeve	O	20.00
Bishops Stortd	V	40.00
Bishop's Stortford	P	5.00
	S	£150

Location	Mark	Price
Bishops Stortford	G	£100
	Y	65.00
	Y erased	40.00
	CC	£100
(see also Bishops Torford below, also Bps Stortford etc)		
Bishopsthorpe	O	40.00
Bishopstoke	CC	65.00
Bishops Torford	D	£200
Bishop Stortford	D	£100
	W	40.00
Bishops Waltham	Y	40.00
	Y erased	20.00
Bishops Waltm	V	40.00
Bissiter	F	£200
Bittern	CC	65.00
Blackburn	C	65.00
	D	65.00
	G	65.00
	M	40.00
	P	8.00
	V	60.00
	W	20.00
	W erased	40.00
	AA	60.00
	BB	65.00
	CC	65.00
	HH	£150
	JJ	75.00
	MM	£150
Blackpool	V	60.00
	CC	40.00
Blackwater	O	60.00
	CC	65.00
Blackwood	CC	20.00
Blakeney	O	20.00
Blandford	C	40.00
	D	45.00
	J	75.00
	P	5.00
	S	£125
	V	20.00
	W	15.00
	Z	20.00
	Z dated	20.00
	JJ	75.00
	MM	£125
Bletchingley	W	65.00
Bletchingly	C	40.00
Blockley	O	20.00
Blofield	CC	40.00
Bloxwich	O	60.00
Blyth	CC	60.00
Bocking	G	£200
Bodedern	CC	40.00
Bodmin	C	40.00
	O	60.00
	P	5.00
	V	40.00
	W	40.00
	Y	20.00
Bognor	C	65.00
	P	10.00
Bolingbroke	V	65.00
	V erased	65.00
Bollington	CC	£100
Bolton	C	£100
	P	8.00
	V	20.00
	X	20.00
	Z	65.00
	JJ oval	£150
Bolton-Le-Moors	E	40.00
	O distinctive	£350

33

Marks of the Provincial Post to 1839 - England and Wales

Place	Mark	Price
Bolton-Le-Sands	CC	60.00
Bookend	CC	£100
Bootle (Cumberland)	C	40.00
	O	20.00
	CC	65.00
Bootle (L'pool)	N	£300
	O	20.00
	CC	60.00
Boreham (Sussex)	C	£100
	O	40.00
Borobridge	P	5.00
	W	15.00
Boroughbridge	D	40.00
	H	40.00
	V	20.00
	W	15.00
Borrough Bridg	D	£150
Boscastle	O	65.00
Boston	C	65.00
	P	6.00
	R	20.00
	S	£120
	W	20.00
	X	20.00
	Z	£100
Botesdale	BB	£100
Botley	CC	40.00
Bourn	C	65.00
	S	£100
	V	40.00
	W	40.00
Bourne	O	40.00
	Y	40.00
	Y erased	40.00
Bournmouth	CC	65.00
Bowes	O	40.00
Bowness	CC	65.00
Boxford	C	£100
	D	£150
	V	60.00
	W	40.00
Bozeat	C	65.00
	V	£100
Bps Auckland	V	20.00
Bps Stortford	Z	40.00
	AA	65.00
	MM	£250
Bp Stortford	D	£150
Brackley	C	£100
	F	£200
	O	20.00
	Q	5.00
	S	£250
	V	40.00
	W	20.00
	W erased	8.00
Bracknell	G	60.00
	O	20.00
	P	10.00
	W	20.00
Bradford-W (Wilts)	C	65.00
	D	60.00
	Q	10.00
	S	£125
	V	40.00
	Y	20.00
	BB	65.00
Bradford-Wilts	P	8.00
Bradford (Yorks)	C	40.00
	D	£125
	W	15.00
	HH	20.00
	MM	£125
Bradford Y	C	40.00
	D	40.00
	P	5.00
	V	20.00
	W	15.00
Bradford Yorks	P	5.00
	AA	60.00
	BB	65.00
	JJ	20.00
	MM	£300
Bradwell	V	£100
	CC	£100
Brailes	O	20.00
Braintree	C	£100
	P	10.00
	V	£100
	W	40.00
	Y	60.00
	Z	40.00
	AA	£100
	BB	£100
Braintrie	D	£200
Braintry	C	£200
Bramfordspeke	CC	£100
Bramham	O	40.00
Brampton (Cumbd)	P	5.00
	W	20.00
	W erased	20.00
Brancaster	CC	40.00
Brandon	C	65.00
	P	10.00
	V	40.00
	W	20.00
	W erased	40.00
Brannston	C	£100
Brasted	O	40.00
Brecknock	C	20.00
	D	60.00
	V	20.00
	W	20.00
Brecknock.L	M (double circ)	£150
Brecon	C	15.00
	O	8.00
	P	5.00
	Y	20.00
	CC	60.00
	JJ	60.00
Breewood	C	60.00
	O	60.00
Brenchley	O	60.00
	CC	60.00
Brentwood	C	£100
	G	60.00
	P	8.00
	S	£200
	V	60.00
	W	60.00
	Y	40.00
	Y erased	20.00
Brereton	C	£200
Bridgend	H	£150
	O	20.00
	P	5.00
	V	40.00
	W	15.00
Bridgenorth	D	40.00
	O	40.00
	P	5.00
	S	£100
Bri.water	B	£200
Bridgewater	C	60.00
	D	40.00
	P	5.00
	S	£125
	V	40.00

34

Marks of the Provincial Post to 1839 - England and Wales

	W	40.00
	Y	40.00
	Y erased	40.00
	Z	40.00
	AA	40.00
	BB	40.00
	CC	40.00
	JJ	£100
	MM	£125
Bridgnorth	C	60.00
	D	60.00
	O	40.00
	V	20.00
	W	15.00
	Y	20.00
	Y erased	20.00
Bridgwater	D	£100
Bridlington	D	65.00
	M	40.00
	O	40.00
	Q	5.00
	V	20.00
	W	20.00
	W erased	20.00
Bridport	C	25.00
	D	£150
	P	5.00
	R (lower case)	£600
	S	£125
	V	20.00
	W	20.00
	Z	40.00
Brierley Hill (Birm'ham)	E	20.00
Brigg	C	60.00
	O	20.00
	P	8.00
	V	40.00
	W	20.00
	W erased	40.00
	BB	60.00
Brighouse	O	40.00
	BB	40.00
Brighthelmstone	D	£100
	G	£100
	S	£220
Brighton	C	£100
	G	65.00
	P	5.00
	Q	5.00
	V	40.00
	W	20.00
	X	15.00
	Z	60.00
	BB	20.00
	CC	65.00
	JJ	£100
	MM	£250
	NN	£200
Bristol	A (capital 'B')	£200
	A (double circle)	£1500
	A (dotted circle)	£175
	C	40.00
	J	£100
	K	65.00
	L	40.00
	P	5.00
	Q	5.00
	S	£200
	V	65.00
	X	20.00
	Z	65.00
	Z dated	20.00
	AA	65.00
	FF	£200

	HH	25.00
	JJ	50.00
	MM	£125
	OO Add half	£300
Bristol St (Birmingham)	C	40.00
Brittell Lane	CC	65.00
Brixham	H	£100
	M	65.00
	P	10.00
	V	60.00
	W	65.00
	Y	40.00
Broadclist	CC	60.00
Broadstairs	N	£500
Broadwas	O	20.00
Broadway	C	65.00
	O	15.00
	P	5.00
	S	£150
	V	40.00
	W	20.00
	X undated	20.00
Brockley (Bristol)	CC	75.00
Bromley	D	£200
	G	65.00
	K	65.00
	O	20.00
	R	£150
	V	20.00
	W	20.00
	W erased	40.00
	BB	£100
Bromley K (Kent)	S	£150
Bromsgrove	D	40.00
Bromyard	C	£100
	D	£150
	J	£100
	O	20.00
	P	8.00
	V	40.00
	Y	40.00
Brooke	CC	£100
Brookland	O	75.00
Broomsgrove	D	40.00
	O	15.00
	P	5.00
	S	£125
	W	40.00
	Y	20.00
	Z	£150
	CC	£100
Broomyard	C	£100
Broseley	C	65.00
	O	20.00
Brough (W'morland)	C	40.00
	O	20.00
	V	20.00
	W	20.00
	W erased	15.00
Broughton (Cumberland)	C	40.00
Broughton (Hants)	O	60.00
	P	10.00
	CC	40.00
Broughton in Furness	O	20.00
Broyntliss	O	40.00
Bruton	C	60.00
	O	40.00
	V	40.00
	W	40.00
Brynmaur	O	40.00
Brynnllis	O	60.00
Bubwith	O	40.00
Buckden	V	40.00
	W	65.00

35

Marks of the Provincial Post to 1839 - England and Wales

Location	Mark	Price	Location	Mark	Price
Buckingham	D	£100		W (erased)	20.00
	F	£200		Z	£100
	P	5.00	Bury Lanc	Q	8.00
	S	£150	Bury Lancashire	Z	60.00
	V	20.00	Bury Lancr	AA	£100
	W	20.00	Bury.S	H	60.00
	W erased	40.00	Bury (Suffolk)	C	£100
	CC	£100		G	60.00
Builth	H	65.00		H	60.00
	O	15.00	Bury St E	V	60.00
	P	8.00	Bury St.Edmds	Z	60.00
	V	20.00	Bury St Edmonds	Q	10.00
	W	20.00		V	60.00
Bungay	C	65.00		W	40.00
	P	8.00	Bury St.Edms	W	40.00
	S	£200	Bury St Edmunds	D	£100
	V	65.00		Q	5.00
	W	40.00		S	£175
	W erased	20.00		W	40.00
Bungey	C	£150		BB three line	£125
Buntingford	G	£100		CC	£100
	P	10.00		MM	£200
	W	40.00	Bushey	CC	£100
	W erased	60.00	Buxted	CC	£150
Burford	C	20.00	Buxton	C	75.00
	D	65.00		O	20.00
	P	5.00		P	8.00
	V	15.00		V	20.00
	V erased	40.00		W	60.00
	HH	£250		MM	£250
Burley	CC	65.00	Caemarthen	D	20.00
Burnham (Berks)	CC	65.00	Caernarvon	P	5.00
Burnham (Nfk)	C	£100	Caerphilly	C	40.00
	D	60.00		CC	£100
	O	40.00	Caistor-L (Lincs)	O	65.00
	V	40.00		V	40.00
	W	65.00		Y inside circle	65.00
	BB	£100	Calderbridge	CC	65.00
Burnham-Somst	O	40.00	Callington	C	40.00
Burnley	C	60.00		P	5.00
	H	60.00		V	20.00
	P	6.00		Y	20.00
	V	40.00		Y erased	20.00
	W	40.00		CC	60.00
	Y	40.00	Calne	C	40.00
	JJ fancy	£300		O	40.00
Burntwood (Essex)	D	£200		P	20.00
Bursledon	CC	65.00		S	£150
Burslem	O	40.00		V	20.00
Burton (Staffs)	C	65.00		V erased	20.00
	Z	65.00	Calverly (T.Wells)	O	40.00
Burton-K (Westm'd)	H	40.00	Cambourn	C	60.00
Burton-L	C	£100	Cambourne	C	20.00
Burton on T (Staffs)	V	40.00		P	5.00
	W	20.00		AA	60.00
Burton on Trent	D	40.00		CC	40.00
	P one arc	5.00	Cambridg	C	£200
	S	£150	Cambridge	C	40.00
	W	20.00		D	40.00
	W erased	20.00		G	20.00
	JJ	£100		P	5.00
Burton-OT (Staffs)	V	60.00		Q	5.00
Burton-W (Westm'd)	M	40.00		R	40.00
	O	20.00		S	£125
	P	8.00		V	40.00
	Y	20.00		W	8.00
	Y erased	15.00		X	8.00
Burwarton	CC	65.00		Y	8.00
Burwash	CC	65.00		BB	£100
Burwaston	CC (error)	£250	Cambridge Gloucr	CC	60.00
Bury (Lancs)	C	65.00	Camden (Glos)	C	£150
Bury.L. (Lancs)	R distinctive	60.00		P	8.00
	V	40.00		X undated	40.00
	W	40.00		X erased	20.00

36

Marks of the Provincial Post to 1839 - England and Wales

Place	Mark	Price	Place	Mark	Price
	CC	£100		W	15.00
	LL	40.00		W erased	20.00
Camelford	C	65.00		AA	40.00
	D	65.00		HH	£200
	O	15.00		JJ	40.00
	P	5.00	Carnforth	CC	60.00
	W	40.00	Carrig-y-Druidion	C	40.00
	Y	20.00	Castle Ashby	D	£200
	Y erased	40.00	Castle Bromwich (Birm'ham)	E	40.00
Cannock	O	60.00	Castle Cary	C	40.00
Can Office (Mont)	Q undated	75.00		D	40.00
Canterbury	C	60.00		O	40.00
	D	40.00		S	£200
	G	40.00		V	60.00
	H	40.00		AA	40.00
	P	8.00		AA erased	£100
	S	£100	Castle Eden	C	60.00
	V	20.00		O	15.00
	W	15.00	Castle Rising	C	20.00
	X	15.00		CC	40.00
	X erased	15.00	Castleton	C	60.00
	AA	40.00	Castleton-Derbys	O	60.00
	CC	60.00	Castletown (IOM)	D	£800
Cardif	C	£150	Castletown Isle of Man	A boxed	£800
Cardiff	C	20.00	Catterick	C	60.00
	D	£100		D	60.00
	H	40.00		P	5.00
	K	40.00		W	40.00
	P	4.00		Y	20.00
	V	15.00		Y erased	20.00
	W	20.00	Catterrick	V	40.00
	X	15.00	Catton	CC	£100
	AA	20.00	Cave N/224	V	40.00
	JJ	40.00	Cave S/224	V	40.00
	MM	£200	Cavendish Bridge	V	60.00
Cardigan	C	40.00	Caxton	B	£200
	P	8.00		C	£150
	V	15.00		O	40.00
	Y	20.00		P	10.00
	Y erased	15.00		S	£220
Carleon	O	15.00		V	60.00
	W	40.00		V erased	£100
	W erased	40.00	Cefn Bedd	C	65.00
Carlisle	C	40.00	Cefn Bychan	C	£100
	D	60.00	Cemmes	C	40.00
	H	40.00	Chaddesley	C	£100
	M	60.00	Chagford	CC	60.00
	P	5.00	Chalford (Glos)	O	40.00
	R	60.00		P	10.00
	U distinctive Scottish type	65.00		AA	40.00
				CC	£100
	V	40.00	Chapel in Frith	D	40.00
	W	20.00	Chapel in Le Frith	O	60.00
	X	15.00	Chapel Le Frith	C	20.00
	X erased	15.00	Chard	C	60.00
	JJ	£150		O	20.00
	MM	£200		P	5.00
	OO	15.00		S	£120
Carlisle St (Hull)	C	40.00		W	20.00
Carlton on Trent	O	40.00		Y	20.00
Carmarthen	C	20.00		Y erased	20.00
	D	20.00		AA	60.00
	H	40.00		CC	60.00
	P	5.00		JJ	60.00
	Q	8.00	Charing	C	40.00
	V	20.00		O	40.00
	W	20.00		V	40.00
	X	15.00		W	40.00
	BB	40.00	Charlton Kings	O	20.00
	MM	£300	Charmouth	C	25.00
Carnarvon	C	40.00		O	40.00
	D	60.00		P	5.00
	P	5.00	Chartham	CC	60.00
	V	20.00	Chatham	C	40.00

37

Marks of the Provincial Post to 1839 - England and Wales

		G	40.00		JJ	40.00
		P	5.00		MM	£150
		V	15.00	Chesterfeild (error)	D	£300
		W	15.00	Chesterfield	C	60.00
Chatteris		C	£150		D	65.00
		O	40.00		G	65.00
		P	6.00		P	5.00
		V	£100		V	20.00
		W	40.00		W	40.00
		W erased	40.00		X	40.00
Cheadle (Cheshire)		O	60.00		X erased	40.00
		BB	£100	Chester le Street	C	60.00
Cheadle (Staffs)		C	60.00		M	15.00
		H	£100		P	5.00
		P	8.00	Chichester	C	60.00
		R	£100		D	60.00
		V	40.00		F	£200
		V erased	40.00		G	65.00
		W	20.00		P	5.00
Cheetham Hill (M'ter)		PP (distinctive)	£200		S	£200
Chelmsford		C	60.00		V	60.00
		D	60.00		W	£100
		G	60.00		X	15.00
		H	60.00		Z	40.00
		P	5.00		AA	£100
		S	£120		BB	40.00
		V	40.00		CC	40.00
		W	20.00		JJ	£100
		Y	60.00		MM	£200
		Y erased	20.00		NN	£250
		Z	£100	Chilbolton	CC	65.00
		CC	£100	Chilham	CC	65.00
		HH	£200	Chimley	D (distinctive)	£220
		MM	£200	Chip.nham	R	£300
		NN	£300	Chip-Norton	W	£100
		PP "Forward From"	£250	Chippenham	C	40.00
Chelmsford/D29		V	£150		D	40.00
Cheltenham		D	40.00		P	5.00
		P	5.00		S	60.00
		S	£120		V	20.00
		V	20.00		W	15.00
		W	40.00		Y	20.00
		X	15.00		Y erased	20.00
		X erased	15.00		Z	60.00
		AA	40.00		AA	65.00
		BB	20.00		CC	40.00
		JJ	50.00		MM	£150
		MM	£150	Chipping Norton	D	60.00
Chepstow		C	20.00		G	60.00
		J	£100		O	15.00
		P	5.00		P	5.00
		V	15.00		V	40.00
		W	15.00		W	15.00
		Y	40.00	Chipping Ongar	O	40.00
		BB	40.00		P	5.00
Chertsey		P	8.00	Chipping Sodbury	O	20.00
		V	20.00	Chirk	C	40.00
		CC	£100		C boxed	40.00
		MM	£225		AA	40.00
Chesham		C	60.00	Chobham	O	60.00
		G	60.00		CC	£100
		V	40.00	Chorley	C	60.00
		V erased	40.00		G	60.00
Chester		A (capital 'C')	£450		O	40.00
		C	40.00		P	5.00
		D	£100		V	60.00
		H	40.00		JJ	£100
		L	60.00	Christchurch	D	60.00
		P	5.00		O	40.00
		R	£100		P	5.00
		V	60.00		V	40.00
		X	15.00		V erased	40.00
		BB	40.00		CC three line	£100
		CC	65.00	Chudleigh	C	£100

38

Marks of the Provincial Post to 1839 - England and Wales

Town	Mark	Price
	D	£100
	K	£100
	P	5.00
	V	60.00
	W	40.00
	W erased	40.00
	Z	60.00
	AA	£100
	CC	65.00
Chumleigh	P	10.00
	V	40.00
	Y	60.00
	Y erased	60.00
Church Stoke	O	60.00
Church Stretton	D	60.00
	V	15.00
Cirencester	D	40.00
	V	20.00
	W	20.00
	Y	20.00
	Y erased	15.00
	BB	60.00
Clare	G	£100
	P	5.00
	W	40.00
	W erased	£100
Clay	O	40.00
	W	60.00
Claydon	CC	£100
Cleckheaton	O	40.00
	BB	60.00
Clenchwarton	CC	£100
Cleobury	CC	40.00
Cleveland Inn	W	60.00
	W erased	60.00
Clifton (Bristol)	O	15.00
Clithero	H	60.00
	P	10.00
	V	60.00
	W	40.00
	W erased	20.00
Clitheroe	P	5.00
Clynnog	N	£500
Coatham Mundeville	CC	£100
Cobham (Surrey)	C	£100
	O	60.00
	V	60.00
	W	60.00
Cobridge Staffs	O	40.00
Cockermouth	C	40.00
	D	60.00
	H	40.00
	M	40.00
	O	20.00
	P	5.00
	S	£150
	V	20.00
	W	15.00
	Y	15.00
	Y erased	40.00
Coddenham	C	£100
Colchester	C	40.00
	D	£100
	G	60.00
	H	£100
	P	5.00
	S	£175
	V	40.00
	W	20.00
	X	8.00
	X erased	8.00
	Z	20.00
	AA	20.00
	CC	20.00

Town	Mark	Price
	NN	£200
Cold Blow	Y	75.00
Colebrooke	D	60.00
Coleford	AA	40.00
	BB	40.00
	HH	60.00
	MM	£200
Coleshill	C	20.00
	P	5.00
	S	£100
	V	60.00
Collingham	O	40.00
Collumpton	C	£100
	H	60.00
Colnbrook	O	40.00
	P	8.00
	S	£250
	V	60.00
	Z	40.00
	AA	60.00
	BB	40.00
Colne	C	40.00
	O	40.00
	P	5.00
	V	40.00
Colsterworth	D	£100
	G	£100
	O	65.00
	P	20.00
	V	40.00
	W	40.00
	Y	20.00
Coltishall	V	65.00
	CC	£100
Columpton	V	40.00
	Y	20.00
	Y erased	20.00
Colyton	CC	£100
Compton (Devon)	CC	£100
Congleton	C	40.00
	D	60.00
	M	40.00
	O	20.00
	P	5.00
	W	20.00
	Y	20.00
	HH	£100
Conway	C	20.00
	O	15.00
	P	5.00
	V	15.00
	Y	20.00
Copplestone	CC	65.00
Corbridge (North'd)	C framed	60.00
Corfe Castle	C	25.00
	D	£100
	V	50.00
Corsham	N	£175
Corwen	C	20.00
	C inside oval	£150
	O	15.00
	P	5.00
	Y	40.00
Cosham	G	40.00
	O	40.00
	V	65.00
Cotherstone	CC	£100
Cottingham	CC	£100
Coventry	C	40.00
	D	65.00
	P	5.00
	S	£150
	V	20.00
	X	15.00

39

Marks of the Provincial Post to 1839 - England and Wales

	X erased	25.00		CC	60.00
	Z	60.00	Cross	O	20.00
	AA	40.00		P	10.00
	CC	65.00		BB	40.00
	JJ	40.00		CC	40.00
	MM	£200	Cross Hills	C	65.00
Cowbridge	H	60.00		D	£100
	O	8.00		O	40.00
	P	5.00	Cross In Hand	CC	£100
	V	20.00	Croyden	C	£100
	W	15.00	Croydon	C	65.00
	Y	15.00		K	65.00
	Y erased	15.00		V	20.00
Cowes (IOW)	O distinctive	40.00		V erased	20.00
	P	8.00		CC	65.00
	W	20.00	Cuckfield	P	10.00
	W erased	20.00		V	20.00
Cowfold	CC	£100		V erased	40.00
Cowley Bridge	CC	£100		W	60.00
Crabtree	CC	£100		Z	40.00
Cranbourn	C	65.00		BB	65.00
	P	10.00	Cullercoats	CC	65.00
	W	50.00	Culliton	V	20.00
	Y	40.00	Cullompton	P	5.00
	Y erased	25.00		CC	40.00
Cranbrook	G	60.00	Cullumpton	Z	65.00
	P	5.00	Curdworth	P.P. (distinctive)	£225
	S	£125	Dagenham	W	65.00
	V	20.00	Darking	C	65.00
	V erased	20.00		D	£150
	W	20.00		G	60.00
	W erased	20.00		S	£125
	CC	65.00		V	40.00
Crawley	P	5.00		W	40.00
	W	20.00	Darlaston	O	60.00
	W erased	40.00	Darlington	C	60.00
	Z	60.00		D	40.00
Crediton	C	£100		P	5.00
	D	60.00		R	£100
	V	40.00		V	15.00
	W	20.00		W	15.00
	W erased	15.00		X	15.00
	AA	20.00		CC	£150
Crewkern	D	65.00	Dartford	C	40.00
	S	£100		D	60.00
	W	40.00		K	60.00
	W erased	40.00		O	20.00
Crewkerne	C	60.00		P	5.00
	D	60.00		S	£150
	P	5.00		V	20.00
	W	40.00		W	15.00
	AA	40.00		W erased	20.00
	FF	£250		BB	40.00
Crickhowell	C	20.00	Dartmouth	C	£100
	O	15.00		D	£100
	P	5.00		H	£150
	Z	60.00		P	5.00
	JJ	60.00		V	20.00
Cricklade	D	£100		Y	20.00
	V	40.00		BB	20.00
	V erased	40.00	Davenham	N	£400
Criklade	C	60.00	Daventry	C	65.00
Crockernwell	CC	£100		D	£100
Crofe Castle (Corfe Castle)	E	£400 (error)		M	60.00
Croft	CC	65.00		P	5.00
Cromer	C	£100		R	20.00
	O	20.00		R erased	60.00
	W	£100		S	£125
	AA	65.00		V	60.00
	CC	£100		W	40.00
Crookhorn	D	£200		Z	60.00
Crosby (IOM)	O	£200		AA	65.00
Crosby (L'pool)	N	£350		CC	40.00
	O	40.00		MM	£150

Marks of the Provincial Post to 1839 - England and Wales

Town	Mark	Price
Dawley Green	CC	£100
Dawlish	O	40.00
	P	5.00
Deal	C	40.00
	G	60.00
	H	60.00
	P	5.00
	S	£120
	V	20.00
	X	15.00
	Z	40.00
Deale	C	£150
Debenham	CC	£100
Deddington	O	20.00
	V	15.00
	Y	60.00
	Y erased	20.00
Dedham (Essex)	O	40.00
	V	65.00
Dedington	D	65.00
Deeping	C	£100
Delph	O	40.00
	AA distinctive	65.00
Denbigh	C	20.00
	D	20.00
	H	40.00
	O	20.00
	P	5.00
	V	20.00
	W	15.00
	Y	15.00
Dent	CC	60.00
Denton (M'ter)	BB	£150
Derby	C	20.00
	P	5.00
	Q	5.00
	R	£100
	S	£150
	V	20.00
	W	20.00
	X	15.00
	Z	40.00
	AA	40.00
	HH	£200
	MM	£125
Dereham	C	60.00
	O	15.00
	P	5.00
	S	£175
	V	20.00
	W	40.00
Deritend (B'ham)	C	40.00
Devils Bridge	C	60.00
	O	20.00
Devizes	C	40.00
	D	£100
	P	5.00
	S	£150
	V	60.00
	W	15.00
	Y	15.00
	Y erased	15.00
	Z	60.00
	AA	40.00
	BB	60.00
	CC	65.00
	HH	65.00
	MM	£200
Devonport	P	5.00
	X	20.00
	X erased	15.00
	Z (dated)	40.00
	AA	60.00
	JJ	40.00
	MM	£150
Dewsbury	O	20.00
	P	5.00
Didsbury (M'ter)	BB	£100
Disley	C	60.00
Diss	C	20.00
	O	15.00
	V	20.00
	W	20.00
	Y	40.00
Distington	CC	40.00
Dobcross	AA distinctive	£100
Dobscross	O	40.00
Dolgelly	C	20.00
	O	15.00
	V	20.00
	W	15.00
	W erased	20.00
	Y	20.00
	Y erased	20.00
	JJ	65.00
Doncaster	C	40.00
	C distinctive	£200
	D	40.00
	G	60.00
	H	40.00
	M	40.00
	P	5.00
	S	£125
	V	15.00
	W	15.00
	JJ	40.00
Donnington Lincolns	CC	£100
Dorchester	C	40.00
	D	50.00
	F	£100
	P	5.00
	S	£100
	V	20.00
	W	20.00
	W erased	20.00
	X	15.00
	AA	20.00
Dorking	O	20.00
	P	5.00
Douglas Isle of Man	P distinctive	50.00
	CC	£2000
Down	O	40.00
Downham	C	£100
	D	£100
	O	15.00
	P	5.00
	V	20.00
	W	15.00
	W erased	60.00
	CC	£100
Downton	C	60.00
Dover	C	40.00
	F	£125
	G	40.00
	P	5.00
	S	90.00
	V	20.00
	W	15.00
	X	15.00
	X erased	20.00
	AA	40.00
Drayton (Shrops)	C	60.00
	D	65.00
Driffield	C	£100
	O	20.00
	P	5.00
	V	20.00
	W	20.00

41

Marks of the Provincial Post to 1839 - England and Wales

Location	Mark	Price
Droitwich	W erased	20.00
	C	40.00
	P	5.00
	S	£100
	S erased	£200
	V	20.00
	W	20.00
	Y	20.00
	Y erased	15.00
Dudeston Row (B'ham)	C	20.00
Dudley	C	40.00
	O	15.00
	P	5.00
	R	20.00
	W	20.00
	X	20.00
	Y	20.00
	BB	40.00
Duffield Derby	O	60.00
Dulverton	O	20.00
	V	20.00
Dunchurch	W	60.00
	W erased	60.00
Dunkirk	C	75.00
	W	65.00
Dunmow	C	£100
	O	20.00
	P	5.00
	V	60.00
	W	40.00
	W erased	60.00
Dunstable	C	60.00
	D	£100
	O	40.00
	P	5.00
	V	20.00
	W	20.00
	MM	£250
Dunster	G	£100
	O	40.00
	W	20.00
	BB	60.00
Durham	C	20.00
	D	60.00
	H	60.00
	Q	5.00
	V	15.00
	W	15.00
	X	15.00
	CC	£150
Dursley	C	60.00
	P	5.00
	V	40.00
	W	40.00
	Z	40.00
	AA	40.00
	BB	20.00
Duxford	O	60.00
Dyffryn	O	40.00
E (for Exeter)	A (cap 'E' dated)	£3000
Eardisley	C	£100
Earsdon	CC	60.00
Easingwold	P	5.00
	V	20.00
	W	15.00
	W erased	15.00
Easingwould	D	60.00
	V	20.00
East Ayton	O	40.00
Eastbourn	G	£100
	V	15.00
	Z	60.00
Eastbourne	P	5.00
	V	60.00

Location	Mark	Price
	CC	£100
East Farleigh	O	40.00
East Grinstead	A (+crown in circle)	£350
	D	60.00
	P	5.00
	V	15.00
	V erased	20.00
	Z	60.00
	CC	£100
East Grinsted	B distinctive	£400
	S	£200
Eastham (L'pool)	C	£100
East Hoathly	CC	£100
East Moulsey	CC	60.00
East Strotten	CC	£150
Eaton Socon	CC	£100
Eccles (Manchester)	PP distinctive	£100
Eccleshall	C	40.00
Eccleshill	CC	60.00
Edenbridge	O	60.00
Edgbaston	BB	£100
Edgeware	C	£100
	S	£175
	V	20.00
	Y	40.00
	Z	60.00
Edgworth	D	£150
Egham	O	65.00
	V	65.00
Eglwyswrw	O	65.00
*Egremont-Cumbrd	O	20.00
E-Griensted	F	£350
Elland	CC	60.00
Ellesmere	O	40.00
	P	5.00
	S	£200
	W	40.00
	Y	40.00
	Y erased	40.00
	JJ	£150
Elmdon	P.P. distinctive	75.00
Elmham	C	£100
	H	60.00
Ely	C	£100
	O	15.00
	P	5.00
	V	40.00
	W	40.00
	W erased	40.00
Emsworth	H	£100
	P	5.00
	V	40.00
	V erased	40.00
Enfield	D	£200
Ensham	O	40.00
	S	£250
Enstone	C	£100
	O	20.00
	P	5.00
	S	£100
	V	40.00
	Z	£100
	BB	65.00
Eping	C	£200
Epping	C	40.00
	G	£100
	K	£200
	O	20.00
	P	8.00
	V	60.00
	W	40.00
	W erased	40.00
Epsom	C	40.00
	K	£100

42

Marks of the Provincial Post to 1839 - England and Wales

	O	40.00	Falkingham	C	£100
	P	5.00	Falm O	A	£200
	S	£150	Falmouth	C	20.00
	V	40.00		D	75.00
	W	20.00		H	20.00
	W erased	40.00		L	60.00
	CC	£100		P	5.00
	JJ	£100		V	20.00
Epworth	O	40.00		X	15.00
Erdington/	PP (distinctive)	£100		X erased	20.00
Ermebridge	O	40.00		JJ	75.00
	P	8.00		MM	£150
	BB	£100		OO	£100
Escrick	C	£100	Fareham	C	40.00
Esher	H	40.00		H	75.00
	P	5.00		O	20.00
	V	40.00		P	5.00
Etal crown	(mail bag seal)	£400		S	90.00
Et Grinstead	G	£100		V	20.00
Eton	V	60.00		W	20.00
Etruria	O	65.00		Z	65.00
Everly (Beverley)	C	£200		AA	40.00
Eversham	D	£100		BB	65.00
Evesham	C	40.00	Farham	C	£150
	D	40.00	Faringdon	C	75.00
	P	5.00		D	£100
	V	20.00		W	20.00
	W	20.00		BB	65.00
	W erased	15.00	Farnborough (Hants)	CC	65.00
Exeter	C	40.00	Farnborough (Kent)	C	60.00
	D	£200		O	40.00
	F (boxed)	£250	Farnham	C	40.00
	H	60.00		V	40.00
	K	£100		X	20.00
	M	40.00		X erased	40.00
	P	5.00		BB	65.00
	R	£100		MM	£225
	V	20.00	Farningham	O	40.00
	W	20.00	Farringdon	C	40.00
	X	15.00		D	60.00
	X erased	20.00		O	15.00
	Z (dated)	20.00		P	5.00
	AA distinctive	20.00		S	£150
	JJ	15.00		V	20.00
	MM	£150		Y	20.00
	OO Add half	£500		Y erased	20.00
Exmouth	H	65.00	Faversham	C	60.00
	P	8.00		BB	60.00
	V	20.00	Fawley	CC	65.00
	W	15.00	Fazeley	O	40.00
	W erased	15.00		Y	40.00
	Z	60.00	Feckenham	C	20.00
Exon	C	£350		V	40.00
Eye	C	60.00		CC	40.00
	O	20.00	Felstead	V	£100
	V	40.00		V erased	60.00
	W	20.00	Feltham	O	60.00
Eynsham	O	40.00 Fairford	Felton (North'd)	O	20.00
C	60.00			P	5.00
	O	20.00	Fenny Stratford	D	£200
	P	5.00		P	5.00
	S	£150		S	£150
	V	60.00		V	40.00
	W	40.00		W	40.00
	X undated	40.00		W erased	40.00
Fakenham	C	60.00	Ferebridge	D	£250
	D	£100	Feribridg	C	£250
	J	60.00	Ferrybridge	C	60.00
	O	15.00		D	40.00
	P	5.00		P	5.00
	S	£125		V	20.00
	V	40.00		V erased	20.00
	W	40.00		W	15.00
	Y	40.00		Y	20.00

43

Marks of the Provincial Post to 1839 - England and Wales

Feversham	C	£100		V	50.00
	D	60.00	Froome	C	£100
	G	60.00		V	50.00
	P	5.00	Gaddesden	V	£100
	S	£125	Gainford	CC	45.00
	V	20.00	Gainsborough	C	60.00
	W	20.00		D	40.00
	W erased	20.00		M dated	15.00
Filby	CC	£100		S	£150
Fishergate (Preston)	C	40.00		W	20.00
Fishguard	W	20.00	Gainsbro	V	40.00
	CC	75.00	Gannick (Middx)	CC	£150
Five Lanes	C framed	60.00	Gardner Street (Sussex)	M	60.00
	O	40.00	Gargrave	C	20.00
	BB	£100		D	40.00
Five Ways (B'ham)	C	20.00		O	20.00
Fleetwood	O	60.00		V	20.00
	CC	£100		W	15.00
Fletchling	CC	75.00		Y erased	20.00
Flint	C	60.00	Garreds Cross	D	£200
	O	15.00	Garstang	D	£100
	BB	60.00		G	60.00
Flixton (Manch'r)	PP distinctive	£100		P	5.00
Folkestone	Z	65.00		V	40.00
Folkingham	C	60.00		W	40.00
	O	40.00		W erased	20.00
	P	5.00	Gateshead	C	£100
	W	40.00		D	65.00
Folkston	F	£100		H	40.00
Folkstone	H	60.00		O	40.00
	P	5.00		P	5.00
	S	£125		R	£150
	V	20.00		W	15.00
	W	20.00		Y	15.00
	W erased	40.00		Y erased	20.00
Footscray	D	60.00		BB	20.00
	K	£100		CC	£100
	P	5.00		JJ	£100
	S	£150	Gateshead High Fell	CC	65.00
	V	20.00	Gedney	CC	65.00
	V erased	15.00	Gee Cross	BB	£125
Fordingbridge	D	60.00	Gerrards Cr	V	65.00
	O	60.00	Gerrards Cross	D	£100
	P	5.00		G	£100
	V	40.00		P	5.00
	W	40.00		W	40.00
Fore Street Hill (Exmouth)	CC	45.00		Y	60.00
Forsbrook	O	60.00		Y erased	40.00
Four Posts	CC	65.00		BB	60.00
Fowey	C	20.00	Gilling	O	40.00
	O	40.00	Gilsland	O	40.00
	P	5.00	Gisburne	CC	65.00
	V	20.00	Glasbury	O	15.00
	Y	15.00	Glastonbury	D	75.00
Framfield	CC	65.00		P	5.00
Framlingham	D	65.00		W	20.00
	V	60.00		AA	60.00
	Z	40.00	Glocester	C	20.00
	BB	20.00		J	60.00
Frampton on Seveon (error)	CC	£250		V	20.00
Frimley	O	40.00	Glossop	O	40.00
Frodsham	C	60.00		Z	60.00
	H	60.00		BB	£100
	W	40.00	Gloster	C	40.00
	Y	40.00	Gloucester	C	40.00
Frogmill	V	65.00		D	40.00
Frome	J	£100		P	5.00
	O	20.00		S	£100
	P	5.00		W	40.00
	R	60.00		X	15.00
	W	20.00		X erased	15.00
	Y	20.00		Z	40.00
	HH	90.00		AA	40.00
Froom	C	£100		HH	40.00

44

Marks of the Provincial Post to 1839 - England and Wales

Location	Mark	Price
	JJ	60.00
	MM	£150
Eastgate Gloucester	F	20.00
Northgate Gloucester	F	20.00
Southgate Gloucester	F	20.00
Westgate Gloucester	F	20.00
Glouster	D	£100
Glyn Neath	O	20.00
Godalmin	D	£100
	P	5.00
	S	£120
	V	40.00
	W	20.00
	W erased	20.00
Godalming	C	60.00
Godmersham	CC	75.00
Godshill (IOW)	O	20.00
Godstone	C	60.00
	P	5.00
	S	£150
	V	40.00
	W	40.00
	W erased	40.00
	Z	40.00
	BB	40.00
Goldhanger	CC	£100
Gomersal	O	20.00
	BB	60.00
Gooch St (B'ham)	C	60.00
Gooderich	CC	65.00
Goodhurst	O	65.00
	CC	65.00
Goole	C (boxed)	£100
	O	20.00
	P	5.00
Goring	CC	60.00
Gorlestone	BB	£100
Gornal	O	60.00
Gorton (Manchester)	BB	£150
Gosberton	Z	£100
	CC	£100
Gosforth	CC	40.00
Gosport	C	40.00
	D	£100
	P	5.00
	S	£100
	V	40.00
	W	40.00
	X	20.00
	X erased	40.00
	BB	60.00
Goudhurst	CC	60.00
Grampound	C	40.00
	O	20.00
	V	20.00
Grantham	C	40.00
	D	60.00
	G	40.00
	O	40.00
	P	20.00
	S	£200
	V	40.00
	W	20.00
	Y	20.00
	Z	40.00
	BB	40.00
Gravesend	C	40.00
	G	40.00
	Q	5.00
	V	20.00
	W	20.00
	X	15.00
	AA	40.00
Grayes	C	£200

Location	Mark	Price
Grays	H	£150
	C	£100
	G	£150
	S	£200
	V	65.00
Greabridge	C	£250
Greatabridge	V	20.00
	W	15.00
Great Barr	P.P. (distinctive)	£100
Great Heywood	M	60.00
Great Malvern	P	5.00
Great Smeaton	C	60.00
Greenacres (M'ter)	BB	40.00
Green Hammerton	O	40.00
Greenhythe	O	60.00
Green Street	CC	60.00
Gretabridge	D	£100
	O	20.00
	P	5.00
	W erased	20.00
Gretna	Z	40.00
Grimsby	C	20.00
	O	20.00
	V	40.00
	W	40.00
	Z	40.00
Groombridge	O	60.00
Gt Malvern	BB	40.00
	MM	£225
Gt Missenden	G	£100
Guernsey	A (scroll)	£450
	G	£575
	P	50.00
Guildford	C	60.00
	D	£100
	G	60.00
	P	5.00
	S	£200
	V	40.00
	W	20.00
	W erased	20.00
	Z	40.00
	BB	40.00
	JJ	£150
Guilsfield	O	20.00
Guisboro	BB	65.00
Guisborough	D	60.00
	O	20.00
	P	5.00
	V	20.00
	W	15.00
	Y	20.00
	CC	£100
Guiseley	O	40.00
	BB	£100
Guist	C	40.00
	C framed	£100
	G	40.00
Gwindee	V	40.00
Gwyndee	H	65.00
Gwyndu	S	£250
H (for Hatherley)	A	£750
Hadleigh (Essex)	CC	£150
Hadleigh (Suf'k)	G	60.00
	O	20.00
	P	5.00
	V	60.00
	W	40.00
	W erased	40.00
	Z	60.00
	AA	40.00
	CC	65.00
Hagley (Worcs)	C	60.00
	O	20.00

45

Marks of the Provincial Post to 1839 - England and Wales

Location	Mark	Price
Hailsham	O	20.00
Hales Owen	C	£100
Halesowen	V	60.00
Halesworth	C	£100
	D	£100
	O	20.00
	P	8.00
	W	60.00
	Y	60.00
	Y erased	20.00
Halfway House	O	65.00
Halifax	C	40.00
	D	60.00
	M	40.00
	P	5.00
	R	£100
	V	20.00
	W	15.00
	X	15.00
	AA	40.00
	CC	65.00
	HH	40.00
	JJ	75.00
	MM	£200
Halstead (Essex)	C	£100
	G	£100
	P	5.00
	V	60.00
	W	40.00
	W erased	40.00
	Z	60.00
	AA	40.00
	BB	40.00
Halstead (Kent)	O	60.00
Halstow	CC	65.00
Haltwhistle	C	20.00
	O	20.00
	W	40.00
	BB	60.00
Hamble	CC	£100
Hambledon	O	60.00
	CC	60.00
Hambrook (Bristol)	O	20.00
Handcross	O	60.00
	CC	£100
Handley	O	40.00
Handsworth (B'ham)	C	20.00
Hanley Staffs	O	40.00
Harborough	C	60.00
	D	£150
	S	£100
Harbour St (Ramsgate)	C	60.00
Harewood	O	40.00
	CC	65.00
Harewood End (Heref)	CC	75.00
Harleston	C	£100
	D	60.00
	P	5.00
	V	20.00
	W	20.00
	HH	£200
Harling	C	20.00
	D	£100
	O	20.00
	P	5.00
	W	20.00
Harlington	O	60.00
Harlow	C	20.00
	H	£100
	P	5.00
	S	£200
	V	40.00
Harrietsham	O	40.00
Harrogate	P	5.00
	W	15.00
	Z	60.00
	HH	£100
	JJ	£100
Harrowgate	D	40.00
	V	20.00
	Y	20.00
	Y erased	20.00
	AA	60.00
	CC	£100
Hartford (Herts)	C	60.00
	E	£200
Hartfordbridge	D three lines	£150
	G	65.00
	M	20.00
	P	5.00
	S	£120
	V	40.00
	W	20.00
Harting	CC	65.00
Hartlebury	CC	45.00
Hartlepool	O	15.00
	P	5.00
Hartley Pans	CC	65.00
Harwich	C	£100
	D	£150
	F	£200
	G	60.00
	P	5.00
	R	£150
	V	60.00
	W	60.00
	X	45.00
	X erased	20.00
	Z	60.00
Haselbury (Som)	CC	65.00
Haslemere	F	£150
	P	5.00
	S	£150
	V	60.00
	W	40.00
	W erased	40.00
Haslingden	P	5.00
	BB	20.00
Haslingdon	H	60.00
Hastings	C	£100
	G	60.00
	P	5.00
	S	£175
	V	20.00
	V erased	40.00
	W	15.00
	BB	60.00
Hatfield	C	£100
	G	£100
	P	8.00
	V	60.00
	W	40.00
	Z	£100
Hatherley	V	15.00
Hathersage	C	50.00
	BB	£100
	CC	60.00
Havant	G	£100
	H	£100
	O	60.00
	P	5.00
	R	£150
	V	40.00
	V erased	40.00
	W	40.00
	CC	£100
	albino bagseal	£500
Haverf.dwest	AA no frame	75.00

46

Marks of the Provincial Post to 1839 - England and Wales

Haverfordwest	C	60.00
	D	20.00
	H	60.00
	M	60.00
	P	5.00
	V	40.00
	Y	20.00
	Y erased	15.00
	Z	40.00
	CC	60.00
	FF	£300
	JJ	40.00
Haverhill	C	60.00
Hawarden	C	20.00
	O	15.00
Hawes	O	40.00
	P	5.00
	BB	60.00
Hawkhurst	O	40.00
	V	40.00
Hawkshead	C framed	£250
	V	£100
	V erased	40.00
	CC	£100
Hay	C	20.00
	O	15.00
	P	5.00
	V	20.00
	W	20.00
Haydon Bge	C framed	60.00
Haydon Bridge	E distinctive	65.00
	P	5.00
Hayes Kent	O	65.00
Hayle (Cornwall)	O	20.00
	P	5.00
Hayling Island	O	60.00
	CC	£100
Haylsham	V	40.00
	V erased	40.00
Hazel Grove	C	£125
Heacham	CC	£100
Heathersett	C	£150
	D framed	£200
Heathfield	CC	60.00
Heavitree	CC	60.00
Hebden Bridge	CC	60.00
Heckmondwicke	O	40.00
Heckmondwike	BB	60.00
Heddon on the Wall	O	40.00
Hedingham	V	£100
Hedon	O	40.00
	V	40.00
	V erased	40.00
Heighington	CC	60.00
Helmesley	D	£100
	W	40.00
Helmsley	G	£100
	W	40.00
	Y	40.00
	Y erased	40.00
Helston	P	5.00
	R	20.00
	V	60.00
	W	60.00
	Y	60.00
	Y erased	20.00
Helstone	C	60.00
	H	£100
	P	5.00
Hemel Hempstead	D	£150
	G	£100
	P	5.00
	V	40.00
	W	40.00

Hemel Hemsted	S	£150
Henfield	O	20.00
	V	60.00
Henley (Oxon)	C	£100
	G	60.00
	K	£100
	S	£150
	Y	20.00
	Y erased	£100
	CC	£100
Henley-A	V	40.00
Henley in A	W	40.00
Henley in Arden	D	40.00
	M	15.00
	JJ	75.00
Henley on Thames	M	20.00
	P	5.00
Henly in Arden	E	40.00
Henly.T	V	60.00
Henly-T	W	20.00
Hereford	C	40.00
	D	60.00
	P	5.00
	S	£120
	V	40.00
	X	20.00
	BB	40.00
	JJ	50.00
	MM	£150
Herne Bay	O	40.00
Hertford	C	60.00
	D	£100
	G	£100
	P	5.00
	V	40.00
	W	40.00
	W erased	60.00
	Z	60.00
	CC	£100
	JJ	£150
Hertfordbridge	G two line	£100
Hesket	CC	40.00
Hevingham	CC	40.00
Hexham	P	5.00
	V	40.00
	W	20.00
	X undated	20.00
	X erased	15.00
	BB	60.00
Heytesbury	P	5.00
	V	60.00
	Y	60.00
	Y erased	40.00
Heytsbury	S	£100
Heywood	O	40.00
H.fordwest	Z	40.00
H.Hempstead	O	20.00
Higham Ferrars	V	60.00
	W	£100
	W erased	£100
Higham Ferrers	C	£100
	O	40.00
	P	5.00
	S	£200
Higham Ferres	W	£100
Higham Ferris	D	£200
Highfield	CC	£100
High Street (Southampton)	C	60.00
High St (Sunderland)	C	40.00
	E	60.00
High Wickham	D	£100
High Wicomb	S	£200
Highworth	C	£100
	D	£125

47

Marks of the Provincial Post to 1839 - England and Wales

Location	Mark	Price
	G	£100
	P	5.00
	S	£120
	V	40.00
	W	40.00
	W erased	40.00
	CC	£100
High Wycomb	D	£100
	W	20.00
	W erased	40.00
High Wycombe	G two line	£100
	O	20.00
	P	5.00
Hilborough	CC	£100
Hinckley	C	60.00
	P	5.00
	V	40.00
	V erased	40.00
	Z	60.00
	BB	60.00
Hinden	CC	60.00
Hindon	C	60.00
	O	40.00
	P	10.00
	CC	60.00
Hingham	CC	40.00
Hitchen	C	£100
	G	£100
	P	5.00
	V	40.00
Hitchin	C	60.00
	G	£100
	O	15.00
	W	40.00
	Z (distinctive)	£250
Hithe	C	£250
	H	60.00
	V	20.00
Hobbs Point	P	60.00
Hockcliffe	CC	60.00
Hockley (Wks)	CC	40.00
Hockliffe	CC	60.00
Hoddesdon	P	5.00
	W	60.00
	W erased	60.00
Holbeach	P	5.00
	W	40.00
	Z	£100
	BB	£100
Holdsworthy	H	60.00
	FF	£500
Holkham	C	60.00
	C framed	60.00
Hollingsgreen	CC	65.00
Hollinwood (M'ter)	BB	£100
Holmes Chapel	O	40.00
	V	40.00
Holmfirth	O	40.00
	Z	40.00
	CC	£100
Holms Chapell	D	£200
Holsworthy	O	40.00
	P	5.00
	V	40.00
	CC	£100
Holt (Norfolk)	C	£100
	O	15.00
	P	5.00
	S	£200
	W	15.00
	W erased	35.00
Holyhead	C	60.00
	H	60.00
	P	5.00

Location	Mark	Price
	V	40.00
	X	15.00
	X erased	20.00
Holywell	C	40.00
	H	£100
	P	5.00
	S	£100
	V	20.00
	W	15.00
	Y	15.00
Honiton	C	60.00
	D	£100
	H	20.00
	P	5.00
	R	£150
	V	60.00
	W	15.00
	Z	£100
	Z (distinctive)	£125
	CC	25.00
	LL	20.00
Honiton Clist	CC	£100
Hood Hill	C	40.00
Hoo Green	CC	60.00
Hook	CC	£100
Horncastle	C	£150
	D	60.00
	O	20.00
	S	£120
	V	40.00
	W	20.00
Hornchurch	W	60.00
Horndean	H	60.00
	P	5.00
	V	40.00
	W	40.00
	X	20.00
	Y erased	20.00
	CC	40.00
Hornsea	O	40.00
Horsebridge	O	50.00
Horse Monden	CC	£500
Horsforth	O	40.00
	BB	60.00
Horsham	C	60.00
	O	40.00
	P	8.00
	S	£150
	V	15.00
	W	15.00
	W erased	20.00
	Z	40.00
	BB	40.00
	CC	60.00
Hot-Wells (Bristol)	O	40.00
Houghton-le-Spring	CC	40.00
Houlsworthy	S	£100
Hounslow	K	£100
	O	40.00
	P	8.00
	V	60.00
	W	60.00
	Y	40.00
	Y erased	40.00
	AA	40.00
	CC	65.00
	MM	£225
Hove	CC	60.00
Howden	D	£150
	P	5.00
	V	20.00
	Y	20.00
	Y erased	20.00
	CC	£150

48

Marks of the Provincial Post to 1839 - England and Wales

Town	Mark	Price
	HH	£125
	MM	£225
Howden Pans	C	60.00
Hubberstone	H	65.00
Huddersfield	D	75.00
	H	65.00
	Q	5.00
	V	15.00
	W	15.00
	X	15.00
	Y	40.00
	Z	60.00
	AA	60.00
	BB	60.00
	CC	60.00
	HH	50.00
	JJ	20.00
	MM	£250
Hull	A (circular with star)	£300
	C	40.00
	H	20.00
	L	60.00
	P	5.00
	X	20.00
	X erased	20.00
	X distinctive	£200
	BB	£100
	JJ	75.00
	MM	£225
Hungerford	C	40.00
	D	40.00
	O	20.00
	P	5.00
	S	£100
	V	20.00
	W	20.00
	Y	20.00
	Y erased	20.00
Hunmanby	O	5.00
Hunsdon	CC	£100
Hunstanton	CC	45.00
Huntingdon	B	£200
	C	60.00
	D	75.00
	G	40.00
	H	40.00
	O	20.00
	P	5.00
	S	£120
	V	40.00
	W	20.00
	X	20.00
	Y	40.00
	AA	40.00
	CC	60.00
Hunton Kent	O	60.00
Hursley	CC	60.00
Hurst	CC	£100
Hurstbourne	CC	£100
Hurstbourne Tarrant	O	60.00
	CC	£100
Hurst Green	C	£100
	D	£100
	P	5.00
	S	£200
	V	40.00
Hurstperpoint	H	£100
	O	60.00
Hurworth	CC	65.00
H Wycombe	Z	40.00
Hyde (Manchester)	CC	£100
Hythe (Hants)	CC	60.00
Hythe (Kent)	C	40.00
	O	40.00

Town	Mark	Price
	P	5.00
	W	20.00
	W erased	15.00
	Z	65.00
Ide	CC	45.00
Idle	CC	60.00
Ightham	O	40.00
	CC	60.00
Ilchester	C	60.00
	O	20.00
	P	5.00
	V	40.00
	W	20.00
Ilfracombe	O	15.00
	P	5.00
	V	20.00
	CC	40.00
Ilkley	CC	60.00
Ilminster	D	£150
	Q undated	20.00
	S	90.00
	V	40.00
	W	40.00
	Y	20.00
	Y erased	20.00
	BB	60.00
	FF	£150
	JJ	75.00
	MM	£150
Ilsley	O	20.00
Ingatestone	D	£100
	G	60.00
	O	40.00
	P	5.00
	S	£200
	V	60.00
	W	40.00
	W erased	40.00
	Y	40.00
	Y erased	40.00
Ipswich	C	40.00
	D	£100
	G	40.00
	R	£100
	S	£125
	V	40.00
	X	20.00
	X erased	15.00
	Y	40.00
	Z	60.00
	BB	40.00
	NN	£200
Ironbridge	C	60.00
	O	15.00
	BB	40.00
	CC	40.00
Isle of Man	C	£200
	D	£500
	H	£200
	O	£150
	P	20.00
	CC	£1500
Isle of Wight	C	£100
	D	£150
	S	£150
Isle of Wight.	N. C	£100
Isleworth	C	£100
	D	60.00
	G	60.00
	S	£200
Itchen	CC	60.00
Ivinghoe	O	40.00
Ivybridge	D	£125
	H	£100

49

Marks of the Provincial Post to 1839 - England and Wales

Location	Mark	Price
	P	5.00
	W	20.00
	W erased	60.00
Ixworth	BB	40.00
Jarrow	CC	60.00
Jersey	A (scroll)	£450
	C	£550
	G	£400
	P	50.00
	BB	£550
	JJ	£150
Jvybridge (error)	AA	£300
K (for Kingsbridge)	A	£750
Kegworth	O	40.00
	V	60.00
Keighley	C	60.00
	H	60.00
	O	20.00
	P	5.00
	W	20.00
	W erased	20.00
Keinton	C	60.00
	F	£150
	V	60.00
	W	60.00
	W erased	40.00
Kelvedon	C	£100
	F	£200
	G	£100
	O	40.00
	P	5.00
	V	40.00
	Y	40.00
	Z	60.00
	BB	60.00
Kempsey	O	25.00
Kemp Town	O	35.00
	BB	£150
Kemsing-Kent	O	60.00
Kendal	C	40.00
	P	5.00
	V	20.00
	W	20.00
	X	20.00
	X erased	35.00
	Z	40.00
	AA	40.00
	JJ	£200
Kenford	CC	60.00
Kenilworth	O	35.00
	CC	£100
Kentchurch	CC	65.00
Kenyon (L'pool)	PP (distinctive)	£100
	O	20.00
Kenyon (Manch'r)	PP (distinctive)	£100
Kessingland	R	£150
Keswick	H	40.00
	P	5.00
	R	60.00
	V	20.00
	W	20.00
	W erased	20.00
Kettaring	D	£250
Kettering	C	£100
	D	£100
	G	60.00
	P	5.00
	S	£200
	V	60.00
	W	40.00
	W erased	10.00
	CC	£100
Keynsham (Som)	O	20.00
Key Street	CC	65.00
Kidderminster	C	40.00
	D	40.00
	P	5.00
	S	£100
	V	40.00
	W	20.00
	X	20.00
	X erased	20.00
	JJ	£100
	MM	£100
Kidwelly	C	40.00
	H	40.00
	O	20.00
Kighley	C	£100
Kildwick	V	40.00
	V erased	40.00
Kilsby	CC	65.00
Kilvedon	AA	£150
Kimbolton	C	£100
	G	60.00
	O	20.00
	P	5.00
	S	£150
	V	40.00
	W	40.00
	W erased	40.00
Kineton	Z	£100
Kingsbridge	D	£100
	P	5.00
	V	20.00
	W	20.00
	Y	15.00
	Y erased	20.00
	Z	35.00
	CC	40.00
Kingscote	Y	40.00
Kings Langley	W	65.00
King's Norton	P.P. (distinctive)	65.00
Kingston (Surrey)	C	40.00
	K	£100
	P	5.00
	Y	40.00
	Z	60.00
	CC	60.00
	MM	£200
Kingston on Tham	S	£150
Kingston on Thames	M	20.00
	W	40.00
Kingston T	V	40.00
Kingswinford	O	40.00
Kington	O	20.00
	P	8.00
	V	60.00
	W	20.00
Kington-H (Heref)	C	40.00
Kinvar	CC	£100
Kippax	O	40.00
Kirby Lonsdale	P	5.00
	V	20.00
	Y	20.00
	Y erased	15.00
	BB	60.00
Kirby Moorside	O	40.00
Kirkby Lonsdale	C	60.00
Kirkby Moorside	C	40.00
Kirkby Stephen	O	20.00
Kirkgate (Wakefield)	C	40.00
Kirkham	V	£100
	CC	40.00
Kirk Oswald	CC	65.00
Kirkstall	O	40.00
	BB	60.00
Kirton Lindsey	O	60.00
Knaresborough	D	£100

50

Marks of the Provincial Post to 1839 - England and Wales

	H	60.00	Launceston	C	60.00
	M	40.00		D	60.00
	P	5.00		P	5.00
	W	15.00		V	20.00
	Y	20.00		Y	15.00
	CC three line	£200		AA	60.00
Knighton	H	40.00		BB	40.00
	O	40.00		HH	£100
	V	20.00	Lavenham	C	60.00
Knot Mill/Manchr	A	£200	Lawton	C	40.00
Knott Mill/Manchester	E	60.00		O	20.00
Knowle (B'ham)	C	40.00		V	20.00
Knowle (Som)	CC	60.00		W	20.00
Knutsford	B	£250	Lea	C framed	£100
	C	£100		O	20.00
	D	£100		BB	£100
	H	£100	Leachlade	D	£100
	P	5.00	Leamington	N	£125
	V	40.00		O	20.00
	W	15.00		P	5.00
	Y	15.00		BB	40.00
	Y erased	15.00		CC	40.00
Laleham	CC	£100		JJ	40.00
Lamberhurst	C	60.00		MM	£200
	D	£100	Leatherhead	C	40.00
	P	5.00		D	£100
	V	15.00		P	5.00
	Z	60.00		S	£200
	CC	60.00		V	40.00
Lambourn	V	20.00		BB	£100
Lambourne	O	20.00	Lechlade	O	15.00
Lampeter	C	40.00		P	5.00
	D	40.00		V	20.00
	H	15.00		Y	20.00
	P	5.00	Lechmere Heath	CC	£100
	V	20.00	Ledbury	C	60.00
	W	15.00		D	60.00
	W erased	20.00		O	20.00
	BB	65.00		P	5.00
Lancaster	C (lower case)	£200		V	40.00
	C	40.00		W	40.00
	D	60.00		X	20.00
	G	60.00		X erased	40.00
	H	60.00		CC	£100
	M	60.00	Leedes	C	£350
	P	5.00	Leeds	C	40.00
	R	£100		G	60.00
	V	40.00		H	60.00
	X	15.00		M	40.00
	X erased	40.00		P	5.00
	BB	60.00		Q	5.00
	HH	60.00		R	£100
	JJ	75.00		V	20.00
	MM	£175		W	15.00
Lancaster St (B'ham)	C	60.00		X	15.00
Lanceston	D	40.00		BB	60.00
Landillo	C	20.00		CC	60.00
Landovery	D	40.00		HH	15.00
	H	60.00		JJ	40.00
Landrake	CC	60.00		MM	£175
Lanfair	C	40.00	Holbeck/Leeds	E	40.00
Langadock	H	40.00	Hunslet/Leeds	E	40.00
Langollen	C	60.00	Marsh Lane/Leeds	E	40.00
Langport	C	40.00	North St/Leeds	E	40.00
	V	20.00	West St/Leeds	E	40.00
Lantwitt	CC	40.00	Leek	A (unframed circular)	50.00
Lapford	CC	60.00		C	40.00
Larlingford	W	40.00		H	40.00
	W erased	20.00		O	20.00
Latchingdon	CC	£100		P	5.00
Laugharne	C	£100		R	40.00
	D	60.00		R boxed	40.00
	V	£100		Y	20.00
	CC	£100		JJ	£100

51

Marks of the Provincial Post to 1839 - England and Wales

Town	Mark	Price	Town	Mark	Price
Leeke	V	20.00		D	£100
Lees (Manch'r)	BB	60.00	Lincoln	C	60.00
Leicester	C	40.00		P	5.00
	D	£100		S	£125
	G	60.00		V	40.00
	P	5.00		W	40.00
	R	£100		X	20.00
	S	£125		X erased	15.00
	V	40.00	Lindal	CC	60.00
	W	40.00	Linton (Cambs)	G	£200
	X	20.00		O	20.00
	X erased	8.00		P	5.00
	CC	£100		V	£100
	HH	60.00		W	60.00
	JJ	50.00	Linton (Devon)	O	60.00
	MM	£125	Linton-Kent	O	60.00
Leigh (Essex)	CC	£100	Liphook	O	60.00
Leigh (Kent)	CC	60.00		V	60.00
Leigh (Manch'r)	PP distinctive	£100		W	60.00
Leighn Buzzard	V	20.00	Liscard (Cornwall)	D	£100
Leighton-Buz	F	£200	Liskeard (Cornwall)	H	£100
Leighton Buzzard	D	60.00		P	5.00
	P	5.00		Z	40.00
	W	20.00	Litchfield	C	60.00
	W erased	20.00		D	£100
Leintwardine	Y	40.00		S	£100
Lenham	O	35.00		V	20.00
Leominster	C	35.00		X	20.00
	D	60.00	Littlebourne	O	60.00
	P	5.00	Little Gaddesden	G	£250
	S	£120	Littlehampton	O	20.00
	V	40.00		W	60.00
	W	40.00	Liverpool	C	40.00
	X	20.00		D	40.00
	X erased	20.00		H	20.00
	BB	40.00		L	20.00
	CC	60.00		P	5.00
	MM	£150		Q	5.00
Leskeard	V	40.00		R	£100
	V erased	20.00		S	£150
Lestwithiel	D	£200		X	15.00
Letherhead	D	£150		AA	20.00
Letton	CC	60.00		CC	40.00
Leverpool	D	£200		HH	15.00
Leverpoole	C	£200		JJ	30.00
	D	£200		MM	£100
Lewes (Sussex)	C	40.00		OO	40.00
	G	60.00	Berry St	E	65.00
	P	5.00	Church St	E	15.00
	Q	5.00	Edge Hill	E	40.00
	S	£175	Everton	E	20.00
	V	20.00	Falkner St	E	60.00
	W	20.00	Kirkdale	E	15.00
	X	15.00	London Rd	E	20.00
	X erased	20.00	Low Hill	E	20.00
	AA	60.00	Oldhall St	E	35.00
	MM	£200	Oxford St	E	15.00
Lewis (Sussex)	C	£150	Park Rd	O	20.00
	S	£175	Regent Rd	E	60.00
Leyburn	CC	£100	St James's	E	20.00
Leyland	O	60.00	Scotland Rd	E	60.00
Lg Stratton	C	£100	Vauxhall Rd	E	60.00
Lichfield	C	40.00	Liverpoole	C	£250
	D	£100	Llanbedr	O	40.00
	J	40.00	Llandillo	V	15.00
	P	5.00	Llandilo	H	20.00
	X	15.00		O	15.00
	CC	40.00		P	5.00
	JJ	60.00		W	15.00
	MM	£225		Y	15.00
Limber	C boxed	£100		Y erased	20.00
	O	60.00	Llandissyl	CC	65.00
Lime	C	£300	Llandovery	D	60.00
Limington	C	60.00		O	8.00

Marks of the Provincial Post to 1839 - England and Wales

	P	5.00		D	65.00
	V	60.00		F	£200
	W	20.00		G	60.00
	Y	20.00		P	5.00
	Y erased	20.00		S	£150
Llandudno	CC	60.00		V	40.00
Llanelly	O	15.00		W	20.00
	P	5.00		W erased	20.00
	BB	40.00		MM	£200
Llanerchymedd	CC	40.00	Loughborow	D	£250
Llanfair	C	20.00	Loughor	CC	20.00
	O	20.00	Louth	C	40.00
Llanfihangel Crucorny	CC	40.00		P	5.00
Llanfyllin	O	15.00		V	40.00
Llangaddock	W	40.00		W	40.00
Llangadock	O	40.00	Lower Wallop	O	60.00
	P	10.00		CC	£100
Llangefni	CC	40.00	Lowestoff	P	5.00
Llangollen	P	5.00	Lowestoffe	S	£200
	Y	20.00	Lowestoft	D	£100
Llanidloes	P	5.00		O	20.00
	V	15.00		V	40.00
Llannelly	W	20.00	Low Harrogate	O	40.00
Llanrhaiadr	O	40.00	Luddenden	C	40.00
Llanrwst	C	15.00	Ludlow	C	60.00
	O	5.00		P	5.00
Llansaintfraid	O	40.00		S	£120
Llansantfraid	O	20.00		V	20.00
Llanyblodwell	O	40.00		W	15.00
Llanydlos	C	40.00		X	15.00
Llanymynech	O	20.00		JJ	£100
Llaugharne	FF	£250	Lugershall	O	30.00
Loddon	O	40.00	Luterworth	D	£100
Lodsworth	CC	£100	Luton	C	60.00
Loe	C	£150		G	60.00
	F	£200		O	20.00
Loftus	CC	£100		P	5.00
London Colney	CC	60.00		S	£120
London Rd. Worcester	O	20.00		V	20.00
Long Benton	CC	40.00		W	20.00
Long Buckly	C	60.00		W erased	20.00
Long Ditton	CC	£100		MM	£225
Longdon	C	60.00	Lutterworth	D	20.00
Long Melford	C	60.00		O	40.00
Longparish	CC	60.00		P	5.00
Longport Staffs	O	40.00		V	40.00
Long Stratton	C	£100		W	40.00
	O	40.00		CC	£100
	P	5.00	Lydd	O	60.00
	JJ	£100		V	20.00
Long Sutton	CC	60.00	Lydney	O	20.00
Longtown	C	20.00		CC	£100
	M double circle	60.00	Lyme	C	40.00
	R framed	20.00		G	75.00
	R framed, mileage etc erased	20.00		O	30.00
	U distinctive Scottish type	20.00		P	5.00
				V	20.00
	V	40.00		W	20.00
Loo	C	£150	Lymington	C	40.00
	BB	£125		D	60.00
Looe	C	£100		O	40.00
	V	£100		P	5.00
	W	20.00		S	£125
Loose	O	60.00		V	40.00
Lostwithiel	O	20.00		W	20.00
	P	5.00		Y	20.00
	W	40.00		Y erased	20.00
	W erased	40.00		AA	40.00
	Z	60.00		JJ	60.00
	CC	60.00	Lympston	H	60.00
Lougharne	C	60.00		CC	40.00
Loughborough	A	£200	Lyndhurst	C	60.00
	C	60.00		P	5.00
				S	£150

53

Marks of the Provincial Post to 1839 - England and Wales

	V	40.00		X	15.00
	V erased	20.00		CC	£100
	W	20.00		JJ	20.00
Lynn	C	20.00	Malvern	C	20.00
	L	£150		Z	40.00
	P	5.00	Malvern Wells	Z	60.00
	S	£120	Manchester	C	60.00
	X	15.00		D	20.00
	X erased	15.00		G	60.00
	Z	20.00		H	20.00
	BB	40.00		L	20.00
	CC	£100		P	5.00
	JJ	60.00		Q	8.00
	MM	£150		X	8.00
Lynn Regis	D	£200		X inverted	75.00
Lynton (Devon)	O	60.00		BB	£200
Lytchett	CC	£100		HH	20.00
Macclesfield	D	60.00		JJ	60.00
	H	40.00		MM	£100
	P	5.00		OO	40.00
	V	40.00	Manningtree	C	£125
	W	20.00		O	20.00
	X	15.00		P	5.00
	JJ	40.00		V	40.00
Machell St (Hull)	C	40.00		V erased	40.00
Machynleth	C	60.00	Mansfield	C	60.00
	D	40.00		P	5.00
Machynlleth	O	10.00		V	60.00
	P	5.00		W	40.00
	Y	15.00		Y	20.00
	Y erased	15.00		Y erased	20.00
	CC	£100	Marazion	C	£100
Madeley	O	40.00		D	£100
Madeley Wood	D	65.00		O	40.00
Maghull (Liverpool)	C framed	£100		P	5.00
	O	15.00		V	20.00
Maidenhead	D	60.00		V erased	20.00
	G	40.00	March	C	£150
	P	5.00		O	60.00
	S	£100		P	5.00
	V	20.00		V	60.00
	V erased	20.00	Marden	O	60.00
	BB	60.00	Margate	A oval with crown	£500
Maidston	D	£200		C	60.00
	F	£100		G	60.00
Maidstone	C	60.00		H	40.00
	D	60.00		P	5.00
	G	40.00		V	20.00
	P	5.00		W	20.00
	S	90.00		X	15.00
	V	15.00	Market Deeping	P	10.00
	W	15.00		V	40.00
	W erased	20.00		Y	40.00
	Z	40.00		Y erased	40.00
	BB	20.00		BB	£100
Malden	C	£125	Market Drayton	O	15.00
Maldon	C	60.00		P	5.00
	H	£100		V	20.00
	P	5.00		W	15.00
	V	60.00		W erased	15.00
	W	40.00		MM	£175
	Z	60.00	Market Harborough	D	60.00
	BB	40.00		P	5.00
Malmesbury	V	60.00		W	20.00
Malmsbury	C	40.00		Y	20.00
	D	£125	Market Raisen	M	20.00
	O	5.00	Market Raisin	D	60.00
Malpas	C	60.00		H	£100
Malten	C	£100		P	5.00
Malton	C	40.00		V	40.00
	P	5.00		W	40.00
	R	20.00		Y	40.00
	V	20.00	Market St (Beds)	Y	60.00
	W	15.00	Market St (Herts)	V	60.00

54

Marks of the Provincial Post to 1839 - England and Wales

Location	Mark	Price
Market Street (Beds)	Y	£100
	C	£100
	G	£100
	P	20.00
	V	60.00
Market Street (Herts)	C	£100
	G	£125
	P	10.00
Market Weighton	P	5.00
	V	20.00
	W	20.00
	Y	20.00
	Y erased	20.00
Marlboro	MM	£200
Marlborough	C	£200
	D	£100
	K	£100
	O	60.00
	P	5.00
	S	£150
	V	40.00
	W	40.00
	Y	20.00
	Y erased	40.00
	CC	60.00
	HH	£100
Marlow	C	40.00
	P	5.00
	V	20.00
	W	40.00
	W erased	40.00
Marsden (Yorks)	O	40.00
Marsefield	CC	60.00
Marsk	CC	£100
Marske	O	40.00
Martock	C	60.00
	Y	20.00
Marton	CC	60.00
Maryport	P	5.00
	W	20.00
	W erased	20.00
Masham	CC	60.00
Matlock	C	60.00
	BB	£100
Matlock Bath	O	20.00
	P	5.00
Matton	C	£200
Mavagissey	C	£100
Mayfield	CC	60.00
M.dean (Mitcheldean)	AA	£100
Meifod	O	20.00
Melbourne	O	60.00
Melksham	C	40.00
	D	60.00
	P	5.00
	V	40.00
	W	20.00
	Y	20.00
	Y erased	20.00
	Z	£100
	AA	60.00
Melton Mowbray	D	60.00
	M	20.00
	V	40.00
	W	40.00
	Y	20.00
	CC	£125
Melton. S	G	40.00
Menai Bridge	O	20.00
Mere	C	60.00
	O	20.00
	V	20.00
	V erased	40.00
Merthyr Tidvil	V	20.00
Merthyr Tydfil	W	15.00
	P	5.00
	BB	40.00
Merthyr Tydvill	M	15.00
Mevagissey	C	20.00
Michldean	C	£125
Middleham	CC	60.00
Middlesborough	O	40.00
MiddlesBro	CC	60.00
Middleton (M'ter)	C	£100
	K	£100
	BB	40.00
Middleton One Row	CC	£100
Middle Wallop	O	20.00
	CC	£100
Middlewich	D	60.00
	O	40.00
	P	5.00
	V	40.00
	W	40.00
	FF	£250
Midhurst	C	40.00
	D	60.00
	O	60.00
	P	5.00
	S	£125
	V	40.00
Midwich	C	£225
Milbrook	CC	60.00
Mildenhall (Suffk)	C	£100
	P	5.00
	V	60.00
	W	20.00
	W erased	20.00
	AA	20.00
Milford (Wales)	C	40.00
	P	5.00
	X	40.00
	Y	40.00
Milford Haven	V	60.00
Millbridge	O	40.00
	BB	60.00
Milnthorp	Y	40.00
	Y erased	40.00
Milnthorpe	H	60.00
	V	40.00
	W	40.00
	BB	40.00
Milverton	C	20.00
	V	20.00
Minchinhampton	D	60.00
	O	20.00
	S	£150
	V	40.00
	W	40.00
	Y	40.00
	AA	40.00
	BB	60.00
Minehead	C	60.00
	D	40.00
	W	20.00
	CC	40.00
Minster	CC	60.00
Mirfield	C boxed	60.00
	O	40.00
Missenden	O	20.00
	V	60.00
	W erased	60.00
Mitcheldean	O	20.00
Mitcheldever	CC	60.00
Mitford (North'd)	CC	60.00
Mk Weighton	W	20.00
M.Lavington	O	60.00
Mochdrai	O	60.00

55

Marks of the Provincial Post to 1839 - England and Wales

Modbury	C	20.00
	W	20.00
	W erased	20.00
Mold	C	60.00
	P	5.00
	V	15.00
	V erased	20.00
	W	15.00
Monksheath	O	40.00
Monk Wearmouth	CC	60.00
Monmouth	C	40.00
	D	40.00
	P	5.00
	S	£150
	V	15.00
	W	15.00
	Y	15.00
	Y erased	40.00
	Z	40.00
	BB	40.00
	JJ	20.00
Montgomery	D	40.00
	P	5.00
	V	20.00
	Y	40.00
	Y erased	40.00
Moreton Hampstead	K	£125
	CC	20.00
Moreton in Marsh	O	15.00
	W	20.00
	Y	20.00
	Y erased	20.00
	CC	60.00
Moreton-in-Mush (error)	BB	£300
Morley	O	40.00
	BB	60.00
Morpeth	C	40.00
	D	60.00
	H	40.00
	O	20.00
	P	5.00
	V	40.00
	W	20.00
	AA	60.00
	CC	60.00
Morton in Marsh	G	60.00
	P	5.00
	S	£150
	V	40.00
	W	20.00
Mottram (Manch'r)	BB	60.00
Mould	C	65.00
Mountgomery	D	£100
Mount Radford	CC	60.00
Mountsorrel (Essex)	B	£100
	V	60.00
M Raisin	C	£100
M.Tidvill	W	15.00
	W erased	20.00
Much Wenlock	O	20.00
Mundford	CC	£100
Mundon	CC	£100
M Weighton	D	£100
	G	60.00
Nailsworth	O	20.00
N Allerton	C	60.00
Namptwich	A (circular)	£300
	C	40.00
	H	40.00
	P	5.00
	R	20.00
	W	20.00
Nantwich	C	40.00
	Y erased	20.00

Narbarth	C	60.00
Narbeth	C	60.00
	O	10.00
	P	5.00
	W	20.00
	Y	20.00
	JJ	20.00
Nayland	C	60.00
	V	60.00
N Castle Unline	D	£250
Neasham	CC	£100
Neath	C	20.00
	F	£100
	H	60.00
	O	20.00
	P	5.00
	R	£100
	V	40.00
	W	15.00
Needham	C	£100
	D	£125
Needham M	V	60.00
Needham Market	W	40.00
	W erased	20.00
Nerbeth	V	20.00
Neston	C	60.00
	O	35.00
	V	40.00
	Y	20.00
Nettlebed	C	£150
	D	£150
	G	60.00
	O	20.00
	P	5.00
	S	£120
	V	40.00
	W	15.00
Newark	C	20.00
	P	5.00
	S	£150
	V	40.00
	W	40.00
	W erased	40.00
	Z	60.00
	CC	£100
	MM	£200
Newbiggin	CC	65.00
Newbridge	CC	40.00
New Brighton (Liverpool)	H	£100
	O	40.00
New Buckenham	CC	65.00
Newbury	C	40.00
	D	60.00
	G	40.00
	S	£100
	V	20.00
	W	20.00
	X	20.00
	X erased	15.00
	Z	40.00
	AA	60.00
	BB	40.00
Newby Bridge	CC	40.00
	O	60.00
Newcastle (North'd)	C	40.00
	D	40.00
	H	40.00
	R	£100
	S	90.00
	V	20.00
	BB	60.00
	CC	60.00
	JJ	20.00
	OO	40.00

Marks of the Provincial Post to 1839 - England and Wales

Place	Mark	Price
Newcastle (Staffs)	FF	60.00
Newcastle S (Staffs)	FF	60.00
Newcastle-Emln	V	20.00
	W	40.00
Newcastle-Emlyn	H	60.00
	O	15.00
Newcastle on Tyne	C	60.00
	H	40.00
	P	5.00
Newcastle-T	W	20.00
	X	15.00
	X erased	15.00
Newcastle Tyne	C	40.00
	M	60.00
Newcastle U.L.	P	8.00
	X	15.00
	W	20.00
	MM	£150
Newcastle-U-Line	V	20.00
Newcastle-U-Lyme	X	15.00
Newcastle Under Lime	X	40.00
Newcastle under Line	A (reversed horseshoe)	£150
	D	40.00
	J	40.00
Newcastle Under Lyme	E	£100
	X	20.00
	JJ	40.00
Newcastle Under Lyne	D	£100
	M	20.00
Newcastle U R Lyne	D	60.00
Newcastle Und.	S	£150
Newcastle Under	C	£100
Newcastle upon Tyne	D	40.00
Newcastle-U-T	V	20.00
	W	20.00
Newcastle-UTE	X	15.00
New Cross/Manchester	E	40.00
Newenden	O	60.00
Newent	W	20.00
New Ferry (Cheshire)	CC	£100
Newhaven	O	40.00
Newick	O	50.00
	CC	£100
Newington Kent	CC	60.00
Newmarket	D	£100
	G	60.00
	P	5.00
	S	£120
	V	40.00
	W	20.00
	Y	40.00
	Y erased	20.00
	BB	40.00
Newnham (Glos)	O	15.00
	P	5.00
	BB	£100
	MM	£125
Newnham-G	Y	40.00
Newnham-Glo.	V	40.00
Newnham Kent	CC	60.00
Newpor Pagnel	S (error)	£350
Newport (Mon)	V	20.00
Newport Isle of Wight	D	£100
	P distinctive	5.00
	CC	£150
Newport I.W.	V	60.00
	W	15.00
Newport.M	D	60.00
	K	60.00
	Y	15.00
	Y erased	40.00
Newport Mon	P	5.00
	BB	20.00
Newport Monmouth	CC	£175

Place	Mark	Price
Newport Pagnel	E	£100
	P	5.00
	S	£200
	V	20.00
	W	20.00
Newport (Shrops)	C	40.00
	D	40.00
	Y	20.00
Newport S.	V	40.00
	W	20.00
	Y	15.00
	Y erased	15.00
	MM	£200
Newport Salop	O	20.00
New Port (Yorks)	C	£100
Newport-Yorks	O	40.00
New Radnor	D	40.00
New Romney	C	20.00
	D	60.00
	O	40.00
	P	5.00
	V	20.00
	V erased	20.00
	CC	60.00
Newton (Lancs)	C	60.00
	CC	40.00
Newton (Lincs)	C	£100
Newton (Liverpool)	C	60.00
	O	40.00
Newton Abbot	C	40.00
	M	20.00
	P	5.00
	R	60.00
	W	40.00
	Y	20.00
	Z	£100
	AA	20.00
	CC	60.00
Newton Abbott	D	40.00
	Z	20.00
	CC	60.00
Newton Heath (M'ter)	BB	60.00
Newton Lancashire	CC	60.00
Newton St Cyres	CC	65.00
Newton St Looe	O	40.00
Newtown	C	20.00
	O	15.00
	P	5.00
	W	15.00
	Y	20.00
	BB	60.00
	JJ	50.00
NHampton	D	£150
N.hampton	V distinctive	75.00
Ninfield	D	£200
	O	60.00
N Isle of Wight	D	£100
	R	£100
Norham (North'd)	O	40.00
Normanton	O	40.00
	MM	£250
Northailerton	D	£150
Northalerton	D	£150
Northallerton	C	60.00
	D	60.00
	H	40.00
	M	40.00
	O	20.00
	P	5.00
	W	20.00
	W erased	20.00
Northampton	C	£100
	D	£100
	G	£100

57

Marks of the Provincial Post to 1839 - England and Wales

	H	£100		W erased	20.00
	P	5.00		X	20.00
	Q	5.00		JJ	20.00
	S	£150	N.Shields	C	40.00
	V	60.00		V	40.00
	V distinctive erased	£150		Z	60.00
				BB	60.00
	X	20.00		CC	40.00
	JJ	90.00	Nursling	CC	60.00
	MM	£150	Nuthurst	CC	£100
North Cave	C	£100	Oakham	C	£125
Northfield.P.P.	(distinctive)	£125		O	20.00
Northfleet	CC	75.00		P	5.00
Northgate (Cantab)	C	75.00		V	60.00
Northiam	O	40.00		W	60.00
	W	£100		W erased	60.00
Northleach	D	60.00		Y	60.00
	O	15.00	Oakhampton	D	£100
	P	5.00		V	60.00
Northleech	S	£125	Odiam	C	60.00
	V	40.00		F	£150
Northop	C	40.00		O	40.00
	H	40.00		P	6.00
	W	15.00		V	20.00
	Z	40.00		W	20.00
	CC	40.00	Okehampton	O	15.00
North Petherton	M	40.00		P	5.00
	O	20.00		Y	40.00
North Shields	C	65.00		Y erased	20.00
	G	40.00		AA	20.00
	H	40.00		FF	£125
	P	5.00	Old Buckenham	CC	£125
	X	20.00	Oldbury (Birm'ham)	C	20.00
	Z	60.00	Oldbury (Shrops)	C	40.00
North Sunderland	CC	40.00	Old-Down	C framed	20.00
North Tawton	CC	40.00		P	5.00
North Walsham	D	25.00	Old Hall Green	CC	£100
	W	15.00	Oldham	A (in double circle)	£225
	Y	15.00		BB	15.00
	JJ	60.00	Old Swan (L'pool)	C	£125
Northwich	D	60.00		O	40.00
	H	40.00	Ollerton	O	20.00
	O	20.00		Q	5.00
	P	5.00		V	40.00
	V	40.00		W	40.00
	W	20.00	Ombersley	O	40.00
	BB	£100	Ongar	C	£100
	JJ	£100		G	£100
Norton	CC	65.00		V	40.00
Norton Sheffield	O	40.00		W	60.00
Nortwich	B	£250		Y	60.00
Norwich	C	25.00	Orford	V	40.00
	D	60.00		W	40.00
	J	60.00		Z	60.00
	P	5.00	Ormskirk	C	40.00
	Q	5.00		D	60.00
	S	£100		P	5.00
	V	20.00		V	60.00
	W	40.00		W	20.00
	X	15.00		Y	60.00
	X erased	8.00		Z	60.00
	Z	£100		BB	60.00
	BB	40.00	Orpington	O	50.00
	CC	20.00	Ossett	BB	60.00
	JJ	50.00	Oswaldkirk	CC	75.00
	MM	£150	Oswestry	C	60.00
Nottingham	C	£100		D	60.00
	D	60.00		P	5.00
	P	5.00		R	£100
	Q	5.00		V	60.00
	S	£200		W	40.00
	U	£100		X	15.00
	V	40.00		Z	60.00
	W	15.00		AA	20.00

58

Marks of the Provincial Post to 1839 - England and Wales

Location	Mark	Price
	JJ	£100
Otford	O	60.00
Otley	G	60.00
	O	20.00
	P	5.00
	V	20.00
	W	20.00
	BB	£150
	CC	£150
	JJ	60.00
Otterbourne	CC	60.00
Otterton	C	40.00
	D	£100
	AA	40.00
	BB	40.00
	CC	60.00
	JJ	£150
Ottery	C	60.00
	W	60.00
Ottery St Mary	CC	60.00
Oulney	C	£150
	G	£100
	O	15.00
	V	40.00
Oundle	C	£100
	O	20.00
	P	5.00
	V	60.00
	W	40.00
	Y	40.00
	Y erased	40.00
Over Darwen	C	£100
Overseal	C	60.00
	CC	£100
Overton (Hants)	C	60.00
	V	40.00
	V erased	40.00
Overton F (Flint)	Y	20.00
Overton-Hants	P	8.00
Oxford	C	40.00
	G	60.00
	P	5.00
	S	90.00
	V	15.00
	W	15.00
	X	15.00
	X erased	15.00
	BB	£150
	HH	60.00
	MM	£150
Oxford Street/Manchester	E	20.00
Oxted	O	60.00
Padiham	O	40.00
Padstow	C	60.00
	O	25.00
	Y	40.00
	Y erased	60.00
Painswick	C	60.00
	O	15.00
	V	40.00
	V erased	15.00
	BB	£100
Panswick	C	£100
Parkgate Kent	O	40.00
Parkstone	CC	60.00
Pateley Bridge	O	40.00
Patrington	O	40.00
Peacock Inn	H	£200
Pearsmarsh	W	40.00
Peasmarsh	O	40.00
	CC	£100
Peeltown Isle of Man	A boxed	£500
Pembrey (Wales)	O	20.00
Pembrock	D	£200
Pembrok	D	£150
Pembroke	C	40.00
	D	20.00
	K	60.00
	P	5.00
	V	20.00
	W	15.00
	Y	15.00
	FF	£200
	JJ	75.00
Pembroke Dock	O	20.00
Pembrook	C	£150
	D	£150
Pembury	CC	60.00
Pencraig	CC	60.00
Penkridge	C	40.00
	O	40.00
	P	10.00
Penny Bridge	CC	60.00
Penrin	C	£200
Penrith	C	40.00
	D	60.00
	G	40.00
	H	20.00
	P	5.00
	R	60.00
	V	20.00
	W	20.00
	X	15.00
	X erased	15.00
	Z	40.00
	Z distinctive framed	£150
	JJ	60.00
Penryn	C	40.00
	H	60.00
	P	5.00
	R	40.00
	V	60.00
	W	20.00
	X no date	15.00
	X no mileage	15.00
Penshurst	CC	60.00
Pentrevoelas	V	40.00
Penybont	D	40.00
	W erased	20.00
Penzance	C	60.00
	P	5.00
	V	40.00
	X no circles	15.00
	BB	£100
	CC	60.00
	JJ	£100
Pershore	C	40.00
	O	20.00
	P	5.00
	V	40.00
	W	40.00
	JJ	30.00
Peterboro	W	60.00
Peterborough	C	£150
	D	60.00
	G	£100
	O	20.00
	P	5.00
	S	£150
	V	60.00
	W	40.00
	Z	£100
	BB three lines	£100
Peterchurch	CC	60.00
Petersfield	C	60.00
	D	£100
	G	60.00
	O	60.00

59

Marks of the Provincial Post to 1839 - England and Wales

	P	5.00	Ponterdulais	M	20.00
	S	£100		O	40.00
	W	40.00	Ponterfract	C	£100
	BB	60.00	Pontfract	C	£250
Petworth	C	20.00	Pontypool	O	8.00
	D	60.00	Pool	C	50.00
	P	5.00		W	20.00
	S	£200		X	20.00
	V	20.00		X erased	20.00
	W	20.00	Pool.D.	S	£200
	Y	60.00	Poole	P	5.00
	Y erased	20.00		V	20.00
Pewsey	C	£100		CC	50.00
	O	40.00	Portchester	O	50.00
	P	5.00	Port Madoc	O	30.00
	V	60.00	Portsea	C	60.00
	Y	60.00		O	30.00
	Y erased	60.00	Portsmouth	C	40.00
	CC	60.00		D	60.00
Pickering	C	40.00		G	60.00
	O	20.00		H	60.00
	P	5.00		P	5.00
	Q	5.00		Q	5.00
	CC	£150		S	£120
Pierce Bridge	CC	45.00		V	40.00
Pinner	O	40.00		X	20.00
Plimpton	R	£200		X inside circle	£100
Plym Dock	X	25.00		Z	£100
Plymouth	C	40.00		AA	40.00
	D	£100		JJ	75.00
	F	£250		MM	£125
	H	20.00	Post Witham (Lincs)	D	£250
	M	20.00	Potton	BB	40.00
	P	5.00	Poulton	CC	40.00
	R	£200	Powick	O	15.00
	S	£200	Prescot	C	60.00
	V	40.00		C lower case	£250
	W	20.00		M	60.00
	X	15.00		O	40.00
	X erased	40.00		P	5.00
	Z	20.00		S	£175
	AA	20.00		V	60.00
	CC	40.00		W	40.00
	JJ	40.00		Y	60.00
Plymouth Dk	V	60.00		Y erased	40.00
	X	20.00		Z	£100
Plymouth Dock	C	£100		BB	60.00
	D	20.00		CC	£100
	H	£100		JJ	60.00
	M	£100	Prestbury (Glos)	O	20.00
	V	75.00	Presteign	C	20.00
	W	40.00		D	40.00
	Z	60.00		H	20.00
Plympton	M	60.00		O	20.00
	P	5.00		P	5.00
	V	60.00		V	20.00
	W	60.00		Y	20.00
Plymton	W	60.00		Y erased	40.00
	W erased	20.00	Prestein	C	£150
Pmouth (Portsmouth)	B	£250	Preston	C	40.00
Pocklington	D	60.00		D	60.00
	H	60.00		G	40.00
	P	5.00		H	40.00
	W	20.00		P	5.00
	W erased	20.00		Q	5.00
Polpero	C	60.00		R	£150
Polperro	N	£200		R distinctive	£250
Pontefract	C	60.00		V	40.00
	D	40.00		W	20.00
	G	40.00		X	20.00
	O	20.00		Z	40.00
	P	5.00		HH	60.00
	W	15.00		JJ	75.00
	Y	20.00		MM	£200

Marks of the Provincial Post to 1839 - England and Wales

Location	Mark	Price
Preston Brook	P	10.00
	BB distinctive	£150
Princes Risborough	O	20.00
Prittlewell	O	25.00
	CC	£100
Puckeridge	CC	£100
Pudsey	O	40.00
	BB	60.00
Pulborough	O	20.00
Pulhely	C	40.00
Purbrook	O	60.00
Pwllheli	O	20.00
	P	5.00
Pyle	O	15.00
Queenboro	G	60.00
Queenborough	D	60.00
	G	£100
	H	60.00
	P	5.00
	S	£120
	V	20.00
	V erased	20.00
	W	20.00
Radcliffe	BB	£150
Radnor	H	60.00
	V	40.00
	W	20.00
	W erased	20.00
Ragland	O	40.00
Rainham	CC	60.00
Raisen (Lincs)	W	60.00
Ramsbottom	O	40.00
Ramsbury (Wilts)	O	40.00
	S	£120
	V	40.00
	V erased	20.00
Ramsey Isle of Man	A boxed	£300
	C	£1500
Ramsgate	C	60.00
	G	60.00
	P	5.00
	S	£125
	V	15.00
	W	15.00
	BB	40.00
	CC	60.00
	MM	£200
Ravenglass	H	40.00
	O	30.00
	P	5.00
	Y	40.00
	Y erased	40.00
	BB	60.00
	CC	60.00
Rawclife	D	£100
Rawcliffe	C	40.00
	D	£100
	H	£100
Rawden	O	30.00
	BB	60.00
Rawtenstall	BB	£100
Rayleigh	C	£100
	O	30.00
	W	60.00
Reading	A (in double circle)	£450
	C	60.00
	D	£100
	F	£150
	G	40.00
	P	5.00
	R	60.00
	V	20.00
	X	20.00
	Z	40.00
	BB	40.00
	JJ	50.00
London St/Reading	E	40.00
Russell St/Reading	E	40.00
Redbridge	CC	60.00
Redburn	G	£150
Redcar	CC	60.00
Redditch	C	60.00
	O	15.00
	V	40.00
	Y	40.00
Redland (Bristol)	CC	25.00
Redruth	C	60.00
	O	20.00
	P	5.00
	Y	20.00
	Y erased	40.00
	JJ	60.00
Reepham	O	40.00
Reeth	O	30.00
Reigate	C	60.00
	O	20.00
	P	5.00
	W	40.00
	Y	60.00
	Y erased	40.00
Retford	C	40.00
	D	£150
	O	20.00
	P	8.00
	V	40.00
	W	20.00
	W erased	40.00
Rewe	CC	£100
Rhayader	D	£100
	H	40.00
	O	20.00
	P	5.00
	V	40.00
	W	40.00
Rhuabon	C	15.00
	O	20.00
	BB	£100
Richmond	C	60.00
	D	£100
	H	60.00
	O	20.00
	P	5.00
	V	20.00
	W	15.00
	BB	60.00
Richmond Y	C	40.00
	H	60.00
Richmond YE	C	60.00
Richmond Yorkshe	D	60.00
Rickmansworth	P	5.00
	V	60.00
	W	40.00
	W erased	60.00
	BB	£100
Ridge	CC	£100
Ringwood	C	40.00
	D	60.00
	O	30.00
	P	5.00
	S	£150
	V	40.00
	W	20.00
	CC	65.00
Ripley (Surrey)	C	£125
	G	£100
	O	30.00
	P	5.00
	S	£200

61

Marks of the Provincial Post to 1839 - England and Wales

Town	Mark	Price
	V	60.00
	W	40.00
	W erased	40.00
	Z	40.00
Ripley Yorks	O	40.00
Ripon	H	40.00
	P	5.00
	R	20.00
	V	20.00
	W	15.00
	X	15.00
	BB	40.00
Rippon	C	60.00
	G	40.00
	R	£100
	V	20.00
Risca	CC	20.00
R.Isle of Wight	D	£200
	R distinctive	£250
Robertsbridge	C	40.00
	O	20.00
	P	8.00
Rochdale	C	40.00
	D	60.00
	M	60.00
	P	5.00
	V	60.00
	W	40.00
	X	60.00
	Z	60.00
	CC	60.00
	MM	£225
Rochester	C	40.00
	D	60.00
	F	£125
	G	40.00
	P	5.00
	Q	5.00
	S three line	£200
	V	20.00
	W	20.00
	W erased	20.00
Rochford	C	60.00
	O	20.00
	P	5.00
	V	40.00
	W	20.00
	Z	60.00
	AA	60.00
	CC	60.00
Rockbeare	CC	£100
Rockingham	D	£150
	W	60.00
	W erased	60.00
Rolvenden	C	20.00
	O	60.00
Romford	PP distinctive	65.00
	P	5.00
	X	20.00
	X erased	20.00
	Z	40.00
	AA	40.00
	BB	40.00
	CC	40.00
Romney	BB	60.00
Romsey	P	5.00
	X	20.00
	X erased	20.00
Ross	C	40.00
	P	5.00
	V	40.00
	W	20.00
	W erased	20.00
	Z	20.00

Town	Mark	Price
	CC	40.00
	HH	£100
	JJ	15.00
Rotherfield	CC	£100
Rotherham	C	40.00
	D	£100
	P	5.00
	S	£150
	V	20.00
	W	15.00
	JJ	20.00
	MM	£225
Rothersbridge	G	£150
Rothwell	O	40.00
Rougham	C	£150
	O	15.00
	P	5.00
	V	20.00
	Z	20.00
	CC	£100
Royston	C	£100
	D	£100
	O	15.00
	P	5.00
	V	40.00
	V erased	40.00
	CC	£100
Rudgeley	C	40.00
Rudgwick	CC	£100
Rugby	C	40.00
	O	20.00
	P	5.00
	V	20.00
	Y	40.00
	Y erased	15.00
	JJ	£100
	MM	£150
Rugeley	C	40.00
	O	30.00
	P	8.00
	JJ	£100
Rumford	C	60.00
	D	£150
	K	£100
	R	40.00
	V	40.00
	W	40.00
Rumney	F	£100
	G	60.00
Rumsey	C	40.00
	G	60.00
	R	£100
	V	40.00
	W	20.00
Rumsy	C	£125
Runcorn	C	40.00
	P	5.00
Rushyford	C	60.00
	D	60.00
	O	60.00
	P	5.00
	W	20.00
	BB	60.00
Ruthin	C	20.00
	P	5.00
	V	20.00
	W	15.00
	X	20.00
	X erased	15.00
	JJ	£100
Ruyton	CC	40.00
Ryde (IOW)	C	60.00
	O	40.00
	Q	5.00

62

Marks of the Provincial Post to 1839 - England and Wales

Place	Mark	Value
	W	20.00
	BB	£200
	JJ	£100
	MM	£250
Ryde IW	W	40.00
Rye	C	40.00
	G	£100
	P	5.00
	S	£150
	V	40.00
	W	40.00
	W erased	20.00
	Z	60.00
	AA	£100
Ryegate	C	60.00
	D	£150
	S	£200
	V	40.00
	W	40.00
Ryton	CC	60.00
Saffron Walden	D	£100
	G	£125
	O	40.00
	P	5.00
	S	£175
	V	60.00
	W	40.00
	Y	60.00
St Albans	C	£100
	D	£150
	G	60.00
	P	5.00
	S	£200
	V	40.00
	W	40.00
	Y	20.00
	Y erased	40.00
	Z	60.00
	CC	£100
	JJ	£150
	MM	£200
St Asaph	C	40.00
	D	60.00
	H	40.00
	O	20.00
	P	5.00
	V	20.00
	W	15.00
	W erased	15.00
	BB	60.00
	CC	£100
	HH	£150
St Austell	O	20.00
	P	5.00
	CC	40.00
	JJ	£100
St Austle	C	60.00
	H	£150
	V	60.00
	W	20.00
	W erased	40.00
	Y	20.00
St Clairs	FF	£150
St Clears	C	£100
	O	20.00
	MM	£200
St Colmbes	C	£250
St Colombe	C	£250
St Columb	C	40.00
	D	£125
	P	5.00
	V	20.00
	V erased	20.00
	Y	20.00

Place	Mark	Value
	Y erased	40.00
	CC	£100
St Cross	CC	40.00
St Davids	CC	60.00
St Davids Hill	CC	40.00
St Faiths	CC	£100
St Germains	H	60.00
St Germans	D	20.00
	CC	£100
St Helens	O	60.00
St Ives (Hunts)	A	£250
	C	60.00
	P	5.00
	R	£125
	V	40.00
	W	20.00
	W erased	60.00
St Ives C(Cornw'l)	C	40.00
	K	£100
St John's Common	CC	£100
St John's Worcester	O	20.00
St Lawrence (Kent)	O	50.00
St Leonards	D	£100
	P	5.00
St Mary Bourne	CC	60.00
St Mawes	C	20.00
	O	20.00
St Maws	C	60.00
St Neots	C	40.00
	O	20.00
	P	8.00
	V	£100
	W	40.00
St Noets (error)	O	£200
St Peters (Kent)	N	£500
	O	40.00
St Sidwell	CC	20.00
St Thomas	CC	20.00
Salesbury	D	£150
Salford/Manchester	E	20.00
Salford/Manchr	A	£200
Salisbury	C	40.00
	D	60.00
	D boxed	£200
	P	5.00
	Q	5.00
	S	£100
	V	20.00
	X	15.00
	Z	40.00
	JJ	30.00
	MM	£100
Salop	C	£100
Saltersgate	D	£150
Salterton	AA	£100
Sandbach	O	20.00
	P	5.00
	V	40.00
	W	20.00
Sandgate	O	30.00
Sandhurst	W	20.00
Sandhurst-Kent	O	50.00
Sandling	O	50.00
Sandpits (B'ham)	C	60.00
Sandwich	C	20.00
	D	60.00
	G	60.00
	O	20.00
	P	5.00
	S	£150
	V	20.00
	W	15.00
Sarre	CC	£200
Sawbridgeworth	O	30.00

63

Marks of the Provincial Post to 1839 - England and Wales

Location	Mark	Price
	P	5.00
	W	60.00
Sawston	O	50.00
Saxmundham	D	60.00
	P	5.00
	W	20.00
	W erased	40.00
Scarboro	W	20.00
Scarboroug	J	60.00
Scarborough	C	60.00
	D	60.00
	H	60.00
	P	5.00
	V	20.00
	W	20.00
	X	15.00
	CC	£125
	JJ	40.00
Scilly	C	£200
	P	£150
Scole	C	£100
	P	5.00
	V	20.00
	JJ	60.00
Scottow	Y	£150
Seacomb (L'pool)	CC	40.00
Seacombe (L'pool)	N	£350
	O	20.00
	CC	60.00
Seaford	G	60.00
	O	30.00
	W	60.00
Seaham	O	50.00
Sea Houses (Sussex)	CC	60.00
Seal	O	50.00
Seaton (Devon)	A (in circle with no.2)	£150
	C	£100
	C (with no.2)	40.00
Seaton (Durham)	CC	60.00
Sedberg	CC	60.00
Sedbergh	C	40.00
	O	30.00
Seddlescomb	CC	40.00
Sedgefield	O	50.00
Selby	C	60.00
	M	40.00
	O	20.00
	P	5.00
	Y	40.00
	MM	£300
Settle	C	60.00
	H	40.00
	O	20.00
	P	5.00
	V	20.00
	W	15.00
	X	20.00
	Y	20.00
	BB	60.00
Sevenoakes	Z	45.00
Seven Oaks	A (inside circle)	£200
	G	60.00
	P	5.00
	V	15.00
	V erased	15.00
	AA	40.00
Sevenoaks	C	40.00
	D	60.00
	G	60.00
	S	£100
Shaftesbury	D	65.00
	P	5.00
	V	40.00
	W	15.00

Location	Mark	Price
	Y	15.00
	Y erased	15.00
	Z	60.00
	AA	20.00
	BB	20.00
	FF	£150
	MM	£150
Shaftsbury	C	40.00
	S	£100
	Z	£100
	FF	£200
Shaldon	O	20.00
Shap	C	£150
	O	30.00
Shardelow	V	60.00
Sheerness	C	60.00
	P	5.00
	V	20.00
	W	20.00
	W erased	20.00
Sheffeild	D	£200
Sheffield	C	40.00
	D	60.00
	G	60.00
	P	5.00
	S	£200
	U	£150
	V	20.00
	W	15.00
	X	15.00
	X erased	20.00
	Z	60.00
	Z small boxed	£100
	AA	£100
	JJ	30.00
	MM	£175
Duke St/Sheffield	D	40.00
Gibralter St/ Sheffield	E	40.00
Glossop Rd/ Sheffield	E	40.00
South St/ Sheffield	E	40.00
The Wicker/Sheffield	E	40.00
Shefford	V	40.00
	W	40.00
	Z	60.00
	BB	60.00
	CC	60.00
Shefield	C	£200
Shefnal	C	60.00
Shefnall	C	£150
Shelton Staffs	O	60.00
Shenley	CC	£100
Sheptn Mallet	FF	£300
Shepton Mallet	P	5.00
	V	40.00
	W	40.00
	JJ	60.00
Shepton Mallett	W	40.00
Sherbone	D	£400
Sherborn	D	£150
Sherborne	A (in circle with Post Office)	£450
	D	40.00
	P	5.00
	S	£120
	V	20.00
	W	20.00
	W erased	20.00
	Z	40.00
	JJ	75.00
Sherbourne	C	£300
Shields-N	V	20.00
Shields.S	V	20.00
Shiere	O	60.00
	BB	60.00

Marks of the Provincial Post to 1839 - England and Wales

Place	Mark	Price
Shiffnal	C	60.00
	P	5.00
	S	£150
	V	40.00
	W	15.00
	W erased	15.00
	X	15.00
	AA	20.00
	BB	£100
	MM	£200
Shiffnall	D	60.00
	Z	40.00
Shifnal	C	£100
Shifnall	C	40.00
	D	£200
Shildon	O	20.00
	CC	40.00
Shipdam	C	60.00
	D	£200
Shipdham	C	20.00
Shipston	C	40.00
	W	40.00
Shipstone on Stour	M	20.00
	P	8.00
	BB	60.00
Shipton (another spelling of Shipston)		
	V	60.00
Shipton Mallet	D	£150
	J	60.00
Shirley	CC	60.00
Shirley Street	PP distinctive	£100
Shirleywich	C	60.00
Shooters Hill	CC	60.00
Shoreham	D	£150
	H	£100
	P	5.00
	V	40.00
	Y	40.00
	Y erased	20.00
	Z	£100
	BB	£100
Shoreham S	D	£150
Shrewsbury	C	40.00
	D	20.00
	H	20.00
	P	5.00
	V	40.00
	X	15.00
	X erased	15.00
	BB	40.00
	JJ	30.00
	MM	90.00
Sidmouth	C	75.00
	D	£100
	O	20.00
	P	5.00
	V	20.00
	W	20.00
Silsoe	G	60.00
	O	50.00
Silverton	CC	50.00
Sittingbourn	D	£100
	V	20.00
Sittingbourne	D	£100
	M dated	15.00
	S	£150
	W	15.00
	W erased	15.00
	Z	60.00
	CC	60.00
Skelton	O	40.00
	CC	60.00
Skipton	C	40.00
	D	£100

Place	Mark	Price
	O	20.00
	P	5.00
	V	20.00
	W	20.00
	Y	40.00
	Y erased	20.00
	BB	£100
Skirlaugh	O	40.00
Slaithwaite	O	40.00
Sleaford	C	£200
	D	£100
	J	£100
	N	£500
	P	5.00
	S	£125
	V	40.00
	Y	20.00
	Y erased	20.00
Sledmere	C	40.00
	C boxed	40.00
	O	30.00
Slough (Bucks)	P	5.00
Smarden	CC	65.00
Smethwick	P.P (distinctive)	40.00
Snaith	M	40.00
	O	30.00
Snettisham	CC	40.00
Sodbury (Glos)	C	£100
Solva	CC	40.00
Somersham	C	£100
	O	30.00
Somerton	C	65.00
	D	£100
	P	5.00
	S	£125
	V	40.00
	W	40.00
	BB	65.00
Sonning	O	30.00
So.Shields	BB	£100
Southall	C	£100
	D	£100
	O	30.00
	P	5.00
	S	£150
	V	40.00
	W	40.00
	BB	£100
Southam	C	£100
	P	5.00
	V	40.00
Southampton	C	60.00
	D	40.00
	G	40.00
	P	5.00
	S	£100
	V	40.00
	W	15.00
	X	15.00
	X erased	15.00
	Z	40.00
	Z dated	20.00
	AA	40.00
	BB	40.00
	MM	£125
Southbourne	CC	60.00
South Cave	C	60.00
	D	75.00
	O	30.00
Southend	O	20.00
	P	5.00
	CC	£100
Southminster	G	£200
	CC	£100

65

Marks of the Provincial Post to 1839 - England and Wales

Location	Mark	Price
South Molton	C	20.00
	M	15.00
	P	5.00
South Moulton	D	25.00
South Parade (Leamington,Wks)	E	40.00
South Petherton	D	60.00
	E	60.00
	P	5.00
Southport	C	£150
	P	15.00
	CC	£100
South Shields	D	£100
	P	5.00
	Q	5.00
	X	15.00
	JJ	60.00
South Teal (error for South Zeal)	CC	£100
Southwell	C	60.00
	O	20.00
	P	5.00
	W	20.00
Southwold	C	60.00
	Z	60.00
	BB	20.00
	CC	20.00
Spalding	C	40.00
	D	£125
	H	£100
	O	20.00
	P	5.00
	R	20.00
	S	£125
	V	40.00
	W	20.00
	Y	20.00
	BB	60.00
	CC	65.00
Spennithorpe	CC	60.00
S.Petherton	O	30.00
Spilsby	C	40.00
	O	20.00
	P	5.00
	S	£120
	W	40.00
	W erased	40.00
	BB	£100
Spittal	O	50.00
Spittal-Durham	O	40.00
S.Shields	C	£100
	R	£150
S Strat	B	£200
S Stratford	D	£150
Stafford	C	65.00
	D	65.00
	O	30.00
	P	5.00
	S	£150
	W	20.00
	W erased	20.00
	Z	65.00
	MM	£200
Staford	C	£250
Staindrop	O	20.00
Staines	C	£100
	G	60.00
	P	5.00
	R	£150
	V	20.00
	W	40.00
	X	20.00
	X erased	20.00
	Z	65.00
	MM	£200
Staleybridge	C	40.00
Staley Bridge	BB	£100
Stalham	CC	£100
Stalybridge	C	40.00
Stamford	C	60.00
	D	£100
	P	5.00
	S	£150
	V	20.00
	W	20.00
	Y	20.00
	JJ	£100
Stampford	D	£100
Standish	O	30.00
Stanes	C	£150
Stanhope	C framed	£250
	O	30.00
Stanmore	P	10.00
Stanstead (Herts)	CC	£100
Stapleford Cambridge	O	65.00
Staplehurst	O	40.00
	P	5.00
Starcross	CC	40.00
Stayning	E	£250
Stevenage	D	£150
	G	£150
	P	5.00
	V	60.00
	V erased	40.00
Stewkeley	CC	£100
Steyning	C	£100
	H	£100
	O	30.00
	P	5.00
	S	£200
	V	60.00
	W	40.00
	Z	£100
	AA	60.00
Stillington	CC	65.00
Stilton	C	£100
	D	£150
	G	£150
	O	40.00
	P	5.00
	V	40.00
	Y	60.00
	MM	£300
Stockbridge	G	60.00
	P	5.00
	V	40.00
	V erased	40.00
	CC	40.00
Stockenchurch	C	£100
Stockport (8 varieties, 1784-1813)	A	£100+
	C	40.00
	D	60.00
	P	5.00
	V	40.00
	W	20.00
	X	20.00
	X erased	20.00
	Y	60.00
	Z distinctive	£100
	JJ	65.00
	MM	£200
Stockton	C	40.00
	D	£100
	H	40.00
	M	40.00
	P	5.00
	V	15.00
	W	15.00
	X	15.00
	BB	£100

Marks of the Provincial Post to 1839 - England and Wales

Place	Mark	Price
	CC	£150
Stockton on T	V	20.00
Stoke (Norfolk)	C	40.00
Stoke-Bucks	O	20.00
Stoke Canon	CC	£100
Stoke Climsland	CC	65.00
Stoke Ferry	C	25.00
	O	5.00
	CC	£100
Stoke-N (Norfolk)	V	40.00
Stokenchurch	O	40.00
	P	5.00
	V	40.00
	Y	60.00
	Y erased	40.00
Stokesley	C	60.00
	P	5.00
	V	20.00
	W erased	20.00
	Y	20.00
	BB	60.00
Stoke under Ham (Som)	C	£100
Stoke upon Trent	O	40.00
Stone	C	40.00
	P	5.00
	S	£150
	V	40.00
	W	15.00
	MM	£150
Stonecrouch	C	£200
	D	65.00
	S	£100
Stoneham	O	40.00
	P	5.00
Stoney Cross	C boxed	£100
Stoney Middleton	H	60.00
Stoney Stratford	M	20.00
	P	5.00
	V	40.00
	W	40.00
	W erased	40.00
Stonham	C	£100
	O	30.00
	V	60.00
	W	60.00
Stony Stratford	D	£100
	G	£100
	S	£200
Storington	O	20.00
Storrington	C	60.00
Stouerbridg	D	£100
Stourbridge	C	20.00
	D	40.00
	P	5.00
	S	£100
	V	20.00
	W	20.00
	Y	20.00
	Y erased	20.00
	Z	60.00
	CC	65.00
	MM	£150
Stourport	C	40.00
	D	40.00
	E inside oval	65.00
	O	15.00
	P	5.00
	W	40.00
	MM	£100
Stow	X undated	65.00
Stowerbridg	D	£150
Stowerbridge	C	£200
	D	65.00
	D inside circle	£200

Place	Mark	Price
Stow in the Wold	M	20.00
Stowmarket	O	20.00
	P	5.00
	V	60.00
	W	40.00
	Y	60.00
	Y erased	40.00
Stratfd on Avon	AA	60.00
	BB	40.00
Stratford	V	60.00
	Z	£100
	HH	60.00
	JJ	60.00
Stratford on A	Y	15.00
	AA	60.00
	BB	60.00
Stratford on Avon	E	60.00
	M dated	20.00
	P	5.00
	S	£150
	W	15.00
	BB	60.00
	CC	£100
	JJ	65.00
	MM	£200
Stratford Upon Avon	E	£150
Strathfield Turgis	M	40.00
Stratton (Cornwall)	H	40.00
	O	15.00
	CC	65.00
Stratton (Norfolk)	V	40.00
	W	65.00
Stretford (Manch'r)	PP (distinctive)	65.00
Stretton	CC	60.00
Stretton on Dunsmore	O	30.00
Stroud	C	40.00
	P	5.00
	V	40.00
	W	20.00
	X undated	20.00
	X erased	20.00
	CC	£100
	HH	£100
Studley	C	20.00
	O	30.00
Sturminster Marshall	O	45.00
Sudbury (Suffolk)	C	£100
	D	60.00
	F	£200
	P	8.00
	V	60.00
	W	20.00
	Z	60.00
	BB	40.00
	CC	40.00
Sudbury-D (Derbysh)	C	65.00
Sudbury-S (Suffk)	C	£100
Sunderland	C	£100
	D	65.00
	H	65.00
	P	5.00
	V	15.00
	W	15.00
	X	15.00
	BB	20.00
	JJ	80.00
Sunng Hill	B framed	£150
Sunninghill	C	60.00
	O	30.00
	CC	65.00
Sutterton	Z	£100
	CC	60.00
	Crown bag seal	£500
Sutton (Yorks)	CC	£100

67

Marks of the Provincial Post to 1839 - England and Wales

Location	Mark	Price
Sutton Coldfield	E	20.00
Sutton-in-Ashfield	CC	£100
Sutton Scotney	CC	75.00
Swaffham	C	20.00
	D	£200
	P	5.00
	S	£200
	V	40.00
	W	20.00
	BB	65.00
	CC	65.00
Swanage	C	40.00
	H	45.00
Swansea	C	20.00
	Q	5.00
	V	15.00
	X	15.00
	X erased	15.00
	JJ	50.00
Swanton	C	£100
Swanwick	CC	45.00
Swanzey (Swansea)	C	20.00
	D	60.00
Swathling	CC	65.00
Swinden	C	£100
Swindon	C	60.00
	D	60.00
	J	60.00
	O	30.00
	P	5.00
	MM	£150
Swineshead (Lincs)	C distinctive	£200
Swineshead Lincolns	CC	£100
Tadcaster	C	40.00
	D	65.00
	O	20.00
	P	5.00
	V	15.00
	W	15.00
Taibach	O	40.00
	P	5.00
	JJ	60.00
Tamworth	C	60.00
	D	£100
	O	40.00
	P	5.00
	V	40.00
	W	20.00
	Y	20.00
	Y erased	20.00
Tanybwlch	M	40.00
Taplow	O	30.00
	CC	60.00
Tarleton	CC	60.00
Tarporley	O	30.00
	P	5.00
	W	40.00
Taunton	C	60.00
	H	60.00
	P	5.00
	R	60.00
	V	40.00
	W	20.00
	W erased	20.00
	X	20.00
	Z	40.00
	Z dated	15.00
	FF	£350
	JJ	50.00
	MM	£200
Tavistock	C	£100
	H	£100
	O	20.00
	P	5.00
	V	60.00
	W	15.00
	Y	15.00
	Z	£100
	AA	£100
	HH (scroll)	£125
	MM	£300
Tean	O	65.00
Tedbury (Glos)	C	60.00
Teignmouth	C	£100
	P	5.00
	V	60.00
	Y	15.00
	Y erased	15.00
	BB	60.00
	CC	60.00
Temple Sowerby	CC	60.00
Tempsford	CC	65.00
Tenbury	C	40.00
	O	20.00
	P	5.00
	S	£200
	V	40.00
Tenby	C	40.00
	P	5.00
	V	40.00
	W	15.00
	Y	40.00
	Y erased	20.00
Tenterden	C	40.00
	D	£100
	P	5.00
	R	£100
	V	20.00
	W	15.00
	Y	20.00
	Y erased	20.00
Terrington (Nfk)	CC	65.00
Tetbury	C	60.00
	O	15.00
	P	5.00
	V	40.00
	W	20.00
Tetsworth	C	40.00
	D	60.00
	O	40.00
	V	15.00
	W	15.00
	Z	60.00
	BB	£100
Tettenhall	O	50.00
Tewkesbury	C	40.00
	D	60.00
	P	5.00
	R	£100
	X	20.00
	BB	40.00
	CC	40.00
	JJ	50.00
Tewksbury	C	40.00
	D	60.00
	V	20.00
Thame	C	£150
	F	£250
	P	4.00
	R	15.00
	S	£200
	V	40.00
	W	20.00
	CC	60.00
Thames Ditton	CC	60.00
Thaxted	BB	£125
Thetford	C	25.00
	D	60.00

68

Marks of the Provincial Post to 1839 - England and Wales

Place	Mark	Price
	R mileage above	£200
	S	£175
	V	15.00
	W	15.00
	Y	15.00
	Y erased	20.00
Thirsk	C	60.00
	G	40.00
	H	40.00
	O	20.00
	P	5.00
	V	20.00
	W	15.00
	Y	20.00
Thornbury (Som)	O	20.00
Thorne	C	60.00
	H	60.00
	O	20.00
	P	5.00
	V	20.00
	W	15.00
Thorney	O	65.00
Thornham	CC	60.00
Thorp-Arch	O	40.00
Thorpe (Essex)	C	60.00
Thorpe (Norfolk)	CC	£100
Thrapston	C	£100
Thrapstone	D	£100
	O	30.00
	P	5.00
	V	60.00
	W	40.00
	Z	£100
	BB	£100
Thropston	D	£150
Thwaite	C	£150
	V	£100
Ticehurst	O	20.00
	CC	60.00
Tickhill	O	20.00
Tid	CC	60.00
Tiddeswell	D	£150
Tideswell	C	£100
	D	£100
	O	50.00
	V	£100
	W	£100
Tillingham	CC	£100
Tintern Abbey	O	65.00
Tipton	C	60.00
Titchfield	O	£100
Tiverton	C	60.00
	D	£150
	H	£100
	K	£100
	P	5.00
	V	60.00
	W	15.00
	Y	15.00
	Y erased	20.00
	Z	60.00
	CC	£100
Tocester	D	£200
Todmorden	CC	40.00
Tolleshurst D'Arcy	CC	£150
Tonbridge Wells	P	5.00
	JJ	£100
Topsham	C	£100
	H	£100
	P	5.00
	V	60.00
	V erased	60.00
Topsham Road	CC	£100
Torquay	C	60.00
	P	5.00
	CC	40.00
	JJ	£150
Torrington	D	£150
	H	60.00
	O	30.00
	P	5.00
Totnes	C	£100
	D	£100
	O	20.00
	BB	£100
Totness	C	60.00
	H	60.00
	P	5.00
	V	60.00
	W	60.00
	Y	60.00
	Y erased	60.00
	CC	60.00
Totton	CC	40.00
Towcester	C	60.00
	D	£150
	G	60.00
	O	20.00
	P	5.00
	S	£200
	V	40.00
	V erased	20.00
Town Malling	D	£150
	S	£200
Towyn	C	40.00
Trecastle	O	50.00
Tredegar	O	20.00
Tregony	C	60.00
	Y	40.00
	Y erased	20.00
Tremadoc	O	20.00
Tring	C	£150
	G	£100
	O	20.00
	P	5.00
	S	£175
	V	40.00
	W	40.00
	W erased	60.00
Trowbridge	C	60.00
	D	60.00
	O	40.00
	P	5.00
	S	£100
	V	60.00
	W	20.00
	W erased	40.00
	MM	£200
Truro	C	20.00
	P	5.00
	V	40.00
	W	20.00
	AA	20.00
	HH	40.00
	JJ	£100
	MM	£200
Truroe	C	£200
Trysall	CC	£100
Tunbridge	C	60.00
	D	60.00
	G	40.00
	O	40.00
	P	5.00
	S	£100
	V	20.00
	W	20.00
	BB	60.00
	CC	60.00

69

Marks of the Provincial Post to 1839 - England and Wales

	MM	£150		Z	60.00
Tunbridge Wells	D	60.00	Uxbridge	C	£100
	G	£100		D	£100
	S	£120		K	£100
	Y	20.00		O	50.00
	Circular mileage	40.00		P	5.00
	Circ mileage erased	20.00		S	£175
Tunb-Wells	A framed	£200		V	60.00
	V	20.00		W	40.00
	W	20.00		W erased	60.00
Tunstall	O	30.00		CC	£100
Tutbury	O	60.00	Ventnor (IOW)	O	20.00
Tuxford	C	£200	Wadebridge	C	40.00
	D	£150		M	15.00
	P	10.00	Wadesmill	CC	£100
	V	40.00	Wadhurst	BB	60.00
	W erased	40.00		CC	60.00
Twycross	CC	£100	Wailingford (error)	D	£200
Twyford (Hants)	CC	60.00	Wakefield	C	40.00
Twyford-Berks	O	40.00		D	60.00
Tynemouth	C	40.00		H	40.00
	O	20.00		P	5.00
Uckfield	C	60.00		R	£100
	G	60.00		V	20.00
	O	20.00		W	15.00
	P	5.00		X	15.00
	V	40.00		X erased	40.00
	V erased	40.00		BB	£100
	Z	60.00		HH	60.00
	AA	40.00		JJ	40.00
Uley (Glos)	C	40.00	Wakering	CC	60.00
	O	20.00	Wallingford	D	60.00
	Y	40.00		M	20.00
Ullesthorpe	O	60.00		P	5.00
Ulverston	C	60.00		V	20.00
	W	20.00		W	20.00
Ulverstone	M	20.00		Z	40.00
	P	5.00		BB	60.00
	V	40.00		CC	60.00
	W	40.00	Wallsend	CC	40.00
	BB	60.00	Walmer	O	50.00
Upper Mill	O	40.00	Walsall	C	40.00
	BB	60.00		O	30.00
Upper Parade/Leamington	E	40.00		P	5.00
Uppingham	C	£100		V	40.00
	D	£200		W	20.00
	O	20.00		Z	£100
	P	5.00	Walsingham	C	20.00
	W	40.00		D	60.00
	Y	20.00		O	25.00
Upton (Liverpool)	N	£200		Y	20.00
	O	65.00	Waltham Cross	D	£100
Upton (Worcs)	O	20.00		P	5.00
	V	60.00		R	£150
	Y	40.00		V	60.00
Upton.C (Liv'pl)	CC	75.00		W	40.00
Upton on S.	C	40.00		W erased	40.00
Upton on Severn	D	40.00		Z	60.00
Usk	C	20.00		AA	£100
	P	5.00		BB	£100
	S	£100		CC	£100
	V	15.00	Walton (Liv)	C framed	60.00
	W	15.00	Wandesford	D	£200
	W erased	20.00	Wandsford	O	20.00
	CC	60.00		P	5.00
	JJ	60.00	Wangford	D	£100
Usworth	CC	£100		P	8.00
Utoxeter	D	£150		W	60.00
Uttoxeter	C	40.00		Z	60.00
	D	65.00	Wansford	V	£100
	P	8.00		W	£100
	V	40.00		W erased	65.00
	W	20.00	Wantage	C	40.00
	W erased	20.00		D	£100

Marks of the Provincial Post to 1839 - England and Wales

		G	40.00	Wavertree (L'pool)		O	20.00
		P	5.00			CC	65.00
		S	£150	Wednesbury		C	40.00
		W	20.00			P	5.00
		W erased	20.00	Weedon		C	£100
Ware		C	60.00			P	8.00
		O	20.00			MM	£300
		P	5.00	Weely		C	£100
		V	40.00	Welchpool		C	40.00
		W	40.00			D	40.00
		Y	40.00			H	40.00
		Y erased	60.00			V	20.00
		Z	£100			W	15.00
		AA	60.00			AA	65.00
		BB	65.00			BB	40.00
Wareham		C	30.00	Weldon Bridge		CC	65.00
		D	75.00	Welford		O	40.00
		P	5.00			P	5.00
		W	20.00	Wellesbourne		O	40.00
		W erased	20.00	Wellingboro		W	40.00
Wareham-D		D	£150	Wellingborough		D	£100
Wargrave		O	20.00			G	£150
		CC	60.00			H	£100
Warminster		C	60.00			P	5.00
		D	60.00			S	£200
		P	5.00			V	60.00
		S	£200			W	40.00
		V	40.00			Y	20.00
		Y	20.00			JJ	£150
		Y erased	40.00	Wellington (Salop)		C	£100
Warrington		B	£200			D	60.00
		C	40.00			V	65.00
		D	60.00			Y	20.00
		H	60.00			Y erased	20.00
		P	5.00	Wellington (Som)		D	60.00
		V	60.00			V	20.00
		X	40.00			V erased	40.00
		X erased	60.00	Wellington Com (error for Som)		CC	£150
		Z	60.00	Wellington Rd. (B'ham)		C	40.00
		BB	65.00	Wellington-S (Salop)		W	40.00
		CC	65.00			Y	40.00
		Crown bag seal	£450	Wellington.S (Som)		D	65.00
Warwick		C	20.00	Wellington-Salop		D	£100
		D	40.00			P	5.00
		F	£150	Wellington Somst		M	40.00
		P	5.00	Wellington Somerset		P	5.00
		S	£125	Wells (Norfolk)		C	£100
		V	20.00			R	£100
		X	15.00	Wells (Som)		C	65.00
		X erased	40.00			W	40.00
		Y	15.00			MM	£225
		Z	40.00	Wells-N		R	£100
		AA	60.00			R erased	20.00
		BB	45.00			V	15.00
		JJ	60.00	Wells Norfolk		P	5.00
		MM	£125	Wells.S.		C	40.00
Watchet		CC	65.00			K	60.00
Wateringbury		O	40.00			V	40.00
Waterloo St (Brighton)		C	20.00			W	40.00
Watford		C	£100			Y	40.00
		G	£150			Z	40.00
		P	5.00			AA	40.00
		S	£200			HH	£200
		V	40.00			MM	£175
		W	40.00	Wells Som.		Z	45.00
		W erased	60.00	Wells Somerset		P	5.00
		Z	£100	Wel.n.borough		B	£200
Wath		C dated	£150	Welshpool		C	40.00
Watton (Herts)		CC	£100			P	5.00
Watton (Norfolk)		C	20.00			Y	15.00
		W	20.00			Z	60.00
Watton-Herts		O	75.00			CC	40.00
Watton Norfolk		O	20.00	Welwyn		C	£150
Waverley St.(Hull)		C	40.00			G	£100

71

Marks of the Provincial Post to 1839 - England and Wales

	O	20.00		V	60.00
	P	5.00		Y erased	60.00
	S	£200	Whickham	CC	65.00
	V	40.00	Whiddon Down	CC	£100
	W	60.00	Whimple	CC	40.00
Wem	C	40.00	Whitby	C	40.00
	O	20.00		H	40.00
	Y	40.00		P	5.00
	Y erased	40.00		R	£150
Wendover	F	£200		V	20.00
	G	£100		W	20.00
	P	5.00		X	15.00
	S	£200		X erased	20.00
	V	60.00	Whitchurch (Hants)	G	£100
	W	60.00		V	40.00
	W erased	60.00		W	20.00
Wenlock	O	20.00	Whitchurch (Shrop)	D	65.00
	W	60.00		G	65.00
Weobley	CC	65.00	Whitchurch H.(Hants)	D three line	£150
West Auckland	O	20.00		G	£100
West Boldon	CC	60.00	Whitchurch Hants	M	15.00
West Bromwich	E	40.00		BB three line	£150
	P	5.00	Whitchurch Herefords	CC	65.00
West Burton	CC	60.00	Whitchurch – Oxon	O	20.00
Westbury	C	60.00	Whitchurch S (Shrops)	D	40.00
	D	£100		H	40.00
	P	5.00		O	20.00
	S	£150		V	20.00
	V	60.00		BB	65.00
	W	40.00	Whitchurch.Salop	P	5.00
	W erased	20.00	Whitechurch (Shrops)	D	£100
Westbury on Trym (Bristol)	CC	20.00	Whitehaven	D	40.00
Westbury Salop	CC	60.00		G	40.00
West Derby (L'pool)	C framed	60.00		M	40.00
	O	30.00		P	5.00
West Drayton	O	50.00		S	£200
West End (Hants)	CC	45.00		V	20.00
Westerham	O	30.00		X	20.00
Westfield	CC	£100		X erased	20.00
Westgate	C	65.00		BB	60.00
West Grinstead	CC	60.00		CC	£100
West Haddon	C	£100		JJ	80.00
West Malling	O	30.00	Whitfield	CC	65.00
West Moulsey	CC	65.00	Whitminster	CC	65.00
Weston super Mare	P	5.00	Whittingham	O	20.00
West Tarring	CC	£100		Y	20.00
West Wycombe	O	20.00		Y erased	20.00
Wetherby	C	60.00	Whittington	CC	£100
	D	60.00	Whittlesea	O	50.00
	G	60.00	Whitwell (Yorks)	O	40.00
	M	40.00	Whitworth	O	40.00
	P	5.00	Wichnor (Staffs)	C	60.00
	R	60.00	Wickford	C	40.00
	V	20.00	Wickham	O	40.00
	W	15.00	Wickham.Mk	C	20.00
	W erased	15.00	Wickham Market	D	65.00
	BB	65.00	Wickwar	C	£100
Weyhill	O	50.00	Widford	CC	£100
	CC	60.00	Wigan	C	65.00
Weymouth	C	40.00		C in oval	£250
	D	60.00		H	60.00
	G	60.00		P	5.00
	Q	5.00		R	£150
	S	£200		V	60.00
	V	40.00		X	40.00
	W	20.00		X erased	40.00
	X	15.00		Z distinctive	£150
	JJ	£150		BB distinctive	£200
	MM	£200		JJ	65.00
Whalton	CC	£100		MM	£200
Wheatley	G	£150	Wiggan	C	£150
	O	40.00	Wigton	C	60.00
	P	5.00		G	20.00
	R	40.00		P	5.00

Marks of the Provincial Post to 1839 - England and Wales

	W	20.00		CC	65.00
	MM	£225	Winkleigh	CC	£100
Wiley (Warwicks)	C	65.00	Winlaton	CC	65.00
Wiley (Wilts)	C	40.00	Winsford	C	40.00
	P	10.00		O	50.00
	CC	£100	Winslow	C	£100
Willenhall	O	30.00		P	5.00
	BB	65.00		V	60.00
Willingdon	CC	60.00		W	60.00
Wilmslow (Manch'r)	Z	65.00		W erased	40.00
	BB	65.00		CC	£150
Wilton	C	40.00	Winwick	CC	60.00
	P	5.00	Wirksworth	C	60.00
Wily (Wilts)	MM	£225		D	£100
Wimborn	D	£150		P	10.00
	K	£150		V	60.00
	S	£175		W	60.00
	V	40.00		Z	60.00
	W	20.00	Wisbeach	C	£100
Wimborne	O	20.00		O	15.00
	P	5.00		P	5.00
	CC	£300		V	£100
Wimbourn	C	£100		W	40.00
Wincanton	C	60.00		Y	20.00
	D	£100		CC	£100
	P	5.00	Wisbich	C	£150
	W	40.00		D	£200
	FF	£250	Witham	C	60.00
	HH	£125		F	£200
	MM	£200		G	60.00
Wincaunton	D	£150		O	20.00
Winchcomb	O	20.00		P	5.00
	Y	40.00		R	£150
	Y erased	20.00		V	60.00
Wincheap (Kent)	C	65.00		W	40.00
Winchelsea	O	50.00		W erased	40.00
Winchester	C	60.00	Witham-Hull	C	40.00
	D	40.00	Witney	C	60.00
	G	65.00		D	60.00
	P	5.00		O	40.00
	Q	5.00		P	5.00
	S	£100		V	40.00
	V	40.00		W	15.00
	W	20.00		Z	60.00
	X	15.00		BB	60.00
	X erased	20.00	Wittersham	CC	60.00
	CC	£100	Witton Le Wear	O	30.00
Windham	C	£150	Wiveliscomb	O	20.00
	F	£150	Wiveliscombe	P	5.00
	S	£225	Wivelscombe	V	20.00
	V	45.00	W. Malling	C	£100
Windlesham	O	40.00	Woburn	C	60.00
	CC	£100		G	60.00
Windsor (Berks)	C	40.00		O	30.00
	D	60.00		P	5.00
	G	40.00		V	40.00
	P	5.00		W	20.00
	S	£120		W erased	25.00
	V	20.00	Woking	CC	£100
	W	20.00	Wokingham	C	40.00
	X	20.00		O	20.00
	Y	20.00		P	5.00
	BB	65.00		V	20.00
	JJ	20.00	Wolseley Bridge	D	60.00
	MM	£200		M	40.00
	NN	£200		O	60.00
Windsor/Manchester	E	75.00	Wolsingham	O	40.00
Wingham	C	60.00	Wolston	O	40.00
	H	60.00		CC	65.00
	P	8.00	Wolverhampton	D	40.00
	S	£150		G	60.00
	V	20.00		J	65.00
	W	20.00		P	5.00
	W erased	20.00		R	£100

73

Marks of the Provincial Post to 1839 - England and Wales

	V	40.00		G	60.00
	X	15.00		O	20.00
	X erased	20.00		P	5.00
	Z	60.00		S	£150
	AA	60.00		V	40.00
	CC	65.00		W	40.00
	MM	£200		Z	£100
Wolviston	O	65.00	Worstead	C	65.00
Woodbridge	C	20.00		O	25.00
	D	60.00	Worthing	C	£100
	P	5.00		P	5.00
	V	60.00		W	40.00
	W	20.00		W erased	40.00
	CC	40.00		NN	£150
	NN	£150	Wotten Bassett	D	£100
Woodbury	CC	£100		V	65.00
Woodhouse Lane (Leeds)	C	40.00	Wotton.G (Glos)	C distinctive	£225
Woodside (L'pool)	C	65.00	Wotton under Edge	D	65.00
	N	£250		O	20.00
	CC	65.00		P	5.00
Woodstock	D	£150		CC	£150
	K	60.00		JJ	40.00
	O	20.00	Wotton un.r.Edge	AA	£250
	P	5.00	Wragby	C	60.00
	S	£150		O	30.00
	V	20.00		V	40.00
	W	20.00		W	40.00
	AA	65.00	Wray	O	40.00
	CC	65.00	Wrentham	V	40.00
Woodyates	O	50.00		W	40.00
	P	20.00		CC	40.00
	CC	£150	Wrexham	C	20.00
Wooler	O	20.00		D	65.00
	X undated	20.00		O	15.00
	X erased	15.00		P	5.00
Woolpit	C	60.00		V	20.00
	O	40.00		W	15.00
	W	60.00		Y	15.00
Woolton (L'pool)	CC	£100		BB	60.00
Woolverhampton	D	£250		JJ	£100
Woolviston	O	20.00		MM	£250
Woore	N	£300	Wrington	C	40.00
Wooten under Edge	D	60.00	Wrotham	O	40.00
	S	£200	Wroughton	O	60.00
	V	20.00	WTR (Warrington)	A	£500
	W	20.00	Wycombe-H	V	40.00
	W erased	20.00	Wye	O	40.00
Wootten Bassett	D	£200	Wykeham	CC	£100
Wootten Bridge (IOW) (spelling error)			Wykeham-Yorks	O	40.00
	CC	£250	Wymondham	C	60.00
Worcester	C	20.00		O	20.00
	D	40.00		P	5.00
	H	20.00		W	15.00
	Q	5.00	Wyndham	C	£100
	S	£100	X Church (Christchurch)	D	£250
	V	40.00	Yalding	O	50.00
	X	20.00	Yarm	C	£100
	X erased	20.00		O	20.00
	Z	40.00		P	5.00
	BB	45.00		V	20.00
	JJ	60.00		W	20.00
	MM	60.00	Yarmouth (Nfk)	C	£150
Wordesley	CC	40.00		D	£100
Workington	C	£150		J	65.00
	D	45.00		P	5.00
	H	40.00		V	20.00
	P	5.00		W	20.00
	V	20.00		X	15.00
	W	20.00		CC	£100
	Y	20.00		JJ	20.00
	Y erased	20.00	Yarmouth I.W.	W	65.00
	BB	65.00		Y	40.00
	CC	60.00		Y erased	80.00
Worksop	C	60.00	Yarmouth-N	C	£100

		S	£125
		V	20.00
Yarmouth Norfk		P	5.00
Yarmouth Norfolk		P	5.00
Yeaden		BB	65.00
Yeadon		O	30.00
Yealmpton		O	40.00
		P	5.00
Yeovil		C	40.00
		P	5.00
		S	75.00
		V	20.00
		W	20.00
		BB	65.00
York		C	20.00
		D	£150
		H	40.00
		P	5.00
		Q	5.00
		R	£100
		V	20.00
		W	15.00
		X	15.00
		CC	£150
		JJ	75.00
		MM	£125
Micklegate/York		C	40.00
Walmgate/York		C	40.00
Yoxford		C	40.00
		H	65.00
		O	20.00
		W	40.00

Visit **SAMWELLS** for _All_ GB Postmark Types
Browse our large stocks at Stampex & York. View selected items online

1936 PARLIAMENT HOUSE/EDINBURGH on FDC

1926 DROGHEDA on Irish Republic 'Seahorse' issues

1916 BY KING'S MESSENGER on WWI cover from The Western Front

1908 WINDSOR CASTLE c.d.s.

1939 WINDSOR ROYAL SHOW r.d.s. in violet

WE CAN NOW TAILOR OUR LISTS TO SUIT YOUR REQUIREMENTS
Simply let us know what you collect & we will return results by e-mail
www.postalhistorygb.com 01225 462429 info@postalhistorygb.com

Visit SAMWELLS for Quality Postal History
Always something special for your collection

1912, April 10th, carried by the S.S. TITANIC. Part cover carried Southampton to Queenstown (Enlarged image)

1864 AUCKLAND Penny 'Star' (SG.40) used in New Zealand. Remarkable Imperf' + Perf' 'Chalon' combination

1845 Hume's Tourist Envelope with 4 margin pair SG.8 (RPS Cert)

1840 Spooner Caricature used at Hanwell prepaid 1d in cash (RPS Cert)

1699 'MVLLINGAR' (Mullingar) remarkable early Irish namestamp. Wonderful exhibition quality rarity

We also offer **FREE** e-mail listings of our selected items over £45
For lower priced items visit Ebay sellers 'generalwrangel' & 'samwells-99p'
www.postalhistorygb.com   01225 462429   info@postalhistorygb.com

4 Early Scottish Marks to 1839

The General Post (G.P.O. Edinburgh)

From the 16th century the Scottish burghs (chartered towns and boroughs) gradually developed Posts within their own areas. In addition, messengers were employed to carry mail between burghs and the seat of government in Edinburgh.

In 1616 the Master of Posts, William Seton, set up a General Post which could be used by the public. In 1657 the English North Post Road (cf. chapter 1) was extended to Edinburgh. Surviving examples of items from this period are rare and bear only manuscript indications of charges to be paid.

In 1693 the Postmaster General of the General Letter Office, Edinburgh, decreed that:
(i) a dated handstamp should be struck on letters to and from London
(ii) letters to other parts of England should receive a name stamp
(iii) letters to other parts of Scotland should not be handstamped at all.

From 1730 only mail going out from Edinburgh was handstamped. From 1758 all mail was handstamped.

Bishop Marks

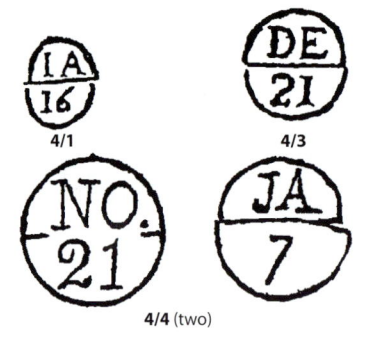

4/1	Small oval, 13x10mm, in two segments, black 1693-1714	£250
4/2	As above but in red 1714-1725	£225
4/3	Single circle, slightly irregular, approx 15mm, red 1725-1757	75.00
4/4	Larger single circle, various sizes and styles, red 1758-1806 (15.00 prior to 1785)	25.00

Later datestamps

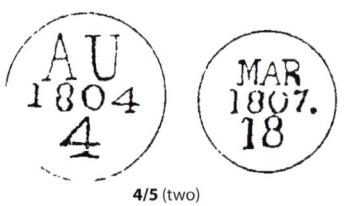

4/5 (two)

4/5	Single circle, year in full, 24 or 20mm, red 1801-1812	6.00
4/6	Double circle, year in 3 or 4 figures, red 1807-1812	6.00
4/7	Octagonal rim, day in centre, year 4 figures, red 1811-1823	6.00
4/8	As above but no rim 1818-1825	8.00
4/9	Single circle, many sizes, red 1812-1839	5.00
4/10	Double circle, approx 26mm, red 1825-1830	5.00

Namestamps

4/11	EDING/BURGH, 2 lines, black or red 1723-1732	£250
4/12	EDIN=/BURGH, 2 lines, black or red 1732-1756	£300
4/13	As above but without =, red -1757	£200

78

Early Scottish Marks to 1839

Paid Marks

4/28	Handstruck "1"	6.00
4/29	Handstruck "2"	15.00
4/30	Crown Inspector's marks, many varieties	30.00
4/31	Time stamps to 1808	50.00
4/32	Time plus date stamps	4.00

Edinburgh Local Posts (Penny Posts)

Williamson's Post 1773-1793

4/14	POST/PAID in single circle, 20mm, red 1790-1796	25.00
4/15	As above but with additional curved lines, 26mm, red 1796-1808	20.00
4/16	POST/PAID in fancy scroll design, red or black 1804-1807	£150
4/17	PAID in upright dated oval, red 1807-1813	20.00

4/18	PAID at EDINBURGH, many types, with or without frame, black or red 1808-1839	4.00
4/19	PAID in dated single circle, many types, red 1814-1821	4.00
4/20	PAID in the COUNTRY, various types, with or without frame, red 1818-1823	50.00
4/21	PAID and date, unframed, red 1824-1831	6.00
4/22	As above but in framed single or double circle 1832-1839	4.00

Instructional Markings

4/23	MISSENT/TO/EDINBURGH (various) 1813-1839	£100
4/24	TOO/LATE in single circle, 20mm, red 1796-1805	18.00
4/25	TOO LATE in various varieties/frames 1806-1839	30.00
4/26	TO PAY/ONE PENNY	25.00
4/27	POSTAGE TO EDINBURGH NOT PAID 1810-1839	40.00

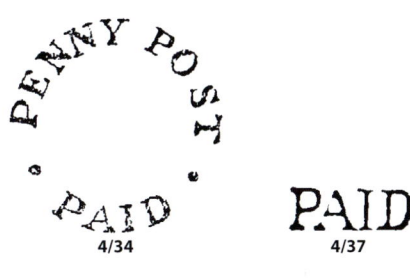

A private Penny Post organised by Peter Williamson for letters within Edinburgh and Leith. It was taken over by the Post Office and a compensation pension paid.

4/33	Straight line EDIN & date & 1d, black 1773	£1250
4/34	Circular PENNY POST/PAID, black or red 1774-1777	£500
4/35	As above but without PAID 1774 1777	£500
4/36	As above but with date in centre 1774-1775	£650
4/37	Straight line PAID, two sizes, black 1781-1793	£450
4/38	Circular E.PENNY POST NOT PAID 1774-1790	£250
4/39	Wavy NOT PAID 1790-1793	£250

Semi Official Posts

Postmasters were officially appointed to handle General Post in three nearby towns, but in addition organised Penny Posts as private ventures.

4/40	Small straight line Dalkeith, black 1776-1797	£125
4/41	As above but Mufsleburgh 1776-1797	£100
4/42	As above buts PreftonPans 1776-1797	£150

Early Scottish Marks to 1839

City Receiving Houses

A 4/43 Double circle with P.P.O

B 4/44 Double circle with PAID

C 4/45 Double circle with UNPAID

D 4/46 One line, with or without frame

E 4/47 Two lines, with or without frame

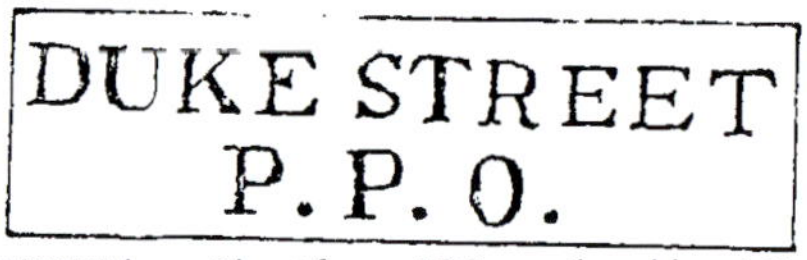

F 4/48 With or without frame, P.P.O., or other abbreviations

G 4/49 With or without frame, PP abbreviations or in full

H 4/50 With or without frame, PP abbreviations or in full

Castle Street	A	£125
	B	£100
	C	35.00
	E	8.00
	F	10.00
Chapel Street	A	£100
	B	£100
	C	35.00
Cross	D	6.00
Duke Street	B	90.00
	C	40.00
	E	6.00
	F	6.00
Dundas Street	E	6.00
	bag seal	£600
Grassmarket	D	6.00
	E	6.00
Hanover Street	B	£100
	C	40.00
	E	6.00
	F	6.00
High Street	E	6.00
Hillhousefield	D	30.00
Holyrood	D	6.00
Howe Street	D	6.00
	E	6.00
	G	25.00
	H	25.00
India Street	E	6.00
Lauriston Place	E	6.00
Leith Walk	E	6.00
	G	25.00
	H	15.00
Leopold Place	D	6.00
Nicolson Street	E	6.00
	F	10.00
Port Hopeton	E	25.00
Port Hopetoun	D	90.00
	E	25.00
Portsburgh	D	25.00
	F	25.00
West Nicolson Street	F (3 lines)	30.00
William Street	E	6.00

Outbounds and District Receiving Houses

Note: Outbounds was a term used to indicate the suburbs of Edinburgh outside the legal city area.

J 4/51 With or without frame

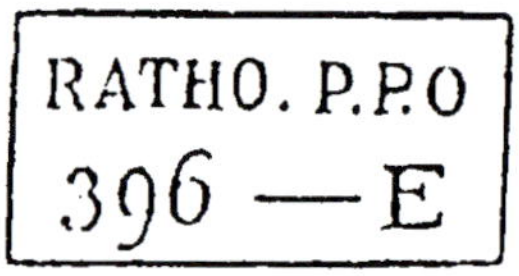

K 4/52 With or without frame

L 4/53

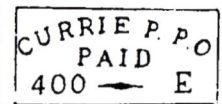

M 4/54

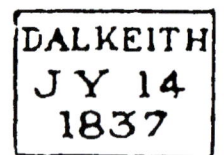

N 4/55 With or without code letter/time

O 4/56 With lines: place name in straight line(s) or curved

P 4/57 Without lines: place name in straight line(s) or curved

Q 4/58 Paid or Unpaid, abbreviations in full

Early Scottish Marks to 1839

Outbounds Receiving Houses

Burrowmuirhead	K (3 lines)	15.00
	W	15.00
	AA	15.00
Newhaven	G	25.00
	H	15.00
	Handstruck "2"	6.00
Newington	AA	25.00
	AA erased	6.00
	Handstruck "2"	6.00
Stockbridge	D	25.00
	AA	25.00
	Handstruck "2"	6.00
Warriston	D	6.00
	AA	25.00

District Receiving Offices

Balerno	AA	30.00
Broxburn	AA	30.00
Colington	H	£150
Colinton	B	30.00
	D with PP	20.00
	K	20.00
Corstorphin	D	20.00
	H	30.00
Corstorphine	B	30.00
	K	30.00
	K erased	15.00
Cramond	D	£200
	D curved	15.00
	H	30.00
	K	18.00
	AA	18.00
Currie	H	30.00
	K	18.00
	L	18.00
	L erased	10.00
	M	25.00
Dalkeith	B	40.00
	C	25.00
	D	12.00
	H	15.00
	J	10.00
	K	10.00
	N	4.00
	AA	15.00
	BB	10.00
	CC	£200
	EE	30.00
	Handstruck "2"	12.00
Duddingston	N	12.00
	AA	60.00
	CC	£150
Fisherrow	D	18.00
Ford	H	30.00
	J	15.00
	K	15.00
	L	15.00
	M	30.00
	N	4.00
	AA	15.00
Hermenston	J	15.00
Hermiston	AA	15.00
Kirkliston	D	12.00
	J	15.00
	L	25.00
	M	35.00
	AA	15.00
Kirknewton	K	15.00
	AA	15.00
Lasswade	B	40.00
	C	25.00
	D	12.00
	H	12.00
	J	15.00

	K	15.00
	O	40.00
	AA	15.00
	Handstruck "2"	12.00
Leith	B	15.00
	C	10.00
	D	25.00
	H	15.00
	J	15.00
	T	4.00
	U with PPO	15.00
	Y	4.00
	BB	6.00
	CC	£100
	DD	40.00
	octagonal d/s	6.00
	circular d/s	4.00
	Handstruck "1"	6.00
	Handstruck "2"	15.00
Libberton	B	30.00
	J	15.00
	K	15.00
	AA	15.00
Loanhead	AA	15.00
Musselburgh	A	40.00
	B	30.00
	C	25.00
	H	18.00
	J	18.00
	K	10.00
	N with PPO	12.00
	AA	15.00
	Handstruck "2"	8.00
Mussleburgh	P	30.00
Pennicuik	Q	65.00
	Q Unpaid	45.00
Pennycuik	H	10.00
	J	15.00
	L	10.00
	M	25.00
	AA	15.00
Portobello	H	30.00
	J	15.00
	K	12.00
	AA	15.00
	AA (fancy)	£400
Prestonpans	A	40.00
	B	25.00
	C	15.00
	G (variety)	40.00
	H	15.00
	H (variety)	12.00
	J	15.00
	K	12.00
	N	4.00
	BB	40.00
	Handstruck "2"	12.00
Ratho	J	15.00
	K	12.00
	AA	15.00
Roslin	N	4.00
	AA	15.00
Slateford	F	25.00
Tranent	B	25.00
	C	18.00
	D	10.00
	G	15.00
	H	12.00
	J	15.00
	N	4.00
	P	40.00
	AA	18.00
Uphall	AA	25.00
Winchburgh	AA	40.00

81

Early Scottish Marks to 1839

The Provincial Post

R 4/59 Many varieties (with or without 1 or 2 arcs)

S 4/60 Many varieties (with or without frame)

Z 4/68 with or without arcs

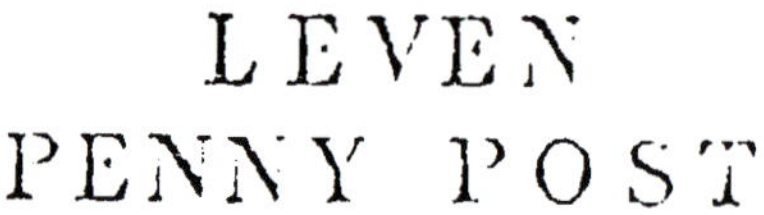

AA 4/69 many types

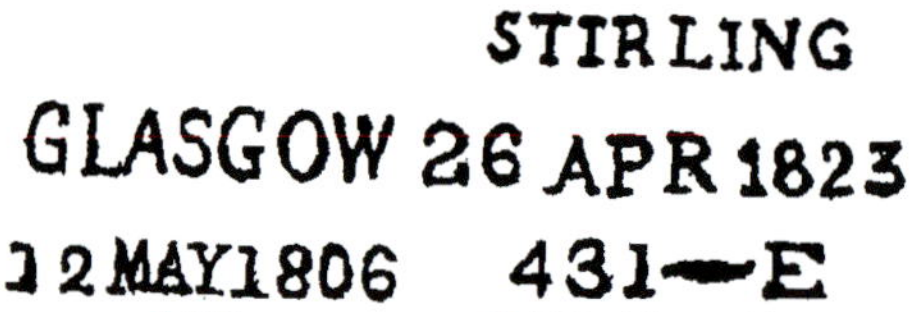

T 4/61

U 4/62 with or without frame (see note below)

BB 4/70 (two) many types

V 4/63 with or without frame (see note below)

CC 4/71 many varieties

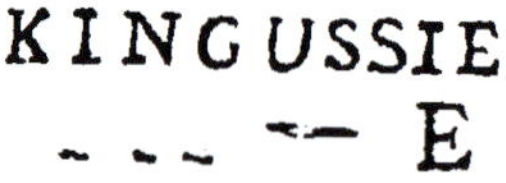

V erased 4/64 (see note below)

DD 4/72

W 4/65 (see note below)

EE 4/73 many varieties/frames

Notes concerning above illustrations:
a) Route letters shown in types U,V,W and X: B(Berwick), C(Carlisle), D(Dumfries), E(Edinburgh), G(Glasgow), L(Leith)
b) The example shown of V erased shows traces of mileage and route letter, but others show no such traces at all

X 4/66 with or without double circle frame (see note below)

Y 4/67 double or single arcs

Abercherder	D	10.00
Aberdeen	D	15.00
	E	15.00
	N	4.00
	O	12.00
	T	6.00
	U	6.00
	U (day mth/year)	25.00
	Y	4.00
	AA	40.00
	BB	6.00
	CC	£100
	Handstruck "1"	20.00
Aberdour	D	15.00

Early Scottish Marks to 1839

Town	Mark	Price	Town	Mark	Price
	D curved	25.00	Aros	D	25.00
	V	10.00		N	6.00
	V erased	10.00		AA	40.00
	W	25.00	Aross	D	50.00
Aberfeldy	D	25.00		V	30.00
	N	4.00		V erased	25.00
	P	15.00		AA	75.00
	V	10.00	Arran	D	30.00
	V erased	10.00	Arrochar	D	10.00
	W	25.00		V	10.00
	AA	25.00		W	15.00
Aboyne	D	10.00	Assynt	D	25.00
	N	4.00	Auchenblae SO	E	30.00
	V	25.00	Auchnacraig	D	40.00
	V erased	15.00		E	25.00
Achterarder	E	25.00		V	25.00
Air	D	35.00		V erased	25.00
	D curved	18.00	Auchterarder	N	4.00
Airdrie	D	10.00		O	25.00
	N	4.00		V	10.00
	O	15.00		V erased	10.00
	V	10.00		W	25.00
	W	15.00	Auchtermuchty	D	10.00
Alexandria	D	15.00		E	10.00
Alford	D	25.00		AA	25.00
	V	10.00	Avemore	D	75.00
	W	15.00	Aviemore	D	60.00
Alloa	D	15.00	Ayr	D	35.00
	O	15.00		N	4.00
	V	10.00		U	10.00
	W	15.00		U erased	10.00
	Y inverted	15.00		V	10.00
	AA	15.00		W	10.00
Alness	AA	25.00		Y	4.00
Alyth	O	15.00		AA	15.00
	V	10.00		CC	£125
	W	15.00		EE	50.00
Anderston (Glasgow)	D	6.00	Ayton	D	10.00
Anderston Walk (Glasgow)	E	15.00		N	4.00
Annan	D	10.00		P	15.00
	W	15.00		V	10.00
	V	10.00		W	15.00
	V erased	10.00	Balfron	V	15.00
	Y	4.00		AA	35.00
Anstruther	D	25.00	Balichulish	D	25.00
	D curved	15.00	Ballantrae	E	15.00
	N	4.00		V	10.00
	V	10.00		V erased	10.00
	V erased	10.00		W	25.00
	W	25.00		AA	25.00
Anwith	D	60.00	Ballater	D	15.00
Appin	D	10.00	Ballindalloch	D	10.00
	N	6.00		N	4.00
	V	10.00		V	10.00
	V erased	10.00		V erased	10.00
	W	15.00	Banchory	N	4.00
	AA	25.00		O	15.00
Arbroath	D	15.00		V	10.00
	E	15.00		V erased	10.00
	N	4.00		W	15.00
	R	25.00		W erased	25.00
	V	10.00	Banff	D	10.00
	V erased	10.00		N	4.00
	W	15.00		O	15.00
	CC	£150		V	10.00
	EE	50.00		V erased	10.00
Ardersier	D	10.00		W	15.00
Ardrie (Airdrie)	AA	25.00		AA	15.00
Argyle Street (Glasgow)	E	10.00	Barrhead	AA	35.00
Arisaig	D	50.00	Barrowfield (Glasgow)	D	25.00
	V	30.00	Bathgate	P	25.00
	V erased	30.00		V	10.00
	W	40.00		V erased	10.00
Arocher	P	25.00		W	15.00

83

Early Scottish Marks to 1839

Location	Mark	Price
Beauly	D	10.00
	N	4.00
	V	10.00
	AA	25.00
Beild	D	15.00
	W	25.00
	bag seal	£350
Beith	D	15.00
	N	4.00
	V	10.00
	V erased	10.00
	W	15.00
	AA	25.00
Bellshill	bag seal	£300
Bervie	D	15.00
	V	10.00
	V erased	10.00
	W	15.00
Biggar	D	10.00
	V	10.00
	W	15.00
Blackburn	D	15.00
Blackhillock	D	10.00
Blackshiells	D	10.00
Blackshiels	O	15.00
	P	35.00
	W	10.00
Blairadam	V	10.00
	V erased	10.00
Blair Athole	V	10.00
Blairgowrie	N	4.00
	O	15.00
	V	10.00
	V erased	10.00
	W	25.00
Boat of Forbes	W	75.00
Bogroy	D	50.00
Bonar Bridge	V	10.00
	V erased	10.00
Bonaw	D	10.00
	V	15.00
	W	15.00
Bo'ness (various spellings incl Borrowstowness)		
	D	10.00
	D curved	50.00
	N	4.00
	V	10.00
	V erased	10.00
	W	15.00
Bowholm	V	40.00
	V erased	40.00
Bowmore	E	75.00
	V	50.00
	V erased	50.00
	AA	£100
Braco	D	50.00
Braemar	V	50.00
Brechin	D	10.00
	V	10.00
	W	15.00
Bridgend of Halkirk	E	50.00
Bridge of Earn	D	30.00
	V	30.00
	W	20.00
Bridge of Erne	E	60.00
Bridge of Halkirk	O	40.00
	S	25.00
Broadford (Skye)	E	50.00
	V	60.00
	V erased	50.00
Brodick	D	40.00
Broomielaw (Glasgow)	D	10.00
Broughton	V	15.00
	W	15.00
Broughton/Tweed	E	30.00
Brucklaw	D	50.00
Buckie	V	15.00
	V erased	10.00
Bunessan	D	90.00
Burghead	AA	25.00
Burntisland	D	10.00
	E	15.00
	V	10.00
	W	15.00
Cairndow	D	10.00
	O	15.00
	V	15.00
	W	25.00
	Y	6.00
	AA	40.00
Cairnish	V	30.00
	W	15.00
Callander	N	4.00
	R	25.00
	V	10.00
	V erased	10.00
	W	15.00
Cambuslang	AA	35.00
Campbelltown (Argyll)	E	40.00
Campbelton (Argyll)	E	50.00
	N	20.00
	V	30.00
	V erased	30.00
	W	15.00
	Y	4.00
Campbeltown (Argyll)	E	40.00
Canonbie	D	15.00
	N	4.00
	EE	25.00
Carinish	D	40.00
Carlinwark	D	25.00
Carluke	D	10.00
Carmoustie (error for Carnoustie)	AA	75.00
Carnwath	D	15.00
	V	15.00
	V erased	15.00
	W	15.00
Carrbridge	D	15.00
Castle Douglas	E	15.00
	N	4.00
	S	25.00
	V	10.00
	V erased	10.00
	W	15.00
	Y	4.00
	AA	15.00
Cathcart	H	60.00
Catrine	AA	50.00
Cawdor	AA	75.00
Chance Inn	D	50.00
	O	50.00
	V	30.00
	V erased	30.00
	W	40.00
Chapel of Seggat	P	£200
Clachan	D	30.00
Cluny	D	30.00
Cockburnspath	N	5.00
Coldingham	D	18.00
	V	18.00
	V erased	18.00
	W	18.00
Coldstream	D	12.00
	E	30.00
	N	5.00
	R	30.00
	V	12.00
	W	18.00

84

Early Scottish Marks to 1839

Town	Mark	Price
	AA	30.00
Colinsburgh	E	18.00
	N	5.00
	O	18.00
	V	12.00
	V erased	12.00
Coll	V	£100
	W	£100
Comrie	D	12.00
	W	30.00
Cornhill	AA	30.00
Coupar Angus	E	15.00
	V	12.00
	W	18.00
Coupar Fife	E	18.00
	V	12.00
	V erased	12.00
	W	18.00
Cowcaddens (Glasgow)	D	18.00
Cowdenburn	D	18.00
	V	18.00
	W	18.00
Cowpar Angus	E	18.00
Cowpar Fife	E	18.00
Craigellachie	N	5.00
	V	12.00
	V erased	12.00
Crail	D	12.00
	V	12.00
	W	18.00
Creetown	D	30.00
	O	30.00
	V	12.00
	V erased	12.00
	W	18.00
Crieff	D	12.00
	N	5.00
	O	18.00
	V	12.00
	V erased	12.00
	W	18.00
Crinan	D	18.00
Crinan SO	D	12.00
	W	18.00
Cromarty	D	30.00
	V	12.00
	V erased	12.00
	W	18.00
Crook	V erased	40.00
Crook on Tweed	V	18.00
Cruden	D	30.00
Cullen	D	12.00
	W	18.00
Culross	D	18.00
	N	5.00
	V	12.00
	V erased	12.00
	W	18.00
Cumbernauld	AA	30.00
Cumnock	D	18.00
	N	5.00
	V	18.00
	V erased	18.00
	W	18.00
	AA	45.00
Cupar Fife	E	45.00
	N	5.00
	O	18.00
	W	18.00
	Y	5.00
	AA	18.00
	CC	£125
	EE	60.00
Daljarrock	bag seal	£600

Town	Mark	Price
Dalmally	P	18.00
	V	12.00
	W	18.00
Dalmellington	V	12.00
Dalry (Ayrshire)	V	6.00
	V erased	6.00
	W	18.00
Denny	D	12.00
	N	5.00
	V	12.00
	V erased	12.00
	W	18.00
Dingwal	D	75.00
Dingwall	D	40.00
	O	40.00
	V	12.00
	W	18.00
	Y	5.00
	AA	75.00
Dornoch	D	18.00
	O	18.00
	V	12.00
	V erased	12.00
	W	18.00
Douglas	D	12.00
	D curved	30.00
	V	12.00
	V erased	12.00
	AA	30.00
Douglas Milln	E	40.00
Doune	N	5.00
	P	18.00
	V	12.00
	V erased	12.00
	W	18.00
	AA	30.00
Drumlanrig	E	30.00
Drumnadrochit	D	18.00
	E	18.00
Drymen	P	30.00
	V	30.00
	W	18.00
Duke Street (Glasgow)	D	30.00
Dumbarton	D	12.00
	E	30.00
	N	5.00
	V	12.00
	V erased	12.00
	W	18.00
	AA	18.00
	CC	£150
Dumfermline	D	18.00
	E	18.00
	V	12.00
	V erased	18.00
Dumfries	D	18.00
	D with mileage 341 boxed below	30.00
	N	5.00
	O	18.00
	P	18.00
	T	6.00
	U	6.00
	U erased	12.00
	V	12.00
	W	18.00
	Y	5.00
	AA	30.00
	BB	12.00
	CC	£150
	EE	40.00
Dunbar	D	12.00
	E	£150

85

Early Scottish Marks to 1839

	N	5.00			V	12.00
	V	12.00			V erased	12.00
	V erased	12.00			W	18.00
	W	18.00	Echt		F	75.00
Dunbeath	D curved	18.00	Eddleston		V	18.00
	O	18.00			W	18.00
	V	12.00	Eddlestone		D	30.00
	W	18.00	Elgin		D	18.00
Dunblane	D	12.00			O	18.00
	N	5.00			V	12.00
	R	30.00			V erased	12.00
	V	12.00			W	18.00
	V erased	12.00			Y	5.00
	W	18.00			AA	18.00
Dundee	D	12.00	Elie		N	5.00
	E	18.00	Elie Fife		O	18.00
	N	5.00	Ellon		D	12.00
	P	18.00			N	5.00
	T	6.00			W	18.00
	U	6.00	Ely Fife		O	30.00
	Y	5.00			V	12.00
	AA	18.00			W	18.00
	BB	6.00	Errol		D	12.00
	CC	£100			O	18.00
	EE	50.00			W	18.00
	Handstruck "2"	12.00	Evanton		V	18.00
	TO PAY/		Exchange (Glasgow)		D	12.00
	ONE PENNY	£100	Eyemouth		R	30.00
Dunfermline	D	18.00			V	12.00
	E	18.00			V erased	12.00
	P	12.00	Eyemouth SO		V	18.00
	W	18.00			W	30.00
	Y	5.00	Falkirk		D	12.00
	AA	18.00			E	18.00
	CC	£150			O	18.00
Dunkeld	D	18.00			V	12.00
	D curved	18.00			W	18.00
	N	5.00			Y	5.00
	V	12.00			AA	30.00
	V erased	12.00			BB	12.00
	W	18.00			EE	18.00
Dunnet SO	E	18.00	Falkland		D	12.00
Dunning	D	12.00			AA	50.00
Dunoon	D (1806 only)	50.00	Farr SO		E	18.00
	N	5.00	Fearn		AA	75.00
	V	12.00	Fenwick		D	18.00
	V erased	12.00	Fettercairn		D	12.00
	W	18.00			V	12.00
	Y	6.00	Findhorn		AA	50.00
Duns mixed face	D	£100	Finhaven SO		E	30.00
Dunse	D	12.00	Focabus		D	18.00
	N	5.00	Fochabers		D	12.00
	O	18.00			E	18.00
	V	12.00			O	30.00
	V erased	12.00			S	30.00
	W	18.00			V	12.00
	Y	6.00			V erased	12.00
	AA	18.00			W	18.00
Dunvegan	D	50.00	Fordoun		D	60.00
	V	50.00	Forfar		D	18.00
	W	75.00			N	5.00
Dysart	D	18.00			V	12.00
	V	12.00			V erased	12.00
	V erased	12.00			W	18.00
	W	18.00			BB	18.00
Eaglesham	D	50.00			EE	30.00
Earlston	D	12.00			Bag seal	£600
	V	12.00	Forres		D	12.00
	V erased	12.00			N	5.00
	W	18.00			O	18.00
	Handstruck "2"	50.00			V	12.00
Easdale	AA	45.00			W	18.00
Ecclefechan	D	12.00	Fort Augustus		D curved	75.00
	E	18.00			E	12.00

Early Scottish Marks to 1839

Location	Mark	Price	Location	Mark	Price
	R	30.00		X	4.00
	V	18.00		X erased	4.00
	AA	30.00		Y	4.00
Fort George	D	18.00		Y with EX	6.00
	D curved	18.00		Z	4.00
	S	30.00		AA	12.00
	V	12.00		BB	4.00
	V erased	12.00		CC	90.00
	W	18.00		DD	45.00
Fortingal	AA	30.00		EE	40.00
Fortrose	D	12.00		Handstruck "1"	8.00
	V	12.00		Handstruck "2"	15.00
	W	18.00		MORE TO PAY	£100
Fort William	D	12.00	Glenlivat	D	12.00
	E	18.00		W	18.00
	N	5.00	Glenluce	D	12.00
	S	30.00		E	18.00
	V	12.00		N	4.00
	V erased	12.00		V	12.00
	W	30.00		W	18.00
	AA	30.00		AA	75.00
	"Thistle" (fancy)	£1500	Glenmoreston	E	£100
Fraserburgh	E	12.00	Golspie	D	12.00
	N	6.00		N	4.00
	V	12.00		V	75.00
	V erased	12.00		W	18.00
	W	18.00	Gorbals (Glasgow)	D	30.00
	AA	45.00	Grangemouth	N	4.00
Fushiebridge	E	12.00		R	45.00
	N	4.00		V	18.00
	W	12.00		V erased	12.00
Fyvie	D	12.00		W	45.00
	BB	£100	Grantown	D	18.00
G (Glasgow)	3 lines dated	4.00		V	12.00
Galashiels	D	12.00		W	18.00
	N	4.00	Greenlaw	D	12.00
	R	30.00		P	18.00
	V	12.00		V	12.00
	V erased	12.00		W	18.00
	W	18.00	Greenock	D	18.00
	CC	£150		E (fancy)	£350
	Handstruck "1"	20.00		O	18.00
	Handstruck "2"	50.00		P	18.00
Gallowgate (Glasgow)	D	12.00		T	12.00
Galston	AA	30.00		U	6.00
Garlieston	D	18.00		Y	5.00
	N	6.00		AA	30.00
Garmouth	AA	50.00		BB	6.00
Gartmore	AA	60.00		CC	£100
Garve SO	E	75.00		Handstruck "1"	40.00
Gatehouse	D	12.00		Handstruck "2"	75.00
	S	45.00	Gretna	AA	30.00
	V	12.00	Haddington	D	30.00
	V erased	12.00		E	30.00
	W	18.00		V	6.00
Gatehouse of Fleet	E	18.00		V erased	12.00
Girvan	D	12.00		W	12.00
	N	4.00		Y	4.00
	V	12.00		AA	25.00
	V erased	12.00		EE	50.00
	W	18.00		Handstruck "1"	30.00
	AA	30.00	Hamilton	D	12.00
	CC	£100		E	18.00
	Handstruck "2"	£100		N	4.00
Glammis	D	18.00		R	30.00
	V	12.00		V	12.00
	V erased	12.00		W	18.00
	W	18.00		Y	4.00
Glasgow	E	£100		Y undated	18.00
	N	5.00		AA	18.00
	P	6.00		CC	£125
	P (fancy frame)	£150	Hauick	D	£100
	T	4.00	Hawick	D	12.00
	U	4.00		V	12.00

87

Early Scottish Marks to 1839

	V erased	12.00			E	30.00
	W	18.00			V	12.00
	Y	4.00			W	18.00
	AA	18.00			Y	4.00
	CC	£150			Handstruck "1"	50.00
	EE	75.00	Johnstone		D	12.00
Helensburgh	D	12.00			AA	30.00
	N	4.00	Jura		V	£125
	V	12.00			V erased	£100
	V erased	12.00	Keith		D	12.00
	W	18.00			V	12.00
	AA	30.00			W	18.00
Helmsdale	V	18.00	Keith Hall		N	6.00
	V erased	12.00			V	18.00
Holytown	D	18.00			V erased	18.00
	N	4.00	Kelso		D	18.00
	V	12.00			N	4.00
	V erased	12.00			O	18.00
	W	18.00			P	18.00
Hope Street (Glasgow)	D	6.00			V	12.00
Howgate	D	30.00			W	18.00
Huna	D	£125			Y	4.00
	V	£100			AA	18.00
	V erased	£100			BB	45.00
	W	£150			EE	75.00
Huntley	D	12.00	Kelty Bridge		E	75.00
	N	4.00			W	50.00
	V	12.00	Kenmore		V	12.00
	W	18.00			V erased	12.00
Inchture	P	30.00	Kennoway		S	30.00
Inveerkithing	E	50.00			V	12.00
Inverary	D	12.00			V erased	12.00
	E	18.00			W	30.00
	R	30.00	Kerriemuir		E	18.00
	V	12.00	Kettle		N	4.00
	V erased	12.00			AA	30.00
	W	18.00			CC	£200
	Y	4.00			EE	75.00
	AA	60.00			Bag seal	£450
	CC	£175	Kilbride		AA	45.00
Invergordon	E	12.00	Killearn		AA	45.00
	R	30.00	Killin		D	12.00
	V	18.00			O	18.00
	V erased	12.00			W	18.00
	W	45.00	Kilmarnock		D	18.00
Inverkeithing	D	12.00			E	18.00
	N	4.00			N	4.00
	R	30.00			R (no frame)	18.00
	V	12.00			S	18.00
	V erased	12.00			V	12.00
	W	18.00			W	18.00
	AA	30.00			Y	4.00
	CC	£175			AA	18.00
Inverkip	AA	30.00			BB	6.00
Inverness	D	18.00			CC	£150
	D curved	45.00	Kilmaurs		AA	45.00
	E	30.00	Kilpatrick		H	30.00
	N	4.00			AA	30.00
	P	18.00	Kilsyth		D	12.00
	V	12.00			D curved	30.00
	W	18.00			O	45.00
	X	12.00			V	12.00
	X erased	12.00			W	18.00
	Y	4.00	Kincardine		D	12.00
	BB	75.00			V	18.00
	EE	18.00			V erased	12.00
Irvine	D	12.00			W	18.00
	N	12.00			AA	18.00
	V	12.00	Kincardine O'Niel		R	30.00
	V erased	12.00			V	12.00
	W	18.00			V erased	18.00
	AA	18.00			W	18.00
	CC	£125	Kinghorn		D	30.00
Jedburgh	D	12.00			N	4.00

Early Scottish Marks to 1839

		V	18.00		V erased	12.00
		V erased	12.00		W	18.00
		W	18.00		Y	4.00
		CC	£200	Largs	D	12.00
Kingorn		D	50.00		N	4.00
Kingussie		D	18.00		P	18.00
		V	18.00		V	12.00
		V erased	12.00		V erased	12.00
Kinross		D	12.00		W	18.00
		O	18.00		AA	40.00
		V	12.00	Lauder	D	12.00
		V erased	12.00		E	18.00
		W	18.00		W	18.00
		Y	4.00	Laurencekirk	E	12.00
		AA	18.00		N	4.00
Kintail		D	18.00		W	18.00
Kintore		D	18.00	Leadhills	D	12.00
		V	18.00		W	18.00
		V erased	12.00	Leith Lumsden	D	40.00
		W	18.00	Leitholm	AA	50.00
Kintra		D	£300	Lennoxtown	AA	75.00
Kippen		V	18.00	Lerwick	E curved	£100
		V erased	12.00		N	4.00
		W	18.00		V	18.00
		AA	75.00		W	30.00
Kippin		P	75.00		AA	75.00
Kircaldy		Y	6.00	Lesmahagow	N	4.00
Kirkaldy		D	45.00		V	12.00
Kirkcaldie		W	18.00		V erased	12.00
Kirkcaldy		D	18.00	Leven	D	12.00
		N	4.00		V	12.00
		P	18.00		W	18.00
		V	12.00		Y	4.00
		Y	4.00		AA	18.00
		AA	30.00		CC	£125
		BB	18.00		Handstruck "2"	50.00
		CC	£150	Linlithgow	D	12.00
		EE	50.00		E	30.00
		UNPAID TO	£125		N	4.00
Kirkcudbright		D	18.00		V	12.00
		E	18.00		W	30.00
		R	30.00	Linton	D	30.00
		V	12.00		V	18.00
		V erased	12.00		W	18.00
		W	18.00	Lismahago	CC	£200
		Y	4.00	Lithgow	AA	18.00
Kirkintulloch		D	12.00	Lochalch	V	30.00
		E	18.00	Lochalsh	D	30.00
		V	12.00		V	40.00
		W	18.00		AA	60.00
Kirkmichael		AA	30.00	Lochcarron	D	12.00
		AA erased	30.00		S	£100
Kirkwall		D	18.00		V	30.00
		E	30.00		W	45.00
		N	4.00	Lochearnhead	R	45.00
		P	18.00		W	18.00
		V	18.00	Lochgilphead	D	12.00
		V erased	30.00		N	4.00
		W	18.00		R	30.00
Kirriemuir		N	4.00		V	18.00
		V	18.00		V erased	12.00
		V erased	12.00		W	18.00
		W	18.00		AA	30.00
Laggan		D	30.00	Lochgylphead	V	18.00
Lairg		D	18.00	Lochinver	D	30.00
Lamlash		D	30.00	Lochmaben	E	18.00
Lanark		D	12.00		W	18.00
		N	4.00		V	12.00
		V	12.00		V erased	12.00
		V erased	12.00	Lochwinnoch	D	30.00
		W	18.00	Lockerby	D	12.00
Langholm		D	12.00		N	4.00
		E	30.00		P	18.00
		V	12.00		V	12.00

89

Early Scottish Marks to 1839

		V erased	12.00		Y (inverted)	£100
		W	18.00		AA	30.00
		EE	50.00		EE	75.00
Longhope		D	75.00	Mortlach	O	18.00
Lossiemouth		AA	75.00		W	18.00
Luib		V	£100	Morvern	D	18.00
Luss		D	50.00		N	6.00
		O	40.00		W	75.00
		V	40.00	Mossat	D	18.00
		W	30.00	Mount Stewart	P	£100
Lybster		D	75.00	Moy	D	75.00
Lynwilg SO		V	75.00	Muirdrum	D	18.00
Markinch		N	4.00		N	6.00
		AA	18.00		O	18.00
		CC	£175		V	12.00
		EE	75.00		W	18.00
Maryhill		F	30.00	Muirkirk	D	12.00
Muchlin		D	30.00		V	12.00
		AA	50.00		V erased	12.00
Mauchline		D	18.00		W	30.00
		N	4.00	Munlochy	D	25.00
		V	12.00		V	30.00
		V erased	12.00		V erased	12.00
		W	18.00		W	45.00
Maybole		D	12.00	Nairn	D	12.00
		N	4.00		N	4.00
		V	12.00		O	18.00
		V erased	12.00		V	12.00
		W	18.00		W	18.00
Meigle		D	18.00	Neilston	P	45.00
		V	12.00		V	45.00
		V erased	12.00		W	45.00
		W	18.00		AA	30.00
Melrose		D	18.00	Newburgh	D	12.00
		V	12.00		N	4.00
		V erased	12.00		AA	30.00
		W	18.00		EE	50.00
		Y	4.00	Newburgh Fife	E	18.00
		Handstruck "1"	18.00		W	18.00
		Handstruck "2"	50.00	New Deer	D	18.00
Melvich SO		E	50.00	New Galloway	E	12.00
Methlic		D	60.00		V	12.00
Mey SO		V	75.00		W	18.00
Mid Calder		D	12.00	Newmills	AA	50.00
		N	4.00	New Pitsligo	D	18.00
		P	18.00	Newport	V	12.00
		V	12.00		V erased	12.00
		W	18.00	Newton Douglas	E	30.00
		AA	45.00		R	30.00
Middleton		D	18.00	Newton Stewart	E	18.00
		W	75.00		N	6.00
Millgavie		F	30.00		V	12.00
Minnhyve		D	30.00		W	18.00
Mintlaw		N	4.00		AA	30.00
		V	12.00	Noblehouse	E	18.00
		V erased	12.00		N	4.00
		AA	30.00		V	18.00
Moffat		D	12.00		V erased	12.00
		N	4.00		AA	30.00
		V	12.00	North Berwick	S	30.00
		V erased	12.00		V	18.00
		W	18.00		W	12.00
		AA	30.00	North Queensferry	D	18.00
		CC	£150		V	12.00
Moneymusk		E	30.00		V erased	12.00
Moniaive		D	12.00		W	18.00
		O	30.00	Novar	O	75.00
		V	18.00		V	40.00
		W	45.00	Oban	D	12.00
Monnigaff		E	75.00		N	4.00
Montrose		D	18.00		V	12.00
		V	12.00		W	18.00
		W	18.00		AA	18.00
		Y	4.00	Old Deer	D	18.00

Early Scottish Marks to 1839

Location	Mark	Price
Old Meldrum	V	12.00
	W	18.00
	D	18.00
	E	12.00
	E (step frame)	£150
	V	18.00
	W	18.00
Old Rain	D	18.00
	V	12.00
	V erased	12.00
	W	18.00
Paisley	D	12.00
	N	4.00
	O	18.00
	T	6.00
	U	6.00
	V	6.00
	W	12.00
	Y	4.00
	AA	18.00
	BB	6.00
	CC	£125
	Handstruck "2"	75.00
Paisly	D	30.00
Parkhead	H	30.00
	AA	30.00
Parkhill	D	12.00
Peebles	D	18.00
	V	12.00
	W	18.00
	Y	4.00
	AA	18.00
Perth	D	18.00
	D curved	18.00
	O	18.00
	T	12.00
	U	6.00
	W	£100
	Y	6.00
	AA	18.00
	BB	6.00
	CC	£125
	EE	50.00
	"Lamb" (fancy)	£1000
Peterhead	D	12.00
	N	4.00
	V	12.00
	V erased	12.00
	W	18.00
	Y	4.00
Pitcaple	D	12.00
Pitlochry	N	4.00
	V	12.00
	AA	30.00
Pitmain	D	45.00
Pittenweem	D	12.00
	E	18.00
	W	18.00
Pollockshaws	F	45.00
	AA	60.00
Polmont	AA	75.00
Poolewe	V	18.00
Portaskaig	D	18.00
	S	75.00
	W	30.00
Port Askeg	E	£150
Port Dundas RH (Glasgow)	Z	18.00
Port Glasgow	D	12.00
	E	18.00
	R	30.00
	S	30.00
	V	6.00
	W	18.00
	Y	4.00
Portland Street (Glasgow)	CC	£125
	E	18.00
Portmahomac	AA	£100
Portnacroich	E	£150
Port Patrick	E	18.00
	W	18.00
	Y	4.00
Portree	D	12.00
	V	18.00
Portsoy	D	12.00
	W	18.00
Port William	E	12.00
	N	6.00
	V	18.00
Poyntzfield	D	18.00
Press	D	30.00
	W	50.00
Prestonkirk	D	12.00
	N	4.00
	R	30.00
	V	12.00
	V erased	12.00
	W	18.00
Rachanmill	V	30.00
	V erased	30.00
Rannoch	AA	30.00
Reay	AA	£100
Renfrew	D	12.00
	V	12.00
	W	18.00
Rhynie	D	50.00
	W	30.00
	W erased	45.00
Rothes	D	30.00
	V	12.00
	W	18.00
Rothesay	D	30.00
	E	18.00
	V	12.00
	W	18.00
	Y	4.00
	AA	75.00
Rothiemay	AA	75.00
Ruthven	D	30.00
St Andrews	D	18.00
	V	12.00
	V erased	12.00
	W	18.00
	Y	4.00
	CC	£150
	EE	18.00
St Boswells Green	E	12.00
	N	4.00
	V	18.00
	W	18.00
St Margts Hope	D	50.00
St Rollox (Glasgow)	D	45.00
Saltcoats	D	12.00
	N	4.00
	V	12.00
	V erased	12.00
	W	18.00
	AA	18.00
Sanday	AA	£100
Sanquhar	D	12.00
	D curved	18.00
	V	12.00
	V erased	12.00
	W	18.00
	AA	30.00
Sauchiehall (Glasgow)	D	18.00
Sconser	D	50.00
	W	50.00
Selkirk	D	12.00

Early Scottish Marks to 1839

	N	4.00	Strontien	E	75.00
	V	12.00	Swinton	AA	75.00
	W	18.00	Tain	D	12.00
	Y	6.00		N	4.00
	Handstruck "2"	50.00		V	12.00
Skene	D	18.00		W	18.00
	V	12.00	Tamnavoulen SO	E	50.00
	W	18.00	Tarbert	D	12.00
	R	30.00		D curved	40.00
South Ferry				P	40.00
South Queensferry	V	12.00		V	12.00
	V erased	12.00		V erased	12.00
	W	18.00		W	18.00
Stage Hall	D	50.00		Y	4.00
	E	40.00	Tarland	D	18.00
	O	40.00		O	18.00
	V	50.00		W	18.00
	W	30.00	Tayinloane	V	18.00
Stanley	AA	50.00		V erased	18.00
Stewarton	D	12.00	Tayn	D	45.00
	N	4.00	Thornhill	D	12.00
	V	12.00		N	4.00
	V erased	12.00		R	18.00
	W	18.00		V	12.00
Stewartton	E	30.00		W	18.00
Stirling	D	12.00	Thornton	AA	30.00
	N	4.00	Thurso	D	18.00
	O	12.00		N	4.00
	P	18.00		O	18.00
	U	6.00		P	30.00
	V	12.00		V	12.00
	W	18.00		V erased	12.00
	Y	4.00		W	18.00
	AA	18.00	Tiry	D	£125
	BB	12.00	Tobermoray	D	40.00
	CC	£125	Tobermorry	D	£100
Stonehaven	D	12.00	Tobermory	N	20.00
	N	4.00		V	30.00
	V	12.00		W	50.00
	V erased	12.00		AA	75.00
	W	18.00	Tomintoul	V	12.00
	EE	75.00	Tomintoul SO	W	30.00
Stornaway	D curved	50.00	Tongue	D	45.00
	V	40.00		R	45.00
	V erased	30.00		V	18.00
	W	50.00		W	18.00
Stow	D	12.00	Tradestown (Glasgow)	D	75.00
	W	12.00	Troon	N	4.00
Stranraer	D	18.00		V	18.00
	E	30.00		V erased	12.00
	O	30.00	Tullick	D	18.00
	V	12.00		W	18.00
	V erased	12.00	Turriff	D	12.00
	W	18.00		N	4.00
	Y	4.00		V	12.00
	AA	30.00		V erased	12.00
Strathaven	V	18.00		W	12.00
	V erased	12.00		AA	40.00
	W	45.00		BB	50.00
Strathblane	V	30.00	Tyndrum	V	30.00
	AA	45.00		V erased	12.00
Strathdon	D	18.00		W	30.00
	W	18.00	Tyree	V	£100
Strathpeffer	E	18.00		W	£125
Strichen	D	15.00	Udney	D	18.00
	W	15.00	UIST to/DUNVEGAN (see chapter 14)	E	£500
Stromness	O	30.00	Ullapool	D	30.00
	V	18.00		V	18.00
	W	30.00		W	18.00
Stronsay	AA	£100	Watten	D	50.00
Strontian	D	30.00	W Kilbride	V	30.00
	N	20.00		V erased	12.00
	V	30.00	Westray	AA	£125
	W	40.00	West Salton	V	75.00
	AA	75.00			

Whitburn	D	12.00
	E	12.00
	N	4.00
	W	12.00
Whitehouse	D	18.00
Whithorn	D	12.00
	E	18.00
	N	4.00
	V	12.00
	V erased	12.00
Wick	D	18.00
	V	12.00
	V erased	12.00
	W	18.00
	Y	4.00
	BB	18.00
Wigtown	D	12.00
	V	12.00
	W	18.00
	Y	4.00
	AA	50.00
Wilsontown	D	60.00
	V	40.00
	W	50.00
Windygates	V	30.00
Wishaw	D	30.00

The Additional Halfpenny

For the 26 years from 1813 to 1839 letters carried by 4-wheeled coaches on roads in Scotland *for any part of the journey* were charged a tax of ½d. in addition to the postage. Letters inside a Penny Post area were exempt as were those re-directed within Scotland and Free Franks.

If the tax was paid by the sender a red manuscript "½" was noted next to the postage amount. When tax was due from the receiver a black manuscript "½ "or a special handstamp was appropriate. Instructions were issued that, should a mark be noticed as indistinct at a transit or arrival office, a second mark must be applied. Hence the existence of letters bearing two different "½" marks.

At first only a few main offices had special handstamps, but their use (with colour variations) was gradually extended to many towns in Scotland, plus some in England and Dublin. Note : the Wales/Ireland manuscript additional halfpenny charge (1836-39) is an unrelated matter.

Further reading: *The Additional Halfpenny Mail Tax* by W G Stitt Dibden (1963).

The Scottish Additional Halfpenny Mail Tax by K Hodgson and W A Sedgewick, second edition 1984.

The main types are illustrated below, but there are very many different sizes and variations.

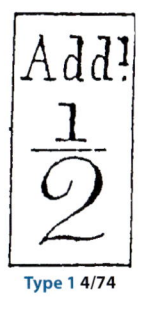

Type 1 4/74 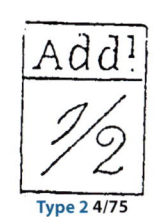 **Type 2** 4/75 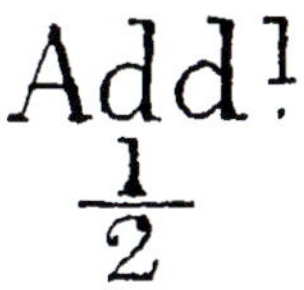 **Type 3** 4/76 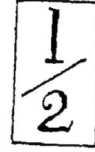 **Type 4** 4/77  **Type 5** 4/78

In the listing that follows each town is followed by the types used (see illustrations) and the colours are shown in brackets. The colours are : b=black, bl=blue, g=green, r=red.

Note: Ballantrae has weak/missing left frame line.

Aberdeen	5 (b,bl)	6.00
Annan	3 (b)	15.00
Arbroath	4 (b)	15.00
Ayr	4 (b,bl)	15.00
Ayton	4 (b)	50.00
Ballantrae	4 (b)	30.00
Blackshiels	4 (b)	£250
Bonaw	4 (b)	£100
Bo'ness/Borrowstouness	5 (b)	50.00
Bridge of Earn	4 (b)	60.00
Campbellton	4 (b)	75.00
Canonbie	4 (b)	30.00
Castle Douglas	4 (b)	30.00
Coldstream	3,5 (b,bl,r)	15.00
Culross	4 (b)	£125
Cumnock	4 (bl)	90.00
Cupar	4 (b,bl,g)	15.00
Denny	4 (bl)	£200
Dumbarton	4 (b)	30.00
Dumfries	1,4 (b,r)	6.00
Dunbar	4 (b,bl)	30.00
Dundee	3,5 (b,bl,g,r)	6.00
Dunfermline	4 (b,bl)	15.00
Duns	4 (b,bl)	15.00
Edinburgh	1,2,3 (b,r)	6.00
Falkirk	4,5 (b,bl)	6.00
Fort William	4 (b)	£150
Fraserburgh	4 (b)	30.00
Galashiels	4 (b)	30.00
Garlieston	4 (b)	60.00
Girvan	4 (b)	30.00
Glasgow	1,2,3,4 (b,bl,r)	6.00
Golspie	4 (r)	£275
Greenock	3,4 (b,bl)	6.00
Hamilton	4 (b)	30.00
Hawick	3,4 (b)	15.00
Inverary	4 (b)	50.00
Inverkeithing	4 (b)	30.00
Inverness	3,5 (b)	6.00
Irvine	4 (b)	£150
Jedburgh	4 (b)	15.00
Kelso	3 (b)	6.00
Kettle	4 (b)	50.00
Kilmarnock	4,5 (b,bl)	15.00
Kinghorn	4 (b)	£125
Kinross	4 (b)	£150
Kircaldy	4 (b,bl,g)	15.00
Kirkcudbright	4 (b)	30.00
Leadhills	4 (b)	£100
Leith	1,3 (b,bl,g)	15.00
Lesmahago	4 (b)	£100
Leven	4 (b,bl,g)	30.00
Linlithgow	4 (b)	15.00
Lochalsh	4 (b)	30.00
Lockerby	4 (b,r)	30.00
Markinch	4 (b)	30.00
Mauchline	1 (b)	£175
Maybole	4 (b)	30.00
Moffat	4 (b)	30.00
Montrose	5 (b)	6.00
Newburgh	4 (b,bl)	15.00

Early Scottish Marks to 1839

New Galloway	4 (g)	£100
Newton Stewart	4 (r)	£275
Oban	4 (b)	75.00
Paisley	1,2,3,4 (b)	6.00
Perth	5 (b)	6.00
Peterhead	4 (b)	75.00
Port Glasgow	3 (b)	15.00
Port Patrick	4 (b)	30.00
Portree	4 (b)	£125
Rothsay	1 (b)	50.00
St Andrews	4 (bl)	50.00
Saltcoates	4 (b)	30.00
Stewarton	4 (b)	£200
Stirling	3 (b,bl,g)	15.00
Stranraer	4 (b)	15.00
Whitburn	4 (b)	50.00
Wigtown	4 (b)	75.00

5 Early Irish Marks

The edditor is grateful both to Stan Challis and to David MacDonnell, of MacDonnell Whyte Ltd of Dublin, for providing the much-needed rewrite of this chapter.

The General Post (G.P.O. Dublin)
Evan Vaughan, an appointee of Oliver Cromwell, is given credit for establishing the Irish Post Office in 1657. The network was based on three great post roads radiating from Dublin; the Munster Road led to Cork with branches to Limerick and Waterford; the Connaught Road crossed the Shannon at Athlone and ended at Galway; the Ulster Road passed through the then small port of Belfast to end at the great castle of Carrickfergus, with branches to the religious capital of Armagh and Donaghadee for the crossing to Scotland. Initially all mail passed through Dublin, unless on the same post road but over time a series of cross posts was developed.

The Irish Post Office was independent in the years 1784 to 1831, at which date, as a result of numerous corrupt practices which had developed, it was 'taken in hand' and put under the control of GPO London.

Forerunners: The first recorded Irish postmarks are small circular marks with the letters D or W inscribed within a circle c15mm diameter. These letters are believed to be the initials of the postmasters and are recorded for the years 1667-1669. It is not possible to price these as most surviving examples are unavailable to collectors.

Bishop marks are known used in Dublin from 1670 but were not consistently applied until after 1700. The first town namestamps date from 1698, Carlow, Mullingar, Strabane and Waterford being amongst the earliest known. The service expanded rapidly so that by 1840 there were 328 (Head) Offices and approximately 370 sub offices and receiving houses. As they are largely considered as a single grouping, all undated marks used at provincial offices, whatever their status, are included here. With a handful of exceptions these markings were all withdrawn by March 1860.

Marks of the Dublin General Post Office

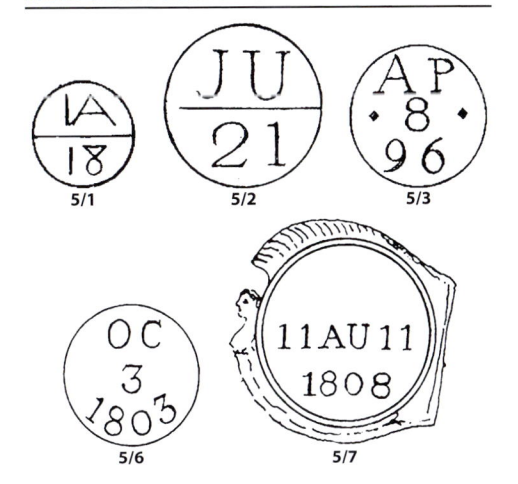

5/1	Small Bishop marks, 1670-1746	75.00
	– do, in two parts (from 1696)	£100
	– do, tête-bêche	£1,500
5/2	Larger Bishop marks, sometimes with dot between letters, 1746-95	30.00
5/3	Circular year marks, dots at sides, 1796	40.00
5/4	– do, dashes at sides, 1796	80.00
5/5	– do, no dots or dashes 1796-99	25.00
5/6	– do, year in four figures 1800-07	20.00
	– do, with sideways 's" at sides, 1796	£750
5/7	Mermaid, various types, red, 1808-14	90.00
5/8	Octagonal, red or black, with or without code letter, 1811-1815	5.00
5/9	– do, rounded corners, 1815-31	5.00
5/10	– do, concave corners, 1822-31	5.00

Early Irish Marks

5/11	– do, Sunday, red, black, green 1815-50	40.00
5/12	Diamonds, rhomboid, double frame, red, with or without code or time, 1820-41	3.00
5/13	– do, single frame, 1820-41	3.00
5/14	Diamonds, upright, double frame, red, with or without code or time, 1842-46	3.00
5/15	- do, single frame 1842-46	3.00
	- do, 'From/To' with times 1841-52	75.00
5/16	Circular, with code and/or letter, red, black, green, 1847-57	2.00
5/17	– do, no code letters 1853-57	4.00

Dublin Paid markings

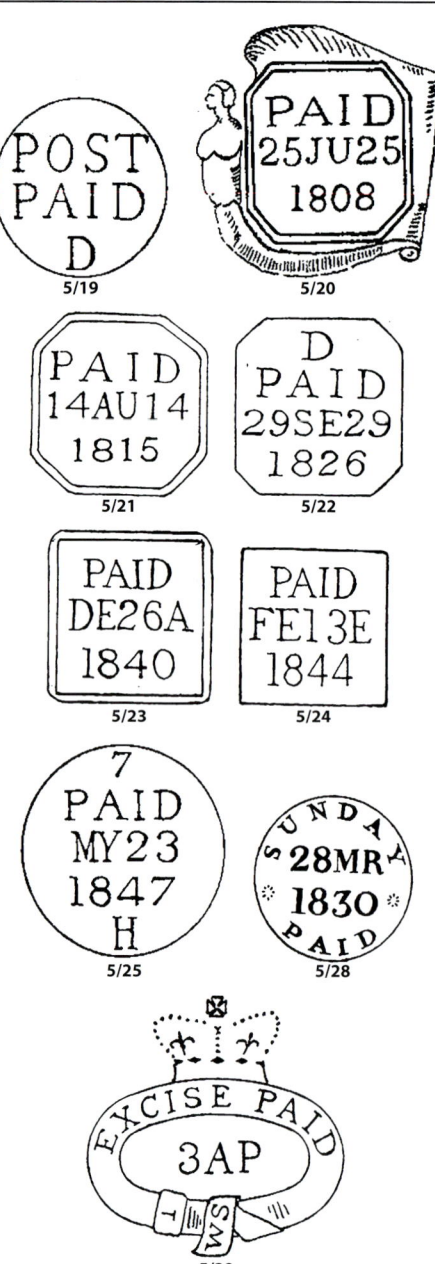

5/18	Post/D/Paid, D in centre, claret, black 1763-68	£150
5/19	Post/Paid/D, red black 1773-1802	50.00
5/20	Paid Mermaid, red, 1808-1815	£150
5/21	Paid, octagonal, double frame, red with or without code, 1815-40	5.00
5/22	– do, single frame, 1815-40	5.00
5/23	Paid, square, double frame, red, with or without code 1840-46	5.00
5/24	– do, single frame 1840-46	5.00
5/25	Paid, circular, red, with codes 1846-57	2.00
5/26	– do, crown at top, red, 1840-57	10.00
5/27	– do, crown at top, Paid below, and Dublin within circle, red, green, 1857	25.00
5/28	Sunday Paid, red, 1830-31	£250
5/29	Excise, Taxes, Customs, Revenue, oval, red, 1819-29	£250

Marks of the Dublin Penny and Twopenny Posts

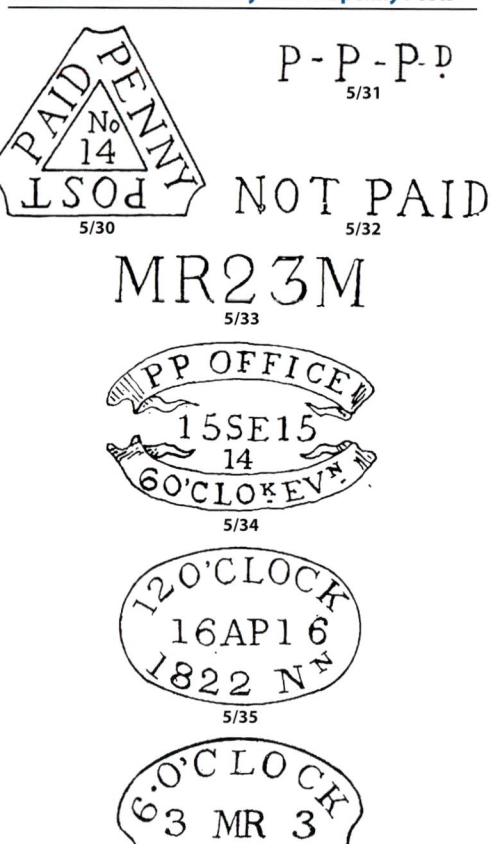

Early Irish Marks

Marks applied to mail between Ireland and Britain (and beyond)

Some of these were applied outside Ireland.

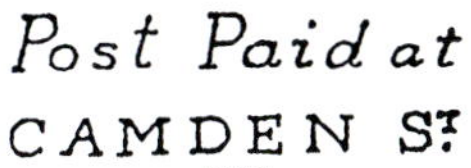

5/45	Dublin Penny Post, circular, black, 1820-45	15.00
5/46	Number/Paid/1d, red, 1840	£100
5/47	To Pay One Penny Only, black, 1820-45	£200

Marks associated with the Cork Mailcoaches

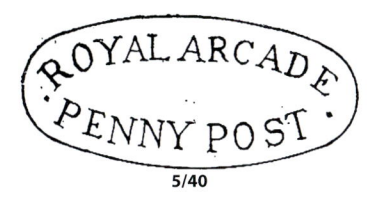

5/48	Octagonal Mid In/ Mid Out, red, 1811-22	50.00
5/49	Midday Mail, red, 1816-41	40.00
5/50	Mid Day mail, 1827-35	25.00
5/51	Post Paid/ Midday Mail, red, 1815-40	£100
5/52	Cork Evg Mail, red, 1822-28	40.00

Marks applied to mail between Ireland and Britain (and beyond), some of these were applied outside Ireland

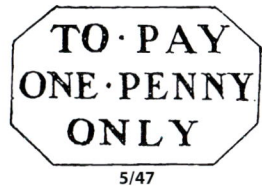

5/30	'Dockwra' type, black, 1782-84	£7,000
5/31	P.P.Pd, various, black, red, 1803-09	£450
5/32	'Not Paid', black, 1788-1809	£500
5/33	Dated, various formats	£100
5/34	Ribbon, red, black, 1814-20	40.00
5/35	Oval, black, 1814-32	18.00
5/36	Oval, concave sides, black, red, 1821-32	40.00
5/37	Genl. Py. P. Office/1 Py Paid, red, black 1810-26	£500
5/38	– do 2 Py Paid, red, 1830-33	£600
5/39	Office name P.P., straight line, red, blue, black, green, 1805-50	30.00
5/40	Oval Penny Post, black, red, 1825-31	£200
5/41	Post Paid at, black, red	£250
5/42	Curved, black	£350
5/43	Office name (Dublin receiving houses) black, 1828-50	15.00
5/44	Enniskerry/ Twopenny post, black, red 1827-40	£250

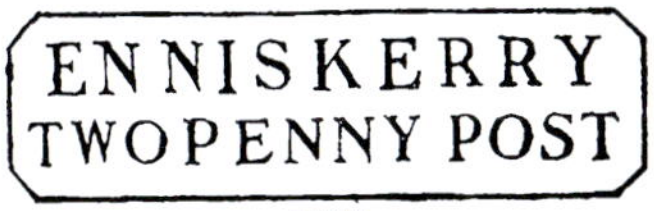

5/53	Straight line DUBLIN, 1720-87	85.00
5/54	CNTRY, 1721-41	£125
5/55	COUNTRY, 1748-1810	£100
5/56	IRELAND, various sizes, red, black 1777-1810	40.00

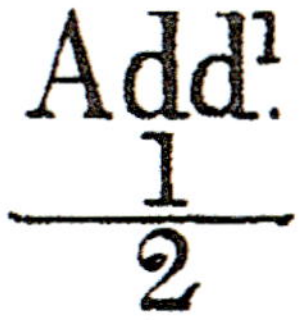

97

Early Irish Marks

5/57	– do, S/IRELAND, red, 1798-1802 (S = Sunday, used at London) Later strikes of these marks are believed to have been applied at the Irish desk at GPO London.	£400
5/58	½d Scottish wheel tax (long bar) additional charge, c1830-39	50.00

Provincial office markings

WATERFORD
A 5/101

BALLYSHANNON
B 5/102

LEIGHIN BRIDGE
C 5/103

A-LONE
D 5/104

R-CREA
E 5/105

BROADWAY 30
F 5/106

N·T·LIMY 137
G 5/107

CORK '124'
H 5/108

CASHEL 79
J 5/109

BELFAST MR23 1820 80
K 5/110

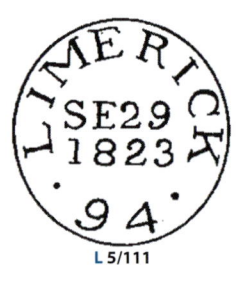

LIMERICK SE29 1823 ·94·
L 5/111

LURGANGREEN 37 *
M 5/112

WATERFORD 13 NO 1830
N 5/113

LOUGHREA DE27 1838
O 5/114

A	5/101	Straight line town namestamp large first letter, 1698-1736	£350
B	5/102	Straight line, some without serifs,1713-1850 (before 1750 add 500%, from 1750 to 1800 +150%)	15.00
C	5/103	– do, two lines	50.00
D	5/104	Small letters, often contracted	75.00
E	5/105	Larger letters – contracted	50.00
F	5/106	Mileage, 1808-57	15.00
G	5/107	Mileage, contracted	30.00
H	5/108	Mileage, curved, Cork, 1828-30	40.00
J	5/109	Mileage, boxed	70.00
K	5/110	Mileage, dated, with ornaments	25.00
L	5/111	Mileage, dated, plain (or dots)	30.00
M	5/112	– do, circular, undated	£150
N	5/113	Circular, year at base, 1829-31	35.00
O	5/114	Circular, arcs at base, 1830-60s	3.00

These marks are generally found struck in black, but certain types can also be found after 1808 in red, blue (both 20% premium) and green (100% premium).

Provincial Paid markings

POST PAID
PA 5/125

POST PAID
PB 5/126

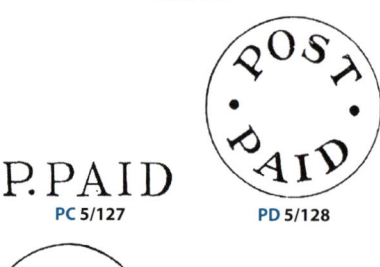

P.PAID
PC 5/127

POST PAID
PD 5/128

POST PAID
PE 5/129

PAID
PF 5/130

P.D C·RAINE
PG 5/131

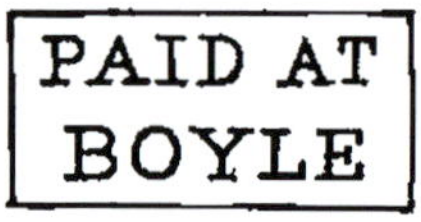

PAID AT BOYLE
PH 5/132

98

Early Irish Marks

PJ 5/133 — PAID AT CORK
PK 5/134 — PAID AT BELFAST
PL 5/135 — PAID at OMAGH
PM 5/136 — PAID at DUNGANNON
PN 5/137 — Paid at Enniskillen
PP 5/138 — PAID AT KELLS
PQ 5/139 — POST PAID AT CARLOW

Many of the types of the 'Paid At' marks were used only at one town. A selection is shown here – see detailed lists for other towns. Inks used, variously, red, black, blue, green.

PA	5/125	Post Paid scroll, various, with/ without ornaments, 1806-40	60.00
PB	5/126	Post Paid, various, 1806-48	30.00
PC	5/127	P.Paid, various, 1797-1850	20.00
PD	5/128	Post Paid, circular, various, c1826-40	80.00
PE	5/129	Post paid, horizontal in circle c1814-36	60.00
PF	5/130	Paid, various, 1817-47	25.00
PG	5/131	P.D/ C.RAINE, 1845-8	20.00
PH	5/132	Paid At … , wide usage, 1834-51 (certain towns considerably more)	15.00
PJ	5/133	Paid At Cork, 1833-39	30.00
PK	5/134	Paid At Belfast, 1832-44	50.00
PL	5/135	Paid At Omagh, 1833-35	£100
PM	5/136	Paid At Dungannon, 1835-42	75.00
PN	5/137	Paid At Enniskillen, 1835-43	75.00
PP	5/138	Paid At Kells, 1846-60	£350
PQ	5/139	Post Paid At Carlow/ Tralee 1834-50	80.00
	5/140	Other distinctive types, 1826-46	80.00

Provincial Penny Posts

PPA 5/151 — BALLYSHANNON PENNY POST
PPB 5/152 — Kanturk Penny Post
PPC 5/153 — Enniskillen Penny Post
PPD 5/154 — CASTLETOWNBERE Penny Post
PPE 5/155 — MAGUIRESBRIDGE P.P
PPF 5/156 — No 1
PPG 5/157 — No 2
PPH 5/158 — No 2
PPJ 5/159 — C

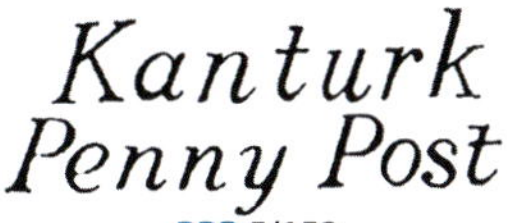

PPA	5/151	Penny Post, capital letters, 1832-50	40.00
PPB	5/152	Penny Post, italics, 1832-53	50.00
PPC	5/153	Boxed, Enniskillen, 1835-45	90.00
		– Monaghan, fancy frame, 1837-41	£250
PPD	5/154	Mixed, capital and italic, 1847-56	£150
PPE	5/155	Maguiresbridge PP, 1840-45	£300
PPF	5/156	Receiving house numbers, capitals	30.00
		– do, boxed	30.00
PPG	5/157	– do, italics	40.00
PPH	5/158	– do, italics and boxed	50.00
PPJ	5/159	– do, letter only (used in Cork)	50.00

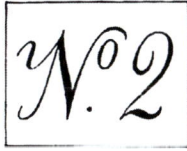

Undated and Receiving House marks

The type numbers are those normally used by Irish collectors

UD1A 5/201 — GLASSLOUGH
UD1B 5/202 — DUGORT
UD1C 5/203 — LAURENCETOWN BANBRIDGE
UD1D 5/204 — CONVOY REC$^{\circ}$ HOUSE

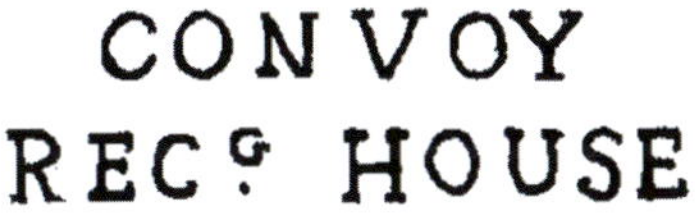

Early Irish Marks

BALLYHAISE RECEIVING·HOUSE
UD1E 5/205

DRAPERSTOWN RECEIVING HOUSE
UD1F 5/206

AHOGHILL R.H
UD1G 5/207

DONAGHMORE R.H
UD1H 5/208

CROSSMOLINA
UD2A 5/209

FEENY   DERRY
UD2B 5/210

CASTLEBRIDGE COREY
UD2C 5/211

Crawfordsburn
UD3A 5/212

Arthur Street RH. Belfast
UD3B 5/213

Ballintra · Ballyshannon
UD3C 5/214

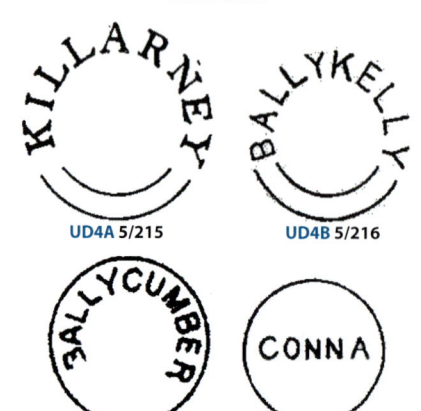

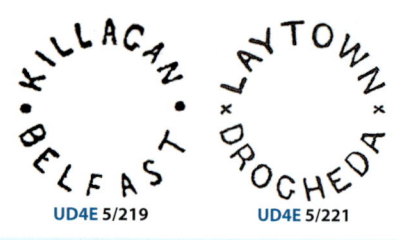

KILLARNEY
UD4A 5/215

BALLYKELLY
UD4B 5/216

BALLYCUMBER
UD4C 5/217

CONNA
UD4D 5/218

KILLAGAN · BELFAST
UD4E 5/219

LAYTOWN × DROGHEDA ×
UD4E 5/221

UD1A	5/201	Straight line, as 5/102 but used at a Receiving House	15.00
UD1B	5/202	Boxed, used only at Dugort	£750
UD1C	5/203	Two line	50.00
UD1D	5/204	RECg HOUSE	£150
UD1E	5/205	RECEIVING HOUSE in full	£150
UD1F	5/206	Octagonal box	£200
UD1G	5/207	With 'R.H'	50.00
UD1H	5/208	Boxed with 'R.H'	£200
UD2A	5/209	Smaller straight line, no serifs	25.00
UD2B	5/210	In one line, with name of Head Office alongside	60.00
UD2C	5/211	Two line	25.00
UD3A	5/212	Italic script, one line	70.00
UD3B	5/213	Two line with 'RH.'	30.00
UD3C	5/214	Two line, italic	25.00
UD4A	5/215	Circular, with serifs	20.00
UD4B	5/216	Circular, smaller, plain script	30.00
UD4C	5/217	Curved in circle	65.00
UD4D	5/218	Straight line across circle	80.00
UD4E	5/219	No frame, dots at sides	90.00
UD4E	5/220	No frame, no dots at side	80.00
UD4E	5/221	No frame, crosses at sides	90.00

Ireland - list of offices

The number after types F to L in the lists below is the mileage from Dublin. Where different mileages are known from the same town, no attempt is made to show a separate value for each. The varying distances can arise through re-routing, re-surveying or the different routings taken by day and night mailcoaches.

Some offices used straight line marks (type B) before 1808 (the introduction of mileage marks) and again as an undated mark in the 1830s (type UD1A) – note Abbeyleix below as an example. No attempt is made to differentiate prices although, in general, where both exist, those before 1808 merit a premium. A number of these marks are only known as a result of examples struck in 1858-59 when samples were taken by some Postmasters to ascertain what markings were in use at sub-offices under their control. Where, as a result of these surviving sample strikes, a mark is known to have been issued but is not recorded in use, a 'P' (Proof) is shown in the valuation column below. Many of those so struck have been recorded in use and it can be assumed that the remainder were also in regular use but examples remain to be found.

The circular datestamps (type O) are not listed here; this type and /or later varieties thereof, had become all but universal by c1855.

Spellings shown are both those actually recorded and, where different, the generally accepted current spelling is used.

Detailed listings of colours used at individual offices are beyond the scope of this catalogue. In addition to Black and Red, various shades of Blue and Green were also used. Other colours can also be found.

Full inscription on the Undated Marks is not given unless it is necessary to provide clarity.

No attempt is made to allocate types PPF, PPG or PPH to the individual Receiving Houses. Many allocations are not known and some Receiving Houses are known to have used more than one number.

Brackets in the Type column indicate that the item is similar to the illustration but a variant thereto.

Early Irish Marks

** after the name of the office indicates two (or more) offices exist with the same name and confirmation is required of the actual office of use; valuations of such items are tentative pending better information.

Marks used at Dublin Penny Post Offices prior to 1840 are excluded but the majority of those of the Twopenny Post Offices are included as some of these offices also served as 'rural' sub-offices.

Office	Type	Value
Abbeyfeale	F 102	50.00
Abbeyleix	B/ UD1A	20.00
	F 47/48	20.00
	PF	30.00
	PPB	60.00
Achill Sound	UD2A	£100
Adamstown	UD4B	50.00
Adair (Adare)	B	30.00
	F102	35.00
Aghadowey	UD1G	50.00
(Agadowey)	UD2C	40.00
	UD4B	40.00
Aghadown	UD2A	75.00
Agher (Meath)	UD4D	£100
Ahascragh	F 75/78	50.00
	PPA	75.00
	UD1A	35.00
Ahoghill	UD1G	50.00
	UD2C	50.00
Andersonstown	UD2C	P
Annahilt	UD3C	40.00
Annalong	UD3B	40.00
	UD3C	30.00
Annalore	UD2C	50.00
	UD4B	50.00
Annamoe	UD1A	50.00
Annascaul	UD2A	50.00
Antrim	B	25.00
	F 93	20.00
with 'squiggle' at sides	(PC)	80.00
two ornaments below Paid At	(PL)	£300
	PPA	75.00
	UD4A	25.00
Archerstown	UD2A	40.00
Ardagh **	UD2A	50.00
	UD4D	80.00
Ardagh (Longford)	UD3C	40.00
Ardara	F 130/132	70.00
	UD1A	40.00
Ardattin	UD2C	40.00
	UD3A	70.00
	UD4B	50.00
Ardee	B/ UD1A	25.00
	F 31/34/35	35.00
	PPA	60.00
	F 40	60.00
Ardfert	UD2A	50.00
Ardglass	F 90	40.00
	UD4A	25.00
Ardkeen	UD2C	P
Ardlogher	UD3B	40.00
(Ardloher)	UD3C	40.00
Ardmore	UD1A	40.00
Ardstraw	UD3B	40.00
	UD3C	40.00
Arklow	B/ UD1A	30.00
	F 36	25.00
	PB	25.00
	PH	60.00
	UD4A	25.00
Armagh	B	20.00
(A.Magh)	G	£100
	F 63/66	20.00
	PH	40.00

Office	Type	Value
	PPA	60.00
Armoy	UD3B	30.00
	UD3C	35.00
	UD4E (5/220)	80.00
Arran Island	UD4C (c1870)	£250
	UD4E (5/220)	£250
Artane	UD1A	40.00
Arthurstown	F 75	50.00
	PPA	80.00
	PPB	80.00
Arthur St (Belfast)	UD3B	30.00
	UD3C	25.00
Articlave	UD2B	P
	UD3C	40.00
Arvagh (Arva)	F 66	35.00
	UD1A	35.00
Ashbourne	F 10	30.00
	Scroll	£150
	PPA	50.00
	UD1A	30.00
	UD4A	30.00
Ashford (Wicklow)	F 21	30.00
	PPB	50.00
Askeaton	F 115	50.00
	J 113	75.00
	UD3C	35.00
Ashfield	UD3B	35.00
Athboy	B	30.00
	F 31/38	30.00
	PH	40.00
	PPB	50.00
	UD1A	25.00
Athea	UD2A	40.00
Athenry	B	30.00
	F 100	25.00
Athleague	F 79	50.00
	UD2A	40.00
Athlone	B	25.00
(A-Lone)	D	£125
	F 59/60	25.00
	PH	35.00
	PPA	50.00
Athy	B	25.00
	F 32/41	30.00
	PH	50.00
	PPA	60.00
Augher	UD3C	25.00
Aughnacloy	B/ UD1A	40.00
	F 71	35.00
unframed	(PH)	£200
	PPA	70.00
Aughnafutten	UD4E (5/220)	£100
Aughrim (Galway)	F 76	60.00
	UD1A	30.00
Aughrim (Wicklow)	UD3C	40.00
Ayle	UD4B	50.00
Bag(e)nalstown	B	25.00
	F 47	20.00
	UD1A	35.00
Bailyborough (Baillieboro)	B	30.00
(BYBoro)	G 43	30.00
	UD4A	35.00
Balbriggan	B	35.00
	F 15	30.00
	PPA	65.00
	UD4A	30.00
Balla	UD2A	40.00
	UD4B	50.00
Ballacolla	UD4A	40.00
Ballaghaderreen (BHAderin)	G 92	30.00
(also Ballaghadireen)	UD1A	30.00
Ballaghy see Bellaghy		
Balli(y)bay	B	30.00
	F 56/57	30.00

101

Early Irish Marks

Office	Type	Value
	UD1A	25.00
Ballickmoyler	UD1A	30.00
	UD2A	40.00
	UD2C	40.00
Ballina	B/ UD1A	30.00
	F 124/144/148	30.00
	PH	18.00
	UD4A	35.00
Ballinacally	UD3C	40.00
Ballinacargy see Ballynacargy		
Ballinacurra	UD2A	35.00
	UD4B	50.00
Ballinagh (Cavan)	UD3C	40.00
(Ballinanagh)		
(Bellanaragh)	UD3C	35.00
Ballinagore	UD3C	40.00
	UD4B	40.00
Ballinahinch see Ballynahinch		
Ballinakill	F 50/74	40.00
(BNAkill)	G 50	35,00
	UD4A	20.00
(Ballynakill)	UD4B	50.00
Ballinalee	UD1A	30.00
Ballinamallard	UD3C	35.00
Ballinamore	F 83	35.00
	UD4A	50.00
Ballinan (Ballylinan)	UD3A	80.00
Ballinasloe	B	20.00
(BNAsloe)	G 71/72	35.00
(Balinasloe)	F 71	30.00
	PPB	50.00
Ballincollig	F 128/131	35.00
	UD4A	40.00
Ballinderry (Antrim)		
(Ballinderry Lower)	F 73	50.00
	UD1A	25.00
	UD4A	40.00
	UD4B	40.00
Ballinderry Upper		
(Upper Ballinderry)	UD2C	40.00
	UD3C	40.00
Ballinderry **	UD2A	40.00
Ballinderry (Tipperary)	UD2C	40.00
Ballindine	UD3C	40.00
Ballinfull	UD2A	40.00
	UD4B	50.00
Ballingar(r)y (Lim'k)	F 113	40.00
Ballingarry (Kilkenny)	UD3C	40.00
Ballinglen	UD2C	35.00
Ballinhassig	UD2A	35.00
Ballinlough	UD2A	40.00
Ballinrobe	F 110/116	35.00
	UD1A	20.00
Ballintra	UD2C	40.00
	UD3C	35.00
Ballintubber(t) (Athy)	UD4B	50.00
Ballisodare	UD2A	30.00
Ballitore	UD1A	25.00
Ballivor	UD4C	65.00
(Ballivore)	UD2A	30.00
Ballon	UD1A	30.00
	UD4B	50.00
Ballyardle	UD4E (5/221)	£120
Ballyaughlis	UD2C	30.00
	UD4B	50.00
	UD4E (5/220)	80.00
Ballybay see Ballibay		
Ballybofey	UD4B	50.00
Ballyboy (BYBoy)	G 59	30.00
Ballyboyne	UD2C	40.00
	UD3C	40.00
Ballybrack (Dublin)	UD2A	40.00
	UD2C	40.00

Office	Type	Value
	UD4A	50.00
	UD4B	50.00
Ballybrack (Kerry)	UD2A	60.00
Ballybrittas (BYBrittas)	G 33	40.00
	UD2C	35.00
	UD4B	50.00
Ballycanew	UD1A	25.00
	UD2C	30.00
Ballycarn	UD1A	40.00
Ballycarry	UD3C	40.00
Ballycassidy	UD2C	40.00
Ballycastle (B.Castle)	E	50.00
	F 114/140	40.00
	PH	30.00
	PPA	60.00
	UD1A	30.00
Ballycastle (Mayo)	UD2C	35.00
Ballyclare	PC	30.00
	UD1A	30.00
	UD3A	80.00
	UD4A	20.00
Ballycogley	UD1A	40.00
Ballyconnell	B	35.00
(BYConnell)	G 67/68	35.00
	PH	50.00
	PB	50.00
	PPA	75.00
	UD4A	40.00
Ballycrissan(e)	UD2A	40.00
	UD2C	40.00
Ballycumber	UD2C	30.00
	UD4B	50.00
	UD4C	75.00
Ballydehob	PPD	£150
	UD1A	40.00
	UD4B	50.00
Ballydugan	UD3B	35.00
Ballyeaston	UD2C	40.00
Ballyfarnon	UD2A	40.00
	UD3A	70.00
(Ballyfarnon/Boyle)	UD3C	40.00
Ballyfeard	UD2A	40.00
Ballyforan	UD2A	40.00
Ballygar	UD3A	80.00
	UD3C	40.00
Ballygawley	F 78	35.00
(Ballygawly)	F 74	40.00
Ballyglass	F 116/130	40.00
	UD1A	30.00
	PPA	65.00
Ballyglunin	UD2A	40.00
Ballygorman	UD2C	P
Ballygowan	UD3C	40.00
Ballygraney	UD3C	40.00
Ballyhaise	UD1A	40.00
	UD1E	£150
	UD4A	40.00
Ballyhalbert	UD2C	40.00
	UD4B	P
Ballyhaunis (BYHaunis)	G 98	50.00
Ballyheelan	UD2A	40.00
	UD4C	75.00
Ballyhooly	UD1A	35.00
	UD4A	40.00
	UD4B	40.00
Ballyhoran	UD3C	40.00
Ballyjamesduff	B	30.00
	F 46	45.00
(BallyJSDuff)	G 44	40.00
	PPB	60.00
	UD4A	40.00
Ballykelly	UD1A	35.00
	UD2A	40.00

102

Early Irish Marks

Office	Type	Value
	UD2B	P
	UD4A	40.00
Ballylinan	UD2A	40.00
Ballylongford	F 129	60.00
	UD1A	18.00
	UD4B	50.00
Ballymacarrett	UD1A	35.00
Ballymacelligott	UD2A	40.00
	UD4B	50.00
Ballymaguigan	UD2C	40.00
Ballymahon	B/ UD1A	20.00
	F 54	30.00
(BYMahon)	G 54	50.00
	PPA	50.00
Ballymakenny	UD2A	40.00
Ballymascanlan	UD3C	40.00
(Ballynascanlan)	UD4B	50.00
Ballymeen	UD4B	50.00
Ballymena	B	20.00
(B-Mena)	D	£250
(B-Menagh)	E	75.00
	F 101	20.00
	PH	25.00
	PPA	40.00
Ballymoe (BYMoe)	G 85	30.00
	UD1A	25.00
Ballymoney	B/ UD1A	20.00
(B.Mone)	E	60.00
	F 108/119	35.00
	J 118	50.00
no fleurons	PA	£140
with fleurons	PA	£220
	PH	35.00
	PPB	60.00
	UD4A	40.00
Ballymore (Ballimore)	B	50.00
	F 56	45.00
(BYMore)	G 48	60.00
	UD2A	40.00
Ballymore Eustace	UD2C	40.00
	UD3C	40.00
Ballymote	B	35.00
(BYMote)	G 94	40.00
(Ballymoate)	UD1A	20.00
	PF	30.00
	PPA	50.00
Ballymurry	UD2A	40.00
Ballynacargy		
(Ballinacargy)	F 45	30.00
(Balnacarig)	F 48	50.00
	UD4A	40.00
Ballynafad	UD3C	40,00
(Ballinafad)	UD4B	50.00
Ballynahinch	B	50.00
(BYNahinch)	E	50.00
	F 74	50.00
(Ballinahinch)	UD4A	40.00
Ballyneen	UD4B	50.00
Ballynure	UD2C	40.00
Ballyporeen	UD1A	35.00
	UD2A	30.00
Ballyragget	F 53	40.00
	UD1A	35.00
	UD4A	35.00
Ballyronan	UD3C	40.00
Ballysax	UD2A	40.00
Ballyshannon	B	30.00
(B.shannon)	E	50.00
	F 101	25.00
(BYShannon)	G 101	50.00
	PH	40.00
	PPA	60.00
Ballytore (BYTore)	F 28	35.00
(Ballitore)	UD1A	30.00

Office	Type	Value
Ballyvary (BYVary)	G 119	40.00
	UD3C	40.00
Ballyvaugh(e)n	UD1A	40.00
Ballyvourney	UD2A	40.00
Ballywalter	UD1G	60.00
	UD4B	P
Ballyward	UD3B	40.00
Balnacarig see Ballynacargy		
Balrath	UD3C	35.00
Baltimore	UD1A	40.00
Baltinglass	B/ UD1A	30.00
	F 40	40.00
(BNGlass)	G 40	40.00
	PPA	60.00
Banagher	B	35.00
	F 64/75/77	40.00
	PB	35.00
	PPA	50.00
	UD4A	40.00
Banbridge	B	30.00
	F 60	25.00
	PH	35.00
Bandon	B	30.00
	F 137/141/146	40.00
	PB	30.00
	PH	30.00
	PPA	50.00
Bangor (Down)	B	35.00
	F 90	40.00
	UD4A	35.00
Bangor (Erris)	UD3C	40.00
Bansha	UD1A	35.00
Banteer	UD2A	40.00
Bantry	B	40.00
	F 164/171/ 172/176	50.00
	PPB	90.00
Barna (Limerick)	UD2A	40.00
Barna **	UD4D	£100
Baronscourt	UD4B	60.00
Barrington's Bridge	UD2C	50.00
	UD3C	40.00
Bawnboy	UD2A	35.00
	UD3C	40.00
	UD4B	50.00
Baylin	UD4B	50.00
Beaufort	UD1A	40.00
	UD4C	80.00
Beleek	UD1A	30.00
	UD2C	40.00
	UD4A	40.00
	UD4D	£100
Belfast	B	15.00
(B.Fast)	D	£250
(BLFast)	E	£100
	F 80	18.00
	K 80	25.00
Scroll (two different)	(PA)	£175
with Irish/British below	(PB)	£500
	PC	35.00
lower case letters	(PC)	40.00
boxed	(PC)	35.00
	PF	60.00
	PK	50.00
	PPA	40.00
	PPB	50.00
	N	25.00
PAID / no date	(O)	75.00
Bellaghy (Ballaghy)	F 92	40.00
	PB	35.00
	UD2A	35.00
	UD4A	40.00
	UD4B	50.00
	UD4E (5/219)	£100

Early Irish Marks

Office	Type	Value
Bellanaragh see Ballinagh		
Belmullet	F 160	60.00
Belrath (Balrath)	UD2A	40.00
Belturbet	F 61/65	30.00
	PH	40.00
	8	50.00
	UD1A	30.00
Benburb	UD3B	35.00
	UD3C	40.00
Bennettsbridge	UD2A	30.00
Beragh	UD1A	30.00
Bettystown	UD1A	40.00
	UD1G	60.00
Birr (see also Parsonstown)	B	50.00
	D	80.00
Blackhill	UD4B	50.00
	UD4E (5/220)	80.00
Blacklion	UD3C	40.00
Blackrock (Dublin)	PPA	60.00
	PPB	50.00
	UD2A	50.00
Blackrock (Cork)	UD2B	60.00
	UD4E (5/221)	£120
Blackwater	UD2C	35.00
Blackwatertown	B	40.00
(BlackwatertN)	G 70	45.00
	PF	40.00
	UD1A	20.00
	UD4A	40.00
Blarney	UD1A	20.00
Bles(s)in(g)ton	F 22	30.00
	PPB	70.00
Blue Ball	UD1A	20.00
	UD1G	60.00
Bohirmeen (Bohermeen)	UD2A	30.00
Bonmahon	UD2C	40.00
Bogay	UD2A	P
Booterstown	PPA	90.00
	UD4B	50.00
Borris	UD2B	60.00
Borris Bagenalstown	UD2C	30.00
Borris Kilkenny	UD2C	40.00
Borrisokane	B	30.00
(Bor.kane)	E	80.00
(BSAkane)	G 72/77	35.00
	PPA	50.00
	PPB	50.00
	UD1A	60.00
Borris-in-Ossory	B	35.00
	C	65.00
(BS in Ossory)	G 54	40.00
Borrisoleigh (BSOleigh)	G 74	40.00
	PB	50.00
	UD2C	40.00
Borrisokane (Burrisakane)	UD1A	25.00
Boyle	B	30.00
	F 84/85	30.00
	PB	30.00
	PH	15.00
	P5	75.00
Brannockstown	UD2C	40.00
Brantry	UD2C	40.00
Bray	B	30.00
	F 10	25.00
	PPA	50.00
	UD4A	35.00
Bready	UD1A	35.00
	UD3C	40.00
Broadway	F 80	40.00
	UD4A	40.00
Bridgetown (Wexford)	UD1A	40.00
	UD2C	40.00
	UD4B	50.00
Brittas	UD2C	45.00

Office	Type	Value
British	UD4B	80.00
Broadford (Clare)	UD1A	25.00
	UD2A	40.00
Broadway (Wexford)	F 80	30.00
	UD2C	45.00
Brookeboro(ugh)	F 73	45.00
	PH	50.00
	UD4A	40.00
Brosna **	UD4B	50.00
Broughshane	F 108	50.00
	UD1A	30.00
	UD2C	40.00
Brownstown	UD2A	40.00
Bruff	B	40.00
	F 105/106	50.00
	PPB	70.00
Bruree	UD2A	40.00
	UD4B	50.00
Bryansford	UD3B	40.00
Buncrana	B	50.00
	F 122/129	50.00
	PH	60.00
	UD4A	40.00
Bundoran	PH	60.00
	UD1A	35.00
(Bundoran/B'Shannon)	UD2C	30.00
(Bundoran/Enniskillen)	UD2C	40.00
	UD3C	35.00
Bunnahow	UD4B	60.00
Bunnanadden	UD2A	70.00
Bunratty	F 100	60.00
	UD1A	25.00
	UD2A	40.00
Burghtown (Burtown)	UD4B	60.00
Burnfoot	UD3B	50.00
Burrisakane see Borrisokane		
Burrin	F 109	60.00
	UD4C	75.00
	UD4D	£100
Bushmills	F 127/128	50.00
	PB	30.00
	UD1A	30.00
Butlers Bridge	UD1A	50.00
	UD4B	50.00
Buttevant	F 122/132/135	35.00
	PB	30.00
	PH	65.00
	UD1A	30.00
Cabinteely	F 6	40.00
	PPA	75.00
	UD3C	40.00
Cahir	B	30.00
	F 87/88/92	30.00
	PB	30.00
	PH	50.00
	UD4A	40.00
Cahirciveen	F 178	50.00
	PPB	85.00
(also Cahirsiveen)	UD1A	40.00
Cahirconlish	F 101	60.00
	UD3C	35.00
Cairncastle	UD1G	50.00
Cal(l)edon	F 72/74	40.00
	UD4A	40.00
Callan	B/UD1A	25.00
	F 64/65	25.00
Camlough	UD3C	40.00
Camolin	F 51	40.00
	UD1A	40.00
Camp	UD4B	70.00
Campsie	UD2C	P
Canningstown	UD3A	80.00
	UD3C	40.00
Cappawhite	UD2A	40.00

104

Early Irish Marks

Office	Type	Value
	UD2C	35.00
	UD3C	40.00
	UD4B	50.00
Cappoquin	F 106/122/126	40.00
Carbury	UD1A	30.00
(Carberry)	UD4B	50.00
Carlanstown	UD1A	40.00
	UD2A	40.00
Carlingford	F 60	50.00
	UD1A	40.00
Carnlough	UD2C	40.00
Carlow (Catherlovgh)	B	£2,000
	B	20.00
	F 39	20.00
	PQ	80.00
Carnmoney	UD3B	60.00
(Carmoney)	UD4B	50.00
Carn(donagh)	B	50.00
	F 132	60.00
	UD1A	40.00
	PPA	50.00
Carnew	F 47	40.00
	UD1A	40.00
Carney (Sligo)	UD3C	40.00
Carrickbue	UD2A	40.00
Carrickfergus	B/ UD1A	40.00
(C.Fergus)	D	75.00
	F 88	40.00
(CKFergus)	G 88/89	40.00
	PPA	55.00
	UD4A	35.00
Carrickmacross	B/ UD1A	30.00
(C.Macross)	D	90.00
(CKMacross)	E	50.00
(C-M-C)	E	£450
(C.K.Mcross)	E	£150
	F 44	35.00
(CKMacross)	G 44/45	35.00
	PPA	50.00
	PPB	60.00
Carrick on Shannon	B/ UD1A	30.00
(C-Rick/ on/ Shannon)	(C)	£350
(CK on Shannon)	F 74	35.00
	PPA	50.00
Carrick on Suir	B/ UD1A	30.00
(C-Rick)	D	75.00
(CK on Suir)	E	50.00
(CK on Suir)	G 78	40.00
	F 86/87/92	30.00
Carrigaholt	UD1A	35.00
Carrigahorig	UD2A	40.00
(Carrighorrig)	UD3C	40.00
Carrigalin(e)	UD2A	40.00
	UD4B	50.00
Carrigallen	UD2A	40.00
Carrigans	UD3C	40.00
Carrigart	UD1A	40.00
Carrigtwohill	UD2A	40.00
Carrowdore	UD3C	40.00
	UD4B	P
Cashcarrigan (Keshcarrigan)	F 80	60.00
	UD2A	40.00
Cashel(l)	B/ UD1A	30.00
	D	75.00
	F 79/94/96/98	35.00
	J79	40.00
	UD1A	30.00
	PB	35.00
Cashelmore	UD2A	40.00
Castlebar	B	40.00
(CLBar)	G 113/122/125	25.00
	F 125	35.00
	PH	40.00
	PPB	60.00

Office	Type	Value
Castlebellingham (C.Bellingham)	G 34	40.00
	M 34	£200
	UD4A	40.00
Castleblaken(e)y	B	50.00
(CLblakeney)	G 84	50.00
Castleblayn(e)y	E	50.00
	F 52	30.00
	PH	70.00
	UD4A	30.00
	UD4B	50.00
Castlebridge (Wexford)	UD1A	35.00
	UD2C	40.00
	UD3C	40.00
Castlecaulfield	UD2C	40.00
	UD3C	35.00
Castlecomer	F 55	40.00
	PB	35.00
	UD1A	25.00
	UD4A	35.00
Castleconnell (CLConnell)	G 88	40.00
	UD1A	35.00
	PPB	60.00
Castledawson	E	50.00
	F 90	40.00
with dash	(PC)	80.00
	UD1A	35.00
Castlederg	F 109	50.00
	UD1A	25.00
	UD4A	40.00
	PPB	75.00
Castledermot	B	50.00
(C.Dermott)	E	60.00
(CLEDermott)	E	50.00
(CLDermot)	G34	40.00
Castle Ellis	UD2C	60.00
	UD3C	60.00
Castlefin	PB	50.00
	UD1A	30.00
Castlefreke	UD4B	50.00
Castleisland	F 154	50.00
	UD1A	20.00
Castleknock	UD3C	35.00
	UD4A	50.00
	PPA	70.00
Castlelyons (C.Lyons)	D	90.00
	UD2A	35.00
Castlemartyr	B	40.00
(C.Matyr)	E	50.00
(CLEMartyr)	G 126	45.00
Castlepollard	B/ UD1A	30.00
(C.Pollard)	E	50.00
(CLEPollard)	G 47	40.00
Castlerea	B/UD1A	40.00
(CLrea)	G 88	30.00
Castlerickard	UD2A	40.00
Castletown (Queen's)	UD2C	30.00
	UD3C	40.00
Castletown (Meath)	UD3B	40.00
Castletown **	UD4B	50.00
Castletown(bere)	B/ UD1A	40.00
	E	60.00
	F 193/198	60.00
	UD2A	35.00
Castletown Delvin	B	40.00
(C.T.Delvin)	E	50.00
(C T Delvin)	G 39	40.00
Castletownroche (C T Roche)	G 114/116/118	45.00
	UD2A	40.00
Castletownshend	UD4B	50.00
	PPD	£200
Castlewellan (C.Wellan)	E	80.00
	F 65	40.00
	UD1A	30.00
	PPA	75.00

105

Early Irish Marks

Office	Type	Value
Causeway	UD2A	40.00
Cavan	B	30.00
(Cauan)	B	£100
	F 54	25.00
	PH	50.00
	PPB	50.00
Celbridge	F 9	40.00
	PPB	50.00
Chapelizod	UD1A	50.00
	UD2A	40.00
	UD4B	50.00
	PPB	80.00
Charleville	B	30.00
(C-Ville)	G 115	40.00
	PB	40.00
	UD1A	35.00
	UD4A	40.00
	PPA	50.00
Chichester St (Belfast)	UD1G	50.00
Churchhill	F 88	75.00
	UD1A	30.00
(Churchill)	UD4A	40.00
Churchtown (Cork)	UD1A	30.00
Churchtown (Wexford)	UD2C	40.00
Clady (Derry)	UD3C	40.00
Clady (Tyrone)	UD3C	50.00
Clane	F 19	35.00
	UD4A	40.00
	UD4B	50.00
Clara	B/ UD1A	20.00
	F 48/49	30.00
	PPA	50.00
Clare(morris)	F 117	35.00
(Clare/Claremorrls)	UD1A	25.00
Clarecastle	UD1A	40.00
Clareen	UD4B	50.00
Claregalway	UD2A	40.00
	UD2C	40.00
Clarina	UD1A	30.00
Clashmore	UD1A	30.00
Clerihan	UD2A	40.00
Clifden	F 144	50.00
	UD1A	40.00
Cliffoney	UD1A	35.00
Cloghan	F 60	40.00
	UD4A	40.00
Clogheen	F 94	35.00
Clogher	F 78/82/83	35.00
Clogher Head	UD1A	30.00
	UD1E	£200
Clo(u)(gh)nakilty	F 151/156	49.00
	UD1A	25.00
Cloghran	UD1A	30.00
	UD4C	75.00
Clonard	B	40.00
	F 26	40.00
	UD4A	40.00
Clonaslie (Clonaslei)	F 47	60.00
	UD2C	40.00
Clonbur	UD1A	40.00
Clondalkin	UD2C	30.00
Clonegal(l)	B	50.00
	F 45/51	40.00
Clones	B/ UD1A	30.00
	F 61/67/68	30.00
	PH	50.00
	PPA	60.00
	UD4A	40.00
Clonevan	UD1A	40.00
(Clonevin)	UD2C	40.00
Clonlara	UD3C	40.00
Clonlost	UD2A	35.00
Clonmel(l)	B	25.00
	B curved	70.00

Office	Type	Value
(CLMell)	D	75.00
	F 82	30.00
no ornaments at sides	K 82/96	80.00
	PB	30.00
	PPA	50.00
Clonmellon	UD3C	40.00
	UD4B	50.00
Clonroche	UD1A	40.00
	UD2A	40.00
	UD4B	50.00
Clontarf	PPA	£120
	PPB	£120
Cloone (Leitrim)	UD2C	40.00
	UD3C	40.00
Clough (Antrim)	UD3C	40.00
	UD4E (5/221)	90.00
Clough (Down)	F 69	40.00
	UD1A	30.00
	PPB	75.00
Cloughjordan (CHJordan)	G 72	40.00
Cloughnakilty see Clonakilty		
Clountain	UD1A	40.00
(Clounthaun)	UD1A	40.00
(now Glounthaun)		
Cloyne	F 125/126	35.00
	PPB	60.00
Coachford	UD4A	40.00
Coagh	UD3C	35.00
	UD4E (5/220)	80.00
Coalisland	F 76	40.00
	UD4A	30.00
	UD4B	50.00
	UD4C	75.00
Colehill	F 57	40.00
	UD1A	40.00
Colerain(e)	B/ UD1A	25.00
	F 121/124	30.00
	PF	25.00
boxed and curved	(PF)	80.00
	PG	20.00
	PH	35.00
	PPA	40.00
Collany (Collaney)	UD3C	40.00
Collinstown	UD2A	40.00
	UD4B	50.00
Collon	B	20.00
	F 29	40.00
	UD1A	25.00
	UD2C	40.00
Collooney	B	40.00
	F 97/98	35.00
(Colooney)	UD1A	30.00
	PPA	65.00
Comber	F 87/91	40.00
	PPB	60.00
	UD4A	40.00
Cong	F 120	45.00
	UD2A	40.00
	UD4B	50.00
Conna	UD2A	40.00
	UD4D	£100
Corboy	UD4B	45.00
Convoy	UD1D	£200
	UD3C	40.00
Cookstown	B	40.00
	F 82/86	35.00
	PH	75.00
	UD4A	40.00
Coolattin	UD2A	40.00
	UD2B	75.00
	UD2C	30.00
Coolkenno	UD1A	40.00
Coolrain	UD1A	40.00
(Coolraine)	UD4B	50.00

Early Irish Marks

Office	Type	Value
Coolsallagh	UD2A	40.00
	UD2C	40.00
	UD3C	40.00
Coot(e)hill	B/ UD1A	25.00
	F 52/58	35.00
	UD4A	40.00
Corboy	UD4B	30.00
Corcreaghy	UD2C	40.00
	UD4B	40.00
Cork	B	15.00
(Corke)	B	£250
	D	60.00
	F 124	15.00
	H 124	40.00
	PJ	50.00
	PPA	40.00
	PPB	50.00
	N	30.00
used at town RHs	PPJ	75.00
Court House (Belfast)	UD2C	40.00
	UD3B	40.00
Courthouse RH	(UD2C)	£150
Courtmacsherry	UD2A	40.00
Courtown Harbour	UD1A	45.00
	UD2C	60.00
(Courtown)	UD4B	60.00
Cove	B	25.00
	F 130/134/136	30.00
	PB	45.00
	PH	45.00
Craigavad	UD2C	P
Cratloe	UD2C	40.00
Craughwell	B	40.00
	F 95	50.00
	PPA	65.00
Crawfordsburn	UD2A	40.00
	UD3A	80.00
	UD3C	40.00
Crebally	UD1A	40.00
Creeslough	UD1A	40.00
	UD4A	40.00
Creggan	UD4B	50.00
Crettyard	UD1A	35.00
Crinkle	UD2C	35.00
	UD4B	50.00
Croghan	UD2A	40.00
Crookhaven	PPD	£150
	UD4E (5/220)	£100
Crookstown	UD1A	30.00
Croom	F 102	40.00
Cross	UD3B	50.00
	UD3C	40.00
Crossakeel(e) (or Crossakiel)	F 36	50.00
	UD2C	40.00
	UD4A	40.00
	UD4B	40.00
Crossdoney	F 58	50.00
	PB	75.00
	PH	75.00
	UD4A	40.00
Crossgar	UD3C	40.00
Cross Keys	UD2C	75.00
Crosshaven	UD2A	40.00
Crossmolina (CSMolina)	F 131	50.00
	UD2A	40.00
Crosshaven	PPA	60.00
	PPB	70.00
	UD2A	40.00
Crumlin	F 78/89	40.00
	UD4A	40.00
Cuffes Grange boxed	(UD1A)	£200
	UD4B	50.00
Culdaff	UD3C	40.00
	UD4E	P

Office	Type	Value
Cullybackey	UD3C	40.00
Culmore	UD2C	P
Curragh Camp	Scroll	£2,000
Currofin (Corofin)	F 110	60.00
Curryglass	UD2A	40.00
	UD4B	50.00
Cushendall	F 109/115	40.00
	UD4A	40.00
Dalkey	UD1A	15.00
	PPA	£125
Dangan	F 90/91	60.00
	UD1A	40.00
Daunts Square (Cork)	UD4B	60.00
Delgan(n)y	F 15	35.00
	UD1A	25.00
	PPB	£125
Derry	B	25.00
(Londonderry)	B	50.00
	D	60.00
(L.Derry)	G	75.00
	F 112/113/115/118/119	35.00
(curved)	(PC)	£100
	PH	35.00
	PPA	40.00
	PPB	50.00
Derrygonelly	UD3C	40.00
Derryhale Corner	UD4B	60.00
Derrylin	UD3C	40.00
Derrymacash	UD2C	40.00
Dervock	F 120/122	40.00
	UD4A	35.00
	UD4B	50.00
Dingle	B	50.00
	F 164/174	60.00
Doagh	UD3C	40.00
	UD4B	60.00
Docks (Belfast)	UD2C	40.00
	UD3C	40.00
Dominick Street (Galway)	UD2B	75.00
	UD2C	35.00
	UD4B	60.00
Donabate	UD3B	30.00
	UD3C	40.00
	UD4B	50.00
Donacloney	UD3B	40.00
	UD4E (5/220)	80.00
Donadea	UD2A	35.00
	UD3C	35.00
Donaghadee	B	40.00
	F 93/94	40.00
Donard	UD2C	40.00
Donegal	B	40.00
	F 111	30.00
	PH	60.00
	PPA	60.00
	UD4A	40.00
Doneraile	B	30.00
	F 122/124/126	35.00
Donnybrook	PPA	£150
Donoughmore (Down)	UD1H	£200
	UD2A	40.00
Donoughmore (Tyrone)	UD3C	30.00
	UD4E (5/221)	90.00
Doolin	UD3C	40.00
Doonbeg	UD1C	75.00
	UD4E (5/221)	80.00
Douglas	UD2B	60.00
Down (Patrick)	B/ UD1A	30.00
(D-Pat)	D	£100
(D-Pat)	E	50.00
	F 74	30.00
	PH	35.00
Dowth	UD2C	40.00

107

Early Irish Marks

Office	Type	Value	Office	Type	Value
Draperstown	UD1F	£200		PM	75.00
Drogheda	B	15.00		PPA	45.00
	F 22/24	20.00	Dungarvan (Kilkenny)	UD1C	£100
	PE	60.00	Dungarvan (Waterford)	B	35.00
	PH	20.00		F 96/97/124	45.00
	PPA	40.00		PB	30.00
Dromahair	F 106/107	60.00		PPB	50.00
(Drumahair)	UD1A	40.00	Dungiven	F 138/139	40.00
	UD2A	40.00		PC	50.00
Dromara(gh)	F 70	60.00		UD4A	40.00
	UD4A	40.00	Dungloe	UD4A	40.00
	UD4B	50.00	Dunkeerin	UD2C	40.00
Dromiskin	UD2A	40.00	Dunkineely (Dunkaneely)	F 117	75.00
(Drumiskin)	UD4C	75.00		UD3C	40.00
Dromod	F 67	60.00		UD4E (5/220)	£100
	UD1A	35.00	Dunlavin	F 27	35.00
Dromore (Down)	B	25.00	Dunleary (Kingstown)	PPA	£250
	D	60.00	Dunleer	B	35.00
	F 66	20.00		D	£180
	UD1A	25.00		F 29/30/31	35.00
Dromore (Tyrone)	UD2C	30.00		PD	£125
	UD3C	30.00	Dunlewey	UD3C	75.00
Dromore **	UD2A	40.00	Dunloy	UD4E (5/220)	£100
Dromore West	B	50.00	Dunmanway	F 152	35.00
	F 111	50.00	Dunmore	F 104/110	40.00
	PPB	70.00		UD2A	40.00
	UD1A	40.00		UD4A	35.00
Drumahoe	UD2C	P	Dunmore East	F 82/83	40.00
Drumcollagher	UD1A	50.00		UD2A	40.00
	UD2A	30.00		UD4A	40.00
	UD4B	50.00		UD4B	50.00
Drumcondra	PPA	£150	Dunmurr(a)y	UD1A	35.00
	PPB	£125		UD2C	40.00
Drumconra(th)	UD3C	40.00		UD4B	50.00
Drumcree	F 43	50.00		UD4E (5/220)	£100
	UD1A	30.00	Dunnamana(gh)	F 106	50.00
	UD2A	40.00	Dunsany	UD2A	40.00
Drumgriffin	UD2A	40.00	Dunshaughlin	B/UD1A	35.00
Drumheglish	UD2C	60.00		F 14	40.00
Drumkeerin	UD2A	50.00		PB	50.00
Drumlish	UD1A	40.00	Durrow	B	30.00
Drumnagoir	UD4B	P		F 52/53/54	30.00
Drumshanbo	UD2A	40.00	Eask(e)y	UD2A	40.00
Drumsna	B/ UD1A	35.00		UD4B	50.00
	F 73/75/85	40.00	Eden	UD2C	50.00
Dugort	UD1B	£600	Edenderry	B/ UD1A	35.00
Duleek	UD3C	40.00		F 32	35.00
Dunadry	UD3C	40.00	Edendork	UD4B	50.00
Dunamanagh	UD4A	40.00	Edern(e)y	UD1G	60.00
	UD4B	50.00		UD2C	40.00
Dunboyne	UD3C	30.00	Edgeworthstown	B	30.00
Duncormick	UD2C	40.00		F 52	25.00
Dundalk	B/ UD1A	20.00		PPA	50.00
(D-Dalk)	D	£125	Eglinton	UD4B	P
	F 40	15.00	Eglish	UD2C	50.00
	PB	30.00	Elphin	B	40.00
	PE	75.00		D	75.00
	PH	50.00		F 74/75	40.00
	PPA	50.00	Emo	B	40.00
	UD4A	40.00		F 34/35	35.00
Dundonald	UD3C	40.00	Emyvale	F 66	40.00
Dundrum (Down)	UD3B	40.00	Enfield	F 19	25.00
	UD3C	40.00		UD1A	25.00
Dundrum (Dublin)	PPA	£100	Ennis	B	25.00
Dundrum (Tipperary)	B	50.00		F 112/114	30.00
	UD2A	40.00		PPC	£140
Dunfanaghy	B	60.00	Enniscorthy	B	25.00
	F 131	40.00		F 60/62	35.00
	PH	70.00	(ESCorthy)	G 60/62	30.00
	PPA	70.00		PPA	50.00
Dungannon	B	20.00	Enniskean	UD2A	40.00
	D	60.00	Enniskeen (Inniskeen, Co Louth)	UD2C	40.00
	F 73/74/75/76	18.00		UD3C	40.00
	PH	30.00	Enniskerry two penny post	5/44	£300

108

Early Irish Marks

Office	Type	Value
	PPA	£200
Enniskillen	B/ UD1A	30.00
	E	50.00
	F 80/82	30.00
	G 79	40.00
	PB	40.00
	PN	75.00
	PPA	60.00
	PPC	90.00
Ennistimon	B	50.00
	E	50.00
(ESTimon)	G 127	45.00
	PPB	£120
Errill	UD2C	35.00
	UD3C	35.00
Eyrecourt	B	40.00
(E.Covrt)	D	80.00
	F 81	35.00
	PF	50.00
	UD4A	40.00
Fahan	UD3C	40.00
Fairview	PH	£250
Fairview Avenue (Dublin)	PPB	£200
Falcarragh	UD3C	40.00
Falls Road (Belfast)	UD2C	50.00
	UD3C	40.00
Farranfore	UD4B	50.00
Feakle	UD1C	£100
Feeny	UD2B	75.00
Fenagh	UD1A	35.00
	UD4E (5/220)	£100
Ferbane (Farbane)	F 50/57	40.00
	UD2A	40.00
	UD2C	40.00
	UD4B	50.00
Fermoy	B	30.00
	F 108/112	30.00
	PH	50.00
Ferns	B/ UD1A	35.00
	F 54/56	35.00
Ferrybank	UD1A	40.00
	UD4B	50.00
Fethard (Tipperary)	B/ UD1A	35.00
	F 88	35.00
(FethD Tip)	G 90	40.00
	PB	35.00
	UD4A	35.00
	UD4E (5/220)	80.00
Fethard (Wexford)	UD1A	35.00
	UD2C	40.00
Finea	UD2C	45.00
Finglas	PPA	£125
Fintona	B/ UD1A	30.00
	F 93/97	40.00
	UD4A	40.00
Finvoy	UD3C	40.00
Five Alley	UD1A	30.00
	UD4B	50.00
Fivemilebourne	UD2A	50.00
Fivemiletown	E	65.00
(Five M Town)	G 78	40.00
	UD1A	30.00
	UD4A	40.00
Florence Court	C	75.00
	F 90	45.00
	UD4A	40.00
	UD4B	50.00
Flurrybridge	F 46	40.00
	PH	£150
Forkhill	F 45	50.00
Foulksmill	UD2C	40.00
(Foulkesmills)	UD4B	50.00
Foxford	F 136	60.00
Foxhall	UD2A	40.00

Office	Type	Value
Foynes	UD1A	25.00
Frankford	F 60	40.00
	UD1A	20.00
Frenchpark	F 86	35.00
	PPA	70.00
	UD1A	25.00
Freshford	B	30.00
	F 64	40.00
Fu(e)rty	UD2A	40.00
Galbally	UD1A	40.00
Galway	B	25.00
(G-Way)	D	90.00
	(B) (italic)	£250
	F 104/105	20.00
	J 104	40.00
	PH	15.00
	PPA	40.00
Garristown	UD3C	40.00
Garronpoint (Garron Point/ Glenarm)	UD2C	50.00
(Garronpoint/ Larne)	UD2C	50.00
Garvagh	F 113	40.00
(Garva)	F 119	40.00
Gaybrook	UD2A	40.00
Geashell	F 49	40.00
(Geashill)	UD1A	20.00
	UD2A	40.00
	UD2C	40.00
Gilford	F 67	35.00
	UD1A	25.00
Glanamadda (see Glenamaddy)		
Glandore	UD1A	30.00
Glaneely	UD2C	30.00
	UD3C	40.00
Glanmire	UD2A	40.00
Glantane	UD2A	40.00
Glanworth	UD1A	25.00
	UD2A	40.00
Glasnevin	UD4C	75.00
	PPA	£150
Glasslough	B/ UD1A	30.00
	F 68/69/70	45.00
	UD4A	35.00
Glasson	UD2A	40.00
Glasthule	UD2A	40.00
Glen (Donegal)	UD1A	50.00
Glenageary (Glenegary)	UD2C	50.00
Glenamaddy (Glenamadda)	UD1A	40.00
	UD2A	40.00
Glenarm	F 106	35.00
	PH	£100
	UD1A	30.00
Glenavy	F 77	40.00
	UD2A	40.00
	UD4A	30.00
	UD4B	40.00
Glenbeigh	UD1A	40.00
Gleneely (Donegal)	UD4E (5/221)	P
Glengarriff	UD2A	40.00
Glenties	UD3C	40.00
Glenville	UD2A	40.00
Glin	F 126	35.00
	UD1A	20.00
	UD4B	50.00
Glounthaun	UD1A	40.00
also see Clountain		
Glyn (Antrim)	UD2C	40.00
Golden	F 80/83	35.00
	UD4D	£100
Golden Ball	UD1A	40.00
	PPA	£250
Goleen	UD2A	40.00
Goresbridge	B	40.00
	F 52/55	40.00
	PPA	40.00

109

Early Irish Marks

Office	Type	Value
Gorey	B	30.00
	F 46/48	30.00
	J 48	40.00
Gormanstown	UD2A	35.00
Gort	B/ UD1A	40.00
	F 98/99	40.00
	PB	35.00
	PH	50.00
Gowran	B	40.00
	F 52	40.00
Gracehill	UD3C	40.00
Graig(namanagh)	F 58	30.00
	UD2C	25.00
Granard	B/ UD1A	30.00
	F 59/60	50.00
	PPA	60.00
Grange (Sligo)	UD2C	40.00
	UD4D	£100
Grange(con) (Wicklow)	UD1A	45.00
Grange Corner	UD2A	40.00
Greencastle	UD4E (5/220)	80.00
Green Island	UD2C	40.00
	UD3C	40.00
Greyabb(e)y	UD1A	40.00
	UD2A	40.00
	UD4A	40.00
	UD4B	P
Greystones	UD2C	40.00
	UD4B	50.00
Groomsport	UD1A	40.00
Gurteen	UD1A	40.00
	UD2A	40.00
Hacketstown (HacketstN)	G 47	60.00
	UD3C	40.00
	UD4B	50.00
Harold's Cross	PPA	£200
Hayes	UD2A	40.00
Headford	B/ UD1A	40.00
(HeadfD)	G 108	40.00
Hill of Down	UD2A	40.00
Hillsboro(ugh)	B	30.00
	F 69/70	25.00
	PB	30.00
	PH	45.00
	PPB	60.00
	UD4A	40.00
Hilltown	UD3B	40.00
Hollyfort	UD2C	40.00
Hollymount	B/ UD1A	25.00
(HYmount)	F 110	50.00
	PC	30.00
	PPA	75.00
Ho(l)lywood	J 84	40.00
	UD1E	£250
	UD1A	35.00
	PB	35.00
Holycross	UD2C	40.00
Horans Cross	UD1A	40.00
	UD2A	40.00
	UD4E (5/219)	£100
Horseleap	UD2A	40.00
Hospital	UD2A	40.00
Howth	B	35.00
	F 8	35.00
	UD4A	40.00
Inch (Donegal)	UD4B	P
Inch (Wexford)	UD3C	35.00
Inchigeela(g)h	UD2A	40.00
Inistiogue	B	40.00
	F 64	40.00
Inniscarra	UD2A	40.00
Innishannon	F 142	50.00
(Innoshannon)	F 130	60.00
Inishcroane (Enniscrone)	UD1A	60.00

Office	Type	Value
Inniskeen		
(also see Enniskeen)	UD2C	40.00
Irvin(e)stown	F 89	35.00
	UD4A	40.00
	UD1A	35.00
Islandmagee	UD3C	75.00
Johnstown	B	35.00
	F 62/63	40.00
	PB	40.00
	PPA	55.00
Julianstown	UD3C	35.00
	UD4B	50.00
Kanturk	F 120/138	40.00
	PPB	50.00
	UD1A	35.00
Katesbridge	UD1G	60.00
	UD3B	35.00
	UD3C	40.00
Keadue	F 88	60.00
	UD1A	15.00
	UD2A	40.00
Keady	F 58	40.00
	UD1A	40.00
Kells (Antrim)	UD3C	40.00
Kells (Kilkenny)	UD2C	30.00
	UD4B	50.00
Kells (Meath)	B/ UD1A	30.00
	D	70.00
	F 30/31/32	30.00
	PB	30.00
	PP	£350
Kenagh	UD1A	40.00
Kenmare	B	40.00
	F 156	40.00
	PPB	80.00
Kennety see Kinnety		
Kenvara see Kinvara		
Kerrykeel	UD2A	50.00
Kilbeggan	B	35.00
	F 44	35.00
	PB	30.00
	PPB	50.00
	UD4A	30.00
Kilbegs (Killybegs)	B	65.00
	F 123	75.00
(KYBegs)	G 123	50.00
	PPA	75.00
Kilane (Killanne)	UD1A	40.00
Kilbehenny	UD2A	40.00
Kilbride (Wicklow)	UD2C	40.00
Kilbride **	UD4C	75.00
Kilcock	F 14	40.00
	PB	40.00
	PH	60.00
Kilcolgan	UD2A	40.00
Kilconnell	F 78	40.00
	UD1A	25.00
Kilcoole	UD2C	40.00
Kilcooley	UD2C	50.00
Kilcreest	UD2A	40.00
Kilcullen	B	40.00
	F 21/23	35.00
	UD2A	35.00
	UD4A	40.00
Kildalkey	UD3C	40.00
Kildare	B/ UD1A	30.00
	F 24	30.00
Kildemo	UD4B	50.00
Kildorrery	UD1A	40.00
	F 134	50.00
	PH	75.00
Kildysart	F 126	60.00
Kiledmond	UD4C	75.00
Kilfinane	UD4B	50.00

110

Early Irish Marks

Office	Type	Value
Kilflyn(n)	UD2A	40.00
Kilgarvan	UD2A	40.00
Kilkee	UD1A	30.00
Kilkeel	F 65	50.00
	UD1A	25.00
Kilkenny	B	25.00
(K-Keny)	D	90.00
	F 57/58	18.00
	30	25.00
	PH	45.00
Kilkishen	UD2C	40.00
	UD3C	40.00
Kill (Kildare)	UD1A	40.00
Killagan	UD4E (5/220)	90.00
Killala	B/ UD1A	40.00
	F 131	50.00
	PPB	60.00
Killaloe	B	30.00
	F 87	35.00
	PPB	60.00
Killaloo	UD2A	40.00
Killargue	UD4B	50.00
Killarney	B	50.00
	F 144/176	45.00
	PPA	60.00
	PPB	65.00
	UD4A	20.00
Killavullen	UD2A	40.00
Killedmond	UD2A	40.00
Kil(l)eigh (Kings)	UD2C	40.00
Killenaule see Killynaule		
Killes(h)andra	B	40.00
	F 64	35.00
	PH	50.00
	PPA	50.00
	UD4A	35.00
Killashee	UD1A	35.00
Killeagh (Cork)	UD1A	30.00
Killetter	UD3C	35.00
Killina	UD4B	50.00
Killinardish	UD1A	25.00
	UD4B	50.00
Killinchy	F 83	35.00
	UD1A	40.00
	UD4A	30.00
	UD4B	50.00
Killiney	UD1A	40.00
	UD4B	40.00
Killinick	UD1A	35.00
	UD4B	50.00
Killorglin	UD2A	40.00
Killough	F 79	50.00
	UD4A	35.00
Killucan	F 32	30.00
	UD2A	35.00
Killurin	UD1A	35.00
	UD1G	60.00
Killybegs see Kilbegs		
Killygordan	UD3C	35.00
Killylea	UD3C	40.00
	UD4C	75.00
Killyleagh	B	40.00
	F 79	40.00
(Killyleigh)	UD4A	40.00
Killyman	UD3C	40.00
Killymore	UD2A	40.00
Killynaule (Killenaule) (KYnaule)	B	30.00
	G 75	40.00
Kilkerrin	UD2A	40.00
	UD4B	50.00
Kilmacow	UD1A	30.00
Kilkmacrennan	UD4B	50.00
Kilmacthomas (KilmacthS)	G 84	50.00
(KilmacthoS)	G 86	50.00

Office	Type	Value
	UD1A	40.00
	PPA	60.00
	PPB	50.00
Kilmaine	UD2A	35.00
Kilmainham	PPA	60.00
Kilmallock	B	50.00
	F 110	50.00
	PPA	50.00
	PPB	50.00
Kilmanagh	UD2C	30.00
	UD4B	50.00
Kilmeaden	UD1A	35.00
	UD4B	50.00
Kilmeague	UD2C	40.00
Kilmessan	UD2A	40.00
Kilmoganny	UD1A	35.00
Kilmore (Armagh)	UD2A	40.00
	UD4E (5/219)	£100
Kilmore (Down)	UD2C	40.00
Kilmore (Roscommon)	UD2A	40.00
Kilmore (Wexford)	UD2A	40.00
Kilmore **	UD1A	40.00
Kilmuckridge	UD2C	40.00
Kilnaleck	UD3C	40.00
	UD4C	75.00
Kilrea	F 100/104	40.00
	UD1A	25.00
	UD4B	50.00
Kilroosky	UD2A	40.00
Kilrush	B/ UD1A	35.00
	F 139/141/159	50.00
	PPA	70.00
	UD2A	40.00
Kilsheelan	UD2C	30.00
Kilskeery	UD2C	40.00
(Kilsherry)	UD2C	40.00
Kiltegan	UD3C	40.00
Kiltormer	UD2A	35.00
Kiltyclogher	UD3C	50.00
Kilworth	F 104	45.00
Kinallen	UD2C	40.00
Kingscourt	F 38	50.00
	UD4A	40.00
Kingstown	5/40	£200
(see also Dunleary)	PPA	£100
	PPB	£120
Kingwilliamstown	UD2A	40.00
	UD4B	50.00
Kinlough	UD2C	40.00
	UD4B	50.00
Kinnagh	UD2A	50.00
	UD4B	50.00
Kinnegad	B	30.00
	F 29	30.00
	UD4C	75.00
Kinnet(t)y	F 64	40.00
(Kennety)	F 67	40.00
Kinsale	B	30.00
with inverted N	D	80.00
	F 136/146	35.00
	PH	50.00
	UD4A	40.00
Kinvara (Kenvara)	UD1A	25.00
	UD2A	40.00
Kircubbin	F 93	50.00
	UD4A	40.00
	UD4B	50.00
Kish (Kesh)	B/ UD1A	30.00
	F 90	40.00
	PPA	55.00
Knock (Clare)	B	60.00
	F 133	60.00
	UD2A	40.00
Knockbridge	UD4E (5/219)	90.00

111

Early Irish Marks

Office	Type	Value
Knockcloghrim	UD3B	40.00
Knocklong	UD2A	40.00
	UD4B	50.00
Knocknacarry	UD1A	35.00
	UD1G	50.00
	UD2B	35.00
	UD4B	50.00
Knocktopher	F 63/64	40.00
	PPB	50.00
Kyle	UD1A	30.00
Lahinch	UD1A	35.00
	UD2A	40.00
Lambeg	UD2C	40.00
Lanesboro(ugh)	F 68	35.00
	UD2A	30.00
Larne	B/ UD1A	35.00
	F 97/98	30.00
Laurencetown	UD1C	50.00
	UD2A	40.00
	UD2C	40.00
	UD3C	30.00
Laytown	UD4E (5/221)	90.00
Lecarrow	UD2A	40.00
Leggs	UD2C	40.00
Leighlinbridge	C	50.00
(LNBridge)	G 45	40.00
	UD1A	30.00
	PPA	50.00
Leitrim St (Cork)	UD2C	35.00
Leixlip	B	35.00
X as back to back Cs	B	£100
	F 8	35.00
	PPB	60.00
Lenamore	UD1A	35.00
Letterfrack	UD2A	30.00
Letterkenny (L.Kenny)	E	50.00
	F 113	40.00
	PH	65.00
	UD1A	40.00
Lifford	UD3C	30.00
Ligoniel	UD2C	40.00
Limerick	B	15.00
(Limrick)	D	75.00
	F 94	20.00
	L 94	30.00
	PB	30.00
	PH	30.00
	PPA	60.00
	PPB	50.00
	N	40.00
Lisbellaw	UD3C	40.00
Lisburn	B	40.00
(L.Burn)	D	75.00
	F 73/75	25.00
	J 73	40.00
	PPA	50.00
Lisdoonvarna	UD1A	40.00
Liskinfere	UD4B	50.00
Lismore	B	35.00
	F 97/109/122	35.00
	PH	50.00
	UD4A	35.00
Lisnacree	UD2C	40.00
Lisnagry	UD1A	30.00
	UD4C	75.00
Lisnarick	UD2C	40.00
	UD4C	75.00
Lisnaskea (LSNaskea)	E	60.00
	B/ UD1A	40.00
	F 70	40.00
	PH	50.00
	PPA	60.00
(Lisnaskee)	UD4A	40.00
Lisryan	UD2A	30.00

Office	Type	Value
	UD4D	80.00
Lissardagh	UD4E (5/220)	80.00
Lisselane	UD2A	40.00
	UD4B	50.00
	UD4C	75.00
Listowel	B/ UD1A	40.00
	F 134/137	50.00
	PH	60.00
Littleton	F 70	35.00
(Lyttleton)	F 70	50.00
	UD4E (5/220)	£100
Lobinstown	UD2B	50.00
Londonderry see Derry		
Longford	B	35.00
(LGFord)	E	70.00
	F 58/59/62	30.00
	PH	30.00
Longwood	UD2A	40.00
Lorra(h)	UD3C	40.00
Loughbrickland (L-Land)	D	£150
(L.Brickland)	E	60.00
	UD1A	35.00
	F 56/58	40.00
	PPA	70.00
	PPB	75.00
Loughgall	F 66	40.00
	UD1A	40.00
	UD4B	50.00
Loughgilly	UD4C	75.00
Loughlinstown	UD2C	40.00
Loughrea (Lochrea)	A	£350
	B	30.00
(L-Reagh)	D	75.00
(LHRea)	G 87	50.00
	F 86/87	25.00
	PF	25.00
	PPA	50.00
	UD1A	40.00
	UD2A	40.00
Louisburgh	UD2A	50.00
Louth	UD2C	35.00
	UD3C	40.00
	UD4A	35.00
	UD4B	50.00
Lower Georges Street	UD4B	50.00
Lowtherstown	PH	£100
Lucan	F 6	40.00
Lurgan	B	35.00
	F 67	25.00
	UD4A	40.00
Lurgangreen	E	65.00
(no date)	M 37 (5/112)	£200
(LNGreen)	G 37	40.00
	PE	£200
(LNGreen)	UD1A	35.00
Macroom	B	40.00
	F 142/145	45.00
Madden	UD2C	20.00
Mageney	UD2C	40.00
Maghera	F 96/97	35.00
	UD4A	40.00
Magherafelt (M.Rafelt)	E	50.00
	F 92/94	30.00
	UD1A	35.00
	PF	30.00
Magheralin	UD3B	40.00
Magheramorne	UD1A	35.00
	UD2C	50.00
Maghery (Tyrone)	UD2C	40.00
Magilligan	UD2C	40.00
	UD3C	40.00
	UD4E (5/221)	P
Maguiresbridge	PPE	£300
	UD1A	30.00

Early Irish Marks

Office	Type	Value
Malahide	UD4A	40.00
Malin	UD3C	55.00
Mallow	B	30.00
	F 130	25.00
	PPA	50.00
	UD4A	40.00
Malone	UD2C	35.00
	UD3C	35.00
Malone Road (Belfast)	UD2B	75.00
	UD2C	30.00
	UD4C	60.00
Manorcunningham	UD3C	35.00
Manorhamilton	F 102	60.00
(MRHamilton)	G 91/114	60.00
	PH	75.00
	UD4A	30.00
Markethill	B	30.00
	F 60/61/63	35.00
	PPA	65.00
Marlfield	UD4B	50.00
Maryborough (M-Brovgh)	D	£150
(MYBurrough)	E	40.00
(MYboro)	F 40	30.00
(P::PAID with lines at top and bottom)	(PC)	80.00
Maynooth	B/ UD1A	25.00
	F 11	30.00
Menlough	UD4B	50.00
(Menlagh)	UD2A	40.00
Merrion	UD2C	35.00
Mid(d)leton	B	30.00
(Midl.Ton)	E	30.00
	F 134	25.00
(MiddletN)	G 122	35.00
	UD1A	30.00
	UD4A	40.00
Middletown	UD3C	40.00
Milford (Carlow)	UD2C	40.00
	UD4E (5/220)	£100
Milford (Donegal)	UD3C	40.00
Millstreet	B/UD1A	35.00
	F 160	50.00
Milltown (Dublin)	UD1A	25.00
	UD1C	£100
Milltown (Galway)	UD1A	40.00
	UD2A	40.00
Mil(l)town (Kerry)	F 160/169	50.00
	UD1A	40.00
	UD2A	40.00
	UD4A	40.00
	UD4B	50.00
Milltown **	UD4C	75.00
Milltownpass	UD2A	40.00
Miltown Malbay (M T Malbay)	J 134	60.00
	UD1A	35.00
Mitchelstown (MTTowne)	E	50.00
(MitchLSTown)	E	50.00
	Γ 109	40.00
(MitchelstN)	G 104/110	40.00
	PB	40.00
	PH	75.00
Moate	B/ UD1A	20.00
	F 52	25.00
Mohill	B/ UD1A	40.00
	F 73	50.00
Moincoin (Mooncoin)	UD4B	50.00
Moira	B	40.00
	F 71/72	40.00
	UD4A	35.00
Monaghan	B	25.00
	F 62/65/66	25.00
	PB	40.00
scalloped at sides	(PPC)	£250
Monamolin	UD4B	50.00
Monasterevan	B/ UD1A	30.00

Office	Type	Value
(Monastereuan)	B	50.00
(MonT.Even)	E	50.00
(MREven)	G 30	30.00
	PB	30.00
Moneygall	B/ UD1A	25.00
(MYGall)	G 66	40.00
Moneymore	B	40.00
	F 89/90	35.00
	PB	40.00
	PPA	50.00
	UD4A	40.00
Monelea (Monilea)	UD4B	50.00
Monivea	F 100	50.00
	UD2A	30.00
Monkstown (Cork)	UD2B	60.00
	UD3C	40.00
	UD4E (5/220)	80.00
Monkstown **	UD1A	25.00
	UD2A	40.00
Moone	UD4A	40.00
Morroe (Murroe)	UD2A	40.00
	UD4D	£100
Mosside	UD3C	25.00
Mountcharles	UD3B	40.00
	UD3C	40.00
	UD4E (5/220)	80.00
Mountfield (Tyrone)	UD3C	40.00
Mountmellick	B	30.00
(MTMellick)	G 40	40.00
	PH	35.00
	PPA	40.00
	UD4A	35.00
Mountnorris	UD2B	75.00
	UD2C	40.00
	UD3C	40.00
Mount Nugent	F 44/46	45.00
	UD1A	40.00
Mount Pottinger	UD2A	75.00
Mountrath	B/ UD1A	35.00
(MTRath)	G 46	50.00
(also Montrath)	F 47	30.00
	PC	30.00
Mountshannon	UD4B	50.00
Mount Talbot	F 81	50.00
(MT Talbot)	G 82	50.00
	UD1A	25.00
Moville	F 132/133	50.00
	F 125	70.00
	PPA	65.00
	UD1A	35.00
Moy	F 69/71	40.00
	UD1A	35.00
Moyallon	UD1G	50.00
	UD2C	40.00
Moycullen	UD3C	40.00
	UD4B	50.00
Moylough	UD2A	40.00
	UD4B	50.00
Moynalty	F 35/36	50.00
	UD2C	40.00
	UD4A	35.00
Moyne (Limerick)	UD1C	£100
Moyne (Tipperary)	UD2C	40.00
Moyne **	UD1A	40.00
	UD4D	£100
Moyvalley	UD2A	40.00
Moyvore	UD1A	35.00
Muff (Muff Don)	UD3C	45.00
Mullagh	UD2C	40.00
	UD4D	£100
Mullenan	UD3C	50.00
Mullinahone	UD1A	40.00
Mullingar (Mvllingar with reversed N)	A	£1,000
(Mvllingar)	A	£1,000

113

Early Irish Marks

Office	Type	Value
	B	25.00
	B (curved)	90.00
(Mullin/Gar)	C	£125
	D	65.00
(M.Gar)	E	£125
	F 38	20.00
	PB	30.00
	PH	30.00
	PPA	50.00
Munster Harbour	UD4C	£100
Murrintown	UD1A	40.00
Myroe	UD2C	P
	UD4D	80.00
Myshall	F 56	50.00
	UD2C	40.00
Naas	B	30.00
	F 16	30.00
	PE	60.00
	PF	25.00
	UD4A	40.00
Narin	B	60.00
(Nairn)	F 134	75.00
Narrow Water	B	£300
Naul	UD3B	30.00
Navan (also Nauan)	B	30.00
	F 23/24	20.00
	PB	30.00
	PH	30.00
Nenagh	B	30.00
	F 74/75	25.00
New Birmingham	F 70	30.00
Newbliss	F 72	40.00
	UD4A	35.00
Newbridge (Kildare)	F 20/21	30.00
	UD1A	25.00
Newbridge (Wicklow)	UD2C	35.00
Newcastle (Down)	UD3C	40.00
Newcastle (Tipperary)	UD1A	35.00
Newcastle (West)	B	30.00
	F 114/116	35.00
New Inn **	UD4B	50.00
Newmarket	UD1A	40.00
Newmarket on Fergus	B	40.00
	E	50.00
(N Mkt on Fergus)	G 107	50.00
	PPA	50.00
Newmills	UD3C	40.00
Newport (Mayo)	B/ UD1A	35.00
	F 122	40.00
Newport (Tipperary)		
(Newport TipY)	E	65.00
(N-Port.C.Tip)	E	£100
	G 90	50.00
	UD1A	40.00
Newry	B	25.00
	D	80.00
	F 50/51/54	20.00
scroll points to top left	(PA)	£150
	PB	30.00
	PE	75.00
	PH	30.00
Newtownards	B	35.00
(N-T-Ards)	G 88	30.00
boxed	(PB)	75.00
	UD4A	40.00
Newtownbarry	F 48/55	40.00
	UD4A	40.00
Newtownbreda	UD1G	50.00
	UD4B	45.00
Newtownbutler	UD3C	35.00
Newtowncromelin	UD4B	50.00
Newtowncunningham	UD3C	40.00
Newtown Forbes	F 61	35.00
	UD1A	40.00

Office	Type	Value
Newtownglens	Scroll	£750
Newtowngorecrossroads	UD2A	60.00
Newtownhamilton	C	50.00
(N T Hamilton)	G 53/56	35.00
	UD1A	35.00
	UD2A	35.00
Newtown Limavady	B	40.00
(N.Lvady)	E	70.00
(N T LimY)	G 124/137	35.00
	PH	75.00
	PPB	£100
	UD4A	40.00
Newtownmountkennedy		
(Newtown.M)	E	60.00
(N T MTKenY)	G 17	75.00
(N T MTKennedy)	G 17	40.00
(Newtown MTKennedy)	G 17	50.00
	PB	35.00
	PPA	£100
	UD1A	30.00
Newtown Sandes	UD2A	40.00
Newtown Stewart	F 94	40.00
(N T Stewart)	G 99	40.00
	UD1A	35.00
	PH	75.00
Newtown Vevay	UD2C	40.00
Nobber (Nobbor)	F 33	40.00
	UD4A	35.00
	UD4E (5/220)	80.00
North Main St (Cork)	UD2C	40.00
O'Briens Bridge	UD2A	40.00
	UD2B	75.00
	UD2C	40.00
	UD4B	50.00
O'Callaghans Mills	UD3C	40.00
Oldcastle	B	35.00
	F 41	30.00
(Old Cl)	G 46	60.00
	UD4A	40.00
Omagh	B/UD1A	30.00
	F 86	30.00
	PF	35.00
	PL	£100
	PPA	60.00
	PPB	60.00
Omeath	UD3C	40.00
Oranmore	B/ UD1A	30.00
	F 101	35.00
	PPB	50.00
Oulart	F 58	40.00
	UD1A	35.00
(Oulart/Gorey)	UD2C	35.00
(Oulart/Enniscorthy)	UD2C	50.00
Ou(gh)terard	F 112/118	45.00
(Oughterard)	UD2A	35.00
Oylgate	UD2C	40.00
	UD4B	50.00
Palatine	UD1A	40.00
Pallasgreen	F 96/111	50.00
	UD1A	30.00
Pallaskenry	F 105	40.00
	UD3C	40.00
	UD4A	25.00
	UD4B	50.00
Park (Derry)	UD2C	P
Parkgate (Belfast)	UD3C	40.00
Parsonstown	B/ UD1A	30.00
(ParsonstN)	G 71	30.00
	F 64/68/71	25.00
	PF	25.00
Passage (East)	F 80	40.00
	UD2C	40.00
Passage West	F 129	35.00
	UD2A	35.00

Early Irish Marks

Office	Type	Value
Patrickswell	UD2A	40.00
Pettigo	UD3C	40.00
Pharis	UD3B	50.00
(Pharush)	UD3C	40.00
Philipstown	B/ UD1A	25.00
(P.Towne)	D	£100
	F 45	35.00
Pil(l)town	F 84	30.00
Pomeroy	UD1A	30.00
	UD2C	40.00
Portadown	B/ UD1A	30.00
	F 66	30.00
Portaferry	F 80/101	35.00
Portarlington	B/ UD1A	30.00
(PTA:L:Ton)	E	£250
(PTArlington)	G 36	35.00
	F 34/35	30.00
	PB	30.00
	UD4A	30.00
	UD4B	50.00
Portglenone	F 102	40.00
(PTGlenone)	G 100	50.00
	UD1A	30.00
	PB	40.00
Portlaw	F 84	35.00
	UD4A	30.00
	UD4B	50.00
Portobello Hotel (P.Bello Hotel)	PPA	£200
Portroe	UD2C	30.00
Portrush	UD2C	30.00
	UD3C	40.00
Portstewart	UD2C	40.00
	UD3C	30.00
Portumna	B	40.00
	F 78/82/89	45.00
Poynt(s)pass	UD3C	40.00
Priesthaggard	UD2C	40.00
	UD3C	40.00
	UD4B	50.00
Priesthall	UD2A	50.00
Puckane	UD1A	30.00
Queensborough	UD2A	40.00
Quigley's Point	UD3C	P
Quin(n)	UD1A	40.00
	UD2A	40.00
Rahan	UD2A	40.00
Raharney	UD2A	25.00
	UD4B	30.00
Ra(t)heny	PPA	£200
	PPB	£150
Railway (Galway)	UD2A	£1,000
Railway Station (Athenry)	UD2A	£1,000
Ramelton	B/ UD1A	35.00
	F 117/123	45.00
	PB	30.00
	PPA	80.00
	PPB	00.00
Randalstown	B	50.00
(RandalstN)	G 97	35.00
	PB	35.00
Ranelagh	PPA	50.00
Raphoe	B/ UD1A	30.00
	F 106/108	40.00
	PH	45.00
	PPA	50.00
Rasharkin	UD2C	50.00
Rasnastraw	UD2C	50.00
	UD4B	50.00
Rathangan	B/ UD1A	30.00
	F 28	40.00
(RHAngan)	G 28	60.00
	PB	50.00
(PAID in circle)	(PE)	£150
Rathcabbin	UD2C	40.00

Office	Type	Value
	UD3C	40.00
Rathcoole (Dublin) (RHCoole)	F 8	40.00
Rathcoole (Wicklow)	UD2C	40.00
Rathcormack (RHcormuck)	G 111	40.00
(Rathcormac)	F 111	35.00
	PPA	60.00
Rathdowney	B	50.00
(RHDowney)	G 59	40.00
	UD4A	40.00
Rathdrum	B	35.00
(RHDrum)	G 32	40.00
	F 29	35.00
	PPB	70.00
Rathfarnham	PPA	80.00
	PPB	90.00
	UD2C	30.00
	UD3C	40.00
	UD4B	50.00
Rathfriland	B/ UD1A	30.00
(R-F-Land)	D	£150
	F 57	35.00
	PH	50.00
Rathgar	UD1A	60.00
	UD2A	60.00
Rathkeale	B	30.00
	F 108	30.00
(RHKeale)	G 108	40.00
Rathlacken	F 136	80.00
(RHLacken)	G 161	80.00
Rathmines	PPA	85.00
	UD1A	40.00
	UD1G	80.00
Rathmore (Kildare)	UD2C	40.00
	UD4A	40.00
Rathmoylon	UD1A	35.00
(Rathmolyon)	UD2A	40.00
Rathmullen	UD3C	30.00
Rathnew	UD1A	35.00
	UD4A	40.00
Rathowen	F 55	40.00
	UD1A	40.00
Ray	UD2C	40.00
Readypenny	UD2A	40.00
Redcastle	UD3C	P
Redcross	UD2C	35.00
Redhills	F 58	50.00
	UD1A	35.00
	UD2C	40.00
Rhode	UD2A	40.00
	UD3C	35.00
Rich(h)ill	B	50.00
	F 64	45.00
	UD4A	35.00
Richmond Harbour	UD2A	50.00
Ringaskiddy	UD2A	40.00
Ringsend	PPA	£180
	UD4A	40.00
Riverside (Newry)	UD2C	£100
Riverstown (Louth)	UD2C	40.00
	UD4E (5/220)	80.00
Riverstown (Sligo)	UD2A	30.00
Robertstown	UD2C	40.00
Robinstown	UD2A	40.00
Rochfortbridge	UD2A	40.00
Rock	UD3C	35.00
Rockbrook	UD3C	40.00
Rockcorry	UD3C	40.00
Rockmills	UD2A	40.00
	UD4B	50.00
Ros(s)carbery	B/ UD1A	40.00
	F 154	40.00
	PPA	55.00
Rosco(m)mon	B	25.00
(R:Comon)	D	£180

115

Early Irish Marks

Office	Type	Value
	F 70/74/75	25.00
Roscrea	B	25.00
	D	90.00
(R-Crea)	E	75.00
	F 59	25.00
	PF	25.00
Rosenallis(Rosenallis/P't'lington)	UD2C	50.00
(Rosenallis/Maryboro')	UD2C	50.00
(Rosenallis/M'tmellick)	UD3C	50.00
Roslea	UD3C	40.00
Ross (New)	B	25.00
	F 68/69/70/71	35.00
(Post. Pd. – wavy)	(PB)	£200
	PB	35.00
	PF	35.00
	PH	£150
Rosses Point	UD2A	40.00
Ros(s)trevor	B/ UD1A	35.00
	F 57/58	40.00
	PF	40.00
Rostellan	UD2A	40.00
Roundstone	UD3C	40.00
Roundtown (Dublin)	PPB	£120
Roundwood	UD2C	60.00
Ruskey (Roosky)	F 66	40.00
	PH	£150
	UD2A	40.00
Rush	UD3C	40.00
Rutland	F 156	£150
St Dolough's	UD3B	75.00
	UD4C	75.00
Saintfield	F 78	50.00
no circle/in two lines	(PE)	£200
	UD4A	40.00
St Johnston	UD3C	P
St Lukes (Cork)	UD2C	60.00
Sallins	UD3C	40.00
Salthill	UD2A	40.00
Sandycove	UD1A	40.00
Sandymount	PPA	£100
	UD1A	35.00
	UD4B	50.00
Santry	UD1A	40.00
	PPB	90.00
Scariff	F 96	50.00
Scarva	UD3C	40.00
Scotshouse	UD3C	40.00
Scrabby	UD1A	50.00
Seaforde	UD3C	40.00
Seskanore	UD2C	35.00
Shan(n)agarry	UD1A	40.00
	UD2A	40.00
	UD4C	75.00
Shanagolden	F 113/115	50.00
	UD1A	40.00
Shanballymore	UD1A	40.00
Shanklin Road (Belfast)	UD2C	35.00
Shannonbridge	UD1A	40.00
Shantonagh	UD3B	40.00
	UD4B	45.00
Sharavogue	UD2A	50.00
Shercock	UD3C	35.00
Shinrone	B/UD1A	25.00
	F 63	30.00
Shrove	UD4E (5/221)	P
Shrule	UD1A	30.00
	UD2A	40.00
Silvermines	UD1A	35.00
	UD4B	50.00
Sixmilebridge	E	55.00
(Six M BR)	F 102	40.00
	UD1A	35.00
Skerries	UD3C	35.00
	UD4C	75.00

Office	Type	Value
Skibbereen	B/ UD1A	35.00
	F 159/160/167	35.00
	PPA	40.00
Skull (Schull)	PPD	£200
Slane	B	30.00
	F 30	30.00
	UD4A	30.00
Sligo	B/ UD1A	20.00
(Sligoe)	B	£100
	F 102/103	25.00
	PB	30.00
	PH	15.00
	PPA	60.00
	PPB	50.00
Smithborough	UD3C	25.00
Sneem	UD2A	40.00
Spanish Point	UD2C	40.00
Speenoge	UD3C	40.00
Spiddal	UD1A	35.00
Stackallen	UD3B	40.00
Staffordstown	UD4E (5/220)	£100
Stewartstown	F 82	45.00
as PB but no dots	(PB)	£150
	UD4A	35.00
Stillorgan	PPA	£100
	UD1A	35.00
	UD2A	40.00
Strabane	A	£3,000
	B	30.00
	F 100	20.00
	PB	30.00
	PH	60.00
	PPA	50.00
Stradbally (Queens)	F 40/45	35.00
	PPB	70.00
	UD4A	40.00
Stradbally (Waterford)	UD2C	40.00
	UD3C	40.00
Stradone	F 49	50.00
	PPB	90.00
	UD1A	35.00
Straffan	UD1A	40.00
Straid	UD3C	50.00
Strandtown	UD4C	60.00
Strangford	B	40.00
	F 79/80	40.00
Stranorlar	F 111	40.00
	UD1A	35.00
	PPA	60.00
Stratford (Stratford/ Ballitore)	UD3C	50.00
(Stratford/ Newbridge)	UD3C	50.00
	UD4B	70.00
Street	UD2A	40.00
Strokestown	B	50.00
(Strokes-Town)	B	65.00
	F 74	40.00
	PPA	60.00
	UD4A	35.00
Summercove	UD4B	50.00
Summerhill	B	45.00
	F 20	50.00
	PPA	60.00
Suncroft	UD2C	50.00
Sundays Well	UD2C	50.00
Swanlinbar	F 75	60.00
	UD2A	25.00
	UD3C	30.00
	UD4B	45.00
Swinford	B	50.00
(SwinfD)	G 127	40.00
	F 127	40.00
Swords	F 7	35.00
	PPB	£100
Sydenham	UD4B	50.00

Early Irish Marks

Office	Type	Value
Taghmon	F 72	40.00
	PPA	60.00
Tagoat	UD1A	40.00
Tallaght	F 7/12	50.00
Tallanstown	F 39	60.00
Tallow	A	£500
	B	30.00
	F 114/118	35.00
	PB	40.00
	PH	£100
Tamney	UD3C	40.00
Tanderagee	B	40.00
	F 63	35.00
	PH	45.00
	UD4A	35.00
Tara	UD1A	35.00
	UD2A	35.00
	UD3C	40.00
	UD4D	80.00
Tarbert	PPA	50.00
	PPB	50.00
	UD1A	30.00
	UD3C	40.00
Tashinny	UD1A	40.00
Tassagh	UD4B	50.00
	UD4E (5/219)	£100
Templemore	F 68	35.00
mixed script	(PB)	£500
	PPA	60.00
Templeogue	PPB	£100
Templepatrick	UD1A	30.00
	UD1E	£200
	PPA	65.00
Templeshambo	UD2C	40.00
Templetuohy	UD2C	35.00
Tempo	F 75	60.00
	UD3C	40.00
Termonfeckin	UD3C	40.00
	UD4C	75.00
The Quay (Westport)	UD2A	50.00
Thomastown	B/UD1A	45.00
(ThoSTown)	E	50.00
	F 58/59	30.00
(ThomastN)	G 59	40.00
	PPA	50.00
	PPB	60.00
Thurles	B	30.00
	F 74/75/82	25.00
	PPB	75.00
Timoleague	UD4E (5/220)	80.00
Tinahely	B	35.00
(Tinnehely)	F 42	40.00
Tipperary	B/UD1A	30.00
(T-Perary)	E	50.00
	F 100/108	30.00
	PH	65.00
	PPA	55.00
Tobermore	F 98	40.00
(Tubbermore)	F 98	60.00
	UD4A	35.00
Toomavara	UD1A	20.00
Toomebridge	F 102	50.00
(Toombridge)	F 100	60.00
(Toome)	F 102	60.00
	UD1A	20.00
	UD2C	40.00
	UD4A	30.00
	UD4B	40.00
Tourmakeedy	UD2A	40.00
Townley Hall	UD2A	40.00
Tralee	B	40.00
(Traley)	D	£180
	F 145/146/151	40.00
	PF	30.00

Office	Type	Value
	PQ	£100
	PPA	£100
	PPB	90.00
Tramore	F 82	40.00
Trillick	UD1D	£150
	UD3B	40.00
(Trillick/Enniskillen)	UD3C	50.00
(Trillick/Omagh)	UD3C	40.00
Trim	B/UD1A	30.00
	F 25	30.00
Tuam	B	30.00
	D	60.00
	F 87/93/98/103	30.00
	PH	40.00
Tubbercurry	UD1A	35.00
Tubbermore see Tobermore		
Tulla	F 111	50.00
	UD1A	40.00
Tullamore	B	30.00
	F 48/49	25.00
star in centre	(PD)	80.00
(Tullamoore)	PH	25.00
	UD4A	40.00
Tullaroan	UD4B	50.00
Tullow	B/UD1A	40.00
	F 46	35.00
Tully	UD2A	40.00
Tullyhogue	UD3C	40.00
Tullyvin	UD3C	40.00
Tulsk	B/UD1A	30.00
	F 75	60.00
	UD4B	50.00
Tynagh	UD1A	30.00
	UD2C	40.00
	UD4B	50.00
Tynan	F 75	50.00
	UD1A	40.00
	PPA	£100
Tyrella	UD3B	40.00
Tyrrells Pass	F 40	40.00
Upper Ballinderry see Ballinderry Upper		
Upper Georges St	UD2C	30.00
	UD3C	30.00
Upper Malone (Belfast)	UD2C	P
Urlingford	UD1A	35.00
	UD2C	40.00
Valentia	F 178	£150
(Valencia)	UD4B	£100
Verners Bridge	UD1A	45.00
	UD3C	50.00
Villierstown	UD2A	40.00
	UD4B	50.00
Virginia	B/UD1A	40.00
	F 40/46	35.00
Waringstown	UD1A	40.00
	UD4A	40.00
Warren(s)point	F 55	35.00
(WNPoint)	G 55	50.00
	PH	60.00
	UD4A	40.00
Waterford	A	£450
	B	30.00
(W-Ford)	D	£100
	F 74/75/76/78	25.00
(WaterfD)	G 78	50.00
both dots and lines at sides	L 74	30.00
	N	40.00
Post Paid in italics	(PB)	40.00
unboxed	(PH)	75.00
	PH	70.00
	PPA	50.00
	PPB	50.00
	UD2A	40.00
Watergrasshill	UD1A	40.00

117

Early Irish Marks

Office	Type	Value
	UD2A	40.00
	UD4B	50.00
Waterside	UD3B	40.00
	UD4E (5/219)	£100
Westport	B	30.00
	F 121/133/138	40.00
	PH	40.00
	PPA	70.00
	PPB	50.00
Wexford	B	30.00
(Waxford)	D	£100
	F 72/74	35.00
	PPA	75.00
curved	(PB)	60.00
	PH	65.00
Whiteabbey	UD2C	40.00
	UD4E (5/220)	90.00
Whitegate (Cork)	UD1A	40.00
Whitegate (Clare)	UD2C	40.00
Whitehall (Whitehall/Bag'stown)	UD2C	40.00
(Whitehall/Kilkenny)	UD2C	40.00
	UD4C	65.00
Whitehouse	UD2C	35.00
	UD3C	40.00
	UD4B	45.00
Wicklow	B	30.00
	F 24	35.00
Wilkinstown	UD3B	40.00
Windsor Avenue (Fairview)	PPB	£175
Woodburn	UD4E (5/220)	80.00
Woodford (Galway)	UD2A	40.00
Woodlawn	UD1G	60.00
	UD2A	40.00
	UD4B	50.00
Youghal(l)	B	30.00
(Y-Hal)	D	£150
	F 124/128	25.00
	N	75.00

Office	Type	Value
Merrion Row	5/43	20.00
Nth King St	5/43	30.00
Northumberland Buildings	5/43	30.00
Penny Post in centre	(5/40)	£150
Phibsboro	5/43	30.00
Queen St	5/43	30.00
Sir John Rogerson's Quay	5/43	50.00
South King St	5/43	30.00
Stephens Green	5/43	30.00
Summerhill	5/43	30.00
Temple St	5/43	20.00
Thomas St	5/43	30.00
Ushers Quay	5/43	40.00
Ushers Island	5/43	40.00
Warrington Place	5/43	50.00

Sources: Feldman and Kane
          Dixon Penny Posts
          Moxter mileage marks
          Kane undated handstamps
          note: some errors in these corrected
(Auction catalogues)

Dublin Town Receiving Houses

Marks used at Receiving Houses before 1840 in conjunction with the Dublin Penny Post are not shown in the list below. Those listed can be found after 1840 and many are frequently seen by collectors. Type **5/43** is the same as the undated mark UD1A.

Office	Type	Value
Amiens St	5/43	30.00
Aungier St	5/43	30.00
Baggot St	5/43	20.00
Baggot St Upr	5/43	30.00
Bride St	5/43	20.00
Brunswick St	5/43	30.00
Camden St	5/43	20.00
Capel St Lr	5/43	30.00
Capel St Upr	5/43	30.00
Castle St	5/43	30.00
Clare St	5/43	20.00
College Green	5/43	20.00
Dawson St	5/43	30.00
Dorset St	5/43	30.00
Four Courts	5/43	45.00
Grafton St	5/43	20.00
Gt Britain St	5/43	30.00
Gt Brunswick St	5/43	30.00
Gt Denmark St	5/43	50.00
Harcourt St	5/43	20.00
High St	5/43	30.00
Holles St	5/43	20.00
Inns Quay	5/43	30.00
James's St	5/43	30.00
Linen Hall (horizontal)	(5/40)	£900
Lower Coombe	5/43	£200
Mecklenburgh St	5/43	40.00

6 The Great Post Office Reforms, 1839-1844

Uniform 4d Post, 5 Dec 1839 - 9 Jan 1840

Despite very heavy postal charges, for years the Post Office was run at a loss. From 5 December 1839, as an experiment, a flat rate of 4d per ½ ounce was introduced on all letters formerly charged at 4d or more, regardless of distance. Most towns marked letters with a black manuscript '4' (unpaid) or in red for those paid in advance. Some towns used handstamps but these are scarce.

6/4 Catterick

6/5 Sherborne

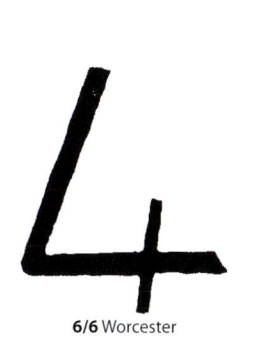

6/6 Worcester

6/7 Scottish standard type

6/9 Galashiels

6/11 Dublin

6/1	Manuscript '4', 'P4', 'Pd 4' or 'Paid 4', black for unpaid letters	£100
6/2	As above but in red for paid letters	£175

★	from 400+	★★★	very rare from 2000+
★★	Rare from 1250+	—	only 1 or 2 known

6/3 Handstruck '4' from English or Welsh towns (several in some cases):

Arundel	★★★	Ipswich	★★
Ashburton	★★★	Kington	★★★
Ashby	—	Leominster	★★
Baldock	—	Manchester	—
Blackburn	★★★	Norwich	—
Carlisle	from 1000+	Nottingham	from 1000+
6/4 Catterick	—	Oxford	★★★
Chester	★★	Rushyford	—
Cullompton	—	Scarborough	★★★
Dorchester	★★★	**6/5** Sherborne	★★
Grimsby	★★★	Stockton	★★★
Guildford	—	Wakefield	from 1000+
Halifax	★★★	Welshpool	—
Hawes	—	Whitchurch	from 1200
Hertford	★★	Woodbridge	★★
Hoddesdon	—	**6/6** Worcester	★★
Horsham	—		

Note: A cover from Nottingham sold for £1430 at auction in 1992.

6/7 Handstruck '4' from Scottish towns (standard type):

Aberdeen	£250	Inverness	£400
Dundee	£250	Leith (blue)	£300
Edinburgh	£125	Perth	£200
Glasgow	£150	Stonehaven	£250
Haddington	£300		

6/8 As above but individual Scottish types:

Ayr	★★	Kirkwall	£600
Coldstream	£600	Lochgilphead	★★
Galashiels **6/9**	★★	Port Glasgow	★★
Golspie	★★	Wigtown	★★★
Hawick	£750		

6/10 Handstruck '4' from Irish towns

Armagh (blue)	★★	Dundalk	£1200
Ballymena	£1000	Dungannon	★★★
Belfast	£1000	Enniskillen	★★
Derry	£1000	Galway	£1000
Down	★★	Newry	£1000
Drogheda	★★	Roscrea	£1200
Dublin **6/11**	£500	Rosscarberry	—

Further reading: "Charge Marks of The 4d Post" (1990) by P.J. Chadwick.

Uniform 1d Post, from 10 Jan 1840

The Uniform 4d Post was such a great success that it soon became clear the charge could be reduced to 1d for a pre-paid letter and 2d when paid by the recipient. The Uniform 1d Post started on 10 January 1840 and the Free Frank system was abolished from that date.

Many post towns introduced handstamps, usually in red, to show that 1d postage had been pre-paid. Similarly there were handstamps, usually in black, to show that 2d was due, from the recipient, for letters not pre-paid. This system continued in

119

The Great Post Office Reforms, 1839-1844

diminishing use after the introduction of adhesive stamps and until the 1850s.

Many towns used thick or thin straight lines sometimes appearing like a red handwritten line without serifs. Some towns used more than one type.

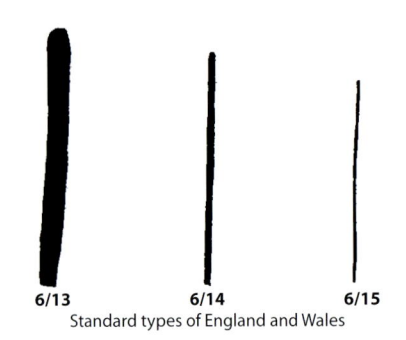

6/13   6/14   6/15
Standard types of England and Wales

6/16 Aberystwyth   **6/17** Burnley   **6/18** Chester

6/12	Manuscript '1' in red, paid letters	5.00
	Handstruck '1' (see 6/13-15), 'pd 1', 'Paid 1d', 'P1', etc. from English or Welsh towns (usually in red):	

Town	Price	Town	Price
Abergavenny	45.00	Brighton	25.00
Aberystwyth **6/16**	60.00	Bungay	£200
Addingham	£150	Buntingford	£150
Amlwch	£100	Burford	£300
Andover	£180	Burnley **6/17**	£400
Arundel	£150	Bury St. Edmunds	50.00
Attleborough	£100	Carlisle	50.00
Aylsham	50.00	Carnarvon	£200
Baldock	£180	Catterick	£150
Banbury	£350	Cawood	£300
Bangor	75.00	Chelmsford	75.00
Banstead	£350	Chertsey	75.00
Barford	£100	Chester **6/18**	50.00
Barnet	£100	Chichester	£150
Barrow in Furness	£300	Colchester	75.00
Barrow on Humber	£150	Coleford	£100
Basingstoke	25.00	Colne	£300
Battle	£200	Conisborough	75.00
Bawtry	75.00	Cranbrook	75.00
Beaconsfield	£100	Crawley	£100
Beaumaris	£300	Croydon	£100
Bedale	£100	Darlington	75.00
Berwick	45.00	Dorking	£150
Beverley	65.00	Douglas IOM	*
Biddenden	£150	Dowlais	£350
Bingham	£150	Edgware	£100
Bishop Auckland	£100	Englefield Green	£150
Bishop's Stortford	£100	Epsom	£100
Blackburn	£100	Esher	£150
Bognor	£150	Falmouth	75.00
Bolton	£150	Folkestone	£150
Bradford	50.00	Gateshead	75.00
Braintree	£150	Goole	£100
Brentford	£175	Gravesend	75.00
Bridgend	£100	Guernsey	*

Town	Price	Town	Price
Guildford	50.00	Rickmansworth	£150
Halifax	30.00	Ripley	£150
Harleston	£150	Robertsbridge	£150
Hastings	£100	Rochdale	£200
Havant	£150	Rochford	£100
Haverfordwest	£200	Romford	£100
Hawes	£100	Romsey	£100
Henfield	£150	Rushyford	£150
Hertford	£100	St.Leonards-on-Sea	£200
Higham Ferrers	£200	Salisbury	15.00
High Wycombe	£100	Sawbridgeworth	£100
Hoddesdon	£150	Scarborough	75.00
Horsham	75.00	Selby	£200
Horwich	£300	Sevenoaks	£100
Huddersfield	50.00	Shaftesbury	£100
Hull	30.00	Sheffield	£150
Hurst Green	£150	Skipton	£150
Ipswich	50.00	Slough	£150
Ixworth	£150	Southampton	30.00
Jersey	*	Staplehurst	£150
Kingston	£150	Stevenage	£200
Lancaster	£250	Swindon	£100
Lamberhurst	£100	Tadcaster	£150
Ledbury	75.00	Thetford	£150
Leeds	15.00	Thrapston	£150
Liverpool	15.00	Ticehurst	£150
London	15.00	Todmorden	£150
Long Stratton	£150	Tunbridge	50.00
Lyndhurst	75.00	Tunbridge Wells	75.00
Maidstone	50.00	Ulverstone	£250
Margate	£100	Uxbridge	75.00
Marlborough	£100	Wadhurst	£150
Merthyr Tydfil	£150	Waltham Cross	£100
Middleham	£150	Warwick	£100
Montgomery	£150	Watton	£100
Nantwich	£100	Wednesbury	£100
Newbury	£100	Weedon	£250
Newcastle on Tyne	30.00	Welwyn	£100
Newcastle-u-Lyme	75.00	West Bromwich	50.00
New Cross (Manchester)	£200	West Burton	*
Newmarket	£100	West Drayton	£150
Newport Pagnell	£150	West Haddon	£300
New Romney	£100	Whitchurch	£100
Northampton	50.00	Whitehaven	50.00
Nottingham	£100	Wigan	£225
Old Down	£350	Wigton	75.00
Oldham	£200	Windsor	75.00
Otley	£300	Wokingham	£100
Oulney (Olney)	£100	Wolverhampton	75.00
Petworth	£100	Workington	£100
Poole	£100	Worthing	£100
Port Madoc	£100	Wrexham	£100
Portsmouth	£200	York	75.00
Presteign	£150		
Pyle	£150		
Ramsgate	£100		

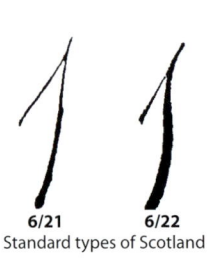

6/20   6/21   6/22   6/23
Standard types of Scotland

The Great Post Office Reforms, 1839-1844

PDI   **d**   **l**

6/24 Ballater   6/26 Ballymena

6/27 Dundalk

6/19 Handstruck '1', etc., from Scottish towns (usually in red): **D = Distinctive types**

Aberdeen	8.00	Fraserburgh	10.00
Aberdour	10.00	Galashiels	10.00
Alloa	10.00	Garliestone	50.00
Annan	10.00	Girvan	15.00
Anstruther	10.00	Glasgow	8.00
Appin	10.00	Glenluce	50.00
Arbroath	15.00	Golspie	15.00
Auchenblae D	£125	Greenock	8.00
Auchnacraig D	£125	Haddington	10.00
Auchterarder	15.00	Hamilton	10.00
Auchtermuchty	10.00	Hawick	10.00
Ayr	10.00	Holytown	75.00
Ayton	15.00	Huntly	10.00
Ballantrae	10.00	Inverkeithing	15.00
Ballater **6/24** D	£250	Inverness	15.00
Banff D	£100	Jedburgh	10.00
Bathgate	10.00	Kelso	10.00
Beith	15.00	Kettle	15.00
Biggar	10.00	Kilmarnock	8.00
Boness	15.00	Kincardine	10.00
Braco	£100	Kinghorn	20.00
Bridge of Earne	50.00	Kircaldy D	£150
Callander	10.00	Kirkcaldy	20.00
Campbelton	15.00	Kirkcudbright	10.00
Canonbie	10.00	Kirkwall	£400
Cockburnspath	25.00	Lanark	10.00
Coldstream	15.00	Langholme	10.00
Collinsburgh	10.00	Largs	10.00
Coupar Angus D	£150	Lauder	10.00
Crail	10.00	Laurencekirk D	£125
Crieff	25.00	Leith	8.00
Culross	15.00	Lerwick	£100
Cumnock	10.00	Lesmahago	50.00
Cupar	10.00	Leven	15.00
Dalkeith	15.00	Linlithgow	15.00
Denny	15.00	Lochgilphead	10.00
Douglas	15.00	Lockerby	8.00
Dumbarton	10.00	Mauchline	10.00
Dumfries	8.00	Maybole	10.00
Dunbar	10.00	Melrose	15.00
Dundee	8.00	Midcalder	15.00
Dunfermline	15.00	Moffatt	10.00
Dunoon	30.00	Montrose	10.00
Dunse	15.00	Musselburgh	10.00
Ecclefechan	10.00	Newburgh	10.00
Edinburgh	5.00	Newport	15.00
Elgin	10.00	Newton Stewart	15.00
Falkirk	8.00	North Queensferry	15.00
Fisherrow	50.00	Paisley	8.00
Forfar	8.00	Peebles	10.00
Forres	10.00	Perth	10.00
Fort William	10.00		

Peterhead	30.00	Stirling	10.00
Pittenweem	10.00	Stonehaven D	£150
Port Patrick	30.00	Stow	15.00
Port William	15.00	Stranraer	10.00
Prestonkirk	15.00	Tarbert D	£100
Rhynie D	£125	Thornhill (Doune)	50.00
St Andrews	10.00	Tobermory	50.00
St Boswells	15.00	Whithorn	30.00
Sanquhar	15.00	Wick	10.00
Selkirk	10.00	Wigtown	30.00
Stewarton	10.00		

6/25 Handstruck '1d', etc., from Irish towns (usually in red):

Abbeyleix	£150	Drogheda	75.00
Armagh	£100	Dublin	30.00
Athlone	£100	Dundalk **6/27**	£125
Athy	£150	Dungarvan	£125
Ballymena **6/26**	90.00	Maghera	£150
Ballymoney	£100	Maryborough	£250
Borrisakane	£125	Navan	£125
Carrickfergus	£100	Parsonstown	75.00
Castleburn	£200	Portarlington	£300
Cookstown	£250	Portglenone	£200
Derry	75.00	Roscrea	50.00
Donaghadee	£125	Tallow	90.00
Down	75.00	Verner's Bridge	£350

6/30 Blackburn   6/31 Colchester

6/33 Kirkcaldy   6/35 Castlebar

6/28 Manuscript '2' or '2d', black, for unpaid letters   8.00
6/29 Handstruck '2' or '2d' from English and Welsh towns (usually black, sometimes blue or green):

Aberayron	£100	Braintree	£125
Abingdon	£100	Bridgewater	£150
Ashburton	£125	Broadway	£125
Attleborough	£100	Buckingham	£200
Bangor	£150	Burnley	£150
Barmouth	£200	Bury (Lancs)	£150
Barnard Castle	£125	Canterbury	75.00
Basingstoke	£100	Carlisle	£150
Bawtry	£100	Carnarvon	£200
Beaumaris	£200	Catterick	£125
Bedale	£100	Chester	75.00
Belford	£100	Cockermouth	75.00
Beverley	£100	Colchester **6/31**	£100
Birmingham	90.00	Darlington	75.00
Bishop Auckland	£100	Derby	£100
Blackburn **6/30**	£100	Dorchester	75.00
Bolton	£175	Douglas	*
Bradford	75.00	Durham	£200

121

The Great Post Office Reforms, 1839-1844

Town	Price	Town	Price
Gilsland	£100	Preston	£125
Gravesend	£150	Reading	£150
Guernsey	★	Richmond (Yks)	£100
Halifax	£100	Rochford	£100
Harwich	£150	Romford	£100
Hastings	£150	Romsey	£100
Haverfordwest	75.00	Ross (Heref)	£150
Hawes	£150	Ryde	75.00
Haydon Bridge	75.00	Salisbury	50.00
Hereford	£150	Scorton	£200
Hertford	£100	Selby	75.00
Holyhead	£150	Sleaford	75.00
Hounslow	£150	Southampton	50.00
Huddersfield	£100	Stafford	£100
Ipswich	£100	Stockport	£100
Isle of Man	★	Stoneham	£125
Jersey	★	Sunderland	75.00
Leamington	£100	Todmorden	£200
Leeds	30.00	Torquay	75.00
Litchfield	75.00	Wakefield	£100
Liverpool	25.00	Waltham Cross	£100
London	10.00	Warwick	£100
Loughborough	£125	Wellington (Salop)	£150
Market Deeping	75.00	Weymouth	£100
Marlborough	£200	Whitehaven	75.00
Middlesborough	£150	Wigan	£150
Newbury	£100	Wigton	£100
Newcastle on Tyne	25.00	Winchester	75.00
Newcastle-u-Lyme	75.00	Windsor	£100
Newport (Mon)	£200	Wolverhampton	75.00
Northampton	£150	Woodbridge	£100
North Shields	75.00	Workington	75.00
Nottingham	75.00	Wrexham	£100
Otley	£100	York	60.00
Portsmouth	75.00		

6/32 Handstruck '2' from Scottish towns (usually black, sometimes blue or green):

Town	Price	Town	Price
Aberdeen D	£150	Irvine	30.00
Alloa	30.00	Jedburgh	75.00
Annan	75.00	Kelso	30.00
Auchtermuchty	20.00	Kettle	40.00
Ayr	75.00	Kilmarnock	20.00
Ayton D	£125	Kinross	30.00
Ballantrae	30.00	Kirkcaldy **6/33**	75.00
Banff D	£125	Kirkwall D	£200
Beith	30.00	Langholme	40.00
Bridge of Earn	75.00	Largs	30.00
Cairnryan	40.00	Leith	20.00
Canonbie	30.00	Lerwick	40.00
Carnoustie D	£100	Leven	50.00
Carsphairn D	£125	Linlithgow	20.00
Cockburnspath	40.00	Lochgilphead	30.00
Creetown	30.00	Mauchline D	£100
Crieff	30.00	Maybole	20.00
Dalkeith D	75.00	Melrose	30.00
Dumbarton	30.00	Moffatt	20.00
Dunbar	20.00	Newburgh	20.00
Dunblane	30.00	Newport	30.00
Dundee	15.00	Paisley	75.00
Dunfermline	20.00	Peebles	40.00
Dunse	30.00	Perth	20.00
Edinburgh	15.00	Pittenweem	30.00
Edinburgh (dated)	£250	Portobello	30.00
Falkirk	30.00	Sanday	75.00
Galashiels	50.00	Selkirk	30.00
Glasgow	30.00	St Boswells	30.00
Glasgow D	60.00	Stirling	30.00
Glenluce	40.00	Stonehaven	£125
Greenock	30.00	Stow	30.00
Haddington	20.00	Stranraer	20.00
Hamilton	75.00	Tranent	75.00
Hawick	20.00	Whithorn	75.00
Inverkeithing	30.00		

6/34 Handstruck '2' from Irish towns (usually black, sometimes blue or green):

Town	Price	Town	Price
Abbeyleix	75.00	Kells	75.00
Armagh	40.00	Kilbeggan	£100
Athlone	75.00	Killucan	75.00
Ballyboro	75.00	Lisnaskea	75.00
Ballyjamesduff	£100	Longford	£100
Ballymena	40.00	Lurgan	60.00
Ballymote	75.00	Magherafelt	75.00
Banbridge	40.00	Maryborough	40.00
Belfast	30.00	Monaghan	40.00
Castlebar **6/35**	£100	Moneymore	40.00
Cookstown	£100	Mullingar	40.00
Derry	40.00	Newry	40.00
Donaghadee	40.00	Newtownlimavady	£100
Donegal	75.00	Portadown	75.00
Drogheda	40.00	Roscrea	75.00
Dublin	30.00	Tipperary	£150
Dungannon	40.00	Tralee	£200
Dundalk	75.00	Tuam	60.00
Enniskillen	50.00	Warren Point	£100

Maltese Cross Cancellations, 1840 - 1844

These were introduced in May 1840 to obliterate the new adhesive stamps and prevent their fraudulent re-use. They appear also on postal stationery - centrally on Mulready sheets, but over the Queen's head on other items.

6/47 General (England)
6/48 General (Scotland)
6/49 Channel Islands
6/59 Kilmarnock
6/61 Leeds
6/63 Manchester
6/64 Mullingar
6/65 & 6/67 Norwich or Plymouth

122

6/73 Wotton-under-Edge

6/74 York

6/80 London No. 6
(Nos. 1-12 were used)

The value of an imperf stamp, on and off cover, varies considerably with the number and width of its margins. The following values are based on a 3 clear-margins stamp of good appearance at our regular 85% (3 star) quality. A 4 wide-margins stamp of fine appearance would be at least double.

Stanley Gibbons

Great Britain Department

BY APPOINTMENT TO
HER MAJESTY THE QUEEN
STANLEY GIBBONS LTD
LONDON
PHILATELISTS

Stanley Gibbons, a name synonymous with quality.

Ever since the birth of our hobby Stanley Gibbons has been at the forefront of GB philately and we invite collectors access to one of the finest GB stocks in the world by registering for our renowned free monthly brochure. Whatever your budget or collecting interests you will find a range of the highest quality material for the discerning collector.

Simply contact Mark Facey on **020 7557 4424** email **mfacey@stanleygibbons.com**
or Michael Barrell on **020 7557 4448** email **mbarrell@stanleygibbons.com** to register

STANLEY GIBBONS
Est 1856

Stanley Gibbons
399 Strand, London, WC2R 0LX
+44 (0)20 7836 8444
www.stanleygibbons.com

The Great Post Office Reforms, 1839-1844

	Colours:	One Penny Imperf 1840 Black ✉	○	One Penny Imperf 1841 Red ✉	○	Two Penny Blue Imperf 1840 No Lines ✉	○	Two Penny Blue Imperf 1841 White Lines ✉	○
6/36	Red	£700	£375	£35000	£4800	£3000	£950	—	+
6/37	Black	£700	£350	40.00	30.00	£2500	£875	£650	£275
6/38	Blue	£30000	£12000	£1700	£650	£50000	£15000	£11000	£5000
6/39	Brown	£9500	£3000	—	—	—	£12000	—	—
6/40	Green	—	—	£40000	£6500	—	—	—	—
6/41	Magenta	£15000	£3000	—	—	£30000	£12000	—	—
6/42	Orange	£2600	—	—	—	—	—	—	—
6/43	Ruby	£4500	£1200	—	—	£14000	£7000	—	—
6/44	Vermilion	£3000	—	—	—	—	—	—	—
6/45	Violet	++	£12000	£40000	£8500	—	—	—	—
6/46	Yellow	—	—	—	—	—	—	—	—

Values: + = more than £20000
++ = more than £30000

	Types:	One Penny Imperf 1840 Black ✉	○	One Penny Imperf 1841 Red ✉	○	Two Penny Blue Imperf 1840 No Lines ✉	○	Two Penny Blue Imperf 1841 White Lines ✉	○
6/47	General	£700	£350	40.00	30.00	£2500	£875	£650	£275
6/48	Scottish	£700	£350	£220	£120	£2500	£875	£1000	£400
6/49	Ch. Isles	—	—	£55000	£10000	—	—	—	—
6/50	Belfast	—	—	£650	£240	—	—	£2200	£750
6/51	Brighton	—	—	£900	£380	—	—	—	—
6/52	Cork	—	—	£1500	£400	—	—	£5500	£1500
6/53	Coventry	—	—	£2800	£1000	—	—	—	—
6/54	Dublin	£9000	£3000	£300	£150	£7000	£2500	£2000	£700
6/56	Greenock	£9000	£3000	£500	£250	£7500	£2500	£2000	£700
6/57	Hollymount	—	—	£17000	£2800	—	—	—	—
6/58	Kelso	—	—	£4000	£800	£11000	£4000	£10000	£3000
6/59	Kilmarnock	—	£10000	£5500	£1700	£35000	£9000	£18000	£3500
6/60	Leamington	—	—	£800	£250	—	—	—	—
6/61	Leeds	£10000	£2800	£2500	£600	£7500	£3000	£5500	£2300
6/62	Limerick	—	—	£1900	£500	—	—	—	—
6/63	Manchester	£4500	£1400	£1100	£350	£7000	£1750	—	—
6/64	Mullingar	—	£10000	£20000	£3600	£60000	£18000	£45000	£12000
6/65	Norwich	£13000	£3800	£1800	£550	£15000	£6000	£4000	£1300
6/66	Perth	£9000	—	£1000	£250	—	—	—	—
6/67	Plymouth	£13000	£3800	—	—	£15000	£5000	—	—
6/68	Settle	—	—	£9500	£1800	—	—	—	—
6/69	Stirling	—	—	£550	£150	—	—	—	—
6/70	Stonehaven	£22000	£4500	£11000	£2400	£35000	£12000	—	—
6/71	Welshpool	—	£4800	£5000	£750	—	—	—	—
6/72	Whitehaven	—	—	£10000	£2200	—	—	—	—
6/73	Wotton	£25000	£6500	£20000	£6000	£60000	£16000	—	—
6/74	York	—	—	£2500	£800	£20000	£5500	£12000	£2500
6/75	London 1	+	£18000	£550	£180	+	£18000	£2250	£700
6/76	London 2	+	£18000	£550	£180	+	£18000	£2250	£700
6/77	London 3	+	£18000	£600	£225	+	£18000	£2250	£700
6/78	London 4	+	£18000	£2000	£600	+	£18000	£2250	£700
6/79	London 5	+	£18000	£550	£180	+	£18000	£2800	£850
6/80	London 6	+	£18000	£450	£160	+	£18000	£2250	£700
6/81	London 7	+	£18000	£450	£160	+	£18000	£3250	£1200
6/82	London 8	+	£18000	£450	£160	+	£18000	£2800	£1000
6/83	London 9	+	£18000	£550	£180	+	£18000	£3200	£1200
6/84	London 10	+	£18000	£1000	£320	+	£18000	£4000	£1500
6/85	London 11	+	£18000	£1100	£350	+	£18000	£2800	£850
6/86	London 12	+	£18000	£1100	£350	+	£18000	£1600	£550

Values: + = more than £25000

Maltese Crosses on piece are worth about 50% above the price for loose stamps.

6A Scots Local Cancellations

As this is the first time we have included this subject in *Collect British Postmarks* we have covered this complex topic as simply as possible, showing most of the types and a SELECTION of locations and their valuations. In a later edition we may go further and, with permission from the authors of the books shown, include a more comprehensive listing. Meanwhile collectors are directed to these books to seek more details. This popular topic has received much attention over the years, with pioneer work from John Anderson and from C W Meredith, whose book was published (see below) in 1953 (second edition 1963) and whose collection was sold in 1971.

Further reading : *Scots Local Cancellations* by C W Meredith, pub. R C Alcock, second edition 1963
Scots Local Namestamps by The Scottish Postmark Group, 1964
The Scots Local Namestamps 1840-1860 by P M Stephens & R S Erskine, pub. the authors, 1994

The need to cancel mail with adhesive stamps of course dated from 1840, and many Scots villages had namestamps from a previous era, which they used to cancel stamps. The single feature of marks in this chapter is that they are undated, largely to avoid the expense of a movable-date datestamp for what may well have been a small volume of mail. In broad terms they were supposed to mark the mail away from the adhesive allowing the Head Office to cancel the postage stamps. This was changed in 1854 when sub-offices and villages were permitted to cancel the adhesives, with the Head Office still stamping the letter sometimes on top of the village mark. Even then a good proportion of these marks have not been found cancelling stamps, but in spite of this we have retained "cancellations" in the chapter title. All came to an end in 1860 when an instruction was issued that local stamping should cease. Valuations are for marks that cancel the stamps: others should be given a lower valuation.

Types of Datestamp (all lettering upper case):

- A1 Seriffed, one straight line, unframed – **6A/1**
- A2 As above but 2 lines
- B1 Sans seriffed, single line above and below – **6A/2**
- B2 As above but double line above/below and name shown twice – **6A/3**
- C1 Circular, sans seriffed, double arc below
- C2 As above but seriffed – **6A/4**
- C3 As C1 but name top/bottom and no arcs
- C4 As C2 but name top, RH at foot, single arc either side – **6A/5**
- C5 As C4 but no arcs
- C6 As C3 but double arcs
- D1 Rectangular frame, sans serif – **6A/6**
- D2 As D1 but italic – **6A/7**
- D3 As D1 but seriffed
- D4 As D2 but two lines
- D5 As D3 but two lines
- D6 Unusual frame – **6A/8**
- D7 As D3 but italic – **6A/9**
- D8 As D7 but two lines – **6A/10**
- D9 As D8 but italic second line only
- D10 As D1 but three lines
- E1 As B1 but double line and italic
- E2 As E1 but seriffed – **6A/11**
- E3 As E1 but two lines of text

6A/1 Type A1 — COWCADDENS

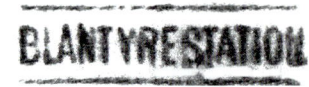

6A/2 Type B1 — BLANTYRE STATION

6A/3 Type B2 — DUROR DUROR

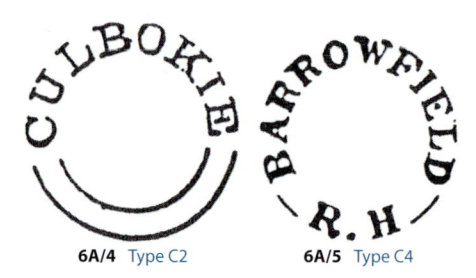

6A/4 Type C2 — CULBOKIE

6A/5 Type C4 — BARROWFIELD R.H.

6A/6 Type D1 — BURRAVOE

6A/7 Type D2 — LHANBRYDE

6A/8 Type D6 — PORT EGLINTON

6A/9 Type D7 — ELM ROW

6A/10 Type D8 — LAURISTON PLACE

6A/11 Type E2 — HANOVER STREET

Scots Local Cancellations

Selection of Offices (usually in black but other colours listed, valuation on whole cover, substantially less for piece – Head Office as shown may not have been a formal HO but town shown is where the mail was sorted)

Office	Head Office	Type(s)	Valuation
Aberarder	Inverness	D1	£120
Acharacle	Strontian	E1	£120
Alford	Aberdeen	C2	40.00
Altnaharry/Altnaharra	Lairg	D1/E1	£120
Anderston	Glasgow	A1/D1	50.00
Ardclach (Nairnshire)	Forres	C1/E1	60.00
Argyle Street	Glasgow	A2/D4	30.00
Arisaig	FtWilliam	C1/B1/E1	£100
Arrochar/Arrochar Village	Glasgow	A1/C1/B1	80.00
Ascog (Isle of Bute)	Rothesay	D1	£120
Assynt	Golspie	A1/C1/D1	£100
Barrowfield RH	Glasgow	C4	80.00
Berriedale	Golspie	D7	60.00
Blantyre Station	Glasgow	B1	£150
Broadford Recg House	Aberdeen	D4/D5	60.00
Burravoe (Shetland)	Lerwick	A1/D1	£200
Cabrach	Aberdeen	D1	80.00
Camptown	Jedburgh	D7	£100
Carridale (later Carradale)	Campbeltown	D1	80.00
Charlotte Place	Edinburgh	D4	30.00
Cowcaddens	Glasgow	A1/D1	30.00
Crinan SO	Lochgilphead	A1	50.00
Croy	Inverness	C1	60.00
Culbokie	Beauly	C2/D7	80.00
Culgower (later Loth)	Golspie	D1	£180
Drumlithie	Stonehaven	C2/D1	50.00
Duffus	Elgin	A1/C1/D2	80.00
Dundonald	Kilmarnock	C1	60.00
Duror Duror	Bonawe	B2	60.00
East Yell	Lerwick	C1/D1	£150
Elm Row	Edinburgh	D7/E1	40.00
Ferryden	Montrose	C1	80.00
Fife Keith	Keith	D1	£100
Forbes	Aberdeen	D7	60.00
Fowlis	Crieff	D1	50.00
Gallowgate (or with WO)	Glasgow	A1/D1/D4	40.00
Glendaruel	Greenock	C1/B1	80.00
Glenelg	Kyle	A1/D1	£150
Govan or Govan Govan	Glasgow	C1/B2/E1	50.00
Grassmarket	Edinburgh	A1/D1/E2	30.00
Gretna	Carlisle	C1/E1	50.00
Halkirk/Halkirk Roadside	Thurso	C2/D1	80.00
Hanover Street	Edinburgh	A2/C1/D4/E2	30.00
Harbour Recg Office	Kirkwall	E3	80.00
Helmsdale	Golspie	C2	60.00
Holyrood	Edinburgh	A1/E2	40.00
Hope Street	Glasgow	A1/D4	30.00
India Street	Edinburgh	A2/E2	40.00

Office	Head Office	Type(s)	Valuation
Innerwick	Dunbar	C1	£120
Invercannich	Beauly	C1	£150
Invergary	Inverness	C2	60.00
Inverie	Mallaig	C2/D1	£150
Isle Ornsay (Isle of Skye)	Broadford	C2/C1	80.00
Juniper Green	Edinburgh	C1	60.00
Keiss	Wick	D1	£120
Kenmore (SO)	Aberfeldy	A2/C2	80.00
Kilchrenan/ Kilcrennan/ Kilchrennan	Inveraray	C1/B1/E1	60.00
Kilninver	Oban	D1/E1	80.00
Kiltarlity	Inverness	C1	50.00
Kingussie	Inverness	A1	£150
Kinlochmoidart	FtWilliam	B1	£120
Kirkpatrick Fleming	Dumfries	C3	40.00
Lamlash (Isle of Arran)	Ardrossan	A1/E1	60.00
Largo	Leven	C1	60.00
Lauriston Pl.	Edinburgh	A2/D8	50.00
Ledaig	Bonawe	C1/B1	60.00
Lhanbryde	Elgin	C2/D2	50.00
Lismore (Isle of)	Oban	C1/B1	£150
Miavaig (Isle of Lewis)	Stornoway	E1	£180
Monkton	Ayr	C1/D1	60.00
Morinish/Mornish (Isle of Mull, later Dervaig, see chapter 17)	Oban	C1/B1	£150
Munlochy	Inverness	D1	£100
New Galloway	CastleDouglas	A2	60.00
Newington	Edinburgh	A1/C1/E2	30.00
Onich Onich	FtWilliam	B2	£100
Osborne Buildings	Glasgow	D4	50.00
Patna	Ayr	C1/D1	60.00
Pitt Street	Edinburgh	C1/D3	30.00
Port Eglinton	Glasgow	D6	£150
Portmahomac(k)	Tain	C1/D1	80.00
Q S Station (Queen St)	Glasgow	D9	£100
St Mary's Holm	Kirkwall	D1	£100
Sandbank	Greenock	C1	80.00
Sauchihall	Glasgow	A1/D7	40.00
Skeabost (Isle of Skye)	Portree	D1	£150
Stanley	Perth	A1/C1	80.00
Struan (Isle of Skye)	Portree	A1	£100
Tayinloan	Lochgilphead	C1/B1	50.00
Ulva Ulva (Isle of Mull)	Aros	B2	£150
Waterton of Echt	Aberdeen	D10	60.00
Whitehouse	Aberdeen	A1/C1/E2	80.00
Windygates	Markinch	C1	80.00

Visit SAMWELLS for All GB Covers
All Postmark Types, Stamp Issues, Themes, Subjects & Periods 1400-2013

1925 WADDON AERODROME/CROYDON on arrival of Cobham's India survey flight (Signed by Engineer)

1905 SHELL GROTTO

1926 LIVERPOOL/LATE FEE c.d.s.

1913 CARLAND/DUNGANNON (Tyrone) temporary 'rubber' datestamp

1944 SALVAGED FROM/AIR CRASH on Airletter ex Canadian Forces FPO/313 (Italy)

1911 FIRST UNITED KINGDOM/2/AERIAL POST/WINDSOR

Browse at Stampex & York Stamp Shows or view selected items over £45 online
SPECIAL OFFER: 10% discount on your first online order QUOTING **CBP**
www.postalhistorygb.com   01225 462429   info@postalhistorygb.com

Visit SAMWELLS for *All* GB Postmark Types

Browse our large stocks at Stampex & York. View selected items online

MULTIPLE DOTS in MX repeated in 3 strikes

1854 BRISTOL spoon Archer trial perf

1840 PETERBOROUGH PENNY POST and 'No4' Receiver on EL ex Thorney Abbey

1843 PILTOWN MX (Co.Kilkenny)

GREENOCK MX

1840 MONAGHAN Irish MX & 'No.2' Receiver on Mulready envelope

1854 TAN-Y-BWLCH undated circle and '032' numeral. This numeral allocated to Festiniog. NEW DISCOVERY

1845 MOUNTSORREL (Leics) double ring distinctive namestamp & '476' numeral

WE CAN NOW TAILOR OUR LISTS TO SUIT YOUR REQUIREMENTS
Simply let us know what you collect & we will return results by e-mail

www.postalhistorygb.com   01225 462429   info@postalhistorygb.com

7 Numeral, Spoon and Duplex Postmarks

Numeral handstamps replaced the Maltese Crosses in 1844, but it was still necessary to place an additional dated postmark on the reverse of each cover. From 1853 the first double, or duplex, handstamps started to appear. Thus the place of origin and the date could be combined into one strike.

Basic Prices for London, England and Wales

	Numeral	Duplex
Queen Victoria: Penny Red Imperf.	10.00	£125
Queen Victoria: Penny Red Perf.	8.00	8.00
Queen Victoria: Penny Lilac	2.00	1.00
King Edward VII: ½d or 1d	2.00	1.00
King George V: ½d or 1d	3.50	1.00
King George VI period	10.00	-
Queen Elizabeth II period	15.00	-

London: Inland Section

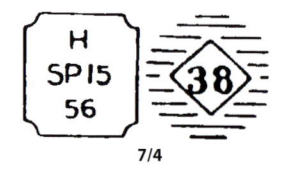

7/1

7/4

7/5

London: District Post and Suburban Offices

7/8

7/9

7/10

7/11

7/13

7/1	Horizontal oval with number in diamond, single, 1-37, 39-44 and 52-75, from 1844	5.00
7/2	As above but twin, 45, 46 or 47	35.00
7/3	As above but triple, 48 or 49	£100
7/4	Duplex, square datestamp with indented corners, from 1853	25.00
7/5	Duplex, circular datestamp, number in diamond, vertical oval, 1-107	5.00
7/6	As above but double circle datestamp	10.00
7/7	Single obliterators with number with or without diamond, vertical oval or circular	5.00
7/8	Horizontal oval with number in circle, 1-98, from 1844	8.00
7/9	Duplex, circular datestamp with vertical oval, 1853-57	5.00
7/10	Single obliterators with District initials, vertical oval or circular	8.00
7/11	Duplex with vertical oval, several series, from 1858	5.00
7/12	Sideways duplexes of London W or SE, 1857-62	10.00
7/13	Duplex with hexagonal datestamps, for late fees	25.00

Numeral, Spoon and Duplex Postmarks

Numbers used in London District Post cancellations

Note - The datestamps sometimes include the "handstamp number" and/or the code for the London District as shown below:

1	Highgate		Manor Park
2	Finchley	45	Portland St
	E. Finchley		Tottenham
3	Whetstone		North Woolwich
4	Hampstead	46	Stepney
5	Hendon	47	Southwark
6	Edgware	48	Shoreditch
	Churton St	49	Sidmouth St
7	Stoke Newington		Royal Hill Greenwich
8	Tottenham	50	Victoria Docks
	W. Brompton	53	Woodford Green
9	Kentish Town		Homerton
10	Edmonton	54	Norwood
	S. Kensington	55	Leyton St
11	Enfield	56	Isleworth
	Chelsea	57	Sutton
12	Bow	58	Wimbledon
13	Stratford	60	Kilburn
14	Leyton	61	Willesden
	St. Martin's Place	62	Harrow
15	Woodford	63	Elstree
	Highbury	64	Cheshunt
16	Chigwell		W. Ealing
	Victoria St, EC	65	Camberwell
17	Ilford	66	Lewisham
	Leytonstone	67	Peckham
18	Deptford	68	Kennington
19	Halfway St	69	Blackheath
	Finsbury Pk.	70	Anerley
20	Greenwich	71	Catford
21	Woolwich	72	Lower Norwood
	Wanstead	73	Shooter's Hill
22	Eltham		WC District office
	Plaistow	74	Tottenham
23	Bexley	75	Edmonton
	Brockley		Paddington DO
24	Dulwich	76	New Cross
25	Sydenham	77	E Dulwich
26	Beckenham	78	SE District Office
	Kensal Town	79	SW District Office
27	Clapham	80	Tottenham
28	Tooting	81	Lower Edmonton
29	Mitcham	82	Leyton
	Forest Gate	83	Upper Edmonton
30	Carshalton	84	Chingford
	Lee	85	Walthamstow
31	Wandsworth	86	NW District office
32	Putney	87	N District office
33	Mortlake	88	E District Office
34	Richmond	89	W District Office
	Earl's Court	90	Muswell Hill
35	Twickenham	91	Cricklewood
	Bethnal Green		
36	Hampton	**B and C Series, issued from 1861**	
	Walthamstow		
	Balham	1B	Ponders End
37	Brompton	2B	Colney Hatch
38	Kensington	3B	Hornsey
39	Hammersmith	4B	Southgate
40	Acton House	5B	Holloway
	of Commons	6B	Clapton
41	Brentford	7B	Loughton
	Barnes	8B	Hackney
42	Paddington	9B	Canning Town
	Walworth	10B	Chadwell
43	Charing Cross	11B	Poplar
	Sutton	12B	Charlton
	Aldgate	13B	Chislehurst
44	North Row	14B	Erith
	Wimbledon	15B	Foots Cray

16B	Lessness Heath	37C	Notting Hill
17B	Lewisham	38B	Paddington
18B	Peckham	38C	Paddington
19B	Penge	39B	Shepherds Bush
20B	Plumstead	40B	Southall
21B	Rotherhithe	41B	St. John's Wood
22B	Welling	42B	Stanmore
23B	Brixton Hill	43B	Sudbury
	Brixton	44B	The Hyde
24B	Camberwell	45B	Barking
25B	Merton	46B	Walham Green
26B	South Lambeth		Fulham
27B	Stockwell	47B	Sunbury
28B	Streatham	48B	Forest Hill
29B	Thornton Heath	49B	Sth Norwood
30B	Walworth	51B	Winchmore Hill
	Maida Hill	52B	Wood Green
31A	New Wandsworth	53B	Upper Holloway
31B	Battersea		Junction Rd.,
32B	Petersham		Upper Holloway
33B	Teddington		
34B	Acton		
35B	Ealing		
36B	Hanwell		
37B	Notting Hill		

England and Wales

7/14 **A** Numeral, horizontal oval

7/15 **B** Numeral, vertical oval

7/16 **C** Spoon, several types

7/17 **D** Sideways Duplex, several types

7/18 **E** Duplex, circular numeral, town horizontal

131

Numeral, Spoon and Duplex Postmarks

7/19 F Duplex, circular numeral town curved

7/20 G Duplex, vertical numeral, town horizontal

7/21 H Duplex, vertical numeral, town curved

Notes
(a) The numbers and thickness of bars vary
(b) Some vertical types have numbers/letters in top and/or bottom bars
(c) Many minor variations in placenames are not listed
(d) Marks for which a value is not at present established (noted as "?" in Fifth Edition) have been omitted
(e) Marks which did not relate to a specific geographical location, eg Railway Sorting Tenders and TPOs, are not listed – see chapter 13 for these
(f) Some numbers and periods of non-geographical use eg in London Chief Office; such additional usages are not listed in this edition.

These prices are current as of Nov 2013.
We are indebted to John Parmenter for permission to use this information.

1	Abergavenny	A	5.00
		B	40.00
		F	12.00
		H	3.00
2	Aberystwith	A	10.00
		B	60.00
		F	5.00
		H	4.00
	Aberystwyth	H	3.00
3	Abingdon	A	5.00
		D	10.00
		H	3.00
4	Wantage	A	5.00
		G	3.00
		H	3.00
5	Accrington	A	15.00
		B	60.00
		F	3.00
		H	3.00
6	Alfreton	A	5.00
		F	8.00
		H	4.00
7	Crich	A	£125
	Longhope	B	£150
8	Alnwick	A	5.00
		E	3.00

		G	8.00
		H	3.00
10	Alresford	A	5.00
		H	4.00
	Alresford/Hants	H	3.00
11	Alton	A	3.00
		G	8.00
	Alton/Hants	H	3.00
12	Altrincham	A	6.00
		B	75.00
		F	3.00
		H	3.00
13	Ambleside	A	6.00
		B	80.00
		H	3.00
14	Amersham	A	5.00
		H	3.00
15	Chesham	A	5.00
		B	60.00
		H	12.00
	Chesham/Bucks	H	3.00
16	Great Missenden	A	6.00
		B	40.00
		H	3.00
17	Amesbury	A	60.00
		B	30.00
		H	3.00
18	Ampthill	A	5.00
		F	15.00
		H	3.00
20	Silsoe	A	60.00
21	Andover	A	5.00
		B	60.00
		G	3.00
		H	3.00
22	Andover Rd.	A	60.00
	Micheldever Station	A	60.00
		B	£200
		F	10.00
		H	10.00
23	Whitchurch	A	20.00
	Senny Bridge	B	£100
		H	20.00
24	Overton	A	40.00
		B	40.00
25	Appleby	A	5.00
		H	3.00
26	Arrington	A	£125
	Cray	B	£150
27	Arundel	A	5.00
		B	15.00
		E	3.00
		G	3.00
		H	4.00
28	Ashbourne	A	5.00
		F	3.00
		H	3.00
29	Ashburton	A	5.00
		B	35.00
30	Ashby de la Zouch	A	4.00
		B	15.00
		H	3.00
31	Ashford	A	15.00
		B	80.00
		E	15.00
		G	15.00
		H	3.00
	Ashford/StationOffice	H	15.00
32	Ashton Under Lyne	A	5.00
		B	40.00
		D	15.00
		F	3.00
		H	3.00
33	Atherstone	A	5.00

Numeral, Spoon and Duplex Postmarks

		B	60.00			H	3.00
		F	3.00	55	Bawtry	A	12.00
		H	3.00			E	3.00
34	Attleborough	A	30.00			H	3.00
		B	15.00	56	Gringley	A	£125
	Attleborough/ Norfolk	H	3.00		Forest Row	B	15.00
35	Axminster	A	6.00			H	4.00
		B	12.00	57	Beaconsfield	A	4.00
		H	4.00	58	Beaumaris	A	6.00
36	Colyton	A	75.00			B	60.00
37	Seaton	A	75.00			H	4.00
	Buckfastleigh	B	12.00	59	Beccles	A	20.00
38	Aylesbury	A	5.00			B	25.00
		B	80.00			G	3.00
		F	3.00			H	3.00
		H	3.00	60	Bedale	A	4.00
39	Aylsham	A	5.00			B	50.00
		B	60.00			E	3.00
		H	30.00			G	3.00
40	Bagshot	A	5.00			H	3.00
	(3 CD)	E	£400	61	Bedford	A	5.00
	Newtown/ Monmouthshire	H	20.00			B	15.00
	Chapel Town/Mon	H	3.00			D	12.00
41	Bakewell	A	5.00			E	3.00
		F	40.00			H	3.00
		H	3.00	62	Belford	A	8.00
42	Baslow	A	40.00			G	30.00
	Chiswick	B	£150			H	3.00
		H	15.00	63	Wooler	A	40.00
	Login	B	75.00			H	3.00
43	Turnham Green	A	£250	64	Belper	A	8.00
	Docking	B	15.00			B	80.00
44	Tideswell	A	£125			E	3.00
	(3 side Arcs, Error)	A*	£300			H	20.00
45	Baldock	A	4.00	65	Berkhemstead	A	3.00
		B	40.00			B	25.00
		E	12.00			H	3.00
		H	2.00		Berkhampstead	H	3.00
46	Banbury	A	5.00	66	Berwick	A	8.00
		B	40.00			B	25.00
		E	3.00			E	3.00
		G	15.00			G	8.00
		H	2.00			H	3.00
47	Bangor	A	12.00		Berwick Station	F	50.00
		D	15.00	67	Beverley	A	3.00
		E	4.00			B	12.00
		G	3.00			F	2.00
		H	3.00			H	2.00
48	Barnard Castle	A	3.00	68	Bewdley	A	5.00
		F	4.00			E	8.00
		H	3.00			G	15.00
49	Barnsley	A	4.00			H	3.00
		B	25.00	69	Bicester	A	3.00
		F	3.00			F	15.00
		H	3.00			H	4.00
50	Barnstaple	A	5.00	70	Bideford	A	5.00
		B	15.00			B	15.00
		D	12.00			F	3.00
		F	3.00			H	3.00
		H	3.00	71	Biggleswade	A	8.00
51	Barton-on-Humber	A	20.00			B	80.00
		F	30.00			F	15.00
		H	3.00			H	3.00
52	Basingstoke	A	8.00	72	Billericay	A	6.00
		H	3.00			B	15.00
53	Bath	A	10.00			H	3.00
		B	40.00	73	Bilston	A	8.00
		D	10.00			E	3.00
		E	3.00			G	12.00
		H	3.00			H	3.00
	Woodford Green (error of Type H)	H	£350	74	Birkenhead	A	8.00
54	Battle	A	4.00			C	£150
		D	£125			D	6.00
		G	3.00			F	3.00

133

Numeral, Spoon and Duplex Postmarks

		H	3.00
75	Birmingham	A	3.00
		A (roller)	£350
		B	12.00
		C	20.00
		D	4.00
		F	3.00
		H	3.00
		H (5 bars)	£275
	Five Ways/ Birmingham	H	3.00
	Gt. Hampton St./ Birmingham	H	3.00
	Smethwick/ Birmingham	H	3.00
76	Campden	A	5.00
		H	3.00
77	Halesowen	A	40.00
78	Henley-in-Arden	A	60.00
	Aldershot	B	30.00
		H	3.00
79	Knowle	A	40.00
80	Bishop Auckland	A	3.00
		B	60.00
		H	3.00
	South Rd./ Bishop Auckland	H	35.00
	Bishops Auckland	H	3.00
81	Stanhope	A	20.00
		B	40.00
82	Bishops Castle	A	6.00
		B	80.00
		H	3.00
83	Bishops Stortford	A	15.00
		B	25.00
		F	3.00
		H	3.00
84	Canterbury	A	5.00
		B	6.00
		D	10.00
		F	4.00
		H	3.00
85	Bishops Waltham	A	12.00
		B	20.00
		H	3.00
86	Blackburn	A	15.00
		B	60.00
		E	3.00
		H	3.00
87	Blandford	A	5.00
		B	40.00
		F	4.00
		H	3.00
88	Bodmin	A	5.00
		G	4.00
		H	4.00
89	Wadebridge	A	8.00
90	Padstow	A	8.00
91	Bognor	A	5.00
		B	100
		G	3.00
		H	3.00
92	Bolton	A	5.00
		B	20.00
		D	10.00
		E	3.00
		H	3.00
93	Boroughbridge	A	10.00
		B	80.00
94	Boston	A	15.00
		B	80.00
		D	30.00
		E	3.00
		G	8.00
		H	3.00
95	Alford	A	8.00
		E	3.00
		G	3.00

		H	3.00
	Alford Linc.	H	3.00
96	Stickney	A	£100
	Aldershot Camp	B	£125
		H	40.00
97	Bury St.Edmunds	A	5.00
		B	25.00
		D	35.00
		F	3.00
		H	3.00
	Bury St.Edmonds	D	30.00
98	Blackburn	A	15.00
		B	80.00
	Dinas Mawddwy	B	20.00
100	Botesdale	A	£125
101	Ixworth	A	30.00
	Alnmouth	B	50.00
		H	3.00
102	Woolpit	A	30.00
	Leyton/S.O.	B	40.00
		H	20.00
	Winfrith	B	£100
103	Bourn	A	15.00
		B	15.00
		E	25.00
	Bourne	H	3.00
104	Brackley	A	5.00
		F	5.00
		H	5.00
105	Bracknell	A	8.00
		H	3.00
106	Bradford on Avon	A	12.00
		H	3.00
107	Bradford Yks	A	3.00
		B	40.00
		D	5.00
		H	4.00
	Bradford/Yks	H	2.00
	Bradford Yorks	F	5.00
		H	3.00
108	Carnarvon	A	8.00
		B	60.00
		D	15.00
		F	4.00
		H	3.00
109	Walthamstow	B	8.00
		H	8.00
	Walthamstow S. O.	H	8.00
	Walthamstow/ Orford Rd	H	75.00
110	Keighley	A	4.00
		B	25.00
		H	3.00
	Ingrow/Keighley	H	£100
111	Bingley	A	4.00
		B	25.00
		H	3.00
112	Braintree	A	5.00
		F	3.00
		H	3.00
113	Brampton	A	40.00
		H	25.00
	Brampton/Carlisle	H	3.00
114	Brandon	A	12.00
		E	3.00
		H	3.00
115	Stoke Ferry	A	40.00
		B	£100
116	Brecon	A	3.00
		B	15.00
		G	3.00
		H	3.00
117	Trecastle	A	£100
	Tottenham	B	£150
		H	30.00

134

Numeral, Spoon and Duplex Postmarks

	Tottenham S.O.	H	12.00
118	Brentwood	A	5.00
		B	20.00
		D	10.00
		F	12.00
		H	3.00
119	Edmonton	H	£110
	Trebanos	B	90.00
120	Bridgend	A	6.00
		F	6.00
		H	4.00
	Ringwood (error)	A	£100
	Bridgend/Glam	H	3.00
121	Pyle	A	30.00
	Morpeth (error)	A	£125
	West Cross	B	£200
122	Bridgenorth	A	6.00
		B	25.00
		C	80.00
		H	3.00
123	Bridgewater	A	4.00
		B	£100
		F	3.00
		H	3.00
124	Bridlington	A	4.00
		H	8.00
125	Bridlington Quay	A	8.00
		B	6.00
		H	8.00
126	Hunmanby	A	75.00
	Spennymoor	H	12.00
127	Bridport	A	6.00
		B	20.00
		F	8.00
		H	2.00
128	Beaminster	A	£300
129	Brigg	A	30.00
		E	3.00
		G	25.00
		H	25.00
130	Caister	A	30.00
		E	60.00
		H	40.00
131	Limber	A	60.00
132	Brighton	A	4.00
		B	15.00
		D	6.00
		F	3.00
		Error of type G		
		(diamond)	£250
		H	3.00
	Brighton/A	H	3.00
	Brighton/A1	F	4.00
		H	2.00
	Brighton/B	H	3.00
	Brighton/B2	F	4.00
		H	4.00
	Brighton/C	H	8.00
	Brighton/D	H	8.00
	Brighton/E	H	8.00
	Brighton/1	H	15.00
	Brighton/2	H	10.00
	Brighton/ H.P.O.	H	40.00
	Alma Terr/ Hove Brighton	H	25.00
	Bedford St./ Brighton	H	40.00
	Dyke Rd./ Brighton	H	40.00
	Hove B.O./ Brighton	H	6.00
	Kemptown B.O./ Brighton	H	20.00
	Lewes Rd./ Brighton	H	15.00
	Preston Rd./ Brighton	H	10.00
	St. Georges Rd./ Brighton	H	£100
	St. James's St./ Brighton	H	40.00
	Victoria Rd./ Brighton	H	25.00
	Western Rd./ Brighton	H	4.00

	Western Rd. B.O./ Brighton	H	4.00
	West Pier B.O./ Brighton	H	20.00
133	Catterick	A	4.00
		B	25.00
		H	3.00
134	Bristol	A	4.00
		C	25.00
		D	8.00
		E	4.00
		G	4.00
		H	3.00
	Clifton/Bristol	F	4.00
		H	4.00
	North St./ Bristol	F	10.00
		H	6.00
	Redcliffe/ Bristol	F	10.00
		H	10.00
135	Caxton	A	£125
	Corbridge	H	15.00
136	Brixham	A	12.00
		H	2.00
137	Broadway	A	52.00
		H	35.00
138	Bromyard	A	15.00
		F	4.00
		H	20.00
139	Bromsgrove	A	4.00
		B	40.00
		F	3.00
		H	3.00
140	Redditch	A	8.00
		H	3.00
141	Studley	A	£100
142	Brough	A	6.00
	Brough/ Penrith	H	20.00
	Brough/ Westd.	H	20.00
143	Temple Sowerby	A	75.00
	Pontardawe	H	3.00
144	Bromley/Kent	A	15.00
		B	15.00
		H	3.00
	Shortlands/ Kent	H	10.00
145	Buckingham	A	5.00
		H	3.00
146	Builth	A	10.00
		B	25.00
		H	10.00
147	Bungay	A	20.00
		B	60.00
		D	75.00
		E	8.00
		G	15.00
		H	6.00
148	Buntingford	A	4.00
		B	15.00
		H	3.00
149	Burford	A	50.00
		G	5.00
		H	2.00
150	Burnley	A	3.00
		D	10.00
		E	2.00
		H	2.00
151	Colne	A	5.00
		B	20.00
		E	15.00
		G	15.00
		H	8.00
	Colne/Lanc	H	8.00
152	Burton upon Trent	C	75.00
	Burton-on-Trent	A	5.00
		B	60.00
		F	8.00
		H	3.00

Numeral, Spoon and Duplex Postmarks

No.	Place	Type	Price
153	Burton/Westmoreland	A	25.00
		H	15.00
154	Bury Lanc	A	5.00
		B	20.00
		D	6.00
		E	3.00
		H	3.00
	Bury/ Lancashire	H	3.00
155	Buxton	A	12.00
		E	3.00
		G	8.00
		H	3.00
156	Chapel en le Frith	A	£100
	Maesycwmmer	B	90.00
		H	10.00
	Ilfracombe	B (error)	£250
157	Calne	A	3.00
		B	50.00
		G	3.00
		H	15.00
	Calne/Wilts	H	3.00
158	Cambridge	A	4.00
		B	25.00
		D	6.00
		F	3.00
		H	3.00
159	Chard	A	5.00
		B	60.00
		G	15.00
		H	3.00
160	Camelford	A	6.00
		H	40.00
161	Five Lanes	A	75.00
	Bardney	B	£200
162	Cardiff	A	10.00
		B	60.00
		D	10.00
		E	4.00
		G	3.00
		H	3.00
	Barry Dock B.O./ Cardiff	H	50.00
	Bute Docks/ Cardiff	H	25.00
	Cardiff/ Ship Letter	H	£850
163	Pontypridd	A	6.00
		H	3.00
	Haford/ Pontypridd	A	£100
164	Cardigan	A	8.00
		B	60.00
		H	3.00
165	Carlisle	A	6.00
		B	15.00
		D	10.00
		E	8.00
		F	4.00
		H	3.00
166	Haltwhistle	A	50.00
		B	£100
167	Carmarthen	A	5.00
		B	80.00
		D	8.00
		F	3.00
		H	3.00
	Stockton	A (error)	£200
168	Kidwelly	A	25.00
		H	3.00
169	Chelmsford	H (error)	£150
170	Newcastle Emlyn	A	12.00
		H	3.00
171	Chalford	A	£100
	Campsea Ash	B	£125
172	Minchinhampton	A	90.00
173	Chatham	A	5.00
		B	80.00
		D	25.00
		E	3.00
		G	20.00
		H	3.00
174	Chatteris	A	£100
	West Felton	B	40.00
175	Cheadle/ Staff	A	5.00
		B	60.00
		H	3.00
176	Chelmsford	A	8.00
		B	10.00
		D	25.00
		F	3.00
		H	3.00
177	Cheltenham	A	3.00
		B	15.00
		C	£2500
		D	10.00
		F	3.00
		H	3.00
178	Chepstow	A	4.00
		F	30.00
		H	3.00
179	Chertsey	A	15.00
		B	15.00
		D	12.00
		E	3.00
		H	2.00
180	Chester	A	5.00
		B	60.00
		C	40.00
		D	6.00
		E	3.00
		G	3.00
		H	3.00
	Chester/R.O.	H	50.00
181	Abergele	A	10.00
		B	50.00
		H	3.00
182	Hawarden	A	£120
	Betchworth	B	75.00
		H	2.00
183	Mochdrai	A	£200
184	Neston	A	£100
	Shipley/Yorks	B	15.00
		H	3.00
	Windhill/ Shipley Yks	H	50.00
185	Northop	A	75.00
		B	60.00
		H	2.00
186	Chesterfield	A	8.00
		B	80.00
		D	12.00
		F	6.00
		H	3.00
187	Staveley	A	£150
	Consett	B	50.00
		H	3.00
188	Chester le Street	A	20.00
		H	3.00
189	Leadgate	B	£200
190	Chichester	A	5.00
		D	6.00
		F	3.00
		H	3.00
	Chichester/ Station Office	H	12.00
191	Chippenham	A	3.00
		B	30.00
		F	3.00
		H	3.00
192	Malmesbury	A	12.00
		H	3.00
193	Chipping Sodbury	A	£100
	Worthing	A (error)	£175
194	Charmouth	A	8.00

Numeral, Spoon and Duplex Postmarks

		B	80.00			F	3.00
195	Chipping Norton	A	4.00			H	3.00
		B	20.00	224	Cowbridge	A	6.00
		F	30.00			H	8.00
		H	4.00	225	Cowes, IOW	A	5.00
196	Chirk	A	12.00			B	12.00
197	Ruabon	A	5.00			G	10.00
		G	6.00			H	3.00
		H	3.00	226	Cranbrook	A	50.00
198	Chorley Lanc	A	10.00		Tutbury	H	15.00
		F	10.00	227	Swadlincote	H	6.00
		H	8.00	228	Crawley	A	5.00
200	Christchurch	A	4.00			G	6.00
		B	15.00			H	3.00
		H	8.00	229	Crediton	A	5.00
	Christchurch/ Hants	H	3.00			B	40.00
202	Chudleigh	A	8.00			H	4.00
		B	30.00	230	Crewkerne	A	5.00
203	Chumleigh	A	75.00			B	12.00
	Bwlch	B	£110			H	3.00
		H	5.00	231	Crickhowell	A	3.00
204	Cirencester	A	5.00			B	60.00
		D	18.00			H	15.00
		F	3.00	232	Cuckfield	A	5.00
		H	3.00			B	60.00
205	Worcester Park	H	3.00	233	Darlington	A	5.00
206	Clare	A	75.00			B	50.00
	Bream	B	£125			D	10.00
207	Clitheroe	A	7.00			F	3.00
		H	3.00			H	3.00
208	Cobham/Surrey	A	10.00	234	Smeaton	A	£110
		B	80.00		Llansamlet	B	£175
		H	3.00	235	Staindrop	A	50.00
209	Cockermouth	A	8.00	236	Dartford	A	5.00
		B	20.00			D	80.00
		F	25.00			F	3.00
		H	3.00			H	3.00
210	Colchester	A	4.00	237	Dartmouth	A	4.00
		B	20.00			H	3.00
		D	15.00	238	Daventry	A	3.00
		F	3.00			H	3.00
		H	3.00	239	Dawlish	A	8.00
211	Boxford	A	£150			B	15.00
212	Coleford	A	10.00			H	2.00
		H	3.00	240	Deal	A	4.00
	Coleford/Glos	H	8.00			B	25.00
213	Coleshill	A	40.00			G	3.00
	Woodville	H	3.00			H	3.00
214	Cullompton	A	4.00	241	Denbigh	A	4.00
		H	2.00			B	25.00
215	Colsterworth	A	90.00			G	4.00
	Repton	H	3.00			H	3.00
216	Congleton	A	3.00	242	Derby	A	4.00
		F	25.00			B	40.00
		H	2.00			D	8.00
217	Monksheath	A	80.00			E	3.00
	Barton-under-Needwood	H	3.00			G	3.00
218	Conway	A	8.00			H	3.00
		E	8.00		Duffield Rd/Derby	H	50.00
		H	3.00	243	Melbourne/Derby	A	8.00
219	Corwen	A	4.00			H	20.00
		B	40.00		Melbourne/Derbyshire	H	3.00
		G	10.00	244	Ticknall	A	40.00
		H	3.00		Talley	B	60.00
220	Bala	A	4.00	245	Dereham	A	20.00
		H	3.00			B	50.00
221	Barmouth	A	10.00			G	8.00
		H	3.00			H	4.00
222	Dolgelly	A	12.00		East Dereham	F	8.00
		B	80.00	246	Briningham	A	£125
		H	3.00		Mountain Ash	H	2.00
223	Coventry	A	5.00	247	Elmham	A	£100
		B	80.00	248	Guist	A	90.00
		D	8.00		Felstead	B	25.00

137

Numeral, Spoon and Duplex Postmarks

249	Devizes	A	6.00			B	60.00
		B	80.00			D	12.00
		D	10.00			E	3.00
		E	3.00			G	3.00
		G	3.00			H	3.00
		H	3.00	268	Seaham	A	40.00
250	Devonport	A	4.00		Broseley	H	3.00
		D	10.00	269	Dursley	A	8.00
		F	3.00			B	25.00
		H	3.00			G	3.00
	Devonport/ H.M.S.	H	£500			H	3.00
251	St. Germans	A	12.00	270	Berkeley	A	5.00
252	Torpoint	A	20.00			B	50.00
	Seascale	H	5.00			H	3.00
253	Dewsbury	A	3.00	271	Eastbourne	A	5.00
		B	25.00			B	60.00
		F	3.00			F	3.00
		H	3.00			H	3.00
254	Diss	A	15.00	272	East Grinstead	A	5.00
		B	40.00			H	3.00
		G	15.00	273	Eccleshall	A	15.00
		H	3.00			B	40.00
255	Doncaster	A	3.00			H	3.00
		B	50.00	274	Ellesmere	A	8.00
		D	8.00			H	3.00
		F	3.00	275	Ely	A	5.00
		H	3.00			E	3.00
256	Dorchester	A	5.00			G	3.00
		B	40.00			H	3.00
		D	20.00	276	Much Wenlock	B	40.00
		F	3.00			H	3.00
		H	2.00	277	Emsworth	A	8.00
257	Dorking	A	10.00			B	60.00
		D	50.00			H	3.00
		E	3.00	278	Enstone	A	10.00
		G	20.00			G	40.00
		H	3.00			H	20.00
258	Dover	A	20.00	279	Epping	A	15.00
		D	15.00			E	10.00
		E	4.00			H	3.00
		G	8.00	280	Epsom	A	5.00
		H	3.00			G	3.00
	Dover/Station Office	H	6.00			H	3.00
259	Walmer	A	50.00	281	Ermebridge	A	£100
	New Walsingham	B	£100		Madeley/Salop	B	20.00
		H	50.00			H	6.00
	Walsingham/ Norfolk	H	8.00	282	Modbury	A	40.00
260	Downham	A	20.00		Dawley	B	£125
		B	40.00			H	25.00
		G	20.00	283	Esher	A	8.00
		H	4.00			H	3.00
261	Driffield	A	4.00	284	Evesham	A	3.00
		B	20.00			G	3.00
		F	8.00			H	3.00
		H	3.00	285	Exeter	A	4.00
262	Droitwich	A	5.00			B	15.00
		B	30.00			D	10.00
		F	35.00			E	3.00
		H	3.00			G	3.00
263	Dudley	A	5.00			H	3.00
		C	£150		Exeter Station	B	- see chapter 13
		D	10.00	286	Exmouth	A	4.00
		E	3.00			B	15.00
		G	15.00			H	40.00
		H	2.00	287	Eye	A	5.00
264	Dunchurch	A	£150			B	60.00
	Woolwich	B	75.00			G	15.00
		H	3.00			H	15.00
265	Dunmow	A	12.00	288	Fakenham	A	15.00
		B	20.00			D	70.00
		H	3.00			F	20.00
266	Dunstable	A	5.00			H	4.00
		H	4.00	289	Walsingham	A	£100
267	Durham	A	3.00		Coalbrookdale	B	40.00

138

Numeral, Spoon and Duplex Postmarks

		H	4.00		Gloster	F	2.00
290	Falmouth	A	6.00			G	1.00
		D	15.00			H	2.00
		F	4.00		Gloster Station	H	15.00
		H	3.00		Gloucester Station	H	25.00
291	Fareham	A	3.00	313	Lea	A	£250
		E	3.00		Mitcheldean	A	£100
		G	3.00		Cromford	H	40.00
		H	3.00	314	Painswick	A	90.00
	Faversham	A (error)	£175	315	Thornbury	A	8.00
292	Farnham	A	5.00			B	30.00
		B	25.00			H	3.00
		E	3.00	316	Godalming	A	5.00
		H	3.00			B	40.00
293	Faringdon	A	5.00			H	3.00
		B	40.00	317	Godstone	A	£100
		F	3.00		Chelford	H	2.00
		H	3.00	318	Bletchingley	A	£125
	Dudley	A (error)	£110		Llanfyrnach	B	30.00
294	Fairford	A	10.00	319	Goole	A	6.00
		H	3.00			E	3.00
295	Highworth	A	4.00			G	25.00
		H	3.00			H	3.00
296	Lechlade	A	5.00		Booth Ferry Rd/ Goole	H	50.00
		H	3.00		Old Goole/Goole	H	90.00
297	Fazeley	A	50.00	320	Gosport	A	3.00
298	Felton	A	40.00			B	15.00
		B	40.00			D	25.00
		H	20.00			E	8.00
299	Fenny Stratford	A	30.00			H	3.00
	Horsehay	B	20.00	321	Grantham	A	15.00
300	Ferrybridge	A	12.00			B	60.00
		H	3.00			D	15.00
301	Faversham	A	15.00			F	3.00
		H	3.00			H	3.00
302	Folkingham	A	25.00	322	Gravesend	A	5.00
		B	60.00			B	25.00
		F	4.00			D	25.00
		H	3.00			F	2.00
303	Folkestone	A	8.00			H	2.00
		B	60.00	323	Grimsby	A	30.00
		D	6.00			B	15.00
		F	3.00			E	12.00
		H	3.00			H	3.00
304	Fordingbridge	A	12.00	324	Guernsey	A	40.00
		B	25.00			B	75.00
		H	3.00			F	15.00
305	Fowey	A	8.00			H	20.00
		B	35.00	325	Guildford	A	10.00
306	Frome	A	5.00			B	80.00
		E	3.00			D	15.00
		G	3.00			F	3.00
		H	3.00			H	3.00
307	Gainsborough	A	15.00	326	Guisborough	A	5.00
		F	8.00			B	50.00
		H	4.00			H	6.00
308	Garstang	A	6.00	327	Greta Bridge	A	£125
		H	5.00		Shrewton	B	30.00
309	Gateshead	A	5.00	328	Hadleigh	A	40.00
		D	10.00		Edgware	H	3.00
		F	3.00	329	Halesworth	A	15.00
		H	3.00			B	20.00
310	Gerrards Cross	A	50.00			H	6.00
	Malpas	B	35.00	330	Halifax	A	3.00
	Malpas/Ches	H	30.00			B	40.00
	Malpas/ Cheshire	H	12.00			D	5.00
311	Glastonbury	A	5.00			E	3.00
		B	20.00			G	3.00
		H	3.00			H	3.00
312	Gloucester	A	3.00	331	Sowerby Bridge	A	25.00
		B	50.00	332	Todmorden	A	12.00
		C	30.00			E	15.00
		D	10.00			H	3.00
		H	3.00	333	Northowram	A	£150

139

Numeral, Spoon and Duplex Postmarks

334	Halstead		A	5.00			H	2.00
			B	40.00	356	Nettlebed	A	£125
			F	3.00		Charing	H	2.00
			H	3.00	357	Hereford	A	6.00
	Halstead/Essex		H	8.00			B	15.00
335	Haverhill		A	80.00			D	10.00
336	Harleston		A	5.00			F	3.00
			B	50.00			H	3.00
			D	£350	358	Eardisley	A	75.00
			H	4.00			B	£150
337	Harlow		A	15.00		Radstock	B	60.00
			B	20.00			H	3.00
			E	15.00	359	Hertford	A	4.00
			H	30.00			B	15.00
338	Harrogate		A	6.00			D	20.00
			B	8.00			F	3.00
			D	20.00			H	3.00
			F	3.00	360	Hexham	A	8.00
			H	3.00			B	60.00
339	Hartfordbridge		A	40.00			G	3.00
340	Harwich		A	15.00			H	3.00
			B	50.00	361	Heytesbury	A	12.00
			G	6.00			B	30.00
			H	8.00		Loughor	B	75.00
341	Haslemere		A	40.00	362	Deptford Inn	A	£125
342	Hastings		A	4.00		Brize Norton	B	£100
			B	15.00	363	Higham Ferrers	A	6.00
			D	6.00			B	15.00
			F	3.00	364	High Wycombe	A	5.00
			H	3.00			B	£100
	Hastings/Station Office		H	8.00			F	3.00
	High St/ Hastings		H	15.00			H	3.00
	White Rock/ Hastings		H	25.00	365	Hinckley	A	15.00
	Kings Rd/ St. Leonards-on- Sea		H	75.00			B	8.00
	St. Leonards-on-Sea/ Kings Rd B.O.		H	6.00			F	3.00
	St. Leonards on Sea/Marina		H	12.00			H	3.00
	St. Leonards-on- Sea/Station Office		H	6.00	366	Hindon	A	10.00
343	Hatfield/Herts		A	3.00			B	40.00
			B	50.00	367	Hitchin	A	5.00
			H	3.00			E	5.00
344	Havant		A	12.00			G	15.00
			D	60.00			H	3.00
			G	12.00	368	Pembroke Dock	A	10.00
			H	3.00			D	75.00
345	Haverfordwest		A	5.00			F	6.00
			B	30.00			H	6.00
			D	10.00	369	Hoddesdon	A	4.00
			F	3.00			H	5.00
			H	8.00	370	Holbeach	A	30.00
346	Hawes		A	25.00			B	25.00
			H	3.00			H	25.00
347	Hay		A	8.00	371	Holt	A	30.00
			B	15.00			B	50.00
348	Bruntless		A	75.00	372	Blakeney	A	£110
349	Glasbury		A	50.00	374	Holyhead	A	5.00
			B	30.00			B	60.00
350	Haydon Bridge		A	£100			H	4.00
351	Helston		A	6.00	375	Holywell	A	12.00
			B	50.00			B	50.00
			D	80.00			H	12.00
			G	6.00		Holywell/Flints	H	1.00
			H	25.00	376	Honiton	A	5.00
352	Hayle		A	6.00			B	40.00
			B	50.00			D	15.00
			G	50.00			G	4.00
			H	4.00			H	3.00
353	Hemel Hempstead		A	3.00	377	Ottery St. Mary	A	3.00
			B	15.00			B	12.00
			F	3.00			H	4.00
			H	2.00	378	Horncastle	A	5.00
354	Kings Langley		A	60.00			F	3.00
			H	3.00			H	4.00
355	Henley-on-Thames		A	5.00	379	Old Bolingbroke	A	£100
			B	30.00		Charlton	B	40.00

140

Numeral, Spoon and Duplex Postmarks

	Church Lane/ Charlton Kent	H	60.00
	Lower Rd/ Charlton Kent	H	40.00
	Old Charlton	H	50.00
380	Horndean	H	25.00
		A	12.00
381	Horsham	H	5.00
		A	6.00
		E	3.00
		G	3.00
		H	3.00
	Horsham/Station Office	H	10.00
382	Howden	A	10.00
		E	3.00
383	Hull	H	3.00
		A	3.00
		B	25.00
		C	20.00
		D	5.00
		E	3.00
		G	3.00
		H	3.00
		H (5 bars)	£350
	Hull S.T.– see chap 13		
384	Filey	A	10.00
		E	10.00
385	Hedon	A	15.00
	Shooters Hill	B	£110
386	Barrow-on-Humber	A	80.00
	Welling	B	£125
		H	3.00
387	Huddersfield	A	4.00
		B	50.00
		D	8.00
		F	3.00
		G	3.00
		H	3.00
388	Marsden	A	35.00
	Bexley Heath	B	80.00
		H	30.00
389	Slaithwaite	A	£125
	Bexley	B	90.00
390	Hungerford	A	8.00
		B	12.00
		F	15.00
		H	3.00
391	Aldbourne	A	£175
	Holt	B (error)	£125
392	Lambourne	A	60.00
		B	60.00
	Dudley	A (error)	£150
393	Ramsbury	A	6.00
		B	5.00
		H	40.00
394	Hounslow	A	4.00
		B	80.00
		F	40.00
		H	3.00
395	Southall	A	£125
		H	3.00
396	Huntingdon	A	25.00
		B	20.00
		D	60.00
		F	3.00
		H	3.00
397	Buckden	A	£100
	Crayford	B	£100
		H	4.00
398	Hythe/Kent	A	8.00
		H	3.00
399	Ilchester	A	5.00
		B	30.00
		H	15.00
400	Ilfracombe	A	15.00
		B	60.00

		H	4.00
401	Ilminster	A	8.00
		B	25.00
		H	8.00
402	Ingatestone	A	8.00
		B	60.00
		H	30.00
403	Rayleigh	A	90.00
	Erith	B	25.00
		H	4.00
404	Wickford	A	£125
	Belvedere	B	£100
		H	60.00
	Ironbridge (error)	H	£175
405	Ipswich	A	5.00
		B	60.00
		D	10.00
		E	3.00
		G	3.00
		H	3.00
406	Ironbridge	A	6.00
		B	50.00
		H	3.00
407	Isle of Man	A	40.00
		D	£200
	Douglas Isle of Man	F	30.00
	Douglas/Isle of Man	H	10.00
408	Ivybridge	A	5.00
		B	50.00
		F	4.00
		H	4.00
409	Jersey	A	25.00
		B	30.00
		E	25.00
		G	25.00
		H	25.00
410	Kelvedon	A	4.00
		B	30.00
		H	3.00
411	Kendal	A	5.00
		B	20.00
		D	6.00
		E	4.00
		G	4.00
		H	3.00
412	Bowness	A	15.00
	Lessness Heath	B	£125
		H	£110
	Picardy Belvedere	H	50.00
413	Keswick	A	6.00
		B	15.00
		G	5.00
		H	2.00
414	Kettering	A	5.00
		B	80.00
		H	3.00
415	Kidderminster	A	5.00
		B	60.00
		C	£200
		D	40.00
		F	3.00
		H	3.00
416	Kimbolton	A	15.00
		B	15.00
		H	3.00
417	Kineton	A	£100
	Hucknall Torkard	H	8.00
418	Kingsbridge	A	6.00
		B	40.00
		H	4.00
419	Kington	A	5.00
		B	40.00
		G	3.00
		H	3.00

141

Numeral, Spoon and Duplex Postmarks

420	Pen Y Bont		A	75.00			B	12.00
			B	90.00			C	50.00
421	Radnor		A	£100			D	6.00
	Long Eaton		H	3.00			E	3.00
422	Kingston		A	10.00		(double circle datestamp)	F	£275
			D	£110			G	3.00
	Kingston on Thames		F	3.00			H	3.00
			H	3.00		Chapeltown Rd. B.O./Leeds	H	6.00
	Norbiton/ Kingston on Thames		H	20.00		Hunslet B.O./ Leeds	H	6.00
423	Kirkby Lonsdale		A	8.00		Hyde Park B.O./ Leeds	H	6.00
	New Charlton		B	80.00		Hyde Park Corner B.O./ Leeds	H	4.00
			H	40.00		Market St. B.O./Leeds	H	£100
424	Knaresborough		A	3.00	448	Leek	A	8.00
			B	8.00			B	60.00
			H	2.00			E	8.00
425	Knutsford		A	5.00			H	3.00
			H	3.00	449	Leicester	A	6.00
426	Lamberhurst		A	£150			B	15.00
427	Hawkhurst		A	30.00			D	6.00
			H	3.00			F	3.00
428	Hurst Green		A	5.00			H	3.00
			D	6.00	450	Leighton Buzzard	A	10.00
			F	3.00			F	3.00
			H	3.00			H	3.00
429	Newenden		A	90.00	451	Lewes	A	5.00
	Broxbourne		B	£125			B	25.00
430	Northiam		A	£100			D	8.00
	Headcorn		H	3.00			E	3.00
431	Peasmarsh		A	£100			G	3.00
	Wye		H	3.00			H	3.00
432	Rolvenden		A	80.00		Lewes/Station Office	H	15.00
	Croesgoch		B	£125	452	Newhaven	A	£110
433	Sandhurst		A	80.00		Porthcawl	B	£100
	Maesteg		B	£100			H	8.00
			H	5.00	453	Seaford	A	£100
434	Lampeter		A	10.00		Llanfairfechan	H	3.00
			H	4.00	454	Leominster	A	8.00
435	Aberayron		A	£125			F	12.00
436	Lancaster		A	5.00			H	3.00
			B	60.00	455	Pembridge	A	30.00
			D	6.00			B	£100
			F	3.00			H	3.00
			H	3.00	456	Shobden	A	£125
437	Kirkby Stephen		A	20.00			B	£150
			H	4.00	457	Lichfield	A	15.00
438	Sedbergh		A	4.00			B	20.00
			H	4.00			F	3.00
	Sedbergh R.S.O.		H	25.00			H	3.00
439	Launceston		A	8.00	458	Lincoln	A	12.00
			B	50.00			B	20.00
			H	3.00			D	15.00
440	Holsworthy		A	12.00			E	3.00
			B	60.00			G	3.00
			H	2.00			H	3.00
441	Stratton		A	8.00		Lincoln Sorting Tender		£300
			B	6.00	459	Kirton Lindsey	A	30.00
442	Bude		A	30.00			F	20.00
443	Lawton		A	50.00			H	3.00
	Aberkenfig		B	80.00	460	Wragby	A	30.00
444	Leamington		A	4.00			E	20.00
			C	£125			G	60.00
			D	25.00			H	3.00
			F	3.00	461	Linton	A	90.00
			H	3.00		Upper Bangor	H	30.00
	Leamington Spa		H	4.00	462	Liphook	A	15.00
445	Leatherhead		A	15.00			H	3.00
			B	80.00	463	Liskeard	A	8.00
			H	3.00			B	60.00
	Ledbury		H (error)	25.00			H	4.00
446	Ledbury		A	3.00	464	Looe	A	25.00
			B	15.00		Hessle	H	4.00
			E	3.00	465	Polperro	A	50.00
			H	3.00		Llangennech	B	£150
447	Leeds		A	2.00	466	Liverpool	A	3.00

142

Numeral, Spoon and Duplex Postmarks

		A (roller)	£300
		B	15.00
		C	15.00
		C Reg	£300
		D (French)	£2500
		E	2.00
		G	3.00
		H	3.00
		H (5 bars)	3.00
	E.D./Liverpool	G	4.00
	Liverpool E	H	12.00
	N.D./Liverpool	G	4.00
	Liverpool N	H	12.00
	S.D./Liverpool	G	4.00
	Liverpool S	H	4.00
	W.D./Liverpool	B	£250
		G	2.00
		H	6.00
	Exchange Liverpool	H	8.00
	Bootle/Liverpool	H	15.00
	Bootle-cum-Linacre/ Liverpool	H	25.00
467	Llandilo	A	12.00
		H	3.00
468	Llandovery	A	12.00
		H	3.00
469	Llanelly	A	4.00
		F	3.00
		H	3.00
	Llanelly Dock	H	£100
	Llanelly Docks	H	75.00
470	Pontardulais	A	60.00
		H	8.00
471	Llangadock	A	30.00
		B	60.00
		H	3.00
472	Llangollen	A	3.00
		B	25.00
		H	3.00
473	Long Stratton	A	20.00
		H	15.00
474	Lostwithiel	A	3.00
		B	30.00
		H	4.00
475	Loughborough	A	10.00
		B	10.00
		F	6.00
		H	6.00
	Loughboro	H	6.00
476	Mountsorrel	A	£125
477	Louth	A	12.00
		E	3.00
		G	4.00
		H	3.00
478	Lowestoft	A	5.00
		B	20.00
		D	12.00
		F	3.00
		H	3.00
479	Ludlow	A	6.00
		B	80.00
		E	4.00
		G	4.00
		H	3.00
480	Knighton	A	8.00
		B	60.00
		H	3.00
481	Leintwardine	A	50.00
	Haslemere	H	3.00
482	Luton	A	15.00
		B	15.00
		E	8.00
		G	3.00
		H	3.00
483	Lutterworth	A	6.00

		B	40.00
		H	3.00
484	Lyme	A	8.00
		B	60.00
		G	8.00
		H	25.00
	Lyme Regis	H	2.00
485	Lymington	A	8.00
		F	8.00
		H	3.00
486	Yarmouth/Isle of Wight	A	30.00
		B	30.00
		H	15.00
	Yarmouth/I.of Wight	H	3.00
487	Lyndhurst	A	15.00
		B	10.00
		H	3.00
488	Lynn	A	5.00
		B	60.00
		D	50.00
		E	3.00
		G	3.00
		H	3.00
489	Burnham	A	£100
	Hildenborough	H	3.00
490	Holkham	A	£100
	Ham Street	H	25.00
491	Macclesfield	A	5.00
		F	3.00
		H	3.00
	Chestergate B.O./ Macclesfield	H	25.00
492	Maidenhead	A	10.00
		B	15.00
		D	40.00
		F	8.00
		H	3.00
493	Maidstone	A	5.00
		B	15.00
		D	8.00
		F	3.00
		H	3.00
	Maidstone/Station Office	H	30.00
494	Maldon	A	5.00
		B	8.00
		E	4.00
		G	2.00
		H	2.00
495	Malton	A	2.00
	NRYORK S	B	8.00
		E	2.00
		G	6.00
		H	2.00
	Norton/Malton	H	30.00
496	Sledmere	A	£110
	Kew	H	6.00
497	Malvern	A	5.00
		D	15.00
		E	4.00
		G	4.00
		H	4.00
498	Manchester	A	4.00
		A (roller)	£500
		B	6.00
		C	20.00
		D	6.00
		D (French)	£2000
		E	3.00
		F	3.00
		F (Beard)	£300
		G	3.00
		H	3.00
	Manchester/E	H	8.00
	Manchester/N	H	8.00
	Manchester/NW	H	4.00

143

Numeral, Spoon and Duplex Postmarks

	Manchester/S	H	4.00
	Manchester/S.D.O.	H	3.00
	Manchester/SE	H	4.00
	Manchester/SW	H	4.00
	Manchester/W	H	6.00
499	Glossop	A	30.00
		G	35.00
		H	15.00
500	Haslingden	A	£100
	Keymer	H	45.00
501	Rawtenstall	A	50.00
		H	50.00
502	Stalybridge	A	15.00
		H	4.00
503	Manningtree	A	5.00
		H	6.00
504	Mansfield	A	15.00
		F	3.00
		H	3.00
	Ipswich	H (error)	£200
505	March	A	5.00
		B	40.00
		G	15.00
		H	3.00
506	Margate	A	8.00
		D	10.00
		E	3.00
		G	3.00
		H	3.00
	Northumberland Rd/ Margate	H	80.00
507	Marazion	A	12.00
		B	30.00
		H	3.00
508	Market Deeping	A	50.00
		H	3.00
509	Market Drayton	A	5.00
		B	25.00
		H	3.00
510	Woore	A	£150
511	Market Harborough	A	5.00
		F	6.00
		H	3.00
	Market Harboro	H	10.00
512	Market Rasen	A	30.00
		F	30.00
		H	10.00
513	Market Street	A	£110
	Merstham	H	3.00
514	Market Weighton	A	10.00
		H	4.00
515	South Cave	A	20.00
	Whyteleafe	H	3.00
516	Marlborough	A	3.00
		B	15.00
		H	3.00
	Marlboro	F	3.00
517	Great Bedwin	A	30.00
518	Marlow	A	5.00
		B	80.00
		E	8.00
		H	6.00
519	Maryport	A	6.00
		H	3.00
520	Matlock Bath	A	5.00
		B	12.00
		F	3.00
		H	3.00
521	Melksham	A	4.00
		H	3.00
522	Melton Mowbray	A	4.00
		B	20.00
		F	10.00
		H	3.00
523	Merthyr Tydfil	A	6.00

		B	50.00
		D	15.00
		F	4.00
		H	3.00
524	Middlewich	A	8.00
		H	3.00
525	Holmes Chapel	A	75.00
		H	3.00
526	Winsford	A	£150
	Boston Spa	H	3.00
527	Midhurst	A	15.00
		B	40.00
		H	15.00
528	Mildenhall	A	£100
529	Milford	A	5.00
		G	12.00
	Milford Haven	H	3.00
530	Milnthorpe	A	3.00
		B	30.00
		H	6.00
531	Mold	A	10.00
		G	15.00
		H	2.00
	Morpeth	E (error)	75.00
532	Monmouth	A	5.00
		B	15.00
		F	3.00
		H	3.00
	Over Monnow/ Monmouth	H	60.00
533	Raglan	A	40.00
534	Moreton-in-Marsh	A	6.00
		B	60.00
		H	3.00
535	Stow on the Wold	A	5.00
		B	60.00
		H	3.00
536	Winchcombe	A	12.00
		H	3.00
537	Morpeth	A	30.00
		E	25.00
		G	12.00
		H	3.00
538	Nantwich	A	10.00
		F	6.00
		H	3.00
539	Narberth	A	5.00
		B	20.00
		H	3.00
540	Neath	A	4.00
		G	6.00
		H	3.00
541	Newark	A	4.00
		B	40.00
		D	12.00
		E	3.00
		G	3.00
		H	3.00
542	Southwell	A	25.00
		F	20.00
		H	3.00
543	Carlton-on-Trent	A	£110
	Liss	H	90.00
544	Newbury	A	8.00
		B	60.00
		D	15.00
		E	3.00
		G	3.00
		H	3.00
545	Newcastle on Tyne	A	3.00
		B	15.00
		D	5.00
		F	3.00
		H	3.00
		H (Scottish)	12.00

Numeral, Spoon and Duplex Postmarks

	Neville St/ Newcastle on Tyne	H	8.00
	Quayside/ Newcastle on Tyne	H	6.00
546	Newcastle-under- Lyme	A	5.00
		F	15.00
	Newcastle, Staff	F	8.00
		H	3.00
	Newcastle/Staff	H	3.00
547	Stoke on Trent	A	12.00
		B	30.00
		C	£400
		F	3.00
		H	3.00
548	Tunstall	A	30.00
		F	30.00
		H	3.00
	Tunstall/Staff	H	8.00
549	Hanley	A	20.00
		G	15.00
		H	3.00
	Hanley/Staff	H	3.00
	Hanley/Stoke on Trent	H	12.00
550	Cobridge	A	£125
	Kenley	B	40.00
		H	8.00
551	Burslem	A	30.00
		E	25.00
		H	3.00
552	Lane Delph	A	£100
	Sandgate	H	3.00
553	Longton Staff	A	8.00
		F	3.00
	Longton/Staff	H	6.00
554	Etruria	A	£110
555	Longport	A	£100
556	Shelton	A	£100
557	Newmarket	A	5.00
		B	60.00
		D	15.00
		F	8.00
		H	3.00
558	Newnham	A	8.00
		G	3.00
		H	6.00
	Newnham Glos	H	6.00
559	Lydney	A	12.00
		G	10.00
		H	3.00
560	Newport/I of Wight	A	10.00
		B	60.00
		F	20.00
		H	5.00
	Newport/I. W.	H	25.00
	Newport/ Isle of Wight	H	5.00
561	Newport/Mon	A	5.00
		B	15.00
		D	10.00
		F	3.00
		H	3.00
	Newport Mon.	F	3.00
		H	3.00
	Newport Docks	H	75.00
	Newport Docks/ Newport Mon	H	15.00
562	Caerleon	A	75.00
		B	60.00
563	Tredegar	A	15.00
		F	8.00
		H	3.00
564	Newport Pagnell	A	3.00
		H	3.00
565	Newport/Salop	A	12.00
		B	60.00
		H	3.00
566	New Romney	A	20.00
		H	3.00
567	Newton Abbot	A	3.00
		B	20.00
		D	10.00
		F	8.00
		H	3.00
568	Newtown Mont	A	8.00
		B	£100
		H	4.00
	Newtown/Mont	H	4.00
569	Northallerton	A	3.00
		F	6.00
		H	3.00
570	Northampton	A	4.00
		B	40.00
		C	75.00
		D	6.00
		F	3.00
		H	3.00
571	Northleach	A	12.00
		H	3.00
572	Andoversford	A	60.00
	Wighton	B	£100
573	North Shields	A	10.00
		B	20.00
		D	15.00
		F	4.00
		H	3.00
574	Northwich	A	15.00
		F	4.00
		H	3.00
575	Norwich	A	3.00
		B	60.00
		D	5.00
		E	3.00
		G	3.00
		H	3.00
576	Acle	A	£110
	Rolvenden	H	3.00
577	Cromer	A	20.00
		B	60.00
		H	25.00
578	Loddon	A	£125
	Appledore/Kent	H	20.00
579	North Walsham	A	20.00
		B	60.00
		H	3.00
580	Reepham	A	£110
	Lamberhurst	H	10.00
	Wednesbury	A (error)	£125
581	Scottow	A	£200
	Burnham (Som)	B	£100
582	Worstead	A	£150
583	Nottingham	A	4.00
		B	40.00
		D	5.00
		F	3.00
		H	3.00
584	Bingham	A	30.00
	Woodchurch/Kent	H	20.00
585	Ilkeston	A	30.00
		H	3.00
586	Stapleford	A	75.00
587	Oakham	A	15.00
		B	40.00
		E	3.00
		G	3.00
		H	3.00
588	Okehampton	A	3.00
		B	20.00
		H	3.00
589	Hatherleigh	A	£100
	Grasmere	B	12.00
		H	3.00
590	Odiham	A	30.00

145

Numeral, Spoon and Duplex Postmarks

	Billingshurst	H	10.00			H	3.00
591	Oldham	A	12.00	615	Fittleworth	A	£150
		B	20.00	616	Pulborough	A	20.00
		E	3.00			H	3.00
		G	3.00	617	Storrington	A	£125
		H	3.00	618	Pewsey	A	4.00
592	Ollerton	A	50.00			B	6.00
593	Ormskirk	A	10.00	619	Pickering	A	5.00
		B	25.00			H	3.00
		H	5.00	620	Plymouth	A	5.00
594	Southport	A	10.00			B	15.00
		B	25.00			C	30.00
		F	8.00			D	10.00
		H	3.00			F	3.00
595	Oswestry	A	6.00			H	2.00
		B	20.00		Stonehouse/ Plymouth	H	45.00
		C	80.00		Plymouth/H.M.S.	H	£500
		F	4.00		Devonport	D	£120
		H	2.00	621	Plympton	A	15.00
596	Cerrig-y-druidion	A	90.00			B	20.00
	Fittleworth	H	3.00			H	3.00
597	Llanrwst	A	10.00	622	Pocklington	A	10.00
		B	40.00	623	Pontefract	A	3.00
		H	3.00			B	20.00
599	Otley	A	4.00			H	3.00
		B	50.00	624	Poole	A	12.00
		E	3.00			B	25.00
		H	3.00			D	18.00
600	Addingham	A	75.00			E	15.00
601	Oundle	A	4.00			G	15.00
		B	12.00			H	3.00
		G	25.00	625	Portsmouth	A	4.00
		H	4.00			B	12.00
602	Ongar	A	4.00			D	6.00
		B	30.00			F	3.00
		H	20.00			H	1.00
603	Oxford	A	3.00		Portsmouth/ H.P.O.	H	30.00
		B	40.00		High St. BO/ Portsmouth	H	8.00
		D	10.00		Landport/ Portsmouth	H	6.00
		E	3.00		Portsea/ Portsmouth	H	3.00
		G	3.00	626	Prescot	A	8.00
		H	3.00			B	25.00
604	Pembroke	A	10.00			G	15.00
		H	3.00			H	3.00
605	Penkridge	A	5.00	627	Presteign	A	12.00
		B	60.00			B	60.00
		H	3.00			H	35.00
606	Penrith	A	4.00	628	Preston	A	5.00
		B	15.00			B	20.00
		D	15.00			D	6.00
		E	4.00			E	3.00
		G	4.00			G	3.00
		H	3.00			H	3.00
607	Alston	A	40.00	629	Fleetwood	A	30.00
608	Penryn	A	8.00			H	3.00
		G	50.00	630	Preston Brook	A	30.00
		H	3.00			B	60.00
609	Penzance	A	6.00			F	8.00
		B	25.00	631	Frodsham	A	£110
		H	3.00	632	Pwllheli	A	15.00
610	Scilly	A	£350			B	60.00
		B	£225			H	3.00
611	Pershore	A	3.00	633	Queenborough	A	60.00
		H	3.00	634	Ramsgate	A	5.00
612	Peterborough	A	15.00			B	80.00
		B	15.00			D	10.00
		D	15.00			F	3.00
		F	3.00			H	2.00
		H	3.00		Addington St/ Ramsgate	H	80.00
613	Petersfield	A	5.00	635	Reading	A	8.00
		F	3.00			B	8.00
		H	3.00			D	10.00
	Oxford	H (error)	20.00			D (biscuit)	£125
614	Petworth	A	5.00			E	3.00

146

Numeral, Spoon and Duplex Postmarks

		G	3.00			B	15.00
		H	3.00			D	40.00
636	Redruth	A	8.00			E	3.00
		B	50.00			G	3.00
		E	4.00			H	6.00
		G	40.00		Royston/Cam	H	15.00
		H	3.00	659	Rugby	A	3.00
637	Reigate	A	6.00			B	15.00
		B	40.00			C (shoe)	£225
		D	20.00			E	3.00
		E	3.00			G	3.00
		G	5.00			H	3.00
		H	3.00		Rugby Station	H	8.00
638	Retford	A	6.00	660	Rugeley	A	5.00
		B	40.00			E	8.00
		E	10.00			H	3.00
		G	3.00	661	Great Heywood	A	75.00
		H	25.00		Rotherfield	H	3.00
639	Rhayader	A	8.00	662	Shirleywich	A	£125
		B	60.00		Sowerby Bridge	B	12.00
		H	8.00			H	2.00
640	Devils Bridge	A	£125	663	Wolseley Bridge	A	80.00
641	Richmond Yorks	A	3.00		Feltham	H	3.00
		H	3.00	664	Rushyford	A	£150
	Richmond/Yorks	H	3.00	664	Ilkley	H	3.00
642	Ravenglass	A	50.00	665	Ruthin	A	4.00
643	Rickmansworth	A	20.00			B	25.00
		F	10.00			G	15.00
		H	3.00			H	3.00
644	Ringwood	A	15.00	666	Ryde, IOW	A	10.00
		B	25.00			B	40.00
		H	15.00			E	4.00
645	Ripley	A	60.00			G	4.00
646	Ripon	A	3.00			H	5.00
		B	50.00	667	Rye	A	5.00
		E	3.00			B	15.00
		H	3.00			H	3.00
647	Robertsbridge	A	40.00	668	Romford	A	4.00
648	Rochdale	A	5.00			B	60.00
		B	20.00			G	3.00
		D	10.00			H	3.00
		F	3.00	669	Saffron Walden	A	3.00
		H	3.00			B	40.00
649	Littleborough	A	£110			H	3.00
649	Snodland	B	30.00	670	St. Austell	A	5.00
		H	30.00			B	20.00
650	Rochester	A	5.00			H	4.00
		B	80.00	671	Grampound	A	8.00
		D	5.00			B	60.00
		F	3.00			H (5 bars)	£175
		H	3.00	672	St. Mawes	A	£110
	Rochester/Kent	H	3.00	673	Mevagissey	A	30.00
651	Rochford	A	3.00			B	60.00
		B	12.00	674	Tregoney	A	£100
652	Rockingham	A	30.00		Great Chesterford	B	£125
	Crymmych	B	£100	675	St. Albans	A	4.00
653	Romsey	A	12.00			B	12.00
		G	8.00			F	10.00
		H	3.00			H	3.00
654	Ross	A	5.00	676	St. Asaph	A	15.00
		B	12.00			H	3.00
		E	8.00	677	St. Clears	A	5.00
		G	30.00			B	40.00
		H	3.00			H	3.00
	Ross/Herefordshire	H	3.00	678	St. Columb	A	6.00
655	Rotherham	A	3.00			B	30.00
		D	10.00	679	St. Helens	A	3.00
		F	3.00			F	3.00
		H	3.00			H	3.00
656	Wath	A	25.00		St. Helens/Lanc	H	3.00
	Bingham/Notts	H	3.00	680	St. Ives Hunts.	A	8.00
657	Rougham	A	£100			B	15.00
		B	50.00			F	3.00
658	Royston	A	3.00		St. Ives/Hunts.	H	3.00

147

Numeral, Spoon and Duplex Postmarks

681	Somersham	A	£110			G	3.00
	Dukinfield	H	3.00			H	3.00
682	St. Leonards	A	3.00	701	Shepton Mallet	A	8.00
		F	2.00			F	3.00
		H	2.00			H	3.00
	St. Leonards-on-Sea	H	3.00	702	Sherborne	A	5.00
	St. Leonards on Sea/Hastings	H	3.00			B	20.00
	Borough Green/Kent	H	8.00			H	3.00
683	Salisbury	A	3.00	703	Queen Camel	A	50.00
		B	40.00		Hatherleigh	B	£150
		D	12.00	704	South Shields	A	8.00
		F	3.00			F	3.00
		H	3.00			H	3.00
684	Downton	A	6.00	705	Shifnal	A	6.00
		B	15.00			H	2.00
		H	10.00	706	Shipston on Stour	A	5.00
685	Wilton	A	8.00			B	25.00
		B	30.00			H	3.00
	Wilton/Wilts	H	3.00	707	Shoreham	A	5.00
686	St. Neots	A	5.00			B	25.00
		B	20.00			H	15.00
		E	3.00		Shoreham/Sussex	H	3.00
		G	25.00	708	Shrewsbury	A	5.00
		H	4.00			C	20.00
687	Sandbach	A	10.00			D	8.00
		H	3.00			F	3.00
688	Sandwich	A	8.00			H	3.00
		B	60.00	709	Church Stretton	A	8.00
		H	4.00			B	60.00
689	Sawbridgeworth	A	10.00			H	80.00
		B	25.00	710	Llanidloes	A	20.00
		H	3.00			H	4.00
690	Saxmundham	A	5.00	711	Wem	A	30.00
		B	25.00			H	3.00
		F	3.00	712	Sidmouth	A	5.00
		H	2.00			B	60.00
691	Aldeburgh	A	20.00			H	4.00
	Eglwyswrw	B	90.00	713	Sittingbourne	A	15.00
692	Yoxford	A	£125			B	20.00
	Velindre	B	£100			H	3.00
693	Scarborough	A	5.00	714	Skipton	A	3.00
		B	8.00			B	8.00
		D	8.00			E	3.00
		F	3.00			H	3.00
		H	3.00	715	Cross Hills	A	£225
	Scarborough	E	3.00			H	3.00
	South Cliff B.O./ Scarborough	H	12.00	716	Sleaford	A	5.00
694	Scole	A	15.00			F	3.00
		E	30.00			H	3.00
		H	3.00	717	Slough	A	5.00
695	Selby	A	4.00			B	80.00
		E	15.00			D	15.00
		G	6.00			E	3.00
		H	5.00			G	3.00
696	Settle	A	3.00			H	3.00
		B	8.00	718	Colnbrook	A	75.00
		H	3.00		Manorbier	B	£100
697	Sevenoaks	A	4.00	719	Solihull	A	20.00
		F	4.00	720	Somerton/Somerset	A	5.00
		H	3.00			B	25.00
	Eden Bridge	H (error)	£120			H	40.00
698	Shaftesbury	A	8.00	721	Langport	A	5.00
		B	25.00			B	40.00
		H	2.00			H	4.00
699	Sheerness	A	20.00	722	Southam	A	75.00
		B	60.00	723	Southampton	A	3.00
		D	£150			B	6.00
		F	4.00			D	6.00
		H	3.00			F	3.00
	Saffron Walden	H (error)	75.00			H	3.00
700	Sheffield	A	3.00			H (5 bars)	50.00
		B	50.00		Southampton H.P.O.	H	6.00
		D	8.00		Oxford St. B.O./ Southampton	H	60.00
		F	3.00	724	South Molton	A	5.00

Numeral, Spoon and Duplex Postmarks

			B	30.00	747	Thwaite	A	£125
			H	3.00		Nantyfflon	B	£175
725	South Petherton		A	8.00	748	Newton Heath	H	10.00
726	Martock		A	15.00	749	Stoney Stratford	A	5.00
727	Spalding		A	10.00			B	40.00
			B	15.00			F	3.00
			D	12.00			H	35.00
			F	20.00		Stony Stratford	H	3.00
			H	3.00	750	Stourbridge	A	5.00
728	Spilsby		A	5.00			D	12.00
			E	3.00			F	3.00
			G	8.00			H	3.00
			H	3.00		Stourbrigde	H (error)	£125
729	Spittal		A	£150	751	Stourport	A	5.00
730	Stafford		A	18.00			F	20.00
			B	£150			H	3.00
			D	8.00	752	Stowmarket	A	5.00
			F	3.00			B	60.00
			H	3:00			H	3.00
	Stafford Station		H	15.00	753	Needham Market	A	5.00
731	Stilton		A	£100			B	25.00
	Spelter Works		B	£250			H	3.00
732	Stockbridge		A	60.00	754	Stratford on Avon	A	5.00
	Stafford		C (error)	£500			F	3.00
	South Stockton		H	15.00			H	3.00
	Thornaby on Tees		H	4.00	755	Alcester	A	75.00
733	Stockport		A	4.00	756	Budleigh Salterton	A	8.00
			B	30.00			B	25.00
			D	30.00			H	6.00
			F	3.00	757	Stroud	A	5.00
			H	3.00			B	40.00
734	Whalley		B	60.00			D	25.00
			H	3.00			E	3.00
735	Hazelgrove		A	£100			G	10.00
	Trecastle		H	3.00			H	3.00
736	Stockton		A	5.00		Stroud Glos	F	10.00
			B	15.00			H	2.00
			F	3.00		Stroud/Glos	H	3.00
	Stockton on Tees		H	3.00	759	Uley	A	£100
	Cecil St./ Stockton on Tees		H	80.00	760	Sudbury	A	5.00
	Norton Rd./ Stockton on Tees		H	80.00			E	5.00
737	Castle Eden		A	6.00			G	4.00
	Broadstairs Station		B	£150			H	20.00
			H	40.00		Sudbury/Suffolk	H	20.00
	Broadstairs/ Station Office		H	20.00	761	Sunderland	A	3.00
	Broadstairs/ Station Office B.O.		H	12.00			B	25.00
738	Stokenchurch		A	40.00			D	10.00
	Byfield		B	25.00			F	3.00
			H	3.00			H	3.00
739	Stokesley		A	5.00	762	Swaffham	A	20.00
			H	3.00			B	20.00
740	Ingleby Cross		A	£150			F	20.00
	Crawley Down		B	50.00			H	3.00
741	Staines		A	10.00	763	Swansea	A	6.00
			B	15.00			B	50.00
			E	3.00			D	12.00
			G	3.00			E	4.00
			H	3.00			G	3.00
742	Stamford		A	5.00			H	3.00
			B	20.00		The Docks/ Swansea	H	15.00
			D	12.00		The Docks BO/ Swansea	H	15.00
			F	3.00		Swansea/ Mumbles	H	35.00
			H	3.00		Swansea/ Walters Rd	H	60.00
743	Stevenage		A	3.00		Walters Rd./ Swansea	H	75.00
			B	8.00	764	Brynmawr	A	20.00
			H	5.00			H	8.00
744	Steyning		A	15.00		Brynmawr/ Breconshire	H	3.00
			B	60.00	765	Reynoldstone	A	£150
			H	15.00		Partridge Green	B	75.00
745	Stone		A	8.00	766	Swindon	A	4.00
			G	8.00			B	80.00
	Stone/Staff		H	3.00			D	25.00
746	Stonham		A	25.00			E	3.00
			G	60.00			G	4.00

149

Numeral, Spoon and Duplex Postmarks

		H	3.00
	New Swindon/ Swindon	H	6.00
767	Cricklade	A	4.00
		H	3.00
768	Wootton Bassett	A	25.00
		B	30.00
		H	5.00
769	Wroughton	A	50.00
		H	4.00
770	Stanmore	A	30.00
		B	60.00
		H	3.00
771	Caerphilly	B	£100
772	Tadcaster	A	3.00
		B	6.00
		F	4.00
		H	4.00
773	Taibach	A	8.00
		G	30.00
		H	50.00
	Aberavon/ Port Talbot	H	75.00
774	Tamworth	A	15.00
		B	15.00
		F	3.00
		H	3.00
775	Tarporley	A	4.00
		H	2.00
776	Taunton	A	3.00
		B	25.00
		D	8.00
		E	3.00
		G	3.00
		H	3.00
777	Williton	A	5.00
		B	12.00
778	Dunster	A	25.00
		B	30.00
779	Minehead	A	8.00
		B	20.00
780	Tavistock	A	5.00
		D	35.00
		F	4.00
		H	2.00
	Stafford	A (error)	80.00
781	Callington	A	8.00
		B	8.00
782	Teignmouth	A	5.00
		B	30.00
		H	3.00
783	Tenbury	A	5.00
		G	8.00
		H	3.00
784	Tenby	A	5.00
		D	10.00
		G	12.00
		H	3.00
785	Tenterden	A	15.00
		H	3.00
786	Tetbury	A	30.00
		E	6.00
		G	8.00
		H	3.00
787	Tetsworth	A	12.00
		F	3.00
		H	3.00
788	Tewkesbury	A	5.00
		F	3.00
		H	3.00
789	Thame	A	6.00
		B	40.00
		E	5.00
		H	3.00
790	Thetford	A	8.00
		B	20.00

		D	£100
		F	3.00
		H	3.00
791	Harling	A	15.00
		B	25.00
		H	60.00
	East Harling	H	3.00
792	Larlingford	A	£125
	New Tredegar	B	£150
793	Shipdham	A	30.00
	Sandringham	B	£100
794	Watton	A	20.00
		B	50.00
	Watton/Norfolk	H	3.00
795	Thirsk	A	4.00
		G	10.00
		H	3.00
796	Osmotherley	A	75.00
797	Thorne	A	25.00
	Kibworth Harcourt	H	12.00
798	Thrapstone	A	4.00
		B	12.00
	Thrapston	H	5.00
799	Tipton	A	20.00
		E	20.00
		G	3.00
		H	3.00
800	Tiverton	A	5.00
		B	60.00
		D	60.00
		F	3.00
		H	3.00
801	Wimbledon	B	60.00
		H	8.00
	Wimbledon Camp	H	£300
	Tonyrefail	H	£100
802	Bampton	A	25.00
		B	50.00
803	Dulverton	A	8.00
		B	12.00
804	Topsham	A	40.00
		B	40.00
805	Torquay	A	3.00
		B	15.00
		D	8.00
		E	3.00
		G	3.00
		H	3.00
806	Torrington	A	8.00
		B	50.00
		H	3.00
807	Totnes	A	5.00
		B	35.00
		G	3.00
		H	2.00
808	Towcester	A	4.00
		B	15.00
		F	15.00
		H	3.00
809	Merton	H	20.00
	Eastgate	B	£125
810	Tring	A	3.00
		B	15.00
		E	3.00
		G	10.00
		H	2.00
811	Montford Bridge	B	£200
812	Princes Risborough	A	40.00
813	Trowbridge	A	4.00
		B	40.00
		F	3.00
		H	3.00
814	Truro	A	5.00
		B	25.00

150

Numeral, Spoon and Duplex Postmarks

			D	45.00	835	Waltham Cross	A	12.00
			E	4.00			H	3.00
			G	4.00	836	Wangford	A	5.00
			H	3.00			B	60.00
815	Camborne		A	6.00			F	8.00
			B	40.00			H	3.00
			H	3.00	837	Wrentham	A	90.00
816	Sunbury Common		H	3.00		Reeth	B	75.00
817	St. Ives/Cornwall		A	8.00	838	Southwold	A	15.00
			B	20.00			H	3.00
			H	2.00	839	Wansford	A	20.00
818	Tunbridge		A	15.00			F	3.00
			B	30.00			H	3.00
			F	3.00	840	Cannock	H	3.00
			H	3.00	841	Weldon	A	£110
	Tunbridge/Station Office		H	10.00		Hednesford	H	3.00
	Tonbridge		H	15.00	842	Ware	A	3.00
	Tonbridge/Station Office		H	10.00			B	15.00
819	Aspatria		H	4.00			E	3.00
820	Tunbridge Wells		A	5.00			G	3.00
			D	12.00			H	3.00
			F	3.00	843	Wareham	A	5.00
			H	3.00			B	40.00
	High St. B.O./ Tunbridge Wells		H	3.00			H	2.00
	High St./ Tunbridge Wells		H	3.00	844	Corfe Castle	A	15.00
	Calverley/ Tunbridge Wells		H	15.00			B	40.00
821	Tuxford		A	90.00	845	Swanage	A	20.00
	Ashford/Middx		B	80.00			B	40.00
			H	6.00			H	2.00
822	Uckfield		A	3.00	846	Warminster	A	3.00
			B	6.00			B	6.00
			H	2.00			E	40.00
823	Hailsham		A	15.00			H	2.00
			B	12.00	847	Warrington	A	5.00
			H	3.00			C	75.00
824	Ulverstone		A	5.00			D	15.00
			B	8.00			F	3.00
			F	3.00			H	3.00
			H	3.00	848	Warwick	A	8.00
	Wrexham		H (error)	£125			E	3.00
825	Uppingham		A	4.00			G	3.00
			H	3.00			H	3.00
826	Usk		A	8.00	849	Watford	A	3.00
			H	3.00			E	3.00
827	Uttoxeter		A	5.00			G	3.00
			B	25.00			H	3.00
			H	3.00	850	Wednesbury	A	8.00
828	Abbots Bromley		A	£100			B	20.00
	Lanchester		B	30.00			F	3.00
			H	3.00			H	3.00
829	Sudbury/Derby		A	30.00	851	Weedon	A	6.00
			H	3.00			B	15.00
	Crowborough		H	60.00			H	3.00
830	Uxbridge		A	5.00	852	Welshpool	A	2.00
			B	40.00			B	10.00
			D	12.00			H	1.00
			F	3.00	853	Machynlleth	A	10.00
			H	3.00			B	60.00
831	Wakefield		A	3.00			H	3.00
			B	20.00	854	Montgomery	A	20.00
			D	8.00			H	20.00
			F	3.00	855	Chirbury	A	£150
			H	3.00		Tylorstown	B	£175
832	Wallingford		A	8.00	856	Churchstoke	A	20.00
			B	60.00		Pumpsaint	B	£100
			H	3.00	857	Welford	A	8.00
833	Chingford		H	40.00		Silloth	B	60.00
	Cowshill		B	£125			H	4.00
834	Walsall		A	12.00	858	Wellingboro'	A	6.00
			B	80.00			B	40.00
			C	£250			F	15.00
			E	3.00			H	30.00
			G	3.00		Wellingborough	H	2.00
			H	3.00	859	Wellington/Salop	A	6.00

Numeral, Spoon and Duplex Postmarks

		B	50.00			H	3.00
		D	12.00	883	Wincanton	A	5.00
		F	4.00			B	12.00
		H	4.00			H	3.00
	Wellington Salop	H	3.00	884	Henstridge	A	40.00
860	Wellington Som.	A	4.00		Aberbeeg	B	£110
		B	12.00	885	Milborne Port	A	40.00
		D	10.00		Abertillery	B	75.00
	Wellington/Som.	H	3.00	886	Crumlin	B	60.00
862	Milverton	A	8.00	887	Stalbridge	A	80.00
		B	30.00		Cwmtillery	B	£150
853	Wells/Norfolk	A	30.00	888	Winchester	A	8.00
		B	80.00			D	8.00
		F	40.00			F	3.00
864	Wells, Somst	A	5.00			H	3.00
		B	15.00	889	Elland	B	40.00
		D	8.00			H	3.00
		H	6.00	890	Windsor	A	8.00
	Wells/Somt	H	3.00			B	20.00
	Wells/Som	H	3.00			D	10.00
865	Welwyn	A	6.00			E	3.00
		B	20.00			G	3.00
		H	3.00			H	3.00
867	Wendover	A	40.00	891	Godstone	H	5.00
868	West Bromwich	A	5.00	892	Chatteris	H	3.00
		F	50.00	893	Wingham	A	30.00
		H	3.00			H	50.00
869	Port Dinorwic	H	20.00	894	Winslow	A	20.00
870	Westbury/Wilts	A	4.00			E	15.00
		B	12.00			H	3.00
		H	3.00	895	Wirksworth	A	5.00
871	Weston-super-Mare	A	10.00			F	40.00
		B	25.00			H	20.00
		D	8.00	897	Wisbeach	A	5.00
		F	3.00			D	15.00
		H	3.00			F	3.00
872	Wetherby	A	10.00			H	3.00
		B	20.00		Wisbech	H	3.00
		H	15.00	898	Brightlingsea	B	£150
873	Weymouth	A	5.00	899	Hunstanton	B	75.00
		B	50.00	900	Witham	A	4.00
		D	12.00			B	20.00
		F	3.00		Witham/Essex	H	3.00
		H	3.00	901	Pangbourne	H	4.00
874	Wheatley	A	20.00	902	Witney	A	4.00
	Godstone Station	H	£100			B	50.00
	South Godstone	H	15.00			G	4.00
875	Whitby	A	3.00			H	2.00
		E	3.00	903	Wiveliscombe	A	5.00
		H	3.00			B	30.00
876	Whitchurch/Salop	A	15.00	904	Wokingham	A	4.00
		F	25.00			H	3.00
		H	4.00	905	Wolverhampton	A	5.00
	Whitchurch Salop	H	4.00			B	60.00
877	Whitehaven	A	6.00			C	60.00
		B	50.00			D	6.00
		F	4.00			F	3.00
		H	2.00			H	3.00
878	Wigan	A	5.00	906	Woburn	A	12.00
		D	15.00			E	15.00
		E	3.00			H	6.00
		G	3.00	907	Woodbridge	A	5.00
		H	3.00			D	35.00
879	Wigton	A	8.00			F	4.00
		B	60.00			H	3.00
		E	6.00	908	Wembley	B	£150
		H	2.00	909	Harrow Station	B	£250
880	Allonby	A	75.00	910	Woodstock	A	4.00
	Didsbury	H	20.00			H	3.00
881	Swindon Station	B	£150	911	Elmham	B	75.00
		H	10.00			H	3.00
882	Wimborne	A	6.00	912	Deddington	A	25.00
		B	30.00		Hebron	B	£100
		F	15.00	913	Woodyates	A	£400

152

Numeral, Spoon and Duplex Postmarks

No.	Place	Type	Price
	Crook Log/Bexley Heath	B	£100
		H	4.00
914	Cranborne	A	15.00
		B	40.00
		H	2.00
915	Wotton-under-Edge	A	6.00
		B	8.00
		H	3.00
917	Wickwar	A	£100
	Askam	B	75.00
		H	3.00
918	Worcester	A	3.00
		B	25.00
		C	25.00
		D	8.00
		F	3.00
		H	3.00
919	Llanfallteg	B	50.00
920	Upton-on-Severn	A	3.00
		H	3.00
921	Workington	A	8.00
		B	50.00
		F	20.00
		H	3.00
922	Worksop	A	15.00
		E	6.00
		G	25.00
		H	3.00
923	Worthing	A	4.00
		B	15.00
		F	3.00
		H	3.00
	Brighton Rd/ Worthing	H	£100
	Brunswick Rd/ Worthing	H	£100
	Chapel Rd. North/ Worthing	H	£100
	Montague St./ Worthing	H	60.00
	Worthing/Station Office	H	12.00
	Worthing Station B.O./Worthing	H	12.00
924	Wrexham	A	5.00
		B	60.00
		C	£150
		D	12.00
		E	3.00
		G	15.00
		H	3.00
925	Wymondham	A	10.00
		B	20.00
		F	25.00
		H	3.00
926	Yarm	A	4.00
		B	25.00
		G	25.00
		H	3.00
927	Yarmouth Nfk	A	5.00
		B	40.00
		D	12.00
	Yarmouth/Norfolk	F	3.00
		H	3.00
	Great Yarmouth	H	3.00
928	Yealmpton	A	20.00
	Crowborough Cross	H	30.00
929	Yeovil	A	5.00
		B	40.00
		G	8.00
		H	2.00
930	York	A	3.00
		B	20.00
		C	60.00
		D	6.00
		E	3.00
		G	3.00
		H	3.00
	Micklegate/York	H	15.00
	Strensall Camp/ York	H	10.00
931	Easingwold	A	6.00
		B	10.00
		H	3.00
		H (side bars)	£225
932	Escrick	A	50.00
	Barnetby	B	80.00
933	Hammerton	A	50.00
934	Helmsley	A	30.00
	Mundford	H	3.00
935	Kirby Moorside	A	50.00
	Castle Acre	B	£100
936	Whitwell	A	50.00
937	Barnet	A	20.00
		B	30.00
		G	3.00
		H	3.00
938	Croydon	A	15.00
		B	30.00
		D	60.00
		E	3.00
		G	3.00
		H	3.00
	Croydon/E	H	6.00
	Croydon/S	H	15.00
	Croydon/W	H	6.00
	New Thornton Heath/Croydon	H	10.00
	Thornton Heath	H	6.00
	Thornton Heath/ High St.	H	10.00
939	Staplehurst	A	20.00
		B	60.00
		D	30.00
		F	3.00
		H	2.00
940	Alne	A (side bars)	£500
	Litcham	B	£150
941	Burton Agnes	A (side bars)	£500
	Three Cocks	B	75.00
942	Sedgefield	A	50.00
943	Beaminster	A	5.00
		B	20.00
		H	2.00
944	Lynton	A	8.00
		B	40.00
945	Runcorn	A	30.00
		G	3.00
		H	32.00
946	Middlesborough	A	3.00
		B	15.00
		F	3.00
		H	15.00
	Middlesbrough	H	2.00
947	Hartlepool	A	3.00
		B	60.00
		F	3.00
		H	3.00
948	Bruton	A	8.00
		R	8.00
949	Castle Cary	A	5.00
		B	8.00
		H	3.00
950	Kenilworth	A	12.00
		F	35.00
		H	3.00
951	Pontypool	A	5.00
		B	60.00
		F	15.00
		H	3.00
952	Hollytroyds	A	£175
	Greenhithe	H	3.00
953	Blackpool	A	8.00
		B	60.00
		F	4.00
		H	3.00
	South Shore/ Blackpool	H	8.00

153

Numeral, Spoon and Duplex Postmarks

954	Longtown		A	50.00			H	3.00
			B	£100	984	Mere	A	25.00
			H	25.00			B	50.00
	Longtown/Cumbd.		H	6.00			H	4.00
955	Otterton		A	75.00	985	Aberdare	A	15.00
	Southborough		H	5.00			F	6.00
956	Hurstpierpoint		A	12.00			H	6.00
			F	3.00		Churston Ferrers	H (error)	50.00
			H	3.00	986	Treherbert	B	£100
957	Nuneaton		A	5.00			H	8.00
			B	25.00	987	Burbage	A	80.00
			F	35.00		Treorchy	B	£100
			H	2.00			H	8.00
958	Leigh/Lane.		A	£250	988	Ystrad Rhondda	B	£150
			H	30.00			H	25.00
	Leigh Lancashire		H	20.00	989	Tonypandy	B	£150
	Fence Houses		A	£150			H	12.00
959	Clifton		A	8.00	990	Collingbourne	A	£100
			D	20.00		Dinas	B	£200
			E	4.00	991	Cymmer	B	£200
	Long Sutton		H	20.00		Porth	B	£100
	Long Sutton/Line.		H	3.00			H	80.00
960	Crewe		A	15.00		Porth/Glam	H	4.00
			B	60.00	992	Tidworth	A	£100
			E	8.00		Pen-y-graig	B	£150
			H	2.00			H	£125
961	Sutton Bridge		H	3.00	993	Cholderton	A	£150
962	Middleham		A	12.00		Blaenllecha	B	£225
			H	3.00		Ferndale	H	6.00
963	Winchfield		A	15.00	994	Axbridge	A	40.00
			B	25.00		Trealaw	B	£225
			F	3.00	995	Brierley Hill	A	20.00
			H	3.00			B	60.00
964	Euston Square Station		A	£225			F	3.00
			B	£125			H	3.00
	Wearhead		B	50.00	996	Sturminster	A	40.00
965	Alderney		A	£500			B	50.00
966	Hadlow		H	10.00	997	Shillingstone	A	£125
967	Edenbridge		A	15.00	998	Charfield	H	3.00
			H	3.00	999	Paulton	B	10.00
	Edenbridge/Kent		H	3.00	001	Pensford	B	£100
968	Winchelsea		H	3.00	002	Ulceby	A	50.00
970	Lynmouth		A	30.00			B	60.00
971	Ventnor, IOW		A	10.00			E	60.00
			G	4.00			G	25.00
			H	3.00			H	5.00
972	Flint		A	15.00	003	Weobley	A	80.00
			G	15.00			B	40.00
			H	3.00	004	Redcar	A	6.00
973	Rhyl		A	10.00			E	4.00
			D	15.00			H	4.00
			G	3.00	005	Corsham	A	30.00
			H	3.00			B	40.00
974	Sedbergh		A	12.00			H	3.00
976	Windermere		A	15.00	006	Temple Cloud	B	60.00
			B	40.00	007	Brough	A	60.00
			F	4.00			E	4.00
			H	3.00		Brough/Yorkshire	H	4.00
977	Ferry Hill		A	20.00	008	Clutton	B	£110
			F	3.00	009	Farrington Gurney	B	£125
			H	3.00	010	Copplestone	A	30.00
978	Littlehampton		A	6.00	011	Hallatrow	B	£125
			B	60.00	012	Highampton	A	75.00
			H	3.00	013	North Tawton	A	20.00
979	Acklington		A	20.00			B	80.00
			F	35.00			H	20.00
			H	3.00	014	Witheridge	A	15.00
980	Rhymney		A	30.00			H	8.00
			B	80.00	015	Milford Junction	A	75.00
			G	60.00		South Milford	B	25.00
			H	4.00			H	3.00
982	Dowlais		A	30.00	016	Brockenhurst	B	£100
983	Soham		A	12.00			H	3.00
			B	40.00	017	Upper Clevedon	A	£100

154

Numeral, Spoon and Duplex Postmarks

	Rainham	B	£125
	Rainham/Kent	H	15.00
018	Egham	H	3.00
019	New Malden	H	3.00
020	Clevedon	A	8.00
		H	3.00
021	St. Just	A	50.00
		B	3.00
022	Ripley Yorks	A	25.00
		F	25.00
	Ripley/Yorks	H	3.00
023	Farnboro' Station	A	80.00
		B	£100
		D	£125
		F	10.00
		H	10.00
	Farnborough Station	H	20.00
	Farnborough/ Hants	H	4.00
024	Stonehouse	A	30.00
	Stonehouse Glos.	F	3.00
	Stonehouse/ Glos.	H	10.00
025	Bletchley Station	A	50.00
		B	£100
		H	25.00
026	Southend	A	7.00
		B	20.00
		H	6.00
	Southend/Essex	H	3.00
	Southend-on-Sea	H	3.00
027	Houghton le Spring	A	£100
028	Ramsey/Hunts	A	60.00
	St. Keyne	B	60.00
029	West Hartlepool	A	10.00
		B	15.00
		F	4.00
		H	3.00
030	Tremadoc	A	£100
		B	30.00
031	Portmadoc	A	15.00
		H	4.00
032	Festiniog	A	80.00
		B	25.00
		H	3.00
033	Tanybwlch	H	10.00
034	Smethwick	F	15.00
		H	6.00
	Oldbury	A (error)	£150
035	Oldbury	E	8.00
		H	25.00
	Smethwick	A (error)	£125
036	Ramsey/I. of Man	A	50.00
		H	25.00
037	Castletown/ Isle of Man	A	80.00
		B	£125
		H	8.00
038	Chathill	A	30.00
		F	25.00
		H	4.00
039	Willenhall	H	3.00
040	Whittlesea	A	60.00
	Duloe	B	60.00
041	Crowland		£100
	Kirkby Thore	B	£150
		H	£100
042	Sandplace	B	£100
043	Yatton Keynell	A	75.00
044	Lacock	A	£100
	Polperro	B	40.00
045	Sutton Benger	A	35.00
	Temple Sowerby	B	80.00
		H	£100
046	Aldershot Camp	A	50.00
		D	£100
		F	30.00

	Trawsfynydd	B	40.00
047	Crewe Station	A	75.00
		B	£150
		H	20.00
048	Normanton	D	15.00
		F	3.00
		H	3.00
	Normanton/ Station Office	H	20.00
	Normanton Station	H	8.00
049	Paddington Station	A	£200
049	St. John's Chapel	B	£100
050	Bampton/Oxon	A	8.00
		H	4.00
052	Shotley Bridge	A	£100
		B	60.00
		H	3.00
053	Heckmondwike	H	3.00
054	Farnworth	H	12.00
	Farnworth/Bolton	H	4.00
055	Beaford	A	20.00
		B	60.00
		H	6.00
056	Bow	A	90.00
		H	80.00
057	Brandis Corner	A	80.00
		B	45.00
058	Bridestowe	A	50.00
		B	50.00
059	Chulmleigh	A	5.00
		H	6.00
060	Newent	B	8.00
061	Eynsford	H	12.00
062	Dolton	A	60.00
		B	30.00
063	Exbourne	A	50.00
		B	£150
064	Lewdown	A	25.00
		B	£150
065	Lifton	A	25.00
		B	25.00
066	Capel Bangor	B	£100
067	Morchard Bishop	A	25.00
		B	40.00
		H	3.00
068	Ponterwydd	B	£175
069	Devils Bridge	B	£150
070	Sampford Courtenay	A	£100
		H	80.00
071	Wembworthy	A	20.00
		B	50.00
072	Winkleigh	A	15.00
		H	3.00
073	Waltham	A	£125
074	Probus	A	15.00
		B	50.00
		H	50.00
075	Newton in Cartmel	A	12.00
	Rhydyfelin	B	15.00
076	Knottingley	A	25.00
		B	40.00
		H	3.00
077	Aston on Clun	A	80.00
		H	3.00
078	Brampton Brian	A	15.00
		B	£125
079	Bromfield	A	20.00
		H	30.00
080	Clun	A	60.00
		H	3.00
081	Castletown	B	50.00
082	Leintwardine	A	40.00
		B	40.00
084	Lydbury North	A	60.00
		B	80.00

Numeral, Spoon and Duplex Postmarks

			H	3.00	B08	St. Mellion	A	20.00
085	Craven Arms		A	£100			B	60.00
			B	£110	B09	Washaway	A	£100
			H	3.00			B	£100
086	Fortuneswell/ Portland		B	60.00	B10	Perranarworthal	A	30.00
			H	3.00	B11	Devoran	A	50.00
087	Onibury		A	£100			B	£150
	Goginan		B	75.00	B12	Bickley Station/ Kent	B	£150
088	Sunninghill		H	12.00			H	80.00
089	Usk		B	60.00	B13	Kingsland	A	80.00
090	Wistanstow		A	£150			B	80.00
			B	£100	B14	Staunton-on-Arrow	A	40.00
091	Kirkby Lonsdale		B	£100	B15	Titley	A	60.00
			H	3.00	B16	Plymouth-Bristol TP	O	- see chap 13
092	Fence Houses		A	40.00	B17	Bronwydd Arms	B	£100
			F	3.00	B18	Mardy	B	£200
			H	3.00	B19	Wolverton	A	25.00
093	Harwell		A	80.00			B	50.00
	Crowthorne		B	£100	B20	Nailsea	A	£100
094	Steventon/Berks		A	15.00			B	£150
			B	60.00	B21	Yatton	A	80.00
			H	8.00	B22	Congresbury	A	25.00
095	Drayton		A	£150	B23	Wrington	A	40.00
096	Colwyn Bay		H	12.00	B24	Langford	A	25.00
097	Shiplake		A	£300	B25	Burrington	A	60.00
	Twyford		A	50.00	B26	Blagdon	A	60.00
			B	40.00			B	60.00
	Mitcheldean		H	3.00	B28	Moreton Hampstead	B	£150
099	Whitchurch/Hants		B	8.00	B29	Chagford	B	£100
			H	2.00	B30	Petersham	B	£150
A16	Newcastle Station		A	£250	B33	Grampound Road	A	40.00
			B	£300			B	50.00
A19	Appledore		A	50.00			H	50.00
			B	80.00	B34	London-Holyhead TP	O	see chap 13
A20	Wickham Market		A	20.00	B35	Shrivenham	A	5.00
			B	40.00			B	60.00
			F	4.00			H	3.00
			H	3.00	B36	Stratton St. Margaret	A	50.00
A21	Red Hill		A	30.00	B37	Longcot	A	30.00
			B	40.00	B38	Pinner	A	30.00
			E	3.00			B	40.00
			F	30.00			H	3.00
			H	10.00	B39	Harpton	A	80.00
	Red Hill/ Station Office		H	12.00		Herne Bay	B	£100
A22	Boxmoor		A	£150			H	8.00
			B	80.00	B40	Hundred House	A	£100
A23	Fremington		A	50.00	B41	Nantmel	A	£150
			B	50.00	B42	Walton (Radnor)	A	£150
A24	Instow		A	15.00		Whitstable	B	80.00
			B	30.00			H	3.00
A84	Brasted		H	4.00	B43	Washington Station	A	£150
A86	Upper Cwmtwrch		B	£150			H	40.00
A87	Forest Fach		B	£150	B44	Flax Bourton	A	40.00
A90	East Liss		H	3.00			B	40.00
A91	Southsea B.O./ Portsmouth		H	3.00	B45	West Town	A	£150
A92	Masham		H	3.00			B	£150
A93	Llanfarian		B	20.00	B46	Rhyddlan	A	£100
A94	Penarth		B	£100		Llandudno	B (error)	£150
			H	5.00	B47	Llandudno	A	30.00
A95	Newport (Yorks)		B	20.00			F	5.00
A96	North Cave		B	8.00			H	3.00
A97	South Cave		B	6.00	B48	Trefriw	A	60.00
A98	South Bank		H	4.00			H	4.00
A99	Chwilog		B	75.00	B49	Amlwch	A	60.00
			H	15.00			H	4.00
B03	Northfleet		B	£100	B50	Llangefni	A	50.00
			H	80.00			H	4.00
B04	Par Station		A	50.00	B51	Menai Bridge	A	20.00
			B	20.00			H	2.00
B05	Scorrier		A	20.00	B52	Hatch End	A	£100
			H	30.00			B	£125
B06	Hatt		A	75.00	B54	Cramlington	A	60.00
			B	15.00			F	25.00
B07	St. Issey		A	30.00			H	3.00

Numeral, Spoon and Duplex Postmarks

B55	Beal	A	10.00		B89	Shanklin, IOW	A	50.00
		B	40.00				B	40.00
		H	5.00		B90	Starcross	A	80.00
B57	Bagshot	B	50.00				B	80.00
		H	35.00		B91	Saltash	A	25.00
B58	Bucknell	A	80.00				B	15.00
		B	60.00		B92	Rainhill	A	40.00
B59	Shap	A	25.00				B	60.00
		H	12.00				H	40.00
	Shap/Westmoreland	H	6.00		B93	Lelant	A	£110
B60	Bournemouth	A	30.00				B	25.00
		B	20.00		B94	Saltburn-by-the-Sea	A	25.00
		H	3.00				H	3.00
	Bournemouth/S.O.	H	3.00		B95	Horrabridge	A	8.00
B61	Gowerton	H	8.00				B	30.00
B63	Blaydon-on-Tyne	A	25.00		B96	Roborough	A	40.00
		F	4.00				B	15.00
		H	3.00		B97	Skegness/Linc.	H	3.00
B66	Briton Ferry	A	35.00		B98	Princetown	A	50.00
		B	60.00				B	£100
		H	8.00		B99	Abermule	A	25.00
	Kibworth Harcourt	F	75.00		C01	Berriew	A	30.00
B67	Winsford	F	15.00				B	25.00
		H	6.00		C02	Borth	A	£100
	Winsford/Cheshire	H	5.00				H	6.00
B68	Lympstone	A	£100		C03	Bow Street	A	20.00
		B	40.00		C04	Caersws	A	20.00
B69	Paignton	A	8.00		C05	Carno	A	25.00
		B	40.00		C06	Cemmaes	A	40.00
		H	2.00		C07	Chirbury	A	40.00
B70	Dalton-in-Furness	A	40.00		C08	Churchstoke	A	£200
		H	3.00		C09	Cemmaes	A	45.00
B71	Barrow-in-Furness	A	40.00		C10	Garthmyl	A	25.00
		B	50.00		C11	Glandovey	A	60.00
		H	2.00				B	80.00
B72	Malvern Wells	F	15.00				H	30.00
		H	8.00		C12	Llanbrynmair	A	80.00
B73	Wylam	A	80.00				B	50.00
		H	3.00		C13	Llandinam	A	25.00
B74	Blyth	A	80.00		C14	Taliesin	A	£100
		H	20.00		C15	Pateley Bridge	H	8.00
	Blyth/Northumberland	H	3.00		C16	Chorley/Cheshire	H	50.00
B75	Bedlington	A	80.00			East Cowes	A	50.00
		B	£100		C17	Brighouse	F	15.00
		H	4.00				H	5.00
B76	Cowpen	A	80.00		C18	Bilton	A	50.00
	Emma Colliery	B	£175		C19	Holmfirth	H	5.00
B77	Cowpen Lane	A	50.00		C20	Great Haywood	B	£150
	Bebside	H	30.00		C21	St. Columb Minor	A	£100
B78	Nedderton	A	£100		C22	Newquay/Cornwall	A	75.00
B79	Boscastle	A	25.00				B	25.00
		B	10.00				H	5.00
					C23	Tywyn	A	£110

Note: Erratic use of B80-B84 in Totnes area, not in accordance with official regulations and lists.

B80	Blackawton (1890--1902)	A	£150		C24	Plymouth & Exeter/ N.M.T. - see chap 13		
	Harbertonford (1868-93)	A	£150		C25	Mostyn Quay	A	£125
B81	Blackawton (1863-66)	A	£150				H	8.00
B82	Harbertonford (1899-1905)	A	60.00		C26	Darwen	B	60.00
	Mounts (1877-80)	A	£150				G	8.00
B83	Harberton (1870-72)	A	£150				H	3.00
	Halwell (1870)	A	£150		C27	Cleckheaton	H	5.00
B84	Halwell (1869-92)	A	£150		C29	Jarrow	B	60.00
	Mounts (1867-99)	A	£150				G	25.00
B85	Malvern Link	B	50.00				H	4.00
		F	8.00		C31	Castleford	B	80.00
		H	6.00				H	3.00
B86	Matlock Bridge	A	30.00		C32	Aberdovey	A	60.00
		H	30.00				B	15.00
B87	Weybridge Station	A	75.00				H	3.00
		B	£150		C33	Towyn	A	40.00
		H	30.00				B	60.00
	Weybridge	H	8.00				H	3.00
B88	Sandown, IOW	A	75.00		C34	Pennal	A	£125
		B	15.00		C44	Fishguard	H	3.00
					C45	Mossley	G	45.00

157

Numeral, Spoon and Duplex Postmarks

Code	Location	Type	Price
		H	15.00
C46	Hoyland	B	£100
		G	50.00
	Everthorpe	B	£100
C47	Mirfield	H	3.00
C48	Chipping Sodbury	A	£200
		H	3.00
C49	Stretford	H	4.00
C50	Ashton on Mersey	H	50.00
	Sale	G	15.00
		H	2.00
C52	Godshill, IOW	A	30.00
		B	15.00
		H	3.00
C53	Rookley, IOW	A	£120
C54	Brading, IOW	A	75.00
		B	25.00
		H	10.00
C55	Wootton Bridge, IOW	A	75.00
C63	Heywood	H	25.00
C65	Heywood	G	40.00
		H	15.00
C66	Woking Station	B	50.00
		H	40.00
	Woking	B	15.00
		H	4.00
C67	Droylsden	H	25.00
C68	London & Dover TP	O	- see chap 13
C69	Newton-le- Willows	H	5.00
	Newton-le- Willows/Lanc	H	3.00
C70	Cosham	A	20.00
		B	60.00
		H	8.00
	Cosham/Hants	H	12.00
C71	Willington/ Durham	B	40.00
		H	3.00
C72	Cheetham Hill	H	80.00
C73	Eccles	G	50.00
		H	12.00
C74	Middleton	H	40.00
	Middleton/Lanc	H	60.00
C75	Newchurch	H	60.00
	Newchurch/ Manchester	H	40.00
C76	Prestwich	H	3.00
C77	Radcliffe	H	15.00
C78	Wilmslow	H	12.00
C79	Purley/Surrey	H	15.00
	Caterham Junction	B	£250
C80	Helperby	B	50.00
C84	Aberayron	H	5.00
C85	Enfield	B	80.00
		G	15.00
		H	3.00
C89	Dudley	B	60.00
	Dudley/ Northumberland	H	4.00
	Dudley/Northd	H	60.00
C90	Burgess Hill	B	40.00
		H	3.00
C91	Harrow	G	80.00
	West Malling	H	3.00
C92	Neyland	G	15.00
	Neyland Pem.	H	10.00
C93	Twickenham	H	3.00
C94	Teddington	B	£100
		H	5.00
C95	Hampton	G	35.00
		H	3.00
C96	Sunbury	G	20.00
		H	15.00
C97	Elstree	B	40.00
		H	3.00
C98	Newhaven	B	20.00
C99	Broughton-in- Furness	B	15.00
		H	5.00

Code	Location	Type	Price
D01	Holborn Hill	B	60.00
	Millom	B	15.00
		H	3.00
D02	Grange	B	60.00
		G	15.00
		H	35.00
	Grange over Sands	H	3.00
D03	Seaford	B	£100
D04	Dowlais	G	50.00
		H	8.00
D05	Chislehurst	H	3.00
	Chislehurst/ Station Office	H	50.00
	Lower Camden/ Chislehurst	H	6.00
D06	Erwood	B	20.00
D07	Llanuwchllyn	B	£150
	Yalding	H	3.00
D08	Llyswen	B	60.00
D09	Rhydymain	B	£150
D10	Gretna	B	£100
D11	Framlingham	B	40.00
		H	6.00
D12	Burgh/Linc.	H	60.00
	Burg	H	30.00
D13	Beckenham	B	60.00
		H	3.00
D15	Aldeburgh	B	50.00
		H	2.00
D16	Leiston	B	£150
		H	2.00
D18	Newbridge-on-Wye	B	60.00
		H	3.00
D19	Burnopfield/Co.of Durham	H	75.00
D19	Bowers Gifford	B	£125
D20	Black Hill /Co.of Durham	B	60.00
		H	8.00
D21	Richmond/Surrey	B	6.00
		H	3.00
D23	Sutton/Surrey	B	60.00
		H	3.00
D24	Mitcham	B	60.00
		G	15.00
		H	8.00
D25	Llandyssil	H	6.00
	Llandyssil/Sorting Tender- see chap 13		
D31	Carn Brea	B	80.00
		H	8.00
D32	Llanfihangel-ar- Arth	B	£100
D33	Newport (Essex)	B	£100
D34	Waterfoot	H	30.00
D35	Talybont	B	£100
D36	Hopkinstown	B	£200
D37	Coggeshall	H	4.00
D38	Earls Colne	H	4.00
D39	Bourton-on- the-Water	H	3.00
D41	Padiham	B	40.00
		H	4.00
D42	Blaenllecha	B	£200
D43	Llanarth	B	60.00
D44	Potters Bar	H	3.00
D46	Cockfield	B	40.00
D49	Treharris	B	20.00
D50	Wroxall, IOW	B	£150
D51	Peel/IOM	B	£125
		H	20.00
D52	Figure Four	B	£100
D53	Llanilar	B	30.00
D54	Crosswood	B	£200
D55	Clydach Vale	B	60.00
D56	Olney	B	60.00
D57	Bute Docks	B	10.00
		H	15.00
	Bute Docks/ Cardiff	H	12.00
	Bute Docks B.O./ Cardiff	H	12.00
D58	Harrington Cumbd	B	60.00

Numeral, Spoon and Duplex Postmarks

		H	3.00	E17	New Inn	B	£100
D59	Marske-by-the-Sea	B	12.00	E18	Llanbyther	B	60.00
		H	3.00			H	3.00
D60	Valley	B	£150	E19	Llanwnen	B	£150
		H	4.00	E20	Talsarn	B	£100
	The Valley	H	50.00	E21	Ciliau Aeron	B	75.00
D61	Barrasford	H	£150	E22	Aberarth	B	60.00
D62	Southwick/Sussex	H	£100	E23	Llanon	B	£100
D63	Nawton	B	50.00	E24	Llanrhystyd	B	£100
D64	Kirby Moorside	B	80.00	E25	Brimfield	B	30.00
		H	4.00			H	6.00
	Kirkby Moorside	H	25.00	E27	Llechryd	B	15.00
D65	Helmsley	B	15.00	E29	South Benfleet	B	20.00
	Yoxford	H (error)	6.00	E31	Little Haywood	B	£150
D66	Gillingham/ Dorset	B	40.00	E32	Pontlottyn	B	£200
		H	6.00	E33	New Barnet	H	3.00
D69	Wingate	B	£100	E34	Landore	B	80.00
D70	Castle Eden Station	B	75.00			H	12.00
		H	50.00	E35	Morriston	B	40.00
D71	Wingate	H	6.00			H	8.00
	Castle Eden Colliery	B	£125	E36	Clydach	B	£150
D72	Coxhoe	B	40.00	E37	Pontardawe	B	£200
		H	5.00	E38	Ystalyfera	B	75.00
D73	Trimdon Grange	B	40.00			H	35.00
		H	8.00	E39	Ystradgynlais	B	60.00
D75	Harrow	B	£100			H	2.00
		G	20.00		Ystradgnlais	H	40.00
		H	1.00	E40	Abergwilly	B	40.00
D76	Buckhurst Hill	B	8.00	E41	Llanarthney	B	60.00
		H	3.00	E42	Nantgaredig	B	90.00
D77	Loughton	B	30.00	E43	Manordilo	B	60.00
		H	10.00	E44	Golden Grove	B	60.00
D78	Brancepeth	B	50.00	E46	Sketty	B	£150
D79	Sandy	B	60.00	E48	Penclawdd	B	£200
	Twyford	B	60.00	E49	Reynoldstone	B	30.00
D80	Potton	B	60.00	E51	Greenhill	B	£200
		H	6.00	E52	Henfield	B	40.00
D81	Bures	B	£150			H	4.00
D82	Llwyngwril	B	25.00	E54	Cross Inn	H	40.00
D83	Blaina	G	15.00		Ammanford	H	15.00
D84	Beaufort	H	40.00	E55	Cwmamman	H	60.00
D85	Ebbw Vale	B	80.00		Garnant	B	£100
		H	3.00	E56	Llandebie	B	£100
D86	Nantyglo	H	6.00		Treforest	B	80.00
D88	Linton	G	40.00			H	15.00
D89	Haverhill	H	40.00	E57	Haughley	B	£150
D90	Long Melford	H	15.00	E59	Llanpumpsaint	B	60.00
D91	Lavenham	H	20.00	E60	Llangunllo	B	£100
D92	Clare	G	30.00	E61	Dolau	B	40.00
		H	3.00	E62	Llandrindod	B	40.00
D93	Shefford	B	60.00			H	8.00
		H	3.00		Llandrindod Wells	H	3.00
D94	Woodford Bridge	B	80.00	E63	Llangammarch	B	5.00
	Penarth Docks/ Penarth	H (error)	£250	E64	Beulah	B	£100
D96	West Drayton	B	35.00	E65	Llanwrtyd	B	15.00
D97	Carshalton	B	40.00			H	3.00
		H	3.00	E66	Hovingham	B	£100
D98	Pentre	B	60.00	E67	Slingsby	B	50.00
		H	8.00	E68	New Quay/Car.	H	25.00
E01	Brimscombe	B	£100		New Quay/ Cardiganshire	H	8.00
E03	Letterstone	H	8.00	E69	Winforton	B	60.00
	Letterston	H	4.00	E70	Whitney	B	£100
E04	Dinas Cross	H	4.00	E71	Clifford	B	60.00
E05	Solva	G	12.00	E72	Talgarth	B	25.00
E07	Newport/Pem.	H	20.00			H	3.00
E08	St. Davids	H	8.00	E73	Carnforth	H	4.00
E09	Tangiers	B	£150	E74	Penmaenmawr	B	60.00
E10	Treffgarne	B	60.00			H	4.00
		H	60.00	E75	Leamside B	B	£100
E11	Wolfcastle	B	60.00			H	15.00
E12	Dwrbach	B	12.00	E76	Didcot	B	60.00
E13	Camrose	B	60.00	E77	Ferryside	B	40.00
E14	Roch	B	60.00			H	15.00
E15	Penycwm	B	30.00	E78	Chigwell Rd	H	4.00

Numeral, Spoon and Duplex Postmarks

	Chigwell Road	H	15.00		F32	Bettwys-y-Coed	H	12.00
E79	Burwash	B	60.00			Bettwsycoed	H	3.00
E80	Mortimer	B	15.00			Bettws Bledrws	B	35.00
E81	Etchingham	B	60.00			Derry Ormond	B	35.00
		H	40.00		F33	Ystrad Meurig	B	20.00
E82	Norham	B	80.00		F34	Llanddewi Brefi	B	£150
		H	5.00		F35	Tregaron	B	60.00
E83	Caterham Valley	B	80.00				H	4.00
		H	5.00		F36	Surbiton	H	6.00
E84	Garth	B	£110			Surbiton/ Kingston-on-Thames	H	6.00
E85	Begelly	B	40.00		F37	St. Leonards/ Gensing Station Rd.	H	15.00
E86	Saunderfoot	B	60.00			Gensing Station Rd./ Hastings	H	15.00
		H	3.00		F38	Stanford-le-Hope	B	35.00
E87	Crook/Co. Durham	H	4.00		F39	Leigh	B	£100
E89	Tyne Docks	H	40.00		F40	Grays	H	4.00
	Tyne Docks/ South Shields	H	15.00		F41	Purfleet/Essex	B	50.00
E90	Pencader	B	60.00				H	4.00
E91	Conwyl Elfed	B	£100		F42	Rainham	B	£150
E92	Burry Port	B	60.00		F43	Hyde	H	3.00
		H	20.00		F44	Denton	H	60.00
E93	Horley	B	£150			Denton/Lanc.	H	25.00
		H	£100		F45	Patricroft	H	15.00
E94	Gloucester Station	H	25.00		F46	Shorncliffe Camp	H	15.00
E95	Brentford	B	80.00		F47	St. Mellons	B	£150
		H	5.00		F48	Criccieth	B	40.00
E96	Pontrilas	B	80.00		F49	Dyffryn	B	25.00
E97	Isleworth	H	8.00				H	3.00
E98	Aberavon	B	30.00		F50	Groeslon	H	20.00
E99	Cwm Avon	B	£100		F51	Harlech	H	3.00
		H	15.00		F52	Llanbedr	H	20.00
F01	Haywards Heath	H	3.00		F53	Penygroes	H	15.00
	Cuckfield	H	4.00		F54	Penrhyn Deudraeth	H	10.00
F02	Bethania	B	£100		F55	Talysarn	H	12.00
F03	Bagillt	B	£150		F56	Alderley Edge	H	3.00
F04	Four Crosses	H	20.00		F57	Leyburn	B	75.00
	Blaenau Festiniog	H	2.00				H	3.00
F05	Rhiwbryfdir	B	80.00		F58	Ponders End	H	3.00
F06	Tanygrissiau	B	80.00		F59	Talysarnau	B	40.00
F07	Ilford	B	60.00		F60	Llangranog	B	90.00
		G	25.00		F61	Blaenyffos	B	£100
		H	35.00		F62	Kilgerran	B	6.00
F08	Barking	G	40.00		F63	Boncath	B	75.00
		H	4.00				H	8.00
F09	Holm Rook	B	60.00		F64	Llanymynech	B	£100
		H	30.00				H	10.00
F10	Chadwell	B	£150		F65	Llanfyllin	B	£100
		H	40.00				H	8.00
F11	Ramsbottom	H	30.00		F66	Sutton Benger	B	40.00
F12	Batley	G	15.00		F67	Little Haven	B	60.00
		H	4.00		F68	Rhydlewis	B	75.00
F13	Wotton	B	£100		F73	Slades Bridge	B	£100
F14	Askrigg	B	6.00		F74	Walton on the Naze	B	40.00
F15	Parkend	B	80.00		F77	Lintz Green Station	H	£150
F16	Falfield	B	40.00			Lintz Green	H	5.00
		H	3.00		F78	Tebay	B	40.00
F17	Alveston	B	80.00				H	8.00
F18	Rudgeway	B	40.00		F79	Sandy	B	80.00
F19	Almondsbury/Glos.	B	75.00				H	4.00
		H	8.00		F82	Warcop	B	£150
F20	Woodford Green	H	10.00				H	£150
F21	Ermington	B	£150		F89	Six Mile Bottom	H	5.00
F22	Whitecroft	B	40.00		F90	Sharpness Point	H	40.00
F24	Whitland	B	60.00		F92	Llantrissant	H	15.00
		H	5.00		F93	Paddock Wood	B	40.00
	Whitland R.S.O.	H	£100				H	3.00
F25	Llanfair Pwllgwyngyll	B	£100		F94	Ripley, Derby	H	3.00
		H	6.00		G01	London & Exeter T.P.O.- see chap 13		
F26	Gaerwen	B	£150		G02	Walton-on-Thames	B	60.00
F27	Llanerchymedd	B	60.00				H	3.00
		H	4.00		G04	Rothbury	H	4.00
F28	Rhosybol	B	40.00		G05	Widnes	H	4.00
F30	Charlbury	B	£100		C07	Bacup	H	6.00
		H	3.00		G08	Highbridge	B	60.00
F31	Maesycrugiau	B	60.00		G09	Stonehouse/Devon	B	£100

160

Numeral, Spoon and Duplex Postmarks

		H	90.00			H	3.00
	St. Mary Cray	H	5.00	G91	Wainfleet/Linc	H	30.00
G11	Llanio Road	B	40.00	G92	Portfield Gate	B	£150
G20	Much Marcle	B	£150	G93	Orpington	H	8.00
G21	Narberth Road	B	75.00	G94	Ebchester	B	£100
G22	Eltham	B	90.00			H	3.00
		H	6.00	G95	Swalwell	H	4.00
G23	Cleator	H	3.00	G96	Wickham	H	30.00
G24	Cark-in-Cartmel	H	6.00	G97	Sarnau	B	75.00
G25	Egremont	H	25.00	G98	Cross Inn	B	8.00
	Egremont/Cumbd	H	6.00	G99	Ffostrassol	B	£100
G26	St. Bees	H	6.00	H01	Cenarth	B	80.00
G27	Cleator Moor	H	6.00	H02	Maesllyn	B	40.00
G28	Garn Dolbenmaen	B	60.00	H03	Tunstall	B	£150
G29	Eastwood/Notts	H	6.00	H04	Orford	B	25.00
G30	Stantonbury	B	£125	H05	Dymock	B	£100
G31	Castle Donnington	H	£100	H06	School Green/ Isle of Wight	H	80.00
G32	Duffield	H	3.00		Freshwater Station/ I. of Wight	H	10.00
G33	Kegworth	H	4.00	H07	Ynysmudw	B	£150
G35	Lesbury	H	8.00	H08	Stanley/Co.Durham	H	4.00
G37	Grosmont/Yorks	H	75.00	H10	Tram Inn	H	25.00
G38	St. Peters/Kent	H	80.00	H11	Birchgrove	B	£200
G39	Rhoshill	B	£125	H14	Llanbadarn Fawr	B	15.00
G40	Rhostryfan	H	20.00	H16	Brotton	H	6.00
G41	Fishponds	B	£150	H17	Carlin How	B	20.00
G42	Gorseinon	H	8.00	H18	Easington	B	20.00
G43	Blaenavon	H	6.00	H19	Staithes	H	3.00
G44	Cookham	B	£100	H20	Loftus	H	3.00
G45	Bourne End	B	£100	H21	Longfield/Kent	H	80.00
G46	Wooburn	B	75.00	H22	Seaton	H	3.00
G47	Birchington	H	3.00	H23	Hassocks/Sussex	H	4.00
G48	Westgate-on-Sea	H	3.00	H25	Wheatley	B	£125
G50	Dolwyddelan	B	8.00	H26	Hinderwell	H	3.00
G51	Morecambe	B	25.00	H27	Pensarn	B	80.00
		H	3.00	H28	Abinger Hammer	H	3.00
G52	Beckermet	B	75.00	H29	Bures	H	4.00
		H	6.00	H30	Pocklington	H	3.00
G53	Frizington	B	30.00	H33	Llandderfel	B	60.00
		H	6.00	H34	Waterlooville	H	3.00
G54	Tilbury/Essex	H	4.00	H35	Mersham	H	£100
	Tilbury Docks/ Essex	H	50.00	H36	Lydd	H	12.00
G55	Gorleston	B	£125	H37	Horley Station/ Surrey	H	70.00
G57	Hollinwood	H	6.00		Horley Station Rd	H	40.00
G60	Hersham Road	H	3.00	H38	Shoeburyness	B	60.00
G61	Cottingham	H	75.00			H	4.00
G62	Haltwhistle	H	3.00	H41	Willesborough	H	10.00
G63	Snettisham	B	20.00	H43	Coalville	H	4.00
G64	Burnham Market	B	15.00	H44	Whitefield	H	40.00
G65	Bankyfelin	B	90.00		Whitefield/Lanc.	H	4.00
G67	Clarbeston Road	H	20.00	H45	Connah's Quay	B	60.00
G68	Marden/Kent	H	3.00			H	4.00
G69	Roche/Cornwall	H	25.00	H46	Carlton Iron Works	H	12.00
G70	Skelton-in- Cleveland	B	£100	H47	Sedgefield	H	4.00
		H	4.00	H48	West Cornforth	H	4.00
	Skelton R.S.O.	H	75.00	H49	Wingate Station	H	35.00
G71	Cleobury Mortimer	H	4.00	H50	Sidcup	H	8.00
G72	Angmering	H	20.00	H51	Heathfield	H	60.00
G73	Angmering Station	H	75.00	H52	Church	H	10.00
G74	New Hampton	H	60.00		Church/Lanc	H	60.00
	Hampton Hill	H	4.00	H53	Nelson-in-Marsden	B	60.00
G75	Ascot	H	8.00			H	50.00
G76	Shillingstone	H	4.00		Nelson	H	3.00
G77	Heytesbury	B	£125	H54	Heathfield Station	H	£100
G78	Upper Edmonton S.O.	H	80.00	H55	Ingleton	H	25.00
G79	Stalbridge	B	£150	H56	Greenfield	B	80.00
G80	Lower Edmonton	H	80.00	H57	St.Dogmaels	H	6.00
	Parton	B	£100	H58	Northiam	H	4.00
G82	Ceinws	B	75.00	H59	Wittersham	H	6.00
G84	Cranbrook	H	3.00	H60	Brandon Colliery	H	40.00
G87	Cemmaes Road	B	75.00	H62	Snaith	H	3.00
G88	Lytham	H	3.00	H64	Seaham Harbour	H	8.00
G89	Corris	H	4.00	H65	Velindre	B	90.00
	Pantperthog	B	40.00	H66	Greatham	H	30.00
G90	Tow Law	B	80.00	H67	Seaton Carew	H	3.00

161

Numeral, Spoon and Duplex Postmarks

H68	Purton	H	6.00
H69	Stratton St.Margaret	H	6.00
	Stratton St.Margarets	H	8.00
H70	Bramley/Yorks	H	3.00
H71	Harrow Weald	B	75.00
		H	8.00
H72	Llandebie	B	£110
H73	Wealdstone	B	75.00
		H	15.00
H74	Parkstone	H	3.00
H75	Hotham	B	6.00
H76	North Newbald	B	8.00
H80	Nunthorpe	B	75.00
H81	Reedness	B	£125
H84	Sancton	B	50.00
H85	Langwathby	H	8.00
H86	Kirkoswald, Cumb.	H	6.00
H87	Lazonby	H	8.00
H88	Dedham	B	£150
H89	Llanfaelog	B	£150
H91	Rhosgoch	B	£150
H92	Baildon	H	8.00
H93	Saltaire	H	15.00
H94	Llanfihangel	B	£150
H95	Hylton	B	20.00
H96	Talysarn	B	60.00
H97	Chelsfield	H	4.00
H98	Glanamman	H	20.00
H99	Thames Ditton	H	3.00
J01	Englefield Green	H	4.00
J02	Butterknowle	B	30.00
J03	Trefnant	B	40.00
		H	12.00
J04	Rhyddlan	H	£110
J06	Upper Brynamman	H	50.00
J07	Oxted	H	40.00
J08	Limpsfield	H	4.00
J09	Wellington College Station	B	£225
J10	Langley Park	B	30.00
J11	Armley	H	8.00
J12	Birstall	H	6.00
J13	Morley	H	25.00
	Morley/Yorks	H	4.00
J14	Pudsey	H	4.00
J15	Jackfield	H	4.00
J16	Farnborough/Kent	H	15.00
J17	Great Harwood	H	4.00
J18	Brierfield	H	4.00
J19	Stoke-under-Ham	H	8.00
J20	Hinstock	B	£150
J21	Tycroes	B	£175
J22	Westerham	H	4.00
J24	Greenstreet/Kent	H	40.00
J25	Addlestone/Surrey	H	4.00
J27	Bissoe	B	75.00
J28	Stamford Bridge	B	£125
J29	Llandrillo	B	75.00
J31	Bethersden	H	15.00
J32	East Molesey	H	4.00
J33	Willingdon	H	4.00
J34	Cranleigh	H	4.00
J35	Burnopfield	H	4.00
J36	Takeley	B	£125
J37	Bramley/Surrey	H	4.00
J38	Llanuwchllyn	B	60.00
J39	East Cowton	H	6.00
J40	Great Ayton	H	4.00
J41	Great Smeaton	H	75.00
J42	Newby Wiske	H	90.00
J43	South Otterington	H	8.00
J44	Thornton-le-Moor	H	4.00
J45	Newtown/ Southborough	H	20.00
J46	Virginia Water	H	4.00
J48	Wickford	B	£175

J49	Ripley/Surrey	H	40.00
J50	Ewell/Surrey	H	15.00
J51	West Tanfield	B	12.00
J52	Broadstone	H	5.00
J53	Llangwyllog	B	90.00
J54	Carnforth & Whitehaven TP	O	- see chap 13
J55	Wrafton	B	£125
J56	Braunton	B	£100
J57	Morthoe	B	£150
J58	Abersychan	B	80.00
J59	Wallsend	H	3.00
J60	Bodorgan	B	£150
		H	6.00
J61	Whitley	H	8.00
J62	Bisley Camp/ Woking	H	10.00
J63	Wallington	H	20.00
	Upper Wallington	H	40.00
J64	Sudbury	B	£125
J65	Camberley	B	40.00
		H	3.00
J66	Ramsey/Hunts	H	3.00
J67	Chapel-en-le- Frith	B	75.00
J68	Wool	H	5.00
J69	Boscombe	B	£125
J70	Shepperton	H	3.00
J71	Hockley	B	90.00
J72	Cambo	H	4.00
J73	Eastleigh	H	4.00
J74	Totton	H	4.00
J75	Blackwater/Hants	H	£100
J76	Horwich	H	4.00
J77	Marton/Yorks	H	6.00
J78	Medomsley	H	3.00
J79	Thatcham	B	£200
J80	Beenham	B	£200
J81	Woolhampton	B	£100
J82	Wadhurst Station	H	£125
J83	Datchet	B	90.00
J84	Ossett	H	6.00
J85	Church Lane/ Old Charlton	B	£125
		H	25.00
J86	Woolwich Rd./ Old Charlton	H	£100
J87	Cloughfold	H	6.00
J88	Haslingden	H	6.00
J89	Summerseat	H	90.00
J90	Luddenden	H	4.00
J91	Luddendenfoot	H	4.00
J92	Mytholmroyd	H	4.00
J93	Yeadon	H	4.00
J94	Ingleby Greenhow	H	4.00
J95	Bradford/Lanc	H	90.00
J96	Bodenham	H	£150
J97	Willington Quay	H	10.00
J98	Eston	H	4.00
J99	Normanby/ Middlesborough	H	25.00
K01	Felling	H	3.00
K02	Hebburn	H	3.00
K03	Walker	H	10.00
K04	Helmshore	H	10.00
K05	Stacksteads	H	50.00
K06	Little Hereford	H	10.00
K07	Shaw	H	25.00
K08	Lymm	H	8.00
K09	Woodborough	B	80.00
K10	Howden-le-Wear	B	50.00
K11	Sinnington	H	25.00
K12	Earlstown	H	£100
K13	Brenchley	H	8.00
K14	Liversedge	H	4.00
K15	Ryton	H	4.00
K16	Brotherton	B	£125
K17	Purston	B	£100
K18	Melplash	H	10.00
K19	Carlton/Yorks	H	4.00

Numeral, Spoon and Duplex Postmarks

K20	Rawcliffe/Yorks	H	8.00
K21	Rawcliffe Bridge	H	20.00
K22	Whitley Bridge	H	10.00
K23	Ravenstonedale	B	20.00
K24	Llanwnda	H	30.00
K25	Plasmarl	B	£100
K26	Bexhill	H	50.00
K27	Bexhill Station	H	75.00
K31	Goudhurst	H	8.00
K32	Gomshall	H	6.00
K33	Coniston/Lanc.	H	5.00
K35	Murton Colliery		
K37	Mumbles	H	5.00
K38	Brayton Station	H	£200
K39	Dalston/Cumbd	H	20.00
K40	Littlestone	H	8.00
K41	Swinton/Lane.	H	6.00
K42	Northwood/Herts	H	£125
K43	Collingbourne Ducis	B	£100
K44	Mayfield/Sussex	H	8.00
K45	Saltford	B	£150
K48	London & Holyhead TP	O	- see chap 13
K49	Minster/Ramsgate	H	10.00
K50	Boot	H	6.00
K51	Eskdale	H	6.00
K52	Gosforth	H	8.00
K53	Ravenglass	H	10.00
K54	Arnside	H	15.00
K55	Silverdale/Lanc.	H	10.00
K56	Bigrigg	H	75.00
K57	Bootle/Cumbd	H	10.00
K58	Bootle Station	H	£100
K59	Silecroft	H	15.00
K60	The Green	H	25.00
K61	Kirkby-in-Furness	H	10.00
K62	Furness Abbey	H	10.00
K63	New Oxted	H	10.00
K64	Lindal	H	30.00
K67	Goring	B	80.00
K68	Littleport	H	10.00
K71	Blockley	B	£175
K73	Newbiggin	B	75.00
K76	Gwaun-cae-Gurwen	B	£200
K78	Witton Park	B	75.00
K79	Lakeside	B	£150
K80	Calderbridge	B	£100
K81	Danby	B	20.00
K83	Aynho	B	75.00
K84	Heyford	B	£100
K85	King's Sutton	B	20.00
K86	Somerton	B	£100
K87	Souldern	B	£100
K88	Hook Norton	B	50.00
K90	Haworth	B	25.00
K91	Silsden	B	£100
K92	Pitsea	B	30.00
K93	Waskerley	B	£100
K94	Clacton on Sea	B	£150
K95	Shipton-under-Wychwood	B	30.00

T01-6 – The precise use of the marks is not known. They are believed to have been used by PO-employed staff on mail boats £250

Scotland

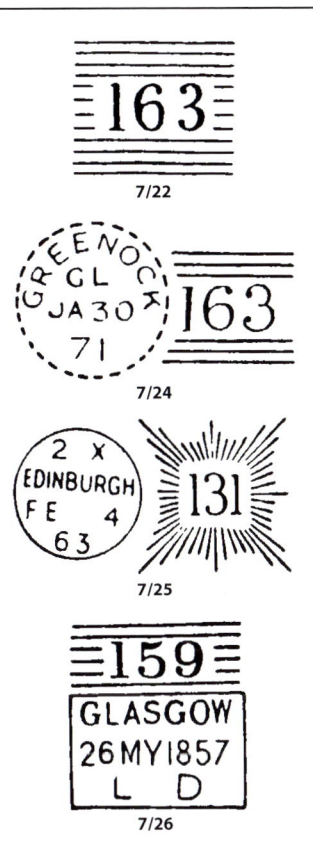

[illustration: numeral "163" between horizontal bars — 7/22]

[illustration: Greenock GL JA 30 71 circular datestamp with "163" — 7/24]

[illustration: Edinburgh 2 x FE 4 63 circular datestamp with "131" Brunswick Star — 7/25]

[illustration: "159" over GLASGOW 26 MY 1857 L D — 7/26]

Basic Prices for Scottish marks

7/22	Numbered cancellations between horizontal barks, from 1844	5.00
7/23	Duplex cancellations, circular datestamp from 1857	5.00
7/24	Duplex cancellations, dotted circle types	12.00
7/25	Duplex cancellations, Edinburgh 'Brunswick Star' types	15.00
7/26	Glasgow 'Madeleine Smith' types	25.00

Numbers used in Scottish numeral and duplex marks

1	Aberdeen	15	Ardrossan
2	Aberfeldy	16	Abington
3	Aberdour Achnacroish	17	Airdrie
		18	Arisaig Ardersier
4	Aboyne		
5	Aberchirdir Abernethy, Strathspey Nethy Bridge	19	Aultbea
		20	Arrochar Avoch
		21	Auchnacraig
6	Alford Advie	22	Anstruther
		23	Aros
7	Alloa	24	Appin
8	Aberlour	25	Auchterarder
9	Alexandria	26	Auchtermuchty
10	Alness	27	Ayr
11	Annan	28	Ayton
12	Auchenblae Ardgour	29	Assynt Auchnasheen Achnasheen
13	Arbroath		
14	Ardersier Fort George Station Gollanfield	30	Alyth
		31	Ballater
		32	Crathie

163

Numeral, Spoon and Duplex Postmarks

	Bannockburn	82	Craigellachie	138	Eyemouth	189	Invergarry
33	Ballantrae	83	Creetown		Fairlie	190	Jura
34	Ballindalloch	84	Crieff	139	Falkirk		Inverkip
35	Banchory	85	Cromarty	140	Falkland	191	Kinaldie
36	Banff	86	Craigellachie Station		Fasnacloich	192	Keith
37	Macduff	87	Cullen	141	Fenwick	193	Kelso
	Birnam	88	Culross		Forgandenny	194	Keith Hall
38	Bathgate		Corstorphine	142	Fettercairn		Inverurie
39	Beauly	89	Crosshill	143	Fochabers	195	Kettle
40	Beith	90	Cumnock	144	Forfar		Kildonan
41	Biggar	91	Cupar Angus	145	Forres	196	Kenmore
42	Blackshiels		Coupar Angus	146	Fort Augustus		Kirkliston
	Bogroy	92	Cupar	147	Fortrose	197	Kennoway
	Blackridge	93	Cluny	148	Fort William		Kilmartin
43	Bervie		Colintraive	149	Fort George	198	Killin
44	Blair Athole	94	Castleton	150	Fraserburgh	199	Kirknewton
	Blair Atholl		Colinton	151	Fushie Bridge	200	Kingussie
45	Dalnacardoch	95	Crinan		Fossoway	201	Kintore
	Bankfoot		Crianlarich	152	Finhaven	202	Kilsyth
46	Blairgowrie	96	Cruden		Finstown		Kirn
47	Blair Adam		Cowdenbeath	153	Farr	203	Kilmarnock
48	Bonaw	97	Cockburnspath		Greenlaw	204	Kincardine
	Bunessan	98	Dalkeith	154	Fyvie		Kilwinning
49	Bonar Bridge	99	Delny	155	Galashiels	205	Kinghorn
	Ardgay	100	Dalmally	156	Garlieston	206	Kinross
50	Bogroy	101	Dalry		Garmouth	207	Kirkwall
	Ballachulish	102	Denny	157	Gatehouse	208	Kippen
	Ballachulish Ferry	103	Dingwall	158	Girvan	209	Kirkcudbright
	Ballachulish Quarries	104	Dornoch	159	Glasgow	210	Kirkcaldy
51	Blackburn	105	Dunbeath		Glasgow-Carlisle	211	Kirkintulloch
	Buckhaven	106	Douglas		Sorting Tender		Kirkintilloch
52	Borrowstouness		Dalmellington		Hope St. Glasgow	212	Kirriemuir
	Boness	107	Doune	160	Glenluce	213	Kirkmichael
	Bunchrew	108	Dumfries	161	Grangemouth		Largs
53	Bowmore	109	Drimnin	162	Greenlaw	214	Kincardine O'Neil
	Bridgend	110	Dumbarton		Gairloch		Lamlash
54	Braco	111	Dunbar	163	Greenock	215	Lanark
55	Blackhillock	112	Dunblane		Iona Steamer/	216	Langholm
	Buchlyvie	113	Dunfermline		Greenock	217	Largs
56	Braemar	114	Dundee		Columba Steamer/		Upper Largo
	Bothwell	115	Broughty Ferry		Greenock – see	218	Lauder
57	Brechin	116	Lochee		chapter 14		Lochgelly
58	Edzell		Drummore	164	Glenlivat	219	Laurencekirk
	Brodick	117	Kincaldrum		Garve	220	Leadhills
59	Broadford	118	Dunkeld	165	Glamis		Larkhall
60	Bridge of Earn	119	Dunphail		Garlieston	221	Leith
61	Buckie	120	Dunning	166	Grantown	222	Leithlumsden
62	Burntisland	121	Dunoon		Grantown on Spey		Lumsden
63	Brucklaw	122	Dunse	167	Golspie		Leuchars
	Burnbank		Duns	168	Brora	223	Lerwick
64	Callander	123	Dunvegan	169	Gartly	224	Lynwilg
65	Campbelton	124	Durness	170	Glenmorriston		Ledaig
	Campbeltown		Dunalastair	171	Haddington	225	Laggan
66	Canonbie	125	Dunnett	172	Halkirk		Lentran
67	Carluke		Dunragit	173	Hamilton	226	Lochcarron
68	Cairnryan	126	Drumnadrochit	174	Hawick	227	Lochearnhead
	Catrine	127	Dysart	175	Helmsdale	228	Lesmahagow
69	Carnwath	128	Eaglesham	176	Helensburgh		Lochgoilhead
70	Carsphairn		Ettrick	177	Harris	229	Leven
	Carstairs Junction	129	Earlston		Holytown	230	Linlithgow
71	Castle Douglas		Elvanfoot	178	Huntly	231	Lochalsh
72	Cairndow	130	Ecclefechan	179	Holytown		Balmacara
	Castle Kennedy	131	Edinburgh		Innellan	232	Lochgilphead
73	Coldingham		Edin-Carlisle Sorting	180	Huna	233	Lockerby
74	Coldstream		Tender		Innerleithen		Lockerbie
75	Carrbridge		Carstairs & Edinburgh	181	Inveraray	234	Lochmaddy
76	Carnoustie		Sorting Tender	182	Inverkeithing	235	Lochmaben
77	Chance Inn	132	Eddlestone	183	Inverness		Lossiemouth
	Crossmichael		Easdale	184	Inchture	236	Lochinver
78	Colinsburgh	133	Elgin	185	Invergordon		Luib
79	Comrie	134	Ellon	186	Irvine	237	Lairg
	Coll	135	Elie	187	Jedburgh	238	Longhope
80	Crail	136	Errol	188	Johnstone		Longniddry
81	Cromdale	137	Evanton		Innerwick	239	Luss

Numeral, Spoon and Duplex Postmarks

240	Lybster	290	Portsoy	345	Loanhead		New Deer
241	Markinch	291	Port William	346	North Berwick	400	Shotts
242	Mauchline	292	Poyntzfield	347	Pennycuick	401	Pollockshaws
243	Maybole		Port Patrick		Penicuik	402	Perth & Aberdeen
244	Melrose	293	Prestonkirk	348	Portobello		Sorting Carriage
245	Meigle	294	Rachan Mill	349	Prestonpans	403	Causewayhead
246	Melvich		Rannoch	350	Slateford	404	Strathyre
247	Mey	295	Renfrew		Tarbolton	405	Murthly Station
	Moy	296	Rhynie	351	Winchburgh		Murthly
248	Mintlaw	297	Rothes		The Mound	406	Johnstone
249	Methlick	298	Rothesay	352	Ferryport-on-Craig	407	Storme Ferry (actual
	Macduff	299	Rothiemay		Altnabreac		spelling used)
250	Moneymusk		Rogart	353	Strachur	408	Currie
	Milnathort	300	St. Andrews		Burghead	409	Larbert
251	Montrose	301	St. Boswell's Green	354	Bonnybridge	410	Dolphington
252	St. Cyrus		St. Boswell's	355	Dalnacardoch	411	Murrayfield
	Monkton	302	Saltcoats		Bo'ness	412	Cambus
253	Mossat	303	Sanquhar	356	Trinafour	413	Woodside N.B.
	Millport	304	Scourie		Inversnaid	414	Cornhill
254	Mortlach		St. Monance	357	Alexandria	415	Dufftown
	Methil	305	Selkirk		Stonehouse	416	Polmost
255	Midcalder	306	South Queensferry	358	Tillicoultry	417	Dreghorn
256	Moffat	307	Stewarton	359	Drem	418	Ringford
257	Moniaive	308	Stirling	360	Lauder	419	Twynholm
	Mossend	309	Stonehaven		Slateford	420	Kirkgunzeon
258	Morvern	310	Stornoway	361	Motherwell	421	Dalry
259	Moy	311	Stow	362	Ratho	422	Prestwick
	Montgreenan	312	Stranraer	363	Liberton	423	Braemar
260	Muirdrum	313	Strathaven		Eyemouth	424	Guthrie
	Munlochy	314	Strathdon	364	Bridge of Allan	425	Port Appin
261	Munlochy		Stanley	365	Ladybank	426	George St.,
	Minto	315	Strichen	366	Insch		Edinburgh
262	Muirkirk		Salen	367	Barrhead	427	Auchinleck
263	Musselburgh	316	Stromness	368	Stobo	428	Reston
264	Nairn	317	Strontian	369	Coatbridge	429	Earlston
265	Newburgh	318	Skene	370	Milngavie	430	Arrochar
266	New Galloway		Strathmiglo		Stevenston	431	Lochawe
267	New Deer	319	St. Margaret's Hope	371	Maryhill	432	Auldgirth
	Newington		Tullypowrie	372	Baillieston	433	Ardrishaig
	Newington R.O./		Strathtay		St. Ninians	434	Abernethy
	Edinr.	320	Tain	373	Whiting Bay	435	Alford
268	New Pitsligo	321	Tarbert (same as 440)	374	Lennoxtown	436	Auchencairn
	Newmilns		Muir of Ord		Upper Keith	437	Lauder
269	Newport	322	Tarland	375	Partick	438	Lamington
	New Cumnock	323	Thornhill	376	Cumbernauld	439	Portaskaig
270	Newton Stewart	324	Thurso		Tarbet,	440	Tarbert, Lochfyne
271	Noblehouse	325	Tobermory		Loch Lomond	441	Bowmore
	Nigg Station	326	Tomintoul	377	Fordoun	442	Port Ellen
272	North Queensferry		Tayport	378	Dalbeattie	443	Wemyss Bay
	Noblehouse	327	Tomnavoulin	379	Aviemore	444	Bonnyrigg
	Mountain Cross		Torphins	380	Ballinluig	445	Lower Largo
273	Oban	328	Tongue	381	Blackford	446	Iona
274	Old Meldrum		Taynuilt	382	Fearn	447	Whitburn
275	Old Rain	329	Tranent	383	Portmahomack	448	Strathpeffer
	Old Aberdeen	330	Troon	384	New Cumnock	449	Roslin
276	Orton	331	Turriff	385	Leslie	450	West Linton
	Pencaitland	332	Tyndrum	386	Kirkcowan	451	Culter Cullen
277	Paisley		Tiree	387	Newton St. Boswells	452	Davidson's Mains
278	Parkhill	333	Udney	388	Menstrie	453	Corrie, Arran
	Kildary		Uddingston	389	Alva	454	Broxburn
279	Peebles	334	Ullapool	390	Dollar	455	Carron
280	Perth	335	Watten	391	Highland Sorting	456	Redgorton
281	Peterhead	336	West Kilbride		Carriage	457	Armadale Station
282	Pitcaple		Windygates	392	Muthill	458	Fife Sorting Tender
283	Pittenweem	337	Whitburn	393	Chirnside		Fife Sorting Carriage
284	Pitlochry		West Kilbride	394	Edrom	459	Kincardine
285	Poolewe	338	Whithorn	395	Grantshouse	460	Carradale
286	Portaskaig	339	Wick	396	Charlotte Place,	461	Clachan
	Parton	340	Whitehouse		Edinburgh	462	Tayinloan
287	Port Glasgow		Walkerburn		Lynedoch Place,	463	Moidart
288	Port Patrick	341	Wigtown		Edinburgh	464	Gourock
	Port of Monteith	342	Wishaw	397	Govan	465	East Wemyss
	Station	343	Ford	398	Hillhead	466	Freuchie
289	Portree	344	Lasswade	399	Greenburn	467	Rousay

Numeral, Spoon and Duplex Postmarks

468	Falkland	536	Fearnan	606	Muthill Station		spelling used)
469	East Grange Station	537	Lawers	607	Newport, Fife		Knockando
470	Fortingal	538	Gullane	608	Cobbinshaw	678	Rannoch Station
471	Armadale	539	Cardenden	609	Coalburn	679	Roy Bridge
472	Blaino	540	Archiestown	610	Kilninver	680	Spean Bridge
473	Laudale	541	Craignure	611	Orton Station	681	Tulloch
474	Ratho Station	542	Connel	612	Lismore	682	Bridge of Orchy
475	New Galloway Station	543	Lochbuie	613	Chapelton	683	Amisfield
		544	King Edward	614	Blackshiels	684	Kirkmuirhill
476	Longriggend	545	Onich	615	Heriot	685	Kinloch Rannoch
477	Bothkennar	546	Staffin	616	Leadburn	686	Maud
478	Guard Bridge	547	Airth Road Station	617	Lamancha	687	Darvel
479	Loanhead	548	Skelmorlie	618	Blackhall	688	Strathcarron
480	Dailly	549	Newmains	619	Cramond	689	Achanalt
481	Roxburgh	550	Stenhousemuir	620	Cramond Bridge	690	Auchnashellach
482	Juniper Green	551	Kilbirnie	621	Fountainhall	691	Lochbroom
483	Gorebridge	552	Lochearnhead Station	622	Crosslee	692	Lochluichart
484	Johnshaven		Balquhidder Station	623	Gordon	693	Forsinard
485	Ormiston	553	Crookham	624	Winchburgh	694	Kinbrace
486	Yetholm	554	New Mills, Fife	625	Uphall	695	Glenfinnan
487	Kettle	555	Sauchie	626	Liberton	696	Blackmill Bay
	Kingskettle	556	Bellshill	627	Polton	697	Plockton
488	Lesmahago	557	Shiskine	628	Rosewell		Berriedale
489	Polmont Station	558	Law	629	Rosslyn Castle	698	Bank
490	Balerno	559	Caldercruix	630	Gilmerton		Latheron
491	Glenbarr	560	North Queensferry	631	Fauldhouse	699	Toberonochy
492	Blairmore	561	Auchterless Station	632	West Calder	700	Cornaig
493	Rowardennan	562	Strone	633	Macmerry	701	Hartwood
494	West Wemyss	563	Kames	634	Milton Bridge	702	Carron
495	Tignabruaich	564	Lonmay	635	King's Cross, Arran	703	Hurlford
496	Monifieth	565	Eskbank, Dalkeith	636	Rumbling Bridge	704	Kilchoan
497	Strichen	566	Avonbridge	637	Fionport	705	Kincardine
498	Brucklay	567	Skeabost Bridge	638	Kirkhill	706	Longmorn
499	Douglas N.B.	568	Denino	639	Tomintoul	707	Balvicar
500	Kilchrennan	569	Tyndrum	640	Drumoak	708	Blackburn, Bathgate
	Kilchrenan	570	Cove, Helensburgh	641	Craighouse, Jura	709	Marchmont
501	Port Sonachan	571	Kilcreggan	642	Howwood	710	New Lanark
502	Renton	572	Struan	643	Kilbarchan	711	Kyle
503	Crianlarich	573	Hollandbush	644	Machany	712	Port Erroll
504	Dalmeny	574	Collessie	645	Dunecht	713	Kinlocheil
505	Beattock	575	Aberfoyle	646	Tarves	714	Crawford
506	Lochinver	576	Uphall Station	647	Balloch	715	Hatton
507	Isle of Whithorn	577	Gateside	648	Conon Bridge	716	Boddam
508	Lilliesleaf	578	Gartmore Station	649	Meikleour	717	Raasay
509	Auchmill	579	Cladich	650	Newcastleton	718	Eskbank, Dalkeith
	Bucksburn	580	Lochwinnoch	651	Ancrum	719	Lochailort
510	Palnure	581	Acharacle	652	Blairadam Station	720	Arisaig
511	Oyne	582	Slamannan	653	Kippen Station	721	Kettleholm
512	Balblair	583	Methven	654	Whitehouse	722	Bonawe Quarries
513	Kinlochbervie	584	Oxton	655	Achluachrach	723	Aberlady
514	Cardross	585	Glendaruel		Glenborrodale	724	Dirleton
515	Castlebay	586	Urray	656	Comrie	725	Achnacarry
516	Lochboisdale Pier	587	Strathcoran	657	Blacksboat	726	Aberchirder
517	Philpstown	588	Abernethy	658	Mindrim Mill	727	Cambuslang
	Philpstoun	589	Aberdour, Fife	659	Shiskine	728	Newton, Glasgow
518	Inverie	590	Thornton, Fife	660	Deanston	729	Shettleston
	Knoydart	591	Tarbolton Station	661	Westfield	730	Carstairs
519	Kinlochewe	592	Row	662	St. Fillans	731	Kenmore
520	Friockheim	593	Garelochhead	663	Springfield	732	Craigmillar
521	Collieston	594	Glenfarg	664	Haywood	733	Rosehearty
522	Cove, Aberdeen	595	Shandon	665	Eddleston	734	Strath
523	Lumphanan	596	Hollybush	666	Grenadier Steamer	735	Findochty
524	Broughton	597	Stravithie	667	Lochmaben	736	Portknockie
525	Old Deer	598	Riccarton, Kilmarnock	668	Auchendinny	737	Langbank
526	Thankerton	599	Carsaig	669	Aros	738	Auchenheath
527	Galston	600	Croggan	670	Port of Monteith Station	739	Netherburn
528	Glenboig	601	Rum			740	Quarter
529	Tynehead	602	Gailes Camp, Irvine	671	Kilconquhar	741	Roseneath
530	Bishopton	603	Galloway Sorting Tender Galloway Sorting Carriage	672	Bridge of Weir	742	Clynder
531	East Calder			673	Glengarnock	743	Cleland
532	Lhanbryde			674	Kilmacolm	744	Colonsay
533	Addiewell			675	Cross Gates	745	Kilmun
534	Ardeonaig	604	St. Margaret's Hope	676	Ardlui	746	Sandbank
535	Ardtalnaig	605	Ruthwell	677	Dalbeallie (actual	747	Toward Point

166

Numeral, Spoon and Duplex Postmarks

748 Inchbare
749 Bieldside
755 Canna

Ireland

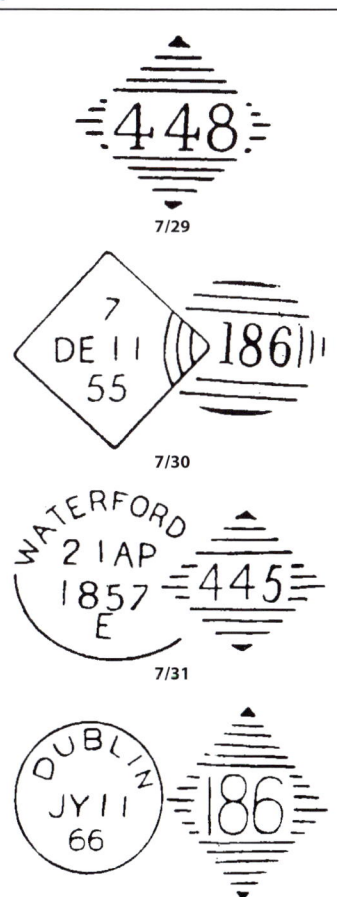

7/29

7/30

7/31

7/32

Numbered cancellations in diamond, from 1844

7/27	186/Dublin	5.00
7/28	62/Belfast, 156/Cork, 172/Derry, 303/ Limerick, 445/Waterford	10.00
7/29	Others	35.00

Spoons 1855-72

		English Type	Irish Type
16	Athenry	£350	-
18	Athlone	£150	75.00
29	Ballina	75.00	-
32	Ballinasloe	£110	50.00
48	Ballymoney	£150	75.00
62	Belfast	30.00	30.00
104	Carrick-on-Shannon	£150	50.00
142	Clonmel	75.00	50.00
156	Cork	35.00	35.00
172	Derry	45.00	40.00
179	Drogheda	40.00	30.00
186	Dublin **7/30**	-	25.00
211	Ennis	£250	-
214	Enniskillen	£125	50.00
232	Galway	40.00	50.00
269	Kilkenny	£110	60.00
272	Killarney	£100	70.00
289	Kingstown	70.00	80.00
291	Ballina (error)	-	£150
303	Limerick	50.00	35.00
321	Mallow	£300	£100
345	Mullingar	75.00	60.00
357	Newry	70.00	40.00
368	Oranmore	£100	£150
397	Roscrea	75.00	50.00
410	Sligo	90.00	80.00
412	Strabane	-	£250
435	Tuam	£100	£125
438	Tullamore	75.00	60.00
445	Waterford **7/31**	75.00	50.00
447	Westport	50.00	-
448	Wexford	£125	75.00
456	Dalkey	£350	£400

Duplex cancellations, from 1860s

7/32	186/Dublin	5.00
7/33	62/Belfast, 156/Cork, 172/Derry, 303/ Limerick, 445/Waterford	10.00
7/34	Others	25.00

Numbers used in Irish numeral and duplex marks

1	Abbeyleix		32	Ballinasloe
2	Adair		33	Ballincollig
	Adare			Ballybrack
3	Ahascragh		34	Ballinderry
4	Ardara			Ballybofey
	Cratloe		35	Ballingarry
5	Ardee			Ballycassidy
6	Ardglass		36	Ballinrobe
	Ardrahan			Ballybrophy
7	Ardrahan		37	Ballycastle
	Abbeyfeale			Ballybunion
8	Armagh		38	Ballyclare
9	Ballingarry		39	Ballyconnell
10	Arklow			Ballylongford
11	Arthurstown		40	Ballybrittas
	Armoy			Ballygawley
12	Arva		41	Ballygawley
	Ashbourne			Ballycastle
13	Ashbourne		42	Ballyglass
	Aghadowey			Balla
14	Ashford		43	Ballyhaise
15	Athboy			Ballyglunin
16	Athenry		44	Ballyjamesduff
17	Athleague			Ballyhaunis
	Ardsollus		45	Ballymahon
18	Ardsollus		46	Ballymena
	Athlone		47	Ballymoe
19	Arva		48	Ballymoney
20	Athy		49	Ballymore
21	Aughnacloy			Ballymore Eustace
22	Aughrim (Galway)		50	Ballymote
	Aughrim (Wicklow)		51	Ballynacargy
23	Antrim			Ballymurry
24	Askeaton		52	Ballynahinch
25	Bagnalstown		53	Ballynamore
	Bagenalstown			Baltinglass
26	Baileyborough		54	Baileyragget
	Baily		55	Ballyshannon
27	Balbriggan		56	Ballytore
28	Ballaghaderin		57	Bangagher
29	Ballina		58	Banbridge
30	Ballybay		59	Bandon
31	Ballinakill		60	Bangor
	Ballinamallard			Barnesmore

167

Numeral, Spoon and Duplex Postmarks

61	Bantry	111	Castleblayney		Corofin	209	Emyvale
62	Belfast	112	Castlecomer	160	Creeslough	210	Enfield
63	Bellaghy		Castleconnell		Craughwell	211	Ennis
	Belleek	113	Castleconnell	161	Crookstown	212	Enniscorthy
64	Belmullet	114	Castledawson		Crossgar	213	Enniskerry
	Beauparc	115	Castlederg	162	Crossakiel	214	Enniskillen
65	Belturbet	116	Castledermot	163	Crossdoney	215	Ennistimon
66	Broadford		Castleknock	164	Crossmolina	216	Eyrecourt
	Bessbrook	117	Castlefin	165	Croome	217	Ferbane
67	Blackwatertown	118	Castlemartyr		Croom		Farranfore
	Blackrock	120	Castlepollard	166	Crumlin	218	Fermoy
68	Blackrock	121	Castlerea		Crossmolina	219	Ferns
	Booterstown	122	Castletown	167	Corofin	220	Fethard, Tip.
69	Blessington		Castletown Bere		Cullybackey	221	Fethard, Wexford
70	Boyle	123	Castletown Delvin	168	Cushendall	222	Fintona
71	Booterstown		Castletown Mullingar	169	Dartrey, Monaghan		Finglas
	Borris		Castletown	170	Dangan	223	Fivemiletown
72	Bray		Geoghegan		Draperstown		Fintona
73	Broadway	124	Castletownroche	171	Delgany	224	Florence Court
	Belfast & N Counties	125	Castlewellan	172	Derry		Fintown
	R.P.O.	126	Cavan	173	Dervock	225	Flurrybridge
74	Brookeborough	127	Celbridge	174	Dingle		Fivemiletown
	Belmullet	128	Charleville	175	Donaghadee	226	Forkhill
75	Broughshane	129	Church Hill		Donaghmore	227	Foxford
	Beragh		Clifden	176	Donegal	228	Foynes
76	Bruff	130	Clane	177	Doneraile	229	Frankford
	Bangor Erris	131	Clara		Donabate	230	Frenchpark
77	Buncrana		Clanabogan	178	Down	231	Freshford
	Belmont	132	Clare		Downpatrick		Geashill
78	Bunratty		Claremorris	179	Drogheda	232	Galway
	Beaufort	133	Clashmore	180	Dromod	233	Garvagh
79	Burrin		Clara		Dromore, Tyrone		Gilford
	Blarney	134	Clifden	181	Dromore (Down)	234	Geashill
80	Borrisakane		Clandeboye		Dromod		Glasslough
	Bruree, Kilmallock	135	Cloghan	182	Dromore West	235	Gilford
81	Borrisoleigh	136	Clogheen		Dromore, Down		Glasnevin
	Brittas	137	Clogher		Drumcree		Glemcolumbkille
82	Borris-in-Ossory		Clonee	183	Drumsna	236	Glasslough
83	Bushmills	138	Cloghnakilty	184	Drumsna		Glenealy
	Bundoran		Clonakilty		Drumcondra	237	Glenarm
84	Buttevant	139	Clonard	185	Draperstown		Garvagh
85	Baltinglass		Cleggan	186	Dublin	238	Glenavy
	Burton Port	140	Clonee	187	Dundalk		Glenties
86	Cabineteely		Clonelly	188	Dunfanaghy	239	Glin
	Cabineteely	141	Clones	189	Dundrum	240	Golden
87	Cahirciveen	142	Clonmel	190	Dundrum		Glenhull
88	Cahirconlish	143	Clough (Down)		Dublin & Belfast	241	Golden Ball
	Rathdowney		Clough, Newry		R.P.O.	242	Gort
89	Camp	144	Cloughjordan		Dunkineely	243	Gorey
90	Cahir		Clonsilla	191	Drumkeerin	244	Gowran
91	Caledon	145	Cloyne	192	Dromara	245	Graig
92	Caledon		Cloughjordan		Dungloe (Don)		Graigue
	Caragh	146	Coachford		Dunmore, Tuam		Graiguenamanagh
93	Callan		Clonbur	193	Dungannon	246	Granard
94	Camolin	147	Coalisland	194	Dungarvan	247	Grey Abbey
95	Cappoquin	148	Colehill	195	Dungiven		Greystones
96	Carlingford		Clogher		Dunkettle Station	248	Goresbridge
	Carbury	149	Coleraine		Glanmire	249	Headford
97	Carlow	150	Collon	196	Dunlavin		Hazelhatch
98	Carey's Cross		Collooney		Dunadry	250	Hillsborough
99	Carna	151	Collooney	197	Dunleer	251	Hollymount
100	Carn		Coachford	198	Dungloe	252	Hollywood
	Carrickmore	152	Cong	199	Dunmurry		Howth
101	Carnew		Comber	200	Dunmanway	253	Howth
	Carrickmines	153	Comber	201	Dunmore		Irvinestown
102	Carrickfergus		Coole		Dunrymond	254	Inistiogue
103	Carrickmacross	154	Cookstown	202	Dunmore East		Inniskeen
104	Carrick-on-Shannon	155	Cootehill		Dunshaughlin	255	Innishannon
105	Carrick-on-Suir	156	Cork	203	Dunshaughlin		Island Bridge
106	Cashel	157	Cove	204	Durrow		Inver
107	Castlebar		Queenstown	205	Edenderry	256	Johnstown
108	Castlebellingham	158	Carrigart	206	Edgworthstown		Inch, Gorey
109	Castlegregory		Courtmacsherry	207	Elphin	257	Kanturk
110	Castleblakeney	159	Craughwell	208	Emo	258	Keady

Numeral, Spoon and Duplex Postmarks

	Kells, Killarney	309	Longford		Newtownforbes		Sixmilebridge
259	Kells, Meath	310	Loughbrickland	360	Newtownforbes	410	Sligo
260	Kenmare		Loughlinstown	361	Newtownhamilton	411	Stewartstown
261	Kilbeggan		Shankhill	362	Newtown Limavady		Scarriff
	Kesh	311	Loughgall		Limavady	412	Strabane
262	Kilcock		Lough Eske	363	Newtownmount-	413	Stradbally
263	Kilconnell	312	Loughrea		kennedy	414	Stradone
	Kilbride	313	Lowtherstown	364	Newtown Stewart	415	Strangford
	Manor Kilbride		Lispole	365	Nobber		Straffan Station
264	Kilcullen	314	Louth	366	Oldcastle	416	Stranorlar
	Kilbrittain		Lucan	367	Omagh	417	Strokestown
265	Kildare	315	Lucan	368	Oranmore		Shanagolden
266	Kildorrey		Lahinch	369	Pallasgreen	418	Stoneyford
	Killorglin	316	Lurgan	370	Pallaskenry		Strafford on Slaney
267	Kildysart	317	Macroom	371	Parsonstown	419	Summerhill
	Kilcar		Lusk		Birr		Stewartstown
268	Kilkeel	318	Maghera	372	Passage West	420	Swinford
269	Kilkenny		Mageney		Philipstown	421	Swords
270	Killala	319	Magherafelt	373	Philipstown		Stranocum
	Killeshandra	320	Malahide		Pettigo	422	Taghmon
271	Killaloe	321	Mallow	374	Piltown		Swords
272	Killarney	322	Manorhamilton	375	Portadown	423	Tallaght
273	Killinardrish		Manorcunningham	376	Portaferry	424	Tallow
	Killiney	323	Markethill		Pomeroy	425	Tanderagee
274	Killeagh		Magheramena	377	Portarlington	426	Tarbert
	Kilfenora	324	Maryborough	378	Portglenone	427	Templemore
275	Killucan	325	Maynooth		Patrickswell	428	Thomastown
276	Killybegs		Maghera	379	Portlaw	429	Thurles
	Killygordon	326	Middleton	380	Portumna	430	Tinahely
277	Killyleigh		Midleton		Portrush		Tinode
278	Killynaule	327	Millstreet	381	Ramelton	431	Tipperary
	Killybegs		Markethill		Portstewart	432	Toome
279	Killeshandra	328	Miltown, Co.Kerry	382	Randalstown		Tinahely
	Killlylea		Milltown, Dublin	383	Raphoe	433	Tralee
280	Killinchy	329	Miltown Malbay	384	Rathangan	434	Trim
281	Killough	330	Mitchelstown		Raheny		Trillick
282	Kilmacrennan	331	Moate	385	Rathcoole	435	Tuam
283	Kilmallock	332	Mohill		Portglenone	436	Tubbermore
284	Kilrea, Co.Derry		Moira	386	Rathcormack		Trim
285	Kilrush	333	Moira		Rathcoole	437	Tulla
286	Kilworth		Moyvore	387	Rathdowney	438	Tullamore
287	Kilmacthomas	334	Monaghan	388	Rathdrum	439	Tullow
288	Kingscourt	335	Monasterevan	389	Rathfarnham	440	Tynan
	Kincasslagh	336	Moneygall	390	Rathfriland	441	Tyrrellspass
289	Kingstown		Monkstown	391	Rathkeale		Urney
290	Kinsale	337	Moneymore	392	Rathowen	442	Valentia
291	Kinnegad	338	Mountmellick		Rathnew		Toombebridge
	Knockloghrim	339	Mount Nugent	393	Red Hills	443	Virginia
292	Kinnitty		Mount Pleasant		Ratoath	444	Warrenspoint
	Rathmore	340	Mountrath	394	Rich Hill		Warrenpoint
293	Kircubbin	341	Mount Talbot		Rockcorry	445	Waterford
294	Kish		Multyfarnham	395	Rochfort Bridge	446	Waringstown
	Knockcroghery	342	Moville		Roundstone		Woodlawn
295	Knock		Muckamore	396	Roscommon	447	Westport
	Kylemore	343	Moy	397	Roscrea	448	Wexford
296	Knocktopher	344	Moynalty	398	Ross	449	Wicklow
	Larne Harbour		Mulhuddart		New Ross	450	Youghal
297	Kinvara	345	Mullingar	399	Rosscarbery	451	Clonegal
	Leixlip	346	Naas	400	Rostrevor		Ward
298	Lanesborough	347	Narin	401	Ruskey		The Ward
	Letter	348	Navan		Rush	452	Dunamanagh
299	Larne	349	Nenagh	402	Saintfield		Tubbermore
300	Leighlinbridge	350	New Birmingham	403	Scarriff		Tobermore
	Laurencetown	351	Newbliss		Sandyford	453	Mount Bellew Bridge
301	Leixlip	352	Newbridge	404	Scrabby		Newton Butler
	Leggs	353	Newcastle		Scarva		Newtown Butler
302	Letterkenny		Newcastle West	405	Shanagolden	454	Ovoca
303	Limerick	354	Newmarket on		Saggart	455	Curragh Camp
304	Lisburn		Fergus	406	Shinrone	456	Templeogue
305	Lismore	355	Newport (Mayo)		Skerries		Batterstown
306	Lisnaskea	356	Newport (Tip)	407	Sixmilebridge	457	Dalkey
307	Listowel	357	Newry		Shillelagh	458	Stillorgan
308	Littleton	358	Newtownards	408	Skibbereen		Ballisodare
	Lixnaw	359	Newtownbarry	409	Slane	459	Baldoyle

169

460	Banteer	521	Leenane
461	Ballinhassig	522	Rusmuck
462	Ballyneen		Rosmuck
463	Castleisland	523	Recess
464	Carrigtwohill	524	Cashel, Galway
465	Clarecastle	525	Letterfrack
466	Clashmore	526	Ballycroy
467	Clondalkin	527	Ballyglass
468	Drimoleague	528	Tourmakeady
469	Drumree	529	The Neale
470	Enniskean		Neale
471	Glounthaune	530	Cong
473	Innishannon	531	Sion Mills
475	Kilkee	532	Dromahair
476	Killeagh	533	Toombeola
479	Knocklong	534	Bangor
482	Leap	535	Holywood
483	Millstreet	536	Strandtown
484	Manorhamilton	537	Donaghadee
486	Little Island	538	Dundrum, Down
487	Maynooth	539	Newcastle, Down
488	Delgany	540	Ardagh
490	St. Margarets	541	Six Mile Cross
491	Templepatrick	542	Maguiresbridge
492	Templeogue	543	Slane
493-8	TPOs	544	Ardfert
499	Welchtown	545	Lisdoonvarna
500	White Abbey	547	Lisselton Cross
501	Doagh		Lisselton
502	Ballinamore	548	Headford, Killarney
503	Doochary	549	Ballincollig
505	Upperlands	550	Ballinskelligs
506	Dervock	551	Glenbeigh
507	Rallinrobe	552	Valencia Island
508	Timoleague	553	Waterville
509	Bailieborough	554	Dunboyne
510	Kingscourt	555	Annascaul
511	Macroom	556	Blennerville
512	Ballinlough	557	Woodenbridge
513	Glenanne	558	Bawnboy
514	Limerick Junction	559	Ballyconnell
515	Hill of Down	560	Bushmills
516	Moycullen	561	Ardara
517	Rosscahill	562	Bruckless
518	Oughterard	563	Carrick
519	Maam Cross	564	Mount Charles
520	Maam		

8 Squared Circle Postmarks

Experiments to find an improvement to the duplex resulted in the introduction of the Squared Circle at Leeds, Liverpool and London EC in 1879. This was so successful that issues were made to many offices throughout England and Wales. They were not used in Scotland or Ireland. Each office mark (known as a "hammer") is described in accordance with the definitive work, detailed below.

There are six main types (Roman numerals I to VI) with varying numbers of arcs (counted at top left/right) or inner circles. If the hammer has an identity letter or number ("H.I.") it is given an additional sub-type designation (capitals A to G) to show the position of the H.I. Sub-type C denotes any position H.I. other than those illustrated.

In the following simplified lists we show the main types and sub-types used at each office, with any H.I.s in brackets. We do not correlate the use of H.I.s with the sub-types in which they are shown.

It is difficult to place general values on the wide ranges of material available. *A strike on a QV cover is usually worth much more than a similar one on a KE VII ppc.* In our lists most of the values below £5.00 apply to offices found mainly on KE VII ppc's. Most of the values above £7.00 apply to offices found mainly on QV covers. * means "few examples known". - means "does not exist" (London Suburban District Offices only).

We strongly recommend to collectors wishing to specialise that they will require "Collecting British Squared Circle Postmarks", details of which are shown in the Bibliography.

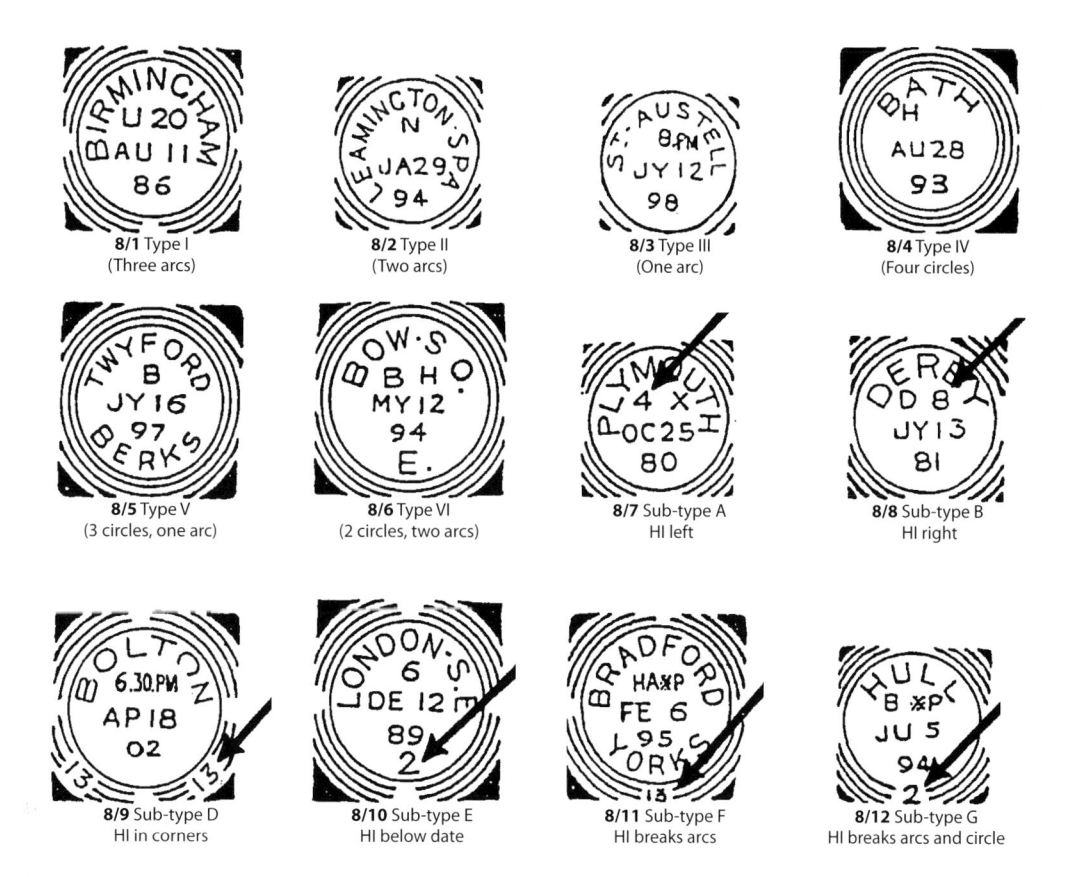

8/1 Type I
(Three arcs)

8/2 Type II
(Two arcs)

8/3 Type III
(One arc)

8/4 Type IV
(Four circles)

8/5 Type V
(3 circles, one arc)

8/6 Type VI
(2 circles, two arcs)

8/7 Sub-type A
HI left

8/8 Sub-type B
HI right

8/9 Sub-type D
HI in corners

8/10 Sub-type E
HI below date

8/11 Sub-type F
HI breaks arcs

8/12 Sub-type G
HI breaks arcs and circle

171

BILL BARRELL Ltd

SPECIALISTS IN POSTAL HISTORY AND
POSTAGE STAMPS OF GREAT BRITAIN

From the Stuarts to the current reign, we have an excellent range of postal history, stamps and cancellations, with wonderful supporting material such as proofs, essays, imprimaturs, as well as maps, and important GB literature.

Please contact us or see our amazing website www.barrell.co.uk

Email: bill@barrell.co.uk

BILL BARRELL LTD
PO BOX 218, HEATHFIELD,
EAST SUSSEX, TN21 0RS
UNITED KINGDOM
TEL: (+44) 01435 408247

Squared Circle Postmarks

London Head District Offices

London E.C.	IA,IIA,VIA (A-L,R)	1.00
London E.	IA,ID,IE,IIA,IID (A-Z) (1-33,41)	1.00
London N.	IA,ID,IIA,IID,IIIA (A-E,P,X) (5,7,9-11,18,19)	2.50
London N.W.	IA,ID,IF,IIA,IID (1-21,24-26)	1.00
London S.E.	ID,IE,IID,IIE,IIIE (1-9,11,12, 18-20,23,24,27-38)	1.00
London/S.W.	IA,ID,IF,IG,IID,IIF,IIID (1-33)	1.00
London W.	IE,IG,IIE,IIG,IIIE (18,19,33, 34,36-38,41,47-53,55,57,60-82)	1.00
London W.C.	I,IA,ID,IIA,IID,IIIA (A-E,H-P,X) (2,5,15,18-30)	1.00
Paddington W	IA,ID,IE,IID (A-K,O,R,V) (8,11,14,21,54,57-72,100)	1.00

London Branch Offices

Aldgate B.O./E	IA,ID (A,B)(1,2)	18.00
Bedford St. S.O./W.C.	IA,ID (1,9-13)	5.00
Charing Cross W.C.	IA,ID,IIA,IID,IIIA (A-F,Z) (1-5)	2.00
London W.C./C.X.	IA,IIA,IIIA (7-11)	2.00
Lombard St. B.O./E.C.	IA (A-E,K,L,O,Q)	6.00
Lombard St. S.O./E.C.	IA (C)	22.00
Mark Lane E.C.	I,IA,II,III (A-H,J,K)	5.00
Stock Exchange /E.C.	I known on postal stationery cut-outs from telegraph forms	£500+ piece
Threadneedle St. B.O./E.C.	I	12.00
Throgmorton Avenue/E.C.	I	*

London Suburban District Offices

The difference in values between QV and KE7 is particularly great for these offices so for this section only, separate prices are given for covers or cards appropriate to the two reigns

		QV	KE7
Blackheath S.O./S.E.	IA (D,E)	25.00	-
	I,ID,II,IID,IIID (1,2)	10.00	5.00
Bow S.O./E.	IA,VIA (A-C)	22.00	-
	ID,VID (1-3)	9.00	3.00
Brockley S.O./S.E.	I	45.00	18.00
Camberwell S.O./S.E.	I,ID,IID,IIID (1,3)	12.00	2.00
Catford S.O./S.E.	I	18.00	4.00
Chingford S.O.	IA (A)	45.00	-
	ID (2)	35.00	18.00
Chiswick	IF,IIF (1-3)	6.00	2.00
Clapton S.O./E	IA (A)	45.00	-
	ID (1)	25.00	5.00
Deptford S.O./S.E.	I	£125	-
Ealing W.	I	12.00	6.00
Ealing Dean/W.	I	50.00	-
East Finchley S.O./N	I	45.00	-
Finchley/Church End N.	I	60.00	-
	ID,IID (1)	18.00	5.00
Finchley/East End S.O. N	I	*	-
Finsbury Park S.O./N.	I	40.00	-
	ID,IID (1,5,6)	8.00	3.00
Forest Gate S.O./E.	IA (B)	85.00	-
	ID (1)	10.00	3.00
Forest Hill/S.E.	I,II	10.00	5.00
Greenwich S.O./S.E.	I	£125	35.00
Hammersmith/W	I	60.00	18.00
Herne Hill S.O./S.E.	I	8.00	8.00
Highbury S.O./N.	I	85.00	-
	ID (1)	45.00	5.00
Highgate/N.	I	80.00	-
	ID (2)	25.00	12.00
Highgate N.	IA (A)	£100	-
	I	35.00	18.00
Homerton S.O./E	IA (A)	30.00	-
	ID (1)	18.00	7.00
Hornsey N.	I	£100	-
	ID (2)	50.00	20.00
Hornsey/N	ID (1,3)	15.00	8.00
Kennington S.O./S.E.	I	80.00	-
	ID (1)	12.00	5.00
Kentish Town N.W.	I,ID,II,IID,IIID (1,3)	4.00	2.00
Lee S.O./S.E.	I,ID (1)	10.00	4.00
Leyton S.O.	IA (A,B)	35.00	-
	ID (2,3)	25.00	6.00
Leytonstone S.O./E.	IA (A)	45.00	-
	ID (1)	18.00	10.00
Lower Edmonton S.O.	I	55.00	-
	ID (1)	18.00	15.00
Maida Hill/W.	I	18.00	-
	ID (1)	7.00	3.00
Manor Park S.O.	IA (A)	75.00	-
	ID (1)	22.00	5.00
New Cross S.O./S.E.	I	25.00	7.00
New Southgate/N	I	£100	-
	ID (1)	30.00	30.00
North Finchley/N	I	90.00	-
	ID (1)	12.00	8.00
North Kensington/W.	IE (1-6)	18.00	2.00
North Woolwich S.O./E	IA (A),ID (2)	£200	60.00
Norwood S.E.	I,II	4.00	3.00
Notting Hill/W.	I	18.00	12.00
Palmers Green S.O./N	I	£100	12.00
Peckham S.O./S.E.	I	90.00	-
	ID,IID (6)	22.00	18.00
Plaistow S.O./E.	IA (A,B)	22.00	-
	ID (1,2)	15.00	4.00
Poplar S.O./E.	IA (D)	70.00	-
	ID (1)	24.00	7.00
St.John's Wood S.O./N.W.	IA (1-4)	9.00	-
	ID,IID (1-4)	6.00	2.00
Shepherds Bush W.	IE (1)	8.00	6.00
Southgate/N	I	80.00	-
	ID (1)	25.00	15.00
South Tottenham S.O.	I,ID,II (1)	6.00	3.00
South Woodford S.O.	IA (A)	£300	-
Stoke Newington S.O./N.	I,IA (A)(2)	35.00	-
	ID (1-3)	12.00	6.00
Stratford S.O./E.	IA (A-D)	25.00	-
	ID,IID (2-5)	15.00	3.00
Tottenham S.O.	I,IA (B)	35.00	-
	ID (1,2)	9.00	3.00
Upper Edmonton	IA (A)	£150	-
Upper Edmonton S.O.	I,ID (2)	£110	20.00
Upper Holloway S.O.	IA (A,C)	30.00	-
	ID (1)	10.00	4.00
Victoria Docks S.O./E.	IA (A)	40.00	-
	ID (1)	15.00	3.00
Walthamstow	IA (A),ID (1)	30.00	10.00
Walworth S.E.	I,IA (2)	15.00	6.00
West Kensington W.	ID,IE,IIE (1-5)	5.00	2.00
West Norwood S.E.	I,II	5.00	3.00
Whetstone S.O./N.	I	£100	-
	ID (1)	15.00	8.00
Willesden S.O./N.W.	I,ID (2)	£100	50.00
Wimbledon	I	6.00	3.00
Winchmore Hill S.O./N	I	40.00	-
	ID (1)	18.00	4.00

Squared Circle Postmarks

Office	Types	QV	KE7
Woodford & South Woodford/Essex	IA (A),ID (2)	50.00	6.00
Wood Green/N	I,ID (1)	30.00	4.00

Provincial Offices

Note: at Birmingham the * is included in the H.I.

Office	Types	Value
Aldbourne	I	40.00
Alford	I	£100
Alfreton	I	4.00
Alton/Hants	I, II	7.00
Ampthill	I, III	3.00
Andoversford	I	18.00
Appledore/Devon	I	30.00
Ardleigh	I	9.00
Armley	I	£125
Arundel	I	3.00
Ashbourne	I	4.00
Ashford/Kent	I, II, III	22.00
Ashley Green	I	75.00
Ashton under Lyne	I	4.00
Aspley Guise	I	28.00
Atherstone	I	18.00
Atherton	I	18.00
Axminster	I, II, III	4.00
Aylsham	I	5.00
Aysgarth Station	I	22.00
Bacup	I	6.00
Bakewell	I	4.00
Baldock	I, II	4.00
Barham	I	£150
Barnet	I, II	15.00
Barnetby	I	18.00
Barnsley	I, ID (1, 2)	2.00
Barnstaple	I, II, III	2.00
Barrasford	I	22.00
Barrow in Furness	I, II	4.00
Barry	I	£175
Bath	I, II, III, IV	4.00
Bawtry	I	6.00
Baydon	I	60.00
Beaworthy	I	4.00
Beckenham	I	22.00
Bedford	I, II	2.00
Beer	I	3.00
Beer Alston	I	60.00
Beeston/Notts	I	3.00
Belper	I, III	3.00
Berkhamsted	I	40.00
Berwick	I, II, III	4.00
Bexley	I, II	4.00
Bicester	I, II	2.00
Bideford	I	8.00
Biggleswade	I, III	3.00
Bildeston	I	18.00
Billinghurst	I	£125
Bingley	I (A-F)	3.00
Birkenhead	IA, ID, IE (4-9)	2.00
Birkenhead: Liscard/Cheshire	IA (A)	£150
Birkenhead: New Brighton/Cheshire	IA (A, B)	£150
Birkenhead: Oxton/Birkenhead	I, IA (A, B)	2.00
Birkenhead: Rock Ferry/Birkenhead	I, IA, ID (A, B) (1, 2)	3.00
Birkenhead: Seacombe/Cheshire	IA (A, B)	£125

Office	Types	Value
Birmingham	IA, ID, IID (A-H, J-N, P-Z, DD, GG, HH, JJ, KK, MM, QQ, SS, YY, C*, D*, E*) (50, 56-60, 63-79, 98)	2.00
Bishop Stortford	I	30.00
Bishops Stortford	I	5.00
Blackheath/Staff	I	5.00
Blackley	I	£225
Blisworth	I	9.00
Bloxwich	I	8.00
Bodmin	I, II, III	2.00
Bognor	I, II	2.00
Bolton	I, ID, II, IID (9, 11-16)	2.00
Boroughbridge	I, II	3.00
Boscastle	I	2.00
Boston	I, II	2.00
Boughton/Kent	I	£250
Bow/North Devon	I	20.00
Box	I	8.00
Boxmoor	I	4.00
Bracknell	I	2.00
Bradford/Lanc	I	£200
Bradford	ID, IE, IF (1-3, 5-9, 12, 13)	2.00
Bradford/Yorks	I, IA, IC, ID, IE, IF (1-13)	2.00
Braintree	I	50.00
Brandis Corner	I	8.00
Braunton	I	6.00
Brentwood	I, IV	2.00
Bridge	I	15.00
Bridgwater	I, II, III	2.00
Bridport	I, II	2.00
Brierley Hill	I, II	3.00
Brigg	I	3.00
Brightlingsea	I	9.00
Brighton	I	£100
Brighton/H.P.O.	I, II, III	10.00
Brighton: Cannon Place B.O.	I	£125
Brighton: College Road B.O.	I	60.00
Brighton: Kemp Town	I	£110
Brighton: Old Steine	I	40.00
Brighton: Western Rd.B.O.	I	20.00
Bristol	I, IA, ID, IE, IG, IID, IIE, IIG, IIID, IIIE, IIIG (A-I, N, R) (1-12)	2.00
Bristol: Clifton	IA, II, IIA (C, D)	8.00
Bristol: Hotwells	I	*
Briton Ferry	I	3.00
Bromley/Kent	I, II	3.00
Brompton	V	£150
Brough/Yorks.	I	90.00
Broxbourne	I	3.00
Bruton	I	2.00
Bude	I	2.00
Budleigh Salterton	I	9.00
Bulwell	I	3.00
Buntingford	I	£125
Burgh	I	60.00
Burnham/Somerset	I	3.00
Bury/Lanc	I, II	2.00
Buryas Bridge	I	30.00
Bury St. Edmunds	I	4.00
Buxton	I, IA, ID, IE (1)	2.00
Cadoxton	I	£175
Caerphilly	I	7.00
Caistor	I	3.00
Callestick	I	30.00
Callington	I	2.00
Calne/Wilts	I, II, III	2.00

Squared Circle Postmarks

Office	Types	Value
Calstock	I	5.00
Camborne	I	3.00
Camelford	I, II	2.00
Canterbury	I, II, III	3.00
Cardiff	I, IA, ID (5-7)	2.00
Cardiff: Barry Dock B.O.	I	35.00
Cardiff: Bute Docks	I	25.00
Carmarthen	I, II, III	4.00
Castleton	V	30.00
Chacewater	I	75.00
Chard	I	30.00
Charlton Kings	I	*
Charmouth	I	3.00
Chartham	I	3.00
Chatham	I, II	2.00
Cheadle/ Cheshire	I	2.00
Chelmsford	I	2.00
Cheltenham	I, II (1)	2.00
Cheltenham-B.P.	I, II	£125
Cheltenham: Pittville	I	£150
Cheltenham: Townsend Place	I	*
Chepstow	I, II	22.00
Chesham.New.Town	I	*
Chester	I	2.00
Chester/Station Office	I, II, III (5)	3.00
Chesterfield	I, II	2.00
Chichester	I	2.00
Chichester/ Station Office	I	5.00
Chigwell Road	I	*
Chilham	I	7.00
Chippenham	I, II	4.00
Chislehurst	I	8.00
Chorley	I	2.00
Chorlton Cum Hardy	I, II	3.00
Church Stretton	I	2.00
Cirencester	I	2.00
Clacton on Sea	I	2.00
Colchester	I, ID, II, IID (1, 2)	2.00
Colyford	I	15.00
Colyton	I	3.00
Conway	I, III	12.00
Copplestone	I	25.00
Cornholme	I	60.00
Cornwall R.S.T.	I	£300
Coventry	I, II	4.00
Cowbridge	I	3.00
Cowes	I, II	4.00
Cradley Heath	I	3.00
Cradley/Staff	I	*
Crediton	I	10.00
Crewe	I, ID (2)	3.00
Crewe Station	I, ID (3)	4.00
Criccieth	I, III	4.00
Crickhowell	I	4.00
Cromer	I	1.00
Cullompton	I	5.00
Cury Cross Lanes	I	8.00
Dagenham	I	50.00
Darlington	I, IA, ID (1-3)	2.00
Darwen	I, II	2.00
Dawley/Salop	I	6.00
Dawlish	I, III	3.00
Deal	I, II	3.00
Deal: Lower Walmer	I	6.00
Deepfields	I	£175
Denton/Lanc	I, II	2.00
Derby	IB, II (8)	£125
Derby: Melbourne/ Derby E	I	£200
Dereham	I, IA, II (1, 3)	2.00
Devizes	I, II	5.00
Devonport	I, IA, IB, II (2, 3)	2.00

Office	Types	Value
Devoran	I	7.00
Didcot	I	3.00
Dinas	I	£150
Diss	I	2.00
Doncaster	I, II	8.00
Dorchester	I, II	10.00
Douglas/ Isle of Man	I, II	4.00
Dover	I, II, III	5.00
Downham	I, II, III	2.00
Droitwich	I, II	2.00
Droylsden	I, II	3.00
Dunmow	I	2.00
Dunstable	I	2.00
Dunster	I	2.00
Eastbourne	I, ID, II, III (4)	3.00
Eastwood/Yorks	I	75.00
Eccles	I, II	2.00
Egloskerry	I	2.00
Eltham	I	2.00
Ely	I, III	2.00
Enfield	I	4.00
Epping	I, II	3.00
Esher	I, II	3.00
Etchingham	I	25.00
Evesham	I, II, III	3.00
Exbourne	I	8.00
Exeter	I, II, III	3.00
Exmouth	I, II	2.00
Eye	I	3.00
Fakenham	I	6.00
Fallowfield	I	20.00
Falmouth	I, II	2.00
Farnborough Road	V	50.00
Farnborough Station	I	30.00
Farnham	I	2.00
Faversham	I, II, III	5.00
Felixstowe	I, V	2.00
Filey	I, II	2.00
Finghall	I	75.00
Fladbury	V	35.00
Folkestone	I, II, III	2.00
Folkestone: Tontine St. B.O.	I	40.00
Foot's Cray	I, II	12.00
Fowey	I	2.00
Frome	I	8.00
Gainsborough	I, II	5.00
Gamlingay	I	6.00
Ganton	V	40.00
Glaisdale	V	35.00
Glossop	I	18.00
Gloucester	I, ID, IG, II, IID (1, 4, 7)	2.00
Gloucester Station	I	15.00
Godalming	I	6.00
Gomersal	I	22.00
Gorton	I	4.00
Gorton Brook	I	£175
Grampound Road	I, III	3.00
Gravesend	I	2.00
Great Somerford	I	6.00
Great Yarmouth	I, II	1.00
Greenstreet/Kent	I	£200
Grimsby	I, IA, II (B)	2.00
Grimsby & Lincoln Sorting Tender	I	15.00
Guernsey	I, II	2.00
Guildford	I, II	4.00
Hadleigh	I	45.00
Hafod/Gla	I	*
Hailsham	I, II	5.00
Halesworth	I, II	2.00
Halifax	I, IA, II, IID, IIID (4)	2.00

175

Squared Circle Postmarks

Office	Types	Value
Halstead	I	22.00
Halstead/Essex	I	40.00
Halstead/Kent	I	12.00
Handcross	I, II	5.00
Hanley	I, II	4.00
Harleston	I, II	3.00
Harlow	I	2.00
Harrogate	I, III, IIIB (A)	3.00
Harwich	I, II	2.00
Hastings	I, II	3.00
Hastings: Gensing Station Rd	I	35.00
Hatfield/Herts	I	3.00
Hatherleigh	I	3.00
Haverfordwest	I	40.00
Haverhill	I, II	2.00
Hawkhurst	I, II, III	5.00
Haxby	I	40.00
Hay	I	3.00
Hayes/Middx	I	20.00
Haywards Heath	I	6.00
Heamoor	I	18.00
Heathfield	I	£100
Hebden Bridge	I, II	12.00
Heckington	I	8.00
Helston	I	4.00
Hereford	I	2.00
Hertford	I, II	2.00
Hetton le Hole	I	5.00
Hexham	I	50.00
Heytesbury	I	6.00
Heywood	I, II	2.00
Higham Ferers	I, II	3.00
Highampton	I, II	3.00
Highbridge	I	2.00
Hingham	I	*
Hinstock	I	12.00
Hitchin	I, II	2.00
Hockcliffe	I	40.00
Hoddesdon	I	2.00
Holbeach	I	2.00
Holsworthy	I	12.00
Holt/Norfolk	I	5.00
Honiton	I, II	8.00
Hoo	I	*
Hornchurch	I	18.00
Horndean	I, II	5.00
Houghton-le-Spring	I	4.00
Hounslow	I, II	2.00
Hoylake	I	3.00
Hull	I, IA, ID, IG, II, IIIG (2, 3, 5)	3.00
Hunmanby	I	3.00
Huntingdon	I, III	3.00
Huttoft	I	75.00
Hyde	I, II	2.00
Ilford	I, II	3.00
Ilfracombe	I, II	2.00
Ilminster	I, II	7.00
Ingatestone	I	3.00
Instow	I	3.00
Ipswich	I, IA, ID, IE, IF, II, IID (1-4)	2.00
Ipswich: St. John's	I	£200
Isleworth	I, II	7.00
Ivybridge	I, II	3.00
Jersey	I, II, III	2.00
Kelvedon	I	3.00
Kettering	I, III	2.00
Kilmington	I	80.00
Kineton	I	7.00
Kingsbridge	I, II, III	3.00
King's Lynn	I, IA, II, III (1-6)	2.00
Kingston-on-Thames	I, II, III	3.00
Kirkby Stephen	I	*
Kirkham	I	60.00
Kirkham Abbey	V	10.00
Kiveton Park	I	30.00
Knockholt	I	12.00
Lakenheath	V	65.00
Lambourn	I, II	2.00
Langport	I	2.00
Launceston	I	2.00
Leamington	I, IA (1-4)	5.00
Leamington Spa	I, IA, ID, II, IID, IIID (1-4)	2.00
Ledbury	I	4.00
Leeds	IA, ID, IID, IIID (A-E, L)	2.00
Leeds: Call Lane B.O.	I	*
Leeds: Chapeltown Rd	I, II	5.00
Leeds: Holbeck B.O.	I	20.00
Leeds: Hyde Park Corner	I	4.00
Leeds: Market St	I	£125
Leeds: Marsh Lane B.O.	I, II	10.00
Leeds: Marsh Lane S.O.	I	20.00
Leicester	I, ID, IID, IIID (1-9)	2.00
Leigh/Lanc	I, II	2.00
Lelant	I	2.00
Levenshulme	I, II	2.00
Lewdown	I	3.00
Lewes	I, II	8.00
Lewes/Station Office	I	5.00
Leyland	I	10.00
Lifton	I	3.00
Lincoln/S.T.	I	12.00
Lincoln/S.C.	I	8.00
Lindfield	I	5.00
Liskeard	I, III	2.00
Littleborough	I	4.00
Liverpool	IA, IB, IIA, IIB, IID, IIIA, IIIB, IIID (A-F, J-L, O, Y, Z, AL, BZ, CL, OL, ZZ) (32, 33, 35, 36, 40)	2.00
Liverpool: Eastern District	IA (ED)	*
Liverpool: Northern District	IA, IIA (N, ND)	3.00
Liverpool: Southern District	IA (SD)	3.00
Liverpool: LX (Exchange)	I, IA, II, IIA, IIIA (A-C, E-G)	8.00
Liverpool: LX (Exchange)	I, IA, IIA, IIIA (B, F)	8.00
Liverpool: N	I	7.00
Liverpool: N3	II	3.00
Liverpool: SD	I, IA (A)	3.00
Liverpool: Aigburth	I	5.00
Liverpool: Blundellsands	I	5.00
Liverpool: Bootle	IA (B, D)	12.00
Liverpool: Bootle-cum-Linacre	IA (D)	10.00
Liverpool: Exchange	IA, II, III (L)	4.00
Liverpool: Garston	I	20.00
Liverpool: Lark Lane	I, IA, II (A, C)	8.00
Liverpool: Liscard	IA (A)	28.00
Liverpool: New Brighton	IA (A, B)	25.00
Liverpool: Old Swan	I	20.00
Liverpool: Rice Lane	I, II	3.00
Liverpool: Seacombe	IA (A, B)	20.00
Liverpool: Seaforth	I	4.00
Liverpool: Walton Rd. Sub D.O.	I, IA, ID (N)(1, 2)	4.00
Liverpool: Waterloo	I, II	4.00
Liverpool: Wavertree	I, IIF (2)	25.00
Liverpool: West Derby (see also Birkenhead)	I	4.00
Liverpool & London T.P.O.	on piece	60.00
	on cover	£350
Llwynypia	I	9.00

Squared Circle Postmarks

Office	Types	Value
Longfield	I	25.00
Longridge	I	35.00
Long Rock	I	7.00
Long Stratton	I	6.00
Looe	I, II	1.50
Loughborough	I, IA, II (1)	2.00
Louth/Linc.	I	2.00
Lower Sheringham	I	£125
Lower Sherringham	I	£175
Luton	I	2.00
Lyme	I	45.00
Lymington	I, II, III	2.00
Lynmouth	I	5.00
Lynton	I	2.00
Mablethorpe	I	4.00
Macclesfield	I	2.00
Macclesfield: Chestergate B.O.	I	30.00
Maidenhead	I, II, III	1.00
Maldon	I	2.00
Malmesbury	I	55.00
Malvern	I, II	3.00
Manchester	IA, IIA, IIIA (A, D, U, X-Z, BX, CX, DX, EX, HX, XX, ZX)	2.00
Manchester: S.W.	I	7.00
Manchester: Barlow Moor Rd	I	12.00
Manchester: Pendleton D.O./ Salford	I, IA, ID (1, 2)	6.00
Manningtree	I	3.00
Marazion	I	£125
March	I	3.00
Margate	I	22.00
Margate: Northumberland Rd	I	£150
Market Harborough	I, II	2.00
Market Rasen	I, III	2.00
Marlborough	I, V	7.00
Marlow	I	2.00
Martock	I	2.00
Matlock Bath	I	8.00
Mawgan	VI	18.00
Melton Constable	I	5.00
Merthyr Vale	I	10.00
Mevagissey	I	12.00
Middleton/Lanc	I	2.00
Midhurst	I, II	4.00
Milborne Port	I	4.00
Milford/Surrey	I	18.00
Minehead	I	2.00
Morchard Bishop	I	4.00
Morpeth	I	3.00
Morthoe	I	60.00
Mossley	I	18.00
Mounts	I	40.00
Narberth	I	4.00
Narborough/ Norfolk	I	60.00
Navigation	I	*
Newbridge/ Cornwall	I	35.00
Newcastle-on-Tyne	I, IE, IIE, IIIE (A-F) (2, 3, 6)	2.00
Newent	I	3.00
Newhaven	I	£125
Newhaven/Sussex	I	3.00
Newington/Kent	I, II	60.00
Newmarket	I, III	3.00
Newnham	I	35.00
Newnham/Glos	I, II	2.00
Newport/Mon	I, III	2.00
Newquay/Cornwall	I	40.00
Newton Abbot	I	4.00
Newton le Willows/Yorks	I	15.00
Newtown/Mont	I	5.00

Office	Types	Value
New Tredegar	I	3.00
Neyland	I	15.00
Normanton	I	*
Normanton Station	I	£500
Northampton	I, II	2.00
North Shields	I	5.00
North Tawton	I	3.00
North Walsham	I	12.00
Norwich	I, ID, IF, IG (A, K) (12, 13)	4.00
Nottingham	I, ID, IE, IG (4, 5, 12)	3.00
Old Brentford	I	75.00
Oldbury	I, II, III	3.00
Old Hill	I	5.00
Ongar	I, II	2.00
Openshaw	I	35.00
Orleton	I	18.00
Orpington	I	35.00
Ossett	I, III	10.00
Ottery St. Mary	I, II	2.00
Oundle	I	3.00
Padstow	I, II	3.00
Par Station	I, II	5.00
Patricroft	I	7.00
Peel / Isle of Man	V	7.00
Penarth	I, II	6.00
Pendlebury	I	3.00
Penryn	I	30.00
Penzance	I, II	40.00
Perranarworthal	I	*
Perranporth	I	2.00
Perranwell Station	I	8.00
Pershore	I, II	3.00
Peterborough	I, ID, II, V (3)	3.00
Peterborough/ Parcel Post	I	75.00
Petersfield	I, II	2.00
Plymouth	I, IA, ID, IF (1-10, 40, 52)	2.00
Plymouth: Stonehouse/ Devon	I	*
Plymouth: Stonehouse B.O.	I	4.00
Plympton	I	*
Polegate	I	8.00
Pontefract	I, II	3.00
Pontlottyn	I	30.00
Pontyclown	I	75.00
Pontyclun	I	5.00
Pontypridd	I	12.00
Portscatho	I	5.00
Portsmouth	IA, IIA, III, IIIA, IIID (1-3)	7.00
Portsmouth: Landport	I	£100
Portsmouth: Portsea	I, II	18.00
Port Talbot	I	2.00
Port Talbot: Taibach	I	*
Poulton Le Fylde	I	3.00
Preston	IA, ID, IG (A)(2)	7.00
Princetown	I	3.00
Radcliffe	I	60.00
Rainham/Essex	I	45.00
Rainham/Kent	I	35.00
Ramsbottom	I	4.00
Ramsey/ Isle of Man	I	45.00
Ramsgate	I, II, III	2.00
Rawtenstall	I, II	5.00
Rayleigh	I	90.00
Reading	I, II, III	3.00
Redruth	I, II	3.00
Retford	I	2.00
Richmond/Surrey	I, II, III	2.00
Rillington	V	30.00
Ringwood	I, III	3.00

177

Squared Circle Postmarks

Office	Types	Value
Robertsbridge	I	4.00
Rochdale	I, IA, ID, IID (A)(1)	2.00
Rochester	I, II, III	2.00
Romford	I, II, III	2.00
Ross	I	10.00
Rowley Regis	I	40.00
Royston/Cambs	I, II	6.00
Royston/Herts	I	2.00
Ruan Minor	I	3.00
Rugby	I, II, III	5.00
Rugby Station	I, II	8.00
Ryde	I, II	3.00
St. Annes on the Sea	I	2.00
St. Austell	I, II, III	2.00
St. Buryan	I	12.00
St. Columb	I, II	3.00
St. Germans/ Cornwall	I, II	3.00
St. Ives/Cornwall	I, II	4.00
St. Ives/Hunts	I	40.00
St. Just	I	2.00
St. Keverne	I	30.00
S. Mabyn	I	18.00
St. Martin/ Cornwall	I	18.00
St. Mary Cray	I	30.00
St. Mawes	I	3.00
St. Neots	I	2.00
St. Tudy	I	4.00
Sale	I	2.00
Saltash	I, II	2.00
Sandown	I, III	2.00
Sandwich	I	4.00
Sandy	I	2.00
Saxmundham	VI	35.00
Scarborough	I, IA, IF, IID, IIF (1, 2)	1.00
Scorrier	I	30.00
Seaford	I, II	2.00
Sedgley	I	18.00
Selby	I	2.00
Sennen	I	2.00
Sevenoaks	I, II	18.00
Shaftesbury	I, III	60.00
Shanklin	I, II	2.00
Sheffield	IA, ID, IE, IID, IIE, IIIE (2, 4, 10-14)	2.00
Sheffield N	IA, ID (A, B) (1, 2)	3.00
Sheffield S.D.O.	IA, ID (A, B) (1, 2)	3.00
Sheffield W.D.O.	IA, ID (A, B) (1, 2)	2.00
Sherborne	I, II	2.00
Shipley/Yorks	I, II	2.00
Shrewsbury	IA, IC, IIA, IIE (1, 2)	2.00
Sidcup	I, II	30.00
Sidmouth	I, II	2.00
Sittingbourne	I, II	15.00
Sittingbourne: Milton	I	£100
Skegness	I	2.00
Slough	I, II	2.00
Snodland	I, II	3.00
Soham	I	6.00
Somerton/ Somerset	I	2.00
Southampton	IA, IIA, IIIA(1, 2)	3.00
Southampton: Oxford St. B.O.	I, II	5.00
Southend/Essex	I	6.00
Southend on Sea	I, II	1.00
South Molton	I, II	3.00
South Petherton	I, II	3.00
Southport	I	1.00
Southport: Birkdale B.O.	I	3.00
South Shields	I	£125
South Stoke	I	*
Southwick/Sussex	I, II	2.00
Spalding	I	3.00
Spennymoor	I	*
Spilsby	I	3.00
Spondon	I	5.00
Staines	I, III	2.00
Stantonbury	I	18.00
Staplehurst	I	3.00
Stevenage	I	3.00
Stockport	I, ID, II (1)	2.00
Stoke on Trent	I, II, IIID (5)	3.00
Stonham	I	35.00
Stony Stratford	I, II	7.00
Stratton/North Devon	I, II	3.00
Strensall	V	20.00
Stretford	I	20.00
Stroud/Glos	I, II	6.00
Sturry	I	3.00
Sudbury/Suffolk	I, II	2.00
Sutton/Linc	I	£100
Sutton in Ashfield	I	3.00
Swaffham	I, II	2.00
Swanley Junction	I, II, III	5.00
Swansea	I	40.00
Tadcaster	I, II, III	3.00
Talybont	I	*
Taunton	I, II, III	2.00
Tavistock	I, II	2.00
Teignmouth	I, IG, II (1, 2)	1.00
Tenby	I	3.00
Terrington	VI	£125
Tetbury	I, II	40.00
Tewkesbury	I	18.00
The Lizard	I	1.00
Thetford	I, II	1.00
Thrapston	I, II	3.00
Tideswell	I	3.00
Tipton Green/ Tipton	I	*
Tredegar	I, II	3.00
Treen	I	15.00
Tregony	I	25.00
Treharris	I	4.00
Trowbridge	I, II	2.00
Truro	I, II	1.00
Tunbridge	I	*
Tunbridge Wells	I	5.00
Tunbridge Wells: Calverley	I	30.00
Tunbridge Wells: Mount Ephraim,	I	30.00
Twyford/Berks	V	5.00
Tyldesley	I	6.00
Upminster	I	60.00
Uppingham	I	3.00
Wadebridge	I, III	2.00
Wakefield	I	7.00
Walmer	I	£125
Walmer Road	I	6.00
Walsall	I	2.00
Walsden	I	£100
Walton-on-Naze	I	1.00
Ware	I	1.00
Wargrave/Berks	I	4.00
Warrington	I	5.00
Washaway	I	75.00
Washford	I	3.00
Waterfoot	I	3.00
Wednesbury	I	18.00
Welburn	V	15.00
Wellington College Station	I	6.00
Wellington/Som.	I, II	2.00
Wells/Norfolk	I	5.00
Wells/Somerset	I	10.00
Welwyn	I	£110

178

Office	Types	Value
Wem	I	15.00
West Bromwich	I, II	3.00
Westbury/Wilts	I, II	4.00
West Hartlepool	I, II, IID (1)	2.00
West Heslerton	V	*
West Kirby	I	3.00
Weston super Mare	I	7.00
Wetherby	I	3.00
Weybridge	I, V	3.00
Weymouth	I, II	2.00
Whitford/Devon	I	90.00
Wickwar	I	5.00
Wigan	I	2.00
Williton	I, II	3.00
Wilmslow	I	3.00
Winchester	I, II, III	5.00
Windsor	I, II, III	1.00
Wirksworth	I, II, III	2.00
Witham	I	28.00
Witham/Essex	I	2.00
Withington	I	30.00
Woburn	I	3.00
Woburn Sands	I	3.00
Woking	I, III	3.00
Wokingham	I, II, III	5.00
Wolverhampton	I, II, IID, IIID (11)	2.00
Wolverton/Bucks	I, II	2.00
Woodford Green	I	5.00
Woolpit	I	5.00
Woolwich	I, ID, IE, IF (2, 6)	5.00
Worcester	I, II	4.00
Worksop	I	2.00
Worthing	I, II	75.00
Worthing Station B.O./ Worthing	I	30.00
Wrexham	I, II, IID (2)	3.00
Wrington	I	6.00
Wroxall	I, II	2.00
York	I, II, III	2.00

London Fancy Geometric Postmarks

During the 1870s efforts were made to produce a handstamp less cumbersome than the duplex. The most successful and popular replacements undoubtedly were the Squared Circles used in about 800 offices throughout England and Wales. However, three offices in London – Inland Branch, Lombard Street Branch and London E.C. – had similar designs, that (but for one) were based on the octagon. The first of these Fancy Geometrics was issued in 1880. They remained in use until the early 1900s. In the listing below, HIs are shown in brackets similar to the Squared Circle listing, followed by recorded dates of use for each entry.

A 125-page study of these attractive postmarks, by M. Barette, was published in December 1994. It lists all types, rarities and value ranges. The illustrations and reference numbers are from that book, with permission.

8/13 Type IA

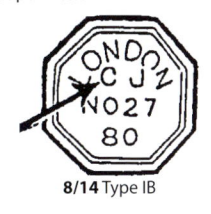

8/14 Type IB

8/15 Type IIA

8/16 Type IIB

8/17 Type IIC

8/18 Type III

8/19 Type IV

8/20 Type V

8/21 Type VI

8/22 Type VII

London Inland Branch

IA (no HIs)	(1.5.1880 to 29.7.1880)	50.00
IB (lower case a-f)	(2.12.1880 to 28.11.1909)	30.00
IIA (capital A,E,F)	(2.8.1880 to 7.12.1882)	25.00
IIB (capital A-F)	(17.2.1883 to 1.3.1890)	35.00
IIC (capital A-R)	(20.2.1882 to 3.12.1895)	15.00

London E.C.

III (capital H-P)	(30.11.1880 to 7.3.1898)	15.00
IV (capital A)	(1.6.1882 to 13.10.1899)	35.00
V (capital A)	(1.6.1882 to 18.6.1897)	35.00
VI (capital A)	(31.5.1882 to 3.6.1885)	60.00

Lombard St Branch Office

VII (capital B,H,I)(7)	(9.5.1882 to 26.3.1906)	25.00

DAVID SHAW

GB & WORLD POSTAL HISTORY AT REALISTIC PRICES
– ESTABLISHED 1981

We trade on eBay.co.uk as Sutherlandladdie – go to our website and it will take you straight in to our eBay shop

DAVID SHAW'S OLD LETTERS where everything is illustrated and added to almost daily.

WE OFFER 1560s to 1960s POSTAL HISTORY TO SUIT BEGINNER TO ADVANCED COLLECTORS -

COUNTY MATERIAL (specialist Scottish section) AND A WIDE VARIETY OF SUBJECTS

Website – www.davidshawpostalhistory.com
e-mail david@davidshawpostalhistory.com
tel. 01653 694953 (24 hr ansaphone)
or you can write to -
QUARRY BANK, BROUGHTON, MALTON,
NORTH YORKSHIRE
YO17 6QG

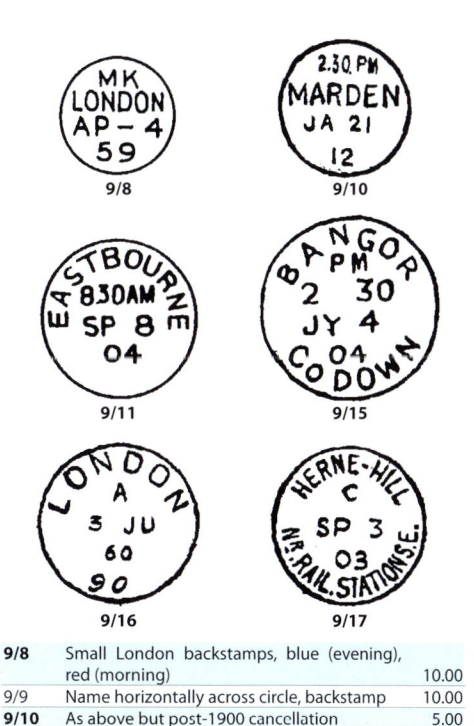

9 Later Circular Handstamps

Although they had been in use from the 1850s it was not until the end of the 19th century that the single and double circles ("circular datestamps" or cds's as dubbed by stamp collectors) came into their own. The double circle, with its thick arcs, was designed to cancel stamps: the single circle was for backstamping, but later for post office counter work. A small single circle, the "thimble", had initially been used for backstamping, later for stamp cancelling. Rubber handstamps, widely known as "rubbers" or "village rubbers", were firstly brought in at "postal order money offices", then used on mail but not on the stamp, leaving the larger sorting office to stamp the stamps. Later, stamps were cancelled with these rubbers. The next generation of rubber handstamps (to the present day) were used, at larger sorting offices, for stamping "soft packets", hence the term "packet handstamp".

Readers should note the distinction between a post office sorting office and a post office counter, even though at small offices these were only a few feet apart! The "standard pattern" for the 20th century is as follows (possibly an over-simplification) :

- a *sorting office* is equipped with double circles (with time, or with code A for morning, B for afternoon) for stamping letters, rubber stamps for "soft packets", and "paid" postmarks (if the office is large enough) plus registered handstamps primarily for receipts on incoming items etc.
- a *counter* is equipped with single circle handstamps (or "SIDs" in modern times) (with no time), with a code identifying the handstamp, used for all paperwork (pensions etc), registered letters and receipts, sometimes used for parcels as well; later if traffic was sufficient a separate parcel handstamp was also supplied.

There are MANY exceptions eg double circles are issued to counters, single circles are used in sorting offices etc etc and some in this chapter are not even circular in spite of the chapter heading! Values are for covers/cards (or large piece if from a parcel), but double for handstamp on postal order counterfoil (pre QEII) and also double, minimum 5.00 for parcel labels.

Further reading : "*Postmarks of England and Wales*" by James A. Mackay

Single Arcs

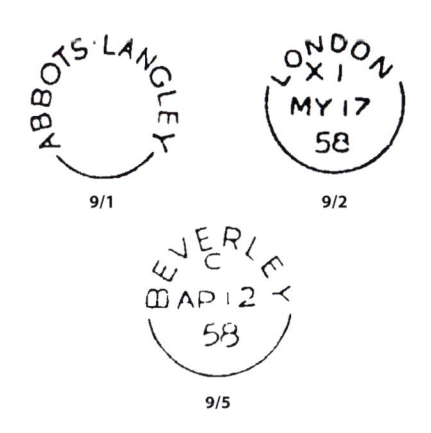

9/1	Undated single arc backstamp, from 1850	25.00
9/1A	Undated double arc datestamps, from 1820-50	25.00
9/2	Dated London single arc backstamp	25.00
9/3	As above but as Edwardian cancellation	10.00
9/4	As above but district initials breaking arc, backstamp	6.00
9/5	Dated provincial single arc backstamp	6.00

Thimbles (small diameter single circles)

9/6	Undated thimble	50.00
9/7	Dated thimble	5.00

Single Circles

9/8	Small London backstamps, blue (evening), red (morning)	10.00
9/9	Name horizontally across circle, backstamp	10.00
9/10	As above but post-1900 cancellation	5.00

Later Circular Handstamps

9/11	Single circle backstamps, usually black or blue	3.00
9/12	As above but cancelling stamps, coded or timed before 1900	10.00
9/13	As above, timed, after 1900	1.00
9/14	As above, with inscription altered, such as R of RSO removed	3.00
9/15	Larger Irish type of single circle	3.00
9/16	London mis-sort stamps (code in italic characters)	3.00
9/17	Single circle used for counter duties	1.00

Double Circles

9/18 9/19

9/20

Early types

9/18	Small double circle types	20.00
9/19	Large London double circle, with or without thick arc	10.00
9/20	Continental type double circle ('Hammer'), London or London E.C. coded 1-6	75.00

Double arc types

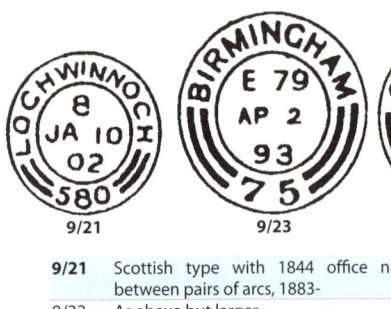

9/21 9/23 9/24

9/21	Scottish type with 1844 office numbers between pairs of arcs, 1883-	2.00
9/22	As above but larger	2.00
9/23	Double arc with English office numbers, from 1885:	5.00
	75 Birmingham	4.00
	466 Liverpool	4.00
	761 Sunderland (single arcs)	10.00
	K34 Haswell (double arcs)	35.00
	(single arcs)	40.00
	K35 Murton Colliery	50.00
	K36 South Hetton	30.00
9/24	As above with blank space, Irish	2.00
9/25	As above with cross or stamp number between pairs of arcs, English, Scottish or Irish	1.00

Later double circle types with single arc

9/26 9/27

9/28 9/32

9/33 9/34

9/35

9/26	Medium arc broken by cross pattee or handstamp number	0.50
9/27	As above, post town, county or district at foot	0.50
9/28	As above with 'Station Office' or other inscription removed	3.00
9/29	As above, arc broken by six pointed star	2.00
9/30	As above, arc broken by eight pointed star	3.00
9/31	Thick arc broken by cross pattee, handstamp no. or unbroken arc, 1920s-	0.50
9/32	As above, post town, county or district at foot	0.50
9/33	As above but circular "spacers" instead of thick arcs.	0.50
9/34	Thin arcs and post-town, county etc. at foot, from c1950 (different letterings) or single unbroken thin arc	0.50
9/35	Unusual type with no side arcs at all	0.50

Later Circular Handstamps

Coded time

Note: This section is relevant to chapters 7, 8, 9 and 19; we include it here for convenience.

For the period 1893-95 time was expressed in a coded form, and this was used in various types of handstamp postmark - duplex, squared circle, single & double circle, and so on. For example, about 15% of the offices that used squared circles used coded time; the same applies to duplex postmarks, but not necessarily the same offices. Full details of the usage of these codes can be found in "The Use of the 1894 Coded Time System in English Provincial Offices" by John A E Moy, published in 1991 by the author in conjunction with the British Postmark Society.

9/36

Simplified details of the codes are as follows, with A-M used to show both hours and minutes:

Code	Hour	Minutes
A	1	5
B	2	10
C	3	15
D	4	20
E	5	25
F	6	30
G	7	35
H	8	40
I	9	45
K	10	50
L	11	55
M	12	–

The normal code consisted of two letters, the first the hour, the second the minutes. A separation device followed, usually an asterisk, alternatively a solid square in Ireland and dots of various sizes in Birmingham. Finally came an A for AM or a P for PM. Thus LI*P = 11.45pm and EF*A = 5.30am. 'Time in clear' officially replaced coded time in March 1895 but at some offices it continued into the 1900s.

Skeletons

Composed of individual characters made up for each temporary use. The terms 'travellers' or 'travelling datestamps' seem to be applied only to the 1840s-1850s usage, see next two entries.

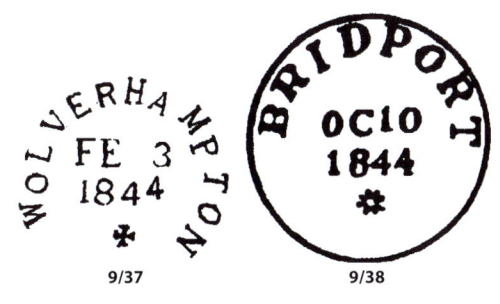

9/37   9/38

9/37	Office name in arc, unframed, seriffed or non-seriffed lettering, cross or index number at foot, 1840s	£120

9/38	Circular 34mm, year in full, seriffed or non-seriffed letters,1840-50's	£100
9/39	Circular, small 23-24mm, year in 2 or 4 figures, 1890s-1910s (These are easily confused with single circle handstamps of same period; in skeletons the lettering is usually irregular and the wording asymmetrical.)	8.00

9/40   9/42

9/43   9/44

9/40	Circular, year in two figures, non-seriffed, chiefly 1885 to 1920, 30-36mm, date in 2 lines (generally no county up to 1906)	8.00
	(values higher for villages, lower for seaside resorts, but pre-1900 20.00)	10.00
9/41	As above but Camp, railway station or RSO (see chapters 13,15, 16)	15.00
9/42	As above but 28mm design from 1914, date in one line	8.00
9/43	As above but with spelling or other errors	30.00
9/44	Rubber skeletons (particularly difficult to find clear impressions)	40.00
9/45	Irish double rim skeletons	25.00

Hooded Circles

Previously known as 'Scrolls'.

9/46

9/46	London or London EC, as cancellation, from 1882 (value higher post-1900)	5.00
9/47	As above but modern receiving marks, usually from abroad, red	5.00
9/48	Liverpool, includes 466, pre-1900	15.00
9/49	Liverpool, without 466, 1900s	6.00
9/50	As above but V. Liverpool S, 466 (Victoria St.)	£100
9/51	As above but E. Low-Hill D., 466	20.00

183

Later Circular Handstamps

Precancel

9/62	Stamford Mercury precancel with 742 numeral QV	50.00
	Other	20.00

Note: For further hooded circles see Aviation and Royalty.

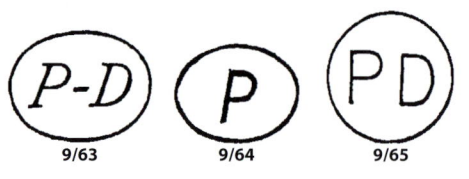

P/PD (Paid) Handstamps (in red)

9/63	Oval P-D or PD on paid letters to Europe, 1840's-1870's, used at Southampton and London, sometimes in blue or black	10.00
9/64	As above but P	20.00
9/65	As above but circular PD or PP	10.00

Note: Unframed or boxed PD marks, all PF marks and most PP marks are French, so mainly are PPPP marks, indicating passed thro' Paris 'Port Payee Passee Paris'.

Rubber handstamps (from 1885)

Climax datestamp

This is distinguished by having the month in three characters and a full stop after month, with the date on revolving wheels.

Period 1

Approx to 1930s, known in this period as "rubbers" or "village rubbers", often with post town horizontally above date:

9/66	Cancelling stamps (or stamped alongside), violet/black, 1907-30 (value higher pre-1900 or on postal order)	12.00
9/67	As above but distorted by oil in black ink	15.00

Period 2

Approx from 1930, in the modern era climax datestamps are plentiful on documents and for "internal purposes" not usually connected with stamping mail. However a good number may also be found used for stamping letters from Post Office departments, usually in black or purple, sometimes in red:

Irish

9/52	Cork	50.00
	Limerick	60.00
	Londonderry	75.00
	Waterford	£100

Used for late fees

9/53	(with 'L' and value d, 1d etc; there are inscription variations, ie with/without B.O, E.C. etc)	
	London (Inland Section)	15.00
	47 Cannon St. B.O. E.C.	20.00
	Eastcheap B.O. E.C.	15.00
	Fenchurch St. B.O. E.C.	20.00
	Fleet St. E.C.	15.00
	49 Fore St. B.O. E.C.	20.00
	Gracechurch St. E.C.	25.00
	Leadenhall St. E.C.	15.00
	Liverpool St. E.C.	75.00
	Ludgate Circus E.C.	50.00
	Mark Lane E.C. .	15.00
	Threadneedle St. B.O. E.C.	15.00
	Throgmorton Avenue B.O. E.C.	18.00
9/54	"Late Box" at Bradford, Leeds, Liverpool, Manchester stations, see chapter 13	

Registered

9/55	Steel h/s, mainly London, or London District Offices (see also 19/53)	4.00
	(also occasional modern usage eg Haywards Heath, Wolverton etc)	4.00
9/56	As above but Official paid, in red (9/55-56 both show month 2 chars)	8.00
9/57	Rubber hooded circle with double rim (month 3 chars)(see also 19/54)	8.00
9/58	As above but modern version with single rim .	6.00

Parcel Post

9/59	G.P.O. London/Parcel Post/Depot	50.00
9/60	South West District/Parcel Post/Depot .	50.00
9/61	Euston, London Bridge, Paddington, Waterloo stations, see chapter 13	

9/68	Modern usage on Post Office letters of handstamps with various "administrative purposes" wordings, often including phone number or "duty" eg "Opening duty", "Datapost duty" etc	1.00

Later Circular Handstamps

Blackwell datestamp

9/70

9/72

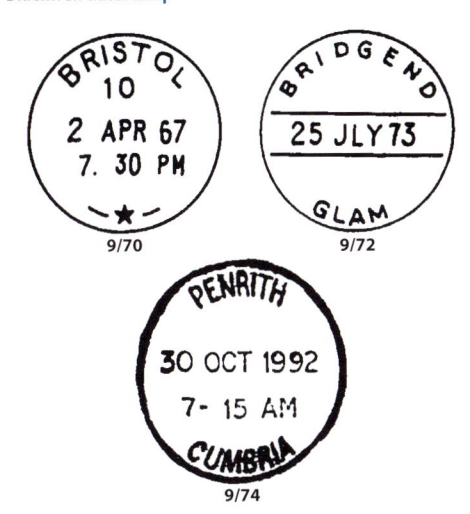

9/74

Exceptional types

9/79

9/81

9/84

9/85

Period 1
Approx 1900 to 1980s - this is distinguished by having the month in three letters, no full stop, year as two digits, and the date is composed of loose type, known more usually as "packet handstamp" or "soft packet handstamp".

9/69	Early packet handstamp, approx 1900-40 (various types)	3.00
9/70	Modern handstamps used for packets, some with star at foot	0.50
9/71	As above but London missort mark (code at foot or below London)	1.00
9/72	With "bridge", no facility for time	0.50
9/73	Modern usage on Post Office letters of handstamps with various "administrative purposes" wordings (see **9/68**)	1.00

Period 2
From 1979 (though period 1 handstamps remained in use until replaced) - this is distinguished by having the month in three letters, no full stop, year as four digits, and the date is on revolving wheels:

9/74	Modern datestamps used for packets, some with star at foot, in seriffed/unseriffed characters and upper/lower case	0.50
9/75	As above with errors (eg "Fylde Wyre Lancs" with no Blackpool)	1.50
9/76	As above but small lettering used approx 1985-88	0.50
9/77	As above but with narrow date, from approx 1992	0.50
9/78	Modern usage on Post Office letters of handstamps with various "administrative purposes" wordings (see **9/68**)	1.00

9/79	Large barred circle eg Liverpool, B.M.(Birmingham) (see similar in chapter 19)	1.00
9/80	Double oval eg Cheltenham 1977, others with star at each end	1.00
9/81	Time included in handstamp inscription eg Enfield and Croydon	1.00
9/82	"Label" parcel marks adapted, words "Parcel Post" removed etc	2.00

185

Later Circular Handstamps

9/93 Swindon trial (device of German manufacture), 1991-94   10.00

Paid Handstamps (in red)

Note: Can include value (from 1968 "1st" or "2nd" etc) or "Official Paid"; the latter existed to about 1985, whence Government Departments were required to pay for their own mail. Generally 20th Century Paid handstamps include "Great Britain" as country of origin since no adhesives used. From 1990 occasional use of black. In about 2009 the facility for "mail prepaid in cash" was bought to an end, and with it the use of "Paid" postmarks (applies to machine postmarks also, see chapter 10), largely as a result of PPIs (see chapter 26) being used in such quantities by commercial concerns.

9/83	Single or double rim oval based on registered design **19/50**	1.00
9/84	Oval "rugby ball" at Bradford or double rim oval at Darlington	1.00
9/85	Double circle (rubber) at Aberdeen, 1993-	1.00
9/86	"24 hour" handstamp (rubber, diff sizes) at Southampton, Darlington	1.00
9/87	Boxed handstamps eg Newmarket, "Tyneside"	1.00
9/88	Unframed NE/SR handstamp at Newcastle upon Tyne, 1996-98.	1.00
9/89	Circular handstamp with "Glasgow" in straight line, 1996-97	1.00

Note: The "exceptional" items shown above serve to show the range of such handstamps used since about the 1960s: they do not represent an exhaustive list.

Rollers

Included here since hand-applied rollers were also used for stamping soft packets, others not shown here were used on parcels; priced for large piece.

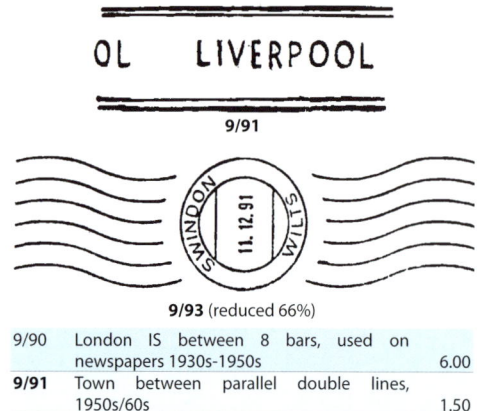

9/93 (reduced 66%)

9/90	London IS between 8 bars, used on newspapers 1930s-1950s	6.00
9/91	Town between parallel double lines, 1950s/60s	1.50
9/92	Swansea trial, 1970-71	8.00

186

Later Circular Handstamps

9/106A	Plain 23mm handstamp, but with date of the distinctive style shown in **9/107** (with dot after day), 1985-86 trial at a few offices	2.50
9/107	23mm handstamp with "fancy" edge (this is the style largely used from 1987), generally known as SID	0.50
9/107A	As **9/107** but 'PO Local' or 'PO Essentials' inscription (from 2008) instead of 'Post Office' as new categories of post office introduced	1.00

Dumb handstamps

"Dumb" meaning they say little and have no date.

The first item is included here for convenience. The others are used for cancelling stamps that have been missed by a stamp cancelling machine; there are a series of these, and the most well known examples are shown here:

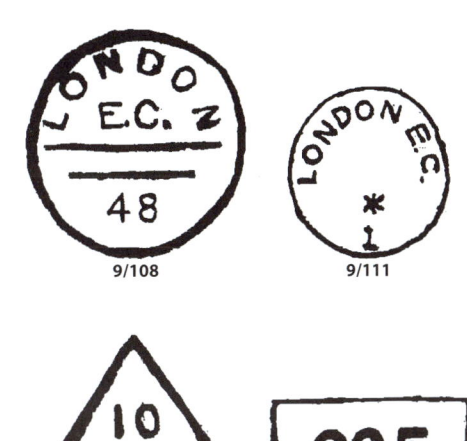

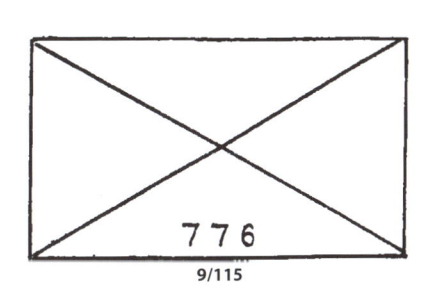

9/94	Single circle "Official Paid" (metal)(variations)	2.00
9/95	Single circle (metal) with PAID across centre, date at foot, 28mm	4.00
9/96	Single circle (metal) with large at centre, PAID above	3.00
9/97	Double circle (metal)	1.00
9/98	Distinctive metal single circle with PAID and value, 32mm (from 1968 1st or 2nd instead of value, or "R" more unusual)	7.00
9/99	Rubber Blackwell Paid handstamps (month 3 characters, year 2 digits)	1.00
9/100	Skeleton Paid handstamps (chiefly 1907-17)	18.00
9/101	Economy wartime undated rubber handstamps, 1940s	2.00
9/102	Large double circle handstamp with revolving date wheels, from 1980 (known as "lifebelt", year 4 digits, centre revolves to show 1st/2nd etc)	1.00
9/103	As above but used in black on normal mail	1.50
9/104	Modern exceptional types eg Bournemouth with "First Class" included	1.50

Other types used for backstamping

9/105	Square backstamps in red or black	10.00
9/106	Foreign Office quartered handstamps (sim to **14/24**) with central N	30.00

Self Inking datestamps (SIDs)

From approx 1985 used for various trials, operationally from 1987, counter datestamps generally applicable where computerisation of counter work (ECCO) has taken place, followed by massive countrywide spread 1993-97, see also page ix).

9/108	Economy wartime undated rubber stamps, 1940s	3.00
9/109	Post-war use of numeral handstamp	8.00
9/110	Barred circle Paddington, similar to **9/79** but smaller	1.00
9/111	London EC, steel single circle undated */1-3, 1960s	1.00
9/112	IS triangle with number (London Mount Pleasant), later ISMLO	1.00
9/113	Reading 635 in box (variations in size and colour)	2.00
9/114	Manchester 498 or 498D in hexagon (variations)	1.00
9/115	Large Taunton 776 envelope design (in green)	3.00

187

Later Circular Handstamps

Charity appeal mailing handstamps

Some senders of large mailings had for some years preferred to affix stamps to their mailings, usually cancelled by machine (see **10/198** for a typical diamond postmark). In the 1990s there seemed to be an increase in these mailings and Royal Mail decided to permit senders of charity appeals and other large mailings to cancel, with approval, the stamps themselves. See **10/208** for a machine postmark so used, and below is a selection of postmarks believed to be handstamps (though it is difficult to ascertain whether handstamp or machine). These continued to grow, applied in a variety of designs and colours, but in the 21st century there has been less handstamping and more machine-applied postmarks, see chapter 10.

9/116

9/117 (in pink)

9/118 (in blue)

10 Machine Cancellations

Growing volumes of mail, along with the desire to get letters to their destination between one evening and the following morning, have been the driving forces behind development of machines to cancel letters. Much effort has gone into machine development over more than a hundred years, to enable speed of cancellation to be combined with a quality readable postmark. Experiments and developments were still taking place in the 1990s, including machines for stamping packets and large letters for "large flats" as they are termed). Machines are listed chronologically in order of the first use of each make. In his book Peach (see Bibliography) uses the term "dater" for the town/date portion: we have used the term "town die" instead for consistency with other chapters.

Pearson Hill Experimental Machines, 1857-58

		✉	△	○
10/1	Without London, first machine, 1857	*	£1000	£125
10/2	With London, coded A or M, second machine 1857-8	£600	£100	30.00
10/3	Opera Glass type, prob 2nd machine modified, 1858	£4000	£300	£100
10/4	As above but twin circle type, prob third machine	£4000	£600	£110

Charles Rideout, from 1858

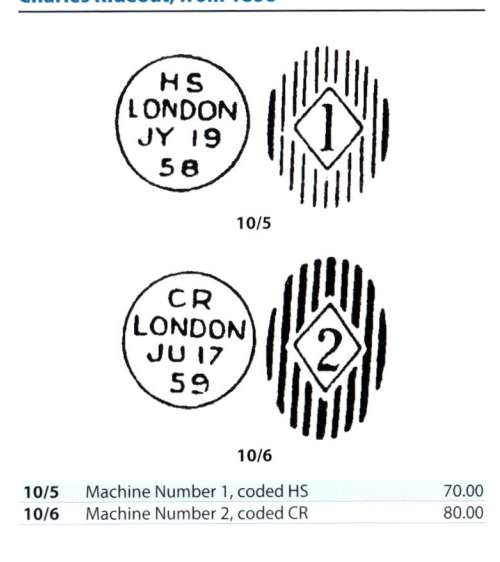

10/5	Machine Number 1, coded HS	70.00
10/6	Machine Number 2, coded CR	80.00

Pearson Hill, from 1858

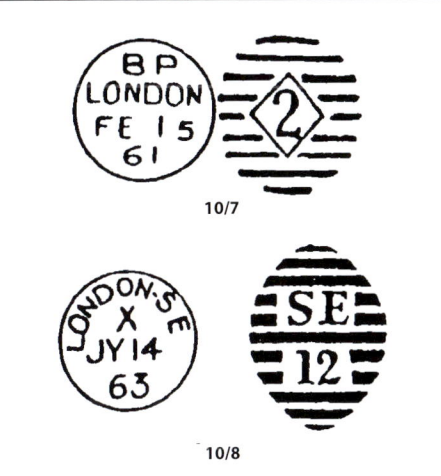

Note: It is difficult to put precise values on the higher priced items since normally sold only at auction or by private treaty. New information is always welcome.

Machine Cancellations

10/7	Parallel Motion machines, London, Nos 1-6, 87, 90-92, 97, 100-101	5.00
10/8	Parallel Motion machines, London District offices	5.00

Note: Pivot machines, listed separately in the Fifth edition, are Parallel Motion machines fixed to special arms; their postmarks are identical.

Azemar, 1869-72 (or Fischer and Maas)

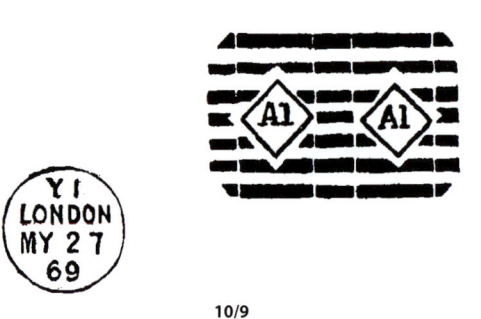

10/9

10/11

10/9	Town die lower at left, dates in 1869 (not used 1870) (bars in 3, 4 or 5 sections, varying in sequence)	£250
10/10	As above but town die level with bars, 1871-72	£100
10/11	Rectangular town die, lower at left, along with 89 in diamond (see illustration), used January 1871 only on postcards	£750

Sloper, 1870-75

10/12	Stamped postcard perforated by single hole (doubts exist as to whether this single hole is made by a Sloper machine)	30.00
10/13	As above but series of holes in shape of arrow	50.00
10/14	As above but series of holes in shape of orb	£750

Hoster, 1882-93

Note: Care should be exercised in the use of the following summary of this complex topic. Inclusion of stars in the town die is not shown, and with two die heads in each machine, only one of each pair has an asterisk or star at the centre. These in turn should not be confused with side stars, and for simplicity some items with these stars are not shown. The term "mirrored" is used to show bars in the NE/SW direction as opposed to NW/SE, and is shown below as (M). (L) denotes corner bars to the left of town die at top and/or bottom.

10/18

10/21

10/30

10/15	Single rim London-EC town die 20mm, 18 thick bars but none at left	£300
10/16	Single rim London/EC town die 28-30mm, 14 bars but none at left	25.00
10/17	As above but (L)	25.00
10/18	Similar but with numbers in bars to bottom right of town die	35.00
10/19	As above but London/NPB, 14 bars	£550
10/20	Single rim London/Offl Paid town die, no bars, red	£250
10/21	Double rim London/E(year)C town die, 18 bars (M) (L)	40.00
10/22	As above but 12/14/15 bars, not (M)	25.00
10/23	Similar but 17 bars and numbers in LH bars	40.00
10/24	Double rim London/EC town die, year above EC, 14 bars (L)	25.00
10/25	As above but with stars and 12 bars	20.00
10/26	Double rim London town die, 12/15/16 bars (L)	20.00
10/27	As above but 16/18 bars (M)	25.00
10/28	As above but square dots for bars	£600
10/29	Double rim London EC town die, no bars, used as backstamp, blk/red	15.00
10/30	Double rim Charing Cross town die, 17 bars	£400
10/31	Double rim Bedford St town die, (M) or no bars	£800

Ethridge, September 1886-April 1887

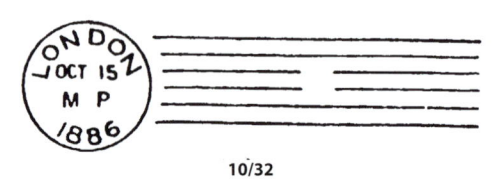

10/32

Machine Cancellations

10/32	Single circle town die, six straight bars with central space)	£500

International, 1893-1933 (or Hey & Dolphin, or Flier)

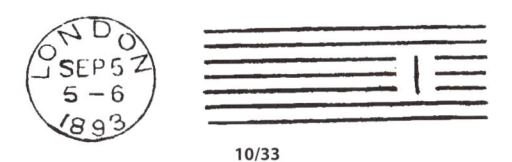

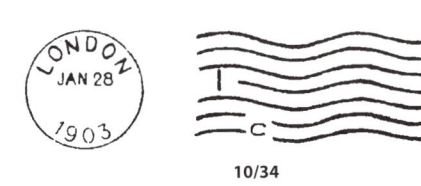

10/33

10/34

10/33	Single circle town die, seven straight bars with 1 (August-September 1893 trials)	£400
10/34	Single circle town die, seven wavy bars with 1/C (1902-03 trials)	50.00
10/35	As above but Paid town die, without bars, red	60.00
10/36	As above but 1911 trials at London EC	90.00
10/37	As above but 1911-12 trials at Liverpool	£125

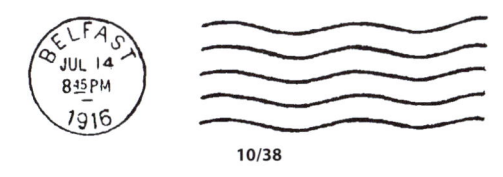

10/38

10/42

10/44 (in red)

10/38	Single circle town die, five wavy bars	1.00
10/39	As above but seven wavy bars	2.00
10/40	Double circle town die, five wavy bars	1.00
10/41	As above but six straight bars	3.00
10/42	As above but seven wavy bars	1.00
10/43	Rectangular Paid die, in red without bars	2.00
10/44	As above but "Official Paid"	3.00

For continuation see "Universal postmarks from 1933 - summary" following **10/171B**.

Imperial Mail Marking, 1897

10/45

10/46

10/45	Victoria Flag: demonstration trial, June 1897	*
10/46	VR Flag: demonstration trial, September/November 1897	£2500

Empire Machine, 1898

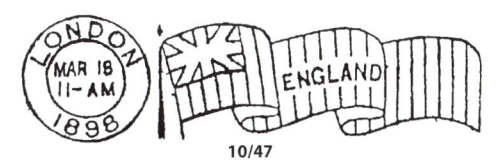

10/47

10/47	England Flag: used on four days in March 1898	£3000

Bickerdike, 1897-1907

10/49

10/53

10/48	V Crown R within bars, non-seriffed, year in full	£500
10/49	As above but larger VR with serifs	£500
10/50	As above but VR without serifs and numbers 1-6 beneath crown	15.00
10/51	As above but year in two digits	15.00
10/52	As above but Liverpool, 1 or 2 beneath crown	50.00
10/53	E Crown R, year in two digits, numbers beneath crown (rounded crown)	8.00
10/54	As above but Victoria crown	50.00
10/55	As above but year in full horizontally, no numbers (rounded crown)	6.00
10/56	As above but year in full round rim, no numbers	8.00
10/57	As above but Liverpool, 1 or 2 beneath crown	40.00

191

Machine Cancellations

Boston, 1898-1907

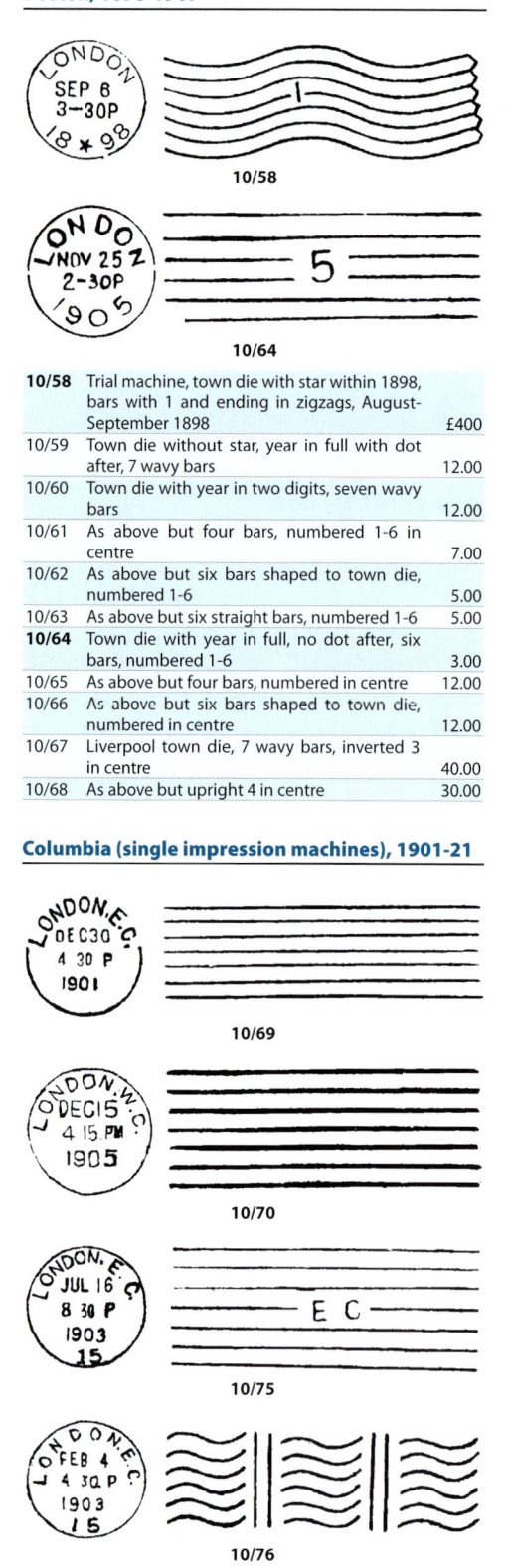

10/58

10/64

10/58	Trial machine, town die with star within 1898, bars with 1 and ending in zigzags, August-September 1898	£400
10/59	Town die without star, year in full with dot after, 7 wavy bars	12.00
10/60	Town die with year in two digits, seven wavy bars	12.00
10/61	As above but four bars, numbered 1-6 in centre	7.00
10/62	As above but six bars shaped to town die, numbered 1-6	5.00
10/63	As above but six straight bars, numbered 1-6	5.00
10/64	Town die with year in full, no dot after, six bars, numbered 1-6	3.00
10/65	As above but four bars, numbered in centre	12.00
10/66	As above but six bars shaped to town die, numbered in centre	12.00
10/67	Liverpool town die, 7 wavy bars, inverted 3 in centre	40.00
10/68	As above but upright 4 in centre	30.00

Columbia (single impression machines), 1901-21

10/69

10/70

10/75

10/76

10/83

10/87

10/89

10/90

10/69	Single arc town die with seven straight bars	12.00
10/70	Single circle town die: London MP, EC, SE, SW, W or WC with seven straight bars	3.00
10/71	As above but with die number in centre of bars	3.00
10/72	As above but London District letters in bars	3.00
10/73	As above but with five wavy bars segmented into three sections, bars above and below and central 3	6.00
10/74	Single circle town die, coded at foot, seven straight bars	2.00
10/75	As above but London District initials in bars	3.00
10/76	As above but with six wavy bars segmented into three sections	4.00
10/77	Paid single circle town die, red, with seven straight bars	6.00
10/78	As above but London District initials in bars	9.00
10/79	As above but with segmented bars	18.00
10/80	As above but with six straight bars and die numbers at left between bars	12.00
10/81	Three line town die, lines above and below, seven straight bars	3.00
10/82	As above but with six straight bars	7.00
10/83	As above but with six straight bars, and die number at left between central bars: London E (18), EC (2), NW (19 and 20), SE (15 and 19), SW (14), WC (16 and 19), W (17), Paddington W (19 and 21), Aberdeen (1), Birmingham (1), Bristol (1), Cardiff (1), Dublin (1), Edinburgh (1), Glasgow (1), Hull (1), Leeds (1), Liverpool (1 and 2), Manchester (1 and 2), Newcastle-on-Tyne (1), Nottingham (1)	2.00
10/84	Three line town die without lines, seven straight bars	3.00
10/85	As above but 4 cuts in top 2 bars or 9 cuts in top 3, 1906-07	4.00
10/86	As above but with six straight bars	2.00
10/87	As above but with six straight bars segmented into three sections	7.00
10/88	As above but with six straight bars and die number at left between central bars from London and provinces, as listed above (10/83)	3.00
10/89	As above but with five wavy bars	2.00

192

Machine Cancellations

10/90	As above but with six straight bars in three pairs	12.00
10/91	As above but with eight straight bars in four pairs	25.00
10/92	As above but with large London district letters in 5 wavy bars	4.00
10/93	As above but town die only, no bars, used as receiving mark	3.00
10/94	Four line Paid town die, 6/7 straight bars or 5 wavy bars, red	6.00
10/95	As above but Official Paid	6.00
10/96	As above with six bars in three pairs, in red	12.00
10/97	As above, six bars, die number at left between central bars	10.00
10/98	As above but Paid town die only, no bars, in red	4.00
10/99	As above but Postage Paid town die only, no bars, in red	8.00
10/100	Posted in Advance for Xmas, Manchester, large X and six bars (see chapter 20 for details)	£120
10/101	Triangular die with telegraphic code (eg S. M., M.T.P.I.) with six, seven bars, or bars with central die numbers	5.00
10/102	Dulwich SE21, four-line town die, eight straight bars, 1920	60.00

For continuation see "Universal postmarks from 1933 - Summary" following **10/171B**.

Krag (continuous impression machines), from 1905

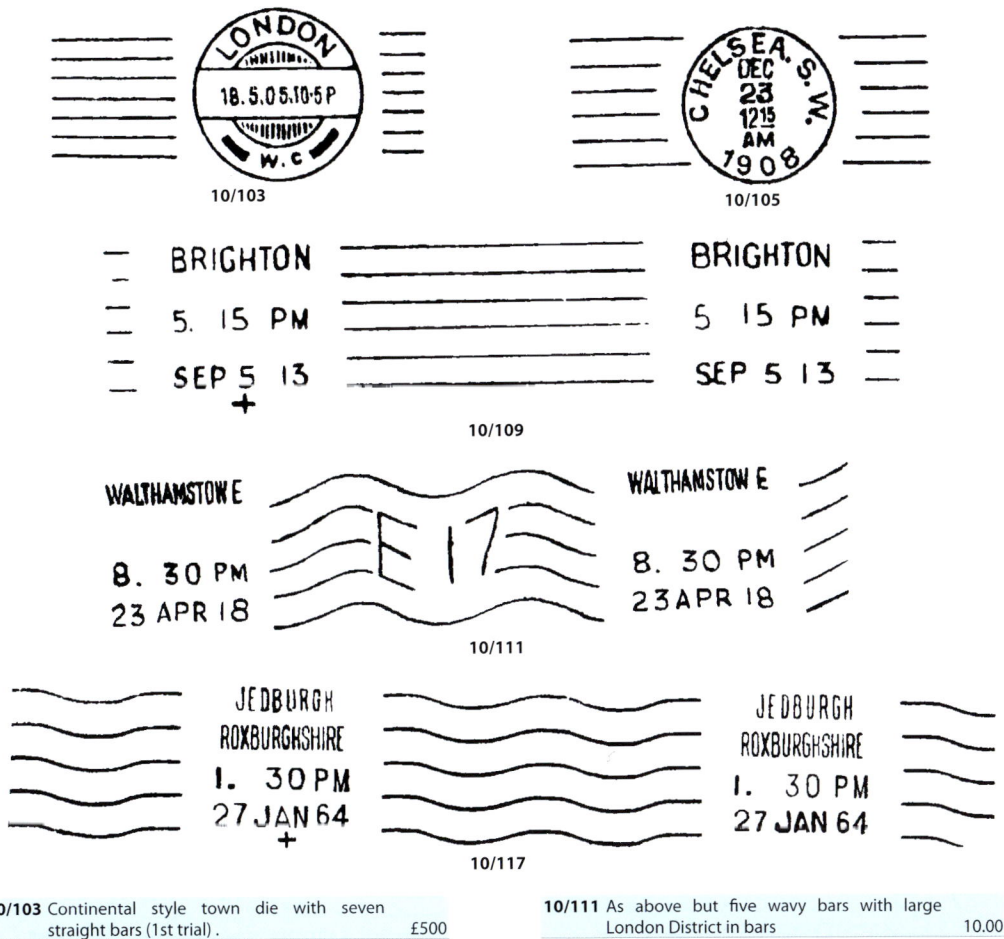

10/103

10/105

10/109

10/111

10/117

10/103	Continental style town die with seven straight bars (1st trial) .	£500
10/104	Single circle, London EC, with six straight bars, shaped ends	4.00
10/105	As above but Chelsea S.W.	4.00
10/106	As above but London F.S.	10.00
10/107	Three line town die, London W, six straight bars and central 3	3.00
10/108	As above but London E.C.	4.00
10/109	As above but six straight bars, London or Provincial	1.00
10/110	Three or four-line town die with five deep wavy bars	1.00
10/111	As above but five wavy bars with large London District in bars	10.00
10/112	As above but wartime dies of bars, crosses or +s, *see chapter 14*	
10/113	Three line Gt Britain town die with Paid & 6 straight bars, in red	2.00
10/114	As above but with five wavy bars, in red	1.00
10/115	As above but Official Paid with five wavy bars, in red	2.00
10/116	Triangular die with telegraphic code and six straight bars	3.00
10/117	Five shallow wavy bars, from 1950s, with 3 or 4-line town die	1.00

193

Machine Cancellations

10/118	As above but Gt Britain town dies and Paid, red (with value, DP etc, sometimes different in the 2 boxes)	1.00
10/119	As above, but Gt Britain die used in black on normal mail	2.00
10/120	As above but with triangular die, code no. or telegraphic code	3.00
10/121	As above but with errors, eg one "box" inverted, dates different	2.00

Sylbe, 1907-08

10/122	Three line London EC town die similar to Krag but with 9 above time, six straight bars	30.00

Columbia (continuous impression machines), 1909-11

Note: Many dies were used on trial basis, not all are covered here.

10/123

10/123	Three line London town die with three straight bars	20.00
10/124	As above but with six bars arranged in three pairs	20.00
10/125	As above but Kensington W, with six evenly spaced straight bars	25.00
10/126	As above but Paid town die, three straight bars	25.00

Universal, from 1910

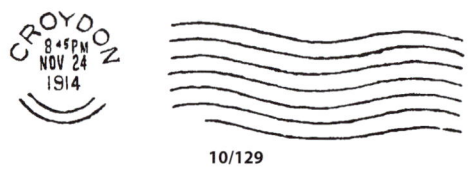

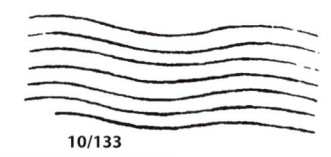

10/129

10/133

10/127	London EC single circle, code H or C, seven wavy bars, 1910-11	12.00
10/128	As above, other towns, without inner arc, approx 1912-15	15.00
10/129	Croydon double arc, seven wavy bars, 1914-15, 1920 (5.00 for 1920)	4.00
10/130	Double circle town die, Stockport 1914-15 (Paid die 1917, 50.00)	12.00
10/131	As above but Margate, 1924-25	3.00
10/132	As above Doncaster Yorks, 1926-28 *	12.00
10/133	Single circle town die with inner arc, and six or seven (or later five) continuous wavy bars, later county at foot (variations)	1.00
10/134	Great Britain circular town die with "Paid" within circle, in red	2.00
10/135	As above but with square Paid die, in red	1.00
10/136	As above but Great Britain die used in black on normal mail	3.00
10/137	Triangular die used for printed papers	2.00
10/138	Census diamond die	1.00

Nos. 10/137 and 10/138 are undated but prices are for pre-1933 period.
*Note: Peach shows as 7 wavy bars, but seen with 5 wavy bars
For continuation see "Universal-style postmarks from 1933 - Summary" following **10/171B**.

Time Mail Marking Machine Company, 1912-13

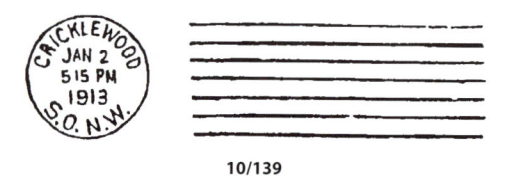

10/139

10/140

10/139	Cricklewood single circle town die with seven straight bars, December 1912-January 1913	£300
10/140	As above but St John's Wood, year in 4th bar, 1913	£500

Alma or Bee, 1912-22 (continuous impression machines)

10/141

10/141	London EC four-line town die (one blank) with six short bars	3.00
10/142	New Cross SE trial, three line town die with six straight bars	30.00
10/143	As above but with five wavy bars from London EC, SW1, Kensington, Woolwich SE18 or Southend-on-Sea	2.00
10/144	As above but with Paid ½d, in red	7.00

Machine Cancellations

Krag (single impression machines), from 1923

10/145

10/146

10/148

10/150 (in red)

10/145	London WC trial, 24mm circular town die with five wavy bars, 1923	£150
10/146	As above but London WC trial, 19½mm diameter, 1925-26	70.00
10/147	As above but London NW1 trial, 1926	£300
10/148	Single circle 22mm town die from elsewhere (not trial) from 1927	3.00
10/149	Double circle town die with five wavy bars	2.00
10/150	Square Paid town die, single or double, with five wavy bars, red	5.00

For continuation see "Universal-style postmarks from 1933 - Summary" following **10/171B**.

Klussendorf (or Standard), 1930-37

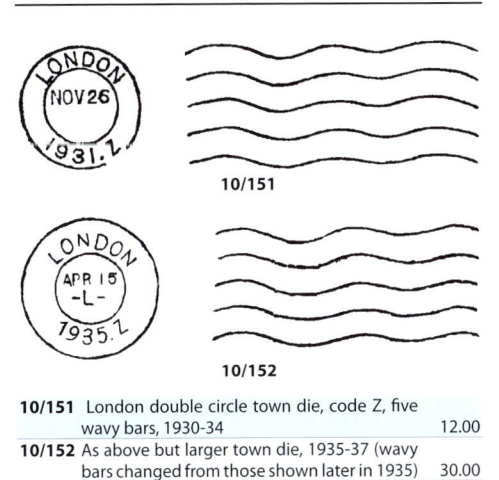

10/151

10/152

10/151	London double circle town die, code Z, five wavy bars, 1930-34	12.00
10/152	As above but larger town die, 1935-37 (wavy bars changed from those shown later in 1935)	30.00
10/153	Double square Paid town die, no bars (with wavy bars - rare), red	30.00

Totometer, 1957-90 (used for stamping magazines/wrappers)

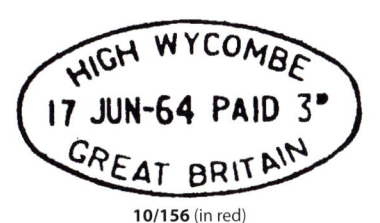

10/155 (in red)

10/156 (in red)

10/154	Postage Paid die in 4 straight lines, lines above and below, red	15.00
10/155	Liverpool/Gt. Britain, circular town die struck sideways, in red	65.00
10/156	Large Paid oval, in red, used to 1980	1.00
10/157	As above but with "Parcel Post" wording	6.00
10/158	As above, exceptional use 1987-90, in black from Bristol	2.00

Machines for stamping "large flats" and/or packets

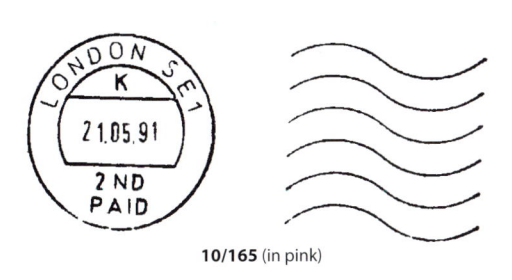

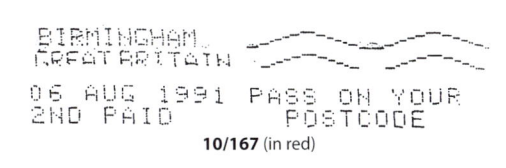

10/165 (in pink)

10/167 (in red)

10/171A (in red)

195

Machine Cancellations

10/171B

10/159	Roddis "Mangle" from 1957, continuous impression similar to Krag (normally struck across centre of envelope), red	1.00
10/160	Krag eg London E1,N1, Croydon in black on adhesives, 1980s-90s	1.00
10/161	Norwich trial 1959 (3 rows of wavy lines, one with town dies)	60.00
10/162	Manchester trial 1963	15.00
10/163	Edinburgh trial 1989-90 (black or red), 2 rows of wavy lines	4.00
10/164	Klussendorf, Liverpool (variations in date layout), 1991-92	1.00
10/165	As above but London SE1 Paid, in "luminous pink", 1991-94	1.00
10/166	Birmingham ink jet postmark with/without slogan, 1992-93, black	4.00
10/167	As above but Paid wording (variations), 1991-92, red	5.00
10/168	London SW "Please use Postcode" (variations) ink-jet imprint, 1991 (this legend is applied at the foot of the envelope, not on stamp)	5.00
10/169	Ink jet messages at foot of large envelopes, black or red, 1993-	1.00
10/170	Oxford trial, August 1992 (used few days only)	18.00
10/171	Perth trial, also used short period August 1992	20.00
10/171A	Pitney Bowes trial at Swindon, 2004, red	3.00
10/171B	NEC Flats cancelling machine, Manchester 2008 (with later variation omitting row of wavy lines)	2.00

Universal-style (unified) postmarks from 1933 - Summary

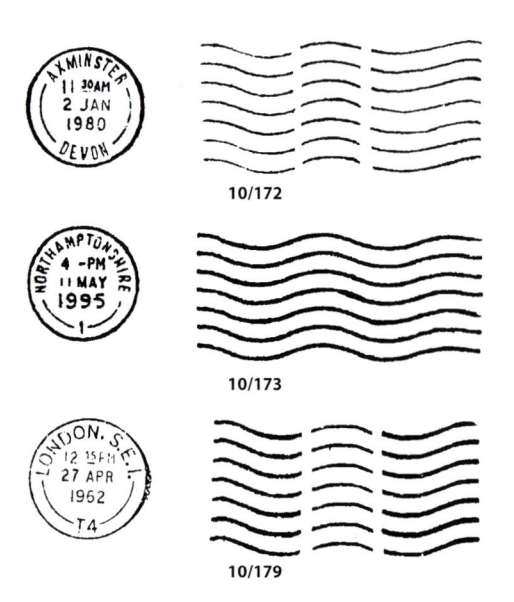

10/172

10/173

10/179

10/183 (in red)

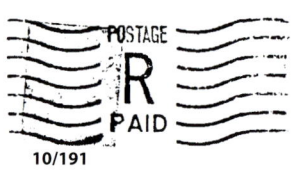

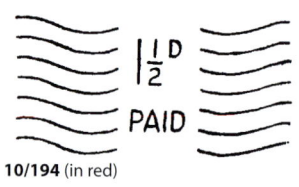

10/191

10/194 (in red)

Note: From 1933 the style of town dies used in Universal machines was adopted for other types of single impression machine, hence the term "unified dies" regardless of the manufacturer of the machine: the manufacturer thus cannot be identified.

10/172	Unified design with wavy lines (3-part wavy lines from 1936) (for details/valuations of individual TOWNS see next section).	0.50
10/173	Post-1950 use of continuous wavy lines (5 or 7 lines)	0.50
10/174	Similar but 6 lines	1.00
10/175	As above but in red, 1990 only (3-part wavy lines)	0.50
10/176	As above but with slogan - see next chapter	0.50
10/177	With double circle town die (eg Bournemouth-Poole to c1950)	0.50
10/178	With London missort die (usually on reverse of envelope)	1.00
10/179	Early ALF dies 1957-62, eg Southampton S, London SE1 T4	1.50
10/180	FCT dies from 1976 with distinguishable codes, eg London EC S1	0.50
10/181	CFC dies from 1989 with distinguishable codes, eg Leicester CFC1 (see glossary of terms at end of chapter 27)	0.50
10/182	Square Paid die with continuous lines or 3-part wavy lines, in red	1.00
10/183	Same but 1960 or later (values higher with slogans)	1.50
10/184	Same but at Guildford, new die 1985-95	0.50
10/185	Circular Gt Brit die with 2d paid/1st paid etc in wavy lines, red (to 2009, see note re "Paid handstamps" in chapter 9)	0.50
10/186	Same but in black on paid mail from 1990 (eg Watford, Dover)	1.00
10/187	Same but NOT Gt Britain die used on paid mail, red	0.50
10/188	Same but Slough/Windsor SL0-9 with octagonal die, red, 1995	1.00
10/189	Circ Gt Britain die in black on normal mail with slogan/wavy lines	1.00
10/190	Similar but with continuous wavy lines	1.00
10/191	Similar on charity mailings eg "R" or "Mailsort" on adhesives	1.00
10/192	Same but "Paid" in town die, eg Hastings, 1963-, in red	1.50
10/193	Triangular die with wavy lines, to 1968 (used on printed papers)	1.00

Machine Cancellations

10/194	Similar but with "ld paid" etc in wavy lines, in red	1.50
10/195	Census diamond (to 1985 when general use ceased)	0.50
10/196	As above but red or with wavy lines, or narrow type, or other varieties including triangle used instead of diamond	1.00
10/197	Same (or triangle in its place) used post-1985	0.50
10/198	Diamond (same but not census!) on charity appeal mailings, 1990s-	0.50
10/199	Dated diamond, first used at Croydon in reserve machines Dec 1996	0.50
10/200	Errors of town die, year inverted, time/date errors etc (Many of these are very common, but others such as "two years" or "two times", possibly inverted as well, are less so)	1.00

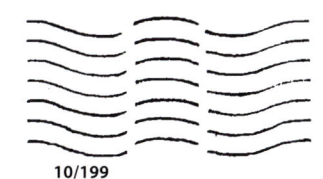

10/199

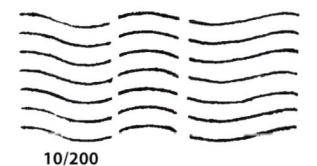

10/200

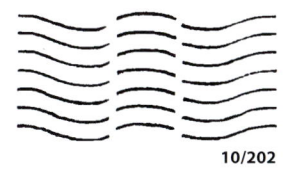

10/202

10/207

10/201	Errors of wavy lines, centre portion inverted etc	£1.00
10/202	-transposed wavy lines (ie to left of town die)	0.50
10/203	Errors of "paid" section eg "2nd paid" in black on normal mail	1.00
10/204	Pre-decimal "ld"/"2d" used post-1971 with d or d removed, red	1.00
10/205	Date removed (or year only shown) after postal strike July 1964	1.50
10/206	Any postal strike machine postmarks 20 January to 7 March 1971	2.00
10/207	Bradford "chess board" design, 1988-93 (used initially for "blacking out" incorrect meter postmarks, later for stamp cancelling)	2.00

Computer produced Postmarks on Bulk Mailings, from 1993

In a major development for posting items in large numbers where the sender preferred to use adhesives, Royal Mail permitted senders to stamp their own mail. Development of computer systems has allowed addresses and postmarks to be applied together, while envelopes are "stuffed" and sealed and stamps affixed all by machine usually in one operation. The undated postmarks are produced in large numbers.

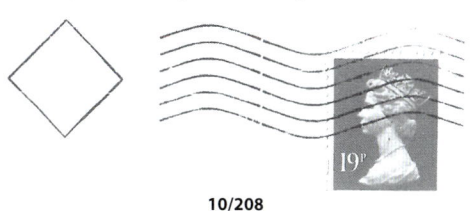

10/208

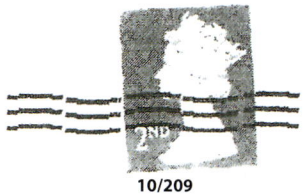

10/209

10/208	Diamond with distinctive wavy lines and small gaps, cf 10/198	0.50

(see note in chapter 9, high density ink jet machine on charity appeals with adhesives affixed, Royal Mail agreeing that senders cancel stamps themselves)

10/209	Other machine postmarks applied by senders (machines developed by bulk mailing companies to "stuff" envelopes, affix stamp, apply address and postmark all in one operation)	0.50

Nos. 10/210-220 reserved for future use.

Ink jet machines, from 1993

10/221

10/224

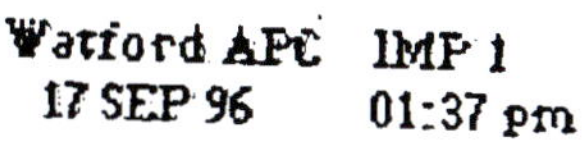

10/225

10/221	Trials at Gloucester, Darlington etc, 1993-94	8.00
10/222	As above but rectangular Paid die, Swindon, 1994, red	5.00
10/223	London FS ink jet machine, Paid mail (variations), pink, 1995-	5.00

197

Machine Cancellations

IMP machines

10/230

10/232

10/224	First use in IMP at Watford (5.00 for early dates Aug-Oct 1996)			1.00
	(Aug-Oct 1996 postmark had no slogan, but imprint on reverse of env) (later used countrywide)			
10/225	same machine but Q of S mark on reverse of meter mail etc, 1996			1.00
10/226	Revised format (there were several revisions from 1998 onwards)			0.50
	(for illustrations of IMP slogan postmarks see **11/14** and **11/15** in chapter 11)			
10/227	"Shallow" version IMP postmark without slogan (used on smaller or "shallow" envelopes)			1.00
10/228	Prepaid mail struck with Royal Mail Franking Service IMP Postmark (modern equivalent of Paid postmark but struck in black)			1.00
10/229	Test postmark used on live mail in error			1.00
10/230	Two halves of postmark "out of sync"			3.00
10/231	IMP slogan postmark, similar to 10/226 but revised version from August 2011			1.00
10/232	As above but with one or two sets of wavy lines at LEFT instead of at RIGHT			1.00
10/233	New IMP postmark of six wavy lines only, no slogan, date or town from January 2012			1.00
10/234	As 10/231 but with "Delivered by Royal Mail" added, 2012-			0.50

Note: along with the new IMP postmark variations in 2011 came the inclusion in the postmark of various symbols -dot, #, +, u etc, indeed two of these are shown in the illustration **10/232** which has a dot under the wavy lines and # at top right. For more details of these see Patrick Awcock's articles in *British Postmark Society Journal*. Patrick has also helped with the following list.

Offices using IMP machines
(generic titles are not shown, see list at end of chapter)

Belfast	2000-	London South	1997-2012
Birmingham	1997-	Manchester	1997-
Bolton	1997-2010	Newcastle upon Tyne	1997-
Bristol	1997-	Nottingham	1997-
Cambridge	1998-	Oxford	1997-2009
Cardiff	1998-	Plymouth	1999-
Carlisle	1997-	Preston	1997-
Chelmsford	1997-	Romford	2010
Chester	1999-	Sheffield	1999-
Crewe	1997-2010	Shrewsbury	1998-2013
Gatwick	1998-	Slough	2001-04
Greenford	2000-	(also Heathrow but Slough postmark)	
(initially Harrow postmark)			
Hull	1999-	Southampton	1998-
Leeds	1998-	Swansea	1998-
Leicester	1997-	Swindon	1997-2008

Truro	1997-	Wolverhampton	1998-
Watford	1996-2011	Worcester	1997-2012

(Nos.10/235-240 reserved for future use)

Inkjet machines used with CFCs/ILSMs

Intelligent Letter Sorting Machines (ILSMs) do not normally produce a postmark but the facility exists to add inkjet printers to them. In the 2009-10 trial (**10/242**) an undated postmark was applied to top left of envelope and the stamp cancelled by a CFC (as usual), but from 2012 the CFC produced no postmark and the ILSM inkjet printer (see **10/243-244**) cancelled the stamp.

10/241

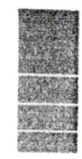

10/242

10/243

10/244

198

Machine Cancellations

10/241	Inkjet trial, Peterborough 2004 (printer attached to CFC) (this item previously shown as **10/230**)	3.00
10/242	Trial at "Jubilee MC", 2009" 10 - postmark top left of envelope (see note above)	5.00
10/243	New postmark used "live", 2012 ("chunky") version used at 6 offices, approx Feb-June 2012)	1.00
10/244	As above but with 4,5,8 or 11 lines, 2012- (see list on next page)	0.50

Mail Centres using 10/244:
The following used the new printers from 2012:
(London) Mount Pleasant
Aberdeen
Croydon
"Dorset & SW Hants"
Edinburgh
Exeter
Glasgow
Home Counties North MC
Jubilee MC
Medway MC
Norwich
Peterborough
South Midlands MC
Swindon
Warrington
(Nos. 10/245-250 reserved for future use)

Baumann (previously Klussendorf) machines, from 2003

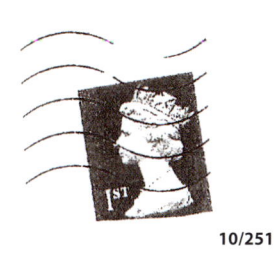

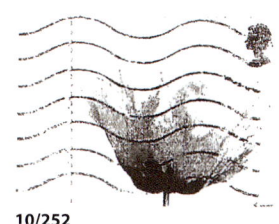

10/251

10/252

10/251	Format 1, approx 6 machines used (variations) (similar to 10/164 – 165 but with "Royal Mail" at top and wavy lines at left, firstly at "London South" in 2003, last remaining machine at Hemel Hempstead to 2011)	1.00
10/252	Format 2, approx 6 machines from 2008	1.00
	(illustration shows machine at Carlisle)	

Towns with Krag and Universal machines from 1933 to 1999

But see note regarding 21st century.
The list that follows is a priced guide to machine postmarks from 1933 (when unified dies started) to 1999, but for completeness the new 21st century Mail Centres of Greenford, "Jubilee", "Thames Valley" (Swindon) and "London East" etc are included. To conserve space it is in compact, heavily abbreviated form. Machines are of the Universal type unless (**K**) for Krag is shown. (**U**) denotes use of the Universal type, usually following (**K**). The following are not specifically indicated in the list :
(a) machine types ie ALFs, FCTs and CFCs,
(b) MLO/APC/Royal Mail inscriptions
(c) GB dies used in black or in red on paid mail (including Krag machines used for paid mail, as late as the 1990s, at offices such as Wisbech and Worthing)
(d) old and new counties before/after the county changes of 1974 in England and Wales (in Scotland the old counties remained unchanged in postmarks). However, use of generic descriptions is shown eg 'North Devon' at Barnstaple.
* denotes towns that still have machines

The following codes show that at the relevant office ONLY the following categories of mail were still stamped (usually for the remaining years of 20th century):
(**P**) paid mail (in red)
(**L**) local and/or missorted items; thus mail stamped at this office is not normally seen outside the local area, but MAY be used at Christmas.
(**M**) missorted items (postmark usually on the reverse of the envelope)
(**R**) restricted collections of outward mail, typically the first morning collection only, or first class mail only; (**R**)/(**L**) means (**R**) later (**L**)
(**X**) mail in the pre-Christmas period

Summary of 21st century machine postmarks (to 2013)
Since about 1997 IMPs (see previous section) were used at about 30 of the country's Mail Centres for stamping normal mail, though normal machines (see 'a' above) are retained for a small proportion of the mail. However, a further 30 Mail Centres retain CFCs and other "non IMPs" and the postmarks are as shown in this section (see * above). This leaves the smaller offices, which are now dedicated solely to mail deliveries, while missorts and locals are no longer stamped at these offices, also with Health & Safety considerations in mind the machines at most of the towns listed below can be considered to have ENDED in 2000 or some time in the years that followed (where no end date shown): it is a shame one cannot be more precise. There are no doubt some exceptions, usage at Christmas each year being one such exception, but by 2009 the concept of "outsourcing" the stamping operation at Christmas seems to have ended. Further exceptions are Amlwch and Llangefni which ended in 2001 but normal mail was being stamped at these two locations up to then.
(**N**) denotes the Mail Centres that used the new postmarks shown at **10/243-244** from 2012. Some of these continued to use "conventional" machines on a residual basis (eg on "large flats" or at Xmas). Similarly some IMP offices (see list after **10/234**) have also retained some "conventional" machines.
For both sets of offices * is thus retained in the list that follows. As at 2013 the Mail Centres still using "conventional" machine postmarks for normal mail were Doncaster, Gloucester, Inverness, Ipswich and Portsmouth.

199

Machine Cancellations

PLEASE - COLLECT MACHINE POSTMARKS COMPLETE WITH WAVY LINES NOT AS SHOWN HERE!

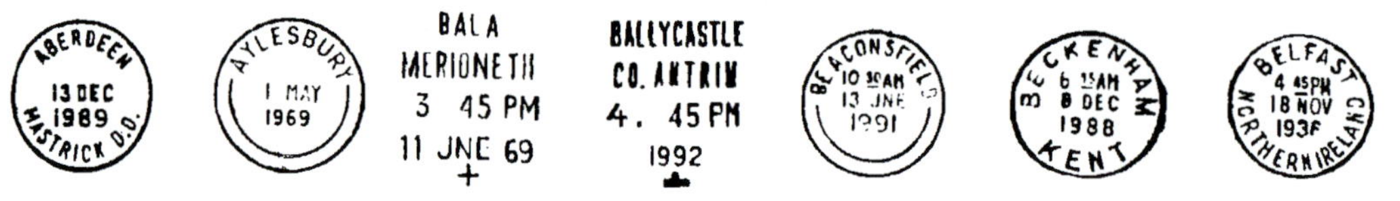

Camp Hill — Blackpool

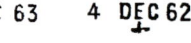

Bolton — Brighton — Brighton

Glasgow — Glasgow South — Grimsby

Lochgilphead

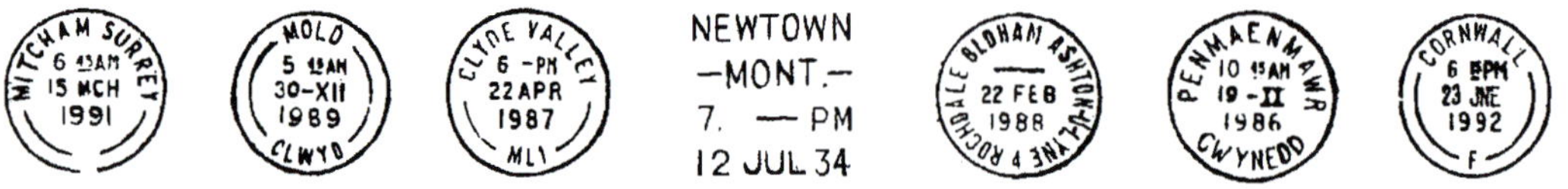

Motherwell — Oldham — Penzance

200

Machine Cancellations

Postmark examples shown (left to right, top to bottom):

- PLYMOUTH & DISTRICT A, 5 AUG 1990
- PORTMADOC CAERNARVONSHIRE, 12 45 PM, 8 SEP 59
- PORTSMOUTH ISLE OF WIGHT, 3 DEC 1991
- REIGATE SURREY RH2, 25 APR 1996
- ROCK FERRY B'HEAD, 11.— AM, 15 MAY 40
- ROSSENDALE LANCS, 21 DEC 35
- SEDBERGH YORKSHIRE —PM—, 18 DEC 69
- SENNEN & LAND'S END PENZANCE, 6 ½PM 2 JNE 1992
- SLOUGH/WINDSOR, 1 ½PM 22 AUG 1991, SLO-9 — Slough
- STAPLEFORD NOTTINGHAM, 10 15 AM, 11 DEC 69
- NORTH HERTS, 16 DEC 1985 — Stevenage
- STOKESLEY MIDDLESBROUGH PAID 1ST, 13 FEB 69
- CROYDON/SUTTON, 6—AM 11 SEP 1991, SUTTON — Sutton
- TRING HERTS, 6 30 PM, 3 DEC 55
- ULVERSTON LANCS., 8.— PM, 5 MCH 36
- VIRGINIA WATER SURREY, 19 DEC 1967
- KLOOVILLE HANTS, 1 ½PM 21 JLY 1990
- WESTBURY ON TRYM BRISTOL, 2. 30 PM, 1 JUL 35
- WHITCHURCH SHROPSHIRE, 4 ?AM 29 NOV 1989
- WISHAW LANARKSHIRE, 7.— PM, 10 MCH 44
- YEADON LEEDS, 1 ½PM 5 SEP 1966
- LONDON IS M.L.O., 10 ½AM 8 MAY 1989
- MOUNT PLEASANT, 6 ½PM 18 MCH 1985 — "error"
- LONDON NORTH A2, 9 FEB 1996
- LONDON N13/N21, 10 ½AM 22 JLY 1991 — Winchmore Hill N21
- GREAT BRITAIN, 14 FEB 1972 — Battersea SW11
- HOME DISTRICT, 6 ½PM 6 JNE 1937
- GUERNSEY POST OFFICE ALDERNEY, 4 -PM JAN 7 1992
- LONDON, B, 16 JLY 1968, JOB — Maida Hill
- KILBURN, B, 14 JAN 1967, 60
- LONDON —75— —A— 16 DEC 63 — Paddington

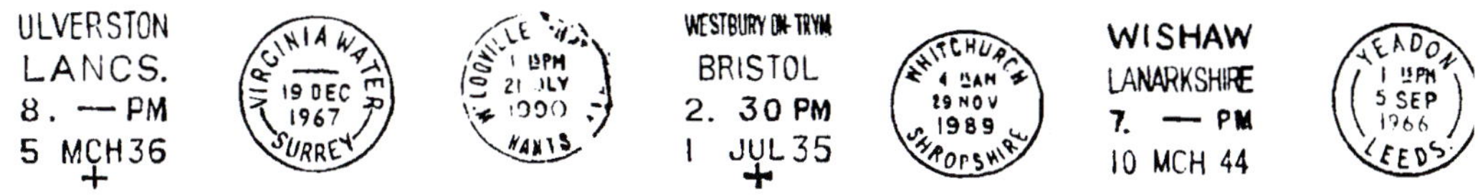

	1933-44	45-60	61-99
Abercarn (L) 94-2001			1.00
Aberdare (K) 27-34	3.00		
then (U) 35-	0.60	0.50	0.50
then 'Cardiff 10' (L) 89-			1.00
then 'Aberdare' (bilingual)(L) 2000 only			2.00
Aberdeen – 2012 (N)	0.50	0.50	0.50
Aberdeen DO (M) 88-91			1.00
Aberdeen Mastrick DO (M) 88-91			1.00
then (X) 94			1.00
Aberdovey (K) 68-72			1.00
Aberfeldy (K) 58-60		1.00	
then (U) 61- later (R)-82			0.50
Abergavenny (K) 36-38	4.00		
then (U) later (R)/(L)-2000	0.60	0.50	0.50
Abergele 50-63, (R, at Rhyl)-71		0.50	0.50
Abertillery (K) 45-		2.00	
then (U) 49- later (R)-99		0.50	0.50
Aberystwyth-97 then (L)-98	0.50	0.50	0.50
also (K) 77 only			3.00
then (U) 'SY23 SY24 SY25' etc (actually at Shrewsbury) 97-98			1.00
with 'SY23-25' at Aberystwyth (L) 98-?99			1.00
then (X, same die) 2002-03			1.00
Abingdon (K) 35-39	2.50		

	1933-44	45-60	61-99
then (U) later (L)	0.50	0.50	0.50
Accrington -75	0.50	0.50	0.50
then 'Lancashire 15' (M) 89-			1.00
Airdrie (K) 35-38	2.00		
then (U)-68	0.60	0.50	0.50
then 'Coatbridge & Airdrie' (X) 82-85			1.00
Alcester (K) 61-71			1.00
then (U,R)/(L)			0.50
Aldeburgh (K) 61-72			1.00
Alderley Edge/Manch (K) 55-56		4.00	
then A Edge/Cheshire (K) 56-63		1.00	1.00
then (U) later (L)-92			0.50
Aldershot -92 (replaced by Farnborough)	0.50	0.50	0.50
Aldershot PDO (M) 89-			1.00
Aldridge ?60-70		1.00	1.00
Alexandria (K) 41-56	1.50	1.00	
then (U) 57-?72 then (X)-86 (spelling 'Dumbartonshire' 57-59 1.00)		0.50	0.50
Alford 57-77		0.50	0.50
Alfreton (K) 49-54		1.50	
then (U)-76		0.50	0.50
Alloa (K) 29-48	2.00	2.00	
then (U)-68		0.50	0.50

201

Machine Cancellations

	1933-44	45-60	61-99
Alnwick (K) 36-49	1.50	1.50	
then (U) later (R)/(L)		0.50	0.50
Alresford (K) 49-58		1.00	
then (U)-?68		0.50	0.50
Alton (K) 36-48	1.50	1.50	
then (U)-73 then (P,X)		0.50	0.50
but all mail again 88-92 then (L)			0.50
Altrincham -86	0.50	0.50	0.50
later (M)-90 then (X) 93-98			1.00
Alyth (K) 64-77			1.00
Ambleside (K) 32-60	1.00	1.00	
then (U)		0.50	0.50
then 'Lancs & S Lakes 17' (M) 93-			1.00
Amersham 'Chesham & Amersham' (K) 33-34 (prev Chesham)	3.50		
then (U) later (L)		0.50	0.50
Amlwch (K) 61-77			1.00
then (U) -2001, then (X) 2001			0.50
Ammanford (K) 43-49	5.00	5.00	
then (U)-94 then (L,X)		0.50	0.50
then 'Rhydaman Ammanf'd' (L) 99-2004			2.00
Andover (K) 32-36	2.00		
then (U) later (L)		0.50	0.50
Annan (K) 52-58		1.00	
then (U) later (R)-93 then (L)		0.50	0.50
Anstruther (K) 64-75			1.00
Antrim (K,X) 68-69			5.00
then (U) later (R)/(L)			0.50
Appleby (K) 60-70		1.00	1.00
Arbroath (K) 32-38	1.50		
then (U) later (R)/(L)		0.50	0.50
Ardrossan 36-71	0.60	0.50	0.50
Armagh (K) 39-54	4.00	3.00	
then (U) 'Armagh Co Armagh'-56		6.00	
then 'Armagh' later (R)/(L)		0.50	0.50
Arundel (K) 39-55	1.50	1.00	
then (U)-77 then again (L) 89-		0.50	0.50
Ascot (K) 29-38	1.50		
then (U) later (L)		0.50	0.50
Ashbourne (K) 50-59		1.50	
then (U)-76		0.60	0.50
Ashby-de-la-Zouch (K) 57-62		1.00	1.00
then (U)-75			0.50
Ashford Kent later (R)	0.50	0.50	0.50
and 'Tonbridge Y' (2nd class) 85-96			0.50
then 'Ashford' again -97			0.50
then 'Tonbridge' -98			0.50
Ashington (K) 38-48	2.00	2.00	
then (U) later (R)/(L)		0.50	0.50
Ashton-in-Makerfield (K) 58-80		1.50	1.50
Ashton-u-Lyne then (R)-91	0.50	0.50	0.50
Atherstone (K) 47-59		1.00	
then (U)-70		0.50	0.50
then 'Nuneaton' (U,X) 74			1.00
then 'Atherstone' again (U,M) 91-			1.00
Atherton (K) 34-55	1.00	1.00	
then (U) later (R)/(L)		0.50	0.50
Attleborough (K) 60-77		1.00	1.00
Auchterarder (K) 57-71		1.00	1.00
Audenshaw (K) 55-69		1.00	1.00
Aviemore (K) 67-74			1.00
then (U)-86			0.60
Avonmouth 57-88		0.50	0.50
Axminster (K) 39-52	1.50	1.00	
then (U)-93		0.50	0.50
Aylesbury -94 then (M)-97	0.50	0.50	0.50
but 'no Bucks' error 69 & 91			2.50
and (K) in black 75 only Paid die			2.50
Aylsham (K) 61-86			1.00

	1933-44	45-60	61-99
Ayr -94 then (L)-96	0.50	0.50	0.50
then (X)-2006			1.00
Bacup (K) 35-49	2.00	2.00	
then (U) later (R)/(L)		0.50	0.50
Baillieston (K) 59-82		1.00	1.00
then (U,R)/(L)			0.50
Bakewell (K) 50-63		1.00	1.00
then (U)-71			0.50
Bala (K) 68-83			1.00
Baldock (K) 58-63		1.00	1.00
then (U)-68			0.50
*Balivanich (K) 77-83			1.50
then (U) later (R)			1.00
but 'Balavanich' spelling error 83 & 92			10.00
Ballater (K) 67-78			1.00
Ballycastle (K) 59-97		1.00	1.00
Ballymena (K) 12-48	4.00	3.00	
then (U) later (L)/(X)-2008		0.50	0.50
Ballymoney (K) 54-58		6.00	
then (U) later (R)/(L)		1.00	0.50
Banbridge (K) 51-59		2.50	
then (U)-93 then (X) 94-2000		0.50	0.50
Banbury later (L)	0.50	0.50	0.50
Banchory (K) no county Dec 63			6.00
then (K) with county 63-78			1.00
then (U,X) 'Aberdeen' 90-92			1.00
then 'Banchory' (U,X) 94-2005			1.00
Banff (K) 56-58		2.50	
then (U)-76 then (X) 83-2005		0.50	0.50
Bangor Caern/Gwynedd later (R)-2001	0.50	0.50	0.50
also 'Gwynedd N' on Sundays 90-97			1.00
Bangor Co Down (K) 26-36	4.00		
then (U)-93 then (L)	1.00	0.50	0.50
Banstead (K) 42-47	2.00	2.00	
then (U)-?61		0.60	0.60
Bargoed (K) 38-55	3.00	2.00	
then (U)-75 (used at Hengoed from 1966)		1.00	0.50
Barking -55	0.50	0.50	
then again 70- later (L)			0.50
then 'Romford G31' (L) 88-			1.00
Barmouth (K) 37-58	1.50	1.00	
then (U) later (R)-2000		0.50	0.50
Barnard Castle 45-71		0.50	0.50
Barnet -94 then (L)	0.50	0.50	0.50
also (K,X) 55 only		2.00	
Barnoldswick (K) 61-69			1.50
then (U,X) 2002 only			1.50
Barnsley later (L)-?93	0.50	0.50	0.50
also 'Sheffield' (X) 87-90 & 94			1.00
then 'Barnsley' again (X) 95-2004			1.00
Barnstaple	0.50	0.50	0.50
then 'North Devon' 70-93 then (R)-98			0.50
Barrhead 55- later (L)		0.50	0.50
Barrow/Barrow-in-Furness -96 then (R)-2001	0.50	0.50	0.50
Barry (K) 15-33	1.50		
then (U)-76	1.00	0.50	0.50
then 'Cardiff 1' (M) 88-96			1.00
Barry Empire Games Village 58		4.00	
Barton on Humber (K) 60-67		1.00	1.00
Basildon 52-later (R)-94 then (L)		0.50	0.50
Basingstoke (K) 28-35	1.00		
then (U)-94 then (L,X)	0.60	0.50	0.50
Bath	0.50	0.50	0.50
and (K, reserve) 38-40	2.50		
then (U) NO Avon 96-99			0.50

Machine Cancellations

	1933-44	45-60	61-99
Bathgate 39-83 then (R)-86	1.00	0.50	0.50
then (X) 87-2002			0.50
Batley (K) 28-34	2.50		
then (U) -70 (at Dewsbury)	0.50	0.50	0.50
then 'Wakefield' (X)/(L)			0.50
Battle 52-84		0.50	0.50
then 'Hastings or Tonbridge' (X) 80-96			1.00
Beaconsfield (K) 39-44	2.00		
then (U)	0.50	0.50	0.50
then 'High Wycombe' (R) 75-			0.50
then 'Beaconsfield' again (M) 91 only			1.00
then 'Hemel Hempstead' (M) 91-			1.00
Bearsden 54- later (L)		0.50	0.50
Beauly (K,R) 65-78			1.00
Beaumaris (K) 64-77			1.50
then (U)-88			0.50
Bebington 56-67		1.00	1.00
Beccles (K) 29-49	1.00	1.00	
then (U)-77, later (L) 85-		0.50	0.50
Beckenham (R)/(L)	0.50	0.50	0.50
Bedale (K) 53-75		1.00	1.00
then (K, paid mail only)-83			1.50
Bedford -93 then (L)	0.50	0.50	0.50
Bedlington Station (K) 57-64		5.00	5.00
then Bedlington (K)-76			1.00
Bedwas Gwent (M) 91-			3.00
then 'Bedwas Newport Gwent' (M) 92-94			2.00
Bedworth 'Nuneaton' (X) 74			1.00
then 'Bedworth' (M) 91-92			2.00
Beeston (K) 33-38	1.50		
then (U)-76	0.50	0.50	0.50
then again (M) 87-92			0.50
Beith (K) 64-75 then (K,X)-85			1.00
*Belfast	0.50	0.50	0.50
but 'Belf N Ireland' 36-40	10.00		
also (K, reserve) 51-55		5.00	
then (U) N Ireland & NIMC 2000- (both inscriptions+Belfast later used)			0.50
Bellshill 51-58, (X) 60-68		0.70	1.00
Belper (K) 39-62	1.00	1.00	1.00
then (U)-75			0.50
Belvedere (K) 55-59		1.50	
then (U)-76		0.70	0.50
Bembridge (K) 65-72			1.00
Benfleet 64- later (R)/(L)			0.50
Berkhamsted (K) 36-38	1.50		
then (U) later (M)	0.50	0.50	0.50
Berwick-on-Tweed (K) 28-38	1.50		
then (U) later (L)	1.00	0.50	0.50
Bethesda (K) 64-68			2.00
Bethlehem Xmas first days 67-76			1.00
Betws-y-Coed (K) 62-73			2.00
also (U) (at Llanrwst) 66-84			1.00
Beverley (K)-38	1.50		
then (U) later (R)-88	1.00	1.00	1.00
also (K) again 60-71 (possibly later(L))		1.50	1.50
Bewdley (K) 60-69		1.00	1.00
then (U,L)-76			1.00
Bexhill-on-Sea -95	0.50	0.50	0.50
also 'Tonbridge' (X) 87-91 & 93			1.00
Bexley 'Dartford' (X) 61-62			1.00
Bexleyheath (K) 32-34	2.50		
then (U)	0.50	0.50	0.50
then 'Dartford H' (R) 76-97 (but H later used at Dartford)			0.50
Bicester (K) 44-56		1.50	1.00

	1933-44	45-60	61-99
then (U)-77		0.50	0.50
then again (M) 91-			1.00
Bideford (K) 32-39	1.50		
then (U)-93	0.50	0.50	0.50
Biggar (K) 61-			1.00
then (K) 'ML12 Clyde Valley' 87-93			1.00
then (K,M)-96			1.00
Biggin Hill 'Sevenoaks' (U,L) 96-			1.00
then 'Biggin Hill' (U,L) 97-			2.00
Biggleswade (K) 39-61	1.50	1.00	1.00
then (U) later (R)-85			0.50
Billericay (K) 53-59		2.00	
then (U)-66		0.50	0.50
then 'Basildon'/'Chelmsfd' (U,X) 74-84			1.00
then 'Billericay' (M) 90-95			1.00
Billingham (K) 40-51	3.00	2.00	
then (U) 54-69		0.60	0.60
Billingshurst (K) 61-68			1.00
Bilston 37-70	1.00	0.50	0.50
then again (M) 92-			1.00
Bingham (K) 69-77			1.00
Bingley (K) 37-49	1.50	1.50	
then (U) later (R)-93		0.50	0.50
but (K) used Feb 74 only			4.00
Birkenhead later (L)-?89	0.50	0.50	0.50
then (X) 96-97			1.00
also (K, reserve) 38 seen	2.50		
Birmingham-?2006	0.50	0.50	0.50
('Birmingham' spelling errors)			2.00
also (K, reserve) 37 seen	3.00		
AM (Aston)-37 then 'ADO'-?84 then see +			
CH (Camp Hill)-?76 then see +			
ED (East)-?86 then see +			
WD/WDO (West)-?86 then see +			
H (Hockley)-?84 then + (H later used at HO)			
- all	0.50	0.50	0.50
Acocks Green (K) 32-37	2.50		
then (U)-?74 then +	0.50	0.50	0.50
Blackheath (K) 39-61	1.50	1.00	1.00
then (U)-67			0.50
Erdington (K) 26-35	1.50		
then (U)-?86 then +	0.50	0.50	0.50
Great Barr (K) 55-58		1.00	
then (U)-?65 then +		0.50	0.50
Hall Green (K) 37-58	1.50	1.00	
then (U)-65 then +		0.50	0.50
Handsworth: 'Birmingham HA' (K) 14-35	1.50		
then 'Handsworth' (U) 38-80 then +	0.50	0.50	0.50
Kings Norton -?65 then +		0.50	0.50
Kitts Green -?65 then +		0.50	0.50
Moseley (K) 29-37	1.50		
then (U) 'DO' -?86 then+	0.50	0.50	0.50
Northfield Birm 31 (K) 45-		1.50	
then (K) without '31' 60-		1.00	1.00
then (U)-64-?65 then +			0.50
Oldbury (K) 34-37	3.00		
then (U)-67 then +	0.60	0.50	0.50
Quinton DO (K) 37 seen	3.00		
then 32 distr no. 39-55	1.50	1.00	
then (U)-?65 then +		0.50	0.50
Rednal (K) 58-72 then +		1.00	1.00
Selly Oak (K) 30-37	1.50		
then (U)-69 then +	0.60	0.50	0.50
but (K) again 55-59		1.50	
Shirley (K) 41-55 then +	1.00	1.00	

203

Machine Cancellations

	1933-44	45-60	61-99
Yardley DO **(K)** 38 seen	3.00		
then **(U)**-?65	0.60	0.50	0.50

NOTES: (1) Beware of December dates. Dies from above offices used at temp Birmingham offices at Xmas in 1960s-80s, eg Acocks Green Dec 1974.

+(2) all the following had machines in use (some were new, some were re-uses) **(U,M)** 87- (++ initially Solihull/Warley dies) (valuation 1.00, but Redfern Park 2.00):

ADO, CH, ED, WDO,
Acocks Green-97
Castle Bromwich
Chelmsley Wood
Coleshill
++Cradley Heath
Erdington
Great Barr-97
Hall Green
Handsworth
++Henley-in-Arden
Hockley (not Birm H)
Kings Norton
Kitts Green DO
++Knowle
Moseley DO
Northfield
++Oldbury
Quinton DO
Redfern Park 97 only
Rednal-?92
++Rowley Regis-96
Selly Oak
Sheldon-97
++Shirley

	1933-44	45-60	61-99
Bishop Auckland **(K)** 29-37	1.50		
then **(U)**	0.60	0.50	0.50
then 'SW Co Durham' 70- later **(L)**			0.50
but 'Darlington' **(X)** 83 only			1.00
Bishopbriggs 65- later **(L)**			0.50
Bishops Stortford **(K)**-37	2.00		
then **(U)** later **(R)**-94/**(L)**	0.60	0.50	0.50
Blackburn **(U)**-75	0.50	0.50	0.50
also **(K, reserve)** 50 only		2.00	
also **(U)** 'Blackb & Accrington' 61-			0.50
then 'Blackb & NE Lancs' 73-			0.50
then 'Lancashire 33' **(L)** 75-			1.00
Blackpool	0.50	0.50	0.50
also **(K, reserve)** 32-33	2.00		
then 'Fylde Coast' (variations) 66-			0.50
and **(K)** 'Fylde Coast' 67-69			4.00
then **(U)** 'Fylde B'pool Wyre' 75-95			0.50
then 'Blackpool' **(U,L,X)** 95-2003			1.00
Blackwood **(K)** 52-53		5.00	
then **(U)** 55-76 then **(L,X)**-?82		0.50	0.50
Blaenau Ffestiniog **(K)** 56-59		3.00	
then **(U)** 60-88		0.60	0.50
Blairgowrie **(K)** 56-59		2.00	
then **(U)** 60-77		0.60	0.50
then 'Perth' **(X)** 83 only			1.00
Blandford **(K)** 33-41	3.50		
then **(U)**-53	0.50	0.50	
then Blandford Forum later **(R)**-87		0.50	0.50
Blantyre **(K)** 55-58		1.50	
then **(U)** 59- later **(L)**		0.60	0.50
Blaydon-on-Tyne **(K)** 48-58		1.50	
then **(U)**-70		0.60	0.50
then Blaydon **(X)** 72-81,**(M)** 87-			1.00
Bletchley 39-73 (then MKeynes)	0.50	0.50	0.50
Blundellsands 45-58		1.00	
Blyth **(K)** 26-48	2.00	2.00	
then **(U)**-76 then **(X)**-85		0.50	0.50
then again **(M)** 88-			1.00
Bodmin **(K)** 36-39	2.00		
then **(U)**-92, **(X)**-99	0.60	0.50	0.50
but 'Cornwall 4' Sundays 90-92			1.00
Bognor Regis later **(L)**	0.50	0.50	0.50
Bolton	0.50	0.50	0.50
then 'Bolton & Bury' 74-			0.50
then 'Bury Bolton Wigan' 81-2008			0.50
but 'Bolton Lancs' Sundays 90-2007(this inscription used other occasions also)			0.50

	1933-44	45-60	61-99
Bo'ness **(K)** 57-58		3.00	
then **(U)** 59- later **(R)**-83, **(X)**-93		0.60	0.50
Bonnyrigg **(K)** 69- later **(R)** then **(M)**-97			1.50
also **(U,X)** 'Edinburgh' 81 & 85			1.00
Bootle/Liv then Lancs -76	2.00	1.00	1.00
then 'Bootle/Merseyside' 76 only			2.50
then 'GSO Bootle' **(M)** 86-90			1.00
Bordon **(K)** 50-58		1.00	
then **(U)**-73 then **(X)**-75		0.50	0.50
then again **(L,X)** 89-91			1.00
Borehamwood ?40-76	1.00	0.50	0.50
then again **(M)** 87-94			1.00
Boston later **(R)** -98	0.50	0.50	0.50
and **(K, ?in reserve)**-63	2.00	1.50	1.50
Boston Spa **(K)** 60-70		1.00	1.00
Bourne **(K)** 51-63		1.00	1.00
then **(U)** later **(R)**-98			0.50
*Bournemouth:			
'Bournemouth-Poole' **(U)**	0.50	0.50	0.50
also **(K, reserve)** 33-35 (earlier B'mouth)	3.00		
but 'Bournemouth Dist' Sundays 90-94			1.00
also 'Royal Mail B'th' July 91 only			1.50
then 'Dorset & SW Hants' 94- **(N)**			0.50
Bourton-on-Water **(K)** 68-91			1.00
Bovington Camp **(K)** 49-50		20.00	
Brackley ?50s- later **(L)**-89		0.50	0.50
Bracknell **(K)** 39-54	1.00	1.00	
then **(U)** later **(R)**/**(L)**		0.50	0.50
Bradford -2012	0.50	0.50	0.50
'Yorkshibe' spelling error 65			1.00
Bradford-on-Avon **(K)** 51-59		1.00	
then **(U)**-85 then **(L)**		0.50	0.50
Braintree 38-93 then **(L)**	0.50	0.50	0.50
and 'Chelmsford' **(X)** 85 only			1.00
Bramhall 'Stockport Z' **(R)** 86-88			1.00
Brampton **(K)** 68-78			1.00
Brandon **(K)** 61-78			1.00
Braunton **(K)** 67-71			1.50
Brechin 50- later **(R)**/**(L)**		0.50	0.50
Brecon **(K)** 36-44	2.50		
then **(U)**-97 then **(L)**-2001	0.60	0.50	0.50
Bredbury 'Stockport W' **(R)** 86-94			1.00
Brentford **(K)** 29-33	2.50		
then **(U)** 36 seen	2.50		
Brentwood **(K)** 26-34	2.50		
then **(U)**-93 then **(L)**-97	0.50	0.50	0.50
and 'Chelmsford' **(X)** 85 only			1.00
Bridge "First day" 29.4.68 only			2.00
Bridge of Allan **(K)** 64-68			1.00
Bridgend 34-88	0.60	0.50	0.50
then 'Cardiff 15' **(M,P)** 90-			1.00
'Pen-y-Bont ar Ogwr B'd' **(L)** 2000 only			3.00
Bridgnorth **(K)** 39-41	3.00		
then **(U)**-?70	0.50	0.50	0.50
then again **(M)** 88-			1.00
Bridgwater **(K)** 26-34	2.50		
then **(U)**-96 then **(R)**	0.50	0.50	0.50
Bridlington later **(M)**-87	0.50	0.50	0.50
Bridport **(K)** 36-39	2.50		
then **(U)**-87	0.50	0.50	0.50
Brierley Hill **(U)** 49, **(U, X)** 45 only	4.00	4.00	
then **(K)** 49-59		1.00	
then **(U)**-?79		0.50	0.50
Brigg ?50s-66		1.00	1.00
also **(K)** 62 only			2.00
Brighouse **(K)** 33-36	2.00		
then **(U)**-67	0.60	0.50	0.50

204

Machine Cancellations

	1933-44	45-60	61-99
Brightlingsea (K) 63-74			1.00
then 'Brightlingsea. Colchester' -75			2.50
then (U) later (R)/(L)			1.00
Brighton 'Brighton & Hove'	0.50	0.50	0.50
also (K, in reserve) 28-34	1.50		
and 48-64		1.00	1.00
then (U) 'Sussex Coast' 76-99			0.50
but 'South Coast' error 89			10.00
*Bristol	0.50	0.50	0.50
then 'Bath Bristol Taunton' 98-			0.50
Bristol NDO 38-71	0.60	0.50	0.50
Brixham (K) 36-49	1.00	1.00	
then (U)-70			0.50
then 'S Devon' (X) ?73-83			1.00
Broadbottom (K) 62-71			1.50
Broadstairs	0.50	0.50	0.50
then 'Thanet C' 71-72			1.00
Broadway (K) 59-66		1.00	1.00
Brockenhurst (K) 57-60		1.50	
then (U)-69			0.50 0.50
Brodick (K) 54-74		1.00	1.00
then (U) later (L)			0.50
'Kilmarnock' on Sats only 83-89			1.00
Bromley (U) 31,39 seen	2.50		
then 'Brom & Beckenham'	0.50	0.50	0.50
then 'Bromley' 70- later (R)/(L)			0.50
Bromsgrove (K) 34-37	2.00		
then (U) later (M)	0.60	0.50	0.50
Bromyard (K) 62-72			1.00
Broughty Ferry (K) 40-72	1.00	1.00	1.00
Brownhills (K) 60-62		3.00	3.00
then (U)-68			1.00
Broxburn (K) 58-65		1.00	1.00
then (U)-75 later (X)-93			0.50
Brynmawr (K) 52 seen		5.00	
then (U) 55-71		1.00	0.50
Buckie (K) 50-59		1.00	
then (U) later (U,X)-2005		0.50	0.50
Buckingham (K) 40-58	1.50	1.50	
then (U) later (R)/(L)-2000		0.50	0.50
Bude (K) 36 only	4.00		
then (U)-92, (X) 94-2001	1.00	0.50	0.50
Budleigh Salterton (K) 50-58		1.00	
then (U)-70		0.50	0.50
then 'Exeter Dist' (U,X) 75-92			1.00
Builth Wells (K) 61-74			1.00
then (U)-99			0.50
(Breconshire short-lived 74-75)			1.00
Bulford Barracks (U) 45-49		15.00	
then (K) -70		3.00	3.00
Bungay (K) 50-63		1.00	1.00
then (U)-77			0.50
Buntingford (K) 63-71			1.00
Burgess Hill (K) 49-56		1.00	
then (U) later (M)		0.50	0.50
Burnham-on-Sea 51-67		0.50	0.50
then 'Bridgwater' (X) 95-97			1.00
Burnley 'Burnley & Nelson'	0.50	0.50	0.50
also (K) 38-42	2.50		
then (U) 'Burnley' 67-			0.50
then 'Burnley & Pendle' 76-93			
then (M)			0.50
Burntisland (K) 59-76		1.00	1.00
then (U,L) 95-			1.00
Burslem (U) later (R)	1.00	0.50	0.50
but (K) 63-64			1.50
Burton-on-Trent-86 then (L)	0.50	0.50	0.50
Bury	0.50	0.50	0.50
then 'Bolton & Bury' (R) 74-			0.50
then 'Bury Bolton Wigan' (M) 81-			1.00

	1933-44	45-60	61-99
Bury St Edmunds-93 then (L)	0.50	0.50	0.50
Buxton (K) 15-34	1.00		
then (U) later (R)-93	0.50	0.50	0.50
Cadishead (K) 55-65		1.00	1.00
Caernarvon (K) 34-35	4.00		
Caernarvon/fon(U) 36-2001	1.00	0.50	0.50
also 'Gwynedd S' Sundays 90-97			1.00
Caerphilly (K) 37-38	4.00		
then (U) -76		0.50	0.50
then 'Cardiff 16' (L) 89-			1.00
then 'Cardiff Newport 16' (L) 95-			1.00
Caldicot (M) 89-99			1.50
Callander (K) 58-61		2.00	2.00
then (U) 62-76			0.50
Calne (K) 40-49	1.50	1.50	
then (U) later (L)-93		0.50	0.50
Camberley (K) 26-33	2.50		
then (U)-76 then (M) 89-	0.60	0.50	0.50
Camborne (K) 35-36 then see Redruth (but 'Camborne Redruth A' later at Camborne)	3.00		
Cambridge-2010	0.50	0.50	0.50
also (K, reserve) 64 and 69			2.50
Cambuslang (K) 50-53		2.50	
then (U)-86 then (L)		0.50	0.50
Camelford (R) 87-92			1.00
Campbeltown (K) 45-49		2.00	
then (U)-93 then (L)		0.50	0.50
Cannock (K) 39-48	2.00	2.00	
then (U)-67		0.50	0.50
then 'Walsall' (X) 79-84			1.00
then 'Cannock' (R)/(L) 87-			1.00
Canterbury -2011	0.50	0.50	0.50
Canvey Island 59- later (L)		0.50	0.50
*Cardiff	0.50	0.50	0.50
then 'Cardiff Newport' 93-			0.50
then 'De Dd Cymru SE Wales' 99- (but all 3 inscriptions later used)			0.50
Cardiff districts E,N,W (M) shown as 'Cardiff 4,5,6' 88 only seen			1.00
Cardigan (K) 42-58	1.50	1.00	
then (U)-94 then (L)		0.50	0.50
then 'Aberteifi/Cardigan' (L) 99-2005			1.50
*Carlisle	0.50	0.50	0.50
also (K, reserve) 40-53	2.50	2.00	
then (U) 'Cumbria Dumf's & Galloway' 93-			0.50
Carluke (K) 55-59		1.50	
then (U)-68 then (X)-75		0.50	0.50
Carmarthen (K) 28-36	2.00		
then (U)-94 then (L)	0.60	0.50	0.50
then 'Caerfyrddin/Carm' (L) 99-2006			1.50
Carnforth (K) 50-60		1.00	
then (U) later (R)		0.50	0.50
then 'Lancs & S Lakes 15' (M) 93-			1.00
Carnoustie (K) 54-63		1.00	1.00
then (U)-84			0.50
Carrickfergus (K) 58-61		3.50	3.50
then (U) later (R)-86			0.50
Carterton (U,M) 97-98			1.50
Castlederg (K) 68- later (R)-94			1.00
Castle Douglas (K) 49-56		2.50	
then (U) later (R)/(L)		0.50	0.50
Castleford (K) 28-38	2.00		
then (U)-69	0.60	0.50	0.50
then 'Wakefield' (X) 70-84			0.50
Caterham (K) 35-39	2.00		
then (U)-70	0.60	0.50	0.50
Catterick Camp 40-64	2.50	2.50	1.50

205

Machine Cancellations

	1933-44	45-60	61-99
Chard 51- later (M)		0.50	0.50
also 'Taunton' (X) 94 only			1.00
Chatham 'Rochester & Chat'	0.50	0.50	0.50
then 'Medway' 70- later (R)-98			0.50
Chatteris (K) 60-66		1.00	1.00
then (U)-89			0.50
Cheadle Cheshire (R)-?92	1.00	0.50	0.50
then (X) 96 only			1.00
Cheadle Stoke on Trent (K) 57-64		1.00	1.00
then (U) later (R)/(L)			0.50
*Chelmsford	0.50	0.50	0.50
then 'SE Anglia' (later both used) 97-			0.50
Cheltenham (U)-93, (L)-98	0.50	0.50	0.50
also (K) seen 37-53	2.00	2.00	
and 'Gloucestershire' (X) 94-			1.00
Chepstow (K) 36-48	2.50	1.00	
then (U) 51- later (L)-72		0.50	0.50
then again (L) 81-90			1.00
Chertsey (K) 40-48	2.00	2.00	
then (U)-?61		1.00	1.00
Chesham (L) 90- (see also Amersham)			1.00
*Chester	0.50	0.50	0.50
also 'Clwyd 1' 72-82 (used for postings in Deeside area)			0.50
then 'Chester Clwyd Gwynedd' 82-			0.50
then ditto with Gwynedd erased			0.50
also 'Chester/Clwyd 1' 87-			0.50
then 'Chester & Clwyd/-1-' 88-			0.50
then 'Chester N Wales' (variations) 99-			0.50
Chesterfield later (R)/(L)-93,(X) 96	0.50	0.50	0.50
Chester le Street (K) 33-51	1.00	1.00	
then (U)-?69, 83 and (M) 92-		0.50	0.50
also 'Durham' (X) 81-87			1.00
Chichester later (M)-98	0.50	0.50	0.50
Chippenham (K) 28-37	2.50		
then (U) later (R)/(L)	0.50	0.50	0.50
Chipping Campden (K) 62-66			2.00
Chipping Norton (K)60-later (L)-73		2.00	2.00
Chipping Sodbury P (K) 62-63			2.00
then 'PDO' (U)-72 (then Yate)			0.60
Chislehurst (K) 48-81		1.00	1.00
then (U,R)-95			0.50
Chorley	0.60	0.50	0.50
then 'Lancashire 40' 75- (R)/(M)			1.00
then 'Chorley Lancs 40' (M) 94-99			2.00
Chorlton-c-Hardy (K) 32-36	3.00		
then (U) later (R)/(L)	1.00	0.50	0.50
Christchurch (K) 30-48	1.50	1.00	
then (U)-71		0.50	0.50
then 'Christchurch Dorset' first day posting 77 only (stamped at Bournemouth)			1.00
Church Stretton (K) 61-64			1.50
then (U,R)-98			0.50
Cinderford (K) 52-57		1.00	
then (U)-68		0.50	0.50
Cirencester (K) 32-38	3.00		
then (U)-?72	1.00	0.50	0.50
then 'Gloucestershire' (L) 89-?92			1.00
Clacton-on-Sea later (R)-97 then (L)	0.50	0.50	0.50
Clarkston (K) 60-79		1.00	1.00
then (U,X) 'Glasgow' 77			1.00
then (U,X) 'Clarkston PSO' 78			1.00
then PSO (U,R) 79-86 then (L)			1.00
Cleator Moor (K) 70-91			1.00
Cleckheaton (K) 26-37	1.00		
then (U)-77	0.50	0.50	0.50

	1933-44	45-60	61-99
then 'Wakefield' (X)-80s			1.00
Cleethorpes (K) 25-49	1.00	1.00	
then (U)-64		0.50	0.50
Clevedon (K) 39-49	1.00	1.00	
then (U)-78		0.50	0.50
Clitheroe (K) 34-50	1.00	1.00	
then (U)-75		0.50	0.50
then (U,M) Lancs 16' 89-			1.00
Clydebank (K) 30-38	2.00		
then (U)-86 then (L)	0.60	0.50	0.50
Coalville (K) 41-57	1.00	1.00	
then (U)-76		0.50	0.50
and (K) on breakdown 70 only			3.00
then (U,X) 'Leicester' 94-95			1.00
Coatbridge -68	0.50	0.50	0.50
then 'Coatbridge & Airdrie' -86			0.50
Cockermouth (K) 51-59		1.50	
then (U) later (R)-91		0.50	0.50
Colchester-97 then (L)	0.50	0.50	0.50
also (K) 39,63,66	2.00		1.50
Coldstream (K) 64-75			1.00
Coleford (K) 53-60		2.00	
then (U)-70		0.50	0.50
Coleraine (K) 37-48	4.00	4.00	
then (U) later (R)/(X)-2006		0.50	0.50
Coleshill (K) 59-64		1.00	1.00
then (U)-?78			0.50
Colne (K) 29-35	2.00		
then (U) -76	0.60	0.50	0.50
then 'Burnley & Pendle' (L,X) 81-			1.00
Colwyn Bay-2000	0.50	0.50	0.50
but 'Llandudno-Colwyn Bay' 60-64, then separate Colwyn Bay & Llandudno machines at CB-84, then (L) 84-87 when mail stamped at Chester and 'Llandud-CB' again (X) 64-83 & 97-99		0.50	0.50
Congleton (K) 37-47	2.00	2.00	
then (U)-75 (at Macclesfield)		0.50	0.50
then (X) 95 only			1.00
Consett (K) 46-48		3.00	
then (U)-?83 then (M)-93		0.50	0.50
Conway (K) 54-60		1.50	
then (U) Conway -72		0.50	0.50
then (U) Conwy -84 then (L)-?92			0.50
Cookstown (K) 51-60		2.50	
then (U) later (R)		0.50	0.50
Corby Kettering (K) 45-48		4.00	
then (K) NO Kettering 48-52		4.00	
then (U) later (M)		0.50	0.50
Corsham -69		0.60	0.50
then 'Chippenham' (X) 83-84			1.00
Corwen (K) 59-63		2.50	2.50
then (U)-83 then (M),(X) -2000			0.60
Cosham ?52- later (R)/(L)		0.50	0.50
Cottingham (K) 61-76			1.00
(N Humberside 75-76 only)			1.50
Coulsdon (K) 24-48	1.00	1.00	
then (U)-?71		0.50	0.50
Coupar Angus in red with 'Paid' 66-70			4.00
Coventry (U)	0.50	0.50	0.50
also (K, reserve) 35-44	2.00		
then 'Coventry & Warwickshire' 80-2010			0.50
Cowbridge (K) 61-72			1.50
Cowdenbeath (K) 54-57		1.50	
then (U) later (R)/(L)-98		0.50	0.50
Cowes (K) 32-37	3.00		
then (U)-77	0.50	0.50	0.50

Machine Cancellations

	1933-44	45-60	61-99
Cradley Heath **(K)** 35-49	1.00	1.00	
then **(U)**-67		0.50	0.50
then see Birmingham entry			
Cranbrook **(K)** 53-59		1.50	
then **(U)**-76		0.50	0.50
then 'T Wells/Tonbridge' **(X)** 80-91			1.00
Cranleigh **(K)** 42-59	1.50	1.00	
then **(U)**-75		0.50	0.50
then 'Guildford' **(X)** 80-86 then **(R)**			1.00
then 'Cranleigh' again **(R)/(L)** 91-			1.00
Craven Arms **(K)** 51-60		2.00	
then **(U)** later **(L)**-87		0.60	0.50
Crawley **(K)** 32-36	3.50		
then **(U)** later **(M)**	0.50	0.50	0.50
Crediton **(K)** 49 only		5.00	
then **(U)**-78		0.50	0.50
then 'Exeter District' **(X)** ?80-92			1.00
Crewe then 'Cheshire' 83-2010	0.50	0.50	0.50
but 'Crewe' **(M,X)** 88-2009 (both inscriptions in use)			1.00
Crewkerne **(K)** 50-59		1.50	
then **(U)** later **(P)**-86		0.50	0.50
then 'Taunton' **(U,X)** 94-97			1.00
Criccieth **(K)** no county 59 only		5.00	
then **(K)** with county 60-77		1.50	1.50
then **(U)**-87			0.50
Crickhowell 67-72 (at Abergavenny)			1.50
Crieff **(K)** 37-38	3.00		
then **(U)**-83 then **(X)**-84	0.50	0.50	0.50
Cromer **(U)** 32-41	0.60		
then **(K)** 43-50	1.00	1.00	
then **(U)**-76		0.50	0.50
Crook **(K)** 53-54		3.00	
then **(U)**-?70		1.00	1.00
Crosby **(U)** 59-?70		0.50	0.50
also Crosby 21 and 23 56-65		0.60	0.60
then Crosby Liverpool **(R)** 2003-			1.00
Crosby 22 **(K)** 64-66			2.50
Cross Keys **(K)** 49-52		3.50	
then **(U)** 57- later **(L)**-94		0.60	0.50
Crowborough **(K)** 36-55	1.00	1.00	
then **(U)**-?72		0.50	0.50
then 'T Wells/Tonbridge' **(X)** 80-91			1.00
and 'Crowborough' again **(M)** 90-			1.00
Croydon	0.50	0.50	0.50
also **(K)** 31-70	1.00	1.00	1.00
then **(U)** 'Croydon/Sutton' 89-(Croydon & Croydon Surrey inscriptions also) - 2012 **(N)**			0.50
and 'SE Div 2' Sundays only 95-2003			0.60
Cullompton **(K)** 57-66		1.00	1.00
then **(U)**-71			1.00
Cumbernauld **(K)** 64-67			1.00
then **(U)**-86 then **(L)**			0.50
Cumnock **(K)** 50-58		1.00	
then **(U)** -71		0.60	0.50
Cupar **(K)** 36-37	4.00		
then **(U)**-76	0.60	0.50	0.50
then 'Kirkcaldy' **(X)** 81-83			1.00
then 'Cupar' again **(U)** 87- later **(L)**			1.00
Cwmbran ?56- later **(R)/(L)**-2001		0.50	0.50
Dagenham -53	0.50	0.50	
then 'Romford A' 70- later **(M)**			0.50
Dalbeattie **(K)** 61-74			1.00
Dalkeith **(K)** 50-56		1.50	
then **(U)** later **(R)/(L)**		0.50	0.50
Dalmuir **(K)** 59-67		1.50	1.50
then **(U,X)** 60-65,71		0.60	0.60
Dalry **(K)** 64-75 then **(X)**-81			1.00
Darlington **(U)** -2013		0.50	0.50

	1933-44	45-60	61-99
also **(K)** 48-53		1.00	
then **(K)** again **(X)** 55		1.50	
Dartford -2011	0.50	0.50	0.50
Dartmouth **(K)** 35-56	1.00	1.00	
then **(U)**-70		0.50	0.50
then 'S Devon' **(X)** 74-83			1.00
Darwen -75 (gap 64-65)	0.60	0.50	0.50
then 'Lancashire 17' **(M)** 89-			1.00
Daventry **(K)** 61-62			2.50
then **(U)** 62- later **(R)/(L)**-99			0.50
Dawley **(U)** 68 only			6.00
Dawlish **(K)** 49-56		2.00	
then **(U)**-70		0.50	0.50
then 'Exeter Distr' **(X)** 75- then **(R)**-93			1.00
Deal -76	0.60	0.50	0.50
then 'Dover' **(X)** later **(L)**			1.00
Deeside **(M)** 88-92			1.00
Denbigh **(K)** 42-52	3.00	2.00	
then **(U)** 53-71		0.50	0.50
Denny 59-68		1.00	1.00
Denton **(K)** 36-38	3.00		
then **(U)** later **(R)/(L)**		0.50	0.50
Derby **(U)** -2013	0.50	0.50	0.50
and **(K, reserve)** 37 & 47	1.50	1.50	
also **(U)** 'R Mail Midlands' Sundays 93-2002			0.50
Dereham **(K)** 39-48	1.50	1.50	
then **(U)**-77		0.50	0.50
then again **(L)** 83-2004			1.00
Derwentside **(M)** 93-			1.00
Desborough **(K)** 69-71			3.00
Devizes **(K)** 32-47	1.00	1.00	
then **(U)** later **(L)**		0.50	0.50
Dewsbury -70	0.50	0.50	0.50
then 'Wakefield' **(X)**-96			1.00
Didcot **(K)** 43 only	3.00		
then **(U)**-78	0.60	0.50	0.50
Didsbury **(U)** 32-36	4.00		
Dingwall **(K)** 50-53		2.00	
then **(U)** ?56- later **(R)/(L)**-2006		0.50	0.50
Diss **(K)** 48-52		2.50	
then **(U)**-94 then **(L)**		0.50	0.50
but **(K,P)** -88			2.00
Dolgelley **(K)** 52-58		3.00	
then **(U)** 58 only		5.00	
then Dolgellau 58- later **(R)**-2000		0.50	0.50
*Doncaster	0.50	0.50	0.50
also **(K, reserve)** 50 & 61		2.50	2.50
then **(U)** various DN-LN inscriptions 94-			0.50
Dorchester then 'Dorch S & W Dorset' 71-94 then **(M)**	0.50	0.50	0.50
			0.50
Dorking **(K)** 29-35	4.00		
then **(U)**-72, **(M)** 96-	0.50	0.50	0.50
Dornoch **(U)** summer only 65-72			2.50
then **(K)**-95			1.00
Dover -95 then **(X)** 96-97	0.50	0.50	0.50
Downham Market **(K)** 57-60		2.50	
then **(U)**-71		0.70	0.50
Downpatrick **(K)** 42-54	6.00	4.50	
then **(U)**-93 then **(L)**		0.50	0.50
Driffield **(K)** 39-43	3.50		
then **(U)** later **(M)**	0.60	0.50	0.50
Droitwich **(K)** 44-47	3.50	3.50	
then **(U)**		0.50	0.50
then 'Worc District' **(L)** 83-			1.00
then 'Droitwich' again **(L)** 89-			1.00
Droylsden **(K)** 35-55	1.00	1.00	
then **(U)** later **(R)/(L)**		0.50	0.50

Machine Cancellations

	1933-44	45-60	61-99
Dudley later **(L)**	0.50	0.50	0.50
Dulverton **(K)** 58-76		1.00	1.00
Dumbarton **(K)** 30-37	2.00		
then **(U)**-86 then **(L)**	0.50	0.50	0.50
Dumfries **(K)** 11-34	1.00		
then **(U)**-93 then **(L)**	0.50	0.50	0.50
Dunbar **(K)** 40-60	2.00	1.50	
then **(U)** later **(L)**-?97		0.50	0.50
Dunblane **(K)** 61-71			1.00
Dundee Angus **(U)**	0.50	0.50	0.50
but **(K, reserve)** 34-49	1.50	1.50	
then **(U)** NO Angus 65-83 then **(L)**-95 then **(X)**,			0.50
then 'Edinburgh' **(X)** 2003			1.00
Dunfermline later **(L)**	0.50	0.50	0.50
Dungannon **(K)** 49-56		3.00	
then **(U)** 57- later **(R)**/(L)		0.50	0.50
Dunmow **(K)** 48-49		4.00	
then **(U)** later **(L)**-90		0.50	0.50
and 'Chelmsford' **(X)** 78-89			1.00
Dunoon later **(L)**	0.50	0.50	0.50
Duns **(K)** 52-58		1.00	
then **(U)** -84 then **(R)**		0.50	0.50
Dunstable -82		0.50	0.50
then 'Luton' **(L)**-98			1.00
Durham -88 then **(M)**	0.50	0.50	0.50
also **SCD (P)** 64-?77 (Savings Certificate Division)			1.00
Dursley **(K)** 49-53		2.00	
then **(U)**-?72		0.50	0.50
Dymchurch **(U)** 62 only			15.00
Earl Shilton **(K)** 69-8?			1.00
Eastbourne-later **(R)**-2003	0.50	0.50	0.50
also **(K, reserve)** 38 &53	1.50	1.50	
East Grinstead **(K)** 28-34	2.00		
then **(U)** later **(R)**/(L)	0.50	0.50	0.50
East Kilbride 58-86 then **(L)**		0.50	0.50
East Kirkby **(K)** 55 only (then see Kirkby-in-Ashfield)		4.00	
Eastleigh **(K)** 35-38	3.00		
then **(U)**-72	0.50	0.50	0.50
then again **(L)** 90-			0.50
East Molesey **(K)** 39-40	4.00		
Eastwood **(K)** 57-63		1.00	1.00
then **(U)**-77			0.50
Ebbw Vale 49-76 then **(L)**-2000		0.50	0.50
but 'Newport Mon NP3' 71-72			1.00
Eccles later **(R)**/(L)	0.50	0.50	0.50
Edenbridge **(K)** 53-59		1.00	
then **(U)**-76		0.50	0.50
then 'T Wells/Tonbridge' **(X)** 80-91			1.00
Edgware -85 then **(M)**	0.50	0.50	0.50
*Edinburgh	0.50	0.50	0.50
then 'Edinburgh Lothian Fife Borders' 82-			0.50
then 'Edinburgh' again 95- **(N)**			0.50
Edinburgh EC, NW, SEDO, SW, W, Dell-DO (EC 59-92, NW 58- SEDO 68-, Dell-DO 67-) - all later **(R)**/(L)	0.50	0.50	0.50
- all later **(R)**/(L)	0.50	0.50	0.50
CDO (Central) 'Edinburgh C' **(R)** 83-			1.00
then 'City & Leith DO' **(M)** 95-			1.00
Leith DO later **(R)**-95	0.50	0.50	0.50
Portobello DO **(K)** 39-49	1.00	1.00	
then **(U)** later **(R)**/(L)		0.50	0.50
Egremont **(K)** 66-69			1.50
then **(U)** later **(L)**-93			0.50
Elgin **(K)** 29-37	2.00		
then **(U)** later **(R)**/(L)	0.50	0.50	0.50

	1933-44	45-60	61-99
Elie **(K)** 61-72			1.50
Elland **(K)** 49-75		1.00	1.00
then **(K,X)** 80,83,84			1.00
Ellesmere **(K)** 52-81, **(K,X)** -84		1.00	1.00
also **(U)** 65-75 (at Oswestry)			1.00
Ellesmere Port **(K)** 39-40	3.50		
then **(U)** later **(L)**-94 (75- 'Wirral' then 78-94 'S Wirral')	0.50	0.50	0.50
Ellon **(K)** 68-76			1.00
then **(U,X)** 'Aberdeen' 89-			1.00
then 'Ellon' **(M)** 93-			1.00
Ely **(K)** 33-38	3.00		
then **(U)**-76	0.50	0.50	0.50
then 'Cambridge E' **(R)**/(L)-96			1.00
Emsworth **(K)** 50-55		1.00	
then **(U)** 57- later **(R)**/(L)		0.50	0.50
Enfield -?97	0.50	0.50	0.50
also **(K)** 53 and 64		1.50	1.50
Enniskillen **(K)** 39-54	3.00	3.00	
then **(U)** 54- later **(R)**/(X)-2009		0.50	0.50
Epping ?49- later **(R)**-93		0.50	0.50
Epsom	0.50	0.50	0.50
then 'Kingston-u-Thames 6,7,8' 87-			0.50
later '9' **(L)**-96 ('9' later used at Kingston-u-Thames)			1.00
Erith **(K)** 32-36	3.50		
then **(U)**	0.50	0.50	0.50
then 'Dartford I' **(R)** 76-96 (Dartford I die later used at Dartford)			0.50
Esher **(K)** 37-39	4.00		
then **(U)** -65	1.00	0.50	0.50
Evesham	0.50	0.50	0.50
then 'Worcester District' **(L)** 83-98			1.00
but 'Evesham' again **(X)** 91 only			1.00
Exeter	0.50	0.50	0.50
also **(K, reserve)** 32-52	1.00	1.00	
then **(U)** 'Exeter District' 70-			0.50
then 'Devon & Exeter' 98- 2012 **(N)**			0.50
also 'Exeter & Devon' 99			0.50
Exmouth later **(L)**-?85	0.60	0.50	0.50
but 'Ex District' **(X)** 82- then **(R)**/(L)-96			1.00
Eyemouth **(K)** 61-72			1.00
then again **(K,L)** 90-92			2.00
Failsworth **(K)** 36-49	3.00	3.00	
then **(U)** later **(R)**/(L)		0.50	0.50
Fakenham **(K)** 39-49	2.00	1.50	
then **(U)**-77		0.50	0.50
Falkirk -88 then **(L)**	0.50	0.50	0.50
also **(K,X)** 63 only			3.50
Falmouth 33-	0.50	0.50	0.50
then 'Cornwall B' **(L)**/(X) 92-99			1.00
Fareham **(K)** 30-38	3.00		
then **(U)** later **(R)**/(L)	0.50	0.50	0.50
Faringdon **(K)** 54-66		1.00	1.00
then **(U)**-68			1.00
Farnborough 59-69		0.50	0.50
then again (replaced Aldershot) 92-			0.50
then 'Farnborough & Basingstoke' 95-			0.50
then 'Farnborough' again 2000-03			0.50
Farnham -76	0.50	0.50	0.50
then 'Aldershot' **(X)** 89			1.00
then 'Farnham' again **(L)** 90-			1.00
Farnworth **(K)** 60-63		2.50	2.50
also **(U)**-62-67			1.00

208

Machine Cancellations

	1933-44	45-60	61-99
Faversham (K) 30-38	3.00		
then (U)-90 then (L)-98	0.50	0.50	0.50
Featherstone (K) 57-70		1.00	1.00
Felixstowe later (L)	0.60	0.50	0.50
Feltham 49-76		0.50	0.50
Ferndale (K) 60-66		2.00	2.00
then 'Rhondda 6' 66-78 then (X)			1.50
then (U,X) 'Ferndale' 80-89			1.00
then 'Cardiff' (X) 90-91			1.00
Ferryhill (K) 49-57		1.50	
then (U)-63		1.00	1.00
Filey (K) 37-38	2.00		
then (U) 39 only seen	1.50		
then (K) again 46-48		2.00	
then (U) -68		0.50	0.50
Fishguard 60-94 then (L,X)-98		0.50	0.50
then 'Abergwaun/Fishguard' (L) 99-and (X) 99-2002			1.50
Fishponds (K) 34-39	3.00		
then (U) 55-85		0.50	0.50
Fleetwood -67	0.50	0.50	0.50
then 'Fylde' (X) 81-82			1.00
Flint (K) 58-59		2.00	
then (U) -71		0.50	0.50
Folkestone -95 then (L)	0.50	0.50	0.50
Fordingbridge (K) 57-67		1.00	1.00
Forfar (K) 34-48	1.00	1.00	
then (U)-83		0.50	0.50
Formby 47- (R) later (L)-93		0.50	0.50
Forres (K) 54-59		1.50	
then (U) later (R)/(L)-95		0.50	0.50
Fort William (K) 40-55	1.50	1.50	
then (U) 55- later (R)/(L)-2001		0.50	0.50
Fowey (K) 55-64		1.00	1.00
Fraserburgh (K) 48-58		1.00	
then (U) later (L,X) -2005		0.50	0.50
Freshwater (K) 49-61		1.00	1.00
then (U)-77			0.50
Frinton-on-Sea ?51-		0.50	0.50
later (R)-94 then (L)			0.50
Frodsham (K) 68-69			2.50
Frome (K) 32-44	2.00		
then (U)-86 then (M)	0.50	0.50	0.50
Gainsborough (K) 26-37	1.50		
then (U) later (L)	0.60	0.50	0.50
Galashiels (K) 30-35	2.50		
then (U)-95 then (L)	0.50	0.50	0.50
and 'Scottish Borders' 92-95			0.50
Garstang (K) 64-65			2.50
then (U)-71			1.00
then 'Lancs' (L) ?94-			1.00
Garston Liv 19 (K) 48-59		1.50	
then (U)-66		0.60	0.60
Gateshead -33 (later see Newcastle upon Tyne)	1.00		
*Gatwick MLO (variations) 88- (at Crawley, previously shown under Redhill)			0.50
Gerrards Cross 40- later (L)	0.60	0.50	0.50
Giffnock (K) 59-63		1.00	1.00
Gillingham Dorset (K) 50-58		1.00	
then (U)-68		1.00	1.00
Gillingham Kent (K) 23-37	1.00		
then (U)-70	0.50	0.50	0.50
then 'BHC' (Bulk Handling Centre) in red on paid mail (P) 89-?93			1.00
Girvan (K) 34-58	1.00	1.00	
then (U) 59-71		0.50	0.50
Glasgow -2012 (N)	0.50	0.50	0.50
also 'blank Ayrshire' (X) 91			1.00

	1933-44	45-60	61-99
Postmans Office Glasgow (M) 80-86			1.00
Exhibition PO 38 only	1.50		
Glasgow SW3 (Savings Bank) 66-			1.00
(all 'paid') then G58 71-?91			1.00
(also Pitney Bowes machine in use)			0.50
Glasgow 2 (Waterloo St) later (R)-85	1.00	0.50	0.50
Districts: E -57	0.50	0.50	
E2 (K) 33-39	2.00		
E3 55- then G33 71- later (M)		0.50	0.50
NDO (K) 28-48	1.00	1.00	
then (U) 50-		0.50	0.50
then G21 71- later (M)			0.50
NWDO 31-	0.50	0.50	0.50
then G20 71-?88			0.50
SDO/S then G41 71- later (M)	0.50	0.50	0.50
S4 (K) 33-38	2.50		
S5 (U,X) 65-66			1.00
SE then G40 71-?88	0.50	0.50	0.50
SWDO/SW then G51 71-later (M)	0.50	0.50	0.50
W then G11 71- later (M)	0.50	0.50	0.50
W3 (K) 29-36	3.00		
and WDO3&4 (U,X) 54-60		1.00	
also (U) W3 56-		0.50	0.50
then G13 71- later (M)			0.50
W4 (K) 36-47	2.50	2.00	
WDO5 (X) 61-65			2.00
then G15 (X) 73-85			1.00
Glastonbury (K) 50-53		3.00	
then (U)		0.50	0.50
then 'Glastonbury & Street' 63-81			0.50
then again (L) 87-			1.00
Glenrothes 64-76			0.50
then 'Kirkcaldy' (X) /8-			1.00
then Glenrothes again (R)/(L) 87-			1.00
Glossop -?87 then (R)-93	0.50	0.50	0.50
*Gloucester	0.50	0.50	0.50
then 'Gloucestershire' 70-			0.50
Godalming (K) 28-37	2.00		
then (U)-77	0.50	0.50	0.50
then 'Guildford' (X) 80-89			1.00
then Godalming again (L) 89-94			1.00
Golspie (K) 65-2000			1.00
Goole (K) 30-37	2.00		
then (U)-76	0.60	0.50	0.50
then again (M) 88-			1.00
Gorebridge (K) 69-?87			1.00
Goring (K) 59-76		1.00	1.00
Goring by Sea (U,L) 91-93			1.00
Gorseinon (K) 54-65		1.00	1.00
then 'Swansea 12' (U,L) 87-93			1.00
Gorton (K) 32-37	3.50		
Gosport (K) 34-37	1.50		
then (U) later (R)/(L)	0.70	0.50	0.50
Gourock (K) 39-64	2.00	1.00	1.00
then (U)-76			0.50
Grangemouth (K) 44-52	2.50	1.50	
then (U) 54- later (R)-95		0.50	0.50
Grange-over-Sands (K) 50-59		2.00	
then (U) later (R)/(M)		0.50	0.50
Grantham (K) 15-33	1.50		
then (U)-95 then (L)	0.50	0.50	0.50
Grantown-on-Spey (K) 61-72			1.00
then (U)-86			0.50
Gravesend -76	0.60	0.50	
then 'Dartford J' (R)-96			1.00
Grays (K) 26-34	2.50		
then (U) later (M)	0.50	0.50	0.50
then 'Romford R91' (M) 88-			1.00
Great Missenden (K) 56-60		2.50	

209

Machine Cancellations

	1933-44	45-60	61-99
then (U) later (L)-97		0.50	0.50
Great Yarmouth later (L)	0.50	0.50	0.50
Greenford (K) 34-35	4.00		
then (U)-?70	0.50	0.50	0.50
then (M) 90-94			1.00
Greenford Mail Centre (U) 2001-?2008			0.50
(also 'Greenford/Windsor')			0.50
Greenock later (L)-?89	0.50	0.50	0.50
then 'Paisley' (X) 90-93 (then see Inverclyde)			1.00
Grimsby (U)	0.50	0.50	0.50
then 'Grimsby & Cleethorpes' 64- later (L)			0.50
Guildford -2004	0.50	0.50	0.50
(then see Jubilee), also -			
(K, reserve) 37,38,51,60	2.00	2.00	
Guisborough (K) 52-62		1.00	1.00
then (U)-69			0.60
Guiseley (K) 59-83		1.00	1.00
Haddington (K) 49-59		1.00	
then (U) 60- later (R)/(L)		0.50	0.50
Hadfield Manchester (K) 58-61		2.00	2.00
then (U) 'Hadfield Hyde' -76			0.50
Hadleigh Ipswich (K) 61-67			1.50
then (U)-73, then again (L) 98-			1.00
Hailsham (K) 38-49	1.50	1.50	
then (U)-76 then (L)		0.50	0.50
Halesowen (K) 37-61	2.00	1.50	1.50
then (U) 'Halesowen Birmingham'			0.50
then (U) 'Halesowen Worcs' 67-(later W Mids) -92 then (L)			0.50
Halesworth (K) 59-68		1.00	1.00
then (U)-93 then (L)			0.50
Halifax (U)	0.50	0.50	0.50
also (K, reserve) 49-55		2.00	
then 'Huddersfield Halifax B' (U,M) 78-			1.00
Halstead (K) 40-53	2.00	1.50	
then (U) later (R)/(L)		0.50	0.50
Hamilton -77	0.50	0.50	0.50
then 'Motherwell' (X) 83-86			1.00
Hampton (K) 48-60		1.00	
then (U)-86		0.50	0.50
Hanley (K) 23-35	2.00		
then (U) 45-49, see also Stoke		2.00	
Harleston (K) 59-86		1.00	1.00
Harlow 53-94 then (M)		0.50	0.50
Harold Hill 'Romford C' 70-72			1.00
then 'Romford R31' (M) 90-			1.00
Harpenden (K) 39-41	4.00		
then (U)-70, then (R) 87-	0.60	0.50	0.50
Harrogate -77 then (L,P)	0.50	0.50	0.50
Harrow	0.50	0.50	0.50
then 'Harrow & Wembley' 65-			0.50
then 'Harrow' again 80-2001			0.50
(then see Greenford Mail Centre)			
Harrow PDO (U,M) 90-			1.00
Hartlepool 'West'	0.60	0.50	0.50
then 'Hartlepool' 67-76			0.50
then 'Cleveland H' (M)-?78			1.00
Harwich later (L)	0.50	0.50	0.50
Haslemere (K) 33-39	2.00		
then (U)-76	0.50	0.50	0.50
then 'Guildford' (X) 80-84			1.00
Hassocks (K) 49-58		1.00	
then (U) later (L)		0.50	0.50
Hastings later (R)-98 then (L)	0.50	0.50	0.50
Hatfield (K) 42-49	1.50	1.50	
then (U)-71 then (X)-75		0.50	0.50
then again (L) 87-			1.00
Hatfield RM Streamline (R) 95-?98			1.00

	1933-44	45-60	61-99
Havant (K) 34-49	1.00	1.00	
then (U) later (R)/(L)-96		0.50	0.50
Haverfordwest (K) 32-37	2.50		
then (U)'Hav/Pembroke' 37-38 (error)	10.00		
then (U)-94 then (L)/(X)	0.60	0.50	0.50
then 'Hwlffordd/Hav' (L)/(X) 99-2010			2.00
Haverhill (K) 58-59		3.00	
then (U)-92 then (L)-99		0.50	0.50
Hawick -92 then (R)/(L)	0.50	0.50	0.50
and 'Scottish Borders' (R) 92-95 (but indistinguishable from Galashiels)			0.50
Hawkhurst 61-72			1.00
Hawthorn 43-47	20.00	20.00	
Hayes Middx -68	0.60	0.50	0.50
and (K) 61 only			2.00
then Hayes PDO Middx (U,M) 90-			1.00
Hayle (K) 50-58		1.00	
then (U) later (R)		0.50	0.50
then 'Cornwall C' (L) 92-93			1.00
Hayling Island ?50s-81		0.50	0.50
Haywards Heath later (L)	0.50	0.50	0.50
Hazel Grove 'Stockport Y' 86-88			1.00
Heanor 58-76		0.50	0.50
Heathfield (K) 59-60		2.50	
then (U) later (L)		0.50	0.50
and 'Tonbridge' (X) 86-91			1.00
then 'Heathfield' (X) 97			1.00
Hebburn (K) 48-58		1.00	
then (U)-77 then (X)-85		0.50	0.50
Hebden Bridge (K) 39-55	1.00	1.00	
then (U)-75, (L)-76		0.50	0.50
(short-lived W Yorks die 75-76)			1.00
Heckmondwike (K) 39-49	2.00	2.00	
then (U)-?70		0.50	0.50
then 'Wakefield' (X)-96			0.50
Hedge End (L) 90-			1.00
Helensburgh (K) 26-47	1.00	1.00	
then (U)-77 then (X)-?85		0.50	0.50
Helston (K) 39-50	1.00	1.00	
then (U)		0.50	0.50
then 'Cornwall D' (L) 92-98, (X) 99			1.00
Hemel Hempstead 32-2012	0.50	0.50	0.50
(then see Home Counties North Mail Centre)			
Hemsworth (K) 60-70		1.00	1.00
Hengoed (K) 52-65		1.00	1.00
then (U)-76			0.50
then 'Cardiff 7' (M) 88- about 94			1.50
Henley-on-Thames (K) 28-35	2.50		
then (U) later (M)-98	0.50	0.50	0.50
Hereford -93 then (L)	0.50	0.50	0.50
also (K, reserve) 57 only		1.50	
Herne Bay later (R)/(L)-98	0.50	0.50	0.50
Hertford later (L)	0.50	0.50	0.50
Hessle (K) 60-75		1.00	1.00
(N Humberside only Feb-March 75)			2.00
Heswall 56- later (R)-?82		0.50	0.50
Hetton-le-Hole (U) 55 and (U,X) 61 seen		10.00	10.00
then 'Durham' (X) 83 only			1.00
Hexham (K) 36-38	4.00		
then (U)-76, then (X)-84	0.50	0.50	0.50
then again (M) ?90-			1.00
Heywood -66	0.70	0.50	0.50
Highbridge (K) 57-60		2.50	
then (U)-66		0.50	0.50
High Wycombe -92, (M)-96	0.50	0.50	0.50
Hinckley -77	0.50	0.50	0.50

210

Machine Cancellations

	1933-44	45-60	61-99
then again (M) 89-95			1.00
Hindhead (K) 35-49	1.50	1.50	
then (U) later (R)-76		0.50	0.50
Hitchin later (R)/(L)	0.50	0.50	0.50
Hoddesdon (K) 35-39 & 53	3.00	2.00	
then (U)-68		0.50	0.50
then again (L) 91-			1.00
Holbeach (K) 50-65		1.00	1.00
then (U)-87			0.50
Holmfirth (K) 50-57		1.00	
then (U)-67		0.50	0.50
Holsworthy (K) 56-61		2.50	1.50
then (U) later (R)-93			0.50
Holt (K) 50-58		1.00	
then (U)-76		0.50	0.50
Holyhead (K) 33-48	1.50	1.50	
then (U) later (R)-2001		0.50	0.50
Holywell (K) 50-55		2.00	
then (U)-71		0.50	0.50
Holywood (K) 'Co Down' 58		10.00	
then (K) 'Holywood/Belfast' 59-60		5.00	
then (U) 60-63		2.00	2.00
then 'Holywood/Co Down' -84			0.50
Home Counties North Mail Centre 2011-12 (N) (new location at Hemel Hempstead, replacing Hemel Hempstead, Stevenage, Watford)			0.50
Honiton 51- later (R)-93		0.50	0.50
Horden (K) 60-62		2.00	2.00
Horley (K) 39-48	2.00	2.00	
then (U)-70		0.50	0.50
then again (M) 92-			1.00
Horncastle (K) 56-58		3.00	
then (U)-73		0.50	0.50
Hornchurch 'Romford B' 70-72 (R)			1.00
then 'Romford R51' (L) 89-			1.00
also 'Romford G41' (X) 90 only			1.00
Horsforth (K) 55-63		1.50	1.50
then (U)-66			0.60
Horsham later (L)	0.50	0.50	0.50
Horwich (K) 60-62		2.00	2.00
also (U, X)-60-?66		1.50	1.50
Houghton le Spring (U)-67		0.60	0.50
then 'Durham' (X) 82-87			1.00
Hounslow -86	0.50	0.50	0.50
then (X) 90 only			1.00
Hove 'Sussex Coast B4' (L) 90-95			1.00
Hoylake (K) 34-48	1.50	1.50	
then (U) later (L)-76		0.50	0.50
Hucknall (K) 50-55		1.50	
then (U)-?76		0.50	0.50
then (U) again (M) ?90-			1.00
Huddersfield (U)	0.50	0.50	0.50
also (K, reserve) 36-61	2.00	2.00	2.00
then 'Hudders Halifax' (U) 76-93			
then (L)			0.50
*Hull	0.50	0.50	0.50
also (K,X) 37-39	3.00		
Hungerford (K) 59-62		1.00	1.00
then (U)-67			0.50
Hunstanton (K) 32-41	2.50		
then (U)-71	0.60	0.50	0.50
Huntingdon (K) 40-44	1.50		
then (U)-92	0.50	0.50	0.50
then again (M) 96-			1.00
also (K, reserve) 59-74		1.50	1.50
Huntly (K) 56-60		1.50	
then (U)-77 then (X)-2005		0.50	0.50
Huyton (K) 43-48	2.50	2.50	
then (U) later (L)-80		0.50	0.50

	1933-44	45-60	61-99
Hyde (K) 25-34	2.50		
then (U) later (R)/(L)	0.50	0.50	0.50
Hythe Kent (K) 30-48	2.00	2.00	
then (U) later (R)/(L)		0.50	0.50
Hythe 'Southampton' (K) 62-63			2.00
then 'Hythe Southampton' (U) 63-69			1.00
then again (L) 90-			1.00
Ilford (U) -55	0.50	0.50	
also (K, reserve) 36 & 47	1.50	1.50	
also (U) 'Ilford & Barking' 36-(R only to 55)	0.50	0.50	0.50
also (K, reserve) 36 only	1.50		
then Ilford again 70- later (L)			0.50
then 'Romford G11' (L) 89-			1.00
Ilfracombe later (R)/(L)	0.50	0.50	0.50
Ilkeston (K) 30-38	2.00		
then (U)-?76	0.60	0.50	0.50
Ilkley ?40- later (L)	0.60	0.50	0.50
Ilminster (K) 54-58		1.50	
then (U)-79		0.50	0.50
Ingatestone (K) 60-65		1.00	1.00
then (U)-68, then (X)-74			0.50
Inverclyde new office used variety of Gourock, Greenock, Paisley dies (X) 94-2004			1.00
Invergordon later (R)-?2000	0.60	0.50	0.50
*Inverness (later City of)	0.50	0.50	0.50
Inverurie (K) 58-76		1.00	1.00
then (K,X) 85-87			1.00
then (U,X) 'Aberdeen' 90-			1.00
then 'Inverurie' (U,X) 94-2005			1.00
*Ipswich (U)	0.50	0.50	0.50
and (K, reserve) 33-53	1.50	1.50	
Irlam (K) 60-67		1.00	1.00
then (U) later (R)/(L)			0.50
Irthlingborough (K) 65-67			1.50
Irvine (K) 45-55		1.00	
then (U)-79		0.50	0.50
Iver (K) 59-61, (K, X) 63		1.50	1.50
then (U)-73			0.50
Jarrow (K) 32-49	1.50	1.50	
then (U)-77 then (X)-85		0.50	0.50
then again (M) ?91-			1.00
Jedburgh (K) 60-75		1.00	1.00
*John O'Groats (K) 67- init summer only			1.00
Johnstone (K) 51-57		1.00	
then (U)-77 then (X)-81		0.50	0.50
*Jubilee Mail Centre (U) 2002- (N) (near Hounslow, covers KT,TW areas, later GU)			0.50
Keighley later (L)-96	0.50	0.50	0.50
also 'Bradford' (X) 84-91			1.00
Keith (K) 58-76 (and later (X)		1.00	1.00
Kelso (K) 39-58	1.00	1.00	
then (U) later (R)/(L)		0.50	0.50
also 'Scottish Borders' 92-95 (R) (but indistinguishable from Galashiels)			0.50
Kempsey (K) 71-72			3.00
then (U,R)-85			0.60
Kendal later (R)	0.50	0.50	0.50
then 'Lancs & S Lakes 18' (M) 94-			1.00
Kenilworth (K) 41-62	1.50	1.00	1.00
then (U)-69			0.50
again (M) 91-			1.00
Keswick (K) 32-37	2.00		
then (U)-94 then (L)	0.60	0.50	0.50
Kettering later (M)		0.50	0.50
Keynsham (K) 56-58		2.50	

211

Machine Cancellations

	1933-44	45-60	61-99
then **(U)**-79		0.50	0.50
Keyworth **(K)** 70-77			1.50
Kidderminster later **(R)**-99	0.50	0.50	0.50
Kidlington **(M)** 90-96			1.00
Kidsgrove ?60-88		1.00	0.50
Kilmacolm **(K)** 66-76 then **(K,R)**-79			1.00
Kilmarnock -96 then **(X)** -2002	0.50	0.50	0.50
Kilsyth **(K)** 54-59		1.00	
then **(U)** later **(L)**		0.50	0.50
Kilwinning **(K)** 59-69		1.00	1.00
then **(U)**-71			1.50
Kingsbridge **(K)** 38-48	1.50	1.50	
then **(U)**-72		0.50	0.50
then 'S Devon' **(X)** 73-83			1.00
Kings Langley 59-78		0.50	0.50
then again **(M)** 85-89, **(X)**-90			1.00
Kings Lynn -97	0.50	0.50	0.50
Kingston on/upon Thames -2002 (then see 'Jubilee')	0.50	0.50	0.50
Kingswood **(K)** 36-38	3.00		
then **(U)**-86	0.50	0.50	0.50
Kington **(K)** 62-71			1.00
Kingussie **(K)** 67- later **(R)**-93			1.00
Kinross **(U)** 61-70			0.50
then **(K,R)** 70-80			1.00
then **(U,R)** later **(M)**-90 & **(X)** 93			0.50
Kirkby Trading Est **(K)** 53 only		3.00	
then **(U)**-59		0.60	
then Kirkby later **(M)**-?91		0.50	0.50
Kirkby-in-Ashfield **(K)** 55-56		3.00	
then **(U)**-77		0.50	0.50
then again **(M)** 87-88			1.00
Kirkby Lonsdale **(K,R)** 61-93			1.00
Kirkby Stephen **(K)** 61-			1.00
then **(U)** 83- later **(R)**-94			1.00
Kirkcaldy later **(R)/(L)**	0.50	0.50	0.50
also **(K,X)** 58-59		2.00	
Kirkcudbright **(K)** 61-74			1.00
Kirkham **(K)** 69-73 (later see Preston West)			2.00
Kirkintilloch **(U)** 54-86 then **(M)**		0.50	0.50
also **(K,X)** 64-65			2.50
*Kirkwall **(K)** 43-54	2.00	2.00	
then **(U)** 55-		0.50	0.50
Kirriemuir **(K)** 58- later **(R)**-88		1.00	1.00
Knaresborough **(K)** 49-59		1.00	
then **(U)**-72		0.50	0.50
Knighton **(K)** 62-72			1.00
then **(U)**-82 then **(R)**-98			0.50
Knottingley **(K)** 65-69			1.50
Knutsford **(K)** 51-57		1.00	
then **(U)** later **(R)**-75		0.50	0.50
Kyle (of Lochalsh) 61- 2012			0.50
Ladybank **(K)** 61-76			1.00
Lairg **(K)** 55-82		1.00	1.00
then **(U)** later **(R)**-2010			0.50
Lambourn **(K)** 65-67			2.50
Lampeter **(K)** 59-60		3.00	
then **(U)** 61-94 then **(L)**			0.50
then 'Llanbedr PS/Lampeter' **(L)** 99-2001			2.00
Lanark **(K)** 36-48	1.00	1.00	
then **(U)** 50-		0.50	0.50
then 'Clyde Valley ML11' 87-96			0.50
Lancaster 'Lancaster & Morecambe'	0.50	0.50	0.50
then 'Lancs & S Lakes 13' **(M)** 93-			1.00
Lancing -66	0.50	0.50	0.50
then again **(M)** 91-97			1.00
Langholm **(K)** 61-93 then **(R)**-2007			1.00
Langport **(K)** 58-81		1.00	1.00
Larbert 58-68		0.60	0.60

	1933-44	45-60	61-99
Largs **(K)** 34-36	3.00		
then **(U)**-71	0.60	0.50	0.50
Larkhall 59-76		0.60	0.50
Lark Lane Liv **(K)** 12-37	1.50		
then with district '17' 51-53		3.00	
then **(U)**-66	0.60	0.50	0.50
then again **(M)** 91-?92			1.00
Larne **(K)** 40s-57	4.00	4.00	
then **(U)** 57-86		0.50	0.50
Launceston **(K)** 36-48	3.50	2.50	
then **(U)**-77		0.50	0.50
then 'Plymouth' **(X)** 80- then **(R)**-92/**(X)**-99			1.00
Laurencekirk **(K)** 65-79 then **(L)**-87			1.00
Leamington Spa : 'Warwick & Leamington Spa' later **(L)**	0.50	0.50	0.50
then 'Leamington Spa' **(M)** 90-			1.00
Leatherhead **(K)** 30-35	2.50		
then **(U)**-86	0.60	0.50	0.50
then 'Kingston-u-T 6,9' **(R)/(L)** 90-			0.50
Ledbury **(K)** 56-58		2.00	
then **(U)**-72		0.60	0.50
then 'Hereford' **(M)** 91-93			1.50
*Leeds	0.50	0.50	0.50
also **(K)** Xmas reserve 59-70		1.00	1.00
Cross Gates 55-65		0.60	0.60
Moortown 'DO 17' ?55-?63		0.60	0.60
(Morley & Yeadon listed separately)			
Leek **(K)** 27-33	3.00		
then **(U)** later **(R)**	0.60	0.50	0.50
Leicester	0.50	0.50	0.50
also **(K, reserve)** 46-60		1.00	
then **(U)** 'Leicestershire' 93-?2006			0.50
Leigh Lancs -71	0.60	0.50	0.50
then again **(M)** 85-90			1.00
Leigh-on-Sea Essex **(M)** 89-			1.00
Leighton Buzzard **(K)** 34-38	3.00		
then **(U)**-92 then **(L)**-99	0.50	0.50	0.50
Leiston **(K)** 60-68		1.00	1.00
then **(U)**-76			0.50
Leominster **(K)** 38-52	3.00	2.50	
then **(U)**-72		0.60	0.50
*Lerwick **(K)** 32-51	2.00	2.00	
then **(U)** 53-		0.50	0.50
Letchworth **(K)** 28-48	1.50	1.50	
then **(U)** later **(L)**		0.50	0.50
Leven **(K)** 32-36	3.50		
then **(U)**	0.60	0.50	0.50
then 'Leven Buckhaven Methil' 64-76			0.50
then 'Kirkcaldy' **(X)**-85			1.00
then 'Leven' **(R)/(L)** 88-			1.00
Levenshulme later **(R)/(L)**	0.60	0.50	0.50
Lewes -75 then **(L)**	0.50	0.50	0.50
Leyburn **(K)** 55-70		1.00	1.00
Leyland **(K)** 35-38	3.00		
then **(U)**-71	0.60	0.50	0.50
then 'Lancs & S Lakes 10' **(M)** 93-			1.00
Lichfield **(K)** 29-38	3.50		
then **(U)** later **(R)**-?94	0.60	0.50	0.50
Limavady **(K)** 58-59		5.00	
then **(U)** 60- later **(R)**-97		0.50	0.50
Lincoln -94 then **(L)**	0.50	0.50	0.50
Lingfield **(K)** 72-75			1.00
then **(U)**-76 then **(L)**-79			0.60
Linlithgow **(K)** 59-68		1.00	1.00
then **(U)**-84 then **(X)**-93			0.50
Liphook **(K)** 59-66		1.00	1.00
then **(U)** later **(R)**-93			0.50
Lisburn **(K)** 41-48	5.00	5.00	
then **(U)** 49-93 then **(L)**		0.50	0.50

212

Machine Cancellations

	1933-44	45-60	61-99
Liskeard (K) 42-51	4.00	2.50	
then (U)-74		0.50	0.50
then 'Plymouth' (X) 80-			1.00
then (R)-92/(L)-96 then (X)-99			1.00
Littleborough (K) 57-60		2.50	
then (U) later (R)-85		0.60	0.50
Littlehampton -77	0.50	0.50	0.50
then again (R)/(L) 84-			1.00
Liverpool-2010	0.50	0.50	0.50
(then see Warrington Mail Centre)			
also (K, reserve) 42-45	2.00	1.50	
(also 54 Lark Lane/Liv with Lark Lane removed)			
Liverpool ED,ND,SD, all later (R)-77		0.50	0.50
Livingston 74-			0.50
then 'HPO West Lothian' 83-94			0.50
Llanberis (Empire Games 58)		6.00	
Llandilo (K) 55-57		3.00	
then (K) 'Llandeilo' 57-59		3.00	
then (U) 59-75		0.60	0.50
Llandovery (K) 60-75		1.00	1.00
Llandrindod Wells (K) 38-55	1.50	1.00	
then (U) later (R)-99 then (M)		0.50	0.50
Llandudno -60	0.50	0.50	
then (at Colwyn Bay) 64-			0.50
then (M, at Llandudno) ?84-96			1.00
Llandyssul (K) 59-73		1.00	1.00
then (U)			0.50
then 'Llandysul' 80-94 then (L)			1.00
then 'Llandysul' no county (L) 99 only			5.00
Llanelly -66	0.50	0.50	0.50
then 'Llanelli' later (R)/(L)			0.50
then 'Llanelli' no county (L) 99 only			5.00
Llanfairfechan (K) 69-77			1.00
then (U) later (R)-96			0.50
Llangefni 57-2001, then (X) 2001		0.50	0.50
Llangollen (K) 39-61	1.50	1.00	1.00
then (U) -83 then (P), (M), (X)-99			0.50
Llanidloes (at Newtown) 64-80			0.60
and philatelic mail only 82			1.00
Llanrwst (K) 56-62		1.00	1.00
then (U)-84 then (L)-89			0.50
Loanhead (K) 69-85			1.00
Lochgelly 57- later (R)/(L)		0.50	0.50
Lochgilphead (K) 58-87		1.00	1.00
then (U) 'GB' die Jan-Apr 87			5.00
then (U) 'Lochgilp' May 87-93			
then (L)			0.50
Lochmaddy (K) 68-69 then in reserve-77			3.00
Lockerbie 50- later (R)/(L)		0.50	0.50
London (see end of listing)			
Londonderry	1.00	0.50	0.50
later (R) then (X)-2008			0.50
Long Eaton (K) 30-38	2.50		
then (U)-77	0.70	0.50	0.50
then again (L) 87-92			0.50
Longridge (K) 65-71			1.00
then (U,L) 'Lancs' no number 94-			1.00
Longton (U) 34-43	3.00		
then (K) 63-67			1.00
then (U) later (R)			0.50
Looe (K) 36-57	1.00	1.00	
then (U)-74 (at Liskeard)		0.50	0.50
Lossiemouth (K) 61-79			1.00
Lostwithiel (K) 60-87		1.00	1.00
then (U)-92			0.60

	1933-44	45-60	61-99
Loughborough later (R)/(L)-96	0.50	0.50	0.50
Loughton (K) 53 only		5.00	
then (U) later (L)		0.50	0.50
then 'Romford G41' (M) 90-			1.00
Louth (K) 32-38	3.00		
then (U)-77	0.60	0.50	0.50
then (U,X) 'Grimsby & Cleeth' 89-92			1.00
Lowestoft later (M)-94	0.50	0.50	0.50
Ludlow (K) 35-48	1.00	1.00	
then (U) later (R)/(L)		0.50	0.50
Lurgan (K) 46-54		3.00	
then (U) 56-, then		0.50	0.50
'Lurgan Craigavon' 73-93 then (L)			0.50
Luton-98 then (L)	0.50	0.50	0.50
also (K, reserve) 47-62		1.50	1.50
Lutterworth Warwicks (K) 60 only		6.00	
then Lutterworth Rugby (K) 61-			1.00
then (U) 'Lutterworth Rugby' 67-			0.60
then 'Lutterworth Leics' 73-76			0.60
Lydney (K) 41-54	2.50	2.50	
then (U)-70		0.50	0.50
Lyme Regis (K) 50-56		2.00	
then (U) later (R)-2001		0.50	0.50
Lymington (K) 33-37	4.00		
then (U)-75	0.70	0.50	0.50
then again (L) 90-			1.00
Lymm (K) 57-64		1.50	1.50
Lyndhurst (K) 51-60		1.00	
Lynton (K) 32-60	1.00	1.00	
then (U) 'Lynton' -65		1.00	0.60
then 'Lynton & Lynmouth' later (R)-98			0.50
Lytham St Annes -?67	0.60	0.50	0.50
then 'Fylde 8' (X) 81- later (L)-?98			1.00
Mablethorpe -64		0.60	0.50
then 'Mableth'pe & Sutton on Sea' -77			0.50
Macclesfield -92 then (L)	0.50	0.50	0.50
Machynlleth (K) 60-63		1.00	1.00
then (U) later (R)-2000 then (L)-2006			0.50
Maesteg (K) no Bridgend 49		4.00	
then (K) with Bridgend 51-52		3.00	
then (U) -77 (at Bridgend from 67)		0.60	0.50
then occasional use -89			1.00
then 'Cardiff 17' (M) 89-2001			1.00
Magherafelt (K) no county 62 only			7.50
then (K) with county 62-68			2.00
then (U) later (R)/(L)-?98			0.50
Maghull (K) 56-61		2.50	2.50
then (U)-74			0.50
Maidenhead -73 later (L)	0.50	0.50	0.50
Maidstone	0.50	0.50	0.50
also (K, reserve) 36-62	1.00	1.00	1.00
then (U) 'Medway & Maidstone' 83- 2012 (then see Medway)			0.50
Maldon 50- later (L)		0.50	0.50
but 'Chelmsford' (X) 78-89			1.00
Malmesbury (K) 52-57		2.00	
then (U)-68		0.60	0.50
then 'Swindon' (X) 81-91			1.00
Malton (K) 32-38	3.00		
then (U) later (L)-87	1.00	0.50	0.50
Malvern	0.60	0.50	0.50
then 'Worc District M' (L) 83-			1.00
but 'Malvern' again (X) 89 only			1.00
Manchester - ?2004	0.50	0.50	0.50
also (K, reserve) 32-36	2.00		

213

Machine Cancellations

	1933-44	45-60	61-99
also (U) 'Manchester IPS' (M) 83-?95 (Inward Primary Sorting)			1.00
Manchester districts, later (R)/(L):			
E, N, NE(66-), SE, SW	0.50	0.50	0.50
S (K) 13-34	1.00		
then (U) later (R)/(L)	0.50	0.50	0.50
and Manch.H (K) 11-54	1.00	1.00	
Manningtree (K) 54-66		1.00	1.00
then (U) later (L)			0.50
Mansfield -94	0.50	0.50	0.50
March (K) 39-49	2.00	2.00	
then (U)-94		0.50	0.50
Margate	0.50	0.50	0.50
then 'Thanet A' 71- later (R)/(L)-93			0.50
then again (X) 96-97			1.00
Market Drayton (K) 39-48	2.00	2.00	
then (U) later (L)		0.50	0.50
Market Harborough (K)34-38	3.00		
then (U) later (R)/(L)-95	1.00	0.50	0.50
Market Rasen (K) 57-59		3.00	
then (U)-73		1.00	0.50
Markinch 58-64		1.00	1.00
Marlborough (K) 37-51	2.00	2.00	
then (U)-68		0.60	0.50
then 'Swindon' (X) 81-91			1.00
Marlow (K) 50-56		1.50	
then (U)-?66		0.50	0.50
then again (L) 86-			1.00
Marple 'Stockport X' (R) 86-92			1.00
Maryport (K) 48-59		1.00	
then (U) later (R)/(L)		0.50	0.50
Matlock (K) 29-34	2.00		
then (U)-78	1.00	0.50	0.50
Mauchline (K) 59-65		1.00	1.00
then (U)-71			0.50
Maybole (K) 60-71		1.00	1.00
Medway MC 2012 only (N) (new Mail Centre at Rochester replacing Canterbury, Maidstone & Tonbridge) (earlier see Chatham)			0.50
Melksham (K) 39-49	3.00	3.00	
then (U) later (R)		0.50	0.50
Melrose (K) 58-65		1.00	1.00
then (U)-68			0.50
Melton Mowbray (K) 32-44	3.00		
then (U) later (R)/(M)-95	0.60	0.50	0.50
Menai Bridge '1st day' 29.4.68 only (machine at Bethesda)			1.50
Merthyr Tydfil (K) 26-33	1.50		
then (U) 34-77 then (L)	0.60	0.50	0.50
then 'Cardiff 11' (R) 89-?2004			1.00
Mexborough (K) 33-38	3.00		
then (U)-66	1.00	0.50	0.50
then 'Sheffield' (X) 71- then (M)			1.00
Middlesbrough	0.50	0.50	0.50
then 'Teesside' 69-			0.50
then 'Cleveland' 74-			0.50
then 'Teesside' again 97- 2013			0.50
Middleton (K) 34-38	2.50		
then (U) later (R)/(L)	0.60	0.50	0.50
Middlewich (K) 55-64		1.00	1.00
then (U)-75 (at Northwich)			0.50
Midhurst (K) 42-59	1.00	1.00	
then (U) later (R)/(M)-94		0.50	0.50
Mid Rhondda Ganol 'Rhondda 3' (L) 99-2000 (new office replacing Porth & Tonypandy)			3.00
Milford Haven (K) 32-43	3.00		
then (U) later (R)-94 then (L)	0.50	0.50	0.50

	1933-44	45-60	61-99
then 'Aberdaugleddau/M Haven' (L) 99-2002			2.00
Millom (K) 57-61		3.00	3.00
then (U) later (R)-96 then (L)			0.50
Millport (K) 61-92 init summer only			1.50
Milngavie (K) 54-79		1.00	1.00
and (U,X) 65-78			1.00
then (U) 79-, then (L) 86-			0.50
Milton Keynes 73- 2010 (also see Wolverton) then (X) 2010 (then see South Midlands Mail Centre)			0.50
Milton Keynes Kiln Farm (M)/(X) 89-96			1.00
Minehead (K) 29-39	1.50		
then (U) later (L)-97	0.50	0.50	0.50
Mirfield (K) 39-59	1.50	1.50	
then (U)-70		0.50	0.50
then 'Wakefield' (X) 71- later (M)			1.00
Mitcham (U) 33-73	1.00	0.50	0.50
then 'Croydon' (R)-76			0.50
then 'Mitcham' again (M) 89-			1.00
Moffat (K) 61-77			1.00
Mold 40-71	1.00	0.50	0.50
then again (L) 89-			1.00
Monmouth (K) 49-53		3.00	
then (U)-76 then (R)/(L)		0.50	0.50
Montrose (K) 29-43	2.50		
then (U) later (R)/(L)-98	0.50	0.50	0.50
Morden 'Sutton' die (M) 87-			1.00
then 'Croydon Sutton / Morden'(M) ?91-			1.00
Moreton Wirral (K) 56-57		3.50	
then (U)-70		1.00	1.00
Moreton-in-Marsh (K) 57-59		3.50	
then (U)		0.50	0.50
then 'Worcester District' (L) 83-?89			1.00
Morley (K) 40-49	3.00	3.00	
then (U)-71		0.50	0.50
Morpeth (K) 31-38	3.00		
then (U)	0.60	0.50	0.50
then 'Mid Northumberland' 69- later (L)			0.50
Morriston (K) 50-55		3.00	
then (U)-58		10.00	
Mossley Manchester (U) 50s-61		1.00	1.00
then (K) 61 only			5.00
then Mossley Ashton-u-L 61-82			1.00
and (U,R) 61-76 (at Ashton-u-L)			1.00
then again (R)/(L) 91-			1.00
Mossley Hill Liv 50s-66		1.00	0.60
Motherwell	0.50	0.50	
then 'Motherwell & Wishaw' 52- but sometimes 'Motherwell' (X)		0.50	0.50
			1.00
then 'Clyde Valley M L 1' 87-96			0.50
then (R)/(X), various dies)-2008			1.00
Mountain Ash 52-77 then (L,(X)		0.50	0.50
then 'Cardiff 9' (L) 89-			1.00
then 'Aberpennar Mountain Ash' (L) 2000-2001			2.50
Mumbles 'Swansea 9' (L) 87-93			1.50
Musselburgh (K) 45-48		3.00	
then (U) later (L)		0.50	0.50
Nairn (K) 55-59		2.00	
then (U) later (R)/(L)		0.50	0.50
Nantwich -82 later (X)-88	0.50	0.50	0.50
Narberth (K) 59-68		2.00	1.00
then (U) later (R)-94 then (L)			0.50
then 'Arberth/Narberth' (L) 99-2005			2.00
Neath later (R)-75	0.50	0.50	0.50
then 'West Glam 8' (R)			1.00

214

Machine Cancellations

	1933-44	45-60	61-99
then 'Neath' again 80-98 **(R)**/**(L)**			1.00
Nelson 'Burnley & Nelson' **(L)** 93-			1.00
Newark -94	0.50	0.50	0.50
Newbridge **(K)** 55-61		1.00	1.00
then **(U)**-76 then **(R)**-94			0.50
Newbury later **(R)**-2002	0.50	0.50	0.50
Newcastle Co Down **(K)** 56-60		3.00	
then **(U)**-95		0.50	0.50
Newcastle Staffs **(K)** 32-43	3.00		
then **(U)** 45-?48		1.00	
again **(K)** 60-64		1.00	1.00
then **(U)** 65- later **(L)**			0.50
Newcastle Emlyn **(K)** 68-77			1.00
then **(U)**-86			0.60
*Newcastle on/upon Tyne	0.50	0.50	0.50
also **(K, reserve)** 33-61	2.00	1.50	1.50
also **(U)** NO upon Tyne error 84-95			0.50
then 'Tyneside NE SR' 95-			0.50
Newcastle districts **(all U,M 90s)**: '3' at Gosforth, '5' at West5, '6' at Heaton, '8' at Gateshead, '9' at Low Fell, '12' at Forest Hall			1.00
Newhaven **(K)** 49-58		1.00	
then **(U)**-75 then **(R)**/**(L)**		0.50	0.50
New Malden **(K)** 32-34	3.00		
then **(U)**-63	0.60	0.50	0.50
then 'Kingston 5' later **(L)**-93			1.00
Newmarket later **(R)**/**(L)**		0.50	0.50
New Milton **(K)** 40-49	2.00	2.00	
then **(U)**-71		0.50	0.50
Newport Isle of Wight -77	0.60	0.50	0.50
(error with '6' at foot 67-68)		4.00	
then 'Isle of Wight' later **(L)**			0.50
Newport Mon	0.50	0.50	0.50
then 'Gwent' 73-93 then **(M)**			0.50
then 'Casnewydd Newport' **(M)** 2000 only			2.00
Newport Shropshire **(K)** 54-59		1.00	
then **(U)** later **(L)**		0.50	0.50
Newport Pagnell 60- later **(R)**/**(L)**		0.50	0.50
Newquay	0.50	0.50	0.50
then 'Cornwall E' **(L)** 92-99			1.00
New Romney **(K)** 57-61		2.00	2.00
then **(U)** later **(R)**-96			0.50
Newry **(K)** 27-45	4.00	4.00	
then **(U)** later **(R)**		0.50	0.50
Newton Abbot -83	0.70	0.50	0.50
then again **(X)** 86-91			1.00
Newton-le-Willows **(K)** 49 only		4.00	
then **(U)** later **(L)**		0.50	0.50
Newton Mearns 65- later **(L)**			0.50
Newton Stewart **(K)** 54-66		1.00	1.00
then **(U)** later **(R)**-93 then **(L)**			0.50
Newtown **(K)** 34-38	3.00		
then **(U)**-82 then **(L)**-99	0.60	0.50	0.50
Newtownabbey 60-83		0.50	0.50
Newtownards **(K)** 52-53		7.50	
then **(U)** 54-93 then **(L)**		0.50	0.50
Normanton **(K)** 62-70			1.00
then 'Wakefield' **(U,X)** -81			1.00
Northallerton **(K)** 33-38	3.00		
then **(U)** later **(M,P)**/**(M)**	0.50	0.50	0.50
and 'Darlington' **(X)** 83-88			1.00
Northampton	0.50	0.50	0.50
also **(K, reserve)** 40 only	2.50		
then **(U)** 'Northamptonshire' 85-2010 (then see South Midlands Mail Centre)			0.50
North Berwick **(K)** 33-58	1.00	1.00	
then **(U)** later **(R)**/**(L)**		0.50	0.50

	1933-44	45-60	61-99
Northenden **(K)** 46-47		2.00	
Northleach **(K)** 84-92			1.00
Northolt PDO **(M)** 90-			1.00
North Shields -?76	0.50	0.50	0.50
then **(X)**-85, then **(M)** 89-95			1.00
North Walsham **(K)** 57-60		1.00	
then **(U)**-76		0.50	0.50
Northwich **(K)** 23-35	1.50		
then **(U)** later **(R)**	0.50	0.50	0.50
Northwood **(K)** 29-38	2.00		
then **(U)**	0.50	0.50	0.50
then 'Harrow & Wembley N' 70-			0.50
then 'Harrow N' 80- later **(L)**			0.50
*Norwich **(U, N)**	0.50	0.50	0.50
also **(K)** 31-42	2.50		
& **(U)** 'Norwich NORFOLK' error 2003			5.00
*Nottingham-	0.50	0.50	0.50
Nuneaton -?85 then **(M)**	0.50	0.50	0.50
Oakengates **(K)** 56-60		2.50	
then **(U)** 'Oakengates Salop'		1.00	1.00
then 'Oakengates Telford' 69 only			2.50
Oakham **(K)** 43-55	1.50	1.00	
then **(U)**-77		0.50	0.50
Oban **(K)** 26-34	3.50		
then **(U)**-93 then **(R)**	0.50	0.50	0.50
Okehampton **(K)** 48-49		4.00	
then **(U)**-93		0.50	0.50
Oldham	0.50	0.50	0.50
then 'Rochdale Oldham Ashton-u-L' 81-2008 (later towns shown in different sequence)			0.50
but 'Oldham' again 92 only			0.50
Old Swan **(K)** 16-48	1.00	1.00	
then **(U)**-66		0.50	0.50
Omagh **(K)** 36-c48	4.00	4.00	
then **(U)** later **(R)**		0.50	0.50
Ongar **(K)** 58-60		2.00	
then **(U)**-75		0.50	0.50
then 'Chelmsford' **(X)** 78-90			1.00
Openshaw later **(R)**/**(L)**	0.50	0.50	0.50
Ormskirk **(K)** 34-37	4.00		
then **(U)**-66	1.00	0.50	0.50
then again **(M)** 89-93			1.00
Orpington later **(R)**/**(L)**	0.50	0.50	0.50
Ossett **(U)** ?40s-?70		0.50	0.50
then 'Wakefield L' **(X)** then **(M)**			1.00
then 'Ossett' again **(X)** 94 only			1.00
Oswestry **(K)** 26-37	2.00		
then **(U)** later **(R)**/**(L)**	0.50	0.50	0.50
Otley **(K)** 37-48	2.00	2.00	
then **(U)**-?70		0.50	0.50
Oundle 50s-80		0.50	0.50
Oxford -2008	0.50	0.50	0.50
also **(K, reserve)** 40-56	2.00	2.00	
(then see Swindon/Thames Valley)			
Oxted **(K)** 38-41	4.00		
then **(U)**-?70	0.60	0.50	0.50
Padstow **(K)** 58-87		1.00	1.00
then **(U)** later **(R)**-92			0.60
Paignton -70	0.50	0.50	0.50
then 'South Devon' **(X)**-96			1.00
Paisley -94 then **(L)**/**(X)** -2008	0.50	0.50	0.50
but **(K, reserve)** 40 &51	2.50	2.50	
Pangbourne **(K)** 46-59		1.00	
then **(U)**-67		0.60	0.50
Par **(K)** 50-63		1.00	1.00
then **(U)**-68			0.60
Parkstone -?33	1.00		
later 'Bournemouth-Poole C' 69-72			0.50
Peebles **(K)** 39-53	1.00	1.00	

Machine Cancellations

	1933-44	45-60	61-99
then **(U)** later **(R)**/**(L)**		0.50	0.50
Pembroke **(K)** 59-65		1.00	1.00
Pembroke Dock **(K)** 54-59		1.00	
then **(U)** later **(R)**-94 then **(L)**		0.50	0.50
&'Doc Penfro/Pembroke Dock' **(L)** 99-2005			1.50
Penarth **(K)** 32-38	2.00		
then **(U)**-67 then **(L)**-69	0.60	0.50	0.50
then 'Cardiff 8' **(M)** 87-94			1.50
Penicuik 61- later **(L)**			0.50
Penlan 'Swansea 11' **(L)** 87-93			1.00
Penmaenmawr **(K)** 59-61		3.00	3.00
then **(U)**-84 then **(L)**-95			0.60
Penrith **(K)** 28-36	2.50		
then **(U)**-93 then **(L)**	0.50	0.50	0.50
Pentre **(K)** 49-52		5.00	
then **(U)**-66		0.50	0.50
then 'Rhondda 4' **(K)**-69			2.00
Penygroes **(K)** 75-77			2.00
then **(U)**-86			1.00
Penzance	0.50	0.50	0.50
then 'Cornwall F' **(R)** 92-99			1.00
but 'Cornwall 1' Sundays 90-92 (see also Sennen, stamped at Penzance)			1.00
Perranporth **(K)** 69-87			1.00
then **(U)** later **(R)**-92			0.50
Pershore **(K)** 54-60		2.00	
then **(U)**-76		0.50	0.50
Perth **(U)**	0.50	0.50	0.50
also **(K, reserve)** 44 & 52	1.50	1.50	
then **(U)** 'Perth Dundee Angus' 83-95			0.50
but 'Perth' **(R,M)** 89-99			0.50
Peterborough Northants **(U)**	0.50	0.50	0.50
also **(K, reserve)** 27-56	1.00	1.00	
then **(U)** NO Northants 65-2012 **(N)**			0.50
Peterhead **(K)** 39-55	1.50	1.50	
then **(U)**-72 then **(M)**		0.50	0.50
Peterlee **(K)** 62-63			2.00
then **(U)**-82			0.50
Petersfield **(K)** 32-38	2.50		
then **(U)**-93 then **(L)**-98	1.00	0.50	0.50
Petworth **(K)** 30-60	2.50	1.50	
then **(U)**-93 then **(M)**-94		0.50	0.50
Pewsey **(K)** 58-68		1.00	1.00
Pickering **(K)** 56-59		2.00	
then **(U)** -?71		0.60	0.50
Pinner ?39-	0.70	0.50	0.50
then 'Harrow & Wembley P' 71-			0.50
then 'Harrow P' **(R)** 80-			0.50
then Pinner again **(L)** 93-			1.00
Pitlochry **(K)** 39-57	1.00	1.00	
then **(U)**-83 & **(X)** 83		0.50	0.50
*Plymouth	0.50	0.50	0.50
also **(K, reserve)** 36-56	2.00	2.00	
then **(U)** 'Plym Cornwall & W Devon' 80-			0.50
but 'Plym & District' Sundays 90-92			1.00
Pocklington **(K)** 49-70		1.00	1.00
Polegate **(K)** 58-67		1.00	1.00
then **(U)**-76 then **(R)**/**(L)**			0.50
Pontardawe **(K)** 57-58		5.00	
then **(U)**-65		1.00	0.60
then 'Swansea 13' **(L)** 89-99 (this machine used at Swansea Dec 99)			1.00
then 'Pontardawe' no Swansea **(L)** 99-2004			1.00
Pontefract **(K)** 28-36	2.00		

	1933-44	45-60	61-99
then **(U)**-70	0.50	0.50	0.50
then 'Wakefield' **(X)** 70- then **(M)**			1.00
Ponteland 65-68			1.50
Pontnewydd **(K)** 53-54		10.00	
Pontyclun **(K)** 59-61		2.00	2.00
then **(U)**-69			0.50
then 'Cardiff 18' **(M)** 89-96			1.00
Pontypool -75 then **(L)**-2001	0.50	0.50	0.50
Pontypridd -77 then **(L)**	0.50	0.50	0.50
also 'Rhondda 1' 66-71			1.00
then 'Cardiff 2,3' **(R)** 88-99			1.00
Poole **(U seen 32)** see Bournemouth			
Portadown **(K)** 22-49	5.00	4.00	
then **(U)** 50-		0.50	0.50
then 'Portadown Craigavon' 83-93 later **(R)**/**(L)**			0.50
Port Ellen **(K)** 69-99			1.00
then **(U,M)** 2000-			1.50
Port Glasgow **(K)** 50-56		1.00	
then **(U)**-72		0.50	0.50
Porth **(K)** 36 only	2.50		
then **(U)** 37-43	1.00		
then **(K)** again 44-49	2.00	2.00	
then **(U)** again 53-66		0.60	0.50
then 'Rhondda 2' 66- later **(R)**			0.50
then 'Cardiff 12' **(L)** 89-99			1.00
Porthcawl 37-77 (stamped at Bridgend 67-77)	0.60	0.50	0.50
then 'Cardiff 19' **(M)** 89 only seen			1.50
Portishead **(K)** 56-74		1.00	1.00
then 'Bristol' **(X)** 94-96			1.00
Portland **(K)** 59-67		1.00	1.00
Portmadoc **(K)** 53-59		1.00	
then **(U)** 60-		0.50	0.50
then 'Porthmadog' 72- later **(R)**-2001			0.50
Portree 60- 2009		0.60	0.60
Portrush 33-90	1.50	0.50	0.50
*Portsmouth			
'Portsmouth & Southsea'	0.50	0.50	0.50
also **(K)** 33-49	1.00	1.00	
then **(U)** 'Portsmouth & IOW' 81-			0.50
also 'Portsmouth' 92-?94			0.50
Port Talbot 33-75	1.00	0.50	0.50
then 'West Glam 9' **(R)** 75-			1.00
then 'Port Talbot' again **(R)**/**(L)** 80-			1.00
then 'Porth Talbot/Port Talbot' **(L)** 99 only			2.50
Potters Bar 65-71			1.00
Prescot **(K)** 39-48	2.50	2.50	
then **(U)** later **(L)**-?77		0.50	0.50
Prestatyn **(K)** 45-49		4.00	
then **(U)**-71(at Rhyl from 63)		0.50	0.50
*Preston	0.50	0.50	0.50
then 'Lancashire' 75-			0.50
then "Lancashire S Lakes' 93- (both inscriptions later used)			0.50
Preston DO '3' then DO 50- **(R,L)**		1.00	1.00
then 'Lancashire 41' 75-?79			1.00
then 'Lancashire 51' **(M)** ?81- (previously used at North DO)			1.00
and SDO 'Lancashire 55' **(M)** ?81-			1.00
then 'Lancs S Lakes 11' **(M)** 94-			1.00
and West DO 'PDO West Lancs' **(M)** 88-			1.00
Prestonpans **(K,X)** 62-63			2.00
then regular use 64-76			1.00
then 'Edinburgh' **(U,X)** 81-84?			1.00
Prestwich 36- later **(R)**	1.00	0.50	0.50
Prestwick **(K)** 39-53	1.50	1.50	

Machine Cancellations

	1933-44	45-60	61-99
then (U)-?70		0.50	0.50
Princes Risborough (K) 56-59		3.00	
then (U)-78		1.00	0.50
then NO Aylesbury (L) 90-93			1.00
Pudsey Leeds (K) 50-57		1.50	
then (U) 'Pudsey Leeds'		3.00	
then 'Pudsey Yorkshire' 58-70		0.60	0.50
Pulborough (K) 56-59		2.50	
then (U)-78, then (L)-92		0.50	0.50
Pwllheli (K) 37 only	5.00		
then (U) 37-later (R)-2001	1.00	0.50	0.50
Radcliffe (K) 32-39	3.50		
then (U) later (R)/(L)	0.60	0.50	0.50
Radcliffe-on-Trent (K) 69-77			1.00
Radlett (K) 49-59		1.00	
then (U)-68		0.50	0.50
Radstock Somerset (K) 52-53		4.00	
then with 'Bath' (K) 53-57		3.00	
then (U)-82 (county later Avon)		0.50	0.50
then again (L) 86-			1.00
then 'Avon removed' (L) 96-			1.00
Rainham 'Romford R61' (M) 89-			1.00
Ramsbottom (U) 'Manch' 50-60		1.00	
then (U) 'Ramsbottom Bury'		1.00	1.00
then (K) 'Ramsbottom Bury' 66-68			2.50
Ramsey Huntingdon (K) 60-		1.00	1.00
then (U) 75-89			0.50
Ramsgate	0.50	0.50	0.50
then 'Thanet B' 71-87			0.50
Rayleigh (K) 51-59		1.50	
then (U) later (R)-92 then (L)		0.50	0.50
Reading -2009	0.50	0.50	0.50
also (K, reserve) 34-35	1.50		
(then see Swindon/Thames Valley)			
and (X), 2009 (used at Swindon)			1.00
Redcar (K) 29-35	2.50		
then (U)-69	0.60	0.50	0.50
(short lived Teesside county 68-)			1.00
Redditch -96 then (M)	0.50	0.50	0.50
also (K,X) 61-62			3.00
Redhill 'Reigate & Redhill'	0.50	0.50	0.50
then 'MLO Redhill' 76-			0.50
then Redhill 80-88 then (R)-99			0.50
also 'Redhill PDO' 78-?80			1.00
(see also Gatwick, RH area's MLO at Crawley)			
Redruth (K) 32-35	2.00		
then (U) 'Camborne Redruth'	0.50	0.50	0.50
then 'Cornwall G' (L) 92-98, (X) 99			1.00
Reigate (M) 96-			1.00
Renfrew (K) 52-58		1.00	
then (U) -68		0.50	0.50
Retford (K) 29-33	2.00		
then (U)-76 then (M) 90-	0.50	0.50	0.50
Rhayader (K) 76-84 (though philatelic items stamped 87)			1.00
Rhosllanerchrugog (K) 64-83			1.00
Rhyl (U)	0.50	0.50	0.50
also (K, intermittent) -39	2.50		
then (U) 'Clwyd'/'Clwyd 2' 72-			0.50
then Rhyl again 83-2000 (but (L) 83-87 when mail stamped at Chester)			0.50
also 'Clwyd 2' again (X) 87-2001			1.00
Richmond Surrey -47	0.60	0.60	
then 'Twickenham' 73-75			0.50
Richmond Yorks (K) 39-49	1.50	1.50	
then (U)-70		0.50	0.50
Rickmansworth (K) 36-39	3.00		

	1933-44	45-60	61-99
then (U)-?83	0.50	0.50	0.50
then again (M) 87-?94			1.00
Ringwood (K) 34-54	2.00	1.00	
then (U)-71		0.50	0.50
Ripley (K) 53-59		2.50	
then (U)-72 then (X) 74		0.50	0.50
Ripon (K) 15-44	2.50		
then (U)-72	1.00	0.50	0.50
Rochdale later (R)/(L) (see also Oldham)	0.50	0.50	0.50
Rochford (K) 59-61		2.00	2.00
then (U) later (R)-92 then (L)			0.50
Rock Ferry (K) 25-44	2.00		
then (U)-67	1.00	1.00	1.00
Romford -54	0.50	0.50	
also 'Romf & Dag' 51-		0.50	0.50
and (K, reserve) 66 only			1.50
then (U) 'Romford' again 70- 2010			0.50
and 'Romford R21' (M) 86-			1.00
Romsey (K) 39-51	2.00	2.00	
then (U)-69		0.50	0.50
Rossendale 'Rawtenstall' (K) 27-32			
then 'Rossendale' (K) 33-36	2.50	1.50	
then (U)-71	0.50	0.50	0.50
then (U,M) 'Lancashire 44' 89-			1.00
Ross-on-Wye (K) 48-49		3.00	
then (U)-72		0.60	0.50
Rotherham later (L)	0.50	0.50	0.50
also (K, reserve) 57-66		3.00	3.00
and 'Sheffield' (U,X) ?75-91			1.00
then 'Rotherham' again (X) 97-2001			1.00
Rothesay later (L)	0.60	0.60	0.60
Rottingdean (L) 90-			1.00
Royston ?49-77		0.50	0.50
then 'Cambridge' (L)-			1.00
Royton Oldham (K) 49-61		1.00	1.00
then (U)-?64			0.60
Rugby later (L)	0.50	0.50	0.50
Rugeley -68	0.60	0.50	0.50
Ruislip (K) 36-38	3.50		
then (U)	1.00	0.50	0.50
then 'Harrow & Wembley R' 71-			0.50
then 'Harrow R' 78-			0.50
but 'Ruislip' again (X) 85			1.00
Runcorn (K) 33-48	2.00	2.00	
then (U) later (L)		0.50	0.50
Rushden (K) 38 only	4.00		
then (U) later (R)	1.00	0.50	0.50
Rutherglen (K) 33-39	3.00		
then (U) 45- later (L)		0.50	0.50
Ruthin (K) 50-55		2.50	
then (U) -71		0.50	0.50
Ryde -77	0.50	0.50	0.50
Rye (K) 36-52	2.00	2.00	
then (U)-66		0.50	0.50
then 'Hastings or Tonbridge' (X) 80-97			1.00
Ryton (K) 59-70		1.00	1.00
Saffron Walden (K) 37-41	3.00		
then (U)-93 then (L)	0.60	0.50	0.50
St Albans later (R)/(L)-97	0.50	0.50	0.50
and (K) in reserve 33-72	2.00	2.00	2.50
St Andrews -76	0.50	0.50	0.50
then 'Kirkcaldy' (X) 81-			1.00
then 'St Andrews' again (R) ?86-			1.00
St Asaph 67-71 (used at Rhyl)			1.50
St Austell (K) 35-38	3.00		
then (U)	0.60	0.50	0.50
then 'Plymouth R,S,T' 80-92, (X)-99			0.50
and 'Cornwall 3' Sundays 90-92			1.00

217

Machine Cancellations

	1933-44	45-60	61-99
St Columb (K) 69-84			1.00
St Helens later (L)	0.50	0.50	0.50
St Ives Cornwall (K) 32-37	3.00		
then (U)	1.00	0.50	0.50
then 'Cornwall H' (L) 92-95 then (X)-97			1.00
St Ives Huntingdon 58-92		0.50	0.50
St Leonards-on-Sea 'Hastings' (L) 90-			1.00
*St Mary's (K) 59-67		2.00	2.00
then (U)-2002 then (L)			1.00
St Neots (K) 53-60		1.00	
then (U) later (R)-97		0.50	0.50
Salcombe (K) 58-69		1.00	1.00
then (U)-72			0.50
Sale (K) 29-38	1.50		
then (U) later (R)/(L)	0.60	0.50	0.50
Salford later (R)/ (L)		0.50	0.50
Salisbury -94 then (L)	0.50	0.50	0.50
Saltash (K) 49-62		1.00	1.00
then (U)-78			0.50
then 'Plymouth' (X) 80-?90 & 95-99			1.00
Saltburn-by-Sea (K) 40-52	1.50	1.50	
then (U)-70		0.50	0.50
Saltcoats 36-80	0.60	0.50	0.50
then (X) 80 only			1.00
Sandbach (later at Crewe)-?72		0.50	0.50
then again (X) 82 only			1.00
Sandgate (U)-34	3.00		
Sandiacre (K) 69-77			1.00
Sandown (K) 32-35	2.00		
then (U)-77	0.60	0.50	0.50
Sandwich (K) 38-58	2.00	1.50	
then (U)-95 then (L)		0.50	0.50
Sandy (K) 60-76		1.00	1.00
Sanquhar (K) 74-79			1.50
Sarisbury Green (L) 90-			1.00
Saundersfoot 67-93 (at Tenby)			0.60
Saxmundham (K) 54-60		1.50	
then (U) later (L)		0.50	0.50
Scarborough -90 then (L)	0.50	0.50	0.50
Scunthorpe later (L)	0.50	0.50	0.50
Seaford (K) 32-38	3.00		
then (U)-76 then (R)/(L)	0.50	0.50	0.50
Seaham (K) 40-55	2.00	1.50	
then (U)-?69		0.50	0.50
Seascale 73-90			0.60
Seaton later(R)-93 then (L)-95	0.60	0.50	0.50
Sedbergh (K) 59-84		1.00	1.00
then (U)			0.60
then 'Lancs S Lakes 20' (M) 94-98			1.00
Selby -72	0.60	0.50	0.50
Selkirk (K) 55-60		1.50	
then (U) later (R)/(L)		1.50	0.50
Sennen & Land's End 57-92 (at Penzance)		1.00	1.00
Settle (K) 58-77		1.00	1.00
also (U) 70 only			1.50
Sevenoaks later (L)	0.50	0.50	0.50
but 'Tonbridge' (L) 84-			1.00
Shaftesbury (K) 39-50	1.50	1.50	
then (U)-69		0.50	0.50
then 'Salisbury' (X) 76-88			1.00
also 'Bath 5' (R) 87-			1.00
then 'Southampton H' (R) 92-93			1.00
then 'Shaftesbury' again (L) 97-			1.00
Shanklin -77	0.50	0.50	0.50
Shaw (K) 50-61		1.00	1.00
then (U) later (R)/(L)			0.50
Sheerness -71	0.50	0.50	0.50
*Sheffield (U)	0.50	0.50	0.50

	1933-44	45-60	61-99
also (K,X) 58-61		1.50	1.50
Sheffield 5 NEPDO (K,R) 64-92			1.50
WPDO Sheffield 10 (K,R) 65-66			2.50
then 'West PDO' (K,R) -69			1.00
Shepperton (K) 49-58		1.50	
then (U)-61		1.00	1.00
Shepton Mallet (K) 42-55	3.00	2.00	
then (U)-86 then (L)		0.50	0.50
Sherborne (K) 36-38	3.00		
then (U) later (R)/(L)	1.00	0.50	0.50
Sheringham (K) 32-41&47	3.00	3.00	
then (U) 53-76		0.50	0.50
Shifnal (K) 60-82		1.00	1.00
Shipley -67	0.60	0.50	0.50
then 'Bradford' (X) 85-91			1.00
Shipston-on-Stour (K) 61-67			1.00
then (U) later (R)/(L)-95			0.50
Shoeburyness (K) 61-72			1.00
Shoreham-by-Sea (K) 32-49	2.00	2.00	
then (U)-71 then (L)		0.50	0.50
Shotts (X) 67-68			3.00
Shrewsbury	0.50	0.50	0.50
also (K) 52-58		1.00	
then (U) 'Salop erased' 80-			1.00
then 'Shropshire & Mid Wales' 82-			0.50
then 'Shropshire & Y Canolbarth' 99-2013			0.50
Sidcup (K) 29-34	3.00		
then (U)-76	0.60	0.50	0.50
then 'Dartford K' (R)-96			1.00
Sidmouth (K) 32-37	3.50		
then (U)-70	0.60	0.50	0.50
then 'Exeter District' (X) 75-85			1.00
then 'Sidmouth' (X) 86- later (L)-95			1.00
Sittingbourne (K) 27-35	3.50		
then (U)-72	0.60	0.50	0.50
Skegness -97		0.50	0.50
Skelmersdale Ormskirk (K) 61-			3.00
then (K) NO Ormskirk 64-73			1.00
Sketty 'Swansea 10' (L) 87-91			1.00
Skipton later (R)/(L)	0.50	0.50	0.50
Sleaford (K) 36-38	2.50		
then (U)-83	0.60	0.50	0.50
then again (M) ?87-93			1.00
Slough	0.50	0.50	0.50
then 'Slough/Windsor SLO-9' 91-2005 (then see Greenford MC)			0.50
Smethwick (K)-37	1.50		
then (U)-67 (then see Warley)	0.50	0.50	0.50
Solihull/Birm (K) 37-49	1.50	1.50	
then (U) -?55		0.60	
then 'Warwicks' -?95 then (L)		0.50	0.50
Southall later (R)-98 then (L)	0.50	0.50	0.50
Southam (L) 89-96			1.00
*Southampton	0.50	0.50	0.50
South Croydon (K) 29-39	2.00		
Southend-on-Sea -2011	0.50	0.50	0.50
also NO on Sea error 93-96			0.50
*South Midlands Mail Centre 2010-12 (N) (new location at Northampton, replaced Coventry, Milton Keynes, Northampton)			0.50
also 'Coventry & Warwickshire' (X) 2011			1.00
South Molton (K) 53-59		1.50	
then (U)-70, then (R) 88-93		0.50	0.50
South Ockendon (R) 67-72 then (X)			1.00
then 'Romford R71' (L) 89-			1.00
Southport (U)	0.50	0.50	0.50
also (K) 42-57	1.50	1.50	

Machine Cancellations

	1933-44	45-60	61-99
then 'Preston 8/9' **(U,L)** 71-			1.00
then 'Lancashire 32' **(U,L)** 76-			1.00
South Shields -76	0.50	0.50	0.50
then **(X)**-85, then **(M)** 89-			1.00
Southwell **(K)** 63-76			1.00
Southwold **(K)** 58-68		1.00	1.00
then **(U)**-73			0.50
Sowerby Bridge **(K)** 40-75	1.00	1.00	1.00
Spalding **(K)** 32-36	4.00		
then **(U)** later **(R)**-98 then **(L)**	0.60	0.50	0.50
Spennymoor **(K)** 49-52		2.00	
then **(U)**-70		0.60	0.60
Spilsby **(K)** 46-56		2.50	
then **(U)** later **(R)**-97		0.50	0.50
Stafford **(U)** later **(M)**	0.50	0.50	0.50
also **(K,X)** 52 only		3.00	
Staines **(K)** 26-37	1.50		
then **(U)**-?71	0.50	0.50	0.50
Stalybridge **(K)** 32-37	2.50		
then **(U)** later **(L)**-95	0.60	0.50	0.50
(also die at Ashton-u-L -77)			
Stamford **(K)** 26-37	1.50		
then **(U)**-89	0.60	0.50	0.50
Stanford-le-hope **(U,X)** 61-64			1.00
then **(K)** 64-67			1.00
then **(U,X)** 'Basildon'			1.00
then 'Stanford-le-hope' again **(L)** 88-			1.00
Stanley **(K)** 46-48		3.00	
then **(U)**-82 then **(X)**-85		0.50	0.50
then again **(L)** ?90-93			1.00
Stanmore **(K)** 38-44	1.50		
then **(U,M)** ?89-			1.00
Stapleford **(K)** 69-74			1.00
Stevenage **(K)** 49-54		1.00	
then **(U)** -2012		0.50	0.50
but **(K)** again power cut 72			5.00
and **(U)** 'N Herts' error 85			8.00
(then see Home Counties North Mail Centre)			
Stevenston **(U)** 59-72		0.60	0.60
Stirling -94 then **(L)**	0.50	0.50	0.50
Stockport-2009	0.50	0.50	0.50
Stockton-on-Tees **(U)**	0.50	0.50	0.50
also **(K, reserve)** 32-34	5.00		
(short-lived Teesside county '68-)			1.00
then **(U)** 'Teesside' 69-74 **(R)**			1.00
then 'Cleveland'-78 then **(L)**-80			
(then see Middlesbrough)			1.00
Stoke-on-Trent-99	0.50	0.50	0.50
also Stoke-Hanley **(M)** 94-			1.00
Stokesley Middlesbro **(K)** 59-		1.00	1.00
then NO Yks 68-69			2.00
Stone **(K)** 48-49		3.00	
then **(U)**-69, again **(M)** 95-		0.50	0.50
Stonehaven **(K)** 57-66		1.00	1.00
then **(U)** later **(L)**			0.50
Stonehouse **(K)** 54-60		1.50	
then **(U)**-71		0.50	0.50
*Stornoway **(K)** 39-54	4.00	2.50	
then **(U)** later **(R)**		0.50	0.50
Storrington **(K)** 60-68		1.50	1.00
then **(U)**-78 then **(L)**			0.50
Stourbridge later **(L)**-96	0.50	0.50	0.50
Stourport-on-Severn **(K)** 50-57		1.50	
then **(U)** later **(R)/(M)**-95		0.50	0.50
Stowmarket **(K)** 39-49	2.50	2.50	
then **(U)**-93 then **(L)**		0.50	0.50
Strabane **(K)** 49-60		3.00	
then **(U)** 60- later **(L)**		0.50	0.50
Stranraer **(K)** 39-43	4.00		

	1933-44	45-60	61-99
then **(U)** 46-93 then **(L)**		0.50	0.50
Stratford-on-Avon **(K)** 30-33	3.00		
then **(U)** 'Stratford-upon-Avon' later **(R)/(L)**	0.50	0.50	0.50
also NO county, stamped at Coventry 92-98			0.50
also **(K,X)** 64 only			1.50
Strathaven **(K)** 59-77		1.00	1.00
Street 58-64		1.00	0.60
Stretford **(K)** 32-35	3.00		
then **(U)** later **(R)/(L)**	1.00	0.50	0.50
*Stromness **(K)** 67-			1.00
then **(U)** 90- later **(R)**			0.60
Stroud -71	0.50	0.50	0.50
then again **(L)** 86-			0.50
Sturminster Newton **(K)** 58-68		1.00	1.00
Sudbury ?40- later **(R)**-96 then **(L)**	0.60	0.50	0.50
Sunbury on Thames **(K)** 48-59		1.00	
then **(U)**-86		0.50	0.50
Sunderland -95 then **(L)**	0.50	0.50	0.50
also **(K, reserve)** 42-47	2.50	2.50	
Sutton	0.50	0.50	0.50
then 'Croydon' **(M)** 86-			1.00
then 'Croydon Sutton/Sutton' **(M)** 91-			1.00
Sutton Coldfield **(K)** 32-37	2.50		
then **(U)** 'Sutton Cd Birm'	0.60	0.60	
then 'Sutton Coldfield Warwickshire' 57 (later W Mids)-92 then **(L)**		0.50	0.50
Sutton-in-Ashfield **(K)** 40-54	1.00	1.00	
then **(U)**-76, then **(M)** 87-91		0.50	0.50
Swadlincote ?60-78		0.60	0.60
Swaffham **(K)** 56-61		2.00	2.00
then **(U)**-/1		0.50	0.50
Swanage -71	0.50	0.50	0.50
Swanley **(K)** 65-81 then **(U,R)**-96			1.00
Swanscombe **(K)** 67-76			1.00
*Swansea	0.50	0.50	0.50
then 'West Glamorgan' 75-			0.50
then 'Swansea' again 80-			0.50
then 'Swansea & SW Wales' 94-			0.50
then 'De Orll Cymru SW Wales' 99-			0.50
(but last 3 inscriptions all used later)			
also 'Pontardawe' **(X)** 2003 at Swansea			1.00
Swindon	0.50	0.50	0.50
then 'Thames Valley MC' 2009-			0.50
then 'Swindon' again 2011-12 **(N)**			0.50
Swinton **(K)** 33-36	3.00		
then **(U)** later **(R)/(L)**	1.00	0.50	0.50
Tadcaster **(K)** 49-59		2.00	
then **(U)**-71		0.50	0.50
Tain **(K)** 64-84			1.00
then **(U)** later **(R)**–2010			0.50
Tamworth **(K)** 33-39	2.50		
then **(U)**-?95 then **(L)**	0.60	0.50	0.50
Tarbert **(K)** 59-93 then **(M)**-2001		1.00	1.00
Tarporley **(K)** 59-61		2.50	2.50
then **(U)**-71			0.50
Taunton later **(R)**-2000	0.50	0.50	0.50
Tavistock **(K)** 39-50	2.00	2.00	
then **(U)**-76		0.50	0.50
then 'Plymouth' **(X)**-86			1.00
Teddington **(K)** 30-44	3.00		
then **(U)**-68	0.60	0.50	0.50
Teignmouth 33-78	0.60	0.50	0.50
then 'S Devon' **(X)**-83			1.00
Telford 69- later **(R)/(L)**			0.50
Tenbury Wells **(K)** 60-82		1.00	1.00

Machine Cancellations

	1933-44	45-60	61-99
Tenby 33-94 then **(L)**	1.50	0.50	0.50
then 'Dinbych-y-Pysgod/Tenby' **(L)** 99-2005			2.00
Tenterden **(K)** 55-59			3.00
then **(U)** later **(R)**-98 then **(L)**-99		0.50	0.50
Tetbury **(K)** 57-66		1.00	1.00
Tewkesbury **(K)** 49-56		2.00	
then **(U)**-70		0.50	0.50
then 'Gloucester G' **(R)**/**(L)** 88-(later Tewkesbury & Gloucestershire dies seen)			1.00
Thame **(K)** 60-62		1.50	1.50
then **(U,L)**-77			1.00
Thetford later **(R)**/**(L)**	0.50	0.50	0.50
Thirsk **(K)** 36-48	1.50	1.50	
then **(U)**-71		0.50	0.50
Thornbury **(K)** 68-78			1.00
Thorne **(K)** 60-76		1.00	1.00
(S Yorks only 75-76)			2.00
Thornhill **(K)** 59-74		1.00	1.00
Thornton Heath **(L)** 88-92			1.00
Thrapston **(K)** 69-74			1.50
Thurso **(K)** 50-59		1.50	
then **(U)**-?95 then **(R)**-2008		0.50	0.50
Tidworth **(K)** 39-76	2.00	1.50	1.00
Tipton **(K)** 26-66	2.00	1.00	1.00
then **(U)** later **(L)**			0.50
Tiverton **(K)** 34-41	2.50		
then **(U)**-?75	1.00	0.50	0.50
then 'Exeter District' **(X)** 79-85			1.00
then 'Tiverton' again **(X)** 94-96			1.00
Tobermory **(K)** 66-99			1.50
Todmorden **(K)** 34-37	3.00		
then **(U)** later **(R)**/**(L)**	0.60	0.50	0.50
Tonbridge	0.50	0.50	0.50
also **(K, reserve)** 65-69			2.00
(mail concentrated on Tonbridge in place of Tunbridge Wells 83-2012)			
but 'SE Division 1' on Sundays 94- (later various 'SE Div' & 'Kent' dies Sat/Sun, Sats only when Suns discontinued, 2007-11)			1.00
			1.00
Tonypandy **(K)** 39-49	3.00	3.00	
then **(U)**-66		0.50	0.50
then 'Rhondda 3' -77 then **(L,X)**			1.00
then 'Cardiff 13' **(L)** 89-99			1.00
Torquay	0.50	0.50	0.50
'Torquay & Paignton' 40s	1.00		
then 'South Devon' 69-98			0.50
Torrington **(K)** 58-80		1.00	1.00
then **(U,R)**-90			1.00
Totnes **(K)** 36-47	1.50	1.50	
then **(U)**-70		0.50	0.50
then 'S Devon' **(X)** ?73-83			1.00
Totton **(U,L)** 90-			1.00
Towcester **(K)** 55-60		1.50	
then **(U)**-?88		0.50	0.50
Towyn **(K)** 60-66		1.00	1.00
then **(U)**			1.00
then 'Tywyn' 68- later **(R)**-2000			0.50
Tranent **(K)** intermittent 75-79			1.50
then 'Edinburgh' **(U,X)** 81 only			1.00
Tredegar **(K)** 50-52		4.00	
then **(U)** 54-76 then **(L)**,**(X)**-99		0.50	0.50
Treorchy **(K)** 49-53		4.00	
then **(U)** 54-66		0.50	0.50
then 'Rhondda 5' -77 then **(L,X)**			1.00
then 'Cardiff 14' **(L)** 89-2001			1.00
Tring **(K)** 49-59		2.00	
then **(U)** later **(L)**		0.50	0.50

	1933-44	45-60	61-99
Troon **(K)** 34-41	3.00		
then **(U)** 45-72		0.50	0.50
Trowbridge later **(R)**/**(M)**	0.50	0.50	0.50
*Truro	0.50	0.50	0.50
then 'Cornwall A' 92-			0.50
but 'Cornwall 2' Sundays 90-98			1.00
Tunbr Wells -83 then **(M)**	0.50	0.50	0.50
and 'Tonbridge' **(X)** 84-91			1.00
and 'Tun Wells' no Kent **(X)** 92-94			1.00
Turriff **(K)** 51-76		1.00	1.00
then **(K,X)** 84-89			1.00
then 'Aberdeen' **(U,X)** 90-92			1.00
then Turriff **(U,L)** 94-2005			1.00
Twickenham	0.50	0.50	
also **(K, ?reserve)** 13-36	1.00		
then **(U)** 'Richmond & Twick' 48- (also this inscription at Richmond)		0.50	0.50
then 'Twickenham' 73-2003			0.50
and 'Hounslow' **(X)** 86 only			1.00
(then see Jubilee)			
Twyford 59-67		1.00	1.00
Tyldesley **(K)** 55-61		1.00	1.00
then **(U)** later **(R)**/**(L)**			0.50
Uckfield **(K)** 35-48	1.50	1.00	
then **(U)** later **(L)**		0.50	0.50
and 'Tonbridge' **(X)** 86-91			1.00
then 'Uckfield' again **(X)** 97			1.00
Uddingston **(K)** 55-79		1.00	1.00
but **(U,X)** 54-79		1.00	1.00
then **(U)** 80- then **(L)** 86-			0.50
Ullapool **(U)** 64-72 summer only			1.50
also **(K)** 65 summer only			4.00
then **(K)** 73-93			1.00
Ulverston **(K)** 32-39	3.50		
then **(U)** later **(R)**/**(L)**	1.00	0.50	0.50
Upminster **(K)** 40-48	3.00	3.00	
then **(U)**-72 then **(M)**		0.50	0.50
then 'Romford R81' **(M)** 89-			1.00
Uppingham **(K)** 64-77			1.00
Upton (Wirral)**(L)** 65-?79			1.00
Upton-upon-Severn **(K)** 71-72			2.00
then **(U)**-85			1.00
Urmston **(K)** 34-38	3.50		
then **(U)** later **(R)**/**(L)**	0.50	0.50	0.50
Usk **(K)** 59-64		1.00	1.00
then **(U)**-76 then **(L)**-?99			0.50
Uttoxeter **(K)** 40-49	3.00	2.50	
then **(U)**-69		0.50	0.50
then again **(M)** 89-94			1.00
Uxbridge -93 then **(L)**	0.50	0.50	0.50
Ventnor **(K)** 28-39	1.50		
then **(U)**-77		0.50	0.50
Virginia Water **(U,X)** 67 only			10.00
Wadebridge 67-92 then **(X)** 92			0.50
then for Cornwall Show 93 only			1.00
Wadhurst **(K)** 60-75		1.00	1.00
but **(U)** Sundays only 53-68		1.00	1.00
(stamped at Tunbridge Wells)			
Wakefield later **(R)**-98	0.50	0.50	0.50
Walkden **(K)** 46-53		1.50	
then **(U)**-66 (then Worsley)		0.50	0.50
Wallasey later**(L)**-91,**(X)** 96	0.50	0.50	0.50
Wallingford **(K)** 51-61		1.00	1.00
then **(U)**-77			0.50
Wallington **(M)** 89-			1.00
Wallsend **(K)** 33-48	1.50	1.50	
then **(U)**-76 then **(X)**-85		0.50	0.50
then again **(M)** ?90-95			1.00
Walsall -94 then **(L)**	0.50	0.50	0.50
Waltham Cross **(K)** 30-38	2.50		

Machine Cancellations

	1933-44	45-60	61-99
then (U)-71	0.50	0.50	0.50
then 'Enfield' (X) 79-82			1.00
then 'Waltham X' (R) 85-95			1.00
Walton Liv (K) 24-46	1.50	1.50	
then (U)-?67		0.50	0.50
then again (M) ?91 only			1.00
Walton-on-Thames (K) 32-38	2.00		
then (U)-?67, (X)-70	0.60	0.50	0.50
Walton-on-the-Naze (K) 58 only		3.50	
then (U)-85,		0.50	0.50
then again (R) 93-97 then (L)			1.00
Wantage (K) 49-56		1.50	
then (U)-77		0.50	0.50
Ware (K) 42-48	3.00	3.00	
then (U) later (M)		0.50	0.50
Wareham (K) 49-52		3.00	
then (U)-71		0.50	0.50
Warley 67-92 then (M) (incl machine at Smethwick 67-76)			0.50
Warlingham (K) 54-70		1.00	1.00
Warminster (K) 38-47	2.00	2.00	
then (U) later (M)		0.50	0.50
Warrington (K) 11-50	2.50	2.00	
but (U) 30- later (L)	0.50	0.50	0.50
Warrington Mail Centre 2010-12 (N) (replaced Crewe and Liverpool)			0.50
Warwick (K) 33-36	2.50		
later (U,M) 91-96			1.00
('Warwick & Leamington Spa' see Leamington)			
Washington (K) 60-69		1.00	1.00
then (U,M) 90-			1.00
Waterlooville, Portsmouth ?59-		0.50	0.50
then 'P'mouth erased' 90 only			1.00
then NO Portsmouth (R)/(L) 90-			1.00
Watford –2011	0.50	0.50	0.50
also (K, reserve) 28-45	1.50	1.50	
(then see Home Counties North Mail Centre)			
Wavertree (K) 13-44	1.50		
then (U)-66	0.60	0.50	0.50
Wednesbury -67	0.60	0.60	0.60
Wellingborough later (L)	0.50	0.50	0.50
Wellington Shropshire-69	0.60	0.60	0.60
Wellington Som (K) 45-50		3.00	
then (U) later (M)-?89		0.50	0.50
then 'Taunton' (X) 94&97			1.00
then 'Wellington' (X) 95&96			1.00
Wells (K) 34-48	1.50	1.50	
then (U) later (M) 87-		0.50	0.50
Wells-next-the-sea (K) 62-76			1.00
Welshpool (K) 46-55		3.00	
then (U)-82 then (L),(X)-98		0.50	0.50
Welwyn (K) 35 only	4.00		
then (U) 'Welwyn' 35-54	0.60	0.50	
then 'Welwyn Gdn City' later (L)-97		0.50	0.50
Wem (K) 61-70			1.00
then (U,R)-87			0.60
Wembley	0.50	0.50	0.50
then 'Harrow & Wembley E,F' 69-			0.50
then 'Harrow E,F' 80- later (L)			0.50
West Bromwich	0.50	0.50	0.50
then 'Birmingham' (R) 93-			0.50
Westbury (K) 48-58		1.00	
then (U) later (L)-85 &(M) 98-		0.50	0.50
Westbury-on-Trym (K) 34-36	4.00		
then (U), later (R)-87	0.60	0.50	0.50
West Derby 57- later (L)-?87		0.60	0.50
West Drayton (K) 35-40	4.00		
later 'West Drayton PDO' (U,M) 90-			1.00

	1933-44	45-60	61-99
Westerham (K) 60-74		1.00	1.00
but (U,X) 70 only			1.50
then 'Sevenoaks' (X) 82-83			1.00
then 'Tonbridge' (X) 84 only			1.00
Westgate on Sea (K) 32-35	4.00		
Westham (Pevensey) (R) 99-			1.00
(W Hartlepool see Hartlepool)			
Westhoughton (K) 61-68			2.50
West Kilbride (K) 62-71			2.00
West Kirby (K) 33-38	4.00		
then (U)-70	0.60	0.50	0.50
West Malling (K) 59-63		1.50	1.50
Weston-super-Mare later (R)-94			
then (X)-96	0.50	0.50	0.50
West Wickham (K) 48-81		1.00	1.00
then (U,R)-95			1.00
Wetherby (K) 50-59		2.00	
then (U)-71, again (U,M) 84-		0.50	0.50
Weybridge	0.50	0.50	0.50
then 'Kingston 2,3,4' (L) 87-91			1.00
Weymouth later (L)	0.60	0.50	0.50
and (K, reserve) 55 only		2.00	
Whitby later (L)-87	0.50	0.50	0.50
Whitchurch Hants (K) 51-60		1.00	
then (U)-69		0.60	0.50
Whitchurch Shrop (K) 40-44	4.00		
then (U) later (L)-95	0.60	0.50	0.50
Whitehaven (K) 29-35	3.00		
then (U)-93 then (R)/(L)	0.60	0.50	0.50
Whitley Bay -76 then (X)-85	0.50	0.50	0.50
then again (M) ?90- (continued at new N Tyneside office 95-)			1.00
Whitstable (K) 28-36	3.50		
then (U) later (R)/(L)	0.50	0.50	0.50
Whittlesey (K) 60-65		1.00	1.00
then (U)-87			0.50
*Wick (K) 35-48		4.00	3.00
then (U)-95 then (R)		0.50	0.50
Wickford ?58-66		0.60	0.50
then 'Basildon' (X) ?80-88			1.00
Widnes later (L)	0.50	0.50	0.50
Wigan -81 then (L)	0.60	0.50	0.50
Wigston ?55-76		0.50	0.50
Wigton (K) 52-59		1.50	
then (U) later (R)-95 then (L)		0.50	0.50
Willenhall 38-65	1.00	0.60	0.60
also (K,X) 55-56		2.50	
Willerby (K) 62-75			1.00
(N Humberside Feb-Mar 75 only)			1.50
Wilmslow Manch'r (K) 38-47	2.50	2.50	
then (U) 'Wilmslow Manchester'		0.50	
then 'Wilmslow Cheshire' later (R)/(L)		0.50	0.50
Wimborne (K) 33-38	3.00		
then (U)-72	1.00	0.50	0.50
then FDCs 77 only (stamped at Bournemouth)			1.00
Wincanton (K) 50-70		1.00	1.00
then (U) later (R)/(L)			0.50
Winchester -92 then (L)	0.50	0.50	0.50
Windermere (K) 28-40	1.50		
then (U) later (R)	0.50	0.50	0.50
then 'Lancs & S Lakes 21' (M) 94-			1.00
Windsor -91 then (R)	0.50	0.50	0.50
Winsford (K) 52-54		3.00	
then (U)-75 (at Northwich)		0.50	0.50
then again (U,L) 86-			1.00
Winslow (K) 62-88			1.00
then (K,P)-94			1.50
Wisbech (U)-98 then (L)	0.50	0.50	0.50
also (K, reserve) 34-57	1.50	1.50	

221

Machine Cancellations

	1933-44	45-60	61-99
Wishaw **(K)** 33-48	1.50	1.50	
then **(U)**-51 (see Motherwell)		1.00	
then **(U,X)** 64-68			1.00
Witham **(K)** 49 only		4.00	
then **(U)**-79		0.50	0.50
then 'Chelmsford W' **(R)**			1.00
& other Chelmsford dies -93			0.50
(note : W later used at Chelmsford)			
Witney **(K)** 38-51	2.00	1.50	
then **(U)** ?54-77		0.50	0.50
Woking **(U)**-84 then **(L)**	0.60	1.00	1.00
also **(K, reserve)** 43-71	1.00	1.00	1.00
Wokingham **(K)** 30-38	3.00		
then **(U)** later **(R)**/**(L)**	0.60	0.50	0.50
Wolverhampton	0.50	0.50	0.50
also **(K, reserve)** 35-36	2.00		
then 'NW Midlands' 98-2007?			0.50
Wolverton **(K)** 40-57	1.50	1.00	
then **(U)**		0.50	0.50
then 'Milton Keynes 12' 73-85			0.50
Wombwell **(K,R)** 50-76		1.50	1.00
Woodbridge **(K)** 37-43	3.00		
then **(U)** later **(R)**/**(L)**	1.00	0.50	0.50
Woodford Green **(K)** 32-34	4.00		
then **(U)** later **(L)**	1.00	0.50	0.50
Woolton ?58-66		1.00	1.00
then again **(M)** 89-?93			1.00
Worcester	0.50	0.50	0.50
then 'Worcester District' 83-			0.50
then 'Hereford & Worcestershire' 93-?2001			0.50
Worcester Park **(K)** 39-45	3.00	3.00	
Workington -93 then **(R)**/**(L)**	0.50	0.50	0.50
Worksop **(K)** 29-36	3.50		
then **(U)** later **(M)**	0.50	0.50	0.50
also 'Sheffield' **(X)** ?73-82			1.00
Worsley 66- later **(R)**/**(L)**			0.60
Worthing later **(R)**-99	0.50	0.50	0.50
Wotton-u-Edge **(K)** 56-62		1.00	1.50
then **(U)**-?69			0.50
Wrexham -2000 (but **(L)** 83-87 when mail stamped at Chester)	0.50	0.50	0.50
& 'Chester Clwyd Gwynedd' **(X)** 83-86			1.00
Wymondham **(K)** 60 only		5.00	
then **(U)**-76		0.60	0.50
Wythenshawe **(K)** 47-48		4.00	
then **(U)** later **(R)**/**(L)**		0.50	0.50
Yate Sodbury 72-78			1.00
(replaced Chipping Sodbury)			
Yeadon **(K)** 61-65			1.00
then **(U)**-70			1.00
Yeovil -92 then **(L)**	0.50	0.50	0.50
York -2012	0.50	0.50	0.50
and **(K, reserve)** 40-56	2.00	2.00	
Ystalyfera 'Swansea 14' **(L)** 89-98 (but this machine used later at Swansea)			1.00

LONDON: (all sub-districts later **(R)**-about 93, some ended earlier ?90, see **(M)** next page) (some reserve **(K)** not shown eg N1, NW1)

Mount Pleasant 'London' (used on "country mail" posted in EC, this segregation only **to** 94)	0.50	0.50	0.50
then 'IS MLO' 80-			0.50
but 'Mount Plesant' error 85			20.00
then 'Mount Pleasant' 96-2012 **(N)**			0.50
E1 then 'E1-E18' 82-	0.50	0.50	0.50

then 'London East' 2002-12 (at new London East Mail Centre, E3)			0.50
districts: E18 **(K)**-35	2.00		
and E2-E18 **(U)**	0.50	0.50	0.50
(E2/9 merged 77-, then E2/8/9 87-93)			0.50
(E16 Victoria Docks no 's' 67-91			0.50
then E14/E16 merged with new inscription:			
E14 'Poplar & Isle of Dogs' 91-93)			0.50
EC -95 (London mail)	0.50	0.50	0.50
FS (Foreign Section) -90	0.50	0.50	0.50
N1	0.50	0.50	0.50
then 'London North' 95-2003			0.50
and 'NE London' (error) 98-2001			1.00
districts: several N used **(K)** to mid-30s (2.00)			
and N2-22 **(U)**	0.50	0.50	0.50
(N13/21 merged 71-93)			0.50
NW1 (Eversholt St)	0.50	0.50	0.50
then 'NWMLO' (St Pancras Way) 86-95			0.50
districts: NW7 **(K)** -36	2.50		
and NW2-11 **(U)**	0.50	0.50	0.50
(incl 'NWMLO' E,F,G,P,S,T,U at these districts)			
SE1 -95	0.50	0.50	0.50
districts: several SE used **(K)** to mid-30s, also SE2 -54, SE18 -50s (all 2.00)			
and SE2-27 **(U)**	0.50	0.50	0.50
(SE11,17 merged 66-93)			0.50
also Thamesmead SE28 **(R)** 92-93			1.00
SW1 (at Howick Place)	0.50	0.50	0.50
then 'SW' 83- (new location Nine Elms)			0.50
(but SW1 continued on **(L)** mail-?94)			1.00
then 'London South' 95- ? 2010			0.50
districts: SW6 **(K)** 36-51	1.00	1.00	
and SW2-20 **(U)**	0.50	0.50	0.50
'Gt Britain' error (SW11) 72			10.00
(SW8 stopped but back as **(L,X)** 91-93, and SW20 stopped but back in use 90-?94)			
W1 -94	0.50	0.50	0.50
W2 **(K)** 30s (later **R**-62)	1.00	1.00	1.00
then **(U)**	0.50	0.50	0.50
then 'Paddington' no district 85-			0.50
then 'West London' 94-2007			0.50
(but Paddington inscription used alongside West)			
districts: W7 **(K)** -35	2.00		
and W3-14 **(U)**	0.50	0.50	0.50
WC -93 (but one m/c at Trafalgar Sq -?97)	0.50	0.50	0.50

Other London Machines

'London Temp Office' 35-49	8.00	8.00	
and 'Home District' 34-37	8.00	(Sundays)	
and 'House of Commons SW1' 65-(See Nos. 21/12-14, then variations from mid-90s when most stamping moved to S London MC.)			2.00

Channel Islands and Isle of Man

(see also chap 17)

Alderney (Pitney Bowes machine) 92-			3.00
then **(U)** 93-			2.00
Guernsey	2.00	1.00	1.00
then 'Guernsey PO' 69-			1.00

Machine Cancellations

then Siemens machine 2002-				1.00
Jersey		2.00	1.00	1.00
then Jersey CI 69-				1.00
then Siemens machine 2001-				1.00
(Guernsey & Jersey both used unique straight line cancellers after postal independence)				
Ballasalla 90-93				2.00
Castletown **(K)** 59-			6.00	6.00
(one-line inscription 75-77)				8.00
then Pit Bowes 76-77 (continuous lines)				8.00
then **(K)** again briefly 77				4.00
then **(U)** 77-93				1.00
Douglas		1.00	1.00	1.00
also Siemens machine 2001-				0.50
Peel **(K)** 58-			4.00	4.00
then Pit Bowes 76-77 (continuous lines)				8.00
then **(K)** again briefly 77				4.00
then **(U)** 77- (wavy lines 1.50)				1.00
Port Erin 66-93 (summer only -77)				1.00
Port St Mary 67-93 (ditto)				1.00
but Pit Bowes 76-77 (continuous lines)				8.00
Ramsey **(K)** 50-			5.00	
then **(U)** 57-			1.00	1.00
Southern DO **(U,X)** 93-2005				2.00

Special thanks, for their help in updating the above list, are due to Patrick Awcock, Paul Carter, Stan Challis (Northern Ireland), O de Rousset Hall, and Paul Reynolds for "Machine Cancellations of Wales" (2nd edition, 2009).

London missort marks

The code denotes the office concerned. These dies were usually applied to the reverse of missorted letters, and Universal style postmarks were normally applied without wavy lines, but sometimes with slogans (occasionally with wavy lines). The same dies were occasionally used for normal stamping purposes also. Some dates are from British Postmark Society Bulletin. As concentration of missort duties progressed MOST OF THESE ENDED BETWEEN 1992-94 and the stamping of missorts had largely ended in London by 2000.

(H) denotes handstamps only seen.

		1933-44	45-60	61-99
1	Highgate N6 68-			1.00
2	E Finchley N2 59-		5.00	1.00
3	Whetstone N20 90-			1.00
3B	Hornsey N8 67-			1.00
4	Hampstead NW3 54-		5.00	1.00
	(later used at SW!!)			
4B	Southgate N14 69-			1.00
5	Hendon NW4 64-			1.00
5B	Holloway N7 57-		5.00	1.00
6A	EC Dist Office 50-95		5.00	1.00
	(EC/-6A- error 63-64)			1.50
6B	Clapton E5 69-			1.00
7	Stoke Newington N16 62-			1.00
8	W Brompton SW10 60-93		5.00	1.00
8B	Hackney E8 60-87		5.00	1.00
9	Kentish Town NW5 70-			1.00
10	S Kensington SW7 56-		5.00	1.00
11	Chelsea SW3 54-		5.00	1.00
11B	Poplar E14 68-			1.00
12	Bow E3 68-			1.00
13	Stratford E15 69-			1.00
14	E Ham E6 68-			1.00
15	Highbury N5 67-			1.00
16	Woolwich SE18 59-		5.00	1.00

		1933-44	45-60	61-99
17	Leytonstone E11 69-			1.00
18	Deptford SE8 68-			1.00
19	Finsbury Park N4 58-		5.00	1.00
20	Greenwich SE10 59-		5.00	1.00
21	Charlton SE7 59-		5.00	1.00
21B	Rotherhithe SE16 58-		5.00	1.00
22	Plaistow E13 70-			1.00
23	Brockley SE4 60-		5.00	1.00
23B	Brixton SW2 54-		5.00	1.00
24	Dulwich SE21 58-		5.00	1.00
25	Sydenham SE26 59-		5.00	1.00
26	N Kensington W10 56-		5.00	1.00
26B	S Lambeth SW8 56-		5.00	1.00
27	Clapham SW4 61-			1.00
27B	Stockwell SW9 56-		5.00	1.00
28	Tooting SW17 69-			1.00
28B	Streatham SW16 68-			1.00
29	Forest Gate E7 68-			1.00
30	Lee SE12 66-			1.00
30B	Maida Hill W9 57-		5.00	1.00
31	Wandsworth SW18 69-			1.00
31B	Battersea SW11 49-		5.00	1.00
32	Putney SW15 69-			1.00
33	Mortlake SW14 69-			1.00
34	Earl's Court SW5 55-		10.00	
34B	Acton W3 59-		5.00	1.00
35	Bethnal Green E2 69-			1.00
35B	Ealing W5 57-		5.00	1.00
36	Balham SW12 69-			1.00
36B	Hanwell W7 60-		5.00	1.00
37	Eltham SE9 86-			1.00
37B	Notting Hill W11 57-		5.00	1.00
38	Kensington W8 57-93		5.00	1.00
39	Hammersmith W6 57-		5.00	1.00
39B	Shepherds Bush W12 60-		5.00	1.00
40	Inland Sect MP 58-		5.00	1.00
41	Barnes SW13 69-			1.00
41B	St Johns Wood NW8 68-93			1.00
42	Walworth SE17 61-66 (then 45)			1.50
43	Golders Green NW11 68-			1.00
44	Manor Park E12 69-			1.00
44B	The Hyde NW9 68-			1.00
45	Kenn/Walworth SE11/17 66-			1.00
46	Palmers Green N13 **(H)**			
46B	Fulham SW6 54-		5.00	1.00
47	Finchley Church End N3 90-			1.00
48	N Finchley N12 69-			1.00
48B	Forest Hill SE23 61-			1.00
49	Abbey Wood SE2 64-			1.00
49B	S Norwood SE25 58-		5.00	1.00
50	Victoria Docks E16 69-91			1.00
51	New Southgate N11 58-		5.00	1.00
51B	Winchmore Hill N21 78-			1.00
52	Herne Hill SE24 61-			1.00
52B	Wood Green N22 68-			1.00
53	Homerton E9 69-87			1.00
53B	Upper Holloway N19 78-			1.00
54	Norwood SE19 60-		5.00	1.00
55	W Kensington W14 56-		5.00	1.00
56	S Woodford E18 69-			1.00
57	Chiswick W4 58-		5.00	1.00
58	Mill Hill NW7 68-			1.00
59	W Wimbledon SW20 69-?80			1.00
60	Kilburn NW6 51-93		5.00	1.00
	(Kilburn-60- error 59-80)		25.00	2.50
61	Willesden NW10 38-	15.00	1.00	1.00
62	S Tottenham N15 68-			1.00
63	Wimbledon SW19 63-			1.00
64	W Ealing W13 60-		5.00	1.00
65	Camberwell SE5 63-			1.00
66	Lewisham SE13 59-		5.00	1.00

Machine Cancellations

		1933-44	45-60	61-99
67	Peckham SE15 58-		5.00	1.00
68	Kennington SE11 62-66 (then 45)			1.50
69	Blackheath SE3 62-			1.00
70	Anerley SE20 (**H**)			
71	Catford SE6 60-		5.00	1.00
72	W Norwood SE27 59-		5.00	1.00
73	WC Dist Office 35-	15.00	5.00	1.00
	(London WC-73- error 60-62)		5.00	2.00
75	Paddington W2 (**K**) 25-64	15.00	5.00	1.50
	and (**U**) 51-		5.00	1.00
76	New Cross SE14 62-			1.00
77	E Dulwich SE22 59-		5.00	1.00
78	SE District Office 51-		5.00	1.00
79	SW District Office 37-	15.00	5.00	1.00
	and (**K**) 54-63		10.00	
79B	SW MLO Nine Elms SW8 83-			1.00
80	Tottenham N17 62-			1.00
81	Lower Edmonton N9 60-		5.00	1.00
82	Leyton E10 69-			1.00
83	Upper Edmonton N18 85-			1.00
84	Chingford E4 68-			1.00
85	Walthamstow E17 68-			1.00
86	NW District Office 45-		5.00	1.00
87	North Dist Office 49-		5.00	1.00
88	East Dist Office 36-	10.00	5.00	1.00
89	West Dist Office 13-	10.00	5.00	1.00
90	Muswell Hill N10 58-		5.00	1.00
91	Cricklewood NW2 54-		5.00	1.00

Index to 'generic' identities

The town where a generic or joint town die is used can be identified from this list, then cross reference may be made to the preceding list. London offices are excluded. * denotes inscriptions still in use (2013). Two further generics only used in "First day of issue" handstamps were Herefordshire (Hereford) and South Lakeland (Kendal). Others are confined to meter marks, while obsolete inscriptions such as Coatbridge/Airdrie lingered on in meter marks. In some cases, a generic identity having been established eg "Plymouth & Cornwall" in the IMP machines, handstamps were then changed eg "Plymouth Devon" to a different inscription – details of these are not shown below. There was also confusion in IMP postmarks in 2008 when new printers were installed and inscriptions reverted for a year or so to the town/city, thus "Newcastle" (note: NO on-Tyne) instead of "Tyneside" until corrected.

Generic/joint description	Town where used
*Bath Bristol Taunton (or Bristol Bath Taunton)	Bristol
Blackburn & Accrington	Blackburn
Blackburn & NE Lancs	Blackburn
Bolton & Bury	Bolton, Bury
Bournemouth-Poole	Bournemouth
Bournemouth District	Bournemouth
Brighton & Hove	Brighton
Bromley & Beckenham	Bromley
Buckhaven Methil Leven	Leven
Burnley & Nelson	Burnley, Nelson
Burnley & Pendle	Burnley, Colne
Bury Bolton Wigan	Bolton, Bury
Camborne Redruth	Redruth
*Cardiff Newport	Cardiff
Chesham & Amersham	Amersham
Cheshire	Crewe
Chester Clwyd Gwynedd	Chester
Chester/Clwyd 1	Chester
Chester & Clwyd/1	Chester
*Chester N Wales	
Caer Gog Cymru (variations)	Chester
Cleveland	Middlesbrough, Hartlepool, Stockton-on-Tees
Clwyd, Clwyd 2	Rhyl
Clwyd 1	Chester
Clyde Valley	Motherwell, Biggar, Lanark
Coatbridge & Airdrie	Coatbridge
*Cornwall	Truro, Bodmin, Falmouth, Hayle, Helston, Newquay, Penzance, Redruth, St Austell, St Ives (*Truro only)
Coventry & Warwickshire	Coventry
Croydon/Sutton	Croydon, Morden, Sutton
*Cumbria Dumfries & Galloway	Carlisle
Derby/Nottingham	Nottingham (Sundays)
Devon & Exeter (or vice versa)	Exeter
*DN-LN (postcode areas)	Doncaster
Dorchester S & W Dorset	Dorchester
*Dorset & SW Hants (Dorset Mail Centre is at Poole)	Bournemouth
Edinburgh Lothian Fife Borders	Edinburgh
Exeter District (or Exeter & District)	Exeter, Dawlish, Exmouth etc
Fylde Coast (variations)	Blackpool
Fylde Blackpool Wyre	Blackpool & other offices in area
Gatwick MLO (later *Gatwick Mail Centre)	Crawley (replaced Redhill)
Glastonbury & Street	Glastonbury
*Gloucestershire	Gloucester etc
*Greenford/Windsor	Greenford (replaced Harrow)
Grimsby & Cleethorpes	Grimsby
Gwent	Newport Gwent
Gwynedd N (North)	Bangor Gwynedd (Sundays)
Gwynedd S (South)	Caernarfon (Sundays)
Harrow & Wembley	Harrow, Wembley, Northwood, Pinner, Ruislip
Head Post Office West Lothian	Livingston
Hereford & Worcestershire later Herefordshire (and) Worcestershire (IMP)	Worcester
*Home Counties North Mail Centre	(new mail Centre at Hemel Hempstead) HP, WD, EN, AL, LU, SG areas
Huddersfield Halifax	Huddersfield, Halifax
Ilford & Barking	Ilford
Isle of Wight	Newport IOW
*Jubilee Mail Centre (+ postcodes)	New office near Hounslow (replaced Kingston, Twickenham, later Guildford too)
*Lancs, Lancashire and Lancashire & South Lakes	Preston & other offices in area (* Preston only)
Lancaster & Morecambe	Lancaster
*Leicestershire	Leicester
Llandudno-Colwyn Bay	Colwyn Bay
Lynton & Lynmouth	Lynton
Mablethorpe & Sutton on Sea	Mablethorpe
Medway	Chatham
*Medway	Rochester (new 2012 Mail Centre)
Medway & Maidstone	Maidstone
Royal Mail Midlands	Derby (Sundays)
Mid Northumberland	Morpeth
Motherwell & Wishaw	Motherwell
Newport Mon NP3	Ebbw Vale
Northamptonshire	Northampton
*North & West Yorkshire	Leeds (IMP) (includes Bradford & York areas)
North Devon	Barnstaple

Machine Cancellations

Generic/joint description	Town where used
North Herts (error)	Stevenage
*NW Midlands	Wolverhampton
Perth Dundee Angus	Perth
Plymouth & District	Plymouth (Sundays)
*Plymouth Cornwall & W Devon	Plymouth, St Austell etc (*Plymouth only)
*Plymouth and Cornwall (IMP)	Plymouth
*Portsmouth & IOW	Portsmouth
Portsmouth & Southsea	Portsmouth
Reigate & Redhill	Redhill
Rhondda	Pontypridd & others
Richmond & Twickenham	Twickenham
Rochdale Oldham Ashton-u-Lyne (variations)	Oldham
Rochester & Chatham	Chatham
Romford & Dagenham	Romford
Scottish Borders	Galashiels, Hawick, Kelso
Sennen & Lands End	(used at Penzance)
Shropshire & Mid Wales later Shropshire & Y Canolbarth (variations)	Shrewsbury
Slough/Windsor SL0-9	Slough
South Coast (error for Sussex Coast)	Brighton
South Devon	Torquay (+ others at Xmas)
*SE Anglia	Chelmsford
SE Division 1 (also 'Kent') (continued on Saturdays when Sunday collections ceased in 2007, only to 2011)	Tonbridge (Sundays)
SE Division 2	Croydon (Sundays)
*SE Wales (bilingual IMP)	Cardiff
*South Midlands Mail Centre (new Mail Centre at Northampton)	CV, NN, MK areas
SW County Durham	Bishop Auckland
*SW Wales (bilingual IMP)	Swansea
Sussex Coast	Brighton, Hove
*Swansea & SW Wales	Swansea
Teesside	Middlesbrough, Hartlepool, Stockton-on-Tees
later Teesside again (after Cleveland)	Middlesbrough
Thames Valley	Swindon
Thanet	Margate, Ramsgate, Broadstairs
Torquay & Paignton	Torquay
*Tyneside-NE-SR	Newcastle upon Tyne
Warwick & Leamington Spa	Leamington Spa
West Glamorgan	Swansea & other offices in area
West Mercia	Wolverhampton (handstamps only)
Worcester District (see also Hereford & Worcs)	Worcester & other offices in area

Gibbons Stamp Monthly

The first choice for stamp collectors since 1890

- The UK's biggest selling stamp magazine
- Consistently over 150 pages per issue
- Written by stamp collectors for stamp collectors
- Monthly colour catalogue supplement
- Philatelic news from around the world
- Dedicated GB stamp section
- Regular offers exclusively for subscribers every month

For your FREE sample, contact us using the details below.

FREE SAMPLE

Est 1856
STANLEY GIBBONS

Stanley Gibbons Limited
7 Parkside, Christchurch Road,
Ringwood, Hants, BH24 3SH
+44 (0)1425 472 363
www.stanleygibbons.com

225

11 Slogan Postmarks

In 1917 the "wavy line" segment of a machine postmark on letters was first used to advertise the Government's War Bond scheme. The idea soon spread to advertising events and Post Office messages eg "Post early for Christmas". The Wembley Exhibition of 1924 was advertised by means of slogans from as early as 1922, then further slogans were used on mail posted at the actual event in 1924 and again in 1925.

In 1956 the first local slogan was used "Rochdale Centenary" then from 1963 the first "local publicity" slogan advertised Hastings, with no event or anniversary involved. Also in 1963 came the first "transposed" slogan with the legend to the LEFT of the town die. But the Post Office remained adamant that no commercial advertising could be involved unless an anniversary or event was included eg "Gibbons Centenary Stamp Show" of 1965. The policy changed in the 1980s and advertising was later permitted, indeed actively marketed, hence, for example, the nationwide "Kit Kat" and "Quality Street" slogans in 1995-96.

By 1999 nearly 7000 slogans had been used. Thus there is ample opportunity for thematic collectors to search the lists for designs representing their own interest. The ever-popular Post Office Savings Bank and meter correction slogans are shown at the end of the chapter.

The reference numbers shown are from the books of Parsons, Peachey and Pearson (for details see Bibliography); these are used with permission. The numbers in brackets show approximate numbers of dies of each slogan (if no number then one die). Listed are all slogans to 1925, then a selection, including most of "the classics".

A pricing guide is shown below. The minimum values are for clean covers, but * indicates a value of the order of £150-£200.

"Strips" or cut outs	One quarter valuation shown
	(slogans separated from town dies should be discarded)
Slogan with square paid die, in red	Six times normal
	(to 1955, modern ones are more scarce; circular paid dies are unusual and impressions with slogans are scarce)
Slogan with diamond census die (generally to 1985)	
Slogan with triangular die (generally to 1968)	Three times normal
Slogan with London missort die (number at foot)	
Early or late use	1½ times normal

11/2

11/3

11/4

1917			
1	War Bonds Now, single **11/1**	(42)	5.00
2	War Bonds Now, continuous, 33mm	(100)	3.00
3	War Bonds Now, 28mm	(8)	6.00
1918			
A4	War Bonds, single	(2)	40.00
4	War Bonds, lines r & l	(30)	1.50
5	War Bonds, lines rt	(20)	2.50
6	Feed the Guns, single	(40)	5.00
7	Feed the Guns, continuous, 34mm	(130)	5.00
7A	Feed the Guns, 38mm	(6)	6.00
1922			
8	BIF 1922	(5)	4.00
9	Cable Canada, boxed	(2)	2.00
10	Cable Canada, unboxed		*
11	Cable Canada, continuous, Leicester		50.00
12	Post Early boxed, single	(25)	1.00
13	Post Early boxed, continuous, Newcastle		10.00
14	Empire Exhibition, single **11/2**	(22)	3.00
15	Empire Exhibition, continuous	(12)	5.00
16	BIF 1923	(10)	6.00
1923			
17	Ulster Pavilion, single	(2)	75.00
18	Ulster Pavilion, continuous (N Ireland)	(3)	£150
1924			
19	BIF 1924	(12)	5.00
A20	Empire Exhibition. 55mm		6.00

11/1

Slogan Postmarks

20	Empire Exhibition Wembley (on mail at exhibition)		10.00
21	Pageant of Empire	(30)	5.00

1925
22	Empire Exhibition	(30)	1.50
23	Ulster Pavilion	(2)	50.00
24	Empire Exhib Wembley (on mail at exhibition)		25.00
24A	Govt. Pavilion		40.00
25	Join the Fellowship	(5)	10.00
26	London Defended	(25)	8.00
27	Torchlight Tattoo, dates Aug-Sept	(25)	10.00
28	ditto to 10th Oct.	(10)	15.00
29	ditto dates removed	(10)	75.00
30A-E	ditto dots, lines etc.	(29)	50.00
31	British Goods, large	(200)	0.80
32	British Goods, small	(15)	2.50
33	British Goods, continuous, London NW1		*
A34	British Made Goods		75.00
34	Christmas -FOR-	(100)	2.00
35	BIF 1926	(12)	2.50

Only a selection of slogans are listed from this point.

1926
36	British Goods, framed	(2)	10.00
37	King's Roll	(50)	8.00
38	Say it by Telephone	(125)	2.00
39	Christmas -FOR-	(100)	1.50

1927
42	BIF Feb 20-March 2	(12)	3.00

1928
44	BIF Feb 18-March 1	(12)	3.00

1929
45	Newcastle Exhibition	(30)	2.00
46	Christmas -FOR-	(100)	1.50

1930
47	BIF Feb 17-28	(12)	3.00

1931
50	BIF Feb 16-27	(12)	4.00
51	BIF Cotton	(30)	5.00
52-62	Series of 10 telephone slogans, 1931-3 then 1934:		
52	Every home a phone	(25)	1.50
53	Telephone habit	(25)	1.50
54	Quicker to telephone	(25)	1.50
55	Shop by phone, dot dash	(25)	5.00
56	Shop by phone, solid	(25)	1.50
57	Best investment	(25)	1.50
57A	'L' removed		3.00
58	Makes life easier	(25)	1.50
59	Sound investment	(25)	1.50
60	Time and money	(25)	1.50
61	Trade follows	(25)	1.50
62	You are wanted	(25)	1.50

1932
65	BIF 1932	(18)	3.00
66	BIF Textiles	(20)	4.00
71	BIF 1933, Textiles	(20)	3.00

1933
72	Christmas -FOR-)	(150)	1.00
73	Christmas FOR)		1.00
74	BIF 1934, 22 mm	(30)	3.00
75	BIF 1934, 19 mm	(3)	6.00
76	BIF Textiles, 22 mm	(15)	5.00
77	BIF Textiles, 19 mm	(8)	6.00

1934
77Ba	Tel. Exhibition		25.00
78	Mt. Pleasant Opening		£400

1935
84	Christmas -FOR-)	(150)	2.00
85	Christmas FOR)		1.00
86	BIF 1936	(35)	2.50

1936
A89	Telephone Habit G.P.O. Exhibition		30.00
91	BIF 1937	(50)	1.50
92	Young People's Exhibition		20.00

1937
93	Post Early sunburst	(200)	0.50
94	Post Early, boxed, Leith DO only		£100
95	As above used at GPO Exhibition		15.00
98	BIF 1938	(50)	2.00

1938
M.4	All letters go by air		10.00
100	Glasgow Exhibition		0.50
100a	- Exhibition		2.50
101	- Pavilion		7.00
102	Christmas -FOR-) **11/3**	(150)	5.00
103	Christmas FOR)		1.00
104	BIF 1939	(50)	2.00

1939
106	Post Early sunburst	(?)	0.50
107	Road Users	(100)	0.80
108	Grow more Food	(75)	0.80
109	Christmas -FOR-)	(100)	10.00
110	Christmas FOR)		1.00

1940
111	Post Early sunburst	(?)	0.50
112	Grow more food	(50)	2.00
113	Kitchen Front	(50)	2.00
114	Save waste paper	(50)	2.00
115	Christmas -FOR-	(3)	10.00
116	Christmas FOR	(100)	1.00

1941
118	Kitchen Front, Cambridge		20.00

1942
122	Post Early sunburst	(?)	1.00
123	Christmas FOR	(50)	2.00

1945
128	Post Early sunburst	(8)	1.50
129	Victory Europe	(400)	1.00
130	Victory Japan	(400)	1.00
	(129-130 more for smaller offices)		
131	Christmas FOR	(50)	2.00
132	Christmas Holly	(100)	0.80
133	United Nations **11/4**	(112)	10.00

1946
134	National Savings	(350)	0.80
135	Don't Waste Bread	(350)	0.80
136	Death off road	(350)	0.80
M.A8	c/o ship owner not GPO		*
137	Britain can make it	(350)	1.00

1947
140	BIF 1947	(50)	0.80
141	Staggered Holidays	(350)	0.80
142	Blood Donors	(350)	0.80
143	Forces Career	(350)	0.80
144	Britain for Holidays	(50)	0.80
145	Silver Lining	(350)	0.80
147	Royal Wedding	(400)	0.80

1948

150	BIF 1948	(50)		0.80
151	Hand on the Land	(350)		0.80
153	Nursing	(350)		0.80
154	As 151 but June	(3)		15.00
155	Edinburgh Festival	(30)		6.00
156	Eisteddfod	(12)		6.00
157	Olympic Games	(2)		3.50
158	Blood Donors	(350)		0.80
159	Save waste paper	(350)		0.80
160	Christmas FOR	(30)		2.00
161	Christmas Holly	(350)		0.80
162	- Rough Holly			2.00

1949

163	Volunteer Forces	(350)	0.80
164	BIF 1949	(50)	1.00
165	Mind how you go	(350)	0.80
166	Edinburgh Festival	(31)	2.00
167	British Air Lines	(350)	0.80
168	Scottish Industries	(30)	2.50
169	Colonial month	(100)	2.00
170	Food Gifts	(50)	2.00

1950

177	Road Users	(350)	0.80
178	Stamp Exhibition	(50)	1.50
179	Edinburgh Festival	(31)	2.50
180	Christmas FOR, Golders Green		60.00
181	Christmas Holly	(350)	0.80
182	- Rough Holly, Stoke		60.00

1951

183	Voters List	(350)	0.80
184	BIF 1951	(50)	0.60
185	Blood Donors	(350)	0.60
186	Festival Britain	(40)	1.50
187	- SE1 used at Festival		2.00
188	Civil Defence	(350)	0.60
189	Christmas Holly	(350)	0.60

1952

190	BIF 1952	(50)	1.00
191	Voters List	(300)	1.00
192	Postage for Europe	(350)	0.80
193	Christmas rough holly, Sheffield		50.00
194	- holly "outline"	(350)	0.60
195	- holly "solid"		0.60

11/5

11/6

1953

196	Voters List	(350)	0.80
197	BIF 1953	(50)	0.80
198	Eisteddfod Rhyl		50.00
199	Coronation (more for smaller offices)	(921)	0.80

202	Check Address	(350)	0.60

1954

204	Voters, no lines	(350)	0.80
205	Voters, lines at rt		6.00
208	Eisteddf Ystradgynlais	(4)	6.00
210	Buy 2½d stamps in books **11/5**	(350)	0.80

1955

220	Eisteddfod Pwllheli	(4)	6.00

1956

227	BIF Earls Court	(50)	0.80
228	BIF Lond & Birmingham	(50)	0.80
230	Rochdale Centenary		8.00

1957

235	Licence for Radio-TV	(350)	0.50
237	Stalybridge Centenary		30.00
239	Elgar Centenary Worcester		5.00
242	TT Races Isle of Man		40.00
244	Jamboree	(50)	1.50
245	- used at Jamboree (on FDC of Scout stamps 25.00)		3.00
251	Johnstone Centenary		10.00

1958

254	TA Jubilee	(59)	0.80
255	Bangor Abbey		5.00
258	Empire Games	(45)	0.80
261	- special (on FDC of Games stamps 85.00)	(4)	3.00

1959

277	Bible Society	(10)	2.50
278	Oldham Carnival		8.00

1960

294	Refugee Year (hand)	(350)	0.80
295	- defaced die, Halifax		*
298	- revised design	(350)	0.50
324	Post early candle	(350)	0.50

1961

341	Aerial Post Windsor	(2)	2.50
347	BBC TV Jubilee	(350)	0.50

1962

373	Eisteddfod	(6)	0.80
375	Norwich addresses long		2.50
390	Post Early, holly Stafford		6.00

1963

LP.1	Hastings We're ready		0.80
LP.8t	Bath Assembly Rooms **11/6**		0.60
403	London Underground	(50)	0.60
416t	Paisley Abbey	(2)	0.80

NB. "t" denotes 'transposed' but after 1963 "t" is omitted to save space

1964

440	Someone wants a letter		1.50
LP111	Bacup welcomes industry		0.60

1965

514	Gibbons Cent'y Show	(30)	0.80
523	Bromsgrove Festival		0.60
LP268	Crawley best new town		0.80

1966

LP298	Basildon faces future		0.60
631	World Cup City Sheffield	(3)	0.60

1967

LP432	Fly Liverpool Jetport		0.60
839	Southend Illuminations	(2)	0.60

Slogan Postmarks

1968
985	Harlow Charity Ball		2.00
LP653	Back Britain Bridlington		0.60

1969
LP767	Whitby guide book 1/-		0.60
1287	Ballymena Civic Week		2.00
1302	East of England Show	(14)	0.60

1970
1459	Vandalism costs money	(2)	2.50
1549	Philympia 70	(4)	0.80
LP963	Prestatyn welcomes you		0.60

1971
1725	Decimal currency (used during postal strike 5.00)	(143)	0.60
LP1101	Londonderry visitors		0.60

1972
1952	Internatl Book Year	(12)	0.60
LP1285	Industrial dev Consett		0.60

LINCOLN city for engineering enterprise

LINCOLN 7-PM 9 DEC 1973 A

11/7

1973
LP1366	Lincoln engineering **11/7**		0.60
2190	Leigh Arts Festival		0.80
2337	Human Rights	(30)	0.60

1974
2392	Chichester Fest Theatre		0.60
LP1587	Southampton shopping	(2)	0.80

1975
2700	Navy Days Portsmouth	(3)	0.80
LP1747	Tenby hol guide 15p	(2)	0.80

1976
2787	Penfold PGA Sandwich	(3)	1.00
LP1786	Scone Palace	(5)	0.80

EDINBURGH 18 AUG 1986 LOTHIAN FIFE

NORTHERN LIGHTHOUSE BOARD 1786-1986

11/8

CAMBRIDGE 10 AM 28 DEC 1987 E

ELY CATHEDRAL Restoration Trust

11/9

HAVERHILL 6-AM 2 JAN 1991 SUFFOLK

PHILIPS A HUNDRED YEARS AHEAD

11/10

1977
2915	Southampton is MLO	(10)	0.50
LP1861	Exeter Speedway		0.60

1978
LP1903	Wimbledon Tennis Mus'm	(2)	0.80
3082	Nat Arts Collection	(6)	0.80

1979
3170	Dutch Week Notts	(4)	0.80
LP1986	Hagley Hall	(2)	0.60
3259	Collect Brit stamps	(100)	0.50

1980
3293	Sustain Scott scouts	(4)	0.60
LP2014	Torquay quality resort		0.60

1981
LP2047	Nat Butterfly Museum		0.80
3387	Wells 800		0.80

1982
3424	Gillette Marathon	(2)	0.80
3437	Milt Keynes Station	(12)	0.60

1983
3500	GLC Thames Barrier	(4)	1.00
LP2119	Glasgow's miles better (in red from NSB 10.00)	(5)	0.60

1984
LP2132	Lincoln Philat Counter	(2)	0.50
3593	Middlesex Cricket Lords		1.00

1985
3620	The Times	(10)	0.60
LP2148	S Yorks day rovers	(4)	0.60

1986
3696	Air Show Sumburgh		1.00
3726	N Lighthouse Board **11/8**		1.00

1987
LP2197	Shanklin all year hol	(4)	0.60
3810	Ely Cathedral **11/9**		5.00

1988
3844	"Jesus is alive!"	(340)	0.60
3857	Wesley 250th Anniv	(115)	0.50
3890	Irish Geology Week	(2)	1.00

1989
LP2222	Victoria Place		0.80
3944	Lead free (in green)	(370)	0.50
3949	Mailing & Comms Show	(2)	0.80

1990
(NB: red ink in general use 5 Jan to 16 Sep 1990)
4078	Stamp World 90	(625)	0.50
4146	Croydon Business Show	(2)	0.60

1991
4180	Philips 100 years ahead **11/10**	(500)	0.50
4196	Sunday collections	(4)	1.00
4200	Crime Line Rugby		1.00

MILTON KEYNES GARDEN SHOW THE BOWL May Day Weekend 2nd - 4th May

MILTON KEYNES 7 30 PM 5 MAY 1992

11/11

SOUTH DEVON 1 15 PM 26 FEB 1994 I

COLIN RICHARDSON THE BIG 40 27th FEBRUARY 1994

11/12

229

Slogan Postmarks

11/13

1996
4898	Recycle used oil		0.80
4922	Snickers sponsor Euro 96	(2)	0.60
4946	Posted at R Welsh Show (6.00 on commercial cover)		1.00
4980	Newcastle '96 stamp exhib		2.00

1997
4998	Crawley New Town		0.60
B.13	BBC Lutoslawski (magenta)		1.50
5007	Quit smoking (Nottingham)		0.80
5041	Regeneration by Railtrack	(7)	0.80

1998
5089	Nescafe gold blend Valentine	(118)	0.50
5097	New Southend Council		0.60
5104	MIB (Men in Black)	(130)	0.50
5139	Burne-Jones Birmingham	(6)	0.80

1992
4364	Tusk Force	(15)	0.60
4368	Garden Show M Keynes **11/11**		1.50
4471	Channel 4 (in green)	(148)	0.50

1993
4524	Safeway open in Newquay		0.80
4544	Three Counties Radio	(6)	0.60
4572	Posted at R Cornwall Show		2.50

1994
4660	Valentines Day	(140)	0.50
4666	Colin Richardson 40 **11/12**		2.00
4670	Le Shuttle **11/13**	(150)	0.50
4754	Happy Xmas (snowman)	(400)	0.50

1995
4792	Oriana super-liner	(140)	0.50
4811	Charter Day Marazion	(2)	1.00
4835	Nat'l Transplant Week	(2)	0.80
4852	Kit Kat	(154)	0.50

1999
5161	Physicians/Surgeons Glasgow	(12)	0.80

At this point Royal Mail policy changed and no further traditional "steel die" slogans were produced, neither were advertising facilities any longer offered to sponsors. However, there was continuing use of postcode-oriented slogans right through the 2000s and in addition Christmas slogan dies held from previous years at sorting offices were re-used each December (with a few uses of "Valentine", "Mother's Day" etc at appropriate times as well).

The only new slogans that were introduced were computer produced and struck by ink-jet printers in IMP machines, and the subject matter of these slogans was concerned with Royal Mail topics only. Three examples are shown below, the third of these (**11/16**) being a test slogan used in error on normal mail.

11/14

11/15

11/16

230

Slogan Postmarks

Save more Spend less

11/17

KEEP ON SAVING

11/18

Other categories of slogans :

Various special purpose slogans are shown in chapters 14, 15, 16, 18.

Post Office Savings Bank Slogans
Used in Pitney-Bowes machines at London W14, Acton W3, Richmond & Twickenham, Harrogate, and Savings Division London N7. All struck in red except S1.

Ref	Description	Price
S1	OHMS Official Paid, 1926-33 (black or red)	15.00
S2	Save More, Spend Less, 1940 **11/17**	30.00
S3	Serve by Saving, 1940-45	15.00
S4	Win by Saving, 1941-45	20.00
S5	Save to win, 1941-45	25.00
S6	Save for Security, 1942-45	25.00
S7-8B	Keep on Saving (variations), 1947-54 (variation shown **11/18** 25.00)	15.00
S9	Keep on Saving (new design), 1946-52 (variations)	2.50
S10	Keep on Saving through the Post Office, 1954-59	1.50
S11	As above but with 7 lines at right, 1957-63	0.80
S12	POSB 1861-1961 and key, 1961	6.00
S13	1966 use of S11, London N7	5.00
S14	As above but Univ machine 1966-67	5.00

... and a postscript to the POSB section, the first "War Bonds" slogan used in red in a Columbia machine at the POSB office in 1917-8 (valuation 75.00).

Meter Correction Slogans
From the mid 1980s Royal Mail took a closer look at the accuracy of the date in meter postmarks, and applied their own postmark to correct the date if appropriate. Handstamps were sometimes used, or machine-applied meter correction slogans as shown below (year indicates year of introduction). The "ref" numbers refer to "Slogan Postmarks of the Eighties" and "Nineties" as this was the main period of use of these slogans, though there was some residual use in the 2000s. The slogans were intended for meter correction duties – value from 1.00 – but some are used for stamping normal mail – value from 2.00 – and in fact the slogans at Kilmarnock, Lincoln and Southend-on-Sea were only used in this manner.

11/19

11/20

Ref	Town	Abbrev wording	Year	Colours used
M.46	Paddington	Paddington meter post processed	1992	black
M.34	Belfast	Belfast posted on date shown	1988	black/red
M.41	Belfast	Belfast posting date corrected	1990	black
M.37	Birmingham	Correct date of posting in black	1988	black
M.30	Birmingham	Incorrectly dated	1990	red/black
M.32	Bolton ("Bury Bolton Wigan" town die)	Incorrectly dated	1993	black
M.32	Bournemouth ("Bournemouth-Poole" town die, later "Dorset & SW Hants")	Incorrectly dated	1988	black/red
M.30	Bradford	Incorrectly dated	1991	black
M.30	Cardiff (later "Cardiff Newport" town die)	Incorrectly dated	1990	black
M.32	Carlisle ("Cumbria Dumfries & Galloway" town die)	Incorrectly dated	1994	black
M.27	Chester ("Chester Clwyd Gwynedd" town die)	Correct date of posting in black	1987	black
M.43	Colchester	Correct date of posting black ink	1991	black
M.39	Crewe	Cheshire meter post	1989	black/red
M.48	Crewe (both the above used with "Cheshire" town dies)	Received in 2nd class postings	1995	red
M.38	Doncaster	Doncaster District posted on date	1988	black
M.49	Edinburgh	This item was actually posted on	1996	black
M.30	Glasgow	Incorrectly dated	1987	black
M.44	Harrow	Harrow meter post posted on date	1992	black
M.30	Huddersfield ("Huddersfield Halifax" town die)	Incorrectly dated	1991	black
M.35	Hull	Hull meter post	1988	black
M.30	Kilmarnock	Incorrectly dated	1988	black
M.31	Leeds	Incorrectly posted in 2nd class	1988	black
M.30	Leeds	Incorrectly dated	1987	black/red
M.38	Lincoln	Doncaster District posted on date	1990	black

231

Slogan Postmarks

Ref	Town	Abbrev wording	Year	Colours used
M.41B	Lisburn	as Belfast M.41 but Lisburn	1990	red
M.27	Liverpool	Correct date of posting in black	1986	black
M.32	Liverpool	Incorrectly dated	1993	black
M.41A	Londonderry	as Belfast M.41 but Londonderry	1992	black
M.26	Manchester	Incorrect meter presentation	1984	black
M.50	Newcastle upon Tyne ("Tyneside" town die)	Tyneside meter post	2000	red
M.51	Portsmouth	Arrived at The Mail Centre	2005	black/red
M.26	Preston ("Lancashire" town die)	Incorrect meter presentation	1986	black
M.30	Preston ("Lancashire" town die, later "Lancashire & South Lakes")	Incorrectly dated	1994	black
M.27	Romford	Correct date of posting in black	1989	black
M.42	Romford	Correct date shown in red	1990	red
M.47	Romford	Incorrect date Received at Romford	1994	black
M.33	Sheffield	Sheffield meter post posted on date	1988	black/red
M.32	Shrewsbury ("Shropshire & Mid Wales" town die)	Incorrectly dated	1993	black

Ref	Town	Abbrev wording	Year	Colours used
M.43	Southend on Sea	Correct date of posting black ink	1991	black
M.32	Stockport	Incorrectly dated	1993	black
M.51	Swindon	Arrived at The Mail Centre	2011	black
M.45	Uxbridge	Uxbridge meter post posted on date	1992	black
M.31	Wakefield	Incorrectly posted in 2nd class	1988	black
M.32	Wakefield	Incorrectly dated	1988	black
M.40	Watford	Watford meter post posted on date	1989	black/red
M.36	York	York meter post posted on date	1988	black/green

Further reading :

"Collecting Slogan Postmarks" by CRH Parsons, CG Peachey and GR Pearson (1986, includes full listing to 1969)
"Slogan Postmarks of the Seventies" by the same authors (1980)
"Slogan Postmarks of the Eighties" by the same authors (1990)
"Slogan Postmarks of the Nineties" Part 1 (1990-1994) and Part 2 (1995-1999) by the same authors (1995 and 2000 respectively)
"The first slogan cancellations in Great Britain 1917-1918" by R A Keneally c1981
"Machine Cancellations of Scotland" by J A Mackay (1986)
"'Jesus is Alive!' - the story of a slogan postmark" by Dr J T Whitney (1988)
"The London 1945 United Nations Slogan Cancellation", supplement to Journal of United Nations Philatelists, Volume 14 No.1, Oct 1990
British Postmark Society Quarterly Bulletins

12 Special Event Postmarks

Up to about 1960, special event postmarks were only used at post offices set up at relevant events. These were in two categories:
(i) those at which ordinary letters and postcards were stamped, such as the popular White City exhibitions in 1908-14 ("Shepherds Bush" in postmarks). Postcards were posted in large quantities and consequently valuations are low.
(ii) those at which special event marks were used only for counter transactions. The only postal items to receive these postmarks were registered letters and their receipts. Ordinary letters and cards received an ordinary postmark. This applied to many of the agricultural shows of the 1920s and 1930s, which is why many of them are so scarce.

A selection is listed including all the early ones to 1925 and those considered to be "classics". Some early marks are only known in Post Office proof books and these are omitted. So are repeat entries: R denotes an item is repeated in later years. Valuations are shown as * or ** where items appear for sale so seldom that pricing is difficult: * indicates in the region of £200-£300 and ** £400 or more. The reference numbers are, with permission, "*Pearson numbers*"; see Bibliography for details of Pearson and other suggested books.

Recent Discoveries

George King was an avid collector who seemingly submitted his covers for the postmarks to every exhibition, agricultural show etc for over 60 years from 1910 onwards coming up with, in the process, items not known to other collectors. He died in the 1980s, and the details of these postmarks only came to light gradually as his vast collection came on to the market. As a result there are fifteen previously unknown Special Event postmarks, and we have included them in this chapter for the first time in this edition. Two of them are illustrated here with the caption "Recent Discoveries" (so as not to spoil the numbering sequence). Details appeared in a 2007 Supplement to *Special Event Postmarks of the UK* volume 1 by George Pearson, mentioned above and published by the British Postmark Society, and which includes much additional new data. See also 2-4 in Introduction.

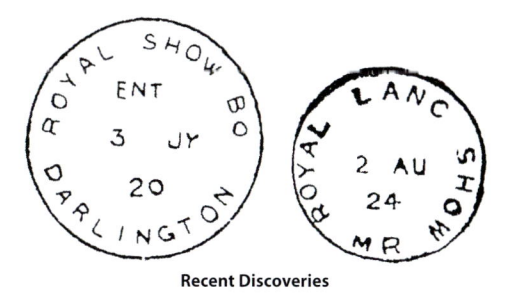

Recent Discoveries

Summary from 1862

12/1

12/2

12/3

12/4

12/5

1862			
1	Internat Exhibition W (duplex) **12/1**		£250
2	do. (single circle, red)		**
A3	do. (killer on reg'd items) **12/2**		**

1883			
6	Fisheries Exhibition SW		**

1884			
7	Health Exhibition SW **12/3**		**

1885			
8	Inventions Exhibition SW **12/4**		**

1886			
10	Colonial & Indian Exhib SW		**

1887			
12	American Exhibition SW **12/5**		**
13	Manchester Exhibition		*

1888			
14	Exhibition Glasgow		*
15	Italian Exhibition SW		**
A16	Irish Exhibition W		**

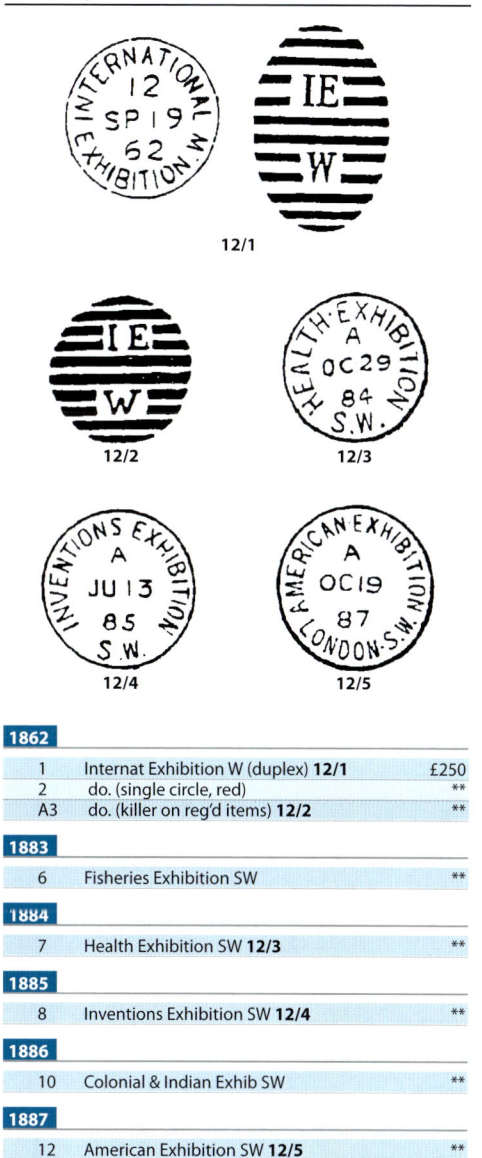

233

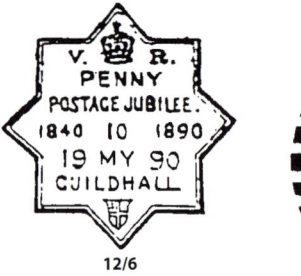

Special Event Postmarks

12/6

12/7

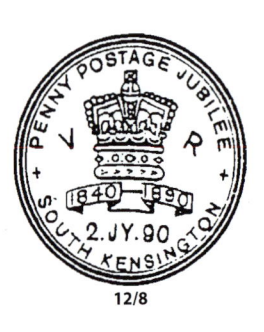

12/11

1893

34	Gardening/Forestry **12/11**	£400
35	Bristol Exhibition	**

1894

36	Royal Show Cambridge	**

1895

37	Show Yard Taunton	**
38	Royal Agric Show Darlington	*

1899

40	Royal Agric Show Maidstone	**

1900

41	Bradford BA	*

1901

42	Exhibition Glasgow	12.00
A43	ditto s/c	*
44	Intl Eng Conf Glasgow	**
43	Brit Assn Glasgow	**

12/8

12/9

12/10

12/12

12/13

12/14

1890

17	Military Exhibition	**
18	1d Post Jubilee, timed **12/6**	25.00
19	ditto, no hour shown	25.00
A20	BAE cachet **12/7**	90.00
20	Edinburgh Exhibition	*
21	1d Post SW7 37mm **12/8**	8.00
22	do. 32mm	18.00
23	do. cachets - 1790 **12/9**	20.00
24	- 1990 **12/10**	20.00
25	- 1d tube post	20.00
26	- 3d tube post	50.00

Nos. 21-26 often together on cover, such "combination covers" 30.00-£150 on 1d Jubilee envelope and/or insert card.

1891

28	German Exhibition SW	£125
29	Royal Naval/Eddystone	90.00
30	ditto s/c	*

1892

31	Horticultural Exhib SW	*
32	Show Yard Warwick	**

1902

	45	Exhib Wolverhampton	£300
R	46	Internat Exhib Cork	**
	47	Botanic Gardens NW	**
	48	Brit Assocn Belfast	**

1903

	49	Henley Regatta	**
	50	Brit Association Southport	**
R	A51	Trades Exhib Plymouth	£125

Special Event Postmarks

1904
A52	Brit Assn Cambridge		**

1905
C52	Showyard Bath		**

1907
53	Exhibition BO Dublin		5.00
53A	ditto s/c		**
A54	Newark Agric Show		**

1908
54	Exhib BO Edinburgh		10.00
55	Franco-Brit Exhib **12/12**		3.00
56	Shepherds Bush (on reg)		£100
57	do. rubber on parcels		*
58	Ballymaclinton **12/13**		3.00

1909
59	Stamp Exhib & Congress		20.00
60	Imperial Internat Exhib		8.00
A61	ditto - machine		£300
61	Ballymaclinton (see 58)		8.00
62	do. rubber on parcels		*
64	Scottish Village		25.00

1910
65	Japan Brit Exhibition		4.00
66	ditto - machine		12.00
67	Royal Agric Show Liverpool		*
A68	Show Ground Spalding		*
68	Lanark (Aviation meeting)		£350

1911
69	Exhibition BO Glasgow		10.00
70	Crystal Palace Fest 1-3 (handstamp 4 60.00)		20.00
71	ditto reg no.7		£150
72	Royal Hortic Ex (see 82)		*
73	Stamp Exhib & Congress		30.00
74	Coronation Exhib **12/14**		20.00
75	Royal Show Norwich		*
76	St Andrews (?golf event)		**
79	Aerial Post London 1-6		35.00
80	Aerial Post Windsor 1-2		50.00

Nos. 79-80 only on special cards/envelopes.

1912
81	Phil Congress Margate		25.00
82	Royal Horticultural Ex London		£120
A84	Royal Show Doncaster		*
84	Royal Society W		**
85	Exhib Shepherds Bush (Latin British)		18.00
86	Stamp Exhibition Jubilee		12.00

1913
87	Phil Congress Edinburgh		30.00
88	Exhibition Liverpool		£150
AA89	Royal Show Bristol		*
A89	Paisley Grandstand		*
A90	Burnley Show Ground		£150
90	Internat Congr Medicine SW		£150

1914
92	Exhib Shepherds Bush (Anglo-American)		15.00
93	Bristol Exhib		50.00
AA94	Showyard Portsmouth		*
A94	UMC (Methodist) Redruth		*
BB94	Show Yard Hawick		*
BC94	Yorks Show Bradford		*

1915
B94	Show Yard Worcester		*
C94	Royal Show Nottingham		*

1917
95	Irish Convention		£100

1919
A96	Lond 213/ R34 (airship)		£3000

1920
96	Phil Congress Newcastle		20.00
A97	Royal Show BO Darlington (two post offices, PAV and ENT)		*
97	Cowes Regatta		£120

1921
98	Phil Congress Harrogate		20.00
A99	Royal Show Ground Derby		*

1922
99	Phil Congress Bath		20.00
A100	Royal Show Cambridge		*

1923
100	Int Stamp Exhibition SW1		5.00
A101	Royal Show B Newcastle Tyne		*

1924
101	Phil Congress Glasgow		25.00
A102	Royal Agric Show Windsor		£150
B102	Royal Show Leicester		*
C102	KCA Ashford (Kent County Agricultural Show)		*
D102	Show Yard Perth		*
E102	Royal Lanc Show MR (Manchester)		*

12/15

12/16   12/17

The Empire Exhibition of 1924 was GB's first commemorative stamp issue. We here introduce valuations of commemorative First Day Covers since the valuation of FDCs with complete sets of stamps (1d and 1½d in the case of the Empire Exhibition) is considerably higher than covers with the same postmark on other dates or bearing one stamp only. We thus include in our selection the "postmark" valuation and the "FDC" valuation on each relevant occasion. The latter is for FDCs with special postmark on illustrated envelopes (except where "plain" noted). For all of 102-123A, covers – or large pieces for the parcel postmarks – would normally bear the Wembley commem stamps, except for "paid" postmarks in red.

102	Empire Exhib Wembley m/c (on Wembley 1d stamp, any date) (FDC with both stamps £300)	5.00
103	do. but red ("paid")	£120
104	do. but large h/s **12/15**	10.00

235

Special Event Postmarks

	105	do. but red ("paid")	£100
	106	do. double rim packet h/s	50.00
	107	do. purple oval regist'd	*
	108	Palace of Engineering	50.00
	109	Engineering parcel	*
	109A	do. but 'British' wording	*
	110	Palace of Industry h/s	50.00
	111	do. parcel	*
	A112	Stadium used on reg'd cover (£2700 on FDC)	**

1925

	112	Empire Exhib Wembley m/c (on Wembley 1d stamp, any date) (FDC, both stamps, plain cover £1000)	15.00
	113	do. but red ("paid")	£150
	114	PO Exhibit h/s (with two parts of souvenir telegram)	£500
	115	PO Exhibit machine	25.00
	116	Empire Exhib large h/s	20.00
	117	do. but red ("paid")	£120
	118	Brit Empire Ex large h/s	60.00
	A119	do. double rim packet h/s	60.00
	119	do. purple oval regist'd	£150
	120	small rubber stamp	*
	121	Brit Empire Exhib parcel	*
	122	Palace of Industry h/s	50.00
	123	do. parcel	£100
	123A	do. parcel with 'British' wording as 109A	*
	C124	Show Ground Watford	*
	D124	Show Yard Maidstone	*
	E124	Portsmouth Show Yard	*
	124	Phil Congress Cambridge	15.00
	125	Railway Congress **12/16**	**
	126	Chester Royal Show	*
	A127	Show Yard Newcastle	**
	B127	S Y (Show Yard) Glasgow	**
	C127	Yorks Show Bradford	**

Selection only shown from this point.

1926

	128	Phil Congress Liverpool	15.00
	A129	Show Yard Kelso	*
	129	Reading Royal Show	£100

1927

	132	Phil Congress Nottingham	15.00
	133A	Newport Mon Royal Show A	£120

1928

R	135	Br Industries Fair Birm	80.00
	136	Phil Congress London NW1	8.00
	B138	Showyard Aberdeen	*
	139	London Stamp Exhibition	6.00
	140	ditto s/c	20.00

1929

	142	Newcastle Exhibition	60.00
	144	Postal Union Congress (FDC ½d-2½d, plain cover £900)	15.00
	145	ditto reg oval in purple	60.00
	146	ditto packet h/s	80.00
	153	Arrowepk Camp	**
	B154	Calshot Aerodrome (Schneider Trophy Race)	*

1930

	154	London Naval Conference	80.00
	157	Margate Sanitary Congress	*
	161	Oxford Esperanto	50.00
	162	SAT London WC1	£100
R	164	Indian Conference	*

1931

	AA167	Chelsea Flower Show	*
	A167	Christian Endeavour	*
	172	Lincs Show	*
	174A	Warwick Royal Show A	80.00
	178	Congr Hall Bristol (TUC)	£120
	182	Burma Conference	80.00

1932

R	184	Telephone Exhib slogan	20.00
R	185	Chelsea Flower Show	50.00
	187	Sutton Coldfield Show	80.00
	A191	Show Yard Leeds (Gt Yorkshire Show)	*

1933

	A194	Bath W of England Show	*
	197	Monetary & Economic Conf	30.00
	198	ditto s/c on reg'd cover	60.00
	199	ditto parcel	*
	200	ditto hooded packet	*
	202A	Derby Show A	*

1934

	204	Air Post Exhib **12/17**	5.00
R	209	Peterborough Show Yard	*
	215	Mildenhall A'dme(Air Race) (more for flown covers)	50.00
	216	Mt Pleasant Opening slogan	£400

1935

R	222	Edinburgh Ch of Scotland	50.00
	B229	Mildenhall Royal Review	£200
	A230	Scientific Management SW1	*

1936

R	232	BIF s/c	15.00
R	233	BIF registered oval	20.00
	235	Phil Congress Paignton	3.00
	240	Royal Show Bristol	£100
	241	Mt Edgcumbe scout camp (look for two different handstamps!)	**
	A243	Jamboree Camp Darlington	**
	244	Stamp Exhibition London	3.00
	245	Young People Exhib slogan	20.00

12/18 BOURNEMOUTH 27TH PHILATELIC CONGRESS GT BRITAIN 6 MAY 1940

12/19 FESTIVAL OF BRITAIN BO 30 MY LONDON S.E.1 1951

12/20 INTERNATIONAL BANKING SUMMER SCHOOL 8 SEP 1955 OXFORD

12/21 46TH PARLIAMENTARY CONFERENCE 12.45PM 12 SEP 1957 LONDON S.W.1

1937

R	252	Henley Regatta (reg label)	£125
	253A	Royal Show Wolverhampton A	80.00
R	E255	Birmingham Dog Show	£100

Special Event Postmarks

1938

	259	Empire Exhib Glasgow slogan	1.50
	260	ditto wavy lines last day	3.00
	261	ditto s/c 1-4	6.00
	262	ditto d/c 5-6	6.00
	263	ditto parcel violet	40.00
	264	ditto packets violet	10.00
	265	ditto PO Pavilion slogan	6.00
	A271	Town Moor Newcastle	*
	274	ILO London W1	**

1939

	282	Phil Congress Liverpool	5.00
	A283	Diss Norfolk Showground	*
	284A	R Windsor Show rectangle	65.00
	286	Dundee Brit Assoc	*

1940

	287	Phil Congr Bournem'th **12/18**	3.00
	288	Stamp Cent'y Bournemouth	3.00
	A289	Pavilion/Bournemouth	£100
	289	Stamp Centy (in red) London (FDC of complete set 55.00)	3.00

1945

	298	CCIF (telephone conf)	*

1946

	299	Phil Congress Brighton	3.00

1947

R	301	BIF s/c 1-3	10.00
R	302	BIF reg oval (purple)	20.00
	A305	Wimbledon skeleton	60.00

1948

	A315	Royal Show York	60.00
	315	Olympic Rings (machine) (FDC whole set 50.00, airletter 30.00)	3.00
	315A	Wembley skeleton (FDC usually with 315, but 315A on stamps missed by machine 70.00)	15.00

1949

R	A316	BIF d/c	15.00
	319	Chelsea Flower MY over date	20.00
	A324	Keswick Convention	*
		Esperanto Congress, Bournemouth skeleton	20.00

1950

	325	Int Stamp Exhib (machine)	1.00
	326	ditto h/s no time	5.00
	327	ditto h/s with time	5.00
	A338	Marine Insurance	*
	338	GATT s/c 1 and 2	40.00
	339	GATT reg oval (338-39 often on same cover)	40.00

1951

	343	Festival of Britain machine	2.00
	344	ditto handstamp **12/19**	3.00
	345	ditto parcel	50.00
	355	Int Air Transport	40.00
	356	Farnborough SBAC	50.00
	357	SBAC Farnborough Hants	50.00
	358	SBAC Farnborough Hts	45.00

1952

	365	Phil Congress Southampton	2.00
	369	Royal Show Newton Abbot	6.00
	370	Int Dental Congress	30.00

1953

	373	Coronation Yr Stamp Exhib	1.00

A	379	Esperanto Bournemouth	40.00
	388	TUC Douglas	*
	390	Canadian PS Exhib	2.00

1954

	392	Table Tennis Wembley	15.00
	397	Int Railway Congress	15.00
	401	Liverpool Show	20.00

1955

R	406	Ideal Home	5.00
R	407	Ideal Home reg	6.00
	415	Royal Highland Show Edinb	10.00
	416	ditto parcel	25.00
	417	Abergeldie Castle	30.00
R	418	Banking Summer School **12/20**	2.00

1956

	A424	Empr of Brit Maiden Voyage	15.00
	427	Health Congress Blackpool	1.00
	A429	SS Reina del Mar M Voyage	30.00
	429	Phil Congress Brighton	1.00
	A430	Showgrounds Helston	*
	433	Fish Docks Grimsby	2.00
	435	Pier Pavilion Llandudno	20.00

1957

R	436	Gifts & Fancy Goods	1.50
	439	Stampex	1.00
	A440	Empr of England Maiden V	20.00
	A441	Mayflower II	2.00
	447	Festival of Women Wembley	5.00
	452	Scout Jamboree slogan (FDC of whole set 25.00)	3.00
	453-454A	4 Sutt Coldf skeletons (difficult to find good impressions)	25.00
	455	Sutton Coldf 'J' parcel	50.00
	456	46th Parliamentary **12/21** (FDC £100, airletter 30.00)	3.00

1958

	462	RHAS Ayr	5.00
	463	Wimbledon Tennis timed	1.50
	464	Empire Games Village m/c (FDC of complete set 85.00)	3.00
	465	Empire Games d/c	5.00
	466	ditto s/c (FDC of complete set 465/66 £225/£275)	6.00
	467	Empire Games packet h/s	50.00
	468	hooded registered h/s	40.00
	469	parcel handstamp	50.00

1959

	A470	Alloway d/c	2.00
	477	Olympex Brighton	1.00

1960

	479	Seaborne Mail SE10	1.00
	481	Rotary Douglas	60.00
	483	Int Stamp Exhib slogan	1.00
	484	ditto large h/s (if clear!) (8.00 if clear on reg letter + GLO set)	2.00
	485	Phil Congress slogan	1.00
	A490	Arlanza Maiden Voyage	80.00

1961

	A492	Empr of Canada Maiden Vyge	10.00
	499	Int Scout Training Reunion	0.80
	500	Midland Stampex Birmingham	0.50

1962

R	511	Royal Highl Show Ingliston	1.00
	514-5	Rhyl-Wallasey Hovercraft (more on flown covers)	2.00
	517/A	Pier Pavilion Llandudno	20.00

237

Special Event Postmarks

From about 1963 the nature of special event postmarks changed considerably. Most since that date have been used to produce philatelic souvenirs rather than to fulfil a postal need at a given location/exhibition/event. Although attractive postmarks, items are not usually stamped at the event and often not on the date concerned. In 1990 seven "Special handstamp centres" were established and since then most covers for stamping have been sent to these locations. In many cases there is now no posting box at the actual events. Many postmarks are associated with stamp issue days as the popularity of First Day Covers has increased.

From 1972 Swiss cancelling machines were used, with a grey but even postmark, then from 1992 "PAD machines" installed to give a black high-definition postmark.

Modern Special Event postmarks are on their own worth little - a standard 0.50 on a small envelope with single stamp; most however can be obtained on a special postcard, souvenir cover or first day cover. Amongst the selection of modern postmarks shown below, valuations of those marked "C" are for postmarks with relevant postcard or souvenir cover etc. For First Day Covers (marked "F") this is with complete set of the appropriate stamp issue and on relevant envelope. There are several specialist publications which will help the collector and give fuller guidance: see Bibliography for details.

Further reading
"*Regus Guide to British Regional Cards and Covers*" (5th edition 1984)
"*Collect Post Office Cards*" by Benham (6th edition 1987)

1963
F	525	Dover Packet Service	25.00
	528	Brownsea Island	1.00

1964
F	542	Shakespeare's 400th Anniv	25.00
	546	Middlesex Philat Socs W3 (first self-inking handstamp)	1.00
F	559-562	S & N Queensferry (but more for the plastic dies)	20.00

1965
	574	Gibbons Centenary	1.00
	585	Wilts Convention Chippenham (first 3-coloured postmark)	2.00
	590	Lincs Show Lincoln skel'n	30.00
	592	Talyllyn Centenary	1.00

1966
	637	Seaspeed Hovercraft Cowes	1.00
C	640-664	World Cup matches (each) (pair of two diff Final h/s 6.00)	2.50
C	665	1d Post repeat of 18	1.50
F	682	Hastings Battlefield	7.00
	694	Stamp Exhib BFPS 1000	1.00

12/22

1967
	717	Sir Francis Chichester Plym	1.00
R	721	Dulwich Millennium	0.50
R	730	BFPS 1000 (Aldershot)	0.50
	A765	Queen Mary (last voyage)	1.50
	A770	Queen Mary (last cruise)	1.50
	A774	Queen Mary slogan	0.50

1968
	820	Rathfriland Civic Week	0.50
C	838	TUC Manchester (4d only)	1.50
	859	Berlin Air lift BFPO 45	0.50
	862	Portsmouth Alec Rose	0.50
	866	RAF Wildenrath Open Day	0.50
	871	Open Golf Final Day	0.50
	891	Philatex Woburn	0.50
	909	Ulster Tattoo BFPS 1072	0.50
F	949	HMS Hermes BFPS 1074 **12/22**	£100

1969
	956	Closure Waverley Route	0.50
F	958	Cutty Sark SE10	25.00
C	969	Investiture Caernarvon (used only on 5/- Caernarvon stamps but 12.00 for 1 March as h/s not announced)	2.00
	973	(League Cup) Swindon	0.50
	1042	Cactus & Succulent Whit Bay	0.50
	A1115	Darlington Show **12/23**	1.50
C	1206	Christm Marshf'd Chippenham	2.50

1970
	1292	(Harbour opening) P Talbot	0.50
	1308	Somerset Jamboree	0.50
	1336	Mayflower Boston	0.50
F	1481	Philympia Opening Day	3.00

Special Event Postmarks

1971
C	1559	R'l Green Jackets BFPS1221	1.00
C	1642	Air Day RAF Henlow BFPS1166	1.00

1972
F	1863	Tutankhamun Exhibition	25.00
	1882	Vaughan Will'ms Down Ampney	0.50
C	2018	John Knox Edinburgh	2.00

1973
F	2139	Westonbirt Arboretum **12/24**	9.00
	2189	David Livingstone Blantyre	0.50
R	2270	Royal Show Stoneleigh s/c	1.50
C	2275	Douglas IOM **12/25** (souvenir cover, IOM regional stamps)	1.50

1974
C	2477	Duddon Valley Post Bus (on postcard with cachet etc)	30.00
	2538	Electric Scots Glasgow	0.50
	2625	Scout Camp Blair Atholl	0.50
	2728	Churchill Centen Woodstock	0.50

1975
F	2777	Chester Heritage City	15.00
	2888	Stephenson Birthplace Wylam	0.50
C	2952	Easy View Sorting Redhill	2.50

1976
C	2973	Concorde 1st scheduled flt	1.50
	3046	Opening Bridge Conwy	0.50

1977
C	3187	MLO Open Day Doncaster	20.00
	3228	Queens Silver Jub Glasgow	0.50
	3418	Liverpool into Europe	0.50

1978
F	3466	Hampton Court Tennis	5.00
C	3522	Barnes Cross Postcard	2.00
	3667	RNLI Stand Boat Show So'ton	0.50

1979
C	3741	Scotland v Wales rugby	2.50
	A3911	Kent County Show Maidstone	40.00

1980
C	4130	To London 1980 by ship	2.00
	4382	Austral v Engl cricket Birm	0.50
C	4460	Welsh rugby centen Cardiff	1.50

1981
C	4564	Victoria Cross Exhib (red)	7.00
F	4838	Royal Wedding Canterbury	5.00

1982
F	5058	Darwin Man of Vision SW7	2.50
	5079	Opening Barbican Centre	0.50
C	5270	S Atlantic Fund Phil Bureau	2.50
C	5291	Blackpool Tram Post Office (postcard with "posted on .." cachet)	2.00

1983
C	5592	Nat Stamp Day	0.50
C	5846	SWDO Nine Elms Opening	1.50

1984
C	5878	Manchester (Kelloggs)	1.00
C	5886	Oxfordshire PO cards (set)	4.00
C	6018	Smallest TPO Garden Fest	1.50
	6208	Last day of the ½p	0.50

1985
	6390	Life-boat Dedic'n Ramsgate	0.50
	6481	Elvis Presley 50th E1	0.50

1986
C	6606	Golf Show Barbican	1.50
C	6702	York PO postcard	0.50
C	6789	Hemel Hempstead PO opening	6.00

1987
	6964	World Snooker Sheffield	0.50
C	6998	Exhib Card 1 + Capex cachet	5.00
C	7063	Victorian Britain Bakewell	6.00

1988
C	7120	TPO Anniv Nat Post Museum (on postcard 88/1,2 or 3)	2.00
F	7335	Edward Lear Knowsley	6.00

1989
C	7444	Stamp Printing Walsall (on £1 stamp book, PO envelope)	5.00
F	7540	Pontcysyllte Aqueduct	5.00
C	7645	Roadside Pillar Box (red)	1.50

1990
F	7649	150th Ann 1d Post London EC (full set definitive stamps)	6.00
F	7747	Opening Day Stamp World N22	6.00
	7868	Benson & Hedges Cricket NW8	0.50

1991
C	8031	Edwardian Exhib EC(set of 4)	3.00
F	8079	Greetings Clowne Derbyshire	6.00
C	8262	Rugby World Cup Twickenham (single stamp, PO souvenir cover)	1.00

1992
	8421	Garden Festival parcel h/s	3.00
C	8433	'People in post' cards(set)	3.00
F	8601	Autumn Stampex	3.00

1993
F	8661	Wildfowl Caerlaverock	5.00
F	8712	£10 Britannia Porth	20.00
C	8827	Postbus 25 years Scotland	1.50
C	8856	Goodwin Sands CT16 1GS	2.00

1994
F	9056	Orlando Marmalade Cat W1	5.00
C	9099	RNLI Boathouse Tobermory	2.00
F	9248	Greg Norman champ Turnberry	5.00
C	9369	Final Despatch Aylesbury	3.00

1995
F	9450	Readers Digest coil Swindon	3.00
C	9478	Edinburgh (magnifying glass)	1.00
F	9503	Glasgow School of Art (first day of aerogramme)	2.50

1996
C	9870	K Edward VIII Sandringham	2.50
F	9913	Cartoon Art Trust London	7.00
C	10067	RHS Chelsea Flower Show	2.50
	10291	Duxford Air Show Duxford	0.50

1997
F	10396	Blooms of Bressingham Norfolk	4.00
C	10484	Railnet Pullman Willesden	6.00
	10516	Man United in Europe	0.50
F	10702	Haroldswick Post Office Shetland	4.00

1998
	10909	Brit Rail 50th Anniv Euston	0.50
F	10964	Kensington (Palace) (Diana)	6.00
F	11045	Defeinitive Portman Sq W1	20.00
F	11065	The Pharos Dover	6.00

Special Event Postmarks

1999
F	11704	Settlers Tale Nile Road E13	7.50
F	11802	Berlin Airlift (label) Br Norton	20.00
C	11831	RHS (Chelsea Flower Show)	2.50
	12108	Centenary Bangor Parish Bells	0.50

2000
C	12329	Dome Greenwich	5.00
F	12353	Millennium Defin Stonehenge	5.00
	12386	Battle of Spion Kop SW1	0.50
C	12829	Public Libraries (coin cover)	6.00

2001
F	13086	Smiles Place SE13	8.00
C	13194	Scottish Congress Falkirk	2.50
F	13237	Submarines (self adhes) Chatham	12.50
C	13272	Festival of Brit 50th Anniv SE1	3.50

2002
F	13606	"Just So" Burwash (silver pmk)	8.00
F	13823	Comet Airliners Hatfield	8.00
C	13896	Philatelic Census (£5 stamp) EC1	4.00
C	13907	Biggin Hill Air Fair BFPS 2680	3.50

2003
F	14200	Hawk & Owl NW1 (silver)	8.00
	14259	Lover Salisbury	0.60
F	14654	Brit Museum Gt Russell St	8.00

2004
F	14860	British Journey Ballymena	8.50
F	15104	Woodland Animals Badger	8.50
F	15144	Holyrood Edinburgh	6.00

2005
F	15308	Charlotte Bronte Museum Haworth	7.50
C	15315	St. Davids Day (coin cover)	9.00
C	15465	Methodist Conference Torquay	2.50

2006
F	15787	Brunel Paddington Station	8.50
F	15867	HM Queen 80th Crathie Ballater	7.50
	15953	Cornish Riviera Cent'y Penzance	1.00

2007
F	16167	Beatles Abbey Rd NW8	9.00
	16292	N of Ireland Philatelic Belfast	1.00
F	16403	Grand Prix Silverstone	7.50
F	16459	Scouts Scout Way NW7	8.00

2008
F	16634	Ian Fleming Ebury St SW1	8.00
	16736	Airbus A380 Heathrow Middx	1.00
F	16774	St. Pauls Cathedral EC1 (error)	9.00

2009
F	17019	Design (Concorde) Filton Bristol	9.00
F	17227	Postboxes Birmingham	7.50
	17352	Flying Scotsman Leeds	1.00

2010
F	17374	Classic Album Covers Glastonbury	7.50
C	17387	Romans left Britain Dover	3.00

2011
F	17722	Genius of Gerry Anderson Pinewood (Iver)	8.50
F	17823	Royal Wedding Westminster London SW1	8.50

2012
F	18053	Roald Dahl Museum Gt Missenden	8.00
C	18056	Rowing Henley-on-T (Olympic 50p coin cover)	9.50

Exhibition sites

Not inscribed for particular events or exhibitions, these marks were usually used only for the duration of such events. Most Crystal Palace marks are extremely scarce. Full details in Pearson, as for special event postmarks.

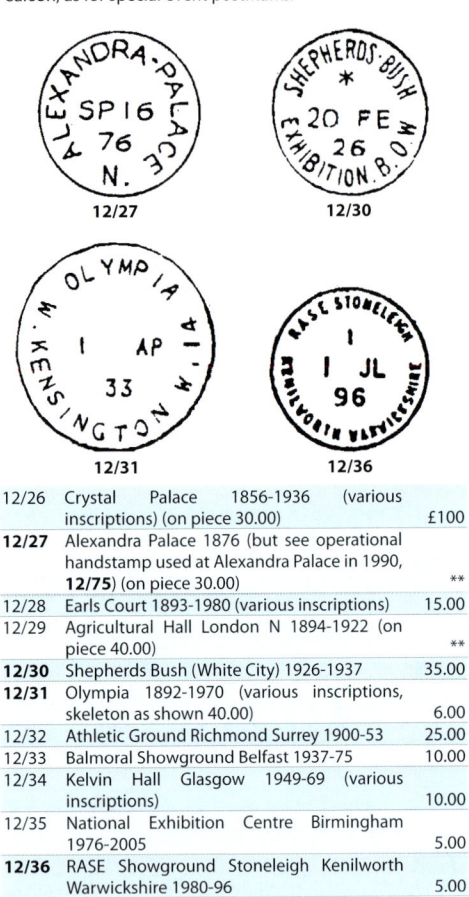

12/27

12/30

12/31

12/36

12/26	Crystal Palace 1856-1936 (various inscriptions) (on piece 30.00)	£100
12/27	Alexandra Palace 1876 (but see operational handstamp used at Alexandra Palace in 1990, **12/75**) (on piece 30.00)	**
12/28	Earls Court 1893-1980 (various inscriptions)	15.00
12/29	Agricultural Hall London N 1894-1922 (on piece 40.00)	**
12/30	Shepherds Bush (White City) 1926-1937	35.00
12/31	Olympia 1892-1970 (various inscriptions, skeleton as shown 40.00)	6.00
12/32	Athletic Ground Richmond Surrey 1900-53	25.00
12/33	Balmoral Showground Belfast 1937-75	10.00
12/34	Kelvin Hall Glasgow 1949-69 (various inscriptions)	10.00
12/35	National Exhibition Centre Birmingham 1976-2005	5.00
12/36	RASE Showground Stoneleigh Kenilworth Warwickshire 1980-96	5.00

"First Day of Issue" postmarks

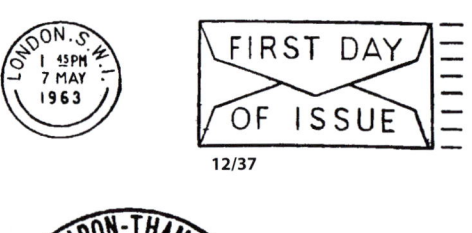

12/37

12/40

12/42

Special Event Postmarks

Introduced in 1963, these are used on stamp issue days but ONLY ON THE NEW STAMPS. The other major feature is that these are Post Office-provided postmarks, unlike most sponsored special event handstamps. However, on stamp issue days all are available for the collector, including "philatelic handstamps" featured in the next section but one. Special posting boxes were provided at initially 30 offices but this was expanded to about 210 offices, later reduced to about 200 offices. Most of these ended in 1998. In addition, pictorial "first day" marks are provided by the Philatelic Bureau (at Edinburgh since 1966) and at (usually) one town or city relevant to the stamp issue. From 1999 the postmark of the "relevant office" was applied to FDCs wherever in the country they were posted. Like modern special event marks, valuations depend largely on the envelope used, the stamps affixed and how the address is written (hand written addresses should be discounted). Valuations shown below are basic prices for clean plain covers with ONE stamp only. For further remarks concerning valuations of FDCs see Introduction.

Technical developments enabled the Philatelic Bureau postmarks and those of the "special offices" to be applied by a combination of "Swiss cancelling machines" (used from 1972), "high speed machine" (from 1985) and "PAD cancellers" (from 1992), though in most cases handstamps have been used as well. Use of these machines is not indicated in the list that follows, which shows the main types (prices are for covers with single stamp).

Further reading :
"Twenty Years of First Day Postmarks" by Brian Pask & Colin G Peachey

12/37	Machine slogan 1963 and CI/IOM 2½d issue 8 June 1964	1.50
12/38	same but later on Medical Mailing or charity mailings (to 1985)	0.50
12/39	same but Regional issue 7 February 1966	0.50
12/39A	same but Bridges issue 29 Apr 1968 at Aberfeldy (also at Bridge and Menai Bridge – bilingual slogan – but these are shown in "towns" list in chap 10)	1.00
12/40	Large handstamp (39mm), 1964-67 (all handstamps are self-inking)	0.80
12/41	Small handstamp (21mm), 14 October 1966 only	1.00
12/42	Medium handstamp (26mm), 1967-91	0.50
12/43	same but in red 1989-90	1.00
12/44	"Posting delayed by strike" cachet Feb 1971 (applied March 1971) ..	1.00
12/45	Philatelic Bureau handstamps (or Swiss machine etc) from 1972	1.00
12/46	Pictorial h/s at PO's selected relevant town for each stamp issue .	1.00
12/47	Domesday bilingual handstamp 17 June 1986	1.00
12/48	New style handstamp without rim from 23 April 1991	1.00
12/49	similar (29mm) but revised by addition of rim from 11 June 1991	1.00
12/50	same but smaller (26mm, with rim) from 10 September 1991	1.00
12/51	same but in green for "green" stamp issue 15 September 1992	1.00
12/52	Other semi-permanent pictorial handstamps	0.50

Special Occasions

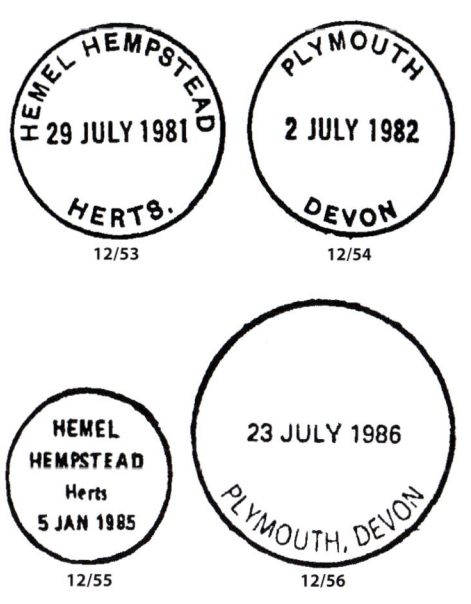

On the four occasions listed below the Post Office offered facilities for purchase of special envelopes and for posting them at the 200-or-so offices countrywide, similar to "first days" but the dates were NOT stamp issue days. Thus, for example, for the wedding of Prince Charles and Lady Diana Spencer the stamps were issued on 22 July 1981 and the "Wedding Day" postmarks were provided on 29 July. Inscriptions do NOT show the events, and datestamps were "fixed date" (prices are for covers with single stamp):

12/53	Royal Wedding 1981 (14p stamp on souvenir cover or PHQ card)	1.50

Special Event Postmarks

12/54	South Atlantic Fund 1982 (15½p Maritime stamp on souvenir cover)	1.50
12/55	Africa Appeal 1985 (31p Xmas stamp on souvenir cover)	1.50
12/56	Royal Wedding 1986 (12p stamp on souvenir cover or PHQ card)	1.50

Philatelic handstamps

These are semi-permanent handstamps which are available for all dates, not just stamp issue dates. Locations are a combination of tourist resorts (hence the alternative term "tourist handstamps") and philatelic counters. All are valued at 0.60 on small envelope with one stamp, but 1.50 for 14 Aug 1972, the (unannounced) first day of Trafalgar Square (shown here) and Chief Office London, or 6.00 each on souvenir cover. Four examples are illustrated.

12/57

12/58

12/59

12/60

12/61 "Green" issue Val. 8.00

12/62 Xmas issue Val. 10.00

12/63 QEII Accession Val. £125

12/64 Sport issue Val. 8.00

12/65 Dogs issue Val. 18.00

12/66 Flowers issue Val. 35.00

Mobile Post Offices

These were introduced in 1936, initially one vehicle but later three, with a full programme of events attended from May-October each year (except 1940-46). We list the events intended for 1936-9 (two MPOs only at this stage) but some may have been cancelled. Datestamps are generally inscribed "MPO" or "MPO 1" for number 1, "MPO 2" and "MPO 3" and lettered A to F in each case. Usually used on registered mail only, valuations are for registered covers; receipts are often offered alone and these are valued at approx one third of the registered cover. Pressure on costs of attending events forced the programme to be cut back in the 1980s. MPO postmarks were last used in 1988, though the vehicles have occasionally been used since.

During the war arrangements were made for temporary post offices to be set up in the event of bomb damage, though not using the same MPO vehicles. A series of 3-digit MPO numbered datestamps were issued, but few were used.

There follows a listing of the 1936-39 events visited by Mobile Post Offices, then a selection of further events from 1947 to 1988.

Additional reading :
"A Priced Catalogue of British Exhibitions 1840-1940" by W G Stitt Dibden
"Mobile Post Offices 1936-1986" article by Cyril Parsons in "Cross Post" Vol 1 No.3 Autumn 1986

Relevant Operational handstamps on FDCs

Although Royal Mail has attempted to satisfy FDC collectors' requirements by providing first day posting facilities (usually at one town relevant to each stamp issue), collectors have an interest in ALL relevant postmarks. FDCs are consequently posted, usually by registered post, and with a full set of stamps, at post offices with names relevant to a specific stamp issue. Obviously such covers have to be addressed, but the other FDC requirements described earlier apply here in order to attract the relevant values. We show here a few examples. A further allied topic is FDCs with relevant SLOGAN postmarks.

Special Event Postmarks

12/67 Golf Event Little Ashton

12/68

12/69

12/71 Horse How Derby

12/67	MPO handstamp on pre-war registered cover (but non-registered cover from initial publicity event on 30 Sep 1936 £150, registered covers from the other 1936 events £100)	40.00
12/68	Edinburgh skeleton 31 Aug 1937 (one-day publicity event)	£100
12/69	Wartime use, London Aug 1941 rubber one-day handstamp	£180
12/70	MPO 121 and similar numbering, wartime use on registered cover	£120
12/71	Post-war events (1.50 for certificate or receipt)	6.00

Notes: AS = Agricultural Show
Also note dates may include day before the event, when MPO arrived.

MPO1- 1936

6-8 Oct	Fruit Show Marden Kent
18-20 Nov	Races Derby
26-28 Nov	Races Manchester
21-22 Dec	Races Derby

1937

18-19 Jan	Races Derby
8-9 Feb	Races Nottingham
15-16 Feb	Races Derby
22-23 Mar	Races Nottingham
31 Mar-1 Apr	Races Leicester
7-9 Apr	Golf Little Aston
20-22 Apr	Races Epsom
28-29 Apr	AS Ayr
10 May	Races Derby
14-15 May	AS Newark
18-19 May	AS Banbury
26-29 May	Bath AS Trowbridge
1-4 Jun	Races Epsom
10-12 Jun	Horse Show Richmond
15-18 Jun	Races Ascot
23-24 Jun	AS Hatfield
25-26 Jun	Cricket Eton
30 Jun- 3 Jul	Henley Regatta
5-6 Jul	Races Nottingham
12-16 Jul	Yorkshire AS York
19-20 Jul	Races Leicester
22 Jul	AS Ampthill
24-27 Jul	Cricket Manchester
29 Jul-2 Aug	Lancs AS Manchester
5 Aug	AS Bakewell
9-10 Aug	Races Nottingham
18-19 Aug	Music&Floral Shrewsbury
27-28 Aug	Highland Games Dunoon
31 Aug	on exhib at Edinburgh (2 hours only)
3-4 Sep	Races Manchester
8-10 Sep	AS Yeovil
14-15 Sep	AS Altrincham
20-21 Sep	Races Leicester
24 Sep-1 Oct	Golf Wadebridge
5-7 Oct	Fruit Show Marden
8-9 Nov	Races Leicester
17-19 Nov	Races Derby
25-27 Nov	Races Manchester
13-14 Dec	Races Nottingham

1938

10-11 Jan	Races Leicester
17-18 Jan	Races Derby
31 Jan-1 Feb	Races Leicester
9-10 Feb	Races Derby
14-15 Feb	Races Nottingham
21-22 Feb	Races Derby
21-23 Mar	Races Lincoln
30-31 Mar	Races Leicester
2 Apr	Hunt Race Meeting Bolton
11-12 Apr	Races Nottingham
19-21 Apr	Races Epsom
27-28 Apr	Cattle Show Ayr
3-4 May	Races Kelso
9 May	Races Derby
13-14 May	AS Newark
18-19 May	AS Wallingford
25-28 May	Bath AS Plymouth
31 May-3 Jun	Races Epsom
9-11 Jun	Horse Show Richmond
14-17 Jun	Races Ascot
22-23 Jun	AS Hatfield
29 Jun-2 Jul	Henley Regatta
5 Jul	Dog Show Richmond
12-16 Jul	Yorks AS Doncaster
19-20 Jul	AS Tunbridge Wells
28-31 Jul	Lancs AS Liverpool
4 Aug	AS Bakewell
8-9 Aug	Races Nottingham
13 Aug	AS Ulverston
17-18 Aug	Floral Fete Shrewsb
25 Aug	AS Sandy
30 Aug-1 Sep	Races Derby
7-8 Sep	AS Yeovil
15 Sep	AS Thame
19-20 Sep	Races Leicester
24 Sep	Races Newark
28 Sep	AS Frome
3-4 Oct	Races Nottingham
22-24 Oct	ditto
7-8 Nov	Races Leicester
16-17 Nov	Races Derby
24-26 Nov	Races Manchester
5-6 Dec	Races Leicester
12-13 Dec	Races Nottingham

1939

9-10 Jan	Races Leicester
16-17 Jan	Races Derby
30-31 Jan	Races Leicester
8-9 Feb	Races Derby
13-14 Feb	Races Nottingham
20-21 Feb	Races Derby
18 Mar	Races Newark
29-30 Mar	Races Leicester
3-4 Apr	Races Nottingham
8 Apr	Races Stockton-on-Tees
15 Apr	Steeplechases, Wrexham
8-10 Jun	R Horse Sh Richmond

243

Special Event Postmarks

	19-24 Jun	Highland Show Edinb
	29 Jun-1 Jul	Milty Displ Aldershot
	5-8 Jul	Henley Regatta
	15-25 Jul	World Scout Moot Crieff
	2-5 Aug	Lanes AS Lancaster
	10 Aug	AS Bakewell
	16-17 Aug	Music&Floral Shrewsbury
	30 Aug	AS Shaftesbury

MP02 - 1938

	16-18 Apr	Races Manchester
	21-30 Apr	Golf Moortown Leeds
	7 May	Races Stratford-upon-Av
	13-20 May	Golf Burnham on Sea
	25-26 May	AS Shrewsbury
	2-3 Jun	Suffolk AS Bury St Ed
	7-9 Jun	AS Helston
	15-16 Jun	AS Midhurst
	21-24 Jun	R Highland AS Dumfries
	28-30 Jun	AS Peterborough
	4-5 Jul	Races Nottingham
	8-12 Jul	Cricket Test Manchester
	18-19 Jul	Races Leicester
	21 Jul	Beds AS Ampthill
	6 Aug	AS Perth
	20 Aug	Highland Gathering Crieff
	26-27 Aug	Cowal Games Dunoon
	2-3 Sep	AS Chester
	6-10 Sep	Races Doncaster
	20-21 Sep	AS Altrincham
	28-29 Sep	Hunt Race Meeting Scone
	4-7 Oct	Horse Sale Lanark
	22 Oct	Races Stockton-on-Tees

1939

	29-31 Mar	D Mail Golf Bournemouth
	8 Apr	Races Newark
	15 Apr	Hunt Races Meeting Bolton
	18-20 Apr	Races Epsom
	9-10 Jun	AS Leicester
	13-16 Jun	Races Ascot
	21-22 Jun	AS Hatfield
	24 Jun	Regatta Marlow
	26 Jun-8 Jul	Tennis Wimbledon
	11-15 Jul	Yorks AS Halifax
	17-18 Jul	Races Leicester
	20 Jul	Beds AS Ampthill
	26-27 Jul	R Welsh AS Caernarvon
	7 Aug	AS Uxbridge
	21-26 Aug	Boys Golf Carnoustie
	4 Nov	Races Stockton-on-Tees

Note: In the list that follows a selection of MPO events are shown. The MPO number is shown in brackets (initially MPO1 showed no number but later '1') while handstamps are lettered A to F. Also single dates are shown, not the whole period for each event.

1947
(2)	27 May	Cheltenham Show

1948
(1)	3 July	Henley Regatta

1949
(2)	4 June	Bath and West Show, Bristol

1950
(2)	26 July	Royal Welsh Show, Rhyl

1951
(2)	4 Sept	Mid-Somerset Ag Show, Shepton Mallet

1952
(1)	12 June	Richmond Horse Show

1954
(1)	23 June	Royal Counties Show, Salisbury
(2)	6 July	Internat Eisteddfod, Llangollen

1955
(2)	6 May	Internat Trophy Race, Silverstone
(3)	27 July	Horse Show, Roehampton

1956
(1)	23 Aug	Southport Flower Show
(1)	12 Sept	Building Construction Exhibition, Newcastle-on-Tyne

1957
(3)	18 June	Lincs Ag Show, Grimsby
(3)	3 Sept	Air Show, Farnborough

1958
(3)	26 Mar	Horse Show, Derby **12/71**
(1)	13 May	Oxfordshire Show, Oxford

1959
(3)	8 May	Newark nad Notts Ag Show
(2)	15 July	Kent Country Show, Maidstone
(3)	1 Sept	Mid-Somerset Ag Show, Shepton Mallet

1960
(2)	6 May	Newark and Notts Ag Show
(2)	8 June	Royal Cornwall Show, Wadebridge

1961
(3)	21 June	Royal Counties Show, Windsor

1962
(1)	4 May	Newark and Notts Ag Show
(3)	6 Aug	Nat Eisteddfod Llanelly

1964
(2)	27 May	Staffs County Show, Stafford
(3)	29 May	Cambs and Ely Show, Ely
(1)	15 Aug	Darlington Show

1965
(2)	2 June	Bath and West Show, Shepton Mallet
(3)	2 June	Suffolk Show, Ipswich
(3)	26 Aug	Monmouthshire Show
(2)	18 Sept	Biggin Hill Air Show

1966
(3)	20 June	Lawn Tennis Championships, Wimbledon
(2)	25 June	Royal Counties Show, Basingstoke
(3)	30 Sept	Kettering Trade Fair
(3)	15 Oct	1066-1966 Celebrations Battle

1967
(2)	15 Mar	Cheltenham Gold Cup
(1)	21 Apr	Badminton Horse Trials
(2)	11 May	Windsor Horse Show
(2)	24 May	Staffordshire County Show, Stafford

1968
(3)	3 May	Oxfordshire Show, Oxford
(2)	23 July	Royal Welsh Show, Builth Wells
(1)	27 July	Northamptonshire Ag Show

1969
(3)	7 June	South of England Show, Ardingly
(1) and (2)	1 July	Prince of Wales Investiture, Caernarvon
(1)	4 Aug	Royal National Eisteddfod Flint

1970
(1)	1 May	Bath Canine Championship Show
(3)	8 May	Newark & Notts Show
(1)	12 Sept	Hampshire Agricultural Show Romsey

Special Event Postmarks

1971
(3)	23 Apr	Horse Trials Badminton
(3)	21 June	Lawn Tennis Championships, Wimbledon
(2)	23 June	Lincolnshire Ag Show

1972
(3)	29 May	Cider Festival, Hereford
(1)	8 June	South of England Show, Ardingly
(2)	20 Sept	Frome and District Ag Show

1973
(2)	16 May	Shropshire Show, Shrewsbury
(1)	4 July	Henley Regatta

1974
(3)	15 May	Shrops and W. Mids Ag Show
(1)	3 July	Internat Eisteddfod, Llangollen
(1)	23 Aug	Southport Flower Show

1975
(2)	26 June	Lawn Tennis Championships, Wimbledon
(3)	11 July	Open Golf, Carnoustie
(3)	28 Aug	Monmouthshire Show, Newport Gwent

1976
(2)	24 June	Lawn Tennis Championships, Wimbledon
(1)	8 July	Open Golf Royal Birkdale, Southport

1977
(3)	9 June	Royal Cornwall Show, Wadebridge
(2)	4 July	Lawn Tennis Championships, Wimbledon

1978
(2)	24 June	Aldershot Army Display
(1)	4 July	Lawn Tennis Championships, Wimbledon

1979
(2)	29 June	Lawn Tennis Championships, Wimbledon

1980
(2)	4 July	Lawn Tennis Championships, Wimbledon

1983
(3)	19 May	Devon County Show, Exeter
(3)	21 July	Royal Welsh Show, Builth Wells
(2)	1 Aug	Nat Eisteddfod, Bangor Gwynedd

1984
(1)	14 July	Kent County Show, Maidstone
(2)	7 Aug	Nat Eisteddfod, Lampeter

1985
(2)	21 July	Kent County Show, Maidstone

1986
(3)	21 July	Royal Welsh Show, Builth Wells

1987
(1)	12 June	Royal Cornwall Show, Wadebridge
(1)	22 June	Royal Highland Show, Ingliston
(2)	11 July	Internat Eisteddfod, Llangollen
(1)	16 July	Open Golf Muirfield Gullane (datestamp reads JU in error)

1988
(1)	18 July	Royal Welsh Show, Builth Wells
(1)	9 Sept	Farnborough International Air Show

Operational handstamps used at events

Operational datestamps are sometimes used at temporary post offices; these can be skeleton, s/c, d/c or rubber stamps. They have replaced MPO handstamps from 1989. A selection is shown here, including one of the "Wood Green" handstamps used at the Mobile Post Office outside "Stamp World 90" at Alexandra Palace. Valuations from 10.00 on registered covers.

12/72

12/73

12/74

12/75

12/76

12/72	White Rock Pav Royal Sanitary Congress (1953)	15.00
12/73	Open Golf Championship (1953)	£100
12/74	World Scout camp (1957)	50.00
12/75	"Stamp World 90" MPO outside Alexandra Palace on FDC	15.00
12/76	Chelsea Flower Show (1991) on souvenir cover	8.00

12/76A

In 2003 Event Office postmarks were introduced and used at a small number of events each year, at Royal Mail sales trailers, effectively the modern successor to Mobile Post Offices.

12/76A	Event Office SID postmark (with/without "Branch", valuation more on Special delivery cover, illustrated is postmark used at Gt Yorkshire Show 2004)	1.50

Seasonal Post Offices (ie summer only)

At one time about 23 offices were open for the summer season each year, largely Butlins Holiday Camps (which later either closed or changed their names). By 1996 about a dozen seasonal offices were still in operation but by the 2000s only Brean Camp remained.

Special Event Postmarks

12/77

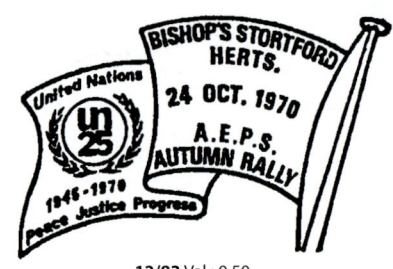

12/78

12/83 Val : 0.50

12/79

Birds/animals

12/84 Val : 0.50

12/77	Single/double circle on cert of posting (pre-1960 5.00) (multiply by 4 for value of registered cover)	2.50
12/78	As above but Douglas Hol Camp/IOM Hol Centre (on registered cover)	80.00
12/79	Parcel handstamp (pre-1960 18.00)	6.00

Thematic collecting

Many stamp/postmark collectors use both SPECIAL EVENT POSTMARKS and SLOGAN POSTMARKS to complement their collecting themes. These themes may be those represented by some of the chapters of this book - Royalty, Islands, Railways etc. Here are some others to show the collecting possibilities.

12/85 Val : 50.00 on reg cover

12/86 Val : 5.00 on FDC

Letter boxes

Music

12/87 Val : 1.00

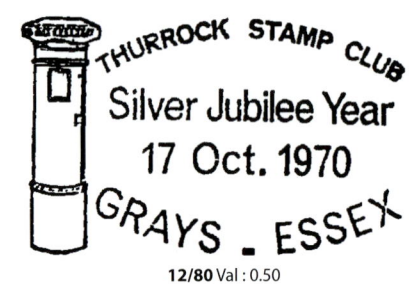

12/80 Val : 0.50

12/81 Val : 0.50 (used 1983 not 1982 as listed in Fifth Edition)

12/88 Val : 3.00 on FDC (Elgar's birthplace)

United Nations

Rugby Football

12/82 Val : 6.00

12/89 Val : 1.00

246

Special Event Postmarks

Christmas

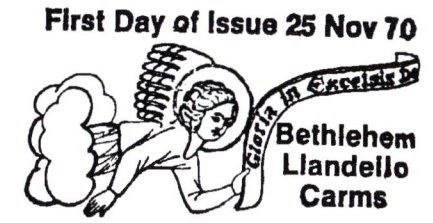

12/90 Val : 2.00 on souvenir cover

12/95 Val : 2.50 on FDC

Scouting

12/96 Val : 2.50 on compliments card (in red)

12/91 Val : 0.50

12/92 Val : 0.50

Police/crime

12/93 Val : 0.50

12/94 Val : 0.80

247

Bill Pipe
The Magpie

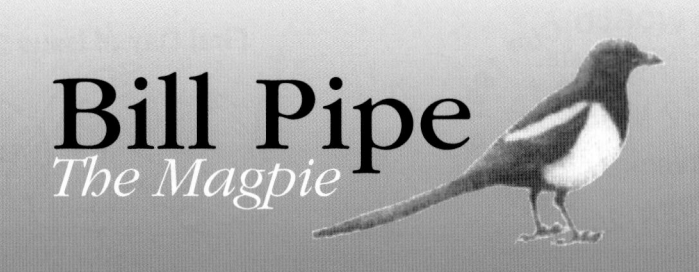

Buying and Selling Postal History and Postcards of the World

Monthly postal auctions of GB, Foreign & Commonwealth postal history-please contact me for a catalogue

7 Richard Close, Upton, Poole, Dorset BH16 5PY

Tel: 01202 623300
Fax: 01202 631149

email: magpiebillpipe@freeuk.com
web: www.magpiebillpipe.com

13 Railway Postmarks

Stations

"Postmarks of British & Irish Railway Stations 1840-1997" by Bill Pipe (see Bibliography) was published in 2004 by the Railway Philatelic Group and permission was granted for inclusion here of some of the data. The Editor is grateful to the RPG, and particularly to Grahame Blackman, Tony Goodbody & Clive Jones who have kindly helped with the careful revision that has been applied to all sections of the railway chapter in this edition.

Many station postmarks are difficult to find. Many are known used on one date only: some are not known at all and these we have deleted. Additional reports of new discoveries are always welcome.

- A Dated double arc
- B Numeral
- C Duplex
- D Squared circle
- E Double circle, Scottish double arc
- F Double circle
- G Single circle
- H Skeleton
- I Rubber handstamp
- S Self-inking handstamp

F 13/6

G 13/7

H 13/8

I 13/9

A 13/1

B 13/2

C 13/3

D 13/4

E 13/5

Station	Type	Price
Aberdeen Station	F	6.00
Addlestone Station	G	15.00
Airth Road Station	E (547)	15.00
Airth Station	F	8.00
	I	20.00
Angmering Station	C (G73)	75.00
	G	3.00
	H	20.00
Annbank Station	F	7.00
	G	4.00
	I	20.00
Armadale Station	E (457)	8.00
Ashford St'n Kent	C (31)	15.00
	G	4.00
	Registered	10.00
	Postage Due	15.00
	Instructional	15.00
Ashford St'n Middlesex	F	3.00
	G	6.00
	H	20.00
Ash Vale Station	F	6.00
	G	3.00
	Parcel	4.00
Auchterless Station	E (561)	10.00
	F	5.00
	G	6.00
Aysgarth Station	D	22.00
	G	18.00
Balcombe Station	G	25.00
Balfron Station	F	4.00
	G	4.00
Balquhidder Station	E (cross)	5.00
Barnham Junction	G	12.00
Bath Station	F	10.00
	G	4.00

249

Railway Postmarks

Beaconsfield Station	G	15.00
Bedlington Station	F	4.00
	G	4.00
	S	4.00
	Krag machine	5.00
	Meter mark	30.00
	Parcel	5.00
Bekesbourne Station	I	25.00
Belvedere Station	F	3.00
	G	3.00
Berney Arms Station	F	20.00
	I	60.00
Berwick Station N'thumbld	A	25.00
	B (66)	50.00
	C (66)	50.00
	G	6.00
Berwick Station Sussex	F	4.00
	G	12.00
Bexhill Station	C (K27)	75.00
	F	10.00
	G	8.00
Bickley Station	B (B12)	£150
	C (B12)	80.00
	G	18.00
Birm'ham New St Stn	G	10.00
Birmingham Snow Hill Stn	G	10.00
Blair-Adam Station	E (652)	25.00
	H	20.00
Blantyre Station	Scots local	£150
Bletchley Station	A	50.00
	A (Single arc)	50.00
	B (025)	50.00
	C (025)	25.00
	F	12.00
	G	7.00
	Registered	35.00
	Parcel	10.00
Bogside Station	F	12.00
	I	20.00
Bootle Station (Cumberland)	C (K58)	£100
	F	4.00
	G	4.00
Bosham Station	F	4.00
	G	4.00
	H	20.00
	S	4.00
	Parcel	5.00
Bournemouth Central Stn	G	12.00
Bournemouth West Station	G	15.00
Station S.O Bournemouth	G	4.00
Bradford Station	"Late box" hooded circle	£400
Braidwood Station	G	8.00
	H	20.00
Brampton Junction	G	4.00
	I	20.00
Brayton Station	C (K38)	£200
	G	30.00
Bridlington Station	F	1.00
	G	5.00
	Krag machine	3.00
	do. with War bonds slogan	4.00
	Postage due	12.00
	Instructional	12.00
Brighton Station	G	20.00
	G "R.L" (returned letter)	20.00
	Registered	20.00
Bristol Station	A	60.00
	G	20.00
	Missent	£225
Broad Clyst Station	F	6.00
	H (rubber skeleton)	£175
Broad Clyst Station	I	20.00
Broadstairs Station	B (737)	£150
	C (737)	20.00
	F	1.00
	G	2.00
	H	18.00
	Registered	15.00
	Parcel	8.00
	Postage due	10.00
	Instructional	10.00
Buckhurst Hill Station	G	18.00
Byfleet Station	G	20.00
Caerwys Station	F	12.00
Cambridge Station	Parcel	10.00
Cannon Street Station	G	20.00
Carlton Station	G	4.00
Carron Station	G	18.00
	Parcel	10.00
Carstairs Junction	B (70)	£100
	E (70)	10.00
	F	5.00
	G	5.00
	H	20.00
Castle Cary Station (Scotland)	G	4.00
Castle Eden Station	A (undated)	75.00
	A (single arc)	30.00
	B (737)	40.00
	B (D70)	75.00
	C (D70)	50.00
	G	8.00
Charing Cross Station	G	12.00
Chester Station (R.O = Railway Office)		
	C (180)	50.00
	D	3.00
	G	3.00
	G (P.P = Parcel Post)	30.00
	Railway Station Straight line	£750
	Registered	15.00
	Parcel	8.00
	Postage due	10.00
	Instructional	10.00
Chichester Station	C (190)	12.00
	D	5.00
	F	3.00
	G	4.00
	Parcel	10.00
	Postage due	10.00
Chislehurst Station	C (D05)	50.00
	G	6.00
	Parcel	15.00
Chollerton Station	I	40.00
Clapham Junction	G	20.00
Clapham Station Lancaster	I	15.00
Craigellachie Station	C (86)	£125
	E (86)	40.00
	G	10.00
Crewe Station	A	40.00
	B (047)	£100
	C (047)	20.00
	D	3.00
	F	2.00
	G	2.00
	G (P.O = Parcels Office)	20.00
	Parcel	8.00
	Postage due	10.00
	Instructional	10.00
	Missent	£300
Crowthorne Station	G	3.00
	S	4.00
	Parcel	5.00
Croy Station	F	8.00
	I	20.00

Railway Postmarks

Station	Mark	Price
Cumbernauld Station	F	5.00
	G	5.00
Custom House Station	G	20.00
Dalston Junction	G	20.00
Derby Station	G	12.00
	Missent	50.00
Dess Station	G	4.00
Douglas Station	G	£100
Dover Station	C (258)	6.00
	G	3.00
	G (P.P = Parcel Post)	20.00
	Registered	35.00
	Parcel	10.00
	Postage due	10.00
	Instructional	10.00
Drymen Station	F	3.00
	G	3.00
Eaglescliffe Junction	G	12.00
Eastbourne Station	G	20.00
East Grange Station	E (469)	25.00
Central Station Edinburgh	G	4.00
	Parcel	5.00
Effingham Junction	G	8.00
	Parcel	5.00
Euston Station	F	5.00
	G	5.00
	I (modern packet stamp)	8.00
	Parcel hooded circle	£300
	Registered	25.00
	Parcel (Euston Central)	5.00
Euston Station Irish Mail	G	£150
Euston Square Station	A (single & double arcs)	60.00
	B (964)	£125
	G	6.00
Exeter Station	A	£600
	G	£100
Farnboro Station	A (single arc)	40.00
	B (023)	40.00
	C (023)	10.00
	S/ways duplex (023) large	£125
	S/ways duplex (023) small	£125
	G	4.00
Farnborough Station	A	20.00
	D	30.00
	G	4.00
Fawley Station (Hereford)	G	4.00
	H	20.00
Fimber Station	G	8.00
	I	20.00
Fishguard Station	G	20.00
Flaxton Station	A (undated)	50.00
	Undated s/c	50.00
	G	5.00
	I	20.00
Folkestone Harbour Stn	G	20.00
Formby Station	G	20.00
Fort George Station	B (14)	60.00
	G	18.00
	H	25.00
	Parcel	10.00
Freshwater Station	C (H06)	10.00
	F	2.00
	G	3.00
	H	30.00
Gartmore Station	E (578)	20.00
Gartness Station	G	12.00
Gillingham Station (Kent)	S	20.00
Gloster Station	C (312)	15.00
	G	4.00
Gloucester Station	A	20.00
	B (312)	25.00
	C (312)	10.00
	E94	25.00
	D	15.00
	G	4.00
	H "traveller"	£250
	Parcel	10.00
Godstone Station	C (874)	£100
	G	20.00
Greenford Station	F	12.00
Gunnersbury Station	G	40.00
Hampstead Heath Station	G	6.00
	Parcel	10.00
Hamworthy Junction	G	5.00
Harperley Station	G	4.00
Harrogate Station	G	20.00
Harrow Station	B (909)	£250
	G	35.00
Haslemere Station (Hants)	G	40.00
Hastings Station	C (342)	8.00
	F	3.00
	G	3.00
	Registered	50.00
	Parcel	10.00
	Postage due	10.00
	Instructional	10.00
Heathfield Station	C (H54)	£100
	G	20.00
Henlow Station	F	5.00
Hereford Station	Registered	8.00
High Peak Junction	I	20.00
Holborn Viaduct Station	G	20.00
Holyhead Station	G	20.00
Holytown Station	G	25.00
Horley Station	C (H37)	70.00
Horsham Station	C (381)	10.00
	G	5.00
	Parcel	10.00
	Postage due	20.00
Hull Station	G	20.00
Ilkeston Junction	G	12.00
Inverness Station	G	12.00
Ipswich Station	G	20.00
Kensington Station	G	20.00
Killearn Station	G	6.00
Kings Cross Station	G	15.00
	H	50.00
Kippen Station	E (653)	10.00
	F	5.00
Kirby Station Liverpool	G	4.00
Kiveton Park Station	F	8.00
	G	8.00
Knapton Station	G	6.00
	I	20.00
Knebworth Station	F	12.00
	G	3.00
	H	20.00
Knowle Station	G	20.00
Laindon Station	F	10.00
	F (Error-Liandon)	25.00
	G	5.00
	H	20.00
Lancing Station	G	25.00
Langwith Junction	F	5.00
Leeds Station	F	20.00
	"Late box" hooded circle	£350
Central Station Leith	G	5.00
	Parcel	5.00
Lewes Station	C (451)	15.00
	D	8.00
	F	4.00
	G	6.00
	Parcel	10.00

251

Railway Postmarks

Station	Mark	Price
	Postage due	10.00
Lintz Green Station	C (F77)	£150
	G	35.00
Liverpool Station (Late Fee)	F	10.00
	G	20.00
	"Late box" hooded circle	£300
Liverpool Lime St Stn (Late Box)	I	25.00
Liverpool St Station	G	4.00
	I (modern packet cancel)	10.00
	Parcel	10.00
Livingston Station	F	8.00
	G	5.00
	I	20.00
Llandudno Junction	F	2.00
	G	4.00
	H	20.00
	S	4.00
	Parcel	6.00
Lochearnhead Station	E (552)	15.00
Lockington Station	G	4.00
London Bridge Station	G	7.00
	H	40.00
	Parcel hooded circle	£300
Lowthorpe Station	G	4.00
Ludgate Hill Station	G	20.00
Maghull Station	G	4.00
Maidstone Station	C (493)	30.00
Manchester Station	G	20.00
	"Late box" hooded circle	£250
Manchester Exchange Stn	G	10.00
Manchester London Rd Stn	F (Late box)	20.00
	G	20.00
	I	30.00
Manchester Victoria Station	G	20.00
Martin Mill Station	F	4.00
	G	4.00
	I	15.00
	Rubber skeleton	£175
Marylebone Station	G	20.00
Meopham Station	F	20.00
	G	4.00
	H	20.00
	S	4.00
Micheldever Station	A	35.00
	B (22)	£100
	C (22)	10.00
	F	6.00
	G	4.00
	H	20.00
	Parcel	10.00
Middleton Junction	F	8.00
	G	4.00
Milford Junction	A	35.00
	A (single arc)	35.00
	B (015)	75.00
	G	25.00
Mintlaw Station	B (248)	75.00
	E (cross)	4.00
	F	3.00
	G	4.00
	H	20.00
	Parcel	10.00
	Meter mail	10.00
Misterton Station	F	5.00
Mitcham Junction	G	35.00
Moorgate St Station	G	20.00
Murton Station	G	5.00
Muthill Station	E (606)	40.00
Newcastle on Tyne Station	B (A16)	£300
	G	50.00
New Galloway Stat'n	E (475)	15.00
	H	40.00
New Killearn Station	G	15.00
New Southgate Station	F	15.00
Nigg Station	B (271)	75.00
	E (271)	10.00
	F	5.00
	G	8.00
Normanton Station	C (O48)	8.00
	D	£500
	G	4.00
	G (P.P = Parcel Post)	20.00
	Registered	10.00
Normanton/Station Office	C (O48)	20.00
Northampton Castle Station	G	12.00
Nottingham Station	G	20.00
Nottingham Victoria Station	G	20.00
Nunburnholme Station	G	5.00
Nunthorpe Station	F	5.00
	G	5.00
	I	20.00
	S	2.00
	Parcel	5.00
Old Steine Station	G	20.00
Orpington Station	F	3.00
	G	15.00
	H	20.00
	I	20.00
	Postage due	15.00
Orton Station	E (611)	5.00
	F	5.00
	G	5.00
	H	20.00
Oxford Station	G	20.00
Paddington Station	A	50.00
	B (049)	£200
	G	5.00
	I (Modern packet cancel)	10.00
	Parcel hooded circle	£350
	Registered	15.00
	Parcel	10.00
L&E T.P.O-P/S-(Paddington Station)	C	£400
Par Station	B (B04)	50.00
	D	20.00
	F	2.00
	G	2.00
	H	20.00
	Parcel	10.00
Park Station	G	3.00
	S	4.00
	Parcel	5.00
Parkeston Quay Station	G	18.00
Penybont Station	F	15.00
	G	4.00
Perranwell Station	D	8.00
	F	4.00
	G	3.00
	S	4.00
	Parcel	10.00
Peterborough North Stn	G	12.00
Pettsborough Wansford Station	Meter mail	4.00
Pettswood Station	G	15.00
Pevensey Station	F	20.00
	G	4.00
Pilmoor Station	G	10.00
Pluckley Station	F	4.00
	G	4.00
Plumpton Station	G	20.00
Plymouth Station	G	20.00
Plymouth Millbay Station	G	20.00
Plymouth North Rd Station	G	20.00
Polmont Station	E (489)	10.00
	G	5.00
Port of Monteith Station	B (288)	£150

Railway Postmarks

Station	Type	Price
	E (670)	10.00
	G	25.00
Preston Station	G	10.00
	G (P.P = Parcel Post)	50.00
	Parcel	10.00
Prudhoe Station	A (undated)	35.00
	F	5.00
	G	6.00
Queensbury Station	G	6.00
Q.S = Queen St Stn Glasgow	Scots local	£150
Rannoch Station	E (678)	10.00
	F	2.00
Rathen Station	G	8.00
Ratho Station	E (474)	10.00
	F	5.00
	G	5.00
	H	20.00
Redhill Station	C (A21)	12.00
	F	8.00
	G	8.00
	Registered	18.00
	Parcel	10.00
	Postage due	15.00
Robin Hoods Bay Station	F	4.00
	G	3.00
	H	40.00
Rugby Station	B (659)	£100
	C (659)	10.00
	D	5.00
	F	2.00
	G	2.00
	H	30.00
	Registered	12.00
	Parcel	10.00
	Postage due	10.00
	Instructional	10.00
St Budeaux Station	F	12.00
	G	4.00
St Leonards on Sea Station	C (342)	6.00
	F	2.00
	G	2.00
	Parcel	10.00
	Postage due	10.00
	Instructional	10.00
St Pancras Goods Station	G	20.00
	I (Modern packet cancel)	10.00
St Pauls Station	G	20.00
Scarborough Station	G	20.00
Semley Station	G	10.00
Sheffield Station	G	20.00
Sheffield Park Station	G	25.00
	I	15.00
Sherburn Station	undated s/c	50.00
Shoreditch Station	G	20.00
Shortlands Station	G	25.00
Shrewsbury Station	G	20.00
Sleights Station	F	4.00
	G	5.00
Southampton Station	G	20.00
	Missent	£300
South Kensington Station	F	10.00
	G	5.00
	H	30.00
	I (Modern packet cancel)	10.00
	S	4.00
	Registered	20.00
	Parcel	6.00
Stafford Station	B (730)	£150
	C (730)	15.00
	F	2.00
	G	2.00
	G (P.P = Parcel Post)	35.00
	Registered	12.00
	Parcel	8.00
	Instructional	10.00
Stoke Newington Station	G	20.00
Stoke upon Trent Station	A	40.00
then Stoke Station	A	40.00
Sunningdale Station	G	10.00
Sutton Station (Surrey)	G	35.00
Swanley Junction	D	5.00
	F	2.00
	G	3.00
	H	20.00
	Parcel	10.00
Swindon Station	A (undated)	75.00
	B (881)	£150
	C (881)	10.00
	F	35.00
	G	3.00
	G (P.P = Parcel Post)	35.00
	H	20.00
	Registered	12.00
	Parcel	10.00
	Postage due	10.00
	Instructional	10.00
Tarbolton Station	E (591)	15.00
Taunton Station	G	15.00
Thorntonhall Station	G	6.00
Thornton Heath Station	F	5.00
	G	5.00
Tilbury Station	G	10.00
Timperley Station	G	3.00
	S	4.00
	Parcel	5.00
Tonbridge Station	C (818)	10.00
(see also Tunbridge)	F	4.00
	G (P.P = Parcel Post)	35.00
	H	40.00
	Parcel	10.00
	Instructional	15.00
Tooting Junction	G	25.00
Trimdon Station	F	6.00
	G	6.00
	Parcel	5.00
Tunbridge Station	C (818)	10.00
	G	8.00
	Registered	18.00
	Parcel	10.00
Udny Station	E (cross)	4.00
	F	6.00
	G	6.00
Uphall Station	E (576)	15.00
	G	6.00
Victoria Station	G	5.00
	I (Modern packet cancel)	10.00
Virginia Water Station	F	20.00
Wadhurst Station	C (J82)	£125
	G	30.00
Warlingham Station	G	18.00
	H	£100
Warrington Station straight line	"Railway Station"	£750
Washington Station	B (B43)	£150
	C (B43)	40.00
	F	5.00
	G	8.00
	H	20.00
	S	4.00
	Instructional	12.00
	Meter mail	15.00
	Parcel	5.00
Waterloo Station	G	4.00
	H	25.00
	I	25.00
	Parcel hooded circle	£250

253

Railway Postmarks

		Registered	15.00
		Parcel	10.00
Watford Station		A (Undated)	£250
Waverley Station		G	20.00
Wellington College Station		B (J09)	£225
		D	6.00
		F	4.00
		G	4.00
		H	20.00
West Ealing Station		G	20.00
West Grinstead Station		I	20.00
West Station Hounslow		G	8.00
		Parcel	10.00
Weybridge Station		B (B87)	60.00
		C (B87)	30.00
		G	5.00
Whitmore Station		A (undated)	75.00
Wingate Station		C (H49)	35.00
		G	15.00
Woking Station		B (C66)	50.00
		C (C66)	25.00
		G	6.00
Wolverton Station		A undated	£400
Woodland Station		G	8.00
Worcester Station		G	20.00
Worthing Station		C (923)	12.00
		D	30.00
		G	6.00
		Registered	25.00
		Parcel	10.00
York Station		G	20.00
		Framed oval "R.W"	50.00

Irish

Athenry Station		Straight line	£1000
Ballycarry Station		F	20.00
		G	20.00
		I	50.00
Dunkettle St'n RSO		B (195)	£250
		G	75.00
Ennis Rly Stn Tel Off (Telegraph Office)			
		G	60.00
Galway		"Railway" straight line in red	£1000
Greenisland Station		G	50.00
Kildare Rail		G	80.00
Limerick Junction		C (514)	£225
		G	12.00
		H	£100
Maryborough Station		G	75.00
Portadown Station		G	6.00
Portarlington Rail		F	75.00
		G	50.00
Portarlington Station		G	75.00
Queenstown Railway		G	£100
Straffan Station		B (415)	£150
		G	20.00
		H	75.00
		I	60.00
Whitehead Station		I	90.00

Travelling Post Offices (TPO's)

A TPO is a specially adapted railway coach (or a "set" of them) in which mail is sorted during the course of a journey. The first one was introduced in 1838 on the Grand Junction Railway. There was much rationalisation of the network during the 1990s and eventually the TPO service was brought to a close on 9 January 2004, after 166 years.

Routes operating in England, Wales and Scotland

If a service runs both ways, it is listed under the first alphabetical reference (e.g. Bangor-Crewe is listed under Bangor but marks also exist worded Crewe-Bangor) and they are marked +. Some of the others, not marked +, ran Up/Down, East/West etc. TPOs for which no marks are known have been excluded: these include Chester-Crewe Parcel TPO, Chester-Holyhead RPO, Dartmoor RST, Gt Western Sunday ST, London-Doncaster ST, London-Dover SC (Ostend Day Mail)(1887), Perth-Dingwall RSC and Shrewsbury & Normanton TPO (1893-94). The rubber handstamps (type R) of 1986 were used for a two-week period of repair to the Birmingham Proof Bridge during which time TPOs were re-routed. "AM index" refers to special arrangements for stamp issue days during 1953-80 when new stamps were on sale from midnight and AM handstamps were used instead of applying to new stamps the previous day's date. Doubts have been expressed about the meaning of "LCR" shown here under "Caledonian"; it now appears to be the "Lancaster & Carlisle" section of the TPO.

The list that follows is a summary of "GB & Ireland Travelling Post Office Postmarks" by Frank J Wilson, published 1991 by the Railway Philatelic Group, who have kindly given permission to use this data.

Further reading

"T.P.O. A History of the Travelling Post Offices of Great Britain" by H S Wilson; published by Railway Philatelic Group, 1996.

Notes on values :

(a) All registered covers, complete with registration labels, are worth a premium; modern registered covers are worth a minimum of 6.00

(b) Bag Tenders (BT) replaced TPOs for the pre-Christmas period each year; mail was not normally postmarked but philatelic "by favour" items were sometimes produced – 8.00

(c) All values given are for the most common marks, generally the most recent; naturally earlier marks are normally priced higher, and Queen Victoria marks at not less than 15.00.

A	Missent types
B	Small circles with initials
C	Unframed circular
D	Star stamps
E	Single circles, many types
F	Numeral and duplex, English type
G	Duplex, Scottish type
H	Double circles, medium or thick arcs
J	Double circles, thin arcs
K	Skeletons
L	Parcel types (**13/20** or **19/11** to **19/13**)
M	'Late fee not paid' seen on this route
N	Squared circles
R	Rubber handstamps

MS᪷I - N-W
R·P·O - NIGHT
A 13/10

E
N.R.
B 13/11

D
FE10
76
C 13/12

L&C
R.P.O
D 13/13

254

Railway Postmarks

E 13/14 — GREAT WESTERN T.P.O. UP, 4 MR 59

F 13/15 — HULL SORTING TENDER, A JU26 74; 383

G 13/16 — HIGHLAND S.T., SP27 70; 391

H 13/17 — HULL SORTING CARRIAGE, 8PM MR 7 06

J 13/18 — CHESTER RELIEF SC, 20 JA 86

K 13/19 — LINCOLN SORTING CGE WEST, 15 MY 14

L 13/20 — BANGOR & CREWE T.P.O. PARCEL S.C., OC 12 93

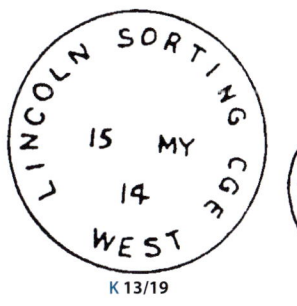

M 13/21 — Posted without late fee 1d to pay

N 13/22 — CORNWALL R.S.T., C OC 9 80

R 13/23 — UP-SPL-T.P.O., 24 FEB 1986, BM SECTION

Aberdeen & Elgin S.C. (1904-16)	E	75.00
+Aberystwyth-Shrewsbury SC(1930-39) (for earlier see Shrews-Aberystwyth)	E	12.00
+Ayr-Carlisle ST/RSC/SC (1874-1969)		
	E (Carlisle-Ayr ST)	18.00
	E (SC/RSC)	4.00
	AM index 1964	6.00
	J	2.00
	M	5.00
+Bangor-Crewe TPO (1870s-1979) (but ran from Holyhead)	E	4.00
	H	2.00
	AM index (C-B)	3.00
	J	2.00
	L (Parcel SC)	£400
	M	2.00
Bangor-Leeds RPO/TPO (1850s-1870s)		
	A (B&N- Bangor & Normanton or Bangor RPO)	£300
	D	£250
	E	60.00
Berwick & Newcastle ST (about 1888)		
	C	£175
	E	£125
+Birmingham-Bristol TPO (1938-49)		
	E	15.00
+Birmingham-Crewe SC/TPO (1885-1967) (& Crewe-Birmingham from 1930)	E	5.00
	J	2.00
	L	*
	M	5.00
+Birmingham-Glasgow (1993-96)	J	2.00
Birmingham-London BT (1986 only)		
	R 'BM-LDN-BT'	10.00
Birmingham-Stafford ST (1856-85)	E	*
Bridlington SC (1892-1916) (+summer service 1919-26)	E Hull ST (BQ index)	15.00
	E Bridlington	£100
Brighton SC - see London-Brighton		
+ Brighton-Hastings SC (1876-1916)	E	60.00
Bristol ST/SC (1895-1914)	E	£300
+Bristol-Derby TPO (1949-88)	H	2.00
	AM index (B-D only)	2.00
	J	2.00
	AM index (B-D only)	2.00
	J no arcs (B-D only)	2.00
	AM index (B-D only)	3.00
	M	5.00
	R (1986)(DY section)	10.00
Bristol-Exeter RPO/TPO (1859-1917)	D	75.00
	E RPO or TPO Day Mail	£125
+Bristol-Gloucester (1910-38)	E	25.00
Bristol-London TPO (1930-40) (earlier London-Bristol only)		
	E	9.00
Bristol-Newton Abbot (1872-95)	E	90.00
Bristol-Penzance (1896-1930)	E	25.00
then +again with Penz-Bristol (1994-2004)	J	2.00

255

Railway Postmarks

+Bristol-Plymouth (1895-1972) (with Plymouth-Bristol from 1930)			
	E	(1896 90.00)	20.00
	J		5.00
	M		5.00
Bristol/Shrews/Normanton (1895-1902)			
	E		75.00
	L		*
Bristol/Shrewsbury/York (1902-10)	E		30.00
Caledonian TPO (1848-1988)	A		£350
	B (CR, LCR etc) or no rim		12.00
	C		22.00
	D "Star"		£500
	E (1872-1957)		6.00
	E (Edinburgh) '-E-'		5.00
	E (Glasgow) '-G.W.-'		5.00
	J		2.00
	J EH Sect		2.00
	J GW Sect		5.00
	E (from 1981)		2.00
	M		5.00
	"P" (Perth) in star missort		£150
Cambridge Dist SC (1863-69)	B		£200
	F		£400
+Cardiff-Crewe RSC/TPO (1920-88)	H RSC		35.00
	E TPO		2.00
	AM index		6.00
	J TPO		2.00
	AM index		3.00
	M		2.00
then again 1994-96	J		2.00
+Cardiff-Glasgow TPO (1996-2003)	J		2.00
Cardiff York TPO (1910-20)	E		50.00
+then again with York-Cardiff 1988-94			
	J		2.00
+Carlisle-Edin SC/ST/TPO (1858-1993)			
	C (Ed-Carlisle)		5.00
	G '131' (Ed-Carlisle)		40.00
	H =S.T.= (Ed-Carlisle)		30.00
	E		5.00
	E 'CESC' for regist'd use		75.00
	J		2.00
	M		4.00
+Carlisle-Peterborough TPO (1991-96)			
	J		2.00
Carmarthen-Newcastle Emlyn SC	E (1895-1904)		£175
Carnforth-Whitehaven TPO (1875-1926)			
	E (Whitehaven ST/SC)		9.00
	F 'J54'		10.00
	H (Whitehaven) (to 1930)		9.00
Chester Relief (1986-94)	J		5.00
	R (1994)		10.00
Cornwall ST (1859-95)	E		90.00
	N		£300
Crewe-Glasgow RSC/SC (1926-93)	E (RSC)		22.00
	E (SC)		5.00
	J		2.00
	AM index 1964		3.00
	M		5.00
Crewe-Liverpool SC (1885-1939)	E		22.00
+Crewe-Manchester SC (1908-39)	H		15.00
+Crewe-Peterborough (1966-91)	J		2.00
	AM index		2.00
	J (Lincoln Section)		2.00
	AM index		2.00
	E		2.00
	K (1974)		*
	M		5.00
Derby-London TPO (1988-95)	J		2.00
+Derby-Penzance TPO (1988-94)	J		2.00
Dingwall-Perth RSC (1917-30)	E		75.00
Doncaster-London TPO (1932-40)	E		30.00
+Dover-London RSC (1922-23)(earlier London-Dover only)			
	H		£100
+Dover-Manchester TPO (1988-96)	J		2.00
Down Special TPO (1923-93)	E		4.00
	H		4.00
	J		2.00
	side A (Aberdeen Section)		5.00
	AM index 1964		5.00
	M		5.00
	R (1939)		80.00
	R (BM sect 1986)		10.00
East Anglian TPO (1929- 2003)	E		10.00
	H		5.00
	J		2.00
	AM index		2.00
	M		3.00
E Anglian K Lynn Section (1929-49)	E		18.00
	H		15.00
E Anglian Peterboro Sect (1949-90)	J		2.00
	AM index		2.00
Edinburgh-Berwick ST (c1866-85)	G numeral '131/ST'		£550
	C		45.00
	E (Edinburgh ST)		25.00
Edinburgh-Carstairs ST (1877-1914)	C		5.00
	G (unframed) '131'		£400
Edinburgh-Glasgow ST (c1869-70)	C		50.00
	G (unframed) '131'		£400
Edinburgh-Newc'le ST/SC (c1869-1922)			
	C		10.00
	E		10.00
Edinburgh-York SC/TPO (1926-85)	E		2.00
	J		1.00
	M		3.00
Exeter-Torrington SC (1906-17)	E		10.00
	K (1906)		£125
Fife ST/SC (1884-1917)	H ST =458=		30.00
	H SC		*
Galloway ST/SC/TPO (1871-1940)	E		15.00
	H ST =603=		35.00
	H TPO		10.00
	M		10.00
Glasg-Carlisle RPO/ST/SC (1858-1914)			
	B (C & G)		30.00
	D on missorts		50.00
	E (incl Glasgow ST)		5.00
	G '159'		30.00
	E registered (Glasgow ST)		50.00
	Reg crown oval (Glasg ST)		£225
+Glasgow-Preston RSC (1914-26)	E		£100
Gloucester-Tamworth RPO (1850-55)	A		£400
Grand Junction Railway (1838)	A		£250
Grand Northern Railroad (1844-59)	B (ENR, MNR)		20.00
Grand Northern RPO (1838-65)	A (no Day)		£250
	A (Day)		£300
Great Northern Night Mail (1910-22)	E		15.00
Great Northern SC Day (1877-1922)	E		8.00
Great Northern ST (1875-1902)	E		30.00
	Box (GNSC, GNST)		£175
Gt N'th'n TPO Midday Mail (1885-1915)			
	E		18.00
Great Western Dist SC (1859-69)	Two line		£225
Great Western RPO (1847-1904?)	A		£400
	B (E/GW)		35.00
Great Western TPO (1896-2004)	E		4.00
	H		5.00
	J		2.00
	AM index		2.00
	M		2.00
Greenock ST (1866-79)	E		35.00
Grimsby-Lincoln SC (1850s-1915)	E		12.00
	H		8.00

256

Railway Postmarks

	N	15.00	
Grimsby-Peterborough SC (1900-17)	E/H (ST)	12.00	
	E (SC)	12.00	
	H (SC)	5.00	
	K (1910)	£125	
	Tax 'K.97'	£125	
Halifax ST (1871-c79)	E	£100	
Helmsdale-Dingwall RSC (1923-30)	E	80.00	
Highland ST/SC/TPO (1870-1978)	G '391'	£300	
	E	20.00	
	H	5.00	
	J	2.00	
	L	£125	
	M	5.00	
Huddersfield, see Liv'l, Whitehaven			
Hull Sorting Carriage (1867-1917)	E (ST 19mm)	50.00	
	E (ST or SC)	9.00	
	F '383'	8.00 minimum	
	H	2.00	
+Hull-Leeds SC (1914-17)	E (Leeds-Hull)	£125	
	H (Hull-Leeds)	18.00	
Ipswich SC/ST (1858-1929)	Box (IST)	£225	
	Two line (DSC)	£400	
	E (ST/SC)	6.00	
+Ipswich-London TPO (1929-31)	E	25.00	
	K (1929)	*	
Lincoln ST/SC (1867-1919)	E 'Tender' or ST/SC	7.00	
	F '458'	£300	
	H (SC)	25.00	
	K (1914)	£200	
	L ('Tender')	£125	
	N (ST)(1891)	12.00	
	N (SC)(1905)	8.00	
+Lincoln-Tamworth SC (1919-40)	E	18.00	
	Registered oval	£125	
Liverpool-Huddersf'd TPO (1899-1965)			
	H (Rly SC)	75.00	
	E	5.00	
	J	5.00	
	M	5.00	
	Liverpool Late Fee	75.00	
	(30.00 for 1930s use)		
Liverpool-London TPO (c1863-1918)	E & N - on piece	60.00	
	on cover	£250	
Llandyssil ST (1875-95)	F 'D25'	£300	
	E	80.00	
	L	£200	
London-Birmingham RPO (1838)	A	£400	
London-Brighton SC Day (1880s-1916)			
	E (incl Brighton SC)	7.00	
London-Brighton SC Night (1864-1916)			
	E	10.00	
London-Bristol SC/ST (1868-1930) (then see Bristol-London)			
	E or box (ST)	£225	
	E (SC)	25.00	
London-Crewe ST/SC (1876-1918)	E (ST)	25.00	
	Box (SC)	£175	
	E (SC)	20.00	
London-Derby SC (1908-18)	Box (1896)	£100	
	E	40.00	
London-Dover SC, Continental Night Mail (1884-1923)			
	E (TPO/SC)	25.00	
	Reg oval FNM	75.00	
	H (+RSC)	£125	
and inscribed Continental Night Mail -			
	F (CS/2 Cannon St)	£100	
	F (CX/1 Charing Cross)	60.00	
	H	40.00	
London-Dover SC, French Day Mail (1860-1918)			
	B (LD/SC)	£100	
	F numeral 'C68'	£250	
	E (FDM)	25.00	
	E (SC)	18.00	
	Reg oval	40.00	
	Tax (hexagon T/C68,72)	12.00	
London-Exeter RPO/TPO (1855-95)	A	£225	
	B	45.00	
	D	45.00	
	Diamond L&E/TPO/E	75.00	
	E (TPO)	22.00	
	F numeral 'G01'	£400	
	L	£125	
L&E TPO - P/S (Paddington Station)	F London type duplex cancel	£400	
London-Folkestone SC (1911-15)	E	25.00	
	Reg hooded circle	75.00	
London-Holyhead Day TPO (1860-1939)			
	A	£350	
	Large X (used with above)	£350	
	E Euston Station Irish Mail	£250	
	F numeral 'B34'	£1250	
	E (TPO)	40.00	
London-Holyhead Night TPO (1860-1940)			
	A & large X	£350	
	Box	£300	
	E	40.00	
London-Holyhead TPO Canadian (1895-1908) & USA Mails (1895-1914)	E Canadian	£550	
	E US + F numeral 'K48'	£300	
	H London-Holyh'd index US	£250	
	Tax (T/L&H)	£300	
+London-Leeds ST/SC/TPO (1901-32)			
	Box L&L/ST	£150	
	E (ST/SC)	35.00	
	H (SC/TPO)	18.00	
+London-Newhaven RSC/SC (1923-39)			
	E	30.00	
+London-Norwich TPO (1931-90)	E (London-Norwich to 1939)	12.00	
	E (Norwich-London)	2.00	
	J (ditto)	2.00	
London-Queenboro ST (1891-1911)	E	35.00	
	Reg hooded circle	90.00	
	Tax (hexagon L.01)	£175	
+London-Shrewsbury TPO (1988-93)	J	2.00	
London-York-Edinburgh (1922-85)	E	5.00	
	H	4.00	
	K (1930)	£225	
	J	2.00	
	M	5.00	
Manchester ST (1864-1908)	E	8.00	
Manchester-Glasgow SC (1951-77)	J	5.00	
	M	5.00	
Midland District SC (1859-69)	Two line	£400	
Midland TPO (1855-2004)	A	£275	
	B (EMR)	25.00	
	D	90.00	
	E	2.00	
	K (South)(1949)	£150	
	H	4.00	
	J	2.00	
	AM index (South)	2.00	
	M	5.00	
Newcastle-on-Tyne ST/SC (1876-1914)			
	E	25.00	
Newcastle-London RSC (1922-26)	H	30.00	
Normanton-Stalybridge (1870s-1893)			
	E	90.00	
North of Scotland SC (1886-1904)	E	£225	
NETPO (Day) (1895-1926)	E	8.00	
	K (South)(1911)	£125	
NETPO Night (1926-95)	E	2.00	
	AM index (Up)	3.00	
	H (Up)	4.00	

257

Railway Postmarks

	H (index K,Z - Leeds Sect)	10.00	
	J	2.00	
	AM index (Down 1964 only)	4.00	
	M	5.00	
NETPO (1995-2004)	J	2.00	
NW District SC (1857-69)	A (boxed)	£150	
NWTPO Day Mail (1847-c1922)	A	£400	
	B (NW/RPO/M)	25.00	
	C	50.00	
	D	45.00	
	Diamond NW/TPO/M	40.00	
	E	18.00	
NWTPO Midday (1883-1915)	Hooded circle	*	
	E	18.00	
NWTPO 10PM Mail (1886-1926)	E	25.00	
NWTPO Night Down (1847-1993)	A	£350	
	Box (NWST)(Sunday)	£300	
	B (NW/RPO/E)	25.00	
	C	25.00	
	diamond NW/TPO/E	50.00	
	D (NW Ry)	25.00	
	E	3.00	
	H	2.00	
	J	2.00	
	AM index	4.00	
	M	5.00	
	R (BM Sect)(1986)	10.00	
NWTPO Night Up (1847-c1918)	E	18.00	
	Diamond NW/TPO/E	35.00	
North West TPO (1993-2004)	J	2.00	
Norwich SC/ST (1869 1929)	E	5.00	
	K (Up)(1909)	£150	
	Tax (L.05, 015)	80.00	
Perth-Aberdeen SC (1871-93)	G '402'	£500	
Perth-Helmsdale RSC (1919)	E on piece	75.00	
Peterborough DSC/ST (1858-1916)	Two line (DSC)	£450	
	E (ST)	25.00	
Peterborough-Ely SC (1908-12?)	E	35.00	
Plym-Bristol(Foreign Mails)(1869-1920s)			
	F numeral 'B16'	£250	
	E	25.00	
	Tax 'B16'	£125	
Plym & Ex'r Nt Mail Tender (1880-94)	F 'C24'	£250	
	E	60.00	
Portsmouth SC (1865-1923)	D/E together	£250	
	E	12.00	
Preston, see Whitehaven			
Rugby-Leeds RPO (1852-62)	A	£450	
Rugby-Newcastle RPO (1845-52)	A	£300	
St Pancras & Derby (1877-1908)	E	75.00	
Scarboro-Whitby SC (c1864)	E (S.W./York in str lines)	25.00	
Shrewsbury-Aberystwyth (1883-1930) then see Aberyst-Shrewsbury	E	10.00	
	H	18.00	
Shrewsbury-Crewe SC (1891-92)	E	*	
Shrewsbury-Hereford SC (1885-1902)			
	E	18.00	
+Shrewsbury-Stafford SC (1985 only)			
	R in red	10.00	
+Shrews-Tamworth SC/TPO (1857-1917) (also Tamworth-Shrewsb'y from 1914)			
	Two line	£400	
	Box (RPO)	£250	
	Box (TPO)	£225	
	E	18.00	
	E (RSC from 1914)	30.00	
+Shrewsbury-York TPO (1920-88)	H (SC)	35.00	
	E	2.00	
	J	2.00	
	AM index	3.00	

	M	5.00	
South East DSC/RPO/TPO (1860-1977)			
	Box (DSC)	*	
	B (E/SE)	*	
	B (SE/RPO)	30.00	
	E	5.00	
	AM index (Down)	3.00	
	F (SE Ry PO)	*	
	H	20.00	
	J	2.00	
	AM index (Up/Down)	2.00	
	M	5.00	
then again (1996- 2003)	J	2.00	
South Wales SC/ST/TPO (1869-2003)	E	2.00	
	H	2.00	
	J	2.00	
	AM index (Down)	2.00	
	R (1988, BT with BT removed)	10.00	
	M	5.00	
S Wales SC/TPO (Nth Mail)(1884-1923)			
	E	18.00	
South Western DSC (1860-69)	Box or 2-line	£300	
South West TPO (Day) (1866-1940)	E	7.00	
South Western Night TPO (1862-1988)			
	Box (RPO)	£125	
	B (L&SW/RPO)	35.00	
	E	4.00	
	AM index (Up)	4.00	
	H	25.00	
	J	2.00	
	AM index (Down)	3.00	
	K (Up)(1910)	£125	
	M	5.00	
Stalybridge, see Whitehaven			
Tamworth-Hereford SC (1902-14)	E	8.00	
Truro-Falmouth ST (1864-1916)	E	60.00	
Up Special TPO (1886-1993)	E 'Mail TPO'	18.00	
	H	7.00	
	E (TPO)	4.00	
	AM index (1953)	5.00	
	J	2.00	
	AM index (1961-)	2.00	
	R (1936,1948)	90.00	
	R (Birm Sect) 1986	10.00	
	J -A- (Aberdeen duty)	5.00	
	M	5.00	
Up Spec Edinburgh Section (1922-93)			
	E	9.00	
	H	5.00	
	J	2.00	
	M	5.00	
Up Spec Glasgow Section (1917-93)	E	5.00	
	H	2.00	
	J	2.00	
	K	£125	
	M	5.00	
West Cornwall Tender (1884-92)	E	*	
Whitehaven ST - see Carnforth-Whiteh'n			
+Whitehaven-Huddersf'd TPO (1966-91)	J	2.00	
	AM index (Hudd-Wh'haven)	2.00	
	M	5.00	
+Whitehaven-Preston TPO (1926-65)	H	4.00	
	J	2.00	
	M	5.00	
+Whitehaven-Stalybridge TPO (1965)			
	J	10.00	
	M	10.00	
York-Newcastle TPO (1853-95)	E	35.00	
York-Scarborough SC (1899-1928)	E	15.00	
Yorkshire TPO (1988-95)	J	2.00	

Railway Postmarks

Irish TPOs (Southern Ireland to 1922)

Ballybrophy ST (1900)		E	£250
Belfast & North'n Counties (1881-1940)			
		Diamond in bars '190'	£500
		E	20.00
		H	25.00
		K (1923)	£225
Dublin-Belfast RPO/TPO (1868-1923)			
		E	12.00
Dublin & Derry TPO (1912-24)		E	25.00
		H	75.00
Dublin-Queenstown TPO (1892-1907)			
		C 'Dublin-Cork American Mail'	£100
		C	50.00
Dublin-Wexford RPO/TPO (1894-1965)			
		E	45.00
		K (1904)	£225
Gt South & West'n TPO (1884-1994)		Diamond in bars 'TPO 498'	£500
		E (Cork TPO, GS&W or Dublin & Cork TPO)	22.00
		K (double rim skeleton)	£150
		R	£125
Kildare ST (1900)		E	*
Limerick ST/SC (1903-18 & 1938-39)		E	50.00
		K (1938-39)	£125
Midland TPO (1893-1994)		E (Midland, MGW or Dublin & Galway TPO)	25.00
		K (double rim)	£125
Mullingar-Sligo ST/SC (1903-76)		E	35.00
		R	£150
Portadown-Derry SC/ST/TPO (1887-1940) (& Derry-Portadown from 1930)		E	20.00
		K (1910)	£125
Ulster TPO (1895-1902)		E (& Portadown-Derry Night)	25.00
		K	£175
Waterford ST/SC (1903-17)		E	75.00

Two further railway postmarks

13/24

13/25

(a) single circle shown as **13/24**; first used pre-war (the one shown here is a 1991 replacement), it was used at TPO publicity events approx 1987-94 (value 8.00) then from 1994 it was made available for collectors as a "philatelic handstamp" (value 2.00) up to 2004.

(b) "Cruise of the Northern Belle" cachet (previously listed in chapter 24) - this train "cruise" first ran from King's Cross 16-30 June 1933 covering 4000 miles, with separate day and night portions accommodating 60 passengers and a crew of 20. Similar trips were made in 1934-39 and the cachet **13/25** was used in purple in 1936 - (valuation £150).

Railway Sub Offices

The story of RSOs is long and complex. The term RSO was originally introduced in 1856 as an accounting device, whereby a number of smaller offices could be down-graded from Head Office status. The original offices were served by TPOs, but the designation was later extended to indicate offices which received the bulk of their mail from a TPO instead of from their own Head Office. Thus towns well away from railways became RSOs. Datestamps generally did not include "RSO", however, until after 1900. The designation was abolished in 1905 but datestamps continued in use after that date, some with the "R" removed. * indicates an item in the list about which we are uncertain, or of which confirmation would be appreciated.

13/26
A Single Circle

13/27
AR Single Circle with R removed

13/28
B Double Circle

13/29
BR Double Circle with R removed

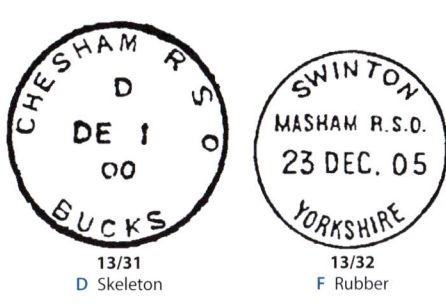

13/30
C Duplex

13/31
D Skeleton

13/32
F Rubber

E Irish Skeleton

G Undated Parcel Types

H Paid Skeleton

259

Railway Postmarks

England, Scotland, Wales

Abbey Cwmhir/Penybont Stn RSO	A	10.00
Abergele RSO/Denbighshire	G	30.00
Abergele/RSO	G	30.00
Aberkenfig/RSO	A	12.00
Abertillery RSO/Mon	A	2.00
	B	2.00
	BR	2.00
	D	40.00
Adelaide Rd/Gillingham RSO Kent	A	15.00
Albert Rd/Farnworth RSO Lanc	A	12.00
Alcester RSO/Warwickshire	G	50.00
Alexandra Rd Morecambe RSO/Lanc	A	12.00
Allendale RSO/Northd	A	2.00
All Stretton/Church Stretton RSO Salop	A	5.00
Alperton/Wembley RSO Middlesex	A	4.00
Alphamstone/Bures RSO/Suffolk	F	50.00
Alveston RSO/Glos	A	4.00
Ancrum RSO/Roxburghshire	A	4.00
Apethorpe/Wansford RSO Northants	A	6.00
	F	40.00
Appin RSO Argyllshire	A	3.00
Appledore RSO/N Devon	A	6.00
	B	2.00
	D	40.00
Ardallie/Mintlaw Station RSO/Aberdeenshire	F	50.00
Ardens Grafton/Alcester RSO/Warwickshire	F	50.00
Ashburton RSO/Devon	B	2.00
	BR	2.00
Ashbury/Shrivenham RSO Berks	A	6.00
Ashington/Pulborough RSO Sussex	A	15.00
Ashurst/Lyndhurst RSO Hants	A	3.00
Ashwater Beaworthy RSO/Devon	A	3.00
Ashwell/Baldock RSO Herts	A	4.00
Aspenden/Buntingford RSO/Herts	F	40.00
Aviemore RSO Inverness-shire	A	2.00
Aylsham RSO/Norfolk	A	3.00
Bainbridge Askrigg RSO/Yorks	A	4.00
Bala RSO/Merioneth	A	4.00
Baldock RSO	D	40.00
Banavie RSO Inverness-shire/+	A	3.00
Barrington/Colliery/Bedlington RSO/Northd	F	75.00
Barton Stacey RSO/Hants	A	4.00
Batley Rd/Heckmondwike RSO Yorks	A	12.00
Bawtry/RSO Yorks	D	35.00
Bawtry RSO/Yorks	D	30.00
Beaconsfield RSO/Bucks	D	40.00
Beal RSO/Northumberland	A	4.00
Beamish RSO/Durham	A	3.00
Beaufort RSO/Brecon	A	4.00
Beaumont/Weeley RSO/Essex	F	40.00
Beaworthy RSO/N Devon	A	3.00
Berkeley RSO/Gloucestershire	A	5.00
Berrow/Burnham RSO Somerset	F	40.00
Betchworth RSO/Sy	D	30.00
Bettws RSO	A	50.00
Beulah RSO/Cardiganshire	A	4.00
Beulah/Garth RSO Brecon	A	4.00
Bexhill on Sea RSO/Sussex	B	2.00
Bexley RSO/Kent	B	2.00
	D	20.00
Bickley RSO/Kent	D	20.00
Billingford/Scole RSO/Norfolk	F	20.00
Billy Row/Crook RSO Durham	A	8.00
Birchgrove/Llansamlet RSO Glam	A	8.00
Birchington RSO/Kent	G	50.00
Birtley RSO/Co Durham	A	5.00
	B	3.00
	BR	5.00

Biscovey/Par Station RSO/Cornwall	F	75.00
Blackhill RSO/Co Durham	A	3.00
	AR	4.00
Blackwater/Scorrier RSO Cornwall	A	4.00
Blaina RSO/Mon	A	2.00
Blisworth RSO/Northants	D	45.00
Bojewyan/Pendeen RSO/Cornwall	F	50.00
Bolam/Heighington RSO/Co Durham	F	40.00
Boldon Colliery RSO/ Co Durham	A	15.00
Bolingey/Perranporth RSO/Cornwall	F	40.00
Borth RSO/Cardiganshire	D	20.00
Boston Spa RSO/Yorks	D	50.00
Bourton-on-the-Water/RSO Glos	G	40.00
Bourton/Shrivenham RSO Berks	F	30.00
Brampton/Wangford RSO/Suffolk	F	40.00
Branch End/Stocksfield RSO/Northumberland	F	50.00
Brandeston/Wickham Market RSO/Suffolk	F	60.00
Brantingham/Brough RSO/Yorks	F	60.00
Broad Haven RSO/Pembrokeshire	A	5.00
Broadway RSO/Worcestershire	A	5.00
Brockenhurst RSO/Hants	A	3.00
	AR	4.00
	G	50.00
Brocklesby/RSO (Lincs)	G	60.00
Brocklesby Village/Brocklesby RSO/Lincs	F	75.00
Bromfield RSO/Salop	A	3.00
Brompton RSO/Yorks	A	3.00
Brompton Regis/Dulverton RSO Som	A	20.00
Broomfleet/Newport RSO Yorks	A	4.00
Brough RSO/Yorks	A	3.00
	B	3.00
Bryncethin/Aberkenfig RSO Glam	A	6.00
Brynna/Pontyclun RSO Glam	A	30.00
Brynsaddler Pontyclun RSO/Glamorgan	A	10.00
	(same but Glam) A	15.00
Bucknell RSO/Salop	A	4.00
Bude RSO/North Cornwall	A	5.00
Builth RSO/Brecon	D	30.00
Builth-Wells RSO/Breconshire	A	2.00
	AR	2.00
Buntingford RSO/Herts	A	6.00
	G	30.00
Burgess Hill RSO Sussex/-1-	B	3.00
	BR	3.00
	G	40.00
Burgh RSO/Linc	A	2.00
	B	2.00
Burgh/Aylsham RSO/Norfolk	F	50.00
Burnham RSO/Somerset	B	2.00
	BR	2.00
	D	25.00
Burnham/RSO Som	D	35.00
Burnham on Crouch RSO/Essex	A	2.00
	AR	2.00
Burry Port RSO/Carmarthenshire	A	3.00
	AR	8.00
Butley/Tunstall RSO/Suffolk	F	40.00
Byron Rd/Gillingham RSO Kent	A	15.00
Byron Rd/New Brompton RSO Kent	A	15.00
Caergeiliog Valley RSO/Anglesey	A	6.00
Callington RSO/Cornwall	G	40.00
Camp/Bridestowe RSO Devon	A	6.00
Campden RSO/Gloucestershire	D	35.00
	G	30.00
Campton/Shefford RSO/Beds	F	50.00
Canterbury St/Gillingham RSO Kent	A	15.00
Capel Celyn/Bala RSO/Merionethshire	F	60.00

260

Railway Postmarks

Location	Type	Price
Carbis Bay/Lelant RSO Cornwall	F	40.00
Cardington/Church Stretton RSO Salop	A	15.00
Cargreen/Hatt RSO/Cornwall	F	60.00
Carharrack/Scorrier RSO/Cornwall	F	50.00
Not For/Carlton RSO/Yorks	A	75.00
Carnetown/Abercynon RSO Glam	A	25.00
Carrbridge RSO Inverness-shire	A	2.00
Carrington/Gorebridge RSO/Midlothian	F	50.00
Castle Cary RSO/Somerset	A	2.00
	B	2.00
	BR	2.00
Castle Eden RSO/Co Durham	A	4.00
	AR	4.00
	B	4.00
Castle Morris/Letterston RSO/Pembrokeshire	F	50.00
Castleton/Grosmont RSO Yorks	A	10.00
Caton RSO/Lanc	BR	10.00
	D (Lancashire)	40.00
Chadwell Heath RSO/Essex	B	3.00
	BR	4.00
Chalfont St Giles/Gerrards Cross RSO	A	2.00
Chapel Amble/WadebridgeRSO/Cornwall	F	40.00
Chappel/Earl's Colne RSO Essex	A	6.00
Chathill RSO/Northd	D	40.00
Chatteris RSO/Cambs	B	2.00
	BR	2.00
Chelsfield Lane/OrpingtonRSO/Kent	F	40.00
Chenies/Rickmansworth RSO/Herts	F	50.00
Chesham RSO/Bucks	D	50.00
Chesham/RSO	G	40.00
Chollerton Station/Wall RSO/Northumberland	F	75.00
Chopwell/Ebchester RSO Co Durham	A	6.00
Church/Freshwater Stn RSO IOW	A	25.00
Church Crookham/Fleet RSO Hants	A	3.00
Church St/Gillingham RSO Kent	A	15.00
Church Stretton RSO/Salop	G	40.00
Clearbrook YelvertonRSO/Devon	A	5.00
Cleckheaton/RSO	G	40.00
Cleckheaton RSO/Yorks	H	50.00
Clydach RSO/Glamorgan	A	4.00
	AR	5.00
Cockfield RSO/Co Durham	A	5.00
Colinsburgh RSO/Fifeshire	B	3.00
Colne Engaine/Earls Colne RSO/Essex	F	40.00
Colwell/Barrasford RSO/Northumberland	F	40.00
Combe Martin RSO/Devon	B	2.00
Commondale Grosmont RSO/Yorks	A	4.00
Coniston RSO/Lanc	A	2.00
	AR	2.00
Consett RSO/Durham	D	50.00
Cootham/Pulborough RSO/Sussex	F	18.00
Copley/Butterknowle RSO Durham	A	15.00
Corbridge RSO/Northumberland	A	3.00
Cosham RSO/Hants	B	2.00
	BR	2.00
	G	40.00
Cotes Heath EccleshallRSO/Staff	A	5.00
Coughton RSO/Warwickshire	A	4.00
Countess Wear RSO/Devon	F	50.00
Court Hill/Swanage RSO Dorset	A	15.00
Cowdenbeath RSO/Fifeshire	B	3.00
Crafthole/St Germans RSO Cornwall	A	4.00
Crapstone/Yelverton RSO Devon	A	4.00
Crawcrook/Ryton RSO Durham	A	4.00
Criccieth RSO/Carnarvonshire	A	4.00
	B	2.00
	BR	2.00
Croggan/+ Craignure RSO +	B	25.00
Crookham/Fleet RSO Hants	A	3.00
Croxley Green RSO/Herts	A	3.00
Crumlin RSO/Mon	A	3.00
Crymmych RSO	D	35.00
Cullercoats/Whitley Bay RSO Northd	A	2.00
Dairsie RSO/Fifeshire	A	3.00
Dale Head/Grasmere RSO Westmd	A	5.00
Dalton-in-Furness RSO/Lanc	A	5.00
Dawley Bank/Dawley RSO Salop	A	6.00
	D	40.00
Denny RSO/Stirlingshire	G	50.00
Devonshire Rd/Bexhill on Sea RSO	A	6.00
Dinnington Colliery/Dudley RSO	A	15.00
Diptford/South Brent RSO Devon	A	5.00
Dornie/Strome Ferry RSO/Ross-shire	F	50.00
Downe/Farnborough RSO Kent	A	7.00
Draycott/Cheddar RSO Somerset	A	6.00
Dulverton RSO/Som	A	2.00
Duncan Rd/Gillingham RSO Kent	A	20.00
Dunphail RSO Morayshire	A	4.00
	AR (whole RSO removed)	8.00
Dyliffe/Llanbrynmair RSO	F	40.00
Eaglescliffe RSO/Co Durham	A	4.00
	AR	4.00
Earls Colne RSO/Essex	G	40.00
Easington/Castle Eden (Stn) RSO	A	20.00
East Boldon RSO/Co.Durham	B	3.00
Eastgate RSO/Co Durham	A	4.00
East Cowick/Snaith RSO/Yorks	F	50.00
	FR (Complete RSO removed)	40.00
Easthope/Much Wenlock RSO/Salop	F	40.00
Eastleigh RSO/Hants	A	3.00
	AR	3.00
Eastleigh RSO Hants/2	A	6.00
	AR	6.00
East Witton/Middleham RSO Yorks	A	5.00
	F	40.00
East Worlington/Morchard Bishop RSO		6.00
Eaudyke/Frisney RSO Linc	A	8.00
Ebrington/Campden RSO Glos	A	7.00
Edwardsville/Treharris RSO Glam	A	15.00
	F	50.00
Efailwen Clynderwen RSO/Pem	A	10.00
Egton/Grosmont RSO Yorks	A	5.00
Egton Bridge/Grosmont RSO Yorks	A	5.00
Ellerker/South Cave RSO/Yorkshire	F	50.00
Elphinstone/Tranent RSO	F	20.00
Elsdon/Otterburn RSO Northd	A	5.00
Elstree RSO/Herts	A	3.00
Euston Rd/Morecambe RSO Lanc	A	15.00
Eversholt/Woburn RSO/Beds	F	60.00
Eydon Byfield RSO/ Northants	A	5.00
Farnworth/RSO	A	20.00
Felinfach RSO/Cardiganshire	A	4.00
	D	50.00
Felixstowe RSO/Suffolk	A	2.00
	AR	2.00
Feltham RSO/Middlesex	A	4.00
Felton RSO/Northd	A	3.00
Feock/Devoran RSO Cornwall	A	4.00
Filey RSO/Yorks	A	2.00
	AR	5.00
	D	40.00
Finstock/Charlbury RSO Oxon	A	8.00
Fishguard RSO/Pem	A	5.00
	AR	6.00
Flax Bourton RSO	F	40.00
Fleet RSO/Hants	D	15.00
Fleet/Holbeach RSO Linc	A	3.00

261

Railway Postmarks

Fleetwood/RSO		G	30.00
Flookborough/Cark in Cartmel RSO/Lanc			
		F	35.00
Fordyce-Portsoy RSO		A	6.00
Four Crosses/Chwilog RSO		A	8.00
Fowey RSO/Cornwall		A	3.00
Freshwater Stn RSO		D	50.00
Frinton on Sea RSO/Essex		A	2.00
		AR	3.00
		B	2.00
Fron/Garthmyl RSO/Montgomeryshire			
		F	60.00
Gainsborough Rd/Felixstowe RSO		A	12.00
Galmpton/Brixham RSO/South Devon			
		F	60.00
Garrigill/Alston RSO/Cumbd		F	50.00
Garstang RSO/Lanc		B	2.00
Garth RSO/Breconshire		A	4.00
Gauldry/Wormit RSO/Fifeshire		F	40.00
Gedney/Holbeach RSO Linc		A	4.00
Gedney Dyke/Holbeach RSO Linc		A	5.00
Gilberdyke RSO/Yorks		A	3.00
Gilberdyke/Brough RSO Yorks		A	10.00
Gillingham RSO/Kent		A	4.00
		B	2.00
		BR	2.00
Glandyfi RSO/Cardigan		A	4.00
Glanton RSO/Northumberland		A	5.00
Glasserton/Whithorn RSO/Wigtownshire			
		F	50.00
Golant/Par Station RSO Cornwall		A	12.00
Golant/Par Station RSO/Cornwall		F	60.00
Golberdon/Callington RSO/Cornwall		F	60.00
Gordon RSO/Berwickshire		A	4.00
Gorran RSO/Cornwall		B	4.00
Graemsay/Stromness RSO/Orkney		F	£100
Grange over Sands RSO/Lanc		B	2.00
Grayingham/Kirton Lindsey RSO/Lincolnshire			
		F	50.00
Grayshott/Haslemere RSO Surrey		B	3.00
Grayswood/Haslemere RSO Surrey		A	5.00
		AR	6.00
Great Alne/Alcester RSO/ Warwickshire		F	50.00
Great Ayton RSO/Yks		D	40.00
Great Broughton/Stokesley RSO Yorks			
		A	5.00
Great Hormead/Buntingford RSO Herts			
		A	12.00
		AR	12.00
Great Missenden RSO/Bucks		A	4.00
Gt Rissington/Bourton-on-the-Water RSO			
		A	5.00
Greenend RSO/Mid-Lothian		A	5.00
Greenside/Ryton RSO Co Durham		A	5.00
Groesffordd Marli/St Asaph RSO/Flintshire			
		F	60.00
Grosmont Pontrilas RSO		A	15.00
Gwytherin/Llanrwst RSO Denbigh		A	6.00
Hacheston/Wickham Market RSO Suffolk			
		A	6.00
Hadleigh RSO/Suffolk		A	4.00
Hailsham/RSO/Sussex		A	4.00
		B	2.00
		BR	2.00
		D	20.00
Hailsham/RSO		G	25.00
Hammer/Haslemere RSO/Surrey		F	50.00
Hamsterley/Witton-le-Wear RSO		A	5.00
Harlech RSO/Merioneth		A	2.00
		B	2.00
Harlech/RSO		D	25.00
Harley/Much Wenlock RSO/Shropshire			
		F	50.00
Harrington RSO/Cumbd		A	8.00
Harrowbarrow/St Dominick RSO		A	7.00
Haslemere RSO/Surrey		A	5.00
		G	40.00
Haslemere/RSO		G	40.00
Hassocks RSO/Sussex		G	50.00
Hatherleigh/RSO		G	40.00
Hay RSO/Hereford		D	40.00
Heckmondwike RSO/Yorks		G	30.00
		H	75.00
Helmsley RSO/Yorks		A	3.00
		D	40.00
Henfield RSO Sussex/1		B	4.00
Henllan RSO/Cardiganshire		A	5.00
Hensall/Snaith RSO/Yorks		F	40.00
Heronsgate/Rickmansworth RSO Herts			
		A	6.00
Herstmonceux/Hailsham RSO Sussex			
		A	4.00
		AR	4.00
Hetton le Hole RSO/Co Durham		A	5.00
		AR	5.00
Higham Rd/Rushden RSO Northants		A	12.00
High Ham/Langport RSO Somerset		A	6.00
		F	50.00
High Wych/Sawbridgeworth RSO/Herts			
		F	20.00
Hill Top/Knottingley RSO Yorks		A	6.00
Hindhead/Haslemere RSO Surrey		B	2.00
		BR	2.00
Hinxworth/Baldock RSO/Herts		F	50.00
Hobson/Burnopfield RSO/Co Durham			
		F	20.00
Holbeach RSO/Lincs		D	20.00
Holborn Hill/Millom RSO Cumbd		A	12.00
Holne/Ashburton RSO/Devon		F	40.00
Holt RSO/Norfolk		A	2.00
		AR	2.00
		D	15.00
Horley RSO/Surrey		B	3.00
		D	20.00
Horndean RSO/Hants		A	4.00
		B	2.00
		D	20.00
Horsehouse/Middleham RSO/Yorkshire			
		F	40.00
Houghton/Stockbridge RSO Hants		A	5.00
Hunstanton RSO/Norfolk		B	2.00
Hunton Bridge/Kings Langley RSO Herts			
		A	5.00
Hutton Bushel/West Ayton RSO/Yorks			
		F	50.00
Inverkeithing RSO/Fife		B	3.00
Irthlingborough/Higham Ferrers RSO			
			12.00
Kearsley Cross/Farnworth RSO Lanc		A	10.00
Kellington/Whitley Bridge RSO/Yorkshire			
		F	50.00
Kelvedon RSO/Essex		G	40.00
Kildale/Grosmont RSO Yorks		A	5.00
Killay RSO/Glamorgan		A	5.00
Kincraig RSO Invernessshire		A	4.00
Kingsland RSO/Hereford		D	40.00
King's Langley RSO/Herts		A	2.00
		AR	3.00
King's Somborne/Stockbridge RSO Hants			
		A	4.00
Kirby Moorside RSO/Yorks		A	5.00
Kirton Lindsey RSO/Lincs		B	4.00
Knockando RSO Morayshire/+		A	4.00
Knottingley RSO/Yorks		A	4.00
		AR	4.00
Lambourn RSO/Berkshire		A	5.00
Lapford/Morchard Bishop RSO		A	5.00

262

Railway Postmarks

Largs RSO Ayrshire/+	B	2.00
Lastingham/Sinnington RSO/Yorkshire	F	50.00
Lauder RSO/+Berwickshire+	B	3.00
Laughton/Shortgate RSO Sussex	A	7.00
Lawrenny/Begelly RSO Pem	A	6.00
Layham/Hadleigh RSO/Suffolk	F	40.00
Leiston RSO/Suffolk	A	12.00
Lelant Downs/Lelant RSO/Cornwall	F	40.00
Leslie RSO/Fifeshire	A	3.00
Leyburn RSO/Yorks	A	3.00
Lilliput/Parkstone RSO Dorset	A	20.00
Linkinhorne/Callington RSO	A	4.00
Lintz Colliery/Burnopfield RSO Co Durham	A	30.00
Liphook RSO/Hants	B	2.00
	BR	2.00
	D (no county)	30.00
	G (no county)	30.00
Little-Dawley/Dawley RSO Salop	A	12.00
Llanarth RSO/Cardiganshire	A	4.00
(Cardingshire spell error)	A	10.00
Llanbedr RSO/Merioneth	A	5.00
Llanbedr/Talycafn RSO/Denbighshire	F	40.00
Llanberis RSO	D	30.00
Llanbrynmair RSO/Mont	A	12.00
Llancarfan/Cowbridge RSO/Glamorgan	F	60.00
Llanddeusant/Llangadock RSO	A	9.00
Llanddeusant/Valley RSO	A	5.00
Llandewi Brefi RSO	A	25.00
Llandinam RSO/Montgomeryshire	A	12.00
	B	6.00
Llandissilio/Clynderwen RSO Pem	A	12.00
	AR	12.00
Llanfachreth/Valley RSO	A	6.00
Llanfairfechan RSO/Carnarvonshire	B	5.00
Llanfallteg RSO/Carmarthenshire	A	5.00
Llanfihangel-ar-Arth RSO/Carmarthen	A	5.00
Llanfihangel/Borth RSO	A	5.00
Llangadock RSO/Carmarthenshire	A	5.00
Llangefni RSO/Anglesey	B	6.00
Llannefydd/Trefnant RSO Denbigh	A	5.00
	*D	60.00
Llangennith/Reynoldstone RSO/Glam	D	70.00
Llanover Rd/Wembley RSO Middx	A	15.00
Llansadwrn/Menai Bridge RSO	A	5.00
Llawryglyn/Llanidloes RSO Mont	A	7.00
Loanhead RSO/Midlothian	B	3.00
Longhoughton/Lesbury RSO Northd	A	5.00
Long Melford RSO/Suffolk	B	2.00
Long Preston RSO/Yorks	A	3.00
Long Rock/Cornwall	A	4.00
Longtown RSO/Cumb	D	30.00
Looe RSO/Cornwall	A	4.00
Lostwithiel RSO/Cornwall	B	2.00
	BR	2.00
	G	30.00
Lower Wallop/Stockbridge RSO Hants	A	8.00
	F	50.00
Lowick/Beal RSO Northd	A	4.00
Low Prudhoe/Ovingham RSO Northd	A	6.00
Luckett/Callington RSO Cornwall	A	3.00
Lydford/Bridestowe RSO North Devon	A	3.00
Lyndhurst RSO/Hants	B	2.00
	BR	3.00
	D	15.00
Maesteg RSO/Glam	D	50.00

Maesycrugiau RSO	A	8.00
Maesycruciau RSO (spelling error)	A	10.00
Maggieknockater/Dufftown RSO/Banffshire	F	50.00
Magham Down/Hailsham RSO Sussex	A	6.00
Marazion RSO/Cornwall	G	40.00
Mare Hill/Pulborough RSO Sussex	A	10.00
Margaretting/Ingatestone RSO Essex	A	5.00
Market St/Eastleigh RSO Hants	A	15.00
Martock RSO/Somerset	F	20.00
Mathry/Letterston RSO Pem	A	5.00
Medway Rd/Gillingham RSO Kent	A	7.00
Mevagissey RSO/Cornwall	B	3.00
Middleham RSO/Yorkshire	A	4.00
Mill End/Rickmansworth RSO/Herts	F	50.00
Mill Green/Ingatestone RSO/Essex	F	40.00
Milnthorpe RSO/Westmorland	A	12.00
	B	2.00
Milton/Steventon RSO Berks	A	3.00
Miltoncombe/Yelverton RSO/Devon	F	40.00
Milton Dameral/Brandis Corner RSO/North Devon	F	50.00
Milverton RSO/Somerset	B	2.00
Minehead RSO	D	15.00
Misson/Bawtry RSO Yorks	A	4.00
Moor-End/Cleckheaton RSO Yorks	A	10.00
Morchard Bishop/RSO	G	40.00
Morcombelake Charmouth RSO/Dorset	A	7.00
Morecambe RSO/Lancashire	B	2.00
Morecambe/RSO	G	30.00
Morriston RSO	D	40.00
Mortehoe RSO/N Devon	A	2.00
	AR	2.00
Morwenstow/Bude RSO N Cornwall	A	3.00
Mullion RSO	G	40.00
Mundesley RSO/Norfolk	A	4.00
Muston/Hunmanby RSO/Yorks	F	40.00
Mydroilin/Felinfach RSO/Cardiganshire	F	50.00
Nassington/Wansford RSO Northants	A	5.00
Newbiggin RSO/Westmorland	B	3.00
New Brompton RSO/Kent	B	2.00
Newcastle/Aston on Clun RSO Salop	A	5.00
Newlands/Morecambe RSO Lanc	A	6.00
Newmarket/Rhuddlan RSO Flints	A	6.00
Newport RSO/Pembrokeshire	A	2.00
	D	25.00
Newport RSO/Yorks	A	3.00
Newton/Porthcawl RSO Glam	A	5.00
Newton by the Sea/Chathill RSO/Northumberland	F	40.00
Newton Rd/Rushden RSO Northants	A	15.00
Newtown/Berkeley RSO Glos	A	4.00
Nomansland/Lyndhurst RSO/Hants	F	40.00
Northam RSO/North Devon	A	3.00
	AR	2.00
North Bovey/Moreton Hampstead RSO/Devon	F	40.00
North Cheriton/Templecombe RSO Somt	A	8.00
Northcliff/Southwold RSO	A	15.00
North Cliff/Southwold RSO	A	12.00
North-End/Burgess Hill RSO Sussex	A	6.00
North Huish/South Brent RSO/Devon	F	50.00
North Litchfield/Whitchurch RSO/Hants	F	40.00
North Wallbottle/Newburn RSO Northd	A	6.00
Northwood RSO/Middlesex	A	2.00

263

Railway Postmarks

	AR	4.00	
	D	25.00	
Norton/Yarmouth RSO Isle of Wight	A	12.00	
Norwood Hill/Horley RSO Surrey	A	25.00	
Oakford/Bampton RSO Devon	A	4.00	
Old Felixstowe/Felixstowe RSO/Suffolk			
	F	50.00	
Old Shoreham/Shoreham RSO/Sussex			
	F	50.00	
Old Town/West Woodburn RSO/Northumberland			
	F	40.00	
Orford RSO/Suffolk	A	3.00	
	AR	4.00	
Ormesby RSO/Yorkshire	A	3.00	
Orpington RSO/Kent	A	4.00	
Orton/Tebay RSO Westmorland	A	3.00	
Ossett RSO Yorks/1	A	3.00	
Ossett RSO Yorks/2	B	3.00	
	BR	3.00	
Otterburn RSO/Northumberland	A	3.00	
Otterburn RSO	D	30.00	
Otterton/Budleigh Salterton RSO/Devonshire			
	F	50.00	
Oulton/Aylsham RSO Norfolk	A	4.00	
Over/Winsford RSO Ches	A	3.00	
Padstow RSO/Cornwall	D	40.00	
Pandy RSO	A	20.00	
Panteg Cross Roads/Maesllyn RSO	A	12.00	
Parham/Wickham Market RSO Suffolk			
	A	5.00	
Parkmill RSO/Glamorgan	A	5.00	
Parkstone RSO/Dorset	A	5.00	
	D	40.00	
	G	40.00	
Parkstone RSO/Dorsetshire	A	3.00	
	AR	3.00	
Park View/Whitley Bay RSO Northd	A	12.00	
Par Station RSO/Cornwall	B	3.00	
Payhembury/Ottery St Mary RSO/Devon			
	F	50.00	
Pelyn Bude RSO/Cornwall	A	12.00	
Pelynt/Duloe RSO Cornwall	A	6.00	
Penllergare/Gorseinon RSO/Glamorgan			
	F	70.00	
Penmaenmawr RSO/Carnarvon	B	2.00	
Penmaenmawr RSO/+	B	2.00	
	BR	2.00	
Penrhiwceiber RSO/Glam	A	5.00	
Penrhyn Deudraeth RSO	D	40.00	
Pentewan RSO/Cornwall	A	4.00	
Pen-y-Banc/Ystradgynlais RSO/Breconshire			
	F	60.00	
Penycae/Ystradgynlais RSO/Breconshire			
	F	70.00	
Penygroes RSO/Carnarvonshire	A	3.00	
	AR	3.00	
	G	50.00	
Perranuthnoe/Marazion RSO/Cornwall			
	F	40.00	
Pondtail/Fleet RSO Hants	A	7.00	
Pont Hirwain/Boncath RSO Pem	A	15.00	
Pont Yates/Kidwelly RSO	A	12.00	
Porteynon RSO/Glam	D	50.00	
Porthcurno/Treen RSO Cornwall	A	4.00	
Port Isaac RSO/Cornwall	G	40.00	
Portmahomack RSO/Rossshire	A	5.00	
Poughill/Bude RSO/North Cornwall	F	40.00	
Poundsgate Ashburton RSO/Devon	A	3.00	
Poundstock/Bude RSO N Cornwall	A	4.00	
Powerstock/Melplash RSO Dorset	A	5.00	
Rackenford/MorchardBishop RSO N Devon			
	A	5.00	
Radcliffe,Acklington RSO/Northd	A	5.00	
Radlett RSO/Herts	G	40.00	

Ravenglass RSO/Cumberland	A	3.00	
Reading Rd/Fleet RSO Hants	A	8.00	
Red Row/Acklington RSO Northd	A	5.00	
Renwick/Kirkoswald RSO/Cumberland			
	F	40.00	
Reynoldston RSO/Glam	B	3.00	
Rhossilly/Porteynon RSO Glam	A	10.00	
Rhydow Merau/Llandilo RSO/Carm	F	60.00	
Rickmansworth RSO/Herts	A	3.00	
Roberton/Abington RSO/Lanarkshire			
	F	40.00	
Robin Hood's Bay Station RSO/Yorks	A	3.00	
Roborough RSO/Devonshire	A	5.00	
Roch RSO/Pembrokeshire	A	4.00	
Roche RSO/Cornwall	A	3.00	
Rock/Wadebridge RSO Cornwall	A	3.00	
	AR	3.00	
Roslin RSO/Midlothian	B	3.00	
Rushall/Scole RSO/Norfolk	F	40.00	
Rushden RSO/Northants	A	5.00	
	B	2.00	
	BR	2.00	
St Agnes/Scorrier RSO Cornwall	A	3.00	
St Anne's on the Sea RSO/Lanc	A	6.00	
	G	40.00	
St Davids RSO/Pembrokeshire	A	2.00	
	AR	2.00	
St Just/RSO	G	40.00	
St Keverne RSO/Cornwall	B	3.00	
St Kew/Wadebridge RSO/Cornwall	F	40.00	
St Martin RSO/Cornwall	B	3.00	
	D	40.00	
St Mellion/RSO	G	40.00	
St Merryn/Padstow RSO	A	4.00	
St Nicholas/Fishguard RSO Pem	A	6.00	
St Teath RSO/Cornwall	D	50.00	
Sandown RSO/Isle of Wight	G	60.00	
Official Paid/Sandringham RSO Norfolk			
	A	45.00	
Sawbridgeworth RSO/Herts	B	3.00	
	G	40.00	
Scorrier RSO/Cornwall	A	3.00	
Scotswood RSO/Northumbd	B	4.00	
	BR	5.00	
Seamer RSO/Yorks	A	3.00	
Seaside/Combe Martin RSO Devon	A	15.00	
Seathwaite/Barrow-in-Furness/RSO/Lanc			
	F	40.00	
Sedbergh RSO	C (438)	25.00	
Seer Green/Beaconsfield RSO/Bucks	F	40.00	
Sennybridge RSO/Breconshire	B	4.00	
Shanklin RSO/IOW	D	50.00	
Shap RSO/Westmorland	A	2.00	
Shap Granite Works/Shap RSO Westmorland			
	A	30.00	
Sharpness/Berkeley RSO Glos	A	3.00	
Shepperton Green/Shepperton RSO	A	5.00	
Shepperton Green RSO	D	40.00	
Sheringham RSO/Norfolk	A	4.00	
	AR	4.00	
	B	2.00	
	G	30.00	
Shermanbury/Henfield RSO/Sussex	F	20.00	
Shortgate RSO/Sussex	A	5.00	
	D	40.00	
Sidcup RSO/Kent	A	6.00	
Six Bells/Aberbeeg RSO Mon	A	12.00	
Skegness RSO/Linc	A	12.00	
Skegness RSO	D	30.00	
Skelton RSO	C (G70)	75.00	
Sleights RSO/Yorks	A	5.00	
Small Dole RSO/Sussex	A	6.00	
	AR	6.00	

Railway Postmarks

Somerford Keynes/Cricklade RSO/Wilts	F	50.00
South Brent/RSO	G	30.00
Southwold RSO/Suffolk	A	3.00
	AR	3.00
	D	40.00
Spreyton/Bow RSO N Devon	A	5.00
Staithes RSO/Yorks	A	3.00
Staithes RSO/Yks	D	40.00
Standford/Liphook RSO Hants	A	6.00
Stanley RSO/Co Durham	A	4.00
Stannington/Cramlington RSO Northd	A	4.00
Stansfield/Clare RSO/Suffolk	F	40.00
Stansted RSO/Essex	A	2.00
Stanway/Winchcombe RSO Glos	A	4.00
Station Rd/Bexhill on Sea RSO Sussex	A	12.00
Station Rd Fowey RSO/Cornwall	A	12.00
Stepaside RSO/Pembrokeshire	A	4.00
Steventon RSO/Berks	G	40.00
Stithians/Perranwell Station RSO/Cornwall	F	50.00
Stockbridge RSO/Hants	A	2.00
	AR	2.00
Stoke Poges RSO/Bucks	D	40.00
Stoke Rivers RSO/N Devon	A	4.00
Stokesley RSO/Yorkshire	A	3.00
Stotfield Lossiemouth RSO/+	A	5.00
Stow on the Wold RSO/Glos	A	4.00
Strachan/Banchory RSO/Kincardineshire	F	40.00
Sudbourne/Orford RSO/Suffolk	F	40.00
Sunnyside/Tow Law RSO	A	5.00
Sutton on Sea RSO/Linc	B	2.00
	RR	2.00
Swanage RSO/Dorset	A	8.00
Swanland/Brough RSO Yorks	A	5.00
Swinton/Masham RSO/Yorkshire	F	40.00
Swinton/Masham RSO	G	40.00
Tanygroes RSO/Cardiganshire	A	4.00
Tavernspite/Whitland RSO/Carmarthenshire	F	50.00
Tebay RSO/Westmorland	A	10.00
Templecombe RSO/Somt	A	4.00
	B	2.00
	BR	2.00
Thakeham/Pulborough RSO/Sussex	F	50.00
The Parade/Wealdstone RSO Middx	A	10.00
The Roe/St Asaph RSO Flintshire	A	8.00
Thornbury RSO/Glos	A	3.00
	B	3.00
Thornley RSO/Durham	D	40.00
Thorpe Abbotts/Scole RSO Norfolk	A	12.00
	F	40.00
Tilbury RSO/Essex	A	8.00
	D	40.00
Tintagel RSO/Cornwall	A	2.00
	AR	2.00
	D (two layouts)	25.00
Tiptree Kelvedon RSO/Essex	A	5.00
	B	6.00
Tisbury RSO/Wilts	A	5.00
	B	4.00
	D	40.00
Toddington/Winchcombe RSO/Glos	F	50.00
Torpoint RSO/Cornwall	A	2.00
	AR	2.00
Towyn RSO/Merioneth	A	2.00
	AR	2.00
Towyn/Abergele RSO/Denbighshire	F	50.00
Trawsfynydd RSO/Merionethshire	B	4.00
Treboeth/Landore RSO Glamorgan	A	5.00
Trefnant/RSO	G	40.00
Tregaron RSO	A	50.00
Treharris RSO/Glamorgan	A	4.00
Trimdon/Trimdon Grange RSO Durham	A	6.00
Trimsaran Kidwelly RSO/Carmarthen	A	5.00
Trusham/Chudleigh RSO	F	40.00
Twatt/Stromness RSO/Orkney	F	£100
Twyford RSO/Berks	D	50.00
Tycroes RSO/Anglesey	A	4.00
Tynllechwedd/Llanidloes RSO/Mont	F	60.00
Ulceby RSO/Linc	A	3.00
	G	40.00
Upton Cross/Callington RSO	A	5.00
Van/Llanidloes RSO/Montgomeryshire	F	60.00
Victoria St/Gillingham RSO Kent	A	15.00
Wainfleet RSO/Lincolnshire	B	2.00
Walberswick/Southwold RSO Suff	A	5.00
Walkden/Farnworth RSO Lanc	B	8.00
Wallbottle/Newburn RSO Northd	A	5.00
Wall-under-Heywood/Church Stretton RSO/Salop	F	50.00
Wansford RSO/Northamptonshire	A	8.00
Washington/Pulboro' RSO	F	40.00
Waterloo Rd./Llandrindod Wells RSO Radnor	A	10.00
Wavendon/Woburn Sands RSO Beds	A	5.00
Wealdstone RSO/Middlesex	A	4.00
	B	5.00
Weeley RSO/Essex	A	4.00
	AR	4.00
Weldon Bridge/Longframlington RSO/Northumberland	F	40.00
Welton/Brough RSO Yorks	A	4.00
Wembley RSO/Middlesex	A	4.00
	AR	4.00
	B	3.00
	BR	3.00
West Cornforth RSO/Co Durham	A	4.00
Westgate on Sea RSO/Kent	A	4.00
	D	40.00
West Mill/Buntingford RSO/Herts	F	50.00
West Pelton/Beamish RSO/Co Durham	F	40.00
West St/Fleetwood RSO Lanc	A	12.00
Westward Ho RSO/North Devon	A	4.00
Whitchurch RSO/Hants	G	30.00
White Colne/Earls Colne RSO/Essex	F	30.00
White Lee/Heckmondwike RSO Yorks	A	6.00
Whitland RSO	A	25.00
	C (F24)	£100
Whitley Bay RSO/Northumberland	A	2.00
	AR	2.00
	B	2.00
	BR	2.00
	D	40.00
Wickham Market RSO/Suffolk	G	40.00
Wickwar RSO (Glos)	D	40.00
Widecombe in the Moor/Ashburton RSO	A	5.00
Willingham RSO/Cambs	A	20.00
Winsford RSO/Cheshire	A	2.00
	B	2.00
	D	40.00
	G	50.00
Wiston/Clarbeston Road RSO Pem	A	6.00
Wiston/Steyning RSO/Sussex	F	50.00
Wiveliscombe RSO/Somerset	B	2.00
	BR	2.00
Woburn Sands RSO/Beds	D	50.00

Railway Postmarks

Wolverton RSO/Bucks	A	4.00
	AR	4.00
Woodleigh Loddiswell RSO/Devon	A	8.00
Wooler RSO/Northd	A	4.00
Wootton/Ulceby RSO Linc	A	8.00
Wotton-under-Edge RSO/Glos	B	2.00
Wragby RSO Lincolnshire	B	5.00
Wykeham RSO/Yorkshire	A	4.00
Yarm RSO/Yorks	D	40.00
Yarmouth RSO/Isle of Wight	A	2.00
Yeoford/Copplestone RSO	A	5.00
Yiewsley RSO/Middlesex	A	5.00
	D	50.00
	G	40.00
Ystrad Meurig RSO	A	6.00
Zelah/Callestick RSO Cornwall	F	50.00

Ireland

Abbeyfeale RSO	B	7.00
Aghadowey RSO/Co. L'derry	A	7.00
Ardagh RSO/Co. Lim'k	A	5.00
Ardrahan RSO/Co. Galway	A	5.00
Ardsollus/RSO	A	20.00
Armoy RSO/Co. Antrim	A	5.00
Askeaton RSO/Co .Lim'k	A	7.00
Augher RSO/Co. Tyrone	A	5.00
Aughnacliffe/Granard RSO/Co. Longford		
	F	60.00
Aughrim RSO/Co. Wicklow	A	6.00
Balbriggan RSO/Co. Dublin	A	5.00
Ballagh/Goolds Cross RSO/Co. Tipperary		
	F	60.00
Ballinamallard/RSO	A	12.00
Ballinamore/RSO	A	25.00
Ballineen RSO/Co .Cork	A	6.00
Ballingarry RSO/Co. Lim'k	A	5.00
Ballinlough RSO Co. Roscommon	B	5.00
Ballintogher/Collooney RSO	A	12.00
Ballybay/RSO	E	75.00
Ballybay RSO/Co. Monaghan	A	7.00
Ballybrophy RSO/Queens Co.	A	20.00
Ballybunion RSO/Co. Kerry	A	6.00
Ballycassidy/Ballinamallard RSO/Co. Fermanagh		
	F	75.00
Ballycastle RSO/Co. Mayo	A	20.00
Ballycroy RSO/Co. Mayo	A	8.00
Ballycumber RSO/Kings Co.	A	8.00
Ballydavid/Dingle RSO	A	25.00
Ballyduff, Lixnaw RSO/Co. Kerry	A	8.00
Ballyglass RSO/Co. Mayo	A	7.00
Ballylanders/Knocklong RSO	A	8.00
Ballymacarberry RSO/Co. Waterford	A	8.00
Baltimore RSO/Co. Cork	A	6.00
Bangor RSO/Co. Down	A	4.00
Bansha RSO/Co. Tip.	A	5.00
Bellaghy/Castledawson RSO	A	8.00
Belleek RSO/Co. Fermanagh	A	3.00
Belmullet RSO/Co. Mayo	A	15.00
Beltra/Ballisodare RSO	A	8.00
Blarney RSO/Co. Cork	A	4.00
Bloomfield RSO/Co. Down	A	4.00
	E (no county)	75.00
Bonmahon/Kilmacthomas RSO	A	7.00
Borris RSO/Co. Carlow	A	5.00
Borris-in-Ossory/RSO Queens Co.	A	6.00
Brosna Abbeyfeale RSO/Co. Limk	A	7.00
Bruckless RSO Co. Donegal	B	7.00
Cabinteely RSO/Co.Dublin	A	6.00
	B	8.00
Cahirciveen RSO/Co .Kerry	A	25.00
Caledon RSO/Co. Tyrone	A	5.00
Caledon RSO/Tyrone	E	60.00
Callan RSO/Co. Kilkenny	A	5.00
Callow RSO/Co. Mayo	A	15.00

Camolin RSO/Co. Wexford	A	7.00
Camp RSO/Co. Kerry	A	8.00
Carah RSO	A	30.00
Carrigtwohill RSO/Co. Cork	A	8.00
Cashel RSO/Co. Galway	A	4.00
Castlecomer RSO/Co. Kilkenny	A	6.00
Castlecomer RSO	E	40.00
Castleconnell RSO/Co. Lim'k	A	5.00
Castlecor/Kanturk RSO	A	9.00
Castledermot RSO/Co. Kildare	A	6.00
Castlegregory RSO/Co. Kerry	A	8.00
Castleisland RSO/Co. Kerry	A	6.00
Castlemahon/Newcastle West RSO/Co. Limerick		
	F	75.00
Castlemaine RSO/Co. Kerry	A	25.00
Castlemaine RSO/-1-	B	8.00
Castlemartyr RSO/Co. Cork	A	5.00
Celbridge RSO/Co. Kildare	A	6.00
Clane RSO/Co. Kildare	A	20.00
Clara RSO Kings Co.	B	7.00
Clarin Bridge RSO/Co. Galway	A	7.00
Cleggan RSO/Co. Galway	A	5.00
Clifden RSO/Co. Galway	A	20.00
Cloghan/RSO	A	30.00
Clonakilty RSO/Co. Cork	A	6.00
Clonbur RSO/Co. Galway	A	6.00
Clondalkin RSO/Co. Dublin	A	5.00
Clooney Glenties RSO/Co. Donegal		
	A	7.00
Cloughjordan RSO/Co. Tip	A	7.00
Coagh/Moneymore RSO	A	8.00
Collinstown/Castlepollard RSO	A	7.00
Cong RSO/Co. Mayo	A	4.00
Coole RSO/Co. Westmeath	A	6.00
Corofin RSO/Co. Clare	A	6.00
Courtmacsherry RSO/Co. Cork	A	5.00
Cratloe RSO/Co. Clare	A	8.00
Creagh RSO/Co. Cork	A	6.00
Cross Cong RSO/Co. Mayo	A	25.00
Crossgar RSO Co. Down	B	6.00
Cullen Mill Street RSO/Co. Cork	A	15.00
Curry RSO/Co. Sligo	A	20.00
Daingean, Philipstown RSO/Kings Co.		
	A	6.00
Dalkey RSO/Co. Dublin	A	20.00
Dartrey RSO/Co. Monaghan	A	6.00
Derinagree/Banteer RSO/Co. Cork	F	75.00
Derrygorry/Aughnacloy RSO/Co. Tyrone		
	F	75.00
Dervock RSO/Co. Antrim	A	5.00
Doonagore Lahinch RSO/Co. Clare	A	7.00
Dromard/Ballisodare RSO/Co. Sligo		
	F	75.00
Dundrum RSO/Co .Down	A	5.00
Dundrum RSO Co. Tip	A	4.00
Dunkettle Stn/-RSO-	A	£125
	Numeral 195	£300
Dunleer RSO	B	15.00
Dunleer/RSO	A	9.00
	E	60.00
Dunmanway RSO/Co. Cork	A	6.00
Edenderry RSO/Kings Co.	A	5.00
Eighter/Virginia RSO/Co. Cavan	F	75.00
Enniskeen RSO/Co. Cork	A	6.00
Ennistymon RSO/Co. Clare	A	6.00
Errill Ballybrophy RSO/Queens Co	A	8.00
Favor Royal/AughnacloyRSO/Co. Tyrone		
	F	75.00
Ferbane RSO/Kings Co	A	5.00
Fiddown Piltown RSO/Co. Kilkenny		
	A	6.00
Foynes RSO Co. Limerick	B	5.00
Garranlahan/BallinloughRSO/Co. Roscommon		
	F	75.00

Railway Postmarks

Garrison/Beleek RSO Co. Fermanagh	A	25.00
Glandore, Leap RSO/Co. Cork	A	4.00
Glanmire RSO/Co. Cork	A	5.00
Glasslough RSO Co. Monaghan	B	7.00
Glenamaddy/RSO	E	40.00
Glenbeigh RSO/Co. Kerry	A	6.00
Glenealy RSO Co. Wicklow	A	6.00
Glenfarne RSO/Co. Leitrim	A	7.00
Glin RSO/Co. Limerick	A	6.00
Gneveguilla/Rathmore RSO	A	25.00
Goold's Cross RSO/Co. Tip	A	7.00
Greenore RSO/Co. Louth	A	4.00
Helen's Bay RSO/Co. Down	A	4.00
Herbertstown Knocklong RSO/Co. Limerick		
	A	8.00
Hillsboro/RSO	C (250)	£250
Hollymount RSO/Co. Mayo	A	7.00
Holywood RSO/Co. Down	A	3.00
	E (no county)	40.00
Hospital/Knocklong RSO	A	12.00
Howe's Strand/Kilbrittain RSO/Co. Cork		
	F	40.00
Innismore/Lisbellaw RSO/Co. Fermanagh		
	F	50.00
Inver RSO Co. Donegal	B	8.00
Kanturk RSO/Co. Cork	A	7.00
Kells RSO/Killarney	A	30.00
	C (258)	50.00
Kells RSO/Co.Kerry	A	20.00
Kenmare RSO/Co. Kerry	A	4.00
	AR	20.00
Kilbrittain RSO/Co. Cork	A	8.00
Kilcock RSO Co. Kildare	B	7.00
Kilfenora RSO/Co. Clare	A	6.00
Kilkee RSO/Co. Clare	A	5.00
Kill/Kilmacthomas RSO/Co. Waterford		
	F	75.00
Killala RSO/Co. Mayo	A	5.00
Killaloe RSO/Co. Clare	A	4.00
Killeagh RSO/Cork	A	5.00
Killinkere/Virginia RSO/Co. Cavan	F	60.00
Killoscully/Newport RSO/Co. Tipperary		
	F	60.00
Killylea RSO/Co. Armagh	A	5.00
Kilmanahan RSO/Co. Waterford	A	15.00
Kilmeedy/Ballingarry RSO	A	5.00
Kilmore/Drumsna RSO	A	8.00
Kilnaboy RSO/Co. Clare	A	6.00
Kilpedder RSO/Co. Wicklow	A	6.00
Kilskeery RSO/Co. Tyrone	A	6.00
Kiltyclogher RSO/Co. Leitrim	A	6.00
Kilworth RSO/Co. Cork	A	5.00
Kingwilliamstown Rathmore RSO/Co. Kerry		
	A	20.00
Knockcroghery RSO/Co. Roscommon		
	A	8.00
Knocklong RSO/Co. Limerick	A	6.00
	E (no county)	30.00
Knocknagashel/Abbeyfeale RSO	A	8.00
Kylemore RSO/Co.Galway	A	6.00
	AR	15.00
Lahinch RSO/Co.Clare	A	5.00
Laurencetown/Gilford RSO	A	6.00
Leap/RSO	A	15.00
	C (482)	£150
Leenane RSO/Co. Galway	A	4.00
Leixlip RSO/Co. Kildare	A	5.00
Letterfrack RSO/Co. Galway	A	5.00
Limerick Junct RSO/Co. Tip	A	35.00
Lisbellaw RSO/Co. Fermanagh	A	5.00
Lisdeen RSO/ Co. Clare	A	6.00
Lisdoonvarna RSO/Co. Clare	A	6.00
Lismore RSO/Co. Waterford	A	4.00
Lisnagry RSO/Co. Limk	A	6.00

Lisnalong/Rockcorry RSO/Co. Monaghan		
	F	60.00
Lisnamuck/Maghera RSO/Co. Derry	F	60.00
Lisnaskea RSO/Co. Fermanagh	A	4.00
Lissleton RSO/Co. Kerry	A	20.00
Listowel RSO/Co .Kerry	A	20.00
Longwood/Moy Valley RSO	A	8.00
Lough Rynn RSO/Co. Leitrim	A	7.00
Louth Inniskeen/RSO	A	8.00
Lucan RSO/Co. Dublin	A	4.00
Maam Cross Roads/RSO	A	30.00
Macmine RSO/Co. Wexford	A	7.00
Madden/Keady RSO/Co. Armagh	F (red)	£150
Manorcunningham RSO/Co. Donegal		
	A	6.00
Manorhamilton RSO/Co. Leitrim	A	5.00
Maynooth RSO Co. Kildare	B	5.00
Mayogall/Knockcloghrim RSO/Co. Londonderry		
	F	75.00
Middletown, Tynan RSO/Co. Armagh		
	A	6.00
Millstreet RSO/Co. Cork	A	5.00
Mitchelstown RSO/Co. Cork	A	8.00
Moira RSO/Co. Down	A	5.00
Monasteraden RSO/Co. Sligo	A	6.00
Monasterevan RSO/Co. Kildare	A	6.00
Mosside/Stranocum RSO/Co. Antrim		
	F	60.00
Mount Bellew RSO/Co. Galway	A	5.00
Mountcharles RSO/Co. Donegal	B	8.00
Mountmellick RSO/Queens Co.	A	4.00
Mountrath RSO Queens Co.	B	6.00
Moycullen RSO/Co. Galway	A	6.00
Mullagh/Milltown Malbay RSO	A	8.00
Murroe Newport RSO/Co. Tip	A	6.00
Narin/Glenties RSO	A	8.00
Neale/RSO	A	5.00
	C (529)	£200
Newbliss RSO Co. Monaghan	B	20.00
Newcastle West RSO/Co .Lim	A	6.00
Newmarket on Fergus RSO/Co. Clare		
	A	6.00
Newport RSO/Co. Tip	A	6.00
Newtown Butler RSO/Co. Fermanagh		
	A	6.00
Oldcastle RSO/Co. Meath	A	6.00
Pallasgreen RSO/Co. Limerick	A	7.00
	(also without county)	
Passage West RSO/Co. Cork	A	4.00
Patrickswell RSO/Co. Lim'k	A	6.00
Philipstown RSO/Kings Co.	A	6.00
Piltown RSO/Co. Kilkenny	A	4.00
Portlaw RSO/Co. Waterford	A	8.00
Portmagee/Valencia Island RSO	A	25.00
Portumna RSO/Co. Galway	A	5.00
Poyntzpass RSO/Co. Armagh	A	5.00
Quin RSO/Co. Clare	A	6.00
Rathaspic/Rathowen RSO/Co. Westmeath		
	F	60.00
Rathdangan/Baltinglass RSO/Co. Wicklow		
	F	75.00
Rathdowney Ballybrophy RSO/Queens Co.		
	A	7.00
Rathfarnham RSO/Co. Dublin	A	5.00
Rathkeale RSO/Co. Lim'k	A	20.00
Rathmore RSO/Co. Kerry	A	6.00
Rathnew RSO/Co. Wicklow	A	6.00
Robertstown RSO/Co. Kildare	A	15.00
Rosmuck RSO/Co. Galway	A	15.00
Rosscahill RSO/Co. Galway	A	7.00
Rosscarbery RSO/Co. Cork	A	20.00
Sixmile Bridge/RSO	A	20.00
Sixmilebridge RSO Co. Clare	B	6.00
	E	30.00

267

Railway Postmarks

Sneem Kenmare RSO/Co. Kerry	A	5.00
Spanish Point/Miltown Malbay RSO	F	75.00
Stamullen/Balbriggan RSO	A	8.00
Stewartstown RSO/Co. Tyrone	A	4.00
Stradbally RSO/Queen's Co.	A	6.00
Street RSO Co. Westmeath	B	8.00
Swords RSO Co. Dublin	B	8.00
Tagheen/Hollymount RSO/Co. Mayo	F	60.00
Tallow/RSO	A	30.00
Tallow RSO/Co. Waterford	A	8.00
Tarbert RSO/Co. Kerry	A	5.00
Tarbert RSO/Co. Limerick	A	9.00
Templeorum/Piltown RSO/Co. Kilkenny	F	60.00
Tourmakeady RSO/Co. Mayo	A	8.00
Tullow RSO Co. Carlow	B	5.00
Tullyvin/Cootehill RSO	A	8.00
Tummery RSO/Co. Tyrone	A	20.00
Tynan RSO Co. Armagh	B	6.00
Union Hall Leap RSO/Co. Cork	A	8.00
Upperlands RSO/Co. Derry	A	6.00
Upton RSO/Co. Cork	A	8.00
Valencia Island RSO/Co. Kerry	A	7.00
Whiteabbey RSO/Co.Antrim	A	7.00
Woodlawn/RSO	E	45.00

London Distribution Centre (initially known as the "Willesden Hub")

13/33

This new large rail/road facility opened in 1996, with road vehicles converging from Mail Centres across the South of England and several TPOs terminating at Willesden instead of at Euston Station as hitherto. Additionally, there was a publicly-accessible Late Posting facility open every weekday evening from 1730 to 2200 allowing letters to catch the relevant TPO (compare this with the "old days" when one could post a letter in the posting box at the side of the train!). At first a rubber handstamp inscribed London Distribution Centre/NW10 7RH was used for such mail, but later a steel double circle was used after the facility had been officially opened by The Princess Royal and named after her, see **13/33**. The late posting facility, with changes at Willesden, fell into dis-use about 2008 though the steel handstamp continued in use to 2010.

Shown at **13/34** is the "special" used for the Royal Opening in 1997

13/34

13A Colliery Postmarks

Colliery Postmarks 1854-1995 by F. W. Taylor was privately published by the author in 1995. Permission has been granted for inclusion here of some of the data from that book. The author has maintained an expanding addendum since the original publication appeared in 1995.

Only postmarks containing the word "colliery", or a similar word such as "drift" (a type of mine), are included in the book. Many villages had collieries but never had the word included in the post office name and are thus not listed. The reason why some post offices had colliery in their name is a separate village often developed around a nearby colliery which was large enough to justify its own post office, eg the Northumberland town of Bedlington had an adjacent colliery and also another a mile away. The latter soon had its own post office which was named Bedlington Colliery to distinguish it from Bedlington post office in the town market place.

Many colliery postmarks are difficult to find and for some examples only single copies have been recorded so far. Amazingly a new unrecorded type of colliery postmark was discovered as recently as 2007. This was a meter paid mark printed in red for Boldon Collliery.

A Circular, Unframed And Undated
B Barred Numeral
C Duplex
D Double Ring
E Scottish Type Double Ring With Numeral
F Single Ring
G Skeleton
H Rectangular Parcel
I Circular Undated Parcel
J Rubber
K Self-Inking Double Hexagon Frame (SID)
L Meter Machine

The following list is simplified and the valuation is therefore based on the commonest example of an office. Some examples are worth more depending on the scarcity which is not necessarily based on age, eg single ring postmarks of Emma Colliery, used on postcards from 1900-1922, are extremely common and more numerous than postmarks of any other colliery post office.

For some types of postmarks several variations of the wording exist as well differences in size, eg, 7 different single ring handstamps are recorded for Pegswood Colliery.
All postmarks are fully illustrated in the above book.

13A/1

13A/2

13A/3

Barrington Colliery	Nld	F	8.00
		G	30.00
Bearpark Colliery	Dur	D	8.00
		F	8.00
Bedlington Colliery	Nld	D	8.00
		F	8.00
		I	30.00
		J	50.00
Bestwood Colliery	Notts	D	8.00
		F	8.00
		J	30.00
Binley Colliery	Warks	D	15.00
		F	15.00
		H	25.00
Blackhall Colliery	Dur	D	8.00
		F	8.00
		H	25.00
Boldon Colliery	Dur	D	8.00
		F	8.00
		G	60.00
		H	25.00
		L	8.00
Brandon Colliery (H40)	Dur	C	75.00
		D	8.00
		F	8.00
		G	30.00
Browney Colliery	Dur	F	8.00
		J	30.00
Cassop Colliery	Dur	A	£200
		D	10.00
		F	10.00
Castle Eden Colliery	Dur	A	£175
		B	£125
		F	8.00
Chevington Drift	Nld	D	8.00
		F	8.00
		J	50.00
Colliery Row	Dur	F	6.00
		H	25.00
Cornsay Colliery	Dur	F	6.00
		H	25.00
Cramlington Colliery	Nld	J	60.00
Croxdale Colliery	Dur	F	10.00
Deaf Hill, Trimdon Colliery	Dur	F	20.00
		J	60.00
Denaby Main	Yorks	D	8.00
		F	8.00
Dinnington Colliery	Nld	D	8.00
		F	8.00
		J	50.00
Easington Colliery	Dur	D	8.00
		F	8.00

Colliery Postmarks

Name	County	Code	Value
		H	25.00
		J	40.00
Easington, Easington Colliery	Dur	D	8.00
		F	8.00
East Howle Colliery	Dur	D	8.00
		F	8.00
		J	50.00
Emma Colliery (B76)	Dur	B	£175
		D	8.00
Esh New Winning	Dur	F	8.00
Esh Winning	Dur	D	8.00
		F	8.00
		K	8.00
Hamsterley Colliery	Dur	D	8.00
		F	8.00
		H	30.00
Hartford Colliery	Nld	D	8.00
		F	8.00
		J	50.00
Harton Colliery	Dur	F	8.00
Hebburn Colliery	Dur	F	8.00
		K	8.00
Newstead Colliery	Notts	D	8.00
		F	8.00
		J	50.00
Hickleton Colliery	Yorks	F	8.00
		J	60.00
High Colliery	Dur	F	8.00
		J	60.00
		K	8.00
High Spen Colliery	Dur	J	75.00
Horden Colliery	Dur	J	75.00
Kiveton Park Colliery	Yorks	F	8.00
		J	60.00
Linton Colliery	Nld	D	8.00
		J	60.00
		K	8.00
Lintz Colliery	Dur	D	8.00
		F	8.00
		J	50.00
Marsden Colliery	Dur	F	8.00
		G	50.00
Meadowfield, Brandon Colliery	Dur	J	60.00
Murton Colliery	Dur	E	25.00
		F	8.00
Nedderton Colliery	Nld	J	60.00
Newbiggin Colliery	Nld	F	8.00
New Brancepeth Colliery	Dur	D	8.00
		F	8.00
Newstead Colliery	Notts	D	8.00
		F	8.00
		J	60.00
Newtown, Boldon Colliery	Dur	F	8.00
North Seaton Colliery	Nld	D	8.00
		F	8.00
Pegswood Colliery	Nld	D	8.00
		F	8.00
		G	60.00
		K	8.00
Ryehope Colliery	Dur	F	8.00
Salters Lane, Shotton Colliery	Dur	D	8.00
		F	8.00
Seaside Lane, Easington Colliery	Dur	F	8.00
Shankhouse Colliery	Nld	D	8.00
		F	8.00
Shincliffe Colliery	Dur	F	8.00
Shotton Colliery	Dur	A	£175
		D	8.00
		F	8.00
		K	8.00
Silksworth Colliery	Dur	F	8.00
Sleekburn Colliery	Nld	J	60.00
Stobswood Colliery	Nld	F	8.00
Team Colliery	Dur	J	60.00

Name	County	Code	Value
Trimdon Colliery	Dur	D	8.00
		F	8.00
Tudhoe Colliery	Dur	F	8.00
Tursdale Colliery	Dur	J	60.00
Usher Moor Colliery	Dur	F	8.00
Usworth Colliery	Dur	D	8.00
		F	8.00
		J	40.00
		H	25.00
Waldridge Colliery	Dur	F	8.00
Wardley Colliery	Dur	F	8.00
		J	40.00
Wearmouth Colliery	Dur	F	8.00
Welbeck Colliery Village Mansfield	Notts	D	8.00
		F	8.00
Westmoor Colliery	Nld	J	60.00
West Sleekburn Colliery	Nld	D	8.00
		F	8.00
		G	60.00
		J	50.00
Westwood, Hamsterley Colliery	Dur	J	75.00
West Wylam Colliery	Nld	F	8.00
Whitburn Colliery	Dur	F	8.00
Widdington Colliery	Nld	F	8.00

14 Maritime Markings

The sections in this chapter, showing some of the varied forms of maritime postal markings of the British Isles, are generally in the sequence of the earliest marking of each section. As well as postmarks there are privately produced cachets which we include only because they form an important element of maritime postal history and where the presence of such cachets (usually on postcards) alters the card's value considerably. Manuscript Ship Letters are known from numerous locations, these are currently beyond the scope of this catalogue but it is hoped to list them in future editions. For further information see "Robertson Revisited" (2012) by Colin Tabeart.

Section I: Ship Letters and India Letters
Applied to mail landed from private trading ships and carried by them from the port of departure, 1760s-1840s.

Note: re type A below: inscription alternatively LRE. or LE. or LETR. 'For 'SHIP' only type marks see type AA.

★	Very scarce and desirable. Auction realisations often vary widely (particularly on distinctive marks)
★★	Rare
★★★	Very Rare - only one or two examples known
★★★★	Proofed but not yet seen in use

SHIP
14/0 AA

DOVER SHIP LRE
14/1 A

DEAL SHIP LRE
14/2 B

SHIP IRE
14/3 C

PORTSMOUTH Ship Lre
14/4 D

PORTSMOUTH SHIP LETTER
14/5 E

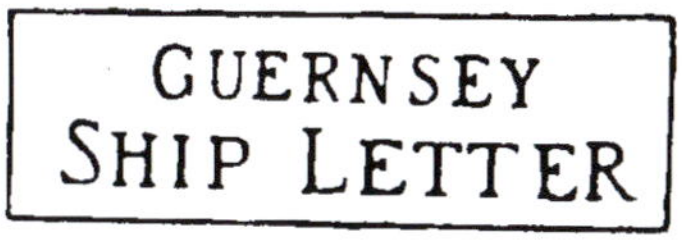

GUERNSEY SHIP LETTER
14/6 F

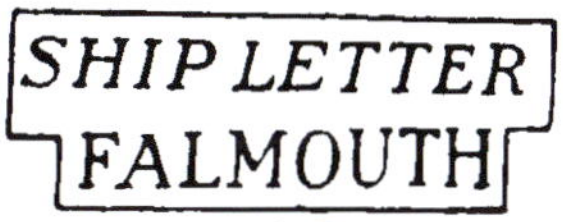

SHIP LETTER FALMOUTH
14/7 G

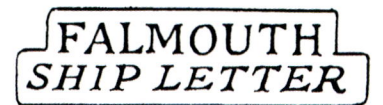

FALMOUTH SHIP LETTER
14/7 GA

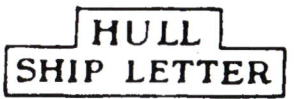

HULL SHIP LETTER
14/8 H

SHIP LETTER LIVERPOOL
14/9 J

SOUTHAMPTON SHIP LETTER
14/10 K

SOUTHAMPTON MR 18 96 SHIP-LETTER
14/11 L

SHIP LETTER 1 JU 1 1836 LONDON
14/12 M

BRISTOL SHIP LETTER
14/13 N

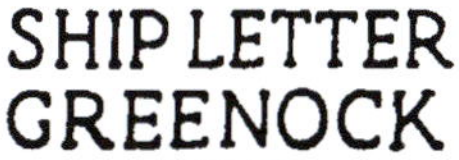

SHIP LETTER GREENOCK
14/14 P

27 JA 44 LIVERPOOL SHIP
14/15 Q

271

Visit SAMWELLS for *All* GB Covers
All Postmark Types, Stamp Issues, Themes, Subjects & Periods 1400-2013

1876 EUSTON STATION/IRISH MAIL c.d.s. cancelling adhesives on EL to New York

1901 F.P.O./BRITISH ARMY S.AFRICA

1866 'C41' numeral of British Post Office GUAYAQUIL (Ecuador) on cover to Peru

1849 GUAYAQUIL/PAID of British Post Office in Ecuador

1863 Bulging CROWN/REGISTERED of Folkestone

1887 'PANAMA/C35' duplex

1859 HOUSES OF PARLIAMENT c.d.s. and 'HP/I' barred London numeral

Browse at Stampex & York Stamp Shows or view selected items over £45 online
SPECIAL OFFER: 10% discount on your first online order QUOTING CBP
www.postalhistorygb.com   01225 462429   info@postalhistorygb.com

Visit **SAMWELLS** for *All* GB Postmark Types
Browse our large stocks at Stampex & York. View selected items online

1820 BING/HAM (Notts) distinctive intaglio namestamp

1799 FREE/CROWN dotted circle (experimental type)

1839 MARGATE/SHIP·LRE and MARGATE/INDIA LETTER on EL ex Callao (Peru). Historic letter re Bernardo O'Higgins

1793 KINSALE/ SHIPLETTER in blue on EL ex Jamaica

1808 WICKLOW Dublin 'MERMAID' in transit

1848 DETAINED for POSTAGE London. Ex India to Madeira

WE CAN NOW TAILOR OUR LISTS TO SUIT YOUR REQUIREMENTS
Simply let us know what you collect & we will return results by e-mail
www.postalhistorygb.com   01225 462429   info@postalhistorygb.com

Maritime Markings

SHIP LETTER.
AVONMOUTH.
BRISTOL.
14/16 R

HARWICH
SHIP LETTER
14/17 S

POST PAID WITHDRAWN SHIP LETTER
II AP II
1815
LIVERPOOL
14/18 SA

INDIA LETTER
PORTSMOUTH
14/19 T

INDIA LETTER
WEYMOUTH
14/20 V

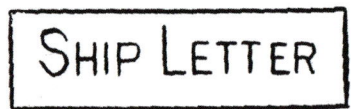

INDIA LETTER
LONDON
14/21 W

SHIP LETTER
14/22 X

SHIP G R 2

SHIP·LETTER

BANGOR SHIPLETTER

Edinbr ShipLre

NEWRY SHIP·LETTER

Type **Z**. Many different types; some illustrated to demonstrate wide variations in design

London Ship Letters:

A	(with or without hyphen)	£125
E		£150
H		75.00
L		25.00
L*	(Paid)	20.00
M		50.00
M	(double circle)	£125
M	(single circle)	£100
SA		£500
T		75.00
W		£125
Paid Ship Letters		75.00
Post Paid Ship Letters		£100
Exempt Ship Letters		£300
Ship Letter/from/India		£2500

Provincial Ship Letters:

Aberdeen	E (dated)	£1000
	F	£500
	H	£400
	X	£200
Aldborough	B	£1250
Anstruther	J	***
Ardrossan	S (dated)	£1100
Arundel	H	£950
	T	£900
Avonmouth	R	£150
Ayr	H	£750
Ballycastle	Z (scroll)	***
Bangor (Wales)	S	£900
Bangor (Ireland)	Z (single line)	***
Barnstable	D	£300
Barnstaple	A	£1250
	D	£1250
	H	£400
Beaumaris	A	£750
	H	£450
	T	***
Belfast	AA	£600
	F	£150
	F* (·Belfast·)	£300
	N	£350
	O	£600
	Z (fancy frame)	£500
Berwick	N ("Letters")	*
Bideford	H	***
	P	****
Birmingham/Ship	L (double circle)	£400
Blyth North.d.	L	****
	P	£500
Bowmore	Ship Lre (2 lines)	***
Bridlington	D	***
Bridport	B (serpentine)	£750
"Bright Helm Stone" (Brighton)	A (4 lines)	£1000
Brighton	B	£400
	E	£500
	G	£125
	H	£200
	K	£150
	N	****
	T (2 sizes)	£150
Bristol	A	£300
	A* (BRISTOLI)	£300
	A (port at top and mileage 129)	£500
	D ("Letter")	£600
	E (port at top)	£500
	G	£150
	H (split frame)	90.00
	K	£175
	K (small)	***
	N	90.00
	S (no frame)	£150

274

Maritime Markings

	SA	★★★	
	T	£350	
Brixham	C	£750	
	D ("Letter")	£350	
	G	£150	
	GA	£100	
	K	£400	
	N (italic)	£300	
	T	£400	
Buncrana	Z (scroll)	★★	
Burntisland	P	★★★	
Caherciveen	Z (oval frame)	★★★	
"Cambleton" (Campbeltown)	A	£750	
"Campbelton" (Campbeltown)	SteamBoat (2 lines)	★	
"Campbleton" (Campbeltown)	S	★	
Cardiff	H	£550	
	L	£300	
	L* (162 duplex)	£850	
Carlisle	H	★★	
Carnarvon	E	★★★	
Carrickfergus	N	★	
Castletown (Ireland)	N	£350	
Castletown (Portland)	R	£400	
Chester	S (no frame)	★★★★	
Chichester	H	★★★	
Colchester	E (dated)	★★★	
	H	£1000	
Coleraine	F	★★★	
Cork	AA	£1000	
	F	£200	
	N	£150	
	O (3 types)	£600	
	T	£225	
Cove (see also "Queenstown")	A	£300	
	N	£125	
	V	£275	
Cowes (see also "Isle of Wight")	A (LRE⁵)	£300	
	G (3 types)	90.00	
	H	£150	
	K	£100	
	T (4 similar)	£150	
Cromarty	E (dated)	★★★★	
	SA	★★★★	
Dartmouth	A	£200	
	D	£300	
	G	£125	
	H	£75	
	L	★★★★	
	P	£350	
	SA	★	
	T	£150	
	T (port at top)	£200	
	V	£225	
Deal	A (4 types)	£125	
	B	£200	
	C	£1250	
	D ("Letter")	£150	
	G (2 types)	90.00	
	H	60.00	
	T (4 types)	90.00	
	T* (port at top)	£150	
Derry	AA	£750	
	D ("Letter")	£500	
Devonport (see also "Plymouth Dock")			
	G (2 types)	£150	
	N	£225	
	T (2 types)	£250	
	V	£300	
	Packet Letter two lines	see 14/26	
Dingle	A	★	
Donegal	F	★	
Douglas (IOM)	A	★★★	
Dover	A (4 types)	£125	

	AA	★	
	B	£175	
	D ("Letter")	£225	
	D* (no port)	£1000	
	E	£150	
	F	★★★	
	G (2 types)	75.00	
	H	75.00	
	P	£200	
	T (5 types)	80.00	
	T (port at top)	£100	
	V	£150	
Dublin	A ("Letter")	£500	
	AA	★	
	J	£500	
	K* (lower case ship letter)	£225	
	N (2 types)	£300	
	R	★★★	
	Z (Family & sided Crown dated)	£400	
Dumfries	J	★★★	
Dunbar	J	★★★	
Dundalk	F	★★★	
Dundee	E (with cypher)	£750	
	H	£500	
	S (port at bottom)	★★★★	
Dunmore East	Z	★★	
Eastbourne	D	£350	
	H	£250	
	T	£300	
Edinburgh	A	£600	
	X (octagonal frame)	£250	
	Z (with ship)	★	
Exeter	A	£750	
	E	£500	
	H	£375	
	T	£450	
Exmouth	H	£450	
	T	£600	
Falmouth	A (2 types)	£250	
	C	£300	
	D	£225	
	E	£250	
	G	60.00	
	GA (port at top)	50.00	
	H	£100	
	L (2 types)	£40	
	P	£200	
	SA	★★	
	T	75.00	
	T* (port in italics)	£100	
	V	£175	
	Circular, dated, double arcs	£500	
	Packet Lre, circ	see 14/32	
	Packet Letter, 2 lines	see 14/33	
	L (Packet)	£350	
Faversham	H	★★★	
Fleetwood	P (no serifs)	★	
Folkestone	D	£350	
	GA (port at top)	£225	
	K	£125	
	T	£225	
Fowey	GA (port at top)	£750	
	T	£1000	
Fraserburgh	J	★★★	
Glasgow	D ("Letter")	£275	
	F (gap below port)	£225	
	F (3-line dated)	£275	
Gloucester	H	★★★	
Goole	H	★	
Gosport	A	★★★	

275

Maritime Markings

Location	Marking	Price
	E	★★★
Grangemouth	E (with cypher)	£900
	F	£750
	X	£400
Granton	S (port at bottom)	£500
Gravesend	A	£300
	AA	£350
	D	£350
	E (single oval)	£750
	G (3 types)	50.00
	GA (port at top)	75.00
	K* (framed lowercase)	50.00
	N (no serifs)	£125
	T (2 types)	75.00
	T (italic lowercase)	75.00
	V	£300
Greenock	C (with ring)	£750
	D	£225
	D* ("Letter")	£250
	E (dated)	£300
	F (dated)	£125
	GA (port at top)	90.00
	J	£300
	N (4 types)	90.00
	P	£200
	P (dated)	£250
	SA (2 types)	£2000
	India (Ship LR)	£250
	T (2 types)	£125
Grimsby	E	★
	L (undated)	★★★★
	N (no serifs)	★
	S	£350
Guernsey	E	★★
	F	£750
	GA	★★
	J	£3000
	T	★★★
Harwich	D* ("Letter")	★★
	G	£150
	H	£300
	S	£150
	T	£600
Hastings	A	£500
	D* ("Letter")	£600
	G	£300
	H	£150
	N (no serifs)	★
	T (italic port)	£175
Haverford West	A (3 lines)	£1000
Helston	G	£600
"Hithe" (Hythe error)	C	★
Holyhead	A	£500
	H (2 types)	£125
	T (italic port)	£250
Holywood	Z	★★
"Hubberstone" (Hubberston)	A	★★★
Hull	C	£1000
	D* ("Letter")	★
	G	60.00
	GA	★
	H	50.00
	K	★
	L	40.00
	N	50.00
	Q* (lozenge)	75.00
	SA	★★★
	T	£350
Hythe	GA (port at top)	£600
Ilfracombe	G (port at top)	£600
	T	★★★
	T (port at top)	★★★
I. Man (I.O.M.)	G	★★★
Ipswich	GA (port at top)	£1000

Location	Marking	Price
Irvine	A	£750
Isle of Wight	D	£650
	G	★
	T (2 types)	£300
Jersey	F	★
	F* (port at bottom)	★★
	GA (port at top)	★
	K	£750
Killybegs	S	★★
Kilrush	N (no port)	★★
Kingsbridge	G	£150
	G*	£150
	H (port at top)	★★★★
	T (3 types)	£200
Kinsale	AA	★
	N	★
Kirkcaldy	J	★
Kirkwall	AA	£600
	J	★
Lancaster	C (circular)	★
	D	£500
	E	£750
	GA (port at top)	£400
Leith	D	★
	D* ("Letter")	£300
	E (with cypher)	★
	E (dated)	£600
	GA (port at top)	£250
	Z (oval, Ship Letter)	£400
	Z* ditto (dated)	£400
	L	75.00
	L* (thimble)	£250
	T	£750
	X (octagonal frame)	£350
Lerwick	GA	£400
	J	★★
Lewes	G	★★
	GA (2 sizes)	£300
	T (2 sizes)	£300
Limerick	F	£300
	Z (scroll)	£750
"Limington" (Lymington)	A	£750
Liverpool	A	£125
	A* (Liverpool/Ship)	£500
	AA	£350
	D	£100
	E	£100
	E (dated)	£450
	F	40.00
	G	50.00
	GA	40.00
	J	50.00
	L (Ship)	40.00
	M	£100
	N	40.00
	Q	40.00
	Q (Paid)	£1000
	S	40.00
	SA	£750
	T	£100
	T (India Ship Lr at bottom)	£125
	Exempt Ship	£300
	Missent to LIverpool/England (Oval)	£3000
Looe	G	£250
"Lowestoff" (Lowestoft)	C	★★★
Lyme	A	£400
	D (Letter)	★★★
	G	£350
	GA	£350
	T	£450
Lymington	A	£225
	D	£1000

Maritime Markings

	G	★★★	
	T (port in italics)	£250	
Lynn	D (Letter)	★★★	
	GA	★★★★	
Maldon	A	★★★	
Marazion	A (no port)	★★★	
	GA	£1000	
Margate	A (2 sizes)	£225	
	G	£150	
	GA	£150	
	SA	★★★	
	T (3 types)	£250	
Mevagissey	GA	£700	
Middlesbrough	L	£500	
Milford (Wales)	A (no port)	£1000	
	D (Letter)	£750	
	GA	£350	
	T	£400	
Montrose	J	£750	
Newburgh	F (dated)	★★★★	
Newcastle (Northd)	D	★★★	
Newcastle on Tyne	R (2 lines)	£300	
	S (unframed)	£450	
Newcastle-Tyne	K (port at bottom)	★★	
Newcastle.u.T.	P	£450	
Newport IOW - see Isle of Wight			
Newport (Mon)	K	★★★★	
New Romney	GA (framed)	£200	
	T (port at top)	£250	
"New Rumney" (New Romney)	D	£900	
Newry	AA	★	
	N	£500	
	Z (oval fancy)	★★	
Newton Abbot	H	£750	
North Shields	E	£1000	
	GA	£750	
	J (port at top)	£500	
Oban	A	★★★	
Padstow	E (Letter)	£1000	
Passage (Ireland)	N	£750	
Pembroke	G	£750	
Penzance	A	★★★	
	D	£350	
	GA (2 sizes)	£175	
	P	£300	
T (double frame)		£400	
	V	£300	
Perth	J	★★★	
Peterhead	P	£700	
	S	£500	
Plymouth	A (4 types)	£225	
	D	£350	
	E	£200	
	G	75.00	
	H (port in bottom line)	75.00	
	J	★★★	
	L (4 types)	20.00	
	L* (double arc)	£225	
	T	90.00	
	V	£125	
Plymouth Dock (Devonport)	C	£1000	
	D	£400	
	GA	£400	
	T	£500	
"Polpero" (Polperro)	S	★★★	
"Pool" (Poole)	A	£350	
	D ("Letter")	£450	
Poole	G	£350	
	GA (2 sizes)	£225	
	J	★★	
	K	£500	
	SA	£1500	

	T	£400	
	V	★★★	
Portaferry	Z (scroll)	★★★	
Portaskaig	Z Ship (single circle)	£1000	
Port Glasgow	D	£275	
	E (dated)	£650	
	E (with cypher)	£300	
	GA	£150	
	N	£125	
	SA	★★	
	T	£200	
Portland Harbour S.O.	R	£750	
Portsmouth	A (5 sizes)	£175	
	A* (small)	£100	
	B	£300	
	D	£125	
	E	£100	
	E (small single oval)	£400	
	G	75.00	
	GA	£125	
	H	50.00	
	K	75.00	
	N	£150	
	SA	★★	
	T (3 types)	75.00	
	T (port at top)	£300	
	T* (double frame)	£150	
Preston	H	£1000	
"Pteerhd Ship letter" (Peterhead)	Z (1 line)	£1000	
"Pt Glasgo" (Port Glasgow)	A	£350	
Pwllheli	S (italic)	£750	
Qn.Borough (Queenborough)	A	£500	
Queenboro (Queenborough)	G	£225	
	T	£700	
Queenborough	B	£650	
	GA	£275	
Queenstown (Cove)	L	£300	
	L* (undated)	£1000	
	R	£300	
Ramsgate	A (2 sizes)	£350	
	E (single oval)	£650	
	G	£450	
	GA	£125	
	T (4 types)	£150	
Rochester	E	£500	
	E* (single oval)	£650	
	G	£450	
	GA	£400	
	K	★★★★	
Rochford	GA	£750	
"Romney" (New Romney)	H	★★★	
	GA	£125	
	P	★★★★	
	T	£225	
	V	★★★★	
Ross (Ireland)	N	£600	
Rostrevor (Ireland)	N	£750	
Rothesay (Bute)	J	£750	
Ryde (Isle of Wight)	E (single oval)	£1000	
	GA	£225	
	K	£200	
	P	£300	
	T	£250	
	T* (no port)	★★	
	V	£200	
	V (port at top)	£275	
	W	£300	
Rye	D ("Letter")	★	
	G	£1000	
	GA	★	
St.Ives	GA	£750	
	T ("corn")	£850	
St.Mawes	G	£400	
Saltcoats	J	★★★	

277

Maritime Markings

Location	Marking	Price
	S (three lines)	****
"Scarbro" (Scarborough)	D ("Letter")	***
Sheerness	B	***
	D	£600
	G	***
	GA	£400
	T	£550
Shoreham	GA	£650
	T	**
Sidmouth	G	£750
Sittingbourne	G	***
Skibbereen	A ("LETR")	£400
	N (italic "Ship letter")	£750
Sligo	N	***
Southampton	A (2 sizes)	£225
	D	£275
	E	£200
	G (2 sizes)	75.00
	GA	£150
	H	£125
	J (port at top)	£125
	K	£150
	L (severed)	15.00
	N	75.00
	P	£125
	S (no frame)	£150
	T (3 sizes)	£150
	V	***
"Sth Shields" (South Shields)	GA	***
South Shields	R (3 lines with "Tyne Dock")	£300
	R* (2 lines "Tyne Dock" removed)	£500
"Southwould" (Southwold)	E	£750
Stornoway (Lewis)	X	£500
Stranraer	A	£600
	GA	*
Sunderland	GA	£750
Swanage	E	£600
	G	£250
	GA	£200
	J	£200
	J* (port at top)	£200
	S (no frame)	£350
	T	£225
	T (port at top)	£225
	W (port at top)	£300
Swansea	GA	£400
	L	£300
	N	£350
	S	***
"Swanzey"	A	£1000
Tarbet	Z (scroll)	***
Teignmouth	G	£600
	GA	£750
	T	**
Tenby	J	**
Thurso	J	***
Tobermory	Z (double circle)	£1000
Torquay	K* (lower case port)	£275
Totness	A	**
	C	**
Troon	E* (single oval with cypher)	£1000
	S (port at bottom)	£350
Tyne Dock (see South Shields)		
Uist to Dunvegan	A*	see 14/85
Warren (Warrenpoint)	N	**
Warrens Pt	N	**
Waterford	AA	£750
	N	£300
Westport	Z (scroll)	***
Wexford	N	***
Weymouth	"from Guernsey"	
	applied at Weymouth, 1826	*
	A	£350
	D	£250
	E (dated)	£600
	G	£125
	GA (split frame)	£100
	H	£125
	T (2 sizes)	£150
	V	£350
	SA	£1500
Whitby	GA	*
Whitehaven	A	£350
	B	£850
	GA	£500
Wick	J (three line)	***
Wicklow	N (no port)	**
"Wisbeach" (Wisbech)	SA	****
Workington	C	***
Worthing	GA	£500
Yarmouth (Norfolk)	A	£650
	D	£500
	GA	£350
Yarmouth Isle of Wight (IOW)	G* (three line with "Sihp" for "Ship")	£750
Yarmouth IW (IOW)	E	£800
Yarmouth.N (Norfolk)	G	£600
	T	***
Youghal	N	£750

Section II: Packet Letters

Carried by vessels hired by the Post Office to carry letters, from 1802.

PACKET-LETTER
14/23

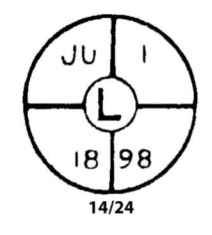

14/24

14/27

14/29

No. 14/22 not used.

London

14/23 Packet Letter, boxed or unboxed, 1802-63   £350

London Foreign Branch

14/24 Quartered handstamp, red or black, 1864-1902, with L (London), D (Devonport), H (Holyhead), I (Ireland - Cork), N (underpaid) - also known with C or blank centre (meanings unclear)   50.00

Maritime Markings

Dartmouth
14/25	Dartmouth Packet Letter, circular unframed, 1857	£500

Devonport
14/26	Packet Letter/Devonport, 1839-50	£350
14/27	Devonport/Packet Letter, circular unframed, 1858-66	£200
14/28	Cape Packet/Devonport, circular unframed, 1858-67	£200
14/29	Paid/Devonport/Cape Packet, 1863-67	£100
14/30	Cape Packet/Devonport, 1869-70	£125

Dublin
14/31	America/Paid/Dublin, with side arcs, black, green or blue, 1856-59	£550

Falmouth
14/32	Falmouth Packt Lre, unframed circular, green or black, 1807-14	£350
14/33	Falmouth/Packet Letter, two line unframed, green or black, 1809-15	£450
14/34	Unframed, with F (Falmouth) in green, 1810-47:	
	America	£600
	Brazil	£500
	Cadiz	£400
	Gibraltar	£1250
	Jamaica	£1000
	Leeward Islands	£1100
	Lisbon	£300
	Malta	£900
14/35	India	**
14/35a	'Fleuron' types:	
	Mexico	£100
	"Columbia" (Colombia)	*
	Buenos Ayres	£750
14/35b	St. Domingo (Haiti)	***
14/35c	Falmouth Packet CDS	£200

Glasgow
14/36	Glasgow Packet/Paid/date, four line unframed, 1860-81	£100
14/37	As above but unpaid, 1865	£200
14/38	Glasgow Packet/Col. Paid/four line unframed, black or blue, 1860-63	£150
14/39	As above but unpaid, 1863	£300
14/40	Packet Letter/Glasgow, oval, 1879-94	90.00
14/41	Paid/Glasgow/Packet, single circle, 1883-90	£150
14/42	As above but unpaid, 1883	*

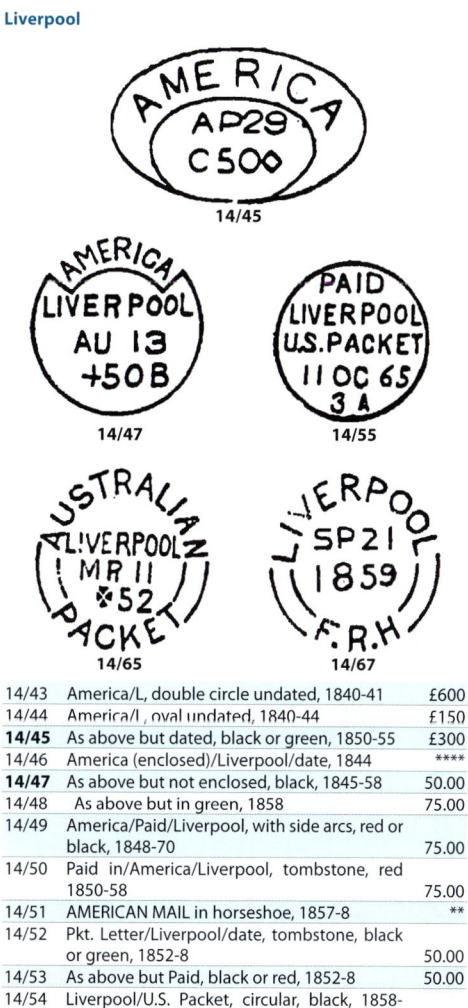

Liverpool
14/43	America/L, double circle undated, 1840-41	£600
14/44	America/L, oval undated, 1840-44	£150
14/45	As above but dated, black or green, 1850-55	£300
14/46	America (enclosed)/Liverpool/date, 1844	****
14/47	As above but not enclosed, black, 1845-58	50.00
14/48	As above but in green, 1858	75.00
14/49	America/Paid/Liverpool, with side arcs, red or black, 1848-70	75.00
14/50	Paid in/America/Liverpool, tombstone, red 1850-58	75.00
14/51	AMERICAN MAIL in horseshoe, 1857-8	**
14/52	Pkt. Letter/Liverpool/date, tombstone, black or green, 1852-8	50.00
14/53	As above but Paid, black or red, 1852-8	50.00
14/54	Liverpool/U.S. Packet, circular, black, 1858-1903	25.00
14/55	As above but with Paid, red, 1858-1903	25.00
14/56	Liverpool/BR Packet, circular, black, 1858-1874	50.00

279

Maritime Markings

14/57	As above but with Paid, red or black, 1858-1902	30.00
14/58	Liverpool/COL. Packet, circular, black, 1859	£100
14/59	As above but with Paid, red, 1859-1903	75.00
14/60	Liverpool/DE Packet, (Londonderry), circular, black, 1859	***
14/61	Paid/Liverpool/LB Packet (Liverpool, Brazil & River Plate Steam Navigation Co.), circular, 1814	**
14/62	Liverpool P.S. Packet (Pacific Steam Navigation Co.), circular 1872	*
14/63	Liverpool.P.L.O. (Packet Letter Office), circular, 1858-1902	50.00
14/64	SOUTH AMERN/Liverpool/Packet, with side arcs, black or green, 1854-55	£450
14/65	Australian/Liverpool/Packet, with double side arcs, black or green, 1852-56	£200
14/66	As above but Paid, red, 1855-57	£200
14/67	Liverpool/F.R.H. (Floating Receiving House), with double side arcs, black, red or blue, 1859-64	£450
14/68	(no entry, for quartered handstamp see **14/24**)	

14/74

14/79  14/80

Londonderry

14/69	Paid/Derry/Col. Packet, circular, black or red, 1862-75	£200
14/70	Londonderry/Paid/Col. Packet, circular, red, 1877-89	£100
14/71	Londonderry Colonial Pkt., circular, black or red, 1897-1906	75.00

Plymouth

14/72	Packet Letter/Plymouth, boxed, 1811-15	£500
14/73	Plymouth/Packet Letter, circular with side arcs, black, red, blue, yellow or green, 1853-56	£100
14/74	Cape Packet/Plymouth, 1870-78	60.00
14/75	Paid/Plymouth/Cape-Packet, 1870	£100

Plymouth Dock (later Devonport)

14/76	Packet Letter/Plym. Dock, boxed, 1813	£400

Portsmouth

14/77	Packet Letter/Portsmouth, unframed, 1847-49	£225

Southampton

14/78	Packet Letter/Southampton, unframed, blue, red, green or black, 1844-55	£100
14/79	Southampton/Packet Letter, circular unframed, black or blue, 1857-67	60.00
14/80	As above but framed, 1881-1917	10.00

Section III: Moveable Box Marks on Mail to France

14/81  14/83

14/84

14/81	Boxed M.B. from 1844: Brighton Dover Folkestone London Southampton from	£250
14/82	Milestone type with year in four digits, from 1856: Dover Folkestone Guernsey Jersey London Newhaven Southampton Weymouth from	£150
14/83	As above but with year in two digits, from 1884	75.00
14/84	Circular MB types, 1893-1939: London Southampton	10.00 10.00

Section IV: British Coastal Steamers

Skye Packet Service

UIST to
DUNVEGAN
14/85

14/85	Uist to/Dunvegan, 1836-41	£500

Fleetwood to Belfast Steamer Service
Circular cachets struck on mail from the 'Prince of Wales' 1843-44

14/86  14/87

280

Maritime Markings

14/86	Prince of Wales,		★
14/87	Fleetwood &/Belfast		£750

Holyhead and Kingstown Service (City of Dublin Steam Packet Co.) 1860-1925

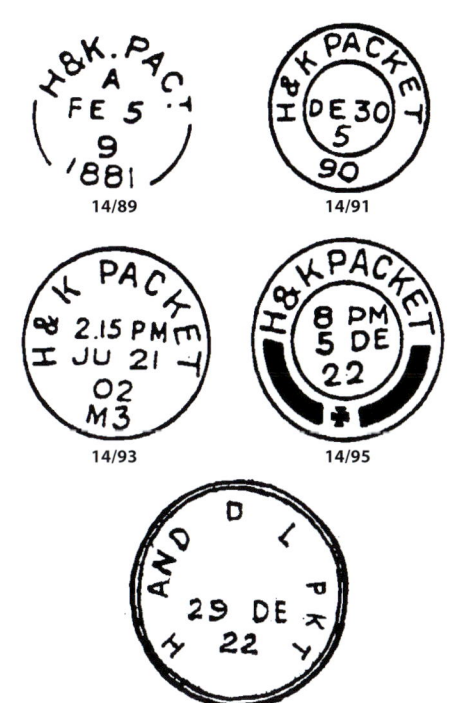

14/88

14/89 14/91

14/93 14/95

14/97

14/88	H & K Pact duplex with diamond numeral 186, from 1860	£500
14/89	H & K Pact, dated, with side arcs (backstamp), from 1860	15.00
14/90	As above but surmounted by 'Night Mail'	£750
14/91	H & K Packet, double circle types, 1884–93	40.00
14/92	H & K Packet, single circle types, 1894–1900	40.00
14/93	As above but larger, C1-4 (Connaught), L1-4 (Leinster), M1-4 (Munster), U1-4 (Ulster), from 1901	50.00
14/94	As above but C5,L5,M5 or U5, rubber, in purple, H & K Packet PO	£150
14/95	H & K Packet, double circle thick arcs broken by cross, from 1919	40.00
14/95A	As above but with adhesives of Irish Free State	50.00
14/96	H and K Packet/Day Boat, double circle, 1914–23	£300
14/97	H and D L Pkt, double-rim skeleton, 1922	£600
14/98	Mis-sent to Hd & Kn Packet, 1862	£500
14/99	Posted without late fee, boxed, 1897-1907	50.00

14/100	Late fee paid, boxed, 1922	50.00

Clyde Steamers

Greenock & Ardrishaig Floating Post Offices (David MacBrayne Ltd), 1879--1917:

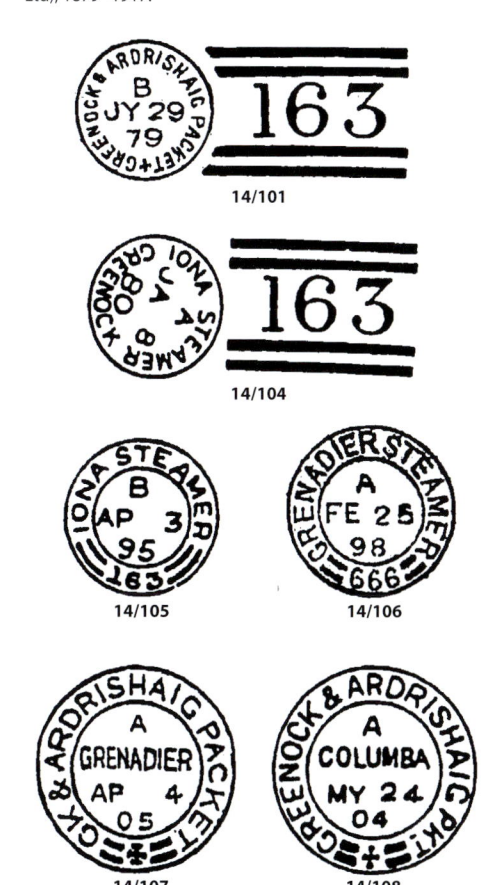

14/101

14/104

14/105 14/106

14/107 14/108

14/101	Greenock & Ardrishaig Packet, duplex 163, 1879 only	£400
14/102	Columba Steamer/Greenock, duplex 163, 1879-1900	£150
14/103	As above but without small side arcs in datestamp	£175
14/104	Iona Steamer/Greenock, duplex 163, 1879-84	£225
14/105	Iona Steamer/163, small double circle, 1884-1900	90.00
14/106	Grenadier Steamer/666, double circle, 1895-1901	£500
14/107	Gk. & Ardrishaig Packet, double circle 29mm, 1901-08 (see note below) - Columba 20.00, Iona 30.00, Grenadier £150, Chevalier	£750
14/108	Greenock & Ardrishaig Pkt, double circle 29mm, 1903-09 (see note below) - Columba 60.00, Iona 30.00, Grenadier	£250
14/109	Gk. & Ardrishaig Packet, double circle 27mm, 1909-15 (see note below)- Columba 20.00, Iona 40.00, Grenadier £175, Chevalier	£750
14/110	As above but without ship's name, 1916-17	£300

Note: Valuations are for index B, afternoon return trip from Ardrishaig to Greenock, used as cancellations. Index A, morning trip, merits a premium. Backstamps should be discounted slightly.

281

Maritime Markings

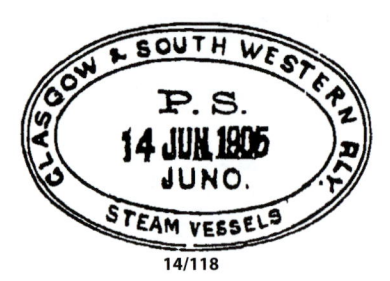

Section V: Private Cachets

D. Hutcheson & Co.

14/111	Posted on Board/"Columba"/date/D. Hutcheson & Co., double oval, 1878	£500
14/112	As above but Iona	£550

Glasgow and Inveraray Steamboat Co.

14/113	Posted on Board/Lord of the Isles/Steamer, unframed, magenta, 1878-79	£400
14/114	Steamer Lord of the Isles, double oval with date, violet, 1903	£250
14/115	R.M.S."Lord of the Isles", oval belt & buckle, violet, 1904-12	£100
14/115A	As **14/115** but black	£125
14/116	Posted on Board S.S."Fairy Queen"/Loch Eck/Argyllshire, 1903-11	£150

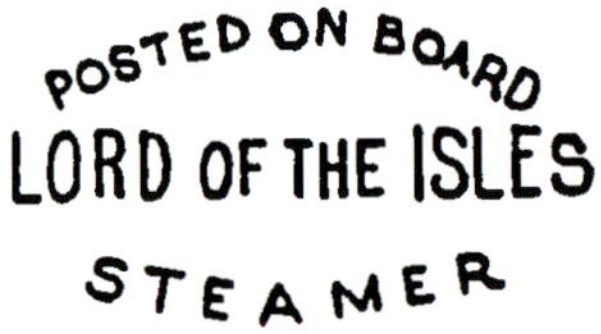

Lochgoil and Lochlong Steamboat Co.

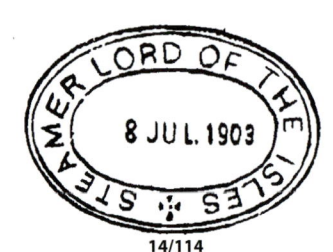

14/117	Posted on Board/"Edinburgh Castle"/Steamer, unframed, violet, 1880-	£550

Glasgow and South Western Railway

14/118	Glasgow and South Western Rly/P.S./Juno/Steam Vessels, 1905–	£225
14/119	As above but P.S. Jupiter, 1904-	£250

Caledonian Steam Packet Co. Ltd.

14/120	Caledonian Steam Packet Co./Limited/Duchess/of Argyll, 1908–	£200
14/121	As above but Duchess /of Rothesay, 1905–	£200
14/122	As above but P.S./Duchess of/Hamilton, 1905-13	£125

(Clyde) Turbine Steamers

14/122A	Turbine/"King Edward"/Steamer, circular, 1903-5	£200
14/122B	Turbine Steamer/"King Edward", oval format similar to **14/122**, 1912	£500
14/122C	New/Turbine Steamer/"Queen Alexandra", boxed, 1905	£200

Loch Lomond

14/123 Posted on board "The Queen", violet, 1892   £750

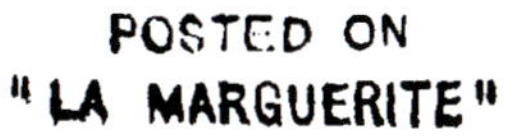

[Cachet: POSTED ON "LA MARGUERITE"]
14/125

[Cachet: POSTED ON ST. ELVIES]
14/128

[Cachet: POSTED ST. TUDNO ON BOARD]
14/131

North Wales Coastal Services

14/124	Per. Passgr. SS 'Trefriw-Belle', small violet cachet, from 1904	£500
14/125	Posted on/"La Marguerite", blue, 1905–10	50.00
14/126	As above but double circle in violet (similar to **14/128**), 1911–14	75.00
14/127	As above but sans-serif letters and crosses, 1911–14	£150
14/128	Posted on St. Elvies, violet, 1912–14	£400
14/129	As above but Posted on Snowdon, 1911-13	£250
14/130	As above but Posted on St. Tudno, 1911 only	£300
14/131	Posted on Board St. Tudno, violet , 1926 only	£225
14/132	St. Tudno, straight line, black, 1926-29	£200
14/133	Passed by Censor HMS *Marguerite*, violet, 1917 only	£150

Tay Pleasure Steamers

[Cachet: TAY PLEASURE STEAMER MARCHIONESS OF BUTE]
14/134

[Cachet: SLIEVE BEARNACH TAY PLEASURE STEAMER P.S.]
14/135

14/134	Tay Pleasure Steamer/Marchioness of Bute, 1911-13	£250
14/135	P.S. Slieve Bearnach/Tay/Pleasure/Steamer, 1913-14	£250

Later period

Of the items shown above in the "British Coastal Steamers" section Nos. **14/86-87** and **14/111-135** are cachets and not Post Office postmarks. We have retained in this chapter the cachets of the "classic period". Subsequent to this there are a wealth of further cachets from steamers all around the UK coasts. We show here six examples, but the listing of these is outside the scope of this book.

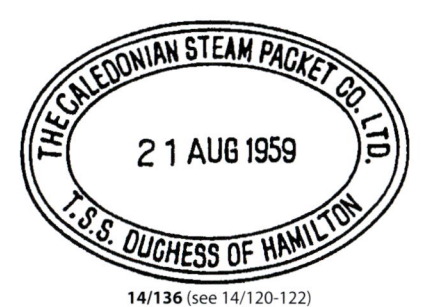

[Cachet: THE CALEDONIAN STEAM PACKET CO. LTD. 21 AUG 1959 T.S.S. DUCHESS OF HAMILTON]
14/136 (see 14/120-122)

MONA'S ISLE
14/137 (Isle of Man, 1963)

[Cachet: PADDLE STEAMER "MAID OF THE LOCH" POSTED ON BOARD Balloch]
14/138 (1981)

RMS HEBRIDES
14/139 (Isle of Skye, 1985)

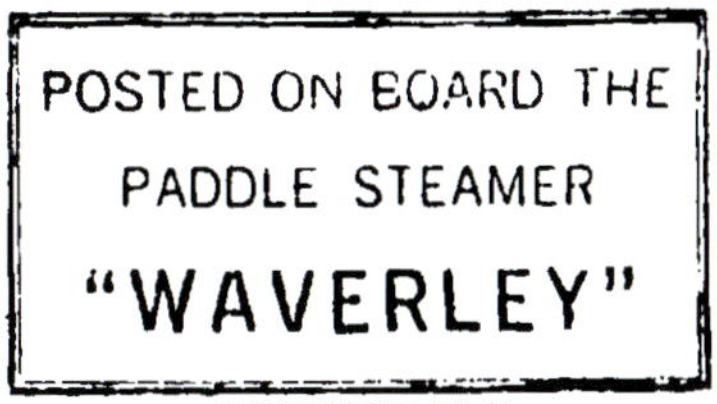

[Cachet: POSTED ON BOARD THE PADDLE STEAMER "WAVERLEY"]
14/140 (IOW, 1979)

AT SEA
m.v. ROYAL EAGLE
14/141 (Southend, 1950)

Section VI: Ocean Going Steamers

The same remark concerning cachets apply here as in the previous section. This is a large topic and we only show here the RMSP Co cachets, thanks to the book by Michael Rego, otherwise this large topic is outside the scope of this book.

Royal Mail Steam Packet Company
Cachets without Ships' names:

[Cachet: THE ROYAL MAIL STEAM PACKET COMPANY Posted on High Seas]
14/142

Maritime Markings

POSTED ON THE HIGH SEAS.
14/144

14/142	Oval belt and buckle cachet, violet or purple-black, 1905-12	8.00
14/143	As above but Posted On/The High Seas in two lines, 1905-09	10.00
14/144	Posted on the/High Seas, 2 lines, violet, purple or black, 1906-09	8.00
14/145	As above but date in second line, blue, 1912	50.00
14/146	As above but single line, no date shown, violet, 1913	50.00
14/147	Posted on the/High Seas, oval, violet or black, 1910-13	8.00

Cachets with Ships' names:

14/148 Straight Line, name of Ship only (1900-04):

Eden	£350
Esk	£200
Solent	£200
Yare and Tagus	£200
Yare	£200

14/149 Dated three or five line cachets (1922-26):

Chaleur	£100
Chaudiere	75.00
Darro	50.00
Teviot	£100

14/150 A. R.M.S.P. above, Ship name below

14/151 B. 'Posted on the High Seas' above, Ship name below

14/152 C. Company name above, 'Posted on the High Seas' below

14/153 D. Ship name above, 'Posted on the High Seas' below

Oval cachets (1908-69) (see 14/150 to 14/153):

Alcantara	C	15.00
	D	8.00
Almanzora	D	8.00
Amazon	A	12.00
	B	7.00
	C	10.00
Andes	D	7.00
Aragon	A	10.00
Araguaya	A	8.00
	B	30.00
	C	12.00
	D	8.00
Arcadian	D	15.00
Arlanza	B	8.00
	D	8.00
Asturias	A	15.00
	D	8.00
Atlantis	D	6.00
Atrato	A	40.00
Avon	A	12.00
	B	15.00
	D	8.00
Beresina	D	8.00
Caraquet	C (large single oval)	£100
Chaleur	D	£125
Chaudiere	C	70.00
	D (single oval)	80.00
Chignecto	C	£100
Clyde	A	30.00
Danube	C	30.00
Darro	B	15.00
	C	10.00
	D	15.00
Demerara	C	15.00
	D	8.00
Deseado	B	15.00
	C	12.00
	D	8.00
Desna	B	12.00
	C	8.00
Essequibo	B	8.00
	C	12.00
Gascony	D	10.00
Highland Brigade	D	8.00
Highland Chieftain	D	15.00
Highland Monarch	D	7.00
Highland Patriot	D	8.00
Highland Princess	D	7.00
Lochgoil	C	20.00
Lombardy	D	20.00
Ohio	D	8.00
Orbita	D	20.00
Orca	D	10.00
Orduna	B	15.00
	D	18.00
Oruba	A	30.00
Sabor	A	50.00
Tagus	A	30.00
Trent	A	30.00

284

Maritime Markings

Section VII: Paquebot

Applied from 1890s to the 1990s to mail posted on board ship. A and B applied either as a cachet or to cancel stamps, but C to H cancelling stamps. This is one of the few circumstances under which stamps of an overseas country may be legitimately cancelled in the country where the ship berths.

A selection of overseas Paquebot marks is shown at the end of the chapter.

14/154 A. Straight Line (size and spacing of letters vary) (or "Paquebots")

14/155 B. Boxed (size of letters and box vary)

14/156 C. Distinctive 'Posted at sea' steel handstamp

14/157 D. Machines (eg. Universal machine with Paquebot slogan or town die or both - Paquebot town die shown as D*)

14/158 E. Double circle with thick arcs

14/159 F. Single circle

14/160 G. Double circle with thin arcs

14/161 H. Rubber stamps (various designs)

Town	Type	Price
Aberdeen	B with port	15.00
Ardrossan	H	10.00
Ayr	A	40.00
Basildon	A	10.00
Belfast	A	20.00
	A	£150
	B	10.00
	C	10.00
	D Hey Dolphin	25.00
	D Universal	10.00
Berwick	A	25.00
Blackpool	A	15.00
Blyth	B	18.00
Boston	A	10.00
	triangular	15.00
Bournemouth	B	8.00
Bridgwater	A 'NAVIRE'	30.00
Bristol	A	20.00
	D Krag	10.00
	D Hey Dolphin	15.00
	D Universal	10.00
Brixham	A	25.00
	D Universal	6.00
	G	12.00
(then see Torquay)		
Buckie	A	75.00
Burnham on Crouch	A	50.00
Burntisland	A	12.00
Campbeltown	A 'PAQUEBOTE'	£100
Canterbury (replaced Dover)	C	5.00
	H	6.00
Cardiff	C	10.00
	D* Krag	20.00
Chatham	A	6.00
	B	6.00
Chelmsford	B	15.00
Cleveland	A	5.00
	B	10.00
Colchester	A	10.00
Coleraine	B	10.00
	H	10.00
Cowes	A	6.00
Craignure	A	15.00
Dartford	A	8.00
	B	8.00
Dartmouth	A	£500
Douglas, IOM	G	£200
Dover	A	£150
	C	10.00
	H red	5.00
	H rectangular, black	8.00
Dublin-Cork TPO	A	35.00
Dublin-Queenstown TPO	A	25.00
	small no rim	45.00
Dundee	B	15.00
Edinburgh	A	50.00
	D/D* Universal	10.00
	D/D^x slogan	20.00
	E	10.00
Erith	A	10.00
Exeter	B	8.00
Falmouth	A	25.00
	F	12.00
Felixstowe	B	6.00
Fishguard	C	8.00
	H (Paquebot Navire)	10.00
Folkestone	A 'PACQUEBOT'	10.00
	A mis-spelt	75.00
	B	5.00
Fort William	A	20.00
	B	10.00
Glasgow	A	50.00
	B	10.00
	D Universal	5.00
Gloucester	A	25.00

285

Maritime Markings

Goole	B	8.00
Grangemouth	A	£225
	B	15.00
Grays	B	6.00
	D* Universal	8.00
Great Yarmouth	A	5.00
Greenock	A	50.00
	D Universal	10.00
Grimsby	A	5.00
Guernsey see St. Peter Port		
Harwich	B	5.00
Holyhead	C	5.00
Hull	A	6.00
	B	10.00
	D Universal	£100
	E	15.00
Ilford	A	50.00
	H	8.00
Immingham	A	5.00
Invergordon	A	20.00
	B	8.00
Inverness	B	20.00
Ipswich	B	6.00
Jersey see St. Helier		
Kilmarnock	A	10.00
	B	5.00
Kings Lynn	A	15.00
Kirkcaldy	B	35.00
Kirkwall	A	40.00
	B	15.00
Lancaster	boxed	6.00
Larne	B	10.00
Leith	A	£225
Lerwick	A	£500
	F without 'Shetland'	£100
	F with 'Shetland'	10.00
Liverpool	A	10.00
	C	5.00
	D Columbia	12.00
	D Hey Dolphin	10.00
	D Universal	10.00
	E	5.00
	F	7.00
London	A	6.00
	D* Krag	5.00
	D Hey Dolphin	5.00
	D Universal (London/London FS) (several)	5.00
	E	6.00
	F	6.00
	G	5.00
	H	5.00
Londonderry	A	25.00
	B	12.00
	H	15.00
Lowestoft	A	25.00
Maldon	A	75.00
Mallaig	A	25.00
	B	15.00
Manchester	A	10.00
Methil	A	£300
Middlesbrough	A	8.00
Milford Haven	G	8.00
	H	8.00
Newcastle upon Tyne	A	20.00
	B	10.00
Newhaven	A	6.00
	D Universal	6.00
	G	6.00
	H	6.00
Newport	A	20.00
	C "Newport Mon"	20.00
	C "Newport Gwent"	8.00
Newry	A	10.00
	B	10.00
North Shields	A	10.00
Oban	A	10.00
Pembroke Dock	H	10.00
Penzance	A	10.00
Peterborough (Wisbech)	B	20.00
Plymouth	A	8.00
	D Columbia	10.00
	D* Hey Dolphin s/c	50.00
	D Hey Dolphin d/c	6.00
	D Krag 'Paquebot'	6.00
'NO PAQUEBOT'	D Krag 'Posted at sea' 1936	£150
	D Universal (several)	5.00
	E	5.00
Port Ellen	B	25.00
Portree (Skye)	A	10.00
	H	25.00
Portsmouth	A	6.00
	B (Portsmouth & Southsea)	5.00
	G no arcs (1953)	50.00
	H	35.00
Port Talbot	F	30.00
	G	30.00
Preston	B	10.00
Queenstown	A	35.00
	E (double arcs)	8.00
Ramsgate	A	6.00
	B	6.00
	H	8.00
Romford	B	10.00
Ryde, IOW	A	15.00
St.Helier (Jersey)	A (1894-1911)	£200
	A (later)	15.00
St.Mary's, Scilly	B	25.00
St.Peter Port (Guernsey)	A (1903-28)	£250
	A (later)	25.00
Saltcoats	A	35.00
Scarborough	A	20.00
Selby	B	20.00
Shoreham by Sea	A	10.00
Southampton	A	12.00
	C	5.00
	D* Columbia	8.00
	D/D* Universal, wavy lines	5.00
	D/D* Universal, with slogans	5.00
	E	8.00
Southend	A	10.00
South Shields	A	25.00
Stornoway	A	30.00
	B	30.00
	F	10.00
Stromness	B	12.00
Sunderland	A	10.00
	B	10.00
Swansea	E	8.00
	G "Swansea"	8.00
	G "West Glam"	10.00
Tayport	with map ref	25.00
Thurso	B	8.00
Tobermory	A	35.00
Torquay ("South Devon")	D	8.00
	G	8.00
Ullapool	A	30.00
Watchet	B 'NAVIRE'	10.00
West Hartlepool	A	25.00
Westray (Orkney)	B	35.00
Weymouth	D* Univ	12.00
	F	12.00

Maritime Markings

	skeleton	75.00	
	H	30.00	
Whitehaven	B	8.00	
Wick	B	12.00	
Wisbech (see Peterboro)	special B	20.00	
Workington	A	15.00	

Section VIII: Sea Post Offices

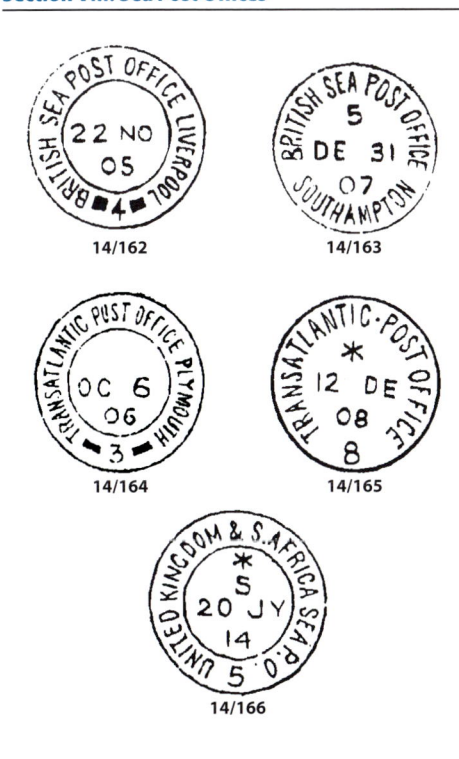

14/162

14/163

14/164

14/165

14/166

Transatlantic Post Offices

In 1904 GB and USA agreed to the establishment of joint post offices on board seven White Star liners and four ships of the American Line. This joint service operated 1905-14. British postmarks were used in the post offices aboard the ships, but tax and mis-sent marks were of the US style on all eleven ships.

14/162 British Sea Post Office Liverpool/number 1-7, double circle, 1905-07 — £100
14/163 British Sea Post Office/Southampton, number 1-10, single circle, 1907-08 — 75.00
14/164 Transatlantic Post Office Plymouth/number 1-4, double circle, 1905-07 — £150
14/165 Transatlantic Post Office/number 1-11, single circle, 1908-14 — 50.00

U.K. & South Africa Sea Post Office

The service operated 1913-14 and was the successor to South Africa administered Ocean Post Offices. One British handstamp was used as shown below, plus tax mark.

14/166 United Kingdom & S. Africa Sea PO/nos. 1-9, double circle (index letters N North or S South above date) — £100
14/167 Tax mark T in hexagon above "UK-SA/Sea Post" — £125

Section IX: Royal Navy

14/169

14/168 Navy Post Office, straight line, unframed, 1840s — £350
14/169 Navy Post Office, circular double arc type, blue, 1850s — £250
14/170 Duplex: Plymouth/H.M.S. with numeral 620, from 1852 — £500
14/171 Duplex: Devonport/H.M.S. with numeral 250, 1860s — £500

World War I period

14/172

14/177

14/180

14/172 Fleet Post Office, single circle, 1914- — 20.00
14/173 Fleet PO, single circle, 1915- — 20.00
14/174 Krag machine, fitted with FPOa dies for anonymity — 8.00
14/175 Krag machine with town dies of bars, crosses or plus signs — 10.00
14/176 Locally made crosses, circles etc, probably rubber or cork — 12.00
14/177 Dumb cancel of seven or eight vertical bars across circle — 5.00
14/178 Received from H.M. Ship./No Charge to be Raised, framed/unframed — 10.00
14/179 As above but machine die (framed or unframed), 1915-20 (see "Collecting Slogan Postmarks" for details) — 8.00
14/180 Received from HM Ships, Krag machine (undated) — 25.00

From 1920s onwards, including World War II period

14/181

287

Maritime Markings

RECEIVED FROM
H.M.S ....
ABROAD.
14/185

14/186   14/188

14/181	Received from H.M. Ships, machine die (framed/unframed, see "Collecting Slogan Postmarks" for details)	8.00
14/182	As above but without town die, 1939-40	5.00
14/183	As above but with census diamond instead of town die, 1939-40	15.00
14/184	London IS/H.M. Ships, rubber handstamp, 1931	10.00
14/185	**Received from/H.M.S. /Abroad, unframed**	**50.00**
14/186	**Received from/H.M. Ships, undated rubber handstamp, 1939**	**10.00**
14/187	Received from/H.M. Ships, single circle, dated, 1939	6.00
14/188	**Received from/H.M. Ships, double circle thick arcs, 1939**	**6.00**
14/189	London/H.M. Ships, double circle thick arcs, 1939	7.00
14/190	As above but Edinburgh, 1939	10.00
14/190A	As above but Southampton, 1938	20.00

Maritime Mail postmarks from 1943

POST OFFICE   MARITIME MAIL
14/191

14/197   14/200

14/201

14/191	Machine die with undated "Post Office" town die, red or black (variations, see "Collecting Slogan Postmarks" for details)	1.00
14/192	As above but dated London town die (& unusually Plymouth), 1968-95	1.00
14/193	Post Office/Maritime Mail, double circle, thick arcs, 1943-	4.00
14/194	Post Office/Maritime Mail, rubber handstamps (various)	7.00
14/195	London I.S./Maritime Mail, rubber handstamp, 43mm diameter, 1967-	5.00
14/196	as above but Plymouth or Portsmouth, 1969-	10.00
14/197	**London I.S./Maritime Mail, rubber handstamps (various) 33mm, 1977-93**	**3.00**
14/198	Maritime Mail/Bristol, steel single circle, 1960s	10.00
14/199	Parcel Post/Post Office/Maritime Mail, parcel handstamp	15.00
14/200	**Town/Maritime Mail, steel double circle 33mm diam, 1968-**	**5.00**
14/201	**Received from Ships, Postage Paid, triangular, red, 1980s (seen used in conjunction with 14/197)**	**10.00**

14/202   14/203 (+ wavy lines)

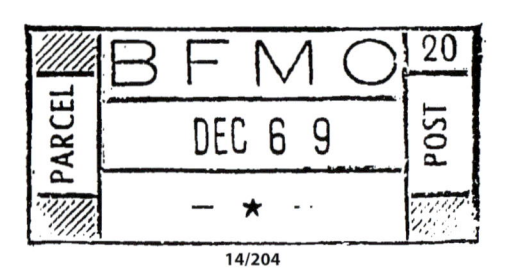

14/204

14/202	British Fleet Mail/number, double circle with thick/thin arcs	6.00
14/203	Base Fleet Mail Office/20, Universal machine die (Singapore), 1960s	6.00
14/204	B F M O parcel handstamp	15.00

Maritime Markings

British Fleet Mail Offices 1941-1982:

1. Ceylon
2. India, Japan
3. Malaya
4. Egypt
5. Australia
6. USA
8. Italy
9. Australia, UK, Hong Kong
10. Malta
11. Germany, Sierra Leone
12. Australia, Palestine, Israel, Greece
13. India
14. USA
15. Gibraltar
16. Australia
17. India
18. Egypt, Germany
19. Kenya
20. Burma, Ceylon, Singapore
22. Netherlands E. Indies
24. Belgium, Italy, Denmark
25. Papua New Guinea
26. Singapore
27. Netherlands E. Indies,
    Ceylon
28. India
29. South Africa
30. Germany
31. India
32. Germany
33. Malaya, Singapore
35. Pakistan
36. Egypt
37. Ceylon
38. Germany
39. Egypt
40. Germany
41. Japan

Note: A large variety of ships' cachets are available on naval covers, either on official use or posted on ships' Open Days (eg HMS Eagle shown on page 176 of the Fifth Edition, used 1936). These are beyond the scope of this handbook.

Naval Censor marks - Second World War

Censorship and censor marks are large topics, and a representative selection of censor marks is shown below, with values. The source of these is "World War Two Censor Marks" edited by John Daynes, see Bibliography. Further censor marks from the same source are included in chapters 15 and 16. To aid cross reference to that book we include the reference numbers used by John Daynes.

14/205 **N100** 0.50 1939-45 (also Suez 1956)

PASSED CENSOR H.M.S. HOOD
14/206 **N201** 25.00 1939 only

14/207 **N216** 60.00 1939 only

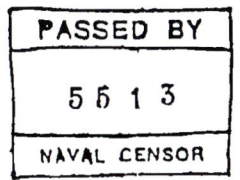

PASSED BY 5613 NAVAL CENSOR
14/208 **N421** 4.00

PASSED BY NAVAL CENSOR
14/209 **N412** 8.00

PASSED BY CENSOR
14/210 **N604** 8.00 1939 only

ON ACTIVE SERVICE PASSED BY CENSOR
14/211 **N802** 15.00 1939 only

PASSED BY SHIP'S CENSOR
14/212 **N904** 12.00

Naval Ships and Establishments

The address BFPO SHIPS was introduced on 12 October 1964 when the Forces Postal Service took over responsibility for mail to HM Ships outside of UK waters. Hitherto it had been the responsibility of the GPO.

In 1968 additional designators were introduced for the despatch of parcels by air to a ship in foreign waters to ensure that the appropriate postage was paid by the sender:

BFPO SHIPS V	HM Ships in European or Mediterranean waters
BFPO SHIPS W	HM Ships in North or South American waters (including the West Indies)
BFPO SHIPS X	HM Ships in foreign waters

With effect from 1 April 1992 the use of the address "BFPO Ships" for Naval mail ceased. Instead each RN ship or submarine, RFA and RMAS vessel and Naval party or shore establishment overseas was issued with its own individual BFPO number. The BFPO numbers used were in the range 200 to 499 and, in the case of RN ships and submarines, have been issued alphabetically according to ship's name. There are gaps between each letter to accommodate new ships and eventually numbers were re-issued. Numbers allocated to RFA and RMAS vessels have also been issued alphabetically, but in one un-interrupted sequence for each Service.

Any vessel or naval party not individually listed below and which previously used the BFPO Ships form of address were to use:
Ships Office London BFPO 200
Not all BFPO listed below are currently active - the Royal Navy has disposed of or mothballed many ships since the introduction of individual BFPO numbers.

289

Maritime Markings

BFPO 200	Ships Office London
BFPO 201	HMS Active
BFPO 202	HMS Alacrity
BFPO 203	HMS Alderney
BFPO 204	HMS Amazon (until c.1993)
BFPO 205	HMS Ambuscade (until c.1993)
BFPO 206	HMS Andromeda
BFPO 207	HMS Anglesey
BFPO 208	HMS Archer
BFPO 209	HMS Argonaut
BFPO 210	HMS Argyll
BFPO 211	HMS Ariadne
BFPO 212	HMS Ark Royal
BFPO 213	HMS Arrow
BFPO 214	HMS Arun (until c.1998)
BFPO 215	HMS Atherstone
BFPO 216	HMS Attacker
BFPO 217	HMS Avenger
BFPO 221	HMS Blyth
BFPO 222	HMS Bangor
BFPO 223	HMS Battleaxe
BFPO 224	HMS Beagle
BFPO 225	HMS Beaver
BFPO 226	HMS Berkeley
BFPO 227	HMS Bicester
BFPO 228	HMS Birmingham
BFPO 229	HMS Biter
BFPO 230	HMS Blackwater
BFPO 231	HMS Blazer
BFPO 232	HMS Boxer
BFPO 233	HMS Brave
BFPO 234	HMS Brazen
BFPO 235	HMS Brecon HMS Portland (from c.1998)
BFPO 236	HMS Bridport
BFPO 237	HMS Brilliant
BFPO 238	HMS Brinton
BFPO 239	HMY Britannia
BFPO 240	HMS Broadsword
BFPO 241	HMS Brocklesby
BFPO 242	HMS Bulldog
BFPO 243	HMS Bulwark
BFPO 248	HMS Campbeltown
BFPO 249	HMS Cardiff
BFPO 250	HMS Carron
BFPO 251	HMS Cattistock
BFPO 252	HMS Charger
BFPO 253	HMS Chatham
BFPO 254	HMS Chiddingfold
BFPO 255	HMS Cleopatra
BFPO 256	HMS Cornwall
BFPO 257	HMS Cottesmore HMS Scott (from c.1998)
BFPO 258	HMS Courageous
BFPO 259	HMS Coventry HMS Severn (from c.2004)
BFPO 260	HMS Cromer
BFPO 261	HMS Cumberland
BFPO 262	HMS Cygnet HMS Scimitar (from c.2003)
BFPO 270	HMS Daring
BFPO 271	HMS Dashe
BFPO 272	HMS Dovey (until c.1998) HMS Shoreham (from c.2002)
	HMS Dauntless (from c.2008)
BFPO 273	HMS Dulverton (until c.2006)
BFPO 274	HMS Dumbarton Castle
BFPO 275	HMS Echo
BFPO 276	HMS Enterprise
BFPO 277	HMS Edinburgh
BFPO 278	HMS Exeter
BFPO 279	HMS Endurance
BFPO 280	HMS Explorer HMS Somerset (from c.1996)
BFPO 281	HMS Example
BFPO 282	HMS Express
BFPO 283	HMS Fearless
BFPO 284	HMS Fencer
BFPO 285	HMS Exploit
BFPO 287	HMS Glasgow
BFPO 288	HMS Gleaner
BFPO 289	HMS Gloucester
BFPO 290	HMS Guernsey
BFPO 291	HMS Grafton
BFPO 292	HMS Grimsby
BFPO 293	HMS Hecla
BFPO 294	HMS Helford
BFPO 295	HMS Helmsdale
BFPO 296	HMS Herald
BFPO 297	HMS Hermione HMS Tyne (from c.2003)
BFPO 298	HMS Humber
BFPO 299	HMS Hunter
BFPO 300	HMS Hurworth
BFPO 305	HMS Illustrious
BFPO 306	HMS Intrepid
BFPO 307	HMS Inverness
BFPO 308	HMS Invincible
BFPO 309	HMS Iron Duke
BFPO 310	HMS Itchen
BFPO 311	HMS Iveston
BFPO 314	HMS Jersey
BFPO 315	HMS Juno
BFPO 316	HMS Jupiter
BFPO 318	HMS Kent
BFPO 319	HMS Kellington
BFPO 320	HMS Kingfisher
BFPO 323	HMS Lancaster
BFPO 324	HMS Ledbury HMS Albion (from c.2001)
BFPO 325	HMS Leeds Castle
BFPO 326	HMS Lindisfarne HMS Ambush (from c.2009)
BFPO 327	HMS Liverpool
BFPO 328	HMS London
BFPO 329	HMS Loyal Watcher
BFPO 330	HMS Loyal Chancellor
BFPO 331	HMS Manchester
BFPO 333	HMS Marlborough
BFPO 334	HMS Mersey
BFPO 335	HMS Middleton
BFPO 337	HMS Minerva
BFPO 338	HMS Monmouth HMS Astute (from c.2008)
BFPO 339	HMS Montrose
BFPO 343	HMS Newcastle
BFPO 344	HMS Norfolk
BFPO 345	HMS Northumberland
BFPO 346	HMS Nottingham
BFPO 347	HMS Nurton
BFPO 350	HMS Ocean
BFPO 351	HMS Opportune
BFPO 352	HMS Opossum
BFPO 353	HMS Oracle
BFPO 354	HMS Orkney
BFPO 355	HMS Orwell
BFPO 356	HMS Osiris
BFPO 357	HMS Pembroke
BFPO 358	HMS Penzance
BFPO 359	HMS Peacock
BFPO 360	HMS Plover
BFPO 361	HMS Polar Circle (until c.1998)
BFPO 362	HMS Puncher
BFPO 363	HMS Pursuer
BFPO 366	HMS Quorn
BFPO 368	HMS Ramsey
BFPO 369	HMS Ranger
BFPO 370	HMS Redpole
BFPO 371	HMS Renown
BFPO 372	HMS Repulse
BFPO 373	HMS Resolution
BFPO 374	HMS Revenge
BFPO 375	HMS Richmond
BFPO 376	HMS Roebuck
BFPO 377	HMS Raider
BFPO 378	HMS Sabre
BFPO 379	HMS Sandown
BFPO 380	HMS Sceptre
BFPO 381	HMS Scylla (until c.1998)
BFPO 382	HMS Sentinel (until c.2002)
BFPO 383	HMS Sheffield
BFPO 384	HMS Sheraton (until c.1997)
BFPO 385	HMS Shetland
BFPO 386	HMS Sirius (until c.1997)
BFPO 387	HMS Smiter
BFPO 388	HMS Soberton HMS Diamond (from c.2008)
BFPO 389	HMS Southampton
BFPO 390	HMS Sovereign
BFPO 391	HMS Spartan
BFPO 392	HMS Spey
BFPO 393	HMS Splendid
BFPO 394	HMS Starling
BFPO 395	HMS Striker
BFPO 396	HMS Superb
BFPO 397	HMS Swiftsure
BFPO 398	HMS Sutherland
BFPO 399	HMS St Albans
BFPO 401	HMS Talent
BFPO 402	HMS Tireless
BFPO 403	HMS Torbay
BFPO 404	HMS Trafalgar
BFPO 405	HMS Trenchant
BFPO 406	HMS Triumph
BFPO 407	HMS Trumpeter
BFPO 408	HMS Turbulent
BFPO 409	HMS Tracker
BFPO 411	HMS Unicorn
BFPO 412	HMS Unseen (until c.1997)
BFPO 413	HMS Upholder
BFPO 414	HMS Ursula
BFPO 417	HMS Valiant
BFPO 418	HMS Vanguard
BFPO 419	HMS Victorious
BFPO 420	HMS Vigilant
BFPO 421	HMS Vengeance
BFPO 423	HMS Walney
BFPO 424	HMS Warspite
BFPO 425	HMS Waveney
BFPO 426	HMS Westminster
BFPO 427	HMS Wilton
BFPO 430	HMS York

Royal Fleet Auxiliary (RFA)

BFPO 431	RFA Wave Ruler
BFPO 432	RFA Wave Knight
BFPO 433	RFA Argus RFA Largs Bay (from c.2003)
BFPO 434	RFA Bayleaf
BFPO 435	RFA Black Rover RFA Lyme Bay (from c.2006)
BFPO 436	RFA Blue Rover (until c.1993)
BFPO 437	RFA Brambleleaf
BFPO 438	RFA Diligence
BFPO 439	RFA Fort Austin
BFPO 440	RFA Fort George
BFPO 441	RFA Fort Grange
BFPO 442	RFA Fort Victoria
BFPO 443	RFA Gold Rover
BFPO 444	RFA Grey Rover
BFPO 445	RFA Oakleaf
BFPO 446	RFA Olmeda (until c.1998)
BFPO 447	RFA Olna
BFPO 448	RFA Olwen RFA Cardigan Bay (from c.2007) RFA Mounts Bay (from c.2004)
BFPO 449	RFA Orangeleaf
BFPO 450	RFA Regent
BFPO 451	RFA Resource
BFPO 452	RFA Sir Bedivere
BFPO 453	RFA Sir Galahad RFA Fort Rosalie (from c.2004)
BFPO 454	RFA Sir Geraint
BFPO 455	RFA Sir Percivale
BFPO 456	RFA Sir Tristram
BFPO 458	RFA Sea Crusader

Royal Maritime Auxiliary Service (RMAS)

BFPO 461	RMAS Arrochar
BFPO 462	RMAS Auricula Operation TELIC 22 January 2003 – -★★-
BFPO 463	RMAS Kinterbury MV Magdalena Green
BFPO 464	RMAS Newton
BFPO 465	RMAS Robust (until c.1997)
BFPO 466	RMAS Rollicker (until c.1997)
BFPO 467	RMAS Roysterer (until c.1998) MV Smit Enterprise MV Eddystone (from c.2002)

Maritime Markings

BFPO 468　RMAS Salmaid
　　　　　MV Stadions Gracht
　　　　　MV Hartland Point (from c.2002)
BFPO 469　RMAS Salmaster
　　　　　MV Tor Anglia
　　　　　MV Hurst Point (from c.2002)
BFPO 470　RMAS Sealyham
　　　　　MV Vikingland
　　　　　MV Langstone
BFPO 471　RMAS Throsk
BFPO 472　RMAS Tormenter
BFPO 473　RMAS Whitehead
　　　　　MV Beachy Head (from c.2003)
BFPO 474　Operation TELIC 22 January 2003 – -★-
BFPO 475　Operation TELIC 22 January 2003
BFPO 476　Operation TELIC 22 January 2003 – -★-
BFPO 477　MV Maersk Baffin
　　　　　MV Anvil Point (from c.2003)
　　　　　MV Passat

Ships taken up from trade (STUFT)
BFPO 478　MV Indomitable
BFPO 479　MV Maersk Ascension
BFPO 480　MV Maersk Gannet
BFPO 481　MV Oil Mariner
BFPO 482　MV St Brandon

Army Vessels
BFPO 483　HMAV Arakan
BFPO 484　HMAV Ardennes

Naval Parties
BFPO 485　Naval Party 1002 Diego Garcia
BFPO 486　Naval Party 1004 HQ Allied Forces Baltic
　　　　　Approaches, Karup, Denmark
BFPO 487　Naval Party 1010 British Defence Liaison Staff,
　　　　　Ottawa, Canada
BFPO 488　Naval Party 1011 Royal Navy Liaison Officer,
　　　　　Autec, Miami, USA
BFPO 489　Naval Party 1022 Royal Navy Liaison Officer,
　　　　　Singapore
BFPO 490　Naval Party 1023 Royal Navy Liaison Officer,
　　　　　Gulf (at Dubai)
BFPO 491　Naval Party 1027 Cyprus
BFPO 492　Naval Party 1242 British Forces Falkland Islands
BFPO 493　Naval Party 1964 HQ Allied Command Atlantic,
　　　　　Norfolk, Virginia, USA
BFPO 494　Naval Party 2010 Naval Party Falklands
BFPO 495　Naval Party 1005 Den Helder, Netherlands
BFPO 496　Naval Party 1016 Inshore Survey
　　　　　Op ATALANTA (from c.2011)

(1)　BFPO 465-470
Transport Ships: MV Anvil Point, MV Beachy Head, MV Eddystone, MV Hartland Point, MV Hurst Point and MV Longstone.
　On contract to the Ministry of Defence (MOD) to provide a strategic sealift service in support of the Joint Rapid Reaction Force (JRRF) until late 2024. As part of the contract four Ro-Ro vessels were in constant use by the MOD whilst the remaining two ships were in commercial use by contractor. However, they could be called upon to support major exercises and operations. The BFPO numbers were only activated when Royal Navy personnel were on board.

(2)　BFPO 478-482
All five vessels had been taken up from trade by 1 April 1991. The MV Indomitable (tug), MV Oil Mariner (supply vessel) and MV St Brandon (ferry) all operated in the Falkland Islands, while the MV Maersk Ascension and MV Maersk Gannet operated as tankers to Ascension Island.

Naval Establishments

14/213

D　Single Circle
E　Double Circle
F　Skeleton
J　Parcel handstamp

Note: The entries are abbreviated, similar to Camps in chap 15.

Admiralty SW	F	75.00
Naval Camp Blandford	E	10.00
	F	30.00
	J	25.00
*HMS Cabbala, Stafford	D	★
	registered	★
Naval Barracks Chatham	D	10.00
	J	20.00
Admiral's office Chatham	D	30.00
Dockyard Chatham	D	15.00
Churchill, Helensburgh	D	10.00
Clyde Submarine Base, Helensburgh		
	D	10.00
	J	20.00
Collingwood (or HMS), Fareham, Hants		
	D	10.00
	J	20.00
Dockyard Devonport	D	15.00
Devonport, Naval Barracks	J	20.00
Naval Barracks Keyham Devonport		
	D	10.00
	F	25.00
Dover Naval Mail Office	rubber	75.00
Drake Hall Stafford	D	15.00
RNC Eaton, Chester	rubber	40.00
HMS Excellent Whale Island	F	50.00
Fort Blockhouse, Gosport, Hants	D	25.00
*Fort Matilda Camp, Greenock	D	★
FMO Greenock	D	10.00
Haslar Hospital, Gosport	D	20.00
Inverness AMDO	E	20.00
Naval Barracks, Lee on the Solent	D	10.00
	J	12.00
(HMS) Nelson Portsmouth	D	10.00
	F	50.00
Plymouth Devon, Naval Barracks	D	10.00
	J	12.00
Portland Dock, Portland Dorset	D	10.00
"Portsmouth, Fort Grange	D	20.00
Portsmouth, Naval Barracks	D	10.00
Raleigh, Torpoint Cornwall	D	5.00
	E	5.00
	J	12.00
Rosyth Dockyard, Dunfermline	E	20.00
Scapa Pier, Kirkwall Orkney	E	50.00
Sultan, Gosport Hants	D	10.00
Whale Island, Portsmouth Hants	D	10.00
	J	12.00
*Woolwich Royal Dockyard SE	D	★

291

Section X: Special Events

A selection of earlier events (see chap 12 for further details).

14/214	Royal Naval Exhibition, London SW, 1891	80.00
14/215	Cowes Regatta, 1920, skeleton	£120
14/216	London Naval Conference, 1930, single circle	80.00
14/217	Marine Insurance Conference Eastbourne, 1950,	*
14/218	SS Empress of Britain Maiden Voyage, 1956, double circle	15.00
14/219	SS Reina del Mar Maiden Voyage, 1956, double circle	30.00
14/220	Fish Docks Centenary Exhib Grimsby, 1956	2.00
14/221	SS Empress of England Maiden Voyage, 1957, double circle	20.00
14/222	Mayflower II Maiden Voyage, 1957, double circle	2.00
14/223	Anglo-Danish Festival (shows Viking ship) Hull, 1957	2.00
14/224	Seaborne Mail Exhibition SE10, 1960	1.00
14/225	Arlanza Maiden Voyage, 1960, double circle	80.00
14/226	Empress of Canada Maiden Voyage, 1961, double circle	10.00

Section XI: Disaster/Wreck and Salvaged Mail

THIS SECTION IS APPLICABLE TO CHAPTERS 14, 15 and 16.

This is a large subject, but in general cachets may or may not be applied to covers that are rescued - THIS APPLIES TO PLANES AS WELL AS SHIPS. Not always is this the case; items may be forwarded with no cachet, or forwarded under cover with an explanatory letter.

DAMAGED BY SEA WATER
14/229

Saved from wreck of s.s. "Eider"
14/239

RECOVERED FROM WRECK OF SS 'LABRADOR'
14/240

General cachets :
14/227 Damaged as a result of enemy action
14/228 Damaged by fire and water

Ship wreck cachets without ships' names:
14/229 Damaged by Sea Water
14/230 Damaged by water
14/231 Damaged by Immersion in Sea Water
14/232 Recovered from the sea
14/233 Salved from submerged mail
14/234 Salved from the sea
14/235 Salved Letter

Wreck cachets from disasters within British territorial waters:
14/236 1833 Brothers
14/237 1838 Lady Charlotte
14/238 1875 Schiller
14/239 1892 Eider
14/240 1899 Labrador
14/241 1900 Ibex
14/242 1907 Jebba
14/243 1915 Hesperian
14/244 1918 Leinster

GPO cachets from disasters outside British territorial waters:
14/245 1799 Lutine
14/246 1846 Great Liverpool
14/247 1858 Ava
14/248 1860 Malabar
14/249 1862 Colombo
14/250 1862 Cleopatra
14/251 1871 Rangoon
14/252 1900 Mexican
14/253 1930 Comorin

All wreck mail bearing cachets with ships' names is scarce.

Particular thanks go to Messrs Cowell, Densham, Frost and Hosking, and to the late John Daynes, for their help with updated listings in this chapter

Appendix - Overseas Paquebot marks

Shown below are some foreign Paquebot marks to be found on mail franked with British stamps. Due to popular demand we have retained this section in this chapter.

Aden:	Boxed Paquebot, from 1894	10.00
	Circular with shaded bottom half, from 1908	8.00
	Paquebot/Aden, shaded background, from 1933	6.00
	Paquebot/Aden G.P.O., single circle, from 1953	5.00
	Paquebot machine marks	5.00
Alexandria:	Boxed Paquebot, from 1902	8.00
	Circular Paquebot/Alexandrie, with Arabic, from 1924	5.00
	Straight line types	10.00
Balboa:	Duplex types, from 1917	15.00
	Straight line types, from 1920	12.00
	Machine types, from 1931	5.00
Bergen:	Straight line types, from 1925	10.00
	Boxed types, from 1905	10.00
	Machine types, from 1938	6.00
Bombay:	Boxed Paquebot, from 1904	6.00
	Straight line types, from 1900	10.00
	Circular Bombay Foreign types, from 1913	4.00
Cape Town:	Circular types, from 1914	5.00
	Machine types, from 1914	5.00
Cherbourg:	Straight line types, from 1920	5.00
	Continuous impression machine, Paquebot between bars, from 1926	5.00
	Machine with tourist slogan, from 1955	8.00
	Machine with boxed Paquebot between wavy bars, from 1965	8.00
Cobh (formerly Queenstown):	Irish skeleton types, 1922	75.00
	British-type double circle, from 1924	10.00
	Machine types from 1963	5.00
Colombo:	Straight line types, from 1894	8.00
	Circular types, from 1912	8.00
	Machine types, slogans or bars, from 1927	6.00
Dublin:	Circular Baile Atha Cliath types, from 1935	6.00
Dun Laoghaire:	Posted at Sea type, from 1923	5.00
Durban	Double circle types, from 1937	8.00
	Machine types, from 1941	8.00
Funchal:	Straight line types, from 1904	10.00
	Paquebot in oval frame, from 1910	25.00
	Boxed Paquebot, from 1913	10.00
	Circular dated type, from 1968	8.00
Gibraltar:	Straight line types, from 1894	10.00
	Gibraltar/Paquebot single circle, from 1910	10.00

	Pictorial mark with ship, from 1967	5.00
Hamilton, Bermuda	Straight line types, from 1907	10.00
	Paquebot/Bermuda, single circles, from 1947	10.00
	Machine with Paquebot boxed, from 1951	20.00
Lisbon	Paquete, straight line types, from 1895	10.00
	Paquebot, straight line types, from 1897	10.00
	Double circle types with Paquete at base, from 1906	5.00
	Double circle types with Lisboa at base, from 1949	4.00
Malta:	All types	10.00
Marseille:	Single or double circle types	4.00
New York:	Straight line types with (N.Y. 2D Div) from 1894	10.00
	As above but (N.Y.P.O. For. Sec.) from 1913	20.00
	Single circle types, from 1905	5.00
	Duplex types, from 1915	4.00
	Machine types, from 1924	4.00
Oslo:	Boxed Paquebot, from 1931	10.00
	Machine type, from 1937	15.00
	Paquebot straight line type, from 1972	8.00
Port Said:	Straight line type, from 1905	10.00
	Pleine Mer, unframed, from 1896	50.00
	Boxed Paquebot, from 1899	4.00
	Circular type, from 1912	4.00
Port Sudan:	Boxed Paquebot, from 1927	10.00
Port Taufiq:	Boxed Paquebot, from 1901	10.00
	Circular type with wording inside arcs, from 1939	4.00
	Circular type with wording across, from 1957	4.00
Quebec:	Straight line types, from 1914	15.00
	Two line, Exempt from War tax, from 1915	75.00
	Boxed, Exempt from War Tax, from 1919	25.00
	Mailed on the High Seas, unframed, from 1920	5.00
	Mailed on High Seas, unframed, from 1923	5.00
	Depose en mer/mailed on high sea, unframed, from 1937	4.00
	Machine with Paquebot/Posted/At Sea, from 1926	4.00
Suez:	Boxed or unboxed Paquebot, from 1902	8.00

Full details of all Paquebot marks are given by Roger Hosking including many not included in the above lists.

15 Military and Camp Postmarks

Section I: Early Wars and Campaigns

15/1

15/2

15/5

War of the Austrian Succession: 1740-48

| 15/1 | Circled AB ('Armee Britannique') | £2000 |

French Revolutionary War: 1799

| 15/2 | Army Bag, circular, in black . | £2200 |
| 15/3 | Post Paid/Army Bag, double oval, in red | £3000 |

Napoleonic and Peninsular Wars: 1803-15

| 15/4 | Lisbon town marks on campaign letters | £250 |
| 15/5 | Transport office oval on Prisoner of War mail | £750 |

Crimean War: 1854-56

15/6

15/7

15/6	Barred type with crown and stars, 1854-55	£750
15/7	Barred type with star and cyphers, 1855-56	£400
15/8	Post Office/British Army, unframed circular types, black, blue, red or green from 1854	75.00

On pieces the first two of the above postmarks are worth about a half of the prices quoted, on loose stamps about a third.

British Expeditions to Egypt (1882) and Sudan (1885)

15/9

| 15/9 | British Army Post Office/Egypt, single circle | £500 |
| 15/10 | Barred type with B.A./E. . | * |

On pieces these postmarks are worth about a third of the prices quoted, on loose stamps about a quarter.

South African War 1899-1902

15/11

15/12

15/19

15/11	Field Post Office B.O./British Army S. Africa, double circle	25.00
15/12	As above but without B.O.	30.00
15/13	Field P.O./British Army S. Africa, single circle	15.00
15/14	Army Post Office/South Africa, large double rim circle with town or code	£100
15/15	Army Post Office/town, double circle	15.00
15/16	Army Post Office/T.P.O. double circle	60.00
15/17	Army PO 43/S. Africa single circle (nos 43-55)	30.00
15/18	Registered/Army Post Office/(place name), hooded circle	80.00
15/19	Octagonal Natal Field Force marks	75.00
15/20	Parcel marks with NFF/FPO etc.	£100
15/21	Instructional marks, 'Not to be found' etc.	75.00

294

Military and Camp Postmarks

Section II : First World War: 1914-19

Most mail passed free and so bears datestamp and censor mark but no stamp. Values vary considerably according to location of unit and date. Some marks were used in more than one theatre of war; Palestine and Russia being highly sought, Western Front, plentiful and cheap. Examination of the censor mark often helps decide from which theatre an item comes. Full details are in Kennedy/Crabb and Proud.

15/22 France 1914-15 Russia 1919 with Suffix R

15/23 France 1914-15 Middle East 1915-16 East Africa 1916-17 Balkans 1916

15/24 France 1915-16 Middle East 1915-19 East Africa, Mesopotamia E. Mediterranean

15/25 France 1916

15/26 France 1916-17 Italy 1917

15/27 France 1917-20 Italy 1917-18

15/28 Salonica, Egypt and Palestine 1917-19, Turkey 1918-20, Balkans, S. Russia 1919

15/29 Italy 1918-19

(Censor illustrations reduced by different amounts)

15/30	Advance Base Post Office, double circle	8.00
15/31	Army Base Post Office, single circle, 1913 manoeuvres only	30.00
15/32	As above but indexes 18-19 at foot (pre-war manoeuvres only)	30.00
15/33	Army Base Post Office, double circle	2.00
15/34	Army Courier Office/S5, single circle, 1920-21	75.00
15/35	Army Letter Office/London, double circle	15.00
15/36	D.A.L.O. London, double circle	15.00

15/37 Army Post Office, single circle with number of infantry brigade at foot (used pre-1914 in England, 1914-15 in France and Belgium):

1	5.00	10		5.00
2	5.00	11		5.00
3	5.00	12		5.00
4	5.00	13		5.00
5	5.00	14		5.00
6	5.00	15		5.00
7	5.00	16		5.00
8	5.00	17		5.00
9	5.00	18		5.00

These APO single circles used pre-1914 are worth from 10.00

15/38	Army Post Office/HD1 (Malta)	10.00
15/39	Army Post Office, double circle with index at foot, and –	
15/40	skeletons, various sizes, chiefly with index at foot:	

Index	Used by	d/c	sk
no index			8.00
1	Base APO 1 Havre	1.00	3.00
2	Base APO 2 Rouen	1.00	
3	Base APO 3 Boulogne	2.00	
4	Base APO 4 Calais	2.00	
19	1 Inf. Div.	3.00	
20	2 Inf. Div.	5.00	
21	3 Inf. Div.	5.00	
22	4 Inf. Div.	2.00	
23	5 Inf. Div.	2.00	
24	6 Inf. Div.	2.00	
25	1 Inf. Div.	2.00	
26	2 Inf. Div.	2.00	
27	3 Inf. Div.	2.00	
28	4 Inf. Div.	2.00	
29	5 Inf. Div.	2.00	
30	6 Inf. Div.	2.00	
31	1 Cav. Bde.	3.00	
32	2 Cav. Bde.	2.00	
33	3 Cav. Bde.	5.00	
34	4 Cav. Bde.	2.00	
35	5 Cav. Bde.	2.00	
36	1 Cav. Div.	2.00	
37	Boulogne	1.00	
38	St.Nazaire	2.00	
39	Army Troops	2.00	
40	?	2.00	
41	I Corps	2.00	
42	II Corps	2.00	

Military and Camp Postmarks

Index	Used by	d/c	sk
43	III Corps	2.00	
44	19 Inf. Bde.	2.00	
45	2 Cav. Div.	3.00	
46	W. Front	2.00	
47	Rouen	1.00	
48	Orleans	2.00	
49	Nantes	1.00	
50	Le Mans	3.00	
51	I Corps Railhead	1.00	
52	II Corps Railhead	2.00	
53	III Corps Railhead	2.00	
54	W. Front	3.00	
55	Lahore Div. Train	4.00	
56	W. Front	3.00	
57	W. Front	3.00	
58	W. Front	2.00	
59	W. Front	3.00	
60	7 Cav. Bde.	2.00	
61	W. Front	3.00	
62	7 Div. HQ	3.00	
63	7 Div. Train	3.00	
64	20 Bde.	3.00	
65	21 Bde.	3.00	
66	22 Bde.	3.00	
67	IV Corps HQ	4.00	
68	8 Div. HQ	3.00	
69	8 Div. Train	3.00	
70	23 Bde.	3.00	
71	24 Bde.	4.00	
72	25 Bde.	4.00	
73	W. Front	5.00	
74	W. Front	5.00	
75	Paris	4.00	
76	W. Front	5.00	
77	W. Front	4.00	
78	Dunkirk	4.00	
79	W. Front	2.00	
80	W. Front	2.00	
81	W. Front	4.00	
82	Etretat	4.00	
83	80 Bde.	7.00	
84	81 Bde.	7.00	
85	82 Bde.	7.00	
86	27 Div. HQ	7.00	
87	27 Div. Train	7.00	
88	W. Front	15.00	
89	W. Front	7.00	
94	W. Front	15.00	
100	Etaples	7.00	
A	Rouen		2.00
B	France		7.00
C	France		6.00
D	France		6.00
E	France		7.00
F2	Abbassia		6.00
G	France		7.00
GR	Germany	15.00	
L1	Italy, Base	3.00	
L2	Italy	4.00	
L3	Italy	5.00	
L4	Italy	7.00	
L5	Italy	7.00	
L6	Italy	7.00	
L7	Italy	6.00	
L8	Italy	5.00	
L9	Italy	6.00	
L11	Italy	6.00	
L12	Italy	10.00	
L13	France	10.00	
L14	Italy	40.00	
L15	Austria	40.00	

Index	Used by	d/c	sk
L16	Yugoslavia	40.00	
PB1	Russia	75.00	
PB2	Russia	75.00	
PP1	Italy		6.00
R1	1 Div Railhead	1.00	
R2	2 Div Railhead	1.00	
R2A	27 Div Railhead	6.00	
R3	3 Div Railhead	1.00	
R4	4 Div Railhead	1.00	
R5	5 Div Railhead	1.00	
Note: R1-5 were initially Corps railheads			
R5A	28 Div Railhead	8.00	8.00
R6	6 Div Railhead	1.00	
R7	7 Div Railhead	2.00	
R8	8 Div Railhead	1.00	
R9	9 Div Railhead	1.00	
R10	10 Div Railhead	20.00	
R11	11 Div Railhead	2.00	
R12	12 Div Railhead	1.00	
R14	14 Div Railhead	1.00	
R15	15 Div Railhead	1.00	
R16	16 Div Railhead	1.00	
R17	17 Div Railhead	1.00	
R18	18 Div Railhead	1.00	
R19	19 Div Railhead	1.00	
R20	20 Div Railhead	1.00	
R21	21 Div Railhead	2.00	
R22	22 Div Railhead	3.00	12.00
R23	23 Div Railhead	2.00	
R24	24 Div Railhead	1.00	
R25	25 Div Railhead	2.00	
R26	26 Div Railhead	3.00	12.00
R27	27 Div Railhead	3.00	12.00
R28	28 Div Railhead	3.00	12.00
R29	29 Div Railhead	2.00	
R30	30 Div Railhead	2.00	
R31	31 Div Railhead	3.00	
R32	32 Div Railhead	3.00	
R33	33 Div Railhead	2.00	
R34	34 Div Railhead	2.00	
R35	35 Div Railhead	1.00	
R36	36 Div Railhead	1.00	
R37	37 Div Railhead	2.00	
R38	38 Div Railhead	2.00	
R39	39 Div Railhead	1.00	
R40	40 Div Railhead	2.00	
R41	41 Div Railhead	2.00	
R42	42 Div Railhead	2.00	
R46	46 Div Railhead	1.00	
R47	47 Div Railhead	2.00	
R48	48 Div Railhead	1.00	
R49	49 Div Railhead	2.00	
R50	50 Div Railhead	2.00	
R51	51 Div Railhead	1.00	
R52	52 Div Railhead	7.00	
R55	55 Div Railhead	1.00	
R56	56 Div Railhead	2.00	
R57	57 Div Railhead	3.00	
R58	58 Div Railhead	2.00	
R59	59 Div Railhead	2.00	
R60	60 Div Railhead	5.00	
R61	61 Div Railhead	2.00	
R62	62 Div Railhead	2.00	
R63	63 Div Railhead	2.00	
R66	66 Div	2.00	
R74	74 Div	3.00	
RA1	1 Ammunition Railhead		1.00
RA2	2 Ammunition Railhead	2.00	
RB	Guards Div Railhead	1.00	
RC1	1 Cav. Div Railhead	2.00	
RC2	2 Cav. Div Railhead	2.00	

Military and Camp Postmarks

Index	Used by	d/c	sk
RC3	3 Cav. Div Railhead	2.00	
RC4	Cav. Div Railhead	6.00	
RG	GHQ Railhead	6.00	
RHD	51 Div Railhead	5.00	
RK	American Div Railheads	18.00	
RK2-8	ditto	18.00	
RL	47 Div Railhead	15.00	
RN	50 Div Railhead	2.00	
RP1-4	Canadian Div Railheads	8.00	
RSM	48 Div Railhead	8.00	
RW	Egypt		15.00
RW1-5	Australian Div Railheads	8.00	
RWR	49 Div Railhead	8.00	
RX	Canadian Div Railhead	8.00	15.00
RX2-4	ditto	8.00	
RX16	XVI Corps Rail	50.00	30.00
RY	59-63 Div	2.00	
RZ	N Zealand Div Railhead	10.00	5.00
S1	Abbeville	1.00	
S2	France	1.00	
S3	France	2.00	
S4	France/Belgium	2.00	
S5	Paris	1.00	
S6	France	1.00	
S7	Marseilles	1.00	
S8	Dieppe	1.00	
S9	Etratat	2.00	
S10	Dunkirk	1.00	
S11	Etaples	1.00	
S12	Harfleur	1.00	
S13	Le Treport	1.00	
S14	France	1.00	
S15	Rouen	1.00	3.00
S16	Serqueux	1.00	
S17	Etaples	1.00	15.00
S18	Camiers	1.00	
S19	France	1.00	
S20	France	1.00	
S21	France	1.00	
S22	France	2.00	
S23	France	1.00	
S24	Calais	1.00	
S25	France	1.00	
S26	France	1.00	
S27	Caudebec	2.00	
S28	St. Saens	2.00	4.00
S29	France	2.00	
S30	France	1.00	
S31	France	1.00	
S32	France	1.00	
S33	France	1.00	
S34	France	2.00	
S35	France	2.00	8.00
S36	Zeneghem	3.00	
S37	France	1.00	
S38	Wimereaux	1.00	
S39	Dannes	1.00	
S40	France/Germany	2.00	
S41	France	1.00	
S42	France	1.00	
S43	France	1.00	
S44	Buchy	2.00	
S45	France	2.00	
S46	France	1.00	6.00
S47	France	1.00	6.00
S48	France	2.00	
S49	France	2.00	
S50	Cherbourg	1.00	5.00
S51	France	1.00	
S52	France	1.00	
S53	France	1.00	

Index	Used by	d/c	sk
S54	France	1.00	
S55	Marseilles	3.00	
S56	France	1.00	6.00
S57	France	2.00	
S58	France	2.00	
S59	France	1.00	4.00
S60	France	1.00	
S61	France	2.00	
S62	France	1.00	
S63	France	1.00	
S64	France	2.00	
S65	France	1.00	
S66	France	1.00	
S67	France	5.00	
S68	France	2.00	
S69	France	12.00	
S70	Italy	4.00	
S71	France	2.00	
S72	France	3.00	12.00
S73	Vendroux	1.00	
S74	France	2.00	
S75	France	1.00	
S76	France	1.00	7.00
S77	France	1.00	7.00
S78	France	1.00	
S79	Le Touquet	1.00	
S80	France	1.00	
S81	France	1.00	4.00
S82	Rue	4.00	
S83	Trouville	1.00	3.00
S84	Lilliers	3.00	
S85	France	4.00	
S86	France	3.00	8.00
S87	France	3.00	
S88	Boulogne	5.00	
S89	France	8.00	
S90	France	3.00	
S91	France	5.00	15.00
S92	France	3.00	
S93	Courban	7.00	
S94	Hesdin	2.00	7.00
S95	St. Pol	5.00	8.00
S97	France	10.00	20.00
S98	France	6.00	
S99	France	3.00	
S100	Taranto	5.00	
S101	Arquata	6.00	18.00
S102	France	5.00	
S103	Aulnois	7.00	
S104	Nancy	15.00	
S105	France	6.00	
-	& Rotterdam (1919)	30.00	
S106	Brussels	7.00	
S107	Belgium	7.00	
S108	France	7.00	
S109	Motteville	9.00	
S110	Antwerp	15.00	
S111	Dieppe	8.00	8.00
S114	Spa	8.00	
S115	Charleroi	7.00	
S116	France	7.00	
S117	Belgium	4.00	
S118	Lille	8.00	
S119	France	6.00	
S120	Germany	8.00	
Note: Usages in France may include Belgium			
SW1	France	5.00	
SW2	Harfleur	8.00	
SW3	France	8.00	
SW4	France	8.00	
SWZ	France	8.00	

297

Military and Camp Postmarks

Index	Used by	d/c	sk
SWZ2	Etaples	8.00	
SX1	Greece	2.00	6.00
SX2	Salonika	3.00	8.00
SX3	Greece	7.00	7.00
SX4	Salonika	5.00	5.00
SX5	Greece	3.00	8.00
SX6	Vertekop	10.00	
SX7	Stavros	10.00	18.00
SX8	Greece	5.00	5.00
SX9	Greece	15.00	18.00
SX10	Greece	15.00	
SX11	Greece	7.00	15.00
SX12	Greece	15.00	15.00
SX13	Eurendzik	10.00	10.00
SX14	Greece	20.00	20.00
SX15	Greece		15.00
SX16	Greece		30.00
SX17	Sarigol		20.00
SX18	Burgas		40.00
SX19	Rupel		30.00
SX20	Hirsova		30.00
SX21	Bulgaria		40.00
SX22	Batum		65.00
SX23	Greece		20.00
SX24	Greece		20.00
SY1	Chanak		20.00
SY2	Turkey		25.00
SY3	Turkey		25.00
SY4	Turkey		20.00
SY5	Turkey		50.00
SZ1	Turkey/Egypt	5.00	5.00
SZ2	Greece/Egypt/Palestine	5.00	6.00
SZ3	Turkey/Egypt	7.00	5.00
SZ4	Turkey/Egypt		4.00
SZ5	Turkey/Egypt/Syria		7.00
SZ6	Greece/Egypt?		8.00
SZ7	Malta/Palestine		8.00
SZ8	Greece/Egypt/Lebanon		15.00
SZ9	Egypt/Lebanon		8.00
SZ10	Cairo		2.00
SZ10T	Cairo		9.00
SZ11	Egypt		8.00
SZ12	Egypt		6.00
SZ13	Egypt/Lebanon		10.00
SZ14	Egypt		8.00
SZ15	Egypt		8.00
SZ16	Egypt/Palestine		15.00
SZ17	Egypt/Palestine		9.00
SZ18	Egypt/Palestine		12.00
SZ19	Egypt		10.00
SZ20	Egypt/Palestine		12.00
SZ21	Egypt		9.00
SZ22	Port Said		3.00
SZ23	Egypt/Palestine		20.00
SZ24	Suez		6.00
SZ24T	Egypt		6.00
SZ25	Egypt		10.00
SZ26	Egypt		15.00
SZ26T	Egypt		20.00
SZ27	Egypt/Palestine		10.00
SZ28	Egypt		10.00
SZ32	Palestine		35.00
SZ33	Palestine		15.00
SZ34	Palestine		20.00
SZ35	Palestine		25.00
SZ36	Egypt		15.00
SZ37	Palestine		15.00
SZ38	Palestine		35.00
SZ39	Palestine		35.00
SZ40	Jaffa		30.00
SZ41	Egypt		15.00

Index	Used by	d/c	sk
SZ42	Egypt		18.00
SZ43	Rafa		20.00
SZ44	Jerusalem		20.00
SZ45	Jaffa		30.00
SZ46	Palestine		40.00
SZ47	Palestine		40.00
SZ48	Palestine		40.00
SZ49	Mulebbis		30.00
SZ50	Turkey		40.00
SZ51	Egypt/Palestine/Syria		30.00
SZ52	Palestine		50.00
SZ53	Palestine		40.00
SZ54	Egypt		25.00
SZ56	Syria		20.00
SZ58	Egypt		20.00
SZ61	Safed		50.00
SZ62	Damascus		30.00
T42	France	2.00	
T62	France	2.00	
X	Greece		3.00
Y1	Turkey	18.00	15.00
Y2	Turkey	25.00	25.00
Y3	Bostanji?		50.00
-	Abbassia		60.00
-	Base X Greece		10.00
-	Cairo		40.00
-	Kantara		50.00
-	Mustapha		60.00
-	Port Said		40.00

15/41 Army Post Office, Krag machines:

POST OFFICE 3
〰〰〰
AUG 15

ARMY POST OFFICE 3
〰〰〰
18 AUG 15

15/41

Army Post Office 1	2.00	17		10.00
Army Post Office 2	2.00	18		10.00
Army Post Office 3	1.00	19		10.00
Army P.O.1	1.00	20		10.00
Army P.O.2	1.00	21		10.00
Army P.O.3	1.00	22		10.00
Army P.O.4	1.00	23		10.00
A.P.O. S12 Harfleur	3.00	24		10.00
Army P.O.S15	3.00	25		10.00
A.P.O. S17	3.00	26		10.00
A.P.O. S40	5.00	27		10.00
A.P.O. S60	10.00	28		12.00
		29		8.00

15/42 Army Post Office (HD), for Home Defence, single ring with index at base:

1	8.00	30	10.00
2	8.00	31	8.00
3	8.00	32	10.00
4	8.00	33	10.00
5	8.00	34	8.00
6	8.00	35	8.00
7	8.00	36	10.00
8	8.00	40	70.00
9	8.00	41	70.00
10	8.00	42	70.00
11	8.00	45	8.00
12	10.00	46	10.00
13	10.00	47	10.00
14	8.00	54	10.00
15	10.00	59	10.00
16	8.00	70	10.00
		A1	10.00
		A3	10.00
		D1	10.00
		D3	8.00

Military and Camp Postmarks

D5	8.00	M8	10.00
D11	10.00	M9	10.00
D12	10.00	M10	10.00
D14	60.00	M11	10.00
D16	10.00	R1	15.00
M6	10.00	R5	10.00
M7	10.00	R19	20.00

15/43	Army Post Office HD/A, skeleton	40.00
15/44	Army R.L.O./London, single circle	20.00
15/45	R.E. Postal Section/R.L.O. single circle	20.00

15/46 Base Army Post Office, double circles with index at base:

1	Le Havre	1.00
2	Rouen	1.00
3	Boulogne	1.00
4	Calais	2.00
W	Brindisi	60.00
X	Salonica	10.00
Y	Greece	10.00
Z	Egypt	3.00

15/47 Base Army P.O. skeletons:

K	Kantara	20.00
T	Port Said	6.00
X	Salonica	10.00
Z	Egypt	5.00

Field Post Office, double circles 15/48 or skeletons with index at base:

15/48

Most Field Post Offices were allotted to formations. A simple number indicated a Brigade, a prefix D or T indicated a Division, H a Corps, and A an Army. Additional codes were B for Guards, C for Cavalry, G for GHQ, K for American, P for Canadian, Q for Tanks, W for Western Frontier Force, Adriatic Mission or Australian, X for Canadian, Y for Yeomanry or Mounted, Z for New Zealand. Territorial formations were at first designated by an abbreviation of their name (eg SM = South Midland) before being numbered. However these descriptions do not hold good throughout, eg on the Western Front from June 1916 to February 1919 datestamps were periodically changed round for security reasons. Example : datestamp FPO DW4 was used initially by 4th Australian Division, then in turn by the 3rd Canadian, 49th, Guards, 63rd and 57th Divisions before reverting to 4th Australian Division.

Index	Used by	d/c	sk
no number	GHQ B.E.F.		3.00
1		1.00	3.00
2		1.00	
3		1.00	
4		2.00	
5		1.00	
6		1.00	
7		1.00	
8		1.00	
9		1.00	
10		1.00	
11		1.00	
12		1.00	
13		1.00	
14		1.00	
15		1.00	
16		1.00	

Index	Used by	d/c	sk
17		1.00	
18		8.00	
19		1.00	
20		1.00	
21		1.00	
22		1.00	
23		1.00	
24		1.00	
25		1.00	
26		1.00	
27		1.00	
28		1.00	
29		8.00	
30		8.00	
31		8.00	15.00
32		8.00	
33		1.00	
34		1.00	
35		1.00	
36		1.00	
37		1.00	
38		15.00	
39		15.00	
40		15.00	
41		1.00	
42		1.00	
43		1.00	
44		1.00	
45		1.00	
46		1.00	
47		1.00	
48		1.00	
49		1.00	
50		1.00	
51		1.00	
52		1.00	
53		1.00	
54		1.00	
55		1.00	
56		1.00	
57		1.00	
58		1.00	
59		1.00	
60		1.00	
61		1.00	
62		1.00	
63		1.00	
64		1.00	
65		3.00	
66		3.00	
67		3.00	
68		1.00	
69		1.00	
70		1.00	
71		1.00	
72		1.00	
73		1.00	
74		1.00	
75		1.00	
76		1.00	
77		3.00	
78		3.00	
79		5.00	
80		2.00	
81		1.00	
82		1.00	
83		1.00	
84		1.00	
85		1.00	
86		1.00	
87		1.00	
88		1.00	
89		1.00	
90		1.00	
91		1.00	

Military and Camp Postmarks

Index	Used by	d/c	sk
92		1.00	
93		1.00	
94		1.00	
95		1.00	
96		1.00	
97		1.00	
98		1.00	
99		1.00	
100		1.00	
101		1.00	
102		1.00	
103		1.00	
104		1.00	
105		1.00	
106		1.00	
107		1.00	
108		1.00	
109		1.00	
110		1.00	
111		1.00	
112		1.00	
113		1.00	
114		1.00	
115		1.00	
116		1.00	
117		1.00	
118		1.00	
119		2.00	
120		2.00	
121		1.00	
122		1.00	
123		1.00	
124		1.00	
125		1.00	
126		1.00	
127		1.00	
137		1.00	
138		1.00	
139		1.00	
140		1.00	
141		1.00	
142		1.00	
143		1.00	
144		1.00	
145		1.00	
146		1.00	
147		1.00	
148		1.00	
149		1.00	
150		1.00	
151		1.00	
152		1.00	
153		1.00	
154		1.00	
155		2.00	
156		2.00	
157		2.00	
158		15.00	
159		12.00	
160		15.00	
161		12.00	
161T			5.00
162		10.00	
163		10.00	
164		1.00	
165		1.00	
166		1.00	
167		1.00	
168		2.00	
169		1.00	
170		2.00	
171		2.00	
172		2.00	
173		1.00	
173		1.00	

Index	Used by	d/c	sk
174		2.00	
175		1.00	
176		2.00	
177		3.00	
178		2.00	
179		2.00	3.00
X179			4.00
180		2.00	15.00
180X			4.00
181		2.00	4.00
X181			4.00
182		2.00	
183		2.00	
184			3.00
185		2.00	
186		2.00	
187		2.00	
188		2.00	
189		2.00	
190		1.00	
197		2.00	
198		2.00	
199		2.00	
200	N. Russia	75.00	
201	Russia	75.00	
202	N. Ireland	75.00	
228	Salonika	20.00	20.00
229		2.00	
230		2.00	3.00
231		3.00	
232		10.00	10.00
233		10.00	30.00
234		10.00	10.00
A1	1 Army HQ	1.00	
A2	2 Army HQ	1.00	4.00
A2A	Adv. Army HQ		3.00
A3	3 Army HQ	1.00	
A4	4 Army HQ	1.00	
A4X	Adv. Army HQ	3.00	
A5	5 Army HQ	1.00	
AD1	1 A.D.O.	1.00	2.00
AD2	2 A.D.O.	1.00	
AD3	3 A.D.O.	1.00	
AD4	4 A.D.O.	2.00	
AD5	5 A.D.O.	2.00	
AGX	Adv. G.H.Q.	40.00	
AH16			8.00
AN8,12-15		40.00	
AR	5 Army HQ	1.00	
AT1	Army Troops	1.00	
1B		1.00	
2B		1.00	
3B		1.00	
4B		1.00	
C1		1.00	
C2		1.00	
C3		1.00	
C4		1.00	
C5		1.00	
C6		1.00	
C7		1.00	
C8		1.00	
C9		1.00	
C10		30.00	30.00
C11		30.00	
C12		30.00	
C13		30.00	30.00
C14		30.00	35.00
C15		?	?
CD3	Kantara	30.00	
CIB	Composite Infantry Brigade		40.00
CZ		50.00	50.00
D1		1.00	
D2		1.00	
D3		1.00	

Military and Camp Postmarks

Index	Used by	d/c	sk
D4		1.00	
D5		1.00	
D6		1.00	
D7		2.00	
D8		1.00	
D9		1.00	
D10		8.00	
D11		1.00	
D12		1.00	
D13		20.00	
D14		1.00	
D15		1.00	
D16		1.00	
D17		1.00	
D18		1.00	
D19		1.00	
D20		1.00	
D21		1.00	
D22		4.00	
D23		1.00	
D24		1.00	
D25		2.00	
D26		4.00	
D27		1.00	
D28		4.00	
D29		1.00	
D30		1.00	
D31		1.00	
D32		2.00	
D33		1.00	
D34		1.00	
D35		1.00	
D36		1.00	
D37		1.00	
D38		1.00	
D39		1.00	
D40		2.00	
D41		1.00	
D42		1.00	
D46		1.00	
D47		1.00	
D48		1.00	
D49		1.00	
D50		1.00	
D51		1.00	
D52		4.00	
D53		15.00	
D54		15.00	
D55		1.00	
D56		2.00	
D57		2.00	
D58		2.00	
D59		2.00	
D60		30.00	6.00
D61		2.00	
D62		2.00	
D63		2.00	
D66		2.00	
66D	APO S66		8.00
D74		4.00	8.00
D75		15.00	
DAN4		6.00	
DAN5		6.00	
DB		1.00	
DC1		1.00	
DC2		1.00	
DC3		1.00	
DC4		6.00	
DC5		30.00	
DHD		2.00	
DK		2.00	
DL2		4.00	
DLL		30.00	
DM		4.00	
DM1		8.00	

Index	Used by	d/c	sk
DM2		8.00	
DM3		50.00	
DM4		40.00	
DN		4.00	
DNL		40.00	
DP1-4		2.00	
DQ		2.00	
DSM		3.00	
DW	Egypt		40.00
DW1-5		4.00	
DWR		5.00	
DX1-4		2.00	
DY		20.00	
2DY			20.00
3DY			30.00
4DY			30.00
DZ	N.Z. Div. HQ	3.00	
EY		50.00	
F1	Eastern Force HQ		40.00
F2	Abbassia		20.00
FD1	Field Depot Italy	6.00	
FD2	Field Depot Italy	12.00	
FD3	Field Depot Italy	12.00	
FD4	Field Depot Italy	12.00	
FD5	Field Depot Italy	10.00	
FD8	Field Depot Italy	10.00	
FD9	Field Depot Italy	10.00	
G	GHQ B.E.F.	3.00	
GM	GHQ B.E.F		10.00
GM1	GHQ E.E.F.		20.00
GM2	GHQ E.E.F.		10.00
GQ	Italy GHQ	8.00	
GQ2	Italy GHQ	8.00	
GX	British Salonika Army	10.00	
GZ	GHQ M.E.F.	15.00	
H1		1.00	
H2		1.00	
H3		1.00	
H4		1.00	
H5		1.00	
H6		1.00	
H7		1.00	
H8		1.00	
H9		1.00	
H10		1.00	
H11		1.00	
H12		4.00	
H13		1.00	
H14		1.00	
H15		1.00	30.00
H16			10.00
H17		1.00	
H18		1.00	4.00
H19		1.00	
H20			20.00
H20T			30.00
H21			30.00
H22		1.00	
HC1		1.00	
HC2		1.00	
HC3		1.00	
1HD		5.00	
2HD		6.00	
3HD		2.00	
HK	II American Corps	3.00	
HM	HQ Desert Column	40.00	50.00
HP	Canadian Corps	4.00	
HR		4.00	
HW		5.00	
HW2		4.00	
HX		4.00	
HY		25.00	20.00
1K-3K	Security purposes	5.00	
4L		3.00	
5L		3.00	

301

Military and Camp Postmarks

Index	Used by	d/c	sk
6L		3.00	
1LL		2.00	
2LL		4.00	
3LL		2.00	
LY	Lowland Mtd. Bde.	50.00	
M1		30.00	30.00
1M		2.00	
2M		2.00	
3M		2.00	
MD1	Anzac Mtd. Div.	50.00	
MD2	Imperial Mtd. Div.	40.00	
MDT1	Anzac Mtd. Div. Train	50.00	
MH2	VIII Corps HQ	40.00	
MH3	IX Corps	40.00	
MX1	Mtd. Bde.	60.00	
1N		5.00	
2N		5.00	
3N		5.00	
NL1		2.00	
NL2		2.00	
NL3		2.00	
NMY		8.00	
1P-12P	Canadian Bde. HQ	4.00	
PB1	Egypt		50.00
PB11	Russia	£100	
PB12	Russia	£125	
PB13	Russia	£100	
PB14	Russia	£100	
PB15	Russia	£125	
PB22	Russia	£100	
PB33	Russia	£100	
PB44	Russia	£100	
PB55	Russia	£100	
PB66	Russia	75.00	
PB77	Russia	£125	
PB88	Russia	£125	
PB99	Russia	£100	
Q1		3.00	
Q2		3.00	
Q3		3.00	
Q4		4.00	
Q5		4.00	
R10	10 Div. Railhead		20.00
S26	France	3.00	
S58	France	5.00	
S62	France	2.00	
S63	W. Front	5.00	
S64	France	5.00	
S66	France		5.00
S74	France	5.00	
S77	France	1.00	
SA1		4.00	
SEY	S.E. Mtd. Bde.	30.00	
1SM		2.00	
2SM		2.00	
3SM		2.00	
SWY2		30.00	
SX2	Greece		10.00
SX3	Salonica		20.00
SZ1	Turkey		5.00
SZ1T	Egypt		5.00
SZ5	Syria		30.00
SZ8	Lebanon		40.00
SZ9	Lebanon		50.00
SZ11	Egypt		6.00
SZ15	Egypt		8.00
SZ16	Haifa		50.00
SZ18	Egypt		30.00
SZ19	Lebanon		40.00
SZ19T	Egypt		10.00
SZ20	Ludd		30.00
SZ21	Egypt		10.00
SZ23	Egypt		20.00
SZ34	Jaffa		30.00
SZ36	Egypt		15.00

Index	Used by	d/c	sk
SZ48	Palestine		50.00
SZ49	Mulebbis		60.00
SZ53	Palestine		50.00
SZ55	Egypt		20.00
SZ57	Haifa		40.00
SZ58	Jericho		50.00
SZ59	Tul Karem		60.00
SZ60	Tiberias		50.00
SZ61	Palestine		50.00
SZ62	Damascus		40.00
T1		1.00	
T2		1.00	
T3		1.00	
T4		1.00	
T5		1.00	
T6		1.00	
T7		2.00	
T8		1.00	
T9		1.00	
T10		8.00	
T11		2.00	
T12		1.00	
T14		1.00	
T15		1.00	
T16		1.00	
T17		1.00	
T18		1.00	
T19		1.00	
T20		1.00	
T21		1.00	
T22		3.00	
T23		1.00	
T24		1.00	
T25		1.00	
T26		3.00	
T27		1.00	
T28		3.00	
T29		1.00	
T30		1.00	
T31		1.00	
T32		1.00	
T33		1.00	
T34		1.00	
T35		1.00	
T36		1.00	
T37		1.00	
T38		1.00	
T39		1.00	
T40		1.00	
T41		1.00	
T46		1.00	
T47		1.00	
T48		1.00	
T49		1.00	
T50		1.00	
T51		1.00	
T52		8.00	
T53		40.00	
T55		1.00	
T56		1.00	
T57		3.00	
T58		3.00	
T59		2.00	
T60		20.00	
T61		2.00	
T62		2.00	
T63		1.00	
T66		3.00	
T74		2.00	
TAN4	4 Aust. Div. Train	3.00	
TAN5	5 Aust. Div. Train	3.00	
TB	Guards Div. Train	2.00	
TC	Cav. Div. Train		4.00
TC4	Cav. Div. Train	3.00	
TG	GHQ Train	2.00	

Military and Camp Postmarks

Index	Used by	d/c	sk
THD	51 Div. Train	10.00	
TK	Spare D/S	2.00	
TL2	47 Div. Train	10.00	
TLL	52 Div. Train	30.00	
TM	46 Div. Train	10.00	
TN	50 Div. Train	10.00	
TNL	RN Div. Train	50.00	
TP1-5		?	
TSM	48 Div. Train	10.00	
TW	W.F.F. Train	40.00	
TW1-5		4.00	
TWR	49 Div. Train	5.00	
TX-TX4		4.00	
TY	Spare D/S	2.00	
TZ		2.00	
W1	W.F.F. Egypt		30.00
W1	B.M.M. Italy	40.00	
W2	W.F.F. Egypt		30.00
W2	B.M.M. Greece		40.00
W2	B.M.M. Greece	40.00	
W3	B.M.M.	40.00	
W4	Greece	40.00	
W9-W11		2.00	
1W-8W		2.00	
12W-15W		2.00	
WBY		10.00	
1WR		4.00	
2WR		4.00	
3WR		2.00	
WSY	Mtd. Bde.	6.00	
1X-12X	Canadian Bdes.	2.00	
1Y	Mtd. Bdes.	25.00	
2Y		50.00	
3Y			10.00
4Y		22.00	
5Y		15.00	
6Y		50.00	
7Y		8.00	15.00
8Y		20.00	
22Y	Mtd. Bdes.	50.00	30.00
1Z-4Z		2.00	

15/49	Instructional marks, 'Present location uncertain' etc., many types		6.00
15/50	Packet handstamp		4.00
15/51	Parcel handstamp (on piece)		6.00
15/52	P.O.W. mail from UK camps with P.C. markings		12.00
15/53	As above but from Isle of Man		20.00
15/54	P.O.W. mail from UK camps with camp cachets		20.00
15/55	As above but from Isle of Man		75.00
	Travelling Post Office markings, see below		50.00

TPO handstamps:
The full inscriptions are not shown here and some include more than one variety, but all include the letters "TPO". Most are skeleton handstamps and many are valued considerably higher than the figure shown:

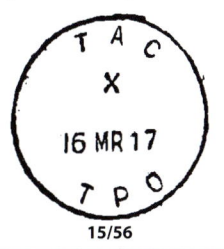

15/56 15/57

15/56	Egypt & Palestine : BAR, RAB, CAT, TAC, DAL, LAD, JAP, PAJ, KAL, LAK, KAR, RAK, LAP, PAL, SAT, TAS, Upper Egypt, Z and W		£200
15/57	France & Germany : BEF Main Line		£125

15/58	Russia : NREF	£750
15/59	Turkey : TPO1	£150

Dublin marks used after Easter rising, 1916
These are civilian marks but are occasionally found on soldiers' mail:

15/60

15/60	Parcel post handstamps	50.00
15/61	Single rim/double rim skeletons	75.00
15/61a	Dublin Roller Cancel	£100

Section III : Between the Two World Wars

In 1921 new styles of postmarks were introduced, rubber stamps **15/63** very briefly and single circle datestamps **15/64**. In Germany single circle Army Post Office datestamps as **15/37** were used, with offices designated S40, or S40A to S40H (with letter above the date or at foot of circle, see below). From 1927 a new series of double circle datestamps came into use, numbered from 1 upwards, 26 being the highest number used before 1939. These new double circle datestamps were the forerunners of the Second World War series, and the earlier datestamps were not used after 1929 apart from some odd exceptions.

Ireland 1920-23

15/63 15/64

15/62	First World War datestamps (as **15/48**) used 1920-23: FPO 202, D41, 3K, T29, W16	75.00
	New rubber datestamps **15/63** (1921) or single circle **15/64** (1921-23): FPO 5,6,7,8,9,10 (not all known used in both types)	80.00

Germany 1922-29
For earlier postmarks see section II. In 1922 the offices were reorganised as sub offices of APO S40, identified by a letter suffix. In 1926 the Army of the Rhine transferred from the Cologne area to Wiesbaden area and the APOs were also moved.

15/65	APO S40, as **15/37** and **15/39**	15.00
15/66	APO S40A to S40C, as **15/37** but with code A,B,C above date	30.00
15/67	APO S40D to S40H, as **15/37** with S40 after Office, codes D-H at foot	30.00
15/68	FPO X, as **15/48**	50.00

Military and Camp Postmarks

Turkey 1922-23:
For earlier postmarks see section II.

15/69	FPO 1,2, as **15/48**	50.00
15/70	FPO 11,12,13,14,15, as **15/64**	50.00

15/71 China 1927-40:

2	Hong Kong as **15/48**	£125
3	Shanghai as **15/48**	£100
4	various as **15/48**	75.00
5	Hong Kong as **15/48**	£100
8	HMT Dorsetshire (single circle)	£125
APO1	Shanghai as **15/39**	50.00
FPO1	Tientsin as **15/48**	75.00

15/72 Egypt 1932-39:
These datestamps were used at Egyptian post offices but on British Forces mail bearing the Army Post stamps (see Gibbons catalogues). They also appear on covers bearing NAAFI seals affixed to the backs of envelopes, which are cancelled with a dotted diamond obliterator.

Abu-Qir	15.00
Abu-Sueir	10.00
Alexandria	2.00
Cairo	2.00
El Daba	*
Mera Matrhu	15.00
Moascar	10.00

15/73

15/73	Port Said	10.00

Saar 1935

15/74	FPO 10, as **15/48**	30.00

Palestine 1936

15/75	FPOs 12,15,16,17,18,20,22,23,24,25,26, as **15/48**	30.00

UK Manoeuvres

15/77

15/76	1925 : FPO 1-16, skeleton as **15/40** but 'Field'	50.00
15/77	1933-7 : Base Army PO 1	25.00
15/78	FPO 1-12, as **15/48**	25.00

Section IV : Second World War 1939-45

Most military postmarks of this period were Field Post Office handstamps type **15/79**, though Krag machines **15/80** were also in use - value 2.00. In the simplified listing on the pages that follow these types are not differentiated. Universal machine FPO 676 **15/81** was used at Inverness where much military mail was handled - value 3.00. Only from 1944 other styles of machine postmarks were used, with Army Post Office wording, see **15/82** and **15/83** though these specimens are from shortly after the end of the war - value 2.00.

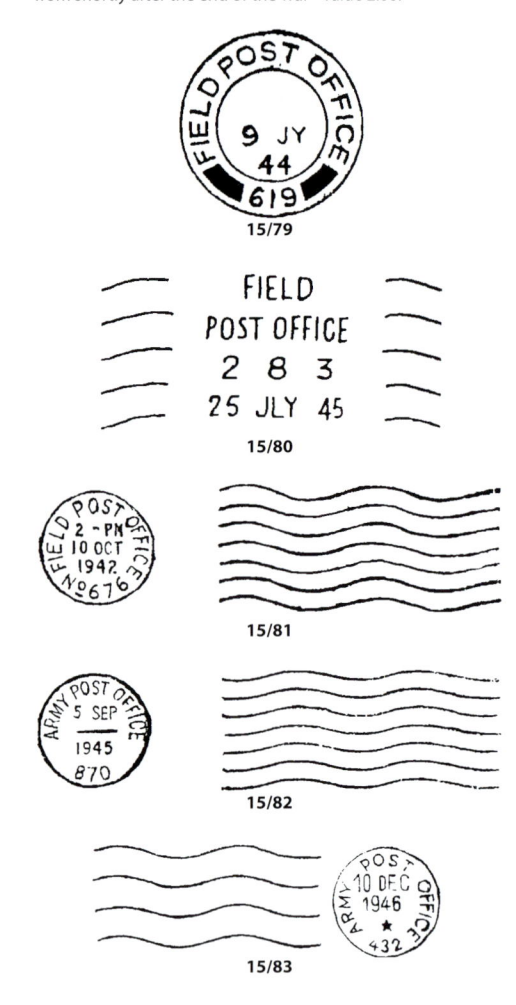

15/79

15/80

15/81

15/82

15/83

Home Depot

15/84	Home Depot R.E.P.S., 1-20, 1939-42	10.00
15/85	Army Post Office, parcel handstamp	10.00
15/86	As above but rubber packet handstamp, 1940	10.00
15/87	Home Depot/A.P.O., rubber packet handstamp, 1941	10.00
15/88	Home Postal Centre, 1-16, 1942-47	10.00
15/89	Home Postal Centre/R.E./A.P.O., rubber packet handstamp, 1942-47	15.00

Base Army Post Offices

15/90

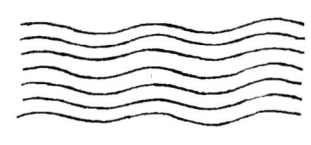

Military and Camp Postmarks

15/92
Either handstamp **15/90** or Krag machine 15/91 similar to **15/80** or Universal type machine as **15/92** but with several different types of town die:

1	France	2.00	(Machine 2.00)
4	Egypt	1.00	
5	Algiers	2.00	(Machine 2.00)
6	Italy	4.00	
7	Rangoon	2.00	
8	Belgium	1.00	(Machine 1.00)
15	Italy	1.00	(Machine 1.00)
17	Singapore	20.00	
18	Dieppe	4.00	

15/93 S.E.A (South East Asia) Base A.P.O. double circle or Krag machine 4.00

British Expeditionary Force in France, 1939-40

No.	Price	No.	Price
5	2.00	54	3.00
6	2.00	55	1.00
7	3.00	56	1.00
8	1.00	57	1.00
9	2.00	58	1.00
10	1.00	59	1.00
11	1.00	60	3.00
12	1.00	61	1.00
13	1.00	62	3.00
14	1.00	63	3.00
15	1.00	64	3.00
16	2.00	65	4.00
17	1.00	66	1.00
18	1.00	67	4.00
19	1.00	68	1.00
20	2.00	69	1.00
21	1.00	70	3.00
22	2.00	71	7.00
23	1.00	72	3.00
24	2.00	73	4.00
25	1.00	74	1.00
26	1.00	75	2.00
27	1.00	76	2.00
28	3.00	77	3.00
29	1.00	78	2.00
30	1.00	79	2.00
31	2.00	80	1.00
32	1.00	81	1.00
33	1.00	82	7.00
34	7.00	85	1.00
35	1.00	86	2.00
36	6.00	87	2.00
37	1.00	88	3.00
38	1.00	89	3.00
39	1.00	100	4.00
40	1.00	101	5.00
41	1.00	102	3.00
42	1.00	103	3.00
43	2.00	104	3.00
44	1.00	110	2.00
45	1.00	111	4.00
46	1.00	112	7.00
47	4.00	113	4.00
48	2.00	114	4.00
49	2.00	130	5.00
50	3.00	132	5.00
51	3.00	135	7.00
52	3.00	136	5.00
53	3.00	137	7.00

No.	Price
140	7.00
181	7.00
182	7.00

Channel Islands Liberation, 1945

138	Guernsey	75.00
302	Jersey	75.00

Cyprus

124	50.00
164	7.00
168	8.00
290	20.00
291	20.00
292	20.00
293	25.00
552	20.00
726	25.00

Egypt

15/94 Military Post Offices, redesignated numeral types M.P.O. or B.P.O., from 1939:

E601	3.00
E602	3.00
E603	4.00
E604	4.00
E605	6.00
E606	6.00
E607	8.00
E608	6.00
E609	18.00
E611	78.00
E611	8.00
E615	6.00

15/94

15/95

15/95 Egyptian Pre-Paid Marks:

1	1.00
2	1.00
3	1.00
4	1.00
5	2.00
6	1.00
7	1.00
8	1.00
10	1.00
11	1.00
12	1.00
13	2.00
14	1.00
15	7.00
16	1.00
17	1.00
18	1.00
19	1.00
20	1.00
21	1.00
22	3.00
23	3.00
24	1.00
25	1.00
26	1.00
27	1.00
28	2.00
29	1.00
30	1.00
31	2.00
32	7.00
33	1.00
34	1.00
35	1.00
36	1.00
37	2.00
38	1.00
39	2.00
40	1.00
41	2.00
42	2.00
43	1.00
44	1.00
45	1.00
46	2.00
47	2.00
48	1.00
49	?
50	2.00
51	1.00
52	1.00
53	1.00
54	2.00
55	1.00
56	1.00
57	1.00
58	1.00
59	?
60	?
61	1.00
62	?
63	2.00
64	1.00
65	2.00
66	1.00
67	3.00
68	1.00
69	1.00
70	?
71	1.00
72	1.00
73	?
74	?
75	1.00
76	1.00
77	2.00
78	?
79	2.00
80	1.00
81	3.00
82	1.00
83	?
84	1.00
85	2.00
86	1.00
87	?
88	1.00
89	1.00
90	1.00
91	2.00

Military and Camp Postmarks

No.	Price	No.	Price	No.	Price	No.	Price
92	?	138	2.00	375	1.00	493	2.00
93	1.00	139	?	394	?	503	3.00
94	2.00	140	2.00	395	5.00	506	1.00
95	3.00	147	5.00	396	?	507	1.00
96	1.00	148	2.00	397	6.00	508	1.00
97	1.00	156	4.00	445	4.00	525	4.00
98	1.00	161	9.00	448	?	533	?
99	?	165	7.00	451	6.00	541	5.00
100	?	167	2.00	481	?	546	2.00
101	?	168	2.00	482	?	584	2.00
102	1.00	169	1.00	503	5.00	605	?
103	1.00	170	1.00	513	2.00	606	2.00
104	?	171	1.00	515	2.00	607	2.00
105	4.00	172	2.00	517	3.00	617	6.00
106	3.00	173	1.00	519	2.00	618	4.00
109	3.00	174	1.00	525	?	620	2.00
111	2.00	177	2.00	530	2.00	660	2.00
112	2.00	178	3.00	531	2.00	660	2.00
113	1.00	186	1.00	533	3.00	690	2.00
114	1.00	187	1.00	546	6.00	692	1.00
115	2.00	188	2.00	550	2.00	706	2.00
117	3.00	189	3.00	551	1.00	716	1.00
118	1.00	190	1.00	554	3.00	734	2.00
121	1.00	191	1.00	555	?	736	2.00
123	1.00	196	1.00	557	6.00	737	1.00
124	1.00	197	1.00	568	3.00	738	1.00
129	1.00	198	1.00	569	2.00	739	2.00
130	5.00	199	1.00	572	1.00	740	1.00
131	1.00	201	2.00	575	5.00	741	2.00
132	1.00	217	3.00	576	1.00	742	2.00
134	4.00	218	2.00	605	?	743	3.00
135	5.00	220	2.00	655	1.00	744	2.00
137	3.00	224	?	659	6.00	792	1.00
139	3.00	225	?	708	?	801	1.00
140	3.00	226	?	716	6.00	809	1.00
141	3.00	232	3.00	717	3.00	810	1.00
142	1.00	233	?	777	3.00	820	3.00
143	2.00	234	4.00			829	3.00
144	3.00	235	2.00			830	5.00
145	6.00	236	3.00			832	1.00
146	3.00	242	2.00			841	1.00
148	1.00	243	2.00			842	1.00
149	2.00	244	2.00			867	1.00
151	2.00	245	2.00			868	1.00
152	2.00	246	2.00			870	1.00
153	2.00	255	2.00			899	1.00
154	2.00	264	?				
155	6.00	265	6.00				

Liberation of Europe (France, Belgium, Germany, Austria), 1944-46

No.	Price
3	2.00
8	2.00
9	2.00
20	1.00
89	2.00
158	2.00
186	2.00
223	1.00
225	2.00
228	2.00
229	2.00
279	2.00
280	2.00
284	4.00
285	2.00
287	4.00
288	4.00
294	2.00
295	2.00
296	3.00
339	2.00
350	1.00
351	2.00
352	3.00
381	2.00
385	2.00
432	1.00
439	3.00
467	?
468	3.00
481	4.00
482	2.00

Field Post Offices, 1939-46 (used in diff locations, some continued later)

No.	Price
13	2.00
15	3.00
17	4.00
35	3.00
36	3.00
37	3.00
38	3.00
39	5.00
67	1.00
68	2.00
69	2.00
74	2.00
76	2.00
96	1.00
113	2.00
123	2.00
124	3.00
129	?
134	?
135	1.00
136	1.00
137	1.00
267	?
284	?
285	?
287	?
288	?
289	?
290	4.00
291	5.00
292	4.00
293	4.00
299	2.00
309	1.00
315	2.00
317	2.00
318	?
319	?
323	?
324	4.00
325	?
326	?
327	?
368	7.00
369	?
370	4.00
371	?
372	3.00

Gibraltar

No.	Price
475	5.00

Greece and Crete

No.	Price
69	10.00
137	5.00
139	12.00
175	75.00
176	?
193	30.00
194	75.00
195	?
250	8.00
264	6.00
265	6.00
266	8.00
267	8.00
285	5.00
286	6.00
287	6.00
288	6.00
400	5.00
402	20.00
454	10.00
514	4.00
567	5.00
654	5.00

Military and Camp Postmarks

709	15.00
727	?
732	?
776	8.00
777	6.00
778	?
782	?
783	2.00

Iceland and the Faroes

2	30.00
3	40.00
89	75.00
128	?
219	?
304	50.00
305	75.00
306	50.00
307	£100
308	50.00
526	50.00
611	£100
695	75.00

India and Burma

6	2.00
8	?
30	2.00
37	1.00
39	2.00
145	1.00
198	1.00
224	?
225	3.00
226	?
259	2.00
260	2.00
261	2.00
262	2.00
263	2.00
352	?
366	1.00
388	6.00
389	2.00
390	1.00
449	1.00
517	8.00
545	4.00
557	3.00
670	5.00
696	1.00
697	1.00
698	1.00
699	1.00
769	3.00
770	1.00
771	5.00
772	3.00
773	1.00
781	?
873	3.00

Iraq

171	1.00
222	?
223	?
224	6.00
225	?
226	?
244	3.00
269	6.00
289	6.00
290	?
291	?

292	?
375	?
394	3.00
395	6.00
397	3.00
398	4.00
533	2.00

Italy and Sicily

1	3.00
16	3.00
32	?
36	1.00
110	1.00
116	1.00
120	2.00
126	2.00
134	1.00
135	1.00
136	?
137	1.00
139	6.00
167	2.00
168	3.00
196	1.00
214	2.00
217	2.00
223	2.00
224	2.00
225	?
232	2.00
236	2.00
238	3.00
239	3.00
250	2.00
254	2.00
255	3.00
256	3.00
257	3.00
258	4.00
265	4.00
266	5.00
267	5.00
284	2.00
285	2.00
286	2.00
287	2.00
288	2.00
290	3.00
291	3.00
292	3.00
300	1.00
315	3.00
317	2.00
323	?
324	2.00
325	4.00
327	1.00
370	1.00
385	1.00
387	1.00
395	2.00
396	3.00
397	2.00
398	3.00
399	3.00
402	1.00
448	2.00
451	3.00
462	2.00
481	2.00
482	2.00
501	2.00
503	?

510	2.00
520	2.00
525	?
530	1.00
531	1.00
533	1.00
546	2.00
550	5.00
558	3.00
568	2.00
570	?
577	?
578	1.00
581	1.00
583	2.00
583	3.00
594	3.00
600	3.00
603	4.00
604	1.00
605	2.00
609	6.00
612	?
613	3.00
614	7.00
615	4.00
627	1.00
629	1.00
632	?
642	1.00
657	?
661	3.00
662	2.00
663	3.00
708	3.00
709	5.00
710	4.00
711	2.00
712	1.00
715	2.00
720	1.00
721	2.00
722	1.00
723	1.00
724	2.00
725	1.00
726	6.00
728	1.00
730	1.00
746	1.00
748	1.00
750	2.00
751	1.00
754	1.00
755	1.00
756	2.00
793	2.00
796	2.00
797	2.00

Lebanon

141	10.00
223	10.00
550	10.00

Libya

33	1.00
40	3.00
51	2.00
111	4.00
134	4.00
135	6.00
156	5.00
168	2.00

178	?
197	2.00
199	10.00
218	7.00
233	3.00
234	3.00
244	4.00
289	6.00
315	3.00
316	4.00
317	2.00
318	4.00
323	4.00
324	5.00
325	8.00
326	8.00
327	?
368	?
369	?
370	8.00
371	?
372	?
394	?
395	?
396	4.00
397	4.00
398	?
448	4.00
451	5.00
499	4.00
515	3.00
516	4.00
518	2.00
571	7.00
572	4.00
653	4.00
656	2.00

Madagascar

226	15.00
596	20.00

Malaya

15/96

1939-42:

SP501 Singapore 15/96	10.00
SP502 Penang	15.00
SP503 Kedah	20.00
SP504 Kelantan	30.00
SP505 ?	30.00
SP506 Perak	30.00

1945-7:

259	10.00
261	20.00
262	20.00

Malta

188	5.00
443	5.00
570	5.00

307

Military and Camp Postmarks

North African Campaign, 1943-45

13	3.00
15	3.00
17	3.00
51	2.00
111	3.00
116	2.00
117	2.00
118	2.00
136	3.00
137	3.00
159	2.00
168	2.00
178	3.00
189	2.00
218	2.00
238	3.00
250	3.00
253	3.00
254	2.00
255	2.00
256	2.00
257	2.00
258	?
264	3.00
265	6.00
266	5.00
267	5.00
284	4.00
285	2.00
286	2.00
288	2.00
289	3.00
317	3.00
323	10.00
324	4.00
325	3.00
326	7.00
327	7.00
370	6.00
385	2.00
395	5.00
397	?
398	5.00
448	?
451	3.00
462	2.00
464	?
481	2.00
482	2.00
497	2.00
500	2.00
520	3.00
525	2.00
532	3.00
546	3.00
568	2.00
571	3.00
572	3.00
580	2.00
581	3.00
582	2.00
583	1.00
589	2.00
591	2.00
594	2.50
601	2.50
603	4.00
605	2.00
632	?
658	3.00
661	6.00
662	6.00
701	2.00
702	2.00
703	2.00
704	2.00
705	?
706	2.00
707	2.00
708	6.00
712	3.00
713	?
720	2.00

Norway
1940:

115	£100
125	£150
127	£125

1945:

150	15.00
343	15.00
785	15.00
786	15.00
787	50.00
788	30.00

Palestine, 1940-48

28	6.00
38	15.00
69	7.00
120	2.00
121	2.00
122	2.00
123	4.00
124	15.00
139	3.00
141	?
143	3.00
146	?
148	3.00
149	3.00
154	3.00
155	5.00
156	7.00
164	3.00
166	10.00
167	10.00
171	10.00
172	10.00
201	7.00
222	10.00
223	10.00
224	?
225	10.00
226	10.00
233	6.00
234	?
254	10.00
256	10.00
257	10.00
258	10.00
284	?
285	?
286	10.00
287	10.00
288	10.00
299	10.00
316	30.00
373	10.00
394	?
395	?
397	?
398	?
448	?
454	15.00
511	40.00
525	25.00
533	?
534	10.00
535	8.00
550	5.00
553	5.00
588	5.00
708	50.00
731	5.00

Persia

222	?
223	8.00
224	8.00
225	8.00
226	8.00
375	?

Sudan

174	4.00
186	4.00
214	5.00
549	3.00
718	2.00
782	6.00

Syria

61	2.00
66	2.00
80	2.00
140	20.00
172	1.00
222	?
223	6.00
224	7.00
225	7.00
226	6.00
257	?

269	10.00
289	6.00
290	6.00
291	6.00
292	4.00
316	?
370	10.00
533	4.00
552	5.00
567	3.00

West Africa

41 Sierra Leone	4.00
45 Gold Coast	4.00
46 Nigeria	5.00
106 Gold Coast	5.00
107 Gold Coast	5.00
108 Gold Coast	5.00
109 Gambia	6.00
536 Gold Coast	10.00
537 Sierra Leone	5.00
538 W.A. Force	5.00
559 Nigeria	4.00
560 Nigeria	10.00
561 W. Africa APS	10.00
562 W. Africa APS	?
563 Nigeria	7.00
564 Gold Coast	20.00
565 W. Africa APS	5.00
670 W. Africa GHQ	5.00
696 W. Africa GHQ	5.00
697 W. Africa GHQ	5.00
698 W. Africa GHQ	5.00
699 W. Africa GHQ	5.00
769 Nigeria	6.00
770 Nigeria	10.00
771 Nigeria	8.00
772 Nigeria	5.00
773 Nigeria	5.00

Army Censor marks - Second World War

See note concerning Censor marks in chapter 14 (Naval censor marks section).

Further marks used throughout the Empire have not been included, but a representative selection is shown here. Prisoner of War and civilian censor marks are included here also.

15/97 A100 Chiefly France 1939-40 1.00

15/98 A200 Chiefly UK 1940-41 1.00

Military and Camp Postmarks

15/99 A300 Egypt 1939-42 1.00

15/100 A500 Worldwide from 1942 1.00

15/101 A600 Worldwide 1944-45 1.00

15/102 A700 Middle East etc 1945 18.00

15/103 B100 North Africa, CMF & NW Europe 4.00

15/104 B403 As **15/103** 2.00

15/105 FC303 Middle East 2.00

UK Prisoners of War

15/106 GBPW100 4.00

15/107 GBPW210 (machine) 7.00

British Civil Censor marks

15/108 GBC3 2.00

15/109 GBC5 2.00

Section V: Post War Operations

An alphabetical listing of FPO locations is shown below. While handstamps of the thick arc type **15/79** continued in use (a more up to date specimen is shown at **15/112**), the thin arcs type **15/113** later took over, with alternative wording as **15/114**. Single circle handstamps **15/115** (alternatively Field Post Office or Forces Post Office) were also plentiful. These are all shown as "steel" in the list. Krag machines **15/116** or Universal machines **15/117** (mostly with continuous wavy lines or with slogans) were also used; there were inscription variations in both cases. Many Field Post Offices also used rubber 'Blackwell' types (see chapter 9), as **15/118** or **15/119** (or other variations). Parcel handstamps (see **15/120** - variations) were also used but are not valued in the list: these are generally about three times the value of the rubber handstamps. The list gives basic values but not dates, thus the address on the envelope (usually

Military and Camp Postmarks

a BFPO number) or contents have to be used to confirm the source of an envelope.

Parcel handstamps were withdrawn from use in British Forces Post Offices around early 2004.

A new series of self inking datestamps (SIDs) were introduced from around 2004 inscribed BFPO and numbered in the 3xxx series (from BFPO 3000 onwards). These have gradually replaced almost, if not all, other steel datestamps that were inscribed FIELD or FORCES POST OFFICE or FPO. The highest number recorded to date is BFPO 3202, but it is likely that higher numbers exist.

A new series of rubber packet handstamps (also known as Blackwell type) was introduced in 2001 inscribed FORCES POST OFFICE and numbered above 200 (highest number seen is 288).

United Kingdom:

United Kingdom FPOs are not included as the list is extensive, also exercises in the UK or overseas, but Northern Ireland is included in the list. FPOs were used at various UK publicity events, also the annual tour of the RE Recruiting Display which over some years used machine 8 and steel handstamps 172 254 258 390 519 643 999 1015 1021 1050 1054 and rubber and parcel handstamps as well.

Gulf War:

Stationary FPOs are listed under the relevant country; under the heading "Gulf War" are listed those FPOs attached to fighting units, some of which travelled from Saudi Arabia into Iraq and/or Kuwait.

We are indebted to the records of the late John Daynes and also to Michael Dobbs of the Forces Postal History Society who have helped with the updated list that follows and with the illustrations.

15/110	Home Postal Depot R.E., 1,4,6,8,16, thick arcs, 1949-53	4.00
15/111	As above but thin arcs, 51-53,63,68, from 1952	3.00

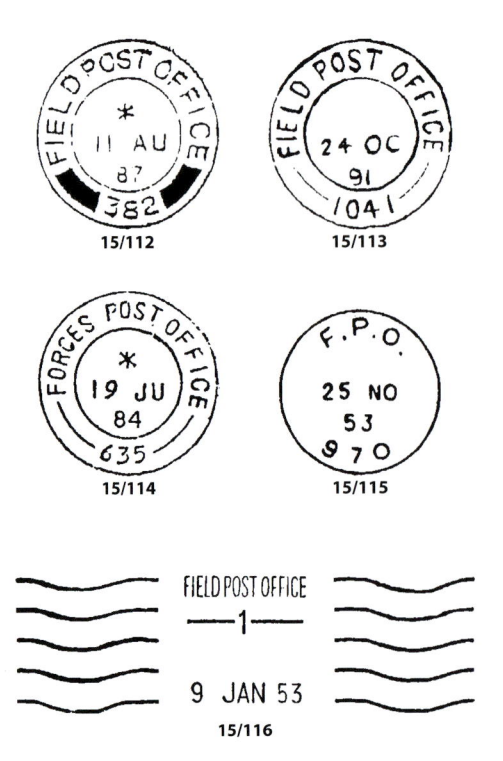

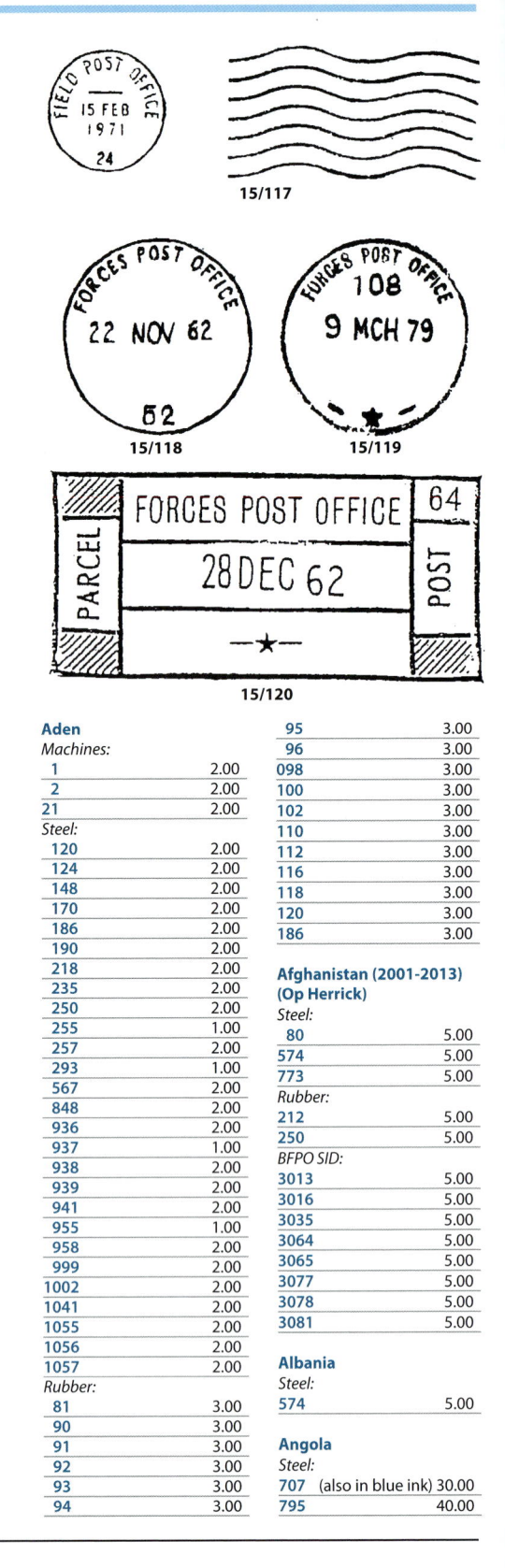

Aden
Machines:
1	2.00
2	2.00
21	2.00

Steel:
120	2.00
124	2.00
148	2.00
170	2.00
186	2.00
190	2.00
218	2.00
235	2.00
250	2.00
255	1.00
257	2.00
293	1.00
567	2.00
848	2.00
936	2.00
937	1.00
938	2.00
939	2.00
941	2.00
955	1.00
958	2.00
999	2.00
1002	2.00
1041	2.00
1055	2.00
1056	2.00
1057	2.00

Rubber:
81	3.00
90	3.00
91	3.00
92	3.00
93	3.00
94	3.00
95	3.00
96	3.00
098	3.00
100	3.00
102	3.00
110	3.00
112	3.00
116	3.00
118	3.00
120	3.00
186	3.00

Afghanistan (2001-2013) (Op Herrick)
Steel:
80	5.00
574	5.00
773	5.00

Rubber:
212	5.00
250	5.00

BFPO SID:
3013	5.00
3016	5.00
3035	5.00
3064	5.00
3065	5.00
3077	5.00
3078	5.00
3081	5.00

Albania
Steel:
574	5.00

Angola
Steel:
707 (also in blue ink)	30.00
795	40.00

Military and Camp Postmarks

Anguilla/Antigua
Steel:
701	20.00
1046	10.00

Rubber:
143	15.00

Ascension
Steel:
777	5.00
998	5.00

Rubber:
163	20.00
242	10.00

BFPO SID:
3031	5.00

Australia
Steel:
51	3.00
67	4.00
69	4.00
80	3.00
80	4.00
146	2.00
149	8.00
155	3.00
155	3.00
233	5.00
234	8.00
385	3.00
708	7.00
1003	3.00
1010	4.00
1014	3.00
1016	4.00
1033	3.00
1035	10.00
1037	7.00
1043	7.00
1046	2.00

Rubber:
71	5.00
75	6.00
138	6.00
157	6.00
159	6.00
186	6.00

Austria
Steel:
286	2.00
431	3.00
482	2.00
594	2.00
710	2.00
746	2.00
751	3.00
754	2.00
766	3.00
795	3.00
797	3.00
893	3.00

Bahrain
Machine:
1	6.00

Steel:
123	5.00
170	3.00
186	2.00
218	2.00
234	3.00
235	3.00

254	2.00
372	5.00
518	3.00
551	3.00
941	3.00
955	2.00
1013	3.00
1056	3.00
1057	3.00

Rubber:
77	5.00
81	5.00
94	4.00
98	5.00
99	5.00
102	5.00
106	5.00
107	5.00
109	5.00
113	5.00
115	5.00
116	5.00
186	5.00

Bechuanaland
Steel:
1002	15.00

Belgium
(for 1990s machine see listing under Germany heading)

Machine:
18	2.00

Steel:
177	1.00
350	2.00
358	2.00
376	2.00
513	1.00
516	1.00
716	1.00
916	1.00
955	1.00
984	1.00
1030	2.00

Rubber:
4	2.00
13	2.00
18	2.00
21	2.00
31	2.00
54	2.00
59	2.00
91	2.00
97	2.00
174	2.00
226	5.00
249	5.00

BFPO SID:
3127	5.00
3140	5.00

Bermuda
Steel:
51	20.00
148	20.00
707	20.00

Bosnia & Croatia (see also Italy)
Steel:
142	3.00
222	3.00
375	4.00

445	3.00
482	5.00
555	3.00
556	4.00
572	4.00
576	3.00
776	2.00
791	2.00
909	3.00
1012	2.00
1027	3.00
1029	3.00
1052	2.00
1057	2.00

Rubber:
32	5.00
44	5.00
95	5.00
108	5.00
119	5.00
132	5.00

British Guiana and Guyana
Steel:
136	15.00
154	6.00
188	3.00
243	3.00
376	8.00
576	8.00
616	4.00
941	6.00
955	3.00
966	8.00
1022	6.00
1043	10.00

British Honduras and Belize
Steel:
188	3.00
293	3.00
939	5.00

Rubber:
177	6.00
193	6.00
200	6.00

BFPO SID:
3043	5.00

British Solomon Islands
Steel:
136	35.00

British Virgin Islands
Steel:
148	20.00
385	30.00

Brunei
Steel:
51	3.00
156	3.00
234	6.00
635	3.00
656	6.00
964	5.00
1034	8.00
1035	8.00
1044	5.00

Rubber:
51	6.00
109	6.00
163	6.00
165	6.00

BFPO SID:
3030	5.00
3032	5.00

Caicos
Steel:
1042	30.00

Cameroons
Steel:
188	10.00
233	50.00
570	30.00
573	10.00
594	15.00
600	30.00
1032	12.00

Canada
Steel:
129	3.00
136	3.00
141	3.00
148	3.00
155	3.00
157	3.00
166	3.00
234	3.00
243	3.00
254	3.00
260	3.00
307	3.00
316	3.00
372	3.00
375	3.00
376	3.00
443	3.00
518	2.00
532	3.00
558	3.00
574	3.00
576	3.00
616	3.00
707	3.00
740	3.00
766	3.00
777	3.00
969	3.00
984	3.00
1012	3.00
1016	3.00
1018	3.00
1021	3.00
1035	3.00
1042	3.00
1045	3.00
1046	3.00
1062	3.00
1063	3.00

Rubber:
15	5.00
166	5.00
190	5.00

BFPO SID:
3075	5.00

Cyprus
Machines:
1 Krag/Univ	1.00
2 Krag/Univ	1.00
3 Krag/Univ	1.00
21	2.00

Steel:
61	1.00

Military and Camp Postmarks

76	1.00	86	2.00	124	1.00	Rubber:	
113	1.00	90	2.00	136	2.00	10	25.00
121	1.00	91	2.00	137	1.00	41	10.00
123	1.00	99	2.00	141	2.00	157	10.00
124	1.00	101	2.00	168	1.00	166	10.00
129	1.00	102	2.00	169	1.00	Meter Style: BFPO	
137	1.00	103	2.00	170	1.00	655	5.00
140	1.00	104	2.00	171	2.00	BFPO SID:	
141	1.00	105	2.00	172	1.00	3021	5.00
147	1.00	106	2.00	174	1.00	3061	5.00
148	1.00	107	2.00	186	1.00		
149	1.00	110	2.00	187	1.00	**Fiji**	
164	1.00	111	2.00	190	1.00	Steel:	
168	1.00	112	2.00	191	1.00	80	10.00
169	1.00	113	2.00	218	1.00	149	10.00
171	1.00	114	2.00	234	1.00	233	15.00
186	1.00	115	2.00	235	2.00	708	15.00
187	1.00	116	2.00	245	1.00	1038	15.00
197	1.00	117	2.00	246	2.00	1044	10.00
201	1.00	118	2.00	255	1.00	Rubber:	
218	1.00	119	2.00	257	1.00	135	30.00
220	1.00	122	2.00	266	1.00		
245	1.00	123	2.00	293	1.00	**France**	
246	1.00	124	2.00	299	2.00	Steel:	
250	1.00	152	2.00	309	2.00	128	3.00
257	1.00	156	2.00	316	1.00	155	3.00
260	1.00	160	2.00	375	1.00	235	3.00
388	1.00	182	2.00	443	12.00	265	3.00
461	1.00	189	2.00	445	1.00	305	3.00
482	1.00	192	2.00	461	1.00	716	2.00
514	1.00	199	2.00	518	1.00	717	3.00
515	1.00	200	2.00	532	1.00	768	2.00
567	1.00	240	5.00	551	1.00	774	5.00
570	1.00	247	5.00	552	1.00	777	3.00
600	1.00	260	5.00	567	1.00	791	3.00
656	1.00	BFPO SID:		576	1.00	815	3.00
658	1.00	3062	5.00	714	1.00	816	3.00
718	1.00	3063	5.00	777	1.00	907	2.00
757	1.00	3068	5.00	938	30.00	915	2.00
775	1.00	3202	5.00	953	30.00	941	3.00
797	1.00			1020	30.00	950	1.00
937	1.00	**Denmark**		Rubber:		951	2.00
938	1.00	BFPO SID:		172	4.00	956	2.00
941	1.00	3025	5.00			968	2.00
942	1.00			**Ethiopia**		975	2.00
943	1.00	**Diego Garcia**		Steel:		979	2.00
944	1.00	BFPO SID:		35	8.00	981	3.00
945	1.00	3033	5.00	143	8.00	989	2.00
946	1.00			375	10.00	1012	3.00
947	1.00	**Dominica**		958	15.00	1045	3.00
949	1.00	Steel:		Rubber:		1046	3.00
966	1.00	558	30.00	50	30.00	Rubber:	
967	1.00					1	5.00
969	1.00	**Dubai**		**Falkland Islands**		2	5.00
970	1.00	Steel:		Machines:		3	5.00
971	1.00	121	20.00	40	5.00		
998	1.00	514	15.00	655	5.00	**Gambia**	
999	1.00	1013	15.00	666	5.00	Steel:	
1000	1.00	1057	12.00	Steel:		129	15.00
1001	1.00	Rubber:		141	10.00	141	15.00
1014	1.05	164	30.00	170	10.00	143	15.00
1025	1.00			252	10.00	243	15.00
1041	1.00	**Egypt**		941	10.00		
1042	3.00	Machines:					
1043	2.00	1 (Krag)	1.00				
1045	1.00	2 (Krag)	1.00				
1053	1.00	Steel:					
1054	1.00	13	1.00				
1055	1.00	15	1.00				
Rubber:		17	1.00	**Germany**			
49	2.00	67	2.00	(excluding Berlin & TPO's) - values 1.00 to 2.00			
68	2.00	76	2.00	Machines of existing design, see **15/117**:			
83	2.00	113	1.00	9, 10, 11, 15, 17, 18, 19, 20, 23, 24, 25, 26, 28, 29, 30,			
85	2.00	123	1.00	31, 32, 33, 774			

Military and Camp Postmarks

From 1994 "meter style" machines **15/121** were used (some initially in red, with/without lines at left & value 000 at right) at the following BFPOs with location shown (except 140) : 15, 16, 17, 22, 25, 26 (Casteau, Belgium), 31, 34, 35, 36, 38, 39, 40 (Rhinedahlen spelling error, slightly different "frank" at right), 140 (also at Rheindahlen), 43 (Laarbruck spelling error), 44, 47
Meter Machines (as **15/132**): BFPO 40, BFPO/105
Steel
76, 116, 128, 137, 154, 168, 172, 177, 209, 218, 220, 222, 223, 230, 235, 245, 246, 251, 256, 262, 264, 265, 266, 267, 280, 283, 286, 299, 305, 307, 308, 309, 318, 319, 328, 331, 339, 340, 350, 351, 352, 358, 359, 361, 382, 383, 414, 424, 431, 432, 445, 461, 463, 493, 501, 508, 521, 530, 535, 556, 575, 588, 594, 606, 607, 619, 620, 694, 716, 717, 718, 729, 731, 734, 740, 746, 748, 752, 755, 764, 768, 774, 783, 790, 791, 792, 798, 800, 813, 816, 841, 843, 850, 867, 870, 893, 899, 901, 907, 909, 911, 914, 915, 916, 950, 952, 954, 956, 957, 958, 959, 960, 961, 962, 963, 968, 973, 974, 975, 976, 978, 980, 982, 983, 984, 985, 986, 987, 988, 989, 990, 991, 992, 993, 994, 995, 996, 1004, 1011, 1015, 1016, 1019, 1020, 1021, 1022, 1023, 1026, 1027, 1028, 1032, 1033, 1035, 1036, 1043, 1044, 1048, 1052, 1053.

Rubber:
1, 2, 4, 5, 6, 7, 8, 9, 11, 12, 13, 14, 15, 16, 17, 18, 19, 20, 21, 22, 23, 24, 25, 26, 27, 28, 29, 32, 33, 34, 35, 36, 37, 38, 39, 40, 41, 42, 43, 44, 45, 46, 47, 48, 49, 50, 51, 52, 53, 54, 55, 58, 59, 60, 61, 62, 63, 64, 65, 66, 67, 68, 69, 70, 71, 72, 73, 74, 75, 76, 77, 78, 79, 80, 81, 82, 83, 84, 87, 88, 90, 92, 95, 96, 97, 98, 100, 101, 105, 108, 110, 114, 116, 117, 119, 120, 122, 123, 127, 129, 131, 135, 136, 137, 140, 143, 146, 148, 149, 180, 183, 187, 188, 192, 197, 204, 205, 206, 207, 217, 219, 220, 221, 222, 223, 227, 238, 239.

BFPO SID:

3123	5.00
3124	5.00
3125	5.00
3126	5.00
3129	5.00
3130	5.00
3131	5.00
3132	5.00
3133	5.00
3134	5.00
3135	5.00
3137	5.00
3139	5.00
3141	5.00
3164	5.00

Germany (Berlin)
Machine:
16
Steel:
128, 359, 382, 493, 606, 737, 909, 911, 916, 987, 994, 1011
Rubber:
37, 45, 60, 65, 66, 114, 128

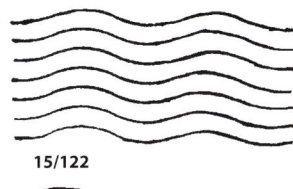

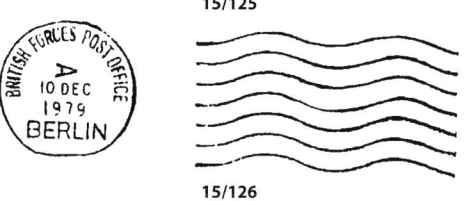

15/124

15/125

15/126

15/122

15/123

15/127

15/128

15/129

BFPO BERLIN (British type)

15/122, 15/123	machine & steel 1-6	5.00
15/124 rubber 1-6		5.00
15/125 parcel 1-2		8.00

(German type)

15/126, *15/127	machine & steel 1-6	2.00
15/128, 15/129	rubber 1-6	2.00

Note: A philatelic version of this handstamp (above date) was used on special covers marking the last date of British Forces in Berlin 16 December 1994.

15/129A	TPOs steel FPO handstamps 908, 910, 912 *each*	20.00

Military and Camp Postmarks

15/130 Special ACE (Allied Command Europe(NATO))
(also smaller lettering) 25.00

15/131

Ghana
Steel:
574	10.00

Gibraltar
(local stamps normally used to 1995 then GB stamps)
Steel:
123	2.00
186	2.00
475	1.00
958	1.00
976	2.00
1061	1.00

Rubber:
52	3.00
130	3.00
133	3.00
145	3.00
169	3.00

Meter Style: BFPO GIBRALTAR
52	5.00

BFPO SID:
3066	5.00

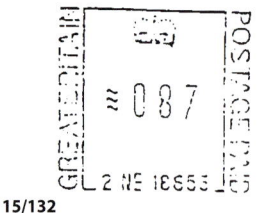

15/132

Gulf War (1990-1992)
See notes at start of listing.
Machine (meter **15/132**):
Gulf 2	8.00

Steel:
40	8.00
222	4.00
375	8.00

Gilbert and Ellice Islands (Christmas Island)
Steel:
158	40.00

15/131 BFPO Christmas Island 10.00

Greece
Steel:
69	5.00
316	5.00
375	5.00
514	3.00
567	5.00
626	5.00
783	2.00
991	5.00
1042	5.00
1043	5.00
1044	5.00
1062	5.00

Rubber:
159	6.00
482	8.00
755	8.00
791	8.00
990	6.00
1012	8.00

Rubber:
7	8.00
46	8.00

Gulf War (2003-2011) (Op Telic)

Bahrain
Rubber:
	5.00

BFPO SID:
3067 (code C)	5.00

Kuwait
Steel:
	5.00

Rubber:
18	5.00
98	5.00
133	5.00
134	5.00
220	5.00
231	5.00

Oman
(includes Ex Saif Sareea in 2001)
Steel:
113	5.00
143	5.00
158	5.00
174	5.00
375	5.00
662	5.00
716	5.00
764	5.00
766	5.00
795	5.00
940	5.00
968	5.00

Rubber:
44	10.00
90	10.00
176	10.00
202	10.00
208	10.00
215	10.00

BFPO SID:
3008	5.00

Qatar
Steel:
142	5.00
710	5.00
790	5.00

Rubber:
	15.00

BFPO SID:
3010	5.00

Saudi Arabia
Steel:
	5.00

Rubber:
228	5.00
229	5.00

Iraq
Steel:
56	5.00
255	5.00
521	5.00
572	5.00
715	5.00
771	5.00

Rubber:
18	5.00
98	5.00

133	5.00
134	5.00
172	5.00
190	5.00
220	5.00
244	5.00

BFPO SID: 3000 to 3007 3011, 3012, 3014, 3015, 3016, 3017, 3018, 3019, 3020, 3037, 3090, 3091 all at 5.00

Hong Kong
Machines:
5 (Krag)	3.00
12 (Univ)	3.00

Steel:
67	3.00
69	3.00
80	3.00
121	3.00
129	3.00
136	3.00
142	3.00
145	3.00
146	3.00
164	3.00
168	3.00
233	3.00
375	3.00
385	3.00
701	3.00
707	3.00
708	3.00
746	3.00
790	3.00
816	3.00
945	3.00
948	3.00
964	3.00
970	3.00
998	3.00
1037	3.00
1038	3.00
1044	3.00

BFPO Hong Kong
15/133 steel 1-8, 10 each 3.00
Rubber:
20	3.00
71	3.00
107	3.00
108	3.00
110	3.00
122	3.00
123	3.00
124	3.00
125	3.00
127	3.00
131	3.00
135	3.00
138	3.00
168	3.00
184	3.00
191	3.00
194	3.00
195	3.00
198	3.00

BFPO Hong Kong rubber
15/134 (large) 1-6   10.00
15/135 (small, with variations) 1-7   8.00

Military and Camp Postmarks

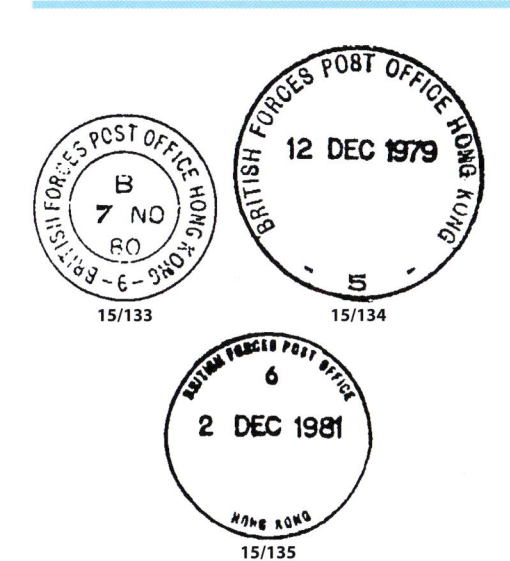

15/133

15/134 — BRITISH FORCES POST OFFICE HONG KONG, 12 DEC 1979, 5

15/135 — BRITISH FORCES POST OFFICE, 6, 2 DEC 1981, HONG KONG

15/136 (layout variations) — BRITISH FORCES POST OFFICE / 28 AUG 1980 / HONG KONG / PARCEL / POST / 6

Iceland
Steel:
316	15.00

Iraq
(see also Gulf War)
Steel:
171	2.00
515	2.00
567	2.00
756	2.00
942	3.00

Israel
Steel:
136	8.00

Italy
(* denotes 1990s FPOs for RAF operations over Bosnia: see also Libya for 2011 operation)
Steel:
136	4.00
148	4.00
164	1.00
174	2.00
186	3.00
190	2.00
243	5.00
246	2.00
534	3.00
558	3.00
*574	2.00
*707	4.00
777	4.00
*795	2.00
*940	4.00
942	1.00
953	1.50
971	1.00
1041	2.00
1051	3.00

Rubber:
57	3.00
87	3.00
*103	5.00
179	5.00
258	5.00

BFPO SID:
3018	5.00
3056	5.00
3053	5.00

Jamaica
Steel:
129	8.00
136	8.00
243	8.00
250	10.00
375	8.00
443	8.00
574	8.00
940	8.00

Rubber:
98	12.00

Japan
Steel:
260	7.00
376	4.00
946	4.00
949	4.00

Jordan
Steel:
61	3.00
113	3.00
121	3.00
137	3.00
140	5.00
149	3.00
155	3.00
174	20.00
201	3.00
575	3.00

Kenya
Steel:
123	1.00
124	1.00
129	3.00
136	3.00
140	3.00
157	3.00
164	2.00
186	2.00
218	2.00
243	2.00
250	2.00
254	2.00
256	1.00
375	3.00
376	3.00
443	3.00
532	2.00
567	2.00
574	5.00
576	1.00
656	1.00
940	3.00
947	3.00
967	3.00
970	2.00
997	2.00
1002	2.00
1039	2.00
1040	3.00
1041	2.00
1055	2.00
1056	2.00
1057	2.00
1063	2.00

Rubber:
096	4.00
098	4.00
099	4.00
100	4.00
115	4.00
121	4.00
134	4.00
194	4.00
198	4.00
200	4.00

BFPO SID:
3041	5.00

Korea
Steel:
80	4.00
121	5.00
136	4.00
406	4.00
707	4.00
734	5.00
740	4.00
746	4.00
766	5.00
790	4.00
798	5.00
948	4.00
1006	4.00
1044	4.00

Rubber:
122	8.00
126	8.00

Kuwait
(see also Gulf War)
Steel:
941	30.00
1039	20.00
1040	15.00
1043	15.00
1062	15.00

Lebanon
Steel:
1055	10.00

Rubber:
102	10.00
172	10.00
174	10.00

Libya
Steel:
1	3.00
28	1.00
61	1.00
76	1.00
113	1.00
141	1.00
142	1.00
147	1.00
149	1.00
168	1.00
171	2.00
174	1.00
190	1.00
191	1.00
197	1.00
246	1.00
257	1.00
258	1.00
267	1.00
461	1.00
518	1.00
532	1.00
534	1.00
552	1.00
550	2.00
576	2.00
656	1.00
658	2.00
756	1.00
757	1.00
782	2.00
942	2.00
944	2.00
953	2.00
971	2.00
998	2.00
1001	2.00
1015	3.00
1019	3.00
1020	3.00
1051	2.00
1062	3.00

Military and Camp Postmarks

Rubber:	
66	5.00
83	5.00
84	5.00
85	5.00
86	5.00
88	5.00

Libya
(Operation Ellamy, 2011 action against Libya, see Cyprus and Italy below:

Cyprus
BFPO SID:
3004	5.00

Italy
BFPO SID:
3143	5.00
3144	5.00
3147	5.00

Malawi
Steel:
443	20.00

Malaya
Steel:
129	5.00
142	5.00
148	8.00
223	5.00
746	5.00
964	8.00
1003	5.00
1004	5.00
1007	5.00
1008	5.00
1010	5.00
1058	8.00

Rubber:
133	10.00
145	10.00

Maldive Islands
Steel:
51	5.00
140	5.00
142	5.50
146	5.00
166	5.00
1000	5.00
1013	5.00
1025	4.00
1048	10.00

Rubber:
129	10.00
140	10.00

Malta
Machine:
21	3.00

Steel:
61	2.00
76	1.00
121	2.00
147	2.00
148	2.00
149	2.00
151	2.00
158	2.00
168	2.00
171	2.00
186	2.00
187	2.00
191	2.00
220	2.00
246	2.00
254	2.00
258	2.00
266	2.00
443	2.00
515	2.00
532	2.00
534	2.00
558	3.00
570	3.00
573	2.00
746	2.00
757	2.00
782	1.00
942	2.00
944	2.00
953	2.00
1001	2.00
1040	3.00
1047	2.00
1051	2.00

Rubber:
82	5.00
84	5.00
88	5.00
89	5.00
103	5.00
107	5.00
109	5.00
112	5.00
152	5.00
156	5.00
161	5.00
167	5.00
169	5.00
189	5.00
Special 1000	15.00

Mauritius
Steel:
255	20.00
1008	20.00

Mozambique
Steel:
	10.00

Namibia
Steel:
940	15.00

Rubber:
189	15.00

Nepal
Steel:
140	10.00
146	10.00
186	12.00
443	12.00
600	12.00

Rubber:
123	20.00
237	10.00

BFPO SID:
3038	5.00

Netherlands
Machine:
18	3.00

Steel:
164	3.00
305	3.00
307	2.00
331	3.00
340	2.00
358	2.00
376	2.00
961	2.00
983	3.00

Rubber:
52	4.00
53	4.00
70	4.00
121	4.00
218	5.00

BFPO SID:
3128	5.00

New Hebrides
Steel:
941	30.00

New Zealand
Steel:
576	10.00
656	10.00
707	10.00
708	10.00
989	10.00

Rubber:
103	20.00

North Borneo
Steel:
154	8.00
166	8.00
169	8.00
450	8.00
573	8.00
766	8.00
948	6.00
1030	10.00
1035	10.00
1061	8.00

Rubber:
146	10.00
164	10.00
190	10.00

Northern Ireland
Machines:
8 (figure 8 damaged, resembles 6)	1.00
27	1.00

Note: "Meter style" machines similar to **15/121** were used in red at Aldergrove, Armagh, Belfast, Holywood and Lisburn from 1996, with/without lines at left

Steel:
316	1.00
385	1.00
551	1.00
552	1.00
553	1.00
554	5.00
576	1.00
658	1.00
659	1.00
714	1.00
770	1.00
771	1.00
772	1.00

Rubber:
3	3.00
53	5.00
72	3.00
116	3.00
158	3.00
159	3.00
161	3.00
162	3.00
170	3.00
171	3.00
175	3.00
176	3.00
177	3.00
179	3.00
181	3.00
185	3.00
187	5.00
203	5.00
210	5.00
211	5.00
230	5.00
232	5.00
233	5.00
235	5.00

BFPO SID:
3022, 3023, 3036, 3069, 3071, 3088, 3119, 3120
all 5.00

Norway
Steel:
129	4.00
136	3.00
141	4.00
148	4.00
157	3.00
158	4.00
172	4.00
190	4.00
222	4.00
234	4.00
243	4.00
375	3.00
376	4.00
443	4.00
532	4.00
707	3.00
740	3.00
777	4.00
797	4.00
867	2.00
941	4.00
951	4.00
1042	5.00
1043	5.00
1044	5.00
1062	5.00
1063	5.00

Rubber:
29	6.00
30	5.00
50	5.00
97	5.00
103	5.00
113	5.00
163	5.00
165	5.00
170	5.00
178	5.00
256	5.00
ACE	15.00

BFPO SID:
3045	5.00

Military and Camp Postmarks

Oman
Steel:
143	8.00
190	4.00
406	4.00
567	4.00
740	8.00
766	5.00
953	4.00

Rubber:
50	20.00
98	15.00

Pakistan
Steel:
	5.00

Rubber
259	10.00

Poland
Steel:
968	10.00

Rhodesia and Zimbabwe

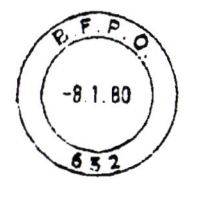

15/137

Machine (meter **15/137**):
632	20.00

Steel:
234	8.00
532	8.00
1053	5.00

Rubber:
94	15.00
191	15.00
194	15.00

Rwanda
Steel:
375	15.00

St Lucia
Steel:
443	25.00

Sarawak
Steel:
67	10.00
69	10.00
136	10.00
156	10.00
948	10.00
964	20.00
1005	20.00
1025	20.00
1035	20.00
1044	20.00
1048	25.00
1059	15.00

Rubber:
131	30.00

Saudi Arabia
Machine:
40	6.00

Portugal
Steel:
67	1.00
157	3.00
186	4.00
221	6.00
464	4.00
558	4.00
574	4.00
718	4.00
791	4.00
1017	6.00

Rubber:
78	6.00
119	6.00
139	6.00

BFPO SID:
3039	5.00

Steel:
190	6.00
234	8.00
574	8.00
764	8.00
1025	8.00
1042	6.00
1058	8.00
1059	8.00

Rubber:
95	10.00
132	10.00
165	10.00
186	10.00

Sharjah
Steel:
186	8.00
190	8.00
234	8.00
235	8.00
255	8.00
293	8.00
514	8.00
936	6.00
1056	8.00
1057	8.00

Rubber:
93	10.00
107	10.00
112	10.00

Sierra Leone
Steel:
	5.00

Rubber
	5.00

BFPO SID:
3040	5.00

Singapore

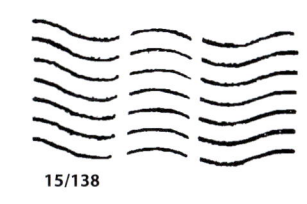

15/138

15/139

15/140

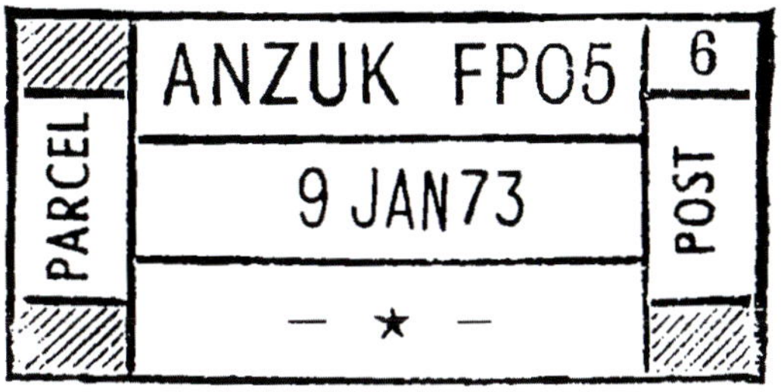

15/141

Machine:
28	2.00
ANZUK **15/138**	6.00

Steel:
66	4.00
123	5.00
142	5.00
154	3.00
156	3.00
254	4.00
258	4.00
514	4.00
570	10.00
965	5.00
ANZUK **15/139**	6.00

Rubber:
26	6.00
27	6.00
145	6.00
154	6.00
156	5.00
188	7.00
ANZUK **15/140**	10.00

Spain
Rubber:
	5.00

BFPO SID:
3054	5.00

Sudan
Steel:
141	8.00
158	8.00
221	15.00
443	8.00
718	6.00

777	8.00
782	5.00

Swaziland
Steel:
124	6.00
656	6.00
997	6.00
1019	8.00
1041	6.00

Tanganyika
Steel:
1062	10.00

Thailand
Steel:
66	4.00
573	4.00
1003	5.00
1005	2.00
1006	3.00
1058	5.00
1061	5.00

Rubber:
147	10.00

Trieste
Steel:
136	4.00
530	5.00
594	4.00
600	5.00

Turkey
Steel:
376	4.00

Military and Camp Postmarks

513	4.00
516	4.00
773	4.00

Uganda
Steel:

201	6.00
218	6.00

Rubber:

112	15.00

USA
Steel:

66	2.00
136	2.00
141	2.00
154	2.50
188	1.00
234	2.00
375	2.00
443	2.00
532	2.00
707	2.00
766	2.00
777	2.00
941	2.00
965	2.00
990	2.00
1043	2.00
1063	2.00

Rubber:

58	4.00
143	4.00
236	5.00
245	5.00

BFPO SID:

3055	5.00
3073	5.00

Yugoslavia (1992-1997)
(UNPROFOR/IFOR/SFOR/EUFOR)
(Croatia, Bosnia & Herzegovina, Macedonia, Kosovo)

Bosnia & Herzegovina
Steel:

76	5.00
222	5.00
445	5.00
482	5.00
555	5.00
556	5.00
572	5.00
576	5.00
909	5.00
1012	5.00
1027	5.00
1029	5.00

Rubber:

32	5.00
108	5.00
246	5.00

BFPO SID:

3058	5.00
3074	5.00

Croatia
Steel:

142	5.00
375	5.00
776	5.00
791	5.00

1052	5.00
1057	2.00

Rubber:

44	5.00
95	5.00
132	5.00
153	5.00

Macedonia
Steel:

56	5.00
67	5.00
798	5.00

Rubber:

50	5.00
98	5.00
179	5.00
200	5.00
225	5.00
243	5.00

BFPO SID:

3067 (code B)	5.00

Kosovo
Steel:

56	5.00
113	5.00
191	5.00
606	5.00

Rubber:

164	5.00
226	5.00

BFPO SID:

3067 (code C)	5.00

Zaire
Steel:

444	10.00

Rubber:

72	15.00

Zambia
Steel:

143	10.00
777	12.00
1018	15.00
1062	12.00

Rubber:

20	20.00
195	20.00

Zanzibar
Steel:

254	15.00
970	15.00
1041	15.00

FPOs used at Sea
Steel:

188	60.00
941	75.00
1020	75.00
1055	50.00

British Forces Self-Inking Datestamps

In 1997-98 the BFPO carried out a trial of self-inking datestamps in four locations around the world – one hot and one cold climate, one static and one exercise BFPO location. The reason given was to bring the BFPO up-to-date with Royal Mail and, for the time being, have the BFPO code incorporated into the design so that they could easily identify which FPO a letter came from. It was the intention to phase out the then current steel datestamps, but for the time being the BFPO retained the rubber packet and parcel datestamps. For the trial the BFPO attempted to disguise the location by using a civil town (CHELSEA) and postcode, but the BFPO number was incorporated into that postcode. The four trial datestamps were as follows:

CHELSEA SW65 5UD (Falkland Islands, BFPO 655)
CHELSEA SW67 7UD (Ascension Island, BFPO 677)
CHELSEA SW1 2UD (Belize, BFPO 12) (not recorded used)
CHELSEA SW1 4UD (British Army Training Unit Suffield, Canada, BFPO 14)

It is reported that the Falkland Islands SID was received on 13 November 1997 and taken into use immediately; it was withdrawn from use on 1 May 1998. However, the Directorate Postal & Courier Services (DPCS) stated the trial ended on 10 April 1998 and all the datestamps were then withdrawn.

The next phase saw the Postal & Courier Service (PCS) Directorate in Germany introduce SID datestamps at a number of FPOs in Germany. These were all inscribed BRITISH FORCES with a location; no BFPO number was included. That for Rheindahlen was issued on 8 May 1998. Datestamps for a further seven FPO's were issued on 1 October 1998.

BRITISH FORCES RHEINDAHLEN (Germany, BFPO 40) (Codes A, B, C &D)
BRITISH FORCES SENNELAGER (Germany, BFPO 16) (Codes A & B)
BRITISH FORCES PADERBORN (Germany, BFPO 22) (Codes A & B)
BRITISH FORCES BRUGGEN (Germany, BFPO 25) (Codes A)
BRITISH FORCES HOHNE (Germany, BFPO 30) (Codes A & B)
BRITISH FORCES OSNABRUCK (Germany, BFPO 36) (Codes A & B)
BRITISH FORCES FALLINGBOSTEL (Germany, BFPO 38) (Codes A & B)
BRITISH FORCES GUTERSLOH (Germany, BFPO 47) (Code A)

BRITISH FORCES JHQ (JHQ Rheindahlen, Germany, BFPO 140) (only code B seen)

The third phase saw new SID datestamps issued to existing and future static British Forces Post Offices from 1999 onwards; but it should be noted that not all BFPOs received a SID. These SIDs include the BFPO number in the datestamp. In all cases, except where stated, only one datestamp was supplied (with the code letter A). In a few locations although a named SID was prepared it was not issued (in one instance the BFPO had closed down before it had arrived). The problem with named SIDs was that once a location had been vacated or closed down there was no further use for that particular named datestamp!

WASHINGTON BFPO 2 (USA)
KATHMANDU BFPO 4 (Nepal)
LISBON BFPO 6 (Portugal)
NAPLES BFPO 8 (Italy)
    (Sorting Office – Code A)
    (Counter – Code B)
GOOSE BAY BFPO 9 (Canada)
    (Counter – Code A)
    (Sorting Office – Code B)
NAIROBI BFPO 10 (Kenya)
SERIA BRUNEI BFPO 11 (Brunei)
BELIZE CITY BFPO 12 (Belize)

Military and Camp Postmarks

SUFFIELD BFPO 14 (Canada)
HERFORD BFPO 15 (Germany) (Codes A & B)
SENNELAGER BFPO 16 (Germany) (Codes A, B & C)
MUNSTER BFPO 17 (Germany)
MAASTRICHT BFPO 18 (The Netherlands)
PADERBORN BFPO 22 (Germany) (Codes A, B, C & D)
CELLE BFPO 23 (Germany)
BRUGGEN BFPO 25 (Germany) (Codes A & B)
CASTEAU BFPO 26 (Belgium)
    (BFPO SHAPE – Code A)
    (BFPO Shopping Centre – Code B)
BRUNSSUM BFPO 28 (The Netherlands)
HOHNE BFPO 30 (Germany) (Codes A, B & C)
HAMELN BFPO 31 (Germany)
KREFELD BFPO 35 (Germany) (before 2002)
ELMPT BFPO 35 (Germany) (prev. RAF Bruggen, to 2002)
OSNABRUCK BFPO 36 (Germany) (Codes A, B, C & D)
FALLINGBOSTEL BFPO 38 (Germany) (Codes A, B, C & D)
BIELEFELD BFPO 39 (Germany)
RHEINDAHLEN BFPO 40 (Germany) (Codes A, B, C & F)
DULMEN BFPO 44 (Germany)
GUTERSLOH BFPO 47 (Germany) (Codes A, B & C)

BRUSSELS BFPO 49 (Belgium)
STAVANGER BFPO 50 (Norway)
WAINWRIGHT/SEATTLE BFPO 51 (Canada/USA)
GIBRALTAR BFPO 52
    (Main FPO – Codes A & C)
    (HMS Rooke – Code B)
EPISKOPI BFPO 53 (Cyprus) (Codes A & B)
REITAN BFPO 55 (Norway)
MADRID BFPO 56 (Spain)
AKROTIRI BFPO 57 (Cyprus) (Codes A & B)
DHEKELIA BFPO 58 (Cyprus) (Codes A & B)
AYIOS NIKOLAOS BFPO 59 (Cyprus)
VERONA BFPO 60 (Italy)
MILAN BFPO 61 (Italy)
VALENCIA BFPO 62 (Spain)
NORFOLK BFPO 63 (Virginia, USA)
ROME BFPO 65 (Italy)

RAMSTEIN BFPO 109 (Germany)
MANSERGH BKS BFPO 113 (Germany)
(later GUTERSLOH MANSERGH BFPO 113)
HEIDELBERG BFPO 115 (Germany) (Codes A & B)
BRITISH FORCES JHQ BFPO 140 (Germany) (Codes A & B)
KARUP BFPO 150 (Denmark)

SIPOVO BFPO 538 (Bosnia & Herzegovina)
LIPPA BFPO 541 (Bosnia & Herzegovina) (Not recorded used)
SARAJEVO BFPO 543 (Bosnia & Herzegovina)
SPLIT BFPO 544 (Croatia)
ZAGREB BFPO 545 (Croatia)
JAJCE BFPO 546 (Bosnia & Herzegovina) (thought SID was not used)
GORNI VAKUF BFPO 548 (Bosnia & Herzegovina) (spelling error for GORNJI VAKUF)
KUPRES BFPO 550 (Bosnia & Herzegovina)
MRKONJIC GRAD BFPO 551 (Bosnia & Herzegovina)
BANJA LUKA BFPO 553 (Bosnia & Herzegovina)
SKOPJE BFPO 555 (Macedonia)

UN NICOSIA BFPO 567 (Cyprus)
GIOIA DEL COLLE BFPO 569 (Italy)
AVIANO BFPO 571 (Italy)
ANCONA BFPO 573 (Italy)
INCIRLIK BFPO 598 (Turkey)
IZMIR BFPO 599 (Turkey) (not thought to have been issued)

RBAF BRUNEI BFPO 605
BAHRAIN BFPO 632
RIYADH BFPO 633 (Saudi Arabia)
AL KHARJ BFPO 634 (Saudi Arabia)
KUWAIT BFPO 635

FALKLAND ISLANDS BFPO 655 (Codes A & B)
ASCENSION ISLAND BFPO 677
KABUL BFPO 758 (Afghanistan)

LISBURN BFPO 801 (Northern Ireland)
BALLYKELLY BFPO 802 (Northern Ireland)
ARMAGH BFPO 803 (Northern Ireland)
OMAGH BFPO 804 (Northern Ireland)
BALLYKINLER BFPO 805 (Northern Ireland)
HOLYWOOD BFPO 806 (Northern Ireland)
LONDONDERRY BFPO 807 (Northern Ireland)
ALDERGROVE BFPO 808 (Northern Ireland) (not issued?)
PORTADOWN BFPO 809 (Northern Ireland)

Section VI : Camps and other military establishments

In this simplified listing some detailed variations in wording are excluded (and BO omitted too), also since there are many variations; the post town or county shown in brackets is sometimes included in the handstamps, sometimes not so. For Naval and RAF/RNAS establishments see chapters 14 and 16 respectively. * denotes entries for which confirmation is required.

Further reading : FPHS are planning in due course to produce an updated version of Kingston's "Camps" book.

A Scroll
B Double Arc
C Duplex
D Single Circle
E Double Circle
F Skeleton
G Krag Machine
H Universal Machine
I Rubbers/Packet handstamps
J Parcel handstamps
K Registered handstamps
S SID (self inking datestamp)

B **15/142** Double Arc

C **15/143** Duplex

D **15/144** Single circle (Several types)

Military and Camp Postmarks

E 15/145 Double circle (Several types)

F 15/146 Skeleton (Irish skeletons are double rim)

I 15/147 Rubber

S 15/148 Self inking datestamp

England, Scotland, Wales

Acreknowe Camp, Hawick	F	25.00
Aldershot Camp	B	75.00
	C (046,96)	£100
	D	6.00
	E	4.00
	J	10.00
Arborfield Camp Reading, (Berks)	D	6.00
	S	3.00
Arncott Depot, Oxford	D	6.00
	E	8.00
Ashley Walk Camp (Hants)	F	30.00
Ashwick Camp (Dulverton or Tiverton)	F	30.00
Auchengate Camp, Troon	D	8.00
Bagshot Moor Camp, Hants (Brockenhurst)		
	F	30.00
Balmer Camp, Lewes	F	40.00
Bangour War Hospital, West Lothian	E	12.00
	F	40.00
Barnstaple Camp	F	50.00
Barry Camp (Dundee or Carnoustie)	D	6.00
Barton Stacey Camp, Winchester Hants	D	5.00
	J	10.00
Bassingbourn Barracks	E	4.00
(for earlier see chap 16)		
Bears Rail Camp, Windsor (rubber skeleton)		
	F	75.00
Beaulieu Camp, Lymington	F	25.00
Beaulieu Heath Camp, Hants	F	40.00
Camp Beauly (Inverness-shire)	F	30.00
Belhus Park Camp, Aveley	E	10.00
	F	30.00
Belton Camp, Grantham	D	8.00
	I	30.00
	J	10.00
Bettisfield Park Camp, Whitchurch	E	6.00
	F	30.00
	J	10.00
Bisley Camp, Woking	C (J62)	10.00
	D	4.00
	E	4.00
	J	6.00
	K	25.00
Blackdown Camp, Aldershot	D	4.00
	E	4.00
	F	20.00
	J	10.00
Blackdown Camp Bridestowe	D	20.00
(see also Camp, Bridestowe listed below)		
Blackpool Military Hospital	D	15.00
	I	50.00
	J	25.00
Blandford Camp, Blandford	D	8.00
	E	5.00
	J	10.00
Blandford Field Force	D	£250
Boards Camp (Denny Stirlingshire)	F	45.00
The Camp, Bodmin	E	10.00
Bordon Camp, E Liss Hants	D	4.00
	E	4.00
Field PO, Bordon	F	20.00
Bourley Camp, Aldershot	E	8.00
	F	20.00
Bovey Tracey Camp, Devon	F	50.00
Bovington Camp	D	4.00
	(Poole or Wareham)	
	E	4.00
	F	35.00
	G	25.00
	"PAID" Krag	75.00
	(in red)	
	I	20.00
	J	8.00
	S (no Camp)	3.00
Bowood Camp	E	10.00
Bow Street Camp	F	15.00
Boyton Camp, Wilts	D	5.00
	E	4.00
	I	10.00
	J	10.00
Bramshott Camp (Liphook)	D	4.00
	E	4.00
	F	20.00
	G	25.00
	J	10.00
Camp, Bridestowe RSO Devon	D	6.00
Brocton Camp, Stafford	D	6.00
	E	4.00
	J	10.00
Brough Camp, Catterick	F	40.00
Buddon Camp (Carnoustie)	D	6.00
	E	6.00
	F	20.00
Bulford Barracks, Salisbury	D	3.00
	E	4.00
	G	3.00
	H	12.00
	I	10.00
	J	10.00
	K	15.00
	Paid handstamp	12.00
Bulford Camp, Salisbury	D	4.00
	E (& FPO)	5.00
	F (& Field PO)	20.00
	J	8.00
Bullswater Camp, Woking	F	20.00
Burley Camp, Ringwood	F	25.00
Burrowhead Camp, Newton Stewart	E	8.00
Bushey Down Camp (Southampton)	F	25.00

Military and Camp Postmarks

Bustard Camp, Devizes	D		6.00
	F (or Salisbury)		20.00
(The) Bustard Field PO	F		25.00
Royal Military College, Camberley	D		15.00
1st Eastern Gen. Hospital, Cambridge	D		30.00
	F		50.00
The Camp, Camelford	E		12.00
Cannock Chase FPO	C (G19)		£1000
Caterham Barracks	D		6.00
	J		10.00
Catterick Camp, Yorks	D		4.00
	E		4.00
	G		15.00
	H		4.00
	J		6.00
	K		15.00
later Catterick Garrison	D		5.00
	E		5.00
	K		15.00
Chelsea Barracks SW	D		8.00
Pimlico Rd Chelsea Barracks SW	D		6.00
Chisledon Camp, Wilts	D		6.00
	E		4.00
	F (and Swindon)		15.00
	J		12.00
Chobham Camp	B		£300
Churn Camp, Oxford	D		7.00
	F		20.00
Chyngton Camp, Seaford	D		6.00
	E		6.00
	F		20.00
	J		10.00
Claughton Territorial Camp (Cheshire)	F		20.00
Cleave Camp, Bude, Cornwall	E		8.00
Clipstone Camp, Notts	E		6.00
	F		35.00
	J		10.00
Clochkeil Camp, Campbeltown	F		50.00
Codford St Mary Camp	J		10.00
Colchester Garrison	E		8.00
Colsterdale Camp, Yorks	E		8.00
	F		20.00
Comrie Camp, Perthshire	E		10.00
Cooden Camp, Bexhill-on-Sea	E		8.00
	J		20.00
Cothill Camp (Forres)	F		20.00
Crookham Camp, Aldershot Hants	D		4.00
	E		4.00
	J		8.00
Crowborough Camp	D		8.00
	F		10.00
	J		8.00
	K		15.00
Camp Hill Camp, Crowboro	F		40.00
	J		10.00
Cuckfield Camp (Sussex)	F		25.00
Darnley Camp (Glasgow)	F		30.00
Dartmoor FPO	C (G17)		£1250
RST	C (G18)		£1500
Deepcut Camp (Aldershot or Farnborough)			
	D		4.00
	E		4.00
	J		8.00
Deganwy Camp (Conway)	F		25.00
Detling Camp, Maidstone	E		10.00
The Barracks, Devizes	D		8.00
Devizes, Military Camp	E		5.00
	J		6.00
Dibgate Camp, Shorncliffe	E		6.00
	F		20.00
Dolphinholme Camp (Lancs)	F		30.00
Doonfoot Camp, Ayr	F		40.00
Duke of York's School, Dover	D		6.00
	E		6.00

Draycott Camp, Swindon	E		8.00
	F		40.00
Dundonald Camp, Troon Ayrshire	D		8.00
	J		10.00
Durrington Camp, Salisbury	D		6.00
	E		4.00
	F		20.00
	J		12.00
East Anstey Camp (Devon)	F		25.00
E Boldre Camp, Brockenhurst	F		25.00
East Down Camp, Devizes	E		6.00
East Marton Camp (Skipton)	I		35.00
Flower Down Camp, Winchester	D		6.00
	E		6.00
Fort George (Inverness)	concave		
	'Fort George'		75.00
	str line		60.00
	Circular		30.00
	circular mileage		25.00
	boxed/unframed		
	mileage		20.00
	mileage removed		10.00
	boxed Too Late		£150
	numeral (149)		50.00
	D		6.00
	E		4.00
	F		20.00
	J		10.00
Fovant Camp, Salisbury	D		6.00
	E		4.00
	F		20.00
	J		8.00
Frensham Camp, Farnham	F		50.00
Frensham Common Camp, Farnham	D		6.00
	E		6.00
	F		40.00
Gailes Camp, Irvine	E (=602=)		8.00
	E (double arc)		20.00
*Gargrave Camp ?	F		30.00
Gipsy Bottom Camp, Aylesbury	F		50.00
Glamis Camp	F		40.00
Glanrheidol Camp (Cardiganshire)	F		40.00
Guards Camp, Goodwood Sx	F		75.00
Gosforth Park Camp, Newcastle-on-Tyne			
	D		8.00
Grazeley Camp, Reading Berks	D		8.00
Greenhill Camp, Sheffield	D		8.00
Hadrian's Camp, Carlisle	E		15.00
Hagley Park Camp (Staffs)	F		25.00
Halton Camp/Tring	D		6.00
(later Bucks or Aylesbury) (Army to 1917 then RAF)			
	E		5.00
	F		25.00
	I		30.00
	J		10.00
	K		15.00
	S (2011)		3.00
Halton Camp North	D		6.00
(see note re Halton above)			
Hampton Court Camp	D		60.00
	F		80.00
(Kingston-on-Thames)	I		40.00
Harrowby Camp, Grantham	D		8.00
	J		10.00
Haynes Park Camp, Bedford	D		8.00
Hazeley Camp, Winchester	D		6.00
	E		5.00
	J		10.00
Heytesbury Camp, Wilts	E		5.00
	I		20.00
	J		10.00
Hindlow Camp, Buxton	F		25.00
Holkham Camp, Wells Norfolk	F		20.00
Hollingbury Camp, Brighton	F		30.00

321

Military and Camp Postmarks

Hollinside Camp NB (Co Durham)	F	50.00
Hollom Dn Barn Camp, Hants	F	30.00
Holmsley Camp, Ringwood	F	30.00
Horsebridge Camp, Hants	F	50.00
Houghton Down Camp, Hants	F	40.00
Hunmanby Camp, Yorkshire	F	20.00
Hurdcott Camp, Salisbury	D	6.00
	E	6.00
(also Hardcott Camp)	F	50.00
	J	10.00
Hursley Camp, Winchester	D	6.00
Hursley Park Camp	D	6.00
	E	6.00
	F	30.00
Ibsley Camp (Ringwood)	F	40.00
Royal Hospital School, Ipswich Suffolk	D	8.00
Kensington Gdns Camp W2	D	20.00
	F	30.00
	K	25.00
King Edward VII Sanatorium, Midhurst	D	7.00
	E	10.00
Kinmel Park Camp, Rhyl	D	6.00
	E	5.00
(Registered/Kinmel Park not Camp)	F	30.00
	J	10.00
Kinross Camp	F	25.00
Knockaloe Camp, Peel (1908)	F	£150
The Camp Knockaloe, Peel (1915 POW Camp)		
	E	75.00
Lamphey Camp, Pembroke (rubber skeleton)		
	F	75.00
Landguard Camp, Felixstowe	E	8.00
Lark Hill Camp, Salisbury	D	5.00
	F	4.00
	F	20.00
	J	10.00
Lathom Park Camp, Ormskirk	D	8.00
	E	8.00
Littlemore Camp, Weymouth	F	30.00
Lodmore Camp, Weymouth	F	30.00
Longmoor Camp, Liss Hants	D	5.00
	E (East Liss)	4.00
	F	20.00
	J	10.00
Lopcombe Camp, Salisbury	F	40.00
Lovesgrove Camp (Aberystwyth)	F	25.00
Lulworth Camp, Wareham	F	25.00
Lydd Camp, Kent	D	8.00
	E	5.00
	F	20.00
Maresfield Park Camp, Uckfield	E	8.00
Marlborough Lines, Aldershot	D	5.00
	E	3.00
	F	20.00
	J	10.00
Camp, Marske by Sea Yk	F	30.00
Martinhoe Camp, Barnstaple	F	50.00
Milford Camp, Stafford	F	40.00
Milton Depot, Steventon Berks	E	6.00
	*I	30.00
The Camp, Minehead Som	D	5.00
Morfa Camp, Conway	D	8.00
	J	8.00
Morn Hill Camp, Winchester	D	5.00
	E	4.00
	F	25.00
Mytchett Camp (Aldershot or Farnborough)	F	30.00
Nettlebed Camp, Henley Ths	F	30.00
*North Denes Camp (Norfolk)	F	?
North Leam Camp NB (Co Durham)	F	50.00
North Sway Camp (Hants)	F	25.00
Norton Barracks, Worcester	D	15.00
Offington Camp, Worthing	F	35.00

Okehampton Camp, Okehampton	D	5.00
	E	6.00
Orsett Camp, Grays Essex	D	6.00
	J	10.00
*Osterley Park Camp, Isleworth	E	?
Otterpool Camp (Kent)	E	8.00
	F	25.00
Oxney Camp, Bordon Hants	F	35.00
Panfield Camp, Braintree	F	35.00
Parham Park Camp (Sussex)	F	25.00
Park Hall Camp, Oswestry	D	5.00
	E	5.00
	F	30.00
	J	8.00
Park Hall West Camp, Oswestry	D	6.00
	E	5.00
	J	10.00
Park House Camp, Salisbury	E	5.00
Park Royal Camp NW	D	50.00
Pease Pottage Camp, Crawley	E	10.00
Peel Camp, Douglas	F	£250
Penkridge Bank Camp, Stafford	E	5.00
Penley Hall Camp, Wrexham Denb	E	8.00
Perham Down Camp, Andover	D	5.00
(& APO/FPO Perham Down)	E	5.00
	F	25.00
	J	10.00
Pewsey Field Force	D	£150
Pirbright Camp, Woking	D	4.00
	E	4.00
Pitt Camp, Winchester	D	8.00
	E	8.00
Plessey Camp, Cramlington	F	40.00
Pond Farm Camp, Devizes	D	8.00
	F (Salisbury)	15.00
Popham Camp, Winchester	F	30.00
Portobello Barracks	F	30.00
Experimental Ground/Stn, Porton Salisbury	E	30.00
Prees Heath Camp, Whitchurch (Salop)		
	D	5.00
	E	5.00
	F	30.00
	J	10.00
Barracks, Preston	D	6.00
	J	10.00
Puddaven Camp (Devon)	F	50.00
Purfleet Camp, Grays	D	6.00
	F	40.00
Ranikhet Camp, Reading Berks	D	6.00
Ravensworth Camp, Gateshead	F	50.00
The Barracks, Reading	D	6.00
	S	4.00
Reedhall Camp, Colchester	D	6.00
	E	6.00
	F	40.00
	J	10.00
Regents Park Camp NW1	F	50.00
Remount Depot, Romsey	D	8.00
	E	15.00
Rhayader Military Camp (rubber skeleton)		
	F	75.00
Richborough Camp, Sandwich Kent	D	8.00
Richmond Camp, Yorks	D	6.00
	E	4.00
	J	10.00
Ripon Camp	D	4.00
	E	4.00
	J	10.00
Rockford Camp (Ringwood)	F	30.00
Roehampton Camp SW	D	8.00
Rollestone Camp, Salisbury	D	5.00
	E	5.00
	F	40.00

Military and Camp Postmarks

	J	10.00	
Romsey Camp, Romsey	E	7.00	
	F	30.00	
	J	10.00	
Roomer Camp, Masham	F	40.00	
Rugeley Camp, Stafford	D	8.00	
	E	5.00	
	F	20.00	
	J	10.00	
Rushmoor Camp, Aldershot	E	6.00	
	F	30.00	
St Anthony Camp, Falmouth	E	10.00	
	I	40.00	
St Giles Camp, Wimborne Dst	F	30.00	
St John's, Crowborough Camp	F	30.00	
	J	10.00	
St Leonards Camp, Ringwood	F	30.00	
Sand Hill Camp, Wilts	E	4.00	
	F	30.00	
	I	25.00	
	J	10.00	
Sandling Camp (Folkestone, Hythe or Shorncliffe)			
	E	4.00	
	F	35.00	
	K	15.00	
Scarborough Race Course Camp	E	20.00	
Seaford Camp, Lewes	F	20.00	
Seaford North Camp, Sussex	D	8.00	
The Camp, Seaford	F	25.00	
Sedbury Camp, Chepstow	E	6.00	
Sheepcot Camp, Wallingford	F	50.00	
Sherrington Camp (Warminster, Wilts)	F	30.00	
Shoreham Camp, Sussex	D	6.00	
	E	4.00	
	F	25.00	
Shorncliffe Camp, Folkestone	C (F46)	15.00	
	D	10.00	
	E	4.00	
	J	8.00	
	K	18.00	
Sling Camp, Salisbury	E	6.00	
	F	25.00	
	J	10.00	
Sling Plantation Camp	F	25.00	
Stanhope Lines, Aldershot	D	5.00	
	E	3.00	
	F	20.00	
	J	10.00	
*Stobs Camp, Hawick	D	15.00	
*Stone Farm Camp, Sandling Hythe	E	?	
Stowe Park Camp, Bucks (or Buckingham)			
	F	30.00	
Strensall Camp, York	C (930)	10.00	
	D	4.00	
	E	4.00	
Summerdown Camp, Eastbourne	D	6.00	
	J	10.00	
Sunningdale Camp, Ascot	E	10.00	
Sutton Mandeville Camp, Salisbury	D	6.00	
	E	8.00	
	J	10.00	
Sutton Veny Camp, Wilts	D	8.00	
	E	4.00	
	F	20.00	
	I	15.00	
	J	15.00	
Swanage Camp, Poole	D	10.00	
	F	20.00	
Tadworth Camp, Epsom	D	8.00	
	E	8.00	
Tain Camp, Ross-shire	F	25.00	
Thetford Camp or Army Camp, Thetford			
	D	6.00	
	E	4.00	

	F	20.00	
Tidworth Barracks, Andover (or Hants)	D	4.00	
	E	3.00	
	F	20.00	
	J	8.00	
Tidworth Park Camp, Andover	D	4.00	
	F (Tidworth or Hants)	20.00	
Tidworth Pennings Camp, Andover	D	5.00	
	J	10.00	
Townfoot Camp, Denny	F	30.00	
Trawsfynydd Camp	D	8.00	
Trenchard Lines (prev RAF Stn Upavon)	D	6.00	
Twezeldown Camp (Aldershot or Farnham)			
	D	5.00	
(or Tweseldown)	E	5.00	
(or Tweseldown)	F	30.00	
Wannock Camp	I	40.00	
Wareham Field Post Office	D	£100	
Welbeck Camp, Worksop	F	40.00	
FPO West Down Camp	E	10.00	
West Down North Camp, Devizes	D (or Salisbury)	6.00	
(or FPO West Down North)			
West Down South Camp, Devizes	D (or Salisbury)	5.00	
(or FPO West Down South)			
West Lavington Camp	E	8.00	
	I	30.00	
West Lulworth Camp, Wareham	E	20.00	
	F	30.00	
West Parley Camp, Wimborne	F	30.00	
Whitchurch Down Camp (Tavistock Devon)			
	F	30.00	
White Hill Bordon Camp, Hants	D	6.00	
Whitmoor Camp, Woking	F	40.00	
Whittington Barracks, Lichfield	D	4.00	
	E	4.00	
	F	20.00	
Wicklesham Camp, Swindon	F	50.00	
Willsworthy Camp (Bridestowe Devon)	F	30.00	
Wiltshire TF Assn Trowbridge	E	50.00	
Wimbledon Camp	C (801)	£300	
	D	40.00	
Wimbledon Common Camp	D	25.00	
Windmill Hill Camp, Andover	D	4.00	
	E	4.00	
	J	10.00	
Wing Camp, Leighton Buzzard	F	15.00	
Witley Camp, Godalming	E	4.00	
Woodbury Camp, Exeter	F (rubber)	40.00	
	F (steel)	40.00	
Woodbury Common Camp	F (rubber)	50.00	
Woodcote Camp, Epsom	E	6.00	
Woodhead Camp (Aberdeen)	F	30.00	
Woolsington Camp, New on T	F	35.00	
Woolwich RA Barracks SE18	D	10.00	
	J	20.00	
Woolwich Royal Arsenal	D	10.00	
Worgret Camp (Poole or Wareham)	D	5.00	
	E	5.00	
	F	20.00	
Worthy Down Camp, Winchester Hants	D	5.00	
	F	25.00	
The Camp, Yarmouth	D	7.00	

Ireland

Aglish Camp, Fermoy	F	50.00	
Ballinvonear Camp, Buttevant	E	10.00	
	F	50.00	
Ballykinler Camp, Co Down	D	8.00	
	E	8.00	
	F	30.00	
	J	20.00	
Bere Island MTO	F	£100	
Clandeboye Camp (Co Down)	F	25.00	
Coolmoney Camp (Co Wicklow)	F	75.00	

323

Military and Camp Postmarks

Cork Barracks Mil Tel Off	D	50.00
Curragh Camp (Co Kildare)	A	£1000
	B	£150
	C (455)	75.00
	D	4.00
with cross pattee	E	8.00
double arc with gap	E	12.00
	F	35.00
	J	20.00
Finner Camp, Ballyshannon (Co. Donegal)	D	30.00
Glen Imaal Camp (Co. Wicklow)	D	20.00
	F	50.00
Glen Imaal Artillery Camp	D	35.00
Gormanston Camp, Co. Meath	D	50.00
	F	40.00
Hare Park, Curragh Camp	D	50.00
Kilbride Camp, Dublin	D	20.00
	F	30.00
Kilworth Camp, Cork	D	12.00
	F	40.00
Lisnegar Camp (Co Cork)	F	40.00
	F (rubber skeleton)	75.00
Magilligan Camp, Londonderry	D	25.00
Malahide Camp, Co Dublin	D	£100
Moore Park Camp (Co Cork)	F	60.00
Palace Barracks, Belfast	D	20.00
Shanes Park Camp, Belfast (single rim skeleton)	F	30.00
Whitefields Camp, Dublin	F	£100

Section VII : Special Events

See chapter 12 for further details.

15/152

15/149	Colonial & Indian Exhibition, 1886	*
15/150	Royal Military Exhibition, 1890	*
15/151	BFPS 1000 (Aldershot Army Display), 1967 (this was the first of many uses of BFPS 1000 handstamps)	2.00
15/152	Royal School of Military Engineering (Open Day), 1967	1.00
15/153	The Royal Tournament BFPS 1068, 1968	2.00

Note: From this point military BFPS handstamps burgeoned including use for Events with RAF, Royal Naval and Royal Marines connections, see chapter 12 and "Special Event Postmarks of the UK" for details.

16 Aviation

The chapter covers air mail postmarks, also Airport and RAF Post Office postmarks though applied to covers that are not normally transmitted by air.

The field of "Aero Philately", connected with study of flown covers, is a large subject beyond the scope of this handbook. This is because first flights, special air meetings and other special flights utilised special envelopes and special cachets, not necessarily with distinguishable postmarks. Listed below, however, are some of the "classic" special postmarks.

16/1   16/4

Air Mail postmarks

16/1	London FS/Air Mail, double circle with thick arcs, from 1930	10.00
16/2	As above but rubber handstamp, from 1931	15.00
16/3	As above but machine die and wavy lines, from 1934	5.00
16/4	As above but hooded registered, rubber, purple, 1948	20.00
16/5	This item (Croydon Air Mail) deleted since shown in Aerodromes section below	
16/6	Airgraph motif with single circle (Dickinson machine) or double circle (Pitney Bowes) datestamp, red, from 1941	20.00

Modern machine marks

16/7	Croydon Air Mail Paid/CR town die, red, 1992	4.00
16/8	London FS/Great Britain, 1st Paid Airmail in wavy lines, 1995	4.00
16/9	Southampton "By air mail" slogan, red, 1996	4.00
16/9A	As above but different designs at Edinburgh (1995), Aberdeen (1996), Mount Pleasant (1998), all red	5.00
16/9B	As above but Hemel Hempstead, black, 1999 (used on bulk mailing with adhesives, but no year shown)	6.00

Note: Details of Nos. 16/9-9B are shown in *Slogan Postmarks of the Nineties part 2: 1995-99*, see Bibliography.

Special Events

A selection of "classic" events, see chap 12 for details.

16/12   16/15

16/10	First United Kingdom Aerial Post London, numbered 1-6, 1911	65.00
16/11	As above but Windsor, numbered 1-2	90.00
	(16/10 and 16/11 only applied to special envelopes and postcards)	
16/12	Airship flight from USA, double circle with R34 above date, 1919	*
16/13	Calshot Aerodrome/Sthmptn, skeleton, Schneider Trophy Race, 1931.	£100
16/14	Air Post Exhibition London SW1, 1934	25.00
16/15	Mildenhall A'drome/Bury St.E, skeleton, UK-Australia Air Race 1934	45.00
16/16	International Air Transport Association 7th AGM London, 1951	50.00
16/17	Farnborough SBAC/Hts Ex (Farnborough Air Display), skeleton, 1951	45.00

Aerodromes and airports

Notes: (1) Croydon name changed from Waddon in 1928 then closed in 1940 and re-opened as "Airport" 1947-60 (2) 16/5 was used at Croydon Head Office (3) Gatwick used from 1936-37 but re-opened in 1958 (4) Heathrow opened 1946 and the PO was located in a hut until the 1960s, and post town had meanwhile changed from Feltham to Hounslow. Later the 3 terminals each had a post office (not shown in handstamps) but rationalisation in 1980s closed two of these, though opening of terminal 4 in 1987 made the total two again, plus Cargo Centre (5) Some data comes from an article in British Postmark Society Bulletin of 1960: it refers to five current post offices including Manchester and Prestwick, thus leaving uncertain the status at that time of postmarks at Dalcross East (Inverness Airport 1941-74, civilian use except 1943-44) and Renfrew (1954-71 then replaced by Glasgow airport) (6) Dates are earliest known not necessarily start dates, but other reports are welcome (7) for Digby see next section (RAF).

16/18   16/19

325

Aviation

16/20 — REGISTERED 23 OCT 50, London Airport, Feltham, Middx

16/21 — LONDON HEATHROW AIRPORT CENTRAL, K 5 JL 87

16/22 — HEATHROW M.S.P.O., N 26 MR 92

16/23 — BELFAST AIRPORT L.S.O., -2 APR 1993

16/24 — GLASGOW AIRPORT.PAISLEY, 15 DE 84, RENFREWSHIRE

16/25 — AIRPORT.MANCHESTER, B 24 SP 92 22

16/26 — PRESTWICK AIRPORT, 9.30 PM 14 JY 60, PRESTWICK 2 AYRSHIRE

16/27 — TEES-SIDE AIRPORT, 30 JU 87, DARLINGTON

(for key see RAF & RNAS Establishments on next page)

Croydon

Waddon Aerodrome (1921)	D **16/18**	£200
Croydon Aerodrome	D (1928)	60.00
	E	50.00
Aerodrome B.O. Croydon, Surrey/ Air Mail	E (1936)	50.00
Croydon Airport	D **16/19**	15.00
(also without BO) (1947, closed 1960)		
	J	40.00

Gatwick

Gatwick Airport/Horley, Surrey	E (1936)	50.00
	D (1958)	20.00
	J (1958)	20.00
London (Gatwick) Airport, Horley, Surrey	D (1961)	6.00
	I	10.00
	J	12.00
Gatwick Airport W Sussex	I (1982)	8.00
Gatwick Surrey	S	5.00
(also Gatwick BO, closed 2004)		

Heathrow

The London Airport, Feltham Middx	D (1946)	75.00
	K (purple) **16/20**	60.00
London Airport North, Hounslow Middx	D (1956-64)	8.00
	J	18.00
	K	25.00
The London Airport, Hounslow Middx	D (1956)	10.00
	E (1956)	8.00
	I	15.00
London Airport	D (1971)	6.00
London (Heathrow) Airport, Hounslow Middx	E (1964)	8.00
	I	12.00
London (Heathrow) Airport Central (variations)	D **16/21**	5.00
	I (L.A Mail Unit)	12.00
	J	10.00
	K	15.00
Heathrow Airport B.O./ Hounslow Middx	D (1983)	5.00
Heathrow Airport/ Terminal 4 (closed 2004)	D (1987)	5.00
	J	6.00
	S	4.00
Heathrow MSPO T2 (terminal 2) (closed 2009)	D (1991) **16/22**	4.00
	I	5.00
	J	6.00
	S	4.00
Heathrow Terminal Three (2009)	S	4.00
Heathrow Airport Cargo Area/ Hounslow	D (1985)	5.00
	J	8.00
	S	5.00

Other airports

Belfast Airport LSO (new sorting office 1990)	I	**16/23**	10.00
Dalcross East/Inverness (Inverness Airport, see note)	E		8.00
Glasgow Airport.Paisley/ Renfrewshire	D	**16/24**	6.00
	J		10.00
Airport.Manchester 22	D (1956)	**16/25**	20.00
	J		12.00
Manchester Airport	S		5.00
Northolt Airport, Ruislip (see RAF listing below)			
Airport.Prestwick/Ayrshire	D		12.00
	J		25.00
Prestwick Airport/Prestwick 2 Ayrshire	E	**16/26**	10.00
Airport, Renfrew	D		40.00
Southampton Airport	D (1937 only)		£100
Tees-side Airport/Darlington	D (1968-92)	**16/27**	8.00

Second World War

16/28 — R.A.F. POST OFFICE, 2 DE 44, 002

Aviation

"Numbered" RAF Post Offices

There were a good number of these; only the initial ones are shown here

RAFPO 001 single circle - Iceland			75.00
002 single circle - Iceland	16/28		75.00
004 double circle - Azores			£100
005 double circle - Iceland			60.00

Air Force Censor Marks

See note in chapter 14.

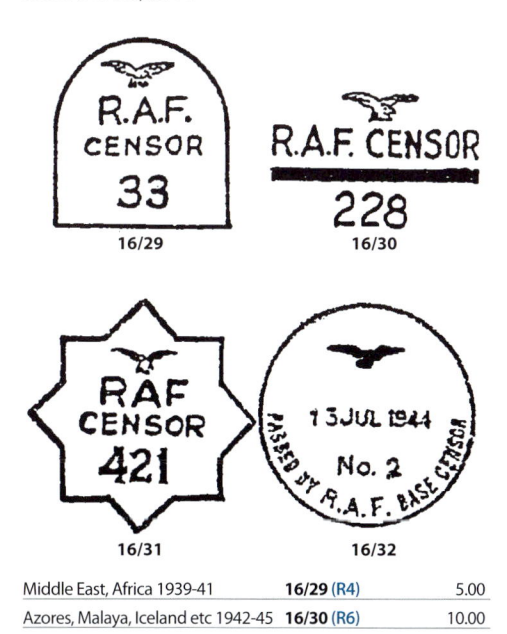

D 16/33 Single Circle **E 16/34** Double Circle

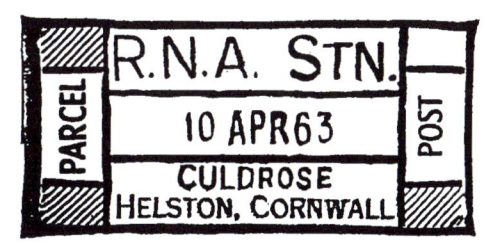

16/29

16/30

J 16/35 Parcel handstamps

16/31

16/32

Middle East, Africa 1939-41	16/29 (R4)	5.00
Azores, Malaya, Iceland etc 1942-45	16/30 (R6)	10.00
Algeria, Sicily 1943-44	16/31 (R14)	15.00
N Ireland 1944	16/32 (R20-3)	12.00

RAF and RNAS Establishments

This list is largely compiled with the aid of "Postal Markings of RAF, RFC and RNAS Stations in the UK 1918-1968" by Bill Garrard, and published by the Forces Postal History Society in 1990. This data is used with permission. Additional data and corrections were kindly provided by Derrick Burney. Inscriptions are abbreviated and shown without punctuation; also not all changes of designation are included eg Aldergrove exists shown both as Lisburn and Crumlin. Some of the post offices are civilian ones but on RAF premises; some are open to the public but others are not.

Most RAFPOs have circular rubber cachets which are easily mistaken for rubber packet stamps but are usually undated; these are RAF Post Room marks and usually only appear on official mail. All values should be DOUBLED for registered covers, and the presence of interesting registration labels and the Post Room cachets referred to here further enhances the value of such covers.

D	Single Circle
E	Double Circle
F	Skeleton handstamps
I	Packet handstamps
J	Parcel handstamps
K	Registered handstamps
S	SID (self-inking datestamp)

England, Scotland, Wales

Abingdon RAFPO/Berks	D	8.00
(later RAF Stn		8.00)
Acaster Malbis RAFPO/York	D	12.00
	E	10.00
Acklington RAFPO/Morpeth, N'thbd	D	8.00
	J	25.00
Alconbury RAFPO Station/ Huntingdon	E	8.00
Alness RAFPO/Alness, Rossshire	D	12.00
Amport RAFPO/Andover, Hants	E	8.00
Andrews Field RAFPO/ Braintree	E	15.00
Ashbourne Dys/RAFPO	D	15.00
Aston Down,Stroud,Glos	D	12.00
	J	40.00
Ayr RAFPO/Ayr	D	15.00
Babdown RAFPO/Tetbury	E	12.00
Balderton RAFPO/Newark, Notts	D	12.00
Balivanich/Lochboisdale (poss used at RAFPO)	D	20.00
then Benbecula RAFPO	E	15.00
Banff RAFPO	D	12.00
Bardney RAFPO/Lincoln	D	12.00
Barrow in Furness RAFPO/ Lancs	D	10.00
Bassingbourn RAFPO/Royston, Herts	E	8.00
then RAF Stn Bassingbourn	E	5.00
	J	25.00
(later Bassingbourn Barracks - see chapter 15)		
Bawdsey Ferry/Woodbridge, Suffolk		
(RAF Bawdsey)	E	6.00
Beaulieu RAFO/Brockenhurst, Hants	E	12.00
Benson RAF Station Benson/Oxford		
(see also Clay Lane below)	D	8.00
Bentley Priory RAFPO/ Stanmore, Middx	D	8.00
Bicester RAFPO/Oxon	D	8.00
	J	25.00
Biggin Hill RAFPO/Westerham, Kent	E	10.00
Binbrook RAFPO/Lincoln	D	6.00
	E	8.00
Bircham Green RAFPO/ Kings Lynn, Nfk	D	8.00
	J	25.00
Blakehill RAFPO/Swindon, Wilts	D	10.00
Blyton RAFPO/Gainsborough, Lincs	D	12.00
Boscombe Down RAFPO/ Salisbury	D	5.00
Bourn RAFPO/Cambridge	E	8.00
Brackla RAFPO/Nairn	D	15.00
Bramcote RAFPO/Nuneaton,Wks	D	8.00
RNAS Brawdy/Haverfordwest, Pembs	D	8.00
Breighton RAFPO/Selby,Yorks	D	12.00
Bridgnorth,Shropshire/RAFPO	D	10.00

327

Aviation

	E	6.00	
Brize Norton RAFPO/Oxford	D	8.00	
Stanmore Cres, Carterton/Oxford (RAF Brize Norton)	D	4.00	
	J	20.00	
Bruntingthorpe RAFPO/Rugby, Wks	D	12.00	
USAF Base, Warrington/Lancs (RAF/USAF Burton Wood)	D	12.00	
Calshot/Southampton (RAF Calshot)	D	6.00	
Calveley RAFPO Nantwich/ Cheshire	D	12.00	
Camelford RAFPO/Cornwall (RAF Davidstowe Moor)	E	10.00	
Carew Cheriton RAFPO/Tenby, Pembs	D	12.00	
Castle Bromwich RAFPO/ Birmingham	D	12.00	
Castle Camps RAFPO/Cambridge	D	12.00	
Catfoss RAFPO/Hull, Yorks	D	8.00	
	I	10.00	
Catterick Camp, see chapter 15			
Charterhall RAFPO/Duns	D	12.00	
Chedburgh RAFPO/Bury St.Edmunds Sfk	D	12.00	
Chicksands RAFPO/Shefford, Beds	D	12.00	
Chigwell RAFPO/Essex	D	12.00	
Chilbolton RAFPO/Stockbridge Hants	D	12.00	
Chivenor RAFPO/Barnstaple, Devon	D	6.00	
Church Fenton RAF Stn/ Tadcaster, Yks	D	10.00	
Church Lawford RAFPO/ Rugby Wks	D	12.00	
Clay Lane, Oxford/- (RAF Benson)	D	6.00	
	E	5.00	
Colerne RAFPO/Chippenham Wilts	D	6.00	
	J	25.00	
Coltishall RAFPO/Norwich, Norfolk	D	8.00	
	E	5.00	
	J	10.00	
	K	50.00	
Compton Bassett Camp/ Calne, Wilts	E	8.00	
	J	30.00	
Cosford Camp, Wolverhampton/ Staffs (or W Mids)	D	6.00	
	J	20.00	
Cottesmore RAFPO/Oakham, Rutland	D	12.00	
	E	5.00	
	J	20.00	
Crabtree RAFPO/Warminster, Wilts (RAF Warminster)	D	12.00	
Cranage RAFPO/ Middlewich, Cheshire	D	12.00	
Cranfield RAFPO/Bletchley, Bucks	D	12.00	
Cranswick RAFPO/Driffield (RAF Hutton Cranswick)	D	12.00	
Cranwell/Sleaford, Lincs	D	6.00	
	E	5.00	
Creca RAFPO/Annan Dumfriesshire	D	12.00	
Crimond RNASPO/Lonmay	E	20.00	
Crosby on Eden RAFPO/ Carlisle	E	15.00	
Crossapol/Isle of Tiree (later RAFPO Tiree)	D	25.00	
Culdrose RN Air Stn/ Helston, Cornwall	D	6.00	
	E	4.00	
	J	20.00	
Culmhead RAFPO/Taunton, Som	D	12.00	
Dalcross East/Inverness (also with RAFPO added) (see Airport listing above)	E	8.00	
Dallachy RAFPO/Spey Bay Morayshire	D	15.00	
Defford RAFPO/Worcester	D	8.00	
Detling RAFPO/Maidstone, Kent	D	12.00	
Digby Aerodrome/Lincoln	D	8.00	
	E	8.00	
	J	30.00	
Dishforth RAFPO/Thirsk, Yks	D	10.00	
(later North Hill	E	5.00)	
	J	30.00	
Downham Market RAFPO/ Norfolk	D	12.00	
Drainie, Lossiemouth/ Morayshire (RNAS Lossiemouth)	D	6.00	
	E	8.00	
	J	20.00	
Driffield RAFPO/Yorkshire	D	6.00
	J	25.00
Duxford Camp	D	20.00
Duxford RAFPO/Cambridge	D	10.00
	E	5.00
Earls Colne RAFPO/Colchester, Essex	D	12.00
East Fortune RAFPO/Drem East Lothian	D	15.00
East Kirkby RAFPO/Spilsby, Lincs	D	12.00
Edzell RAFPO/Brechin, Angus	D	8.00
Elgin RAFPO/Morayshire	D	15.00
(also Bogs of Mayne	E	12.00)
Elsham Wolds RAFPO/Barnetby, Lincs	D	12.00
Elvington RAFPO/York	E	15.00
Errol RAFPO/Perth	D	12.00
Eshott RAFPO/Morpeth, Nthbd	D	12.00
Evanton RAFPO/Evanton Rosshire	D	12.00
Exeter RAFPO/Devon	D	12.00
Fairford RAFPO/Fairford, Glos	E	8.00
Faldingworth RAFPO/Lincoln	D	12.00
Fauld RAFPO/Burton-on-Trent, Staffs	D	12.00
Fazakerley RAFPO/ Liverpool 9	D	12.00
Feltwell RAFPO/Thetford, Norfolk	D	6.00
	J	30.00
Fenton Barns, Drem/East Lothian (RAF)	J	40.00
Butlins Camp/Filey, Yorkshire (RAF Filey)	E	25.00
Filton RAFPO/Bristol	D	12.00
Finningley RAFPO/Doncaster, Yks	D	5.00
	E	6.00
	J	25.00
Fiskerton RAFPO/Lincoln	D	12.00
Ford RNAS, Arundel/Sussex	D	12.00
Forres RAFPO/Morayshire	D	15.00
Foulsham RAFPO/Dereham, Nfk	D	8.00
Fulbeck RAFPO/Grantham Lincs	D	12.00
Full Sutton RAFPO/York	E	8.00
Fylingdales RAFPO/Pickering, Yks	E	8.00
	J	20.00
Gamston RAFPO/Retford, Notts	D	12.00
Gaydon RAF Stn/Leamington Spa, Wks	D	8.00
	E	8.00
Graveley RAFPO/Huntingdon	D	12.00
Gt Dunmow RAFPO/Dunmow, Essex	D	15.00
	E	15.00
Gt Massingham RAFPO/Kings Lynn, Nfk	D	10.00
Grimsby RAFPO/Lincs	D	12.00
Halfpenny Green RAFPO/ Stourbridge	D	12.00
Halton Camp - see chap 15		
Harrowden/Bedford (RAF Cardington)	D	6.00
	E	6.00
Harwell RAFPO/Didcot, Berks	D	12.00
Haverfordwest RAFPO/Pembs	E	15.00
Hawarden RAFPO/Chester	D	8.00
Hednesford Camp, Hednesford/ Staffs	D	8.00
	J	25.00
Hemswell Aerodrome/Lincoln	E	12.00
later RAFPO Gainsborough, Lincs	E	5.00
Henlow Camp/Henlow, Beds	D	5.00
	E	5.00
	J	20.00
	S	3.00
Hinton in the Hedges RAFPO/ Brackley	D	12.00
Hixon RAFPO/Stafford	D	12.00
Holme Moor RAFPO/York	E	12.00
Holmesley Sth RAFPO/ Christchurch, Hants	D	12.00
Honeybourne Grounds/ Evesham, Worcs	D	15.00
Honington RAFPO (later Camp)/ Bury St. Edmunds Sfk	D	6.00
	E	6.00
	J	30.00
Hornchurch RAFPO/Romford, Essex (later South Hornchurch)	D	15.00
Horsham St.Faiths RAFPO/ Norwich	D	8.00
Houndstone Camp, Yeovil/ Somerset	D	8.00
	J	30.00

328

Aviation

Hullavington RAFPO/ Chippenham,Wilts		D	6.00	Milton RAFPO/Abingdon,Berks		D	12.00
		J	25.00	Mona RAFPO/Holyhead,Anglesey		D	25.00
Husbands Bosworth RAFPO/ Rugby,Wks		D	12.00	Moreton RAFPO/Moreton-in-Marsh, Glos		D	12.00
Ingham RAFPO/Lincoln		D	12.00	Netheravon RAFPO/Salisbury, Wilts		D	8.00
Jurby RAFPO/Ramsey, Isle of Man		D	80.00	Newton RAF Station/ Nottingham		D	8.00
parcel **17/191**			80.00	North Cotes RAFPO/Grimsby, Lincs		D	8.00
Keevil RAFPO/Trowbridge, Wilts		E	10.00			J	30.00
		J	30.00	North Creake RAFPO/Egmere Wells, Nfk		D	15.00
Air Ministry Unit RAF/ Kenley,Surrey		D	15.00	North Killingholme RAFPO/ Grimsby		D	12.00
Kidlington/Oxford (RAF Kidlington)		D	5.00	North Luffenham RAFPO/ Oakham,Rutland		D	8.00
		E	5.00	Northolt Airport,Ruislip/ Middlesex (RAF Northolt)		D	15.00
Kinloss RAFPO/Forres, Morayshire		D	8.00	North Weald RAFPO/Epping, Essex		D	8.00
		J	20.00	Norton Disney RAFPO/Lincoln		D	12.00
Kirkham Camp/Preston,Lancs		D	8.00	Oakington RAFPO/Cambridge		D	8.00
		J	30.00	Old Sarum RAFPO/Salisbury, Wilts		D	12.00
Lakenheath Camp/Brandon, Suffolk		D	5.00	Ossington RAFPO/Newark,Notts		D	12.00
		E	5.00	Oulton RAFPO/Norwich,Norfolk		D	12.00
Langar RAFPO/Barnstone, Nottingham		D	12.00			K	30.00
Larton RAF Camp,Wirral/ Cheshire (RAF W Kirby)		D	10.00	Ouston RAFPO/Newcastle-on-Tyne		D	8.00
		E	5.00			J	30.00
(no RAF Camp)		F	50.00	Padgate Camp/Warrington,Lancs		D	8.00
Leconfield RAFPO/Beverley,Yks		D	10.00	(also Cowlane RAFPO)		D	8.00
		K	50.00			J	20.00
Leechmoor Cross/Cowbridge, Glam				Pembrey RAFPO/Burryport, Carm		D	12.00
(RAF Llandow)		D	12.00	Pembroke Dock RAFPO/ Pembroke Dock		D	12.00
Leeming RAFPO/Northallerton, Yks		D	10.00	Penrhos RAFPO/Pwllheli, Caern		D	15.00
(later Gatenby RAF Stn		E	8.00)	Peplow RAFPO/Market Drayton, Salop		D	12.00
Lee-on-Solent - see chap 14				Pershore/Worcs,RAFPO		D	8.00
The Leys/Oxford (RAF Upper Heyford)		D	8.00	Peterhead RAFPO/Aberdeenshire		D	15.00
		E	8.00	Pocklington RAFPO/York		E	12.00
Lichfield RAFPO/Lichfield, Staffs		D	8.00	Port Ellen RAFPO/ Isle of Islay		D	20.00
Lindholme RAFPO/Doncaster, Yks		D	8.00	Rattlesden RAFPO/ Bury St Edmunds,Sfk		D	12.00
		J	30.00	Rednal RAFPO/Oswestry, Salop		D	12.00
Linton-on-Ouse RAFPO/York		D	10.00	Redruth RAFPO/Cornwall		D	12.00
Lissett RAFPO/Driffield,Yks		D	12.00	Riccall Common RAFPO/Selby, Yorks		D	15.00
Little Onn RAFPO/Stafford		D	12.00	Rivenhall RAFPO/Witham, Essex		D	12.00
Little Rissington RAF/ Cheltenham,Glos		D	10.00	Rufforth RAFPO/York		E	10.00
(also Rissington RAFPO		D	8.00)	St.Athan Main Site/Barry, Glam		D	5.00
		J	30.00	(also St. Athan Station		D	10.00
Little Staughton RAFPO/ Huntingdon		D	12.00	and RAF Stn		D	10.00)
Loch Doon Camp/Ayrshire (RNAS)		E	20.00			J	30.00
Locking Camp,Weston-super-Mare/ Som		D	8.00	St.David's RAFPO/ Haverfordwest Pemb		D	15.00
		J	30.00	St.Eval RAFPO/Wadebridge, Cornwall		D	6.00
Long Marston RAFPO/Stratford on-Avon		D	15.00			E	6.00
Longparish RAFPO/Andover, Hants		D	12.00			J	30.00
Ludford Magna RAFPO/Lincoln		E	12.00	St.Mawgan RAFPO/Newquay, Cornwall		D	8.00
Lyneham RAFPO/Chippenham, Wilts						J	20.00
(later RAF Stn)		D	10.00	Saltby RAFPO/ Melton Mowbray Leics		E	12.00
		J	20.00	Sandtoft RAFPO/Doncaster,Yks		E	12.00
Machrihanish RAFPO Campbeltown/Argyll		D	8.00	Scampton RAFPO/Lincoln		D	6.00
Machrihanish North/ Campbeltown (RAF)		D	8.00			J	20.00
		E	8.00	Scapa RAFPO/Kirkwall,Orkney		D	30.00
Manby/Louth,Lincs (RAF)		E	8.00	Sculthorpe RAFPO Fakenham/ Nfk		D	6.00
RAF Stn/Manston,Ramsgate		D	8.00			E	8.00
Marham RAFPO/Kings Lynn, Nfk		D	5.00	Sealand RAFPO/Chester		D	10.00
		E	5.00			J	30.00
		J	20.00	Seighford RAFPO/Stafford		D	12.00
Market Harborough RAFPO/ Leics		D	12.00	Shenley Rd RAFPO Bletchley/ Bucks		D	20.00
Marston Moor RAFPO/York		E	12.00	Silloth RAFPO/Cumberland		E	12.00
Marsworth RAFPO/Tring		E	12.00	Silverstone RAFPO/Towcester, N'thants		D	12.00
Medmenham RAFPO/Marlow, Bucks		D	6.00	Skeabrae RAFPO/Kirkwall, Orkney		E	35.00
Melbourne RAFPO/York		E	12.00	Skitten RAFPO/Wick,Caithness		D	15.00
Melksham Camp/Melksham,Wilts		D	6.00	Sleap RAFPO/Shrewsbury, Shropshire		D	12.00
		J	20.00	Snailwell RAFPO/Newmarket, Sfk		D	12.00
Metheringham RAFPO/Lincoln		D	12.00	Snitterfield RAFPO/Stratford on-Avon		D	12.00
Methwold RAFPO/Thetford, Norfolk		D	12.00	South Cerney RAFPO/ Cirencester		E	6.00
Middleton St.George RAFPO/ Darlington		D	12.00	South Down RAFPO/High Wycombe, Bucks		D	12.00
		J	30.00			J	30.00
Middle Wallop RAFPO/ Stockbridge,Hants		E	6.00	(later RAFPO/High Wycombe, Bucks		D	8.00)
Mildenhall RAFPO/Bury St. Edmunds,Sfk		D	12.00	Spilsby RAFPO/Spilsby,Lincs		D	12.00
Milfield RAFPO/Alnwick		D	15.00	Spitalgate RAFPO/Grantham, Lincs		D	10.00
Mill Green RAFPO/Hatfield, Herts		D	12.00	Stafford RAFPO/Stafford		D	8.00
Millom RAFPO/Cumberland		D	12.00			J	25.00
Milltown RAFPO/Elgin, Morayshire		D	15.00	Stoke Heath RAFPO/Market Drayton, Salop		D	10.00

329

Aviation

Stoke Orchard RAFPO/ Cheltenham	D	15.00
Stoney Cross RAFPO/Lyndhurst, Hants	E	12.00
Stormy Down RAFPO/Pyle,Bridgend, Glam (RAF Porthcawl)	D	12.00
Stornoway RAFPO/ Isle of Lewis	D	35.00
Stradishall Camp/Newmarket Suffolk (also RAFPO)	D	6.00
	E	4.00
	J	20.00
Stretton Sugwas/Hereford	D	5.00
	J	20.00
later RAF Stn/Hereford	D	8.00
Strubby RAFPO/Alford,Lincs	D	12.00
Sturgate RAFPO/Gainsborough Lincs	D	15.00
Sullom Voe RAFPO/Lerwick, Shetland	D	35.00
Sutton-on-Hull RAFPO/Hull, Yks	D	10.00
Swannington RAFPO/Norwich, Nfk	D	12.00
Swanton Morley RAFPO/ Dereham,Nfk	D	8.00
	J	20.00
Swinderby RAFPO/Lincoln	D	8.00
	J	25.00
Syerston RAFPO/Newark,Notts	D	8.00
	J	25.00
Tain RAFPO/Ross-shire	D	12.00
Talbenny RAFPO/Haverfordwest, Pembs	E	12.00
Tangmere RAFPO/Chichester, Sussex	D	12.00
	J	30.00
Tarrant Rushton RAFPO/ Blandford	D	12.00
(then Tarrant Rushton/ Blandford Forum used with Tarrant Rushton Airfield registration label)	E	15.00
Tealing RAFPO/Dundee,Angus	D	12.00
Tempsford RAFPO/Sandy,Beds	E	12.00
Ternhill RAFPD/Market Drayton, Salop	D	6.00
	J	20.00
Thorney Island RAFPO/Emsworth, Hants	D	8.00
Tinwald Downs RAFPO/ Dumfries (RAF Dumfries)	D	10.00
Titchfield RAFPO/Fareham, Hants	D	12.00
Topcliffe RAFPO Thirsk, Yorkshire	D	8.00
(later Thistle Hill	E	5.00)
Tuddenham RAFPO/Bury St.Edmunds, Suffolk	D	12.00
Turnberry RAFPO/Girvan, Ayrshire	E	12.00
Turnhouse RAFPO/Edinburgh 12	D	12.00
Central Flying School/Upavon (variations)	D	50.00
	F	£150
RAF Station/Upavon, Marlborough,Wilts	E	8.00
(later Pewsey)		6.00
	J	25.00
later Trenchard Lines see ch 15		
Upwood RAFPO/Huntingdon	D	6.00
	E	8.00
Uxbridge Common/Uxbridge, Middx (RAF Uxbridge)	D	12.00
Valley RAFPO/Holyhead, Anglesey	D	8.00
	E	8.00
	J	30.00
Waddington RAFPO/Lincoln	D	8.00
	E	5.00
Warboys RAFPO/Huntingdon	D	12.00
Watchet RAFPO/Watchet, Somerset	E	12.00
Waterbeach RAFPO/Cambridge	D	8.00
Watton RAFPO/Thetford, Norfolk	D	8.00
	E	8.00
	J	20.00
Weeton Camp,Preston/Lancs	D	8.00
	J	25.00
Welford RAFPO/Newbury,Herks	E	12.00
Wellesbourne RAFPO/Warwick (RAF Wellesbourne Mountford)	D	8.00
Westcott RAFPO/Aylesbury, Bucks	D	12.00
West Freugh RAFPO/Stranraer	D	18.00
West Malling RAFPO/Maidstone, Kent	D	8.00
West Raynham RAFPO/Fakenham, Nfk	D	8.00
	E	6.00
	J	20.00
West Wickham RAFPO/Cambs	D	12.00
Wickenby RAFPO/Lincoln	D	12.00
Wigbay RAFPO/Stranraer	E	12.00
	J	30.00
Wigsley RAFPO/Newark,Notts	D	12.00
Wigtown RAFPO/Wigtown	D	10.00
Wilmslow RAFPO/Manchester (later Cheshire)	D	8.00
	J	30.00
Windrush RAFPO/Oxford	D	12.00
Wing RAFPO/Leighton Buzzard, Beds	D	12.00
Winthorpe RAFPO/Newark,Notts	D	12.00
Wittering Camp RAFPO/ Peterborough	D	10.00
Woodbridge RAFPO/Woodbridge, Sfk	D	10.00
Woodside/Arbroath,Angus (RNAS Arbroath)	D	8.00
Woodvale RAFPO Formby/Liverpool	D	12.00
Woolfox Lodge RAFPO/Oakham, Rutland	D	12.00
Worksop RAFPO/Worksop,Notts	D	8.00
Wratting Common RAFPO/ Cambridge	D	12.00
Wroughton RAF Hospital/ Swindon,Wilts	D	15.00
	F	50.00
Wymeswold RAFPO/Loughborough, Leics	D	12.00
	J	30.00
Wythall RAFPO/Birmingham	D	10.00
	J	25.00
Wyton RAFPO/Huntingdon	E	6.00
(later RAF Station)	J	30.00
Yatesbury Camp/Calne,Wilts	D	6.00
(RAF Camp)	E	12.00
	J	20.00
Yeovilton/Yeovil,Som	D	6.00
(later RNA Stn)	D	8.00
	J	30.00

Ireland

Aldergrove/Crumlin, Co.Antrim	D	15.00
	E	12.00
Ballyhalbert RAFPO/-	D	50.00
Ballykelly RAFPO/ Londonderry	E	40.00
Bishops Court RAFPO/ Downpatrick	D	15.00
	E	12.00
Castle Archdale RAFPO/ Enniskillen	D	30.00
HQ RAF/Northern Ireland	D	30.00
Killadeas RAFPO/Enniskillen, Co.Ferm	D	30.00
Limavady RAFPO/Londonderry	E	30.00
Long Kesh RAFPO/Lisburn, Co Antrim	D	40.00
Newtownards RAFPO/Co.Down	D	15.00
	F	75.00
Nutts Corner RAFPO/ Co.Antrim	E	50.00

Instructional and other markings

16/39

16/40

16/41

330

AIR MAIL
16/42

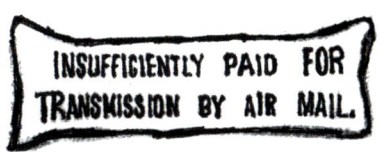

INSUFFICIENTLY PAID FOR TRANSMISSION BY AIR MAIL.
16/46

16/36	Air Mail/Express, unframed two line cachet, 1919	£100
16/37	As above but single line Air Mail, 1920	30.00
16/38	No Flight/sent by/ordinary service, c1920	50.00
16/39	Air Mail/London FS, undated rubber stamps (various sizes), 1940s	25.00
16/40	As above but Reading, 1960s-80s, purple	4.00
16/41	Air Mail or By Air Mail, applied by machine (Glasgow 1935-36) (see "Collecting Slogan Postmarks" for details)	5.00
16/42	As above but symbol "not filled in", handstamp used on registered	50.00
16/43	"All letters go by air" slogan-type marks 1938-39 on incoming mail (note : this and the next item - both Empire Air Mail - were applied by machine, for details see "Collecting Slogan Postmarks")	25.00
16/44	Please Advise Sender that letters should be prepaid 1½d for each half ounce (see above)	40.00
16/45	Over ....oz Insufficiently Prepaid for Transmission by Direct India Air Mail	50.00
16/46	Insufficiently paid for transmission by air mail	10.00
16/47	Postage Deficiency/Paid/(Reading Dutch Scheme)(claimed from sender)	20.00

Disaster or Crash cachets

SALVAGED MAIL AIRCRAFT CRASH PRESTWICK 25-12-54
16/48

See end of chapter 14 for general remarks concerning disasters and crashes. Shown as **16/48** is an example of a cachet used on salvaged mail - value 30.00

17 Islands

The first part of the chapter covers the Channel Islands and the Isle of Man, both before and after their separation from the British PO from 1 October 1969 (Channel Islands) and 5 July 1973 (Isle of Man). The chapter continues with islands of England, Wales, Northern Ireland and Scotland.

The Channel Islands

There have been differing opinions concerning the locations and use of (possibly) two distinctive Maltese Crosses. For a long time they were associated only with Alderney. It is now known there was only one distinctive cross and it is referred to as the "Channel Islands Cross". Its use is recorded between 1843 and 1845. It is very scarce and has a current value of approx £6000. Parcel post labels (from 1890) are generally beyond the scope of this handbook, but it is worthy of note that those of Channel Islands sub-offices are valued from £150, and Alderney and Sark £400.

Codes used in detailed listings in this chapter
A Undated double arc
B Single circle without Island name
C Single circle with Island name (or post town)
D Single circle with Island name and Ch. Is. (or post town & island name)
E Rubber handstamps
F Double circle with thick arcs
G Double circle with thin arcs
H Skeleton handstamps
J Undated double circle parcel mark
K Label type parcel handstamp
L Guernsey PO lower case s/c
L* As L but upper case lettering
M As L but larger
N Boxed parcel mark, Guernsey PO
O As N but unboxed
S Self inking datestamp

Jersey
This page shows "Jersey" postmarks used at St Helier(s).

17/4

17/12

17/15

17/17

17/42

17/1	Concave Jersey, 1794-99	£450
17/2	Straight line Jersey, 1797-1810	£400
17/3	Ship letter types, 1802-53	£650
17/4	Scroll types, 1810-30	£450
17/5	Jersey/Penny Post, boxed, 1831-40	£350
17/6	Double arc handstamps, 1830-58	30.00
17/7	Handstruck numerals: 1, 2 etc (red, black), 1842-68	£350
17/8	Skeleton ("travelling") handstamps, 1843-45	£600
17/9	Maltese cross, 1840-44	£125
17/10	Numeral handstamps (409), 1844-1904	35.00
17/11	Duplex handstamps (409), 1858-86	20.00
17/12	Squared circles, 1881-1905	10.00
17/13	Crown registration marks, 1855-70	£500
17/14	Double circles with cross or 1 at base, 1897-1929	3.00
17/15	Double circles with or without "St. Heliers" in brackets, 1930-	3.00
17/16	Single circles, 1858-1926	8.00
17/17	modern single circle counter handstamps, 1935-	3.00
17/18	Parcel handstamps, barred circle, 1886-1911	75.00
17/19	similar but double circle, 1892-1915	30.00
17/20	rectangular types with/without "St. Heliers" in brackets, 1915-	8.00
17/21	Paid handstamps, with/without Channel Islands at foot, red, 1919-	8.00
17/22	Rubber packet handstamps, 1893-	6.00
17/23	Oval registered handstamps, 1879-	8.00
17/24	Paquebot marks, 1896-1908 (less for 1970s usage)	£180
17/25	Krag machine marks, 1923-30	4.00
17/26	similar but Paid die, red	15.00
17/27	Universal machine marks, 1930-	2.00
17/28	with Square Paid die, red, 1932	15.00
17/29	with circular town die, "Paid" within wavy lines, red, 1937-	5.00
17/30	with triangle 409 and wavy lines or slogan	8.00
17/31	with Telephone slogan, 1931-32	4.00
17/32	with other slogans, 1946-63	2.00
17/33	with Holiday slogans, 1963-73	1.00

From 1969 (postal independence):

17/34	Machine postmark with boxed lines	1.00
17/35	with "Jersey stamps worth collecting" slogan 1978- or "Jersey Post First Class" 1989-	1.00
17/36	with other slogans (most were short lived), 1970-	2.00

17/37	with circular town die, "Paid" within wavy lines, red		2.00
17/38	with "Air Mail Postage Paid" slogan type mark, 1991-, red		4.00
17/39	Rubber packet handstamps		3.00
17/40	Circular rubber "Parcel Post" handstamps		6.00
17/41	Paid steel handstamp, or "Postage Paid" rubber on parcels, red		6.00
17/42	Continental style handstamp (used at Philatelic Bureau), 1984-		2.00
17/43	Handstamps inscribed "Philatelic Bureau" or "Philatelic Service"		1.00
17/44	"Stamp Invalid xxp to pay" surcharge mark (UK stamp used)		4.00

Other Instructional marks and "First Day of Issue" handstamps are not listed.

Other Jersey Offices

For code details see beginning of chapter. S introduced at all offices in 1996 – value 2.00

Augres (1894-1980)	C undated	£300
	C	15.00
	D	6.00
Beaumont (1853-)	A	£350
	C	6.00
	F	4.00
Beresford St. (1909-72)	C	70.00
	D	6.00
	mailbag seal	£300
	K	12.00
Carrefour Selous (1891-1978)	B	12.00
	F	6.00
Central Market (1972-2010)	G no arc	5.00
	K	6.00
Cheapside (1888-)	C	70.00
	D	6.00
Colomberie (1905-20)	C	£350
Conway Street (1903-10)	C	£350
David Place (1874-1914)	C	65.00
Don Street (2010-)	S	3.00
Faldouet (1893-1972)	B	6.00
	F	8.00
First Tower (1885-2002)	B	5.00
	D	5.00
	H	£600
Five Oaks (1889-)	C	8.00
	F	5.00
George Town (1882-)	C	£120
	D	5.00
Gorey (1830-)	A	£450
	Jersey Penny Post	£350
	C (20mm)	65.00
	C (22mm)	6.00
	F	4.00
	H	£550
	K	8.00
Gorey Village (1893-1940)	C	6.00
	D	£100
Grande Marche (2001-)	S	2.00
Grands Vaux (1960-1982)	D	8.00
Great Union Road (1903-24)	C	£500
Greve d'Azette (1927-74)	D	8.00
	mailbag seal	£300
Grouville (1853-2008)	A	£550
	B	8.00
	D	6.00
	F	6.00
Havre-des-Pas (1889-1962)	C	£100
	D	8.00
La Rocque (1892-1988)	C	8.00
	F	5.00
Le Squez (1974-)	D	6.00
Maufant (1983-)	D	6.00

Millbrook (1851-)	A	£375
	B	£225
	C	6.00
	F	6.00
Pier (1891 only)	C	none known
Pontac (1898-1904, 2001-)	E	£750
	S	3.00
Quennevais (1950-)	G	8.00
Roseville St (1962-)	D	8.00
	K	8.00
Rouge Bouillon (1889-2001)	C	£100
	D	6.00
St.Aubin (1830-)	Jersey Penny Post	£350
	A	£400
	C	8.00
	F	6.00
	H	£300
St.Brelade's Bay (1890-1977)	C	35.00
	E	£200
	G	6.00
St.Clements (1852-1860s)	A	none known
St.John's (1852-1932)	A	£550
	C	12.00
St.John's Church (1891-1996, then St. John)		
	B	10.00
	D	5.00
	F	8.00
St.Lawrence (1854-60)	A	£550
St.Martin's (1850-1983)	A	£400
	C	8.00
	F	5.00
St.Mary's (1853-2008)	A	£550
	C	12.00
	F	6.00
St.Owens/Ouen's (1852-)	B	5.00
	C	12.00
	C (code P)	£250
	F	5.00
St.Peter's (1851-)	A	£550
	C	8.00
	D	6.00
	F	8.00
	H	£500
Samares (1887-1999)	B	8.00
	F	6.00
Sion (1932-77)	D	25.00
	F	15.00
Stopford Road (1914-73)	C	£100
	mailbag seal	£400
	D	10.00
	G	8.00
Town Mills (1903-21 & 1973-1997)	C	£250
	D	5.00
Trinity (1852-)	A	£500
	E	£150
	F	6.00
Val Plaisant (1997-)	S	2.00

Islands

Guernsey
This page shows "Guernsey" postmarks used at St Peter Port.

GUERNSEY
17/45

(324)
17/52

27 AP 70
17/81

23 AP 70 Registered
17/85

From 1969 (postal independence), marks inscribed "Guernsey Post Office"

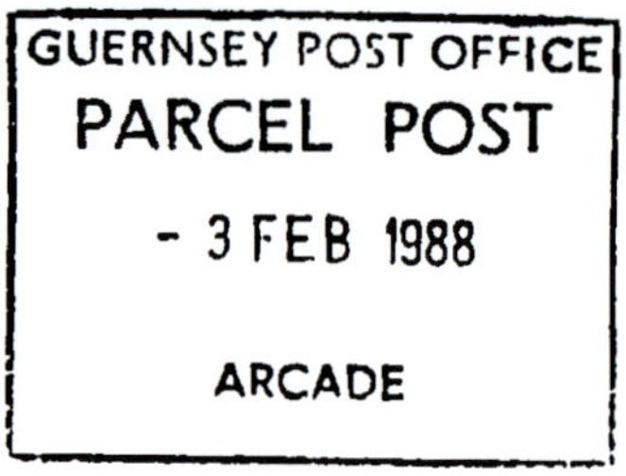

GUERNSEY POST OFFICE
PARCEL POST
-3 FEB 1988
ARCADE
17/90

23 MR 92 L'Islet
17/91

B 23 MR 92 ROHAIS
17/92

17/75	Universal machine postmark with two horizontal bars	1.00
17/76	with "Paid" in wavy lines, red	1.00
17/77	with "New stamps" slogans 1974-75 only in red on paid mail	12.00
17/78	with long running slogans, ie "Collect Guernsey Stamps", "First Class", "Stamps & Coins", "St Peter Port" (pictorial)	1.00
17/79	with other slogans, 1970-	2.00
17/80	with 7 continuous wavy lines, 1990s	1.00
17/81	New style handstamps in lower case lettering (type M)	1.00
17/82	Paid handstamps in lower case lettering, red	5.00
17/83	Rubber packet handstamps in lower case lettering, 1969-71	5.00
17/84	Rubber packet handstamp, upper case, 32mm/40mm diam, 1980s/90s	1.00
17/85	Oval registration marks in lower case lettering	8.00
17/86	Boxed parcel handstamps, "Head Office"/"Sorting Office" (type N)	6.00
17/87	Postal Museum handstamp 1971-82	2.00
17/88	"Stamp Invalid xxp to pay" surcharge mark (UK stamp used)	5.00
17/89	"Accepted after last collection at sender's request", 1980s	10.00

Other Instructional marks and "First Day of Issue" handstamps are not listed.

Other Guernsey Offices

Arcade (1987-2008)	G		5.00
	L*		5.00
	N	17/90	5.00
Bouet (1888-1902)	E		£550
Braye Road (1938-76)	D		50.00
	L		6.00
	N		10.00
Bridge (1988-)	L*		5.00
	N		5.00
Camp du Roi (1925-40)	F		£150
Catel (1849-1986)	A		£600
	B		12.00
	D		5.00
	L		25.00
	N		5.00
Cobo (1888-)	E		£100
	F		8.00

17/45	Concave Guernsey, 1794-1803	£450
17/46	Scroll types, 1802-30	£450
17/47	Ship letter types, 1802-49	£450
17/48	Handstruck numerals: 1, 2 etc (red or black), 1843-47	£350
17/49	Maltese cross, 1840-44	£125
17/50	Double arcs, 1830-58	25.00
17/51	Skeleton ("travelling") handstamps, 1843 & 1847	£600
17/52	Numeral 324 types, 1844-1890s	40.00
17/53	Duplex 324 types, 1858-88	30.00
17/54	Small single circles, 1858-1900s	6.00
17/55	Squared circles, 1887-1905	4.00
17/56	Oval Express mark, 1891	£150
17/57	Paquebot marks, 1903-28 (also 1960s, value less)	£500
17/58	Double circles with cross at base, 1905-27	4.00
17/59	Double circles with/without "St Peter Port" in brackets, 1929-69	3.00
17/60	Paid handstamps, with/without Gt Britain at foot, red, 1920-69	5.00
17/61	Rubber packet handstamps, 1932-69	4.00
17/62	Single circle, counter stamp with "St Peter Port" in brackets	3.00
17/63	Krag machine marks, 1923-31	3.00
17/64	similar but Paid die, red	12.00
17/65	Universal machine marks, 1931-	1.00
17/66	with triangle 324 with wavy lines or slogan	8.00
17/67	with Royal Wedding slogan, 1947	4.00
17/68	with 'British Holiday Abroad' slogan 1966-69	1.00
17/69	with other slogans, 1950-69	2.00
17/70	Parcel handstamps, barred circle type, 1886-89	40.00
17/71	similar but double circle types, 1889-1915	20.00
17/72	similar but rectangular label types, 1915- (with/without "St Peter Port" or "Smith St" in brackets)	8.00
17/73	Oval registered handstamps, 1938-	10.00
17/74	Note : covers/cards with 2d bisects Dec 1940 - Feb 1941	12.00

Islands

	H	£500
	L	5.00
	L*	5.00
	N	4.00
Collings Rd (1974-86)	H	£225
	L	5.00
	N	10.00
Forest (1899-)	E	£125
	F	10.00
	H	£650
	L	5.00
	N	5.00
La Vrangue (2009–)	S	4.00
Les Baissieres (1952-68)	D	£100
Les Gravees (1890-1986)	C	8.00
	D	35.00
	L	5.00
	N	5.00
L'Islet (1891-)	C	8.00
	E	£400
	F	12.00
	L **17/91**	5.00
	N	5.00
Market Place (1883-1987)	C	80.00
	D	10.00
	J	£200
	K	25.00
	L	5.00
	L*	5.00
	M	5.00
	N	5.00
	O	8.00
Mount Row (1895-96)	E	£650
Pleinmont Rd (1958-65)	D	65.00
Quay BO (1932-53)	D	50.00
	F	50.00
Rocquaine (1966-68)	D	60.00
Rohais (1985-)	L* **17/92**	5.00
	N	5.00
St.Andrew(s) (1887-1989)	B	£150
	C	6.00
	F	10.00
	H	£550
	L	5.00
	N	5.00
St.Johns (1935-86)	D	20.00
	L	5.00
	N	5.00
St.Martin(s) (1849-)	A	£550
	C	15.00
	D	15.00
	F	15.00
	L	5.00
	M	5.00
	N	5.00
St.Peters (1852-)	A	£500
	C	£100
then St.Peter-in-the-Wood (1886-)		
(St.Pierre-du-Bois 1994-)	B	10.00
	F	10.00
	L	5.00
	N	5.00
St.Sampson(s) (1849-1987)	A	£450
	B	6.00
	C	£120
	D	15.00
	F	10.00
	J	£150
	K	30.00
	L	5.00
	M	5.00
	N	5.00
St.Saviour(s) (1906-2000)	E	£100
	F	12.00

	L	5.00
	N	5.00
The Vale/Vale (1893-1988)	B	8.00
	F	6.00
	H	£500
	L	5.00
	N	5.00
Torteval (1911-2000)	F	20.00
	L	5.00
	N	5.00
Vale Road (1895-1988)	C	12.00
	D	12.00
	E	£400
	F	15.00
	L	5.00
	N	5.00
	O	12.00
Ville au Roi (1936-2000)	D	12.00
	L	5.00
	N	5.00

Alderney (1843-)

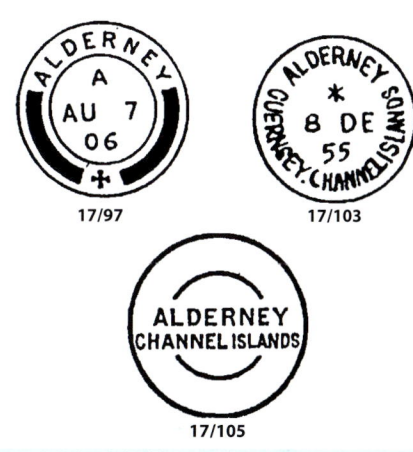

17/97   17/103

17/105

17/93	Undated double arc, 1848-55	£3000
17/94	Numeral 965, 1848-60s	£500
17/95	Dated double arc, 1851-60	£700
17/96	Alderney single circles, 1860-98	£250
17/97	Alderney double circle with cross at base, 1895-1900	50.00
	After 1900	15.00
17/98	Oval Post Office/R.E.Office/Alderney c1907 (probably used by Royal Engineers detachment)	£600
17/99	Alderney skeleton handstamp, 1922	£1250
17/100	Alderney/Ch. Is., double circle, thick arcs, 1930-66	8.00
17/101	Alderney/Guernsey Channel Islands, double circle no arcs, 1966-69	10.00
17/102	Alderney/Ch. Is., single circle, 1936-55	12.00
17/103	Alderney/Guernsey, Channel Islands, single circle, 1955-69	8.00
17/104	Rubber packet handstamps, various wordings, 1955-69	12.00
17/105	Parcel double circle, Alderney or Alderney/Ch'l Islands, 1911-12	£150
17/106	Parcel handstamp, rectangular label type, 1947-69	60.00
17/107	Post-1969 new style single circle (type L)	8.00
17/108	As above but larger (type M)	8.00
17/109	As above but upper case lettering (type L*), 1985-	5.00
17/110	As above but boxed parcel marks (type N)	8.00

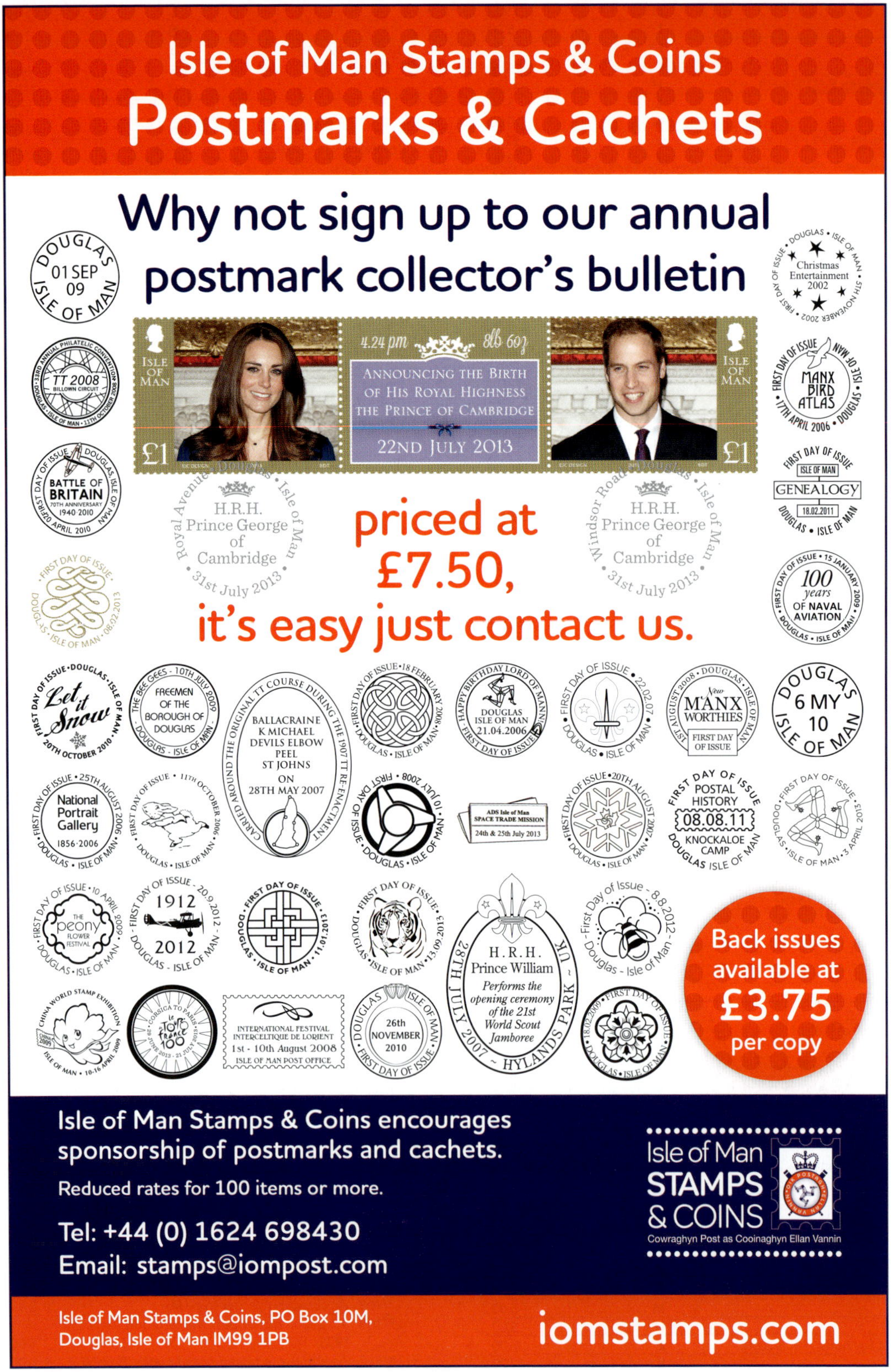

Isle of Man Stamps & Coins
Postmarks & Cachets

Why not sign up to our annual postmark collector's bulletin

priced at £7.50, it's easy just contact us.

Back issues available at £3.75 per copy

Isle of Man Stamps & Coins encourages sponsorship of postmarks and cachets.

Reduced rates for 100 items or more.

Tel: +44 (0) 1624 698430
Email: stamps@iompost.com

Isle of Man STAMPS & COINS
Cowraghyn Post as Cooinaghyn Ellan Vannin

Isle of Man Stamps & Coins, PO Box 10M, Douglas, Isle of Man IM99 1PB

iomstamps.com

Islands

17/111	Rubber packet handstamps, upper case lettering, 1970-	5.00
17/112	Guernsey Post Office/Alderney double circles, 1975-(with or without arcs)	4.00
17/113	Large rubber handstamp, 1990s	4.00

Note: For 1990s machine postmarks see chapter 10.

Sark (1857-)

17/116   17/119

17/126

17/114	Undated double arc, 1858	£5000
17/115	Sark 29mm rubber handstamp, 1888	£750
17/116	Sark single circle, code A, 1885-1940	8.00
17/117	As above but code B	£450
17/118	As above but code C	£850
17/119	Sark, Guernsey/Channel Islands, double circle thick arcs, 1926-66	6.00
17/120	Double circle, thin arcs, 1966-69	5.00
17/121	Sark.Guernsey/Channel Islands, single circle, 1960-69	10.00
17/122	Post-1969 new style single circle (type L)	5.00
17/123	As above but larger (type M)	6.00
17/124	As above but boxed parcel marks (type N)	6.00
17/125	Rubber packet handstamps, upper case lettering, 1970-	5.00
17/126	Guernsey Post Office/-Sark- double circle, 1979-	4.00
17/127	Guernsey Post Office/Sark single circle, 1996-	4.00
17/127A	SID Sark Guernsey/Post Office	5.00
17/127B	SID Sark 'Guernsey Post'	5.00

Herm (1925-)

17/128    17/130

17/128	Herm Guernsey/Channel Islands, d/c, thick arcs, 1925-38	£450
17/129	Meter postmark, 1948	£500
17/130	Post-1969 new style single circle (type L)	8.00
17/131	As above but larger (type M), 1971-	5.00
17/132	As above but boxed parcel mark (type N)	8.00
17/133	Rubber packet handstamps, upper case lettering, 1970-77	18.00
17/134	Guernsey Post Office/Herm single circle, 1996-	5.00
17/134B	SID Herm Guernsey/Post Office	5.00

Isle of Man

The first section shows postmarks used at Douglas, inscribed Isle of Man or Douglas or Regent Street.

ISLE OF MAN
17/135

P1
17/140

17/145

17/187

17/135	Isle of Man, straight line handstamps, 1767-1829	£225
17/136	Isle of Man, horseshoe, blue or black, 1796-1808	£300
17/137	Ship letters, 1802-43	£3500
17/138	Isle of Man, double arc types, undated, 1829-39	£175
17/139	Penny Post types, 1838	£1250
17/140	1840 Penny Post, P1 or 2 in red, 1840-49	£300
17/141	Double arc types, dated, Douglas or Isle-of-Man, 1839-57	25.00
17/142	Maltese Cross, 1840-44	£150
17/143	Skeleton ("travelling") handstamp, Douglas or Isle of Man, 1843	£1000
17/144	Numeral 407 types, 1844-79	50.00
17/145	Duplex 407 types, 1857-1900	25.00
17/146	Oval registered handstamps, 1880-	25.00
17/147	Squared circles, 1892-1901	8.00
17/148	Single circles with Isle of Man or I of Man at foot, 1858-	8.00
17/149	similar but modern counter handstamps, 1940-	4.00
17/150	Double circles with Isle of Man, I of Man or cross at foot, 1901-	2.00
17/151	Rubber packet handstamps, 1903-	5.00
17/152	Paid handstamps, red, 1905-	8.00
17/153	similar but skeleton, 1947	£250
17/154	Posted in Advance for Xmas, 1906-09 (beware of forgeries)	£500
17/155	Parcel handstamps, single circle with PP, 1883	75.00
17/156	barred circle, 1886-88	25.00
17/157	similar but double circle types, 1889-1909	25.00
17/158	similar but rectangular label types, 1895-	10.00
17/159	Krag machine postmarks, 1910-25	4.00
17/160	similar but Paid die, red, 1922-25	£100
17/161	similar but with "Feed the Guns" slogan, 1918	£150
17/162	Hey Dolphin machine postmarks, 1925-33	2.00

337

Islands

17/163	rectangular boxed Paid die without wavy lines, red, 1926-33		50.00
17/164	Universal machine postmarks, 1933-		1.00
17/165	with square Paid die, red		20.00
17/166	Universal, with triangle 407		15.00
17/167	with circular IOM or GB die, with Paid in wavy lines, red		15.00
17/168	Slogans : some examples - British Goods 1926		5.00
17/169	- Join The King's Roll 1926 .		75.00
17/170	- Post Early 1937-39		5.00
17/171	- V-bells, Royal Wedding, Fest of Britain		45.00
17/172	- Jubilee TT Races 1957		30.00
17/173	- Holiday/Retirement slogans 1963-		2.00

From 5 July 1973 (inscribed Douglas unless shown otherwise) :

17/174	Slogans : "First day" 1973 (Douglas, more for Ramsey)		6.00
17/175	"Manx Decimal coins" 1975-76		7.00
17/176	"Congratulations" (birth of Pr William/Harry 1982/84)		3.00
17/177	long-running slogans, 1973-		1.00
17/178	Paid machine postmarks, in red		1.00
17/179	New style double rim/single rim circular parcel marks, 1973-		6.00
17/180	ditto but rectangular, Douglas or "Regent St" inscription		6.00
17/181	Packet handstamps, rubber, 1980s-,		2.00
17/182	Paid handstamp, rubber, 1990s, in red		2.00
17/183	Philatelic Bureau handstamps		1.00
17/184	Postal Museum handstamps		2.00
17/185	Paquebot handstamp, double circle with thin arc, 1973 and 1977 only		£125
17/186	Surcharge mark "Stamps invalid" (various)(UK stamps used)		5.00
17/186A	SID with "Regent St" inscription (Head Office)		4.00

Other Instructional marks and "First Day of Issue" handstamps are not listed.

Douglas Town Offices

Anagh Coar (1990-)	D	4.00
	K	8.00
Athol St (1887-91)	D	£150
Brunswick Rd (1898-2006)	D	6.00
	K	8.00
	S	6.00
Bucks Rd (1885-1965)	C	25.00
	D	10.00
Circular Road (1996-2004)	S	2.00
Crosby Terrace (1941-)	D	10.00
	K	8.00
	S	2.00
Derby Road (1933-65)	D	20.00
Duke St (1858-80)	A	£500
	Undated s/c	£150
	D	75.00
Falcon Street (1886-97)	E	£100
Governors Hill (1998-)	E	2.00
	K	4.00
Grandstand (1972-99)	H	75.00
	special	5.00
Holiday Camp (1949-63)	D	80.00
IOM Holiday Centre (1964-66)	G	80.00
Kirk Onchan (1855-)	B	45.00
	C	10.00
	D	4.00
	G	4.00
	K	8.00
Market Place (1884-1912)	C	75.00
Prospect Hill (1895-1984)	C	20.00
	D	8.00
	G	8.00
	K	8.00
Pulrose (1930-)	D	6.00

	E	60.00
	K	8.00
	S	2.00
Royal Avenue (1911-)	C 17/187	6.00
	E	£100
	K	8.00
Saddlestone (1996-2013)	E	15.00
	S	5.00
St Ninians (1931-36)	D	50.00
	E	£200
Shore Road (1857-1915)	undated	£250
	C	80.00
	D	40.00
South Quay (1874-1913)	C (The Quay)	£100
	D	£100
Station (1889-1940)	C	75.00
	D	75.00
Strand Street (1880-87)	C	£150
The Crescent (1851-1989)	A	£450
	D	5.00
	K	8.00
The Esplanade (1928-33)	D	60.00
The Palace (1907-15)	C	60.00
Victoria Street (1884-1921)	C	50.00
	D	75.00
Villa Marina (1936-89)	D	5.00
	K	8.00
Willaston (1954-)	D	5.00
	K	8.00
Windsor Rd (1975-)	G no arcs	6.00
	G	6.00
	H	£100
	K	8.00
Woodburn Rd (1857)	A	£500
Woodbourne Rd (1965-75)	D	6.00
	K	8.00
York Road (1912-40)	D	60.00

17/188

17/189

17/190

17/191

338

Islands

17/192

17/193

17/194

Other IOM Offices

Abbeylands (1898-1941)	E		£125
	F		60.00
Baldrine (1897-2008)	E		£100
	F		40.00
	G		4.00
Baldwin (1884-1946)	E		£110
	F		60.00
Ballabeg (1862-2006)	C		20.00
	E		£125
	F		6.00
	G		4.00
	K		5.00
	S		6.00
Ballafesson (1907-73)	D		12.00
	E		70.00
Ballasalla (1848-)	A		£350
	single arc		£250
	C		15.00
	F		25.00
	G		4.00
	H		£100
	Univ + slogans		1.00
Ballaugh (1845-)	A **17/188**		£350
	B		80.00
	C		4.00
	F		10.00
	G		4.00
Castletown (1832-)	boxed **17/189**		£800
	unframed		£700
	A seriffed		£100
	A dated		75.00
	Numeral 037		80.00
	Duplex 037		15.00
	B		50.00
	C		4.00
	E		30.00
	F		5.00
	G		2.00
	Paid h/s		15.00
	Krag		6.00
	Krag Paid		30.00
	Krag (one line)		8.00
	Univ + slogans		1.00
	Pitney Bowes m/c		8.00
	J		40.00
	K		6.00
Colby (1858-1999)	undated **17/190**		£500
	C		15.00
	F		8.00
	G		4.00
	K		6.00
Crosby (1854-2010)	A		£350

	C		4.00
	E		£100
	F		8.00
	G		4.00
	S		5.00
Derbyhaven (1898-1974)	E		70.00
	F		10.00
Four Roads (1904-81)	D		4.00
	E		£125
Foxdale (1858-)	undated		£500
	C		25.00
	F		10.00
	G		4.00
	S		2.00
Glen Auldyn (1930-44)	D		70.00
	E		£125
Glenmaye (1858-2002)	undated (Glenmoy)		£500
	D		5.00
	E		£100
	S		2.00
Jurby (1856-1909 & 1983-)	A		£500
	G		4.00
Jurby RAFPO (1951-63)	D		80.00
	parcel **17/191**		80.00
Kirk Andreas (1855-)	A		£400
	B		50.00
	D		25.00
	G		4.00
	S		2.00
Kirk Bride (1858-1990 & 1998-)	small B		£180
	D		4.00
	E		£100
	F		4.00
Kirk Maughold (1858-2010)	undated		£500
	E		£125
	F		5.00
Kirk Michael (1845-?2010)	A		£300
	C		6.00
	F		5.00
	G		3.00
	H		£125
	S		2.00
Knockaloe Camp (1908)	H		£160
The Camp, Knockaloe (1915)	F		60.00
Laxey (1853-)	A		£350
	C		4.00
	F		5.00
	G		4.00
	H		£125
	K		5.00
Lower Foxdale (1896-1978)	D		8.00
	E		£150
North Ramsey (1887-1999)	D		10.00
	E		£150
	G		4.00
Old Laxey (1905-93)	D		5.00
	E		£125
	G		6.00
Peel (1832-)	boxed Peeltown		£500
	A Peeltown IOM		£225
	A Peeltown		£225
	A Peel		£150
	Numeral D51		£125
	Dupl D51 **17/192**		20.00
	B		40.00
	C		8.00
	D		3.00
	Sq circle		8.00
	E		30.00
	F		5.00
	G		2.00
	Paid h/s		20.00
	Krag		4.00
	Univ		1.00

Islands

	Pitney Bowes m/c	8.00	
	J	40.00	
	K	5.00	
	S	2.00	
Peel Camp (1908)	H	£250	
Port Erin (1858-)	undated	£400	
	B	12.00	
	C	4.00	
	E	30.00	
	F	4.00	
	G	2.00	
	H	£200	
	J	40.00	
	K	4.00	
	Univ + slogans	1.00	
Port Lewaigue (1913-16)	none known		
Port St Mary (1852-)	A	£225	
	B	40.00	
	C	4.00	
	E	4.00	
	F	8.00	
	G	2.00	
	H	£150	
	J	40.00	
	K	8.00	
	Pitney Bowes m/c	8.00	
	Univ + slogans	1.00	
Port Soderick (1886-1979)	C	18.00	
	E	80.00	
	F	8.00	
Quarter Bridge (1855-63)	A	£600	
Queen's Pier (1900-13)	none known		
Ramsey (1832-)	Boxed	£300	
	Unframed	£1200	
	A undated	£225	
	A **17/193**	75.00	
	dated single arc	80.00	
	Num 036 **17/194**	50.00	
	Duplex 036	25.00	
	C	4.00	
	Sq circle	40.00	
	E	30.00	
	F	3.00	
	G	1.00	
	Paid h/s	15.00	
	Triangle RAX h/s	60.00	
	Krag	5.00	
	Univ + slogans	1.00	
	+ triangle 036	25.00	
	+ GB die	25.00	
	J	35.00	
	K	5.00	
	circ parcel(1973)	8.00	
	S	2.00	
Regaby Gate (1898-1977)	E	£100	
	F	10.00	
St John's (1853-)	A	£300	
	C undated	£150	
	C	20.00	
	F	5.00	
	G	2.00	
	H	£100	
	S	2.00	
St Marks (1857-1978)	A	£450	
	D	10.00	
	E	80.00	
Sandygate (1909-68)	E	80.00	
	F	80.00	
Santon (1857-2002)	undated (St Anns)	£300	
	C (St Anns)	50.00	
	C (Santon)	30.00	
	E (St Anns)	80.00	
	E (Santon)	30.00	
	G	4.00	

	S	2.00
Southern PDO (1993-2005)	E	30.00
	G	5.00
	Univ + slogans	2.00
Sulby (1853-2006)	A	£350
	C	25.00
	D	5.00
	E	£125
	F	10.00
	S	2.00
The Green (1855-63)	A	£500
Union Mills (1853-)	A	£400
	B	50.00
	C	5.00
	E	£150
	K	5.00
	S	3.00

Isles of Scilly

Note: The main office is on the island of St Mary's (1804-) and "Scilly" postmarks were used there, but replaced by "St Mary's Isles of Scilly" postmarks from 1925.

17/201

17/201A

17/202

17/203

17/195	Straight line, Scilly, 1804-40	£500
17/196	Scilly double arc, 1840-	£225
17/197	Numeral 610, horizontal, 1844-75	£350
17/198	Numeral 610, vertical, 1878-93	£225
17/199	Scilly, single circle with Scilly across centre, 19mm, 1859-60s	£250
17/200	Scilly, single circles, 20-26mm, 1878-?1925	30.00
17/201	Scilly, double circle with cross at foot, 1895-1925	30.00

Bryher (1888-2010 & 2011-)	E	£100
	F	20.00
	G	4.00
	C (Isle of Scilly, 2011) **17/201A**	3.00
St Agnes (1880-)	C	50.00
	F	20.00
	G	4.00
St Martin's (1879-)	C	40.00
	F	8.00
	G	3.00

Islands

St Mary's (see above)	C		4.00
	E		25.00
	F	17/202	5.00
	G		2.00
	Krag		2.00
	Universal		1.00
	K		5.00
Tresco (1868-)	B		50.00
	F		15.00
	G	17/203	2.00
	S		3.00

Isle of Wight

17/204

17/205

17/206

17/207

Note: (1) Dates are years of offices' opening, not necessarily when postmarks recorded (2) Ship letters not included for IOW, see Chapter 14 for these.

Apse Heath (1937-)	C	5.00
Arreton (1843-)	A	£100
	C	8.00
	E	40.00
	G	2.00
Bembridge (1834-)	A	75.00
	B	25.00
	C	2.00
	F	6.00
	G	3.00
	H	60.00
	K	5.00
	Krag	3.00
Blackwater (1843-1995)	A	80.00
	E	8.00
	G	2.00
	H	75.00
Brading (1834-2012 then *Outreach)	A	60.00
	B	8.00
	numeral C54	75.00
	duplex C54	10.00
	C	3.00
	F	6.00
	K	5.00
Brighstone (1843-)	C	6.00
	F (circ spacers)	5.00
	H	40.00
Brook (1886–)	C	5.00
	E	80.00
	G	4.00
Calbourne (1843-2008)	A	80.00
	C	10.00
	E	40.00
	G	5.00

Chale (1849-1997)	A	90.00
	B	30.00
	F	4.00
Chale Green (1912-2009)	E	25.00
	F	15.00
	G	4.00
Chillerton (1853-1999)	A	£100
	E	35.00
	F	5.00
	G	2.00
Cowes (1769-)	mileage	25.00
	A undated	50.00
	A dated	15.00
	numeral 225	12.00
	duplex 225	10.00
	B	4.00
	C	2.00
	E	2.00
	F	4.00
	G	2.00
	H	75.00
	J	15.00
	K	5.00
	registered oval	10.00
	Paid h/s	2.00
	Krag	4.00
	Univ + slogans	1.00
	Univ Paid	2.00
Arctic Road (1894-1923)	B	15.00
	E	£100
Medina (1918-2008)	B	12.00
	C	3.00
	K	5.00
Medina Road (1876-1918)	B	15.00
Pallance Road (1921-)	C	5.00
	E	£100
Tennyson Road (1923-2003)	B	5.00
Victoria Road (1886-1983)	B	8.00
	C	5.00
	K	8.00
Cranmore (1952-2004)	G	5.00
East Cowes (1843-)	A	£100
	B	8.00
	C	2.00
	E	£100
	F	5.00
	G	2.00
	J	15.00
	K	5.00
Clarence Road (1898-1917)	E	40.00
Meadow Road (1957-2008)	C	5.00
Freshwater (1843-93 & 1933-)	A	60.00
	B	5.00
	C	2.00
	F	3.00
	G	2.00
	K	5.00
	Paid h/s	4.00
	Registered oval	4.00
	Krag	1.00
	Krag Paid	8.00
	Univ + slogans	1.00
	Univ Paid	2.00
Church (1902-34 & 1950-2008)	C	4.00
	E	30.00
School Green (1848-93)	A	75.00
	B	15.00
	duplex H06	80.00
Station Road (1934-50)	C	8.00
Freshwater Bay (1893-2013)	C	8.00
	F	4.00
	G	4.00
	H	80.00
Freshwater Gate (1843-60)	A	none known

341

Islands

	B	20.00		F	8.00
Freshwater Station (1893-1933)	C	3.00		G (no arcs)	3.00
	duplex H06	8.00	Osborne (1904-22)	C	8.00
	F	2.00	(see also chap 22)	F	6.00
	H	30.00	Porchfield (1887-2005)	E	75.00
Godshill (1838-)	A	75.00		F	8.00
	numeral C52	30.00		G	4.00
	duplex C52	15.00	Rookley (1853-)	C	22.00
	B	25.00		E	75.00
	F	6.00		F	4.00
	G	2.00	Ryde (1786-)	str line	60.00
Gurnard (1866-2005)	C	8.00		A double	50.00
	F	4.00		A single	20.00
Haven Street (1853-2008)	B	18.00		mileage	20.00
	C	4.00		penny post	£180
Horsebridge Hill (1859-61)	none known			too late	70.00
Nettlestone (1893-2007)	B	8.00		missent	£200
	C	5.00		numeral 666	10.00
	E	80.00		dupl 666 **17/206**	5.00
Newbridge (1899-)	E	75.00		sq circle	3.00
	F	5.00		B	4.00
	G	3.00		C	2.00
Newchurch (1852-)	C	5.00		E	15.00
	E	60.00		F	3.00
	F	8.00		G	2.00
Newport (1673-)(includes "Isle of Wight" to 1762				H 'traveller'	£200
and 1977-c2000)	str line	75.00		J	15.00
	mileage	15.00		K	5.00
	A serif **17/204**	30.00		Krag	2.00
	A	10.00		Univ + slogans	1.00
	penny post	£125		Univ Paid	2.00
	H 'traveller'	£125	Binstead (1853-)	A	80.00
	numeral 560	10.00		B	15.00
	duplex 560	5.00		C	2.00
	C	2.00		F	2.00
	E	15.00		H	80.00
	F	4.00	Elmfield (1884-)	C	4.00
	G	2.00		G	4.00
	H skeleton	50.00		K	5.00
	J	15.00	Esplanade (1871-1900)	C	20.00
	K	5.00	George St (1900-80)	B	8.00
	Krag	2.00		C	5.00
	Krag Paid	5.00	Haylands (1895-2003)	C	3.00
	Paid handstamp	2.00		E	75.00
	Univ + slogans	1.00	High St (1880-)	B	15.00
	Univ '6' error	8.00		C	2.00
	Univ square paid	5.00		K	5.00
	Univ circ Paid	1.00	Oakfield (1853-2004)	A	£100
Carisbrooke (1843-)	A	75.00		B	10.00
	B	8.00		C	3.00
	C	4.00	Strand (1881-2008)	C	4.00
	E	30.00		F	30.00
	K	5.00		K	5.00
Castle Road (1903-85)	C	5.00	Upper West St (1871-80)	B	15.00
Coppins Bridge (1885-1982)	C	5.00	West St (1880-2008)	C	3.00
Hunny Hill (1885-2008)	B	15.00		G	3.00
	C	4.00		K	5.00
Pan (1982-)	C	3.00	St Helens (1834-)	C	2.00
Parkhurst (1903-2003)	C	3.00		F	5.00
Shide (1892-2002)	C	3.00		G	5.00
	E	60.00	St Lawrence (1889-)	B	15.00
	G	6.00		E	75.00
Upper St James St (1877-1985)	C	5.00		F	4.00
	K	5.00	Sandown (1835-)	A	50.00
Whitepit Lane (1936-81)	C	5.00		numeral B88	15.00
Ningwood (1920-52)	none known	–		B	5.00
Niton (1838-)	A dated	70.00		sq circle	2.00
	A single	75.00		C	2.00
	C **17/205**	4.00		E	15.00
	F	8.00		F	3.00
Niton Undercliff (1912-1997)	B	6.00		G	2.00
	G	3.00		J	15.00
Norton (1844-1919)	E	75.00		K	5.00
Norton Green (1897-2002)	C	10.00		Krag	3.00

Islands

Location	Type	Price
	Univ + slogans	1.00
Avenue Road (1894-2004)	B	8.00
	C	4.00
Lake (1843-)	A	£100
	C	3.00
	E	75.00
	K	5.00
Station Avenue (1909-82)	C	8.00
	G	3.00
	K	5.00
Seaview (1834-)	A	75.00
	B	6.00
	C	3.00
	F	4.00
	G	2.00
	H	40.00
	K	5.00
Shalfleet (1843-1903 & 1947- 2011 then *Outreach)	B	12.00
	G	3.00
Shanklin (1843-)	A undated	50.00
	A dated	25.00
	numeral B89	50.00
	sq circle	2.00
	B	4.00
	C	2.00
	E	2.00
	F	3.00
	G	2.00
	H (RSO)	50.00
	J	15.00
	K	5.00
	Registered oval	5.00
	Univ + slogans	1.00
Atherley Rd (1908-70)	C	8.00
Esplanade (1892-1904)	B	15.00
Hope Road (1889-1908)	B	15.00
Regent St (1934-78)	C	5.00
Wilton Pk Rd (1940-2008)	C	3.00
Shorwell (1843-)	B	10.00
	E	40.00
	F	8.00
	G	2.00
	H	50.00
Totland Bay (1880-2008 then *Outreach)	B	7.00
	C	2.00
	F	5.00
	K	5.00
Ventnor (1837-)	A undated	50.00
	A dated	25.00
	B	5.00
	numeral 971	10.00
	duplex 971	4.00
	C	2.00
	E	20.00
	F 17/207	2.00
	G	2.00
	J	15.00
	K	5.00
	Registered oval	5.00
	Paid h/s	5.00
	Krag	3.00
	Univ + slogans	1.00
	Univ Paid die	1.00
Bonchurch (1843-2009)	A	75.00
	B	10.00
	C	3.00
Lowther (1884-2007)	C	5.00
	E	50.00
Madeira Rd (1880-1980)	B	20.00
	C	8.00
Wellow (1899-)	E	50.00
	F	8.00

Location	Type	Price
	G	4.00
Whippingham (1843-)	A (or St)	£100
	C	4.00
	E	40.00
Whitwell (1851-2005 then *Outreach)		
	C	8.00
	E	75.00
	F	2.00
Wootton Bridge (1837-)	Penny post	£200
	B	8.00
	numeral C55	75.00
	C	2.00
(also with circ spacers)	F	5.00
	H	60.00
	K	5.00
Wroxall (1853-)	B	10.00
	sq circle	5.00
	C	2.00
	F	3.00
	J	25.00
Yarmouth (1800-)	mileage str	35.00
	mileage circ	15.00
	A dated	20.00
	numeral 486	30.00
	duplex 486	3.00
	C	2.00
	F	3.00
	G	2.00
	H	50.00
	K	5.00

OTHER ENGLISH ISLANDS

In this section are listed the relevant offices with dates of opening/closing but without details of the postmarks used. The start dates shown are "earliest known listed" dates, for which we thank Ken Smith. The list is restricted to genuine islands, thus Isle of Dogs, Grain and Thanet are excluded.

Foulness (Essex) (1857-2007)
Holy Island (Northumberland)(1847-)
Lundy (1887-1927, local stamps and postal service from 1929)
Whale Island (RN)(Portsmouth) (1907-85)

17/208

17/209

17/210

17/211

Barrow in Furness
Barrow Island (1885-1985) (part of Barrow Docks)
Ramsden Dock Road (1905-) (also on Barrow Island)
Piel (1895-1990) (post office not on Piel island, but on nearby Roa island, and deliveries to Piel were made from this PO)

Walney Island
Douglas Street (1924-2008, see note)
Mikasa Street (1924-, see note)

Islands

Mill Lane (1981-)
Vickerstown (1902-24)
Vickerstown South (1904-24)
Note: The last two offices were replaced in 1924 by Douglas St and Mikasa St, possibly in same locations

Canvey Island (Essex) (1896-)
Canvey on Sea (1907-)
Canvey Village (1931-)
Dovervelt Road (2000-)
Furtherwick (1941-60)
Maurice Road (1951-2003)
Winter Gardens (1955-72, 1978-)

Hayling Island (Hants) (1838-)
Eastoke (1896-)
Gable Head (1893-1946/55)
Manor Road (1901-1997)
Sandy Point (1955-85)

Sea Front (1955-78)
Stoke (1894-)
West Town (1891-2007)

Mersea Island (Essex)
East Mersea (1851-2009 then *Outreach 2010–)
West Mersea (1851-)

Sheppey (Kent)
Eastchurch (1845-)
East Minster (1973-)
Halfway Houses (1904-)
Leysdown-on-Sea (1926-)
Minster-on-Sea (1850-)
Queenborough (1726-)
Sheerness (1799-)
   Blue Town (1876-1984)
   High St E (1921-2003)
   Marine Town (1878-1921)
   Mile Town (1845-76)
   Queensway (1957-2003)
   Warden Point (1931-1989)
   West Minster (1905-76)

WALES

Barry Island (1898-)
Caldy (1896-), later Caldey Island

Anglesey
In bringing the Anglesey listing up to the same standard of detail as that of Channel Islands and Isle of Man (earlier in the chapter) we are delighted to have had the assistance of John Cowell, of the Welsh Philatelic Society, in providing much of the detailed data. Many of the dates were provided by Ken Smith, as with English islands shown on the previous page. Spellings can vary at one location over the years eg "Penny post" at Llan(n)erchymedd pictured below.

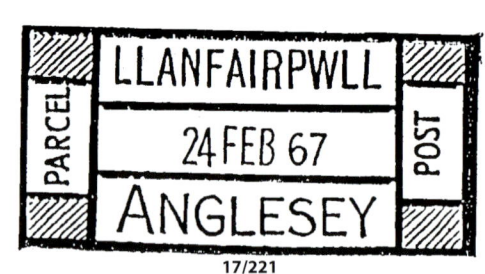

Codes used in Anglesey listing
A   Undated double arc
B   Single circle without Island name
C   Single circle with Island name (or Gwynedd from 1976)
E   Rubber handstamps
F   Double circle with thick arcs
G   Double circle with thin arcs
H   Skeleton handstamps
K   Label type parcel handstamp

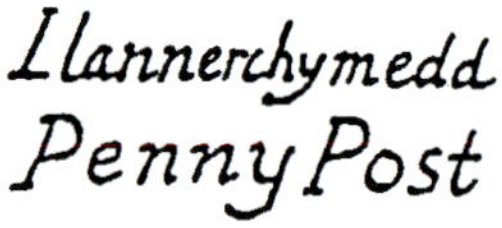

Islands

17/223 — VALLEY R.A.F. STATION HOLYHEAD / 13 MY 65 / ANGLESEY

17/224 — WYLFA CEMAES BAY / 25 FE 67 / ANGLESEY

Aberffraw (1843-)	A		£100
	B		5.00
	C		4.00
	F		2.00
Amlwch (1826-)	Penny post		70.00
	Boxed No.5		20.00
	H/struck 1		45.00
	Numeral (B49)		£100
	Duplex (B49)		5.00
	B		3.00
	C		2.00
	E		1.00
	F		2.00
	G		2.00
	H		12.00
	Krag		1.00
	Univ		1.00
	K		5.00
	registered		5.00
Amlwch Port (1891-1985)	B		8.00
	C		4.00
Beaumaris (1705-)	str line		18.00
	st line mileage		18.00
	circ undated		12.00
	circ dated		4.00
	h/struck 1		£250
	h/struck 2		£175
	Paid 1		£200
	Traveller		80.00
	Missent		£180
	Ship Lre		£400
	Ship letter		£300
	India lett		£400
	A		25.00
	A dated		4.00
	Num'l (58) vert		50.00
	Num'l (58) horiz		6.00
	Duplex (58)		4.00
	B		2.00
	C		2.00
	E		1.00
	F		1.00
	G		1.00
	H		12.00
	Krag		1.00
	Univ		1.00
	K		5.00
	Registered		8.00
Benllech (1975-)	C		3.00
Bethel (1850-1990 &1972-)	A		75.00
	B		8.00
	C		2.00
Bodedern (1833-)	Penny post		45.00
	Boxed No.3		40.00
	B		6.00
	C		3.00
	F		5.00
Bodffordd (1868-)	B		8.00
	C		5.00
	F		4.00
Bodorgan (1887-1972)	Numeral (Horizontal) J60		£100
	Duplex (J60)		12.00
	B		4.00
	C		2.00
	F		2.00
	K		5.00
Bryngwran (1852-2006)	A		£100
	B		6.00
	C		3.00
	F		3.00
Brynllanfair (1845-55) (renamed Llanfairpwll)	A		£100
Brynsiencyn (1850-)	A		£125
	B		4.00
	C		2.00
	G no arcs		2.00
Brynteg (1884-1998)	E		15.00
	F		5.00
	G		5.00
Bull Bay (1896-1993)	B		6.00
	C		2.00
	E		15.00
	F		2.00
Caergeiliog (1895-2008)	C		4.00
	F		4.00
Capel Gwyn (1930-77)	C		5.00
	F		4.00
Carmel (1912-76)	C		5.00
	F		4.00
Carreglefn (1877-2001 then *Outreach 2011-)	B		8.00
	C		4.00
	E		15.00
Cemaes (1843-1912) (renamed Cemaes Bay)	A		60.00
	B		2.00
Cemaes Bay (1912-)	C		2.00
	F		2.00
Cerrigceinwen (1864-1978)	B		8.00
	C		5.00
	G no arcs		3.00
Dulas (1873-?1977)	B		8.00
	C		5.00
	F		4.00
Dwyran (1857-2008)	A		75.00
	B		5.00
	C		3.00
	F		2.00
Four Mile Bridge (1914-2008)	B		8.00
	C		5.00
	E		30.00
	F		3.00
Gaerwen (1846-)	A		75.00
	Numeral (F26)		£100
	B		6.00
	C		3.00
	F		2.00
	K		5.00
Glyn Garth (1887-1946)	B		4.00
	F		4.00
Gwalchmai (1852-)	A		60.00
	B		5.00
	C		3.00
	F		2.00
Gwyndy (1785-1867)	266 Gwyndu		£150
	H'shoe (Gwyndee)		80.00
	Gwindee 266		50.00
	Boxed No.2		25.00
Holyhead (1780-)	A		75.00
	Str line		65.00
	Mileage		35.00
	Circ mileage		15.00
	Erased		20.00
	Horseshoe		75.00
	Circ dated		4.00
	H/struck 2		£100

345

Islands

	Ship Lre	£400	
	Ship letter	£200	
	India lett	£250	
	Numeral (374)	5.00	
	Duplex (374)	4.00	
	B	2.00	
	C	2.00	
	E	1.00	
	F	1.00	
	G	1.00	
	H	12.00	
	Krag	3.00	
	Univ	1.00	
	K	5.00	
	registered	5.00	
Alderley Terrace (1938-77)	C	5.00	
Church Terrace (1892-2009)	B	9.00	
	C	5.00	
Kingsland (1924-66)	C	5.00	
Llaingoch (1852-2008)	A	75.00	
	B	8.00	
	C	5.00	
	F	3.00	
London Road (1902-1973)	B	10.00	
	C	5.00	
Morawelon (1973-)	C	4.00	
Porthyfelin (1928-)	F	4.00	
Llanbedrgoch (1886-2008)	B	6.00	
	C	3.00	
	E	15.00	
	F	4.00	
Llanddaniel (1864-)	B	8.00	
	C	4.00	
	E	15.00	
Llanddeusant (1860-1999)	B	6.00	
	C	3.00	
	F	3.00	
Llanddona (1874-2000)	B	8.00	
	C	5.00	
	E	15.00	
	F	4.00	
Llandegfan (1859-2008)	B	8.00	
	C	5.00	
	E	15.00	
	H	15.00	
Llandyfrydog (1949-93) (previously Tynypwll)	C	4.00	
Llanedwen (1897-1971)	B	8.00	
	C	5.00	
	E	15.00	
Llanerchymedd (1828-)	Penny post	45.00	
	Boxed No.4	30.00	
	Numeral (F27)	60.00	
	Duplex (F27)	4.00	
	B	5.00	
	C	3.00	
	F	2.00	
	K	5.00	
Llanfachraeth (1859-)	A	60.00	
	B	6.00	
	C	3.00	
	F	3.00	
	H	25.00	
Llanfaelog (1868-)	Numeral (H89)	£100	
	B	8.00	
	C	4.00	
Llanfaethlu (1849-)	A	60.00	
	B	8.00	
	C	3.00	
Llanfairpwllgwyngyll (1855-) (previously Brynllanfair) (various abbreviations eg Llanfair PG, for full name see chapter 24)			
	A	£100	
	Numeral (F25)	60.00	
	Duplex (F25)	6.00	

	B	6.00	
	C	3.00	
	F	3.00	
	K	5.00	
Llanfairynghoronwy (1859-1999) (later Llanfairynghornwy)			
	A	£100	
	B	8.00	
	C	5.00	
	E	15.00	
	F	4.00	
Llanfechell (1858-2012)	A	£100	
	B	8.00	
	C	4.00	
	F	4.00	
	H	15.00	
Llanfihangel (1857-67)	A	75.00	
Llanfwrog (1935-1989)	F	4.00	
Llangaffo (1881-)	B	8.00	
	C	5.00	
	F	4.00	
Llangefni (1827-)	Penny post	40.00	
	Boxed No.1	25.00	
	Numeral (B50)	30.00	
	Duplex (B50)	4.00	
	B	4.00	
	C	2.00	
	E	1.00	
	F	2.00	
	G	2.00	
	H	15.00	
	Univ	1.00	
	K	5.00	
	registered	5.00	
Llangoed (1853-)	A	75.00	
	B	5.00	
	C	3.00	
	F	3.00	
Llangristiolus (1978-1989)	C	3.00	
Llangwyllog (1890-1990)	Numeral (J53)	£100	
	B	8.00	
	C	5.00	
	F	4.00	
Llanrhyddlad (1904-2003) (later Llanrhuddlad)			
	B	8.00	
	C	5.00	
	E	15.00	
Llansadwrn (1887-1987)	B	8.00	
	C	5.00	
	F	4.00	
Maenaddwyn (1933-1998)	C	4.00	
Maldwyn (1946–)	C	4.00	
Malltraeth (1912-2008)	B	8.00	
	C	4.00	
	E	15.00	
Marianglas (1896-2001)	E	8.00	
	F	3.00	
Menai Bridge (1841-)	A	75.00	
	Numeral (B51)	20.00	
	Duplex (B51)	4.00	
	B	3.00	
	C	2.00	
	E	1.00	
	F	2.00	
	G	2.00	
	Univ (29.4.68 only)	2.00	
	K	5.00	
	registered	5.00	
Moelfre (1851-2008)	A	90.00	
	B	5.00	
	C	3.00	
	F	3.00	
Mynydd Mechell (1933-)	C	3.00	
Newborough (1850-)	A	75.00	
	B	7.00	

346

Islands

		C	3.00
		F	3.00
Paradwys (1909-75)		B	8.00
		C	5.00
Pengorphwysfa (1897- later Pengorffwysfa -1991)			
		B	8.00
		C	5.00
Penmon (1931-76)		F	4.00
Penmynydd (1863-2003)		B	8.00
		C	5.00
		E	50.00
Pentraeth (1845-)		A	50.00
		B	3.00
		C	2.00
		E	2.00
		F	3.00
		G	2.00
		K	4.00
Penysarn (1855-)		A	75.00
		B	8.00
		C	3.00
Rhoscolyn (1888-1984)		B	6.00
		C	3.00
Rhosgoch (1887-1970)		Numeral (H91)	£150
		B	6.00
		C	4.00
		F	4.00
Rhosneigr (1895-)		B	4.00
		C	2.00
		F	2.00
		K	5.00
Rhostrehwfa (1992-2001)		C	6.00
Rhosybol (1852-)		A	75.00
		Numeral (F28)	40.00
		B	6.00
		C	4.00
		E	15.00
		F	4.00
Rhydwen (later Rhydwyn) (1867-1998)			
		B	6.00
		C	3.00
		F	3.00
Talwrn (1886-2009)		B	8.00
		C	5.00
		E	50.00
Trearddur Bay (1898-)		B	3.00
		C	2.00
		E	50.00
		F	2.00
		H	60.00
Tregele (1933-77)		F	4.00
Trevor (later Trefor) (1883-1981)		B	8.00
		C	5.00
Ty Croes (1888-2000)		Numeral (J21)	£175
		B	6.00
		C	3.00
		F	2.00
		K	5.00
Tynlon (1895-2000)		B	8.00
		C	5.00
		E	50.00
		F	4.00
Tynygongl (1855-1975)		A	90.00
		B	3.00
		C	2.00
		F	2.00
		H	50.00
		K	5.00
(then renamed Benllech)			
Tynypwll (1897-1946)		E	75.00
(then Llandyfrydog)			
Tynyrefail (1857-67)		none known	
Valley or The Valley (1857-)		A	£100
		Numeral (D60)	£150

		Duplex (D60)	4.00
		B	6.00
		C	3.00
		F	2.00
		K	5.00
Valley RAFPO/RAF Station (1943-2004)			
		C	12.00
		G no arcs	8.00
		K	20.00
Wylfa (1964-73)(power station construction)			
		C	25.00

NORTHERN IRELAND

Rathlin Island (1882-)
Note: Greenisland, Carrickfergus is not an island, and is not to be confused with the uninhabited Green Island near Greencastle.

SCOTLAND

Pricing Guide

Postmarks from these island post offices vary in value considerably, some of them being extremely scarce. In the 20th century many post offices in the Scottish islands have handstamped mail (also with machines in some major towns). Remember theses are "from" prices, thus postmarks of smaller locations are worth substantially more.

EASDALE PENNY POST
17/225

MORNISH
17/226

17/231 (EASDALE MY 25 1856)

17/233 (ROTHESAY 3 30PM JY 18 05)

17/234 (BLACK MILL BAY 8 AU 14 696)

17/236 (KERRYCROY 10 APR.06 ROTHESAY)

17/237 (FOULA 30 NO 72 SHETLAND)

347

Islands

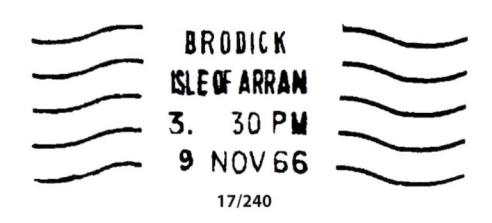

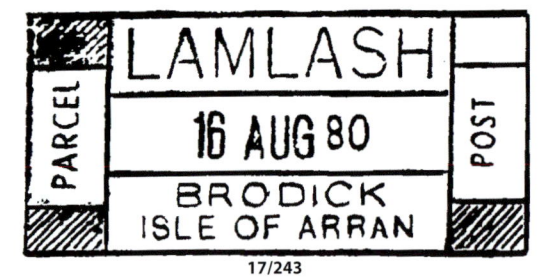

```
BRODICK
ISLE OF ARRAN
3. 30 PM
9 NOV 66
```
17/240

```
PARCEL
LAMLASH
16 AUG 80
BRODICK
ISLE OF ARRAN
POST
```
17/243

```
REGISTERED
7 AU 80
BRODICK, ISLE OF ARRAN
```
17/244

17/225	Penny Post, boxed/ unboxed	75.00
17/226	Scots local stamps, various	£100
17/227	Ship letters – Kirkwall, Lerwick, Tobermory	£300
17/228	Handstruck '1' eg Tobermory	50.00
17/229	Handstruck '2' eg Kirkwall, Lerwick	75.00
17/230	Duplex handstamps	15.00
17/231	Circular dated, double arcs	30.00
17/232	Baltasound (Isle of Unst) mailbag seal used as handstamp	£100
17/233	Single circle, various sizes, value for 1890-1920 specimens	10.00
17/234	Double circle, incl Scottish types, value for 1900-1930 specimens	10.00
17/235	Skeleton handstamps	50.00
17/236	Rubber handstamps, value for 1900-1930 specimens	40.00
17/237	Double circle, modern, on ordinary mail	3.00
17/238	As above, on registered cover	8.00
17/239	Krag machine, pre 1950 (see also Chapter 10)	2.00
17/240	As above, but post 1950	1.00
17/241	Universal machine, pre 1950 (see also Chapter 10)	1.00
17/242	As above, but post 1950	1.00
17/243	Parcels handstamps	10.00
17/244	Registered oval handstamps	5.00
17/245	SID handstamps	1.00

The list that follows shows Scottish island post offices, along with dates, but not details of their postmarks.

SCOTLAND
(some "individual" islands then approx south to north)
Canna (1878-)
Coll (1805-)
Colonsay (1873-)
Eigg (1874-)
Gigha (1859-)
Kerrera (1879-1969)
Rum/Rhum (1891-)
St Kilda (1900-30, but used 1957-62 on forces mail, latterly used at Nunton)
Stroma (1898-1958)

Arran
Blackwaterfoot (1883-)
Brodick (1806- init Arran)
Corrie (1853-2003)
Dippen/Dippin (1946-69)
Kildonan (1880-1946 then Dippen)
Kildonan Shore (1934-2010)
Kilmorie/Kilmory (1849-)
Kings Cross (1880-1978)
Lamlash (1827-)
Lochranza (1854-2004 then Outreach* 2005-)
Machrie (1901-77)
Pirnmill (1872-)
Shannochie (1898-1977)
Shiskine (1854-1983)
Sliddery (1898-1981)
Whiting Bay (1860-)

Islay
Ballygrant (1854-2010 then *Outreach)
Bonahaven (1895-1987)
Bowmore (1774-1859 renamed Bridgend)
Bowmore Village (1847-59 renamed Bowmore)
Bridgend (1859-)
Bruichladdich (1883-)
Gruinart (1862-1977)
Kildalton (1895-1975)
Portaskaig (1767-)
Port Charlotte (1847-)
Port Ellen (1854-)
Portnahaven (1867-)

Jura
Craighouse (1876-)
Inverlussa (1947-84)
Jura (1812-68 then Lagg)
Lagg (1868-1963)

Cumbrae
Millport (1835-)

Bute
Kerrycroy (1900-17)
Kilchattan Bay (1881-)
Kingarth (1848-1946)
Rothesay (1767-)
Ardbeg Road (1889-)
Ascog (1845-1968)
Barone Road (1903-14)
Columshill St (1914-72)
Craigmore Pier (1884-1980)
Gallowgate (1896-2008)
High St (1903-19, 1942-75)
Port Bannatyne (1834-)
Straad (1907-82)

Mull
Aros (at Salen) (1803-)
Auchnacraig (1792-1965 then Lochdon)
Bellochroy (1830-40)
Bridge of Lussa (1864-77 then Lochbuie)
Bunessan (1804-)
Calgary (1888-1967)
Carsaig (1891-1961)
Craignuire/Craignure (1881-)
Croggan (1900-65)
Dervaig (1880-)
Fionnphort (1873-) (various spellings)
Gribun (1909-71)
Gruline (1886-1965)
Iona (Isle of)(1851-)
Lochbuy/Lochbuie (1877-2008)
Lochdon (1965-2012)
Mornish/Morinish (1830s-80 then Dervaig)
Pennyghael (1869-)
Tiroran (1893-2000)
Tobermory (1791-)
Torloisk (1898-1974)
Ulva (island)(1839-72)
Ulva Ferry (1884-)

Lismore
Achnacroish (1881-92 then Lismore)
Bachuil (1898-1940)
Lismore (1892-)
Point (1945-55)

Seil
Balvicar (1897-)
Clachan Seil (1897-1989)
Easdale (1825-2005)
North Easdale (1901-59) (Easdale island)

Luing
Blackmill Bay (1896-1929)
Cullipool (1896-)
Toberonochy (1896-1983)

Tiree
Balemartine (1894-)
Cornaig (1896-)
Crossapol, see chapter 16
Middleton (1934-2000)
Ruaig (1898-2000)
Scarinish (1898-)
Tyree/Tiree (1804-98 then Scarinish)

Skye
Ardvasar (1863-)
Armadale (1829-39)
Arnisort (1857-2000)
Bernisdale (1892-2006)
Borreraig (1884-2000)
Bracadale (1835-44)
Breakish (1879-2008)
Broadford (1820-)
Camustinivaig (1899-1989)
Carbost (1842-)
Culnacnock (1887-1998)
Dunan (1881-1986)

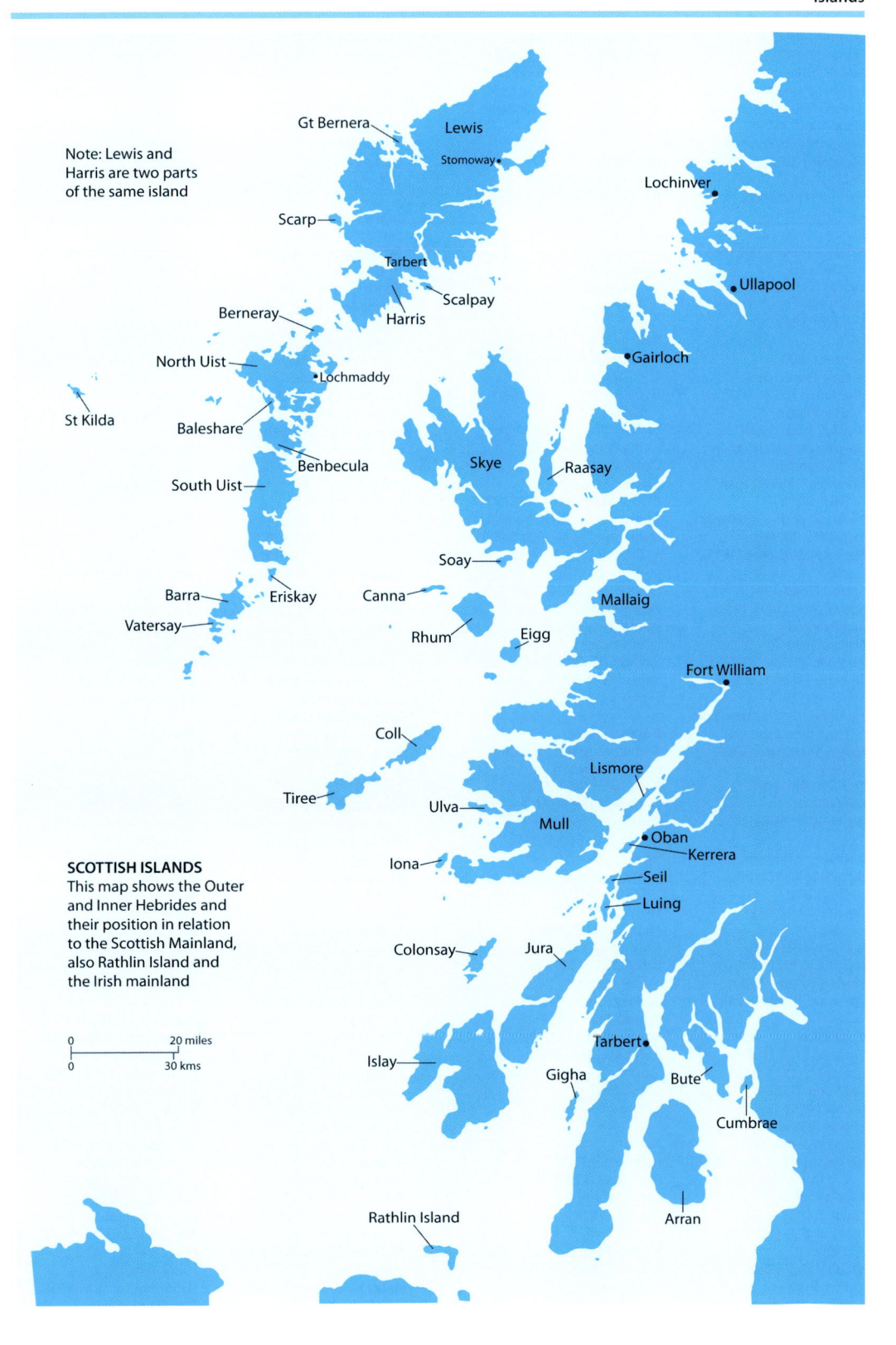

Islands

SCOTTISH ISLANDS
This map shows the Outer and Inner Hebrides and their position in relation to the Scottish Mainland, also Rathlin Island and the Irish mainland

Note: Lewis and Harris are two parts of the same island

349

Islands

Duntulm (1868-1985)
Dunvegan (1741-)
Earlish (1898-2008)
Edinbane (1857, 1877-2008 then *Outreach 2009-)
Elgol (1880-2006)
Glenbrittle (1937-1994)
Glendale (1855-)
Hallin (1935-)
Harlosh (1868-2006)
Isle Ornsay (1829-)
Kilmuir (1830-1994)
Kyleakin (1843–2009 then *Outreach)
Linicro (1955-2005)
Ose (1938-76)
Penifiler (1899-2011)
Portnalong (1924-2007)
Portree (1809-)
Raasay (Isle of)(1833-)
Rhudunan (1884-1937 then Glenbrittle)
Roskhill (1937-1999)
Sconser (1769-2010 then *Outreach)
Skeabost (1855-92 then Bernisdale)
Skeabost Bridge (1889-2001)
Skinidin (1900-87)
Sligichan/Sligachan (1875-1965)
Snizort (1868-1994)
Soay (island)(1891-1953)
Staffin (1868-)
Struan (1835-)
Tarskavaig (1898-2001)
Teangue (1898-2005)
The Braes (1873-)
Tighlone (1855-57 then Edinbane then Arnisort)
Torran (on Raasay)(1898-1967)
Torrin (1898-2001)
Uig (1855-)
Waternish (1855-2008)

Barra

Barra (1855-1921 then Northbay)
Borve (1897-2001)
Castlebay (1875-)
Eoligarry (1931-78)
Northbay (1921-2009)
Skallary (1930-1979)
Vatersay (island) (1928-)

South Uist

Bornish (1916-2000)
Bualdubh (1956-66)
Daliburgh (1888-)
Eochar (1878-1976)
Eriskay (island)(1885-)
Grogarry (1890-1972)
Howmore (1843-1951, 1965-2011 then *Outreach)
Kilbride (1839-2004)
Linique (1935-2000)
Lochboisdale (1878-88, 1909-)
Lochboisdale Hotel (1880-81 then Pier)
Lochboisdale Pier (1881-1909 then Lochboisdale)
Lochcarnan (1937-88)

Lochskipport (1912-68)
North Boisdale (1949-2000)
South Lochboisdale (1926-2001)
Stoneybridge (1951-2001)
West Gerinish (1935-77)

Benbecula

Balivanich (1943-44 & 1972-)
Benbecula RAFPO (1944-46)
Creagorry (1878-)
Gramsdale (1935-74)
Griminish (1938-)
Nunton (1843-1972, used at several locations then Balivanich)

North Uist

Balishare (Baleshare island) (1885-2001)
Bayhead (1877-1994 then Paible)
Bernera (island)(1880-, spelling Berneray 1962-)
Carinish (1802-1990)
Clachan (1988-)
Claddach Kirkibost (1935-71)
Grimsay (island)(1880-)
Locheport (1881-1988 then Clachan)
Lochmaddy (1829-)
Lochportan (1926-2007)
Newtonferry (1878-2001)
Paible (1994-2009 then *Outreach)
Sidinish (1934-2008)
Sollas (1879-2006)
Tigharry (1851-2008)

Harris

Amhuinnsuidh (1950-2009 then Outreach*)
Ardhasaig (1950-2005)
Drinnishadder (1930-)
Finsbay (1914-2005)
Harris (at Tarbert)(1836-)
Kyles Scalpay (1930-) renamed Kyles Harris (1953-2003)
Leverburgh (1921-)
Manish (1879-1989)
Northton (1930-2008)
Obbe (1873-1921 then Leverburgh)
Scalpay (Isle of) (1887-)
Scarista (1951-2007)
Scarp (island)(1931-69)
Seilebost (1946-2003)
Stockinish (1896-2009 then *Outreach)
Strond (1950-2001)

Lewis

Achmore (1927-)
Arivruaich (1950-1994)
Back (1874-)
Balallan (1878-)
Barvas (1855-)
Bayble (1928-2011)
Bernera (1880-) (on Gt Bernera)
Borve (1903-2008)
Bragar (1910-2008)
Breasclete (1950-2008)

Callanish (1884-)
Carloway (1875-2006)
Cromore (1912-2004)
Crossbost (1874-)
Crulivig (1949-1979)
Eneclate (1931-1993)
Galson (1950-)
Garrabost (1855-)
Garrynahine (1873-84 then Callanish)
Gravir (1884-)
Gress (1888-91, 1950-2008)
Grimshader (1947-2008)
Islivig (1892-2000)
Keose (1901-)
Kershader (1925-)
Knock (1892-2008)
Laxay (1884-)
Laxdale (1897-1989)
Lemreway (1928-)
Leurbost (1950-2008)
Marvig (1929-)
Miavaig (1857-1988 then Valtos)
Ness (1875-)
North Tolsta (1879-)
Portnaguran (1888-)
Port of Ness (1888-)
Sandwick (1935-1979)
Sandwickhill (1897-1901)
Shader (1913-2008)
Shawbost (1883-)
Skigersta (1950-2008)
South Dell (1952-2008)
Stornoway (1756-) Bayhead (1951-)
Stornoway RAFPO (1943-47)
Timsgarry (1933-)
Tolstachaolais (1909-)
Tong (1911-1996)
Valtos (1988-2005)

Orkney

Backaland (1898-1970 then renamed Eday)(on Eday)
Balfour (on Shapinsay) (1848-)
Birsay (1849-)
Burray (1858-2008)
Burwick (1800-)
Deerness (1857-)
Dounby (at Downby)(1873-)
Eday (island)(1857-, at Backaland 1970-)
Egilshay/Egilsay (island) (1878-)
Evie (1844-)
Finstown (1844-)
Flotta (island)(1860-)
Graemsay (island)(1882-)
Harray (1849-2008)
Holm (1934-)
Hoy (island)(1879-)
Kirkwall (1746-)
Lady (on Sanday)(1890-)
Longhope (on Hoy)(1835-)
Lyness (on Hoy)(1940-2009 then *Outreach)
Melsetter (on Hoy)(1902-69)
Mire (on Sanday)(1935-82)
North Ronaldshay (island) (1855-, then N Ronaldsay 1966-)
North Shapinsay (on Shapinsay)(1935-75)
Orphir (1848-)
Papa Westray (island)(1879-)
Quivals (on Sanday)(1898-2003)
Quoyburray (1898-1934 then Toab)
Quoyloo (1879-)
Rendall (1869-2008)
Rousay (island)(1854-)
Rusness (on Sanday)(1898-2006)
St Margaret's Hope (on S Ronaldsay)(1826-)
St Mary's Holm (1856-1934 then Holm)
Samson's Lane (on Stronsay) (1884-2001)
Sanday (1839-) (on Sanday at Kettleftoft)
Sandwick (1858-2003)
Sourin (on Rousay)(1879-1969)
Stenness (1875-)
Stromness (1797-)
Stronsay (island)(1839-)
Swannay (1885-2008)
Tankerness (1893-)
Toab (1934-)
Twatt (1879-2008)
Valdigarth (on Westray) (1898-)
Veira (on Wyre) (1885-1933 then Wyre)
Wasbister (on Rousay) (1898-1969)
Westray (island)(1839-)
Wyre (island)(1933-)

Shetland

Aith (1911-)
Baltasound (on Unst, most northerly PO after Haroldswick closed)(1827-)
Bigton (1907-)
Bixter (1884-)
Boddam (1827-39)
Brae (1827-)
Bressay (island)(1857-)
Brettabister (1896-2001)
Bridge-end (Burra islands) (1943-74)
Bridge-of-Walls (1884-1998)
Brough (on Whalsay) (1936-94)
Buness (on Unst)(1839-57)
Burra (island)(1873-1943 then Bridge-end)
Burravoe (on Yell)(1839-)
Camb (on Yell)(1933-2008)
Cullivoe (on Yell)(1839-)
Cunningsburgh (1847-2001)
Dalsetter (on Yell)(1878-1910 then Sellafirth)
Dunrossness (1847-)
East Yell (on Yell)(1845-)
Eshaness (1895-)
Fair Isle (island)(1877-)
Fetlar (Isle of)(1858-)
Foula (Isle of)(1879-)
Garderhouse (1839-1981)
Gott (1943-1997)
Graven (1941-43 then Sullom Voe RAF PO)

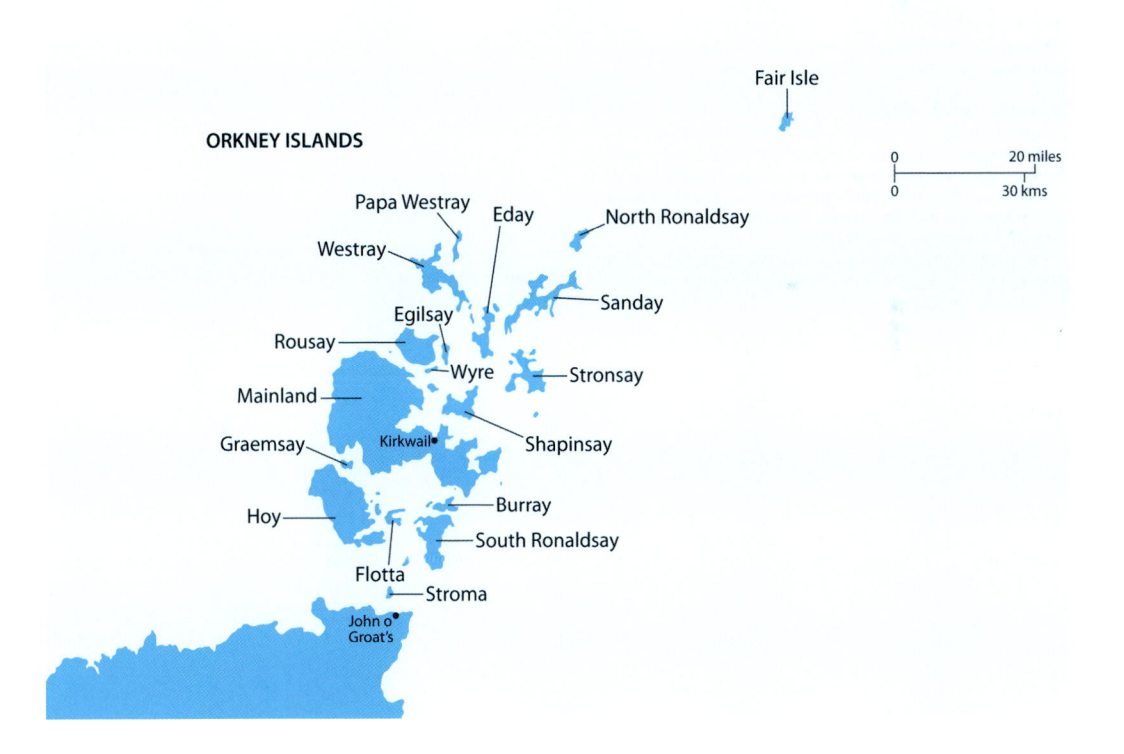

Islands

SHETLAND ISLANDS

ORKNEY ISLANDS

Islands

Grutness (1885-93 then Sumburgh)
Gutcher (on Yell)(1885-2005)
Hamar (1903-72)
Hamnavoe (Burra islands) (1898-)
Haroldswick (on Unst, most northerly PO until its closure) (1827-1999)
Heylor (1892-2001)
Hillswick (1839-2008, then Outreach*)
Hillwell (1933 then Quendale)
Lerwick (1763-)
Freefield (1906-)
Levenwick (1884-2008)
Linkshouse (on Yell, 1827-81 then Mid Yell)
Lochend (1906-2004)
Mid Yell (on Yell)(1881-)
Mossbank (1839-)
Nesting (1865-66)
North Roe (1880-)
Ollaberry (1827-)
Papa Stour (island)(1880-2005)
Quarff (1898-1995)
Quendale (1933-73)
Reawick (1884-)
Sandness (1839-2002)
Sandwick (1847-)
Scalloway (1856-2007)
Scousburgh (1896-1996)
Seafield (on Yell)(1843-49)
Sellafirth (on Yell)(1910-82)
Skellister (1897-)
Skerries (islands)(1889-)
Sullom (1880-2001)
Sullom Voe RAF (1943-46)
Sumburgh (1893-1969)
Symbister (on Whalsay) (1942-)
Tangwick (1826-46)
Tingwall (1869-1943 then Gott)
Tresta (1856-2001)
Ulsta (on Yell)(1827-)
Uyeasound (on Unst) (1827-1998)
Vidlin (1891-2006)
Virkie (1866-)
Voe (1827-2000)
Walls (1827-)
Weisdale (1839-)
Wester Skeld (1930-)
West Sandwick (Yell) (1839-1997)
Whalsay (island)(1866-1942 then Symbister)

Whiteness (1850-2012)

*At Outreach offices services are provided from another office so the postmark of original office rarely survives.

Orkney and Shetland Islands

This map shows the relative positions of the Orkney and Shetland islands, in relation also to John O'Groats on the north coast of Scotland's mainland, and to Stroma which is just off the mainland. Also shown are the individual islands on which post offices exist or once existed. Note that in both cases the main island is referred to as "Mainland".

Haroldswick, the northernmost post office, is also shown in chapter 12.

18 Charge, Instructional and Explanatory Marks

This chapter shows a representative listing of these marks. It does not pretend to be a complete listing, partly as in modern times there are many non-standard marks as local post offices produce handstamps of their own layouts. From the 1980s self-adhesive labels have largely taken over. Meter date correction marks are not included; these are shown in chapter 27, with machine-applied slogans in chapter 11.

Charge Marks

18/1 From 1860s Scottish types often have a Roman letter with full stop beneath. Irish types often have a capital D above a double line

18/2 From 1870s With office number or London District initials above or below value

18/3 Circular Frame and office numbers

18/4 Oval frame and office numbers

18/5 Unframed with 'To Pay' Scottish or Irish are prefixed S or I

	18/1	18/2	18/3	18/4	18/5
½d	10.00	8.00	20.00	10.00	4.00
1d	1.00	0.75	15.00	2.00	0.60
1½d	10.00	10.00	20.00	15.00	3.00
2d	3.00	1.00	15.00	4.00	1.25
2½d	30.00	30.00			
3d	3.00	3.00	15.00		1.00
3½d	4.00		75.00		
4d	12.00	5.00	50.00		1.00
4½d	60.00				
5d	10.00	4.00	15.00		2.00
5½d	£150		40.00		
6d	12.00	5.00	25.00	15.00	2.00

	18/1	18/2	18/3	18/4	18/5
6½d					25.00
7d	30.00	15.00	50.00	20.00	
7½d	75.00			60.00	
8d	15.00	6.00	50.00		3.00
8½d	£100				
9d		18.00	60.00	12.00	
9½d	£225				
10d	20.00	10.00	50.00		
11d	35.00	18.00	50.00		
1/-	8.00	8.00	30.00		
1/1	£150				
1/1½	£350				
1/4	£250				
1/5	£250				
1/7			35.00		
1/8			15.00		
1/9			35.00		
1/10			35.00		
1/11			35.00		
2/-	75.00				
2/3	£300			25.00	
2/6			25.00		
3/-			30.00		
4/6	£350				
5/-	£350				

18/6	Circular frame without office numbers, late Victorian	from	10.00
18/7	Oval frame without office numbers	from	50.00
18/8	Square or rectangular frame without office numbers	from	20.00
18/9	Square or rectangular frame with office numbers	from	15.00
18/10	Charge marks with NPB (Newspaper Branch)	from	50.00
18/11	--------D TO PAY/Number	from	10.00
18/12	Hexagonal frame with TO PAY and office number	from	25.00
18/13	Cross shaped frame with TO PAY and office number	from	25.00

Note: Circular types with H.C.S.W. (House of Commons) - see chapter 21

Boxed T shaped

Marks with office numbers or London District Initials. Black, purple or green (double prices for red), from 1870s - these are difficult to value since some were still in use 100 years later. Clearly earlier specimens are worth more than the values stated:

18/34

353

Charge, Instructional and Explanatory Marks

18/45 — *Gone Away 763B*

18/61 — *Liable to Letter Rate 407*

Ref	Description	Price
18/14	1D to pay	10.00
18/15	4D to pay	30.00
18/16	1D to pay/above … oz	10.00
18/17	1D to pay/contains a letter in/Typewritten characters	50.00
18/18	1D to pay/Liable to/Postcard Rate	2.00
18/19	2D to pay/Liable to/Letter Rate	2.00
18/20	Above … oz/More to pay	5.00
18/21	Above 1oz/1d/More to pay	6.00
18/22	Above 1oz/2d/More to pay	6.00
18/23	Above 2oz/3d/More to pay	15.00
18/24	Above 3oz/1d/More to pay	25.00
18/25	Above 4oz/1d/More to pay	40.00
18/26	Above … oz/ /More to pay	6.00
18/27	Address Contrary to rule	30.00
18/28	Book Post/over	£150
18/29	Charged for/re-direction	40.00
18/30	Circular in imitation type/writing. Posted out of course	50.00
18/31	Closed against inspection	20.00
18/32	Closed against/inspection	15.00
18/33	Closed against inspection/contrary to Regulations	20.00
18/34	Closed contrary/to regulations	10.00
18/35	Closed contrary to/regulations	10.00
18/36	Compulsorily Registered	75.00
18/37	Contains a communication/of the nature of a letter	30.00
18/38	Contains a letter in/type-writing characters	60.00
18/39	Contains writing in/the nature of a letter	30.00
18/40	Contrary to Regulations	1.00
18/41	Contrary to Regulations/Exceeds limits of size	10.00
18/42	Deceased	10.00
18/43	Exceeds limits of size	5.00
18/44	Firm not known	30.00
18/45	Gone Away	1.00
18/46	Gone No address	2.00
18/47	House empty	50.00
18/48	Imitation typewriting/posted out of course	50.00
18/49	Improper enclosure	60.00
18/50	Inadmissible at ½d rate	10.00
18/51	Inadmissible at printed paper rate	30.00
18/52	Inadmissible at … rate	3.00
18/53	Incorrectly Addressed	2.00
18/54	Insufficient Address	1.00
18/55	Insufficiently Addressed	1.00
18/56	Insufficient Paid	10.00
18/57	Insufficiently paid	3.00
18/58	Insufficiently prepaid	4.00
18/59	Insufficiently Paid/over …oz	6.00
18/60	Letter Rate/Above … oz	30.00
18/61	Liable to Letter Rate	0.50
18/62	Liable to/Letter Rate	3.00
18/63	Liable to postcard rate	6.00
18/64	Misdirected	3.00
18/65	More to Pay/Above…oz (line beneath 'More to Pay')	2.00
18/66	As above but without line	2.00
18/67	No Such Street	30.00
18/68	No Such Street in	30.00
18/69	No Such Street in Liverpool	6.00
18/70	No Trace	4.00
18/71	Not called for	4.00
18/72	Not certified as official	75.00
18/73	Not found	2.00
18/74	Not known	1.00
18/75	Not known as addressed	3.00
18/76	Not known at	4.00
18/77	Not paid in stamps	75.00
18/78	Not to be found	2.00
18/79	Not transmissible at the/Rate of Postage	4.00
18/80	Of the nature of a letter	40.00
18/81	Of the nature/of a letter	30.00
18/82	Over … oz	6.00
18/83	Over … ounces	6.00
18/84	Over … oz/More to pay	6.00
18/85	Posted out of course	5.00
18/86	Posted out/of course	5.00
18/87	Posted without Late Fee	50.00
18/88	Posted without/Late Fee	50.00
18/89	Prohibited enclosure	75.00
18/90	Property demolished	30.00
18/91	Re-issued	50.00
18/92	Reposted more than one/clear day after delivery	£100
18/93	Undelivered for reason stated/Return to Sender	10.00
18/94	Unpaid	3.00
18/95	Unpaid/above … oz	15.00

Rectangular types

In black, purple or green (Double prices for red).

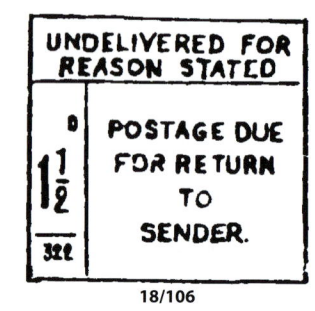

18/96 — *1D / 2 POSTAGE DUE FOR RETURN TO SENDER*

18/101 — *1D TO PAY. LIABLE TO LETTER 407 RATE.*

18/106 — *UNDELIVERED FOR REASON STATED / 1½ 322 / POSTAGE DUE FOR RETURN TO SENDER.*

Charge, Instructional and Explanatory Marks

18/96	½D/Postage/due/for/return/to/Sender, boxed	10.00
18/97	As above but 1d	15.00
18/98	As above but 1½d	25.00
18/99	As above but 2d	30.00
18/100	As above but 3d	50.00
18/101	1D/to pay/Liable/to/Letter/Rate, boxed with office number	10.00
18/102	As above but 2d	25.00
18/103	More to Pay, Above…oz types	20.00
18/104	Undelivered for/reason stated/½D/Postage Due/For Return/To Sender, boxed with office number	10.00
18/105	As above but 1d	10.00
18/106	As above but 1½d	15.00
18/107	As above but 2d	10.00
18/108	As above but 2½d	15.00
18/109	As above but blank value for completion	15.00
18/110	Unpaid 2D to pay/Posted too late for ½D rate, boxed	30.00

Boxed marks

Incorporating charge and explanation in brass or rubber. Value inserted by separate brass piece, by hand or fixed rubber above office number or London District Initials - black, violet, green or red.

Double frame from 1924

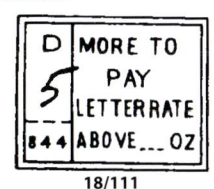

18/111

18/111	More to / Pay / letter rate / above … oz	1.50
18/112	More to / Pay / Printed Paper Rate / above …oz	10.00
18/113	More to / pay / letter rate / above …oz	1.50
18/114	More to / pay / Newspaper / rate / contains newspapers	50.00
18/115	More to / pay / rate / above … oz .	1.50
18/116	To pay / contrary to / regulations / liable to / …rate	2.50
18/117	To pay / Form not / appropriately / printed / Liable to / Letter rate	40.00
18/118	To pay / inadmissible / Sample rate / liable to / letter rate / above … oz	50.00
18/119	To pay / liable to / letter rate	1.00
18/120	To pay / liable to / postcard / rate	1.50
18/121	To pay / Posted / unpaid	1.00
18/122	To pay / Posted / Out of / course	5.00
18/123	To pay / posted / unpaid / above …oz	1.50
18/124	To pay / Posted / unpaid	1.00
18/125	To pay / Posted / Unpaid / Too Late For /½d Rate	20.00
18/126	To pay / Contrary to / Regulations / Liable to / …rate	2.50

Single frame: 1931-69

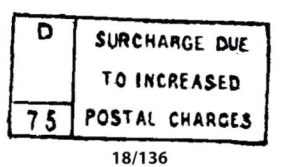

18/132

18/136

18/145

18/127	More to/Pay/Letter Rate/Above … oz	1.00
18/128	More to/pay/letter rate/Above … oz	1.00
18/129	As above but 1 oz	2.00
18/130	As above but 2 oz	3.00
18/131	More to/Pay/ …rate/Above 2 oz	3.00
18/132	More to/Pay/ …rate/Above … oz	2.00
18/133	More to/Pay/Insufficiently/Prepaid	2.00
18/134	More to/pay/Printed Paper/Rate/above oz	5.00
18/135	More to/Pay/Newspaper/Rate/Contains… / Newspapers	10.00
	More to/Pay/Late Fee/Unpaid (see chapter 13)	
18/136	Surcharge Due/to Increased/Postal charges	1.50
18/137	To Pay/closed/contrary to/Regulations/Liable to/Letter rate	20.00
18/138	To pay/contrary to/regulations/liable to … rate	2.00
18/139	To pay/imitation type/circular, not/specially posted/liable to/ … rate	40.00
18/140	To pay/liable to/letter/rate	0.50
18/141	To pay/liable to/letter rate/… oz	1.00
18/142	To pay/Liable to/postcard/rate	1.50
18/143	To pay/liable to/Printed Paper/rate/above … oz	3.00
18/144	To pay/posted/underpaid	1.00
18/145	To pay/posted/unpaid	0.50
18/146	To pay/posted/unpaid/above … oz	0.75
18/147	As above but without office number	1.00
18/148	To pay/Posted Unpaid/Too late for 1d rate	20.00
18/149	To pay/Posted Unpaid/Too late for 2d rate	20.00
18/150	To pay/Posted/Unpaid/Too late for 3d rate	40.00
18/151	To pay	2.00
18/152	To pay/Inadmissible/Sample Rate Liable To/Letter Rate/above … oz .	50.00
18/153	To Pay/Posted in/T.P.O./Late Fee/Not Paid	5.00
18/154	To Pay/Posted/Out of/Course	5.00
18/155	Undelivered for Reason/Stated/Postage Due For/Return to Sender	3.00

Boxed marks: Decimal currency from 1971

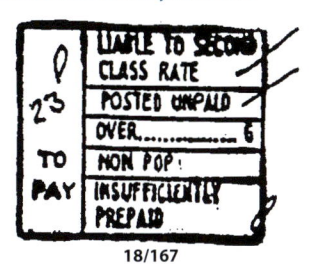

18/167

18/156	3p/More to/Pay/over … oz, with office number	0.50
18/157	P/More to Pay/… Rate/Above … oz., as above	0.50

355

Charge, Instructional and Explanatory Marks

18/158	P/More to Pay/… Rate/Above … Grms., as above	0.50
18/159	P/Surcharged/To Increased/Postal charges	1.50
18/160	Surcharge due/To Increased/Postal charges	1.50
18/161	P/To pay/Insufficiently prepaid	1.00
18/162	P/To pay/More to/Pay over/… oz	0.50
18/163	P/To pay/Posted/Unpaid, blank panel above office number	0.50
18/164	Multipurpose charge box with fixed value	0.75
18/165	As above but blank panel for insertion	0.30
18/166	As above but oz removed after metrication	1.00
18/167	As above but with G or Gms	0.50

Inland Section and Foreign Section

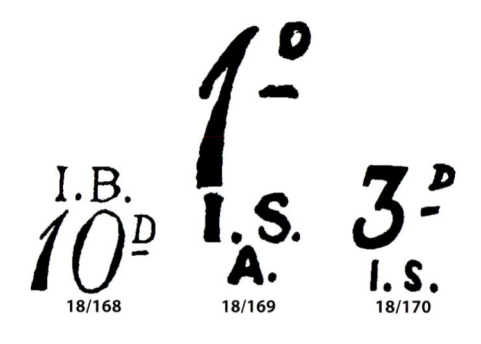

	18/168 Small IB	18/169 Large IS	18/170 Small IB/IS	18/171 Small FB	18/172 Large FB	18/173 Small FS	18/174 Decimal FS
6½d				25.00			1.20
7d	25.00	6.00		25.00	6.00	6.00	1.00
7½d		10.00				10.00	1.20
8d		6.00				6.00	1.00
8½d							2.00
9d		6.00		25.00	6.00		
9½d						30.00	
10d	20.00	10.00			6.00		
11d	40.00	10.00			10.00		
1/-	40.00	10.00			12.00	1.00	
1/0½d					£175		
1/1d		£100			£100		
1/2d		20.00			20.00		
1/3d		£100			£100		
1/4d		60.00			60.00		
1/5d		60.00			60.00		
1/5½d					£175		
1/6d		15.00		15.00	15.00		
1/7d		30.00		30.00	20.00		
1/7½d	£200						
1/8d	30.00			8.00	20.00		
1/9d	60.00						
1/10½d	£225						
2/-	50.00						
3/-	50.00						

Note: Other values of each of the five small types of charge marks probably exist.

Inland Section

18/168	18/169	18/170	18/171	18/172	18/173	18/174
Small IB	Large IS	Small IB/IS	Small FB	Large FB	Small FS	Decimal FS
½d 15.00	3.00		10.00	3.00		3.00
1d 10.00	0.50	3.00	3.00	0.50	2.00	1.00
1½d	15.00			1.00		1.00
2d 10.00	1.00	3.00		1.00	2.00	1.00
2½d 30.00	3.00			3.00		1.00
3d 12.00	1.00	3.00		1.00	2.00	1.00
3½d	6.00				4.50	1.00
4d 12.00	2.00	6.00		5.00	2.00	1.00
4½d	10.00	2.00		2.00	1.00	
5d 15.00	2.00	3.00		2.00	2.00	1.00
5½d	15.00					1.00
6d 25.00	4.00	6.00		4.00	2.00	

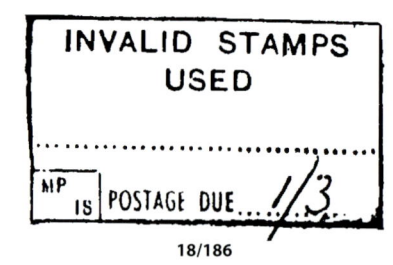

18/175	Above … oz/1D/More to pay/I.S, boxed, T-Shaped	5.00
18/176	Address illegible/I.S. boxed. T-shaped	10.00
18/177	Charge not paid/I.S. boxed, T-shaped	15.00
18/178	Contrary to Regulations/I.B. boxed, T-shaped	2.00
18/179	Damaged by/Sea-water/M.P./I.S.	40.00
18/180	Delayed through being/posted in a letter box/for 'Country' letters/ please advise sender, crinkly frame (used at ECDO)	10.00
18/181	Delayed through being/posted in a letter box/for 'London' letters/ please advise sender, crinkly frame	10.00
18/182	Express/Fee Partly/Paid/To Pay/MP I.S.	30.00
18/183	Found Torn/and enclosed at/Inland Section, boxed, in purple	6.00
18/184	Insufficient Postage 1st Class/Transferred to 2nd Class, boxed	1.50
18/185	Insufficiently Addressed/I.S. boxed, T-shaped	2.00
18/186	Invalid Stamps/Used/MP I.S., Postage Due	10.00
18/187	I.S. in triangle, Inspector's mark (see **19/67**)	2.00
18/188	3D/I.S./More to pay/ rate/above … oz, boxed, in green	10.00
18/189	10D/I.S.M.P./To Pay/posted/underpaid, boxed in green	15.00
18/190	Liable to Letter Rate/I.B., boxed, T-shaped	5.00
18/191	Liable to Letter Rate/I.S., boxed, T-shaped	1.00

Charge, Instructional and Explanatory Marks

18/192	Liable to 2nd class rate/Unpaid Underpaid/Over … grammes/I.S.M.L.O.		2.00
18/193	More to pay/above oz/I.S., boxed, T-shaped, in green		3.00
18/194	Multipurpose charge box		0.50
18/195	8D/M.P.I.S./to pay/posted/unpaid/boxed		5.00
18/196	Not on board/Return to Sender, not boxed		40.00
18/197	Posted on Board Ship Abroad/I.S., T-shaped		20.00

Nos.18/180 and 18/181 were machine applied from 1927–68. For full details see "Collecting Slogan Postmarks", see **18/206** for "This Item", also applied by machine

18/206

18/214

18/198	Posted on board ship abroad/I.S., T-shaped		30.00
18/199	Posted on H.M.S./Abroad/I.S., boxed		75.00
18/200	Posted out of course, boxed		3.00
18/201	Posted/out of/course/I.S. boxed		3.00
18/202	Received/Posted Out of course/London I.S.M.L.O.		15.00
18/203	R.L.D.I.S./Surcharge Duty/To pay, boxed		10.00
18/204	Return to Sender/Address Insufficient/I.S., boxed, T-shaped		3.00
18/205	Stamp Disallowed/By Office of Posting/M.P. I.S./To Pay		3.00
18/206	This item was not posted into the correct posting box…delay		2.50
18/207	To Pay/I.S. boxed		4.00
18/208	To pay/R.L.D.I.S., boxed		15.00
18/209	To Pay/Liable to Letter Rate/Posted Too Late/for Inclusion In/ Printed Matter On/Day of Posting/D/I.S., boxed		20.00
18/210	To pay/Postage cannot be/prepaid by means/of an incomplete/franking impression/liable to…rate/I.S.		2.00
18/211	1/- To pay/R.L.D.I.S., boxed		30.00
18/212	Undelivered for/Reason Stated/2D/Postage due/for return/to/Sender, in green		1.50
18/213	Unpaid 2D to pay/Posted too late for ½d rate/I.S. boxed		8.00
18/214	W/X/Y/Z London ISMLO "lifebelt" style delayed code handstamp		2.00

No. 18/206 applied by machine at ECDO before transfer to IS, see "Slogan Postmarks of the Eighties" for details of this and variations.

18/216

18/222

Foreign Section

18/215	Contrary to Regulations/F.B., boxed, T-shaped		5.00
18/216	Delayed - not fully paid, FS, "lifebelt" style handstamp (various)		10.00
18/217	Exceeds Limits of size/F.S., T-shaped		6.00
18/218	Express Fee Paid, boxed		5.00
18/219	Insufficient/Address, boxed		2.00
18/220	Insufficiently Addressed, boxed, FS in panel at right		2.50
18/221	Liable to Letter Rate/F.S., boxed, T-shaped		2.00
18/222	Missent to/Great Britain/London Foreign Section, boxed		15.00
18/223	More to Pay/F.S.		2.50
18/224	More to/Pay/… Rate/above … /oz with F.S. and blank panel to left		5.00
18/225	No service/Return to sender, boxed, divided horizontally, purple		30.00
18/226	Not transmissible unpaid/Postage required, boxed		10.00
18/227	Postage stamps required/for overseas addresses (on Official Paid)		50.00
18/228	Posted out/of course, boxed		10.00
18/229	Returned for/better address, boxed, with FST inside right panel		10.00
18/230	Return to Sender/Open Panel F.S./Contrary to regulations, see page … P.O. Guide, boxed, purple		5.00
18/231	Return to sender/No Transport links available/because of/Middle East Situation (1990) (variations)		10.00
18/232	Service suspended, boxed		30.00
18/233	Stamp not valid for overseas mail, boxed (uncertain where applied)		50.00
18/234	Stamps not valid, with F.S., boxed		6.00
18/235	This item stopped in transit. Postage stamps required…overseas mail		40.00
18/236	Too Late/F.B.G.P.O., small circle		10.00
*18/237	T/15c (or manuscript value) in hexagon, with L for London beneath		1.00
*18/238	T/1d in hexagon, with FS beneath (see note below)		3.00

*Other values exist.

357

Charge, Instructional and Explanatory Marks

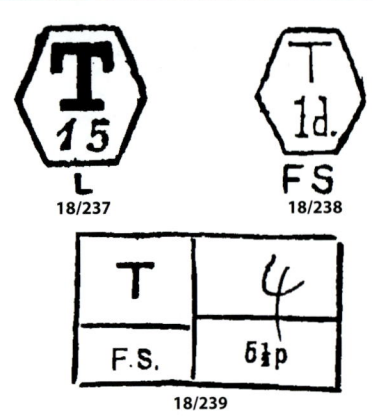

18/237 (hexagonal T/15/L)
18/238 (hexagonal T/1d./FS)
18/239 (T/F.S./5½p in 4-part box)

Note: The system for calculating surcharges on overseas underpaid mail varied over the years, the basis being the centime to 1965 (though sterling marks are also known, see above), then a fraction system took over with new surcharge marks of which the following is an example; the marks applied did not apply to FS alone, see next section.

18/239	T/F.S./5½p in 4-part box	2.00
18/240	Undelivered for reason stated/Returned to Sender, with FSR inside panel to right	2.50

Charge and other marks confined to mail from abroad (incl Channel Is)

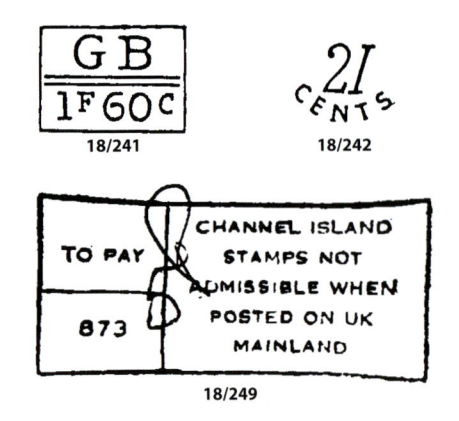

18/241 (GB/1F 60C)
18/242 (21 CENTS)
18/249 (TO PAY / 873 / CHANNEL ISLAND STAMPS NOT ADMISSIBLE WHEN POSTED ON UK MAINLAND)
18/250 (21 SEP 1979 1 6 P TO PAY)

18/241	Accountancy Marks (to 1875)	25.00
18/242	Cents marks used at Liverpool	15.00
18/243	Hexagonal marks with L for London (see note above, similar to outgoing mail, these hexagonal marks also seen on incoming overseas mail)	2.00
18/244	Insufficiently Paid …… to pay 258 (Dover)	6.00
18/245	Over… grammes …d more to pay/258 (Dover), boxed	6.00
18/246	It is regretted that/this item could not be/delivered because the/addressee is reported/missing, boxed, purple	15.00
18/247	This Letter formed Part of Undelivered/Mails which fell into the hands of/The Allied Forces in Germany. It is/Undeliverable as addressed, and is/Therefore returned to you, boxed (W War II)	40.00
18/248	This letter has been returned by/The Swiss Post Office who were/unable to forward it to Germany/because of the interruption of/communications, boxed (World War II)	60.00
18/249	To pay / Channel Island / Stamps not / admissible when…873 (Weymouth)	20.00
18/250	To Pay, plus value, dated or undated, 1970s-	2.00

Charge Marks used countrywide

See note at end of section.

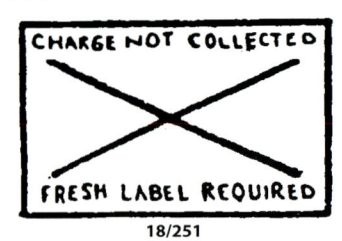

18/251 (CHARGE NOT COLLECTED / X / FRESH LABEL REQUIRED)
18/266 (Liable to Letter Rate)
18/271 (MORE TO PAY / T)

18/251	Charge Not collected/X/Fresh label required, boxed	3.00
18/252	CH, in circle (Clifton, Bristol)	60.00
18/253	Contains enclosure liable to letter rate Manchester F.S.	25.00
18/254	…D to Pay, boxed	2.50
18/255	Delayed not fully paid, Manchester FS, "lifebelt" style handstamp	10.00
18/256	Imperfect impression/6d to Pay, boxed	2.00
18/257	Insufficiently stamped	5.00
18/258	Insufficiently Prepaid for airmail, boxed	4.00
18/259	Insufficiently Paid/For Transmission by Air Mail, boxed	4.00
18/260	Insufficiently Paid boxed	5.00
18/261	Insufficiently paid/…d to pay, boxed with or without office number, in green	1.00
18/262	Insufficiently paid/…, to pay, boxed with office number, in green	1.00
18/263	Insufficient Postage 1st Class/Transferred to 2nd class, boxed, green	1.00
18/264	Invalid Revenue/Stamp, boxed, in green	50.00
18/265	Invalid Stamps Used/Postage Due, boxed	15.00
18/266	Liable to Letter Rate, boxed	5.00
18/267	Liable to Postage surcharge/imperfect Meter franking, unframed in green	5.00
18/268	Liable to Surcharge / Imperfect/Meter franking, boxed with office number	5.00
18/269	LSD stamps/Now Invalid, boxed in green	15.00
18/270	£sd stamps/invalid/… to pay	15.00
18/271	More to pay (many types)	10.00
18/272	OS in double or single circle for 'Old Stamp'	£2500

Charge, Instructional and Explanatory Marks

18/273	Over Grammes/…d More to Pay, with office number	5.00
18/274	Postage cannot be/prepaid by means/of incomplete/franking impressions (variations, framed/unframed, usually in green)	2.00

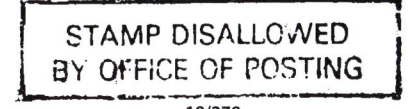

STAMP DISALLOWED BY OFFICE OF POSTING
18/278

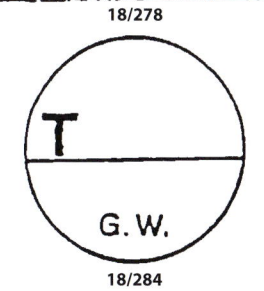

(circular mark with T above G.W.)
18/284

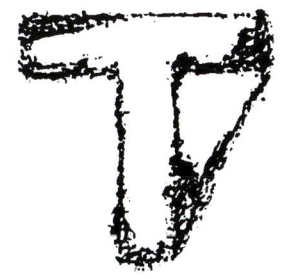

(large T mark)
18/285

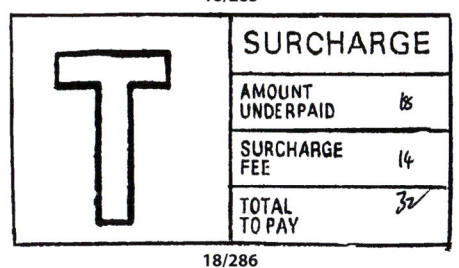

(T with SURCHARGE table: AMOUNT UNDERPAID 18, SURCHARGE FEE 14, TOTAL TO PAY 32)
18/286

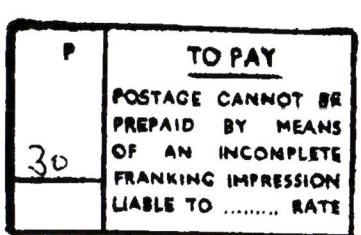

(TO PAY box with POSTAGE CANNOT BE PREPAID BY MEANS OF AN INCOMPLETE FRANKING IMPRESSION LIABLE TO ……. RATE, value 30)
18/293

18/275	Short-Paid / Posted Unpaid/over… g/T, with office number	10.00
18/276	Stamp Invalid, unframed	10.00
18/277	Stamps/Missing in/Transit, boxed, in red	20.00
18/278	Stamp disallowed/By office of posting, boxed	10.00
18/279	Surcharged/Amount underpaid etc	0.50
18/280	Surcharged/Stamps invalid, boxed	4.00
18/281	Surcharge/No licence held/Licence cancelled (on business reply)	15.00
18/282	Surcharge Fee/10p boxed	1.00

18/283	T/15c in small hexagon, with or without office number beneath (used on overseas items, see note above under FS listing)	2.00
18/284	T/G.W., overseas "fractional" tax system from 1960s (Glasgow), but variety of designs from other offices	2.00
18/285	T marks (large), used largely in NE England, solid, outline or boxed, to indicate underpayment on INLAND mail, usually green	0.50
18/286	T incorporated into other surcharge marks, (NE England)	3.00
18/287	To Pay/13p, boxed green (and other values)	0.50
18/288	To Pay/Ldn. RLB unframed 1d, 3d, etc.	6.00
18/289	20p to Pay (and other values), some dated	0.50
18/290	14p/to Pay/Posted/Unpaid/Second Class, boxed (and other values)	0.50
18/291	To Pay/liable to/Postcard Rate, rectangular with blank panel for amount and office number	2.50
18/292	To pay/on return/to sender/Postage/deficiency, in three sections with blank panel for amount and office number	6.00
18/293	To Pay/Postage cannot be/prepaid by means/of an incomplete/ franking impression/liable to … rate, boxed with blank value tablet to left and office number or London District letters, green, black or purple	2.00
18/294	To Pay/amount/Postage Unpaid, boxed	0.50
18/295	Underpaid/Diverted to/Second Class	2.00
18/296	Unpaid, boxed or unboxed	3.00
18/297	Unpaid/Postage/And Fee/Due, boxed	4.00

Note: Modern surcharge marks are often produced locally and have no standard pattern and examples are shown below - **18/302** is a standard type in E. Anglia however (usually red) from 1995. All value from 0.50. From 1983 the surcharge system of "double deficiency" was replaced by the raising of a surcharge fee, initially 10p, added to the deficiency (and p rounded down). Details of later surcharge fees are given in the Postal Rates section at the end of this book. Illustration **18/303** shows a surcharge mark with a spelling error - value 2.50.

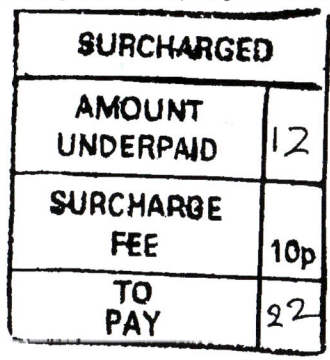

(SURCHARGED table: AMOUNT UNDERPAID 12, SURCHARGE FEE 10p, TO PAY 22)
18/298

(36 TO PAY / POSTAGE UNPAID / POST OFFICE FEE 14p / & DEFICIENT POSTAGE / REVENUE PROTECTION)
18/299

359

Charge, Instructional and Explanatory Marks

Instructional & Explanatory Marks used countrywide

```
TO PAY
23p
```
18/300

SURCHARGED	TOTAL TO PAY
ITEM POSTED UNDERPAID	
10p SURCHARGE FEE	23p

18/301

ROYAL MAIL Norwich -5 MAR 1997 Postage Underpaid SURCHARGE

18/302

TO PAY	
DEFICIENT POSTAGE	18
SURCHAGE	14
TOTAL TO PAY	32

18/303

AVOID DELAY
UNDELIVERED MAIL IS RETURNED WITH GREATER SPEED (and unopened) IF THE SENDERS NAME, ADDRESS AND POSTAL CODE ARE SHOWN ON OUTSIDE OF ENVELOPE OR WRAPPER.

18/306

```
ITEM FOUND IN OFFICIAL
POSTAL SYSTEM.
RETURNED TO SCOUT
MOVEMENT FOR DELIVERY
```
18/331

```
POSTED IN
SECOND CLASS POUCH

30 MAR 1993

HULL APC HU7 0AA
```
18/351

18/304	Actually Posted on/date/Incorrectly Dated By/Sender. Use Correct/Date for L.I.S. Sampling, boxed	5.00
18/305	Address Defective/Please advise sender, boxed, in purple	5.00
18/306	Avoid delay - Undelivered mail…senders name etc	2.50
18/307	Business reply and/Freepost correspondence/ docketed and charged	6.00
18/308	Correct Endorsement/Please, T-shaped	15.00
18/309	Deficient postage on this item/has been raised at Newport, Gwent	10.00
18/310	Delay Regretted - Found/with Second Class letters/at Shrewsbury, boxed	10.00
18/311	Delayed through posting in local box (Plymouth 1969) (also similar at Newport Isle of Wight)	15.00
18/312	Demolished	10.00
18/313	Do not charge/Mistreated in Post	35.00
18/314	Endorse and dispose, boxed	50.00
18/315	Exceptionally this letter must <u>not</u> be redirected etc	15.00
18/316	For correct/Endorsement please, boxed	15.00
18/317	Found Damaged In/A Pillar Box Fire/At…, boxed	30.00
18/318	Found-in-FNO (Foreign Newspaper Office)/ without contents	50.00
18/319	Found in mixed/bundle of first/and second class/meter items	30.00

Charge, Instructional and Explanatory Marks

18/320	Found in WCDO/without contents, boxed	50.00
18/321	Gone away, boxed or unboxed	3.00
18/322	Gone away/Address Not known, boxed	3.00
18/323	Gone away/1/2, boxed	3.00
18/324	Gone away/Left No Address	3.00
18/325	Gone away/Return to Sender	3.00
18/326	Gone away/Not known/Demolished, boxed	5.00
18/327	House/Unoccupied, boxed	20.00
18/328	Insufficiently Addressed, boxed	3.00
18/329	Irregularly included by posted/in a bundle of late posted/meter- franked printed papers, framed in green	10.00
18/330	Item delayed due to/vague address, boxed	10.00
18/331	Item found in Official/Postal System./Returned to Scout/Movement for delivery, boxed (Sheffield)	10.00
18/332	Items delayed/underpaid/Extra Revenue collected/by Derby Finance Dept	8.00
18/333	Late Fee/Paid, boxed	5.00
18/334	Liverpool MLO/Trapped in Machinery, dated single circle	40.00
18/335	Mail opened and disposed/of at Liverpool (etc), boxed	40.00
18/336	Misdirected To, unframed	5.00
18/337	Moved/Please return/to sender	8.00
18/338	No longer in residence/Return to sender	10.00
18/339	No post town, boxed or unboxed	5.00
18/340	No such street/Greenford Middx, many similar types, boxed or unboxed	5.00
18/341	No such street/(or place) in … unframed	5.00
18/342	Not called for, boxed with office number	3.00
18/343	Not known, boxed or unboxed	0.50
18/344	Not known at address stated/Forwarding particulars not available, boxed	5.00
18/345	Not known/Southport,/Lancs, many similar types, boxed or unboxed	3.00
18/346	Open Panel/Return to sender/Inadmissible for/Transmission Abroad, boxed purple	10.00
18/347	Please inform sender/of your correct address, boxed	2.00
18/348	Postage Refunded, straight line .	50.00
18/349	Posted after the last/collection of the Date/shown on the Postmark, unboxed (see chapter 27 for more related marks on meter mail)	2.00
18/350	Posted in/Post Office/Posting Box/liable to surcharge	30.00
18/351	Posted in/Second Class Pouch/Hull APC HU7 0AA (1993)	4.00
18/352	Posted Out of Course, with London initials, boxed	5.00
18/353	Premises boarded up/Unable to gain access/Date etc	10.00

THE POST OFFICE REGRETS THAT THIS ITEM HAS BEEN DELAYED AS A RESULT OF INDUSTRIAL ACTION WHICH AFFECTED THE LIVERPOOL/BELFAST FERRY.

18/367

THIS ITEM WAS INCORRECTLY INCLUDED WITH 2ND CLASS ITEMS BY THE SENDER AND MAY BE DELAYED

18/370

THIS UNDELIVERABLE LETTER WOULD HAVE BEEN RETURNED TO YOU
(A) MORE QUICKLY
(B) UNOPENED

IF YOUR NAME AND ADDRESS HAD BEEN SHEWN ON THE REVERSE SIDE OF THE COVER

18/372

UNDELIVERED FOR REASON STATED

RETURN TO SENDER

18/378

18/354	Present Location Uncertain (World War I)	8.00
18/355	Property boarded up/Initials Badge no. Date, boxed	25.00
18/356	P.T.O., boxed or unboxed	3.00
18/357	Received at Post Office London, in an otherwise empty bag *from*	50.00
18/358	Repaired in R.P.S. London Overseas Mail Office, boxed	30.00
18/359	Returned letter	10.00
18/360	Returned for/Endorsement please, boxed	15.00
18/361	Return sender/moved, boxed	5.00
18/362	Return to delivery officer/for endorsement/badge no. etc	15.00
18/363	Return to sender/Not known at this address, unboxed	3.00
18/364	Return to sender/Undelivered for reasons stated, boxed, without horizontal division, purple	3.00
18/365	Ship Sailed, boxed	50.00
18/366	Sorting Office (town name)/Returned for Endorsement, boxed	10.00
18/367	The Post Office regrets…delay…Liverpool/Belfast ferry (1981)	30.00
18/368	This item has been/franked in Excess. For/Adjustment of the Account/ Please return cover to:-/District Postmaster (PB27) W.D.O. London, W1P 1AA/via your postman/Post Office	10.00
18/369	This item was found with with/2nd class items causing delay	4.00
18/370	This item was incorrectly included with 2nd class items (variations)	4.00
18/371	This item was posted/After the last collection/on the date shown, boxed (see "Posted after last collection" 18/349)	2.00
18/372	This undeliverable letter…name & address on reverse side	8.00
18/373	Too late - ship sailed, unframed in black	40.00
18/374	Transferred to Second Class/Insufficient postage for first/class service 367	2.00
18/375	Unable to Deliver/Return to Sender, boxed	1.50
18/376	Unaddressed	5.00
18/377	Unclaimed, boxed or unboxed	2.00
18/378	Undelivered for reason stated/return to sender, boxed in two horizontal sections in purple, black or green (red 0.80)	0.50
18/379	As above but 'reasons' (see next section)	0.50
18/380	As above but unboxed	1.00

361

Charge, Instructional and Explanatory Marks

18/381	As above but also Returned from R.L.O. London	8.00
18/382	Undelivered for reason stated/to be returned to sender/at the address shown on cover, boxed in two horizontal sections	5.00
18/383	Undelivered for/reasons stated/Return to Sender/PHG Intls No, boxed	5.00
18/384	Word Postcard Omitted/Liable to Letter Rate, used Southampton 1905	£225
18/385	Writer of a letter addressed/to	5.00
18/386	Wrongly Dated By/Poster Not to be/Sampled Under L.I.S., boxed	15.00
18/387	Your correct postal address is/Any other form of address may lead/to delay. Please advise sender	5.00

Multipurpose marks explaining non-delivery, framed or unframed

Illustrations **18/388** to **18/394** show examples of the range of these marks, some of which show the office name or number, or refer to the office in the text (see Ipswich in **18/393**); wording usually starts with "Return to sender" or "Undelivered for reason stated" - value 1.50.

18/388

18/389

18/390

18/391

18/392

18/393

Charge, Instructional and Explanatory Marks

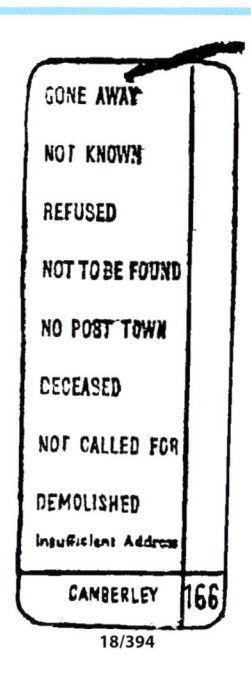

(label showing:)
GONE AWAY
NOT KNOWN
REFUSED
NOT TO BE FOUND
NO POST TOWN
DECEASED
NOT CALLED FOR
DEMOLISHED
Insufficient Address
CAMBERLEY 166

18/394

RLB/RLO Handstamps

The marks described in this chapter are often accompanied by handstamps confirming details of location and date. Frequently these are specially inscribed and examples are shown at **18/395** to **18/399**. Value 1.00 for modern items but rising to 15.00 for some pre-1930 items.

EDINBURGH A JU 22 05 R.L.O.
18/395

RETURNED LETTER BRANCH 6 DEC 7 1 BELFAST
18/396

PORTSMOUTH 14 OCT 1992 SURCHARGE
18/397

REWRAP SECTION M.L.O. 21 SEP 1992 GLASGOW
18/398

LETTER DISTRICT OFFICE, LIVERPOOL L8 1AA
REVENUE PROTECTION
3 0 NOV 1992
051 242 4336
SPL
EXAMINER
18/399

19 Newspaper, Parcel, Registered, Express and Triangular Postmarks

Newspaper Branch

Prices are for large pieces or Newspaper Wrappers.

19/1 *19/2*

19/3 *19/4*

19/1	London NPB obliterators, many similar types	5.00
19/2	London circular marks with bars, several similar types (position of bars shows time of posting)	5.00
19/3	London circular marks with distinctive shading round rim	5.00
19/4	London types with number or letter at top	5.00
19/5	Edinburgh NPB types	10.00
19/6	Dublin NPB types	15.00
19/7	Provincial NPB types (8.00 used on postcards)	10.00
19/8	NPB Surcharge marks	15.00
19/9	Boxed NPB with date, 1880s	20.00

Parcel Postmarks

Prices are for large pieces.

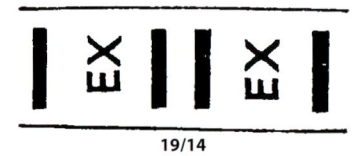

19/10 *19/11*

19/12 *19/13*

19/14

Undated/dated rubber types

19/10	Barred circle (but some are oval), from 1886	50.00
19/11	Double circle type with inscription in straight lines, from 1889	20.00
19/12	Vertical bar types (various sizes), from 1915	20.00
19/13	Dated rubber handstamp with various PP inscriptions (see **19/15**) (this example "Foreign & Colonial Parcel Post")	10.00
19/14	Roller cancellation, various types (see chapter 9 for rollers used for stamping packets)	20.00

Dated steel types

19/15 *19/17*

19/15	Single circles with 'Parcels Office', 'Parcels Depot', 'Parcels Post', 'Parcel Depot', P.P., P.P.O., etc. from 1883	15.00
19/16	Double circle eg NW Parcel Office NW10, 1971 seen	6.00
19/17	Hooded circle handstamps (see also chapters 9 & 13)	£100

Rubber Parcel handstamps

Termed "label types" for **19/19** onwards since based on a facsimile of parcel labels used previously.

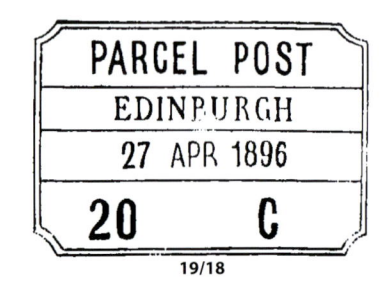

19/18

Newspaper, Parcel, Registered, Express and Triangular Postmarks

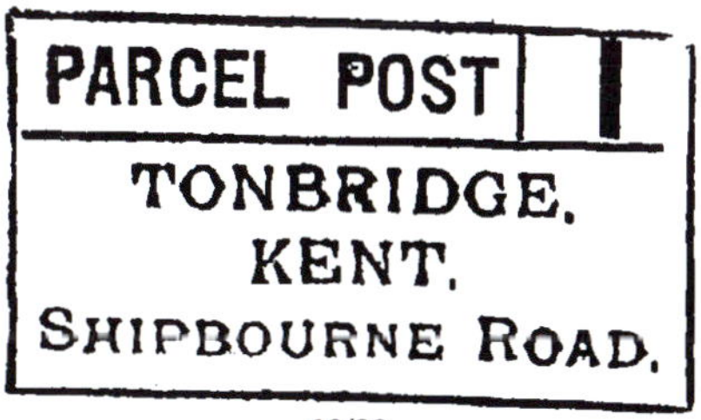

19/18	Concave corners	25.00
19/19	Label type, usually in violet (variations), from 1887	5.00
19/20	Revised design, from 1915, without arms but with telegraphic code	8.00
19/21	Revised design, from 1925, no arms or telegraphic code	5.00
19/22	Undated wartime "economy" parcel handstamp, 1940s	8.00
19/23	Revised design, from 1958, with date at centre, Parcel/Post at ends (date composed of loose type, year 2 digits)	3.00
19/24	Shorter design, from 1979, with revolving date wheels, year 4 digits	2.00
19/24A	As above but blue with date in red, 2000s	3.00

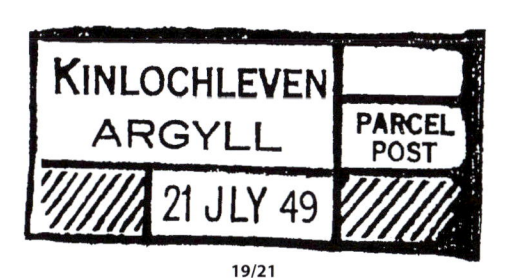

Paid Parcel rubber handstamps (in red)

19/25	Concave corners	25.00
19/26	Large oval double rim design, from 1892, with coat of arms at top	15.00

Newspaper, Parcel, Registered, Express and Triangular Postmarks

19/27	As above but without coat of arms, from 1940	10.00
19/28	Undated wartime "economy" handstamp, 1940s	20.00
19/29	Label type, similar to **19/24**, with PAID, from 1979 (only briefly used, PPIs having largely taken over the function)	8.00

Registration

19/30	Money-Letter, straight line, 1830s	£500
19/31	Crown with 'Registered' above, Foreign Office from 1820s	£125
19/32	As above but crown above Registered, London and Provincial, 1836-71	75.00
19/33	As above, European Country above, 1850s-60s in red	£200
19/34	Registered, straight line, from 1850s	£150
19/35	As above but also with town name, e.g. Registered Scarbro oval	£200
19/36	Single circle marks struck alongside numeral obliterator, from 1850s	£100
19/37	Liverpool 466 registered spoon (see chapter 7)	£300
19/38	Double circle marks, alongside obliterators or as obliterators, from 1860s	75.00
19/39	As above but with thick arcs, Scottish offices, from 1920s	30.00
19/40	As above but R breaking thin arcs	20.00
19/41	Oval, Registered/GPO and side arcs, 1856-7	£100
19/42	Oval Registered marks, steel, from 1860s (date composed of loose type, month 2 characters, year 2 digits)(value higher pre-1930, at least 20.00 pre-1900)	10.00
19/43	As above but incorporating reference to 2d fee	25.00

Note: The following 3 items normally accompany other postmarks on cover, thus the value has to be "combined" with that of these marks.

19/44	R in circle or oval, from 1885	10.00
19/45	As above but with Fee Paid, from 1892	10.00
19/46	Registered 2d straight line, boxed or unboxed	30.00
19/47	Single circle marks incorporating reference to 2d fee	40.00
19/48	Oval Registered marks, rubber, from 1890s (cf. steel **19/42**) (date composed of loose type, month 3 characters, year 2 digits)(see valuation comments for "steel" above)	4.00
19/49	Undated wartime "economy" registered handstamp, 1940s	8.00
19/50	Oval double-rim rubber handstamps from 1980, date on revolving wheels, year four digits	3.00
19/51	Circular Registration handstamps, rubber (Climax, see **9/66**)	18.00
19/52	Skeleton Registration handstamps	40.00
19/53	Hooded Registration handstamps, steel (month 2 characters)	10.00
19/54	same but rubber (month 3 characters), double-rim, black/purple	10.00
19/55	Small oval A.R. ('Avis de Reception') to denote reply required under the 'Advice of Delivery' service	20.00

Newspaper, Parcel, Registered, Express and Triangular Postmarks

Express

Also "Priority Services", new term from 1993 to cover Guaranteed Delivery and Registration Services.

19/57

19/58

19/56	Express - straight line types	50.00
19/57	Express - oval types	20.00
19/58	Priority Services rubber handstamps, from 1993	3.00

Triangular Handstamps

Used to denote posting under specific printed paper regulations to 1968.

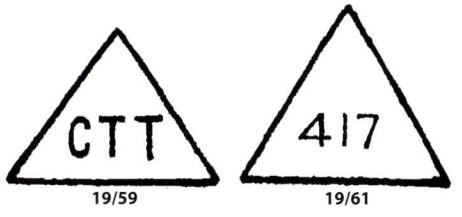

19/59   19/61

19/59	With telegraphic code letters	10.00
19/60	With London District initials or London Head Office initials eg S.M., K.E., M.T.P., F.B., F.S., I.S.	2.00
19/61	With provincial office numbers (including S prefix for Scotland or I for N. Ireland).	2.00

Inspectors' marks

Usually denoting an irregularity has been noted.

19/64   19/67   19/68

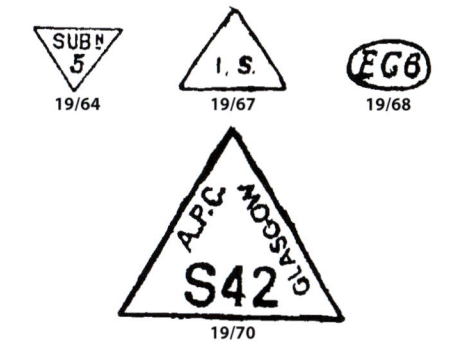

19/62	Diamond marks at Manchester, L.C. and L.C.O. at Letter Carriers' Office, H.O. at Head Office, 1876-1912	8.00
19/63	Diamond marks with London District Office initials or I.S. c1900	6.00

Note: Small inverted triangles denoting mail missorted to wrong stream (values higher pre-1902)

19/64	G.E, MID, N.W, S.E, S.W, SUBN, all with numbers or +	30.00
19/65	G.W, with numbers	15.00
19/66	SCOTCH, WELSH or IRISH with numbers	35.00
19/67	Small triangle (still in use 1980s)	2.00
19/68	Small oval, district initials plus numbers	5.00
19/69	Rubber triangle, MR (Manchester), 1970s	3.00
19/70	similar sized rubber triangle, S42/APC/Glasgow, 1996	3.00

See chapters 9, 14 and 27 for further triangular handstamps.

19/70

367

20 Posted in Advance for Christmas Postmarks

In the late 1800s, Post Office officials became concerned about annual increases in the number of postings at Christmas. Their problem was the need to effect next day delivery for normal business mail as well as the large amount of seasonal greetings. Several alternative proposals were considered and in 1902 it was decided to experiment at Rochdale. For six days prior to Christmas week, greetings to local addresses could be handed in, for delivery on Christmas Day. Green ½d stamps were cancelled in red: red 1d stamps were cancelled in black. Special handstamps were designed for the purpose.

In 1903 the scope of the scheme was extended to a total of 28 towns. It was not a success, so in 1904 only 14 towns were included in the experiment. In 1905 the number dropped to 6. Further special efforts were made during each of the years 1906-9 by 27 offices, but after a total of eight years of modifications and trials, the experiment was eventually abandoned.

Known examples of the special handstamps (and one machine postmark) are listed. We are indebted to (the late) John Swanborough for a detailed analysis of auction realisations and dealers' prices. Only two specimens of the Cheltenham undated postmark are known to us, and the year is thought to be 1903 though not confirmed by the envelope contents.

20/1 Type 1

20/2 Type 2

20/3 Type 3 (parcels)

20/4 Type 4

20/5 Type 5: Columbia Machine

20/6 Type 6

Posted in Advance for Christmas Postmarks

Town	TC	Year	Type	Colour	Val'n
(TC = telegraph code, type 2 only)					
Altrincham	ADJ	1903	2		£350
		1904	2		£300
		1905	2		£300
		1906	4		£350
		1907	4		£350
		1908	4		£350
		1909	4		£350
Ashton Under Lyne		1906	4		£450
		1907	4		£450
		1908	4		£350
Birkenhead		1906	4		£250
		1907	4		£180
		1908	4		£180
		1909	4		£120
Bolton	BL	1903	2		£250
		1904	2		£250
Bradford	BD	1904	2	red	£500
Bury	BC	1903	2	red	£600
Carlisle	CE	1904	2		£600
Cheltenham *(see note above)*		1903	6	red	£750
Douglas IOM		1906	4		£400*
		1907	4		£400
		1908	4		£400*
		1909	4		£400*
Dover	DR	1903	2		£900
Dukinfield		1909	4		£600
Eccles		1906	4		£350
		1907	4		£350
		1908	4		£250
		1909	4		£250
Glasgow	GW	1904	2		£250
Glossop		1907	4		£600
		1908	4		£600
Hull	HU	1903	2	red	£500
Hyde		1906	4		£700
		1907	4		£700
		1908	4		£600
		1909	4		£600
Knutsford		1906	4		£600
(see note at end of list)		1907	4		£600
Leicester	LE	1903	2	red	£350
		1904	2	red	£350
		1908	4		£250
Leigh, Lancs		1907	4		£500
Liverpool		1906	4		£125
		1907	4		£125
		1908	4		75.00
		1909	4		75.00
Macclesfield	MC	1903	2	red	£750
Manchester	MR	1903	2		£150
		1904	2		75.00
		1905	2		75.00
		1905	3	violet	£500
		1905	3	black	£200
		1906	3	black	£250
		1906	4		75.00
		1906	5		£125
		1907	4		75.00
		1907	5		£150
		1908	4		75.00
		1908	5		£125
		1909	4		75.00
		1909	5		£125
Newton Le Willows		1906	4		£600
		1907	4		£600
Norwich		1907	4		£400
		1908	4		£250
Oldham		1906	4		£350
		1908	4		£250
		1909	4		£350
Ormskirk		1906	4		£600
		1909	4		£500

Town	TC	Year	Type	Colour	Val'n
Prescot		1907	4		£600
		1909	4		£600
Preston	PR	1904	2		£500
Reading		1908	4	red	£750
		1908	4	black	£400
Rochdale	RO	1902	1	red	£600
		1902	1	black	£800
		1903	2	red	£400
		1904	2	red	£350
Runcorn		1907	4		£600
St. Helens		1906	4		£350
		1907	4		£350
Sale	SCR	1903	2		£450
		1904	2		£300
		1905	2		£300
		1906	2		£250
		1907	2		£250
		1908	2		£200
		1909	2		£200
Southport	SP	1903	2		£500
Stalybridge		1907	4		£600
Stockport		1906	4		£250
		1907	4		£350
		1908	4		£250
		1909	4		£250
Wakefield	WF	1903	2	red	£400
Walsall	WL	1903	2	red	£500
Warrington	WA	1903	2		£350
		1904	2		£350
		1905	2		£250
		1906	4		£250
		1907	4		£250
		1908	4		£250
		1909	4		£200
Widnes	WIP	1904	2		£500
		1905	2		£500
		1906	4		£600
Wigan	WI	1903	2		£300
		1904	2		£250
		1905	2		£250
		1906	4		£200
		1907	4		£250
		1908	4		£200
		1909	4		£200

*Beware of forgeries

Note: In the Sixth Edition the Knutsford listing included a type 4 handstamp used in 1907, 08 and 09 in addition to 1906. Due to doubts about the authenticity of these three years they were not included in the Seventh/Eighth editions. However a "genuine" 1907 impression has now been seen thus 1907 is reinstated. In the specimen seen the 07 is shown at an unusual angle, see **20/7**, but the 19 has not "impressed" at all.

369

21 Parliamentary

For many years members of both Houses of Parliament were able to post letters without charge, using the Free Frank system. This system ceased upon the adoption of the Uniform Penny Post. Thereafter, to have the benefit of free postage, Members were required to use specially printed envelopes which could be posted only from Parliament. Letters were bagged and taken to the Post Office, where they received a Crown Paid handstamp. Later, special postmarks were introduced.

21/1	House-of-Commons double arc, undated, from 1820s	£750
21/2	Houses of Parliament "killer" numbers 1 and 2, from March 1859	£700
21/3	Houses.of.Parliament/S.W. handstamp from March 1859	£400
21/4	H.C.S.W., circular charge marks from 1870s	£1000
21/5	House.of.Commons/40 duplex from 1882	£100
21/5A	House of Commons/S.W., single circle, 1889 (then see **21/10**)	30.00
21/6	House of Commons S.W.1, double circle, thick arcs (several), 1912-60	7.00

370

Parliamentary

21/7	As above but -1- and -2-, with thin arcs	3.00
21/8	House of Commons skeleton handstamp, 1928	£300
21/9	House of Commons B.O. S.W.1./Official Paid, double circle, red	3.00
21/10	House of Commons B.O./S.W.1. single circle (variations)	8.00
21/11	As above but SID handstamp, from about 1995	4.00
21/12	House of Commons/S.W.1 (later SW.1.) universal machine, 1965–	2.00
21/13	As above but with Official Paid sideways in bars, red	4.00
21/14	As above but 'House of Commons/SW', red, from 1991 (used on mail from outstationed parliamentary offices in Westminster)	3.00
21/15	House of Commons B.O. rubber parcel handstamp (variations)	50.00
21/16	House of Commons/B.O./S.W.1, rubber packet handstamp (variations)	5.00
21/17	Registered/1/House of Commons B.O. oval handstamp (variations)	50.00

21/18 21/19

21/20 21/21

21/18	H.P (House of Peers), small with dot between letters, 1820s/30s	£750
21/19	H:P (ditto), larger with 2 dots between letters, 1830s-1843	£1000
21/20	House of Lords S.W.1./-1-, double circle with thin arcs (variations)	5.00
21/21	House of Lords S.W.1/Official Paid, double circle, red	6.00

Cachets

21/23

21/27

21/28 21/31

21/37

21/22	House of/Commons, oval certifying stamp with crown from 1909	8.00
21/23	House of Commons/Speaker, upright oval with crown (varieties)	4.00
21/24	Vote Office/House of Commons, oval with coat of arms	10.00
21/25	Parliamentary Counsel/Office, double oval	10.00
21/26	Office of / Parliamentary / Commissioner, triangular	10.00
21/27	Clerk of the Parliaments / House of Lords, oval with coat of arms	10.00
21/28	As above but small double circle, crown above (two diff crowns)	5.00
21/29	Black Rod/House of Lords, oval with central coat of arms	10.00
21/30	Staff Superintendent/House of Lords, with central coat of arms	10.00
21/31	Lord Great Chamberlain/House of Lords, double circle (varieties), black or red	8.00
21/32	The Lord Chancellor, straight line script lettering (various colours)	4.00
21/33	Fees Office/House of Commons/London SW1A OAA	10.00
21/34	Postmaster/House of Commons, 1960s-	25.00
21/35	Parliamentary Sound Archives 1984-	8.00
21/36	Opposition Whips Office, / House of Lords, 1987-	8.00
21/37	Screened by Houses of /Parliament contractor, 2005-, various colours	8.00

Nos. 21/38 to 21/50 reserved for future use.

371

Parliamentary

Note: It is difficult to give values to the above cachets since some were used over many years. Some, though still in use in the late 20th century, are not easy to find. Suggested valuation scale is as follows:

    1960 to date – as listed above
    1940-1960 – above values times 2
    1930s – above values times 3
    1920s – above values times 5
    prior to 1920 – scarce
    prior to 1910 extremely scarce

More Modern Postmarks

21/51

21/52   21/55

21/57

21/51	Hasler machine (used for House of Commons or House of Lords mail stamped at London South Mail Centre), red, 1997- (largely replaced 21/13 & 21/14 but there appears to have been an overlap)	5.00
21/52	House of Commons philatelic handstamp (double circle) (or House of Lords)(available at House of Commons post office) (variations inluding time/no time), 1997- (normally on FDCs, valuation higher for complete sets of stamps)	5.00
21/53	House of Commons RMLS (Royal Mail London South), rubber packet handstamp, usually in red, 1998- (probably replaced 21/16 as postmark operation moved to Mail Centre, see **21/51**)	5.00
21/54	Portcullis House London SW1, SID handstamp, 2000- (Parliamentary offices in Bridge St, PO not accessible for public use, used in parallel to **21/11**)	6.00
21/55	House of Commons SW1A 0AA, 39mm double circle rubber handstamp (or House of Lords SW1A 0PW), 2001- (may have replaced 21/53)	6.00
21/56	Similar but large double oval (also House of Lords), 2002- (may have replaced **21/55**)	6.00
21/57	Meter machines, House of Commons & House of Lords, red, 2004-	5.00

Ireland

Irish Parliamentary Mark

21/58	Above/Number/Privileged, in red, 1829	£500

372

22 Royalty

Throughout the developments of the mails described in earlier chapters, Royal letters were carried free in the post. But Queen Victoria paid postage on many of her letters after abolition of the Free Franking system on 10 January 1840. Edward VII also paid postage on some of his letters. In the 20th century most royal covers bear a cachet, usually featuring the royal cypher, as a means of authorising the mail as official. This includes personal letters from the royal family as well as business mail from the Royal Household. Postmarks are mainly "Official Paid" handstamps or machine marks. There are also special handstamps which include a crown or the name of a royal residence. * denotes items of rarity.

Royal Residences (some for short visits only)

Queen Victoria

First two items used on mail from London royal residences.

22/1	London hooded circle handstamp, code A, with VR (serif) at centre	£300
22/2	similar but with VR (serif) at base, 1882-1900	£175
22/2A	Hampton Court, 27 mm single circle, 1880 (issued for telegraphic use but seen on reverse of postally used envelope)	£125
22/3	Osborne/I. of Wight, single circle, 1897-1901 (not Osborne BO/Cowes, which opened 1904)	£300
22/4	Sandringham/Norfolk, single circle, 1900-19	75.00

Note: The background to these single circles is not totally clear: they were probably issued for telegraphic purposes around 1880 though they have been seen used on postcards in the 1904-10 period (the messages do not suggest they come from "royal sources"), and the valuations are for such postcards - royal usage would attract a higher valuation. A Hampton Court handstamp is also seen on postcards in the same period but these have no royal connection

King Edward VII

22/5	London hooded circle handstamp, code A, with ER (non serif) at base	*
22/5A	Balmoral castle, single circle with crown at base 26mm, 1903 -, with or without code, then replacement handstamp, 24mm, 1950- (latest seen 1997)(previously listed as 22/12).	75.00
22/6	**Buckingham-Palace, single circle, 1903-23 (but also seen used on registered letters)	£100
22/7	**Frogmore, single circle, 1907	*
22/8	Official Paid/Sandringham RSO Norfolk, single circle, red, 1902-24	30.00
22/8A	Official-Paid / Windsor, single circle, red, 1903– (previously listed as 22/20; then see 22/26)	25.00
22/9	**Windsor Castle, single circle, 21mm, 1903-26	£100
22/9A	** Cumberland Lodge, Windsor, single circle, 21mm, 1904-	75.00

King George V

373

Royalty

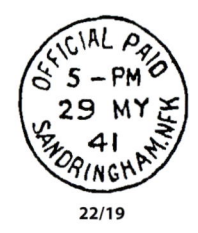

Postmarks listed under King Edward VII at approx same values.

Additional marks:

22/10	London hooded circle handstamp, code A, with GR at base	£500
22/11	Royal Pavilion, Aldershot, single circle with crown, red, 1915	£1000
22/12	This item now shown as **22/5A**	75.00
22/13	Registered/Buckingham Palace, oval, 1920- (or with SW1 1938-)	75.00
22/14	London SW1 (later SW) Official Paid, double circle thick arcs, red	20.00
22/15	Dublin Castle, single circle with cross at base, 1911 only	£500
22/16	Holyrood Palace, single circle with cross at base, 1911-	£250
22/17	Sandringham/Norfolk PAID handstamp, red, 1924	£100
22/18	Sandringham/Norfolk, double circle (long/short arcs), 1934-68	30.00
22/19	Official Paid/Sandringham.Nfk., single circle, red, 1925-62	25.00
22/20	This item now shown as **22/8A**	
22/20A	Official Paid/ Balmoral castle, single circle, red, 1919-(with dots, replacement handstamp no dots 1948-90)(previously listed as 22/31)	25.00

King Edward VIII

Postmarks listed under King George V but approx double values.

King George VI

Postmarks listed under King George V but approx 50% of value.

Additional marks:

22/21	Official Paid/Ballater, double circle with thick arcs, red, 1940-91	30.00
22/22	Balmoral Castle/Aberdeenshire, label type parcel handstamp (various)	75.00
22/23	Buckingham Palace/S.W.1., single circle, 1951-	30.00
22/24	Buckingham Palace S.W.1./Paid, undated univ machine die, black, 1940	75.00
22/25	Buckingham Palace/SW1, label type parcel handstamp, 1951- (various)	75.00
22/25A	Windsor Castle Windsor/Berks, single circle, 1938- (but issued earlier)	30.00
22/26	Official Paid/Windsor Berks, double circle & thick arcs, red, 1937-	10.00
22/27	Windsor Great Park, Windsor/Berks, single circle, 1949-	40.00

Queen Elizabeth II

Postmarks listed under King George VI but approx 50% of value.

Additional marks:

22/28	Registered/Buckingham Palace SW1, double rim oval 1987- (as 19/50)	25.00
22/29	As above but large (55mm long) rubber oval 1990-	25.00
22/30	Abergeldie Castle/Aberdeen, skeleton, 1955 only	25.00
22/31	This item now shown as 22/20A	
22/32	Registered/Balmoral Castle, oval, 1952-	75.00
22/33	Official Paid/Ballater, rubber, red, 1991- (replaced 22/21)	15.00
22/34	Official Paid/King's Lynn, single circle, red (on Sandringham mail)	15.00
22/35	Sandringham House/Norfolk, double circle, 1968-	15.00
22/36	Official Paid/Sandringham House.Nfk, single circle, red, 1972-	20.00
22/37	This item now shown as 22/25A	
22/37A	Buckingham Palace or Windsor Castle, large oval handstamp, 1992- (used on Guaranteed Delivery, successor to "registered")	20.00
22/37B	Buckingham Palace or Windsor Castle PPI style postmark "W7047", applied in blue by meter-style machine, including royal cipher (or not so), 1999-	5.00

374

Royalty

		22/37D

22/37C	Similar but changed to rectangular format, used black/purple at Buckingham Palace, also seen Windsor Castle, Highgrove, Sandringham House & Holyroodhouse, 1999-	10.00
22/37D	New format "W7047" and used in red, applied by meter style machine, 2004- (Buckingham Palace and Windsor Castle)	8.00
22/37E	As **22/37D** (Buckingham Palace) but with "Royal Mail" box at right replaced by "wavy lines", used to cancel adhesives used on Jubilee and Royal Birth "thank you" responses in 2012-13	8.00

Royal Cachets

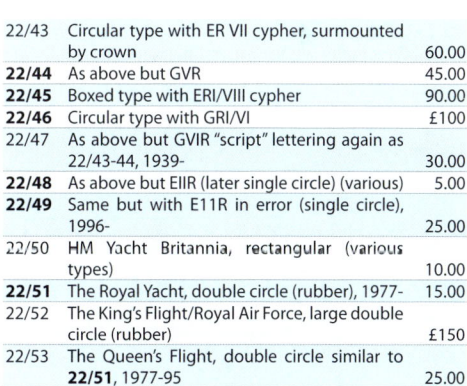

22/44    22/45

22/46    22/48

22/49    22/51

22/43	Circular type with ER VII cypher, surmounted by crown	60.00
22/44	As above but GVR	45.00
22/45	Boxed type with ERI/VIII cypher	90.00
22/46	Circular type with GRI/VI	£100
22/47	As above but GVIR "script" lettering again as 22/43-44, 1939-	30.00
22/48	As above but EIIR (later single circle) (various)	5.00
22/49	Same but with E11R in error (single circle), 1996-	25.00
22/50	HM Yacht Britannia, rectangular (various types)	10.00
22/51	The Royal Yacht, double circle (rubber), 1977-	15.00
22/52	The King's Flight/Royal Air Force, large double circle (rubber)	£150
22/53	The Queen's Flight, double circle similar to **22/51**, 1977-95	25.00

Other Royal Postmarks:

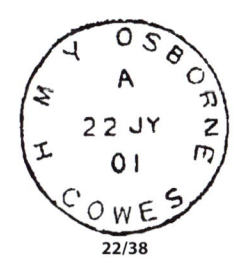

22/38   22/40

22/41   22/42

22/38	HMY Osborne/Cowes, skeleton for Cowes Regatta, 1901	£1250
22/39	His Majesty's Yacht, single circle with crown at base, 1903-35	£400
22/40	King's special wire, as above, 1904-23	£600
22/41	Official-Paid, single circle with crown at base (variations, with or without hyphen), red (or * in black), 1901-11	£150
22/42	Westminster Abbey, 1911 double circle with cross (B rarer than A) (probably issued for telegraphic use but known used on covers, usually unaddressed and probably stamped by favour. Specimen on single stamp sold on ebay in 2011 for 75.00)	£1250

22/55

375

Royalty

22/59 (Lord Chamberlain / St. James's Palace cachet)

22/64 (Office of HRH The Duke of Gloucester, Kensington Palace, London W8 cachet)

22/54	Privy Purse/Buckingham Palace, oval with crown, 1902-52	8.00
22/55	PH/EIIR/Buckingham Palace, oval with crown, 1953-	5.00
22/56	Lord Steward/M.H./Buckingham Palace, oval with crown, 1904-42	8.00
22/57	Master of The Horse/(The) Royal Mews, S.W., oval with crown, 1902-	8.00
22/58	Buckingham Palace Court Postmaster, rubber, 31mm, 1993-	25.00
22/59	Lord Chamberlain/St James's Palace, oval with crown, 1902-	6.00
22/60	Central Chancery of the Orders of Knighthood/8 Buckingham Gate/London SW1, oval with crown 1960- (later St James's Palace, larger oval)	10.00
22/60A	Office of/Marlborough House/ HRH Duchess of Kent, double oval, 1953-	40.00
22/60B	Office of/ St. James' Palace / HRH The Princess Royal, double oval, 1960-	25.00
22/61	Office of/Kensington Palace/HRH Princess Marina Duchess of Kent, double oval, 1961-	20.00
22/62	Office of / Kensington Palace / HRH The Princess Margaret, oval, 1976-	12.00
22/63	Office of/St James's Palace/HRH The Duke of Gloucester, oval, 1958-	12.00
22/64	Office of/HRH The Duke of/Gloucester/Kensington Palace/London W8, 1971- (later with post code W8 4PU)	12.00
22/65	Office of the/Court Postmaster, double circle with GVR cypher used on mail ex Royal Yacht, magenta, 1933-	£750
22/66	Master of the Horse/The Royal Mews Windsor, oval with crown, 1940-	15.00
22/67	Master of the Household's Department/Windsor Castle, double oval with crown, 1941-, later single oval	20.00
22/68	Privy Purse/Windsor, oval with crown, 1908-40	20.00
22/69	Royal Gardens/Windsor, oval with crown, 1964-90	35.00
22/70	HM's Representative/Ascot Office/St James's Palace SW1A 1BP, 1978-	15.00
22/71	The Royal Collection/St James's Palace SW1A 1JR, 1988-	10.00
22/72	Estate office/Sandringham, oval, 1978-	15.00
22/72A	The Royal Studs / Sandringham, double-rimmed circle, 1979-	15.00

Note: The above cachets are difficult to price since some were used over many years. Most, even if still in use in the late 20th century, are not easy to find and are thus priced higher than "EiiR" and "PH" (Paymaster of the Household) which are comparatively common. Uses of 22/54 onwards (exc 22/65) pre-1940 should be priced at double the figures shown and for pre-1920 prices should be trebled.

For further cachets not shown above see Glenn Morgan's book listed in Bibliography

Meters at Royal Residences/Estates

See chapter 25. All in red.

22/74

22/76

22/73	Meters used "incognito" at London W8 (Kensington Palace), Sandringham, Windsor (see Morgan for details), 1984- (no indication of source, town only shown, no slogan)	5.00
22/74	"Aberdeen" meter with Crown EiiR ex Balmoral Estate, 1983-94	8.00
22/75	"Forfar" meter with Glamis Castle slogan, 1986-88	8.00
22/76	"Kings Lynn" meter with "The Royal Studs Crown EiiR" slogan, 1990-	8.00
22/77	"Sandringham" meter & "The Estate Office Sandringham" slogan, 1990 (note this is the Sandringham meter from 22/73 with slogan added)	8.00
22/78	"Slough" meter with "St George's School Windsor Castle" slogan, 1993	8.00

Nos. 22/79 to 22/90 reserved for future use.

Court Post Offices (modern FDCs)

22/91

22/92

There has always been a demand for First Day Covers stamped at Buckingham Palace, Windsor Castle and the other royal residences. The post offices were not accessible by the public, but court staff were able to prepare FDCs. From at least 1966 to 1993 these were sent by registered post in order to satisfy PO regulations. In the 1990s the post offices were closed, leaving each establishment with a Court Post Office, which was run with its own rules, not those of Royal Mail. Under the new system Court staff were able to prepare a small number of FDCs for each issue, and rubber handstamps were used solely on these items. Some of these covers have come on to the market quite legitimately and are valued at 25.00 for covers with a single stamp and up to £150+ for complete sets, depending on the set of stamps used. Shown here are two examples at **22/91** (Buckingham Palace, initially struck in purple, later without 'Court Post Office', purely with inscription at foot of handstamp) and **22/92** (Sandringham House), with a similar handstamp available at Windsor Castle (see **12/63**).

Stanley Gibbons

Great Britain Department

BY APPOINTMENT TO
HER MAJESTY THE QUEEN
STANLEY GIBBONS LTD
LONDON
PHILATELISTS

Stanley Gibbons, a name synonymous with quality.

Ever since the birth of our hobby Stanley Gibbons has been at the forefront of GB philately and we invite collectors access to one of the finest GB stocks in the world by registering for our renowned free monthly brochure. Whatever your budget or collecting interests you will find a range of the highest quality material for the discerning collector.

Simply contact Mark Facey on **020 7557 4424** email **mfacey@stanleygibbons.com** or Michael Barrell on **020 7557 4448** email **mbarrell@stanleygibbons.com** to register

Est 1856
STANLEY GIBBONS

Stanley Gibbons
399 Strand, London, WC2R 0LX
+44 (0)20 7836 8444
www.stanleygibbons.com

23 British Post Offices Abroad

In colonies and countries lacking efficient postal administration, some British Consulates were authorised to provide postal services (some from the late 1700s) and later to supply GB stamps. By 1890, most of these arrangements had officially been terminated, although a few continued until the 1920s.

This chapter now lists only markings used as cancellations on complete covers franked solely with GB adhesive stamps ie NOT GB overprints nor mixed GB and foreign.

Collectors requiring a more detailed account of this subject are advised to refer to John Parmenter's book shown in the Bibliography.

Ovals with codes C, G, M and S

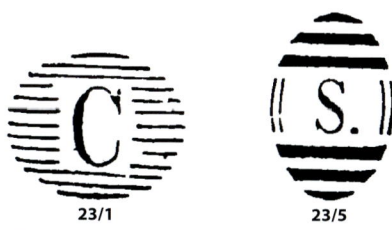

23/1	"C." horizontal oval - Constantinople	75.00
23/2	As above but upright oval	£500
23/3	"G" horizontal oval - Gibraltar	£150
23/4	"M" horizontal oval - Malta	£150
23/5	"S." upright oval (with full stop) - Stamboul	£125

Ovals/duplexes with numeric and alpha-numeric codes

		Horizontal Oval	Upright Oval	Circular duplex	Oval duplex
247	Fernando Po		??		
582	Naguabo, Porto Rico		£14000		
942	Larnaca, Cyprus		£750		
969	Nicosia, Cyprus 23/6		£1500		
974	Kyrenia, Cyprus		£6000		
975	Limassol, Cyprus		£2500		
981	Papho, Cyprus		£5000		
982	Famagusta, Cyprus		£6000		
A01	Kingston, Jamaica 23/7	£150		£200	
	("twin" horizontal oval	£900)			
A02	St John's, Antigua	£600			
A03	Demerara/ Georgetown, Br Guiana	£500			
A04	Berbice/New Amsterdam, Br Guiana	£800			
A05	Bahamas	£750			
A06	Belize, British Honduras	£750			
A07	Dominica, Leeward Is	£800			
A08	Montserrat	£6000			
A09	Nevis	£1000			
A10	St Vincent, Windward Is	£700			
A11	St Lucia	£2500			
A12	St Kitts	£1000			
A13	Tortola, Virgin Is on stamp	£2000			
A14	Tobago	£750			
A15	Grenada	£300			

379

British Post Offices Abroad

		Horizontal Oval	Upright Oval	Circular duplex	Oval duplex
A18	English Harbour, Antigua on stamp	£1000			
A25	Malta **23/8**	£125	£125	50.00	75.00
A26	Gibraltar	75.00	£700	75.00	75.00
A27	Alexandria, Jamaica	£600			
A28	Annotto Bay, Jamaica	£450			
A29	Bath, Jamaica	£450			
A30	Black River, Jamaica	£300			
A31	Brown's Town, Jamaica	£600			
A32	Buff Bay, Jamaica	£600			
A33	Chapelton, Jamaica	£450			
A34	Claremont, Jamaica	£625			
A35	Clarendon, Jamaica	£600			
A36	Dry Harbour, Jamaica	£600			
A37	Duncans, Jamaica	£600			
A39	Falmouth, Jamaica	£300			
A40	Flint River, Jamaica	£450			
A41	Gayle, Jamaica	£450			
A42	Golden Spring, Jamaica	£600			
A43	Gordon Town, Jamaica	£600			
A44	Goshen, Jamaica	£300			
A45	Grange Hill, Jamaica	£400			
A46	Green Island, Jamaica	£450			
A47	Highgate, Jamaica	£1000			
A48	Hope Bay, Jamaica	£600			
A49	Lilliput, Jamaica	£300			
A51	Lucea, Jamaica	£450			
A52	Manchioneal, Jamaica	£600			
A53	Mandeville, Jamaica	£300			
A54	May Hill, Jamaica	£300			
A55	Mile Gully, Jamaica	£600			
A56	Moneague, Jamaica	£450			
A57	Montego Bay, Jamaica	£300			
A58	Montpelier, Jamaica	£400			
A59	Morant Bay, Jamaica	£300			
A60	Ocho Rios, Jamaica	£450			
A61	Old Harbour, Jamaica	£300			
A62	Plantain Garden River, Jamaica	£300			
A64	Port Antonio, Jamaica	£450			
A65	Port Morant, Jamaica	£300			
A66	Port Maria, Jamaica	£300			

		Horizontal Oval	Upright Oval	Circular duplex	Oval duplex
A67	Port Royal, Jamaica	£600			
A68	Porus, Jamaica	£300			
A69	Ramble, Jamaica	£450			
A70	Rio Bueno, Jamaica	£450			
A71	Rodney Hall, Jamaica	£550			
A72	Saint David, Jamaica	£600			
A73	St.Ann's Bay, Jamaica	£950			
A74	Salt Gut, Jamaica	£450			
A75	Savanna-la-Mar, Jamaica	£300			
A76	Spanish Town, Jamaica	£400			
A77	Stewart Town, Jamaica	£800			
A78	Vere, Jamaica	£550			
B01	Alexandria, Egypt	75.00	75.00		£100
B01	Cairo, Egypt	£400			
B02	Suez, Egypt	£150			
B32	Buenos-Ayres, Argentina	£400	£500	£2500	
C28	Montevideo, Uruguay	£750			
C30	Valparaiso, Chile		£300		£400
C35	Panama, Colombia	£400			£300
C36	Arica, Peru	£1800	£1800		
C37	Caldera, Chile	£850			
C38	Callao, Peru	£450	£350		£1200
C39	Cobija, Bolivia	£3000	??		
C40	Coquimbo, Chile	£750			
C41	Guayaquil, Ecuador	£550			
C42	Islay, Peru	£750			
C43	Paita/Payta, Peru	£2000			
C51	St.Thomas, Danish W Indies	£350	£400		£350
C56	Cartagena, Colombia	£500			
C57	Grey-town, Nicaragua **23/9**		£250 on stamp		£1000
C58	Havana, Cuba	£550			£450
C59	Jacmel, Haiti	£350			
C60	La Guayra, Venezuela	£600			
C61	Porto Rico	£400	£900		£350
C62	Santa Martha, Colombia	£750			
C63	Tampico, Mexico	£750			
C65	(error) Cartagena, Colombia	£900			
C81	Bahia, Brazil		£650		
C82	Pernambuco, Brazil		£650		
C83	Rio de Janeiro, Brazil		£550		
C86	Porto Plata, Dominica		£1200		
C87	San Domingo, Dominica		£1200		
C88	St.Jago-de-Cuba (Santiago), Cuba		£2000		
D22	Ciudad Bolivar, Venezuela		??		
D74	Pisco, Peru		£7500		
D87	Iquique, Peru		£2500		

380

British Post Offices Abroad

		Horizontal Oval	Upright Oval	Circular duplex	Oval duplex
E53	Port-au-Prince, Haiti		£550		
E88	Colon, Colombia		£1000		
F69	Savanilla, Colombia		£900		
F83	Arroyo, Porto Rico		£1400		
F84	Aguadilla, Porto Rico		£1500		
F85	Mayaguez, Porto Rico		£750		
F87	Smyrna		£150		
F88	Ponce, Porto Rico		£650		
G06	Beyrout, Levant		£150		

Postmarks in "clear English"

– in alphabetical sequence

23/10	Ascension, single circle (until 1922) £150
23/11	Beyrout/British Post Office, hooded circle (until 1906) 75.00
23/12	British Post Office/Constantinople, single circle (until 1923) 15.00
23/13	Grey-Town, Nicaragua, single circle (until 1882) £500
23/14	Jacmel, Haiti, single circle (until 1850) £1250
23/15	British Post Office/Salonica, single circle (until 1905) 50.00
23/16	As above but double circle (until 1905) 40.00
23/17	Smyrna, small single circle (until 1893) 60.00
23/18	British Post Office/Smyrna, single circle (until 1905) 25.00

381

24 Tourist Cachets

Cachets are normally rubber stamps applied to an envelope or postcard away from the stamp. They are NOT postmarks. We have limited the scope of the listing below to the popular tourist cachets, excluding:
(a) cachets used on official mail from Government departments
(b) slogan type messages advertising political parties or "protest messages" eg "Permit Sunday trading"
(c) the plethora of modern cachets used on philatelically prepared covers, including Postal Museums "Posted at " or "carried on mail coach" etc.

This chapter is restricted to privately produced "tourist cachets" which are or were available on postcards posted by visitors at the appropriate location, not on a "one off" occasion or connected with a special or philatelic posting. Some cachets that do not strictly meet this definition were in the fifth or sixth edition but are now excluded. Some cachets are applied to cards before purchase, hence unused cards are available and these can be posted at other locations. Cacheted cards should ideally bear local postmarks, otherwise values should be reduced by half, which applies also to unused cards. Values given are for cards or covers with stamps, local postmarks, and clear cachets. Dates shown are for the earliest known specimen in each case though a range of years is shown particularly where the cachet was used over a long period. It is not intended to maintain a complete listing of locations producing too many modern cachets, but a listing of recent Land's End cachets has kindly been provided by John Holman and this is included.

Some cachets are *printed* on postcards; these are *excluded*. Some are applied only to, or intended for use with privately produced labels, eg Caldey Island and Llechwedd Caverns and these too we have excluded along with those intended for use on or with railway letter stamps. The 1987 Snowdon Summit entry is, however, retained. Cachets produced primarily for use on "tourist passports", but which can also be used on postcards, we have excluded. This includes National Trust and National Trust for Scotland cachets listed in the Sixth Edition. Of the Dartmoor cachets only the Cranmere Pool cachets are listed, not the hundreds of other "log book" cachets.

We acknowledge the considerable assistance given by John Holman (once again) in checking details and adding some entries. John Owen, who produced the recent Land's End book (see Bibliography), has kindly provided a summary for inclusion here.

Beachy Head

24/1	Beachy Head, straight line, with seriffed or sans serif lettering, unframed, purple/black, 1905	30.00
24/2	Watch Tower/on/Beachy Head/England/Harry Randal, circular, black, 1909	15.00
24/3	Watch Tower/Beachy Head/year, 3 straight lines, purple/black, 1910-11	20.00
24/4	The Watch Tower/Beachy Head, belt/buckle design, purple/black, 1911	15.00
24/5	Watch Tower/Beachy Head, double framed diamond, black/purple 1920	5.00
24/6	Watch Tower/*Beachy Head*, oval, purple or black, 1930	6.00
24/7	As above but with lighthouse in centre, purple, 1931	6.00
24/8	Posted at/Beachy Head Hotel, framed, purple, 1954	6.00
24/8A	Posted/on/Beachy/Head, black, 1989	5.00
24/8B	Beachy Head/Countryside Centre (pictorial with lighthouse), black, 1999	5.00

Blackpool Tower

382

Tourist Cachets

24/9	Tiny Town/Post Office/Tower Blackpool, double oval, purple, 1933	40.00
24/9A	Same but with Tower Blackpool removed, used at MARGATE, purple, 1935	50.00
24/10	Posted at John Lester's/Midget Town/The Tower/Blackpool, boxed (?date)	50.00
24/11	Posted from Top of/Blackpool/Tower/518 feet high, double rim oval, red, black, purple or magenta, 1949	2.50
24/12	Posted/from/the/top/of/Blackpool/Tower/Height 518 feet (pictorial), purple, red, black or blue, 1957-	2.50
24/13	Similar to **24/11** but Centenary Year, turquoise, 1994	5.00

Cranmere Pool and other Dartmoor cachets

Note: Cranmere Pool is Britain's remotest letter box and the only one marked on Ordnance Survey maps - cards usually bear postmarks of Bridestowe, Sticklepath, Okehampton or Plymouth.

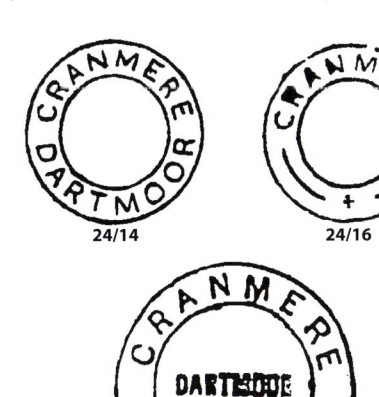

24/14	Cranmere/Dartmoor double circle, 25mm, black, 1900s	50.00
24/15	Cranmere, double rim circle, 20mm, purple/black, 1914-18	75.00
24/16	Cranmere/+, double circle, 24mm, red/purple/blue/black, 1916-30s	40.00
24/17	Cranmere/Pool/Dartmoor, double rim circle, 35mm, purple, 1938-47	30.00
24/18	Cranmere/=Pool=/Dartmoor, double circle, 35mm, blue/purple, 1940-56	10.00
24/19	Cranmere Pool/Dartmoor, large, two straight lines, purple, 1953	10.00
24/20	Cranmere/Pool/*Dartmoor*, double circle, 30mm, purple, 1959	10.00
24/20A	similar but Pool in centre (no stars) not at foot, 36mm, black, 1980	8.00
24/21	Cranmere Pool/*Dartmoor*/1825 feet, black/red/purple, 1960s-1970s	4.00
24/22	similar wording but rectangular, red, 1966	5.00
24/23	Cranmere Pool/Dartmoor, hexagonal, black, 1991	7.50
24/24	Other Dartmoor cachets eg Duck's Pool, 1939-73 oval, or 1960 circle, and others arranged by scouts in 1970	6.00
24/25	Museum of Dartmoor Life Okehampton, circular 73mm, blue or red, 1988-93	7.50

Note: There are many hundreds of Dartmoor cachets but they are designed for applying to "log books" or other documents and are seldom used on postcards.

Island Cachets

24/26	Ailsa Craig, single circle with star, violet, 1908	£100
24/27	similar but without star, violet, 1920	75.00
24/28	Ailsa Craig in oval (different sizes), violet, 1928	30.00
24/29	Ailsa/Craig in oval, black, 1952	20.00
24/29A	Ailsa Craig, straight line, violet, 1959	20.00
24/29B	Posted at Blackgang Chine IOW/*, in oval, blank centre, purple, 1948	30.00
24/30	Burgh Island/Bigbury-on-Sea/South Devon/TQ7 4AU UK, large double rim oval, black or violet, 1989	5.00
24/31	Posted at/Ettrick Bay, Bute, boxed, purple, 1906	75.00
24/32	Posted at/date/Ettrick Bay, larger than 24/31, purple, 1909	60.00
24/33	Fingal's Cave Staffa, large double circle, purple, 1969	10.00
24/33A	Osborne House/Queen Victoria's Home, IOW, purple or black, 1999	5.00
24/34	St. Kilda/date, unframed, 1931	£200
24/35	As above but boxed with indented corners, purple	£150

Tourist Cachets

24/36	St. Kilda/The furthest station west, circular with puffin, violet, red, black, purple-blue, blue, 1959-2000s (variations in size & details)	15.00
24/37	As above but double rimmed circle (variations), similar range of colours, 1970s-2000s	10.00
24/37A	St Kilda/World Heritage Site black & blue, 2001, used on labels	3.00
	(applied on island with NTS permission, but philatelic postmark also applied on mainland)	
24/37B	St Kilda 70th Anniversary of Evacuation 1930-2000, black, 2000	3.00
24/37C	St Kilda 75th Anniversary of Evacuation 1930-2005, black, 2005	3.00
	(also philatelic use on labels, blue or red)	
24/37D	St Kilda 50th Anniversary of Re-Occupation 1957-2007, black 2007	4.00
	(also philatelic use on labels, blue or red)	
24/37E	Posted at St Kilda/The St Kilda Club, NTS, blue or black, 1999-	5.00
24/37F	St. Kilda World Heritage Site, 1986-2011 25th Anniversary	5.00
24/38	St. Mary's Island Whitley Bay, shows lighthouse, pink or blue, 1991	5.00
24/39	St. Michael's Mount., boxed, with decorative border, 1935	20.00
24/40	Honeybills/South Stack Tea Rooms/Holyhead, double box, black, 1935	50.00
24/41	As above but pictorial shield design, showing lighthouse, 1937	20.00
24/41A	Posted on Brownsea Island, Girl Guide Camp, black, 1990	5.00
24/41B	Isle of/Ulva (off Mull, shows wolf's head), 1996	7.00

Island Cachets - Channel Islands

24/42	Herm, single line, black, 1903	£350
24/43	Wolf Caves, Jersey, double circle, violet or red, 1905	50.00
24/44	Jethou Island/date, straight line, black, 1907	£300
24/45	Jethou Island/Chan.Isles, circular, violet, 1909	£250

Island Cachets - Isle of Man

24/46	Posted at Cunningham Holiday Camp Douglas IOM boxed, purple, 1923	£120
24/47	Peel Castle/Isle of Man, horizontal diamond, purple, 1908	£100

Snaefell Summit

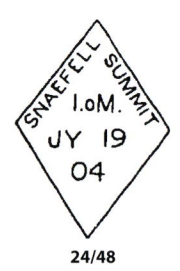

24/48

24/48	Upright diamond in black 1904 (first year 20.00), or violet 1907-32	10.00
	(but 1907-08 30.00, 1922-25 15.00, 1929-32 40.00, all violet)	
24/49	As above but green 1926, or red 1927-33	50.00

24/50	Horizontal diamond, 1928 violet, or (diff cachet) 1933-34 in red, 1934, 35, 39 violet	50.00
24/51	As above in violet 1946-49	20.00
24/51A	As above in black 1950- (variations) (also 1935-38 30.00)	5.00
24/51B	As above but seriffed lettering 1966 only	25.00
24/52	As above (non-serif) in blue, 1977-78	8.00
24/53	As above plus height 2036FT, red or violet, 1992	6.00
24/54	As above but with "Centenary 1895-1995" added, pink, 1995	8.00
24/55	As 24/54 but with "Centenary" and "1995" removed, 1996-99, red or black	6.00
24/55A	Oval design 2036FT Hotelier Ken Whipp, blue 1983 or red 1984	8.00
24/55B	Snaefell Summit Snaefell Mountain Railway, circular, 2001 (used concurrently with diamond design 24/51A)	6.00
24/55C	Summit Railway Station Isle of Man, circular, black, 2008	5.00
24/56	Tholt-y-will/Sulby Glen, upright diamond, black/purple, 1908	£200
24/57	As above in green, 1922	£225
24/58	As above but horizontal diamond, black or violet, 1995	6.00
24/59	Laxey Post Office, shows wheel, black, 1989	5.00

Nos. 24/60-80 reserved for future use.

John O'Groats

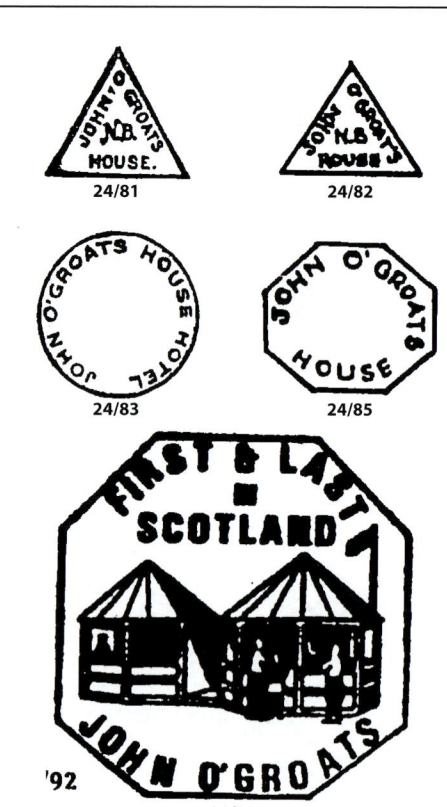

24/81

24/82

24/83

24/85

24/92

24/81	John O'Groats/N.B./House, NB in script, in triangle, black, 1898	75.00
24/82	John O'Groats/N.B./House, in triangle, black/purple, 1903	40.00

Tourist Cachets

24/83	John O'Groats House Hotel, single circle, purple, 1931	6.00
24/84	John O'Groats House, single circle (diff sizes), purple, 1930s	3.00
	(24/83 with "Hotel" removed, also later new cachets without Hotel)	
24/85	John O'Groats/House, octagonal, purple, 1950	3.50
24/86	John O'Groats House Hotel, straight line, purple, 1957	4.00
24/87	As above but small circle, purple, 1970	4.00
24/88	As above but oval (variations), purple/black, 1978	4.00
24/89	John O'Groats/Scotland, double rim circle, purple, 1959	10.00
24/90	As above but oval with space for inserting date, black, 1984	4.00
24/91	Last House, John O'Groats, straight line, violet or blue, 1961	3.50
24/92	First & Last in Scotland, large octagonal pictorial, black, 1989	5.00
24/93	The Last House/in Scotland/John O'Groats, three straight lines, purple or black, 1991	3.50
24/93A	As above but smaller, purple or blue, 2001	4.00
24/93B	Last House Museum, single line, purple, 1994	6.00

Land's End

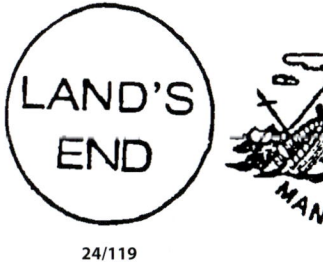

24/95 (triangle with LAND'S END)

24/95	Land's End, triangle with blocked border, black, purple or blue, 1901-78	2.00
24/96	Land's End/Hotel,/Cornwall., rectangle with indented corners, purple, 1903	10.00
24/97	First and Last Refreshment House/By E. James/Lands End, double oval, black, 1905	8.00
24/98	As above but without words 'By E. James', black, 1907	8.00
24/99	Lands End, small double circle, black, 1905	10.00
24/100	Lands End/Post Office, large double circle, black, 1913	15.00
24/101	Lands End, small double rim oval, blue, purple or green, 1911-13	4.00
24/102	As above but large single oval, purple, 1920 .	6.00
24/103	As above but large double rim oval, 1921-25	5.00
24/104	First & Last House/Lands End, unframed 2-line, purple, 1912-25	6.00
24/105	As above, variety of cachets, diff sizes/colours, 1929-35 (many versions of this cachet were printed, not listed here)	4.00
24/106	Sennen/Post Office/Lands End, single circle, black, 1924	8.00
24/107	Lands End, single triangle, purple, 1925-29	2.00
24/108	Lands End, boxed with blocked border, 1928	8.00
24/109	First & Last House/Lands End, two lines, boxed, red/black, 1931-76	2.50
24/110	First and Last House/In England/Land's End, 3 lines, boxed, red, 1931-38	3.50
24/111	Lands End, shield with lighthouse, scroll below, purple, 1935-39	3.00
24/112	Lands End between pairs of 4 wavy lines, black, 1939-47	3.00
24/113	As above but pairs of 2 wavy lines, black, 1947-49	3.00
24/114	Lands End, double triangle (apex downward) with scrolls, black, 1950-64	2.50
24/115	Last/Inn/Lands/End, boxed, purple, 1953-54	5.00
24/116	The Land's End Hotel Ltd/Land's End, 38mm circle with shield, black, 1950	5.00
24/117	The First & Last House/In England/Lands End, 3 straight lines in two colours, Lands End in red, remainder in blue, 1976-77	5.00
24/118	Breathtaking/Lands End, large boxed, 51mm wide, black, 1982	8.00
24/119	Land's End, single circle, 31mm, black, 1982	5.00
24/120	Land's End/Man & the Sea, with waves, lighthouse and shipwreck, blue, 1983	3.00
24/121	Lands End, unframed with star attached to E, black/blue, 1984-88	3.00
24/122	Lands End, large 71mm oval with picture of house within, black, 1985	3.00
24/123	Lands End, semi-circle + lighthouse & rays of light, red, blue or black, 1989-93	2.00

The modern Land's End cachets that follow are difficult to value. On the one hand a nominal 2.00 each would appear appropriate (to contrast with the older "classic" material, though the long-lived **24/95** is one of the easiest to find), but they each had such a limited life they would be difficult for collectors to locate so that a higher value would appear suitable!

24/111 (shield with lighthouse, LANDS END)
24/115 (LAST INN LANDS END boxed)
24/119 (LAND'S END circle)
24/120 (MAN & THE SEA, LANDS END)
24/123 (LAND'S END semi-circle)

24/94	From the/Old Man at the/Land's End, rectangle with indented corners, purple, blue or green, 1901-10	6.00

24/124 (LANDS END 14 MAY 1992 'YOU KNOW THE WAY')

385

Tourist Cachets

24/124	Lands End/date/You know the way, large oval, black, 1992-94	
24/125	Land's End, mermaid design, blue, 1994	
24/126	Posted at Land's End Cornwall England, red, 1994 (two types)	
24/127	Land's End/Cornwall England, framed, flying bird design, red, 1994-	
24/128	Holiday Greetings from Land's End (pictorial), red, 1995	
24/129	Land's End Cornwall (circular, bird design), red, 1997	
24/130	Special Greetings from Land's End Cornwall, circular, red, 1996	
24/131	Posted at Land's End (framed, bird design), red, 1996	
24/132	Posted at Land's End Cornwall England (framed Land's End rocks design), 1997	
24/133	Posted in the Famous Land's End Post Room (eclipse design), red, 1999	
24/134	The Land's End Post Room (circular), red, 1999	
24/135	Duchy of Cornwall/Land's End (coat of arms design), red, 1999	
24/136	Posted at Land's End "stamp shaped" (pictorial), red, 2000	
24/137	Land's End Post Room (circular, bird design), red, 2000	
24/138	The Land's End Post Room Millennium Year 2000 (circular), red	
24/139	The Land's End Post Room Cornwall 2001 (circular), red	
24/140	Our Cachet Mark Centenary/The Land's End Post Room, framed, red, 2001	
24/140A	Celebrating the Centenary of Using Cachet marks 1901-2001, circular, red, 2001	
24/140B	The Land's End Post Room (circular, bird design), red, 2002	
24/140C	Posted at Land's End in the Duchy of Cornwall (circular, heraldic), red, 2003	
24/140D	Posted at Land's End Cornwall (circular, lighthouse design), red, 2003	
24/140E	The Land's End Post Room 2004 (circular bird design), red, 2004	
24/140F	similar but '2005', red, 2005	
24/140G	Posted at Land's End 2006 (large rectangular flag & bird design), red, 2006	
24/140H	Posted at Land's End 2007 (rectangular), red, 2007	
24/140I	Posted at Land's End Cornwall England 2008 (circular), red, 2008	
24/140J	Posted at Land's End 2009 (circular), red, 2009	

Llanfair P.G.

24/141	Village name round rim of double circle with 'Posted at' or 'Post Office' in centre, many types, blue, black or violet, 1956	3.00
24/142	As above but map or dragon in centre	3.50
24/143	Village name round rim of single circle (some with double rim), dragon at centre (variations), several types/colours, c1960.	3.00
24/144	As above but 'Posted From', 'Posted at' or blank centre (variations, sizes vary 27-37mm), 1961	3.00
24/145	As above but picture of station at centre, red/black, 1985	5.00
24/146	As above with dragon and "Siop Betsan" inscription, several types, red, 1983, and 2-colour version red/green, 1990	6.00
24/147	Village name, unboxed straight line, several sizes/colours, 1964	5.00
24/148	Village name round rim of double oval with blank centre, ?1968	5.00
24/149	As above (vertical) but large "Marquess of Anglesey's Column", black, 1980	7.50
24/150	As above (horizontal) but "Siop Garnedd Wen" at centre, purple, 1985	5.00
24/151	Large unframed 95x40mm "Siop.Betsan" with 2 dragons, pink, 1990	6.00
24/152	Large vert oval with "Siop Betsan" & "longest named railway station in the world", green, & red/black Welsh lady at centre, 1990s	6.00
24/153	Circular village name in single circle with "Siop Betsan" at centre, Wales at foot, red, 1995	6.00
24/154	Village name (lower case) round rim (but no rim) with added wording "Isle of Anglesey Ynys Mon", and either "James Pringle", 1990, or dragon (used in Pringle shop), black (different sizes), 1991	4.00

Nos. 24/155-170 reserved for future use.

LLANFAIRPWLLGWYNGYLLGOGERYCHWYRNDROBWLLLLANDYSILIOGOGOGOCH

24/147

24/141

124/150

24/154

Tourist Cachets

Snowdon

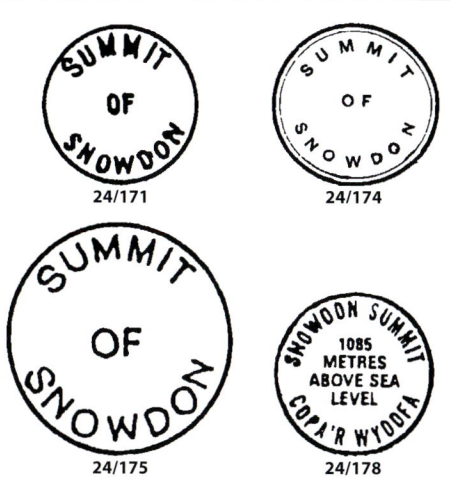

24/171
24/174
24/175
24/178

24/171	Summit/of/Snowdon, single circle, 23mm, blue/purple, 1902-38	5.00
24/172	As above but double rim circle, 37mm, purple/black/red/green, 1925-33	4.00
24/173	As above, single circle, 21mm, purple/black/red, 1930s	5.00
24/174	As above, double rim circle, 24mm, purple/red, 1945-52	4.00
24/175	As above, single circle, 32-35mm, variations, purple or black, 1950s-80s	2.00
24/176	Half-way House/G. Williams/Snowdon, double oval, blue, 1930s-50s	6.00
24/177	Mount Snowdon, violet, straight line 45mm, 1946	20.00
24/177A	From Snowdon Llanberis, circular, violet, 1957	8.00
24/178	Snowdon Summit 1085 metres etc, circular (on labels), black/red, 1987	3.00
24/179	Snowdon/Railway, circular 25mm, green, ?1930s	30.00
24/180	Snowdon/blank, possibly above item with "Railway" removed, green, ?1930s	25.00

Ship's cachets

All are static displays open to the public, except SS "Sir Walter Scott" which sails on Loch Katrine, Scottish Trossachs.

24/186
24/190 
24/192 

24/181	Posted on board HMS Belfast (River Thames London), 40mm double rim circle, black, 1973	3.50
24/182	Cutty/Sark 1869 (Greenwich), circular, black, 1967-71	6.00
24/182A	as 24/182 but Off. No. 63557 added, 1978	7.00
24/183	as 24/182A but London added, black, 1991	5.00
24/184	SS Great Britain Bristol (ship pointing right), black, 1978	4.00
24/185	similar, ship pointing left, black/blue/violet, 1985 (variations)	3.50
24/186	similar but "150 Years 1843-1993" wording, violet, 1993-94	2.50
24/186A	Brunel's SS Great Britain, ship at right, black, 2007	5.00
24/186B	Posted on board ., large design with ship in central circle, black, 2009	5.00
24/186C	SS "Sir Walter Scott" Launched 1899, 2011	6.00
24/187	The Frigate Unicorn/Victoria Dock Dundee, pictorial, black, 1989	5.00
24/187A	RSS Discovery/Dundee 1901 2001 Centenary, large pictorial oval, blue, 2001	7.50
24/187B	Posted Beneath/HMS Royal Oak (Plymouth), black, 1938	30.00
24/188	Posted In/H.M.S. Victory (Portsmouth), blue, unframed, 1949, or Posted/in H.M.S. Victory, purple, 1954	2.50
24/189	Illustration of HMS Victory, no wording, blue, 1951	3.50
24/190	As above but smaller with Posted/on board/H.M.S. Victory wording (variations), blue, violet, purple or black, 1952	2.00
24/190A	Similar with "Posted on board" but no ship's name, green, 1974	4.00
24/191	Large boxed ship illustration with name of HMS Victory Commanding Officer, red, 1978	2.50
24/192	Posted on board/HMS Victory, circ, 35mm, violet/blue/black/red, 1982	2.00
24/192A	Similar but smaller, 30mm, black, 2001	4.00
24/193	HMS Warrior/1860 (Portsmouth), double rim oval, black, 1988	4.00
24/193A	as above but rectangular, 2011	5.00

Other cachets – England

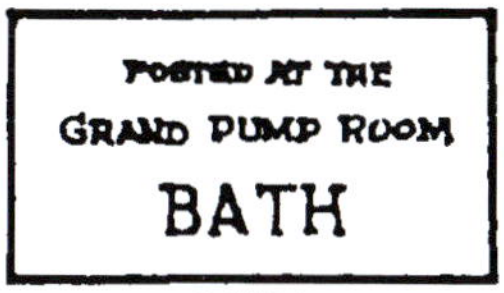

24/194 
24/195 
24/212

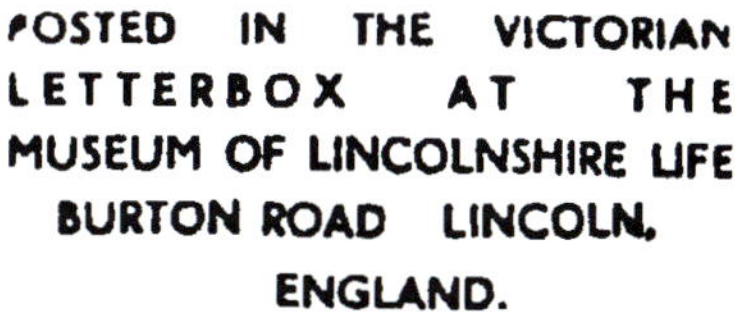

POSTED IN THE VICTORIAN LETTERBOX AT THE MUSEUM OF LINCOLNSHIRE LIFE BURTON ROAD LINCOLN, ENGLAND.

24/214

387

Tourist Cachets

24/217   24/222

24/193B	Posted at Anderton (Northwich)/Home of the Anderton Boat Lift, red, 1996	4.00
24/193C	Posted at Attingham Park (Shrewsbury) (large pictorial), black, 1995	5.00
24/194	Posted at the/Grand Pump Room/Bath, boxed (variations), 1912	40.00
24/195	Posted at the/Pump Room/Bath, England, boxed, purple/black, 1958-75	3.00
24/196	Posted at/Cape Hill/Brewery/Birmingham, pictorial, pink, 1938	30.00
24/196A	Blackpool (Sands) S Devon (near Dartmouth), circular pictorial, 1966	8.00
24/196B	Carbis Bay (near St Ives Cornwall), within triangle, violet, 1906	20.00
24/197	Chatterley Whitfield Mining Museum (Tunstall Stoke on Trent), circular, dated, black, 1981 .	4.00
24/198	Central Spa/Town Hall, rectangle with indented corners, used at Cheltenham (details of dates required)	25.00
24/199	Posted in Coronation Street (TV studio set, Manchester), 1970s	2.00
24/200	Posted at Crewe Heritage Centre, circular, red, 1991	2.50
24/201	Posted at Tramway Museum Crich (Derbyshire), circular, red, 1974	4.00
24/201A	similar but large "stamp shaped", red or green, 1973	5.00
24/202	Carried by tramcar (same location), pictorial, red, 1989	3.00
24/202A	Devil's Dyke (near Brighton), circular, violet, ?1928 (year not clear)	30.00
24/203	Small Relics Museum Didcot, triangular, red, 1982	5.00
24/203A	Posted at The Dover Cruise Terminal, green, 1998	5.00
24/204	Posted at the Black Country Museum, Dudley, black, 1987	5.00
24/205	Haddon Hall/date/Bakewell, single circle, black or violet, 1953	4.00
24/206	Royal Pump Room Museum (Harrogate), circular, black, 1970	7.50
24/207	Royal Pump Room Museum/Harrogate Yorkshire, circular, 1982	5.00
24/208	Hell's/Mouth/Cornwall, triangular, pink, 1951	10.00
24/208A	same wording but words outside triangle, violet, ?1950s	10.00
24/209	Holmfirth/Postcard/Museum, framed in square, black, 1987	3.00
24/210	Posted on the World's First Cast-Iron Bridge, Ironbridge, red, 1989 (on souvenir cover with full set of Industrial Architecture stamps 8.00)	3.00
24/210A	similar but smaller design, black, 2009	4.00
24/211	Posted at Blists Hill Ironbridge Shropshire, red or black, 1989	3.50
24/211A	Similar but larger design, black or red, 2009	4.00
24/211B	Jamaica Inn (Cornwall), large pictorial, black, 2008	5.00
24/212	Posted at Jodrell Bank, circular, 25mm, 1967 (also dated version used 19 Sept 1966, Technology stamp issue day)	3.50
24/213	similar but large unframed 52mm, pictorial, 1972	4.00
24/214	Museum of Lincolnshire Life Lincoln, black, 1978	4.00
24/214A	The Lizard Cornwall/date/Britain's Most Southerly Post Office, black, 2008	5.00
24/214B	Mouse/hole Penzance, triangular, black, 1952	10.00
24/214C	North Lowestoft/Gt Britain's most easterly/Post Office, black, 1998	5.00
24/214D	Geevor Tin Mines plc Tin Mining Museum Pendeen (Cornwall), ?1980s	5.00
24/215	Penny Park/House/Coventry, double circle, 1970s	4.00
24/215A	Obtained at/Couch's House/Polperro/Cornwall (Sir Arthur Quiller-Couch), circular, green, ?1960s	8.00
24/216	Portsmouth City Museum/Dickens Birthplace, circular, 1969	5.00
24/217	Ragley/Hall, small double rim circle, blue/black/violet, 1960s	3.00
24/218	RAF Museum Hendon, circular, 1970s	3.00
24/219	Ryedale Folk Museum/Posted at, with wheatsheaf, black, 1991	4.00
24/220	Posted End of Pier/Southend, red, 1913	50.00
24/221	Tan Hill, England's Highest Inn, purple, 1930s-58 (Kendal pmk)	10.00
24/222	The Old Post Office/Tintagel, large circle (variations), green/black/blue, 1971-1990s (also used on labels)	4.00
24/223	as above but with "NT Centenary 1895 1995" added	8.00
24/223A	The Old Post Office/Tintagel/NT/100 Years of Ownership, green, 2003	8.00
24/224	Underground Post Box / Wheal / Roots / Mine / Wendrow, oval, black, 1979	5.00
24/225	Poldark/Mining Ltd/Posted/Underground, black, 1979	5.00
24/226	Posted underground / at Poldark Mine, circular, black or blue, 1992	5.00
24/226A	Posted underground / Poldark Mine Cornwall, circular, black, 2002	5.00
24/227	Upleatham Old Church, smallest church in England, black, 1960s	6.00
24/228	Posted at the Upminster Windmill, purple, 1949	12.00
24/229	Posted at/Wannock (gardens at Eastbourne), unframed, violet, 1936-39 .	15.00
24/230	Posted at the/Wedgwood/Visitor/Centre, circular, black/blue, 1982	5.00
24/230A	Westminster Cathedral/St Edward's Tower/London, black, 1936	60.00
24/231	Posted in / Wookey/Hole (near Wells), boxed, witch on broomstick, blue, black, green or red, 1960	4.00
24/232	Wrekin Hill/Wellington Salop, decorated two line cachet, ?date	50.00
24/232A	A Birrell/The Wrekin Cottage/Wellington Salop, large oval, violet, 1911	30.00
24/233	NRM (National Railway Museum, York), small, black, 1979	4.00
24/234	Posted at Tyneham Post office (Dorset, ghost town') circular black, 1973	30.00

Nos. 24/235-259 reserved for future use.

Tourist Cachets

Other cachets – Scotland

24/266 CAIRNGORM CHAIRLIFT POST BOX HIGHEST IN BRITAIN

24/269 CULLODEN BATTLEFIELD NTS

24/278 SHELL GROTTO

24/260	Burns' Cottage (Alloway), various sizes, blue or violet, 1987-	5.00
24/261	Aonach Mor, Fort William, Britains Highest Postbox, boxed, 1993	4.00
24/261A	similar but "posted at 2150ft", black or blue, 1998 .	5.00
24/261B	New design, cable car/trees "Highest postbox in Western Highlands", black, 2009	4.00
24/262	Santa Claus Land/Aviemore Centre, double circle, red, 1983	4.00
24/263	Tam O'Shanter/Museum/Ayr, oval, black, ?1960s	7.50
24/264	Ben Nevis/Observatory, double oval with centre blank, purple, 1903	50.00
24/265	Ben Nevis Summit/J. Miller/Hotel, double oval, purple, 1905-13	15.00
24/266	Cairngorm Chairlift/post box/highest in Britain, framed, black, purple, green or red, 1963-94	5.00
24/267	Cairngorm Chairlift/Car Park 2150ft/Top Station 3647ft, unframed, blue, violet, black, red or green, 1969-82	4.00
24/267A	Cairngorm Mountain/UK Highest Postbox/1097M, unframed, black, 2009	3.50
24/268	Culloden Battlefield NTS, circular 26mm pink, 1969	3.50
24/269	similar but 28mm, black or blue, 1974-1990s	2.50
24/269A	Scotland's First & Last Post Office Drummore Wigtownshire, black, 2003	5.00
24/269B	Dunoon/Castle House Museum/=121=, black, 2002	5.00
24/270	Glasgow Museum of Transport, Oldest Pillar Box in Scotland, unframed, red, 1968	5.00
24/271	similar but framed, black, 1978-1990s	5.00
24/271A	Glamis Castle, black, 2005	5.00
24/272	First House in Scotland/Sark Bridge/Gretna, boxed, violet, 1973	6.00
24/272A	First House/in Scotland (Gretna), black, 2001	4.00
24/273	Posted from Livingstone Memorial Blantyre, black, red or green, 1971-93	3.50
24/274	Loch Ness Visitors Centre, Drumnadrochit, pictorial, black, 1989	5.00
24/275	Loch Ness Official Exhibition Centre, circular, black, 1993	4.00
24/276	Posted at / Sanquhar / The Oldest / Post Office / in Britain / Est 1763, unframed, red, 1986	8.00
24/277	Sanquhar the world's oldest working post office, pictorial, black or green, 1993	8.00
24/277A	Similar but oval design with year 1712 (variations), black, 1997	5.00
24/278	Shell Grotto (Burns Memorial Gardens, Alloway), black, 1905 only	75.00
24/279	Nat Trust for Scotland/White Lady Shieling 2525 feet, black, 1966	5.00

Other cachets – Wales

24/281 Bought on Cader Idris Summit, Pror. H. Jones, Aberynolwyn, Towyn, REFRESHMENT ROOM

24/282 THIS CARD WAS POSTED ON LLANDUDNO PIER

24/280	Llythyrdy/Bethlehem (old post office), circular, red/black, 1991-2002 (with/without date across centre)	3.00
24/281	Bought on Cader Idris Summit, Refreshment Room, oval, violet, 1939 .	15.00
24/282	This card was/posted on/Llandudno Pier, three straight lines, red, 1987	7.50
24/283	This Card was Posted/at the Summit of the/Great Orme, Llandudno, boxed, blue, black, purple or red, 1964	3.50
24/284	Posted from the/Great Orme Summit (variations), boxed, red, 1986	5.00
24/285	Llywernog Silver Lead Mine, circular, c1984	5.00
24/286	similar but with Ponterwyd location included, pictorial, with "Posted underground in Mid-Wales", 1985	3.50
24/287	St. Davids "Britain's smallest city", boxed, 82x23mm, 1970	7.50
24/288	Garden Festival of Wales	5.00

Nos. 24/289-300 reserved for future use.

Other cachets – Northern Ireland

24/301	Giant's Causeway Northern Ireland, pictorial circular, red, 2002	3.00

Note : The "Sark Quatercentenary" item has been omitted since it is a Post Office cachet: the "Cruise of the Northern Belle" railway cachet is listed in chapter 13.

Further reading :
"A Guide to the Postcard Cachets of Land's End" by John D B Owen, 1994
"The Postal History of the Manx Electric Railway" by A Povey & J T Whitney, 1979

Articles as follows :
J Holman on *"British Souvenir Stamps and Cachets"* in *"Stamp Collecting"* 1978-84
J Sherwood on *"Other than the postage stamp"* in *"Stamps"* 1983-92
G Crabb on *"The Land's End Cachet - and others"* in *"Gibbons Stamp Monthly"* 1967 and similar 1968 and 1970.
O W Newport on *"St Michael's Mount"* in *"Stamp Collecting"* 1984
J Holman under *"New Collector"* heading in *"Gibbons Stamp Monthly"* 1994 et seq

25 Meter Marks

Companies, local authorities and other users purchase or license meter machines to stamp their own mail, making appropriate payments to the Post Office. They were first used in the UK in 1922 and in general they are struck in red to denote "prepaid mail" and contain the inscriptions "Great Britain" (except Channel Islands & Isle of Man after postal independence) and "Postage paid". They should not be confused with Post Office "Paid" postmarks struck in red by means of handstamps or machines (see chapters 9, 10, 11, 21 and 22) on Post Office premises.

Since used only for the mail of one company, advertising slogans or patriotic and "appeal" legends can be used freely within the normal bounds of acceptability. Covers with slogans are priced at up to 10 times the value of postmarks without slogan though for low value post-1950 items this will only apply to slogans with a particular thematic appeal.

In the early days there were three manufacturers of meter machines but after 1968 the number increased. Letters and numbers included in the postage paid emblem (termed "frank") distinguish the manufacturer and/or the machine model but the initial Pitney Bowes series had none. Once in use in a machine the frank can remain unchanged for years. Thus, for example, a GviR frank may be found used during the reign of EiiR. We show here most of the types used showing manufacturers but not machine models. For further reading see Mann's book (listed in Bibliography) and articles by Jack Peach in Postal Mechanisation Study Circle Newsletters. Alastair Nixon has kindly provided the update shown in section starting 25/37 and his efforts are appreciated: for more details see Alastair's website mentioned at the end of the section.

For convenience parcel post labels are included at the end of the chapter, also the postmark of the 1912 Wilkinson "penny in the slot" machine.

Early meters

25/1

25/2

25/4

25/5

Meter Marks

25/7

The Universal Midget 3
PRINTS FRANK-POSTMARK
& *YOUR OWN* ADVERT.

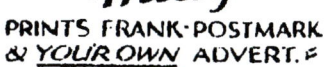

25/8

25/9   **25/11**

25/16

25/1	Pitney Bowes 1922 (valuation is for 1922, 2.00 from 1923)	7.00
25/2	Universal NZ 1922, frank 25x25mm, town die black 5 bars, spaced at distance to left	75.00
25/3	Closer spaced, town die black 6 bars, frank 25x22mm, from 1923	5.00
25/4	similar but town die red	3.00
25/5	As above but special Wembley town die in black or red, 1924-25 (used in NZ Pavilion at Wembley exhibition)	£225
25/6	As above but circular town die within 6 wavy lines, from 1923	50.00
25/7	similar but within 7 wavy lines ("High speed"), from 1923	4.00
25/8	Neopost machine with N below number in centre, or Universal "Midget" (M), circular town die, from 1925 (valuation higher with slogan as shown at **25/8**)	1.50
25/9	New frank - manufacturers and codes were Pitney Bowes (PB,H), Universal (M, NZ, NZA), Neopost (N)	1.00
25/10	As above but with small cypher at foot, from 1932 - Universal (U) from 1932, Pitney Bowes (P) from 1935 (Note : there are other variations in the frank design eg position of "Post Paid" wording", which are not listed here)	0.50
25/11	EviiiR cypher, from 1936 - Pitney Bowes (PB,P), Universal (M,U), Neopost (N), (8.00 with slogan of thematic appeal)	2.00
25/12	GviR cypher, from 1937 - Pitney Bowes (PB,H), Universal (NZ,M), Neopost (N)	0.50
25/13	As above but with small cypher at foot, as 25/10 - Pitney Bowes (P), Universal (U, UA etc, S, SA)	0.50
25/14	EiiR cypher, from 1953 - Pitney Bowes (PB), Universal (NZ,M), Neopost (N)	0.50
25/15	As above but with small cypher at foot, as 25/10 - Pitney Bowes (P,PA), Universal (U,UA etc, S, SA, SB, SV, SX, SY, SZ, SL, A, AA), Neopost (NA-ND)	0.50
25/16	As any of 25/12-25/15 with slogan of thematic appeal	1.00

Meter Marks

25/17

25/18

25/17	New floral emblems frank design, from 1959 - Universal/Pitney Bowes (P, PA-PC, RT, S, SA etc, U, UA etc, AA-AH), Roneo-Neopost (N, NA-NR, J, TN)	0.50
25/18	New frank design, from 1967 - Postage & Revenue Franking Machines (fml)	1.50

New Frank, 1968

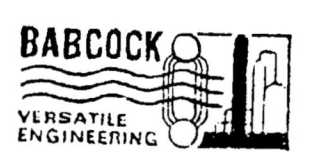

25/19

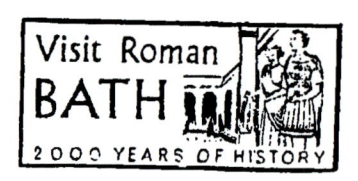

25/32

25/33

Meter Marks

From 1968 a new frank design was introduced in readiness for decimalisation with values in pence/ ½pence only. Suppliers as follows:

25/19	a)	Acral (Francotyp machine) (AC.A, ACA)	4.00
25/20	b)	Addressing Systems International (Secap machine)(ASA, ASM)	0.50
25/21	c)	Envopak/Francotyp-Postalia (EGS, ENV, EMD, EFS)	0.50
25/22		as above but (T) printed by *thermal transfer, from 1992	0.50
25/23	d)	Friden (G)	1.50
25/24	e)	Hasler/Ascom Hasler (HGB, HAS, HF, HM, HB, HT, HS)	0.50
25/25	f)	Mailing & Mechanisation (Frama machine) (MMC)	1.50
25/26	g)	Pitney-Bowes (PBC, PBS, PBA, PBR, PBT, PBL, PBE, PB, PBT, PBD, PBH, PBK, PBM, PBN, PBF, PBG, PBO, PBV, PBW, PBC, PBJ, PBP, PBQ, PBB, PB9)	0.50
25/27		as above with coloured slogan (black, green, blue)	0.50
25/28		similar but colour error eg slogan/frank reversed	3.00
25/29	h)	Postage & Revenue Franking Machines (Hasler m/c)(fml, FML)	1.00
25/30	i)	Roneo/Alcatel/Neopost (N, J, JA-JZ, NA-NZ, PX, TN, RN, RM, RR, RV, W, 2N, 1-9NE incl 4NE by *thermal transfer from 1996)	0.50
25/31	j)	Scriptomatic / Cheshire Mailing / Frama (FSC, 5 or 6 digits)	0.50
25/32		Any of the above with slogan matching a Post Office slogan	1.50
25/33		Pitney Bowes "Post Perfect" (PB7) printed by *thermal transfer, and encrypted code to left of town die, from 1995	0.50
25/34		New designs for Channel Islands, 1969- , and Isle of Man, 1973-	0.50

*Note: thermal transfer postmarks have a glossy finish

New "bar code" Design

Has bar code in place of Great Britain/Postage Paid, "United Kingdom" in town die, and "Royal Mail" above value.

25/35	Sample postmarks for collectors provided by Royal Mail (seen dated Feb-Aug 1996, with Watford town die, one machine only, not to be confused with test mail since these items passed through mail)	5.00
25/36	Trial in Watford/St Albans/Hatfield area, 1996-2002 (used in 100 meter machines in the area, in connection with IMP trial at Watford, see chapter 10, illustration shows earliest date seen)	3.50

Meter Marks

Ink-Jet Printed Meters

The following section covers 1998-2010. With the exception of 25/37, all new machines during this period used Ink-jet printing technology. Those shown as using blue ink refer to "Advanced mail" which provides discounts for large users.

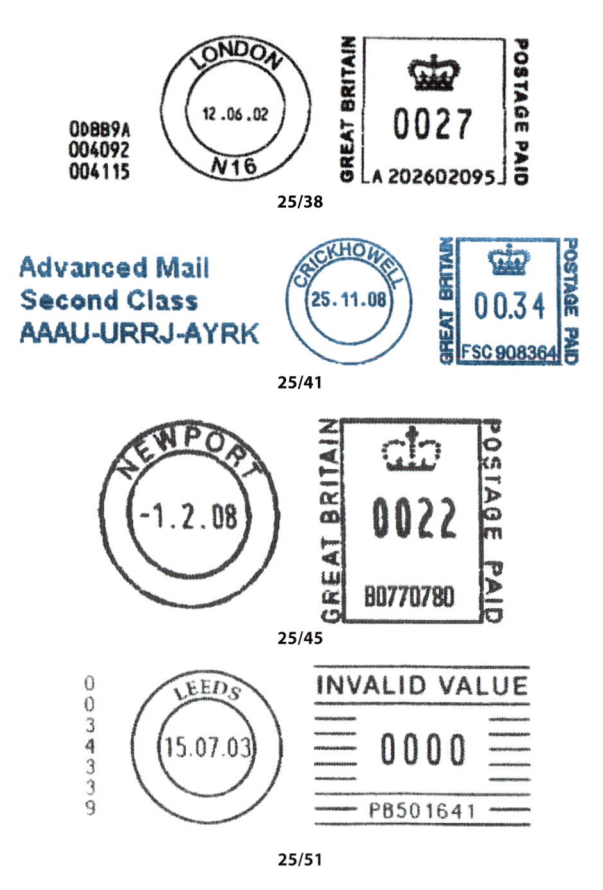

25/38

25/41

25/45

25/51

25/37	Ascom Hasler HS, HT series refurbished machines by Neopost with Z suffix, 2004-05	2.50
25/38	Ascom Hasler Ink-jet printed, 'A20' prefix, 2002	35.00
25/39	Frama Ink-Jet printed, FSC2, FSC3, FSC7, FSC9, F1, 2000-	0.50
25/40	as above in but blue ink, 2006-	0.50
25/41	as 25/40 with Advanced Mail slogan	0.50
25/42	Francotyp-Postalia Ink-jet printed, F04, FC, FJ, FM, FU, 2001-	0.50
25/43	as above but in blue ink, 2006-	0.50
25/44	as 25/43 with Advanced Mail slogan	0.50
25/45	as 25/42 but with 'B' prefix (error), 2008	15.00
25/46	Neopost Ink-jet printed, N10, N11, N12, N13, N3, 2000-	0.50
25/47	as above but in blue ink, 2006-	0.50
25/48	as 25/47 with Advanced Mail slogan	0.50
25/49	as 25/48 but in red ink (error)	2.50
25/50	Pitney Bowes Ink-jet printed, PB0, PB1, PB2, PB3, PB4, PB5, PB6, PB8, 1998-	0.50
25/51	as above but with "Invalid value" die	1.00
25/52	as 25/50 but in blue ink, 2006-	0.50
25/53	as 25/52 with Advanced Mail slogan	0.50
25/54	as 25/53 but in red ink (error)	2.50
25/55	SECAP Technologies, Ink-jet printed, 'ST' prefix, 2001-02	0.50

For further details of meters of this period see http://www.meterfranking.co.uk
Nos. 25/56 to 25/80 reserved for future use.

Delivered by Royal Mail

Delivered by

25/81

25/81 "Delivered by Royal Mail" added by machine, in black, at Mail Centre, 2013- (used in combination with the meter postmark, thus valuation dictated by the meter postmark) 0.50

Nos. 25/82 to 25/86 reserved for future use.

Parcel post labels

All are in red on white gummed paper, dimensions refer to printed area.

25/88

25/89

25/91

25/92

25/87 Parcel post labels sold at PO counters, 1947-48, Romford/Cambridge (first trial of TIM "Ticket Issuing Machines Ltd", approx 55x22mm, inscribed "Parcel Post") 50.00
25/88 as above but large and different design, approx 55x35mm, 1947-50 (Westinghouse-Garrard trial at Cambridge, same machine later at Birmingham) 75.00
25/89 as above, two-part design with "stamp" at left, circular town die at right, 1950- (trial of Universal Postal Frankers Ltd machine, Birmingham/Romford initially, lesser valuation for other offices, 1952-59) 50.00
25/90 as 25/87, trial of Setright, 43x21mm, Birmingham/Cambridge, 1951-(first design to include "Parcel Post Paid" wording, applies to later designs) 50.00
25/91 as above, TIM machines, 53x22mm, operational from c1950-69 (also coloured magenta or orange in mid 1950s) (supposedly a "Wembley/Middlesex" machine at 1948 Olympic Games but no specimens known) 25.00
25/92 as above but special design at Festival of Britain, 1951 75.00
25/92A as 25/90, Setright machines, approx 50x22mm, operational 1959-69 (design similar to 25/91 with larger crown but no royal cipher, trial at Remnant St London WC2 1958-59 valuation 20.00) 10.00

Wilkinson "Penny in the slot" machine

25/93

25/93	Wilkinson "Postage Paid" postmark on cover, dated 25 January 1912	£150
25/94	As above, other 1912 dates	£200
25/95	As above but London EC handstamp (see note below) in red	£120

Note: No date is shown in the machine impression and all were struck towards the centre of the cover, in red, but all were additionally handstamped "London EC" etc, dated between 25 January and 31 August when the sole machine was withdrawn.

Note: Listing of Horizon labels and other Modern postal labels, previously listed as 25/101 to 25/117, have been moved to Chapter 28.

26 Printed Postage Impressions

For large companies and magazine distributors, the postmarking of mail, either by the customer (meter mail) or by the Post Office (Paid mail) is a time-consuming process. This could be avoided by means of regulations introduced in 1965, whereby a "Printed Postage Impression" could be printed beforehand on the envelope. Later, magazine plastic wrappers were developed and PPIs were printed on these too. PPIs heralded what later became known as "junk mail".

The principle of a PPI is that the words "Postage paid" are shown, along with a town name and a "serial" that identifies the sender. A "PHQ" series (Postal Headquarters) is used for major users, printers and magazine distributors with multiple outlets. Although there are some standard types, there are many exceptions, in terms of design and inscription. Colourful variations followed as senders attempted eye-catching designs, and to avoid their mailshots being discarded as unwanted "junk mail" by the recipient.

Although most PPIs are printed, others are applied by rubber stamp or machine. Charities often use adhesive stamps on their appeal envelopes, again to avoid being discarded as junk mail, and from 1992 PPIs applied to adhesive stamps are known. In 1996 PPI rubber stamps were seen used for pre-cancelling stamps on charity mail (ie the postmark appeared on the stamp not on the envelope as well).

The first PPI type was used up to the introduction of the "two tier" system in 1968, and shows no "1" or "2" - see **26/1**. **26/2** is one of various types used on some of the Post Office's own mail. These are not really PPIs but, like PPIs, such envelopes do not usually attract another postmark.

26/1

26/2

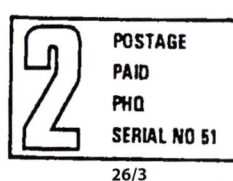

26/3

26/4

26/5

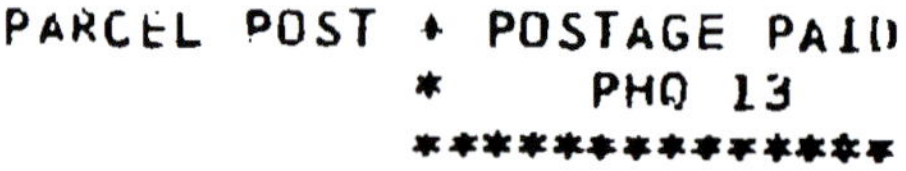

26/6

26/7

26/8

26/9

26/10

26/11

Although all PPI designs require to be approved, from the outset there were many non-standard designs. Type **26/4** shows a "stamp simulation", and **26/5** was probably machine applied and is struck in red. Type **26/6** shows an early (1968) computer-printed PPI for parcel post. In the post-1968 PPIs, "1" and "2" denote first and second class mail, "R" mail which attracts a rebate, and "P" parcel mail.

In the 1970s a series of about eight standard designs was developed, and these included triangular and octagonal designs as well as the long format shown at **26/10**. There

26/1	1965-68 First type, with serial number but without "class"	0.50
26/2	from 1960s Other "Post Paid" symbols used on Post Office envelopes	0.50
26/3 to 26/13	from 1968 as 26/1 but with "1" or "2" etc.	0.50

Printed Postage Impressions

are many exceptions to these layouts, and in some cases simulations of "normal" Post Office postmarks are used. Type **26/12** shows a machine postmark simulation. Similarly, the Chester example (**26/13**) is printed (in black) as a simulation of a meter postmark (though this would have been in red).

From 1989 Mailsort was introduced for bulk mailings, and this is usually indicated by the "stylised M", the Mailsort logo, and this, as shown in **26/9** and **26/11**, replaced R. MHQ (Mailsort Headquarters) (as in **26/12**).

26/12

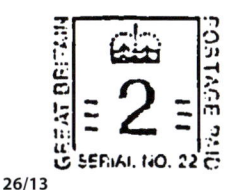

26/13

26/14
POSTAGE PAID LONDON
PRINTED PAPER SEALED UNDER PERMIT LONDON F.S. 175

26/15
1 POSTAGE & REGN. FEE PAID EDINBURGH SERIAL NO. 135

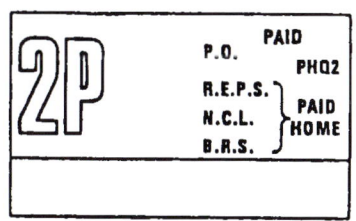

26/16

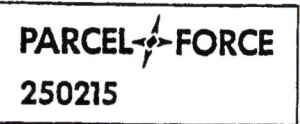

26/17
PARCEL-FORCE 250215

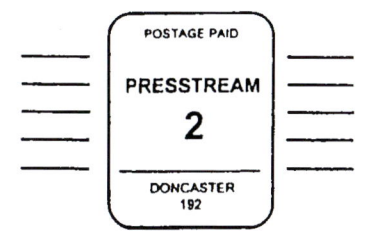

26/19
POSTAGE PAID PRESSTREAM 2 DONCASTER 192

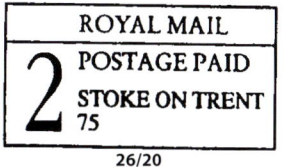

26/20
ROYAL MAIL POSTAGE PAID 2 STOKE ON TRENT 75

26/21
2 ROYAL MAIL POSTAGE PAID GB BRIGHTON 456

26/21A
Delivered by Royal Mail 2 ROYAL MAIL POSTAGE PAID GB HQ44814

Three further variations are shown at **26/14** – **26/16**. One is the inclusion of "Sealed under permit" inscriptions; these sometimes show a different location from the PPI location. Second is inclusion of a registration fee. The "multiple carrier" parcel PPI is shown at **26/16**; here "P.O." (this is pre-"Parcel Force") is shown as one of a number of options for carriage of the parcel concerned.

26/14	Sealed under permit marks, usually with PPIs	0.50
26/15	PPI with recorded delivery or registration fee	1.00
26/16	Multi-carrier parcel marks	0.50
26/17	Parcel marks with contract number, "Parcel Force" 1990s	0.50
26/18	Mailsort marks with "stylised M" (see **26/9** or **26/11**)	0.50
26/19	Presstream mark, 1990s, another new service, development of Mailsort	0.50
26/20	PPIs with "Royal Mail", 1994-	0.50
26/21	New layout including GB, 2004 -	0.50
26/21A	"Delivered by Royal Mail" added to wording, 2012-	0.50

Further reading: PPI listing produced as supplements to British Postmark Society Bulletin 1987-94, thanks to the efforts of Dr Michael Gould.

Printed Postage Impressions

Alternative Carriers – Condition 9 Access Mail

26/22

26/23

26/24

From 2004 licences were issued for mailing companies to handle the bulk mailings of commercial concerns as Royal Mail lost its monopoly on this class of mail. The companies had access to Royal Mail in that the mail was handed over, at pre-determined rates, for Royal Mail to complete delivery, sometimes termed "the final mile". The marks are invariably printed on the envelopes, usually in black and include the name of the carrier (see UK Mail in **26/22**, one of the first such carriers) along with a symbol including C9, as shown here also in **26/23**. Such envelopes have become the norm for most bills and "junk mail" in the 21st-century.

From 2012 the wording "Delivered by Royal Mail" was included, a new policy of Royal Mail and to emphasise the "final mile" point made above. An example is shown at **26/24** with "One Post" in this case an Alternative Carrier, 'C9 10031' the detail of the licence, and with "Delivered by Royal Mail" added.

26/25

| 26/25 | Explanatory marks with "Condition 9 Access Mail" wording, red or black, 2008- | 1.00 |

Additionally a machine "slogan" with similar wording has been seen used, in red, from 2009.

398

27 Postal Mechanisation

Successful automation of the postmarking process spurred the Post Office to mechanise the letter sorting process. This chapter summarises developments from the 1930s up to the massive changes to letter handling that have followed from about 1970. Test/dummy mail and philatelic covers are omitted. After listing the "marks" to be found on envelopes, some other mechanisation oriented postmarks are then shown. A glossary of terms complete the chapter.

Transorma Marks

Trials of a Transorma machine started at Brighton as early as 1935. Operator identity codes A to Z, later lower case letters and numerals, were applied to the front of envelopes.

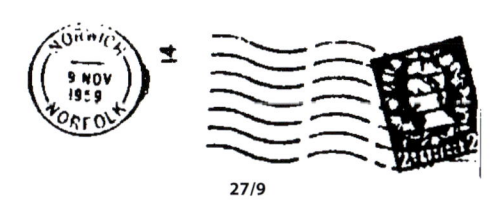

27/9

27/4   27/11

27/1	Trials prior to 7 October 1935	£100
27/2	Operational in red, 1935	20.00
27/3	Similar, 1936-37	5.00
27/4	Similar, 1938-45	3.00
27/5	Used in black or red/black mixture, 1945-46	30.00
27/6	In red, 1946-50	2.00
27/7	In red, 1951-68 (when use of machine ended)	1.00

Other Early Sorting marks

Between 1952 and 1956 trials took place at Mount Pleasant of a six-position Letter Sorting Machine (LSM) with Roman numeral idents I to VI. From 1955 single position machines (SPLSMs) were used at several offices.

27/8	Six-position LSM idents (roman I to VI) at London (Mt Pleas) 1952-56	£150
27/9	SPLSM with operator code, 1959-64 (red, black, or violet)	75.00
27/10	similar but later double-digit codes at London Foreign Sec, 1971	£125
27/11	single character (diff sizes) at London Foreign Section, 1977-89	6.00

Dots representing postcodes and related idents

In 1959 a 2-stage sorting system was introduced at Luton. At a coding point phosphor dots were printed vertically on envelopes, which were then sorted mechanically. A similar system was later used at other mechanised offices, as postcodes were introduced countrywide, to apply two rows of dots horizontally in binary code representing the two halves of the postcode.

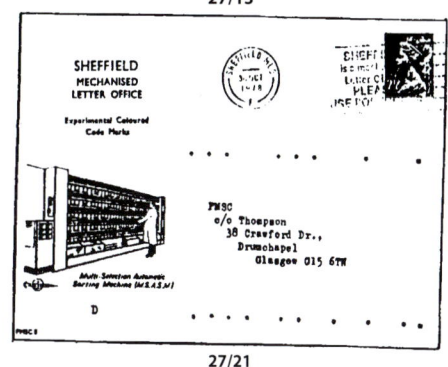

27/13

27/21

27/12	Coding dots at Luton - vertical at right, clear, 1960-65	£150
27/13	Similar with added red SPSLM operator marks	£200
27/14	Horizontal dots at foot of envelope, 1965-68	40.00
27/15	Coding dots at Norwich - rectangular, clear, 1966-68	60.00
27/16	Experimental white raised dots, 1966	*
27/17	Similar but "wax" dots, 1966-67	£200
27/18	Large clear dots eg London EC, Croydon, 1970-	2.00
27/19	Rectangular dots (but London EC 20.00)	2.00
27/20	Small dots	1.00
27/21	Blue dots, early dates (first used Sheffield 30 Oct 1978) (illustration is of a philatelic item, value 2.00)	1.00
27/22	Later blue dots	0.50
27/23	Colour variations : turquoise .	1.00
27/24	Turquoise opacified	0.50

399

Postal Mechanisation

27/25	Blue opacified	0.50
27/26	Upper row of dots only, overseas mail, 1991-	2.00

Idents are usually black, the following are variations:

27/27	Clear "phosphor" ident at right : Cardiff, 1977-78	8.00
27/28	Similar from Chelmsford, 1983-84	4.00
27/29	Ident inside start dot eg London IS, 1980	25.00
27/30	Coloured idents eg red/black at Romford, magenta at Huddersfield	1.00
27/31	Commem ident T/50 in red at Brighton, 1985 (on PO postcard SEPR46) (this is a philatelic item, commercial *)	5.00
27/32	Q of S ident eg 3 figures at Birmingham	1.00
27/33	Italic ident at London Mt Pleasant (London and incoming overseas mail destined for the provinces)	1.00
27/34	Large ident from Slough, top of envelope, repeated 58mm, 1995-97	1.00

Further marks from "manual" coding

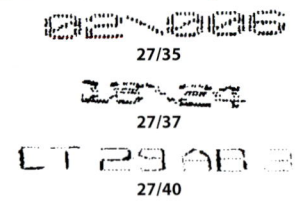

27/35

27/37

27/40

27/43

27/35	Coding desk ink-jet ident at top left - Reading inland mail, 1987	*
27/36	similar but without zeros, 1987-88	5.00
27/37	similar without zeros, London FS (overseas mail), 1988-	2.00
27/38	similar at FS but pink or yellow (ditto), 1989	40.00
27/39	similar on Jersey mail to UK, 1991-	1.00
27/40	similar at Canterbury, March 1990 (office+day+operator+desk)	25.00
27/41	Ink-jet pre-sorter slogan imprints at Liverpool, 1989-93	1.00
27/42	same but blue, June-July 1989	5.00
27/43	short-lived messages eg Valentine 1990-92	4.00
27/44	spelling errors eg CAMCER (note: 27/41-44 are on front of env'pe)	5.00

Bars from OCR process

Following an extended trial at London EC, the automatic, or optical, reading of postcodes on letters soon became operational; the process prints bars as opposed to dots, on the envelopes, but the bars are composed of a number of minute dots.

27/53

27/45	OCR trials - clear ink-jet bars at Guildford, 1980	*
27/46	London EC trial, blue, 1983	8.00
27/47	Operational use at London EC & other offices, blue, 1984-	1.00
27/48	Revised (thinner) bars, 1992-95	0.50
27/49	As above but one-eighth inch pitch instead of ¼", 1994-	0.50
27/50	As above but red (more for red/blue on one envelope), 1995-	0.50

27/51	Four-state OCR bars in blue, Preston trial (and others), 1994	*
27/52	As above but operational at Glasgow, April-May 1995	1.00
27/53	As above but in red, Scotland & Belfast 1995-, others 1996-	0.50
27/54	As above but colour variations eg red-brown, purple	0.50
27/55	As above but bright orange bars, 1997-	0.50

Nos. 27/56- 27/80 reserved for future use.

Other marks from OCR process

27/82

27/83

27/86 Total length (day number + hour) 43mm and 65mm

27/87

27/89

27/81	Ink-jet imprint top left, firstly Reading 1988 (RG + day of week)	2.00
27/82	Other offices eg GL (office + day of month) 1989-93	0.50
27/83	Extended print for engineers but used on live mail	8.00
27/84	Q of S imprints at Liverpool on reverse of envelopes, black, 1991 (size varies, also printed is "Liverpool MLO" in phos blue at left)	3.00
27/85	As above but in clear phosphor, 1991	8.00
27/86	As above but in phosphor blue (almost invisible) 1991	8.00
27/87	"Serial product counter" blue phos messages (used at 6 towns), 1991 (eg IIItownIII or "this letter was processed at W1" on reverse)	5.00
27/88	Slogan imprints or date/time at Liverpool and others, 1991-	0.50
27/89	Same but short-lived or with spelling errors	3.00
27/90	Same but used in error eg "Get your message across here", 1991	5.00
27/91	Reading bar code trial, black, 1990 (on reverse of envelope)	*

Note: No. 27/88 is similar to 27/41 pre-sorter marks at Liverpool but leaning to left; these were printed at a number of towns, London SE1 and some at Dartford on the front, leaning to right, but generally on reverse of envelopes, and some are in red eg Croydon; see Patrick Awcock's Volume 2 in Bibliography for lists.

Nos. 27/92-120 reserved for future use.

For ink-jet messages on "large flats" see chapter 10. Later 4-state bars (as in **27/53**) were added to large flats often on a self adhesive label.

Postal Mechanisation

Mechanisation oriented postmarks

27/121 Early ALF machines.
Value: 1.50 each

27/122 Generic postmarks used at MLOs.
Value: from 0.50

27/123 MLO machine and handstamp postmarks.
Value: from 0.50

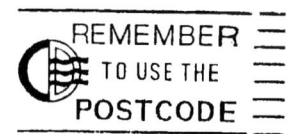

27/124 Postcode slogans. *Value:* 1.00 (Aberdeen) and 0.50 (Tredegar)

27/125 Philatelic handstamps on postcode theme.
Value: 2.00 each on souv cover

Postal Mechanisation

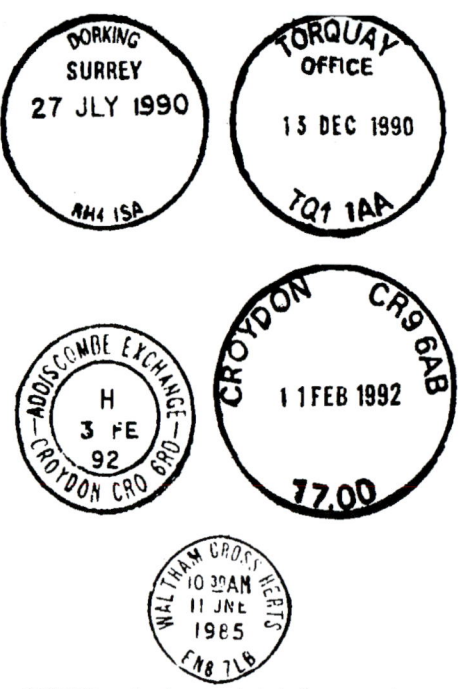

27/126 Operational postmarks including postcodes.
Value: from 0.50 each

Quality of Service explanatory cachets - used to correct dates on meter mail, alternatively machine applied slogans carry out the same duty, for these see chapter 11; for further explanatory marks see chapter 18.
Value: 2.00 each

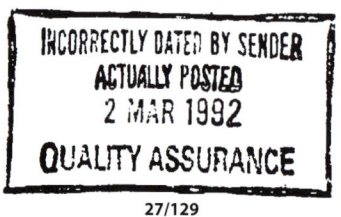

27/127

27/128

27/129

27/130

27/131

27/132

Glossary of some mechanisation-related terms/abbreviations

ALF -	Automatic Letter Facing machine, first introduced 1957 at Southampton
APC -	Automated Processing Centre, the latest (1992-97) term for MLO (then "Mail Centre" used instead)
ASM -	Automatic Sorting Machine, uses the phosphor dots/OCR bars once applied
CFC -	Culler Facer Canceller, 1990s generation of automated cancelling machine
clear -	colourless "phosphor" marks only visible if held at angle to light
Coding desk-	the machine which, when an operator keys postcode, applies dots (unlike OCR, see below, which is automatic and an operator is required only when the OCR is unable to confirm the postcode)
Coding dots -	rows of dots which represent the postcode (or town) in binary code
FCT -	Facer Canceller Table, 1970s generation of semi-automated cancelling
Ident -	numbers/letters showing either coding desk or operator or both, or date!
IMP -	Integrated Mail Processor
Imprints -	other Q of S messages printed on envelopes
Ink jet -	fast modern printer using small jets to form characters from dots
MLO -	Mechanised Letter Office, the result of concentration of letter traffic in the relevant

402

	catchment area (term introduced 1976)
MTT -	Mail Transport ie the mechanism for passing mail through sorting equipment
OCR -	Optical character recognition, resulting bars on envelopes are ink jet printed (larger on brown or dark envelopes), unlike blue coding dots; bars generally of same size, later 4-state code bars of diff sizes see 27/53
Opacified -	added to the blue dot is a white chalky-looking substance to make blue dots opaque when applied to window envelopes & shiny substances
Phosphor blue -	pale blue barely visible colour used for some marks on envelopes
Q of S -	Quality of service, postmarks to show date/time of stages of letter sorting, or confirmation of date of posting (eg of meter mail)
SPLSM -	Single position letter sorting machine
Transorma -	name of sorting machine at Brighton (name means "TRANsporting" and "SORting", plus MA = design company Marchand-Andriessen Engineering Co.)

Although this chapter summarises a complex topic, we have covered it without mention of third generation, tag codes, OCR/VCS, AEG or transitional coding. Readers who wish to delve further should contact the Postal Mechanisation Study Circle.

28 Modern Postal Labels

In the 21st century the Post Office have introduced several new alternatives to postage stamps as means of paying postage (this chapter written by Colin Peachey). None of these labels requires a postmark though they are occasionally postmarked.

The driving force behind introducing Horizon labels was to reduce the time-consuming necessity to handstamp large letters and packets as required when stamps are affixed. The reasoning behind the Smart stamps and Post & Go labels (the subsequent sections in this chapter) was quite different. It was purely the advantages that "self help" or "self service" bring, both convenience for the sender along with the avoidance of queuing and thus the use of a counter clerk's time as a result. The Post & Go machines have become so popular, however, that at busy times a queue for these develops at some major offices!

All these labels are self-adhesive, the only exception being Smart Stamps, which can (optionally) be printed direct on to envelopes.

Horizon Labels

Collectors have debated what is a "stamp" and what is a "label". Broadly speaking a stamp includes the Queen's head and is undated, but some labels show the Queen's Head so the distinction is not crystal clear. As post office counter functions became computerised, "Horizon" was the name of the system producing postage labels and receipts. The Horizon label is dated and is printed and affixed to the letter/packet by the post office counter clerk: the sender normally does not handle the label, unlike in the sections that follow. Ideally collected with receipt, though not practicable for most used specimens (ie the receipt will be retained by sender!). The parcel post labels shown in chapter 25 were 1940s forerunners of these labels.

28/1

28/1	White Horizon label printed/affixed at post office counter(first used 2002, rolled out countrywide soon after, generally restricted to letters over 100gms – also Large Letters from 2006 – Special Delivery, Recorded Delivery and overseas – used to 2010, residual use in 2011)	0.50
28/2	Similar but Welsh bilingual- to 2010, residual use in 2011	1.00

Note : in later years there were several design changes including changes to the service indicator eg "1st class large" changed from "1LL" to "1LG" – there are about 30 different service indicators, too many to list here, for details see *British Philatelic Bulletin* dated September 2011 page 14, article by John Newcomb – and many of these have a higher valuation

28/5

28/3	2004 experiment at Albemarle St (London W1), Special Delivery only, printed Horizon details unchanged but large white label incorporating "Special Delivery" details in violet	10.00
28/4	2009 experiment at Camden Town (London NW1), large GOLD label shows Queen's Head background, security features & simulated perforations, with printed Horizon details as 28/1 but used on Special Delivery only (valuation 50.00 for first/last day)	20.00
28/5	Gold label, with Queen's Head as 28/4, but used as 28/1 (valuation 20.00 for earliest dates 20-21 April 2010, gradually rolled out countrywide)	0.50
28/6	As above, used at "Festival of Stamps 2010" Exhibition (8-15 May 2010, London N1 but no special inscription, ideally collected on "special cover" and with receipt)	10.00

404

Modern Postal Labels

28/7 Similar to 28/5 but Welsh bilingual, printing as 28/2 (valuation 20.00 for earliest dates 20-21 April 2010) 1.00

Note : new software called "Online Horizon" was introduced in 2010, initially at one (English) office later rolled out countrywide from May 2010, the printing being of a narrow font, with other minor changes; naturally this is available with either white labels (28/1-2) or gold (28/5 & 7) and was in use countrywide by the time of the next change, see 28/8-9

28/8 Similar to 28/5 but gold label has straight edges, not "simulated perforations" (referred to as type 2; for "first day" "English only" at Old St London EC1V on special envelope, 23 August 2010 60.00; later spread countrywide) 0.50
28/9 Similar to 28/8 but Welsh bilingual, printing as 28/2 (from Sep 2010) 1.00
28/10 As 28/9 but 2011 variety – final "l" of "Post Brenhinol" MISSING 3.00

28/12 (white label)

28/11 As 28/8 but with lower case letter added after "Royal Mail" to show "service code" eg c for 1st class large letter, y for Special Delivery, from Sep 2011 (valuation 10.00 for first day with receipt) 0.50
28/12 As 28/11 but Welsh bilingual, printing otherwise as 28/2 (valuation 10.00 for first day with receipt) 0.50

Notes : (1) Stocks of white labels (28/1-2) overlapped with the use of gold labels (28/5-7), then stocks of both white (28/1-2) and gold (28/5 & 7) overlapped with 28/8-9. The result is that 28/11 & 12 can be found with straight edged gold labels and the older "serrated edge" labels also, white labels too (higher valuation).

(2) 28/11 & 12 normally with "4" on lower line after UK (meaning 'no VAT') but other codes used to indicate appropriate VAT charge is included.

(3) Further changes to the gold labels themselves are not detailed here. However, from 2 April 2013 the terms "packet" (PK on the labels) and "standard parcel" (SP) were discontinued and replaced by small parcel (1SP or 2SP) and medium parcel (1MP or 2MP). See also 28/55 and Chapter 30.

(Nos 28/13 to 30 reserved for future use)

Smart Stamps

28/31

28/32

Royal Mail's on-line postage service permits "self help" computer users or small businesses to "sign up" for use of the relevant software. Details of an item to be posted are then printed on to the label or direct on to an envelope. A "post by" date is shown as with Post & Go labels (see overleaf) which is the day after production, even if a Sunday or Bank Holiday. The system permits overseas items and also Special Delivery or Recorded Delivery, though such items require to be handed in at a post office counter.

28/31 "Smart stamps", "first type" from early 2004 (printed in black, source/town not shown but optional coloured "slogan" shown at left) 1.50
28/32 New design including Royal Mail "indicia", from about Sep 2004 1.00
28/33 As above without value, designed for E Bay vendors (optional) 1.50

(Nos. 28/34 to 50 reserved for future use)

405

Modern Postal Labels

Post & Go labels

A self-service facility permitted the weighing and posting of letters/packages, initially known as "Weigh and Pay", though "Automated Postal Service" was inscribed on the initial machines. The term "Post & Go" was used later, probably from 2008. The customer purchases labels using a "touch screen", then affixes the labels to the items, which are then posted. Two trials took place before eventual "live operation" from 2008. The machines are located almost exclusively in "crown offices" ie the Post Office's own premises. Labels, either mint or on cover, are ideally collected with receipt showing details of date and location of purchase.

28/51

28/51 "Weigh & Pay" labels, first trial at three locations, 2004 only(wide label of horizontal format; inland & overseas mail accepted including Special Delivery, Recorded Delivery etc, manufacturer Bowe Bell & Howell; date shown is date of purchase, also branch code is shown and labels are individually numbered) 10.00

Note: the illustration shows a date of 26 March 2004, but this was the first day of a trial machine at Broadgate, London EC (second of the three machines), but it was 25 March and the entire day's labels were mis-dated – valuation 30.00 for first day with receipt

28/52 As above but second trial 2007-08, eventually at nine locations (narrower label of vertical format, inland letters/packets accepted but not overseas, Special Delivery nor Recorded Delivery; machines from two manufacturers, Fujitsu and Pitney Bowes, with slight differences in labels and receipts) 5.00

28/53

28/55

28/53 "Post & Go" "live" installation at over 100 locations, from 2008 (first office was The Galleries Bristol, 8 October 2008, though Royal Mail described this installation as a trial), label in horizontal format 1.50

Note: manufacturer Wincor-Nixdorf; inland/overseas letters/packets accepted but not Special Delivery nor Recorded Delivery – see 28/59 - label shows a "post by" date, which is the day after purchase, even if a Sunday or Bank Holiday; labels "straight-edged" with rounded corners, residual use after 28/54 introduced

28/54 As above but serrated edges (no rounded corners) from Jan 2009, then withsmaller text from approx 30 June 2009 1.00

28/55 New design with Royal Mail "indicia" (similar to 28/32) from July 2009(included were two locations in Wales from Sep/Oct 2009 (later two more) where only receipts optionally printed in Welsh, labels in English) 0.50

Note: from 2 April 2013 the terms "parcel" (Pcl on Post & Go labels) and "packet" (Pkt) were discontinued and replaced by "small parcel" (Sml.P) and "medium parcel" (Med.P), similar to 28/11 & 12, see note 3. On overseas items the indicator Sml.Pkt seems to have continued however. See also chapter 30.

28/56 Label with "scrambled" text on bottom line, used at about six branches(the "post by" date is absent and "indicia" smaller) 1.00

Note: the specimen of 28/56 illustrated is from Manchester (Nov 2009): the branch code 003422 is shown at the centre of bottom line and the item number 03944 is shown at bottom right and bottom left)

28/56

28/59

406

Modern Postal Labels

28/57	As **28/55** but used at "Festival of Stamps 2010" Exhibition(8-15 May 2010, London N1 but no special inscription, though "office" code shown as 2010, machine no. shown as zero, two types of label, straight-edged "prototype" label – valuation 10.00 - and serrated edge)	6.00
28/58	As above but used at "Autumn Stampex" Exhibition (15-18 Sep 2010, London N1 but no special inscription, though "office" code shown as 2010, machine no. 9 (month), serrated edge labels. Note the "Fast stamps" issued by this machine were of Queen's Head design 15-16 Sep but Birds designs – see next section below – for 17-18 Sep; no labels were produced at Stampex exhibitions in 2011 as Hytech machines were introduced – also see next section – producing stamps only)	6.00
28/59	As **28/55** but fairly "plain" design label used for Special Delivery (other "priority services" too) as part of new software system (termed 'V2') first used October 2011 (Recorded Delivery also available but this label is of the "indicia" design as **28/55**) (note : higher valuation for higher tariff services eg"Special Delivery by 9am" or for first day of use)	5.00

(Nos. 28/60 to 80 reserved for future use)

Post & Go Handstamps

From 2012 small handstamps (some larger) were introduced inscribed "Post & Go". These are intended for use by staff who help customers at Post & Go machines and are intended for stamping receipts produced by the Post & Go machines. The specimen shown (Arndale) at **28/81** is from Luton. Valuation 1.00

28/81

Fast Stamps

The machines producing the labels shown at **28/53** onwards above also have a "Buy stamps" option which provides "Fast stamps", as they are termed, stamps printed on demand (five different services, "1st class up to 100gms", "1st Large up to 100gms" etc) on a self-adhesive label pre-printed with a background pattern and the Queen's Head (or "Machin"), this aspect being similar to "Frama labels" (a one year experiment in 1984-85, gummed not self-adhesive, labels which are still valid for postage!). They are not dated, but collectors require specimens, particularly mint ones, to be WITH the receipt, giving details of date of purchase. Indeed the receipts themselves, with all the details of the branch and variations in printing, are themselves collectable!

A philatelic "pack" of five different valued stamps, not from a "Post & Go" machine but gravure printed, was made available in 2009. This was followed in 2010-11 by several issues of six Birds designs, initially from the machines at selected offices only, and gravure-printed in "pack" form. In addition the text printed on to each stamp by the machine was made smaller to accommodate the design of the Birds stamps. There have been many font errors, for example sporadic use of the large font after the change to small!

At Spring Stampex 2011 stamps were available from machines of a new manufacturer, Hytech, and at Autumn Stampex 2011 several new items were produced, including a Machin overprint and a '40g worldwide' stamp.

The '40g Worldwide' stamp, but from the Wincor-Nixdorf system, then became available countrywide as part of the V2 system mentioned in **28/59** (from October 2011), which additionally produced a "collectors' strip" of the six values that the system offered.

Once again Hytech machines were in use at Spring Stampex 2012 where a stamp (of Queen's Head design) with Diamond Jubilee overprint was available, as well as the first of the Animals stamps mentioned below.

The Birds stamps were followed by an Animals series in 2012, also produced in both forms ie from machines and in "pack" form, However, for the first time the February 2012 Animals "pack" available from Royal Mail contained stamps in strips printed by Hytech machines, see above.

Neither Fast Stamps, which are closer to being stamps than labels, nor the 1984 Frama labels, are listed here.

29 "A-Z of Interesting Places".

For much of this book we have concentrated on TYPES of postmark. Many collectors are interested in postmarks of specific post offices regardless of type, collecting specific towns, counties or post offices of their home locality, or even of the area where they spent their holiday.

So in this brief A-Z overview we have included a pretty haphazard selection of interesting locations and topics! This list was compiled by Colin Peachey, co-Editor of two previous editions of this book, and for the Ninth Edition Colin has come up with a new list compared to the Eighth Edition. So, says Colin, a reader can now compile his/her own list, possibly the basis of a future collection or of a "fun" philatelic display.

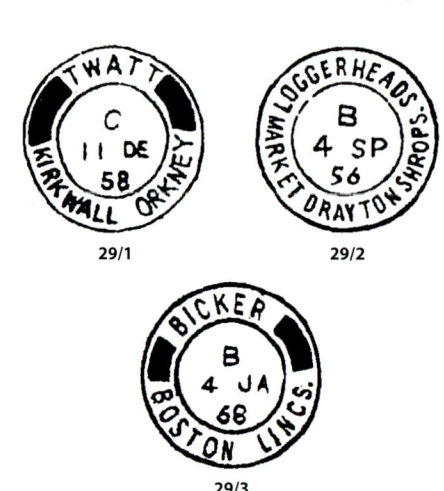

29/1

29/2

29/3

29/4

29/5

A is for "Amusing Placenames". Freezywater, a post office no longer open, brings a smile to the face! Other examples are Bicker, Loggerheads, Barking, Foxholes, Beer, Wool, Horrabridge, Nomansland and Piddletrenthide. Then there are those typically English village names of Sampford Peverell, Cheriton Bishop, Kingsbury Episcopi and Wootton Fitzpaine.

29/6

A is also for Ae, without doubt the shortest place-name. In lovely Dumfriesshire countryside, with a post office that was open from 1967 to 2001, one imagines Ae post office were well used to requests from collectors for impressions of their datestamp.

29/7

A is also for Aerial Post. In 1911 the first Aerial Post took place, with the flimsy aeroplanes of the time being flown by brave pilots from Hendon to Windsor and back with bags of mail on board (about 26 pounds per bag) which one would imagine the planes could hardly carry. Only special envelopes and postcards pre-purchased at various stores in London were carried, but these seemed to catch the public imagination at the time and sales boomed. Likewise the event is a popular collecting area now, with different coloured envelopes and postcards, then there are the Windsor ones too, and the advertising cards, then there are the cards that have travelled overseas, and so on. My wife Valerie and I visited Windsor for the 50th anniversary of this event in 1961 (posting covers for the special slogan postmark) and I was delighted my covers received what has been termed the "reserve die" of the slogan used at Windsor for that day only, shown here. Then we visited Hendon in 2011 on "centenary day" to witness Tony Buckingham - a well known dealer and cover producer - take off in his hired helicopter to re-enact the 1911 flight.

29/8

408

A-Z of Interesting Places

B is for **Baltasound,** now the most northerly post office in the UK, and there is a special postmark to say so. There are in fact two identical postmarks, one held at the Glasgow Special Handstamp Centre (where postal requests for stamping of collectors' items should be sent, but in 2012 Tallents House has taken over this task) and the other is held at Baltasound. Previously Haroldswick was the most northerly post office, but on the closure of this post office Baltasound took over!

29/9

B is also for **Bridge of Orchy,** which is one of several Scottish post offices where the post office is (or was) on the station, much to the excitement of the railway postmark collectors. Having said that, the word "station" doesn't appear in the Bridge of Orchy postmark thus it doesn't appear in chapter 13. Valerie and I were fortunate enough to "catch" the post office in 1991 when it was on the station, though it was moved by 1994 to the house alongside the station or (to be precise) to the Portakabin-type building next door, where it remained until 2009 when the post office closed. Luckily, Outreach arrangements took over at the church "down" on the main road, which we have also visited. The once-weekly post office service then operated thanks to a lady who visited from Dalmally and she used a "Dalmally Outreach" postmark. This unfortunately means (as with most Outreach arrangements, see "O") the Bridge of Orchy name has disappeared from postmarks.

29/10

C is for **Canary Wharf,** a newly opened post office in 1992, but a strange postmark in that it included neither "London" nor the postal district. Later, in 2006, a second post office, Churchill Place opened as part of the Canary Wharf complex. It's good to see post offices opening in one part of London. Compare this with Central London post offices that have closed, see V for Victoria Street.

29/11

C is also for **Chelsea Flower Show.** In the 1990s Valerie and I used to attend this annual show, largely since as well as a "special" postmark (obtainable by post from the Special Handstamp Centre) there was also a counter datestamp, which I considered of more interest even though it was usually borrowed from the Chelsea office and carried no special inscription, see the illustration here for an example.

In spite of these two postmarks, there was a temporary post box supplied, but what used to irritate me was that mail posted in it received neither of these postmarks. The mail instead went straight to the Mail Centre for an "ordinary" postmark! I think this was misleading for visitors who were posting items at the Flower Show post office postbox EXPECTING to get a relevant postmark. Postmarks at the Wimbledon Tennis each year were similar.

29/12

C is also for **Chelsea Hospital.** A modern SID postmark is in use, though the status of the post office there is not clear. One could hardly expect to "march in off the street" and use the post office there as one would any other, and one would assume it is for the use of the residents!! It is in the grounds of the Hospital where the Flower Show is held each year.

29/13

D is for **Diss.** First Day Covers have to be prepared on or before the day of issue of the relevant stamps and one of the problems for the First Day cover dealer is how many to prepare, since once the day has passed - too late! An enterprising dealer in Diss in 1966 had the idea of preparing his own postmark so he could stamp envelopes when the orders turned up, and I purchased one of these (by post) thinking it was a genuine Diss postmark, as indeed it was a good copy of what a "First Day" postmark should look like. First Day postmarks only started in 1963 and at this time the number of towns providing such postmarks was growing rapidly, so to find another, Diss, was no great surprise. I only found out when I wrote to Diss post office for the next stamp issue only to find they had no such postmark! Later I was a witness at the forgery trial of "our Diss friend", on the basis I had purchased the items "that purported to be genuine". The Diss postmark (one of several "forged" postmarks used) is shown here.

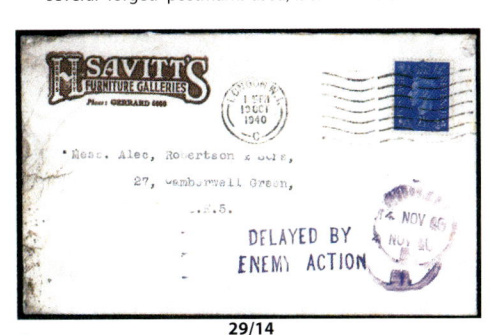

29/14

D is also for **Delayed by Enemy Action.** There were a variety of cachets with this or similar wording used in London during

409

A-Z of Interesting Places

World War II, and all genuine covers bearing these cachets are now desirable. If only the envelope could tell its story, as there is inevitably a story attached to each use of this cachet!

29/15

E **is for Errors.** I could probably fill a small chapter with various errors in machine and handstamp postmarks. Most errors I could describe are of modern postmarks, so it is a nice change to find "an old one". Creagan, a lovely spot on the Argyll coast, is marked on most road maps as Creagan Inn. There is little more there than the Inn, but it had a post office up to 1934, and there is now no clue as to where the post office was. I was not only delighted to purchase a postcard with the Creagan postmark but even more pleased to find it is clearly spelt Greagan. I should add that Creagan Inn is on the north side of Loch Creran whereas the late Jim Mackay's excellent *Scottish Post Offices* confirms the post office was on the south side. The railway bridge across the loch fell into disuse after closure of the Connel-Ballachulish line, but it was rebuilt as a road bridge in the 2000s cutting some 10 miles off the road route as a quick look at a road atlas will soon confirm.

29/16

F **is for Fire.** In this case we refer to a Pillar Box Fire, showing this unusual cachet, the source of which is not known as it was applied to a cover but with no town or date, and the cachet was incorrectly used to cancel the stamp. Surely, if the office was large enough to have such a rubber stamp, they should have known the correct procedure even though a pillar box fire is an unusual event. Clearly the bottom line was meant to be completed, possibly in manuscript, to show the date, and a postmark applied to show the town! All we know is that the item was sent in June 2002, in the era of the short-lived "Consignia" name. I doubt if many postmarks (or explanatory marks) were produced containing the Consignia name.

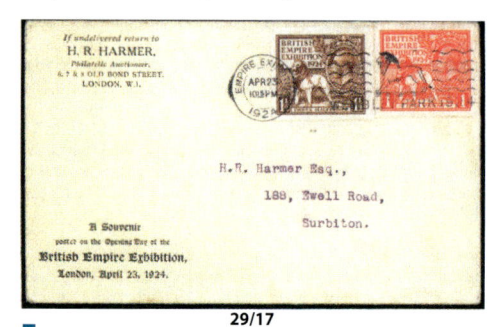

29/17

F **is also for First Day Covers.** This is a big topic, and one which has "changed its spots" over the years. The first commemorative issue was in 1924 and, although special envelopes were not printed, the "Harmer cover" shown here is the nearest one can get to a pictorial envelope and it is a very desirable cover. Pictorial envelopes were printed from the Olympic issue of 1948 onwards (some before that were "hand drawn") but they were not generally available until about 1952. So although plain covers are "frowned upon" by FDC collectors in modern times, at the time the typical schoolboy stamp collector produced his first day covers on plain envelopes with handwritten addresses and many such covers are available "in the marketplace". I think it is a shame they appear not to be "loved" any more, selling for a few pence and often not selling at all! In later years the purist collector seemed to require address labels (or no address as the labels were peelable!) and the whole cover had to be in perfect condition as if it has not gone through the mail at all - biro-written addresses were definitely not acceptable!

29/18

F **is also for Forton Services** (near Lancaster). As far as I know this is the only post office at a motorway service area. I often find that visiting post offices provides a parking problem but not at motorway service areas, so why aren't more post offices at these locations? By chance I was travelling north on the M6 on the day that this post office opened, 23 March 1982, so I was able to "do" the first day of the datestamp. Unfortunately, after a few years, business did not warrant the post office continuing and it closed in 1988.

29/19

G **is for Giggleswick.** Though I have not visited this Yorkshire village, I would prefer the Giggleswick name to be used in special postmarks for the real attributes of the village not just because it sounds amusing and I don't feel the village should be "used" in this way, though I am sure the residents are used to it! The picture shown here (with the post town Settle missing!) is of a philatelic postmark used for the Comics stamp issue in 2012. I really don't approve of ANY postmarks (not just Giggleswick) based just on the NAME of the village. The pioneer of these was Bethlehem in South Wales, used by Royal Mail for the "First Day" postmark for the first Christmas issue in 1966, and for every Christmas issue since. I don't think Royal Mail meant to suggest Christ was born in South Wales, merely that the village name sounds relevant. I wish they'd grow up and think again, but with a habit that's now well established I don't see things changing!!

410

A-Z of Interesting Places

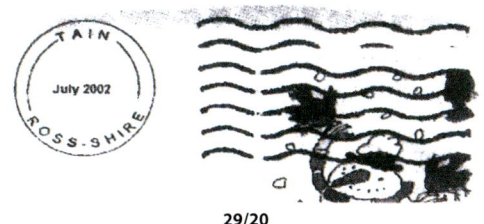

29/20

G is also for **Glenmorangie**. This refers to the whisky distillery at Tain in the Scottish highlands. In chapter 10 we refer to the bulk mailings where, in the 21st century, Royal Mail permits the sender to stamp their own mail, and in this case the distillery, as part of a 2001/02 marketing campaign, affixed stamps to the envelopes and applied postmarks one of which is shown here. The unusual thing about it is that it shows the town of posting, Tain (most such postings are anonymous, see J for junk mail), and indeed the postmark bears a faint resemblance to the normal Tain machine postmark!

29/21

G is also for **Gleneagles Hotel**. This was a "summer only" post office (see chapter 12) and was open from 1924 to 1999. Valerie and I had an enjoyable day there in 1994, though we were only spectators at the golf, not players! This was the stamp issue day for the golf stamps: after all it seems such an obvious place to get Golf First Day Covers stamped!

29/22

H is for **Hotels**. This is one of many themes that are quite difficult to collect as there are probably none still in use. They thrived early in the 20th century at a few London hotels, also at department stores (I could have had H is for Harrods!). As for a modern example to illustrate, apart from Gleneagles (see above) we'll have to settle for Grand Hotel Buildings!

29/23

I is for the **Iona**. Islands have a fascination for collectors. Iona is a small island off the western tip of Mull and it is shown in the Mull list of post offices in chapter 17. It is reached by a short ferry trip from Fionnphort. One attractive feature about Iona is that its postmarks even on early 20th century postcards are not difficult to find, and the double arc handstamp used for many years is shown here.

29/24

I is also for **Inverted slogans**. A slogan is fitted to a "die hub" and to appear inverted the slogan has to be screwed in upside-down! This does happen occasionally and once in use may not be noticed as there are instances of such an error continuing for days or even weeks! "Amazing Glazing" used in 1995 is shown here.

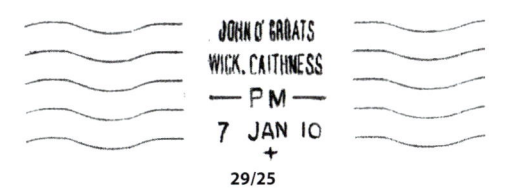

29/25

J is for **John O'Groats,** generally thought to be the most northerly post office on the mainland, and with cachets (see chapter 24) to confirm this! The terrain is generally windswept and treeless, and the post office stands almost alone, about a mile short of the hotel which marks the end of land! The good news is that this post office has the last remaining Krag stamp-cancelling machine in the country, and a 2010 impression is shown here.

29/26

J is also for **Junk mail**. No-one likes it but it deserves a mention and the true postal historian (in my view) collects any items that have passed through the mail, even though most junk mail looks unattractive and does not get retained. The marketers go to great lengths to ensure recipients do NOT destroy the items immediately and one way of doing this, so results tell us, is to affix adhesive stamps, making the item look less like junk mail. Pioneers of this in the UK were Readers Digest in the 1970s, but modern "mailers" use the same technique, with machinery developed to affix stamps, print addresses and cancel the stamps all in one operation, all acceptable to and authorised by Royal Mail (see chapter 10) who do not have to cancel the stamps (since the sender has done so) and who offer discounts for bulk mailings pre-sorted into postcode areas.

411

A-Z of Interesting Places

29/27

K is for Knoydart. A marvellous spot on the western coast of Scotland that, without a long hike across the hills, is generally only accessible by sea even though it is on the mainland. A boat service from Mallaig serves the remote village of Inverary, where the post office still uses a Knoydart postmark.

29/28

L is for Llanfairpwll (see chapter 24 for its full name) which is known for being the longest place name in the country. It has a post office but the postmark does not bear the full name, this privilege being left to the cachets, which over the years have been provided both at the post office and at different shops in the village.

29/29

L is also for London Chief Office. This is another post office that disappeared in the 1990s. The grand architecture of the post office in St Martins-le-Grand was there for postal customers to enjoy, but in 1994 it closed, though the counter area was taken over for a while (until 1998) by the National Postal Museum for display purposes. Meanwhile the post office was moved to Wood Street, in modern "anonymous looking" premises off Cheapside (the post office was named "Cheapside"), with 33 Cannon Street having closed at the same time. The philatelic counter was squeezed into the confined Lombard Street post office much to the chagrin of staff and customers alike. Cheapside and Lombard Street continued for a number of years, then Cheapside closed in 2005 leaving, of course, reduced post office facilities in the area. At neither the Wood Street nor the Cannon Street premises do any indications remain that these locations were once home to famous post offices!! In Cannon Street the block was demolished and re-developed and the Lombard Street premises (the post office closed in 2001, the philatelic counter moved to the new "City" office) later became a coffee bar! However the nearby plaque in Post Office Yard commemorating the early Lombard Street post office has so far survived!

29/30

M is for Mount Edgcumbe. One of the scarcest of Special Event marks is the Mount Edgcumbe Scout Camp of 1936. Scout events seem to be particularly popular and this one is one of the "star" items of any collection. Just to make it more difficult for the collector (a) it appears normal items posted in the box at the event received a normal Plymouth machine mark (b) there were TWO double circle postmarks, one of which is on the cover shown here and probably used on normal mail but only when handed over the counter; the second handstamp was used for counter transactions including registereds - if you can find one (H is for Hen's teeth!!) - and has no time above the date (code letters A and B instead), also with circular spacers at each side not the rectangular ones in the handstamp shown here.

29/31

N is for Northern Parliament. A small post office housed for some years in the Stormont building in Belfast.

29/32

O is for Outreach. Many post offices have unfortunately closed in recent years, though the good news is that limited services have returned to many villages that lost their post office under the guise of "Outreach", whereby the service is provided for a few hours per week from another office. The specimen shown here is that of the Outreach service provided at Drumbeg, whose identity is not shown in the postmark, instead the postmark shows the name of Lochinver, the host office (this is because the host office may serve several satellites and only one datestamp is thus required).

A-Z of Interesting Places

29/33

P is for postal stationery. The normal definition is stationery (envelopes, postcards, airletters etc) sold by the post office and with stamps already printed on them. They have a special attraction, and a large collector following, with or without a postmark. The lovely specimen shown here is a King George V 1d. postcard with an attractive stamp exhibition postmark.

29/34

P is also for postbus cachet. Starting at Llanidloes in 1967, postbuses flourished in the 1970s and so did the postcards which Royal Mail produced. The postcards covered many postal themes, including postboxes, post office buildings but none more popular than postbuses including attractive rural views. Collecting Royal Mail postcards is easy and fun, and although the issue of such cards largely stopped when the postal regions ceased in 1986 (the National Postal Museum continued to the 1990s), many are still available and are inexpensive and attractive. Shown here is a Penrith "posted on the bus" cachet used chiefly (if not exclusively) on Royal Mail postcards. The postbus route ran from Penrith to Martindale and unfortunately the route ended in 2006. Valerie and I visited the Penrith Delivery Office on the last day of the service. The staff, to their credit, had maintained a small "private museum", as they termed it, and the "treasures" included the original cachet probably not used since the 1980s, which they were able to apply to "last day" postcards! More cut-backs to the service saw the last English route end in 2012 (the Welsh ones had already ended) leaving only a handful of routes running in Scotland.

See also "R is for Rannoch Station" below.

29/35

Q is for Quinton DO (District Office) Birmingham 32. This is the only machine die listed in chapter 10 beginning with Q. The Birmingham DO's get little coverage so a chance to mention them. Most, including Quinton, started with a Krag machine then changed to a Universal die (shown here), but with the march of concentration these ended in the 1960s. Amazingly, machines were re-installed at all the DOs in 1987 but only for stamping missorts and locals. The original dies had probably been destroyed and new ones were provided. However the procedure for stamping missorts changed around 2000 so this machine, in common with hundreds of others, was removed about that time.

29/36

R is for Rannoch Station. Stations have a special collector following and so do post offices that are less easy to access. Rannoch Station is both of these! It is accessible of course by train (but the post office closed in 1999) but only on a service that runs a couple of times a day from Fort William or Oban. The alternative is a twenty mile or so drive west from Pitlochry. The road ends at Rannoch Station so there is no alternative but to turn round and come back! An alternative was the postbus service, but these have been cut back so there are only a handful remaining (see P for Postbus above) and the Pitlochry-Rannoch Station service ended in 2011. The bus route passed several ex-post offices en route - Loch Tummel, Dunalastair, and Bridge of Gaur to mention three. Kinloch Rannoch post office was another post office on the Rannoch road and for a while was within the cafe called "Post Taste" (which Valerie and I enjoyed!), but the post office then closed. Fortunately it re-opened in 2010 in the "mini supermarket" but it has no cafe.

29/37

S is for Stock Exchange. An anonymous concrete tower block housed the "old" Stock Exchange in Throgmorton Street and a post office was open there from 1970 to 1996. The building was demolished soon afterwards and a modern "glass tower block" is now in its place, while the Stock Exchange moved to a new building in Paternoster Square - with no post office! Naturally there is no trace of the old post office!

413

A-Z of Interesting Places

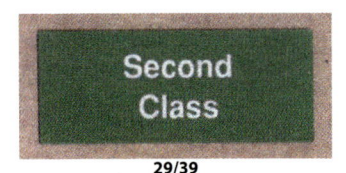

29/38

29/39

S is also for SPSO. A trial was run at SPSO's (sub post offices) in the HP and CB postcode areas in 1997, the idea being that packets handed in over the counters (a) were handstamped and (b) had a first/second class label affixed, both in order to save time and effort when the items arrived at the sorting office. The handstamps were rubber and were used alongside the normal counter datestamps. They were very strange in that the identity of the office was shown but not the full address. One shown here is Halton Camp (see chapter 15, but this item is additional to those in the "Camps" listing) but with no post town (Aylesbury) or county (Bucks). Also shown here is a "second class" sticker in green. Even stranger were High St Amersham Bucks, only shown in the handstamp as 'High Street SPSO', and Waddesdon, which was spelt wrongly as 'Waddeson'. The trial lasted for six months but some of the handstamps remained in use thereafter, at one office at least for stamping parcels.

29/40

T is for Thames Valley. A typical "generic" title but it didn't last long. The catchment area included the whole of the Reading and Oxford areas which were concentrated on to Swindon in 2009, including an area as far north as Banbury area to the north of Oxford - a substantial area! Apparently an administrative postal region was then named Thames Valley (presumably with a different area) so it was no longer appropriate that Swindon should use the title in its postmarks, so it was terminated after only a year or so and postmarks reverted to Swindon!

29/41

U is for University, another popular theme. Shown here is the postmark of Liverpool University.

29/42

V is for Victoria Street (110), a London post office closed in 2003 for redevelopment, in this case for the Cardinal Place Shopping Centre which opened in 2008. Luckily for the post office customer, Broadway post office is quite close! Other London post offices befalling the same fate include Euston Centre, Stock Exchange and Theobalds Road, all closed in the last thirty years and of which there is now no trace.

29/43

W is for Waterloo Station. The London termini all had their own post offices up to the 1960s and full details can be found in an earlier chapter. The specimen shown here is from a receipt for a registered letter posted at Waterloo Station.

29/44

X is for "Xmas extra" machine dies. This phenomenon resulted from a requirement for extra capacity, so that Mail Centres utilised the services of outlying offices to help with the stamping of pre-Christmas volumes of mail. Sometimes such offices used postmarks that disguised the location, meaning a certain amount of detective work was necessary to ascertain where the "extra" postmarks were used. I visited a number of these locations, as this was the best way of telling what was used and where. For example, the picture shown here is a Swindon die used at Malmesbury (another was used at Marlborough). The alternative was to write, as I did for the relevant Scottish towns, but I had to be careful to write the identity on the reverse of the envelopes (for example with several towns in the Paisley area) or when they were returned I would not know which was which! These arrangements continued into the 21st century, largely in Scotland, and only in 2010 (the last office was Haverfordwest in West Wales) have we waved farewell to Xmas extras, as reduction in volumes allowed Mail Centres to cope without the need for "outsourcing". I remain grateful to the Royal Mail staff who helped with my enquiries each December over the years.

414

29/45

Y is for Yell. This is an island in the Shetland group, with several post offices, see chapter 17. The handstamp impression from one of them is shown here. I have been reading an article in *The Scots Magazine* concerning life on this island, where in the summer the focus is on peat cutting in order to stay warm in the winter. The summer evenings, still daylight up to midnight, lend themselves to this activity enjoyed by residents who may well have carried out a "day job" earlier in the day. Life isn't easy on the island!

29/46

Z is for Zennor. This is a pretty village on the north coast of Cornwall and although its post office closed in the 1960s, the illustration here shows a "rubber" (see chapter 9) from 1932.

We acknowledge the use in this chapter of pictures from old auction catalogues, also from the *British Postmark Society Bulletin*.

30 Postal Rates

Inland Letters Rates 1638-1839

All rates quoted are for single letters, i.e. letters written on a single sheet of paper tucked round as an 'Entire'. Double and treble letters were charged at double and treble rates. Quadruple rates applied per ounce.

1638
- 2d under 80 miles
- 4d 80-140 miles
- 6d over 140 miles
- 8d London to Scotland
- 9d London to Ireland

1653
- 2d under 80 miles
- 3d over 80 miles
- 4d London to Scotland
- 6d London to Ireland

1711
- 3d 80 miles
- 4d over 80 miles
- 6d London to Edinburgh
- 6d London to Dublin

1765
- 1d One Post Stage
- 2d between one and two Post stages
- 3d between two Post stages and 80 miles
- 4d over 80 miles
- 6d London to Edinburgh

1784
- 2d One Post Stage
- 3d between one and two Post stages
- 4d between two Post stages and 80 miles
- 6d 80-150 miles
- 7d London to Edinburgh

1796
- 3d 15 miles
- 4d 15-30 miles
- 5d 30-60 miles
- 6d 60-100 miles
- 7d 100-150 miles
- 8d over 150 miles

1801
- 3d 15 miles
- 4d 15-30 miles
- 5d 30-50 miles
- 6d 50-80 miles
- 7d 80-120 miles
- 8d 120-170 miles
- 9d 170-230 miles
- 10d 230-300 miles

1805
- 4d 15 miles
- 5d 15-30 miles
- 6d 30-50 miles
- 7d 50-80 miles
- 8d 80-120 miles
- 9d 120-170 miles
- 10d 170-230 miles
- 11d 230-300 miles
  1d each additional 100 miles or part

1812
- 4d 15 miles
- 5d 15-20 miles
- 6d 20-30 miles
- 7d 30-50 miles
- 8d 50-80 miles
- 9d 80-120 miles
- 10d 120-170 miles
- 11d 170-230 miles
- 1/- 230-300 miles
  1d each additional 100 miles or part

1838
- 2d 8 miles
- 4d 8-15 miles
  Other rates as for 1812

Scotland

1710
- 2d under 50 miles
- 3d 50-80 miles
- 4d over 80 miles
- 6d Edinburgh to London

1765
- 1d One Post stage
- 2d between one Post stage and 50 miles
- 3d 50-80 miles
- 4d over 80 miles
- 6d Edinburgh to London

1784
- 2d One Post stage
- 3d between one Post stage and 50 miles
- 4d 50-80 miles
- 5d 80-150 miles
- 6d above 150 miles
- 7d Edinburgh to London

1796
- 3d One Post stage
- 4d between one Post stage and 50 miles
- 5d 50-80 miles
- 6d 80-150 miles
- 7d above 150 miles
- 8d Edinburgh to London

1801
  Scottish rates made same as English

Ireland (1660-1839)

Rates were for Irish miles except for a brief period Jan 1826-July 1827.

1660
- 2d 40 miles
- 4d over 40 miles
  (1/- per ounce over 40 miles, raised to 1/4 in 1711)

1765
- 1d One Post stage
- 2d between One Post Stage and 40 miles
- 4d over 40 miles

Postal Rates

1768
2d One Post stage
4d over 40 miles

1773
Dublin local post established

1784
2d under 15 miles
3d 15-30 miles
4d over 30 miles

1797
2d under 15 miles
3d 15-30 miles
4d 30-50 miles
5d 50-80 miles
6d over 80 miles

1805
3d under 15 miles
4d 15-30 miles
5d 30-50 miles
6d 50-80 miles
7d over 80 miles

1810
4d under 15 miles
5d 15-30 miles
6d 30-50 miles
7d 50-80 miles
8d over 80 miles

1813
2d under 10 miles
3d 10-20 miles
4d 20-30 miles
5d 30-40 miles
6d 40-50 miles
7d 50-60 miles
8d 60-80 miles
9d 80-100 miles
10d over 100 miles

1814
2d under 7 miles
3d 7-15 miles
4d 15-25 miles
5d 25-35 miles
6d 35-45 miles
7d 45-55 miles
8d 55-65 miles
9d 65-95 miles
10d 95-120 miles
11d 120-150 miles
1s. 150-200 miles
1s.1d 200-250 miles
1s.2d 250-300 miles
1d each additional 100 miles

1826 (6 Jan)
English rates and currency introduced.
Previous Irish rates reduced by 1d

1827 (July)
Irish rates of 1814 restored but in English currency.

1832 Provincial Penny Posts

1832
Provincial Penny Posts established throughout the U.K.

By the 1830s postal charges had become insupportable. To send a single sheet from London to Edinburgh cost 1½d while sending a letter the same weight as the 1990 minimum charge cost 8½d. About 2 weeks pay was required to send a letter of the same weight inside Great Britain! Opposition came from the newly enfranchised middle classes and the agitation led by Robert Wallace MP and Rowland Hill. A House of Commons Select Committee, appointed November 1837, reported in August 1838 and recommended the adoption of Hill and Wallace's proposals. A uniform rate was to be charged, regardless of distance. After a brief experimental rate of 4d, a penny rate was introduced from 10th January 1840. Handstamps were used from this date, adhesive stamps and printed stationery being issued on 6 May 1840. In 1890 an anniversary publication commented, 'one of the greatest social reforms ever introduced was, to speak plainly, given as a bribe by a tottering Government to secure political support'.

1839-1968

1839 (5 Dec)
4d ½ oz
4d per ½ oz; the 2d rate still applied up to 8 miles; pre-paid London local letters were charged at 1d, unpaid at 2d or 3d

1840 (10 Jan)
1d ½oz
1d for next ½oz, 2d for each subsequent ounce (or part) to maximum of 16 oz; unpaid letters were charged double

1847
16 oz limit abolished

1865
1d for next ½ oz and each succeeding half oz

1872
initial weight step raised to 1 oz,
½d for each succeeding 2 oz (or part) to 12oz, thereafter 1d per oz

1882
12 oz limit abolished

1897
initial weight step raised to 4 oz,
½d for each succeeding 2 oz (or part)

1915
initial weight step reduced to 1 oz;
2d between 1 oz and 2 oz;
½d for each succeeding 2 oz (or part)

1918 (3 June)
1½d 4 oz ½d for each succeeding 2 oz

1920 (1 June)
2d 3 oz ½d for each succeeding ounce

1922 (29 May)
1½d 1 oz
2d for 3 oz; ½d each succeeding ounce

1923
initial weight step raised to 2 oz;
½d each succeeding 2 oz

1940 (1 May)
2½d 2 oz
½d each additional 2 oz

1952
½d for next 2 oz,
1d for each 2 oz thereafter

1957 (1 Oct)
3d 1 oz
1½d for each succeeding 2 oz

1965 (17 May)
4d 2 oz
2d for each succeeding 2 oz up to 1lb, then 3d per 2 oz

417

Postal Rates

1968-2013

In 1968 Two Tier postage was introduced, allowing senders to choose first or second class mail (first class generally delivered in one day, second class two days or more). The second class service also replaced the previous printed paper rates, and bought to an end the use of triangles (see 10/193-194)

Date of new charge		Max weight for minimum charge	First class minimum charge	Second class minimum charge
1968	16 September	4 oz.	5d	4d
1971	15 February (decimalisation)	4 oz.	3p	2½p
1973	10 September	2 oz.	3½p	3p
1974	24 June	2 oz.	4½p	3½p
1975	17 March	2 oz.	7p	5½p
1975	29 September (metrication)	60g	8½ p	6½p
1977	13 June	60g	9p	7p
1979	20 August	60g	10p	8p
1980	4 February	60g	12p	10p
1981	26 January	60g	14p	11½p
1982	1 February	60g	15½p	12½p
1983	5 April	60g	16p	12½p
1984	3 September	60g	17p	13p
1985	4 November	60g	17p	12p
1986	20 October	60g	18p	13p
1988	5 September	60g	19p	14p
1989	2 October	60g	20p	15p
1990	17 September	60g	22p	17p
1991	16 September	60g	24p	18p
1993	1 November	60g	25p	19p
1996	8 July	60g	26p	20p
1999	26 April	60g	26p	19p
	(but rates increased for weights over 60g)			
2000	27 April	60g	27p	19p
2003	8 May	60g	28p	20p
2004	1 April	60g	28p	21p
2005	7 April	60g	30p	21p
2006	3 April	60g	32p	23p

On 21 August 2006 "Pricing in Proportion" (PIP) was introduced, and under the system large letters were priced separately (and packets too), with initial prices of 41p. (first class) or 37p. (second class) for large letters of 100–250 grams. At the same time the limit for "basic letters" was raised from 60g to 100g:

2006	21 August	100g	32p	23p
2007	2 April	100g	34p	24p
2008	7 April	100g	36p	27p
2009	6 April	100g	39p	30p
2010	6 April	100g	41p	32p
2011	4 April	100g	46p	36p
2012	30 April	100g	60p	50p
2013	2 April	100g	60p	50p

From 2 April 2013 letter and large letter rates remained unchanged, but the terms "packet" (for items thicker than 25mm) and "parcel" were discontinued and replaced by "small parcel" and "medium parcel". This affected the indicators in labels shown in Chapter 28. For overseas mail both "printed papers" and "small packet" were discontinued, becoming "small parcels". There was also a name change to the Recorded Delivery service, becoming "Royal Mail Signed For".

Postcards:
1870	½d
1918	1d
1921	1½d
1922	1d
1940	2d
1957	2½d
1965	3d

A separate postcard rate disappeared with the advent of Two Tier post in 1968.

Surcharges on unpaid/underpaid mail

Until 1983 unpaid/underpaid mail was subject to a surcharge equal to double the deficiency, and this was charged to the recipient. Subsequently a new system was introduced, with a surcharge fee added to the deficiency and ½p (if there was one) then rounded down. Thus, for example, with a rate of 12½p at the time (underpaid items always charged as second class), and with a surcharge fee of 10p, on an unpaid item 22p would have been charged. The surcharge fees were as follows:

1983	5 April	10p
1988	5 September	11p
1989	2 October	12p
1990	17 September	13p
1991	16 September	14p
1993	1 November	15p
1996	8 July	20p
2001	2 January	50p
2002	4 July	80p
2003	8 May	£1

From 1914 "To pay" labels were used as a receipt for surcharges paid, but from the mid 1990s these seem to have been discontinued with little publicity. Shown here is a 1997 "Surcharge paid" marking which has the same purpose. The amount involved is shown in the "to pay" marking shown elsewhere on the envelope.

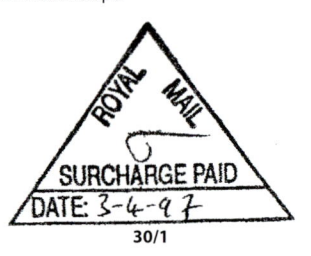

TPO late fees
1860		2d
1880		½d
1969	1 July	1d
1971	15 February	½p
1974	24 June	1p
1976	27 September	no fee payable (but service for 1st class letters only)

418

31 Abbreviations

Care should be taken in interpreting abbreviations in postmarks; for example there are two meanings of FPO! This list omits abbreviations of place names (eg IOW = Isle of Wight) and telegraphic codes (eg BHK = Bishop Auckland). Other abbreviations, such as UPF ("Univeral Postal Frankers", the former name of a manufacturer of stamp cancelling machines), have not to our knowledge appeared in operational postmarks. Others, however, are shown in Chapter 27.

ADO	Aston District Office (Birmingham)
ALF	Automatic Letter Facer
AM/AMDO	Aston Manor (District Office Birmingham)
AMDO	Army Mail Distribution Office
APC	Automated Processing Centre
APO	Army Post Office
BA	British Association
BAPO	Base Army Post Office
BC & FPP	British Colonial and Foreign Parcel Post (prev I & FPP)
BFPO	British Forces Post Office
BFPS	British Forces Postal Service
BMM	British Military Mission
BO	Branch Office
BP	Bulk Posting
BT	Bag Tender
CDO	Counters District Office
CF	Compensation Fee
CFC	Culler Facer Canceller
CH	Clearing House or Camp Hill (District Office, Birmingham)
CL	Late Matter Collection
CO	Chief Office
Co.	County
CP	Competition Posting (football pools)
CR	Caledonian Railway
CS	Church of Scotland Assembly
CX	Charing Cross
DALO	Director of Army Letters Office
DLS	Dead Letter Section
DO	District Office
DOM	Delivery Office Manager
DP	Deferred or Discount Posting
DSC	District Sorting Carriage
EC	East Central
ED	Eastern District
EDO	Eastern District Office
EX	Exchange
F & CPP	Foreign and Colonial Parcel Post
FB	Foreign Branch
FBO	Foreign Branch Office
FC/FCT	Facer Canceller Table
FD	Foreign Dept (of PO)
FMO	Fleet Mail Office
FNM	French Night Mail? Foreign Night Mail?
FNO	Foreign Newspaper Office
FNS	Foreign Newspaper Section
FO	Flag Officer, also Foreign Office (dept of PO)
FPO	Field Post Office or (modern) Franchised Post Office
FRH	Floating Receiving House
FS	Foreign Section
GNR	Great Northern Railway
GP	General Post
GPO	General Post Office
G(R)SD	Giro (Remittance) Services Dept.
H	Hockley (District Office Birmingham)
H & K	Holyhead and Kingstown
HD	Home Depot
HMY	His/Her Majesty's Yacht
HO	Head Office
HP	House of Peers
HPO	Head Post Office
JMC	Jubilee Mail Centre
IB	Inland Branch
IE	International Exhibition
IPS	Inward Primary Sorting
IS	Inland Section
IVO	Inward Vouching Office
KE	King Edward St.
L	Late
LB & SC	London, Brighton and South Coast
LDO	Letter District Office (1986-92)
LIS	Letter Information Sample
LOMO	London Overseas Mail Office (E16)
LPD	Local Parcel Depot
LPR	London Postal Region
LPS	London Parcel Section
M	Mailsort
MB	Movable Box
MC	Mail Centre
MHQ	Mailsort Headquarters
MLO	Mechanised Letter Office
MO & SB	Money Order & Savings Bank
MOO	Money Order Office
MP/MTP	Mount Pleasant
MPO	Mobile Post Office
MPPO	Mount Pleasant Parcel Office
MS	Missent
MSPO	Modified (contract) Sub Post Office
MT	Motor Transport
MTO	Military Telegraph Office
MTP	Mount Pleasant
NB	North Britain
NDO	Northern District Office
NE(TPO)	North Eastern TPO
NILD	Northern Ireland Letter Dist
NMT	Night Mail Tender

Abbreviations

NPB	Newspaper Branch		SDO	Southern District Office or Sub District Office
NR	Northern Railway		SDSO	Sub-District Sorting Office
NSB	National Savings Bank		SEDO	South Eastern District Office
NSD	National Savings Dept.		SM	St Martins Le Grand
NWTPO	North Western TPO		SMP	St Martins Place
			SO	Station Office or Sub Office or Sorting Office
OCR	Optical Character Recognition		SPDO/SPSO	Scale payment Delivery Office/Sub-Office
OCS	Old Cavendish Street		SSO	Station Sorting Office
OS	Old Stamp		ST	Sorting Tender
OVO	Outward Vouching Office		SW(R)	South Western Railway
			SWDO	South Western District Office
P (in PPIs)	Parcel		SY	Show Yard
PB	Parcel Branch			
PC	Prison Censor		T	Taxe (ie postage underpaid)
PCO	Parcels Concentration Office		TD	Telegraph Department
PD	Paid to destination or Paid		TO	Telegraph Office
PDO	Postmen's Delivery Office, or Parcel Delivery Office		TP	Two Penny
			TPO	Travelling Post Office
PHG	Postman Higher Grade		TSO	Town Sub-Office
PHQ	Postal Headquarters			
PL	Paid Late		W	Window Letter
PO	Post Office		WC	Western Central
POC/POOC	Posted Out Of Course		WDO	Western District Office
POW	Prisoner of War		WR	Willesden Ride
PP	Penny Post or Parcel Post or Post Paid			
PPI	Printed Postage Impression			
PPO	Parcel Post Office			
PS	Parcel Section			
PSC	Parcel Sorting Carriage			
PSO	Postmen's Sub Office			
PTO	Please Turn Over			

The following abbreviations refer only to Horizon labels from 2002. Some also apply to the early "Weigh & Pay" labels from 2004, later "Post & Go", those marked * only being used for this purpose. "Post & Go" labels changed to the "indicia" design in 2009 so these abbreviations were subsequently no longer applicable. Horizon labels, however, continue to show "service codes", as they are termed. See Chapter 28.

R	Rebate or Registered			
RDO	Rural/Railway Distribution Office		A	International Airmail
RH	Receiving House		AAX/AX	Airsure
RHAS	Royal Highland Agricultural Society		BF	Forces parcel
RHS	Royal Highland Show		BL/BLG/BLL	Forces letter/large letter
RL	Ride Letter		BPK	Forces packet
RLB	Returned Letter Branch		FF	"Free" Forces mail
RLE	Registered Letter Enclosure		FP	Make-up of deficient postage on overseas mail
RLO	Returned Letter Office		HM	* Forces mail
RLS	Returned Letter Section		L	Letter (usually 1L or 2L denoting 1st or 2nd class)
RNAS	Royal Naval Air Service		LG/LL	Large letter
RNC	Royal Naval College		MOR	Mail Order Return
RO	Receiving Offices or Railway Office		MP	Medium parcel
RPO	Railway Post Office		P	*Parcel
RRH	Rural Receiving House (Office)		PE	International Parcel (Economy)
RSC	Railway Sorting Carriage		PF	Parcel (Parcelforce)
RSO	Railway Sorting Office or Railway Sub Office		PK	Packet
RST	Railway Sorting Tender		PS	International Parcel (Standard)
RWPO	Railway Post Office		RPR	Mail Order Returned Recorded Signed For
			S/SU	International Surface Mail
SC	Sorting Carriage		SD	Special Delivery
SCM	Stamp cancelling machine		SP	Standard parcel, later Small Parcel

Bibliography

"The Classics"

Modern writers, including ourselves, are greatly indebted to the research and scholarship of the writers whose works are listed below. These early publications still have much of interest and value to collectors wishing to specialise. Our background knowledge and many of our illustrations come (with permission) from them. The books are collectable in their own right and collectors search for them at book sales, auctions etc.

The History of the Early Postmarks of the British Isles, J.G. Hendy, 1906
The History of the Postmarks of the British Isles 1840-1876, J.G. Hendy, 1909
The Postmarks of Great Britain and Ireland, R.C. Alcock and F.C. Holland, pub. R.C. Alcock, 1940
(Note : an abridged version of the whole work is : **British Postmarks: A Short History and Guide**, R.C. Alcock & F.C. Holland, Revised Edition, pub. R.C. Alcock, 1977)
The Encyclopaedia of British Empire Postage Stamps, Vol. 1 Great Britain and The Empire in Europe, written and published by Robson Lowe, Second Edition 1952, reprinted in two parts by HJMR as Billig Philatelic Handbook Vols 34 & 35
The Postmark Slogans of GB, George Brumell, pub. R.C. Alcock Ltd, reprinted from The Philatelic Adviser, 1938
The Maltese Cross Cancellation of the United Kingdom, R.C. Alcock and F.C. Holland, pub. R.C. Alcock Ltd, Second Edition 1970
British Post Office Numbers 1844-1906, G. Brumell, originally pub. 1946, reprint pub. R.C. Alcock Ltd, 1979
The Local Posts of London 1680-1840, G. Brumell, 1938
Postal Cancellations of London 1840-1890, H.C. Westley, pub. H.F. Johnson, 1950
Naval Mails 1939-49, J. Goldup, pub. TPO and Seapost Society, 1950
British Army Field Post Offices, 1939-1945, Locations and Assignments, G.R. Crouch and N. Hill, pub. Lava, 1951
A Christmas Story, C.W. Meredith and C. Kidd, pub. R.C. Alcock, 1954
The Spoon Experiment, 1853-58, R.M. & R.W. Willcocks & W. Bentley, pub. the authors, 1960, then similar but R.M. Willcocks and W.A. Sedgewick, pub. the authors, 1980
The Maritime Postal Markings of the British Isles, A. Robertson, pub. the author, 1958. Reprinted in 2 vols by James Bendon Ltd., 1993
British Slogan Cancellations 1917-1958, V. Swan, pub. the author, No.3 in series "The British Specialist", 1959
The Skeleton Postmarks of Great Britain, G.F. Crabb, pub. British Postmark Society, 1960
Handbook and Catalogue of the Stamps and Postmarks of the Islands of Great Britain, pub. Woodcote Stamps, 1961
The Coronation Aerial Post 1911, Francis J Field & NC Baldwin, pub. FrancisJ Field Ltd, 1934
A Priced Catalogue of British Exhibitions 1840-1940, W.G. Stitt Dibden, pub. Argyll Stamp Co. Ltd, 1962
Current Machine Postmarks of the United Kingdom, J. Bruce Bennett, C.R.H. Parsons, G.R. Pearson, pub. British Postmark Society, 1963
Early Stamp Machines, W.G. Stitt Dibden, pub. The Postal History Society, 1964
Squared Circle Postmarks, W.G. Stitt Dibden, 1964, reprinted Harry Hayes, 1974
A History of Wreck Covers originating at Sea, on Land and in the Air A.E. Hopkins, pub. Robson Lowe, c1968
Fifty Years of British Air Mails, 1911-1960, N.C. Baldwin, pub. F.J. Field, reprinted 1969
Camp Postmarks of the United Kingdom, R.A. Kingston, pub. Forces Postal History, 1971. Supplement 1974
Newspaper Branch Cancellations, W.G. Stitt Dibden, pub. The Postal History Society, 1971
Meter Stamps of Great Britain and Ireland, John C. Mann, pub. the author, Second Edition 1972
Posted in Advance for Delivery on Christmas Day, C. Kidd, pub. Robson Lowe, 1974

"The Moderns"

This section is grouped approximately in line with preceding chapters.

Most of "The Classics" are out of print and have been superseded and updated by more recent works. In the preparation of the recent editions we have drawn extensively (with permission) on many of them. Naturally many of these are, in turn, out of print.

There are more works of James A. Mackay than indicated here. All were published by the author except the 2006 work published by British Postmark Society.

Postmarks of England and Wales, James A. Mackay, Second Edition 1988
Irish Postmarks since 1840, James A. Mackay, 1982 - both with supplements in Postal History Annual published each year 1979-89
Scottish Postmarks from 1693 to the Present Day, James A. Mackay, Second Ed 1995
England's Postal History to 1840, R.M. Willcocks, pub. the author, 1975
The Postal History of Great Britain and Ireland, A Summarised Catalogue to 1980, R.M. Willcocks and B. Jay, pub. the authors, Second Edition 1980
Postal Markings of Scotland to 1840, Second Edition, Bruce Auckland, edited by Ron Stables, pub. Scottish Postal History Society,1995
Handbook of Irish Postal History to 1840, David Feldman and William Kane, pub. D. Feldman Ltd, 1975
Herewith my Frank, J.W. Lovegrove, pub. the author, Second Edition 1989
The Provincial Local Posts of England 1765-1840, G.F. Oxley, ?date
Welsh Post Towns before 1840, P. Scott Archer, 1970
The Scottish Additional Halfpenny Mail Tax, K. Hodgson & W.R. Sedgewick, pub. the authors, Second Edition 1984
The Scots Local Namestamps 1840-1860, P M Stephens & R S Erskine, pub. the authors, 1994
The Early Days of the Postal Service, Tony Gammons, pub. Nat Postal Museum, 1986
The Early Days of the Postal Service: The Masters of the Post – The Authorised History of the Royal Mail, Duncan Campbell-Smith, pub. Allen Lane, 2011

British County Catalogue, R.M. Willcocks & B. Jay, Vols 1/2 (combined & updated) 1996; Vol 3 1983; Vol 4, 1988; Vol 5, 1990

Wiltshire and its Postmarks, J. Siggers, pub. Sandcliff Press, 1982

Encyclopaedia of the Maltese Cross Cancellations of Great Britain and Ireland, Rockoff & Jackson, Volume 1 2006, Volume 2 2008

Postmarks of the Date Impression Books, Section one (Vols. 1 and 2), W. Raife and H. Wellsted 1979; Section Two (Vols 3 and 4) by E.W. Proud 1983, pub. Proud-Bailey Co. Ltd

A Provisional Guide to the Valuation of the Numeral Cancellations of the British Isles, Part 1 England and Wales, M.R. Hewlett, Picton Philatelic Handbook No.1, 1979

The Use of the 1894 Coded Time System in British Post Offices, J A E Moy, 1997 and Supplements 1 (2004) & 2 (2007), pub. the author

The Sideways Duplex Cancellations of England and Wales, R.G. Traill and F.C. Holland, pub. R.C. Alcock, 1975

Priced check list of horizontal oval single cancellations with the number in a circle, J.C. Parmenter, pub. the author, 1974

London Cancellations, L. Dubus, pub. Robson Lowe Ltd., 1969-70

British Post Office Numbers, 1924-69, J.A. Mackay, pub. the author, 1981

British Post Office Numbers by County, K. Chapman, pub. Harry Hayes, 1985

Scottish Numeral Postmarks, J.A. Mackay, pub. the author, 1987

Barred Numeral Cancellations, J. Parmenter, Vol One, Wales 1984; Vol Two, England, Bedfordshire to Durham 1985; Vol Three, Essex to Kent, 1986; Vol Four, Lancs to Notts 1986; Vol Five, Oxfordshire to Sussex, 1987; Vol Six, Warwicks to Yorks, 1988, all pub. the author

Barred Numeral Cancellations, the above six volumes gradually being updated; vol 1, Wales, J Parmenter with Prof C Prys-Roberts & Ken Smith, 2011; vol 2 Bedfordshire to Durham, J Parmenter with Ken Smith, 2011, both pub. J Parmenter

Spoon Cancels 1853-1870, The Spoon Study Group, pub. Richard Arundel Ltd, 1992

Brunswick Star Cancels, R. Arundel, pub. Richard Arundel Ltd, 1993

Collecting British Squared Circle Postmarks, Second edition, Parts 1 & 2, S.F. Cohen, M Barrette, J Hine & A M Williams, pub. S F Cohen, 2006

London Fancy Geometric Postmarks, M. Barette, pub. London Postal Hist Grp, 1994

Sub Office Rubber Datestamps of England and Wales, James A. Mackay, 1986

Sub Office Rubber Datestamps of Scotland, James A. Mackay, 1985

Sub Office Rubber Datestamps of Ireland, James A. Mackay, ?date

Official Mail of the British Isles, James A. Mackay, 1983

Scottish Post Offices, James A. Mackay, 1989

Skeleton Postmarks of Scotland, James A. Mackay, 1978

Skeleton Postmarks of England and Wales, James A. Mackay, compiled by Patrick G Awcock and John R Frost, pub. British Postmark Society, 2006 (with later supplements)

UK Machine Marks, J. Peach, pub. Vera Trinder Ltd, Second Edition 1982

Machine Cancellations of Wales 1905-2009, Paul Reynolds, Second Edition, pub the author, 2009 (first edition was "1905-1985")

Machine Cancellations of Scotland, James A. Mackay, 1986

English Provincial Krags, James A. Mackay, 1987

Krag Machine Postmarks of GB & Ireland, Paul T. Carter, pub. British Postmark Society, 2012

Collecting Slogan Postmarks, Cyril R.H. Parsons, Colin G. Peachey & George R. Pearson, pub. the authors, 1986 (includes full listing to 1969)

Slogan Postmarks of the Seventies, details as above, 1980

Slogan Postmarks of the Eighties, details as above, 1990

Slogan Postmarks of the Nineties: part 1 1990-94, details as above, 1995

Slogan Postmarks of the Nineties: part 2 1995-99, details as above, 2000

(Note : Supplements to the above in Bulletins of British Postmark Society)

In-depth UK Slogan Postmark Listings (four volumes covering 1960-99), 10 years each vol), Colin G. Peachey, pub. the author : Vol 1 The Sixties, 1996; Vol 2 The Seventies, 1997; Vol 3 The Eighties, 1997; Vol 4 The Nineties, 2000

Special Event Postmarks of the United Kingdom: Vol 1, George R. Pearson, Fourth Edition, compiled by Colin Peachey and John Swanborough, pub. British Postmark Society, 1991 (covers years 1851-1962); Vol 2, 1996 (covers years 1963-83); Vol 3, 1994 (covers years 1984-93), Vol 4, 2004 (covers years 1994-2003); (vol 5 due 2014, covers years 2004-13); vols 2-5 compiled by Alan Finch and Colin Peachey (based on earlier work by George R. Pearson), pub. British Postmark Society

(Note : Supplements to the above in Bulletins of British Postmark Society)

The Lion roars at Wembley (The British Empire Exhibition 1924-25), Donald R. Knight and Alan D. Sabey, pub. D.R. Knight, 1984

Twenty Years of First Day Postmarks, Brian Pask and Colin G. Peachey, pub. British Postmark Society, 1983 (covers years 1963-83)

(Note : Supplements to the above in Bulletins of British Postmark Society)

Collect GB First Day Covers, The Booth Catalogue, 30th edition, First Day Publishing Co, 2009

Collect British First Day Covers, Adrian Bradbury, 31st edition, pub. the author, 2012

Regus Guide to British Regional Cards and Covers, 5th edition, Regus Publications, 1984

Railway Station Postmarks, D.P. Gowen, pub. Railway Philatelic Group, 1978

The Railway Sub Offices of Great Britain, A.M. Goodbody, pub. Railway Philatelic Group, Second Edition 1983

An Introduction and Guide to the Travelling Post Offices of Great Britain, A.M. Goodbody, pub. Railway Philatelic Group, Second Edition 1983

History of Travelling Post Offices of Great Britain & Ireland, H.S. Wilson, pub. Railway Philatelic Group, 1996 (previously in three volumes)
The Railway TPO's of GB & Ireland 1838-1975, Norman Hill, pub. Harry Hayes Philatelic Pamphlets, 1977
GB & Ireland Travelling Post Office Postmarks, Frank J. Wilson, pub. Railway Philatelic Group, 1991
TPO Postmarks of Great Britain 1962-1990, R.M. Stubbs and G.P. Roberts, pub. TPO & Seapost Society, 1992
TPO Postmarks of Great Britain 1990-2004, R. M. Stubbs, pub. TPO & Seapost Society, 2007
Mail by Rail – The History of the TPO and Post Office Railway, P Johnson, pub. Ian Allan Publishing, 1995
Postmarks of British Railway Stations, W.T. Pipe & G.J. Blackman, pub. Railway Philatelic Group, 1994
Postmarks of British & Irish Railway Stations 1840-1997, W.T. Pipe with special acknowledgement to G. J. Blackman, pub. Railway Philatelic Group, 2001
Paquebot Cancellations of the World, Mike Dovey & Keith Morris (4th edition based on Roger Hosking work), pub. TPO & Seapost Society, 2012
Floating Post Offices of the Clyde, James A. Mackay, 1979
The Transatlantic Post Office, Roger Hosking, pub. the author, 1979
Royal Mail Steam Packet Company, Michael Rego, Cockrill Series Booklet No.49, 1987
Early Forces Mail, Barrie Jay, pub. Stuart Rossiter Trust Fund, 1997
The Postal History of the British Army in World War I, A. Kennedy and G. Crabb, pub. Forces Postal History Society, 1977
History of British Army Postal Service, Vol. 1 1882-1902, Vol. 2 1903-27, Vol. 3 1927-63, E.B. Proud, pub. Proud-Bailey Co. Ltd, 1982
Field Censor System of the Armies of the British Empire, 1914-18: Unit Allocations, i. War Office Based types 1,2,3,4 and 7, F.W. Daniel, pub. the author, 1984
World War II Censor Marks, J.A. Daynes, pub. Forces Postal History Society, 1984
British Forces Machine Postmarks 1940-1983, M Dobbs, pub. Forces Postal History Society, 1983
The Royal Naval Air Service, Dr M.H. Gould, pub. Forces Postal History Society, 1984
Postal Markings of RAF, RFC and RNAS Stations in the United Kingdom 1918-68, W. Garrard, pub. Forces Postal History Society, 1990
The Channel Islands Sub-Post Offices and their Postmarks, David Gurney, pub. CISS Publishing, 1983; update 1990
The Post Office in the Smaller Channel Islands, David Gurney, pub. CISS Publishing, 1993
Channel Islands Postal History Catalogue, Stanley Gibbons Publications Ltd, 1991
Isle of Man Stamps and Postal History (YPM4), Dr J.T. Whitney, pub. BPH Publications, Third Edition 1978
Isle of Man Postal Slogans and Machine Cancellations, 7th edition by P Britnell & revised by G M Jarand, pub. Isle of Man Sales Ltd 1996 and supplement to 2013
Islands Postal History - Series of 12 volumes, J.A. Mackay
Catalogue of Great Britain Surcharge and Explanatory Dies, C.M. Langston, pub. the author, 1964
Surcharged Mail of the British Isles, J.A. Mackay, 1984

UK Taxe Marks for International mail 1875-2000 Usage and Listing, K Snelson, 2007 and amendments issued 2009 and 2011, pub. the author
Telegraphic Codes of the British Isles, 1870-1924, J.A. Mackay, 1981
The Parcel Post of the British Isles, J.A. Mackay, 1982
Registered Mail of the British Isles, J.A. Mackay, 1983
Express Service 1891-1971, H A Wellstead, pub. Postal History Society, 1986
Royal Household Mail, G. Morgan, pub. British Philatelic Trust, 1992
GB Used Abroad: Cancellations and Postal Markings, John Parmenter, pub. the author, 1993 and updated 2009
The Postal History of the Manx Electric Railway, A. Povey and J.T. Whitney, pub. the authors, 1979
A Guide to the Postcard Cachets of Land's End, J.D.B. Owen, pub. the author, 1994, an update of previous book of similar name by G. Beckwith and J. Lawrence, Second Edition 1982
Dartmoor Letterboxes (and others), Anne Swinscow, pub. BPCC Wheatons Ltd Exeter, 1984, revised 1987
An Introduction to British Postal Mechanisation, D.N. Muir & M. Robinson, pub. Postal Mechanisation Study Circle, 1979 with supplements 1981, 1983, 1992
British Postal Mechanisation, edited by Douglas N. Muir, pub. Postal Mechanisation Study Circle, 1993 with amendments to 2006
Automatic Letter Sorting in the UK, P.G. Awcock, pub. the author; Vol 1, 12th (final) edition, part 1 1996, part2 1999, part 3 2003; Vol 2, 2nd edition, 1996
Brighton Transorma 1935-1968, Patrick G. Awcock, pub. the author, 1996
Colliery Postmarks 1854-1995, F.W. Taylor, pub. the author, 1995
Post Offices of the United Kingdom, The Post Office (last edition 1977)
Postal Directory 1850, reprint by London Postal History Group, 1987
Irish Post Offices 1600-1990, H. Frank & K. Stange, pub. F.A.I., 1990
Robertson Revisited, Colin Tarbrart, pub. James Bendon, 1997

"General"

Postmark Collecting, R.K. Forster, pub. Stanley Paul, 1960
Collecting Postmarks, R.K. Forster, pub. Stanley Gibbons Guides, 1977
Introducing Postal History, A. Branston, pub. Stanley Gibbons Guides, 1978
The Guinness Book of Stamp Facts & Feats, James A. Mackay, pub. Guinness Superlatives Ltd, 1982
Three Centuries of Scottish Posts, A R B Haldane, pub. Edinburgh University Press, 1971
Royal Mail: The Post Office since 1840, M J Daunton, pub. The Athlone Press, 1985

Visit SAMWELLS for *All* GB Postmark Types
Browse our large stocks at Stampex & York. View selected items online

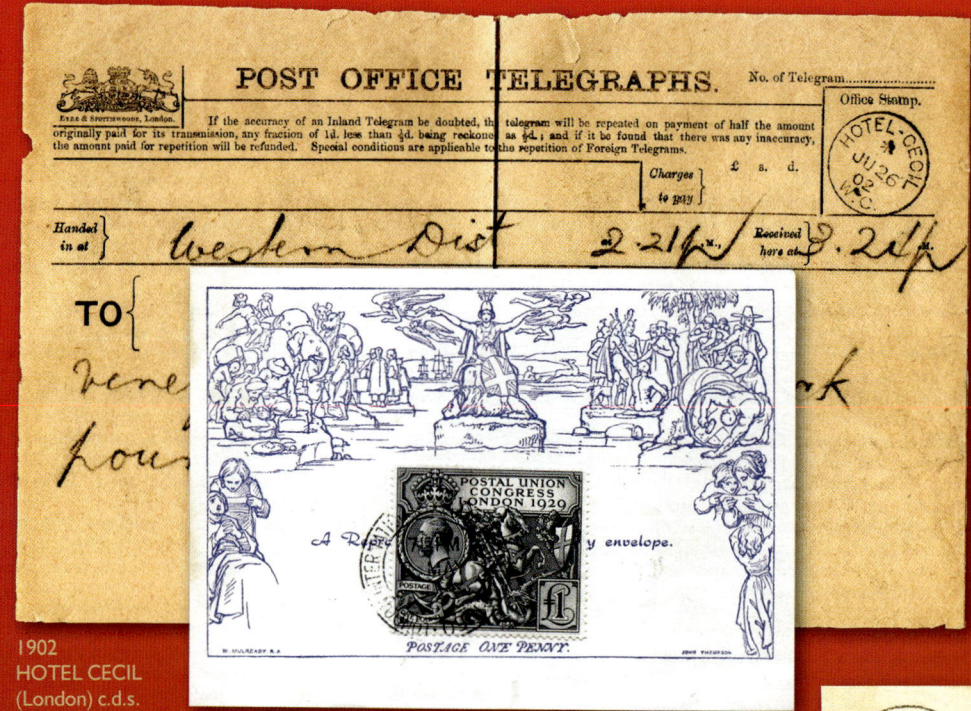

1902 HOTEL CECIL (London) c.d.s.

1950 LONDON INTERNATIONAL STAMP EXHIBITION c.d.s.

1924 EMPIRE EXHIBITION WEMBLEY/ STADIUM proof strike

Unrecorded machine trial

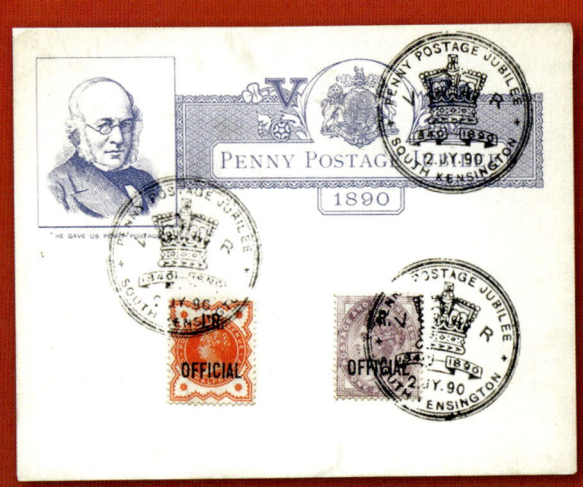

'1769' of St.Malo

'30' of Carshalton

Pearson Hill trial machine

1890 PENNY POSTAGE JUBILEE/SOUTH KENSINGTON

Bombay numeral

1870 Parcel Post trial cancel

WE CAN NOW TAILOR OUR LISTS TO SUIT YOUR REQUIREMENTS
Simply let us know what you collect & we will return results by e-mail

www.postalhistorygb.com   01225 462429   info@postalhistorygb.com

Everything for the Stamp Collector

Over 5000 items for the discerning collector

- **Albums and Leaves**
  - Peg-fitting • Springback • Ring-fitting • Coin
  - Luxury • One-Country • First Day Cover
  - Postcard • Junior • Booklets • Supplements

- **Catalogues and Books**
  - Great Britain • Commonwealth
  - Foreign • Specialised • Reference

- **Accessories**
  - Microscopes • Watermark Detectors
  - Ultraviolet Lamps • Tweezers
  - Lamps & Magnifyers • Colour Keys

- **Stockbooks**
  - Wide range of colours and sizes

- **Mounts and Hinges**
  - Huge Selection

- **Frank Godden**
  - Binders • Leaves • Protectors

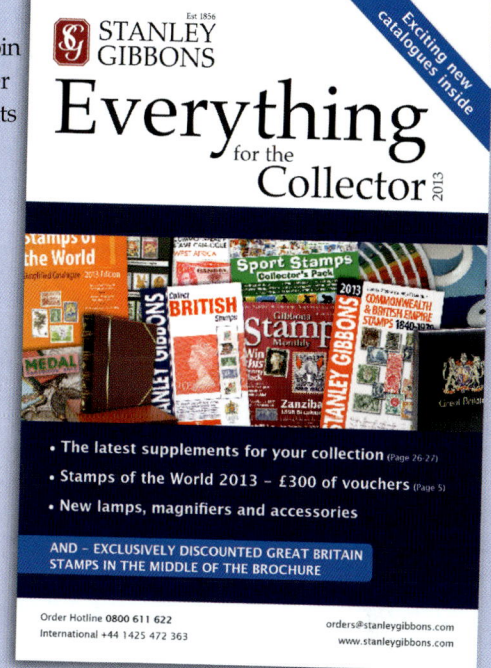

- **Great Selection of Children's Starter Kits**

For all your collecting needs or to request a brochure, contact us on

☎ Customer Service **0800 611 622** (UK)
   +44 1425 472 363 (Overseas)

@ email
   orders@stanleygibbons.com

Or write to us at the address below

Stanley Gibbons Limited
7 Parkside, Christchurch Road,
Ringwood, Hampshire, BH24 3SH
www.stanleygibbons.com

Est 1856
STANLEY GIBBONS

Stanley Gibbons
Microscopes

Stanley Gibbons always have something to enhance your collection

USB Digital Microscope - SG UM05 *Magnification 1x80*

The Stanley Gibbons UM05 USB Digital Autofocus Microscope is the first USB microscope we have sold that allows you to capture an image of the whole stamp with ease and is ideal as a quick and simple alternative to scanning.

The autofocus option allows you to automatically zoom with a magnification ratio of 1-80x, allowing you see any object at 320x on a 22" monitor. This feature removes the hassle of trying to focus in on fine details such as errors, plate numbers and flaws.

Once the operating software is loaded on your computer, simply plug the UM05 into your PC and, with one click of the focus button on-screen, you will quickly receive the clearest images automatically.

You can also take photos, record videos and adjust the brightness of the microscope's 4 inbuilt LEDs from your PC, allowing you to set the microscope up on its stand and take multiple images without having to reposition anything.

WITH AUTO FOCUS

| RUM05 | SG UM05 Digital Microscope | £150 |

USB Digital Microscope - SG UM02 *Magnification 1x60*

The SG UM02 USB Microscope offers the same image quality and hardware as the UM05 in a lightweight unit with the magnification ratio of 1x60. Ideal for any philatelic use, the UM02 has dials for manual optical focus and brightness control and you can capture images and video with a single touch of the 'snapshot' button on the top of the microscope.

The UM02 also comes with the same software package as the UM05, allowing you to measure the length, angle, circumference and area of anything you choose to view. Both microscopes come with stands but can also be operated and held in the hand.

A versatile and well priced addition to your philatelic toolkit.

PERFECT FOR COMPLETE STAMP IMAGES

| RUM02 | SG UM02 Digital Microscope | £74.95 |

Prices correct as of October 2012 and are subject to change

To order, call **0800 611 622** or email **orders@stanleygibbons.com**

Est 1856
STANLEY GIBBONS

Stanley Gibbons
7 Parkside, Christchurch Road, Ringwood, Hants, BH24 3SH
+44 (0)1425 472 363
www.stanleygibbons.com

Stanley Gibbons
399 Strand

BY APPOINTMENT TO
HER MAJESTY THE QUEEN
STANLEY GIBBONS LTD
LONDON
PHILATELISTS

Unsure how to progress your collection?

Visit 399 Strand to get advice from our experienced and knowledgeable staff. They will help to choose philatelic products that will enhance and develop your collection as well as advising on techniques for the care and storage of your stamps and catalogues.

We have one of the largest ranges of albums and philatelic accessories in the world.

We pride ourselves in having possibly the most comprehensive range of philatelic accessories and albums available. We strive to cater for every need a collector might have, and if we don't have the exact item you need, we will recommend an equivalent or an alternative.

Come in, browse our range and choose what's best for you.

Before you commit to a particular album, take the time to talk to our staff who will help you weigh up the pros and cons before you make your decision. We are always happy to demonstrate anything we sell from tweezers to Frank Godden luxury albums.

OUR PROMISE TO YOU!

If anything is out of stock when you visit, we will ship it to you free of charge.

Scan the QR code for directions to our shop

Please contact Wayne Elliott - shop@stanleygibbons.com
399 Strand opening hours Mon-Fri 9am-5pm Sat 9:30am-5pm Sun Closed

Est 1856
STANLEY GIBBONS

Stanley Gibbons Limited
399 Strand, London, WC2R 0LX
+44 (0)20 7557 4444
www.stanleygibbons.com

Gibbons Stamp Monthly

The first choice for stamp collectors since 1890

Subscribe TODAY!

Gibbons Stamp Monthly offers you:

- Great value, usually 20-30% more pages than other stamp magazines
- More news
- More articles
- More on Great Britain and Commonwealth
- A magazine written by stamp collectors for stamp collectors
- Comprehensive catalogue supplement every month

The UK's No.1 stamp magazine

"The premier philatelic magazine available anywhere – it's difficult to improve on perfection"
— Everett L. Parker, Global Stamp News

3 easy ways to read Gibbons Stamp Monthly

POST
Call our Subscription Hotline or complete the form facing this page to recieve your monthly issue straight to your door:

0800 611 622 (UK)
+44 1425 472 363 (Overseas)

ONLINE
Subscribe and view online:

stanleygibbons.com/view/content/sg_gsm_subscribe

APP
View via our APP and view anytime or anywhere:

stanleygibbons.com/app

www.stanleygibbons.com

STANLEY GIBBONS
A Stanley Gibbons Publication